Y0-BXR-609

The Edinburgh Companion to Ancient Greece and Rome

Edited by

Edward Bispham,
Thomas Harrison and
Brian A. Sparkes

Edinburgh University Press

Edinburgh University Press Ltd
22 George Square, Edinburgh

Typeset in 10 on 12pt Ehrhardt
by Servis Filmsetting Limited, Manchester, and
printed and bound in Great Britain by
Antony Rowe Ltd, Chippenham, Wilts

A CIP record for this book is available from the British Library

ISBN-10 0 7486 1629 2 (hardback)
ISBN-13 978 0 7486 1629 9 (hardback)

Contents

C. Periods

Introduction

The study of classics and ancient history in universities in Europe and North America is, contrary to expectation, not dying but thriving. However, as Greek and Latin are unavailable to the majority of students and the range of modern foreign languages through which study of classics is disseminated is remarkably wide, much of the literature that students are asked to read and the secondary evidence they are urged to use is currently inaccessible to them. The purpose of this *Edinburgh Companion* is to help bridge the gap between students and scholars by providing a reliable, accessible and up-to-date source of practical reference for students of classics and ancient history, and one which their teachers may also find valuable.

The book aims to impart basic information clearly and concisely: it will help students to navigate the sometimes tricky landscape of the ancient world and should enable them to value and enjoy the contrasting perspectives and methods of several disciplines that seek to interpret the world of ancient Greece and Rome.

The book is divided into four parts. Part One gives an overview of modern approaches to the various aspects of the classics. Study, understanding and interpretation are constantly changing; emphases alter and the appearance of fresh evidence, original ideas or influence from the contemporary world may open up new avenues for research and investigation. The civilisations of Greece and Rome are currently seen, rather more than they used to be, in the context of their relationships with neighbouring peoples, and the chronological spread of the subject is much wider than was usual in past scholarship.

Part Two looks at the material background to the two peoples. This denotes the land, the sea and the built environment, together with the surviving material evidence, whether that be in the form of architecture, sculpture, metalwork, or texts that continue to be unearthed: papyri or inscriptions (usually on stone and metal, but occasionally on wood). Part Three covers the wide spectrum of literary genres, from Greek epic at the start of the history of Greek literature to the more rarely studied Latin and Greek technical, scientific and legal textbooks, giving a taste of the full range of Graeco-Roman culture.

Finally, Part Four is intended to provide a practical resource: guides to such items as names, measures, writing systems or metre, as well as maps, time-charts, a glossary of ancient and modern terms, details of textbooks and other (print and web) resources for the study of the classical world, and a full list of abbreviations – all intended to help readers to find their own way through publications in the various disciplines of classics.

The *Edinburgh Companion* is a gateway to the fascinating world of ancient Greece and Rome. Wide-ranging in its approach and pragmatic in its method, it reveals the multifaceted nature of the classical enterprise and shows something of the rewards and satisfactions to be gained by drawing together the perspectives and methods of different disciplines, from philosophy to history, poetics to archaeology, art history to numismatics, and many more.

Spelling

All authors grappling with the classical world find themselves face to face with the problem of the spelling of transliterated Greek and Latin names and terms. Complete consistency is impossible to achieve and unwise to attempt. The editors have adopted a relaxed attitude but in the main have chosen the Latin forms. This means that readers will meet Polyclitus more often than Polukleitos, and Achilles rather than Akhilleus, and so on. However, there are many Greek names and technical terms that were not adopted into Latin and/or look more comfortable in their Greek guise, e.g. *euthunai*, Palladion, *peplos*, *phoros*, Telekleides, *xoanon*. Some will be found here in both Greek and Latin forms. Keen-eyed readers will also notice Virgil and Vergil, and *virtus* and *uirtus*.

Here is a selected list of the major differences in spelling:

Greek		**Latin**	
ai	Athēnai	ae	Athenae
e	nautēs	a	nauta
ei	Mēdeia	e	Medea
ei	Iphigeneia	i	Iphigenia
ion	sumposion	ium	symposium
k	krātēr	c	crater
kh	kheirourgia	ch	chirurgia
oi	oistros	oe	oestrus
on	stadion	um	stadium
os	skuphos	us	skyphus
ou	Ekklēsiazousai	u	Ecclesiazusae
u	gumnasion	y	gymnasium

It would be pedantic to convert anglicised names such as Homer and Ovid back to their Greek or Latin form, and proper names such as Aiskhulos and Ianus and words like *psukhē*, when left in strictly transliterated form, are not easy to recognise at first blush as Aeschylus, Janus and psyche.

None of the variations in this book is likely to lead the reader astray.

Acknowledgements

The editors wish to thank the following for their practical help or advice: Professor Moshe Amit, Professor Kai Brodersen, Dr Mark Pobjoy, Professor Neil Smith, Sue Willetts and the Joint Library of the Hellenic and Roman Societies, Institute of Classical Studies, London; Carol Macdonald, James Dale, Ann Vinnicombe and Fiona Sewell of Edinburgh University Press, for overseeing production with professionalism; and above all, John Davey, who first conceived the idea of the Companion, who put the editors together, and whose name should by rights appear alongside theirs.

The editors are grateful to a number of institutions and individuals for permission to publish works in their care and to reproduce their photographs. We apologise for any permissions that we have failed to record.

Athens, Acropolis Museum (Aesthetics 3); American School of Classical Studies, Alison Frantz Archive AT24 (Landscape 1); Epigraphical Museum 7279 (Inscriptions 1); German Institute of Archaeology inst. neg. 822 (Hege) (Aesthetics 3); Kerameikos Museum (Pottery 4); National Museum 743 (Dress 2)

Basel, Antiken Museum (Pottery 5); Berlin, Staatliche Museen zu Berlin BKP (Sculpture 5); Boston, Museum of Fine Arts (Landscape 4); Bristol, University of Bristol Sicily Expedition (Marine 2)

Cambridge, Fitzwilliam Museum (Gems 1–2); Museum of Classical Archaeology, photo Nigel Cassidy (Sculpture 1)

Derek Content (Gems 5); Dublin, Trinity College (Papyri 1–4)

Eccles Excavation Committee (Gems 3)

Florence, Alinari 27289 and 38033 (Landscape 6 and 5), Alinari Archives-Anderson Archive (Sculpture 8)

London, British Museum, Department of Coins and Medals (Coinage 2, 4, 6–8, 10); Department of Greek and Roman Antiquities (Aesthetics 1; Sculpture 2; Painting 6; Gems 8–9); Los Angeles, Getty Research Library, Wim Swaan collection 96.P.21 (Painting 7); The J. Paul Getty Museum (Pottery 2 and 3)

Madrid, Museo Arqueológico Nacional (Music 1, 3 and 5); Manchester, The Whitworth Art Gallery, The University (Dress 4); Munich, Staatliche Antikensammlung und Glyptothek (Landscape 2, Aesthetics 2 and 4)

Naples, National Archaeological Museum (Landscape 7 and 10; Sculpture 6; Painting 1); Newcastle-upon-Tyne, The Shefton Museum of Greek Art and Archaeology (Armour 1–2); New York, Metropolitan Museum of Art (Sculpture 3; Pottery 9 and 10; Dress 1)

Ostia, Museum (Sculpture 10); Oxford, Ashmolean Museum (Pottery 7; Gems 6–7, 10; Measures 1); Centre for the Study of Ancient Documents (Inscriptions 4)

Palestrina, Palazzo Barberini (Landscape 6); Paris, Musée de Louvre (Music 2 and 4); Piraeus, Museum (Measures 2a)

Reggio, Museo Nazionale di Reggio (courtesy of the Ministero per i Beni e le Attività Culturali n. 23, 9/04/2003) (Sculpture 4); Rome, British School at Rome (Sites 5); Fototeca Unione 3247F and 4737 (Dress 3; Sites 2); German Archaeological Institute inst. neg. 57.843, 58.1447, 59.1992, 61.2297, 66.1831 (Koppermann), 72.654A (Singer), 80.3236 (Schwanke) (Painting 2 and 1, Landscape 7, Aesthetics 5, Sculpture 6, 7, 10); Palazzo Massimo alle Terme (Landscape 8); Vatican Museums (Landscape 5; Sculpture 8)

Thessaloniki, Archaeological Museum (Pottery 11); Tunis, Bardo Museum (Painting 9); Tyne and Wear Museums (Inscriptions 3)

Adapted from published works: M. I. Finley (ed.), *Atlas of Classical Archaeology* (Chatto and Windus, 1977) 74, 127, 134, 164, 174, 242 (Sites 11, 10, 4, 7, 6, 8); *Gallia*, Supplement 16 (1962), fig. 26 (Sites 3); K. Miller, *Die Peutingersche Tafel* (1916) segment VI 3–5 (Sites 1); R. V. Schoder, S. J., *Ancient Greece from the Air* (Thames & Hudson, 1974) 209, top (Landscape 9); M. Ventris and J. Chadwick, *Document of Mycenaean Greek* (2nd edn), Cambridge: Cambridge University Press, 1973, p. 385 (Writing Systems 1); A. Heubeck, 'Schrift' (*Archaeologica Homerica* III, x), Göttingen: Vandenhoek and Ruprecht, 1979, p. 103 (Writing Systems 2); M. Panfolfini and A. L. Prosdocimi, *Aflabetari e insegnamento della scrittura in Etruria e nell'Italia antica*, Florence: Olschki, 1990, p. 20 (Writing Systems 3); M. Cristofani (ed.), *Civiltà degli etruschi*, Milan: Electa, p. 343 (Writing Systems 4)

Photos: Félix Bonfils, c. 1870 (Architecture 3); Jon Coulston (Armour 3–4); Bruce Frame (Gems 5); Roger Ling 45/3, 36/29, 19/7, 98/5, 90/7, 6/33 (Painting 4–6, 8–10); Institute for Exploration/Institute for Archaeological Oceanography-URL/GSOG (Marine 3); Lloyd Morgan (Architecture 8); Peter Stewart (Sculpture 9); Richard Tomlinson (Architecture 1–2, 4–7, 9–11); Robert Wilkins (Gems 1–4); Jonathan Williams (Coinage 9)

Drawings: C. Brandon (Marine 1); Susan Grice (Marine 8, after J. P. Joncheray); A. J. Parker (Marine 4, from a reconstruction model by R. Roman); (Marine 5, and Susan Grice, after P. Pomey, M. Rival and others); (Marine 6 and 7, and Susan Grice, after J. P. Joncheray); (Marine 9, after P. and J. Throckmorton); (Marine 10, and Susan Grice); William D. Creese (Music)

Diagrams, maps and profiles: the staff of the Cartographic Unit of the Geography Department, Southampton University (Tim Apsden, Bob Smith, Andy Vowles) (Coins 5; Pottery 1 and 6; Measures 2b; Maps)

Part One: Classics and the Classical World

A. Classics in the Twenty-First Century

Study, understanding and interpretation of the classical world are constantly changing; emphasis alters and new avenues are revealed. Each generation gives the kaleidoscope a fresh twist, and a new pattern is formed. The chapters in Part One A present some of the new ideas and views on the major aspects of the study of the classics: history and historiography, archaeology, philology, literature, philosophy and art. Subjects also touched on comprise religion, economics and gender; the introductory and concluding chapters address, respectively, the history of classical scholarship and the study of classical reception, that is, the ways in which down the centuries the classics have been manipulated (translated, transformed, appropriated, etc.).

1. The History of the Discipline

Christopher Stray

Classical scholarship began in classical antiquity: in the Hellenistic period texts of Homer and other authors were being collected in libraries. In Alexandria, scholars like Aristarchus were studying, comparing and annotating manuscripts of what were already 'classical' Greek writers. Alexander and his successors ruled large areas inhabited by non-Greek speakers: the need to teach them Greek led to the formation of explicit linguistic rules, and so to the systematic study of grammar and syntax (already pioneered by the Sophists). After the Roman conquest of Greece, the construction of a corpus of 'ancient' Greek was in a sense replicated by the Romans. Disdain for the political weakness of the Greeks was accompanied by reverence for the literary achievements of their ancestors, and a long line of Roman scholars studied Greek language and literature as well as their own. A similarly ambivalent relationship towards the Graeco-Roman classics obtained in the case of Christianity. The new religion emerged in an empire whose official language was Latin, and in whose Eastern half Greek was commonly spoken. When the second/third century AD theologian Tertullian asked rhetorically, 'What has Athens to do with Jerusalem? What has the Academy to do with the Church?', he wrote this in elegant Latin. In the ninth century the grammarian Ermenrich of Ellwangen, defending his many quotations from Virgil, claimed that 'even as dung spread upon the field enriches it to a good harvest, so the filthy writings of pagan poets are a mighty aid to Divine eloquence'. After the fall of the Roman Empire in the fifth century, Graeco-Roman culture was transmitted through the Middle Ages (c. 600–1300 AD) largely by the Christian church, and especially in the monasteries founded all over Europe from the sixth century onwards. Most of our modern texts of classical authors derive from manuscripts written by monks in the cells and scriptoria of these monasteries. The discipline of classical philology developed out of their attempts to decipher manuscript readings of texts, and to choose between variant readings in different manuscripts (see chapter 33).

The Renaissance

In the fourteenth century, a power vacuum in Italy created by the simultaneous weakness of the papal and Hohenstaufen regimes led to the creation of secular republics, and these became the seedbed of the Renaissance. This 'rebirth' looked to the rediscovered literature of the Romans, and especially the Greeks, for examples of moral and aesthetic theory and practice. Italian scholars and their patrons searched libraries and monasteries for manuscripts. Greek scholars fleeing Constantinople after its sack by the Turks in 1453 were engaged to teach their language and to decipher manuscripts. The new scholarship was spread, and an international academic community assembled, with the help of the newly invented printing press using movable type. Aldus Manutius was a leader in both fields: he set up an academy for the teaching of Greek, and established a press in Venice which produced the 'Aldine' editions of the classics. It is difficult now to imagine the excitement men of the fourteenth and early fifteenth centuries like the Italian humanists Francesco Petrarch, Coluccio Salutati and Poggio Bracciolini must have felt when their searches in monastery libraries revealed the manuscripts of Latin and Greek authors whose works they had never previously read. Their discoveries created a vividly detailed past with which they identified – Petrarch, after finding manuscripts of Cicero and of Homer, wrote Latin epistles to both of them. The new discoveries were communicated to England in the sixteenth century both by printed editions and by correspondence and visits. Poggio spent five years in England, while Thomas Linacre of Oxford visited Florence and Rome, studying manuscripts and learning Latin and Greek. Linacre and his friends William Grocyn and William Latimer were the founders of modern English scholarship. Their younger contemporary William Lily, first High Master of St Paul's School, wrote for it a Latin textbook which as the 'common' or 'royal' grammar became a standard work; revised versions were still in use in the nineteenth century.

England and Germany: criticism and *Wissenschaft*

The outstanding classical scholar in Europe in the early eighteenth century was Richard Bentley (1662–1742), Master of Trinity College, Cambridge, with whose Fellows he conducted a long and bitter legal battle. Arrogant and disputatious Bentley may have been, but his work on classical authors was brilliantly perceptive. He is best known for his demonstration that the *Epistles of Phalaris* (the supposed letters of a sixth-century Sicilian tyrant) were a forgery, but he should also be remembered as the discoverer of the digamma, an early Greek letter which had dropped out of texts of Homer leaving their scansion askew. Bentley is remarkable too for his range: he dealt with a large number of Latin and Greek texts, and was happy to investigate historical as well as linguistic questions. The next outstanding English classicist, Richard **Porson** (1759–1808), who became Professor of Greek at Cambridge in 1792, stood in marked contrast. His scholarship was focused entirely on Greek, and in particular on the editing of Greek drama, though like Bentley he made his name by proving a text (in this case, from the Bible) to be spurious. After his death a kind of Porson cult developed, his pupils (J. H. Monk and C. J. Blomfield) following his narrow interests; his fine Greek handwriting became the basis of a standard Greek font – used, for example, in the Oxford Classical Texts (1900–).

In Germany, Porson's contemporary Friedrich **Wolf** (1759–1824) was laying the basis of an encyclopaedic programme of classical scholarship far removed from the narrow Porsonian style. Wolf's definition of 'philology' was 'knowledge of human nature as exhibited in antiquity' – this was an Enlightenment project which sought to create a totality of knowledge and a unity of theory and practice. The new programme of *Altertumswissenschaft* ('the study of antiquity') was to rest firmly on the understanding of literary texts, but to include the whole of Graeco-Roman culture. (The other civilisations of the ancient world were dismissed by Wolf as unimportant.) The programme was only sketched by Wolf himself, but it was given systematic exposition by his pupil August Boeckh (1785–1867). Boeckh produced two pioneering works which laid the foundation for work in their fields: *Die Staatshaushalting der Athener (The Public Economy of Athens*) (1817) and the first two volumes of the *Corpus Inscriptionum Graecarum* (1825–43). This latter was severely criticised by Gottfried **Hermann** (1772–1848), whose own work was, like Porson's, much more narrowly linguistic. The methodological debate between the two men contrasted not only the narrower and broader (*Altertumswissenschaft*) styles of classical scholarship, but also conceptions of their subject matter: either a fixed source of timeless value, or a culture subject to historical change.

Wolf's claim to be the founder of modern classical scholarship rests not only on his vision of *Altertumswissenschaft*, but on his establishment at Göttingen in 1786 of a philological seminar. This was a specialised institution for the training of classical teachers; it became one of the principal features in the increasingly professionalised study of classics in nineteenth-century Germany. Napoleon's invasion of Prussia in 1806, which brought to an end Wolf's career at the University of Halle, prompted the reconstruction of German education a few years later. The architect of this reconstruction was Wolf's friend Wilhelm von Humboldt (1767–1835), who served in the Prussian education ministry and was instrumental in founding the University of Berlin (1810). This served as an exemplar for later German universities, which adopted both the powerful research training device of the seminar and the ideology of *Altertumswissenschaft* (Humboldt's reforms also created a demand for classical texts to which the publishing firm of B. G. Teubner responded in founding its celebrated series (1824)). The seminars in German universities became the power bases of leading professors, whose students tended to form schools, following their masters' lead in subject matter and methodology. Competition between universities and between professors often led to intense rivalry and mutual criticism, while a student who dared to criticise the god-professor was liable to be cast out, and would then be denied the master's patronage. Professors were technically civil servants, chairs being filled by a 'call' from the Ministry of Education in Berlin; but such calls were often the outcome of struggles behind the scenes between the backers of rival candidates.

Among the most successful professors in this system was Theodor **Mommsen** (1817–1903), professor of ancient history at Berlin from 1848 till his death. Mommsen organised and contributed to the *Corpus Inscriptionum Latinarum* (1867–), and was also heavily involved in the German records series, *Monumenta Germaniae Historica*. His career did not begin smoothly, however, since his involvement in liberal protests during the 1848 revolution led to his leaving Germany for Switzerland. The experience prompted and coloured his famous *History of Rome* (1854–5), not only in the text but also in the popularist avoidance of footnotes: on this ground another exile, Arnaldo **Momigliano**, memorably assigned Mommsen to the 'naked school of historiography'. Mommsen's output was enormous – over 1,000 items are listed in the bibliography compiled after his death. In 1902 he was awarded the Nobel Prize for literature – so far, the only classical scholar to be so honoured.

A different kind of impact on the discipline was made by Mommsen's son-in-law Ulrich **von Wilamowitz-Moellendorff** (1848–1931), who became recognised as the outstanding Hellenist of his period. Wilamowitz's output covered a very wide range and brought together language, literature, philosophy and history. He was concerned to resist the canonisation of the Greeks, and instead painted a vivid historicist picture of a culture and society, warts and all. He was capable of hasty and careless work (the American classicist Basil **Gildersleeve** (1831–1924) called him 'the rough rider'), but his enormous technical skill was acknowledged even by so severe a judge as A. E. **Housman** (1859–1936), who described him as 'a very great man, the greatest now living and comparable with the greatest of the dead'.

The career of Wilamowitz's schoolfellow Friedrich Nietzsche (1844–1900) began promisingly, with a classical chair at Basle at the age of 24. Influenced by the German philosopher Arthur Schopenhauer (1788–1860) and the German composer Richard Wagner (1813–83), he published *The Birth of Tragedy* in 1872, highlighting the wild Dionysiac spirit which he claimed had been overcome by a taming Apollonian influence (Arrowsmith, 'Nietzsche'). The book's advocacy of a 'philology of the future' (*Zukunftsphilologie*) brought a fierce rejoinder from Wilamowitz, who denounced Nietzsche's new science as 'backside philology' (*Afterphilologie*). Nietzsche's radical vision of a new scholarship which would cut through the accretions of Roman, Christian and modern assumptions deserves to be taken seriously. His *We Philologists* (*Wir Philologen*) of the mid-1870s should be compared with Wolf's notes for a projected encyclopaedia of *Altertumswissenschaft* of nearly a century before. Both men sought an intense vision of moral value; both found it by excluding all of the ancient world except the Greeks.

Scholarship as an institution

Nietzsche's concern with the distorting effects of traditions of pedagogy and scholarship reminds us that the history of classical scholarship has often been written as the history of individual achievement (e.g. by Pfeiffer, *Classical Scholarship* (two vols), and Brink, *English Classical Scholarship*). This is to ignore the increasing influence of groups and 'schools' such as the Porsonians and the members of German professorial seminars. The emergence of Germany as the international powerhouse of classical scholarship in the nineteenth century reflected the development of a massive institutional system of gymnasia, seminars, institutes, journals and professional careers. It was this system which was imported into the USA from the 1850s by Americans who studied in Germany (Winterer, *Culture of Classicism*), and to some extent into France after its military defeat by Germany in 1870. During the nineteenth century the emergence of an academic career (Germany again being well ahead) led to increasing publication by scholars for other scholars, rather than for an audience of amateur gentlemen or for the general public: books addressed to this last audience, like J. C. Stobart's *The Glory that was Greece* (1911), belonged in fact to a reaction against a separation of academic and popular audiences, and increasing specialisation within scholarship. England had till this point been the home of amateur gentlemen and clerical scholars. Non-Anglicans were excluded from jobs at Oxford and Cambridge, while talented Anglican scholars were liable to be diverted into ecclesiastical careers (Stray, *Classics Transformed*). Classical journals, well established on the continent, tended not to survive in England for more than a few years. The first British classical journal, which is still published today, the *Journal of Hellenic Studies*, was founded only in 1880. This was followed by *Classical Review* (1886), *Classical Quarterly* (1906) and the *Journal of Roman Studies* (1911); together these developed complementary coverage of an increasingly specialised field.

JHS and *JRS* were both founded as the organs of societies (the Hellenic and Roman Societies), both of which concentrated largely on history and archaeology. These areas of scholarship had developed in the second half of the nineteenth century as organised fields of study, underpinned by the inclusion of ancient history in the Oxford curriculum (Literae Humaniores or 'Greats') since 1850, and of ancient history and archaeology in the Classical Tripos at Cambridge since 1881 (compare Germany: Marchand, *Down from Olympus*). They signalled the end of the domination of 'classics' by traditional philology. (The pioneering work of the Oxford scholar John **Beazley** (1885–1970) on Greek vases drew both on technical art history and on connoisseurship; see chapter 3.) The development of classics in England is reflected in the metamorphosis of the *Classical Review* from a 'review' in the Victorian sense – a cultural journal, like the great literary reviews – to a journal devoted to scholarly reviews of academic books, written by members of a specialist body for each other.

Publication – now often a prime and mechanically measured indicator of academic achievement – has long constituted an important aspect of classical scholarship, though some genres are now almost defunct – for example, the polemical 'letter', like Bentley's *Epistola ad Millium* (1695). Not surprisingly in a field where much of the evidence lies in ancient texts composed in dead languages, the commentary has been a thriving genre, and has recently become an object of study in its own right (Gibson and Kraus, *Classical Commentary*). A few outstanding commentaries have themselves become classics: an example is Wilamowitz's on Euripides' *Heracles*. Others include Gildersleeve's edition of Pindar (1885), the Sophocles (1883–96) of Sir Richard **Jebb**, and the edition of Euripides' *Bacchae* (1944, 2nd edn 1960) by E. R. Dodds (1893–1979). Just why these books have lasted while others are forgotten is a question worth pondering, not least for anyone who contemplates an edition. Another enduring genre is that of the reference work; here pride of place must go to the *Real-Enzyklopädie der Altertumswissenschaft* (first published 1839–52, revised edition 1893–1978 – a Wolfian enterprise, but broader and more inclusive), but the great lexica should not be forgotten: the *Thesaurus Linguae Latinae* (issued on CD-ROM in 2002) and the *Thesaurus Linguae Graecae* (issued on CD-ROM in 1992, with later updates). The dictionaries of Liddell and Scott (1843) and Lewis and Short (1846) were also collaborative efforts, but of only two authors; though in both cases, others contributed to revised editions. The nineteenth-century dictionaries edited and partly written by William Smith (1813–93), beginning with the *Dictionary of Greek and Roman Antiquities* (1842), belong to a style of scholarship, centred on University College London, which was open to continental influences but free from the religious restrictions of Oxford and Cambridge. The term 'classics' itself, denoting the study of Graeco-Roman antiquity, as opposed to 'the classics' = classical literature, probably derives from the newly examining University of London (1836). 'Classics' is usually taken to include the whole of

Graeco-Roman antiquity, but its beginning and end dates as conventionally defined have varied, and have often been contested. And even within an agreed chronological range, some periods and areas have in practice often been marginalised or ignored. In the eighteenth century, Augustan Rome was seen as central to classical civilisation; by the mid-nineteenth, Periclean Athens had taken its place. In either case, the Hellenistic period and late antiquity received little attention. One of the notable features of twentieth-century scholarship was the opening up of these neglected periods, and also of areas like Egypt and Asia Minor. Modern ideological agendas have consciously turned away from the traditional centres of attention; similarly they have impelled the exploration of dark areas such as sexuality and, in the early twenty-first century, education. What needs to be remembered is that each generation's new illumination brings its own blindness.

Another notable development in scholarship has been the blurring of disciplinary boundaries. Within classics this has led to the bringing together of literary texts and epigraphic and archaeological material, which previously tended to be studied separately. Some scholars have also made contact with other disciplines and used their insights to interpret classical material. Anthropology, which had hardly emerged as a discipline in its own right by 1900, was already being drawn on by Jane **Harrison** in her *Prolegomena to the Study of Greek Religion* (1903) and *Themis* (1912). Her approach was left stranded by the development of anthropology away from history and psychology and towards fieldwork, but the connection was re-established by E. R. Dodds in his *The Greeks and the Irrational* (1951), and by Moses Finley in *The World of Odysseus* (1955). They were atypical of an increasingly specialised scholarly profession; as was Gilbert **Murray** (1866–1957), textual and literary critic, translator, man of the theatre, radio personality, psychic researcher and internationalist.

Harrison, as a woman, and Murray, as an Irish Australian, might be seen as outsiders, as might the powerfully influential New Zealander Ronald Syme (1903–89), especially in the historiography of Rome. The life and career of another outsider, Moses Finley, offer a stimulating yet chastening example to budding classical scholars. Born in New York City in 1912, he was a childhood prodigy, gaining a BA at Columbia at 15 and a PhD at 19 – neither degree being in classics. Involvement with the exiled members of the Frankfurt School of neo-Marxists and editorial work on social science publications broadened his theoretical and practical horizons, and he was encouraged by W. F. Westermann of Columbia to work on ancient slavery. Forced by the McCarthy witch-hunts of the early 1950s to leave the USA, he settled in Cambridge, where his methodological acumen and comparativist analysis came as a breath of fresh air. The example of Finley's influence reminds us of the role of outsiders in shaking up home traditions – wherever 'home' might be. The outstanding example is that of the refugees from Nazi Germany in the 1930s, who injected the values and learning of the later generation of the *Altertumswissenchaft* tradition into British (and especially Oxford) classics. Men like Charles Brink, Eduard **Fraenkel**, Felix **Jacoby**, Paul Maas and Rudolf Pfeiffer brought the intensity and weight of German scholarship into contact (and sometimes collision) with the more urbane and amateur style of Oxford and Cambridge.

The present and future of the past

Where does the discipline stand now? It has survived batterings both from state intervention (e.g. the National Curriculum of 1988, which removed classics from the official map of knowledge) and from the near-disappearance of linguistic teaching in schools. The successive waves of postmodernist theory have been digested, and in some cases excreted. It is notable that Latinists have been especially receptive to literary theory, Hellenists to anthropology. Tensions between literary theory and philological tradition persist, as do those between an introspective professional style and a popularist engagement with contemporary culture. This latter has been buoyed up by the increased popularity of classical literature in translation and especially by modern productions of Greek drama. Poets like Tony Harrison, Ted Hughes, Christopher Logue and Derek Walcott have engaged at length with classical literature. The ancient world is much in evidence in radio, television and film. All these areas have much to offer classical scholars, who can both find avenues for talking about the ancient world, and experience (and play with) the cultural resonances of their work and its objects (see chapter 11).

Is classics one discipline or many? One traditional justification for classics is that it is not a discipline, but a field in which many disciplines interact. There is much to be said for this, remembering that the definition of 'discipline' is itself often ideologically saturated. Classics no longer has a stable home in elite culture or as a bulwark of a religious establishment, but it may well have a future in which rigorous analysis is at home with an engagement with contemporary culture and the expanding and accessible resources of the web. Why, finally, should we study the history of 'the discipline'? Because it is part of a wider history which also deserves to be studied. And because the record of past achievements, failures and disagreements helps us to put our own work usefully in perspective – just as contemporary comparison does, both within and across disciplines.

Further reading

NB: Names in bold type are of scholars with entries in Briggs and Calder.

W. Arrowsmith, 'Nietzsche: notes for "We Philologists",' *Arion* n.s. 1.2 (1973/4), 279–380 – still the best guide for classicists wishing to examine their navels and/or consciences.

W. W. Briggs and W. M. Calder III (eds), *Classical Scholarship: A Biographical Encyclopedia*, New York: Garland, 1990 – variable quality, and some surprising omissions, but on the whole a useful and detailed source, with bibliographies.

C. O. Brink, *English Classical Scholarship: Historical Reflections on Bentley, Porson and Housman*, Cambridge: Clarke, 1985 – a detailed study by a scholar who identified with the 'philological' tradition; includes a chapter on Victorian amateur classics. The author's early attachment to Hegel is reflected in occasionally cloudy prose.

R. K. Gibson and C. S. Kraus, *The Classical Commentary: Histories, Practices and Theory*, Leiden: Brill, 2002 – a collection which gives a wide range of perspectives on the why and how of writing commentaries, with a thoughtful introduction.

S. Marchand, *Down from Olympus: Archaeology and Philhellenism in Germany, 1750–1970*, Princeton: Princeton University Press, 1999 – a detailed study of the German archaeological projects, largely in Asia Minor, putting them in political and ideological context.

R. Pfeiffer, *History of Classical Scholarship: From the Beginnings to the End of the Hellenistic Age*, Oxford: Clarendon Press, 1968 – the standard and authoritative treatment; weak on institutional traditions and thin on the final period.

R. Pfeiffer, *History of Classical Scholarship from 1300 to 1850*, Oxford: Clarendon Press, 1976.

C. A. Stray, *Classics Transformed: Schools, Universities, and Society in England 1830–1960*, Oxford: Oxford University Press, 1998 – examines the shift from amateur to professional scholarship, the role of classical knowledge in social exclusion, and some neglected subjects such as school textbooks.

R. B. Todd (ed.), *Dictionary of British Classicists, 1500–1960* (3 vols), Bristol: Thoemmes Continuum, 2004 – aims to be comprehensive, including minor names not listed elsewhere.

F. M. Turner, *The Greek Heritage in Victorian Britain*, New Haven: Yale University Press, 1971 – a detailed and systematic study of the role of ancient Greece in Victorian culture and society. Especially good on political philosophy.

C. Winterer, *The Culture of Classicism: Ancient Greece and Rome in American Intellectual Life, 1780–1910*, Baltimore: Johns Hopkins University Press, 2001 – a crisp and well-organised survey, useful for orientation and for comparison with Britain.

2. *History*

Alastair Blanshard

History's greatest rival is imagination. Although many historians disagree (often violently) about what constitutes history, almost all would agree that history is not fiction. It is easy to underestimate the importance of this, seemingly obvious, statement. For example, such a distinction influences the range and format of the stories that can pass for history. It has been crucial in determining where ancient history has been generated, by whom it has been practised, and how it has been consumed. It has led to the denigration of projects not rooted in true fact (e.g. counterfactual history). As a by-product, it has meant that statements that are included in histories are often uncritically accepted as true.

This desire to escape fanciful speculation lies at the centre of most of the problems for, and disputes in, the discipline of ancient history. The historian who wishes to write a true history, or even a plausible one, faces a problem. Although Nietzsche overstates the case when he claims that 'there are no facts, only interpretation', it is soon apparent to the historian that our 'facts' about the ancient world fall far short of being able to provide us with a coherent narrative of its events, places and people. The response to this deficiency from historians has traditionally been twofold. First, they have attempted to ensure that the information they have at their disposal is complete and accurate. Material (both texts and objects) needs to be correctly collected, described and understood. Second, historians have attempted to develop a series of rules ('a methodology') for filling in the gaps in this information. These two processes have constantly fed into each other, driving innovation and promoting further scholarship. New material prompts advances in methodology, while advances in methodology help us to understand new and old material correctly.

So far, this discussion of history has pretended that ancient history occurs in an isolated environment, where the rules of the game are set by a group of dispassionate individuals committed to the same agenda to the same degree. However, we lose an important dimension of the practice of the ancient historian if we pretend that it has only been (or currently is) an intellectual endeavour purely to seek the truth. The truthful understanding of the classical past may be the ancient historian's stated goal, but the pursuit of that goal has been driven by fashion, politics and economics. Radically different subjects, stories and conclusions have been, at different times and places, in practical terms what constitutes ancient history. This state of affairs is not the result of historians lessening their commitment to truth or abandoning their senses. The greatest mistake that historians of scholarship can make is to assume that their subjects are fools or shysters. Rather, it is a recognition of the fact that one of the greatest influences on the truth is acceptability. Truth is unlikely to be recognised (or, as more radical thinkers would argue, produced) unless it falls within the expectations of its audience. This doesn't mean that ancient history has always produced narratives that are popular or conventional. Rather, it recognises that there are limits imposed by society on ancient history, and that these limits may change over time. Perhaps part of the hostility that history has borne towards fiction has stemmed from this similarity. Like fiction, ancient history has a market.

The raw materials of ancient history

The collection, description and systematisation of ancient material are tasks that occupy many ancient historians. The impetus for this task came from a realisation that the surviving works from antiquity that are conventionally called 'histories' are inadequate sources for the modern historian.

Despite the enormous debt that modern historians owe to the histories written by Herodotus, Thucydides, Livy and Tacitus, their histories all exhibit features that make them unable to stand as the complete and definitive encapsulation of their periods (see chs 49, 50). They are inevitably selective in the subject matter that they treat. The value-system of the author and his time ensures that large segments of the population (e.g. women and slaves) are rarely mentioned. Demands of style and genre mean that elements such as speeches are almost never verbatim quotations of speakers, but rather artful products that are considered fitting for the moment. Personal and cultural biases influence description of events, actions and characters. Ignorance about the processes of the natural world often leads to misleading descriptions of events and attribution of causes. For example, it is almost impossible, despite numerous attempts, to work out from the description of symptoms in ancient authors the precise pathogen involved in outbreaks of plague (e.g. Thuc. 2.49) or identify the toxin in descriptions of poisoning. Disease and poisoning no doubt occurred. For example, medical archaeology increasingly points towards the important impact of malaria on the ancient world. However, even at the level of straight reportage of observable symptoms, we see the accounts of our ancient witnesses coloured by their own beliefs and expectations. Although, as we shall see, often these 'mistakes' are useful to the historian in developing an idea about the system of beliefs that underpin the classical world, it is undeniable that their first effect was to increase suspicion over the reliability of historians in antiquity. The harder we look at these texts, the more we realise that writing history in the classical past is a very different project from that practised by the modern historian.

This sense of disillusionment with the ancient historians ushered in the era of 'scientific approaches' to history. Prior to this period, the writing of ancient history had largely consisted of the abridgement of the most prominent classical authors. As suspicion grew over the reliability of these authorities, it became important to 'prove' or 'disprove' the existence of their claims. This discussion of 'proof' is not accidental. The vocabulary of this movement was largely derived from science, whose standards of accuracy became the benchmark for this new history. This movement is often associated with nineteenth-century German scholarship. However, this attribution to Germany overstates the case. As diaries, letters and lecture notes reveal, the movement had adherents in every major European capital. Under this movement the quantity and quality of sources became important criteria for historical scholarship. The ideal was independent corroboration by a reliable source. The establishment of the dual criteria of independence and reliability became the aim of scholarly endeavour.

The pursuit of these two elements drove historians both inward towards the close study of texts and outward towards the collection of new material. The study of historical texts became an imperative. It was believed that truth lay behind these texts. All one needed to do was make allowances for the biases and distortions of the author, and the truth would be revealed. Coupled with an examination of an author's bias was an interest in his sources. As a preliminary step to revealing the truth that lay behind the accounts, scholars attempted to reconstruct the texts that these authors had digested. The priority in time of these earlier historians was often translated into a priority in believability. In addition, the study of sources allowed historians to trace competing traditions, and could be used to weed out corrupt ones. A similar process had been undertaken in biblical scholarship, and its successful results proved encouraging to ancient historians. Genealogical trees were established for individual narratives. Texts were filleted to construct collections of fragmentary historians. Indeed, the overzealous nature of much of this work has recently been the focus of scholarly concern. Historians have realised that a lot of this initial work was too confident in its ability to ferret out the works of earlier historians. The attribution of fragments to authors and works was often based on only very thin knowledge of an author and the genres in which he worked. Additionally, the quest for fragments has often blinded historians to the sophistication of the later texts (see chapter 33). Rather than just being repositories of other texts, these works have come increasingly to be seen as artful constructions that skilfully knit these pieces (often with considerable tweaking) into complex arrangements that speak to their own time and place.

As well as looking inward onto the historical texts, the desire for corroboration led to the search for other sources to confirm the picture provided by the literary texts. Documentary evidence (coins, papyri, inscriptions etc.) was prized because it was conceived as lacking rhetorical exaggeration (see chapters 25, 32 and 34). Likewise, archaeology was valued for its ability to provide material that was unmediated by personal bias. However, in all these cases, such information was ancillary to the main texts. Ideally, they provided footnotes to confirm the picture of the historians. When they gave an alternate view, it was particularly troubling. Moreover, the tendency for literary histories to set the agenda meant that periods for which there were strong pre-existing historical narratives were privileged over periods and regions for which there was no literary history. Thus, fifth-century Athens and late Republican and early imperial Rome dominated the output of narrative histories. It was only in the mid- to late-twentieth century that this attitude of subservience to literary histories started to dissipate. Archaeology was the first discipline to break away and renegotiate its position with literary texts. The realisation, derived from the experience of prehistoric and non-classical archaeology, that classical archaeology could in itself provide complete and sufficient narratives of historical change meant that the discipline was freed from dependence on literary sources (see chapter 3). Similarly, we have seen the study of papyri, inscriptions and coins develop into disciplines, all based on an appreciation that the objects under examination are valuable materials in their own right with their own particular rules of composition and problems of interpretation. This revaluation of material has in turn led to an expansion in the chronological range of historical investigation. With the agenda no longer set by literary texts, it is possible to focus on periods that are poor in literary sources, but rich in other material such as archaeological remains (e.g. 'Dark Age' Greece; see chapter 15) or inscriptional evidence (e.g. the Hellenistic kingdoms; see chapter 17).

In practice the establishment of a verifiably true history has been much harder than scholars initially believed. Part of the problem has been that 'truth' has proved a much more difficult concept than first thought. Increasingly scholars realised that it was impossible to treat human affairs as if they were some branch of physics or chemistry. A number of the questions that historians have traditionally asked have proved impossible to answer. Some questions have failed because they require access to criteria that are impossible to establish. For example, questions such as 'Who was responsible for the outbreak of the Peloponnesian War?' or 'Was Nero a "bad" emperor?' immediately involve the interrogator in insoluble difficulties. The first question requires us to establish with certainty issues of causation, responsibility and intention. Can we usefully speak of Athens and Sparta intending anything? Or should we limit our discussion to specific groups or individuals? To what extent could anybody foresee the consequences of their actions? In such a complex set of events, how should we apportion responsibility? Finally, even if we could determine responsibility, what would that tell us about ancient Greece? The second question is no easier. Once again we find ourselves involved in further questions involving the establishment of evaluative criteria, the weighing-up of competing interests, and the attribution of responsibility for actions (e.g. 'How much credit or blame should we give to an emperor for events in his reign?'). Even questions of fact have proved difficult either because they often require us to be able to read an individual's mind (e.g. 'Did Alexander consider himself a god?'), or because accurate data were never collected (e.g. 'How successful was Augustan moral legislation?'), or because the issue is such that any individual who would know the answer couldn't be trusted to speak truthfully (e.g. 'Did Messalina cuckold Claudius?'). The realisation that no matter how closely we study the pieces, we will be unable to answer a large number of historical questions has led a number of historians to change or adapt their approach. First, there has been a realisation that we will only ever succeed in answering certain questions about the ancient world, and we need to think very carefully about the types of questions that we want answered. Second, the reconstruction of the ancient world must rely on an independently derived model. Evidence may be used to confirm, deny or modify the model, but the chances of evidence 'speaking for itself' are slim.

Fitting the pieces together

One of the important developments in the study of ancient history was the realisation that it might be easier to study institutions and mentalities rather than individuals. Too often our sources lack the precision or the certainty required to study great men and deeds. In contrast, they are often invaluable witnesses to the cultural mores of their own time. Influential in developing this idea have been changes in the field of literary criticism.

Given the importance attached to texts in the discipline of classics it is not surprising that changes in the field of literary criticism should flow onto ancient history. Particularly influential has been the idea that language has less to do with conscious intervention by the author and rather should be viewed as a product of social forces and a reflection of systems of thought. At the same time, the concept of 'text' has been expanded to include not only literature, but also non-literary texts and artworks. Historians have been keen on such ideas because they expand the range of available sources to potentially every work of literature and art from the ancient world, and they also mean that elements previously thought to be problematic in sources (e.g. rhetorical exaggerations, overblown characterisation, dramatisation of narratives) now become just as valuable as unembellished statements of fact, perhaps even more so. Studying our sources from this angle involves a shift of focus. Suddenly, Livy becomes not a source for the early republican period, but rather a source for attitudes to the past in the early empire. Similarly, Herodotus stops being an authority on Egyptian and Scythian practices, and becomes an example of the complex series of negotiations whereby Greeks defined their ethnic identity. A similar story can be told about Strabo and his *Geography* in Rome.

Political movements have also been important for introducing categories beyond individuals onto the scholarly agenda. Socialism demanded that historians take an interest in non-elite groups. Feminism encouraged historians to seek out the history of women. This was a history that could not be effectively written purely by focusing on the few prominent women mentioned in our historical sources. Inevitably, scholars were forced to examine the life of 'ordinary' women, and the attitudes that they confronted and dealt with. The drive for homosexual equality ensured that the issue of sexuality in the ancient world could not be ignored. The dissection of racism, the fall-out of colonialism, and the politics of identity have meant that categories such as race, ethnicity and imperialism have all been the subject of historical investigation.

To satisfy these intellectual and political pressures a variety of methodologies has been employed. Most of these methodologies have been borrowed from other disciplines. In fact, one of the noticeable features of recent scholarship is the scarcity of historical methodologies that have been generated within ancient history. The recent trend has been for adaptation, rather than invention. Perhaps the one notable exception is prosopography, where scholars use onomastic evidence (i.e. evidence related to the study of names) to discuss regional and familial influence on affairs and individuals. Although the term is used in other disciplines, nothing quite like the practice of prosopography in Greek, and especially Roman, history exists outside the discipline of classics (see chapter 61).

Almost every discipline in the humanities has provided something useful to the field of ancient history. For example, military historians have benefited from developments in the study of war in other arenas of combat. In particular, the recent focus on the experience of battle in modern warfare has directed the study of ancient warfare away from the study of strategy to how battle was experienced by the hoplites and legionaries who conducted it. The weight of armour, the effect of wear and tear, the influence of nutrition, and even the trauma of combat have all now become important areas for understanding ancient battle. Similarly, legal historians have benefited from developments in social jurisprudence. Legal realism has encouraged them to look beyond law to how law was practised (see chs 57 and 58). Historians of religion have benefited from developments in their field that have collapsed previously rigid distinctions such as Christian/pagan, religion/magic and superstition/belief (see chapter 4).

Beyond such subject-specific contributions, some developments have had a wider and more general impact on the field. Models derived from the social sciences have proven invaluable in creating a framework for understanding some of the pressures that were placed on ancient populations. An important breakthrough was the realisation that irrespective of cultural conditions, certain fundamentals must have operated in the ancient world. Populations experience birth and death in a predictable manner. Each human being requires a minimum number of calories to survive. Land is able to produce certain numbers of crops. Food generates a fixed number of calories. Using such basic information, it is possible to calculate maximum and minimum populations as well as predict survival pressures that will influence the form that cultures take and the decisions that they will make. The application of certain economic fundamentals allows us to make similar predictions about trade, population movements and deployment of resources. The complexity of such arrangements may be debatable; their existence is not (see chapter 5).

While such studies have been useful in establishing the broad outline of societies, they are less helpful in understanding the behaviour that makes cultures distinctive. For example, demographic models may tell us that it will be unusual to have parents surviving into old age, and that orphans will be common. Yet this information will not explain the particular form that arrangements for adoption and guardianship took in the Graeco-Roman world. Nor will it explain why Greek adoption differs so much from Roman adoption. We may make plausible guesses about male and female life expectancies and fertility rates, but this will tell us nothing about the nature of Greek or Roman marriage or the ceremonies used to mark the event.

In order to understand the distinctive and peculiar, scholars have regularly sought answers through comparative anthropology. By looking for cultures with similar rituals or ideologies, it is possible to gain insight into rituals or living arrangements that appear initially opaque. Ultimately, the success or failure of such a project depends on the appropriateness of the example chosen as the comparison. A number of societies, particularly in the Mediterranean, seem to share important features with the cultures of Greece and Rome (e.g. the importance of honour and shame, a strong distinction between public and private, and a well-demarcated gender division). However, no culture exactly replicates classical Greece and Rome, and anthropological approaches have been criticised for their tendency to reduce antiquity to pale simulacra of pre-existing cultures.

All models enjoy a constant state of refinement. However, the issue of individuals and their actions remains a problem. For example, we may know everything about the life expectancy, ritual outlook and social expectations of the Roman male, but Augustus remains an enigma, still capable of polarising views. Perhaps the greatest challenge awaiting historians is understanding individuals within a broad structural framework. We still await an approach to command universal acceptance that combines a sense of individual agency with an appreciation of the complexity of the power and influence of societal ideology.

Further reading

M. Bettini, *Anthropology and Roman Culture: Kinship, Time, Images of the Soul*, Baltimore: Johns Hopkins University Press, 1991.

M. I. Finley, *The Use and Abuse of History*, London: Chatto and Windus, 1975 – an important collection of essays that encourage critical thinking about writing about the ancient past.

M. I. Finley, *Ancient History: Evidence and Models*, London: Chatto and Windus, 1985.

K. Hopkins, 'Rules of evidence', *Journal of Roman Studies* 68 (1978), 178–86 – a provocative review that set the agenda for the sociological study of the Roman world.

S. C. Humphreys, *Anthropology and the Greeks*, London: Routledge and Kegan Paul, 1978 – a work that pioneered the application of modern anthropological techniques to the Greek world.

A. Momigliano, *Essays in Ancient and Modern Historiography*, Oxford: Blackwell, 1977 – a series of essays which established Momigliano as one of the important critics of the practice of ancient history.

A. Momigliano, *The Classical Foundations of Modern Historiography*, Berkeley and Oxford: University of California Press, 1990.

N. Morley, *Writing Ancient History*, London: Duckworth, 1999 – a useful introduction that addresses a large number of the issues involved in writing ancient history.

T. P. Wiseman (ed.), *Classics in Progress: Essays on Ancient Greece and Rome*, Oxford: Oxford University Press, 2002. See esp. ch. 4 by R. R. R. Smith, 'The use of images: visual history and ancient history', pp. 60–102, and ch. 9 by J. K. Davies, 'Greek history: a discipline in transformation', pp. 225–46.

3. Archaeology

James Whitley

The scope of classical archaeology

Archaeology is both a broad subject and an ambiguous term. A preliminary definition of archaeology as it affects the Greek and Roman worlds might be the study of all material evidence relating to the ancient world with a view to addressing historical questions. By historical questions I do not mean 'questions that arise through the study of our textual sources'; the fact that both archaeology and text-based history are primarily historical does not mean that the one is handmaiden to the other. Rather, both ancient texts and material evidence throw various kinds of oblique light on the history and culture of the ancient world. Often, text and material evidence do not make for a neat fit, and archaeology throws up some very strange cases indeed. What makes archaeology distinctive is the range of approaches and methods required to address such basic historical questions as 'how densely populated was classical Greece?' or 'what was the settlement pattern (and manpower) of late republican Italy?' Archaeology uses material means, and looks primarily at material evidence, to answer such questions. One thinks of such evidence as being recovered primarily from excavations, but in fact material from survey, scientific analyses and re-study of material in museums form an equally important part of archaeological research. 'Material evidence' is also usually taken to exclude that covered by the other material subdisciplines (numismatics, epigraphy, papyrology). But here there are ambiguities, since material evidence has both content and context. Traditionally, numismatists, epigraphers and papyrologists have attended strictly to the identification and the content of coins, inscriptions and papyri. Increasingly, however, such scholars are interested in context, and in this sense numismatics, papyrology and epigraphy are becoming more archaeological (see chs 25, 32 and 34).

If archaeology is an ambiguous term, classical archaeology is now a contested one. The term itself implies that there is something essentially different about the material evidence from Greece and Rome that distinguishes it from European prehistory on the one hand and the archaeology of the Near East on the other. The traditional subjects of classical archaeology (sculpture, public architecture, mosaics, gems, 'vases') constitute a class of objects superior to those studied by other archaeologies. The distinctiveness (and implied superiority) of classical archaeology is built into its basic terminology. There is a hierarchy of terms, and the more 'classical' a class of object, the more elevated the term. So, while both the British Iron Age and the Roman ceramic specialist deal in wares (haematite coated ware, Çandarli ware), experts on Greek painted pottery of the seventh to early third centuries BC study vases. Those of superior sensibility (if not sense) study not the vases themselves, but their surfaces – vase-painting.

But if classical archaeology has given the impression that it is a superior and rather exclusive club, it is one that many now seem eager to leave. The Aegean Bronze Age used to be thought of as part of 'classical archaeology', its practitioners dealing with a similar class of objects (frescoes, palaces, engraved gems). Increasingly, however, younger scholars of this period refer to themselves as Aegean prehistorians, and find they have more in common with European prehistorians or scholars of 'complex societies' in Mesopotamia or Mesoamerica than they do with experts in fifth-century Attic vase-painting. Similarly, specialists in the northwest provinces of the Roman Empire feel less and less inclined to affirm that Roman Britain was a part of the classical world, but rather seek to open up a dialogue with British prehistorians as to the likely effects on a conquered people of incorporation into a cosmopolitan empire. Colonisers and empire-builders are now viewed with suspicion, and terms such as 'romanisation' and 'hellenisation', once processes thought to be natural, inevitable and good, have become problematic.

All this is to say that classical archaeology is losing its innocence. Such innocence was, of course, always slightly contrived. Neither classics nor classical archaeology can avoid wider intellectual currents that have questioned both the political and the intellectual foundations of their disciplines. Classical archaeology is facing something of a crisis of identity. Is the subject primarily a branch of classics or of archaeology? Should it deal with a defined universe of objects? Or should it be defined, not by its objects, but by its research questions and its research methods?

Classical archaeology and classical art history

One apparent solution to this dilemma is to engage in a 'rebranding' exercise by coining a new term, 'classical art history', and thereby affirming the traditional objects of classical archaeology. For many, 'classical art history' has the advantage of keeping the subject classical and within classics. Just as classics remains, for many, an endless subject with a totally definitive set of texts, so classical art history proposes a similarly definitive universe of classical 'art' objects to study, reinterpret and reevaluate. It also gives classical scholars more familiar with the study of literature leave to apply a variety of semiotic approaches to the interpretation of ancient art.

There are difficulties with this proposal, however. The first is that 'classical art history' demands an almost Orwellian rewriting of the history both of classics and of archaeology. J. J. Winckelmann, once regarded as the 'father of archaeology', becomes the father of art history, and J. D. Beazley, the great scholar responsible for the attribution of thousands of Attic and Etruscan black- and red-figure pots to individual painters unknown to the historical record, becomes a 'classical art historian'. This label is, to say the least, anachronistic. Beazley's art-historical contemporaries, Bernard Berenson and Erwin Panofsky, knew nothing of 'classical art history'. For them, Beazley and his contemporaries were either classical archaeologists or classical scholars.

The major difficulty with 'classical art history' is its arbitrariness. Art history deals with art, and how one abstracts a definitive universe of art objects from the mass of ancient material culture will necessarily be a subjective procedure. We cannot simply make use of the ancients' view of art, since they had no such concept, and, in so far as they selected out certain objects for study or appreciation, these objects are now either in a very fragmentary state, known only from copies or entirely lost. A 'classical art history' based on what ancient authors mentioned or appreciated could study the pediments of the Parthenon, but not the metopes or the frieze. 'Classical art history' deals, on the one hand, with many more objects than the ancient authors considered, but far fewer than we actually have from the ancient world. It is not clear why, for example, Attic painted pottery for the most part falls within the purview of 'classical art history', but Hellenistic Megarian bowls and Roman *terra sigillata* do not. The decision is based on nothing more than arbitrary aesthetic judgement and inherited prejudice. There is, in truth, no rational principle for distinguishing between art and material culture. Since all art is material culture, and not all material culture is art, the only rational solution is to accept that 'classical art history' is no more than an aspect of classical archaeology.

What form should classical archaeology then take? There is no single answer to this question. But it is clear that the major challenge facing ancient history and archaeology today is to cope with the explosion of new information about the ancient world that has come to light in recent years. Most of this new information is archaeological, and it really does change the picture quite radically. To take one example: until the mid-1970s, ancient Macedon was little explored and the emergence of a powerful Macedonian monarchy was a quite mysterious process. Since then Balkan politics, the energy and commitment of such figures as Manolis Andronikos (former Professor of Archaeology at the University of Thessalonike and excavator of Vergina, ancient Aegae) and Julia Vokotopoulou (former Director of the Archaeological Museum of Thessalonike), and a huge programme of rescue excavation in advance of road-building have all combined to expand our information about Iron Age, archaic and classical Macedon quite enormously. The inconclusive debate about the identity of the person buried in 'Philip's tomb' at Vergina should not obscure the major facts that have emerged. First, there are many more cemeteries in Macedon than in southern Greece, and the cemeteries are generally richer in finds, especially in the archaic period. Second, there are correspondingly fewer sanctuaries, and far fewer metal votives. Third, a kind of 'weapon burial ritual' survives in Macedon when it has disappeared in southern Greece, and such a ritual remains a particularly important aspect of royal burials. Fourth, Macedonian houses of the late fourth century (such as those at Pella) are much grander and more richly decorated than those further south. Now, of course, it could be argued by the committed 'textual' historian that none of these new facts actually settles anything – that is, none of them arbitrates decisively one way or another on the issues that have, so far, engaged the scholarly energy of historians. But that is to miss the point. Such facts emphasise the great social, cultural and political gulf that divided the northern and southern Aegean. However we may wish to interpret them, any new social history of archaic and classical Macedon would have to seek to explain them. It is in this way that ancient history becomes more archaeological and less textual.

Space and context

It is for reasons such as these that a convergence of interests have developed between archaeologically minded historians and historically minded archaeologists. And indeed many of the more promising new developments in the study of ancient material culture have been initiated by historians. The primary purpose of Andrew Wallace-Hadrill's study of Pompeian houses is to investigate *domestic space*, that is the social dimensions of how and why houses are so designed. The study of architecture, wall-painting and other finds is thereby integrated with textual evidence to produce a new kind of social history. These themes have been taken up by classical archaeologists working on Greek material such as Lisa Nevett. Such an integrated approach to houses requires that greater attention be paid to *context*. A wall painting or a mosaic floor can no longer be considered as simply decoration. Similarly, the decision taken by numerous Roman aristocrats of the first century AD to furnish their houses with marble copies of the bronze statue of Demosthenes by Polyeuktos is of more than passing political interest.

This is all part of a wider trend in the study of ancient material culture and art: the greater emphasis given to *context*, whether that context is political, social or archaeological. So scholars of classical art now pay much more attention to the setting of, let us say, the pediments and metopes of the temple of Zeus at Olympia than they did before. The sculptures of the Parthenon (chryselephantine cult statue, frieze, metopes and pediments) are seen as an ensemble, whose 'meaning' can to some degree be interpreted by cross-referencing between themes and images on each of its various parts. Similarly, new interpretations of the 'meaning' of Orientalising pottery in seventh-century BC Attica or Corinth have paid much more attention to the archaeological context in which it was found, and new interpretations of well-known archaic statues, such as the Anavyssos *kouros* or the *korē* inscribed 'Phrasikleia', pay much greater regard not only to the setting of such statues, but to the relationship between statue and inscription.

It is, however, the political and social context that has received most attention from scholars of Attic black- and red-figure pottery. Sometimes simple correlations are sought between, let us say, the frequency of portrayals of Heracles on sixth-century Attic pots and the political interests of the tyrant Pisistratus; images of women on red-figure and white-ground vases are scrutinised to yield a variety of interpretations as to the status of 'wives, whores and maidens' in classical Athens; and, at other times, more 'nuanced' readings of complex scenes are held to provide insights into the emergence of Athenian democracy. Such interpretations are supported by considerations of the social setting of the pots based on their shape (that is, the symposium in the case of 'political' images), but unfortunately often wilfully ignore the actual archaeological contexts (findspots) of the pots they discuss; for many of the best, or at least the most discussed, examples of archaic and classical Attic painted pots have been found, not near Athens, but in Italy, particularly Etruria. Such evidence ought to raise a whole host of questions, not merely about the nature of 'trade' in painted pottery, but also about what we understand by the process of 'hellenisation' in the Mediterranean. Anthropological studies of material culture have underscored the fact that pots and their images are never simply 'commodities'; rather, they are vehicles for cultural ideas and a range of cultural competences (of which the ability to 'read' images along with inscriptions may be the most important). Certain basic questions about the nature of the relationship between Etruscan consumers and Attic producers remain to be addressed. Were Etruscans simply ignorant consumers, grateful for any 'Hellenic' product they could lay their hands on? Or did Etruscan demand affect, to some degree, both the shapes and images that Attic painters and potters produced? Such questions can only be addressed by a more rigorous consideration of the final *contexts* of such pots. Such work has barely begun (see chapter 28).

Archaeology and identity

The Etruscan appropriation of the Greek 'symposium package' was only one of the ways in which material culture mediated the negotiation of identities (class, gender, political and ethnic) in the Mediterranean world, and this too is a developing theme in archaeological research. It has long been recognised that the Greek appropriation of Near Eastern ideas, images and technologies (of which alphabetic literacy is the most important) – what we call the 'Orientalising' process – was a creative one, but it is only recently that this recognition has been extended to other Mediterranean peoples. Only in the past few years have striking variations between the regions of Attica, Euboea, Corinth and Crete in the course of this 'Orientalising' clearly emerged, and only recently has it become clear that the 'Orientalising' never really stopped. Athenians continued to appropriate aspects of Persian material culture even in the fifth century BC. The politics of the Near East have impeded research into the opposite process of 'hellenisation' in the areas conquered by Alexander the Great; the spectacularly 'Greek' site of Aï Khanum in Afghanistan remains in splendid isolation (see chapter 23). 'Romanisation' by contrast has received a great deal of attention. Here again there is much variation. The material expression of 'becoming Roman' in Italy in the third to first centuries BC differed in important respects from the 'romanisation' of the northwest provinces of the Roman Empire, such as Britain, a province divided quite sharply into military and civilian zones. Particular ambiguities arise in the 'romanisation' of Greece and Asia Minor. The Roman appropriation of, and respect for, Greek art and the Greek past led to considerable regional variations in 'romanisation'. Especially under the Antonine and Severan emperors, the Greek past in Athens, Sparta and the plain of Troy was 'improved' – touched up in order more closely to resemble what it ought to have been. The modification of Greek theatres at Dodona and Philippi to accommodate beast fights and gladiatorial contests, by contrast, demonstrates the victory of the Roman present over the Greek past in early imperial Epirus and Macedonia.

The sine qua non of any such 'archaeology of identities', and indeed of any attempt to draw inferences about long-distance transactions by archaeological means, is to separate the local from the exotic. Ideally, we should be able to distinguish products in all materials, from metalwork to glass to stone. In practice, however, traditional methods of typology and attribution are most successful when the material is abundant, that is, with pottery. Here much had been achieved by the early 1970s, particularly with Greek pottery of archaic and classical date and the various production centres (Italian and Gaulish) of Roman *terra sigillata*. Pots could often be pinned down to the individual workshop, potter or painter. Recently attention has concentrated on Hellenistic and Late Roman pottery, and on plain wares of various dates, giving us a ceramic sequence of fine wares that covers the whole of antiquity. In the early 1970s, however, it became clear that there were some questions of provenance that traditional methods could not answer. Were the abundant archaic fine wares found at the Greek *emporion* at Naucratis in Egypt local products, or imports from Chios? Similarly, were the 'Hadra *hydriae*', the characteristic cinerary urn of Hellenistic Alexandria, local products or imports? In principle, such questions could be answered though chemical analyses of the fabrics, making comparisons with the chemical 'signature' of defined clay beds. In both cases, it was established that both classes of objects were in fact imports (the Hadra *hydriae* were made in Crete). Such work became the particular strength of the Fitch Laboratory of the British School at Athens, which also began to look more closely at coarse wares. Chemical analysis here is less useful than ceramic petrology, the close scrutiny of the mineral inclusions, often looked at through thin sections. Particular advances have been made in recent years in understanding the economy of the Bronze Age Aegean palace states (states which invested heavily in ceramic storage) by such means.

Archaeology and landscape

Good local ceramic sequences are also absolutely essential for that other area of endeavour in which Mediterranean archaeology excels: surface survey. Survey began as an extension of topographical exploration, and developed from two basic observations; ancient pottery survives in large quantities on ancient sites, and surface pottery can often be used to date sites. Survey rapidly became the primary means of understanding changing patterns of settlement through time, and thereby of addressing demographic issues (see chapter 23). There was a time in the early 1980s when almost every valley in northern and central Italy was being studied by a British or American survey team. Projects such as the south Etruria survey revealed a huge increase in rural sites (variously interpreted as *villae rusticae* or *latifundia*) in late republican and early imperial times. It was in Greece, however, that the major methodological advances took place. During the late 1970s and 1980s, in Ceos, the southern Argolid and Boeotia, survey became both more systematic and more intensive, as it was appreciated that small sites could often be missed and that the carpet of 'background' material was something that had to be explained. In Greece too survey has had a major impact on our view of ceramic evidence, and has provided a major stimulus for a closer examination of coarse wares. So, in Crete for example, the sequence of painted fine wares which has engaged so much of the attention of traditional 'Minoan' archaeologists is of limited use in survey archaeology. What survey archaeologists need is rather a sequence, based on shape and fabric, of the coarse 'cooking wares'. Consequently most current survey projects try to produce their own fabric sequence, and this has yielded impressive results in at least one case. It is now possible to arrive at relatively precise dates, based largely on the study of their fabrics, for the prehistoric coarse wares found on the Kythera project. This is an example of how advances in ceramic petrology and survey go hand in hand.

Poleis and prospects

Survey has also stimulated an interest in landscape archaeology, and attempts at explaining why sites are where they are. Particular attention has been focused on the location of sacred sites, and the emergence of 'sacred place' in both Greece and Italy in the archaic period. Here the terms of the debate have been set by a historian, François de Polignac. De Polignac has argued that early sanctuaries are often placed on borderlands, in two senses of that term; a 'symbolic' border, between land and sea or between the wild and the sown; or a political border, at the very limit of a city's territory (see chapter 23). De Polignac's work also signals a new interest in 'phenomenological' approaches to landscape by both historians and archaeologists.

De Polignac's arguments also mesh with those of archaeologists interested in explaining the rise of 'polis states' in the Iron Age Mediterranean. Analytical techniques and arguments familiar to the 'social archaeologist' of European prehistory have been applied to Greek and Italian cemeteries. So Ian Morris has argued that the differing absolute numbers and proportions of adult and child graves in Early Iron Age and archaic cemeteries in Athens reflect not so much demographic change as differing principles of inclusion or exclusion, through which we can detect the emergence of a 'polis ideology'. Similar kinds of analyses (if not similar arguments) have been applied to Early Iron Age and archaic cemeteries in Etruria, Latium and Campania, notably M. Bietti Sestieri's work on the cemetery of Osteria dell'Osa. Despite this, comparative work on the similarities and differences between the emergence of 'states' in Iron Age Greece and Italy on the one hand, and between the palaces of the Aegean Bronze Age and the 'poleis' of the Aegean Iron Age on the other, has been notable by its absence.

In many primers on archaeology and histories of archaeological thought, classical archaeology is often treated as a strange relic, a living fossil, as it were, of eighteenth-century antiquarianism. There are, to be sure, areas where classical archaeologists need to make better use of scientific techniques. Faunal and seed analyses have yet to become routine in the excavations of classical sites; radiocarbon and dendrochronology remain underused; and the full potential of new techniques such as micromorphology (essential for defining 'activity areas' within houses) or lipid analysis (for identifying the contents of transport amphoras) remain to be realised. But, if classical archaeology is in some ways a problematic field, it is also a uniquely lively one, and one that is at least as innovative as any other branch of archaeology or classics.

Further reading

S. E. Alcock and R. Osborne (eds), *Placing the Gods: Sanctuaries and Sacred Space in Ancient Greece*, Oxford: Clarendon Press, 1994 – a very important collection of papers that applies and also critiques de Polignac's ideas.

J. F. Cherry, 'Archaeology beyond the site: regional survey and its future', in J. K. Papadopoulos and R. M. Leventhal (eds), *Theory and Practice in Mediterranean Archaeology: Old World and New World Perspectives*, Los Angeles: Cotsen Institute of Archaeology, University of California, 2003, pp. 311–18 – the most recent and complete overview of the impact of survey on Mediterranean archaeology and the future prospects for this technique.

T. Cullen (ed.), *Aegean Prehistory: A Review* (American Journal of Archaeology Supplement 1), Boston: Archaeological Institute of America, 2001 – an invaluable series of papers that summarises developments in studies of the Aegean Bronze Age since the mid-1980s.

O. Dickinson, *The Aegean Bronze Age*, Cambridge: Cambridge University Press, 1994 – the most authoritative synthesis of the Aegean Bronze Age.

M. Millett, *The Romanization of Britain: An Essay in Archaeological Interpretation*, Cambridge: Cambridge University Press, 1990 – a groundbreaking study of the effect of Roman rule in Britain that makes a clear break with the pro-imperialist accounts of earlier British writers.

I. M. Morris, *Burial and Ancient Society: The Rise of the Greek City State*, Cambridge: Cambridge University Press, 1987 – the most thorough attempt to apply sociological principles and statistics to specific archaeological and historical questions.

R. Osborne, *Archaic and Classical Greek Art*, Oxford: Oxford University Press, 1998 – differs from the standard accounts in trying to understand Greek art in its original and social setting.

T. W. Potter, *The Changing Landscape of South Etruria*, London: Paul Elek, 1979 – the earliest attempt to synthesise the results of survey and apply them to specific historical problems.

A. Wallace-Hadrill, *Houses and Society in Pompeii and Herculaneum*, Princeton: Princeton University Press, 1994 – the most systematic attempt to place Roman, particularly Pompeian, houses in a social context.

J. Whitley, *The Archaeology of Ancient Greece*, Cambridge: Cambridge University Press, 2001 – it does exactly what it says on the tin (it is not an 'art' book).

Note: Archaeological information about the Mediterranean world increases all the time. For summaries of the situation, especially in the Aegean, see *Archaeological Reports*, published annually as a supplement to the *Journal of Hellenic Studies*. *Archaeology in Greece* 2003–4, published in *Archaeological Reports*, gives details of how new finds are changing our picture of ancient Macedon.

4. Religion

Richard Gordon

To read Homer, Hesiod or Herodotus is to grasp that the religions of the Greeks – and Romans, for that matter – were seriously different projects from modern Christianities. The Archaic poet Hesiod, for example, names well over 1,100 Greek gods, nymphs and heroes, and could certainly have recounted a significant story about most of them, besides being able, had he been pressed, to name very many more; and Roman scholars of the late republican period, such as Varro and Granius Flaccus, were familiar with the names, and usual epithets, of hundreds of *indigitamenta*, spirits who oversaw the myriad tasks and incidents of everyday life, from Abeona Adeona to Vervactor. However, even if we could discover the names of all ancient divine beings – and no ordinary individual in antiquity knew more than a handful – we would only have established that polytheisms imagine many gods, which we knew already, and yet know nothing about how they functioned as religions.

Greek religion

There have been two main approaches to archaic and classical Greek religion since the 1960s, both building upon older ideas. The achievement of the Historical school is to have shown that significant features of polis-religion (inspection of the liver of sacrificial animals, foundation deposits, belief in the power of the dead over the living), as well as numerous myth-narratives, were introduced into the Greek world from the Near East during the archaic period, mainly by itinerant craftsmen and ritual experts. At the same time, it is agreed that we are unlikely ever to be in a position to retrace the processes by which the Greek pantheon, as represented by Homer and Hesiod, was constructed: the events themselves are too complex, the break between the Mycenaean age and the archaic period too complete. The achievement of the Paris school, on the other hand, has been to demonstrate the central place of animal sacrifice in the Greek imagination. Not only did sacrifice provide the normal means of communication between this world and the other world as well as constituting the core event of all festivities, but it enshrined a positive, rational and quasi-contractual relationship to that other world. This insight has effectively come to dominate modern approaches: Greek religion, and ancient religion more generally, are today seen primarily as a matter of action. Of course the divine world was more or less fully imagined, but it is ritual that formed the hinge between mental representations and the social order, and sustained the intensely and overtly instrumental character of the entire system.

The Greek religious system was 'embedded': it was not available as an object of inquiry for those whose lives it informed. They understood much more about what constituted *eusebeia*, conduct in conformity to the wishes of the gods, about *asebeia*, its inverse, and about *deisidaimonia*, 'superstition' – that is, unbecoming, unmanly behaviour in relation to the gods – than we ever can, and they certainly could think intelligently within the terms it offered, but, with the possible exception of the Cynics, even intellectuals such as Aristotle's pupil Theophrastus could not distance themselves from it further than to imagine that the religion of primitive times knew no blood-sacrifice. Such distance required the radical challenge of early Christianity: in the third century AD,

Neoplatonists such as Porphyry could argue that blood-sacrifice was actually a form of *asebeia*, action against the wishes of the gods. But they could not say so very loudly; and in public they continued to sacrifice as became members of their class.

We can think of Greek religion heuristically as a series of complex grids superimposed on one another. One grid is topographic: each city possessed its own unique sacred geography, arranged in a notional hierarchy from the main temple of the main divinity – Apollo at Corinth, Zeus Soter at Megalopolis – forming the ideal centre, down through lower-ranking civic temples for other Olympian divinities, to street-corner shrines to Heracles, say, or Hecate or Hygieia (Health), and out into the *chōra* (rural territory of a polis), with its smaller, humbler shrines, scattered in villages, along roads, and then out, away from the cultivated land, into the rough pasture-land and the mountains. Each such spot had its own anchorage in myth or myths. Sacred topography thus mapped a divine hierarchy, from high Olympian gods, to their restricted manifestations (such as Apollo Boedromios, who helped in law suits), to panhellenic heroes such as Heracles, and local (founder-)heroes, such as Battos at Cyrene, to stream- and meadow-nymphs. The rules for each such cult, its festivals, sacrifices and priesthoods, were commonly formalised in public decrees, inscriptions that provide some of our most important and detailed knowledge of Greek cult practice. Topography, but not cult, distinguished between Olympian and 'chthonian' divinities (the gods of the Underworld), and between Olympians and heroes (there were also demonic child-killing entities such as Mormo and Gello, and the 'undead', not associated with particular places or worshipped, but only placated as necessary). This civic grid could be transferred to colonies, thus marking their dependence upon the mother-city; and was itself notionally fitted, at least hazily, into a panhellenic grid, which acknowledged the ideal religious unity of Hellas – as represented schematically by the poems of Homer and Hesiod, and practically by the oracles of Dodona and Delphi, and the panhellenic games. It will thus be clear that the term 'Greek religion' is just a handy modern simplification (and anyway there is no Greek word for our term 'religion' – *thrēskeia*, for example, means 'cult').

The second grid is temporal: every cult place, high and low, became active through a calendar of ritual observances, sometimes associated with fairs or markets, throughout the year (or less frequently); these sacred calendars were often inscribed (see chapter 64), especially on the occasion of some alteration, and provide some of our most important evidence for Greek religious practice. This knowledge was likewise arranged in a hierarchy of accessibility: every citizen knew what was done at the great festivals of the high gods, but only the local initiate women knew, say, what went on in the cave of Rhea at Methydrion in Arcadia – or why. Except for that deployed by the major oracles, significant religious knowledge, precisely because it was practical and contextual, not theoretical or book-bound, was not the property of a restricted group of specialists but – at least in principle, which left room for a number of secret, unrevealed cults – the common possession of the adult male citizens.

The third grid is social, the traditional system of rules according to which civic cults are prior to, and model, those of subunits, including the family; aristocratic cults privileged over popular cults; male religious roles considered prior to those of women and children; citizens' roles prior to those of resident aliens and slaves. This grid, however, cannot be thought of as purely social: the cult of the nymphs, for example, linked landscapes (caves, mountains), genealogies, patterns of mythic narrative, women's rites of passage, and themes of wildness and domestication, destruction and fertility. In other words, it arranged important cultural themes into associative patterns; the cognitive sense it made could not be directly articulated in words, could only be communicated through ritual experience, music, dance and snatches of incidental narrative. Moreover, even a minor cult such as that of the nymphs has itself a complex history, extending from the archaic period into late antiquity.

Innovation, of divinities or cults, deemed to be compatible with the dominant politico-cultural interests was continual and unproblematic, which meant that the religious system could easily adjust to changing circumstances and perceived needs, for example by introducing specialist healing cults, such as that of Asclepius, at springs, hot or cold, which had always been there, but whose religious value, if marked at all, had been understood differently. The topographic grid could thus, as it were, be partially recomposed. Private innovation by individuals, especially by women and foreigners, could be, and often was, punished by execution or exile. There was no right of private conscience: the 'ancestral religion' was an intensely political matter, stoutly defended, as one of its essential domains, by the community of adult male citizens. Pollution, whether through crime, direct contact with the dead, sexual intercourse or some other cause, was the major threat posed by the individual to the divine order, and so to the social order it maintained – indeed pollution (not 'sin') is to be seen as the stress- or fault-line which best reveals the character of the entire system: pollution, the fears it aroused, and the misfortunes it provoked, are the obverse of the Homeric image of grandly talking, grandly feasting Olympians. The fact that in Greek cult the chief means of purification was sacrificial blood neatly makes the point that in religious contexts all meanings depend upon the system that generates them: we see the blood as filthy if not foul; the polluted Greek saw it as a means of liberation.

Roman religion

In its essentials, Roman religion worked in much the same manner as Greek: it too can be analysed mutatis mutandis in terms of these grids. But three further points must be made. First, thanks to Jerome's translation of the Bible into Latin, many key Roman religious terms, such as *religio*, *superstitio*, *sacer*, *religiosus*, *profanus*, *sanctus*, *pius*, *impius*, *caerimoniae* and *ritus*, also occur in English religious language, but in every case their meaning is significantly different. Second, the aristocratic character of the Roman political system ensured that control of the state always also meant control of the religious system by the Senate through the lawful actions and decisions of the magistrates and the major priestly colleges, the pontiffs, the augurs, and the *decemviri* (later *quindecimviri*). Third, the astonishing politico-military success of this regime, in subjecting first Italy and then the entire Mediterranean world to its rule, led to numerous attempts, formal and informal, to reproduce the religious system of Rome outside the *pomerium*, but finally, with the inauguration of the principate, there was nothing for it but to appeal to the ritual language of the cult of the emperors. From the Flavian period (late first century AD), worship of the living emperor(s) and the *divi* provided the hinge between the traditional religion of Rome and the innumerable religions of the cities and settlements of the empire.

Further reading

M. Beard, J. North and S. R. F. Price, *Religions of Rome* (2 vols), Cambridge: Cambridge University Press, 1998 – an outstanding illustrated history and sourcebook, but requires some previous knowledge.

L. Bruit Zaidman and P. Schmitt Pantel, *Religion in the Ancient Greek City*, trans. P. Cartledge, Cambridge: Cambridge University Press, 1992 – a brief, lively, presentation of the ideas of the Paris school.

S. I. Johnston (ed.), *Religions of the Ancient World: A Guide*, Cambridge MA: Harvard University Press, 2004 – an excellent thematic survey of Near Eastern, Greek, Etruscan and Roman religions, and early Christianity.

R. Lane Fox, *Pagans and Christians*, Harmondsworth and New York: Viking, 1986 – a well-written survey of later Graeco-Roman religion and Constantine's fateful endorsement of Christianity.

J. D. Mikalson, *Ancient Greek Religion*, Oxford: Blackwell, 2005 – a solid, illustrated introduction.

J. Rüpke, *Roman Religion*, Cambridge: Polity, 2007 – a more penetrating follow-up to Scheid's book.

J. Scheid, *An Introduction to Roman Religion*, trans. J. Lloyd, Edinburgh: Edinburgh University Press, 2003 – a clear, but rather static, account of the central themes and concepts of Roman religion.

5. Economy

Lisa Bligh

The economy forms just as fundamental a part of a society's structure as the political, social and cultural elements, so it is natural that historians should be interested in the economic basis of the ancient world. However, there are difficulties, chiefly provided by problematic source material and an acute sensitivity to previous work among contemporary scholars. In order to understand current approaches to this somewhat complicated field, it is necessary to appreciate both these issues fully.

The source material is problematic for two reasons. First, neither Greek nor Roman culture seems to have encouraged sophisticated economic thought or to have expressed it in complex terms. Ancient literary and documentary evidence chiefly provides lists of goods and services involved in commerce (e.g. Diocletian's Price Edict; see chapter 58) or highly superficial descriptions of economic and financial activity (e.g. Cicero *Att.* 5.21.10–13). It is therefore of limited use to us, because it is not even trying to convey the kind of detailed information that modern scholars need in order to make a proper assessment. Second, there is the abundant archaeological evidence (a wide range, from amphorae to factory sites). Correct interpretation of this material is both the key and the problem; unresolved issues are many and various. Commercial and industrial premises are difficult to identify and assess accurately, so the scale and nature of economic activity are hard to gauge. When an artefact is found at a distance from its probable point of production, was it moved by commerce (monetary trade or barter?) or as a gift (free or socially enforced?)? How is the volume of trade, or its relative importance to the economy as a whole, to be deduced from finds of individual artefacts? Preservation is erratic and selective: for example, ceramic goods survive, foodstuffs do not. As a result of the state of the evidence, attempts to understand the economies of ancient societies are largely concerned with creating theories into which to slot the fragmentary and problematic evidence. Theories allow gaps to be plugged by inference and allow maximum use to be made of available material.

The first serious attempts to apply the relatively new science of economics to past societies occurred during the mid-nineteenth century, as supporters of communism and socialism looked to history for lessons about socio-economic elitism. The earliest writer of any influence on the subject was Karl Marx; later Max Weber made ancient societies a specialised focus of attention. What both men actually published were theories of how ancient economies *might* have functioned based on the fragmentary evidence available and, of course, both found a basis for their theories in their political philosophy. Both Marx and Weber depicted an ancient world where individualistic capitalism appeared to be a factor, but not a dominating one. Weber's influential theory of the 'Consumer City' suggested that a simple subsistence economy functioned through an unequal exchange between major rural agrarian production and minor urban services (justice, security, manufacturing etc.). From the very beginning, therefore, the study of past economies was bound up with contemporary political, social and economic doctrines.

This shadow has continued to accompany the economic study of the ancient world. For example, between the 1920s and 1940s Michael Rostovtzeff rejected theories depicting economic simplicity in the ancient world, arguing that it had been economically and fiscally complex, on a similar level to his own day. Rostovtzeff had left Bolshevik Russia to work in Western universities; he was naturally keen not to bolster the arguments of Communist Party heroes. Furthermore, a return of support for economic simplicity in the ancient world during the 1970s, typified by the work of Moses Finley and subsequently modified by Keith Hopkins, may not have been unconnected with concerns among some contemporary economic theorists about potential dangers in the rise of vast multinational corporations.

Since the 1920s, at least, the study of ancient economies has tended to polarise between two diametrically opposed camps, usually known as 'primitivist' and 'modernist'. Drawing on the same pool of information, the primitivists theorised that the Graeco-Roman world possessed only a basic economy, while the modernising school hypothesised that complex economic structures and concepts were in use. This emphasis on schools of thought has made scholars in this field acutely aware of their own past, since every primitivist drew on the ideas of Weber and Finley and every modernist looked back to Rostovtzeff's work. Scholarship from the early 1990s onwards has been struggling to get clear of this polarised morass, with interesting results. While primitivism in its most extreme forms has been broadly rejected, there has been no rush to embrace modernising tendencies either. Most have attempted to steer a moderate course while still drawing on the past; the work of Weber, Rostovtzeff, Finley and others remains relevant and actively discussed.

There are still plenty of conflicting viewpoints, but there are now some broad areas of agreement. The most important is a rejection of the monolithic approach of both primitivists and modernists, who often treated the ancient world as one single economy. It is now recognised that each ancient society had its own economy, and the economies of large entities like the Roman Empire were clearly composed of many component sub-economies. The local economy of the city of Rome, for example, would have made a startling contrast to that of the desert province of Arabia Felix. Some generalisations can be agreed upon, however: the economies of all ancient societies were overwhelmingly dominated by agriculture at, or barely above, the subsistence level; though large operations did exist, most commercial activity from farming to manufacturing occurred on a small scale; economic and technological change tended to occur slowly; economic and financial concepts were basic but functional. Small-denomination coins available in imperial Rome and classical Athens suggest that some ancient societies were highly monetarised and that barter was not routinely important even in small transactions. However, this cannot be said of all societies, and even at the height of the Roman Empire the use of money was probably far less common in rural areas.

It is important to remember too that ancient economies were not influenced, as we are, by economic science. Recent scholarship has drawn heavily on primitivist ideas about the importance of the social dimension in commercial issues. Modern capitalism emphasises the importance of profit above all else, but this was not necessarily the case in the ancient world, where patronage, ritual friendship and customary practice could override such concerns. It may sound as though the primitivists are still in the ascendant. Their ideas are certainly influential but not overwhelmingly so; we have learnt from the modernists too. Weber's 'Consumer City' is not dead, but most agree it is a problematic and oversimplified model. Probably the most useful lesson taken from the modernists is that 'primitive' systems are not necessarily inefficient or unsuccessful – the financial services industries of Rome and Athens are a case in point. The modernist emphasis on a significant trade in luxury goods as well as basic food staples has also been taken on board, but most scholars would now take a broader view of the term 'luxury' than previously. To a community in an area of soft sandstone bedrock, a granite millstone is as much of a luxury as exotic perfume.

Current consensus sees the economies of the ancient world as at once more complex than the primitivist view and less sophisticated than the modernist view. Equally, most agree that there is an economic spectrum with highly urbanised imperial powers, like the Roman Empire and classical Athens, at one end of the scale, and non-expansionist, predominantly rural communities, like those of northern Gaul in the fifth century AD, at the other. Consensus only takes you so far, however, and different scholars can still produce very different results from the same evidence. At present two important and active areas of study concern the issue of mechanisation in the Roman Empire and the role of mass production in ancient societies generally. Debate concerning the relative economic importance of both these factors is heated and ongoing.

Despite high levels of interest in recent years, economic study of the ancient world remains in its infancy. Roughly speaking, we are at the toddler stage: moving under our own steam, keen to explore, but with only very basic ideas of what is sensible (and with a tendency to persist with things that are clearly a bad idea). The fact that in the past this field has been prone to influence from contemporary social, economic and political trends remains a concern. These influences can be helpful – after all, these are what started investigation in the first place – but can also cloud our vision. Worse, these influences can usually only be appreciated in retrospect. We seem to have fought clear of the polarisation that marred much of the twentieth century and no longer seem influenced by the communist/capitalist debate, but who knows what influence we may be under now?

Further reading

Significant older views of ancient economies

M. I. Finley, *The Ancient Economy*, London: Chatto and Windus, 1973 – the archetypal primitivist study.

M. I. Rostovtzeff, *The Social and Economic History of the Roman Empire*, Oxford: Clarendon Press, 1926 – the fundamental modernist study.

M. Weber, *The Agrarian Sociology of Ancient Civilizations*, trans. R. I. Frank, London: Verso, 1998 – a complete edition of all Weber's ancient writings in English.

Recent work on issues of current interest

P. Cartledge, E. Cohen and L. Foxhall (eds), *Money, Labour and Land: Approaches to the Economies of Ancient Greece*, London: Routledge, 2002 – up-to-date and wide-ranging.

R. P. Duncan-Jones, *Structure and Scale in the Roman Economy*, Cambridge: Cambridge University Press, 1990 – a useful statistic-based (rather than theory-based) study.

K. Greene, *The Archaeology of the Roman Economy*, London: Batsford, 1986 – the ideal beginner's introduction.

K. Hopkins, 'Introduction', in P. D. A. Garnsey, K. Hopkins and C. R. Whittaker (eds), *Trade in the Ancient Economy*, London: Chatto and Windus, 1983 – seminal modification of primitivist theory; other articles will also be of interest.

D. Mattingly and J. Salmon (eds), *Economies beyond Agriculture in the Classical World*, London: Routledge, 2001 – the latest in the mass-production debate.

W. Scheidel and S. von Reden (eds), *The Ancient Economy*, Edinburgh: Edinburgh University Press, 2002 – useful collection of very recent research.

C. Smith and H. Parkins (eds), *Trade, Traders and the Ancient City*, London: Routledge, 1998 – important discussion of the 'Consumer City' model and other trade theory.

A. Wilson, 'Machines, power and the ancient economy', *Journal of Roman Studies* 92 (2002), 1–32 – an influential contribution to the mechanisation debate.

6. Gender

Mark Golden

'Hanging is a man's choice for death.' So writes a woman in a novel written by a man (Richard Wright, *Clara Callan*, Toronto: HarperCollins, 2001, p. 23). But Greek tragic playwrights, themselves male, thought of the noose as a woman's way. Both beliefs concern gender, the social construction of sexual difference. This was an important Greek and Roman means of organising their world and has become crucial to our understanding of it. As my opening suggests, it requires us to map and negotiate complex divisions, not just between men and women but between the ancients and ourselves. In few fields is a survey of scholarship so essential.

It was once accepted that Greek and Roman men and women belonged to separate spheres. Men's took in public life, the open spaces of the city and countryside and the activities they framed: warfare, politics, law, large-scale production and exchange. The house was the province of women. Some scholars saw them as domestic prisoners, not just private but deprived; for others, there was plenty of evidence for affection and female authority within the home, where they managed what men brought into it. But this model, developed as it was during the eighteenth-century struggle for liberty, equality, fraternity – the Rights of Man – had tendentious origins: men sought to justify their monopoly of newly-opened civic space by appeal to classical precedent. It also contained numerous contradictions. While the city might be male in theory, Aristotle knew that poor women (the majority) had to go out to work, and much agricultural labour was done by women. On the other hand, philosophers, medical writers and myths of the birth of Asclepius, Dionysus and Hephaestus combined to denigrate or deny women's role in reproduction. Religion fitted awkwardly if at all, too important to be regarded as an anomaly, pervasive in both public and private life, and women's work as well as men's in both. The division of public and private was itself problematic. At Rome, for example, women (despite their legal limitations) controlled property, influenced elections, demonstrated in the Forum and appeared at the head of armies in life, while their *imagines* (likenesses) and eulogies featured in funerals after it. The elite Roman house was a place for public reception and display as well as for quiet domesticity and might be razed for crimes against the community; some have argued that the city itself was marked by the incorporation of images of male genitalia into the layout of Augustus' Forum.

The present paradigm builds on the work of Michel Foucault, himself much influenced by the British classicist K. J. Dover. It too identifies two genders among the Greeks and Romans. But rather than merely mirroring the self-evident categories of men and women, they are created through sexual acts, penetration and passivity in particular. So a boy or even an adult male could be feminised by the sexual roles they played – here there is overlap and interplay with other dichotomies (child/adult, slave/free, Greek/barbarian). On the other hand, too much virility could likewise unman someone who was in the thrall of his passions or of the woman who provoked them. (Heracles and Mark Antony were examples.) Furthermore, far from belonging to separate spheres, male and female are now everywhere seen entwined: Greek and Roman societies are read as a knot of gendered codes, in which right stood for male and left for female; literary genres, occasions for speech and words themselves were masculine or feminine; and trees were classified, not simply on the basis of producing fruit, but by the character of their wood. (Male trees were tough and knotty; female, pliable and easy to shape.)

There can be no doubt of the productivity of this approach. It has encouraged the close reading of neglected texts (rhetoricians, medical writers, physiognomists; see chapters 45 and 56) and the development of fresh themes for research (performance, humour, the body). The new attention to masculinity is noteworthy: long regarded as the norm from which women's specificity might be measured, maleness too turns out to be notional, man-made, subject to challenge and change. (Homer's heroes weep without shame, Socrates' companions check unmanly tears at his deathbed.) Yet it too raises questions which are hard to answer. Anomalies such as the Amazons can be explained as reversals, object lessons in the risks of transgressing the rules. The gods, however, are more problematic. Athena is a warrior, Hera no mother, Dionysus (despite his coterie of randy satyrs) remarkably uninterested in sex. Divinity trumps gender. Among mortals, Romans may be more unlike Greeks than is generally recognised. The pathic *cinaedus* (catamite) may have made up a third gender, a self-conscious subculture identifiable by distinctive costume, hairstyle, haunts and habits. (Other candidates for this category, hermaphrodites and eunuchs like the *galli*, priests of the goddess Cybele, cross linguistic boundaries as well as genders.)

Weeping was not the only fashion which changed over time. Private, domestic activities become more prominent on Attic gravestones after Pericles' citizenship law of 451/0 BC required mothers as well as fathers of citizens to be Athenian; women receive public recognition as benefactors in Hellenistic inscriptions. Above all, our sources hide as much as they reveal. They introduce biases of genre and context. (The paean, a male preserve in Greek society, is associated with women on the tragic stage; Cicero is as respectful of Clodia's business acumen in his letters as he is scornful of her independent lifestyle in his speech in defence of Caelius.) And they efface women's perceptions and experiences almost entirely. (We never hear Clodia's side.) Did they share whatever view of gender men operated with or the identity it gave to them? Perhaps so, if – among their other contributions to funerary practices – they selected the goods we find deposited in ancient graves. Perhaps not, if Sappho and Sulpicia subvert conventional codes and speak for their sisters when they do. We will never be sure, especially as we must be prepared to accept that here as elsewhere in this sketch the terrain was contested in antiquity too. Octavian's propaganda made much of the influence Cleopatra held over Antony. When he became emperor, he ensured that Livia remained in his shadow. Yet he seems to have tried to fashion a more prominent role for her after his death, only to have Tiberius resist in his turn. At any rate, we can endeavour to see that our own assumptions (that men would not attend the sick, that Apollo's priestess at Delphi spoke only through male intermediaries) do not utterly mislead us.

Further reading

J. H. Blok, *The Early Amazons: Modern and Ancient Perspectives on a Persistent Myth*, Leiden: Brill, 1995 – full discussion of early evidence and modern approaches.

M. Delcourt, *Hermaphrodite: Myths and Rites of the Bisexual Figure in Classical Antiquity*, trans. J. Nicholson, London: Studio Books, 1961 – a psychoanalytical classic.

N. Demand, 'Gender studies and ancient history: participation and power', in S. M. Burstein, N. Demand, I. Morris and L. Tritle, *Current Issues and the Study of Ancient History*, Claremont: Regina Books, 2002, pp. 31–43 – reviews recent work.

E. Fantham, H. P. Foley, N. B. Kampen, S. B. Pomeroy and H. A. Shapiro, *Women in the Classical World*, New York and Oxford: Oxford University Press, 1994 – well-illustrated textbook.

L. Foxhall and J. Salmon (eds), *When Men were Men: Masculinity, Power and Identity in Classical Antiquity*, London and New York: Routledge, 1998 – this and the following contain collections of essays on roles and representations of men.

L. Foxhall and J. Salmon (eds), *Thinking Men: Masculinity and its Self-Representation in the Classical Tradition*, London and New York: Routledge, 1998.

M. Golden and P. G. Toohey (eds), *Sex and Difference in Ancient Greece and Rome*, Edinburgh: Edinburgh University Press, 2003 – collection of 250 years of modern scholarship on sexuality and gender.

M. R. Lefkowitz and M. B. Fant, *Women's Life in Greece and Rome: A Source Book in Translation* (2nd edn), Baltimore: Johns Hopkins University Press, 1992 – standard sourcebook.

L. A. McClure (ed.), *Sexuality and Gender in the Classical World: Readings and Sources*, Oxford: Blackwell, 2002 – includes ancient sources.

S. B. Pomeroy, *Goddesses, Whores, Wives and Slaves: Women in Classical Antiquity*, New York: Schocken Books, 1975 – pioneering work still worth reading.

7. *Philology and Linguistics*

Philip Burton

Definitions

The terms 'philology' and 'linguistics' refer to the systematic study of language. The term 'philology' (Greek *philologia*) originally referred more generally to the study of language and literature. The Graeco-Latin hybrid 'linguistics' is not attested before the 1850s. In English use, the term 'philology' is relatively rare, though consecrated in the names of certain societies, journals and university chairs, and still used sometimes to refer to the historical study of certain languages or language families (e. g. Greek, Celtic, Romance, Germanic philology).

The position of linguistics vis-à-vis classics is not unlike that of archaeology. Both arose largely from the study of classical antiquity; both have subsequently become independent disciplines, whose interests may now be some way removed from the classical world. The following branches of linguistics are particularly important for the formal study of Greek and Latin.

Phonetics, phonology, morphology, lexicology and syntax

Phonetics is the study of the sounds of language. Our assumptions on how Greek and Latin were pronounced are based on three main sources. First, the evidence of 'daughter-languages' (modern Greek, the Romance family); second, explicit statements by ancient writers on language; third, the evidence of puns, of language games and of instances of mishearing. The value of these sources varies considerably. Word-plays may be very hard to interpret (what makes a good pun?). Explicit statements by grammarians differ considerably in quality. The orator Quintilian's description of a letter pronounced 'with a barely human voice . . . by blowing out through the gap between the teeth' is distinctly impressionistic; however, the /f/-sound is instantly recognisable from the fourth-century Marius Victorinus' statement that it is pronounced 'by putting the upper teeth on the lower lip, and breathing out gently'. (/f/ is an instance of the modern typological means of expressing a phoneme; see below.) Reconstruction based on subsequent forms of the language is in many ways the best evidence we have. This is not a simple retrojection of more recent states of language into the past. Most linguists would see it as scientifically acceptable to reconstruct the value /k^{w}/ for the Latin letter *q* not only in words where the /k^{w}/ sound is well attested in Romance (for instance, Latin *qualis* 'what sort' > Italian *quale*, Spanish *cual*), but also where the Romance languages have a /k/ (Latin *quid* 'what?' > Italian *che*, Spanish *qué*). But even such a simple example raises intellectual issues. What we have reconstructed is arguably not classical Latin, but a notional ancestor of Italian and Spanish; and that is before we consider other Romance languages. More radically, some linguists would argue that we cannot reconstruct any phonetic value at all; we can only say that the sound represented in Latin by *q* was different from that represented by *c*.

Phonology seeks to distinguish patterns in the distribution of sounds in a language and to draw inferences from them about the way these sounds are systematised in the mind of the speaker. Central to phonology is the concept of contrast between certain distinctive features. The basic unit of sound is a phoneme. Thus the classical Greek letter φ represents a phoneme /pʰ/, which has the distinctive features of being a voiceless aspirate, a labial, and a stop (see appendix to this chapter). All these three features are also found in other combinations in other Greek phonemes. Most phonologists would see this as a form of economy on the number of different ways the speakers of a language need to configure their mouth and throat when speaking. Phonological theory is useful for explaining certain sorts of language change. The phoneme /h/, for instance, is weak and liable to loss in both Greek and Latin as well as English. Why? Phonologists would point to two facts. First, there is the restricted distribution of the /h/ phoneme in all three languages (rarely found outside word-initial position). This makes the phoneme /h/ less useful in all three languages than (say) /s/ or /n/ or /r/, all of which can occur in a far wider range of contexts. In phonological terms, then, /h/ has a relatively low functional yield. Second, there is the fact that /h/ is phonologically asymmetrical. In formal terms, it is a voiceless glottal fricative; and it is unusual in Latin and English at least for a voiceless consonant not to be 'paired' with a corresponding voiced consonant (in English, for instance, /f/ and /s/ may be paired respectively with /v/ and /z/).

Morphology studies the forms of words. It is conventional to distinguish inflectional and derivational morphology. Inflectional morphology deals with those additions or modifications to the root which convey information about grammatical form. So, for instance, the Greek *leloipa* 'I have left' (present tense *leipō* 'I leave') has three distinctive morphological modifications: the reduplicated *le-* and the *o*-grade of the root (-*loip-*), both marking the perfect tense, plus the first person active ending *-a*. Derivational morphology deals with those additions to the root which serve to create new words. So in English *establishment* it seems easy to isolate the *-ment* morph, which produces nouns from verbal roots (compare *fulfilment*, *retirement*, *agreement*); but what about words like *complement* or *document*? And what of the element-*ish* (compare *finish*, *polish*, *cherish*)? Derivational morphs may also convey some quasi-lexical information about the meaning of a word: contrast, for instance, *verbose* and *verbal*.

Lexicology is concerned with the word-stock of a language. It is concerned in particular with how words enter a language, how they may evolve in meaning over time, how they may become associated with particular registers of the language, and ultimately how they may pass out of use. As the lexicon of a language is potentially vast, studies tend to be confined to particular sorts of words (e. g. the *-skō* verbs in Greek, or the development of the Latin medical vocabulary). There is an obvious sense in which the lexicon is particularly likely to reflect the speakers' culture and values. For instance, Latin has two terms for 'uncle', *avunculus* 'mother's brother', literally 'little grandad', alongside *patruus* 'father's brother'. It has been claimed that *avunculus* is more affectionate, and that it reflects a conceptualisation of that relative as being somehow one of the child's ancestors; the *patruus*, in contrast, is proverbially grumpy and interfering.

Syntax is the study of the processes by which speakers organise words into more complex units, up to the level of the sentence. In Greek and Latin linguistics, this is generally done on an empirical basis, by the analysis of specific examples of certain sorts of syntactic units (for example, conditional clauses, or the various sorts of absolute construction). Syntactic studies in general linguistics were heavily influenced in the late twentieth century by the generativist approach, which emphasised the capacity of the individual speaker to generate novel but still grammatical sentences. This approach has influenced the work of some Greek and Latin linguists also, while others have been less impressed (see chapter 47).

It should be clear even from this brutally short taxonomy that the divisions between these subject areas are often not distinct. Note also that there is no neat borderline between linguistics and other ways of approaching ancient texts. At units larger than the sentence, we move into the branch of linguistics known as discourse analysis, or into stylistics, or into avowed literary criticism; and at this point the pure linguist will lose all professional interest.

The Indo-European hypothesis

In 1786 the Chief Justice of India, Sir William Jones, advanced the hypothesis that Greek, Latin and the sacred Indian language of Sanskrit, along with Gothic, Celtic and Persian, were all descendants of a single original language (for writing systems, see chapter 63). The implications of this theory were eagerly taken up by scholars in Europe. Increasing numbers of correspondences were observed between words of similar meaning with similar phonetic shape. Consider the following:

Indo-European	***duoh**$_1$	**'two'**
Sanskrit	*dvā̆(u)*	
Greek	*duō*	
Latin	*duo*	
English	*two*	

Indo-European	***méh**$_2$***ter**	**'mother'**
Sanskrit	*mātā̆*	
Greek	*méter*	
Latin	*mater*	
English	*mother*	

Indo-European	***h**$_3$***dónt(s)**	**'tooth'**
Sanskrit	*dán* (stem *dant-*)	
Greek	*odón* (stem *odónt-*)	
Latin	*dens* (stem *dent-*)	
English	*tooth*	

Indo-European	***dhuer**	**'door'**
Sanskrit	*dváras*	
Greek	*thúrai*	
Latin	*fores*	
English	*door*	

Indo-European	***tnh**$_2$**-(e)u**	**'thin'**
Sanskrit	*tanú-*	
Greek	*tanaós*	
Latin	*tenuis*	
English	*thin*	

(The asterisks mark reconstructed forms, not directly attested. The character [h] when followed by a numeral represents a class of consonants known as laryngeals. The Indo-European forms are reconstructed according to a late-twentieth-century consensus.)

The first consonants of the last three examples (English *tooth*, *door* and *thin*) illustrate a rule of sound-change known as Grimm's Law, which describes the relationship between the stop-consonants of Indo-European and their reflexes (= descendants) in the Germanic languages. The principle that sound-changes operate according to set laws was canonised by a group of Leipzig scholars (the neo-Grammarians) in the late 1860s. This 'regularity hypothesis' allowed linguists to move beyond mere similarity of sound as a criterion of relatedness. Its value was dramatically demonstrated by the work of Ferdinand de Saussure, who, in 1879, aged 21, reconstructed two Indo-European sounds not directly attested in any daughter-language. This hypothesis was vindicated when the Hittite language of Eastern Asia Minor was deciphered in 1915: subsequent analysis showed that Saussure's 'coefficients' occurred in precisely the sort of contexts he had predicted.

Over the twentieth century, Indo-European linguistics became an increasingly independent discipline. The subject advanced along three main fronts. First, the Indo-European family grew with the decipherment of Hittite and the discovery of the Tocharian languages of Western China. Second, advances in physiology and sound technology led to more accurate descriptions of the operation of the human voice. Third, the rise of general linguistics led to increasingly sophisticated theoretical accounts of language and accounts of language change. A particular contribution has been made by the discipline of typology, which analyses the co-occurrence of specific features across large numbers of languages, not necessarily related. Indo-European studies are now far more than a subset of classics, even when they are practised within a classics department or programme. Greek and Latin represent just two branches of the Indo-European family, the Hellenic and the Italic. Most linguists would add Celtic, Germanic, Baltic, Slavonic, Albanian, Armenian, Anatolian, Indo-Iranian and Tocharian, though different groupings and divisions have been advanced. However, the classical languages remain important for their early date, the extensive volume of extant material and our relatively good understanding of them.

'Vulgar Latin' and imperial Greek

In turn, Greek and Latin linguistics are not confined to Indo-European studies. Since the nineteenth century there has been a flourishing industry of so-called 'Vulgar Latin' studies, which calls attention to the non-literary varieties of Latin, and to the relationship of Latin to the Romance languages. How, for instance, do we get from Latin *equum emi* ('I have bought a horse') to French *j'ai acheté un cheval*? Some 'Romance' features are already apparent in our 'Vulgar Latin' texts: for instance, the breakdown of the Latin case system, the rise of the new perfect tense, the replacement of large parts of the classical lexicon. Some changes, however, remain obstinately invisible. For example, the classical passive forms, completely absent from Romance, are widely found even in very sub-literary documents. In recent years the focus of attention has shifted away from the catch-all category of 'Vulgar Latin' towards the study of special areas of the language (scientific, medical or theological registers) or towards studies of wider linguistic and social phenomena (bilingualism, language contact, the conceptualisation of Latin, pragmatics).

In Greek studies the situation is different. Classical Greek existed in various dialectal forms, whose origins, development and classification have been extensively studied. These dialects were largely superseded in the Hellenistic age by the *koinē* (common, shared) variety, essentially based on Attic Greek. This supra-regional standard inevitably underwent various changes, most notably to its sound system; these changes are relatively well attested, largely thanks to the number of extant papyri which contain Greek writing of all levels of literacy. *Koinē* Greek did not undergo the same dialectalisation as Latin. The absence of a 'Hellenic language family' parallel to Romance has given Greek linguistics a quite different cast to Latin. However, there has been recent interest in the role of Greek as a language of imperial administration, with suggestive comparisons to imperial English, Spanish or Russian.

Appendix

Characters in square brackets are phonetic symbols as distinct from letters; so b is the letter b, [b] the sound made at the start of *bit*.

aspirate stop pronounced with an audible release of breath, such as the sound at the start of *pit*; the sound [h]

fricative produced by constricting the vocal tract (the passage from lungs to mouth) without complete closure to give a noisy flow of air, such as [f], [s], [v]

glottal pronounced with the glottis, that is, the vocal cords and the gap between them; [h] is a glottal fricative, and the sound made instead of [t] in many pronunciations of *butter* or *water* is a glottal stop [ʔ]

labial formed by the lips, such as [p], [m]

laryngeal produced by or with constriction of the larynx; a conjectured sound reconstructed for Indo-European

stop produced with lips, tongue, etc. completely blocking the flow of air from the lungs, such as [k], [t], [b]

voiced produced with vocal fold vibration, like the [z] in *hazy* or the sound at the start of *thy*

voiceless produced without vocal fold vibration, like the [s] in *miss* or the sound at the start of *thigh*

Further reading

J. Aitchison, *Language Change: Progress or Decay?* (3rd edn), Cambridge: Cambridge University Press, 2001 – lively and informative; an excellent introduction.

W. S. Allen, *Vox Graeca: A Guide to the Pronunciation of Classical Greek* (3rd edn), Cambridge: Cambridge University Press, 1987, and *Vox Latina: A Guide to the Pronunciation of Classical Latin* (2nd edn), Cambridge: Cambridge University Press, 1978 – two standard works, offering a modest presentation of the key facts and arguments.

P. Baldi, *An Introduction to the Indo-European Languages*, Carbondale and Edwardsville: Southern Illinois University Press, 1983 – a basic survey of the main language groups.

R. S. P. Beekes, *Comparative Indo-European Linguistics*, Amsterdam and Philadelphia: John Benjamins, 1995 – attractive combination of the technical and the accessible; highly recommended.

D. Crystal, *A Dictionary of Linguistics and Phonetics* (5th edn), Oxford: Blackwell, 2002 – a useful guide to the terminology, if not infallible.

J. Herman, *Vulgar Latin*, University Park PA: Pennsylvania State University Press, 2000 – a brief, plain account by one of the great authorities on the subject; translation of French original of 1967.

G. C. Horrocks, *Greek: A History of the Language and its Speakers*, London and New York: Longman, 1997 – good survey work, especially useful in its analysis of specific passages of Greek from the Bronze Age to the 1980s.

L. R. Palmer, *The Latin Language*, London: Faber and Faber, 1954, and *The Greek Language*, London: Faber and Faber, 1980 – rather dated, but readable and appealing.

A. G. Ramat and P. Ramat (eds), *The Indo-European Languages*, London and New York: Routledge, 1998 – authoritative presentation of late-twentieth century views; not an introductory work.

8. Literature

David Konstan

That there should be a section on current approaches to literature in a companion to ancient Greece and Rome in itself points to an important characteristic of contemporary criticism: it is methodologically self-conscious. Nowadays, it is not assumed that we can simply report faithfully what a text says or means, and count on taste to evaluate its aesthetic merits. Rather, scholars are increasingly aware that what we bring to a work to a great extent conditions how we perceive it. Not everyone will agree with Stanley Fish's dictum, 'Interpreters do not decode poems; they make them', but it captures a key feature of what is called postmodern theory.

The interest in literary theory has given rise to a bewildering variety of approaches and some daunting terminology, for example semiotics, structuralism, deconstruction, formalism, narratology, New Criticism and reader-response criticism, along with methods inspired by Marxism, psychoanalysis, feminism, Bakhtin, Foucault and much else. All have been profitably applied to classical texts. A potted survey of these systems would be dull and indigestible, however. Instead, I have chosen to illustrate how current approaches have changed the way we read with reference to a couple of well-known Latin poems (see chapter 42).

Catullus' story

Catullus wrote two lyrics in the Sapphic metre. They are poems 11 and 51 in the MS tradition (the translations are by Carl Sesar, *Selected Poems of Catullus*, 1974):

11

Furius, Aurelius, right with Catullus
if he'd go out past the limits of India
where the Eastern ocean pounds upon the shore
with far sounding waves,
or to the soft lands, Arabia, Hyrcania,
through Sacia, Parthian bowman country,
into regions the seven-fingered Nile stains
dark with its waters,
or if he marched across the towering Alps
to look out over great Caesar's monuments
from Gallic Rhine to the farthest removed
wild tribes of Britain,
companions ready to brave all this with me
and whatever else heaven's will has in store,
just deliver this brief message to my girl,
meant not to be kind.
Let her enjoy herself with her cheap lovers,
clamp them up between her legs by the hundreds,
say it's love, while one after another she
breaks them inside her,
but let her not look to my love anymore.
After all she's done, it fell, like a flower
at the edge of a field that the plow
barely touches in passing.

51

To me, that man seems to be one of the gods,
or to tell the truth, even more than a god,
sitting there face to face with you, forever
looking, listening
to you laughing sweetly, while poor me, I take
one look at you and I'm all torn up inside,
Lesbia, there's nothing left of me, I can't
make a sound, my tongue's
stuck solid, hot little fire flashes go
flickering through my body, my ears begin

ringing around in my head, my eyes black out,
shrouded in darkness . . .
This soft life is no good for you, Catullus,
you wallow in it, you don't know when to stop.
A soft life's already been the ruin of both
great kings and cities.

Although the woman in 11 is not named, most readers assume she is the Lesbia addressed in 51 and several other passionate poems. Apuleius, writing in the second century AD, reports that 'Lesbia' was Catullus' name for Clodia, a member of a powerful aristocratic family. Here is what one scholar wrote about these poems a little over a century ago: 'Clodia was seven years older than Catullus; but that only made their mutual attraction more irresistible: and the death of her husband in the year after his consulship, whether or not there was foundation for the common rumour that she had poisoned him, was an incident that seems to have passed almost unnoticed in the first fervour of their passion. The story of infatuation, revolt, relapse, fresh revolt and fresh entanglement, lives and breathes in the verses of Catullus' (J. W. Mackail, *Latin Literature*, London: John Murray, 1895; repr. 1995). For Mackail, these poems are the record of a real-life romance: 51 presumably comes early in the affair, 11 at or near the end. There is no distance between the poet's biography and the events mentioned or alluded to in his poems; as Steele Commager put it, the poet goes 'from bed to verse', and what Mackail most values is the immediacy and authenticity of Catullus' poetry.

Back to the text

Mackail's reading of Catullus is a world apart from current approaches. Today, a poem is first of all a verbal artefact or 'icon'; its relation to the poet's personal life is doubtful and in any case irrelevant to its artistry, and naive inferences like Mackail's exemplify what Harold Cherniss called the 'biographical fallacy' (although the method is far from extinct). Several currents helped bring about this shift in perspective. The so-called New Critics in the United States, along with William Empson and others in Britain, emphasised the specifically literary meaning of a poem, residing in patterns of imagery and paradoxical associations that resist what Cleanth Brooks called 'the heresy of paraphrase'. For earlier critics, the contrast in 51 between the intimate party where Catullus sits opposite Lesbia and the reference to kings and cities in the final stanza was a sign of disunity; the New Critics, on the contrary, might see the point of the poem precisely in the ironic tension between private and public life.

A focus on form and technique as opposed to alleged references to the poet's life also encouraged attention to allusions, both to other poems within the Catullan corpus and to Greek precedents. This was not the old-fashioned hunt for sources or *Quellenforschung*. Rather, the world of a poem was now seen to be the whole of poetry, a space where words and meanings interpenetrate in a permanent flux that Julia Kristeva dubbed 'intertextuality.' Viewed this way, 'Lesbia' is not a pseudonym for a Roman matron but a reference to Sappho of Lesbos, and indeed 51 is (apart perhaps from the final stanza) a translation of one of Sappho's poems (31). Here, then, is another conundrum: Catullus occupies the place of Sappho, but he applies her epithet to his beloved. Does this mean that Catullus imagines her to be a learned woman, Sappho's peer in poetry? Not necessarily: the reference may be rather to Sappho's later reputation for lasciviousness, which would square with the image of the woman in 11. Rather than tell a story, even a fictional one – we recall that 11 precedes 51 in the sequence – the poems may be designed simply to titillate, according to Niklas Holzberg. As for 'Furius' and 'Aurelius', these too may be symbolic names suggesting thievishness (Latin *fur* = 'thief') and greed (Latin *aurum* = 'gold').

What is woman?

In dispensing with an imagined chronology for the poems, critics have become more open to seeking thematic (as opposed to narrative) connections among them. For example, Catullus represents a woman in 51 as virtually a goddess – only a god can sit tranquilly at her side – but as a monster in 11. If we read these two images as simultaneous, what do they tell us about Catullus' attitude towards women? The answer to this question depends in part on what we think Catullus is feeling in 51.

A majority of critics believes that, in Catullus 51, the poet is jealous of the man conversing with Lesbia. If so, then 51 intimates that Lesbia is fickle, and this squares with the character of the woman in 11. But the symptoms Catullus describes were traditionally associated with infatuation rather than with jealousy; in this case, the other man seems like a god because he, unlike the poet, is apparently immune to her charms. The problem in analysing the symptoms reminds us that our intuitions may not be reliable even in so basic a matter as recognising an emotion in a Greek or Latin text. Michel Foucault and others have pointed to disparities between ancient and modern concepts which, though they appear similar, may in fact belong to distinct universes of discourse or 'epistemes'. In this, they resemble words in foreign languages that look like English terms but differ subtly in meaning (so-called 'faux amis', false friends).

Catullus, then, both loves and hates together, as he puts it in a famous epigram (85). Psychoanalytic theory, particularly that associated with the French theorist Jacques Lacan, has insisted on the male imaginary's contradictory relation to the feminine: whether the antagonism between the sexes takes the form of misogyny or idolatry, 'the motivation is the same', writes Micaela Janan. Catullus' image of Lesbia as a sexual monster and goddess are two sides of the same coin, the over- and under-evaluation of the beloved. Instead of representing an evolution from infatuation to betrayal, 11 and 51 are in fact complementary and simultaneous.

Catullus and Rome

Like 51, with its abrupt change of tone in the last stanza, 11 has an odd shape: four stanzas illustrate the professed devotion of the friends who are to serve as Catullus' messengers, while the final two contain the brutal message itself. Again, older critics, their attention fixed on the love narrative, have regarded the poem as poorly constructed: it cannot have been a difficult task to deliver those few words (where is the lady, if not in Rome?), and the elaborate geographical excursus seems irrelevant – unless perhaps it is Catullus' way of building suspense. But the reference to Caesar's expedition into Britain in 54 BC, and to the Parthians, against whom Crassus was marching in that same year (he was defeated in 53 BC), evokes a moment in which Rome's armies seemed poised to conquer the entire known world (Pompey, the third member of the 'triumvirate', was planning a campaign in Spain). Here too, as in 51, Catullus combines a personal theme with an allusion to empire, sketching a map of Rome's military operations in the guise of lauding the commitment of his friends.

Mikhail Bakhtin's idea of polyphony or the 'dialogic principle', like intertextuality, encourages us to recognise that multiple levels of discourse may co-exist in a text, even in so personal a genre as lyric, however strange this may appear to modern sensibilities nursed on Romanticism. A New Critic might defend the unity of 11 by observing the ironic echo in the final stanza, where Catullus locates himself at the edge of a ploughed field, of the earlier references to the outermost limits of Roman expansion. But the fusion of the sexual and the political points to a fundamental quality of ancient erotic poetry that current approaches to the history of sexuality have illuminated. Sex was conceived in terms of power, and sexual penetration was imagined as domination. The image of Romans entering (Catullus uses the word *penetrare*) India and 'soft' Arabia is thus homologous to sexual dominance: power relations based on gender, ethnicity and social class intersect within classical ideology itself.

Deconstructing gender

There is a difficulty with this interpretation: it is the woman who is analogised to the plough and to Rome's virile armies, while Catullus is the vulnerable flower at the margins of the meadow. Catullus seems to have reversed conventional gender roles. Recent theories, however, treat gender as an essentially unstable category, as much a consequence as a cause of behaviour (see chapter 6). As Judith Butler puts it, 'there is no performer prior to the performed'. Gender does not express our inner nature, it is a function of how we dress, walk, behave. These insights make intelligible the image of a sexually dominant woman who crushes men as she is penetrated and Catullus' own passivity. As a relation of power, 'gender' was itself mutable.

We may observe that gender is also deconstructed in 51: for in translating a poem of Sappho and assuming her voice, Catullus casts himself in the position occupied, in his model, by a woman. Gender distinctions are here collapsed in the intertextual transfer of Sappho's symptoms and helpless ardour to a man. The final stanza on the dangers of a 'soft life' or life of leisure (*otium* in Latin) can now be read as a critique of Catullus' self-feminisation, but it also threatens kings and cities, and by implication Rome itself. The poem seems to leave no stable locus of masculinity as it elides the contrast between public affairs and private *otium*. Under the microscope, the surface coherence of the text dissolves. This is the method of deconstruction: as Paul de Man writes, a 'reading has to check itself at all points, in quest of cues that puncture the surface of the discourse and reveal the holes and the traps concealed underneath'. Poetic unity is not a virtue but a mystification.

Performing Catullus

Catullus undoubtedly read Sappho's poem, but in the seventh century BC she probably composed it to be recited or sung to the accompaniment of a lyre (see chapter 41). She herself may have written it down, but it survived not only as a literary text but in a performance tradition, possibly in symposiastic contexts. The symposium was chiefly a male institution, and we may perhaps imagine men in their cups chanting Sappho's poetry. If so, the crossing of gender roles was already implicit in these performances. Oral traditions, which, it is now recognised, may continue alongside writing for centuries, convert the listener – and even the reader – into a reciter (one moves one's lips), encouraging identification with the speaker in a text. It is possible that Catullus too composed for recitation, perhaps at a *convivium* or dinner party, as well as for reading. Since women were present at such occasions, his experiments in gender crossing might have been further complicated – or was he writing mainly for men in the kind of 'homosocial' pissing contest in which women serve as tokens of men's sexual achievements?

In any literary work, perspective depends on who is speaking, and recent trends in narratology have called attention to the nature of such focalisation. In assigning to friends the task of communicating to his beloved his pain and disgust at her behaviour, Catullus states in the first person ('let her not look to my love') what the messengers will state in the second and third ('do not look to his love'). To what extent should we hear the voice of the messengers in this reproof? In another poem (21), Catullus accuses Aurelius of attempting to seduce a boy he loves, and it is plausible that he and Furius are among the hundreds who have had relations with the voracious woman in 11. Do they share Catullus' view of her behaviour? Having recognised the possibility of another view of the affair, it is difficult to be certain that Catullus' version represents the whole truth. The interference between different voices, particularly in performance, could alter the tone of the speech that Furius and Aurelius are to deliver and even introduce a note of self-ironic humour. So too, when the poet, in the final stanza of 51, suddenly stands back and admonishes himself, does this voice reveal Catullus' own perspective or merely tempt the reader to create a framing narrative?

Sex and class

If sexuality in antiquity is isomorphic with relations of power, then a destabilisation of gender roles may also disrupt class affiliations. By situating himself at the edge of a field in 11, Catullus questions the privileged position of an aristocratic male at the centre of the empire. Catullus came from the north Italian city of Verona; does he speak as an outsider to the old Roman nobility? He seems to have felt the need for a patron; at all events, he wrote a dedicatory poem (1) to Cornelius Nepos (interestingly, as much an outsider as Catullus himself), whom he may have addressed as *patronus*. He is also apparently prepared to follow Caesar to Britain and beyond the Rhine, presumably in his entourage. Yet elsewhere (29, 57) he is fearless in his attacks on Caesar and Pompey. Anthropological and sociological approaches to the ancient world have emphasised the complex dynamic between friendship and the asymmetrical relationship of inferior and superior in the Hellenistic kingdoms and Rome, and even in democratic Athens. This has led, in turn, to a new sensitivity to literary patronage and its concealment. Literature naturally tends to muddle conventional roles, and Catullus' own social allegiances remain ambiguous.

Crossing boundaries

Just as politics intersects with so intimate a phenomenon as sexuality, there are also other crossings in classical literature that have been illuminated by new approaches. Greek and Roman writers were highly conscious of genre, for instance, and ancient rhetorical manuals describe the conventions for forms such as greetings and farewells. As usual, poets subverted the norms. Thus 11 opens as a poem of praise but concludes as a petition for a favour. Writers also elided the boundaries between art forms by including descriptions of sculptures and paintings, called 'ecphrases', in their compositions ('poetry is like a picture', Horace wrote in the *Ars poetica*). Catullus' catalogue of physical symptoms in 51 and the survey of far places in 11, while not 'ecphrases' in the narrow sense, also suspend the narrative with their vivid maps of the body and geography. Longinus (*On the Sublime* 10.3), the critic to whom we owe the preservation of the poem by Sappho that Catullus translated in 51, remarks on the clinical detachment with which Sappho describes her dissociated condition. The poet's eye (or 'I') stands back from the subject position of the persona and gazes, along with the reader, at the image that she or he has created: a body so numb it seems impossible it should be the bearer of erotic feelings at all.

Whose Catullus?

In imitating Sappho, is Catullus also gazing at her, thus reproducing a transitive visual relation between male and female even as he assumes (or 'colonises') the woman's position? The gendered nature of the gaze is a central issue in modern feminist criticism, and it raises the question of what Catullus 'saw' when he read Sappho's poem. The problem pertains to the transmission of literature generally, as it is treated in modern reception theory. Catullus' Sappho was not the Sappho of her contemporaries; our Sappho is again different, as is our Catullus, who was read for several generations as a proto-Romantic poet before being subjected to the critical methods outlined above. It is something of a mystery how poetry continues to live and breathe through these successive filters, but awareness of them enriches our response by providing a sense of palimpsestic layers in a work. Such readings, however, go beyond what the author can possibly have intended. Responsibility for the meaning of a work is thus shifted to the reader, as reader-response theory and certain phenomenological approaches to literature also propose. We have come round again to Stanley Fish's aphorism that 'Interpreters do not decode poems; they make them.'

In this breathless survey, I have been unable even to mention various new methods in the study of classical literature. Important work is being done on cross-influences between Greece and Rome and neighbouring cultures; on the way ritual shapes narrative (the castrating woman of 11 may have been inspired by the image of Cybele); on the evolution of the poetry book, in which Catullus himself may have played a major role; on the application to dialogue of linguistic techniques such as discourse analysis, to name just a few areas. Critics have adapted rhetorical tropes such as metaphor and metonymy (Gk. 'name change', i.e. 'the substitution of the name of an attribute for the thing itself') to new styles of interpretation, and traced the emergence of the classical canon and its relation to the institutionalisation of classics in the university (when did Catullus become more popular than Plutarch?). But I hope I have communicated a sense of some major theoretical currents and of their power and importance as critical instruments. Thanks to them, ancient literature has assumed a new look. It no longer appears straightforwardly moral or autobiographical, but neither is it a self-contained aesthetic object. Rather, it is engaged with the ambient ideology, probing its contradictions and exhibiting its indeterminacies. Because the culture that nourished it differs from ours, the values that inform it are also dissimilar and must be recovered by modern criticism. And although these techniques may seem to be more concerned with ideas than with beauty, there is also a renewed interest in formal aesthetics and the conditions under which taste itself is formed. The student who approaches classical texts in the critical spirit that animates these methods will find in them new pleasures that are no less valuable or exciting for the changes that time has inevitably wrought on the way we read antiquity.

Further reading

General

J. D. Culler, *Literary Theory: A Very Short Introduction*, Oxford: Oxford University Press, 1997 – lively and basic.

T. Eagleton, *Literary Theory: An Introduction* (2nd edn), Oxford: Blackwell; Minneapolis: University of Minnesota Press, 1996 – sound and comprehensive.

J. Rivkin and M. Ryan (eds), *Literary Theory: An Anthology*, Malden MA: Blackwell, 1998 – a good collection of sources.

On classical literature

S. Goldhill, *The Poet's Voice: Essays on Poetics and Greek Literature*, Cambridge: Cambridge University Press, 1991 – clever and engaging.

I. J. F. de Jong and J. P. Sullivan (eds), *Modern Critical Theory and Classical Literature* (*Mnemosyne* supplement 130), Leiden: Brill, 1994 – covers the territory.

N. S. Rabinowitz and A. Richlin (eds), *Feminist Theory and the Classics*, London: Routledge, 1993 – see how feminism revolutionised the classics.

T. Whitmarsh, *Ancient Greek Literature*, Cambridge: Polity, 2004 – wide-ranging and fun to read.

9. *Philosophy*

Catherine Osborne

'Ancient philosophy' – often known as 'Greek philosophy' because the most famous schools of thought all arose (originally) in the Greek world – has a special place in the background to contemporary Western civilisation. Indeed it is unique in being the one area of classics which, though optional in many classical courses, remains central to its modern counterpart. You would not expect to complete a degree or A-level in philosophy without having encountered the Greeks, and in many cases you would be required to study some Greek philosophy in considerable detail. By contrast, in a classics or classical studies degree you might be offered very little exposure to the thought of these most influential stars of the ancient world, and it is unlikely that you would be forced to study them to an advanced level. Nevertheless, for those who do take the opportunity to explore some ancient philosophy, the riches to be found are highly rewarding; the ancient thinkers ask some of the greatest questions humankind has ever raised, and with respect to many of these questions, they identify most, if not all, the plausible ways of trying to answer them (see chapter 48).

What is philosophy?

The description 'philosophy' tends to be used in every age to cover those areas of intellectual inquiry that have not been clearly marked off as belonging within some other science. In the earliest period there were no clear disciplinary boundaries between science and arts, between literary theory and political thought, logic and mathematics, theology and physics and so on. Those engaged in the search for wisdom would offer their views on any topic whatever, whether it was financial planning, legislation or the nature of the gods. Many of the earliest Greek philosophers wrote widely on all kinds of scientific and theoretical subjects; to some extent this remained true of the great classical philosophers, Plato and Aristotle, whose work ranged over scientific, rhetorical and literary topics alongside logical, mathematical and metaphysical enquiries. However, as science and mathematics became more technical in the post-classical period they were more explicitly marked off from philosophy; eventually 'philosophy' came to mean what it now means. It covers the more abstract and speculative areas of thought, together with ethical and political theory, theory of knowledge and philosophy of religion.

Whose work are you most likely to meet?

Plato and Aristotle

The two great names are Plato (c. 427–347 BC) and Aristotle (384–322 BC). There is also Socrates (c. 470–399 BC), a figure of extraordinary stature who inspired much of what Plato wrote, though he wrote nothing of his own. These three are the leaders in the field during the classical period. You are most likely to be introduced to ancient philosophy via the works of Plato, probably those of his 'middle period' in which he developed the key themes that are labelled 'Platonism': ideas about the structure of the psyche, its survival after death, its knowledge of reality, and the inferior status of the physical world in relation to the world of eternal metaphysical entities known as 'Forms'. Among these middle-period works, the great work in ten books known as the *Republic* has pride of place in the canon, together with shorter dialogues such as the *Phaedo*, *Symposium* and *Phaedrus*. For more detail on these and other works of Plato, see below and chapter 48.

Plato's middle-period work is a relatively easy route into ancient philosophy for two reasons. One is that he writes in the dialogue form. This means that the work is not a continuous presentation of a single position, but rather two or more characters are portrayed holding a discussion. In Plato's dialogues a semi-fictional Socrates often figures as the main character, discussing a specific question with one or more quasi-historical companions (his 'interlocutors'). By writing the dialogue in a chatty style with entertaining asides and much witty and ironic characterisation, Plato sweetens the pill and leads us into questions of fundamental significance, without our realising that they were at all hard. The easy style leads us to see the flaws in positions that we might have been tempted merrily to endorse; yet once Plato's Socrates has shown, in the dialogue, that there are problems with that way of thinking, we are invited to reject our earlier views, without ourselves feeling threatened (in the way that the interlocutor in the dialogue often does). And by giving us both sides of the argument, or considering several competing solutions to a puzzle, Plato helps us to learn to *do philosophy*, since doing philosophy is a matter not simply of putting forward a theory, but of exploring why it does or does not work as an answer to the problem.

A second reason why Plato's work is a good starting point for philosophy more generally is that he antedates the invention of philosophy's technical terminology. Because he is the first person ever to ask most of the questions that have bothered philosophers ever since, his work is free of the great weight of accumulated theoretical background, such as may sometimes seem to obscure the later stages of the history of philosophy and make it inaccessible to one who does not have an extensive training in the field. Plato's language, by contrast, is the everyday language which ancient Greeks spoke in the market-place, and it translates readily into the everyday language that we speak in the cappuccino bar. It is a salutary lesson to realise that thinking about fundamental issues, issues which in one form or another are still with us 2,500 years later, does not necessarily require fancy terms of art or years of training in arcane theory; indeed we can often discover, by reading Plato, where we have become confused over the last two millennia. Plato, standing at the beginning of the development of Western philosophy, can help us to strip away the centuries of complex theory and return to asking the bald questions. This route invites the beginner to make progress towards reaching his or her own informed conclusions, at no major disadvantage compared to the advanced scholar.

Aristotle is generally thought to be a more difficult philosopher than Plato. He is less likely to figure in the elementary parts of a classics or philosophy curriculum, but he is immensely important both as a thinker in his own right and for his subsequent influence on medieval philosophy and thence on modern Western thought. Aristotle was a student and scholar in Plato's Academy (roughly the equivalent of a university). His ideas were developed in response both to Plato's teaching (with which he often disagrees) and to other views, including the more primitive ideas found in philosophers and non-technical thinkers before Socrates. (On Presocratic philosophy, see below.)

Whereas Plato is reasonably accessible to the beginner, both in his style and in his relative freedom from theoretical baggage, by contrast Aristotle is relatively obscure by reason of the opposite habits. His style is problematic largely because the works that we possess are, in the main, not properly written up for publication, but rather notes relating to lecture courses which may have been delivered orally to his own students in the Lyceum. They are not designed to be understood by a reader with no prior knowledge of what is intended. The result is that for us, thousands of years later and way out of touch with the hot topics of discussion that provoked him to think that way, it is often hard to work out what the issue is really about. This is aggravated by the fact that his method often involves considering, and accepting or rejecting, some alternative views, to which he may allude in just a word or two. Unlike Plato, Aristotle does not write a dialogue in which a second character puts the other view. Yet his own work is still a kind of dialogue with others who have thought otherwise. In Aristotle's works it is often quite difficult to disentangle the bits where he is presenting *his own view* from the bits where he is trying to work out the implications of *someone else's view* (with which, perhaps, he is about to disagree). And even if we can do that, we may find it very hard to reconstruct what exactly his answer is.

Aristotle also develops a technical philosophical vocabulary. Although, as we noted earlier, Plato's direct and unpretentious vocabulary has many advantages, there can also be merit in inventing and defining a more precise set of terms, in order to disentangle things where ordinary language conceals an important distinction. Ambiguities in Plato's terminology occasionally prevented him from seeing solutions that Aristotle was able to draw out more clearly, using language devised for the purpose; but this gain is at the expense of easy readability to the uninitiated.

Among the most widely read (and relatively straightforward) works of Aristotle, the *Nicomachean Ethics* and the *Politics* are often chosen for study; both these works reflect on the ideal life for human beings in society and they consider how that society, and its constituent affiliations, within the family and beyond, should be structured for the best. The *Poetics*, famous for its account of what makes a tragedy great, is also relatively accessible without the rest of the Aristotelian edifice. On these and other works of Aristotle, see below and chapter 48.

Presocratic philosophy

While Plato and Aristotle still figure most prominently in the field, they no longer eclipse the rest of the Greek and Roman world entirely. Looking back to the earliest beginnings, Presocratic philosophy (so called because it includes thinkers who show no knowledge of Socrates or his characteristic slant on things) has its own special fascination, partly because it traces the most primitive origins of speculative thought in the Western world: here we can ask what prompts the Greeks (or these Greeks in particular) to begin to ask a special kind of abstract question, instigating that pure inquiry which will culminate in what we know as philosophy. The early period is also fascinating because the evidence is so tricky to handle: there are no complete texts, and every little scrap must be pieced together from what later writers record when they discuss or report their predecessors' views (with the occasional input from some tattered papyrus or inscribed artefact that turns up in an excavation). Often the context of the quotations is lost and the archaic language may be difficult to reconstruct or, once reconstructed, hard to understand. There are difficulties in studying this material in translation, since the translator will already have had to resolve problematic issues of interpretation to decide how best to render each word, but for readers working with the Greek texts there is ready scope for entering into the nitty-gritty of controversy.

Hellenistic and late antique philosophy

'Post-Aristotelian philosophy' is a term that can be used to cover everything after Aristotle up to the official closure of the pagan philosophical schools in Athens in AD 529. This entire period had been relatively neglected until recently: the reawakening of interest in developments from this period is one of the key trends in recent scholarship. The Hellenistic period, from around the death of Aristotle, is characterised by a marked polarisation of groups of philosophers into named schools. Each school was defined by doctrines originally drawn up by the founder and adopted as authoritative by subsequent adherents of the school: the most famous of these are the Epicurean school (also known as 'the Garden'), founded by Epicurus (341–270 BC); the Stoic school (also called 'the Stoa' or 'the Porch'), founded by Zeno of Citium (c. 334–262 BC); and the Pyrrhonian Sceptics, who traced their doctrines (or lack of them) to Pyrrho of Elis (c. 365–275 BC), although the foundation of the school is really the work of Aenesidemus (first century BC). Less prominent and less intensively studied in current literature are the continuing schools founded by Plato and Aristotle – the Academy, founded by Plato, which develops a sceptical line under Arcesilaus (c. 316–242 BC) and Carneades (c. 214–129 BC), during the period called the Middle Academy; and the Lyceum or Peripatetic school, following Aristotelian doctrine, which was headed by Theophrastus until c. 287 BC but was thereafter undistinguished until it underwent something of a revival in the first century AD.

Although the very notion of official school doctrines, and of the authority of a founder figure, seems to go against the spirit of philosophy – with its emphasis on open inquiry and the search for truth as opposed to dogma – closer inspection of the evidence for this period (which is often problematic and indirect) has demonstrated that members of the schools were engaged in a kind of dialectical debate with the rival schools on major issues of ethics, logic, epistemology and metaphysics. Despite the predominant sense (in our rather late and often somewhat pedestrian Roman sources) of towing a party line, there seems to have been room for inspirational leaders to innovate and modify or extend the school doctrines while adhering to the general principles of the founder's vision. Chrysippus (c. 280–207 BC), heading the Stoa after Zeno of Citium, is the classic example of this.

In the later Roman period, these typically Hellenistic schools take second place, overtaken in significance by the revival of Platonism and Aristotelianism, which become the dominant influences up to the sixth century AD, with thriving centres of study in both Athens and Alexandria. From this period we have considerable quantities of complete surviving works. Most influential from the Neoplatonist school are the *Enneads* of Plotinus (c. AD 205–70). There is also a large body of surviving Neoplatonic commentaries on the works of Aristotle, from the school at Alexandria in the sixth century AD.

Socrates: the historical Socrates and Plato's Socrates

In this exploration of what lies beyond the central texts of Plato and Aristotle we have so far omited the third of our great classical figures, Socrates. In terms of approaches to the study of ancient philosophy, Socrates represents a special case, because he figures so prominently as a fictional character in Plato's texts. Other sources of evidence for the historical Socrates (most notably Xenophon's *Memorabilia* and Aristophanes' *Clouds*) give a picture somewhat different, and a good deal less exciting philosophically, than the portrait we find in Plato. There are two ways of approaching the enigmatic nature of the evidence about Socrates. One is to try to reconstruct a historically reliable account of the man who actually died in 399 BC at the hands of the Athenian courts, charged with corrupting the sons of respectable citizens with his disturbing doubts about conventional values. This can be a primarily historical project, rather than a philosophical one: it may involve preferring evidence that is philosophically less exciting over more interesting views that have less historical plausibility. W. K. C. Guthrie's book *Socrates*, from his *History of Greek Philosophy*, is a judicious example of the historical approach. Alternatively it can be a primarily philosophical endeavour, exploring the viability of ideas that are perhaps authentic views of the real Socrates. Gregory Vlastos is well known for his inspiring work in this area. Both approaches rely on the idea that, among Plato's dialogues, those conventionally supposed to have been written early in his career must provide a moderately accurate picture of the historical Socrates and of his approach to philosophical enquiry.

Another approach is to recognise that the extraordinarily provocative character that was the historical Socrates is irrevocably lost to us, except in so far as his ghost lives on in the brilliant fiction created in Plato's best dialogues. Plato was writing in an established genre, the quasi-historical dialogue, in which 'Socrates' is imagined in discussion with some other (perhaps also quasi-historical) personality, and Plato devises an imaginative reconstruction of how the conversation might have gone. Recent work by Kahn and Beversluis has encouraged us to be more circumspect about using Plato's Socratic dialogues as simple historical sources. We cannot simply take them as a record of genuine historical events or conversations, nor do they necessarily provide an accurate portrait in any detail of how Socrates actually proved his points. But they may still be designed to convey a lively sense of the kind of views that Socrates proposed, the kind of philosophical puzzles that they opened up, and features of his most notorious procedure, known as the *elenchus* (refutation, cross-examination), whereby he systematically demolished his opponents' views by bombarding them with counter-arguments and problem-cases designed to shake their confidence (even though sometimes the arguments that Socrates uses are really less good than the opponent in the dialogue supposes).

So it may be that we can get a real sense of Socrates' philosophical passion from Plato's dialogues, though we must not be seduced into thinking we have encountered a factual record of his life. It may be relatively unimportant whether Plato has pressed Socrates' views beyond what the real Socrates actually saw. Indeed if he has done so, Plato has surely done the first part of our work, which is always to investigate the claims of a philosopher and see if they are any good. The puzzles to which Plato alerts us, even if they are not historically Socrates' own contribution, may indeed be the logical consequences of views initially suggested by Socrates.

Plato's dialogues: chronological approaches

Any attempt to use the dialogues of Plato as a means to think about Socratic methods and positions will need to operate with a distinction among Plato's dialogues that has become fairly standard in current scholarship. This is the idea that we can classify the dialogues as 'early', 'middle' or 'late' according to the style, content and philosophical approach that Plato develops in each. Typical early dialogues, such as the *Euthyphro*, *Laches* and *Charmides* – the *Apology* is also early but atypical – are simple in form, have Socrates asking one interlocutor to engage in one simple attempt to define a concept ('What is holiness?' or 'What is courage?'), and end with a state of impasse (*aporia*) as all attempts at definition fail. These so-called *aporetic dialogues* may reflect the pattern typical of Socrates' own discussions. Middle dialogues are more complex: Socrates is portrayed experimenting with theoretical solutions to puzzles about knowledge, about how concepts relate to their instances, and about the nature of things in the world (solutions that would resolve some of the definitional puzzles about relational concepts that figured in the aporetic dialogues). These proposed solutions are usually thought to be Plato's own ideas, and he tries them out, by offering them in response to difficulties encountered in answering the traditional Socratic questions. Late dialogues (including the *Parmenides*, *Sophist*, *Politicus*) tend to throw up further problems and difficulties which cast doubt on the solutions proposed in the middle dialogues. They explore instead some complex issues of logic and the structure of language, to explain away those apparent puzzles that had first fascinated Socrates, and that the middle dialogues had seemed to solve.

This division of Plato's dialogues is important not just for the study of Socrates but for Plato too. For years it has been fashionable to tell a chronological story of Plato's philosophical development, assuming that the 'early/middle/late' division of the dialogues is a record of Plato's advancing maturity and his changing interests. According to that deeply engrained view, the young Plato started off mesmerised by Socrates' ideas and the Socratic method, and he faithfully and piously attempted to encapsulate his great teacher in action in the early dialogues, adding nothing of his own that was not authentic to the spirit of Socrates. However, as he matured he came up with some famous theories of his own – knowledge is recollection of disembodied experience, things in this world are mere copies of the genuine Forms in reality, the psyche is made up of three parts with different desires, the best city would be ruled by philosopher kings – only then to go on and find, in his old age, that things were not so simple and that his earlier theories were flawed. Like several more recent philosophers, Plato in his later life is seen as rejecting views that he had proposed in his prime; instead he reinvents himself as less of a 'Platonist' and more of an Aristotelian.

Approaches to Plato: the dialogue form

More recently, the chronological story has receded slightly into the background, with increasing attention paid to the dramatic and literary aspects of Plato's writings. There are indeed different categories of dialogue, but do they define successive periods of Plato's writing? The different nature of the enterprise in each dialogue may be sufficient to explain variations in the literary and philosophical character: we need not suppose that Plato's own views have changed when he creates characters with different concerns. We should not assume that Plato necessarily endorses the positive theories that are offered by the 'Socrates' in dialogues of the middle period; we do not have to think that Plato endorses the criticisms and revisions of those theories that figure in the later dialogues. We are not obliged to believe that he was unable to see any of the difficulties when he wrote the Socratic dialogues, or that he thought the objections in the late dialogues were unanswerable. Indeed the dialogues in general may be written more to provoke the reader or student to respond than to satisfy their desire for a definitive conclusion. This approach encourages us to be less concerned with reconstructing what Plato believed at any particular stage of his life, and more interested in working out what any particular dialogue might have to offer in clarifying the philosophical issues that it addresses.

Philosophical and historical approaches to ancient philosophy

These alternative ways of approaching the work of Socrates (do we look for historical records or do we look for Socrates' philosophical legacy?) and the work of Plato (do we reconstruct Plato's development or do we read each dialogue for its philosophical insights?) prompt us to observe a bigger general pattern in the study of ancient philosophy as a whole. It relates significantly to the observation with which we started this chapter. Ancient philosophy is alive and well in two contexts: it is part of the study of philosophy and it is part of the study of the classical world. By and large it might seem that this leads in two slightly different directions: philosophers, on the whole, will approach the texts seeking a judgement on their value as philosophy; classicists, on the whole, will be interested in an authentic reconstruction of the past, with close attention to the social and historical context, and a desire to avoid attributing anachronistic views to the ancient thinkers or to face them with questions that were not theirs.

Although this dichotomy is oversimple, as I shall go on to suggest, it does have some truth to it. Philosophers generally seek to engage with ancient philosophers as partners in the same enterprise. They are interested in those aspects that speak directly to the debates current today, and they wish to see whether the ideas suggested by ancient philosophers turn out to solve problems that we are still seeking to solve. Because 'virtue ethics' is a fashionable alternative to Kantian and Utilitarian approaches to ethics, Aristotle's ethical treatises loom large in the required reading for any current scholar working in the field of ethics. They figure there not for mere historical curiosity but because they are serious contenders in the contemporary debate, included because they come up with genuinely promising contributions. Stoic logic is studied not because it is an outdated curiosity from the past but because it questions certain assumptions usually favoured by modern logicians: it shows another way of dealing with tricky issues as a result. Plato's ideas about knowledge are interrogated with a view to discovering how we might avoid falling into the traps that he lays for us.

We might add that there has been a tendency since the early twentieth century to assume, on the whole, that Plato (at least in the middle period) gets things wrong – and is to be studied as a kind of student exercise for spotting the fallacies or as a warning on how not to make the same mistakes – while Aristotle generally (it is assumed) gets things right. This shamelessly arrogant approach to Plato is gradually (and not before time) being laid to rest with the rise of the more sympathetic literary and philosophical appreciation of the dialogue form, and a wider realisation of the need to avoid negative caricatures of the considerations that Plato is putting forward, which may often be rather more subtle and challenging than we cared to notice. Most scholars now would recognise and seek to apply what we call the 'principle of charity': if in doubt, one should attribute to an ancient thinker the argument that seems strongest, rather than assume the worst of him. It remains true, however, that the fashion in current philosophy is more Aristotelian than Platonic in its preconceptions, and some recent work on Plato has tended to 'Aristotelianise' him in the process of seeking a more sympathetic and positive reading. See, for instance, the work of Terence Irwin for the latter approach, while for the critical tradition that dwells on Plato's failures as a philosopher, see the several helpful but rather less charitable works by David Bostock.

Classicists, by contrast with philosophers, have preferred a rather more sympathetic and contextualised approach to the ancient thinkers, exploring the lines of development and influence from one thinker to another and building up a historically sensitive evaluation of the nature of the evidence. Where the texts are fragmentary, classicists have taken pains to develop a methodologically sound assessment of the extent to which we can get back to an authentic account of the facts. For instance, one might contrast the cautious accounts of Heraclitus' thought presented in current work on the Presocratics (such as Richard McKirahan, for example), with the way in which Heraclitus was used as a figure of inspiration by continental philosophers in the Nietzschean and Heideggerian tradition. Classical scholars are likely to spend considerable effort on ensuring that empathy with the spirit of the ancient world governs their reading of a text, rather than questions brought to it from the modern philosophical agenda.

Nevertheless, although this dichotomy between classical and philosophical approaches has some truth to it, the reality is rather less divergent. A good classical interpretation is impossible without passing some philosophical judgements on the merit of the arguments and ideas under consideration. The process of interpreting involves reading with understanding. It is impossible to decide in the abstract what is the most plausible agenda that might explain Aristotle's allusive remarks without reference to what makes the resulting proposal a good or a bad answer to the proposed philosophical problem. It is impossible to work out what problem might be at issue without passing judgement on what is an interesting problem, and it is impossible wholly to free oneself from the preoccupations of the contemporary world in looking for important material among the ancient texts. Classicists too bring an agenda from the modern world to their reading of the texts. Similarly it is part of the contemporary philosophical agenda to recognise that texts mean different things to different readers, that the reader brings certain preconceptions to the text, and that sensitivity to a writer's literary style and historical context (including understanding the opponents against whom he was writing and the socially determined limits on what counted as thinkable at the time) is vital if one is to extract any genuine insight from the text.

These factors bring the two approaches to ancient philosophy together in the common search for a sympathetic and positive understanding of the contribution made by a text to a philosophical agenda that was alive for the ancients and is still alive for us today. There is indeed an impetus, within current approaches, for philosophers as well as classicists to break free from uncritical dogma, such as the longstanding caricature of Plato as a dogmatic peddler of 'noble lies' and racist political views, and to engage directly with the texts. Each of us, whether motivated by philosophical ambitions or by sheer curiosity about the past, needs to tease out the underlying point at issue, whether in Plato's famous *Republic* where his fictional 'Socrates' so shockingly toys with those deliberately outrageous thoughts, or in any other text from the beginnings with Thales to the late antique world of Plotinus and Augustine.

Further reading

J. Annas, *Ancient Philosophy: A Very Short Introduction*, Oxford: Oxford University Press, 2000 – an engaging introduction, sympathetic and philosophically motivated; it includes a fascinating chapter on the history of interpretation of Plato, with reference to the *Republic*.

J. Beversluis, *Cross-Examining Socrates: A Defense of the Interlocutors in Plato's Early Dialogues*, Cambridge: Cambridge University Press, 2000 – a contribution to the debate about how to read Plato: Beversluis explores how Plato (mis)treats the other characters besides Socrates in the philosophical argy-bargy.

D. Bostock, *Plato's* Theaetetus and *Plato's* Phaedo, Oxford: Clarendon Press, 1988 and 1986 – two detailed and helpful commentaries on individual dialogues of Plato, illustrating the Oxford tutorial style, which takes Plato as a dialectical partner.

W. K. C. Guthrie, *Socrates*, Cambridge: Cambridge University Press, 1971 – part of Guthrie's six-volume *History of Greek Philosophy*; the approach is focused on historical accuracy.

M. Heidegger and E. Fink, *Heraclitus Seminar1966/67*, trans. C. H. Seibert from *Heraklit* (1970), Alabama: University of Alabama Press, 1979.

T. Irwin, *Plato's Ethics*, New York and Oxford: Oxford University Press, 1995 – treats one aspect of Plato's thought in Irwin's distinctive style: the principle of charity is applied with somewhat Aristotelian results.

C. H. Kahn, *Plato and the Socratic Dialogue: The Philosophical Use of a Literary Form*, Cambridge: Cambridge University Press, 1996 – shows how Plato's work belongs to an established literary genre: supports the current literary approach to Plato and fuels scepticism about the strict historicity of the portrait of Socrates.

R. McKirahan, *Philosophy before Socrates*, Indianapolis: Hackett, 1994 – translated texts (for Presocratic philosophy) very clearly set out, with discursive commentary focused on both reconstruction and philosophical significance.

F. Nietzsche, *The Pre-Platonic Philosophers*, Urbana and Chicago: University of Illinois Press, 1995.

M. Nussbaum, *The Fragility of Goodness*, Cambridge: Cambridge University Press, 1986 – the most famous example of Nussbaum's approach, distinctive for harnessing Aristotle and Hellenistic philosophy to a modern philosophical project of her own.

C. Osborne, *Presocratic Philosophy: A Very Short Introduction*, Oxford: Oxford University Press, 2004 – includes reflections on the history of discovery and interpretation of Presocratic thought.

G. Vlastos, *Socrates: Ironist and Moral Philosopher*, Cambridge: Cambridge University Press, 1991 – sympathetic treatment of Socrates, philosophically oriented.

10. *Art History and Aesthetics*

Zahra Newby

Ever since the Renaissance, the art of antiquity, and in particular that of the classical Greek world, has been seen as the standard against which all later art could be measured. Its portrayal of the human body provided a model of beauty which was consciously 'rediscovered' in Renaissance art and has affected artistic conceptions of the human body and, especially, the nude ever since. The *naturalism* of ancient art – its ability to present a life-like and realistic (if also idealised) copy of the observed world – has come to be seen as its defining characteristic. Many histories of ancient art are thus dominated by discussion of the development of naturalism and the contribution of various individual artists. Yet in more recent years other approaches to the subject have also emerged, looking at ancient art less in terms of its stylistic development and instead with a focus on its reception by ancient viewers and the roles which it played within cultural, social, political or religious contexts.

The rhetoric of rise and decline

In their concentration on naturalism as the supreme aesthetic for ancient art, scholars have received support and encouragement from the writings about art produced during the Greek and Roman periods. One major source for such views is the *Natural History* of the elder Pliny, written in the first century AD. Within this encyclopaedic work, Pliny's books on metals, minerals and stone (*HN* 34–6) include a number of discussions of the development of sculpture (in both bronze and marble) and painting, apparently drawing on earlier Greek writings on art. In his accounts of the life and works of famous artists, Pliny often suggests a continuing development towards more and more lifelike creations achieved by the technical innovations of individual artists. Thus in bronze sculpture, Pythagoras of Rhegium is said to have been the first to show sinews and veins (*HN* 34.59) while Polyclitus of Sicyon is credited with the discovery of making statues throw their weight onto one leg (*HN* 34.56). Similar discussions of the development of naturalism in sculpture and painting can also be found in the writings of the orator Quintilian (*Inst.* 12.10.2–9).

In these texts the history of Greek art is portrayed as one primarily centred upon the innovations of individual artists, whose rivalries are recorded in a number of memorable anecdotes. One of the most famous is recorded by Pliny and tells of a competition between two painters of the fourth century BC, Parrhasius and Zeuxis. Zeuxis exhibited a painting of a bunch of grapes so realistic that a flock of birds flew up to try to eat them. However, Parrhasius won the competition by displaying a painting of a linen curtain whose naturalism so deceived Zeuxis that he asked for it to be removed and the painting revealed (*HN* 35.65). The worth of these paintings is shown to lie in their naturalism (see chapter 27).

Pliny describes the various networks of teachers, pupils and rivals among Greek sculptors and painters. Yet at one point in his account of bronze sculpture he suddenly stops, declaring that at the start of the third century BC 'art ceased' only to be revived in a rather inferior form in the mid-second century BC (*HN* 34.49–52).

Pliny's account incorporates two strands that have been influential upon the later history of ancient art. One is the concentration on individual artists and their works, a model of art history which was later adopted in the sixteenth century by Giorgio Vasari for his *Lives of the Artists*, a series of biographies of the lives and works of great artists of the Renaissance. According to this model of history, developments in sculpture and painting can be seen as the direct result of individual personalities, who can thus be characterised by certain peculiarities of style or technique. This in turn leads to the practice of *connoisseurship*, whereby it is believed that through a close analysis of individual works of art one can attribute them to particular named artists. The other strand which runs through Pliny's account is summed up in his famous comment 'cessavit deinde ars', 'then art ceased' (*HN* 34.52). It suggests that the history of ancient art is one of rise and decline. According to this model, the arts reached a peak of naturalism in the fifth and fourth centuries BC before entering upon a gradual decline throughout the Hellenistic period, which finally reached its depths in the non-naturalistic and schematic art of the late Roman Empire. As will be clear, this model is heavily value-laden, prizing naturalism as the best form of art and seeing all other styles of representation in relation to it as either steps on the way or indications of decline.

This model of art history as a story of development was first fully worked through in the eighteenth century by the German scholar Johann Joachim Winckelmann (1717–68), who has become known as the 'father of art history'. Winckelmann wrote a number of works on ancient art and was familiar with the collections in Rome through his posts first as librarian and advisor to Cardinal Alessandro Albani (who had a large sculpture collection) and then as papal antiquary and director of antiquities in Rome. In 1764 he published the work for which he has become best known, the *Geschichte der Kunst des Altertums* (= *History of Ancient Art*). In this work Winckelmann considered Egyptian and Etruscan art as well as that of Greece and Rome, but his clear focus was Greek art. His aim, as he says in the preface to the work, was 'to show the origin, progress, change and downfall of art'. He thus divided Greek art into stages. After the 'ancient' style, equivalent to the archaic and early classical period, he defined the art of the fifth century BC as 'grand' or 'lofty' and that of the fourth as 'beautiful', before art then began to decline in the 'period of the imitators'. While Winckelmann links these different stages in art to different artists (Phidias belongs to the 'grand' style, Lysippus and Apelles to the 'beautiful'), he also made clear links between the style of art and the conditions in which it was produced. Greek art is superior, we learn, because it was produced in a temperate climate in conditions of independence and freedom. According to this model, a particular style of art is not primarily the result of the decisions taken by individual artists, but reflects the culture in which it was produced. Greek art is superior because Greek culture too represents the heights of civilisation.

Winckelmann's *History of Ancient Art* is of course more detailed and complex than this brief survey suggests. However, his basic model of the development of ancient art as one of rise and decline with its height firmly placed in the fifth and fourth centuries BC has exerted a powerful effect on the later historiography of ancient art. In particular, it led to the privileging of the study of classical Greek art over that of the Hellenistic or Roman periods, which were generally neglected until the twentieth century. The stress on naturalism as the apogee of artistic styles has also led to this aspect dominating the study of Greek art. Scholars' approaches to this, however, have varied, some examining it from the Plinian perspective and evoking the contributions of various great individuals, whereas others have looked instead at the cultural and political factors which may have fostered this sudden change in style.

Shadowy presences: the search for great masters

The texts of the Roman period are littered with references to various great Greek sculptors and painters. The names of Polyclitus, Lysippus, Zeuxis and Apelles have passed down through the ages to become as famous as those of Raphael, Botticelli or Michelangelo; but none of their original works actually survive. They are known only from literary references and from the copies or echoes which can be perceived in artworks created in the Roman period. Since literary texts reveal the canonical status of these great masters, it has become imperative to find traces of them. Yet, to focus on sculpture, we are hampered by the lack of original Greek statues from the classical period. Apart from a few lucky finds from shipwrecks, such as the Riace bronzes (see chapter 26, fig. 26.4), the majority of bronze statues from classical Greece have been lost, melted down, looted or destroyed through the course of history. What is left is a series of inscribed bases, in which the footprints of statues can sometimes be seen, a series of textual accounts, and a wealth of idealising Roman statuary in marble.

The basic procedure for identifying a canonical Greek statue has been to look for a match between the subjects represented in Roman replicas and

Fig. 10.1 Roman copy of Myron's Discobolus from Hadrian's Villa, Tivoli. Original c. 450 BC. London, British Museum, Sc. 250 (photo: © museum).

those mentioned in literary sources. This has led to the successful identification of a number of famous Greek statues such as Myron's Discobolus (figure 10.1) and the Doryphorus (see chapter 26, figure 26.6) and Diadumenus statues by Polyclitus, all of which are described in some detail in the literary texts and exist in a number of replicas (see chapter 26). Once a famous type has been identified, scholars have then attempted to recreate the exact appearance of the original through a technique known by the German word *Kopienkritik*. This involves grouping together all the replicas of a particular type and attempting to distinguish which of the features that they present goes back to the original statue.

Through these means scholars have attempted to produce an accurate picture of the famous statues of classical Greece and the development of Greek sculpture. Yet in many cases the attempt to find echoes of Greek statues is fraught with difficulties. Recent scholars have pointed out that the different forms of evidence present their own problems. Many of the textual references are no more than simple lists of the statues made by a particular sculptor, without detailed descriptions, and there is always the possibility that authors have merged together the works made by two different artists of the same name (a particular problem for Polyclitus). Inscriptions on statue bases may indicate the sculptor or dedicator of a statue, but again the number of artists sharing the same name often makes it difficult to ascertain which particular one is meant, and many of the footprints would fit a number of different statues.

The evidence presented by Roman idealising statuary needs equal care. It is now widely recognised that many of these statues should be seen as new creations broadly modelled on classical forms rather than as accurate and exact copies of an original Greek statue. Even those which were close copies of a particular original may betray signs of their Roman production, for example in the modelling or finish of the flesh. Other scholars have even expressed doubt over the extent to which the most famous Greek statues would have been available to be copied, particularly if they were set up as sacred votives in a religious sanctuary. While the practice of studying Greek sculpture and its creators through copies and texts continues, the recent trend in this area is for greater caution in contrast to what is often seen as the over-optimism of the past.

Connoisseurship

One characteristic of the artist-centred approach to ancient art is the detailed examination of individual artworks in order to gain a deeper understanding into the style and development of a particular artist. This is closely related to the practice of connoisseurship. This approach was first fully developed in the study of post-classical painting by the nineteenth-century Italian art historian Giovanni Morelli (1816–91). Morelli believed that the close analysis of paintings, and in particular the unconscious rendering of minute details such as hands or ears, could lead one to the identity of the painter. It could thus be used as a means for attributing disputed paintings to particular individual artists.

The same technique was adopted in relation to Greek vase-painting by Sir John Beazley, Lincoln Professor of Classical Archaeology and Art at Oxford University 1925–56. Beazley's achievement was to assign vast numbers of Greek vases to different hands according to close observation of their styles of drawing. Some of these vases could be assigned to a particular painter, through the presence of a painter's signature on one of his works (see chapters 3 and 24). Other anonymous painters were given pseudonyms based on either the location or the subject matter of one particularly famous piece (e.g. the Berlin Painter, the Penthesilea Painter). This methodology dominated the study of Greek vases throughout much of the twentieth century and still continues. Through the concentration on individual artists and their development it allows one to look into the interactions and rivalries between individual vase-painters as well as their associations with different potters. One particularly neat example of this rivalry is a vase inscribed 'as Euphronius never [did]' next to a three-quarters view of a man (figure 10.2). One interpretation of this inscription is that the artist, Euthymides, is here asserting his superior artistic skills in a manner familiar from the anecdotes recorded in Pliny's *Natural History*.

However, recent scholars have also begun to suggest different ways to study vases, cautioning

Fig. 10.2 Red-figure amphora from Vulci, signed by Euthymides. c. 520–500 BC. Munich, Antikensammlung inv. 2307 (photo: © museum).

against imposing too great an artistic status on everyday objects. Instead they suggest that vases (or 'pots', since the terms we use reveal our attitudes towards the status of these objects) should be viewed within their cultural or social contexts, examining, for example, the situations in which they were used and the choice of scenes portrayed upon them. Nevertheless, the search for artists, personalities and workshops continues in the study of ancient art, whether in the identification of different (almost always anonymous) hands in Roman wall paintings (see chapter 27, figures 27.1–27.4), or of different schools of mosaicists (see chapter 27, figures 27.1 and 27.7–27.10).

The Greek revolution

One consequence of seeing ancient art as a story of rise and decline around a peak of naturalism is to privilege the period in which naturalistic art emerged in the fifth century BC. This has led to a plethora of studies questioning why, in the early years of the fifth century BC, sculptors suddenly turned from the rigid postures of archaic statues to more relaxed, supple, naturalistic poses such as that of the Critius Boy from the Athenian Acropolis (figure 10.3). In particular, scholars have sought to identify the events that created the situation in which naturalistic art could emerge. The sudden emergence of lifelike figures has been given a number of names – the 'Great awakening', the 'Greek revolution' and the 'Greek miracle' among them. All are heavily laden with an ideology that sees art as an expression of the values of the age as a whole. One of the clearest examples of this was an exhibition called 'The Greek Miracle: Classical Sculpture from the Dawn of Democracy', held in Washington and New York in 1992–3. Here, the rise of naturalistic Greek art was closely associated with the emergence of the 'best' form of government – democracy. While a variety of other

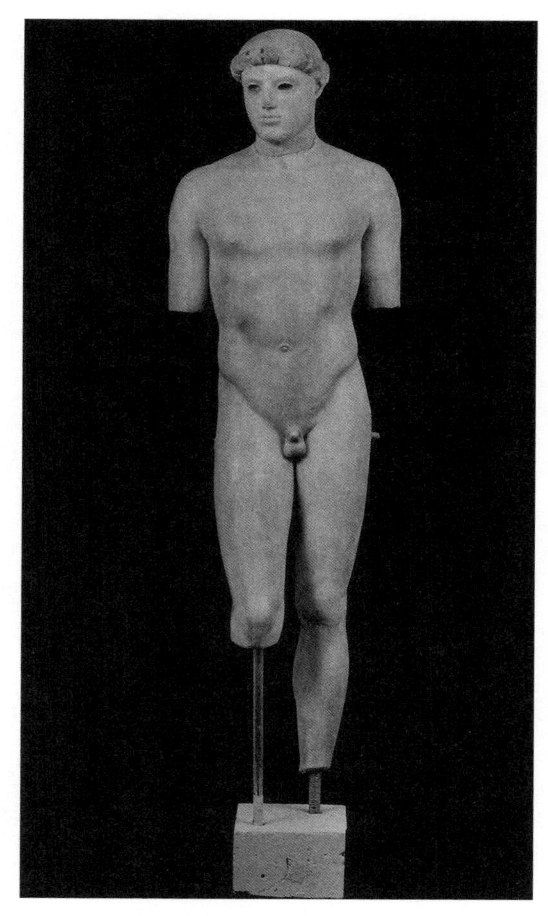

Fig. 10.3 The Critius Boy, from the Athenian Acropolis. c. 490–480 BC. Athens, Acropolis Museum, inv. 698 (photo: © DAI(A)).

explanations has been offered, covering politics, science, narrative and theatre, the emergence of naturalistic art has often been associated with those elements of Greek culture which appear most worthy of praise to contemporary society.

The centrality of naturalism within the study of ancient art has also led to a search for glimpses of it in earlier sculpture. The numerous examples of archaic *kouroi* and *korai* (see chapter 26, figures 26.1 and 26.3) have been placed in a chronological schema which arranges them from least to most naturalistic. While this ordering of the material may be broadly correct, it is also teleological. It starts from a knowledge of the endpoint of the development and works back from that, underplaying the fact that at the point of creation the final stage of development was still in the future and thus unknown.

Hellenistic and Roman art

This model of the rise and decline of naturalism has had its effect on the study of other periods of ancient art too. The hyper-realism of some Hellenistic art (e.g. figure 10.4) was seen by Quintilian as the effect of taking naturalism to its extremes (*Inst.* 12.10.9). Modern scholars have also been influenced by the story of artistic development in later Western art, using terms such as 'baroque' or 'rococo' (styles of art which post-date classicising Renaissance art) to characterise strands of Hellenistic art. More recently, however, scholars of Hellenistic art have begun to suggest that a simple story of stylistic development does not work in this period, whose art is instead characterised by a multiplicity of different styles used for different contexts and purposes.

A similar story can be told of Roman art. While the idealising sculpture created in the Roman period has long been used to recreate lost Greek originals, many other areas of Roman art, such as veristic portraiture and historical reliefs (see chapter 26, figure 26.7), were generally neglected. It was only at the end of the nineteenth century that Roman art began to rise to attention as a period worthy of study in its own right. This was due in particular to the work of Alois Riegl and Franz Wickhoff. These men differed in their approaches and interests, yet both sought to free Roman art

Fig. 10.4 Drunken old woman; Roman copy of a Hellenistic statue. Original c. third century BC. Munich, Glyptothek inv. 437 (photo: © museum).

from the accusation of 'decay'. Instead they asserted that the stylistic developments within Roman art could be seen not as a decline from the naturalistic ideal but rather as a stage in the development of later Christian and medieval art.

However, the tyranny of naturalism has proved hard to avoid. In 1954 Bernard Berenson clearly asserted his belief that the art of late antiquity was characterised by a debased and inferior style in a book brutally titled *The Arch of Constantine or the Decline of Form*. Berenson argued that the re-use on the arch of elements taken from earlier monuments was a clear sign of the artistic impoverishment of the Constantinian age, also manifested in the schematic fourth-century reliefs which contrast so sharply with earlier styles (figure 10.5; see also chapter 26, figure 26.9). While the contrast in styles is undeniable, recent scholars have instead drawn attention to the ideological motives behind the re-use here of particular monuments, all of

Fig. 10.5 Arch of Constantine, Rome, north facade. c. AD 312–15 (photo: © DAI(R)).

which were associated with 'good' emperors of the second century AD.

In an essay first published in the 1950s, the scholar Otto Brendel outlined the historiography of Roman art. As he saw so well, the challenge for Roman art historians has been to encompass both the naturalistic and abstract strands in Roman art and to explain what it is that makes Roman art unique. This may involve looking at the classicism of much Roman art with a view both to how such images were used in their Roman context, for example in the decoration of villas, theatres or baths, and how they reflect Roman attitudes towards Greek culture. Alternatively the non-naturalistic strands of Roman art have been looked at with a view both to how they relate to non-Greek, Italic or popular artistic traditions and to how these stylistic forms came to dominate the art of late antiquity and early Christianity. One particular recent approach has suggested that different artistic styles reflect the different functions which art is seen to serve, arguing that when art was used to convey religious or spiritual truths naturalism became much less important (see chapter 26).

New approaches

As will be evident by now, the study of ancient art has long been dominated by the aesthetic of naturalism, by the belief that it is on its qualities of *mimesis* or imitation that art can best be judged. Yet, more recently, scholars have sought to re-examine ancient art by looking at other criteria, moving away from style and development to focus on art's functions and its reception by ancient viewers. Studies have considered art's role in creating and asserting senses of identity at all levels of society, from the tombstones of Roman freedmen to the propagandist use of art by Hellenistic dynasts or Roman emperors (see chapter 26, figure 26.8). The examination of art in relation to society has also led to studies considering the ways in which images reveal and construct ancient notions of gender and sexuality.

Another recent area of research has been the ways in which the visual arts interact with other creative arts, particularly literature. Scholars have looked at how images can present their own forms of narrative and at how images and texts influence and overlap with one another. A further trend in scholarship, which also urges caution about the extent to which we can ever fully recover ancient art, is to look at the ways in which it has been received, reinterpreted and recreated in post-classical times (see ch. 11). The many restorations and reworkings of ancient statues, which took place from the Renaissance onwards, inevitably influence our own attempts to get back to an 'original' image, which may, in any case, never have existed in one unified or static form. Images change their meanings according to those who see them and the circumstances in which they are displayed. The challenge and excitement for today's historian of ancient art is to select from all these possible approaches, with all their advantages and limitations, those which allow us as far as possible to enter into the visual culture of the ancient world.

Further reading

M. Beard and J. Henderson, *Classical Art: From Greece to Rome*, Oxford: Oxford University Press, 2001 – a provocative reappraisal, particularly good on reception issues.

J. Boardman, *The History of Greek Vases: Potters, Painters and Pictures*, London: Thames and Hudson, 2001 – a good overview.

O. Brendel, *Prolegomena to the Study of Roman Art* (ed. J. J. Pollitt), New Haven: Yale University Press, 1979 – an analysis of the previous historiography.

A. A. Donohue and M. D. Fullerton (eds), *Ancient Art and its Historiography*, Cambridge: Cambridge University Press, 2003 – a collection of articles exploring the historiography of ancient art. See esp. the articles by Lapatin (on the 'minor arts') and Fullerton (on the influence of Winckelmann and *Kopienkritik*).

J. Elsner, *Art and the Roman Viewer*, Cambridge: Cambridge University Press, 1995 – a viewer-focused reading of Roman art.

E. K. Gazda (ed.), *The Ancient Art of Emulation: Studies in Artistic Originality and Tradition from the Present to Classical Antiquity*, Ann Arbor: University of Michigan Press, 2002 – a collection of articles on the theme of copying. The article by M. Koortbojian is particularly useful on the Roman display of classicising statuary.

S. Goldhill and R. Osborne (eds), *Art and Text in Ancient Greek Culture*, Cambridge: Cambridge University Press, 1994 – articles examining different relationships between art and text.

C. Hallet, '*Kopienkritik* and the works of Polykleitos', in W. G. Moon (ed.), *Polykleitos, the Doryphoros, and Tradition*, Madison: University of Wisconsin Press, 1995 – a balanced defence of the use of Roman copies in the study of Greek art.

D. Irwin, *Winckelman: Writings on Art*, London: Phaidon Press, 1972 – extracts showing Winckelmann's attitudes to ancient art.

N. Kampen (ed.), *Sexuality in Ancient Art: Near East, Egypt, Greece, and Italy*, Cambridge: Cambridge University Press, 1996 – a collection of articles examining the representation of sexuality and gender.

M. Marvin, 'Roman sculptural reproductions of Polykleitos: the sequel', in A. Hughes and E. Ranfft (eds), *Sculpture and its Reproductions*, London: Reaktion Books, 1997 – criticises the tendency to see Roman idealising statues as copies of famous Greek originals.

B. S. Ridgway, *Roman Copies of Greek Sculpture: The Problem of the Originals*, Ann Arbor: University of Michigan Press, 1984 – a good survey of the evidence.

J. Tanner, *The Invention of Art History in Ancient Greece*, Cambridge: Cambridge University Press, 2005 – examines the position of artists and theories of art in classical Greece.

11. Classical Legacies

Lorna Hardwick

The curving sickle is beaten into the sword that yields not
(curvae rigidum falces conflantur in ensem).

This agonised line about the impact of war comes from the closing sequence of the first of Virgil's *Georgics* (trans. C. Day Lewis, 1966). The words were found at random by the classical scholar Bernard Knox when in the closing days of World War II he made a 'sors Vergiliana', following the medieval tradition of opening a Virgil text and pointing to a passage, which would then be seen to have prophetic force. At the time Knox was fighting with the Italian partisans and the line seemed to him to express the reality of the shattered environment in which he was living. Yet the line had been interpreted very differently by Joseph Goebbels when he chanced on it in 1926. When serving as gauleiter of Berlin he, according to his biographer, saw in the line a clarion call to arms (Thomas, 'Georgics of resistance', p. 118). These episodes are revealing about perspectives on the classical world – the continuity of tradition through ancient and medieval to modern; the desire to find consolation or inspiration in classical texts and images, allied with a tendency to read them as speaking to one's own condition; the resistance of artistic works to any one exclusive interpretation.

An important strand in classical scholarship has been that of the 'classical tradition'. This studies the transmission of classical culture through history, usually with the emphasis on its direct influence. However, uncritical belief in this transmission of influence and value was interrupted at least from the seventeenth and eighteenth centuries by 'The Battle of the Books', disputes about the relative value of classical and 'modern' culture and about the relationship of classical models to concepts of progress (Highet, *Classical Tradition*; Bolgar, *Classical Heritage*). More recent scholarship has emphasised diversity within classical culture itself and has investigated ways in which some aspects were selected and adapted in order to give value and status to subsequent practices. There have been important studies of the changing role of the classical in education and therefore in patterns of knowledge about the ancient world (Stray, *Classics Transformed*), about analysis of ways in which classical texts may be read in modern literary contexts (Martindale, *Redeeming the Text*) and of how particular texts and images become prominent in different contexts (Edwards, *Roman Presences*). These combine to show that the history of the reception of classical culture is also part of the history of broader cultural shifts. This chapter focuses on four key aspects of this relationship – translation, appropriation, intervention and hybridity – and discusses how they reveal the continuing active role of classical culture in the modern world.

Translation

Many of the modern debates about the nature and purposes of translation parallel those within antiquity. Translation and adaptation from Greek provided an important stimulus to the development of Latin literature. Livius Andronicus produced versions of Greek comedy and tragedy at the Ludi Romani as early as 240 BC (see chs 38, and 40). Translating Greek texts and transplanting Greek ideas into Roman contexts were major occupations of Cicero, who drew a contrast between the different techniques involved in translating word for word and in communicating style and effect 'in language which conforms to our ways' (46 BC). Horace took this a stage further and emphasised the creative impact on the receiving language.

Thus from the earliest times, the selection of classical texts for translation influenced how the source literature would be regarded, shaped its cultural influence, determined who had access to it, and provided a stimulus for adaptation and the creation of new works. The relationship between the source and the translation was sometimes remarkably free. For example, in the twelfth century Virgil's *Aeneid* was translated into Irish prose, as were Lucan's *de Bello Civili* and Statius' *Thebaid*. None of these was a literal or even close translation. Versions of classical texts included new material, some of it from other ancient authors, some from indigenous traditions such as Middle Irish hero tales. This suggests that a wide audience was catered for and that classical material was enriching and being enriched by interaction with a vigorous cultural environment.

From the early Renaissance onwards, translators and critics increasingly reflected on translation practices. Gavin Douglas used his prologue to book 1 to discuss the poetic capacity of the Scots language in relation to the Latin of Virgil's *Aeneid*, although with a slight apology for roughness. Douglas' work (1513, published posthumously in 1553) was an early example of the vernacular revival in which translations of classical works were thought to add status and authority to the receiving language. Douglas' translation produced a new work which later became a landmark of literature, as did those of George Chapman (*Iliad*, 1598–1600), John Dryden (*Aeneid*, 1697) and Alexander Pope (*Iliad*, 1715–20, *Odyssey*, 1725–6) (Underwood, *English Translators*). In the preface to his translation of Ovid's *Epistles* (1680), Dryden reflected on different kinds of translation and their capacity for 'making poetry into poetry'. His three categories were 'metaphrase' (word by word and line by line), 'paraphrase' (keeping the original author in view but concentrating on sense rather than words) and 'imitation', which amounted to creative adaptation. Since this last could do 'the greatest wrong . . . to the memory and reputation of the dead', Dryden's preference was for paraphrase, although the dedication to his translation of the *Aeneid* inclines towards the literal because of his desire not to lose the beauty of Virgil's words.

In the nineteenth century, debates about translation intensified. There was a vigorous argument between F. W. Newman and Matthew Arnold. Newman's edition and translation of the *Iliad* (1856) reflected his view that to be 'faithful' a translation should produce an effect on the reader equivalent to that experienced by the ancient audience. In Homeric terms this included a sense of distance from the society represented in the poems, so Newman consciously archaised, using alliteration, rhythm and words from Anglo-Saxon poetry. In his Oxford lectures *On Translating Homer* (1860–1) Arnold reacted strongly against this 'foreignisation', accusing Newman of creating cultural differences and failing to universalise meaning.

Thus translation practices and debates have been central to the transmission, interpretation and appreciation of classical culture. The most significant issues have been the border between translation and new work, the impact of translation on the receiving language and improvement of access to classical texts for new readers. E. V. Rieu's popular prose translations of the *Odyssey* (1946) and the *Iliad* (1950) for the Penguin Classics series sold over four-and-a-half million copies, while the more scholarly 'canonical' translations by R. L. Lattimore, R. Fagles and R. Fitzgerald have influenced the classical perceptions of thousands of students and general readers as well as poets and dramatists. Translation for the stage raises additional issues of speakability and the relationship between verbal and non-verbal aspects of staging (Hardwick, *Reception Studies*, chapter 4), while notions of equivalence of experience between ancient and modern audiences and readers require cultural as well as linguistic investigation of both ancient and modern contexts. Above all, translation requires a continuing dialogue between ancient and modern, source and receiver. George Steiner has identified four aspects of this transactional process – *trust* that the source has something to say, *aggression* in seizing this, *incorporation* into the receiving language and culture, and a sense of *reciprocity*, that something has been lost and something gained

(Steiner, *After Babel*). Steiner's remarks were made in the context of translation, but they go far beyond linguistic limits and provide an interpretative framework for much of the rest of this chapter.

Appropriation

Appropriation means taking an ancient image, text or idea and using it to justify or sanction subsequent ideas or practices, whether explicitly or implicitly. Thus in terms of Steiner's four aspects of 'translation', the first three could be said to come together in practices of appropriation. In its 'hard' and most direct form, appropriation can imply using the culture and values of the ancient world as propaganda in the modern. However, there are also more subtle kinds of appropriation, 'soft' practices which embed the Greek or Roman source in a new context which derives status or artistic authority from its association with the ancient (see chapter 10).

An example of appropriation for propaganda purposes is Benito Mussolini's association of Italian fascism with Roman ancestry – in both the literal and figurative senses. In 1922, at the time when he was preparing to march on Rome with his fascist militia, he made a speech in which he claimed not only that the Italians were descended from ancient Romans but that they should look to the Romans as models of political and military organisation and unity – 'wise and strong, disciplined and imperial . . . the fasces are Roman, Roman our organisation of combatants, Roman our pride and our courage. *Civis Romanus sum* [I am a Roman citizen]' (Wyke and Biddiss, *Uses and Abuses*, pp. 167–86).

Mussolini's appropriation of ancient Rome in the fascists' cause illustrates a number of the main features of appropriation – the invocation of direct ancestry or similar types of 'foundation myth', the use of ancient models in authorising contemporary values and achievements, and the assimilation of ancient cultural examples into modern practice. He did this through a programme of archaeological excavations and exhibitions and by incorporating into the public face of his regime the visual imagery of ancient Rome, such as fasces, eagles, the wolf which suckled Romulus and Remus, and the triumphal arches and columns which framed public spaces and directed the gaze of the spectators. He even paired his own statue with that of Augustus at the 1937 celebration of Augustus' birthday, while the wars between Rome and Carthage were exploited as a source of anti-semitic propaganda (Hardwick, *Reception Studies*, pp. 43–50).

Rome also provided a source of public imagery and cultural justification for British imperialism, including the analogy between the *pax romana* and the *pax britannica* (the Roman peace and the British peace, i.e. the 'peaceful' states imposed by the two empires; Majeed in Edwards, *Roman Presences*). Visual images of Peace are powerful statements. One example of fusion of the appropriation of classical values and artistic styles may be seen in the allegorical marble figure of Peace, now in the National Museum of Kiev, Ukraine (with a terracotta model in the National Gallery of Scotland, Edinburgh, NG 2649). The statue was commissioned from Antonio Canova in 1811 by the Russian chancellor Count Nicolai Romanov. Peace is depicted as a winged female figure, associated in Roman iconography with Victory. She is resting her hand on a truncated column, which bore inscriptions celebrating a series of peace treaties negotiated by the Russians.

The most difficult examples of appropriation to evaluate are those which are so embedded as to be barely noticed or which appear to domesticate classical material into other contexts. For example, the Caribbean poet Derek Walcott in his long poem *Omeros* (1990) uses classical names for his characters – Achille, Hektor, Helen, Philoctete – in a way that seems to domesticate classical figures into a modern Caribbean cultural context. However, the domestication is not as simple as it first seems. The classical names bring with them allusions to the fact that plantation owners sometimes gave such names to their slaves, blotting out the associations carried by their African names. Furthermore, Walcott domesticates the Homeric simile and the classical names for poor fishermen into a language which combines Caribbean vernacular with the diction of the English poetic tradition. This acts as a reminder that appropriation also involves challenging the idea that there are exclusive links between classical sources and any one subsequent tradition (Hardwick, *Translating Words*, chapter 6).

Thus the role of appropriation in the relationship between ancient and subsequent cultures may vary from propaganda to cultural interaction. At its 'hardest' it represents a ruthless seizure of the ancient to justify the contemporary. At its most subtle, appropriation may be part of a process of cultural migration which moves towards the fourth of Steiner's aspects of 'translation' – a recognition of the cultural energy implicit in the interplay of commonalities and differences between ancient and modern.

Intervention

The previous section on appropriation emphasised the ways in which seizing on classical models can be part of the justification or celebration of power. However, exploitation of classical material has also played a major role in challenging established power, both political and cultural. Intervention involves reworking the source in a way which creates a political, social or aesthetic critique of the receiving society. Use of classical texts as coded forms of challenge has occurred in all periods but was recognised as having a special impact in the twentieth century. The technique was refined by the German poet and dramatist Berthold Brecht, whose work emphasised the distance and difference between ancient and modern and yet also pointed to parallels and resonances which encouraged readers and audiences to criticise the modern as well as the ancient. An early example is a poem in which Brecht adapted the form of the epic simile to set up an ironic comparison between the Roman emperor Nero, who played music as Rome burned, and the German leader Hitler, who sketched a plan for a new building after the Reichstag fire of 1934 – 'So – in the manner of their art – the two differed.'

Predictably, Brecht went into exile, but after his post-war return to Europe his 1948 version of Sophocles' *Antigone* identified Creon with Hitler and explored how a principled individual like Antigone might resist tyranny (Macintosh in Easterling, *Cambridge Companion*). The production raised two main issues which are important for other interventionist examples. First, some plays and paradigms are particularly adaptable in such contexts. Second, so far as drama is concerned the set design and acting styles may work in different ways to raise audience awareness. In the case of Brecht's play the design was formal and minimalist. Its aim was to avoid intervening between the audience and the words. A similar technique was used in 2003 by Verse Theater Manhattan in their performances of Christopher Logue's *War Music*, a version of books 16–19 of the *Iliad*. This tour took place when the invasion of Iraq by the USA/UK/Australian coalition was imminent, and the company resisted suggestions that they should use staging, costume and revisions of the script to indicate the work's relevance to the forthcoming violence. Their argument was that nothing should force the audience to a restricted interpretation of the words. So far as selection of plays is concerned, it has been argued that in the USA performances of Greek plays peak during times of conflict, with Euripides' *Women of Troy* and Aeschylus' *Oresteia* particularly prominent (Hartigan, *Greek Tragedy*). In all traditions, plays which address issues of political or gender oppression or alienation, such as *Antigone*, *Medea* and *Philoctetes*, have had notable productions.

Another important issue is the relative success with which productions of classical plays evaded the twentieth-century censor. In Eastern Europe during the period of Soviet oppression, productions of the plays seem to have been allowed because they were part of the European cultural tradition and were perceived as remote from current concerns, even compensating for the lack of permitted new plays. Research on productions in the former Czechoslovakia has shown, however, that when censorship was particularly severe, plays such as *Antigone* and Aristophanes' comedies were regarded as suspect, as the censors feared the impact on audiences. As the power of the regime weakened, censorship became more benevolent. In order to outwit the censors, old translations were often used and contemporary relevance was signalled less by the words and more by visual aspects such as make-up, costumes and acting style. As the censorship relaxed in the 1980s, a production of Aristophanes' *Birds* broke new ground with its dialogue and characters, using the utopian theme to satirise the political climate of the 1950s, when (before the 1956 Soviet invasion of Hungary) the Communist youth movement aimed to build an ideal state. Ironically, it seems that under the more severe censorship productions had to be nuanced and sophisticated in their political allusions, whereas when the censors became more permissive the characterisation and acting scripts became more crude and one-dimensional.

Productions of Greek plays have also had a major interventionist role in South Africa. Under the apartheid regime, productions in Afrikaans were originally seen as an attempt to enhance the cultural status of the language, but they also had the effect of exposing audiences to radical ideas. A significant example was the 1981 Cape Performing Arts Board production of the *Oresteia*, which addressed the question of how to progress from a cycle of revenge towards a more harmonious society. *Antigone* predictably had a prominent part in expressing opposition to apartheid, notably when from the 1960s the Serpent Players, a group of black actors, began to include Greek tragedy in their repertoire and then co-operated with Athol Fugard in staging *The Island* (first performed in 1973). This includes a play-within-a-play, the *agon* between Antigone and Creon, as rehearsed and staged by political prisoners on Robben Island.

The interventionist function of classical works is by no means confined to resistance to totalitarian regimes. In supposedly liberal or barely censored societies, translations and adaptations have been created as critiques of aspects of modern values and practices and have challenged unexamined assumptions. There have been many adaptations of Greek drama by Irish dramatists who have addressed the relationship between North and South as well as issues of cultural change and gender (McDonald and Walton, *Amid our Troubles*; Hardwick, *Translating Words*, chapter 5). Seamus Heaney and Michael Longley have integrated classical episodes and themes into their poetry, linking the personal and the political (Hardwick, 'Shards and suckers'). A major interventionist writer is Tony Harrison, who, unlike many poets and dramatists, works directly from the original languages. Harrison created *Phaedra Britannica* (1975), based on the Phaedra/Hippolytus plays of Euripides and Seneca, and placed it in an Indian setting to explore the racial and political attitudes of the British Empire. He also wrote the (as yet unperformed) *Medea: A Sex-War Opera*, with music by Harrison Birtwistle (1985), and the film-poem *Prometheus* (1998), based on Harrison's desire for a public poetry. This adapted Aeschylus' treatment of the classical myth to represent the impact of the collapse of the mining communities and by extension that of the British working-class ethos and the socialist ideal in Europe (Hall, 'Tony Harrison's *Prometheus*'; Hardwick, *Translating Words*, chapter 8). In 2005, Harrison's new translation of *Hecuba* was staged by the Royal Shakespeare Company in London and the USA. Although it followed Euripides' text closely, including parody of the workings of democracy, it was widely criticised as anachronistic because of its allusions to the invasion of Iraq by the West. It remains to be seen whether this reaction marks a general fatigue with the use of the past to critique the present or is symptomatic of a specific unwillingness by liberal audiences to accept challenges to their own deep-seated values and practices.

Hybridity

The role of classical material in the cultural politics of intervention and witness has highlighted two main aspects of cultural change. The first was the disruption of the almost automatic association of classical culture with ruling groups and the 'high culture' of Western Europe. The second was a reaching out to new audiences, people who were unlikely to be steeped in classical learning or even to be aware of the basic aspects of the poems, plays and iconography. Such audiences required the development of innovative techniques in translation and staging. These changes fed into the development of hybrid adaptations of classical texts and images which have provoked vigorous critical argument both inside and outside the classical community.

In the technical sense 'hybrid' is a term which denotes cross-fertilisation between different categories or (in the animal and plant worlds) breeds. The *Shorter Oxford English Dictionary* includes in its definition a suggestion of incongruity and loss of purity; yet 'hybrid vigour' is a scientific term which values outcrosses as a source of energy. Increasingly, this model is being applied to the crossing of cultural boundaries. The development of hybrid forms of classical material has been strongly evident in terms of genre, language and theatrical production techniques. It has also been instrumental in the development of 'double consciousness' – an awareness of the aspects which classical mythology, themes, images and texts share with other cultural contexts, as well as those in which they differ.

An important type of hybrid creativity is the genre crossover. This may take the form of transplantation of one genre into another, as in Ted Hughes' *Tales from Ovid* (published 1997 and subsequently staged) and Derek Walcott's *A Stage Version of the Odyssey* (1993), in which epic poetry was given a performance context which drew on Caribbean art forms such as Carnival. It may also take the form of a fusion of genres, as in the film-poem which focuses on the interplay of language, moving image and the horizons of experience of the audience. Tony Harrison has explained how in cinematic construction experiencing and feeling the rhythm of the shots is like responding to metre in literature. In communicating to those who are not classically knowledgeable, Harrison integrates narrative and explanation of the myth into the fabric of the film, using the boy who learns about the myth at school and explains it to his father. The implications are highlighted by Hermes, the cynical spin-doctor who comments on the dangers of popular dissemination of the poetry and ideas of the myth – 'How can Olympus stay intact / if poetry comes to Pontefract?' (Harrison, *Prometheus*, 23).

A related technique used in drama in order to cross cultural boundaries is to situate several languages alongside one another. In the Mark Fleishman and Jennie Reznek production of *Medea*, performed in South Africa 1994–6, the spoken script was multilingual, including Xhosa, Tamil and Afrikaans as well as English. This represented a situation in which in the new South Africa, with its eleven official languages, a representative audience would inevitably understand only parts of the spoken script, a metaphor for the new nation's difficulties in building understanding. The technique was integrated with the use of mime and dance to suggest meaning through the body language and movement of the cast. Elsewhere in Africa and in the Caribbean, poetic collages and hybrid theatrical techniques have produced a new classically-oriented literature and theatre, which has moved beyond the interventionist expression of anti-colonialist ideas and has become a forum for the exploration of new debates about the relationship between diverse aspects of postcolonial cultural identity (notably in the work of Wole Soyinka, Kamau Brathwaite, Ola Rotimi, Femi Osofisan and Christopher Okigbo).

Critics have not always welcomed this hybridity. Some postcolonial critics have deplored the extent to which classical material persists in postcolonial literatures. Some classicists have called for 'authenticity' to be re-established (in so far as it can be reconstructed), and some scholars have expressed discontent with much contemporary staging of ancient drama on the grounds that it privileges modern resonances or places insights from other traditions, such as Japanese Noh, Balinese or African Yoruba theatre, alongside the Greek. In stressing purity and essentialism such approaches perhaps overlook the fact that ancient culture was itself hybrid, both formally and contextually, for example in the response of epic poetry to the *koinē* culture of the Mediterranean and in Roman interaction with the Greek world. Furthermore, it is now being argued that non-European theatrical practice has paradoxically restored to the staging of ancient drama the prominence of visual spectacle, colour, song, dance and movement which were repressed in Western theatrical tradition (Wiles, *Greek Theatre*; Hardwick, 'Greek drama'). Such debates are a useful reminder that classical culture has been dispersed from its original location and contexts and that successive forms of neoclassicism have involved interaction with receiving cultural traditions. In that sense classical texts and images are diasporic. Awareness of their migration patterns and their encounters with other cultures prompts us to try to understand what has been added, adapted, marginalised or lost (Hardwick, 'Remodelling receptions'). In that investigation, Steiner's concept of reciprocity is likely to be a better guide than is the Virgilian lottery.

Further reading

R. R. Bolgar, *The Classical Heritage and its Beneficiaries*, Cambridge: Cambridge University Press, 1954 – a study of the relationships between classical and European high culture.

P. E. Easterling (ed.), *The Cambridge Companion to Greek Tragedy*, Cambridge: Cambridge University Press, 1997 – the best starting point for study of Greek tragedy with chapters on modern reception, including drama and opera.

C. Edwards (ed.), *Roman Presences: Receptions of Rome in European Culture, 1789–1945*, Cambridge and New York: Cambridge University Press, 1999 – includes essays on art, architecture, revolution and imperialism.

E. Hall, 'Tony Harrison's *Prometheus*: a view from the left', *Arion* Spring/Summer, Third Series, 10 (2002), no. 1 – a vigorous analysis of Harrison's art and ideology.

E. Hall, F. Macintosh, and A. Wrigley (eds), *Dionysus since '69*, Oxford: Oxford University Press, 2004 – a collection of essays examining late-twentieth-century performances of Greek drama and their cultural impact.

L. Hardwick, *Translating Words, Translating Cultures*, London: Duckworth, 2000 – discusses nineteenth- and twentieth-century developments in translation practice and the adaptation of classical texts across boundaries of cultural and literary tradition.

L. Hardwick, *Reception Studies* (*Greece and Rome* New Surveys in the Classics 33), Oxford: Oxford University Press, 2003 – an introduction to the methods and subject matter of reception studies, within antiquity and subsequently.

L. Hardwick, 'Greek drama and anti-colonialism: decolonising Classics', in E. Hall, F. Macintosh and A. Wrigley (eds), *Dionysus since '69*, Oxford: Oxford University Press, 2004, pp. 219–42 – discusses Greek drama as a catalyst in cultural politics.

L. Hardwick, 'Shards and suckers: modern receptions of Homer', in R. Fowler (ed.), *The Cambridge Companion to Homer*, Cambridge: Cambridge University Press, 2004 – discusses reception of Homer in relation to cultural change.

L. Hardwick, 'Remodelling receptions: Greek drama as diaspora in performance', in C. Martindale and R. Thomas (eds), *Classics and the Uses of Reception*, Oxford: Blackwell, in press – discusses the migration of Greek texts and performances.

K. Hartigan, *Greek Tragedy on the American Stage: Ancient Drama in the Commercial Theater, 1882–1994*, Westport CT and London: Greenwood Press, 1995 – discusses trends in the selection and staging of classical plays in the USA.

G. Highet, *The Classical Tradition: Greek and Roman Influences on Western Literature*, Oxford: Oxford University Press, 1949 – emphasises unity rather than diversity in Greek and Roman culture, but also anticipates modern links between classical reception and popular culture.

C. Martindale, *Redeeming the Text: Latin Poetry and the Hermeneutics of Reception*, Cambridge: Cambridge University Press, 1993 – argues that classical texts are read through the filter of subsequent cultural traditions.

C. Martindale and R. Thomas (eds), *Classics and the Uses of Reception*, Oxford: Blackwell, in press – discusses a range of classical receptions and their contexts.

M. McDonald and J. M. Walton, *Amid our Troubles: Irish Versions of Greek Tragedy*, London: Methuen, 2002 – includes studies of individual plays and adaptations as well as material on Irish cultural politics.

G. Steiner, *After Babel: Aspects of Language and Translation* (3rd edn), Oxford: Oxford University Press, 1998 – seminal work for the study of the relationships between translation and culture.

C. A. Stray, *Classics Transformed: Schools, Universities and Society in England, 1830–1960*, Oxford: Oxford University Press, 1998 – traces the history of classics in education.

R. F. Thomas, 'The Georgics of resistance from Virgil to Heaney', *Virgilius* 47 (2001), 117–47 – examines receptions of Virgil in subsequent literature and challenges the view that Virgil idealised rural life.

S. Underwood, *English Translators of Homer from George Chapman to Christopher Logue*, London: Northcote House, 1998 – good introduction to literary translations of Homer.

D. Wiles, *Greek Theatre Performance: An Introduction*, Cambridge: Cambridge University Press, 2000 – the best starting point for the study of performance.

M. Wyke and M. Biddiss (eds), *The Uses and Abuses of Antiquity*, Bern, Berlin, Brussels, Frankfurt and New York: Peter Lang, 1999 – examines many types of appropriation and includes essays on material culture and film.

B. The Regions of the Ancient World

Classical scholarship has increasingly recognised the need to see the civilisations of Greece and Rome in the context of their relationships with neighbouring peoples. It would clearly be impossible to survey all those peoples in any detail. Chapters 12 and 13, however, introduce the history of two especially important groups of bordering civilisations: those of the Near East and of Iron Age Europe. Chapter 14 introduces the many regions, and levels of region, that *make up* the classical Greek and Roman worlds; importantly, it also emphasises the extent to which geographical units, like distinctions between historical periods, are 'constructed' (i.e. one's idea of a region depends upon one's own perspective) and, consequently, the extent to which ancient and modern regions often fail to correspond. For relevant maps, see chapter 67 below.

12. The Ancient Near East

Tom Boiy

The Near East includes Egypt, the Arabian peninsula, the Levant (Syro-Palestine, modern Israel, Jordan, Lebanon and Syria west of the Euphrates), Asia Minor (Anatolia, modern Turkey), Mesopotamia (modern Syria west of the Euphrates and Iraq) and Iran. The study of the ancient Near East traditionally went up until the breakdown of the Achaemenid Empire with the arrival of Alexander the Great in the late fourth century BC. Near Eastern scholarship of the last few decades, on the other hand, has recognised the value of the Oriental sources for the reconstruction of history after Alexander the Great. The traditional study of the ancient Near East was therefore extended to include, in co-operation with classicists and ancient historians, the history of Seleucid and Parthian Mesopotamia and Ptolemaic and Roman Egypt.

Geography

The vast area of the ancient Near East shows a large variety of landscapes: the Nile valley in Upper Egypt, the alluvial plain of Mesopotamia, the delta in Lower Egypt, marshes in lower Mesopotamia, mountain ranges (e.g. Taurus, Zagros), deserts in Egypt, Arabia, Syro-Palestine and Iran, the Iranian and Anatolian plateaux and the coastal plains of the Mediterranean. The earliest agricultural experiments, dry farming agriculture, took place around 10,000 BC on the lower parts of the mountain ranges. Especially in the Levant and Upper Mesopotamia, the 'Fertile Crescent', the climate was favourable (enough rain, at least 200 mm/year evenly spread over the year). A second advantage of these regions was the presence of wild barley and wheat which were used to start experimenting and cultivating.

In historical times people used the water system of the important rivers in the ancient Near East to multiply the harvest in the fertile plains of Egypt and Mesopotamia. In Egypt, nature provided, with the Nile, a marvellous agricultural tool. The Ethiopian rains in summer caused the water level to rise and in August–September the whole of Egypt along the Nile was inundated. After the Nile receded to its normal channel in October-November a fertile layer of silts was left on the land. Crops were sown and a rich harvest could be reaped in spring. Therefore, the ancient phrase 'gift of the Nile' is an appropriate description for Egypt. The situation in Mesopotamia is completely different. The Euphrates and Tigris reached their highest water level in spring after the snow of the Anatolian mountains melted. This means that enormous amounts of water entered Mesopotamia just before harvest time and the crops had to be protected from this. At inundation, deposits of silt were dropped next to the river and after several inundations the deposits formed levees (or natural embankments) around the river channel, and the aggrading Euphrates eventually flowed above the surrounding plain level. Irrigation was therefore an easy task: an irrigation channel cut through a levee was enough to get irrigation water from the Euphrates to the fields. Water control was, on the other hand, necessary to get the water to all the places where it was needed (also those far away) and to protect the crops from destruction when the water level was at its highest just before harvest time. The Tigris was not slow and meandering like the Euphrates. The fast

Tigris cut through the landscape and this meant that irrigation here was difficult and labour intensive. It is therefore no surprise that agriculture (and population) in Mesopotamia was in the first place concentrated around the Euphrates and its network of channels.

Chronology

Because of its vast territory, the diversity of peoples that inhabited and invaded it, the number of empires that existed and the large time-span involved, it is impossible to present here a short sketch of the history of the ancient Near East (for some general and introductory summaries of the history of the ancient Near East, see the further reading list below). Presenting the structure of ancient Near Eastern history, on the other hand, is possible, in the form of a schema of the different periods in the ancient Near Eastern regions. It offers an outline of ancient Near Eastern history and makes sure that we do not get lost in the labyrinth of peoples, dynasties and empires. Already in antiquity some reference frameworks were introduced that created some order in the history of the ancient Near East. A periodisation of Egyptian history into thirty dynasties can be found in the writings of the Hellenistic historian Manetho, and this kind of systematisation is present also in Mesopotamia in the form of the Babylonian king lists. Modern scholarship partly followed Manetho's division by introducing larger entities combining several dynasties. For Egypt this means:

Early Dynastic Period (dynasty 1–2)	3000–2700 BC
Old Kingdom (dynasty 3–6)	2700–2200 BC
First Intermediate Period (dynasty 7–10)	2200–2020 BC
Middle Kingdom (dynasty 11–12)	2020–1790 BC
Second Intermediate Period (dynasty 13–17)	1790–1550 BC
New Kingdom (dynasty 18–20)	1550–1069 BC
Third Intermediate Period (dynasty 21–5)	1069–664 BC
Saite Renaissance (dynasty 26)	664–525 BC
Late Period (dynasty 27–31)	525–332 BC
Alexander the Great and Ptolemaic Period	332–30 BC

For Mesopotamia several king lists are preserved. The so-called 'Sumerian king list' presents the cities ruling Mesopotamia during the third millennium BC together with the kings of these places. Babylonian history is divided into dynasties in the so-called king lists A and B. The Assyrian king list, on the other hand, was a running list from mythological kings up to the king ruling at the time that the copy of the list was written. There was no attempt in antiquity to divide this list into dynasties. Although it must be noted that these lists served ideological purposes and that they were not created as a historiographical tool, several elements from this list were retained in the modern periodisation of Mesopotamian history (Early Dynastic Period means the period when the first Mesopotamian dynasties existed according to the Sumerian king list; Ur III means the third dynasty ruling from Ur according to the Sumerian king list). For Babylonia too, modern scholars created larger entities by combining several dynasties. For Assyria a periodisation similar to the one in Babylonia was made:

Early Dynastic Period	2900–2350 BC
Old-Akkadian/Sargonic Period	2350–2100 BC
Ur III	2100–2000 BC
Old-Babylonian Period (dynasty of Isin, Larsa, first dynasty of Babylon)	2000–1595 BC
and Old-Assyrian Period	2000–1800 BC
Middle-Babylonian Period (Kassite dynasty)	1595–1155 BC
and Middle-Assyrian Period	1400–1050 BC
Neo-Babylonian Period (second dynasty of Babylon after several less important dynasties)	626–539 BC
and Neo-Assyrian Period	883–610 BC
Persian/Achaemenid Period	539–331 BC
Alexander the Great and Seleucid Period	331–141 BC
Parthian/Arsacid Period	141 BC–AD 242

Finally, the Hittite empire in second-millennium Anatolia must be taken into account. Hittite history is subdivided into three periods named like the main periods of Egyptian history. The following division is a modern convention and does not reflect an original Hittite historiographical tradition:

Old Kingdom	1650–1500 BC
Middle Kingdom	1500–1420 BC
Empire	1420–1200 BC

The dates mentioned above are very reliable for the first millennium BC. An absolute chronology for the period before 1500 BC, on the other hand, is a risky and difficult undertaking. For Mesopotamia no fewer than three chronological hypotheses are used, the so-called 'high', 'middle' and 'low' chronologies, and a still lower chronology has been added recently (see Gasche et al., *Dating the Fall of Babylon*). Therefore the dates before 1500 BC have to be used with care. Changes to any of the periods of a Near Eastern civilisation have to take the other cultures into account so that attested relations between the cultures are not dated to different periods. Each chronological intervention in any Near Eastern culture is therefore a complex problem. Renewed interest has been shown recently in the chronological problems of the ancient Near East, and an interdisciplinary approach, combining historical information from Egypt, Mesopotamia and the Levant with archaeology, astronomy and dendrochronology, may provide interesting new chronological material (see Bietak, *Synchronisation of Civilisations*).

Sources

Apart from the archaeological remains, our knowledge of the ancient Near East and its history is primarily based on written sources. Information on the basis of classical authors and biblical writings was, after the decipherment of the Near Eastern scripts and languages, supplemented and replaced to a large extent by original Near Eastern documents. These writings show a wide diversity: for example, from simple notes, letters, legal contracts and expenditure lists to religious songs and rituals, royal edicts, omens, lexical and scientific material, school texts and literary masterpieces. The distribution of this written documentation in time and space is very uneven: whereas some periods and regions are well represented in preserved writings, other centuries and places are completely undocumented.

The oldest Egyptian hieroglyphic texts date to the end of the fourth millennium BC. Cursive writing, so-called hieratic, was used on papyri, a forerunner of our paper made from the papyrus reed, and *ostraca*, pieces of potsherd (see chapter 32). From the second half of the first millennium BC Egyptian was written in the so-called Demotic script, and the last stage of Egyptian writing was Coptic (basically the Greek alphabet with some additional signs; from third-fourth century AD onwards). During Macedonian rule in Egypt (Alexander the Great and the Ptolemaic period, 332–30 BC) a large number of Greek papyri and *ostraca* present plenty of information on Egyptian history.

Cuneiform documents from Mesopotamia, written in Sumerian and Akkadian, are preserved in large numbers. The oldest records date from the end of the fourth millennium BC, and cuneiform script was still in use in the first century AD for astronomical tablets.

A large majority of the cuneiform Hittite tablets originate from the Hittite capital Hattusa. Only since the 1990s have excavations at some other sites exposed cuneiform tablets. Far less numerous are Luwian inscriptions on stone and seals.

Written sources from the Levant are, apart from the cuneiform tablets in Eblaite (Ebla, second half of the third millennium BC) and Ugaritic (Ugarit, second half of the second millennium BC), much scarcer, and most of the documentation dates to the first millennium BC. The number of Aramaic, Phoenician and Hebrew inscriptions and *ostraca* is far smaller than that of cuneiform tablets from Mesopotamia. As for papyri and parchments, the finds in the Qumran caves, with both biblical and non-biblical material, deserve special mention.

Contacts with the Graeco-Roman world

Certain evidence of encounters between the Greek and Near Eastern worlds dates to the second millennium BC. Commercial relations between both regions are regularly attested in archaeological records: Minoan and Mycenaean pottery in Levantine and Egyptian sites, and Near Eastern seals and Egyptian objects in mainland Greece and Crete. Textual evidence provides the same picture: on the one hand, the appearance of Near Eastern place names in Linear B tablets; on the other hand, the appearance of Crete, for example, in Egyptian and Ugaritic sources and the attestation of Greeks ('Achaeans') in Hittite tablets.

Also in the first millennium BC trade constituted a major part of Greek–Eastern relations. Apart from the Greeks themselves, Phoenician traders especially are credited with this. Eastern influence in Greece is especially apparent in an 'Orientalising' style found in Greek art and in the introduction of an alphabetic system for the Greek language. New encounters were not the result of friendly trade, but originated in war: Greek mercenaries in Babylonian and Egyptian pay appear sporadically in the sources from the end of the seventh century onwards. The role of Greek soldiery in the East reached a peak without doubt in the second half of the Persian period (roughly the second half of the fifth and the fourth centuries BC): not only did pretenders to the Achaemenid throne hire Greek professional soldiers (Cyrus the Younger and Xenophon's 10,000), but the same mercenaries' services were also used by Persian satraps (provincial governors) and by the Egyptian pharaohs who fought Persian attempts to reincorporate Egypt into the Persian Empire.

The final breakdown of the Persian Empire and the conquest of the Near East by Alexander the Great meant a completely new phase in the relations between the Greeks and the Near Eastern regions. A large number of colonists moved from mainland Greece and the Greek cities of the Western coast of Asia Minor into the newly conquered East, and the people there were more intensively confronted with Greek culture and Greeks than ever before. Greek culture and Greek lifestyle were imported into the newly conquered territories because Greeks and Macedonians were primarily interested in continuing their life as it was in Greece, Macedonia or the Greek cities of Asia Minor. The autochthonous people were without doubt to some degree influenced by the habits of their new masters, but this does not mean that the inhabitants of the ancient Near East during the Hellenistic period were more or less 'hellenised' (willingly or not), or that they adopted a Greek way of life. The Babylonian evidence, for example, reveals that, apart from a few Greek features, not much changed for the Babylonians and that Babylonian culture remained, often with the active support of the new rulers, largely the same as before.

Rediscovery and afterlife

Several elements of ancient Near Eastern culture, religion, science and literature survived in classical and Islamic writings and thinking. Most Near Eastern languages and scripts, on the other hand – with Hebrew and Aramaic being the most important exceptions – were lost after antiquity. The ancient Near East was therefore known in the West almost exclusively through the Bible and the writings of classical authors. Travel stories of late medieval and Renaissance adventurers and the souvenirs they brought home added to the general picture of the ancient Near East. A large increase of knowledge was not possible before the nineteenth century, when several of the ancient Near Eastern scripts and languages were rediscovered, large numbers of antiquities were shipped to Europe and the first scientific excavations of the material remains took place. The discovery of multilingual inscriptions facilitated the deciphering of Egyptian hieroglyphs (Rosetta stone, deciphered 1822) and Persian and Akkadian cuneiform (Behistun rock inscription, deciphered 1830s–1850s) and presented scholars with the tools to read an enormous amount of primary documentation. The European and later American interest, from both individuals and museums, in Near Eastern art, artefacts and writings resulted in a booming antiquities market, and finally scientific methods were applied at excavations to create a historical reconstruction that was as exact as possible (Petrie in Egypt and Palestine, Koldewey in Mesopotamia). During the twentieth century archaeological activity, often in recent years by international missions, multiplied in all Near Eastern countries, and the sources collected by the museums all over the world were explored. Still, the number of sites in the Near East that require further investigation and the quantity of unpublished documentation hidden in the reserves of the museums today is enormous.

The rediscovery of the Ancient Near East resulted in a real Egyptomania in the West (Ucko et al., *Encounters with Ancient Egypt*). This fashion was largely inspired by the French invasion of Egypt at the end of the eighteenth century. Egyptianising elements (hieroglyphs, obelisks, sphinxes, pyramids) found their way into Western art and architecture, and Egyptian themes were used in modern literature and music (e.g. Verdi's *Aida*). Mesopotamia and Babylonia have never influenced modern Western life to such a degree, but some echoes of Babylonia can be found in Western paintings, literature and music (most of the references illustrate Babylon's role in the Bible; see the 'Tower of Babel' paintings by e.g. Pieter Bruegel the Elder, and e.g. Verdi's *Nabucco*).

Further reading

J. Baines and J. Málek, *Atlas of Ancient Egypt*, Oxford: Phaidon, 1980.

M. Bietak (ed.), *The Synchronisation of Civilisations in the Eastern Mediterranean in the Second Millennium BC* (Österreichische Akademie der Wissenschaften. Denkschriften der Gesamtakademie 19), Vienna: Verlag der Österreichischen Akademie der Wissenschaften, 2000.

H. Gasche, J. A. Armstrong, S. W. Cole and V. G. Gurzadyan, *Dating the Fall of Babylon: A Reappraisal of Second-Millennium Chronology (A Joint Ghent–Chicago–Harvard Project)* (Mesopotamian History and Environment Memoirs IV), Ghent: University of Ghent, 1998.

B. Kemp, *Ancient Egypt: Anatomy of a Civilization*, London and New York: Routledge, 1989.

A. Kuhrt, *The Ancient Near East c. 3000–330 BC* (2 vols), London and New York: Routledge, 1995.

C. Lambrou-Phillipson, *Hellenorientalia: The Near Eastern Presence in the Bronze Age Aegean, ca. 3000–1100 B.C. Interconnections Based on Material Record and the Written Evidence plus Orientalia. A Catalogue of Egyptian, Mesopotamian, Mittanian, Syro-Palestinian and Asia Minor Objects from the Bronze Age Aegean*, Göteborg: Paul Åströms Förlag, 1990.

Lexikon der Ägyptologie, Wiesbaden: Otto Harrassowitz, 1975–92.

E. M. Meyers (ed.), *The Oxford Encyclopedia of Archaeology in the Near East*, Oxford: Oxford University Press, 1997.

M. van de Mieroop, *A History of the Ancient Near East ca. 3000–323 BC*, Oxford: Blackwell, 2003.

Reallexikon der Assyriologie, Berlin and Leipzig: Walter de Gruyter, 1928–.

D. B. Redford (ed.), *The Oxford Encyclopedia of Ancient Egypt*, Oxford: Oxford University Press, 2001.

M. Roaf, *Cultural Atlas of Mesopotamia and the Ancient Near East*, New York: Equinox, 1990.

J. Sasson (ed.), *Civilizations of the Ancient Near East*, New York: Scribner, 1995 – reference work collecting essays dealing with all aspects of life in Near Eastern societies.

P. Ucko et al, *Encounters with Ancient Egypt* (8 vols), London: UCL Press, 2003.

13. *Iron Age Europe*

J. D. Hill and Jonathan Williams

For Greeks and Romans, the Mediterranean Sea was the centre of the world, its culture of cities, wine, corn and olive oil the perfection of human existence. But they were aware that they lived on the edge of a very different world in central and northern Europe. The peoples who lived there seemed not to dwell in towns, or practise agriculture, or have any of the refinements of civilized life. Far from being political animals, they appeared little more than wild animals – nomadic, not fully human, and rather terrifying. Despite this apparent gulf, Greeks, and especially Romans, had a lot to do with a number of these peoples: as unwelcome invaders of both Greece and Italy in the fourth and third centuries BC, as mercenaries in Hellenistic armies, then as subjects after the Roman conquest of large parts of northern Europe in the first centuries BC and AD, as fellow citizens of the Roman world empire, and finally as invaders again in the fifth century as the Roman frontier in the West gave way before the dreaded hordes from barbarian Europe.

In this chapter, we will look at some of the terms used by scholars to describe the chronology, peoples and cultures of non-classical Europe, examine the different kinds of evidence on which its study is based, and finally give an overview of its complex history.

Terms: defining the subject

One of the biggest problems for specialists and non-specialists alike is the wide variety of terminology in use to describe prehistoric European peoples, cultures and periods of time. The term 'prehistoric' itself can be confusing. For the general public, it probably means dinosaurs rather than anything else. For archaeologists it refers to peoples, and their cultures, dating to before the production of written historical sources about them.

The Iron Age

The term 'Iron Age' was invented in the nineteenth century by Danish scholars as an element of the Three Age System, which ordered human cultural evolution according to the materials used in the making of tools and weapons – stone, bronze and iron successively. This system has been largely abandoned as a means of understanding human prehistory. As an adjective to describe peoples and things, Iron Age nowadays means 'pre-Roman' and/or 'prehistoric'. In central and northern Europe, the Iron Age denotes the period between the rise of iron-working (800–700 BC) and the Roman conquest. In Britain, for instance, Iron Age means from about 800 BC to AD 43, whereas in Ireland, which was never invaded, it extends right down to the Christian early medieval period, which begins around AD 450. In Scandinavia, which was also never invaded by Rome, the Iron Age runs up to the Viking period, which starts c. AD 800. The term has become popular in English as a substitute for what are now generally regarded as unsatisfactory ethnic terms inherited from classical authors, such as 'Celtic'.

Ethnic terms: Celts et al.

Greeks and Romans often used generic terms to describe the variety of peoples and cultures they knew (rather little) about in northern Europe, terms such as Celts or Gauls, Germans, Scythians, Sarmatians and so on. These terms are still in use among classical historians and some archaeologists. They are useful labels to some degree, but we need to remember that their origins lie in the more or less ill-informed works of historians and geographers in antiquity whose understanding of local realities among the distant and generally unloved peoples of Iron Age Europe was limited. There has been considerable debate on the value of such blanket ethnic terms. Some argue that, as the creations of an external and, under the Romans, imperial viewpoint, they have about as much usefulness as ethnic categories imposed by colonial outsiders in the modern period, such as 'American Indians' or 'Australian Aborigines', which serve only to mask the tremendous cultural and linguistic variety of the different peoples gathered under such simplistic headings.

Archaeological culture names: Hallstatt and La Tène

In addition to these ancient ethnic names, archaeologists have also coined quasi-ethnic terms for prehistoric cultures. These are derived from the names of archaeological sites whose material culture was regarded as typical of a wide area, and hence of a large group of people. In Western Europe, the two most important of these are Hallstatt (Austria) and La Tène (Switzerland). These Iron Age sites gave their names to whole cultural complexes, and also to the periods of Western European history to which they were dated (see figure 13.1). Archaeologists came to

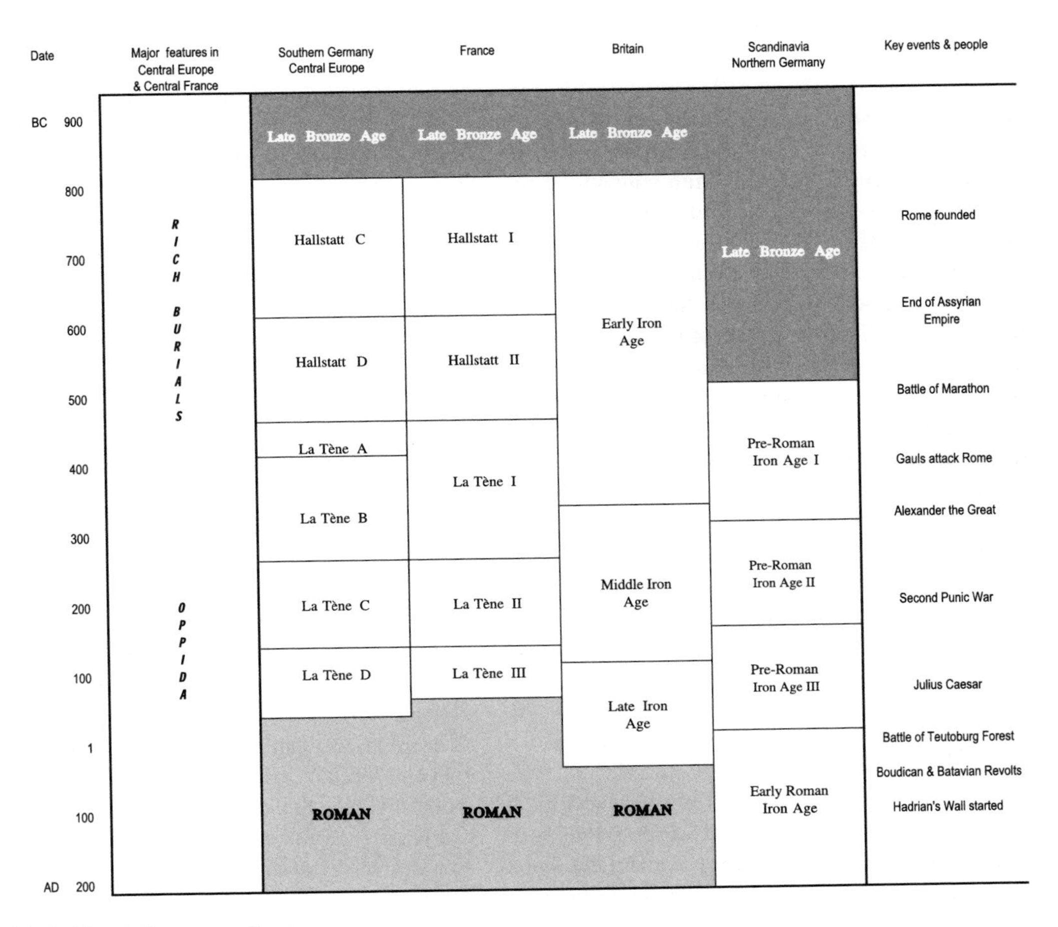

Fig. 13.1 Prehistoric European cultures

believe, wrongly, that the material cultures which these terms encompassed represented the remains of concrete ethnic groups, and they often understood 'Hallstatt' and 'La Tène' as synonymous with the pre-Roman history of the Celts. Nowadays, terms like these are used more carefully, either as labels for artistic styles or to denote a chronological phase.

Greeks and Romans looking at Iron Age Europe

Greek writers thought they had some understanding of the peoples of Iron Age northern Europe although, apart from the voyages of Pytheas of Massalia (Marseille) in the late fourth century BC, who sailed as far as Britain, there seem to have been few active attempts to find out very much about them. In place of hard knowledge, Greeks populated the north with figures from their own mythical traditions or with catch-all ethnic terms of uncertain origin. The fourth-century BC historian Ephorus famously divided up the world surrounding the world known to the Greeks into four quarters: Ethiopians in the south, Indians in the east, Scythians in the north and Celts in the west. These were little more than generic designations to help Greeks distinguish between vast, and virtually unknown, regions filled with far-off barbarians. But Celts and Scythians came to play an extremely important part in ancient and modern conceptions of the European Iron Age. Both came to Greece in various guises – as slaves, as mercenaries and sometimes as invaders – but by and large Greeks, or at least Greek writers, did not return the compliment. In consequence, Hellenistic Greeks knew little about northern Europe.

The second-century BC Greek historian Polybius (see chapter 49) rightly remarked that the West had been opened up to investigation by the Romans just as Alexander had opened up the East. He, together with the Roman statesman and historian Cato the Elder, set a new standard in the investigation of the Iron Age peoples of the Iberian peninsula, northern Italy, the south of France and transalpine central Europe. Polybius was a believer in autopsy, even retracing the footsteps of Hannibal back over the Alps into France.

Posidonius (c. 135–51 BC), one of the major intellectual figures of his day, seems to have visited Gaul and Spain in the 90s BC, where he made observations on the indigenous peoples and worked these results into his influential, but lost, *History* of the period from 146 BC onwards.

The next major leap forward in Roman knowledge of the north came with the phase of conquest begun by Julius Caesar's invasion of Gaul in the 50s BC, which continued under Augustus when the empire's northern frontier was established on the Rhine and the Danube. It was this period that yielded the kind of detailed information about the peoples and places of the north which was displayed in the writings of Caesar himself and, later, Tacitus on Gaul and Germany respectively.

This period also gave rise to two important ethnic categories – Gauls and Germans. Before Caesar's conquest, Romans who looked north across the Alps used the term *Galli* of all the different peoples who lived there, and they understood it to be equivalent to the Greek word *Keltoi* – Celts. After the appearance of Caesar's *Gallic War*, the Rhine emerged as a dividing line between the conquered Gauls and a new group whom Caesar called the *Germani*, a name which emerged as a generic term for all barbarians over the river. Whether the Rhine really was an ethnic, linguistic or cultural boundary as Caesar claimed is still a matter of debate. Once again, though, ethnic categories created in classical antiquity went on to become crucial in the modern rediscovery of the history and archaeology of Iron Age Europe.

Modern Europeans looking at their Iron Age past

What were in fact Roman collective terms for a host of more or less unfamiliar groups living beyond their frontiers were misunderstood by scholars in the nineteenth and twentieth centuries as ancient nations with unifying cultures and languages. They were also made into national ancestors. The French became the descendants of the Gauls, modern Deutschland of ancient Germania. These eighteenth- and nineteenth-century idealised views of the past still have a very strong hold on popular (mis)conceptions of the past. This is especially true for the way the Celts are portrayed in films, comics and even some serious academic books. Whenever words such as Celts, Gauls, Germans and Ancient Britons are used in books, the media or museums, great care needs to be taken to distinguish what are modern prejudices, what are ancient classical stereotypes, and what is based on fact.

Ancient literary evidence was until very recently absolutely fundamental to modern archaeology. It provided ethnic categories such as Celts and Germans, historical characters who often became national heroes for their resistance to the Romans – Boudica in Britain, Vercingetorix in France, Arminius in Germany – and geographical focuses for excavations which were often places where battles had been fought against the Romans – Numantia in Spain, Alesia in France, and the Teutoburg Forest in Germany. Ancient texts also endowed the peoples of Iron Age Europe with a whole host of admirable character traits, despite the fact that most Greek and Roman writers regarded them with extreme distaste. Classical prejudice was filtered out, and scholars set about excavating their ancestors, who, unsurprisingly, turned out to have been plain-living, non-materialistic and utterly heroic. The idea of the pre-Roman northern European as the archetypal 'noble savage' has considerable appeal to this day, particularly in the guise of the Celtic druids. Asterix the Gaul is perhaps its most appealing manifestation.

It is important to realise that there is, in fact, very little evidence from Latin or Greek literature for the peoples of Iron Age Europe. Even in the first century BC when most of the well-known literature was written, by Julius Caesar, Strabo etc., 80–90 per cent of Iron Age Europe merits little more than one or two short mentions in the classical sources, and the sources are themselves not prolific. There are probably fewer surviving words written about Iron Age France and Britain in Latin or Greek than would fill a modern Sunday newspaper and its supplements. For most of Iron Age Europe, then, the only direct evidence for these peoples is archaeological evidence. Even where there are some references in the classical sources, archaeology is still the prime source of evidence for most aspects of life and society. This is also the case for Roman Britain, France and Germany.

Over the twentieth century, archaeology developed itself as an autonomous discipline as techniques of excavation, dating and interpretation were progressively refined. Increasingly archaeologists no longer see Iron Age Europe from the classical, literary perspective. They rely instead on the evidence provided from excavations and surveys (see chapter 3). The archaeological evidence for Iron Age Europe is prolific. Iron Age farms and cemeteries were so common that they are regularly found during archaeological excavations, and they can produce large quantities of animal bones, potsherds, tools and other material. Archaeological evidence provides immediate evidence for daily life, types of settlement, crafts and trade. There is also often direct evidence for burial rites, shrines and religious offerings. Since the 1960s, archaeology has also developed increasingly sophisticated theoretical tools for reaching areas of Iron Age life such as political organisation, religious belief systems and, sometimes, the motivations behind people's actions. Archaeological evidence has to be used with care and rigour. It is no more easy to use, and gives you no more direct access to the past, than literary evidence from Greek and Latin texts.

A brief history of Iron Age Europe

Iron Age Europe was a world of farmers who were warriors and warriors who were farmers. Across Europe away from the Mediterranean coast, from 1000 BC onwards, you would have found a world of farms and villages. These were communities that did not need towns or cities, monumental sculpture, temples, writing, money or large numbers of slaves. There existed large cultural groups sharing their own variations of similar burial rites, house shapes and styles of objects. These groups the Greeks and Romans called Celts, Germans, Iberians, Britons etc. This section provides an introduction to these societies located in temperate Europe north of the Alps and Massif Central, but similar societies also existed in most of Iberia (modern Spain and Portugal), parts of Italy, and the Balkans as far south as northern Greece. To the East a very different way of life existed on the Russian steppes as far as the borders of China. Here there were nomadic groups of horse-herders called over time by different names, such as Scythians, Sarmatians and Huns.

While there were great differences in objects, burial rites and language across non-Mediterranean Europe during the Iron Age, there were some common features. Key among these was that they lived in small but successful farming communities scattered across the landscape in farmsteads or villages. In some areas they built hill-forts, which could be permanent large villages or empty strongholds and gathering places. Society everywhere was based on growing cereals and raising cattle, sheep and pigs. There was considerable trade to provide the basics of life: metal, grinding stones, pottery and salt. Almost everyone was a full- or part-time farmer, even if they were also craftspeople, warriors or leaders. There were extensive networks of trade, marriage and political alliances stretching hundreds of miles. The population was very large: in 1 BC, one or two million people probably lived in Britain and Ireland. The basic social unit was often a group of farms or villages perhaps cultivating an area of 10–20 km across. These local communities formed parts of larger, shifting groups that are the 'tribes' and 'peoples' mentioned in the classical sources. Despite the long-distance links, life tended to focus on the local, and neighbouring 'tribes' could have quite different objects, rituals or settlement patterns from one other.

These communities lacked the defining characteristics of classical Mediterranean life. There were almost no large settlements that might be called towns or cities and they did not need the political institutions associated with the Greek or Roman city in order to operate. Equally, there were neither many large estates of land owned by one family, nor were there large numbers of slaves. In many Iron Age societies, differences in wealth and rank between people appear to have been far less marked than in classical Greece and Rome, though in some places individuals and their families were able to establish themselves as rulers for several generations. These Iron Age societies should not be seen as inherently weaker or less complex than those of Greece or Rome. Certainly, they could not withstand the might of the Roman or Macedonian empires. Yet at earlier times they were probably more powerful than many Mediterranean city-states. 'Barbarian' Iron Age societies of these kinds also existed right on the doorstep of classical societies all over the Mediterranean, even in Greece and Italy. Both Macedonians and Romans were originally 'Iron Age' societies.

Against this constant background there were a number of important changes over the period. Some of the most important are often overlooked, such as the introduction of the rotary quern stone for grinding corn, the ship's sail, chickens, domestic cats, and iron itself. Iron replaced bronze to make tools and weapons etc. in about 800 BC in most areas, but the age of iron really only started in 300/200 BC when iron objects became increasingly common.

From 900 BC to 450 BC – the so-called Hallstatt period – the areas just north of the Alps from France to Slovenia saw many very rich burials, often containing wagons and objects used in lavish drinking parties, some of these having been made in northern Italy, Etruria or the Greek world. These burials suggest the existence of a competitive world of 'princes' and 'kings' whose success rarely lasted more than three or four generations, as other areas rose to power. At this time there were very strong links and similarities between Etruria and northern Italy and those living north of the Alps. These similarities weakened considerably as Etruria and Rome adopted elements of classical lifestyles and the city-centred life.

These burials disappeared after 500/450 BC and from this time temperate European peoples increasingly feature in the classical literature, in the archaeological period known as La Tène. Incursions by 'Celts' are recorded in the histories, including a major raid said to have almost destroyed Rome in 390 BC (or 386 BC) and the sack of the shrine at Delphi in 279 BC. Most of these incursions were military raids, but some were mass migrations by men, women and children in search of new lands. Migration became an increasingly important factor of life in Europe. This usually involved small numbers of people moving relatively short distances to establish new permanent settlements in previously relatively empty or marginal parts of the landscape. The agricultural communities of Europe became increasingly productive, and household industries making metal tools, pottery and other items increased. In some areas, coinage was adopted from Mediterranean prototypes. From c. 200 BC in those areas immediately north of the Alps a new type of settlement appeared. Known as *oppida* by modern scholars, these are settlements surrounded by massive earth and timber ramparts up to 5–9 km long. Some people have argued these were the first towns or cities in temperate Europe. If so, then they represent a distinctly temperate European take on the idea of the 'city', as they lack the defining features of Mediterranean city life. Settlements such as these existed in central France at the time of Caesar's conquest of Gaul.

The Roman conquest of parts of temperate Europe had a major impact on peoples both inside and outside the Roman Empire. For the conquered peoples all areas of life were transformed; politics, religion, economics, land-ownership, houses, everyday objects and language. Towns and cities modelled on Mediterranean prototypes became central to the ordering and functioning of society, major industries were established, and economic exchange increasingly relied on coined money. These processes are described as 'romanisation', a term that makes the point that it was the local people who became Roman, whereas very few Italians ever migrated north.

For those peoples outside the frontiers of Rome there were still more important changes to come. By AD 200/300 new 'peoples' appeared and societies were increasingly dominated by 'lords' and their mounted warrior followers. It was these lords and their war bands who led the barbarian peoples, such as the Goths, Vandals and Franks, that invaded the Roman Empire in the third, fourth and fifth centuries. The same lords and war bands would also make up most of the Roman armies that fought the 'barbarians'. This was now a very different world.

Further reading

J. R. Collis, *The European Iron Age*, London: Routledge, 1997.

J. R. Collis, *The Celts: Origins, Myths, Inventions*, Stroud: Tempus, 2003.

B. W. Cunliffe, *The Oxford Illustrated Prehistory of Europe*, Oxford: Oxford University Press, 1994.

B. W. Cunliffe, *The Ancient Celts*, Oxford: Oxford University Press, 1997.

S. James, *The Atlantic Celts: Ancient People or Modern Invention*, London: British Museum Press, 1999.

S. James and V. Rigby, *Britain and the Celtic Iron Age*, London: British Museum Press, 1997.

P. S. Wells, *The Barbarians Speak: How the Conquered Peoples Shaped Roman Europe*, Princeton: Princeton University Press, 1999.

P. S. Wells, *The Battle that Stopped Rome*, New York and London: W. W. Norton, 2003.

J. H. C. Williams, *Beyond the Rubicon: Romans and Gauls in Republican Italy*, Oxford: Oxford University Press, 2001.

14. Regions of Antiquity

Nicholas Purcell

Understanding regions

A region is a subjective subdivision of space. There are no regions in nature. Regions cannot be helpfully defined scientifically. 'Region' is the basic brick with which the fabric of conceptual geography is built – theirs and ours. The apparent cases of natural regions – an isolated mountain, a tightly bounded plain, even an island – turn out to depend on contingent, cultural values (see chapters 21 and 23). The Romans started hills at the base, whereas we tend to limit them to the tops. Plain-dwellers form part-societies with hill-people. How much of the underwater shelf and shoals around an island goes with the island politically?

All comprehension of space – even within a building or a back garden – works through subdivision. But the subdivision of space into smaller spaces – what topologists call 'tessellation' – is only one form of breaking down the larger to make it more comprehensible. A study of regionalism must include the less obvious 'regions' which are composed of groups of points, often scattered – sets such as the daughter-settlements of Miletos, or the Kalaurian amphictyony – and of lines, the space defined by a transit through rather than a boundary – as when a coastline was defined by the *periplus* or journey along it, or when the highways of Roman Italy gave their names, Flaminia or Aemilia, to whole districts. And it is in the case of making sense of space beyond what you can readily intuit that regional thinking becomes most complex and most important. If you can imagine further than you can see, if places more than a day's walk away matter, then to make sense of diversity, complexity, abstraction and remoteness requires splitting, a subdivision of place. That is regional thinking. Historians' horizons are always wider than what we can see or reach: history can therefore not do without regional classification. The regions of the ancients and ours are not by any means always the same, but they are a similar cognitive manoeuvre.

Regions in ancient thought

Subdivisions of the most basic kind, such as 'our land' or the 'sea in our area', are no doubt basic to human reasoning. One of these had an unexpected future: in an arch fashion, the Greeks and Romans referred to their corner of the map of the world, when they began to know how very extensive that was, in terms appropriate to the most parochial of countryfolk speaking of their valley: 'our sea – our bit of land' (*hē kath'hēmas thalassa* or, more rarely, *gē*). This was their main way of identifying the region of the world in which they lived, and the sea which we call Mediterranean.

In fact, in the Mediterranean world, horizons broad enough to demand regional concepts far antedated Graeco-Roman history. We know nothing of most of the ideas that resulted. In Bronze Age states where political and economic organisation transcended localities, and created quite complex webs of interdependence, regions naturally served to describe subdivisions of those webs. Some names for such regions survive in Hittite records from Anatolia, or in the Linear B tablets, especially those of Pylos. Conservatism in regional onomastics, itself always a phenomenon worthy of note, sometimes makes it possible for us to relate the names of these regions to approximate localities, but not to delve into how people thought of the spaces that they named. Another important impulse for regional thinking was as a means of inventorying and displaying the places in which a military power had achieved noteworthy successes, and in this respect the catalogues of defeated enemies compiled for rulers in the Fertile Crescent and in Egypt are the direct precursor of much Greek and (especially) Roman regional thinking. In this case we see an important ambiguity in regional thought. It is perhaps always easier to reason from people than from more abstract topography, and regions were very often imagined through and named from the people who lived there. On the one hand this is an easy way in to thinking of places which you have not seen, but on the other this encourages a certain level of sophistication in conceptual geography, in that the region you have in mind – Caria, Liguria, Mauretania – will usually be a set of dwelling-places of members of those communities which have little or no topographical unity.

The Homeric epics, by their nature, can hardly reflect the regional conceptions of any one place or time more than fleetingly, but they gave poetic colour and the authority of antiquity to two views which remained highly influential: that familiar, largely sea-oriented world which the readers and reciters of Homer called 'ours', beyond which all was strange and mostly bad; and a polarised division between Greeks and others understood through the conflict around Troy, but also – in a very inchoate fashion – as a stand-off between what would later be identified as East and West. Beyond that, although the Homeric tradition knows some remarkable geography (above all perhaps in the Catalogues), regional thinking as such is not highly developed here (see chapter 51).

As part of the revolution in thought about social organisation which accompanied the first poleis in Greece, the invention of the community territory, or *chōra*, deserves a prominent place in a history of ancient regional ideas. Through this idea, a basic tool for subdividing space was acquired which remained widespread and axiomatic until the end of antiquity. The cellular space around a community centre, the *chōra* was also linked to complex and important ideas about the resource-base needed by the community, and its interdependence or autarky. It also led to the careful mapping of boundaries, through social forms such as the *ephēbeia*, and later through the maintenance of lines of markers which literally marked the edges of these regions. Further, communities came to reflect on what made up the *chōra* and on the interaction of differentiated sub-regions within it. A well-known and precocious instance is the division of Attica into plain, shore and hill in the sixth century BC. The interest here is that the underlying concept is physical, rather than reflecting the name of a subsidiary social group: it is an alternative to thinking by means of kinship relations, real or invented.

There are two major problems with regional identity based on social formations, which echo down the centuries. First, social communities, based as they are on cultural construction and institutions such as kinship, are not primarily spatial entities, and there is always something approximate and arbitrary about pretending that they can be mapped. Second, they are notably labile through time, and a regional label derived from a family group or a larger notionally kinship-based entity, a 'tribe' or a 'people', is particularly apt to become obsolete, to turn into a misnomer. It is often difficult to discover whether a given label is actually a mainly spatial conception drawing its name from a community, or a description of a community that is only incidentally regional. The theorists – whoever they were – of the Athenian *politeia* of the sixth century were clearly unusually aware of the conceptual difference between the physical and the human landscape, as they were of the differences between birth, wealth and location as criteria for community membership. That precision of thinking was by no means normal during the next millennium.

It was also in the archaic period, as far as we know, that the first attempts were made to deploy regional theory as a means of intuiting the whole surface of the earth: though in this the cultures of Mesopotamia, which combined a sophisticated astronomy with wide geopolitical contacts, may have provided models. 'Continent thinking' is the most enduring legacy of this moment: and Asia, Europe and Libya (Africa) became conceptual units at least as early as Hecataeus of Miletus at the turn of the sixth and fifth centuries BC (see chapter 49). This three-way division rapidly became embellished with a very wide range of cultural and social ideas about the nature of the peoples of these areas, loosely based on a set of geographical and historical determinisms into which we cannot enter here: the savagery of Libya, the servility of Asia, and so on. In assessing ancient regional consciousness, one of the most serious problems is, of course, guessing how widespread which levels of sophistication in regional subdivision were. One importance of the notion of three continents is that it offered an easy way of understanding world space, and it is not unlikely that it was a widely disseminated way of thinking.

Alongside the continents, two other global conceptions helped subdivide a world which was recognised from an early date as being immensely large: latitude and longitude. Elementary meteorological observation led to a recognition of hot, cold and temperate zones, arranged according to latitude, and these shaped thought from Herodotus' ethnography to the geographical description of Roman provinces. Spanning more than one of these *klimata* (whence 'climate') became a marker of imperial achievement. The identification of North and South was easy; the more contingent identification of an East and West was made possible by the accidents of Mediterranean topography. The Ionian and Adriatic Seas represent a North-South divide, and the significance of their line of longitude was already expressed in the division of the Roman Empire in the Civil War which brought Augustus to power. The same line divided Eastern and Western empires in late antiquity. Of the compass points, South, East and North all labelled major conceptual regions, partly because they mapped nicely onto Africa, Asia and Europe. All four also labelled cultural stereotypes, partly based on climatic determinism, but in the case of East and West drawing on the tradition which led from Troy through the Persian Wars to Alexander and the Seleucids, and eventually to the Roman and Byzantine construction of Eastern adversaries.

Closely related to this style of thought was the last important macroregional division: inside and outside, our world and Beyond, the other ultimately Homeric – Odyssean – legacy. The stereotypes were used to identify versions of barbarism, in the frosty North, baked South or effete East, and these in turn calibrated the edges of the familiar world both in a more introverted and defensive spirit and for the needs of military aggression.

Something rather different is visible in the Roman state of the Republic, which developed a novel and distinctive interest in spatiality. It was believed that the last king but one had instituted a reform analogous to that in Attica at the end of the sixth century, in which the social divisions of the body politic acquired an identity based on the territory rather than on kinship. More historically, Rome made its own the techniques of surveying and subdividing a *chōra* into lots. This practice was used in certain cases of conquest in archaic Greece, above all by the Spartans, and similarly became widespread in the aggressive settlements of Greeks beyond their homeland. As a transformation of the landscape which imposed a dramatic uniformity on a very large scale, this land division was a potent ingredient in the formation of regional identities. Roman dependent settlements from the fourth century BC until the imperial period made use of it on an enormous scale. The Roman practice of surveying took the distinctive form of a religious procedure connected with divination and carried out by the augurs, whose lines of sight formed another important principle for the division of space and the formation of regions: indeed the term *regio* itself probably derives from this milieu. The doctrine that resulted was linked both with the layout of the cardinal points and with the qualitative separation of domains of different status in religious, and later in civil, law. Road-building and boundary law were both strongly affected by these ways of thinking. It has recently been discovered from a commemorative bronze cup that the linear fortified routeway-cum-frontier which we call Hadrian's Wall was commonly understood in surveyors' argot as being arranged according to a *rigor* – the linear sequence of a formal legal boundary.

It is not surprising that this spatial language made possible some complex regional manipulations, which were to grow in intricacy with the development through the second century BC of new legal and administrative languages, the great expansion of the geographical reach of the Roman state, and the gradual drift towards centralisation and the imposition of more of what we might recognise as 'government', especially linked, from the Augustan period, with the imperative to tax, and to register in order to tax. We are still surprised by new documents such as the Tessera Paemeiobrigensis, a ruling of Augustus given (*AE* 1999, p. 915) from his HQ at Narbo (Narbonne) in 14 BC, which reveals subdivisions of the remoter parts of newly conquered northwest Spain of a kind not previously attested, such as 'the province across the Douro river'. In a certain sense all these tendencies culminated in the administrative reforms of the tetrarchy, a *ne plus ultra* of virtuoso regional subdivision.

Administrative regionality was only one among several forms of making sense of a world with notably wide horizons. From the Hellenistic age onwards, a regional self-consciousness at a cultural level can be discerned, with reflections in institutions such as federal organisations, but not primarily deriving from them. Under Rome it is clear that clusters of provinces – Iberian, Gallic, Aegean Greek – as well as individual areas with marked characteristics, such as the cities of Tripolitania or the Black Sea, came to regard themselves as sharing certain characteristics, and it is the pursuit of these elusive regional identities that is currently preoccupying most historians of the Roman imperial provinces. It is clear that these identities were shaped by patterns in the Roman superstructure and in the chemistry of relationships between 'Roman' outsiders and 'indigenous' locals as much as by the traditional self-consciousnesses of the latter; but they were distinctive enough to be both observed in antiquity and apparent to us in the archaeological record.

It should be remembered that these 'dispersed regionalisms' which do not form contiguous blocks when mapped, but rather scatters of dots or splodges, are as significant in ancient regional thought as tessellations. Already the archaic Greek amphictyonies display a unity which defies topographical rationality, and ancient federal institutions were patterned by the accidents of political and economic independence, their cohesion being expressed as often by mythical or historical narrative ('colonisation', kinship, alliance) as by geographical logic. The closeness of the Phoenician cities of Tyre, Carthage and Gades, measuring the length of the Mediterranean, is an extreme example. Since regions exist in the mind as much as on the map, such networks are certainly regions too.

Somewhat more precise in their definition are the regions which were defined by the heirs of the ancient amphictyonies, the 'leagues' of the classical and Hellenistic period and their Roman successors. On the largest scale, institutions such as the Achaean or Aetolian league, although they defied precise mapping, coloured the regional geography of wide areas. When the Romans formed provinces, these, like kingdoms, were convenient regional templates. Achaea owed its name to the league of that name; Macedonia and Asia were derived very closely from the territories of former kingdoms. Many smaller scale *koina* had a vigorous role in the shaping of provincial territories, and one which transcended the geography of cities. The *koinon* of Cyprus, for instance, conspicuously honoured not the poliadic deities of the famous Cypriote cities, but those of the prominent landmarks of Cyprus' four coasts. And reference points drawn from physical geography were important in Roman regional thinking too: the province in what is now Andalucia was named Baetica from the Augustan period after the great river Guadalquivir (then called the Baetis) whose basin this substantially is.

Ancient history: modern regions

This brings us to the differences between the prevailing patterns of regionality in antiquity and those through which we regard the ancients. Among these, perhaps the most startling has been the invention of the Mediterranean.

We saw that the Greeks and Romans labelled this inland sea just as 'the sea in our area'. Although 'Mare Nostrum' ('our sea') has become strongly suggestive of thalassocracy and imperialism in general, the terms were, as we have seen, parochial rather than proprietorial (there are examples of an equally unambitious use of the 'land in our area'). It was under the influence of continent thinking, and after many generations of world maps, that the idea of the whole Mediterranean as a single inland sea developed, and the term 'Mediterranean' is not actually attested until late antiquity. But it was not until the Enlightenment that this term in turn became not just a label for a body of water in the geography of the earth, but the identifier for all the lands around it. Such a metonymy was characteristic of the beginnings of modern scientific thinking, and called into existence a new object of political and cultural appropriation. The Greeks and Romans had no equivalent.

Less surprising than this development, and underlying it in many ways, is the imposition, overt or subliminal, on the ancient world of subdivisions deriving from post-classical political preoccupations. The division of the space occupied by the Greeks and Romans into Christian and Islamic domains from the eighth century has had one kind of legacy: the subjection of substantial parts of it to a range of essentially colonial regimes, especially from the middle of the nineteenth century. The practical separation of the area into tiers of extremely rich and rather poor states which persists today perpetuates some of these tendencies. Above all, however, it is the ideology of the nation-state which has done most to impose a sclerotic and mostly artificial regionalism on the study of the area. These national ideologies have been imposed, often disastrously, at the expense of highly complex community topographies, and also seldom replicate or render comprehensible ancient regional subdivisions – even when they refrain from perverse, and often deliberately fraudulent, manipulation of history.

Far more useful to the historian are the regional subdivisions of modern historical geography. Here there have been doctrinal debates about the definition of a region – whether it is generated by a central place, or whether it takes its characteristics from ecology – which have been subsumed in the last generation by the understanding that cognitive manoeuvres and heuristic devices such as regional definitions can be fluid, multiple and diverse. We do not have to choose! In Mediterranean history, for instance, ecological zones such as blocks of uplands (the Alps, or Pisidia and Isauria), or major plains (Cisalpina, or the Copaic basin), make natural subjects for social and economic history. Zones whose ecological conformity is provided by maritime communications may be included too (the Balearic islands, or the Corinthian Gulf). The mismatch between ancient regional thinking and this type of analysis may be very fertile. But it is equally interesting to study the generation of a changing region around a centre such as Antioch, Jerusalem or Alexandria. Here ancient thought is likely to converge with the modern analysis, but the region generated by the city will differ in interesting ways in the periods after (or sometimes before) the picture which we can reconstruct for antiquity. The recognition of how interesting conceptually the identification of regions can be has also finally laid to rest the older critiques of regional geography as an unreflectively descriptive pursuit, characterised by the accumulation of untheorised detail.

The sense of perspective which derives from a two-thousand-year gap combines with modern conceptual geography to help identify the differences between whole systems of regional thinking in the ancient world – differences of scale, and differences of ideology. Regionality is patterned by the conceptual distances between places, which in turn are shaped by the speed and ease of transportation, and the ease and dissemination of information and imagination about other places. Thus pre-Roman Italy, as the set of territories of small population groups loosely configured into bigger groupings – the Frentani and the Hirpini and the Pentri, adding up to the Samnites – was radically different from the Augustan *regiones*, patterned by the roads of Italy, and made up of the territories of chartered towns. In many places, the regions which were used by the authorities were deliberate impositions, representing a claim that the conquering power knew better than its subjects how to subdivide their space and organise their populations. An excellent instance is the 'tribal' or 'cantonal' system deployed by Rome in the northwestern provinces, taking a careful selection of the names of Gallic communities from before the conquest, and converting them – beyond all recognition – into more or less equal city territories.

The coherences of the regions discerned by modern geographical approaches are most conspicuously displayed in archaeological evidence. Since the middle of the twentieth century it has been, above all, survey archaeology that has made it possible to develop this form of study. Regions with similar settlement patterns and settlement history, characterised by similar distributions of diagnostic ceramics, have emerged in many different parts of the Mediterranean. At the same time, the continuing publication and study of excavated materials make it easier to trace regional cultures which shared funerary practices or temple decoration. This revolution in our understanding has led to a willingness to look for regional differentiation and an increasing awareness that the homogeneities of elite culture concealed a world which was far more locally diverse. That in turn leads us to revisit the other evidence, epigraphic and literary, and revise earlier opinion. To give one instance: economic differences which are readily deduced from archaeology illustrate a Roman legal text which assumes that regions will vary notably one from another in the availability and price of credit. The charting of such regions and their changing configuration, and the relevance of this to other forms of history, is an exciting challenge for the future.

Against regionalism: the blurs and messes

As we respond to this challenge, however, the constructedness of the region must always be prominent in our thinking. It would not be appropriate to suggest that regional thinking, convenient though it remains and historically central as it genuinely has been, is the only, or even the best, way of coping with diversity, complexity, abstraction and remoteness. In antiquity, it is above all the phenomenon of small-group mobility that renders it unhelpful, giving rise to spatial patterns which are better modelled dendritically or as scatters of points than through tessellations. Diaspora-like movements, whether of Phoenician or Greek overseas settlement, or the settlement of traders or mercenary soldiers or the mass-enslaved, can be occluded by an excessively regional approach. The ethnic map of the Mediterranean before the triumph of the nation-state and the arbitrary cleansings it undertakes is precisely one in which the attempt to impose regional concepts may be actively malign, and that was, as we have seen, often true in antiquity too. This tension itself is an important subject for academic reflection.

Further reading

General surveys

J. B. Harley and D. Woodward (eds), *The History of Cartography, Volume One: Cartography in Prehistoric, Ancient and Medieval Europe and the Mediterranean*, Chicago: University of Chicago Press, 1987.

C. Nicolet, *Space, Geography, and Politics in the Early Roman Empire* (Jerome Lectures, 19), Ann Arbor: University of Michigan Press, 1991.

K. Brodersen, *Terra Cognita* (2nd edn) (Spudasmata, 59), Hildesheim and New York: Olms, 2003.

Some specific topics

J. B. Campbell (ed.), *The Writings of the Roman Land Surveyors: Introduction, Text, Translation and Commentary*, London: Society for the Promotion of Roman Studies, 2000.

O. A. W. Dilke, *The Roman Land Surveyors: An Introduction to the Agrimensores*, Newton Abbot: David and Charles, 1971 (repr. Amsterdam: Hakkert, 1992).

K. Geus, 'Space and Geography', in A. Erskine (ed.), *A Companion to the Hellenistic World*, Oxford: Blackwell, 2003, pp. 232–45.

Modern theoretical approaches

W. V. Harris, *Rethinking the Mediterranean*, Oxford: Oxford University Press, 2005.

M. W. Lewis and K. E. Wigen, *The Myth of Continents*, Berkeley: University of California Press, 1997.

I. Malkin (ed.), *Mediterranean Paradigms and Classical Antiquity*, London and New York: Routledge, 2005.

N. Purcell and P. Horden, *The Corrupting Sea: A Study of Mediterranean History*, Oxford: Blackwell, 2000.

C. Periods

This section provides a narrative background to the phenomena and themes dealt with elsewhere in the *Companion*, allowing the reader to situate these in their proper chronological context. Each chapter gives an overview of the period concerned, to draw out its main developments and characteristics, and the themes which give it special significance when compared to earlier or later periods. The various chapters also try to draw attention to current scholarly preoccupations in the study of those periods.

Part One B showed that the geographical context within which Graeco-Roman civilisations deserve to be studied is one that vastly exceeds any strict definition of 'Greece' or 'Rome'. The chronological limits of what can recognisably be seen as Greek or Roman are equally subject to constant debate. So too are the divisions commonly applied within the overall chronological range. This problem, of *periodisation*, is a recurrent one: by moving the starting points and endpoints for periods of study we bring in or exclude segments of the evidence, generate new views on the causation and consequences of events, or offer new perspectives on degrees of continuity and innovation.

15. The 'Dark Age' of Greece

Irene S. Lemos

The term 'Dark Age' is generally used to describe the archaeological period which starts with the collapse of the Mycenaean palatial system (roughly 1200 BC) and ends with the rise of the Greek city-states (around 770 BC).

The influential and comprehensive studies by Snodgrass (*The Dark Age of Greece*) and Desborough (*The Last Mycenaeans and their Successors* and *The Greek Dark Ages*) remain valuable for the definition of the period. Both scholars justify their use of the term 'Dark Age' in terms of describing the post-Mycenaean period as one which was marked by destruction and abandonment of sites, depopulation and a general fall in living standards. This gloomy picture of Greece was further accompanied by the loss of certain skills in architecture and art and most importantly by the loss of writing (Snodgrass, *Dark Age of Greece*, p. 2; Desborough, *Greek Dark Ages*, pp. 15–18). It was also believed that during this period contacts with areas outside Greece were severely interrupted and even within the Aegean communication was limited. The surviving communities appeared to be isolated when compared to the 'international spirit' which characterised their Mycenaean predecessors.

Since the publication of those studies, understanding of the 'Dark Age' has been enhanced by a number of important archaeological discoveries, and by more surveys of the period. First, the chronological subdivisions within the period are now better understood, especially for that part of it which is still assigned to the Late Bronze Age. Advances have also been made in defining culturally the crucial period following the collapse of the Mycenaean palatial system. This period, which coincides with the last stage of the Late Bronze Age, is called Late Helladic IIIC (c. from 1200 to 1100 BC); it is followed by a short transitional period, the Sub-Mycenaean period (c.1100–1025), the end of which finds Greek communities practising newly introduced iron-working technology. The Early Iron Age in Greece coincides with the beginning of the so-called Protogeometric period (c.1025–900); both Protogeometric and the successive Geometric styles are named after the characteristic geometric motifs employed to decorate the pottery produced in most Greek regions (see also chapter 28). This is followed by the Early and Middle Geometric stages, c. 900–770 BC, which cover the last stages of the so-called 'Dark Age'. The final Geometric stage (the Late Geometric period) is believed to mark the beginning of the recovery in the Greek world and thus is not included in the 'Dark Age'. By this time Greeks had already adopted the alphabet for writing (see also chapter 63).

The importance of Late Helladic IIIC (LH IIIC) emerges from recent research which has shown that this period was not as impoverished as once thought. At the beginning of the period some of the Mycenaean citadels appear still to be occupied and to have served as the seats of local rulers who replaced the Mycenaean *wanaktes* (rulers). This is especially notable in the case of Tiryns, where the Mycenaean *megaron* (central hall) was probably remodelled on a smaller scale to meet the needs of an administrative centre. The population in the Lower Citadel also appears to have increased during this period, indicating that refugees from destroyed or abandoned sites might have found safety at Tiryns.

Another important observation is that a number of sites which were either newly founded (such as Perati in East Attica) or which were insignificant under Mycenaean rule (such as Lefkandi in Euboea and Kynos in east Locris) now appear to be more important. This becomes more apparent during the middle part of this period when a number of sites located along the coasts and the islands of the Aegean show signs of a short recovery. This is reflected in the deposition of grave offerings found in tombs (for example in the tombs at Perati, and on the islands of Naxos and Rhodes) and in the appearance of a pictorial style of decoration on vases (Deger-Jalkotzy, 'Aegean islands'; 'Last Mycenaeans'). The repertoire of this pictorial style includes monsters, such as griffins and sphinxes – fantastical images which continue to be imported from the Near East – and also octopuses, birds and most importantly scenes with warriors (Rutter, 'Cultural novelties'). The most celebrated example of such scenes is the Warrior Krater from Mycenae (French, *Mycenae*, pp. 135–40), while kraters found at Kynos in east Locris and Lefkandi in Euboea, depicting scenes with warriors fighting on ships, are an innovation of the period (Dakoronia, 'Representations of sea battles'). The popularity of warriors' iconography indicates clearly their importance in the running of the affairs of the surviving communities (Deger-Jalkotzy, forthcoming).

Despite, however, the apparent presence and protection offered by a society of warriors, many of the LH IIIC settlements were destroyed or abandoned at the end of the period. Some of them were abandoned for good, but most only for a short period of time. For example, Koukounaries on Paros and Emporio on Chios are both abandoned after the end of the Late Bronze Age but then reoccupied late in the Iron Age. Other sites such as Kastri at Palaikastro and Chania in Crete appear to be abandoned for good. Perati in Attica was also abandoned, while Athens, Lefkandi and Argos survived, even if, according to the present archaeological picture, living standards seem to have deteriorated (Popham, 'Collapse of Aegean civilization'). In fact, if we want to find a period to which the term 'Dark Age' could apply, then this short period at the end of the Late Bronze Age and the beginning of the Sub-Mycenaean period is probably the best candidate.

The following stage is called the 'Sub-Mycenaean' period by experts, in order to suggest that the pottery produced during this period is made and decorated in a debased version of Mycenaean style. But pottery apart, the Sub-Mycenaean phase introduces a number of new features which will become more prominent at the beginning of the Iron Age. In addition, scholars have rightly commented that it is not only the new features which made the difference in the archaeological picture of the period but also the complete rejection of important Mycenaean ones (Desborough, *Greek Dark Ages*, pp. 64–79). One of the most important changes taking place is in burial practices: in some of the core areas of Mycenaean culture, such as the Argolid, central Greece, Euboea and the Cyclades, single burials in cist tombs and pits completely replaced the Mycenaean rite of multiple burials in chamber tombs. Multiple burials in *tholoi* or chamber tombs, however, continued in Thessaly, Phokis, Messenia and Crete. Desborough suggested that such a change in burial rites could only have happened with the arrival of new people, most probably from areas where cist tombs were in use such as Epirus (*Greek Dark Ages*, pp. 106–11). Others put more emphasis on the changing social and political conditions, which required a more economical way of burying the dead (Mee and Cavanagh, 'Mycenaean tombs', pp. 45–64). Snodgrass saw in these changes a revival of similar practices in the Middle Helladic period which preceded the Mycenaean era (*Greek Dark Ages*, pp. 177–84). Whatever the reasons for such a change, the fact remains that in the areas where the rite of single burials appears, there was no return to previous Mycenaean practices. At the same time most regions, including Crete, adopt more extensively the practice of cremation which, although it first appeared in the previous (LH IIIC) period, became gradually more common during this period and the ensuing Early Iron Age (Lemos, *Protogeometric Aegean*, pp. 184–6).

Therefore, the Sub-Mycenaean period should be seen merely as a short transitional period from the last stages of the Late Bronze Age to the beginning of the Early Iron Age. The main sites of this period that have produced settlement deposits or cemeteries continued to be important centres in the Early Iron Age. It is in such important sites, such as Athens, Knossos, Lefkandi, Argos and Tiryns, that the first iron weapons appear in the burials of elite groups during the early stages of the Protogeometric period, marking the beginning of the Early Iron Age in Greece. Snodgrass and others have argued that the new technology arrived from Cyprus, an island which maintained close links with Greece throughout the period (Snodgrass, *Dark Age of Greece*, pp. 228–31; Pickles and Peltenburg, 'Metallurgy', pp. 67–100).

It is unfortunate that most of the archaeological evidence for Early Iron Age Greece comes from cemeteries rather than settlements. It is indeed only from burial practices that attempts have been made to understand the social structures and developments of these early Greek communities (Morris, *Burial and Ancient Society*). From study of the mortuary evidence from major sites, scholars have proposed that diversity is a major characteristic of Early Iron Age societies. Such diversity is clearly reflected in the variety of burial rites practised in Greece during this period (Whitley, 'Social diversity', pp. 341–65; Lemos, forthcoming). There are, however, a number of common practices. For example, it is clear that elite members are buried with the status of warriors; such burials occur mostly in Athens, Knossos and Lefkandi. Care is also taken to differentiate gender and age. Another helpful observation is that in most sites, burials are organised in separate plots, indicating that each one of them may have belonged to a specific kin group or, as Coldstream suggested, that each one of them may have been the family seat of a *genos* or elite descent group (Coldstream, 'Rich lady of the Areiopagus'). Such plots can be found, for example, in the Kerameikos in Athens, in the cemetery of Toumba at Lefkandi, and in several burial plots in the area around the palace of Knossos, where a number of cemeteries have been located, such as Fortetsa, Tekke and the North Cemetery.

Insights into the complexity of the burial rites of the period were spectacularly revealed with the discovery of a male and a female burial under a building at Toumba, in Lefkandi. This discovery left no doubts about the complexity of the funeral rites of the period and of the society which practised them. The building itself, apsidal in plan, as was the norm for the period, is of monumental dimensions (50 m × 10 m = 164 ft × 32.8 ft); under the floor, in the central room of the building, elaborate rites were offered to a male who was cremated and buried with his iron weapons. Next to him was found the burial of a woman, heavily adorned with gold jewellery. In another shaft next to them four horses were buried. Subsequent to these burials, other individuals continued to be buried in front of the building, indicating that they belong to the same kin group (Figure 15.1). The main characteristic in the Toumba cemetery is the rich offerings given to the dead. Apart from the local and imported pottery and the metal ornaments which were the usual offering for the time, exotic goods imported from the Near East and Egypt were also offered (see also chapter 12). The presence of exotic goods clearly indicates that contacts with the Eastern Mediterranean were well established, while the discovery of Euboean pottery in the East suggests that Euboeans might have also played a part in this exchange (Lemos, *Protogeometric Aegean*, pp. 161–8, 202–3).

Conspicuous consumption was also a feature of the burials at Knossos, a site with contacts with the East, especially with Cyprus. Crete also produced evidence of Phoenician presence at the site of Kommos on the south coast, where around 800 BC, a small stone temple was constructed which housed a structure made of three *stēlai* (stone slabs) on a base, resembling similar cult arrangements found later in the Punic world. Cypriot and Near Eastern imports are also found in the cemetery at Eleutherna in Western Crete (Coldstream, *Geometric Greece*, pp. 99–102, 381–5).

Athens and Argos also catch up with the offering of imported goods during the Early and Middle Geometric periods. In Athens, one exceptional woman was buried in the area of Areopagus with imported faience beads and ivory ornaments. In addition to the local fine pottery and elaborate jewellery, she was given a clay chest representing model granaries. This last offering might have symbolically signified the wealth of her family in arable land (Coldstream, 'Rich lady of the Areiopagus'; *Geometric Greece*, pp. 55–61).

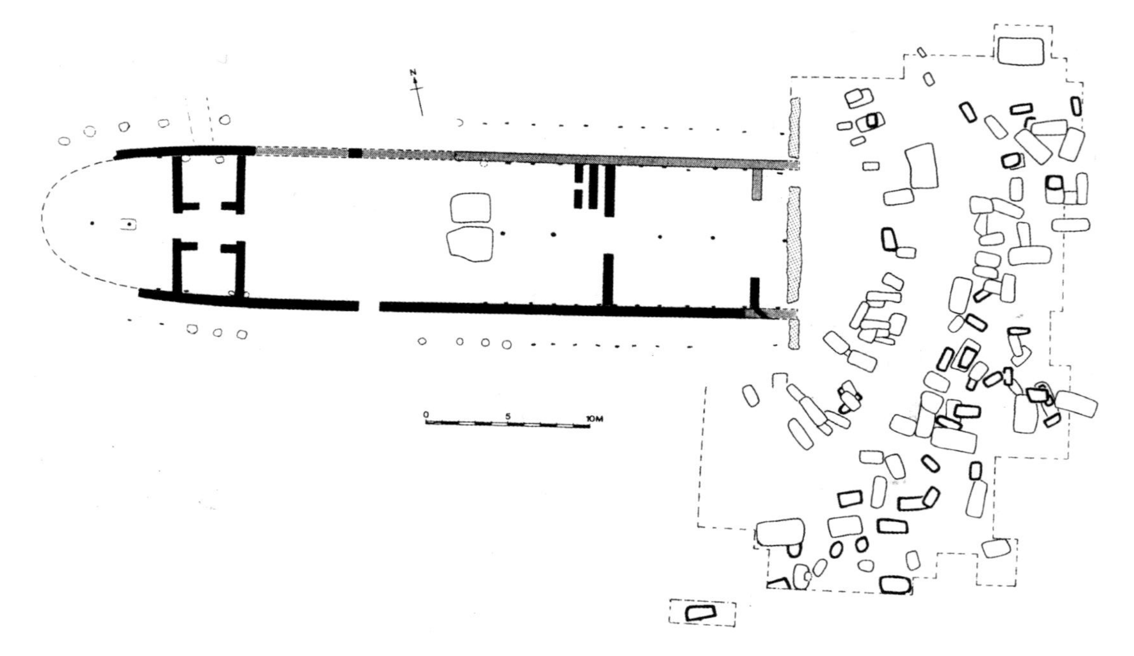

Fig. 15.1 The Protogeometric building and the cemetery at Toumba Lefkandi (after Mervyn Popham and Irene S. Lemos, Lefkandi III: The Toumba Cemetery, London: British School at Athens, 1996).

Athens is also responsible for developments in the Geometric style of pottery. The style finds its first expression in the Attic workshops which profoundly influenced the production of pottery in other centres. Euboea, Thessaly and the Cyclades, however, although keen to import Attic products, stubbornly continued to produce a Sub-Protogeometric style of pottery. It is not until later that these areas joined Athens and the Argolid in the production of the Late Geometric style of pottery.

Recent archaeological discoveries also suggest that the emergence of sanctuaries cannot any longer be considered to be a post- 'Dark Age' phenomenon. Excavations at Kalapodi in Phokis and Poseidi in Chalcidice, and research at Isthmia and Olympia, show that these sanctuaries were receiving offerings during this period (Morgan, *Isthmia VIII*; Lemos, *Protogeometric Aegean*, pp. 221–4). In addition, the study of the architectural remains of the period indicated to Mazarakis Ainian that rituals associated with cults were taking place inside or outside the chieftains' houses (see also chapter 4). He further suggested that in those settlements where such evidence existed, cult activities connected with the chieftain's dwelling were gradually moved to a city temple (Mazarakis Ainian, *From Rulers' Dwellings to Temples*).

The study of the so-called 'Dark Age' has been advanced by archaeological discoveries and research (see also chapters 2 and 3). Compared with what came before it, and what came after, this period can no longer be considered 'dark', only different. It is clear that a number of features which in the past were thought to post-date the 'Dark Age' had already appeared during its course. One of the most important is that communication within and outside Greece had already revived, stimulating an improvement in living conditions, which brought with it changes in the social structures of early Greek communities. The understanding of these social structures can – at present – be observed only in the diversity and complexity of burial practices. The discovery of more settlements dating to this period will offer further insights as to the degree of their sophistication.

One of the most important innovations of this period, however, is the introduction of a superior technology: iron-working (see also chapter 28). Its application at a number of sites demonstrates that Greek communities were ready to experiment with it, and that they did so successfully. At the same time, it appears that most Greeks took an important decision to reject for good the failed palatial system, which had proved to be unsuitable for their requirements, and to start looking for more suitable solutions in the form of smaller but more flexible political units. It is at least misleading not to recognise that, during the so-called 'Dark Age', archaeology reveals the rise of the processes which led towards the formation of the city-states.

Further reading

J. N. Coldstream, 'The rich lady of the Areiopagus and her contemporaries', *Hesperia* 64 (1995), 391–403.

J. N. Coldstream, *Geometric Greece* (2nd edn), London: Routledge, 2003.

F. Dakoronia, 'Representations of sea battles on Mycenaean sherds from Kynos', *Tropis* 5 (1993), 119–28.

S. Deger-Jalkotzy, 'The Aegean islands and the break-down of the Mycenaean palaces around 1200 BC', in V. Karageorghis and N. Stampolidis (eds), *Eastern Mediterranean Cyprus, Dodecanese, Crete 16th–6th cent. BC*, Athens: University of Crete and A. G. Leventis Foundation, 1998, pp. 105–20.

S. Deger-Jalkotzy, 'The last Mycenaeans and their successors updated', in S. Gitin, A. Mazar and E. Stern (eds), *Mediterranean Peoples in Transition, Thirteenth to Early Tenth Centuries BCE, in Honor of Professor Trude Dothan*, Dubuque: Kendall/Hunt, 1998, pp. 114–28.

S. Deger-Jalkotzy, 'Late Mycenaean warrior tombs', in S. Deger-Jalkotzy and I. S. Lemos (eds), *Ancient Greece from the Mycenaean Palaces to the Age of Homer: Proceedings of the 3rd Leventis Conference from Wanax to Basileus*, Edinburgh: Edinburgh University Press, 2006.

V. R. d' A. Desborough, *The Last Mycenaeans and their Successors: An Archaeological Survey c.1200–c.1000 BC*, Oxford: Oxford University Press, 1964.

V. R. d' A. Desborough, *The Greek Dark Ages*, London: Ernest Benn, 1972.

E. French, *Mycenae: Agamemnon's Capital*, Stroud: Tempus, 2002.

I. S. Lemos, *The Protogeometric Aegean: The Archaeology of the Late Eleventh and Tenth Centuries BC*, Oxford: Oxford University Press, 2002.

I. S. Lemos, 'Athens and Lefkandi: a tale of two sites', in S. Deger-Jalkotzy and I. S. Lemos (eds), *Ancient Greece from the Mycenaean Palaces to the Age of Homer*.

A. Mazarakis Ainian, *From Rulers' Dwellings to Temples: Architecture, Religion and Society in Early Iron Age Greece (1100–700 BC)* (*SIMA* CXXI), Jonsered: Paul Aströms Förlag, 1997.

C. B. Mee and W. G. Cavanagh, 'Mycenaean tombs as evidence for social and political organisation', *Oxford Journal of Archaeology* 3 (1984), 45–64.

C. Morgan, *Isthmia VIII: The Late Bronze Age Settlement and the Early Iron Age Sanctuary*, Princeton, NJ: American School of Classical Studies at Athens and Princeton University Press, 1999.

I. Morris, *Burial and Ancient Society: The Rise of the Greek City-State*, Cambridge: Cambridge University Press, 1987.

S. Pickles and E. Peltenburg, 'Metallurgy, society and the bronze/iron transition in the east Mediterranean and the Near East', *Reports of the Department of Antiquities, Cyprus* (1998), 67–100.

M. Popham, 'The collapse of Aegean civilization at the end of the Late Bronze Age', in B. Cunliffe (ed.), *The Oxford Illustrated Prehistory of Europe*, Oxford: Oxford University Press, 1994, pp. 277–303.

J. Rutter, 'Cultural novelties in the post-palatial Aegean', in W. A. Ward and M. S. Joukowsky (eds), *The Crisis Years: The 12th century BC*, Dubuque: Kendall/Hunt, 1992, pp. 61–78.

A. Snodgrass, *The Dark Age of Greece*, Edinburgh: Edinburgh University Press, 1971.

J. Whitley, 'Social diversity in Dark Age Greece', *ABSA* 86 (1991), 341–65.

16. *Archaic and Classical Greece*

Robin Osborne

Archaic Greek history is traditionally held to begin with the first Olympic Games in 776 BC, and to run to the Persian Wars of 480/79. The period from 479 to the death of Alexander the Great is then known as the classical period. Like all periodisations (see also chapters 15 and 19), these terminal points are open to challenge on the grounds that they obscure continuities between periods and create false assumptions of changelessness within periods, but there are real differences in both evidence and major themes between the two periods.

Archaic Greece: evidence

Although the Homeric poems contain stories which had been in the epic tradition for several centuries before the *Iliad* and *Odyssey* were written, along with references to objects of Bronze Age date, and although some writers attempted to put dates back into the second millennium BC onto such mythological events as the Trojan War, no written source records historical events earlier than the eighth century. From the eighth century onwards both contemporary writing and stories in later sources can be related to events of more or less certain historicity. All contemporary allusions, however, to events of the archaic period come in poetry; no prose accounts of either contemporary or past events were written in the seventh or sixth centuries BC, and what we are told by fifth- and fourth-century writers depended almost entirely upon oral tradition, not upon earlier texts. This is by contrast to the classical period, for the events of which we have the testimony of contemporary or near-contemporary historians (Herodotus for the Persian Wars themselves, Thucydides for the events between the Persian and Peloponnesian wars, and for the latter war, Xenophon for the end of the Peloponnesian War and the first forty years of the fourth century). It has often been convenient for scholars to treat the traditions about the archaic period as comparable to the contemporary accounts of the classical period, but, as recent scholarship has emphasised, both the nature of the material preserved and comparative evidence for the nature of oral tradition in other societies strongly suggest that this is not a viable historical practice. Stories about the past get handed on only in as far as they offer something that the person narrating the story has an interest in telling or their audience an interest in hearing. What does, and what does not, get *remembered* therefore says more about the successive interests of those through whom the story has been handed down than it does about what originally happened. The picture of the archaic period which we get from classical writers is itself a picture of the classical period as much as or more than it is a picture of the archaic period.

If the nature of oral tradition means that it is impossible to write a coherent historical narrative of the archaic period, we are nevertheless richly informed about archaic Greek society from the archaeological record and from contemporary poetry. The surviving lyric and elegiac poetry of the seventh and sixth centuries reveals the world and concerns of the wealthy, their social prejudices and their attitudes towards each other and the world outside. In different ways the inscribed texts of archaic laws and the imagery of painted pottery complement these literary texts, while the material traces of settlements and sanctuaries literally enable the presence and activities of Greeks to be mapped. Any history of archaic Greece has to be *total* history.

Archaic Greece: themes

The archaic Greece that is revealed by these diverse sources is itself diverse. When Greeks adopted and adapted writing from the Phoenicians in the eighth century (see also chapter 63) they chose to write not in one but in various local alphabets, for the letter-forms and the number of letters used varied from place to place. This regionalism is paralleled by the regionalism displayed in the forms and decoration of painted pottery and in the nature and forms of other artefacts. These stylistic *regions* only sometimes correspond with political boundaries: regional identities were already in the eighth century, and continued until the end of the sixth century, to be co-extensive neither with political (e.g. Theban or Parian) nor with ethnic identities (e.g. Dorian or Ionian). At the same time it is clear that there were also cultural preferences which were primarily a matter of social status rather than region. Recent scholarship has stressed that in the later eighth century there was something of a common culture among the elite throughout the Eastern and central Mediterranean, a culture marked by the importation of precious items, including gold and silver plate and jewellery, from the Near East and by the imitation of such products. The inhabitants of archaic Greek communities identified themselves in many ways, besides as members of a particular political unit.

One aspect of the diversity of the archaic Greek world is that it was getting bigger. This was true both in straightforward demographic terms, where a more or less steady, if slow, growth of population saw the largest communities of the eighth century, unlikely to number more than 5,000 or 6,000 inhabitants, grow to communities of upwards of 30,000 or, in the case of Athens, perhaps 50,000 inhabitants by the time of the Persian Wars. It is also true in terms of settlement numbers. Archaeology records increasing numbers of settlements in the areas where Greeks were already settled in 750 BC, but also, and most spectacularly, a very great increase in the so-called colonies, the numerous settlements scattered widely around the Mediterranean, from the northeastern coast of Spain and southern coast of France, through southern Italy and Sicily to North Africa, and the littoral of the Black Sea (see also chapter 14). Almost all these settlements came to be claimed by a mother-city (*mētropolis*), but the extent to which they were indeed planned foundations has recently been questioned; many, at least, seem to have been founded by adventurers led by some charismatic individual and out for profit from climates more favourable to agriculture than that of the Greek mainland and Aegean, or from the exploitation of local mineral or other resources.

A second aspect of the diversity is the determination by individual communities of their own political organisation, acts of state-formation often talked of as the 'birth of the polis', where the Greek word *polis* is part of a claim that this was a unique political formation. Whether there had been a general prevalence of kingship during the Dark Age is unclear (see also chapter 15), but there is good evidence, including from contemporary inscriptions on stone, of communities in the seventh and sixth centuries regulating access to magistracies and the duties of magistrates by means of rules to which the community as a whole signs up and in which the role of that community itself may be defined. Evidence for such law-making activity comes not only from both Sparta and Athens in this period, but also from small communities such as Dreros in Crete and Tiryns in the Argolid. The formation of these rules about officials depended upon the prior formation of rules of belonging to the community, and in the course of the archaic period there are signs that it became gradually more difficult for a man from one community to move into, and become a full member of, another community. Political identity came to dominate other identities, whether locally, class- or kin-based, narrower or wider. In Athens this is appropriately signalled by the constitutional changes at the end of the sixth century that resulted in what we call Athenian democracy.

The making of laws was parallel with, and perhaps in part a response to, the phenomenon of tyranny. Tyranny, as defined in the archaic Greek world, was the extra-constitutional rule of a single man, whether harsh or beneficial. In archaic poetry tyranny is associated in part with non-Greek practice, in particular with the rule of Gyges in Lydia. Stories about tyrants have been subjected to increasingly intense scrutiny in recent scholarship. They tend to stress ways in which tyrants deceived their subjects, and the tyrants' inability to set reasonable bounds to their power, particularly when it came to their relations with women. What these stories explore above all are the tensions involved in establishing government for a community in which interests are diverse, and the questions and problems which arise with regard to the exercise of power over groups that do not themselves have a place in the taking of decisions.

The tensions between unity and diversity within the archaic Greek world are well reflected in religious developments, to which scholars have come to devote much attention (see also chapter 4). The eighth century sees both the earliest building of monumental temples to the gods and the first big interstate, and soon interregional, festival, the Olympic games. By the end of the eighth century, the Olympic games were attracting competitors, and craftsmen eager to sell their wares, from all over the Peloponnese. In the sixth century, Greek cities in Sicily, as well as those in the Greek mainland, were putting up buildings at Olympia to house treasures that they dedicated to Zeus, and were also using it as a place to display not only monuments advertising victories achieved but also treaties which they had made with their neighbours. Against this common Greek participation in the worship of a single deity, however, stands both the way in which individual cities marked the borders of their territories by placing temples there and the way in which cities worshipped members of the Olympian pantheon under numerous different epithets, often epithets with local reference. Greek polytheism allowed for both distinction and unity.

Classical Greece: evidence

The interest which Greeks took in the political events of their own times, and their conviction that these events were of more than passing significance, means that we are richly informed about the political and military history of the fifth and fourth centuries. In addition there survive from Athens both a large number of speeches given in Athenian political assemblies and law-courts and more than thirty tragedies and a dozen comedies performed as part of the festivals of Dionysus there. Even more substantial in bulk are the writings of Plato and Aristotle, which manifest a critical interest not so much, as do the fragments which survive of sixth- and fifth-century philosophical inquiries, in the natural world as in social, moral and political issues. These literary texts can be supplemented by a substantial body of texts inscribed on stone, texts which reveal something of the day-to-day workings of corporate bodies operating within the city as well as of the city as a whole.

For all this abundance, however, there are ways in which we are less well informed about the classical than about the archaic world. In particular our classical evidence is dominated by Athens, whereas no single city dominates the evidence from the archaic period. For the archaic period we have substantial fragments surviving of the work of two Spartan poets, Alcman and Tyrtaeus, but from the classical period nothing more than a meagre clutch of inscriptions survives from Sparta, and we are condemned to see it almost entirely through Athenian eyes. Similarly something, at least, survives of the work of sixth- and fifth-century Greek philosophers working in Ionia, the north Aegean, Sicily and southern Italy, but the philosophical works surviving from the fourth century are all from the pens of philosophers working in Athens, and clearly influenced by Athenian practice, even if two of them, Aristotle and Theophrastus, were natives of other Greek cities (see also chapter 48). Although archaeological evidence from the fifth and fourth centuries survives from many places other than Athens, the material upon which classical archaeology has traditionally focused its attention is very much dominated by Athens. By 500 BC the Athenians were the only Greeks producing decorated pottery in any quantity – and they were producing it in very great quantities indeed. The massive programme of temple building undertaken by the Athenians during the fifth century dominates any account of classical architecture or classical sculpture, and the thousands of carved gravestones put up in Athens during the fourth century constitute the largest single body of sculpture from anywhere in the Greek world at any period. It is only when one looks at other classes of material evidence, for example at evidence for settlements themselves, large or small, or for rural fortifications, that the Athenian dominance is seriously challenged. The dominance by Athens of our classical source material is not, however, fortuitous, but reflects very strongly the changed political and economic structure of the classical Greek world.

Classical Greece: themes

The Persian Wars mark a watershed in Greek history both because of what did not happen – it is clearly important that the cities of Greece did not come to be ruled by Persian governors or Greek puppets of Persia – and because of what did. What did happen is that the effort of defeating Persia led to two cities becoming enormously predominant in the Greek world – Athens and Sparta. Although the story of the Persian Wars is often told as if the numerous independent cities of the Greek mainland united to defeat the foreign foe, the reality is that only a small minority of cities took part in the resistance. Of the cities that did take part two were crucial. One was Sparta, whose importance lay partly in its unique possession of something close to a professional army, seen at its most disciplined in the self-sacrificial battle at Thermopylae in 480, and partly in the large number of Peloponnesian cities that were allied to it, whose combined forces constituted the major part of the army that resisted the Persians. The other was Athens, which, partly because it had been engaged in sporadic hostilities with the island of Aegina in the Saronic gulf, and partly because it possessed rich silver mines in the southern part of its territory at Laurium, had formed a navy very much larger than the navy of any other Greek city. The success of the essentially Athenian navy at the battle of Salamis in 480, and of the Spartan-led army at Plataea in 479, not only drove the Persians out of the Greek mainland, but revealed to Athenians and to others the potential power of their navy. To liberate the Greeks of the East Aegean and coastal Asia Minor, who had been under Persian rule, a league was formed under Athenian leadership. The military successes of this league led to the incorporation of the newly liberated city-states into the league, which the Athenians maintained in existence, even once all threat of Persian reaction had receded, as what we call the Athenian empire. This empire came to include more than two hundred cities obliged to make annual payments to Athens with which the Athenians maintained an enormous fleet. So large an empire, the use of force by Athenians to prevent cities leaving it, and the bureaucratic structures which the Athenians created to govern it were unheard of in the Greek world, and inevitably caused anxiety among Greek cities outside it, and particularly among the Spartans and their allies. Athenian power caused, indeed, a polarisation within the Greek world: few cities felt confident enough of their independence not to seek the friendship of one or other of the big powers. At various points in the middle of the fifth century Athens clashed with Sparta or with cities closely linked to Sparta or to its allies, and in 432 the Spartans decided to pre-empt further Athenian expansion by declaring war and, in 431, invading Athenian territory. Invasion and ravaging crops were regular techniques of land warfare, but they were far less effective against a power that controlled the sea and was wealthy enough to import all the food that it might need, and whose 'Long Walls', joining the town to the sea, had made it virtually an island. The Athenians, however, had no land army sufficient to defeat the Spartans and their allies in the field, and so, despite a number of engagements, with variable results, this proved to be largely a competition between the elephant and the whale. An uneasy truce after ten years of war, and the colossal failure of an attempt by Athens further to extend its power by invading Sicily, left both sides in much the same position, and a further ten years of hostilities (413–404) ended only when the Spartans acquired the financial support of Persia and formed a fleet able to defeat the Athenians at sea.

The defeat of Athens was very far from returning the Greek world to the conditions of the period before the Persian War. The dominance of Sparta, which took over the Athenian empire, exacting tribute and installing governors and garrisons, precipitated even various of its traditional allies into opposition. Within ten years there was general war in Greece once more, and Spartan success in that war led only to the reformation of Athenian power in the Second Athenian League and to the resurgence of Theban power at the head of a reformed Boeotian confederacy. The constant realignment of power blocks to give Sparta, Athens or Thebes the upper hand was ended with the rise to prominence of Macedon. This kingdom had vast resources of manpower and natural resources (silver and gold, but also timber for ship-building), but had played only a minor part in earlier Greek history because of internal dissension. Philip II (359–336) managed to unite Macedon, turn its army into the most effective fighting force in Greece, and crush the opposition of the cities of southern Greece at the battle at Chaeronea in Boeotia in 338. Despite continued resentment in those cities at the loss of their freedom, Macedonian control was sufficient to enable Alexander the Great to spend practically the whole of his reign crushing and taking over the Persian empire of Darius III. Greek history was turned into a minor chapter of the history of the rule by Greeks and Macedonians over the eastern Mediterranean and Near East.

The development in the fifth century of Athenian power over others had gone hand in hand both with mass slavery and with a developing ideology of freedom and of popular rule. The constitutional reforms of the end of the sixth century had moved power into the hands of a popular assembly, and a Council of 500 selected by lot, and further reforms after the Persian Wars, consolidated popular control over magistrates and the law-courts. Epigraphic as well as literary sources make it clear that active participation in Athenian political life, speaking in and not merely attending the Assembly, was widespread and not limited to a small class of politicians (see also chapter 60). Scholars have increasingly stressed that the debate over the merits and weaknesses of democracy that is revealed in the ideas floated in the run-up to the replacement of democracy briefly in 411 and 404/3, the reform of democratic procedures in 403, and the writings of such critics as Plato is testimony to the way in which Athenian democracy, in marked contrast to Spartan kingship, was both self-conscious and self-critical. Far less subject to critical assessment was the mass use of foreign slaves to sustain both the Athenian economy, through their involvement in the Athenian silver mines and probably also in agriculture, and the Athenian lifestyle and claims to citizen equality.

It is against the background of both Athenian imperialism and Athenian democracy that Athenian dominance of the cultural remains of classical Greece has to be seen. Directly or indirectly it was the wealth of empire and the self-confidence that came from prolonged, if not uninterrupted, success that enabled both the building of so lavishly decorated a temple as the Parthenon and the intense scrutiny of human social and political relations, whether in the tragedies performed at the festival of Dionysus or in the history written by the Athenian general Thucydides. Even after the collapse of Athenian political supremacy, the size and cultural achievements of the city continued to attract Greeks: both Plato and the orator Isocrates drew pupils from a wide area, and one of those attracted by Plato, Aristotle, further enhanced the educational appeal of the city by adding his own school at the Lyceum to the Academy established by Plato (see also chapter 48). The central place of Athens in Greek culture would long outlast the political conditions that had made it possible in the first place.

Not all the significant political and cultural developments in classical Greece occurred in Athens. The roots of Hellenistic kingship lay in Macedon and in the tyrannies that re-emerged in fourth-century Sicily. Most important, both for its immediate legacy in Greek history and for its later influence, was the development of the federal state. Several of the loose associations of communities of the archaic period developed more or less sophisticated federal structures in the fifth and fourth centuries, structures which combined extensive local autonomy for individual communities with concerted foreign policies both defensive and aggressive. Although such structures proved unable to resist Roman aggression in the Hellenistic period, they shaped the form that that aggression took and proved inspirational to later political theorists.

Further reading

Archaic Greece

O. Murray, *Early Greece* (2nd edn), London: Fontana, 1993 – an eloquent summation of the traditional view of early Greece.

R. G. Osborne, *Greece in the Making 1200–479 BC*, London: Routledge, 1996 – a highly informative account that attempts to treat later historical accounts as tradition and to give priority to contemporary literary and archaeological evidence.

A. M. Snodgrass, *Archaic Greece: The Age of Experiment*, London: Dent, 1980 – the first account to make extensive use of archaeological data and a landmark in the study of the eighth century.

Classical Greece

J. K. Davies, *Democracy and Classical Greece* (2nd edn), London: Fontana, 1993 – a basic guide to the period that is also full of ideas.

S. Hornblower, *The Greek World 479–323 BC* (3rd edn), London: Routledge, 2002 – densely packed with information and remarkable for its coverage of places other than Athens and Sparta.

J. Ober, *Mass and Elite in Classical Athens: Rhetoric, Ideology and the Power of the People*, Princeton: Princeton University Press, 1989 – a highly influential account of the working of Athenian democracy, stressing the importance of communication and ideology in democracy, as against traditional study of the constitutional mechanisms.

R. G. Osborne (ed.), *Classical Greece: Short Oxford History of Europe*, vol. 1, Oxford: Oxford University Press, 2000.

P. J. Rhodes (ed.), *Athenian Democracy*, Edinburgh: Edinburgh University Press, 2003 – a collection of important articles on Athenian democracy.

P. J. Rhodes, *A History of the Classical Greek World*, Oxford: Blackwell, 2005 – a detailed narrative of the central events.

M. Whitby (ed.), *Sparta*, Edinburgh: Edinburgh University Press, 2002 – a collection of important articles on Spartan political and social history.

17. The Hellenistic World

Thomas Harrison

The Hellenistic period runs from the reign (or death) of Alexander the Great (336–323 BC) through to the final Roman conquest of the Greek world – an endpoint traditionally dated to the defeat (31 BC) or death (30) of Mark Antony and Cleopatra VII of Egypt (see also chapter 19).

The scramble for power

It is the period, first, of the consolidation – after an immensely complex process of shifting alliances and jockeying for position – of the kingdoms of the 'Successors' (that is, the Graeco-Macedonian lieutenants of Alexander, who came to inherit the parts of his kingdom). Most prominent were the dynasty of the Ptolemies (named after their first king, Ptolemy I) in Egypt; of the Seleucids (named from their first king, Seleucus I) in the Near East; and of the Antigonids (from Antigonus I, whose power base was elsewhere, in Asia Minor) in Macedonia. Of these major successor kingdoms, it was only Egypt that was under the unbroken rule of one dynasty from the death of Alexander. Seleucus' rule in Asia, by contrast, was only confirmed by a peace treaty of 311 – after he had been restored from exile with Ptolemaic help. The fate of Macedonia took longer still to be settled. It had initially been under the rule of Alexander's lieutenant Antipater, then (after some instability) his son Cassander from 317 to 298/7. The following years, however, saw Macedonia change hands repeatedly until Antigonus II Gonatas took control – as it happened, permanently – in 277.

It could all have fallen out very differently. At the time of the death of Alexander, Antigonus II's grandfather, Antigonus I Monophthalmus (the 'one-eyed'), had been satrap (i.e. governor) of Phrygia in Asia Minor; at the settlement at Triparadisus (320) he had been appointed general of Asia. In the following years, together with his son Demetrius, he made a concerted bid to reunite the various limbs of Alexander's kingdom, only to be defeated and killed (by the combined armies of Cassander, Lysimachus and Seleucus) at the battle of Ipsus in 301. Lysimachus was one of a number of rulers (another prominent example is Eumenes of Cardia) who fell by the wayside but whose defeat was far from inevitable. Initially assigned Thrace, he came to dominate much of Asia Minor and Macedonia before being killed in battle in 281. Though often portrayed as a brutal and unsophisticated ruler (on account of his murder of his son), recent scholarship has sought to rehabilitate him, showing how he acted in similar fashion to other Hellenistic rulers (promoting cults, founding cities, surrounding himself with a court of *philoi* or 'friends'), and setting his murder of his son against the background of similar disputes over succession in other dynasties. Other casualties were the two possible legitimate heirs of Alexander: Philip III Arrhidaeus, Alexander's half-brother, and allegedly half-witted, and Alexander IV, Alexander's posthumously born son by his wife Roxane. Both were too vulnerable to stand any long-term chance of inheriting real power: the conceit was sustained that the successors were ruling in the name of Alexander's heir until the two were finally killed, in 317 and 310 respectively.

A consequence of such military-political turmoil was a certain fragility in the claims to legitimacy of the first-generation kings. It was only in 306, in the aftermath of a major victory, that Antigonus I and his son Demetrius first claimed the title of king. But king of what? In their case, it is possible that the title constituted a claim on the whole of Alexander's empire. When others – Ptolemy, Seleucus, Cassander and Lysimachus – took the plunge in the following year, the title of king more clearly became a matter of personal status, detached from any defined kingdom. A common theme in portrayals of Hellenistic kingship was that it depended on deeds rather than on descent. This ideology, however, did not mark such an abrupt break from the past (after all, Alexander had ruled Asia by right of conquest). The new kings, moreover, were swift to reinforce their own dynasties by a variety of means: the co-regency of fathers and sons (as in the case of Antigonus and Demetrius); dynastic cult (that is, the officially sponsored worship of a king's predecessors; see also chapter 4); and, in the case of the Ptolemies at least, brother–sister marriage.

The boundaries of the Hellenistic kingdoms were never firmly or finally settled. They continued to be fought over, not least in the series of six 'Syrian Wars' (the first c. 274–271, the last 170–168 BC) between the Seleucids and the Ptolemies; all the dynasties were disturbed also by in-fighting and intrigue. Hellenistic history, moreover, is not merely the sum total of the history of the three main kingdoms (Ptolemaic, Antigonid and Seleucid). The Attalid kingdom (centred on Pergamum in northwest Asia Minor) developed out of the local fiefdom of a certain Philetaerus to become a major power, crucial to the introduction of the Romans to the Greek world. Philetaerus had initially been a subordinate of Antigonus and Lysimachus, before transferring his loyalty to Seleucus I; his successors – notably Eumenes I (263–241) and Attalus I (241–197, the first to give himself the royal title) progressively asserted their independence from the Seleucid empire, as well as expending their energies in artistic patronage (most famously, the Pergamene altar). The region of Bactria (in the far east of the Seleucid empire, modern Afghanistan) likewise distanced itself from Seleucid influence at some point in the mid-third century, becoming a distinct Hellenistic kingdom. Meanwhile, on the Greek mainland, two leagues (the Achaean, centred on the Peloponnese; and the Aetolian, centred on the northwest of the mainland, though it came to incorporate members as far away as Asia Minor, Thrace and Crete), by creating a structure for common decision-making and a unified military command (see also chapter 60), ultimately turned a number of smaller cities into powerful enemies and allies (respectively) of Rome. Agis IV and Cleomenes III, third-century kings of Sparta, attempted – and failed – to restore the power and status of their city through a return to the imagined simplicity of archaic Sparta; Sparta was incorporated into the Achaean League in 192.

Roman expansion

The second main plot-line of the period is the progressive domination and dismantling of these political units by the power of Rome. Whether Roman intervention in the Greek world was reluctant or the result of relentless opportunism has been the matter of great dispute. Preceded by generations of contact and trade, Roman progress eastwards gathered pace from early interventions across the Adriatic, such as the First Illyrian war (230–228), through successive defeats of the kings of Macedonia (Philip V at Cynoscephalae, 197; Perseus at Pydna, 168) and of the Seleucids (Antiochus III at Apamea, 188), to the eventual annexation of the Hellenistic kingdoms as provinces of Rome (Macedonia, 146; Syria, 64; Egypt, 30). The Hellenistic kingdoms were isolated and neutered by degrees. The Antigonid kingdom of Macedonia, for example, on its best behaviour (under punitive treaty terms) after its defeats in the First and Second Macedonian Wars (211–205, 200–197) was divided into four republics after the Third (171–168) – a moment seen by the historian Polybius (from Megalopolis in the Achaean League) as the completion of Rome's conquest – only to be converted into a province a little over twenty years later. Rome was never without its friends in the Greek world – indeed a repeated pattern of Roman expansion was of friendship (rewarded by the award of territorial gains) turning cold as soon as an alliance had outlived its usefulness: this can be seen in the cases of the Aetolian League, the Attalids and then Rhodes.

Themes and sources

The name 'Hellenistic' derives from the term 'Hellenismus', first used by the German historian J. G. Droysen (1833) to denote the diffusion of Greek culture into the areas conquered by Alexander. The Hellenistic period, according to this model, is the period of the 'hellenisation' (that is, making Greek) of the successor kingdoms. This process can be seen arguably in a range of contexts: in the creation of magnificent festivals, on the model of the Pythian, Olympian and other Greek games, in the lands conquered by Alexander (pre-eminently the Ptolemaea in Alexandria, replete with exotic animals, representations of the Greek cities under Ptolemaic rule, and a giant phallus of 120 cubits, c. 62 m = 202.5 ft); in the patronage shown by kings, outstandingly by Ptolemy II and the Attalids, to 'classicising' poets (e.g. Theocritus, Callimachus), public art (e.g. the Pergamene altar), or to the collection and systematisation of earlier Greek literature (the Library of Alexandria; see also chapter 46); or in the foundations of cities on the Greek model, most strikingly perhaps that of Aï Khanum (complete with gymnasium, theatre, and inscriptions of Delphic maxims, such as 'know yourself') on the banks of the river Oxus at the eastern edge of the Seleucid Empire in modern Afghanistan. Increasingly, however, as in the case of 'romanisation' (see chapter 13), the one-sided nature of this model of hellenisation has been appreciated, and there has been a greater emphasis on, for example, the role played by non-Greeks in the royal courts, the spread of Eastern cults (such as Serapis or Cybele) across the Mediterranean, or the debt owed by the Seleucids and Ptolemies (in their style of government, in their architecture, and in other areas) to their 'Achaemenid' Persian or Egyptian predecessors.

Our picture of the Hellenistic age is strikingly dictated by the nature of our evidence. Our main narrative histories are those of Polybius (200–118 BC), Livy (writing in the age of Augustus) and Appian (second century AD), both the latter in part reliant on Polybius. They illuminate only certain passages of time: the period from 301 BC down to 229 (the date at which Polybius starts up) is one in which any overarching military-political narrative must be constructed by patchwork; for the independent kingdom of Bactria (roughly modern Afghanistan), we are for large stretches reliant on the evidence of coins alone. We are also lacking, with the partial exception of the Athenian 'New Comedy' of Menander, any large body of literature (such as Athenian oratory or drama in the classical period) which, by virtue of the broad audience it presumes, sheds light on popular social or religious attitudes. Though writers such as Demosthenes and Euripides (together with Homer) were very widely read in the Hellenistic period, the Hellenistic writers par excellence, Theocritus, Callimachus and Apollonius Rhodius, were altogether more self-consciously 'literary' authors, writing highly wrought, seemingly intimate and allusive poetry for elite audiences.

By comparison with the classical period, however, we are awash with papyri and inscriptions. Papyri give us evidence (hitherto undreamed of) of the relentless economic exploitation of the Egyptian countryside by the Ptolemaic administration, of the cumbersome and unresponsive nature of that administration, or of the diffusion of Greek texts (and of literacy) among Greeks and Egyptians. By contrast to the classical period with its disproportionate emphasis on Athens and Sparta, inscriptions draw our attention to smaller centres: Magnesia-on-the-Maeander in Asia Minor, Itanos in Crete, or Antioch-in-Persis on the Persian gulf (to name just a few examples). The themes that stand out differ correspondingly: the relationship (couched in highly complimentary diplomatic language) of cities with kings, in particular the grant of divine honours (or 'ruler-cult') to kings and to their families; the increasing role of private patronage ('euergetism') in ensuring a regular supply of grain or in the financing of public works (see also chapters 19, 34 and 60); a city's demand for the status of *asylia* (inviolability); or the time, expense, and dangers (whether of piracy or weather) involved in diplomatic missions. Although the Hellenistic period is also the era of federalism – that is, of leagues such as the Achaean and Aetolian, sometimes established as counterweights to royal power, sometimes under royal patronage – the picture that emerges is one in which the Greek city and its institutions continued to flourish, albeit under the shadow of disproportionately powerful kings. Inscriptional evidence combines, finally (sometimes jarringly), with that of historians to tell the story of Roman conquest – whether the Romans engineered or were drawn into their foreign interventions, a story rich in diplomatic euphemism and the cynical expression of power.

Further reading

Sourcebooks

M. M. Austin, *The Hellenistic World from Alexander to the Roman Conquest: A Selection of Ancient Sources in Translation* (2nd edn), Cambridge: Cambridge University Press, – an exemplary sourcebook.

R. S. Bagnall and P. Derow, *The Hellenistic Period: Historical Sources in Translation* (2nd edn), Oxford: Blackwell, 2003 – an excellent collection of epigraphic and papyrological evidence.

Secondary literature

A. E. Astin, M. W. Frederiksen, R. M. Ogilvie and F. W. Walbank (eds), *Cambridge Ancient History*, vol. 7, pt 1: *The Hellenistic World* (2nd edn), Cambridge: Cambridge University Press, 1984 – a concentrated collection of chapters of narrative.

A. Chaniotis, *War in the Hellenistic World: A Social and Cultural History*, Oxford: Blackwell, 2005 – a richly rewarding account of the role of warfare.

A. Erskine (ed.), *A Companion to the Hellenistic World*, Oxford: Blackwell, 2003 – an excellent collection on all aspects of Hellenistic history.

J. Ma, *Antiochus III and the Cities of Western Asia Minor*, Oxford: Oxford University Press, 1999 – on the relationship of cities and kings, and on the nature of Hellenistic kingship more generally.

D. Ogden, *Polygamy, Prostitutes and Death: The Hellenistic Dynasties*, London: Duckworth, 1999 – a detailed study of Hellenistic dynasties and dynastic disputes.

S. Sherwin-White and A. Kuhrt, *From Samarkhand to Sardis: A New Approach to the Seleucid Empire*, London: Duckworth, 1993 – argues against a 'Hellenocentric' view of the Seleucid empire.

G. Shipley, *The Greek World after Alexander*, London: Routledge, 2000 – a good, up-to-date introduction to the period; an excellent starting point.

F. W. Walbank, *The Hellenistic World* (3rd amended imprint), London: Fontana, 1992 – an excellent, brief introduction, less up-to-date, and less dense or detailed, than Shipley.

18. The Roman Republic

Mark Pobjoy

The Roman Republic endured for approximately four and a half centuries, until the period of civil wars which ended with the victory of Octavian (later Augustus) over Antony and Cleopatra (see also chapter 19). At its beginning (c. 500 BC), Rome was probably the most prominent of the Latin-speaking city-states in central western Italy, controlling an important junction of land routes at a naturally strong position which enjoyed a good water-supply. However, although apparently being one of the west Italian communities which had a trading agreement with Carthage (Polybius 3.22–3), Rome lacked discernible influence beyond the region. By the end of the Republic, Rome's territorial control extended from the English Channel to southern Spain, northern Africa and the Syrian desert, and Roman coinage and the Latin language were in use across the Mediterranean world. Rome's growth in the intervening years, by no means a story of continuous or steady expansion, can be seen as being based on four interlocking factors, all the subject of lively modern debate: (1) the evolution of its political system and social structure; (2) its military prowess by land and sea; (3) the effectiveness of its foreign policy; and (4) its success in agriculture, and more generally in economic management.

Political system and social structure

For information about the early political development of the Republic we depend on much later literary sources, which can be of dubious value even for the general character of the events which they purport to relate, let alone for matters of detail. But it is at least clear that following the collapse of the monarchy, the Republic's magistracies, Senate and popular assemblies evolved without a written constitution, sometimes swiftly in response to crisis or opportunity. The developed system of the third and second centuries was described by the Achaean Greek Polybius as a combination of the basic types of constitution familiar to Greek political theorists, containing monarchic, aristocratic and democratic elements – the consuls, Senate and People respectively (6.11).

The system is characterised by balance and interdependence. The magistrates, headed by the two consuls (the power of each balancing the other's), were the officials who conducted the military, political, judicial and administrative business of the state. The Senate, a council composed essentially of former magistrates, was strictly only an advisory body to current magistrates, but effectively controlled many aspects of domestic and foreign policy and finance. The People (adult male citizens), in assemblies varying in composition and structure passed legislation, decided on making war or peace, annually elected the magistrates, and sat in judgement in certain legal cases (see also chapter 60). Interdependence is seen in various ways. For example, a consul on campaign required the support of the Senate for finance and supplies, and it was the Senate that would decide whether to extend his period of command, and whether to award him a triumphal procession; the Senate needed to be wary, as the tribunes of the plebs (i.e. the plebeians, constituting the vast majority of Roman citizens) could bring virtually any public business, including senatorial meetings, to a halt with their veto, and could propose legislation to the plebs; and a citizen would not want to antagonise a consul under whose power he might fall on campaign. So it was difficult for any individual or body to disregard the other elements of the system.

In such a system there is room for disagreement even about which body is sovereign, as is seen both in divergent Roman attitudes to the authority of the Senate's decrees, with some maintaining that in an emergency a senatorial decree could override the People's laws and others that it could not do so under any circumstances, and in modern attempts to define the system as fundamentally aristocratic, oligarchic or democratic. Fissures in this system developed and broadened with time, and in its final decades it was characterised by imbalance and strife. But, when Polybius wrote, that lay in the future. To him, Rome's complex political system merits our attention because it largely explains Rome's survival of the war against Hannibal and subsequent conquest of much of the Mediterranean world in little more than 50 years (Polybius 1.1, 6.2).

Harder to discern than the formalities of Roman political life are its interrelationships with social structure. Roman society never ceased to be hierarchical, and was formally stratified according to property, as assessed by the censors (two senior officials appointed every five years). But once the stranglehold which the original aristocratic families, the patricians, had gained on high office and priesthoods was released and these positions became open also to plebeians (this long dispute over access to power is known as the Struggle of the Orders), all citizens were in theory eligible to hold them. Although in practice few families at any one time had a serious chance of such prominence, there were always families rising up the ladder (though not necessarily to the highest offices) and families declining. At times, families might strengthen themselves by arranging marriage alliances or adoptions.

A Roman possessed *nobilitas* ('nobility') if a direct ancestor had held high office, so acquisition of this distinctive social status depended on popular favour, in particular election by the People. Competition between wealthy families for this favour could benefit the state, in offering a choice of able candidates who, if successful, would want to justify the people's confidence in them. With pressure from an expanding citizen body and from recently acquired wealth, there were possibilities for the talented but relatively undistinguished to advance politically and socially. However, the influence of aristocratic lineage should not be underestimated. By the first century, few patrician families remained, but the status still counted: it is not pure coincidence that the dictators (emergency leaders) Sulla and Caesar, and the would-be revolutionary leader Catiline, were not merely noble, but patrician.

The degree of 'downward' social control which could be exercised is much debated. Wealthy Romans did act as *patroni* (patrons) to poorer *clientes* (clients) for mutual benefit, but it is not clear how much influence they exerted over them. On the other hand, Polybius regarded the pervasive rituals of Rome's polytheistic religion as themselves a means of controlling the masses (6.56). However, following the secret ballot laws of the 130s, it is unlikely that unequal social relationships, even if highly significant for daily interaction, could affect political decision-making as directly as they had before, and the emphasis in the latter years of the Republic was very much on *persuading* an electorate to vote one way or another. A wealthy Roman's house, where he greeted visitors in the morning and held meetings and social gatherings at other times, his oratorical skill, and the reputation for virtue of the male and female members of his family, past and present, were among the key elements in the ceaseless competition to impress and persuade.

Military prowess

For most of the republican period, Rome's army was a force of citizen soldiers, with the duty (and privilege) of service restricted to the propertied, and one's rank in the army depending on one's property-rating in the census. The cavalry was formed from those with the highest property-rating (the *equites*), the infantry from the five property bands (*classes*) beneath them, each *classis* armed according to the wealth of its members. Roman citizen soldiers, organised into legions, were regularly supported from the late fourth century by auxiliary forces drawn from the Latins and

Italian allies, until the aftermath of the Social War (= 'war against allies') in the first century saw these communities acquire Roman citizenship and their citizens serve in the legions. The Roman army's success over the centuries owed much to its adaptability, with important changes being made to its battle-order (particularly the shift from a solid phalanx to maniples, and subsequently from maniples to cohorts) and its equipment. There was also flexibility in respect of commanders, who might be continued beyond their term of office by the Senate or replaced. By contrast, army discipline was strict and punishments were severe. Furthermore, the army was not just a highly organised fighting force, but also a formidable construction team.

By the early first century, Rome had ceased to employ citizen cavalry, and effectively relied on auxiliary forces from overseas. For the provision of naval forces also, Rome came to depend on her allies, first those in Italy and then those overseas. There was no substantial standing fleet during the Republic, and fleets of various sizes were gathered for particular purposes. Nevertheless, Rome could enjoy significant successes at sea, most strikingly Pompey's devastating campaign against pirate forces in 67.

Although it has often been claimed that the Roman army became 'professionalised' in the last decades of the Republic, it is perhaps not until the reign of Augustus that soldiering can properly be regarded as having become a regular career for Roman citizens. However, the late Republic did see considerable changes in the composition of the army, which in turn had dramatic social, economic and political consequences. The minimum property qualification for service was lowered until the point was reached at which citizens with no property at all, who had previously been barred from military service, were enrolled in the army. Complex changes in Roman society lay behind this development. Its result was a more powerful bond between troops and their general, a bond which at times superseded any loyalty they felt for Rome's traditions of government. These men did not have property to return to on the completion of their military service, and came to look to their general and his political associates to secure land on which they could settle.

Foreign policy

The extent of Rome's territorial conquests under the Republic was remarkable. For more than a century and a half Rome's wars were fought relatively close to home, but defeat of the fellow members of the Latin League (a federation of the Latin-speaking communities of west central Italy, of which Rome was one) in 338 left Rome the predominant force in the region. Expansion northwards and southwards followed, such that by 264 all of Italy south of the Po valley was under Roman control, its communities being Roman (with full or attenuated citizenship), Latin or allied. Involvement with Messana in Sicily brought conflict with the Carthaginians (264–241), following which Sicily, Sardinia and Corsica successively came into Roman hands. Hannibal's attack on Rome's ally Saguntum in Spain was the spark for the Second Punic War (218–201), after which Rome began to gain control over Spain, Greece and Asia (in Roman terms, western Turkey) and pushed further north into the Po valley. An intensification of Roman hegemony is seen in the physical destruction of recalcitrant cities – Carthage and Corinth in 146 (partly with an economic motive), Numantia in Spain in 133, and Fregellae in Italy in 125.

Further expansion followed, including the first move into Transalpine Gaul, but Rome faced difficult times in the late second and early first centuries, with the migrations of the Cimbri and Teutoni in the north, and the Social War and the first Civil Wars (88–82) in peninsular Italy itself. Although the shockwaves of these conflicts were felt at the furthest ends of the empire, Rome maintained control, and even more expansion accompanied the Republic's politically contentious final years, most notably Pompey's conquests in Asia and Syria and Caesar's conquest of Gaul. The Romans' acquisition of such an empire changed them in various ways, their adoption of many facets of Hellenic culture being among the most notable. Of the foreign policy which helped to secure it, the effectiveness of which is all the more remarkable given the complexity of political decision-making behind it, four aspects stand out: Rome's diplomatic relationships with other states, organisation of Italian manpower, willingness under certain circumstances to extend its citizenship, and skilful deployment of colonies.

Rome's control of Italy was facilitated by the employment of an individual treaty of alliance with each community, thereby making concerted opposition more difficult. Great care was taken to put a fair face on military action, so that expansion would always be represented as in some sense a defensive measure. After defeating Philip V of Macedon, Rome proclaimed the freedom of Greek cities, and left them free of taxation and garrisons. Rome's claim of beneficence was (and sometimes still is) believed, but it gradually emerged that Rome expected obedience to its orders everywhere, and that its empire was more pervasive than might appear at first sight. Inscriptions in Latin and Greek (see also chapter 34), recording for example laws for the recovery of property misappropriated by Roman officials, can be interpreted as at least partly a continued effort to convey an image of Roman rule as a noble endeavour.

The exploitation of Italian manpower played a central role in Rome's territorial expansion, both in Italy and overseas. Latins and Italian allies were obliged not just to contribute troops to fight in Rome's wars but also to pay for their upkeep, and on campaign these forces might equal or even exceed the size of the Roman legionary forces. The Latins enjoyed certain rights in Roman law (which the Italian allies did not), but the burdens on all these communities were heavy and deeply resented: the revolt of Fregellae, a Latin colony, in 125 was probably in part over the demand for troops. This system was ultimately not sustainable, and the rebellion of the Italian allies (and one Latin colony) in the Social War brought Rome so near catastrophe that there was judged to be no alternative to extending Roman citizenship to all communities in Italy south of the Po. But the scale of Rome's empire at this time owed much to the use of these valuable resources over a long period of years.

By comparison with other states in antiquity, Rome was generous with grants of citizenship. Besides communities of Latins or allies in Italy, there were communities of full Roman citizens, and communities of citizens without the vote (the desirability of this last status is somewhat unclear). The citizenship was highly valued, and grants were made carefully in specific circumstances, generally as a reward for support or loyalty. While extension of Roman citizenship can be seen as a generous policy, it is worth noting a particular consequence of this and of the settlement of Roman citizens in central Italy, which was that by the time that the conquest of peninsular Italy was complete in the mid-third century, there was a solid band of Roman territory running northwards from the Tyrrhenian (western) coast of Italy to the Adriatic. This divided off from one another Rome's potential opponents in the north and south of the peninsula, who had earlier co-operated, and helped secure Rome's supremacy.

Colonies are among the most important means whereby Rome established territorial control. The foundation of a colony usually involved the establishment of a town with associated territory in a conquered area. This was often accompanied by road-building. Besides colonies of its own citizens, Rome established Latin colonies (even though the Latin League was no more), which had a subordinate status but were closely bound to Rome through shared legal rights and cultural traits. Both Roman and Latin colonies were generally founded on the best available land, and provided a means whereby the landless might be settled and enjoy prosperity while providing Rome with a bulwark against hostile communities. The success of the policy was seen most clearly in the Hannibalic War and in the Social War. Colonies are to be distinguished from provinces, the term used for Rome's overseas territories (though not exclusively for them). Until the dictatorship of Caesar, Rome had founded only a handful of colonies outside Italy (where settlement was less popular), and it is one of the most extraordinary features of Rome's overseas empire that it survived so long without large-scale colonisation.

Agriculture and economic management

Roman control helped to maximise the agricultural productivity of Italy's diverse territory and, in due course, of land in the provinces. The spread of Roman power itself transformed the available markets for various kinds of produce, and taxation of provincial land naturally affected its agricultural regimes. But the management of land that came directly under Roman control and was then settled greatly facilitated its exploitation. Plains were often centuriated, that is, divided up by (sometimes huge) rectilinear networks of roads into squares of just over 700 m (= approximately 2,300 ft) per side, often still visible in aerial photography or even from nearby mountains. This immeasurably improved the transportation of people, farm equipment, produce and animals, and made the marking out and maintenance of boundaries far easier. In respect of land use, Cato the Elder's second-century manual *de agricultura* (*On Agriculture*; see also chapter 59), a work of strong moral colouring, offers guidance for owners of large estates about how to gain the greatest profit from their land, through choice of crop (for example, whether vine, olive, grain or fruit-trees), equipment purchase, use of time for economically valuable tasks, and treatment of the labour force (in particular selling off old or sick slaves). The extent to which large estates came to dominate republican Italy is disputed, but the output that resulted from the application of such techniques and ideas to conquered territories was clearly immense.

The organisation of labour is one of the most striking aspects of Rome's economic management. Vast numbers of slaves were in use, both in agriculture and in manufacturing, although economic considerations would often make the use of free labour preferable in certain circumstances. Some control of the slave population was achieved by the manipulation of slaves' hopes and fears: slaves had the hope of becoming freedmen (*liberti*) in due course and enjoying some of the rights of Roman citizens, and their children might then be full Roman citizens, while in the other direction, it was usually possible for a slave, if disobedient, to be given a worse existence than the current one, in terms of treatment or employment. So slave revolts, although never entirely avoidable, were reduced in frequency, at the expense of an increase in the size of the citizen body. Well-organised workforces, servile and freeborn, often of substantial size, were required for mining (mostly outside Italy), stone-quarrying and tree-felling, for working in metal, stone and wood, for producing ceramics, textiles and leather goods in bulk, and for working in the construction industry (on public and private buildings, roads, bridges and aqueducts). In the latter case, the engineering skill and building techniques evident in many of the constructions give further testimony to the high level of organisation required.

Private enterprise benefited enormously from the interconnected markets and monetary systems of the empire, and huge fortunes were amassed. Rome made use of contractors for many of its needs (Polybius 6.17), the most familiar being tax-collecting. Roman citizens in Italy had been subject to tax (*tributum*), but that liability ceased in 167, whereafter Roman Italy benefited even more than before from taxation of the provinces. The employment of contractors (from the equestrian order) for much of the vast labour of securing these tax payments relieved Rome of complex administrative problems. Private enterprise played its part too in securing Rome's food supply, alongside state intervention (such as the Sicilian grain tithe). The growth of the city of Rome had led to the need to import a large quantity of grain from overseas (not an indication that Italy was agriculturally unproductive), and there were fixed-price grain distributions from the late second century and free distributions from 58 (following a law proposed by the tribune Clodius). Although there were considerable problems with supply from time to time, the overall management of this task is nevertheless impressive. The use of private enterprise for aspects of such important matters as food supply and tax collection was not without difficulties and dangers, but the scale of Rome's activities might not have been possible without it (see also chapter 60).

The end of the Republic

The factors for growth outlined above might be considered as representing the success of the Roman Republic, but from another point of view they may be seen as resulting in its failure. From the tribunate of Tiberius Gracchus onwards (134–3), violent civil dissension was from time to time a major feature of the political landscape, as was arguably predicted by Polybius (6.57). Behind the competitive aspirations of prominent Romans who championed measures for land distribution or debt relief lay deep problems, with increasing poverty and dislocation marching hand in hand with the increasing wealth of the beneficiaries of Rome's empire and their lavish private dwellings and lifestyles, attested by both literature and archaeological remains. Italy was troubled by serious debt problems at times in the late Republic – for example in 63 (Cicero *de officiis* 2.84), when it was a major grievance behind Catiline's failed coup. The composition of the army and the bond between landless soldiers and their commanders, together with the scale and duration of campaigns, were a recipe for disaster. The expenses of election campaigns, for which many candidates would have to borrow large amounts of cash, the increasing ferocity of the competition, and the great potential for enrichment if successful meant that while the rewards of success in political competition were great, the consequences of failure were dire. Competition was completely out of hand, and there was no means for any central authority to exert control and stabilise the system. All sense of the Republic's balance was gone, and it finally collapsed when civil war broke out between Caesar and his opponents, Pompey among them; Caesar's victory ushered in autocracy, followed shortly by his assassination at the hands of disgruntled nobles, and further civil war. The result of twenty years of conflict was that monarchy returned, and the empire was held together at the expense of Rome's political freedom.

Further reading

P. A. Brunt, *Social Conflicts in the Roman Republic*, London: Chatto and Windus, 1971.

P. A. Brunt, *Italian Manpower* (repr. with postscript), Oxford: Oxford University Press, 1987.

P. A. Brunt, *The Fall of the Roman Republic*, Oxford: Oxford University Press, 1988.

T. J. Cornell, *The Beginnings of Rome*, London: Routledge, 1995.

T. J. Cornell and J. F. Matthews, *Atlas of the Roman World*, Oxford: Phaidon, 1982.

M. H. Crawford, *The Roman Republic* (2nd edn), London: Fontana, 1992.

M. H. Crawford and M. Beard, *Rome in the Late Republic* (2nd edn), London: Duckworth, 1999.

L. J. F. Keppie, *The Making of the Roman Army* (2nd edn), London: Routledge, 1998.

R. Morstein-Marx and N. S. Rosenstein (eds), *A Companion to the Roman Republic*, Oxford: Blackwell, 2006.

R. Syme, *The Roman Revolution* (2nd edn), Oxford: Oxford University Press, 1952.

19. The Roman Empire

Olivier Hekster

The beginning of the Roman imperial period is usually dated to the battle of Actium in 31 BC, when Octavian (later Augustus) defeated Antony and Cleopatra. Its end is less clear, though the deposition of the last emperor, Romulus Augustulus, in AD 476 is conventionally used (see also chapter 20). Before then, however, major reforms by Diocletian (AD 284–305) had already transformed the empire beyond recognition.

Outline of events

The early Roman Empire is, ironically enough, characterised by emperors pretending not to be in sole control. The assassination of Julius Caesar (44 BC) had shown that suspicion of tyranny could be fatal. Augustus' sole reign, therefore, had a Republican façade, in which he was *princeps* or 'first citizen'. A few years after gaining absolute control at Actium, Octavian returned power to the Senate (28–27 BC). In return, the Senate gave Octavian the name 'Augustus' ('consecrated one'), and *imperium* (sacrally imbued executive power) in those provinces where most of the legions were based. Augustus was also elected consul every year until 23 BC. This, however, restricted career opportunities for senators, and he accepted instead the powers of tribune of the *plebs* (*tribunicia potestas*) and supreme *imperium* in the provinces over which the Senate had not yet delegated authority to him.

It was important to keep senators happy. Not only did they occupy key political and administrative positions, the Senate as a whole bestowed powers and honours on the emperor. This was crucial for appearing a legitimate ruler. Losing the consulship made Augustus' position in the city of Rome weaker, though his *tribunicia potestas* still gave him much power. However, in 19 BC the Senate gave him consular power in Rome itself, though Augustus preferred to stress his *tribunicia potestas*, emphasising his protection of the people of Rome. He also held various priesthoods, further strengthening his moral authority (*auctoritas*). He controlled the legions and was immune from trial. Thus, Augustus had complete control of the Roman Empire. The reality of power, however, was given shape through standard republican offices. In Augustus' own words: 'I excelled all in *auctoritas*, though I possessed no more official power (*potestas*) than others who were my colleagues in the several magistracies' (*Res Gestae* 34.3). This made it easier for the traditional elite to accept Augustus' position: he paid them proper respect. This amalgamation of traditional powers and magistracies formed the basis of imperial power for the duration of the empire.

There had been a real sense of gratitude towards the first *princeps*, who had restored order after years of civil war. Augustus ruled for forty-one years and outlived his opponents. His immediate successors, collectively known as the Julio-Claudian dynasty, who continuously emphasised their link to Augustus, were not so lucky. Like him, they were given key powers by the Senate, but they lacked his *auctoritas*, for which they compensated in different ways. Tiberius (AD 14–37) hid behind Augustus' example. His successor Gaius (Caligula) was only 25 when he came to power. He presented himself as all-powerful, disregarded Rome's traditional elite and was murdered within four years. Ancient literary sources, all written by the elite, portray him as insane. The accession of Claudius (AD 41–54) was a result of support from the emperors' guard, the Praetorians, who had been concentrated in barracks on the outskirts of Rome in AD 22. This had increased their importance to the extent that they could ignore the Senate and decide that Claudius, Caligula's uncle, was the true heir.

Claudius' accession shows the importance of dynastic considerations. He had a limp and a speech defect, and Tiberius had refused him a magistracy twice. But he was a member of Augustus' dynasty, and soldiers liked that. He took possession of the enormous wealth and status of the imperial household. In return, he gave large donatives to soldiers and strengthened his military reputation by conquering Britain. He was much less openly monarchical than Caligula. The last Julio-Claudian was Claudius' adopted son Nero (AD 54–68). He started by showing respect for the senatorial elite, adhering to the advice of his tutor Seneca. Later he became very autocratic and paid more attention to the *plebs* than to the Senate. Rebellion in the provinces allowed the Senate to declare him an enemy of the state. Nero has been blamed for all kinds of evil behaviour, including the Great Fire of Rome (AD 64). He was not even in Rome at the time, but senatorial authors blamed him all the same. Emperors who showed disrespect for the Senate were not remembered fondly.

Nero's suicide was followed by civil war and, after a year of fierce fighting, the establishment of a new dynasty; a pattern repeated several times in the next centuries. Some generations into a dynasty, a young emperor would come to the throne who disregarded the Senate and based his power on the soldiers and/or *plebs*. Eventually he was assassinated and the dynasty brought to an end. The end of a dynasty brought instability that only the use of legions would end. Provincial governors in control of legions (mainly based near the Rhine, Danube and in the Eastern provinces) were in those circumstances instant contenders for the throne. In AD 69 Flavius Vespasianus (Vespasian), who had been fighting a war in Judea, was victorious. When the Flavian dynasty that he started fell through the anti-senatorial behaviour of his younger son Domitian, with the inevitable conspiracy (AD 96) and ensuing eradication of his name and image from official records and buildings (*damnatio memoriae*), the Senate chose their own favourite, the elderly Nerva. He lasted just over a year in sole control. By then his position was so weak that he had to adopt Trajan, governor of Upper Germany, the general whose armies could reach Rome most rapidly. Under Trajan, the empire reached its largest size. Serious campaigns against the Dacians and Parthians led to the creation of new provinces, and ensured Trajan's reputation as 'the best ruler' (*optimus princeps*). The empire had probably overstretched itself: Trajan's successor Hadrian (AD 117–38) gave up some of the newly conquered territory and focused on fixed frontiers. Notwithstanding this policy, Hadrian, like all emperors, had to present himself as a capable warrior.

Trajan did not establish a dynasty as such. Like his predecessor and his two immediate successors, Hadrian and Antoninus Pius (AD 138–61), he had no son (in all cases coincidence not choice). These emperors therefore adopted male relatives and made them heirs. Dynastic considerations always ruled supreme. The last of these 'adoptive emperors', Marcus Aurelius (AD 161–80), did have a son, Commodus, who, inevitably, succeeded him. Lack of respect for the Senate, conspiracy, assassination (AD 192) and an unenviable posthumous reputation followed the established pattern. The Senate then chose the elderly Pertinax, who was killed by the Praetorians, and in the ensuing civil war the legions from the Rhine and Danube provinces, led by Septimius Severus (AD 193–211), were victorious.

When the Severan dynasty, including some odd emperors even by Roman standards, ended (AD 235), no new dynasty replaced it, although not for want of aspirants. Rather, different legions continually put forward their own generals. Military preference for dynastic succession, a tradition reaching back to Augustus, also led to the appointment of child-emperors, hardly ever lasting long. Gordian III (AD 238–244), for instance, was only 13 when he came to power and was only chosen because his grandfather and father (Gordian I and II) had been joint emperors for a year (AD 238). He lasted just over five years, followed by twenty-two more or less acknowledged soldier-emperors in fifty years. The crisis ended with the accession of Diocletian, another general-turned-emperor. His twenty-one-year reign saw many administrative, economic and army reforms. His government, more than that of any previous emperor, constituted military despotism. He appointed a co-emperor and two deputies, who were to succeed and appoint deputies in turn. The power to appoint successors lay with the emperors alone. This system (the 'tetrarchy') marked the end of the 'principate', in which the emperor nominally was 'first citizen', and the introduction of the 'dominate' – rule through unambiguous direct control (see also chapter 20). The position of emperor had travelled a long way from Augustus' *civilis princeps* (polite first citizen) to Diocletian's *dux* (leader), though the voyage had been a gradual one.

Governing the Empire

Ultimate authority in all respects lay with the emperor. Individuals or groups could turn to him with requests; cities regularly sent embassies for decisions on controversial issues. Responding to these various local problems, and similar requests from people in Rome, was a time-consuming imperial occupation, and it increased the importance of the imperial household tremendously. Those directly surrounding the emperor regulated his accessibility, and it was through direct access to the emperor, at the court, that many important decisions were taken. Thus imperial freedmen became important political entities through their influence on emperors (which senatorial historians tended to exaggerate). What happened at court happened outside the public domain, and could never be checked. This partly explains the emphasis on court gossip in imperial literature.

The emperor owned land in many provinces, with imperial estates growing at an astonishing rate. Like any Roman noble, he expected gifts and inheritances from *amici* (friends) – he simply had more of them. He could also acquire land, mines and quarries himself. Nero is said to have confiscated half of Africa by executing six wealthy landowners (Pliny *HN* 18.35). To what extent these estates, or imperial property in general, were public or private is open to debate. Whatever the exact status of the property, much of it was run by procurators, direct appointments by the emperor, who by their proximity to the *princeps* gained disproportionate influence in a province. But Roman bureaucracy was limited in size, which constrained its day-to-day impact on society. Local elites in provincial communities remained crucial for administration. Villages and towns retained much autonomy through councils and magistrates, for instance in constructing and managing public buildings, associations for trade and cult, and the food supply. They also did much of the tax-collecting. Essentially, Rome governed its provinces in order to receive taxes and manpower, and to avoid rebellions. These local magistrates – the old aristocracy in much of the East of the empire, a newly created upper class in substantial parts of the West (this is only one of the differences between East and West) – had good reason to appreciate good relations with Rome. They also wanted to emphasise their superior status in their city and the superior status of that city over neighbouring cities, spending much money on public buildings and festivals in the process (*euergetism*; see also chapters 17, 34 and 60). They formed the glue that held the empire together.

The autonomy of local government was restricted. Roman officials could and did interfere directly in disputes within a community's elite or between different communities. Sometimes these disputes were taken all the way to the emperor. The correspondence between Trajan and Pliny the Younger, who was dispatched by the emperor to govern the province of Bithynia-Pontus (AD 110–12), illustrates the level of Roman interference, and how often the emperor was called upon to reach a decision. The spread of Roman citizenship further limited the importance of local laws and customs, since the privileges of Roman citizens could not be ignored: Roman citizens lived by Roman law. Local grandees, who had been of assistance to Rome, gained these privileges on being granted citizenship. Ultimately, however, the rise of local elites to citizenship, and sometimes even equestrian or senatorial status, made them less interested in their cities of origin, and caused real problems at the local level. The administrative reforms of Diocletian were partly aimed at solving those problems. Earlier, the emperor Caracalla, son of Septimius Severus, had granted citizenship to all free inhabitants of the Roman Empire through the *Constitutio Antoniniana* (AD 212). There may have been fiscal reasons for this: more Roman citizens meant more tax revenues.

The *Constitutio Antoniniana* was the culmination of an ongoing extension of the citizenship reaching back into the Republic, but accelerating under the Empire. It had major consequences. One was to make Roman law universal, leading eventually to its codification: the resulting legal system is perhaps the Romans' most influential legacy (see also chapters 20 and 58). Bestowing citizenship was furthermore a gift that could never be completely repaid. In this way, the emperor bound the inhabitants of the empire to him: he had directly enhanced their status, so they owed him loyalty. Second, after AD 212 the relations between the inhabitants of Rome and those of its provinces appeared more egalitarian. This went hand in hand with an increasing difference between emperor and subjects. The emperor ruled openly supreme over all his subjects, which made differences between the subjects themselves less important.

Roman religion and Christianity

Caracalla expressed the hope that universal citizenship would unite the people under the Roman state gods, and guarantee good relations between men and gods (*pax deorum*). This emphasis on religion is characteristic of the Roman Empire. Religion permeated Roman life, with boundaries between religion and politics impossible to draw. The emperor himself was a prominent member of the pantheon, and the specific focus of various rituals. These imperial cults (various localities worshipped the emperor through different rituals) were a unifying factor for the heterogeneous empire. The emperor formed a recognisable focal point, whose worship could be incorporated within existing religious contexts. That does not mean that the imperial cult was organised from Rome as a political tool. Gods in the Roman world were worshipped for what they could do. People sacrificed to specific gods for specific favours. Someone as far elevated above his subjects as the emperor, who could bestow almost limitless favours, was easily equated with the divine: in an unlimited pantheon, there was always room for a new divinity. Similarly, normal honours would not do justice to someone who had done so much for the peace and abundance of everyday life. No other repayment than divine honours would suffice. Equating the emperor with the gods was a way of coming to terms with someone in such a supreme position.

Sacrificing to the emperor and the gods of Rome ensured the *pax deorum*. Refusal to do so jeopardised the state's safety. This lies at the heart of the occasional persecution of Christians. Christianity had, almost from the outset, presented itself as a universal religion, disallowing participation in other cults. It could thus be interpreted as anti-Roman. Still, persecutions were rare in the first two centuries AD. Legal procedures and an attempt to avoid harassment are prescribed by the emperor Trajan in a famous letter to Pliny (10.69). Judaism, from which Christianity originated, was similarly monotheistic, but Roman decrees, a result of good relations between Jewish leaders and Augustus, protected its customary practices. Judaism was also a cult of respectable antiquity – something which Romans valued greatly. When the empire itself became less stable in the third century AD, loyalty to the state gods was deemed more important than ever before – and Christians, therefore, more suspect (see also chapter 20). Indeed, Caracalla's emphasis on unity under the gods after the *Constitutio Antoniniana* shows how participation in the worship of those gods was now formally expected. By then Christianity had become too large a religion to be seriously threatened by intensified persecutions. Constantine (AD 306–37) was the first Roman emperor to turn to Christianity, and in AD 391 it was made the state religion by Theodosius I (AD 379–95). Tellingly, they are the only emperors to be named 'the Great' in our late antique sources.

Problems of periodisation

Roman imperial history is a vast subject; most studies inevitably focus on specific chronologically- or topographically-defined aspects. Yet definitions of time and space carry with them certain preconceptions. Division of the period into different dynasties, for instance, or the analysis of individual reigns in imperial biographies places much emphasis on changes and events at the centre, and on the personal influence of the ruler. Classical authors, almost all of them upper-class, were fascinated by the secret dealings behind closed doors which characterised imperial decision-making (see also chapter 50).

During the reign of Hadrian, furthermore, there was a remarkable interest in succession lists: the list of bishops of Rome (later the popes) represented by the *Liber Pontificalis* started in this period, as did reconstructions of the two main schools (Sabinian and Proculean) of jurists (civil lawyers). And Suetonius (c. AD 77–140) wrote biographies of Roman grammarians and poets, and, most importantly, his *Lives of the Caesars*. Succession and continuity seem to have been important topics at the time, perhaps a result of the lack of imperial sons (see above). Suetonius' *Lives* have greatly influenced later scholarship. Even his near-contemporary Tacitus, who wrote more analytical history, placed much emphasis on individual reigns. The fourth-century *Historia Augusta*, a continuation of Suetonius by an unknown author, almost completes the series of imperial lives for the entire period. This has been a major factor in encouraging reign-by-reign, or dynasty-by-dynasty, views of Roman imperial history.

An emphasis on emperors often leads to a focus on the city of Rome; only a few classical authors described the further regions of the empire. Crucial are the priceless survey of the Mediterranean by the geographer Strabo (60s BC–AD 20s) and the Jewish author Flavius Josephus (AD 37/8–100), a leader of a great Jewish revolt against Rome in AD 66–70, who changed sides and was given Roman citizenship. His writings on the *Jewish War* and *Jewish Antiquities* are our only literary texts written by someone combining provincial and Roman points of view. Finally, the prolific Aelius Aristides, born in Mysia, northwest Asia Minor (AD 117 – c. 181), wrote a speech, *To Rome*, which shows how an admiring provincial might view Rome's accomplishments. But these are exceptions, and most literary sources say little on the empire at large and even less on the provincials' points of view.

There are also more recent, now almost canonical, influences on our notions of the Roman Empire. Thus, for instance, Edward Gibbon's magisterial *The History of the Decline and Fall of the Roman Empire* (1776-88) famously describes the period from the death of Domitian to the accession of Commodus as 'the period in the history of the world, during which the condition of the human race was most happy and prosperous' (I, 78), words still echoed in modern literature. Similarly, the notion of a general 'third-century crisis' derives partly from systematic blackening by the tetrarchs of the period preceding their reforms, but partly also from authoritative nineteenth- and twentieth-century scholarship following ancient commonplaces. Methodologically, scholarship in the twentieth century was heavily influenced by prosopography: the tracing of origins, career tracks and family connections of individuals. Of special importance here are Hans-Georg Pflaum and Sir Ronald Syme, who waded through masses of data on officials, illustrating how the Roman Empire worked. But prosopography should never be an aim in itself and cannot be used to analyse all relevant areas of Roman imperial history. At a much more popular level, Hollywood has been a major influence on common assumptions about individual reigns, and the Roman Empire in general.

Recent scholarship has been addressing these and similar problems. Material evidence has been crucial in this respect, with archaeological site reports and reinterpretations of Roman imperial art balancing the literary evidence. The negative senatorial descriptions of the reigns of 'bad' emperors, for example, have recently been challenged by looking at the way they are represented in art and architecture. Modern sociological, economic and anthropological theories form interesting bases for analysis of the evidence, as do new literary and visual theories. There is now more focus on the periphery of the empire, and on understanding the period by looking inwards from the provinces, rather than outwards from Rome. Much of the documentary and epigraphic evidence is, in fact, found in frontier regions (e.g. Egypt, or Vindolanda, near Hadrian's Wall). The increasing use of several types of evidence and theoretical frameworks in which literary evidence is placed in an ever-wider context leads to a continuous evaluation of many aspects of the Roman Empire. History continues.

Further reading

Sourcebooks

B. M. Levick, *The Government of the Roman Empire: A Sourcebook* (2nd edn), London and New York: Routledge, 2000 – extremely useful, conveniently organised by themes.

Secondary literature

M. Beard, J. North and S. Price, *Religions of Rome* (2 vols), Cambridge: Cambridge University Press, 1998 – up-to-date and authoritative account of Roman religion(s), including a volume of source material.

A. K. Bowman, E. Champlin and A. Lintott (eds), *Cambridge Ancient History*, vol. 10: *The Augustan Empire, 43 B.C.–A.D. 69* (2nd edn), Cambridge: Cambridge University Press, 1996.

A. K. Bowman, P. Garnsey and D. Rathbone (eds), *Cambridge Ancient History*, vol. 11: *The High Empire, AD 70–192* (2nd edn), Cambridge: Cambridge University Press, 2000.

M. Goodman, *The Roman World 44 BC–AD 180* (*Routledge History of the Ancient World*), London and New York: Routledge, 1997 – recent survey on a substantial period of Roman imperial history.

I. Gradel, *Emperor Worship and Roman Religion*, Oxford: Oxford University Press, 2002 – innovative new interpretation of the role of emperor and religion in the Roman Empire.

J. E. Lendon, *Empire of Honour: The Art of Government in the Roman World*, Oxford: Oxford University Press, 1997 – interesting and readable thesis on how the Roman Empire functioned, bringing together several strands of recent scholarship.

A. W. Lintott, *Imperium Romanum: Politics and Administration*, London and New York: Routledge, 1993 – a systematic account of the practical and legal aspects of administering the Roman Empire.

F. G. B. Millar, *The Emperor in the Roman World: 31 BC–AD 337* (2nd edn), London: Duckworth, 1992 – monumental study of what the emperor did and how the Empire worked.

D. S. Potter, *The Roman Empire at Bay AD 180–395*, London and New York: Routledge, 2004.

C. Wells, *The Roman Empire* (2nd edn), London: Fontana Press, 1992 – lucid and concise analysis of the period up to AD 235. Probably the best place to start.

20. Late Antiquity

Richard Lim

'Late antique' history

Late antiquity is the period during which the classical civilisation chiefly identified with the ancient Greeks and Romans transformed itself into the medieval societies of Byzantium, Islam and Latin Christendom. Scholars still debate its chronological parameters but AD 250–800 seems safe enough. In geographical terms, the world of late antiquity is not confined within the political boundaries of the Roman Empire, but extended to the Near East, and more ambitious scholars want to see it encompass even Scandinavia in the north, Ethiopia and Yemen in the south, and Iran in the East (see also chapter 14).

Outline

The two great superpowers of the ancient world, Rome and Parthia, were both in a bad way in the early third century. Following the reign of Marcus Aurelius (161–80) and the outbreak of a devastating pandemic, political and military unrest destabilised many regions in the empire, leading to spiralling social and economic problems. Referred to by historians collectively as the Crisis of the Third Century, the unrest threatened both the imperial system established by Augustus and the integrity of the empire itself. In the east, the Parthian kings were toppled in mid-century and replaced by fellow Iranians who claimed descent from the Achaemenid Persians of old (see also chapter 12). The new Sassanian Dynasty (AD 241–651) warred against the Romans with great energy. Their recurrent and costly wars, moderated only by the annual rhythm of the seasons, and the constraints of geography and imperial finances, remained a perennial feature of the international scene until the rise of Islam and its conquest of the Sassanian Empire in the mid-seventh century. Still, despite their apparent hostility, similarities existed between Rome and Persia. They were both organised, bureaucratic states with sophisticated revenue-extracting institutions and cultural foundations that integrated local native traditions with the values of an assertive imperial civilisation. Both also faced challenges in combating their own tendency towards fragmentation and in dealing with tribal ethnic communities on their borders. Aside from this stand-off in the Near East, the Romans concentrated their resources on the Rhine–Danube frontiers while the Persians kept a close watch over the open expanses of the steppelands to their north. The overriding need to prevent civil war and to guard their frontiers consumed the bulk of state resources and set the political agenda for these two imperial civilisations.

Roman political authority meanwhile continued to devolve to the provinces and the army groups on the frontiers. Septimius Severus (193–211), the 'African emperor' from Lepcis Magna in present-day Libya, was briefly able to re-establish Roman stability, while his son Caracalla (198–217) extended Roman citizenship to all free inhabitants of the empire in 212 by a law called the Antonine Constitution (*Constitutio Antoniniana*; see also chapter 19). But after the Severan dynasty ended in 235, the Roman state was again engulfed in protracted civil wars. Local communities rallied around military leaders who promised them effective protection. Thus Gaul and Britain found themselves asserting local autonomy under Postumus (258–73) and Carausius (286–93) respectively. Even former allies such as Palmyra, a caravan city (i.e. one located on and deriving its prosperity from location on a major trans-desert trade route) in modern Syria, took advantage of the uncertain times to grab Egypt and large chunks of what had been the Roman Near East. The rise of military emperors was a response to these dire circumstances. Aurelian (270–5) retook Egypt in 271 and sacked Palmyra two years later, ending the reign of its remarkable queen Zenobia. With Aurelian also ended the tendency for imperial power to be worn with its Augustan mask. No longer did the emperor need to maintain a semblance of parity with the aristocracy: he stopped presenting himself as a *civilis princeps* (between citizen and ruler) and *primus inter pares* (first among equals) with respect to senators; instead he lorded over everyone as *deus et dominus*, god and master. The Roman principate had given way to the dominate.

The re-establishment of order under Diocletian (284–305), another soldier-emperor, brought important and abiding changes to Roman state and society. Claiming to restore the *mos maiorum* ('way of our forebears'), the emperor revamped administrative and socio-economic structures in major ways. His invention of a college of four emperors, comprising two Augusti, or senior emperors, and two Caesars, or junior emperors, gave the name of tetrarchy ('rule of four') to this period. He reorganised the provinces, separating out military and civil functions, for the sake of greater efficiency. But this efficiency came at a high cost: a sharply increased bureaucracy and military establishment, which naturally claimed an even greater portion of revenues, became a fixture of the late Roman and Byzantine state. To combat inflation, Diocletian issued edicts controlling local prices and wages. To prevent economic pressures from driving peasants off the land, artisans out of their professions and city councillors from their municipal service, he limited the social mobility of groups whose functions he deemed vital to state interests. Overall his laws saw the fixing of the status quo as the solution to the empire's woes. In this way, peasants in the countryside became tied to the land in a way that prefigures the later medieval land-tenure system, while various workers, such as armourers, mint-workers, bread-makers and public entertainers, were made to serve in what became hereditary professions. The tendency towards greater centralisation and conformity also turned the state into a persecutor of religious non-conformists, establishing a pattern for future generations to follow. Manichaeans (a group that adhered to the teachings of Mani, whose beliefs were characterised by the conflict of good and evil, and predestination to heaven for the chosen few) were Diocletian's first target; ironically he attacked them as Persian (hence enemy) fifth-columnists even though the founder of their religion had himself but a few years earlier been executed by the Persian king in 277. Christians were next, as they were deemed 'bad Romans' who had forsaken the worship of the ancestral gods, angering them. But if this official persecution was meant to create a greater consensus in Roman society it fell wide of its mark. Christian martyrs who resisted to the death became inspirational heroes and every day Christians increased in numbers.

In Persia, administrative and tax reforms akin to those undertaken by Diocletian were under way only in the late fifth/early sixth century, after the Sassanians recovered from a devastating incursion by the Turkic or Tibetan Hephthalites, or 'White Huns', from the north. But the growing alliance between the state and an official religion took place much sooner than in Rome. Already at the inception of Sassanian rule in the mid-third century, Zoroastrianism was installed as Persia's state religion and the *magi*, priests who tended the fire-temples that came to be built throughout the land, were highly honoured throughout the empire. The two multi-ethnic empires, constantly reacting to changes their counterpart adopted, increasingly rallied around a state religion to promote a greater sense of internal coherence.

To the west, the tetrarchy was brought to an end by yet another soldier-emperor, Constantine, who along the way embraced Christianity (in 312) but otherwise completed and even in some cases extended many of Diocletian's administrative reforms. Thus Diocletian and Constantine should both be seen as the founders of the late Roman state. Constantine, however, took steps to recruit local Christian bishops as his helpers in creating a better-run empire. He followed his official recognition of Christianity as a legal religion with generous private gifts of lands and estates, as well as the first Christian public buildings: great basilicas, the design originating from that of civil law-courts, which would soon become a standard feature of the landscape of late antique Roman cities. Constantine also founded Constantinople (consecrated 330), an imperial capital named for himself, on the site of the Greek city of Byzantium overlooking the Bosporus. It was at first not a *new* Rome meant to replace the original but a *second* Rome. But later on it indeed became the political centre of the Eastern Roman (or Byzantine) Empire.

The fourth century remained a period of civil wars and foreign conflicts. But now a new historical narrative – one that deals with affairs of the Christian church – also comes into view. The alliance between the Christian church and the Roman state deepened in the years following Constantine. Aside from Julian the Apostate (361–3), who converted from Christianity back to an idiosyncratic form of Neoplatonist polytheism (see also chapter 48), all emperors after Constantine were Christians, who took public stances that favoured Christians and Christianity more and more. But there was not to be a straightforward process whereby the Roman Empire would become a Christian Roman Empire. The establishment of Christianity as *the* religion of the empire happened only in the later fourth century. As the Roman state began to turn into a Christian state, both non-Christians (such as Jews) and non-conforming Christians (such as Arians) came to suffer stiff legal penalities, as seen in laws preserved in the great fifth-century legal compilation, the Theodosian Code (see also chapter 58).

The Roman engagement with the Germanic tribes on its northern frontier complicated this process, for many of the so-called barbarians had been converted prior to their entrance into the empire to an Arian brand of Christianity, which the Roman state later deemed heretical. In 378, refugee Goths fleeing from the Huns crossed the Danube, defeated a Roman army and killed its emperor, Valens, at the battle of Adrianople. This allowed subsequent large-scale migrations to flow into Roman domains, resulting in many unassimilated tribal groups entering the Balkans and the Western provinces. Romans in those regions soon faced a situation whereby they were dominated not only by barbarians but, in their own eyes, by heretics professing the wrong kind of Christian beliefs. Two dominant features of late antique history, then, are the rise of the barbarian kingdoms that gradually emerged in the West, and the story of how Romans and non-Romans, conquered and conquerors, lived with each other within them.

Did Rome fall? Rome was sacked for ten days by Visigoths in 410 and Romulus Augustulus, last emperor of the West, was deposed by the barbarian warlord Odoacer in AD 476. But in practice little changed as a result of these famous 'events'. Besides, Roman cultural, social and political institutions continued to function and develop in the West even while no Roman emperor ruled there. New regimes ruled by 'barbarians' co-existed with what remained of the empire, now centred on Constantinople. But at this time, from out of the steppes, a nomadic confederation began to emerge on the frontiers. The Hunnic empire Attila built on the Hungarian plains extracted annual tribute, or protection money, from Romans and barbarians alike, resulting in a coalition between Romans and Visigoths that defeated the Huns at the battle of the Catalaunian Plains in 451. In this campaign, the Germanic peoples showed themselves to have incorporated fully the most fundamental values and interests of the *pax romana* (Roman peace): they acted as inhabitants of a settled landscape who resisted the demands of their nomadic neighbours.

The fourth and fifth centuries are still commonly regarded as the 'heart' of late antiquity and yet the lesser-known period of the sixth and seventh is now receiving increasing recognition and treatment. The foremost personage from the sixth century was the emperor Justinian, both on account of his long and eventful reign (527–65) and also owing to the large number of historical writings from that period. Chief among the latter is the *History of the Wars* that Procopius of Caesarea, a contemporary, wrote about the great reconquest that the emperor undertook. With great daring and able military leadership, the Romans managed to reconquer North Africa from the Vandals, Italy from the Ostrogoths and Spain (partially) from the Visigoths. For a brief time, and at tremendous cost to local economies and the imperial treasury, the Roman state managed to reverse the process of barbarian domination of the West. But much had also changed in the meantime so that local 'Romans' did not always welcome the return of the empire, which brought haughty Greek-speaking administrators, higher taxes and generally unpopular imperial rule to the recovered provinces.

Neither was Justinian's reign received well in the East, the heart of his empire. Like Diocletian and Constantine he was an energetic ruler who sought to impose order through legislation and reforms. He ordered the codification of Roman civil law (see also chapter 58), and the resulting works (the *Codex*, the *Digest* and the *Institutes*) have remained the most significant Roman legal documents, underlying much modern European law. In ecclesiastical affairs he at first favoured the reconciliation of Christians who were hotly debating the nature of Christ, with rival positions championed by the bishops of Alexandria and those of Antioch and Constantinople; but he soon resorted to sterner measures that made him few friends. Justinian's earnest but heavy-handed approach alienated segments of the imperial population and made many Roman Christians and Jews eager for relief from the outside. The Monophysite Christians of Egypt and Syria saw the rule of an imperial state that championed a Chalcedonian form of Christianity, named after the earlier Council of Chalcedon in 451 which they rejected, as an unbearable tyranny (in early Christianity the 'nature' of the Trinity – three separate natures, three in one, or just one? – was fiercely debated). Thus the stage was set for the later Persian victories in Syria, Palestine and Egypt and for a similar lack of resistance in Egypt and elsewhere to the subsequent arrival of Islamic Arab armies.

Justinian's reign is sometimes seen as the watershed, where the history of Rome ended and that of Byzantium began. Whether the sixth century was an ending, a beginning or neither remains the subject of scholarly discussion. The great plague of the 540s, which few would actually blame on Justinian himself, decimated the population of the Mediterranean and Near East, accelerating the process of de-urbanisation in places, and the pace of social and economic changes that were already well under way.

The wars between Rome and Persia continue to occupy centre stage from the reign of Justinian to the early seventh century, when a spectacular set of Persian victories briefly won them virtually the entire Roman Near East. Heraclius (died 641), the Roman emperor at the time, allied himself with the nomadic Khazars and struck back, deep into Persian territory. The balance of power was rudely restored but the wars completely debilitated both imperial states. Their mutual obsession with each other created a ripe opportunity for desert nomads in Arabia, who, rallying to the teachings of Muhammad of Medina (died 632), set aside their traditions of feuding and united in a new religious and national campaign of conquest. The rapid progress of Islamic Arab armies through Roman provinces in the Near East and North Africa further reduced territories held by the empire. These lands, with their large Christian populations, left imperial control for the last time. To the east, the Arabs defeated the Persians and took over the entirety of their empire, and, after extending their reach to Central Asia, they further defeated a T'ang Chinese army at the battle of Talas in 751, a victory that decisively checked the westward ambitions of one of the most successful Chinese imperial dynasties. Sassanian refugees including members of the royal house fled to China, bringing the Far East closer still to the world of late antiquity.

The late antique world yet again shifted ground. The Roman Empire endured in its enclave, centred on the Eastern Mediterranean world. The Western barbarian kingdoms continued to develop cultures that blended Germanic traditions, Roman civilisation and Christianity. Spain, North Africa, Egypt, Iraq and Iran all came under the rule of Islam and began to look eastwards, first to Damascus under the Ummayad Dynasty (660–750) and later to Baghdad (founded 762) during the Abbasid Caliphate (750–1258). These three main political blocs may be further distinguished by their different religious outlooks: the Roman or Byzantine state professed Orthodox Christianity, the Germanic kingdoms a Latin Christianity based on communion with the Pope in Rome, and the Islamic lands revered God's revelation to the Prophet Muhammad in Arabia as a sacred touchstone.

Themes and sources

The term 'late antiquity' (German *Spätantike*; French *antiquité tardive*) is commonly used to designate the transitional period between the classical antiquity of Greece and Rome and the European Middle Ages. It comes with considerable baggage, as the period was until recently seen by many scholars as a time when the sophisticated, refined classical culture of the Greeks and Romans 'declined', reaching a low point in the 'Dark Ages' and the Middle Ages, only to be partially and imperfectly revived during the Renaissance, the 'rebirth' of classical culture. This way of looking at late antiquity privileges subjective aesthetic judgements to such a degree as to be essentially ahistorical – it is a question of taste, not history. Current scholars now see late antiquity as a period worthy of study in its own right on account of the important transformations that took place. In the empire, the main social and political changes that marked the transition to late antiquity happened during the reigns of Diocletian and Constantine, if not sooner. The state's gradually tightened embrace of Christianity helped along 'Christianisation', which introduced important cultural changes that make the period of late antiquity unique and worthy of study. Just as the complex processes of 'hellenisation' and 'romanisation' in time created the Hellenistic and Roman worlds (see also chapters 13 and 17), Christianisation shaped the late antique societies of the later Roman Empire and the Western barbarian kingdoms (just as a measure of 'Iranisation' was used to increase the cultural coherence of the multi-ethnic Sassanian domains). Christianisation is capable of several definitions, and in any event was an ongoing process; there was no point in time at which the later Roman Empire became fully Christianised. Theodosius I (379–95) famously declared orthodox Christianity the official religion of the empire, but changes in social mores and institutions did not happen overnight by fiat; the triumphal narratives describing Christianity's progressive victory over paganism in Christian writings do not always offer an accurate understanding of what took place 'on the ground'. How the growing Christian majority population adapted the classical heritage remains an important part of the story of Christianisation, as it was generally accepted that much of Graeco-Roman culture was worthy of salvage once the most obvious forms of polytheistic worship such as sacrifice were abolished. But Christianisation also involved the reinvention of public symbols and rituals, conceptions of time and space, notions of authority and sacrality, and a sense of past, present and future. Thus Christianisation, perhaps the most important topic in the study of late antiquity, tells a much richer tale than just how Christians reacted to and appropriated classical literary and artistic traditions.

How Christian communities developed within the empire's civic communities and later replaced those communities remains a key aspect of Christianisation. It involved the creation of new elites, especially the bishops of cities and towns, and new cultural heroes such as the martyrs at the time when Christians were persecuted, and ascetics and monks afterwards. The cult of the saints that grew up around the martyrs, whose deaths were annually celebrated on their 'birthdays' at their shrines (see also chapter 64), gave Christians a new model of the human community and a source of semi-divine patronage. Likewise, living saints – ascetics and monks – who at first inhabited deserted landscapes on the fringes of human communities, but were soon found in even the largest cities, became the new cultural heroes of the day. Even emperors and bishops were seen as seeking the help and advice of these usually unlearned, even illiterate, men and women of God. Both dead martyrs and living ascetics had the ability to form communities around themselves and confer a sacral aura on a landscape. Urban bishops began to take advantage of the charisma that these heroic Christians projected, and co-opted their spiritual power to increase the bishops' own authority within the Christian community. Religion and authority were now closely connected in a way rather different from what had existed before.

Graeco-Roman cities did not disappear overnight, to be sure. Municipal elections continued in places through the fourth century and significant civic institutions were generally maintained. But side by side with civic leaders and traditions one finds the figure of the bishop and the local church. By claiming to be feeders of a city's poor, bishops claimed to represent a significant part of the urban population that earlier had no such representation, thus altering how people imagined the ancient city. Many of these bishops were not only themselves holy men or caretakers of the urban poor but also ecclesiastical and imperial politicians. The history of the Christian church became an integral part of the story of late antiquity, and church councils, which were invariably convoked by imperial or state authority, were called to help resolve Christian theological disputes. But these proceedings appeared to exacerbate existing differences. If the empire gained internal coherence around an increasingly well-defined orthodox theological position, leading to the creation of a Christian Roman Empire, it inevitably also gave rise to disaffection and dissent among those whose beliefs were not embraced by the state.

If one truly wishes to, it remains possible to study late antiquity in the Graeco-Roman Mediterranean in much the same way as one would the earlier periods, since the kinds of sources that exist for the study of Hellenistic and Roman history are available for late antiquity too. While the number of public inscriptions diminished after the third century, the large numbers of surviving late antique literary and non-literary sources still mean that late antiquity remains one of the most richly documented periods in the ancient world. Literary texts, histories, biographies, philosophical treatises, novels and letter collections abounded. Moderns who judge a civilisation by the quality of its works are sometimes led to conclude that late antiquity was a period of decline. But historians do not resort to such criteria and, in any event, late antique writers continued to produce classicising Greek and Latin texts.

Overall, students of late antiquity are well advised not to regard the period with 'classical' lenses as a fading civilisation but rather judge it on its own terms. The richness of the surviving evidence is striking once we move away from traditional literary sources to documentary and non-literary sources. There are the two great late Roman law codes of Theodosius II and Justinian. Papyri continue to come down in large quantities from late Roman Egypt, together with some from Palestine and Italy. The archaeology of late antique sites all throughout the Mediterranean and Near East has given historians a keener sense of the strong regional characteristics of communities that gravitated towards emerging local or regional centres, even those that did not leave behind a discernible literary or written documentary tradition. Mosaic decorations from houses enliven our understanding of the perception of everyday life as well as the self-representations of villa-owners. Mosaics from churches and synagogues reveal the outlooks of the religious communities that built them. And even those villa sites that do not yield mosaics can be studied through improved archaeological survey and remote-sensing techniques to determine the nature of human settlement and activities in the surrounding countryside.

Last but not least, we now have many Christian texts, which match or even surpass in quantity the whole corpus of surviving classical Greek and Roman works. These have come down in a variety of languages. Students of late antiquity confront not only texts in Greek and Latin, but those in Coptic, Ethiopic, Syriac, Armenian and Old Church Slavonic, among other languages. Some of these writings belong to new genres, such as saints' lives and popular sermons, which, being cast in a simple style, allow us to take a closer look at the non-elite strata of ancient society as never before. Used in combination with the epigraphic, archaeological and visual material, these Christian sources make possible the recreation of 'total histories' for regions or cities over a fairly long period of time.

Further reading

Sourcebooks

M. R. Maas, *Readings in Late Antiquity: A Sourcebook*, London and New York: Routledge, 2000 – a useful anthology of annotated primary historical documents.

Secondary literature

G. W. Bowersock, P. Brown and O. Grabar (eds), *Late Antiquity: A Guide to the Postclassical World*, Cambridge MA: Harvard University Press, 1999 – an innovative array of topical essays paired with encyclopedia entries.

P. R. L. Brown, *The World of Late Antiquity, A.D. 150–750* (2nd edn), New York: Norton, 1989 – a penetrating analysis of important cultural and social trends in late antiquity.

P. R. L. Brown, *Augustine of Hippo: A Biography* (rev. edn), Berkeley and Los Angeles: University of California Press, 2000 – the classic biography of an important late antique intellectual and bishop, now updated with new epilogue.

A. Cameron, *The Later Roman Empire: A.D. 284–430*, Cambridge MA: Harvard University Press, 1993 – a useful overview of the history and major institutions of the late Roman state.

A. Cameron, *The Mediterranean World in Late Antiquity: A.D. 395–600*, London and New York: Routledge, 1993 – a valuable survey that takes historiography and archaeology seriously into account.

A. Cameron and P. Garnsey (eds), *Cambridge Ancient History*, vol. 13: *The Late Empire, A.D. 337–425* (2nd edn), Cambridge: Cambridge University Press, 1997 – a collection of important thematic essays with extensive bibliographical references.

A. H. M. Jones, *The Later Roman Empire, A.D. 284–602: A Social, Economic, and Administrative Survey*, Oxford: Blackwell, 1964 – still the authoritative guide to the history and institutions of the late Roman state.

S. Mitchell, *A History of the Later Roman Empire, AD 284–641*, Oxford: Blackwell, 2006.

D. S. Potter, *The Roman Empire at Bay AD 180–395*, London and New York: Routledge, 2004.

Part Two: Material Culture

Comprehension of the classical world is based on a diverse assortment of evidence. Texts provide the written foundations for this understanding but are buttressed by the material setting out of which they rise. The first half of this part looks at the landscape and marine background, the focal points of living and the built environment within which many citizens and slaves dwelt, where sacred rituals were conducted, where athletic competitions were mounted, where political life was organised. In the second half attention is drawn to the major artefacts that were essential elements in the lives of the Greeks and Romans: economic, social, religious, military. These features help to give visual dimensions and depth to our picture of the classical world.

21. Landscape

Nicholas Purcell

There is no such a thing as a natural landscape. The idea of landscape entails a human observer; observation means interpretation, and often goes with intervention. Landscape is therefore never 'out there': it is in the mind of the beholder as much as beauty, and it is never still, because ideas are fluid, and because the observer so often intervenes. The term is used first of the set of ingredients in the wider spatial framework in which human behaviour takes place (hills, streams, villages, farms); second, the framework itself (the scene, the vista, the region); third, what people think about the set of ingredients and the framework (wilderness, prosperity, harmony with nature, disorder); and fourth, what they deliberately make out of those perceptions and ideas (planning, control, literary and artistic representations).

Nature and culture

In the Mediterranean world, and its adjacencies, by the beginning of the Iron Age, there were no wildernesses. Every mountain and island had been visited. Every forest and wetland, however wild it appeared, owed its ecology at least in part to human intervention. Agriculture and pastoralism, practised over the millennia since the Neolithic revolution, had had ample time to influence geomorphological process. Human intervention was everywhere, but by no means uniform, being adapted to local conditions and patterned by social diversity; nor did it tend in a single direction. Cultivated landscapes had been abandoned to forest and the forest cleared again, wetland edges improved only to revert to reedbed and to be reclaimed once more. That was to be the story throughout Graeco-Roman antiquity too, though the interventions were in many cases more thoroughgoing than anything previously seen, and the formation of Greek and Roman overarching cultural continua allowed patterns to develop within the diversity. In this period, too, landscape can be studied in a new way by comparison with prehistory because much of what Mediterranean people thought about the world around them is recorded, and the record has been deeply influential on the notion of landscape as it has developed over the last millennium and a half.

There are certain givens of geology and climate which underlie the human landscapes of the Mediterranean world: most significantly, this is a zone of geologically recent mountain-building, so that relief is steep, altitudes often great, and topography fractured. The commonest rocks, and in many ways the most distinctive, raised into Mediterranean mountain chains are ancient hard limestones. Around them are often found extensive belts of softer, more recent, sedimentary rocks, heavily eroded and dissected into tumbled hill country. The mountains have been built by a complex of colliding continental plates, large and small, and so notable areas of igneous rocks, with some celebrated active volcanoes, are characteristic too. Where plate-edges are descending deeply into the earth's mantle, deep troughs form, and the Mediterranean and its extremely ancient precursor ocean Tethys occupy such a depression. The sea derives some of its character from the depth that results, but the more familiar coastal landscapes are the product of the great rise in sea-level which has drowned great areas of coastal lowland, especially in the Aegean, since the end of the last glaciation some 10,000 years ago. The combination of this drowning with the tangled and mountainous topography has been to create deeply indented coastlines and numerous islands. The relatively high winter rainfall and the rivers that flow from beyond the region have, on the other hand, produced deltas and alluvial plains; the river valleys and the wetlands that form where river sediments meet the sea are an important feature of Mediterranean landscapes unfamiliar today because of reclamation and urbanisation. The impact of agriculture in the Graeco-Roman period and its frequent abandonment in the early Middle Ages have greatly intensified the alluviation of Mediterranean coasts and valley floors.

The position of the Mediterranean at the hub of the old world land-mass has given it a notable diversity of flora, and much of the area is apt to form forest if left to itself; in drier and rockier areas characteristic scrubland floras are found, known by various local names such as maquis, tomillares, phrygana (figure 21.1) Areas of wood and scrub could appear wild and inaccessible in historic times, but were always in fact the site of various human activities which transformed their ecologies. That is also true of the other inaccessible area of the coastlands, the marshes and lagoons of the alluvial plains; but like forests, despite their reputation as a margin, these zones played a vital role in local economies.

Human subsistence activity has profoundly marked the environment. The Mediterranean climate delivers rainfall almost exclusively in the winter months. In the summer drought, before the fruits of autumn, only animal foodstuffs, derived from hunting and fishing, are readily available fresh. Human production has concentrated on extending and managing the rainy season through the conservation of soil moisture for cultivation of a diverse range of food crops, especially those, such as cereals and pulses, which may be stored for summer use; on the maintenance of trees and bushes whose fruit is nutritious and can be processed for storage, above all the vine and the olive (figure 21.2); and on the careful husbandry of

Fig. 21.1 The sanctuary of Rhamnous (Attica) with the scrub from which it derived its name (photo: © Alison Frantz).

Fig. 21.2 Olive trees on Corfu (Corcyra).

domesticated animals which may take advantage of environments less suited to cultivation and which also provide a food-resource against times of shortage, predictable or not. This 'agrosystem' has a number of effects on the landscape; careful, often horticultural, cultivation creates a patchwork of very small units of intensively cropped garden ground around nucleated centres of population; hill-slopes are improved (often by extensive terrace-systems) for the retention of soil-moisture; animal husbandry helps to integrate the niches of most favourable conditions for cultivation with wider and less tractable landscapes. The management of production in the Greek and especially the Roman period extended provision for these basic requirements by the creation of far-reaching systems of reclamation, allotment, road-building and drainage. Finally, the need to store, and where possible to exchange, produce encourages the formation of nuclei, especially in places with year-round water-supply. The landscape may also be modified in the pursuit of resources other than food, above all timber and stone for building and fuel. Woodlands have been substantially reduced by the need for fuel for winter warmth: the Graeco-Roman period also saw a great increase in demand because of the expansion of technologies heavily dependent on fuel, especially metallurgy and ceramics. The extraction of minerals, and above all metal ores, had locally (in southern Spain, for instance) an effect on landscapes not paralleled until the nineteenth century. In this period too, complex social organisation began to make a significant impact on landscapes through urbanisation, the formation of elaborate architectural schemes in and around settlements, and the provision of sometimes extensive cultural facilities for at least certain segments of the population.

Representations

Elements of the world described so far appear in the Homeric epics, glimpses of agriculture and pastoralism, often in similes, but sometimes in set pieces such as the Shield of Achilles (*Il.* 18.478–607) or the scenes set on Ithaca in the later books of the *Odyssey* (such as *Od.* 24.220–34). When the poet wishes to evoke the myriad camp-fires of the Trojans on the plain, he describes the stars visible on a moonlit night above tangled hills and valleys as seen by a shepherd, rare inhabitant of these remoter tracts, and a common observer of nature in Homeric simile (*Il.* 8.555–9). Or we may get a sense of the opportunities to be seen in an under-exploited landscape, as when Odysseus describes the coast of the Cyclopes (*Od.* 9.116–30). And it is as glimpses, vignettes and snippets that a sense of landscape continues to appear in classical Greek literature – sometimes because the work is itself fragmentary, but more because this is how the environment was observed, imagined and depicted. The wider generalities of landscape in the collective sense are not found in this literature. Mountains, springs, caves, harbours, towns, sanctuaries, farms may be evoked, but in the same way that they were portrayed in relief (figure 21.3) or on painted ceramics (figure 21.4), with an emblematic suggestion of a greater whole. The overview is missing.

The emphasis is also strongly on the figures, usually human, sometimes divine, active in the landscape. And inasmuch as humans active in the landscape were usually hard at work, and work was rapidly acquiring connotations of low status, agricultural scenes are less common than might be expected in a society which was overwhelmingly oriented towards the production of food for survival. The successors of Homer's shepherd or the loyal retainers of Odysseus are comic if they are to be found at all, and many of the limited allusions to landscape which survive from classical Athens, especially on painted pottery, have a certain comic realism (figure 21.4). The wilder parts of the environment are imagined as the place of wild animals, and are represented in depictions of royal or aristocratic hunting: in the Persian tradition, the *paradeisos* or hunting-park adapts these links in a special variety of landscape architecture.

Fig. 21.3 A peasant driving his cow to market. A Hellenistic marble relief of the first century BC. Munich, Glyptothek inv 455 (photo: © museum).

Fig. 21.4 A sacrifice in a country landscape on an Athenian red-figure bell-krater. Late fifth century BC. Ht. 41 cm; diam. 41.7 cm. Boston, Museum of Fine Arts 95.24, C. P. Perkins Fund (photo: © museum).

Otherwise, places which are linked with the divine, the equivalent in the wilds of sanctuaries in towns, are evoked in a rather different spirit of awe in the presence of the gods and of nature, a sense of which developed with the theories of philosophers in Ionia and in Sicily from the late sixth century. Thus Empedocles of Acragas was especially impressed by and concerned with the volcanic landscapes of Sicily and south Italy. Wonders will continue to play a prominent part in ancient perceptions of the environment. But despite the diasporas of Mediterranean peoples across the sea, to Egypt or to south Russia, and in some cases beyond it, eastward along the Fertile Crescent to Persia, the classical Greek sense of landscape remains rather parochial: Scythia, says Herodotus, is the only place in the world where the rain falls in the summer rather than the winter.

In literature, the impact of the widening horizons of many Greeks is apparent in the geographical scope of Aristotle and Theophrastus, who show a clearer awareness than their predecessors of the different environments to be found, especially to the east. The nearer but already alien environments of Egypt and Mesopotamia were, after Alexander's conquests, centres of Greek population, and a sense of the Egyptian landscape begins to be felt - not so much among the subjects of the Ptolemies who lived there as among those for whom Ptolemaic rule in Egypt made it a possible concept, to be visualised as well as understood as a political fact. Hellenistic art expands the framework of the individual scenes traditional before, and begins to attempt to construct landscape as a setting for events, for instance in the tradition repre-sented for us in the Roman *Odyssey* paintings (figure 21.5). At the same time there is a new sense of the power to alter the arrangements of nature; long familiar to the Greeks as a hallmark of Eastern despotism, this now becomes a sign of the monarchy of the heirs and conquerors of Persia, and through them, a part of the repertoire of Greek architecture. Greek cities in particular are now planned to exploit and to adapt the givens of the natural environment. A text from the third century (Pseudo-Dicaearchus, *GGM* i, 97) shows how these changes have made possible a complete realistic landscape description, though it remains of a type that has its origins in comedy.

The fourth century BC changed attitudes to landscape. The changes were promoted by and reflected in the investigations into nature of Aristotle and Theophrastus and their followers. These changes had an economic dimension, since agricultural technique made steady progress in a period when opportunities for exchange were generally increasing and when elites were increasingly interested in improving returns on their land. The changes had a philosophical and artistic dimension, as new kinds of representation and new kinds of naturalism began to appear. The changes had a political component, since there can be no doubt that the expeditions of Alexander, and perhaps still more, the establishment of Greek communities in the kingdoms of his successors in Egypt and in Mesopotamia, began to change perceptions of what was normal in the environment. Ill-fated attempts to transplant botanical specimens between different climatic zones demonstrate the interest, which is reflected also in the beginnings of a landscape art which for the first time makes

Fig. 21.5 Odysseus in the land of the Laestrygonians. Detail of the frieze from the Esquiline (section 2). c. 50–40 BC. Ht. 1.16 m. Rome, Vatican, Museo Profano (photo: © Alinari).

generalisations about whole environments. Not surprisingly, Egypt is one of the first landscapes to be depicted in the new spirit. But at this time, parallel with the scholarship which reordered and clarified the texts of the epic poems, a scenery was imagined for the *Odyssey* appropriate to its wonders.

Both the scenery of Egypt and the Odyssean landscapes are best known to us through derivatives in Roman contexts, of which the Nilotic mosaic at Palestrina (figure 21.6) and the *Odyssey* frescoes from the Esquiline in Rome are the outstanding examples. There is a wry verisimilitude in these depictions which is the descendant of the comic vignettes of earlier generations; picturesque Egyptian agriculturalists or characters from the *Odyssey* lost in fantasies of rock and water are part of an interest in the realistic delineation of human conditions, which was most developed in Stoic thought. City-planning now also seeks to set the city in a wider context, adapting even major physical features to provide an appropriate context; and within the city, the human townscape is the subject of witty and generally affectionate poetic representation. Contrasted with the city, the world of the Homeric shepherd now cross-fertilises with the marvels of the mythological world to form a pastoral landscape of rustic ideals, remote from both the gritty conditions of the cities and the realities of the productive countryside, but incorporating those emblems and moments which had been the subject of landscape vignettes in earlier times – shrines, sacred groves, springs, rustic altars. In Roman decorative schemes these will become the popular genre which we know as 'sacro-idyllic' (figure 21.7).

From the Hellenistic period on we have a number of vivid descriptions of landscape in a

Fig. 21.6 The Nile mosaic. Detail of the mosaic from the sanctuary of Fortuna Primigenia, Praeneste. Early first century BC. Palestrina, Palazzo Barberini (photo: © Alinari).

Fig. 21.7 A sacro-idyllic landscape. Detail from the red room (16), east wall of the Boscotrecase villa. c. 10 BC. Naples, Archaeological Museum inv. 147501 (photo: © DAI(R)).

very broad sense, a vision of a prosperous, bustling and diverse inhabited world, teeming with cities. These evocations begin in the philosophical tradition of writing 'on the universe' ([Aristotle,] *de Mundo*; Apuleius, *de Mundo*), and come to serve as a self-congratulatory vision of Roman power, not the least ingredients in the favourable view of an imperial golden age which has been prevalent in modern views of the Roman world. This vision of a populated world is also found in the geographical tradition, which is unlike modern geography in taking a worldwide view; regional studies ('chorography'), which might have entailed a more specific sense of landscape, have seldom survived. But despite its very broad remit, it was influential on what powerful and cultivated Greeks and Romans of the imperial age wanted to see in more local views - plenty of human activity, nicely cultivated land, well-maintained and attractive cities, evidence of prosperity and taste.

This comforting vision was not altogether a mirage. The levels of urbanisation and the extent of intensively managed landscape of the age of the Antonines were indeed higher than ever before across the Roman Empire, and would not be attained again until the nineteenth century. The gaze is selective; it takes little account of the status or expectations of the figures in the landscape; it continues to prefer, like its counterparts in literature, a traditional image of rural felicity to a realistic evocation of the intensively farmed villa or the formally allotted terrains of new cities like Chersonesus in the Crimea, or the colonial settlements of the early Roman emperors. These prospects are also proprietorial; as in later phases of landscape history, delineating is close to appropriating. Control of the landscape was becoming more sophisticated. Roman property-lawyers, tax-officials, land-allotment commissioners, hydraulic engineers, agricultural theoreticians and surveyors changed the way in which space, and therefore landscape, were conceived (see chapters 14 and 51). We see land differently when we have mapped it. Although little Roman chorographical mapping survives, it is clear that it takes its place in this list of ways in which landscape-sensibility changed – rather as it was to do for related reasons in Britain in the sixteenth and seventeenth centuries. At the same time, spatial allegiances, the idea that this is what our territory looks like, were reduced with the submersion of communities in the fabric of the provincial Roman Empire. New ways of thinking about regions developed (see chapter 14), with wider definitions and more general characteristics. This paved the way for the sense of sacred space which was adopted by Christians in the fourth century as a way of establishing the venerability of the Holy Land, a kind of landscape which had not hitherto been seen in Graeco-Roman antiquity.

At the same time, moreover, the essential fictional portrayal of 'romantic' landscapes continued to develop - both in actual literary fiction, and in the closely related rhetorical genre of 'explanation of place'. Aelian's description (*VH* 3.1) of one of the stock natural wonders and beauty spots of the ancient world, the Peneus gorge at Tempe in Thessaly, may stand for all:

> ivy in abundance, and wonderfully thick-fleeced, thrives and flourishes there, and like the vines of fine grapes climbs up and grows into the tall trees; thick honeysuckle ramps up to the heights, shading the rock, which is scarcely visible, while all the greenery is on display, a festival for the eyes. In the lower, flat areas are intricate groves, and walks beneath them throughout, lovely retreats to stop at for travellers in summertime. Many springs flow through it ... birds sing, one taking over from another, some specially musical, entertaining the ear of the traveller and sending him on in untroubled enjoyment. . . . Through the middle flows the river, quietly and gently, like a stream of olive-oil.

No wonder the emperor Hadrian decorated his rural villa at Tibur (Tivoli) with a replica.

The term 'beauty spot' is right: among the developments of Hellenistic thought had been aesthetic theory, and the vocabulary of beauty, which had once been rather vaguely applied to landscape, now acquires specific meanings, mostly connected ultimately with the intrinsic beauty of the works of the beneficent nature which was studied in the treatises on the universe. Alongside the development of landscape painting, accordingly, we now find the invention for nearly the first time in antiquity of a garden art which concerned

Fig. 21.8 Garden paintings. A wall of the Villa of Livia at Prima Porta (detail of north wall). c. 20 BC. Ht. 2 m. Rome, Palazzo Massimo alle Terme.

itself with the echoing, imitation and bettering of what was admired in real landscapes, human or natural. This art was itself reflected in landscape painting, of which the most splendid example is the fantasy-grove of trees, flowers and birds from an underground summer dining-room in Livia's villa at Prima Porta north of Rome (figure 21.8).

Some examples

Let us finally consider a trio of specific instances to exemplify some of the points that have been made.

The island of Thasos in the north Aegean seemed to the early poet Archilochus like a donkey's backbone, composed of rocky ridges; his judgement amazed later observers, for whom Thasos was a type of fertility, renowned for its wine. The polis of Thasos during the fifth century managed its territory and agricultural production with care; subsidiary harbours, rural settlements, quarries and vineyards were connected by a road which ran around the coast of the island. Islands were known as centres of potential high productivity, and Thasos was a precocious example of how the transformations which might be associated with that were managed. It forms a special example of a Greek city landscape (figure 21.9).

The plains of Campania, in west-central Italy, well watered and mineral-rich from volcanic activity, were another landscape of intense productivity, which again benefited from easy communications by sea. Here wealth combined with the unusual

Fig. 21.9 Aerial view of Thasos (after Raymond V. Schoder SJ, *Ancient Greece from the Air*, Thames and Hudson, 1974, p. 209, top).

natural landscape to offer opportunities to the powerful of Hellenistic and Roman Italy to develop islands, coasts and hills with lavish villas which took full advantage of the scenery, and themselves formed part of the beauty of the view, which was depicted in turn on their walls (figure 21.10). The remains of these villas (especially those buried by the AD 79 eruption of Vesuvius) form one of our richest insights into Roman landscape.

Writing for leisured upper classes like those of Campania, the orator Dio Chrysostom developed set-piece descriptions of landscape, one (*Oration* 7) of which gives an extended evocation of what purports to be another Greek island, Euboea, where he sets an idyllic and heavily idealised rustic life, in a setting of conventional charm like the beauties of Tempe, whose protagonists scarcely understand the life of the (gradually decaying) small cities which in theory manage their countryside, but are actually parasitic upon it. The cities are again the abode of comic caricatures; a formerly rich human landscape has given way again to scenery in which the huntsman is the principal figure.

The three cases encapsulate the realities of the human landscapes of the ancient Mediterranean, and the way in which they were turned into scenery by and for the cultured wealthy, being distorted and sometimes ruined in the process, but on the way creating a lively, varied and often very beautiful art and literature of landscape, which has been highly influential in later European art.

Further reading

R. Biering, *Die Odysseefresken vom Esquilin*, Munich: Biering and Brinkmann, 1995.

R. Buxton, *Imaginary Greece: The Contexts of Mythology*, Cambridge: Cambridge University Press, 1994 – for Greek ideas about the environment.

A. T. Grove and O. Rackham, *The Nature of Mediterranean Europe: An Ecological History*, New Haven: Yale University Press, 2001 – for the Mediterranean world and the human impact on it.

P. Horden and N. Purcell, *The Corrupting Sea: A Study of Mediterranean History*, Oxford: Blackwell, 2000 –

Fig. 21.10 Wall painting of Campanian villa beside the sea. c. AD 70. Diam. 25 cm. Naples, Archaeological Museum inv. 9511, from Stabiae.

for reflections on how the human impact should be related to writing history.

W. F. Jashemski, *The Gardens of Pompeii, Herculaneum and the Villas Destroyed by Vesuvius*, vol. 1, New York, New Rochelle: Caratzas Brothers, 1979 – a good starting point for Roman gardens.

E. W. Leach, *The Rhetoric of Space: Literary and Artistic Representations of Landscape in Republican and Augustan Rome*, Princeton: Princeton University Press, 1988 – for the connection with literature and Roman ideas about landscape in general.

R. Ling, *Roman Painting*, Cambridge: Cambridge University Press, 1991, pp. 142–53 – for Roman landscape in painting.

R. Osborne, *Classical Landscape with Figures: The Ancient Greek City and its Countryside*, London: George Philip, 1987 – an excellent evocation of the environmental setting of Greek cities.

22. Marine Archaeology

Anthony Parker

The significance of the sea, economic, political and symbolic, was recognised in ancient times; however, marine archaeology can add a new dimension to our understanding of the sea in antiquity, for it deals with a resource for study which, thanks to submergence, is only now being discovered and exploited. This resource comprises harbours, shipwrecks and landscapes.

Harbours

The massive remains of Graeco-Roman harbour works in stone or concrete are among the most impressive architectural survivals from antiquity; however, only a minority of the monuments which once existed are visible, let alone useful, today. This is in part due to the tectonic instability of the Mediterranean region: thus, the Roman harbour of Cenchreae (near Corinth) was drowned in a succession of earthquakes starting in late antiquity, while the Hellenistic port of Phalasarna (Crete) has been left high and dry by coastal uplift. In more gentle conditions, harbour works have still been degraded by wave action, built over by later developments, or left buried inland by silting (as with the Roman harbours of Ostia and Portus). Moreover, at all periods, but especially in pre-classical times, boats did not require artificial harbour facilities, but could be loaded and unloaded off a beach, or in a rock-bound creek or cove, especially if only water and rest for the crew, or refuge from rough weather, were required: such uses leave scant archaeological trace.

At some stage (perhaps in the Middle Bronze Age, to judge by the size of stone anchors of that period) ships became too large to be beached conveniently, and so anchorages in the shelter of offshore islands came into use, for example at Tyre and Sidon. Not till the classical period can one identify the moles, quays, lighthouses, boathouses and warehouses which are the mark of a port. In the low-lying coast at Carthage, two large basins were excavated and developed in the fifth to third centuries BC; the circular basin, with an island in its centre, was fringed with ranks of boathouses as a secure base for war-galleys, while the rectangular harbour was lined with quays for handling cargo ships. Elsewhere, for example at Piraeus, natural inlets and headlands were augmented with moles, quays and fortifications to achieve the same ends. Harbour developments served more than economic and strategic purposes for Graeco-Roman rulers; they also provided opportunity to display munificent expenditure on a grand scale. This is well seen at Caesarea Maritima, where the largest and most intensive archaeological study of an ancient harbour is still under way (Figure 22.1). Caesarea was the gateway from Rome and the Mediterranean in general to the client kingdom of Herod the Great, and was emphatically provided (no doubt in conscious imitation of the great harbour at Alexandria) with moles and towers to make a harbour – on a straight coast without natural shelter – temples and storehouses to form the port, and a town behind for the workers involved in the port. The sheltering moles were constructed initially by filling great box-shaped barges with concrete, which were sunk off shore to form platforms at key points, and which were then linked by structures of stone or concrete to form the harbour. It seems that the moles were topped by quays and

Fig. 22.1 Caesarea Maritima: a reconstruction view from the northeast, showing the main harbour structures and the layout of the city (drawing: © C. Brandon)

buildings, and the whole complex, rising against all odds from an often hostile environment, impressed all who saw it. However, the harbour works were apparently constructed across geological fault-lines, running parallel to the coast, and by the end of the first century AD, probably less than 100 years from their construction, part of the moles had slumped below sea-level and no longer served its original purpose. At other harbours, problems of construction and maintenance could be overcome, but at a cost: in Marseilles, the naturally enclosed ancient harbour silted up continuously from the sixth century BC till medieval times, but the process was held at bay in the period of the early Roman Empire by dredging; both special dredger boats, and also the traces of their buckets cutting into the mud, have been found in what has long since been dry land. Changing conditions of maritime trade, rather than technical inadequacy, led for the most part to the decay of ancient harbour works.

Shipwrecks

Sometimes, in clear, shallow water, the remains of ancient ships' cargoes can be seen from the surface (e.g. the 'Church Wreck' of Marzamemi, Sicily), but no archaeological investigation of submerged sites took place till diving apparatus came into widespread use (Figure 22.2). Ancient ships, sometimes with cargo still on board, lost or abandoned in silted-up harbours or remote lagoons, have been found in dry-land situations (e.g. 'Caesar's Galley', a Roman ship found, and partly salvaged, in the former harbour of Marseilles in 1864). Sponge-fishermen using 'hard-hat' apparatus came across sunken ships on the seabed in the nineteenth and earlier twentieth centuries, and their discoveries brought about the important recoveries of sculpture and other finds from Antikythera and Mahdia in 1900 and later years. These discoveries drew scholarly attention to the potential of marine archaeology, but proper systematic exploration, even of shallow sites, was not possible until the development and widespread adoption of self-contained underwater breathing apparatus, the 'aqualung', after World War II.

In the Mediterranean, despite the efforts of F. Benoit (France) and N. Lamboglia (Italy) to record underwater sites and have the new technique recognised by scholars, properly controlled diving archaeology did not emerge as a coherent discipline until the excavation of the Titan wreck by P. Tailliez in 1957 and of the wreck at Cape

Fig. 22.2 SCUBA archaeology: a student wearing sport-diving equipment balances over a fourth-century BC wreck site to make a plan, using pencil, tracing-film and planning-frame (photo: © University of Bristol Sicily Expedition).

Gelidonya by G. F. Bass and others in 1960. Some 1,500 prehistoric, Phoenician, Greek and Roman wrecks have now been reported from the Mediterranean and Black Sea region, as well as from Egypt, the Red Sea, the Atlantic coast and the rivers and lakes of the northern Roman provinces; most Mediterranean and northern European countries have an inspectorate of underwater archaeology and maintain a register of their maritime heritage sites. Advances in diving techniques, and the accrued experience and increasingly widespread education of divers, mean that more information is now recovered from sites within diving range. Wrecks are also now more frequently found at deeper depths (from 60 m to over 1,500 m deep) with the aid of satellite navigation, sonic ranging, sonar detection and imaging, underwater video and three-dimensional visualisation, operated with either manned or unmanned submersibles (Figure 22.3). In the deeper, anoxic waters of the Black Sea some spectacularly well-preserved ancient ships' structures have recently been discovered, and important wreck-cargoes, lying at depths too great for scuba divers to plunder them, have been found and studied off the coasts of Egypt, Italy and France by various investigators. On land, too, more expertise and resources have made significant contributions to understanding ancient ship construction, both in the pre-Roman period and under the Roman Empire.

The earliest substantial watercraft so far found in the Mediterranean region is not the sunken wreck of a seagoing ship, but the disassembled, votive remains of a large river-boat, deposited near the Great Pyramid of Giza in Egypt c. 2600 BC. The 43 m-long boat was built using a complicated technique, obviously already well developed, which employed interlocking planks, a broad plank in place of a keel, and lashings which ran from side to side in place of wooden frames. The same general approach to ship construction is seen in the Late Bronze Age ship of Ulu Burun, datable to the late fourteenth century BC, excavated in southern Turkey by G. F. Bass and C. Pulak. The ship and the crew appear to have

Fig. 22.3 Deep-sea archaeology: a robot submersible hovers over a Roman wreck in the Black Sea (photo: © Institute for Exploration/Institute for Archaeological Oceanography-URI/GSO).

come from Canaan or Cyprus; the ship had a central plank which was thicker than the rest, but projected inboard, leaving the bottom smooth externally. The planking was fastened edge to edge with draw-tongue joints, formed of free tenons fitted into mortises cut in the thickness of the planks and then fixed snugly with pegs (Figure 22.5); in the case of the Ulu Burun ship the planking joints are arranged in line athwartships, like the lashings of the Khufu ship 1,000 years before, as if to stiffen the hull. There were no frame timbers in the Ulu Burun ship, it seems, and so its construction bears a closer relation in concept to Egyptian boats than to classical ships. This wreck is also outstanding in the richness and variety of its cargo, including ingots of copper and tin, resin, glass, ivory, and rare woods and shells; there was also a rich variety of weapons, stores and personal possessions on board. Although some earlier sites (not well preserved) are known, Ulu Burun, together with the much smaller and poorly preserved wreck at Cape Gelidonya of c. 1200 BC, forms a rather isolated predecessor of the great mass of ancient Mediterranean shipwrecks.

Fig. 22.4 Stitched construction: partial reconstruction of the sixth-century boat from Marseilles (wreck Jules-Verne 9). The planking, positioned by dowels, is edge-fastened by continuous stitching, and the frames (each comprising several pieces joined together) are bound to the inboard face of the planking by ropes which pass through V-shaped holes in the thickness of the plank (drawing: © A. J. Parker, from a reconstruction model by R. Roman).

No excavated wrecks, and no remains of ships, are known from the 500-year period between the twelfth and the sixth centuries BC. After c. 600 BC, however, a number of archaic wrecks have been studied in the Western and central Mediterranean, for example at Marseilles (wreck Jules-Verne 9, a small fishing-boat). These ships all have hull-planking fastened edge to edge by continuous stitching, built on a rigid keel, and reinforced by jointed timber frames (Figure 22.4). Associated finds and cargo leave open their cultural affiliation – Phoenicio-Punic, Greek or Etruscan; the same technique of ship construction is found in the North Adriatic region in Roman and medieval times, exemplified by the Augustan coastal trader stranded at Valle Ponti, Comacchio. Over most of the Mediterranean, however, stitching was replaced by draw-tongue joints – not, at first (in the later sixth century and the fifth century BC), at the bow and stern, but for the rest of the Graeco-Roman period over the whole of the hull (Figure 22.5). This technique, if

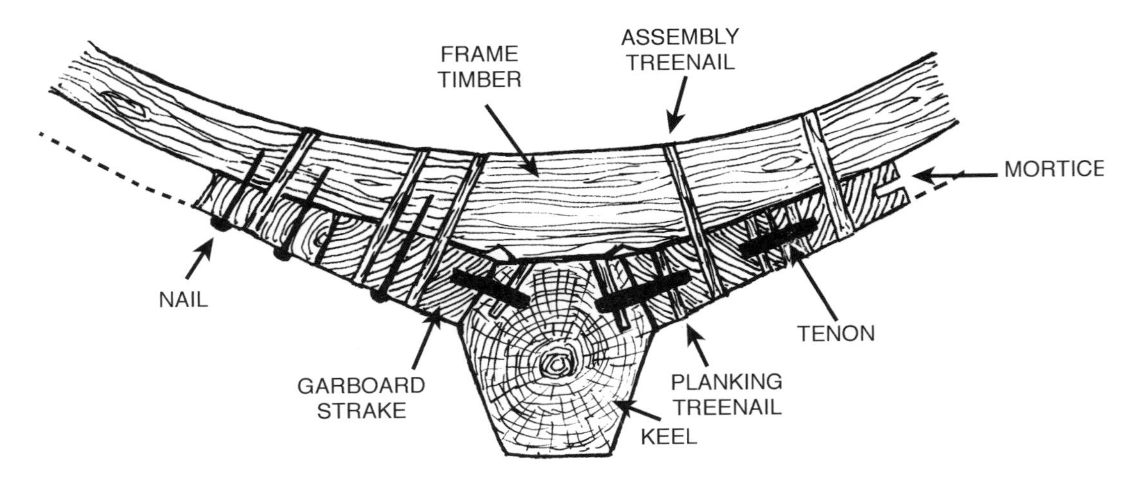

Fig. 22.5 Classical ship construction: a generalised part cross-section of a Graeco-Roman ship. The planks are held tightly together edge to edge by free tenons, pegged firmly in mortises by planking treenails (drawing: © A. J. Parker and Susan Grice, after P. Pomey, M. Rival and others).

suitably reinforced internally by ribs and cross-beams, resulted in a stiff, watertight hull, likely to give a good return on investment – but expensive (in materials and labour) to build, difficult to repair, and best suited to relatively small ships, such as the late fourth-century BC wreck of Kyrenia.

The thorough study of the Kyrenia ship, including trials of a full-scale reconstruction, has shown that even a small cargo-vessel of this kind would perform quite efficiently in most weather conditions. Similar information is, unfortunately, lacking for oared warships, for no wreck of such a ship has yet been found; *Olympias*, a full-scale reconstruction of a classical *triērēs* ('trireme', a Greek warship), is based on inferred dimensions, structure and rigging. Fragments of warships, and traces of merchant galleys, have been found in the Mediterranean, but actual examples of Roman oared ships are known only from the Danube and Rhine frontiers, as at Oberstimm and Mainz. These frontier patrol craft were slender and lightly built, but Hellenistic war-galleys were built of strong, heavy timbers, fully jointed like merchant ships of the time.

No statistics of sea trade survive from classical antiquity, but the archaeological record of shipwrecks shows that more than half of the ancient and medieval sites known from the Mediterranean date from the period c. 200 BC–AD 200. This, the high period of ancient Mediterranean navigation, was no doubt sustained both by the prosperous conditions of the principate and by exports (especially of wine) from the landed proprietors of late Republican Italy. Over a hundred such wrecks are known, mostly in the Western Mediterranean, and whole series of such cargoes were wrecked at hazardous sites in southern Gaul such as the headland of Cap Dramont, the beacon of La Chrétienne, or the islands near Marseilles, which include Le Grand Congloué. An especially important excavation was carried out in 1970–3 by J. P. Joncheray at wreck C of La Chrétienne, datable to the second quarter of the second century BC (Figure 22.6). Here, although the ship's hull was only partly preserved under the cargo of Italian wine-amphoras (of the type called 'Graeco-Italic', but very probably from central Italy), careful excavation and thorough post-excavation enabled both the layout of the ship, its equipment and cargo (Figure 22.7), and also the lines of the ship (15½ m long overall) to be reconstructed. The form of the hull, with a high, rounded stern and relatively low bow, replicates the typical profile of a Roman ship as seen in sculpture, coins and paintings (Figure 22.8). The assemblage of finds from the site reflects a small ship's complement of poor men (whether free or

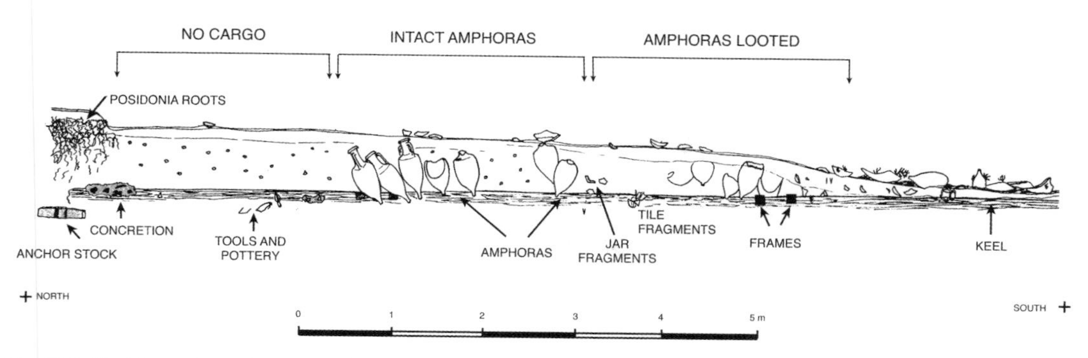

Fig. 22.6 Chrétienne C wreck: a section through the second-century BC wreck as excavated by J. P. Joncheray. Archaeological analysis of the site shows how it was formed, and how the different categories of finds are related to one another and to the original ship's hull (drawing: © A. J. Parker and Susan Grice, after J. P. Joncheray).

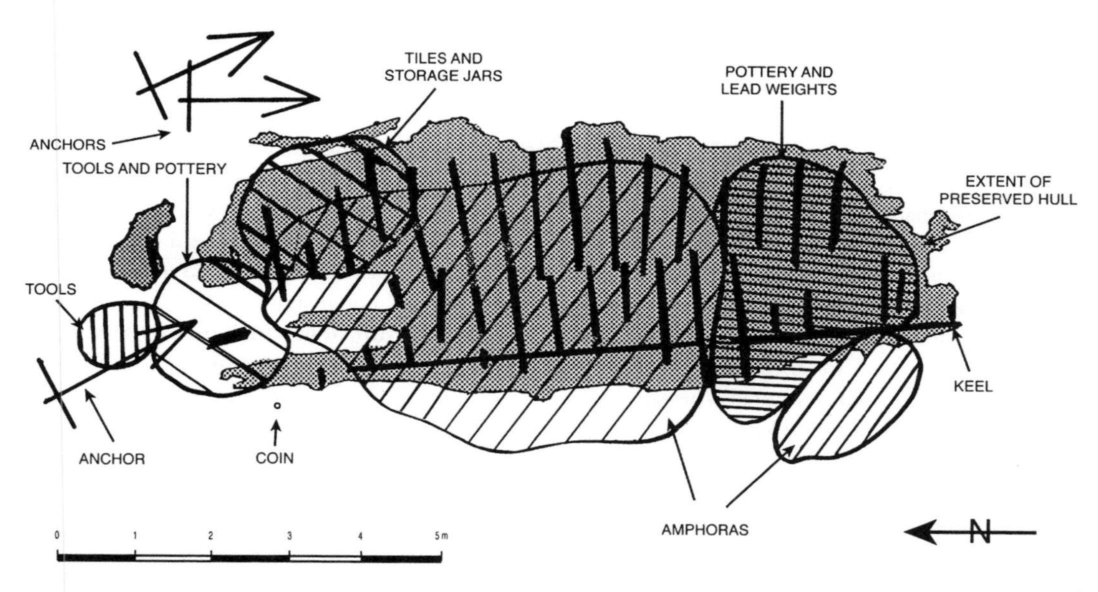

Fig. 22.7 Chrétienne C wreck: an analytical summary plan of the excavated finds, showing how their grouping enables a reconstruction of life on board (drawing: © A. J. Parker and Susan Grice, after J. P. Joncheray).

slave). Wine cargoes, such as that at Chrétienne C, might represent the produce of a single estate or group of estates, even though the ships sometimes carried merchants who marked the amphoras with their seal as they sailed along; although sumptuary legislation limited the size of a vessel which a Roman nobleman could himself own, it seems likely that landowners (no doubt through agents) owned seagoing ships which could transport their household to and from distant postings, or convey their own supplies from one house to another, or gifts to allies or clients. The 'phaselus' (a light passenger ship that derives its name from the Greek for 'beanpod') of Catullus (4.1) was one such ship, and so was the ship which sank at La Madrague de Giens c. 60 BC. This latter (the largest Graeco-Roman wreck to be excavated) was 40 m long and carried about 400 tons of cargo; the ship was strongly built of high-quality materials, with a deep keel and a long forefoot which would have made the ship a fast and impressive sailor. There can be no doubt that prestige, as well as

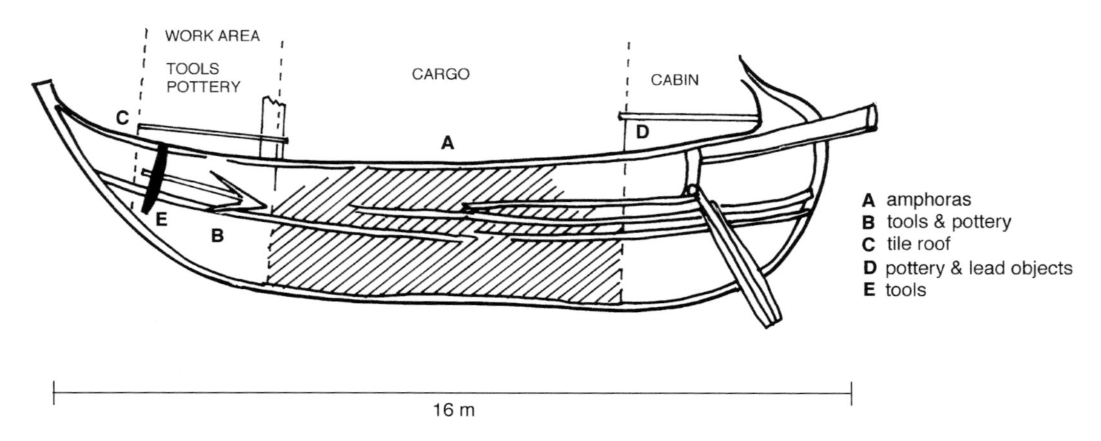

Fig. 22.8 Chrétienne C wreck: a restored profile of the ship, based on the analysis of the finds and the reconstruction of the hull remains (drawing: © Susan Grice, after J. P. Joncheray).

profitability, was part of its concept. Stamps on the cargo amphoras indicate that the wine came from the Caecuban region of Latium, even though samples of the surviving contents suggest that the wine was not white (as the choice Caecuban wine probably was) but red, broadly similar to modern claret, as also found in other Roman wine-cargoes. Other goods carried in amphoras throughout Graeco-Roman antiquity included especially olive oil, and fish or meat preserved in brine (see chapter 28). Cargoes of stone, bricks or metal are less frequent, and textiles, leather, wood and grain (whether loose, or in skins or sacks) are not normally preserved under water, though grain, especially, was economically very important. Animals, too, and indeed humans (passengers) travelled frequently aboard ancient Mediterranean ships, but archaeological evidence is almost entirely lacking.

Many cargoes were composite, assembled in at least one entrepôt along a voyage; such was the amazing variety of goods on board the ship which sank at El Sec (Majorca) in the mid-fourth century BC. The cargo amphoras alone originated in at least ten different parts of the whole length of the Mediterranean, and even the heavy grinding-stones which were also on board must have been grouped together by a merchant from widely separated sources. Graffiti on pottery show that the merchants involved were Carthaginians and Western Greeks; however, there is no definite evidence for the home port of the ship, or for where it was built. The same is true for most Graeco-Roman wrecks: there is no clear identification of origin, and this makes it difficult to discern regional variations in ship construction. For instance, some six ships have now been identified in which the planking is fastened to the frames partly by rope lashings, as well as by treenails: some, but not all, of these ships have links with northeastern Spain. Flat-bottomed ships, which were suitable for loading while beached in shallow water, may also have links with northeastern Spain in some cases, but in others were merely coastal barges, heavily built to carry building materials or giant wine-jars. The only definite regional grouping seems to be that around the head of the Adriatic, exemplified by the Valle Ponti (Comacchio) stitched ship mentioned earlier.

In the Roman provinces of Europe, however, a rich variety of boats and ships has been found. Although native entrepreneurs certainly developed shipping routes on the Swiss lakes, the Danube, the Rhine and the English Channel before the Roman conquest, most archaeological finds indicate development of boat types and boat-construction technology in response to Roman military needs. Romano-British sailing craft, such as the ship found at Blackfriars in London, are in almost every way different from contemporary

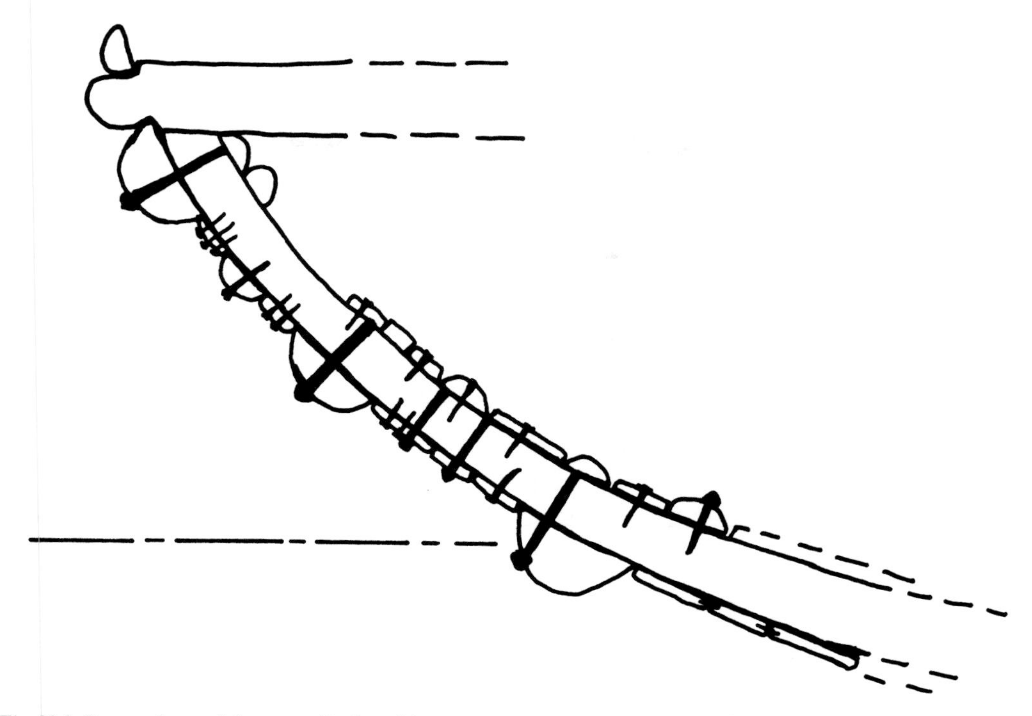

Fig. 22.9 Pantano Longarini: a generalised partial cross-section of the seventh-century AD ship. Loosely fitting tenons position the edges of planks below the waterline; nails attach planks to the heavy frames above water, and the thick, rounded wales are fastened with bolts (drawing: © A. J. Parker, after P. and J. Throckmorton).

Mediterranean ships, but it is not clear whether they belong to a pre-Roman (Celtic) tradition or are the product of a Romanised provincial culture. It is a pity that no seagoing warships have been found, for the range of cargo vessels and of river craft already discovered reflects an empire fully equipped for transport and warfare on both inland waterways and the Eastern Atlantic.

Archaeological evidence of every kind suggests that commercial activity, for whatever reasons, declined markedly from the mid-second century on: the incidence of shipwrecks reflects this. Not only were fewer ships sailing the Mediterranean in the third, fourth and fifth centuries AD (to judge by wreck finds), they were also cheaper to build, repair and operate. For example, the Dramont E ship, lost c. AD 425, used short lengths of wood, bent into shape and caulked where there were gaps, in contrast with the more sculptural, cabinet-like approach of earlier Graeco-Roman shipwrights. Sixth and seventh-century Mediterranean ships, although still using free tenons to edge-join the planking, relied for their shape and rigidity on the framing timbers, to which the planks were fastened with iron bolts and nails, as in the Byzantine ship of Pantano Longarini (Sicily) (Figure 22.9). By this date, the busy Mediterranean trade in foodstuffs and raw materials had dwindled away, and scarcely revived till the sixteenth century.

Marine archaeology has made an interesting contribution to technological history in the case of ancient anchors. The earliest anchors were of stone, and, in the Mediterranean Bronze Age, ships (e.g. Ulu Burun) carried numbers of well-carved tombstone-shaped anchors, intended to lie flat on the seabed; the Homeric term *eunē* means both 'bed' and 'anchor stone'. During the archaic period, anchors with wooden shank and arms, weighted down by a stone stock, came into use; their hook-like shape, intended to dig into the seabed, is reflected in the classical term *ankura* ('bent object'). From the fifth century BC to the second century AD, stocks were made of

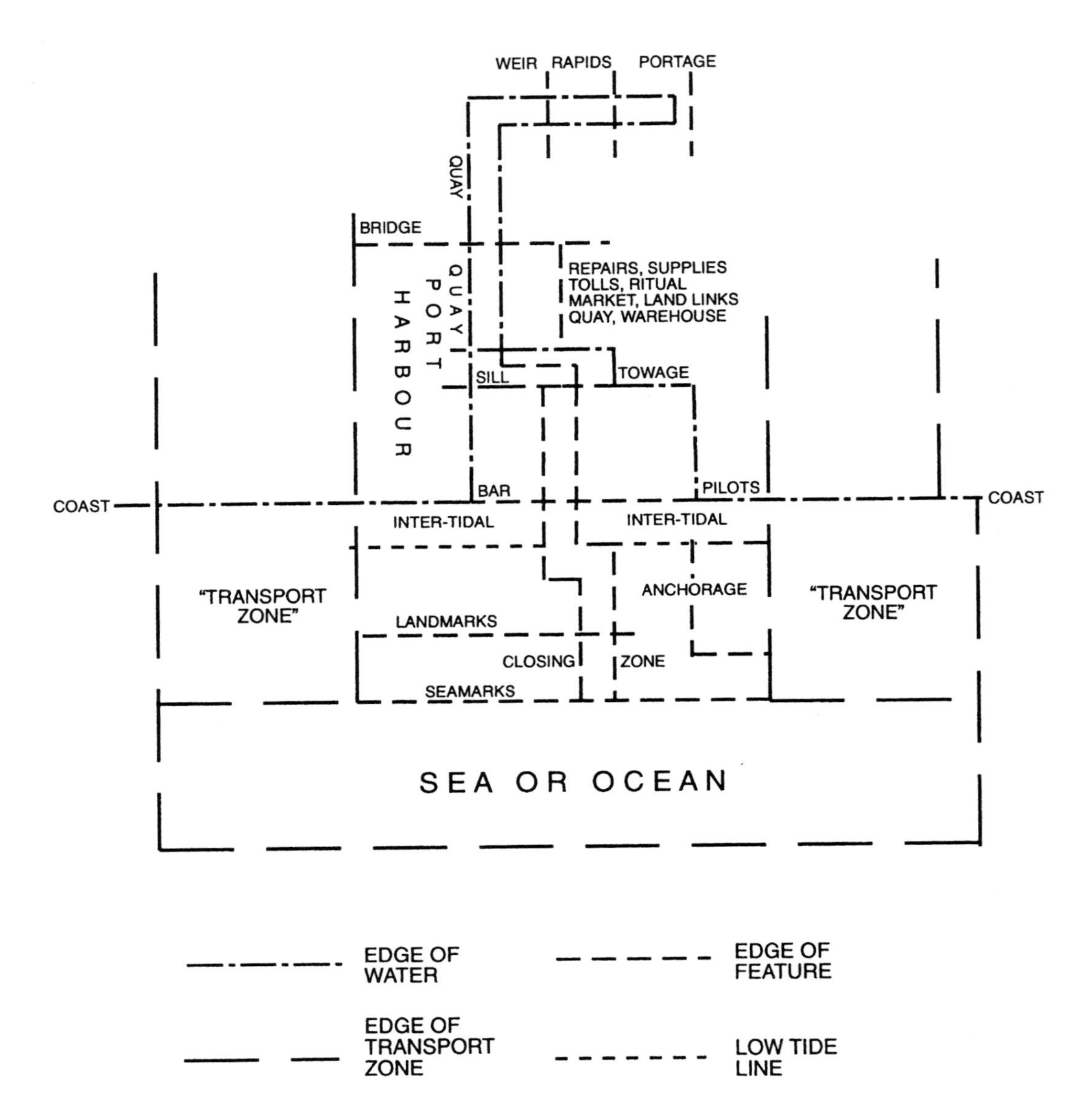

Fig. 22.10 A maritime landscape: the sea-coast as perceived by a mariner, in schematic form. Not all the features shown would be found in every part of the Graeco-Roman world, but a model such as this enables marine archaeological discoveries to be fitted on to theories of ancient cultural interaction (drawing: © A. J. Parker and Susan Grice).

lead, not stone; but from the third century BC iron anchors came into use, and were the only type in the late empire and Byzantine period. During this long period, iron anchors changed from a pointed, dart-like form to a Y-shape with downward-pointing arms: this was probably intended to reduce the length of the iron components, thus reducing the cost of metal and forging, and (hopefully) the tendency for the anchor to break under strain. The archaeological finds which document this technical progression are, in many cases, well dated by association with shipwrecks. The cargo amphoras of the Roman period also show a progression (as well as regional variation) in their ratio of filled weight to packaging (technically 'tare'), though the dating of amphoras is not derived principally from wreck finds.

Networks and landscapes

Marine archaeology has been dominated by the 'traditional' processual archaeology of the 1970s or earlier, but more recently it has come to respond to more interpretative concerns (Figure 22.10). Emphasis has been placed on 'the maritime perspectives of archaeology', and this blends with those ancient historians who stress connectivity by sea as a distinctive characteristic of the Mediterranean region. Political control and ritual observance are important cognitive elements in the landscape on which networks of connectivity are built (see chapter 21); this maritime cultural landscape can be recovered from wrecks and loose finds under water as well as from seamarks, temples, castles and ports on the seacoasts. Such a study needs to be based, not just on topography, ethnography and history, but also on structured interpretative models.

Further reading

L. Casson, *Ships and Seamanship in the Ancient World* (2nd edn), Baltimore and London: Johns Hopkins University Press, 1995 – a comprehensive, authoritative overview, with extensive coverage of ancient sources and references to modern archaeology.

J. P. Delgado (ed.), *Encyclopaedia of Underwater and Maritime Archaeology*, London: British Museum Press, 1997 – brief but mostly well-informed summaries of classical topics and sites, as well as the wider picture.

A. M. McCann and J. Freed, 'Deep water archaeology: a late-Roman ship from Carthage and an ancient trade route near Skerki Bank off northwest Sicily', *Journal of Roman Archaeology*, Supplementary Series 13 (1994) – the first academic account of deep-water archaeology.

S. McGrail, *Boats of the World from the Stone Age to Medieval Times*, Oxford: Oxford University Press, 2001 – includes a thorough survey of Graeco-Roman ships.

J. S. Morrison, J. F. Coates and N. B. Rankov, *The Athenian Trireme: The History and Reconstruction of an Ancient Greek Warship* (2nd edn), Cambridge: Cambridge University Press, 2000 – an accessible account of ancient warships and a hypothetical 'reconstruction'.

A. J. Parker, *Ancient Shipwrecks of the Mediterranean and the Roman Provinces*, Oxford: British Archaeological Reports (Int. 580), 1992 – includes summaries and bibliography for wreck sites and marine archaeology.

Websites

Mystic Aquarium, www.mysticaquarium.org/latest-discoveries/iferesearch/mabs2000.asp – news of recent exploration led by R. D. Ballard.

NAVIS I, www1.rgzm.de/navis/home/frames.htm – an international database of Roman ships and boats, especially those found in northern Europe.

Pisa, www.navipisa.it – an example of the rich finds which can be made in silted-up sites.

23. Sites and Features

Brian A. Sparkes

At the beginning of the period covered by this book (c. 1000 BC) the settlements spread across Greece and Asia Minor, Italy and Sicily, were at the mercy of the physical conditions prevailing: the nature of the landscape, the fertility of the soil, the climate, the difficulty of land and sea travel. They were small in size and closed to all but their neighbours. Their strategy relied on subsistence farming and the ability of the inhabitants to defend themselves against raids and invasions. Before the end of the period (c. AD 500) the Graeco-Roman world had expanded over three continents, to embrace Britain and Spain in the west, North Africa and Egypt in the south, the Black Sea littoral in the northeast, and Syria in the east. Population had increased, and many settlements had grown into large cities with sophisticated architecture, public amenities, and complex political and social administration. Sea and land communications were extensive.

Evidence for sites

As is to be expected, the evidence is of a very wide and varied character within the broad division of texts, landscape and archaeology.

Of the writers of technical treatises (see chapter 59), there are geographers such as Strabo (fl. 30 BC), who wrote a descriptive account of the length and breadth of the Mediterranean, and Ptolemy (fl. AD 150), who was the first to use latitude and longitude as co-ordinates. Vitruvius (fl. c. 30–20 BC) was an architect and military engineer and wrote the influential *de architectura*, which opens with an account of town-planning. Frontinus, one-time governor of Roman Britain (AD 73/4–7), compiled a treatise *de aquis urbis Romae* on the aqueducts of Rome and may have written some of the manuals on land-surveying preserved in a collection (*Corpus Agrimensorum*) which contains works by various anonymous authors on categories of land, and its measurement and division. The traveller Pausanias (fl. AD 150) confined himself to a detailed and largely accurate, if partial, account of sites on the Greek mainland. Information on the location and relationship of sites is also provided by land itineraries and by their maritime equivalent the *periploi*; the best known of the former is the Antonine Itinerary (third century AD) and of the latter *The Periplus of the Erythraean Sea* (first century AD). The itineraries give names of places and lists of distances along main roads throughout the Roman Empire.

The survival of Greek and Roman maps has been small; those that are extant have survived in medieval manuscripts. The best known is the Peutinger Table, a Roman road map that exists in a copy of c. AD 1200 (figure 23.1), with an elongated form that fits the length and breadth of the Roman Empire into a height of only 34 cm (c. 1 ft). Others of less usefulness are the Ravenna Cosmography (c. AD 670) and small drawings that accompany the *Corpus Agrimensorum* and the *Notitia Dignitatum* (based on an original of AD 395), the latter ('List of Offices') a register of military and civil officials in the late Roman Empire. A few examples of inscribed town plans survive, of which the most important is the *Forma Urbis Romae*, a marble plan from the early third century AD at a scale of 1:250 (figure 23.2); although it exists only in fragments, it provides incomparable evidence for the layout of the capital. Plans of a

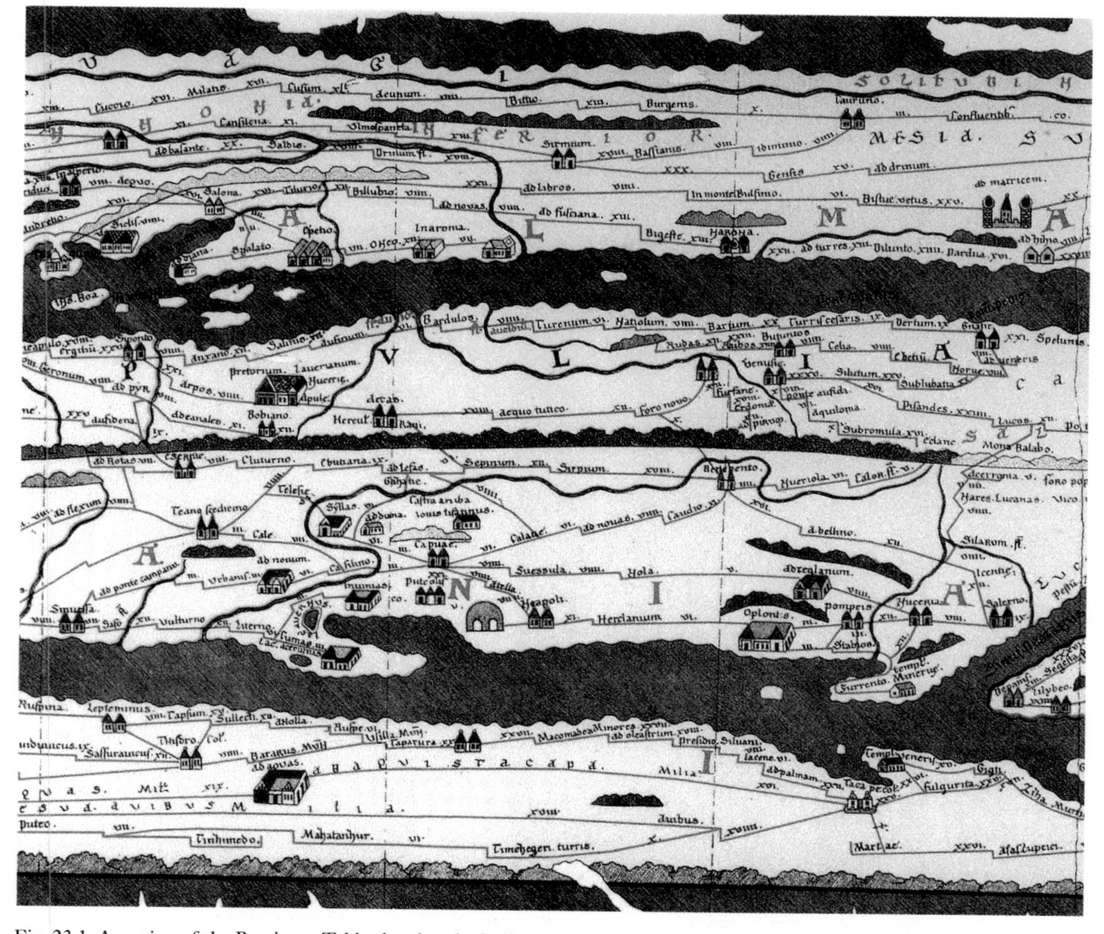

Fig. 23.1 A section of the Peutinger Table showing the Italian coast from Sinuessa to Salerno (from K. Miller, *Die Peutingersche Tafel* (1916), segment VI 3-5).

different form and purpose are the cadasters. The best, though fragmentary, set of these stone tablets is the one that marks out the land around Roman Arausio (Orange); the territory is divided up in a system of centuriation (squares and rectangles) as holdings for the veteran soldiers settled on land taken from the local inhabitants subject to Rome (figure 23.3); the tablets show the main intersections and rivers and the various holdings.

Epigraphy (see chapter 34) is also invaluable: some inscriptions are foundation texts; some give details of building construction and choice of architect; some explain the organisation or enlargement of a settlement; some show the workings of the administrative, commercial and political systems; and some spell out the relations between urban centres and their surrounding territories. Boundary stones within settlements and milestones between them provide evidence of names and distances.

In comparison with the evidence from technical works and inscriptions, Greek and Roman literary texts provide a 'softer' set of support. Historians supply a narrative of events and political background, and may contribute vital facts in helping us both to pinpoint specific sites and the buildings within them and to locate battlefields and other scenes of combat, but rarely with much detail and not totally reliably. Philosophers, whilst often constructing ideal communities (e.g. Plato and Aristotle; Cicero), nonetheless provide us with a rough guide to understanding the nature and size of settlements of their time.

Fig. 23.2 Fragment of the *Forma Urbis Romae* (*regio* ix), showing the Porticus Octaviae. Early third century AD (photo: © Fototeca Unione 4737).

On the archaeological side, we are similarly at the mercy of the evidence that has survived the wreck of classical antiquity (see chapter 3). Many of the important cities of antiquity continued their success in the post-classical centuries and now overlie their predecessors (e.g. Athens, Rome, Alexandria, Byzantium/Constantinople/ Istanbul and many Roman provincial sites), and this makes access to them difficult and gives only a partial view. Those centres that failed before or at the end of antiquity continue to provide excavators with more extensive evidence of their identity and layout, but this evidence may not present a typical picture. Non-excavation techniques have developed rapidly over the past generation and supply much new information. Aerial photography has revealed new sites and unexcavated sections of sites already dug; it has also revealed areas beyond the built settlements such as roads, field systems, farms and camps. For example, aerial photographs revealed the town plan of the Greek site of Metapontum in South Italy, and the field systems outside the settlement (figure 23.4) were also brought to light. The field systems date from the archaic period and may preserve the original arrangement for the division of the farm

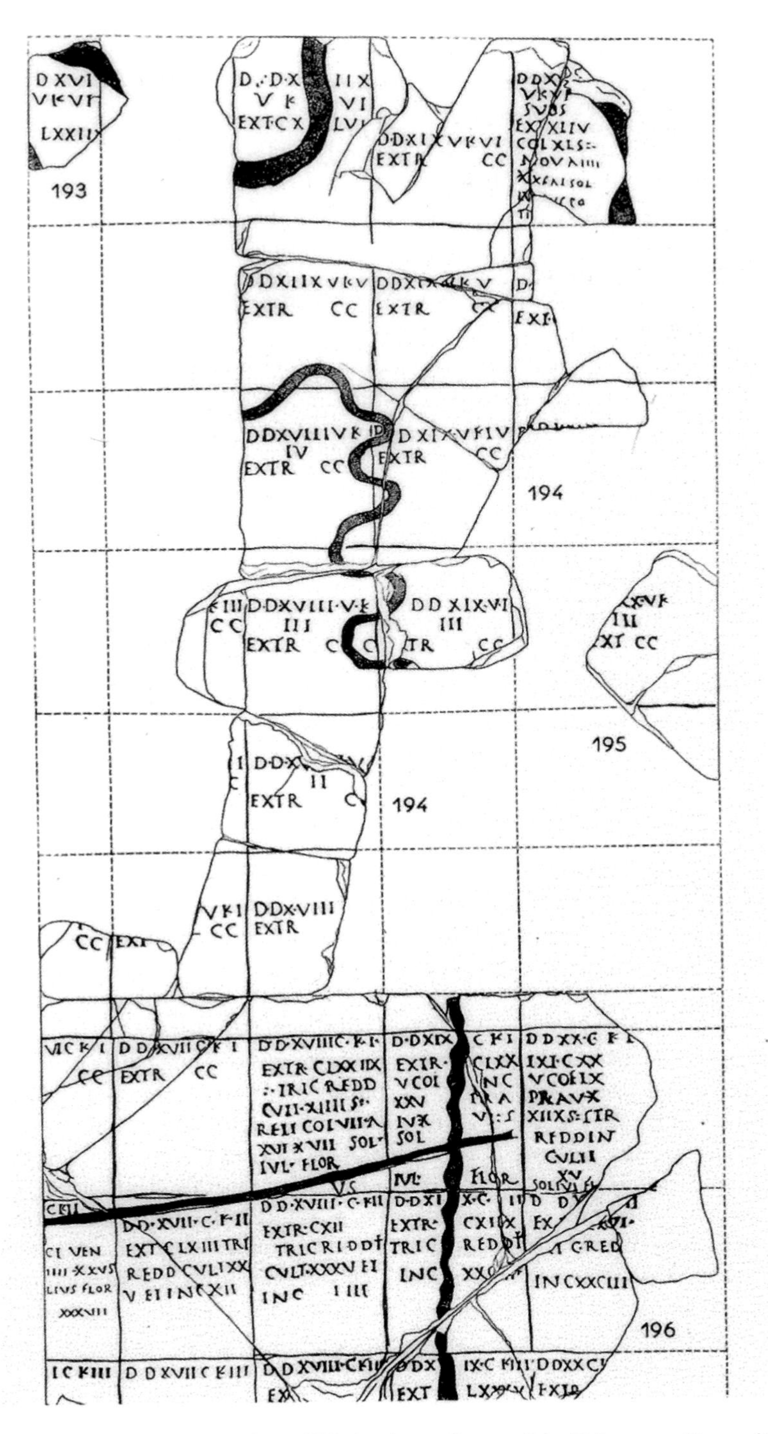

Fig. 23.3 Section of the Orange cadaster B, plaque III J, showing a tributary of the Rhône crossed by an old road closed by centuriation. After AD 77 (from *Gallia*, Supplement 16 (1962), fig. 26).

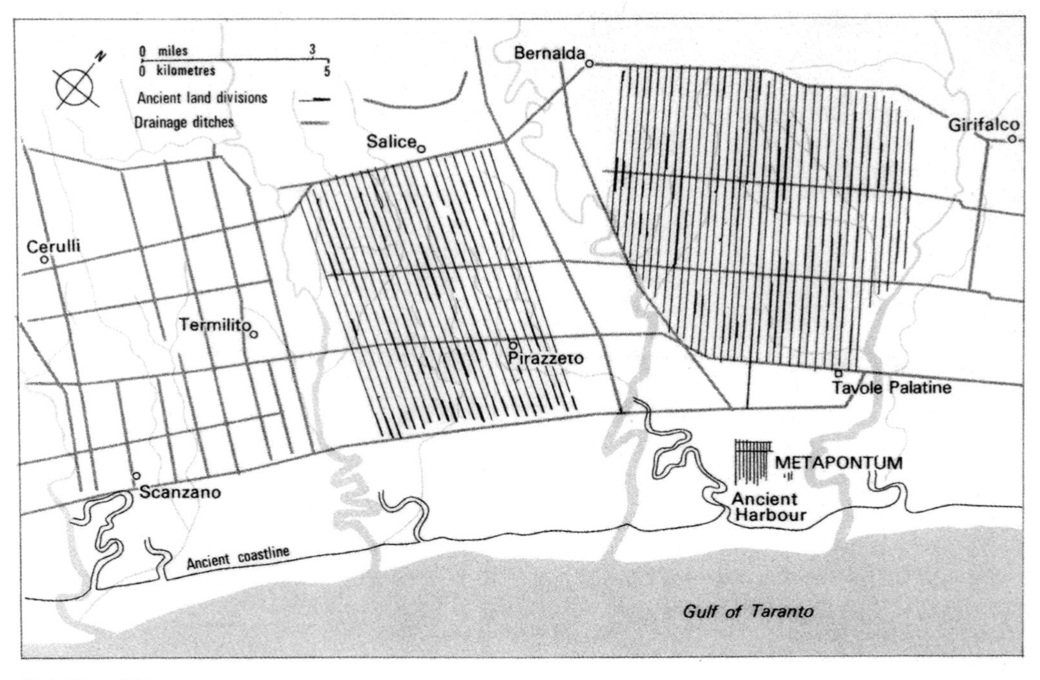

Fig. 23.4 Plan of Metapontum and its associated field systems (adapted from Finley, *Atlas*, 134).

land at the time of the foundation of the Greek colony (c. 600 BC).

Field surveys (e.g. in Messenia, Boeotia, south Etruria and the Tiber Valley) have now provided a valuable supplement to stratigraphical excavations and, with their emphasis on the total picture, have encouraged a move away from the old prominence given to the urban scene and have been helpful in filling in the blanks in the countryside, repopulating it and reassessing the relationship between town and country (see chapter 3). More recently, surveys that use magnetometers and resistivity meters have enabled researchers to form images of whole towns without excavation. Falerii Novi, north of Rome, is an early example of the success of this technique; it has uncovered the whole plan of the settlement within the walls: forum, baths, temples and private houses (figure 23.5). Such a survey as this enables the overall organisation of the urban space and the relation between public and residential layout to be understood in a way that piecemeal excavations cannot. Work on Portus, the port of imperial Rome, is taking this technique further.

Greece

For some generations after the collapse of the Bronze Age palace system, Greek society and sites were reduced to small groups, living a hand-to-mouth existence, with little contact beyond their borders and restricted connection outside the Greek orbit (see chapter 15). The siting of the settlements was dictated partly by the previous locations but more by the availability of resources (land for agriculture and husbandry, water, timber, ores) and by the need for defence against adversaries, whether from nearby or from across the sea. The settlements show little planning and are to be numbered in tens or hundreds of inhabitants in mud-brick and wooden huts on foundations of field stones; some boasted a large dwelling to house the 'big man' of the village and to be used for community gatherings.

During the archaic period (down to 479 BC), the Greeks developed their polis system by which an urban centre and its surrounding countryside (*chōra*) became a unified political whole (see chapter 16). Far from being empty, as was once

Fig. 23.5 Magnetometer layout of Falerii Novi, Latium (© British School at Rome).

thought, the countryside that surrounded the urban centre had a strong network of rural settlements that supported the centre. As conditions improved, the population grew, settlements expanded, and for various reasons people migrated from the old Greek world to south Italy and Sicily, North Africa, the Propontis and the Black Sea. The foundations that were made in these new territories involved planning on the ground, with fair division of house plots and the arable land; this had an obvious effect on the formal layout of towns both abroad and back home in Greece, though already established foundations had little chance of radical reconstruction in the built-up area.

Settlements were established on or near elevated land (*acropolis*), to serve first as a living area, then as a safe place to which to repair in case of attack, and finally as a religious focus; the traditional example of this is Athens (see plan in chapter 67). On the lower level an area was left open in which public business of various sorts, whether commercial, legal or political, was conducted. As business increased, buildings were erected in which meetings could be held, such as council-chambers and varieties of colonnade; old temples were rebuilt or new ones consecrated. For recreation, there were gymnasia and *palaestrae*, stadia, theatres, taverns and brothels. Private houses contrasted with the expensive public buildings ('public splendour, private squalor'). Workshops for craft production, such as those for fulling, pottery-making, milling etc., were usually to be found in one patch of the living area, often as part of a house. Fortifications were still considered a necessity. The dead were buried in cemeteries that lay outside the living area, usually on the roads leading out of town beyond the walls.

By the fifth century BC some major centres such as Corinth and Athens had grown into large cities; some estimates calculate the population of classical Athens at over a hundred thousand inhabitants. However, the vast majority of sites were still small. A helpful example of a modest settlement in the classical period is Olynthus in northern Greece (figure 23.6) (see chapter 24). In 432 BC it was enlarged and made a centre for the members of the Chalcidic League; Philip of Macedon destroyed it less than a century later (348 BC). The town stood on a hill encircled by a mud-brick wall on a stone foundation. The grid pattern of streets (on a north–south orientation, except in the southwest) had been a fairly standard feature of newly established Greek towns since the archaic period. The blocks of houses were divided by a narrow lane, making two rows of five houses. Rooms surrounded an open space with a colonnade and an upper storey; some houses boasted black-and-white pebble mosaics with figured scenes. Water was piped through an underground channel from seven miles away. On one estimate the town had room for about 15,000 inhabitants.

Through recent investigation of rural areas, the Greek countryside is now better understood. Besides the farms with their fields, orchards, vineyards and olive trees, threshing floors and presses, any territory might house small forts and look-out towers, and war memorials that marked the sites of battles (e.g. Marathon, Chaeronea). Sanctuaries are also found that were built at the borders of a state's land, to define the territory symbolically and to act as places where representatives from neighbouring territories could meet to discuss interstate matters in a sacred, safe context (see chapter 3).

Panhellenic sanctuaries at Olympia, Delphi, Nemea and Isthmia were established early and developed over the centuries; other major sanctuaries were organised and run by individual states. We may take Olympia (figure 23.7) as an example of a panhellenic sanctuary. Olympia comprised two areas: the sanctuary itself and the sports ground at the edge of it. The sanctuary contained the standard range of buildings and other structures: altars, temples, treasuries, fountain house, administrative buildings and colonnades, and a few that are particular to the site: the burial place of Pelops (the 'Pelopion') and a round temple known as the 'Philippeion', initiated by Philip of Macedon after the battle of Chaeronea in 338 BC. The sports ground was very slowly enlarged by new structures; initially the emphasis was on the

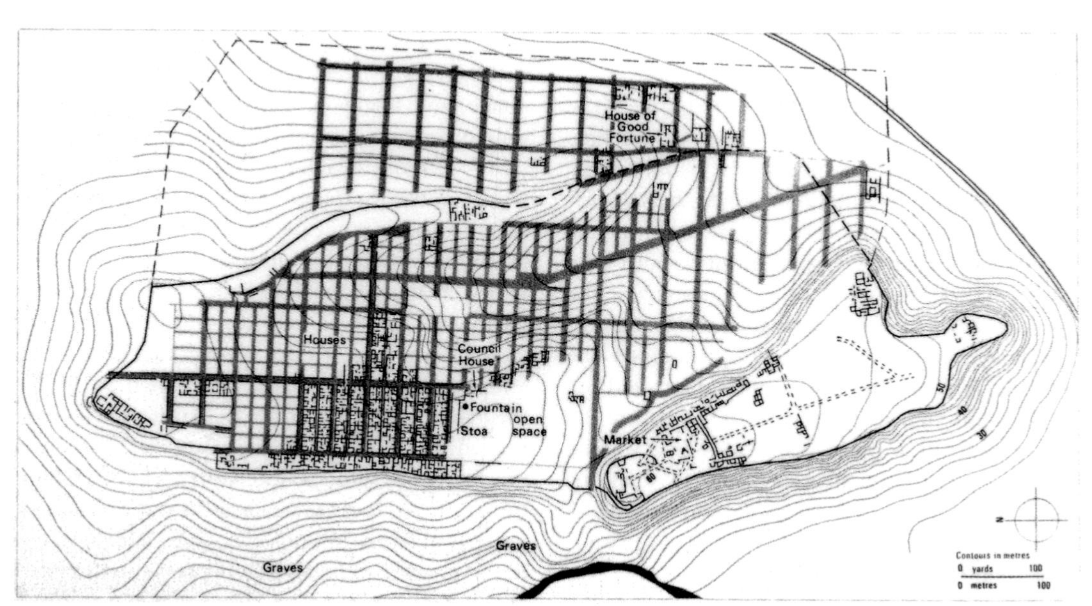

Fig. 23.6 Plan of Olynthus, northern Greece (adapted from Finley, *Atlas*, 174).

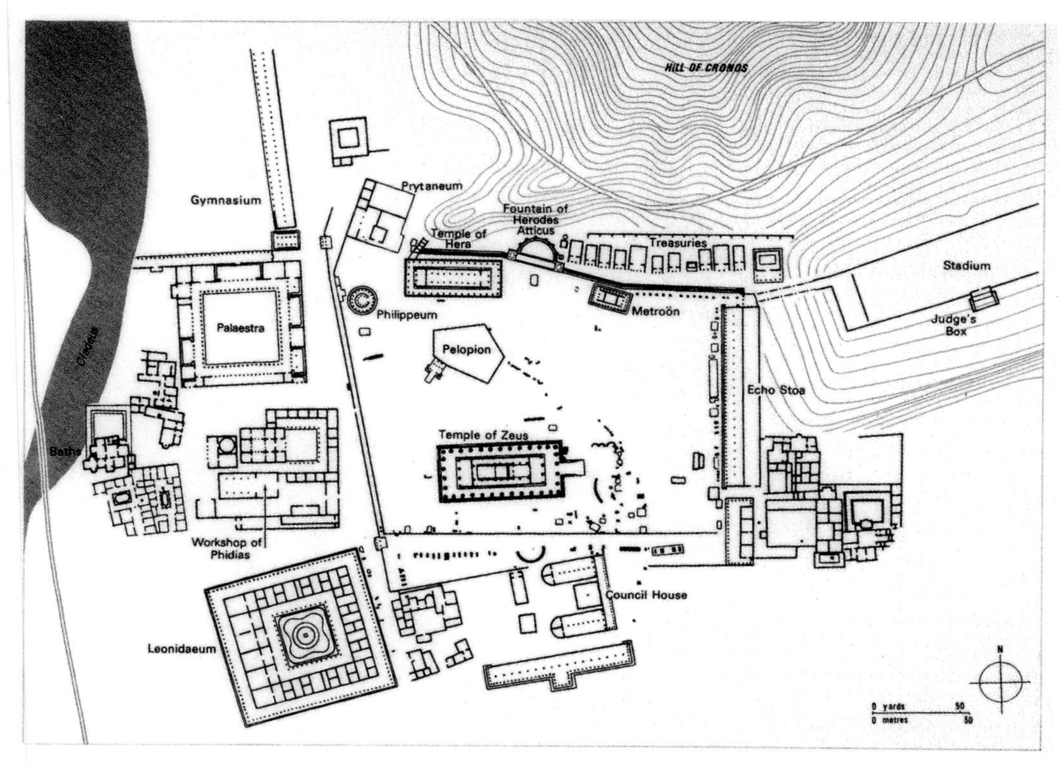

Fig. 23.7 Plan of Olympia, southern Greece (adapted from Finley, *Atlas*, 164).

stadium, and it was only later that amenities for the athletes (palaestra, gymnasium), and eventually for important visitors (the 'Leonidaeum', a sumptuous guesthouse), were put in place.

During the Hellenistic period (323–31 BC) political power was centralised, Graeco-Macedonian territory was extended, and wealth increased. The spread of Greek-based sites is mainly found in the East, following Alexander's successful campaigns against the Persian Empire. Many of the sites were military posts; some failed, others developed into thriving cities. Alexandria itself (founded in 331 BC) is the most outstanding success, with Antioch (founded 300 BC) not far behind, both numbering up to a quarter of a million inhabitants. Further east, excavations have given glimpses of the Hellenic character of both thriving and deserted sites. One of the latter is Aï Khanum (figure 23.8), situated north of Kabul at the confluence of the Amu Drya (the ancient Oxus) and Kokcha rivers in the northern region of Hellenistic Bactria (what is now Afghanistan). It was one of the furthest eastern outposts of Greek settlement (see chapter 24). Founded c. 300 BC, it may be one of Alexander's military settlements; it was overrun c. 140 BC by Yueh-Chi (the 'five tribes'). There is an acropolis and a plain alongside the Oxus where excavators unearthed, within a perimeter wall, Greek-style buildings, Corinthian columns, pebble mosaics, classical statuary and Greek inscriptions.

Of the capital cities that came into being during the Hellenistic period, the most spectacular today is Pergamum near the west coast of Asia Minor (figure 23.9). The site was of no consequence in the pre-Hellenistic period, but successive rulers of the Attalid dynasty spent lavishly on their city and attracted men of culture to their court. The city was built on the summit of a high, precipitous hill overlooking the Caicus valley. On the acropolis were the palace, temples, a library and an altar to Zeus, with a theatre built to take advantage of the steep slope. Lower down was a very large gymnasium on three levels and a market building. Water was piped by a

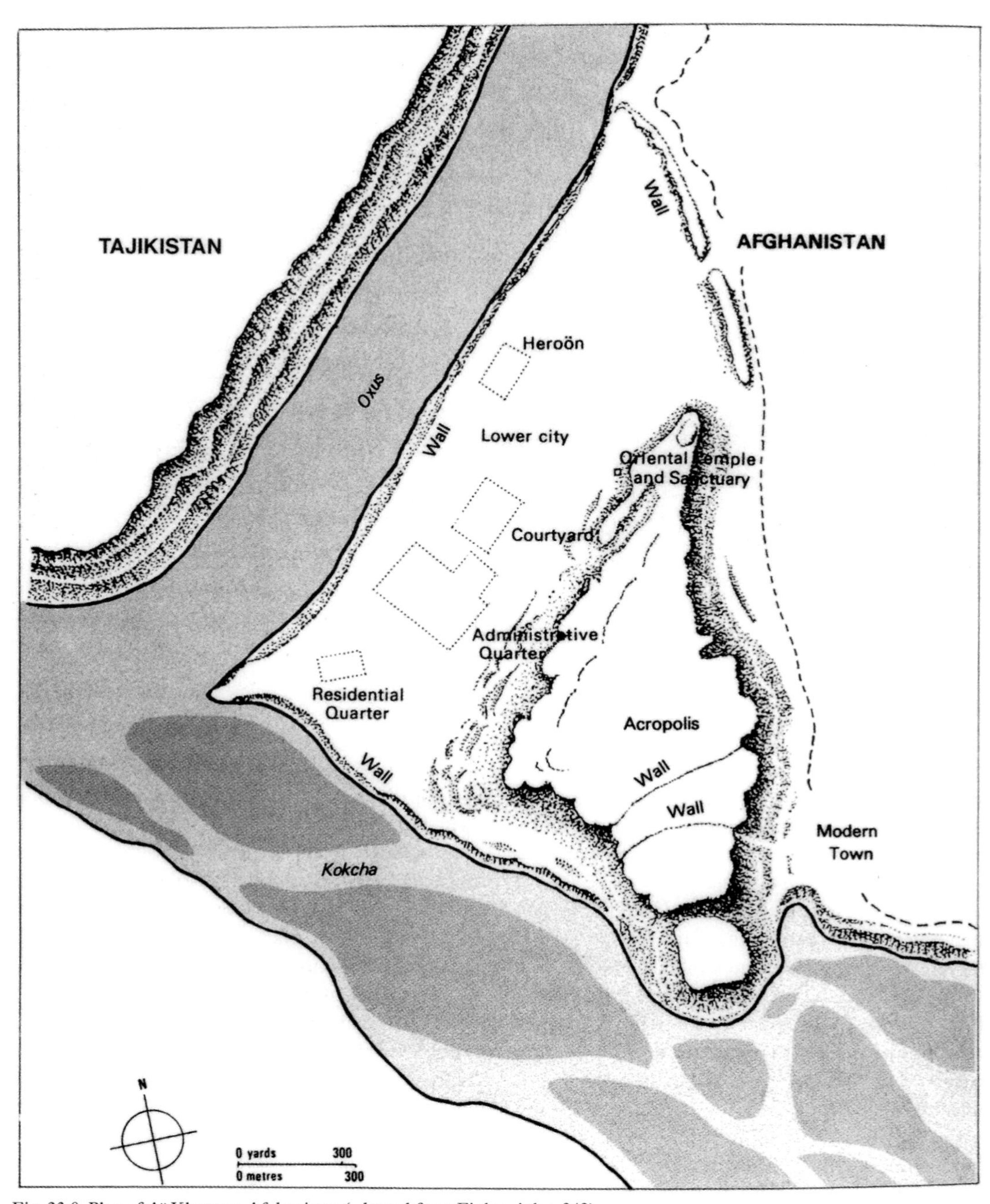

Fig. 23.8 Plan of Aï Khanum, Afghanistan (adapted from Finley, Atlas, 242).

Fig. 23.9 Model of Pergamum, Asia Minor.

high-pressure system from the nearby hills. The whole complex was a demonstration of the technical ability of the town-planner and the self-confidence of the rulers.

Rome and the provinces

The settlements in Italy that came under Roman domination shared some of the elements we have listed above as characteristic of Greek cities. There was often a defensible hill (*arx* or *capitolium*), a gathering ground (*forum*), colonnaded basilicas for use as law-courts, and *comitia* for political meetings. But there were other amenities that were not to be found in classical Greek cities. One such was the amphitheatre for spectator sports such as wild beast shows and gladiatorial combats; the Amphitheatrum Flavium ('Colosseum') is the best known. Another building that marks many Roman towns is the hot-baths; these were a major focus of Roman social life. Pompeii (figure 23.10), destroyed in the eruption of Vesuvius in AD 79, provides evidence for the layout of a small Italian town with a population of c. 12,000. Sulla refounded Pompeii as a Roman colony c. 80 BC. The original area can be recognised in the southwest, and the enlarged and more regularly planned area lies around it on a slightly different orientation. The town boasts the full complement of building types: forum with triumphal arch, temples, baths, basilica, brothels, theatres, palaestra, amphitheatre. The private houses ranged from large palatial mansions ('private luxury, public magnificence') to small apartments; the shops opened directly on to the streets, with bars serving hot and cold drinks and food (see chapter 28, figure 28.8). Gardens for pleasure and profit were a marked feature. Along the roads leading away from the town lay the cemeteries.

The countryside, both in the area of the bay of Naples and elsewhere, was dotted both with holiday villas of wealthy Romans and with working farmsteads. The imperial period saw the concentration of land into fewer, larger estates (sometimes called *latifundia*). Also in the country, at a higher social level, palaces were built such as Hadrian's Villa at Tivoli (ancient Tibur) outside

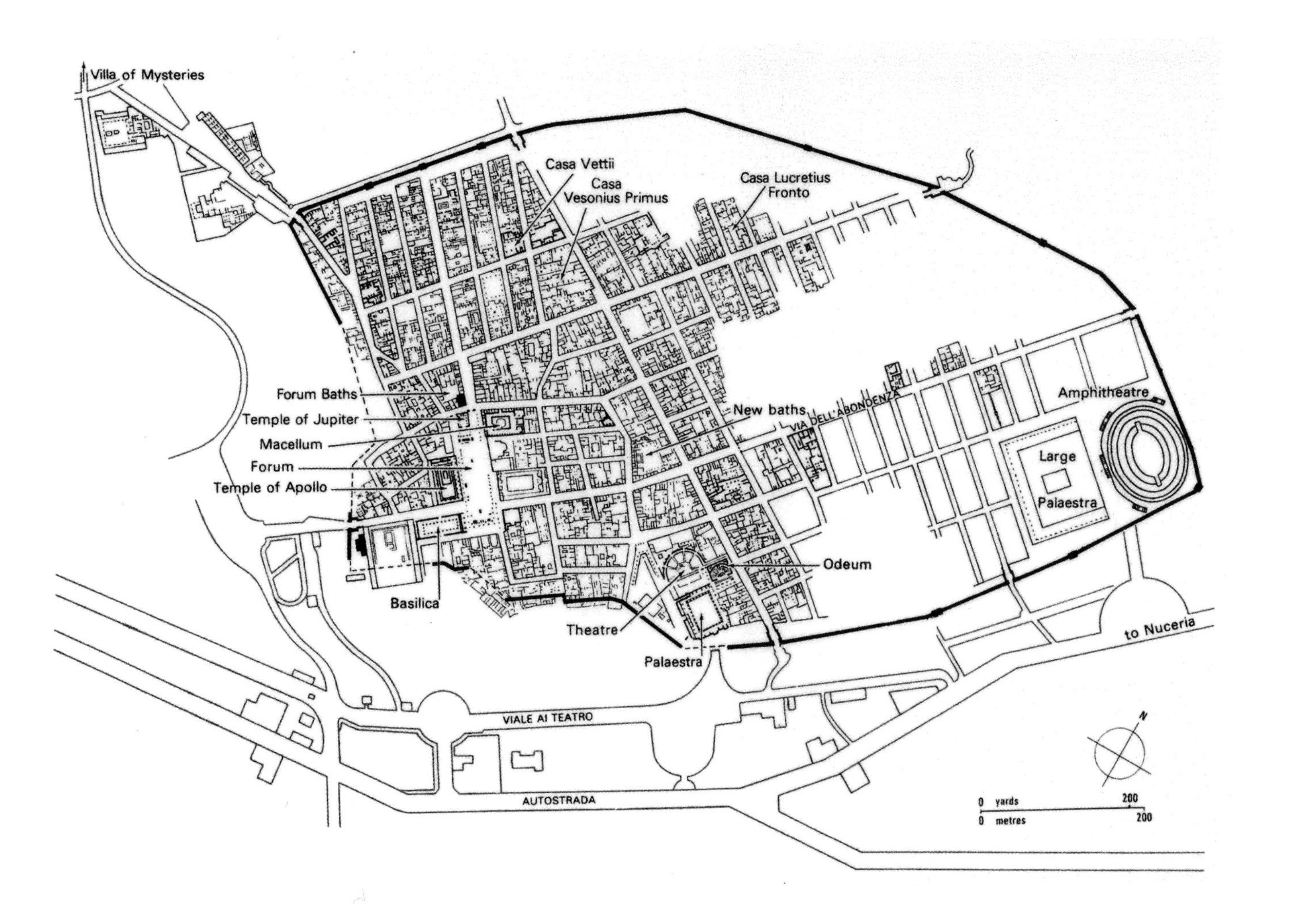

Fig. 23.10 Plan of Pompeii, Italy (adapted from Finley, *Atlas*, 127).

Rome (see chapter 29, figure 24.10), the imperial residence at Piazza Armerina in Sicily, Diocletian's palace at Spalatum (Split) and the Romano-British palace at Fishbourne.

In different areas of the empire famous victories were marked by the erection of monuments such as La Turbie above Monaco (to mark Augustus' victory over Alpine tribes in 15 BC), and memorials at Nicopolis (for Augustus' victory at Actium in 31 BC) and Adamklissi (southwest of Constanza, Romania), where a local monument was raised after AD 106 to commemorate Trajan's victory in the Dacian Wars, a small provincial counterpart to Trajan's Column in Rome.

Unlike the classical Greeks, the Romans had a standing army, and this necessitated the building of military forts and legionary fortresses to police the outlying provinces of the empire (e.g. Syria, North Africa, Spain, Germany and Britain). Some were temporary, others permanent, while some with the addition of civilian extra-mural settlements (*vici*) developed into well-established towns. The Roman leaders also had *coloniae* built to house their retired army veterans (cf. Arausio; see above), and many later towns developed from the original colonial foundation (e.g. Lin(dum) col(o)n(ia) became Lincoln). As an example of a successful *colonia* we may take Timgad (ancient Thamugadi) in Numidia (figure 23.11). In AD 100 on Trajan's orders this *colonia* was built 30 km east of Lambaesis, the site of the legionary fortress of the Legio III Augusta, and the legionaries carried out construction of the *colonia* on strictly military and rectilinear lines. Timgad was one of a series of foundations ranged east and west to act as a defensive line against attack from the south. Once again there were the major public buildings (forum, basilica, *curia* (local Senate house), theatre, temples, latrines etc.), and there were small blocks for housing and also industrial zones with bronze-foundries and pottery-shops as well as large-scale textile businesses that must have worked chiefly for export. Soon there was construction work outside the original rectangle, including a temple to the Capitoline triad (Jupiter, Juno and Minerva) and a vast bath building; these new buildings were not placed with the same regard to military order as the original plan. A few generations later (c. AD 200) the site was enlarged to four times its original size and new gateways were constructed at east and west.

Features

Besides the built environment, there were places and areas that attracted attention, worship and fear because of associations that had left them dangerous, numinous and liminal, no-go areas to be avoided or at least appeased (see chapter 21). Most were connected with the presence of gods or dead heroes, and some associations may have been triggered by the misunderstood ruins and remains from earlier periods. Caves and grottoes were linked to stories of divine assignations, births and the nursing of infants (e.g. the Dictaean Cave at Psychro on Crete, famed as the birthplace of Zeus); rivers, lakes and springs were a vital resource but held monsters or attractive nymphs who would lure the vulnerable young (e.g. Narcissus and Hylas) into their depths. Lonely, rocky places were the haunt of Pan, who could cause panic. There were also, in areas where the ground was unstable, earthquakes and volcanoes (Thera, Ischia, Etna, the Phlegraean Fields, Vesuvius) that exerted their terror and were linked to divine explanations such as defeated enemies of the Olympian gods that were struggling to emerge (Cyclopes, Typhon). Holes in the ground might lead to the Underworld (e.g. Pallene, Enna, Cumae). Forests hid wood nymphs, clefts in the rock were signs that Zeus had hurled his thunderbolt or Poseidon his trident. Rock formations were linked to myths such as Scylla and Charybdis (between Sicily and Italy), the Symplegades (the Clashing Rocks at the north end of the Bosphorus), or the petrified Niobe in sorrow (on Mt Sipylus, Lydia). There were few places without their holy or mythical associations.

Further reading

R. Buxton, *Imaginary Greece: The Contexts of Mythology*, Cambridge: Cambridge University Press, 1994 – looks at the landscape of mythological narrative.

O. A. W. Dilke, *The Roman Land Surveyors*, Newton Abbot: David and Charles, 1971 – a useful study that is packed with detailed research.

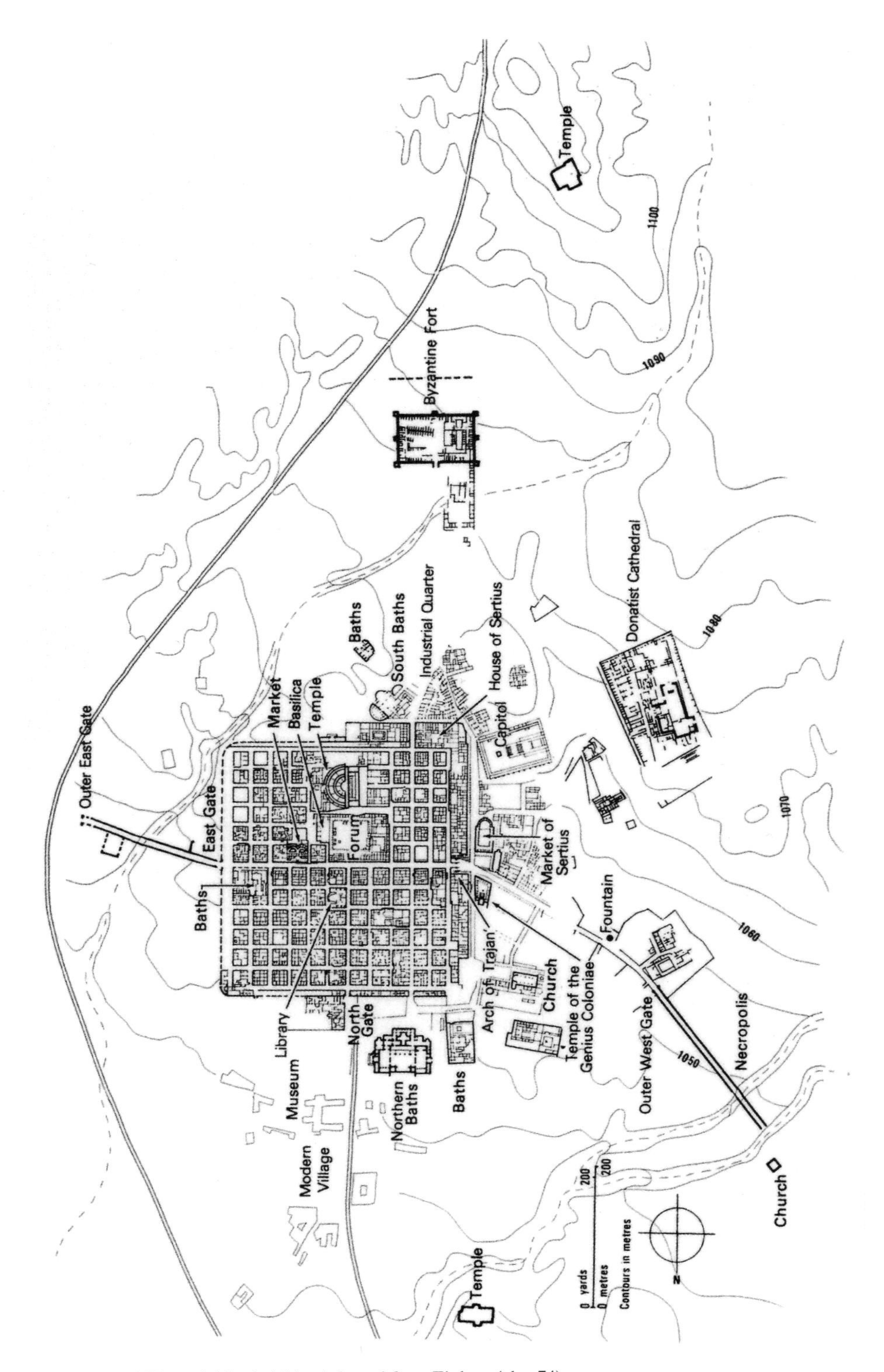

Fig. 23.11 Plan of Timgad, North Africa (adapted from Finley, *Atlas*, 74).

O. A. W. Dilke, *Greek and Roman Maps*, London: Thames and Hudson, 1985 – a well-arranged introduction to the subject.

M. Finley (ed.), *Atlas of Classical Archaeology*, London: Chatto and Windus, 1977 – a well-illustrated survey of some of the major classical sites.

P. Grimal, *Les Villes romaines* (2nd edn), Paris: Presses Universitaires de France, 1966 = *Roman Cities*, (trans. and ed. G. M. Woloch), Madison: University of Wisconsin Press, 1983 – a brief but well-documented study of some sites.

O. Murray and S. Price (eds), *The Greek City, from Homer to Alexander*, Oxford: Clarendon Press, 1990 – essays on the geography and institutions of the Greek city.

R. Osborne and S. Alcock (eds), *Placing the Gods: Sanctuaries and Sacred Spaces in Ancient Greece*, Oxford: Clarendon Press, 1994 – a variety of essays on locating sanctuaries.

E. J. Owens, *The City in the Greek and Roman World*, London and New York: Routledge, 1991 – a useful, straightforward account.

F. de Polignac, *La Naissance de la cité grecque*, Paris: La Découverte, 1984 = *Cults, Territory and the Origins of the Greek City-State*, trans. J. Lloyd, Chicago and London: University of Chicago Press, 1995 – a ground-breaking study of the siting of Greek sanctuaries.

T. W. Potter, *The Changing Landscape of South Etruria*, London: Elek, 1979 – an innovative historical survey of the area based on excavation and survey.

J. Rich and A. Wallace-Hadrill (eds), *City and Country in the Ancient World*, London and New York: Routledge, 1991 – pioneering essays on the relation between town and country.

R. Stillwell (ed.), *The Princeton Encyclopedia of Classical Sites*, Princeton: Princeton University Press, 1976 – a massive compilation.

J. B. Ward-Perkins, *Cities of Ancient Greece and Italy: Planning in Classical Antiquity*, London: Sidgwick and Jackson, 1974 – a useful compendium of city plans with a brief text.

24. *Buildings and Architecture*

Richard Tomlinson

The communities of the Greek and Roman world, whatever their size, existed within a built environment. Most buildings were traditional in form, in a vernacular style and using locally available materials. With the growth of wealth and power, significant structures employed more expensive materials and careful design, in which mere construction – building – was elevated into art – architecture. Building responds to practical needs, architecture to wealth, politics and (inevitably in the ancient world) religion.

Greece has an abundance of good-quality building stone, but this was not available in all localities. In Italy, the quality of local stone is more variable. The best stone was prized and often transported some distance where an important building was to be constructed, adding greatly to its cost. White marble, quarried in relatively few places, came to be particularly valued. Even in important buildings, size was restricted by the problem of roofing and supporting the heavy baked clay (or, in really important buildings, marble) tiles. This required heavy timbers, resting on the walls, with columns or posts as intermediate supports if a wider span was needed. In Greece, six metres is the general optimum span, rising to ten or twelve only in the greatest of temples, such as the Parthenon. This was improved in Roman buildings by developing more elaborate systems of woodwork.

Lime mortar was used from the earliest times (it was known in Bronze Age Greece) for plaster coatings, to disguise or protect cheap materials, such as unbaked brick, or to provide waterproofing when needed, for example in cisterns. The potential of mortar and cement was vastly improved by the Roman discovery of *pozzolana*, found at Puteoli (modern Pozzuoli), a natural cement powder formed by volcanic activity. This greatly reduced the cost of mortared work, and made possible solid, durable construction in mortar and rubble without the need for carefully and expensively quarried stone. It could also be used for roofing.

Most buildings received at least some decoration. The more important of the earliest temples on the Greek mainland, with walls of mud-brick and wooden columns, included in their wooden superstructures (entablatures) over the colonnades square panels of terracotta with painted figure decoration in the technique employed in vase-painting. In the sixth century BC these entablatures were translated into a stone form, the panels (metopes) alternating with rectangles decorated with vertical grooves (triglyphs) the origin of which is disputed, but which recall decorative patterns found also in ivory-work and painted vases of the preceding century. In the east Greek area continuous friezes were often given painted or carved figurative decoration, accompanied by mouldings whose patterns also seem to derive from the minor arts.

These systems rapidly developed into the standard forms of Greek architecture, 'the orders'. The mainland developed the system using friezes of metopes and triglyphs in their entablatures. As early as the fifth century BC this was called Doric, since in its stone form it was probably first created by the Dorian Greek cities of the Peloponnese, Corinth and Argos in particular. It is a misleading name, since it was also the traditional form in other mainland cities which were most certainly not Dorian, above all in Athens (figure 24.1). In the

Fig. 24.1 The Greek Doric order: the Parthenon, Athens, before the recent conservation work. Note the curved profile (entasis) of the columns (photo: © RAT).

east Greek area the alternative form (Ionic, though again it was also employed by non-Ionian cities) developed more slowly (figure 24.2), and displayed some regional variations: the frieze in some places consisted of a series of projecting rectangular blocks (dentils) rather than figure decoration, and it was not until the Hellenistic period that the standard form evolved, with dentils surmounting a continuous, often carved frieze. The columns also differed. Doric was sturdier, with plain, spreading capitals but no base, while Ionic was more slender, having moulded bases and elaborate capitals with linked volutes. In the Hellenistic age a third order of classical architecture, Corinthian, was developed (figure 24.3), with ornate acanthus-leaf capitals, which found particular favour in Roman architecture (figure 24.4).

Temples

These systems were employed in the temples of the gods, the most important structures in any city. Quality of design and workmanship were crucial, and depended on the responsible architects and craftsmen. The names of many Greek architects were recorded in the ancient literature, though fewer Roman; others are known from inscriptions. Craftsmen were infrequently named, unless they were individuals of artistic reputation. How designs were made is uncertain. Rather than making preliminary plans, design work was carried out on site and at full scale. For Greek buildings, particularly temples, this was made possible by the fact that the architect knew before he started what the building would look like, within the usual, defined types. The plan could be laid out on the ground with rope, and subdivided to give the required sizes of the constituent elements, column diameter, spacing and, in Doric, the width of the decorative parts of the frieze. Full-scale drawings (in the form of incisions on flat rock surfaces rather than ink on papyrus) or three-dimensional exemplars – *paradeigmata* – were made as templates for particular parts such as capitals, and the required detail translated in situ to the building stone.

Fig. 24.2 The Greek Ionic order: temple of Nike at the entrance to the Athenian Acropolis, as restored, before the present dismantling (photo: © RAT).

Equally important is the development of mathematics. Measurement, ratios and geometry all have vital contributions to make to the increasingly sophisticated architectural drawings (see chapter 54). By the Hellenistic period the concept of scale drawing – but still incised in stone – had evolved. At the temple of Apollo, at Didyma, near Miletus, a drawing showing how to mark out the curving profile (entasis) of its enormous columns was incised on one of the temple walls, using full size for the horizontal measurements but a scale of 1:16 (one dactyl to the foot) to show the vertical separation. In Roman times the development of more complex plans and the rise of more curvilinear layouts show that preliminary planning on papyrus by ruler and compass was carried out.

Until then evolution of design was slow, handed on from one generation to the next, rather than by the sudden introduction of revolutionary concepts. The influences on Roman temple architecture, and the forms the temples took, are more varied. The Romans themselves attributed their earliest temples to the time when

Fig. 24.3 The Corinthian order: temple of Olympian Zeus, Athens. Hellenistic, completed by the Roman Emperor Hadrian (photo: Félix Bonfils, c. 1870).

Fig. 24.4 The Maison Carrée, Nîmes. Typical Roman Corinthian podium temple, essentially of metropolitan Roman design, but built in local hard limestone rather than white marble (photo: © RAT).

they were ruled by Etruscan kings – the Etruscan temple of Jupiter Capitolinus survived until it was destroyed by fire in the Sullan civil war (83 BC). Etruscan temples, though influenced by the early Greek temples of southern Italy, stood on high podia approached from the front alone, with wooden columns supporting heavy terracotta tile roofs. As in Greece, their early forms were eventually translated into stone construction, but retaining local peculiarities – the primary importance of the front, the podia and roofs which were pitched more steeply than on developed Greek temples. The emergence of Rome as a Mediterranean power, ruler of the Hellenistic East, created a desire to emulate Hellenistic architectural form, and there is an influx of Hellenistic concepts, the use of Ionic and, above all, Corinthian orders, and the importation of white marble. Whatever other revolutionary methods of construction and design evolved in imperial times, Roman temples still retained much the same forms as their predecessors, for reasons of religious conservatism.

Houses I

The earliest houses of the Greek and Roman communities were of the simplest types. A good example is the hillside settlement at (modern) Emporio on Chios, where the houses are small huts. A more developed stage is represented by another small settlement at (modern) Lathouresa in Attica. Here the houses consist of collections of hut-like rooms grouped round central open spaces or courtyards. These early house types illustrate the two basic principles of design found in the buildings of classical Greece: the first, free-standing buildings whose architectural development is concentrated on their exteriors; the second, buildings arranged round a central space, where the architectural interest is in the interior, and inward looking.

Early building in Italy appears to show the same distinctions. The earliest structure at Rome (which was carefully preserved and renewed) was a simple wooden framed hut, the so-called House of Romulus, similar to the hut-like forms used for the ash-urns of contemporary cremation burials. Such huts were soon superseded by the Italic variation of the courtyard house, where the central space has become the specialised (but still centrally open-roofed) atrium.

Specialised structures

As the early communities developed into cities with larger populations, their architectural requirements became more complex. The first call on their available wealth remained the temples, but with a growing need for other, more secular specialised structures; these too became architecture, and the architectural forms evolved for the temples were naturally transferred to them.

For these, the most important single architectural element is the extended colonnade. Small temples employed columns only in their fore-porches, but larger temples were soon surrounded by colonnades. From these it is a logical development to extend colonnades along walls that delimit, whether partially or completely, defined open spaces, whether courtyards, sanctuaries of the gods, or the areas used for political and commercial purposes by the citizens. These porticoes (*stoa*, pl. *stoai*, is the Greek term) are first found providing shelter at religious sanctuaries such as that of Hera at Samos and then extended into the civic sphere.

Such colonnades do not merely line walls or boundaries. From the fifth century BC, in Athens and elsewhere, they were being constructed with rooms, or series of rooms, behind them, to which they provided a convenient covered anterior space (figure 24.5). Such rooms could be put to a variety of purposes such as law-courts, record offices and shops. In the Agora at Athens the South Stoa, built at the end of the fifth century, with stone colonnades but mud-brick walls, had a series of rooms laid out for formal feasting in the Greek manner, reclining on couches. (Similarly arranged rooms are also found in private houses.)

Fig. 24.5 North wing of the stoa at the Sanctuary of Artemis, Brauron, in Attica. End of fifth century BC. This fronted a series of formal dining rooms. Local limestone, with Pentelic marble metopes. Three metopes and triglyphs to each bay (contrast with the Doric temples, fig. 24.1) (photo: © RAT).

The largest stoas are quite complex, with two or even three or more floors, and sets rather than single rooms behind, while the colonnades are often double, with exterior and interior rows, the inner being Ionic, taller and more widely spaced than the exterior Doric, to support the ridge of the roof.

In Roman architecture this leads to a distinctive building type, the basilica, a colonnaded hall, usually situated in the forum, and designed either as a free-standing building or incorporated into a system of courtyard colonnades. The name may reflect the Royal Stoas (*Basilikai Stoai*) of the Hellenistic monarchies. The buildings are rectangular, with external walls and internal colonnades, usually two, occasionally more, forming a nave and two aisles, to use the architectural terminology of the Christian churches which derive from them. They serve as law-courts, with the tribunal or platform for the presiding magistrate at one end, but also as places of commerce and finance.

All these structures greatly increase the monumentality of a Greek or Roman city, with many more buildings of architectural quality, but built more cheaply. Local materials were preferred to expensive imports. The workmanship was less careful and precise. In the Greek cities, the Doric order is inevitably preferred to the more expensive Ionic, even where Ionic is normally used for temples, while the stone is of poorer quality. There are other economies. Columns are more widely spaced, entablatures correspondingly lower, all requiring less work and materials. In the Roman period, where competitiveness between cities led to greater expenditure on building – mostly funded by wealthy landowners rather than the community – Corinthian is used extensively, probably following on from Hellenistic precedent at Alexandria (the best-preserved Hellenistic examples are – or were, until the Soviet invasion of 1979 – at Aï Khanum in Afghanistan, the ancient Bactria; see chapter 23). In the West, though, the simplified Roman Doric column is more usual. It is this extension of architecture, as opposed to vernacular building, which gives the developed classical cities their essential form.

Increasingly, other specialised buildings were needed. By the time of the democracies in the classical Greek cities, such as Athens, political meeting places were given a degree of monumentality, with closed, roofed buildings for the councils (where attendance was limited, and privacy required) and open-air seated spaces for citizen assemblies. The development of drama, in whatever form, similarly required seated space for the larger numbers that attended religious festivals in which drama played a part, and these became the monumental open-air theatres, first perhaps with wooden seating, subsequently, and expensively, stone, with permanent buildings for the performances (figures 24.6 and 24.7). These, too, could be used for political gatherings of the citizen body. An extension of this concept is found in the specialised structures – stadia – for athletic contests, and the hippodromes for horse racing.

Houses II

With the general improvement in architectural quality in the public buildings of the Greek cities, it was inevitable that domestic architecture also improved, particularly with the increase in personal wealth, in at least some sections of society, resulting from the extension of Greek influence into the areas conquered by Alexander the Great. In the classical cities, vernacular forms were maintained for the ordinary houses. Walls were still normally of mud-brick or ordinary, unworked field stone. But plans were more regular, though dependent on the size and shape of the available building plot, and roofs were tiled, at least in the mainland cities (the islands continued to use flat roofs of clay on timbering). Rural houses, when the shape of the plan was not constrained by neighbouring properties, tended to be regular and rectangular in layout; and throughout, even from the archaic period, when new cities were founded in new localities, square or near-square plots were carefully demarcated for each house, resulting in the repetition of standard plans – invariably round a courtyard – and standard dimensions. Examples survive in fourth-century Olynthus (see chapter 23), and have been postulated elsewhere, for example in fifth-century Piraeus. Such forms are normal in the new cities of the Hellenistic world.

Fig. 24.6 Seating (more than a semicircle) and circular orchestra, theatre at the Sanctuary of Asklepios, Epidauros. Late fourth/third century BC. The columnar link (restored) to the ruined stage building on the left is a later addition (photo: © RAT).

Fig. 24.7 Roman theatre at Bostra, Syria. Local black stone with white marble decoration to the stage building (largely restored). Well preserved because it was incorporated into a medieval castle (Photo: © RAT).

In the classical Greek cities the houses, whether regular or irregular in layout, were generally modest in dimensions. House plots at Olynthus are around 250 square metres, and elsewhere (Delos, Priene) sizes are similar (see chapter 23, fig. 23.6). At Pella, however, houses of much greater dimensions have been excavated (the 'House of Dionysus' covering 3,160 square metres, the 'House of the Abduction of Helen' at 2,350 square metres); the palace of the Macedonian kings there is even vaster, of course. By the fourth century, the houses at Olynthus were given internal decoration. The walls were plastered and painted with bands of colour, the floors of important rooms where guests were entertained to dinner were decorated with mosaic made out of coloured pebbles. The Pella houses were far more magnificent, though details of the wall decoration are uncertain. Their courtyards, though, had stone colonnades in the Doric or Ionic order, and far more of the floors were given mosaics, on an altogether grander scale than those found in the houses at Olynthus. Such magnificence is carried to even greater lengths in the palace at Vergina (ancient Aegae); that at Pella itself is less well preserved. Elsewhere, Hellenistic houses tend to be more solidly built and lavishly decorated than their classical predecessors. Those on the island of Delos frequently have stone colonnaded courtyards and mosaics (now made of tesserae, cut pieces of coloured stone), while their walls, though constructed of untrimmed stone, have this relatively cheap material concealed under plaster with mouldings and lavish paintwork (see chapter 27).

Single-storey courtyard houses were wasteful of ground space. In most cities, built on non-agricultural land, this did not matter, but the emergence in Hellenistic times of ultra-large cities such as Alexandria, and, later, Rome, made denser housing more necessary (see chapter 67, map 9). This was achieved by building multi-storey tenements, some with internal light wells, but many with outward-looking windows to give air and light. They were built of stone, or, in Rome, more often of timber frames with timber flooring – highly inflammable, these were the practical cause of the great Neronian fire at Rome in AD 64. Eventually, brick-faced concrete for the walls and concrete floors brought greater safety.

However, the Greek courtyard houses demonstrate an increasing tendency to concentrate architectural interest on the interiors rather than on the exteriors of buildings. This is continued in Roman and Italian building. Roman temples remained outwardly conservative in form. External architectural interest still concentrated on the facades, the front colonnades above the stepped approach to their high podia. More complex systems of woodwork were developed, though, to support the roofs, allowing a wider uninterrupted interior space. The decoration of this space became more important, and the treatment of the wall surfaces more elaborate, often with systems of engaged colonnades and related architectural forms (figure 24.8).

Concrete and Baths

The development of concrete techniques enhanced this architectural movement. While timber construction remained the prestigious form for the roofs of temples and basilicas, the potential of concrete vaulting was to have revolutionary consequences for other, less conservative structures, both for roofs and for supporting substructures, as in Roman theatres. Nowhere is this more apparent than in the great bath buildings, or *thermae*, developed in Rome in the first two centuries AD. The bath buildings were social centres, providing accommodation for lounging and relaxation, as much as for the complex sequence, cold to warm to hot and back to cold again, of the actual bathing. The buildings and the water had to be heated, with furnaces providing hot air which was ducted under and through the structures, and it was concrete which provided the required safety and durability in the presence of fire and damp. Within a relatively short period, perhaps some fifty years during the first century BC at the most, technical developments made it possible to construct concrete vaults for far greater widths than any timber roof, and the resulting unobstructed space within the building made it inevitable that architectural interest would be concentrated on that.

For these buildings, architecture involved two aspects: the technique and expertise in planning and forming the concrete walls and roofs, and the application of decorative schemes to the surfaces of the walls and ceilings. The exteriors were generally left with the brickwork visible, usually combined with occasional courses of stone to break up the monotony of the vertical surfaces, otherwise punctuated only by decorative door- and window-frames. Inside, various systems were employed and combined into elaborate decoration. Hellenistic architects, particularly, it would seem, those working in Alexandria, had developed a system of fixing to walls built of more ordinary materials thin sheets of finely cut and polished stone of varying colours and patterns. This system was taken over by Roman architects to adorn concrete walls and hide their basic construction. Other methods were also used. Though ceilings no longer needed interior columns to support them, decorative columns or half-columns would be placed against the walls, giving the appearance of holding up the roof. The vaulted ceilings would be decorated with complex coffer patterns, moulded into them.

Thus even more than in the conventional temples, the architectural interest was concentrated on the interiors, on the decoration and form of interior spaces. Three examples typify this. The *thermae*, such as the baths of Caracalla and those of Diocletian, conform to a developed and symmetrical ground plan, whose central feature was the great cool room, the *frigidarium*, a vast vaulted hall, a magnificently decorated place of congregation,

Fig. 24.8 House of Amor and Psyche, Ostia. Marble veneer on brick- and stone-faced concrete walls, *opus sectile* floor (photo: © G. Lloyd Morgan).

Fig. 24.9 The baths of Diocletian, Rome. The exterior of the upper part of the great central hall is at the right (photo: © RAT).

with cold pools at either end, and openings in the sides leading to other facilities, the swimming pool to one side, the suite of warmer rooms to the other (figure 24.9). A second example can be found in the great, rambling country house that Hadrian had built for himself at Tibur (near modern Tivoli). This was set in carefully laid-out gardens, but the architectural interest, apart from some re-creation of earlier, even Greek forms, was concentrated on the interiors of the various halls and dining pavilions. Curvilinear plans abound. One dining structure has a vaulted inner hall, opening at the sides onto unroofed spaces with an alternation of shade and light, filled with works of art, sculpture and, almost certainly, plants. Another pavilion, with sinuous lines of wall and colonnaded openings, was surrounded by a circular moat, cooling and reflecting light (figure 24.10).

The third example, the acme of this architecture, is the Pantheon (figure 24.11), the temple dedicated to all the gods, originally built by Agrippa (whose dedication was kept over the front porch) but rebuilt for Hadrian. Externally this has much of traditional form. There was a colonnaded forecourt, with, at one end, the temple porch above its flight of steps, a façade of eight granite Corinthian columns 50 Roman feet in height (but originally intended to be 60 feet). So far, conventional enough, and probably echoing Agrippa's original structure. But on passing through the porch the visitor entered a different world – a huge circular room, 150 Roman feet in diameter, covered with a single dome, apparently resting on a wall which was in fact a sequence of concrete piers with columnar screens between them. The vertical surfaces were decorated with applied veneers of coloured stone, niches and pilasters in the lower storey, a series of imitation window openings in the upper (replaced in the eighteenth century by a different scheme). At the centre of the dome is a circular opening which is the sole actual source of light. Its architect is unknown, despite guesses that it was Apollodorus, architect of Trajan's forum and baths. Whoever it was, he was a master of construction technique, a designer of high mathematical sophistication, comparable to Ictinus at the Athenian Parthenon. If his name is lost, his achievement survives.

Fig. 24.10 The island dining pavilion ('Maritima') at Hadrian's Villa, Tivoli. Set in a circular moat, with curving colonnades and walls defining open spaces (photo: © RAT).

Fig. 24.11 The Pantheon, interior, with crowds showing the scale of the structure. Veneered wall decoration (the restored original upper storey visible to the right) (photo: © RAT).

Further reading

J-P. Adam, *Roman Building: Materials and Techniques*, London: Batsford, 1994 (translation of *La Construction Romaine*, Paris, 1989) – detailed, well-illustrated study, covering all aspects of construction.

A. Boethius, *Etruscan and Early Roman Architecture* (Pelican History of Art), New Haven and London: Yale University Press, 1994 – comprehensive account of surviving evidence, with full bibliography.

P. Connolly and H. Dodge, *The Ancient City: Life in Classical Athens and Rome*, Oxford: Oxford University Press, 1998 – good reconstructions of the buildings, appearance and conditions in the two major ancient cities.

J. J. Coulton, *Greek Architects at Work*, London: Paul Elek, 1977 – an analysis of the practical approaches to design and construction.

W. Hoepfner and W-L. Schwandner, *Haus und Stadt im Klassischen Griechenland* (2nd edn), Munich: Deutscher Kunstverlag, 1994 – detailed accounts of the arrangement of selected Greek cities, with full plans.

A. W. Lawrence, *Greek Architecture* (5th edn), rev. R. A. Tomlinson (Pelican History of Art), New Haven and London: Yale University Press, 1996 – comprehensive account, including prehistoric, with updated bibliography.

R. A. Tomlinson, *Greek and Roman Architecture*, London: British Museum Press, 1995 – general overview, including Hellenistic continuity into Roman times.

J. B. Ward-Perkins, *Roman Imperial Architecture* (Pelican History of Art), Harmondsworth: Penguin, 1989 – comprehensive account of building during the Roman Empire, in Rome and Italy and in the individual provincial regions.

M. Wilson Jones, *Principles of Roman Architecture*, New Haven and London: Yale University Press, 2000 – discusses how Roman buildings were designed; excellent bibliography.

R. E. Wycherley, *How the Greeks Built Cities* (2nd edn), New York and London: W. W. Norton 1976 (1st edn, London: Macmillan, 1962) – an analysis of the layout of Greek cities and building types.

25. Coinage

Jonathan Williams and Andrew Meadows

Because of its apparent familiarity coinage is prone to trip up the historian of the ancient world who would use it as a source. Ancient coinage is different to modern coinage in its methods of manufacture, in the organisation of that manufacture and in its behaviour once in circulation. These facts require methodological sophistication in the handling of ancient numismatic material, but at the same time create a fertile ground for historical inquiry.

Ancient coinage was hand-made in two senses. The dies from which coins were struck were hand engraved, often by craftsmen of considerable skill. The process of striking was also carried out by hand (figure 25.1). A blank piece of metal was placed on the anvil (obverse) die, a punch (reverse) die was placed on top of the blank and hit hard with a hammer. But for all the labour that went into the creation of an ancient coin, coinage is a rare incidence of mass production in the ancient world. Just one worker could produce thousands of coins in a working day. Indeed, vast numbers of coins were produced in antiquity and millions of them still survive today, either in collections around the world or in the ground still waiting to be discovered. Ancient coinage is a large and potent body of evidence.

The rationale behind the production of ancient coinage is not always easy to deduce. Much of the large-scale minting from antiquity can convincingly be linked with periods of crisis and heavy expenditure on the parts of the issuing bodies. Many Greek states went for long periods without issuing coins. It is clear that in general coinage was produced to facilitate the making of payments on a large scale by the issuing body. When such payments were not being made, coinage was not produced. There was, in any case, no concept in the ancient world of a 'money supply' that needed to be maintained or that could be manipulated to economic effect (see chapter 5).

Once it had entered circulation coinage did create a supply of money that could be used in a number of economic and social spheres, but several aspects of the nature of ancient coinage guarantee that it could not behave in the same way as modern coinage. Ancient coinage was made either of precious metal (electrum, gold or, most often, silver) or of base metal (generally bronze or brass). Precious metal coinage took its value from its weight, and while at certain times and in certain places coins were produced that were small enough to act as a form of small change, the overwhelming majority of precious metal coinage produced in

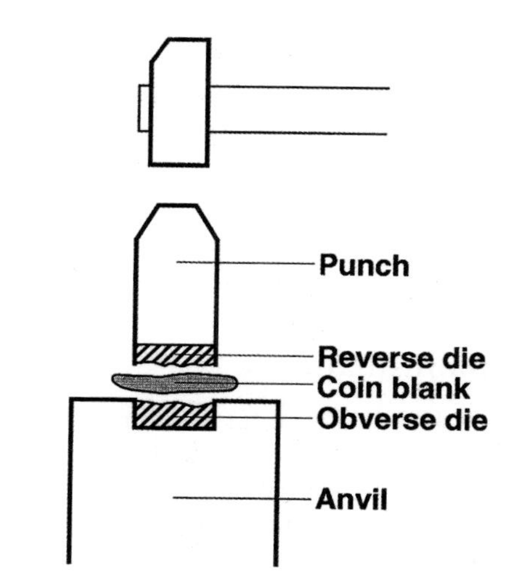

Fig. 25.1 Hand-striking a coin.

Fig. 25.2 Three obols of Athens from the fifth century BC. The Athenian denominational system was exceptional, well supplied with fractional coinage. Diams 7 mm (BMC 104, 99 and CM 1949-4-44-461; © London, British Museum).

antiquity had the value of a day's wages or more for the average worker (figure 25.2). Such coinage could not by itself facilitate the working of a market economy at the level we experience today. Base metal coinage was rare before the Hellenistic period, and before the Roman Empire was essentially a local phenomenon, providing the means for low-level transactions only within individual cities. It was perhaps not until the third century AD that a substantial quantity of low-value coinage was produced to fulfil the needs of the Roman Empire for small change. It is necessary also to be aware that coinage as a form of money could find itself utilised in the same contexts as other non- or pre-coin monetary objects, such as ritual deposits, that do not conform to our expectations of monetary behaviour.

The study of ancient coinage can be divided into a number of different categories.

Pure numismatics

The principal challenge for numismatists is the basic ordering of the material. Essentially this occurs at two levels. At the higher level much effort has been expended to create overviews of minting activity across geographical areas and time by the creation of corpora of types of coinage. For Rome the standard works are Crawford's *Roman Republican Coinage* (*RRC*) and for the empire Mattingly et al., *Roman Imperial Coinage* (*RIC*). There is no modern equivalent in the field of Greek coinage. For the Greek mints of the imperial period *Roman Provincial Coinage* (publication ongoing) will provide complete coverage. At the lower level numismatic study concentrates on the activity of individual mints. The classic reconstruction of such activity comes in the form of a die-study. This consists of an attempt to identify every die used by a mint to strike coinage, to arrange the dies in a relative chronological sequence and to provide an absolute chronology for the period of production. The relative chronology emerges from detailed study of the dies and the fact that obverse and reverse dies had different lifespans. By reconstructing the use of obverse dies against reverse dies, it is possible to establish a sequence of die-links (figure 25.3).

Absolute chronology may be ascertained in a number of ways. Dates may be derived from external historical sources (e.g. city foundation dates or regnal years; see chapter 64) to provide fixed points for the beginnings or ends of die-sequences for certain coinages. The majority of Greek coinages are not so well keyed into the historical record, however, and must be dated by relation to the few

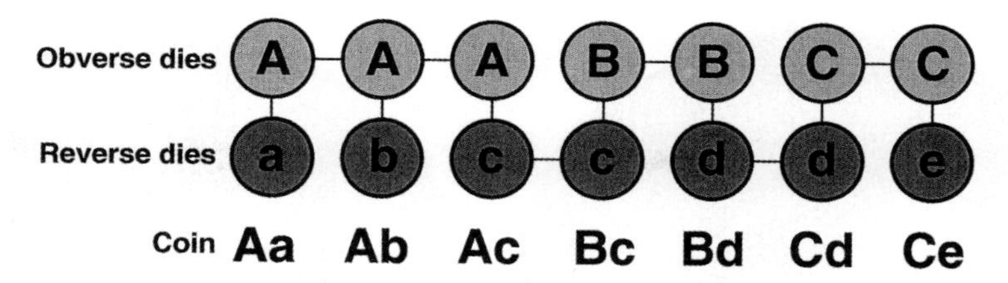

Fig. 25.3 Constructing a die-study.

whose chronology is more secure. The principal methods for the establishment of relationships between different mints are stylistic comparison and hoard evidence. Style of coins is often a reasonable guide to relative chronology, whether it be the artistic style of the die-engraver, or the style of workmanship that went into the physical manufacture of the coinage (e.g. preparation of blanks), but does not permit high degrees of accuracy. Hoard evidence is potentially far more powerful. Hoards are collections of coins taken out of circulation in antiquity and secreted, generally with a view to recovery. In many cases, though not all, hoards will therefore provide a 'snapshot' of coins from different mints that were in circulation at one point in time. From such snapshots, a picture of the chronologies of different mints relative to each other can be generated. The more hoards that are known, the more precise the chronology may become. For much of archaic and classical Greek coinage it is currently possible to establish dates by these means that are precise to within a decade or so.

The ancient economy

The various methods developed by numismatists to study coinage also have potential value in efforts to reconstruct the position of coinage within the ancient economy (see chapter 5). The die-study can provide quantification of the coinage produced by a particular state, at least in terms of the number of dies used. If the number of coins struck from a die can be estimated, then potentially the quantity in terms of value of coinage produced can be calculated. In practice, the number of coins that could be struck from a die was probably subject to variation from time to time and from place to place. None the less, broad estimates are possible of the amount of coinage produced by well-studied mints at certain periods. They tend to suggest that new coinage formed a relatively small element in state expenditure. At Rhodes, in the fourth century BC, for example, there was not enough new coin produced in a year to maintain the harbours (figure 25.4). We may infer that much state expenditure took place in old coin recovered through taxes and other payments back to the state.

There is a certain amount to be gleaned about levels of monetisation from studies of ancient mints too. The extent to which cities produced coinage of low enough value for use in small-scale transactions has been a matter for debate. To settle such disputes it is necessary to have a clear view of the whole production of a given state or mint, to determine the overall amounts of coinage minted at different denominations.

The collection of hoard evidence not only allows greater precision in the dating of coinages, but also provides valuable evidence for patterns of circulation of coinage in antiquity. The spread of the Roman coinage across the Mediterranean and into continental Europe during the late republic and the early imperial period can be charted through the coin-hoard record. Coin hoards from the fringes of the Greek world in the fifth century BC, on the other hand, contain a large number of chopped-up silver coins circulating alongside bullion. In these cases the hoards attest not to a spread of the use of coinage, but rather to its return to bullion status.

Scientific analysis of the metal-contents of ancient coins together with patterns of hoarding also have much to tell about the fluctuations in money supply, particularly within the Roman

Fig. 25.4 A silver tetradrachm of Rhodes of the fourth century BC, with Helios on the obverse and a rose on the reverse. Diam. 22 mm (BMC 16; © London, British Museum).

Empire. Patterns of debasement in the Roman coinage from the first century AD onwards (figure 25.5) may be combined with other testimonia such as levels of wages or prices of goods for changes in the economy of the empire. The reactions of the users of coin to such changes in precious metal emerge also from the hoards, as better-quality coins disappeared from circulation or coins withdrawn from use appear more frequently in unrecovered hoards.

Coins and authority

Coins attest to the military and political history of antiquity in at least two important ways. First, they are themselves the material consequences of political decisions to issue coin on the part of cities, empires and other kinds of community. Coins do not happen by accident. Second, coins and their designs can provide important information on historical events, and on the structures and 'culture' of politics and identity among the groups that issued and used them.

In the city-state culture of the Graeco-Roman ancient Mediterranean, coins were a publicly authorised financial instrument. Their production and circulation were sanctioned and regulated by legal authority. The source of this authority was commonly identified in coin legends. In the Greek city-state, this was mostly expressed as the community of citizens (see chapter 16). Their ethnic name would be inscribed, either abbreviated or in full, in the grammatical form denoting possession, stating that the coin was one 'of the Rhodians', say, and implying that they as a body were the issuing authority (see figure 25.4 above). The later kings of the Hellenistic period similarly expressed their authority over the coinage by imposing their personal names on it in the same form. All the coins in the name of Alexander the Great identify themselves as 'Alexander's' (figure 25.6). Royal authority succeeded to civic (see chapter 17).

The Roman emperors, by contrast, refrained from identifying themselves as the legal owners or issuers of the Roman coinage. Their names were simply written out in the form identifying them as the subject of the imperial portrait on the front (figure 25.7). However absolute a Roman emperor's rule, in theory – and the theory was important – the Roman state remained a republic, and the coinage was issued for and in the name of the Roman people, not the emperor. The official term for what we call the Roman imperial coinage was 'the money

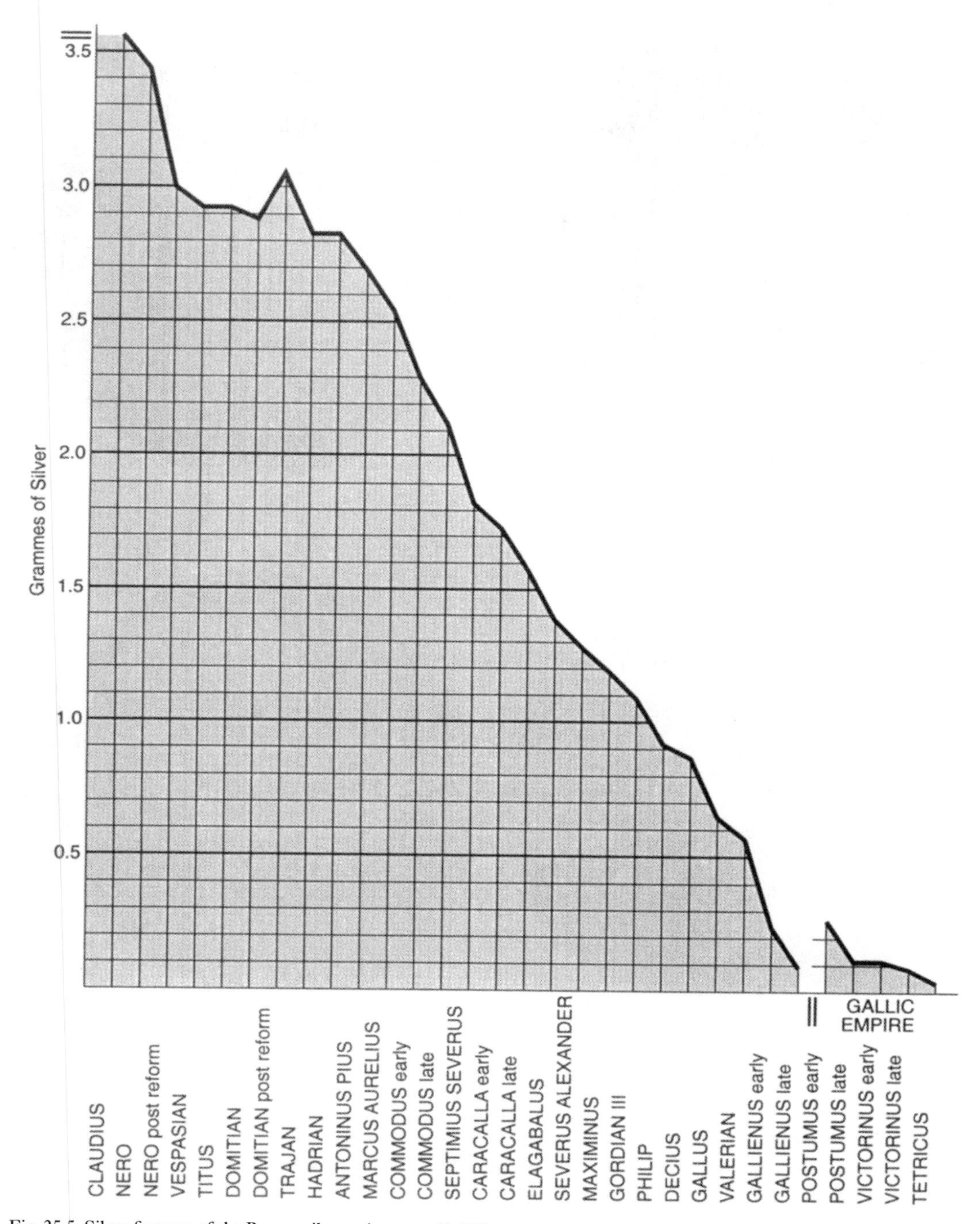

Fig. 25.5 Silver fineness of the Roman silver coinage AD 43–273.

Fig. 25.6 A silver tetradrachm of Alexander the Great (336–323 BC), minted in Macedonia. The obverse has a portrait of Herakles, the reverse the seated figure of Zeus. Diam. 24 mm (BMC 4f; © London, British Museum).

Fig. 25.7 Silver denarius of Augustus with the obverse inscription in the nominative, CAESAR AVGVSTVS. Diam. 21 mm (BMC Augustus 32; © London, British Museum).

struck with the public type of the Roman people', exactly what it had been under the republic.

The issuing of coin was the responsibility of different officials in different cities. Often these magistrates put their names and, in the case of late republican Rome, their family emblems on the coins they produced (figure 25.8). Aristocratic or wealthy individuals of the sort that dominated high political positions in most ancient cities were extremely prone to self-advertisement. Turning the coinage into a long-lasting, and widely circulating, inscribed memorial to their tenure of office was an opportunity too good to miss. That it also assists in writing the history of the city by allowing us to relate individuals named on coins to ones mentioned in literary texts or inscriptions is a considerable bonus for historians, but not the original intention.

Fig. 25.8 Silver denarius made by M. Brutus in the 50s BC depicting his ancestor L. Brutus, first consul of the Republic, attended by lictors. Diam. 20 mm (BM CRR 3861; © London, British Museum).

As a material expression of public authority, coin-legends and designs provide important insights into the dominant visual and symbolic culture of ancient communities. The city-states of archaic and classical Greece typically chose types that refer to the presiding deity of the city: Athena in Athens and Corinth, Poseidon in Poseidonia, or Helios the sun god at Rhodes (see figure 25.4 above). Gods like these feel like communal symbols in which all citizens shared equally. However, we should not forget that some humans positioned themselves closer to the gods than others, by such means as claims to divine descent on the part of aristocratic and royal families. Alexander the Great's choice of Zeus and Heracles as the gods to appear on his coinage reflected not just their status as two of the most widely worshipped of the Greeks' gods, but also their roles as Alexander's divine parent and ancestor of the Macedonian royal house respectively (see figure 25.6 above).

Coins and identity

As manifestations of public authority, however constituted, coins could also serve as symbols of ethnic identity. One of the principal motors behind the spread of coinage in archaic Greece was arguably the attraction, to those states with both the resources and the need to produce one, of having a circulating currency with their own public type rather than using the coins of another city. This sentiment was clearly not universally present, however. Few of the cities of the Peloponnese issued coins in their own name before the fourth century BC, whether through lack of perceived need or of the metal from which to make them (the availability of metal supplies was an important factor; the Athenians were extremely fortunate that they had a large silver-mine within their territory (figure 25.9)). The Spartans seem to have taken things a stage further. In their case, a principled rejection of precious-metal coinage became a marker of difference from coin-using societies elsewhere in the Greek world.

The role of coins as a marker of identity could play an important role in the spread of one coinage at the expense of others. The expansion of the Roman Empire was accompanied by the geographical extension of the Roman currency and the death of local coinages. But there is little evidence that the Roman state ever had a concerted policy of extinguishing indigenous coinages. It is more likely that they petered out through a combination of three factors: a lack of material resources as the invasive Roman state progressively took control of metal supplies within newly conquered areas; the

Fig. 25.9 Entrance to one of the Athenian silver-mines at Thoricus (photo: J. Williams).

consistent quality of the Roman coinage, which made it reliable and attractive to use; and, importantly, a positive desire on the part of conquered peoples to use Roman coin as a sign of their desire to become Romans. In the Western part of the Roman Empire, local civic coinages died out by the reign of Claudius (AD 41–54). They were superseded by the production of local copies of Roman base-metal coins, found throughout the Western provinces from Spain to Britain. This remarkable development has been interpreted as an expression of provincial ambitions to become Roman.

Coins and art history

In many ways the study of coins began as an aspect of the study of ancient art. In the Renaissance coins were prized and collected, along with gems, statues and other worked antiquities, as supreme examples of the art of antiquity (see chapter 10). As the study of coins became more advanced, especially the study of the chronology of undated coin-series including most classical Greek coinages, art historical considerations came to play an important role in ordering the coins and assigning accurate dates to them. Coin styles seemed to follow the same datable progression from archaic to classical to Hellenistic as was observable in other areas. The problem, as was later realised, is that styles do not always change simultaneously across different media, and coins can be particularly conservative. From hoard evidence we now know that Athenian coins preserved the archaic style in the depiction of the head of Athena throughout the fifth century BC.

Coins provide important information on the history of ancient art in other ways. Coins may bear images of famous lost works of art (such as the statue of Zeus at Olympia by Phidias) or buildings (e.g. Herod's temple in Jerusalem, destroyed by the Romans in AD 70 (figure 25.10)), though sometimes in a schematic fashion which may not permit an accurate reconstruction. Named portraits on coins of individuals, Cleopatra for instance, may permit the identification of otherwise anonymous portrait busts, while the evidence of stylistic changes in

Fig. 25.10 Jewish silver shekel of the Second Revolt (AD 132–5) with an image of the temple of Jerusalem, destroyed in the First Revolt (AD 66–70). Diam. 26 mm (BMC 18; © London, British Museum).

the portrayal of an individual on datable coins may provide a structure for the dating of portraits in other media. The changing portrait of Octavian/Augustus is the classic example. Many busts of him survive in a variety of different styles, but their ordering and chronology ultimately rest on the evidence of the dated coins.

Coins and archaeology

The study of large numbers of coin findspots has generated important information on major themes like the spread of the phenomenon of coinage itself, or the expansion of particular coinages like the Roman *denarius*.

More specifically, coin-finds have played an important role in the dating and interpretation of particular archaeological sites. Traditionally, excavators have sought to use coins as a means of dating buildings or other archaeological features within which they are found. This was done on the presumption that coins are more accurately datable than other kinds of artefact usually found on Greek or Roman sites, such as pottery. There are two problems with this: coins are not always easier to date than other kinds of artefact, and it is clear from hoard evidence that coins also remained in circulation sometimes for very long periods of time. A silver *denarius* of the emperor Hadrian (AD 117–38) found underneath a Roman bath-house does not allow us to date the building to his reign. All we can actually conclude is that the building was put up in the century or more after AD 117 during which Hadrian's coins continued in circulation.

Rather than dating archaeologically recovered structures or deposits from coins, it is often the case that coins need to be dated with reference to the archaeological context within which they appear. A revolutionary study of this sort redated the earliest appearance of coinage in Iron Age central Europe to the mid-third century BC, over a century earlier than the previously preferred chronology, which had been based on irrelevant historical and art historical considerations.

In the past, coins found in excavations were studied in isolation and interpreted in the light of what was known, or thought to be known, about the history of the site in question. More recently, coin-finds have been interpreted within the context of similar finds from other sites and against the background of an average picture for the whole region. This comparative method allows the individual characteristics of different sites to come out more clearly and is now the standard approach, especially in the interpretation of Roman coin-finds in Britain and the western empire. The next stage in its refinement, still to come in many ways, will be the integration of the interpretation of coin-finds with other kinds of artefact. Seen archaeologically, it becomes obvious that coins are just another sort of material artefact. It is becoming increasingly clear that they can no longer be studied in isolation from the material world within which they were made, and within which they circulated.

Further reading

R. A. Abdy, *Romano-British Coin Hoards*, Princes Risborough: Shire Archaeology, 2002 – succinct and up-to-date introduction to hoards and what they can tell us.

A. M. Burnett, *Coinage in the Roman World*, London: Seaby, 1987 – all you need to know to get started in 160 pages.

A. M. Burnett, M. Amandry, and P. P. Ripollès, *Roman Provincial Coinage* (2 vols and supplement), London: British Museum Press and Paris: Bibliothèque Nationale de France, 1992 – revolutionary project collecting together all the non-imperial provincial coin-types from the Roman Empire.

K. Butcher, *Roman Provincial Coins*, London: Seaby, 1988 – exemplary introduction.

M. H. Crawford, *Roman Republican Coinage* [*RRC*] (2 vols), Cambridge: Cambridge University Press, 1974 – the standard work of reference.

C. J. Howgego, *Ancient History from Coins*, London and New York: Routledge, 1995 – does exactly what it says on the tin; full of intellectual stimulation.

C. J. Howgego, A. M. Burnett and V. Heuchert (eds), *Coinage and Identity in the Roman Provinces*, Oxford: Oxford University Press, 2005 – new collection of essays on coins as sources for local identities in the Roman Empire.

C. M. Kraay, *Archaic and Classical Greek Coinage*, London: Methuen, 1976 – still the best introduction from one of the greatest authorities on the subject.

H. Mattingly, E. A. Sydenham, *Roman Imperial Coinage* [*RIC*] (10 vols), London: Spink, 1923–94 – the standard reference to all Roman imperial coin-types from Augustus to Romulus Augustulus.

A. R. Meadows and K. Shipton, *Money and its Uses in the Ancient Greek World*, Oxford: Oxford University Press, 2001 – how were coins used? This collection of essays suggests some ways of thinking about the question.

O. Mørkholm, *Early Hellenistic Coinage from the Accession of Alexander to the Peace of Apamea*, Cambridge: Cambridge University Press, 1991 – the best way in to this complex and important period.

R. Reece, *The Coinage of Roman Britain*, Stroud: Tempus, 2002 – the latest condensation of a lifetime's work from the father of archaeological numismatics. Readable, accessible and, this time, no statistics.

26. *Sculpture*

Peter Stewart

The range of material

No Greek or Roman artistic medium is better known or more studied than sculpture. In fact, to a large extent any general history of classical art *is* a history of sculpture, for sculpture survives relatively well and is frequently mentioned by ancient writers. It is therefore important to remind ourselves that the surviving material actually amounts only to an unrepresentative fraction of what once existed.

Most extant Greek and Roman sculpture is carved in stone, especially in marble (which is hard, attractive, and abundant in parts of the Mediterranean), though other stones like limestone were often used in particular areas and periods. A great deal of marble sculpture was lost in antiquity or the Middle Ages, particularly because marble can be burned in lime-kilns to make mortar. Other materials for ancient sculpture proved even more vulnerable.

Numerous ancient works were cast in bronze. The processes were rather different from marble sculpture because they normally started with the modelling of clay or wax (either as the core of the sculpture or as the basis for moulds) rather than chipping away at a block of stone. Some spectacular ancient bronze sculptures do survive (see figure 26.4 below), but most ended up in furnaces because the metal had its own intrinsic value and was readily recycled. Baked clay itself (terracotta) was also an important material for the modelling of ancient sculptures, while others were made in such perishable materials as wood, wax, ivory and precious metals.

Even those sculptures that do survive can be very deceptive. We are used to seeing Greek and Roman works carved in white marble. Their paleness has long accorded with modern ideas of the 'purity' and ideal simplicity of classical art, and it has been imitated in the sculpture of recent centuries. But bleached white sculpture would have made little sense to Greeks and Romans. Enough evidence survives to show that marble sculptures were routinely painted, at least in parts: features like clothing, lips and eyes, hair and other details were coloured to make them appear more realistic (figure 26.1). Bronzes were also colourful and varied because eyes were usually inlaid in glass and coloured stone, copper was inlaid on lips and nipples, teeth and eyelashes were inserted in different metals etc. (see figure 26.4 below). Specially honoured sculptures in both marble and bronze were frequently gilded as well. Besides these there were impressive statues covered in ivory and gold (chryselephantine statues) or composed from different materials such as contrasting varieties of coloured marble or combinations of marble and wood (acrolithic statues).

Not counting the Bronze Age (i.e. approximately the second millennium BC), the earliest surviving, large-scale, Greek sculpture was made in the seventh century BC and was evidently influenced by much older Near Eastern artistic traditions. The Greeks and then the Romans used sculpture continuously thereafter, though in late antiquity (especially from around the fifth century AD) the manufacture of significant sculptures in the round, such as statues and busts, petered out. Broadly speaking, throughout this period sculpture served a fairly consistent range of functions. It should be noted that although artistic skill

Fig. 26.1 Painted plaster reconstruction of the Peplos Kore. c. 530 BC. Ht. 1.21 m. Cambridge, Museum of Classical Archaeology, inv. 34A (photo: Nigel Cassidy. © Museum of Classical Archaeology, Cambridge).

was acknowledged and respected, and wealthy Romans 'collected' old Greek works of art, sculpture was generally not made purely to be admired for its own sake or for the artist's self-expression. Ancient sculpture was required for other purposes, including the following:

1. *Representing gods*: sculptures of gods were venerated as cult-images, customarily placed within a temple or shrine. Sculptures were also dedicated as offerings in sanctuaries (not necessarily portraying the god concerned).
2. *Funerary commemoration*: besides commemorative statues, busts, etc., representations of the dead were carved on grave *stēlae* (tombstones) and other funerary reliefs. Particularly in the Roman world from the second century AD onwards, marble sarcophagi were used. They were often carved with mythological or other scenes as well as, or instead of, a portrait.
3. *Honorific monuments*: particularly from the fourth century BC onwards, portrait-statues (and later busts) were set up in public places in honour of important individuals. They were erected by those who had benefited from the help or generosity of those portrayed. In effect it was often Greek or Roman communities who used these honours to thank and please their benefactors or patrons, including kings or emperors. Inscriptions on statue-bases identified the subject and explained the honour, though these have usually become separated from their sculptures and are too often ignored by art historians.
4. *Architectural adornment*: this does not just mean 'decoration' but also the reliefs and statues that were used as appropriate embellishments for such buildings as temples. Mythological sculptures (usually) appeared on the roofs and in the gables of temples, or as continuous friezes or metopes above the colonnades of the different styles of temple. Tombs, treasuries and other monuments were also adorned with sculpture.
5. *Domestic sculpture*: this is primarily a Roman phenomenon, though it owes something to the traditional Greek decor of sanctuaries, gymnasia, etc. Affluent Romans liked to give the gardens of their houses and villas an appropriate ambience by displaying sculptures of Greek gods, Dionysiac figures and animals, busts of famous men and so on.

These were the main functions, but decorative or figurative sculptures appeared in other contexts too. The main forms of sculpture have already been mentioned. Besides free-standing statues there were the busts and herms (heads of gods or portraits on pillars) which the Romans liked, and there were reliefs. Reliefs are sculptures in which the figures are rendered projecting from, but attached to, a background: they are three-dimensional but they are not free-standing, so they are particularly effective in an architectural setting. The depth of relief sculpture varies considerably. Sometimes the figures almost break free of their background, but sometimes they project only a few centimetres, in which case the sculptor has to use 'painterly' illusionistic techniques to suggest greater depth. The Parthenon – classical Greece's most famous temple – offers examples of all kinds of relief sculpture including the highly skilful low-relief carving of its frieze (figure 26.2). Here a continuous low relief around the top of the walls of the temple building is used to represent a profile view of a religious procession. Although it is never more than a few centimetres deep, the frieze depicts up to eight overlapping cavalrymen, conceived as riding side by side.

It will be clear that there are many ways of studying such a rich and varied body of material. The energies of those studying the field have largely been devoted to the investigation of individual works: dating, identification and interpretation. Such research will no doubt continue to be the foundation of the discipline, as newly discovered sculptures are published and existing works are reassessed. But there are larger patterns in the study of ancient sculpture.

The story of Greek sculpture

There exists, and can exist, no comprehensive or definitive account of Greek and Roman sculpture. As we have seen, this is partly due to the fragmentary nature of the evidence. There are other, less obvious, obstacles. Not all surviving ancient sculptures are on display, or even accessible, in museums. Not all of them have been published, and new discoveries may take a long time to become widely known. Not all sculptures have been photographed, and museums sometimes charge high fees to allow scholars to reproduce the photographs that do exist. Moreover, the greatest attention is inevitably devoted to those sculptures which are considered more attractive or impressive, so that the academic interest of ugly and

Fig. 26.2 Parthenon frieze, north slab XLVII (132–6). c. 447–438 BC. Ht. 1.06 m. London, British Museum (photo: © museum).

fragmentary works is neglected. Above all, different scholars and different generations of scholars ask different questions about Greek and Roman sculpture as they try to make sense of it in their own terms. Nonetheless, it is possible to make some further generalisations about the shape of the subject and the parameters within which its study occurs.

It was only from about the middle of the eighteenth century that Greek and Roman sculptures started to be distinguished from each other and set within a relatively reliable historical framework. The story of sculptural development within which these works were inserted had its roots in Renaissance and Roman writings about art. It was implicitly (and often explicitly) a story of rise and decline. Greek sculpture emerged and began to mature in a primitive, 'archaic' period. In the fifth and fourth centuries BC it reached 'classical' perfection with the optimum balance of realism and idealism. Finally, the Hellenistic period, from the late fourth century BC onwards, was one of decadence, which finished with the Romans' derivative and inferior imitations of earlier art.

Whatever they think in private, most scholars today are no longer quite so concerned to make judgements about the excellence or otherwise of ancient sculpture in different periods. But we have inherited this basic art historical framework, including its value-laden terms. 'Archaic' and 'Classical' (often with a capital 'A' and 'C') are still used as conventional labels for sculpture produced in the Greek world in around the seventh to early fifth and the fifth to fourth centuries BC, respectively. There are art-historical subdivisions as well: early classical (or the 'severe style'); high classical (c. 450–400 BC); late classical.

Particular attention has always been paid to the transition from archaic to classical Greek sculpture. Artists are considered to have cast off a highly conventional, conservative, schematic kind of representation that relied on traditional forms and formulae rather than observation of nature. When they appear to imitate real people and things in a plausible way, 'naturalism' is born. Such naturalistic sculpture had never been developed, or at least it had never been fully exploited, in the other cultures of the Mediterranean. Figures 26.3 and 26.4 demonstrate how profoundly the Greek conception of sculpture changed between about 600 BC and 450 BC. The first statue is a *kouros* ('youth'), an archaic male statue-type, used to commemorate the aristocratic dead and to represent gods. It owes a lot to Egyptian models, as is clear from its stiff pose, impassive face, wig-like hairstyle and proportions. The anatomy and proportions appear unrealistic to modern eyes. The *korē* ('maiden') is its elaborately clothed female counterpart (see figure 26.1 above). In contrast, the slightly over life-size bronze warrior from Riace (figure 26.4) is a classical, naturalistic statue. It is highly idealised, certainly, and its individuality is limited. But the rendering of the naked body demonstrates a much greater interest in convincing proportions and the workings of a real body.

Fig. 26.3 Kouros from Attica. c. 600 BC. Ht. 1.93 m. Metropolitan Museum, New York, Fletcher Fund 1932 (32.11.1) (photo: © museum).

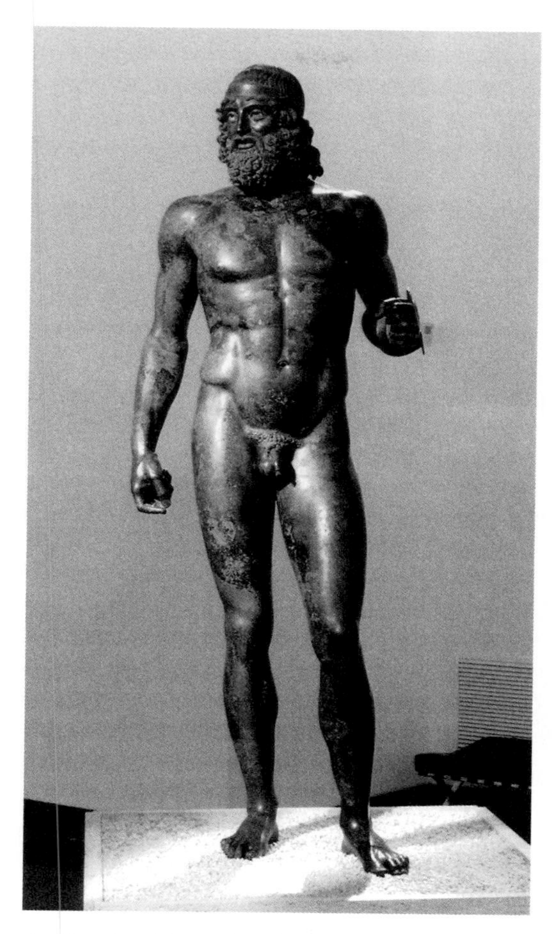

Fig. 26.4 Riace 'Bronze A'. c. 450s BC. Ht. 1.98 m. Museo Nazionale, Reggio Calabria (photo: courtesy of the Ministero per i Beni e le Attività Culturali n. 23, 9/04/2003, Museo Nazionale di Reggio Calabria).

One very distinctive classical innovation is the balanced and harmonious pose of the statue called *contrapposto*, whereby the weight is placed on one leg, the shoulders and hips tilted to lend the figure a measure of dynamism (see figure 26.6 below).

The emergence of this sort of naturalistic sculpture was a gradual process, but the most rapid developments occurred around the late sixth and early fifth centuries BC, which is (coincidentally?) the period in which democracy was developed in Athens and the Greeks repelled invasions by the Persians. It has been called variously the 'Greek Revolution', the 'Greek Miracle' and the 'Great Awakening'. These romantic terms reflect the deeply rooted respect that is still felt for naturalistic representation in art. But not all scholars are happy with the idea of a Greek sculptural revolution. The dating of sculptures, the speed of the transformation and the notion of progress towards greater naturalism have all been questioned. At the same time no thorough explanation for the change has been devised. Technological advances, a shift in artists' narrative intentions and some kind of (usually ill-defined) connection with the birth of democracy and social change have been discussed as contributing factors.

The style of Greek sculpture continued to evolve along with Greek society (see chs 16 and 17). If its subsequent development could be characterised in a few words (which it cannot), then we should note ever greater acknowledgement of anatomical detail and individuality, as well as a more sophisticated concern with movement and illusionism. An extreme manifestation of this trend is the so-called Hellenistic 'baroque' style, best illustrated by the Great Altar at Pergamum (see chapter 23). It is surrounded by a high-relief frieze that represents an old and conventional mythological subject: the battle between the gods and the giants. However, the figures are animated as never before (figure 26.5). They almost seem to burst out of the frieze. Their poses are complex and tense as they tangle in battle, and the faces of the struggling giants are contorted with anguish.

This general story of Greek sculptural change is unusual, compared with many other periods of art history, because it seems to neglect the specific contributions of major artists. In fact, we do know something about the famous sculptors of ancient Greece. They are mentioned in Greek and Latin literature, their names survive on some inscribed pedestals, and their works are reflected in later copies (see below). But it is difficult to do much with them because their sculptures rarely survive. Every time high-quality Greek classical sculptures like the Riace bronzes are discovered, scholars optimistically rush to attribute them to the 'big names'. Yet the fact remains that no extant works can be attributed without dispute to any of the most famous Greek sculptors like Myron, Phidias, Polyclitus or Praxiteles. So, in spite of the undoubted academic interest in famous artists, the

Fig. 26.5 Athena fighting giant, from east frieze, Great Altar at Pergamum. c. 190–150 BC. Berlin, Staatliche Museen (photo: © museum (BKP, Berlin, 2003)).

study of sculpture has tended to dwell more on general stylistic development over time, or contemporary regional differences, rather than personal styles and innovations.

The problem of Roman sculpture

The situation is even trickier when it comes to telling the story of Roman sculpture. First, the Romans write a lot about past Greek artists, but they seem to have virtually no interest in the artists of their own period. Second, there is no very clear story to be told. Roman sculpture (and, to an extent, Hellenistic sculpture before it) is very hard to interpret in terms of progressive development. It is eclectic, stylistically diverse, and in fact it usually makes use of styles, subjects and genres which had already been devised in the Greek world. (This retrospective character often makes Hellenistic and Roman sculpture hard to date.) Moreover, nearly all the 'Roman' sculptors we do know about have Greek names: they are either from the Greek lands or of Greek extraction. In short, Roman sculpture does not have any very clear-cut cultural identity of its own. This phenomenon has been called 'the problem of Roman art'.

For more than a century there have been repeated attempts to identify some distinctive essence of Roman sculpture: something that sets it apart from the Greek tradition. For example, some scholars sought a spark of native creativity in works which eschew Greek ideal naturalism or in the convincing representation of space (e.g. figure 26.10 below). But attempts of this kind have never been very successful, and nowadays the tendency is to approach the material on its own terms. So, if Roman sculpture looks unoriginal and derivative, then do not waste time complaining about its aesthetic poverty or trying to redeem it. Instead, ask *why* it is derivative, and how Greek models or

Greek styles are being used in a new Roman social and political context.

A good example of changing priorities in the study of ancient sculpture is offered by the controversy over Roman copies. Many Roman sculptures are regarded as copies of lost Greek originals. Often there is little evidence to support the idea except that they *look* very Greek. Some works are more precisely identified as copies of famous classical Greek originals like Polyclitus's Doryphorus or Spear-Bearer (figure 26.6; cf. chapter 10, figure 10.1). Such copies have had an essential role in reconstructing the history of *Greek* sculpture. But even when they do provide accurate evidence for lost works there is growing doubt about whether the Romans intended them as copies in the modern sense, or whether they were more interesting for their general appearance and subject matter. The *Roman* context is acquiring greater importance in scholarship.

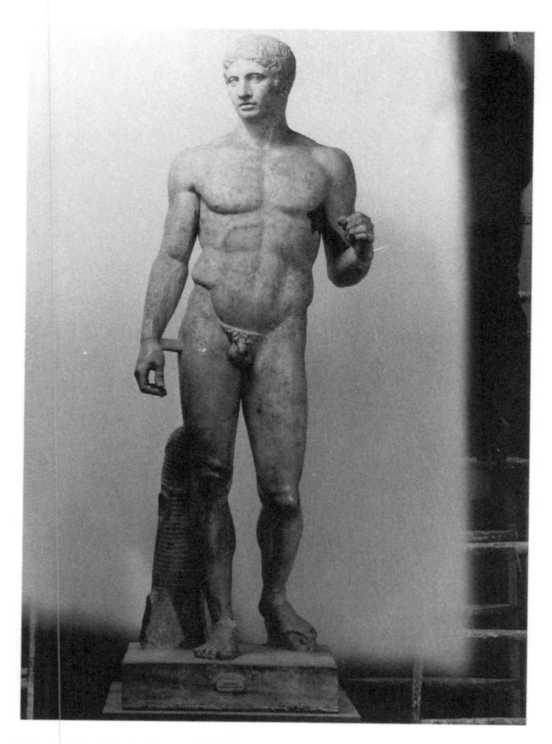

Fig. 26.6 Early imperial Roman copy of the Doryphorus of Polyclitus, from Samnite Palaestra, Pompeii. Original c. 440 BC. Ht. 2.12 m. Museo Nazionale, Naples, inv. 6011 (photo: © Deutsches Archäologisches Institut, Rome, inst. neg. 66.1831 (Koppermann)).

Similarly, there is now much interest in the possible values and meanings that Romans attached to the Greek styles that they used – such as the dignity and decorum of high classical styles – and in how these styles were deployed in Roman works. One of the most famous illustrations is the enigmatic Ara Pacis (Altar of Peace) in Rome (figure 26.7). The sculptures on the walls that enclose it are complex and eclectic, but evidently designed with great care. The low-relief processional friezes on each side of the structure are obviously classicising in their representation of drapery and in the superimposed figures that engage with each other while retaining their ideal impassivity. In fact, these reliefs are often likened to the frieze of the Parthenon.

Most people see the same kind of classicism in the portraiture of the emperor Augustus as well as some of his successors and contemporaries. The best-known example is the statue from Prima Porta near Rome, which depicts him as a youthful, heroised Roman general (figure 26.8). Note that it is not only his head that evokes classical Greek precedents. The whole body, stripped of its armour, closely resembles Polyclitus' Doryphorus: another demonstration of Roman artists' capacity for manipulating and transforming Greek models.

There are no 'revolutions' in Roman sculpture to match the 'Greek Revolution'. But there is a change of comparable significance. Gradually, and noticeably from about the third century AD if not earlier, the underlying assumptions of Greek naturalistic representation start to diminish in Roman sculpture. In this period of 'late antiquity', the skills required to make sculptures that plausibly imitated nature almost disappeared, and there is not much indication that they were missed. The sculptures on the Arch of Constantine in Rome (figure 26.9; cf. chapter 10, figure 10.5) are often taken to illustrate how things had changed by the fourth century (though in fact the monument is not exactly typical). Here a variety of highly naturalistic sculptures from the second century AD have been reused alongside new creations which are schematic and unrealistic (see chapter 10). Traditionally this change has been seen as decline, just as the Greek revolution was 'progress'. But nowadays scholars tend to see it

Fig. 26.7 South side of Ara Pacis, Rome (photo: © Deutsches Archäologisches Institut, Rome, inst. neg. 72.654 A (Singer)).

as a symptom of changing tastes and expectations. Naturalism is not the only way of representing the world, nor is it necessarily the most effective.

Some of the characteristics of 'late antique' sculpture are prefigured in earlier imperial works ('popular' and provincial works) which belong to an alternative artistic tradition, less profoundly influenced by Greece. Figure 26.10 shows a rather crude shop-sign relief from Ostia (Rome's seaport) depicting a poultry-seller's shop. The representation is actually much clearer and more effective than a more sophisticated, naturalistic sculpture would have been.

New directions

Of course, many studies of Greek and Roman sculpture are relatively uninterested in narratives of stylistic change over centuries, and their approaches cut across the accounts outlined above. Recent research is often concerned to understand sculptures in their various contexts: physical/archaeological context, political context, social context. Many studies are interdisciplinary and do not focus on sculpture per se. There are attempts to understand different bodies of evidence – like inscriptions and sculptures – together.

As with other branches of classical scholarship, the study of sculpture has felt the influence of broader developments in other disciplines. There is an increasing application of theoretical models borrowed from literary criticism, anthropology, sociology, feminist and gender studies, etc. Such approaches do not treat the kinds of sculptures illustrated here as isolated works of art; rather, they interpret them as manifestations of Greek and Roman culture, ideology and social relationships. What, for example, is the implication of the fact that the *kouros* could be used equally to depict gods and aristocratic

Fig. 26.8 Statue of Augustus from Prima Porta. Ht. 2.04 m. Vatican Museums, Braccio Nuovo 2290 (photo: © Alinari Archives-Anderson Archive, Florence).

Fig. 26.9 Arch of Constantine, Rome, north facade. c. AD 312–15. Hadrianic (second-century) tondi with scenes from a hunt, and Constantinian frieze showing emperor speaking from Rostra (photo: author).

men? What values are embodied in the nudity of Greek male statues, which we take so much for granted?

One very notable development is the interest in reception; that is, not just what sculptures were *intended* to convey or do, but how they were *actually* viewed. How were they seen? How did ancient viewers 'read' them? How were they treated subsequently? This is often a matter of considering different viewers' perceptions and 'ways of seeing', but it also involves thinking about the original setting. The Parthenon frieze is one of the best examples. Academics are used to studying it in great detail; it is displayed at eye-level in the British Museum and it is accessible through photographs. But in antiquity it was set 12 m high in a dark colonnade, so that the ancient Greek view of it would have been fundamentally different. Does our interpretation have to change accordingly? Naturally, the interest in reception includes modern responses to ancient sculptures: their academic study, their display in museums, their appropriation in popular culture and so on.

While the character of these newer approaches is often broadly theoretical, some scholars swear by the close study of the artefacts themselves rather than abstract explanatory models, and 'theory' is sometimes used, quite literally, as a term of abuse. There are pitfalls along both paths. But suffice it to repeat that there is no consensus about how to explain or use Greek and Roman sculpture, and different stories will continue to be told.

Further reading

J. Boardman, *Greek Sculpture: The Classical Period*, London: Thames and Hudson, 1985 – a rather traditional survey: a good and concise source of information and illustrations.

T. Hölscher, *The Language of Images in Roman Art*, Cambridge: Cambridge University Press, 2004 – translated from an influential German essay, this explains the aesthetic principles underlying Roman sculpture.

D. E. E. Kleiner, *Roman Sculpture*, New Haven and London: Yale University Press, 1992 – good, well-

Fig. 26.10 Shop-sign relief representing poultry-seller's shop, Ostia. Second century AD. Ht. 0.21 m. Ostia Museum inv. 134 (photo: © Deutsches Archäologisches Institut, Rome, inst. neg. 80.3236 (Schwanke)).

illustrated, introductory discussion of selected sculptures, this also contains 'background' history and useful bibliographies.

C. C. Mattusch, *Greek Bronze Statuary: From the Beginnings through the Fifth Century BC*, Ithaca and London: Cornell University Press, 1988 – an authoritative overview of ancient techniques.

R. Osborne, *Archaic and Classical Greek Art*, Oxford: Oxford University Press, 1998 – as an example of regard for the viewer, etc. Not a traditional handbook: more thematic and informed by theory.

P. Rockwell, *The Art of Stoneworking: A Reference Guide*, Cambridge: Cambridge University Press, 1993 – excellent introduction to the techniques, which makes much use of ancient sculpture.

R. R. R. Smith, *Hellenistic Sculpture: A Handbook*, London: Thames and Hudson, 1991 – concise overview.

N. J. Spivey, *Understanding Greek Sculpture: Ancient Meanings, Modern Readings*, London: Thames and Hudson, 1996 – a very readable survey of the subject and different approaches to various works, though not so good for illustrations.

A. F. Stewart, *Greek Sculpture: An Exploration*, New Haven and London: Yale University Press, 1990 – companion volume to Kleiner's (above), but with much broader consideration of Greek ideas, values and social context. Less down-to-earth than Kleiner. Includes many translated extracts from literary sources.

A. F. Stewart, *Art, Desire and the Body in Ancient Greece*, Cambridge: Cambridge University Press, 1997 – stimulating and innovative use of different theoretical approaches.

P. Zanker, *The Power of Images in the Age of Augustus*, trans. A. Shapiro, Ann Arbor: University of Michigan Press, 1988 – a highly respected and influential study, putting early imperial sculpture and other art in cultural and political context.

27. Painting, Stucco and Mosaic

Roger Ling

Among the most distinctive arts of the Greek and Roman worlds are those designed to embellish architectural surfaces and especially, in Roman times, interiors. At the top of the scale of prestige, used first in Hellenistic palaces and later in a wide range of public buildings of the Roman period, were wall veneers in fine stone, notably varieties of coloured marble. Below these, and found not only in public buildings but also in houses and villas, came painting, stuccowork and mosaic.

Painting

In Greek times painting was a major art form. Practitioners such as Polygnotus, Zeuxis, Parrhasius, Apelles and Protogenes enjoyed international reputations and commanded the kind of fees that put them on a par with the great sculptors, architects, gold- and silver-workers and gem engravers. But their work was executed almost entirely on perishable wooden panels, and nothing of their output has survived the ravages of time. For the achievements of Greek painters we are dependent on references in ancient writers, especially Pliny the Elder (died AD 79), the thirty-fifth book of whose *Natural History* summarises the history of painting down to his time. Other authors, notably Lucian, who describes one or two works in detail, the Roman rhetorician Quintilian, who makes passing references to artistic style, and the 'guidebook' writer Pausanias, who describes works visible in Greece in his day (mid-second century AD), add more detail. From their comments we learn that Greek painters step by step mastered the techniques of pictorial illusionism (shading, foreshortening, perspective and chiaroscuro), until by the end of the fourth century BC they were able to create complex compositions which closely imitated real appearances. The so-called Alexander Mosaic from Pompeii, which is thought to reproduce a painting of this time, gives a vivid glimpse of what could be accomplished (figure 27.1).

The wooden panels of the Greek masters were designed to be attached to walls, whether in the form of large mural compositions in public buildings or as isolated pictures like those hung in modern houses and art galleries. The smaller pictures could, of course, be more easily detached and transported, which gave rise to a flourishing art market similar to the one that came to exist in sculpture and the luxury arts. In Roman times there was a mania for collecting 'old masters': originals by famous artists were bought for astronomical sums, and a vigorous copying industry grew up to satisfy the demand for reproductions.

For the techniques of painting on wood we obtain information from ancient writers and from surviving examples, particularly a series of portraits set in mummy cases in Egypt during Roman times. The pigments could be applied directly to the wood with brushes, using some form of binding medium such as animal-size (the 'tempera' technique), or they could be applied to the surface with metal spatulae or burins, using hot wax as a medium (the 'encaustic' technique). Alternatively they could be painted on plaster spread over the wooden surface. In addition to panels of wood, we also have surviving examples of paintings on ivory or stone, for which the normal technique must have been encaustic. Certain famous artists, such as Pausias of Sicyon and the fourth-century

Fig. 27.1 Battle of Alexander against the Persians. Mosaic from Pompeii VI 12 (House of the Faun), *exedra* 37. Late second or early first century BC, based on a wall painting of the late fourth century BC. Ht. 3.42 m. Naples, Archaeological Museum 10020 (photo: © Deutsches Archäologisches Institut, Rome, 58.1447).

Athenian Nicias, apparently specialised in this form of painting.

Alongside paintings on panels of wood and stone there were also paintings executed directly on wall surfaces. Here it was recognised, as it had been in Minoan and Mycenaean times, that the best results were obtained by applying the pigments on a coating of plaster, and preferably on plaster that was still soft. This was the 'fresco' technique. The plaster used in Greece and Rome was based on lime (calcium oxide), which was mixed with sand or some form of calcite, together with water, to create a gritty paste which, after spreading, dried slowly as the moisture within it escaped to the surface. This moisture contained lime, and a chemical reaction with carbon dioxide in the air produced a web of calcium carbonate crystals which fixed the pigments in a highly durable layer.

Paintings on plaster have survived much better than those on wood. Applied to walls and ceilings, they have often been reduced to fragments as a result of buildings collapsing, but they can be recovered in archaeological excavations and sometimes reconstructed. In certain circumstances, notably in underground structures such as tomb chambers, or in archaeological sites where the nature of the destruction was favourable to their preservation, they have been found largely complete. From the Greek period the best-preserved paintings are murals from the chamber tombs of Macedonia (Leucadia, Vergina and other sites), dated mainly to the late fourth and third centuries BC. From Roman times the fullest material comes from the cities buried by the eruption of Vesuvius in AD 79 (Pompeii, Herculaneum and Stabiae) (figure 27.2).

Whereas most of the great Greek panel paintings were of figure subjects, many painted wall-decorations adopted schemes of a more abstract kind, and especially ones based on architectural

Fig. 27.2 Second Style wall paintings. Pompeii, Villa of the Mysteries, bedroom 16 (southwest angle). Second quarter of first century BC (photo: © Deutsches Archäologisches Institut, Rome, 57.843).

motifs. The Macedonian tombs certainly favoured figures, representing either the lifetime interests of the deceased or mythological scenes relating to death and the Underworld. But in Hellenistic houses, such as those of the trading emporium on Delos, the predominant mode of decoration in the best-appointed rooms was inspired by ashlar masonry or marble veneer, using relief and bright colour to create patterns of blocks. The only significant role for figure paintings was in a narrow frieze at eye level.

In the Roman age, however, the architectural formulae became looser and more imaginative, with plays of perspective producing grand vistas or scarcely credible fairy-tale pavilions, and figures came to play an ever more prominent part (figure 27.3). The impressive series of mural decorations from houses in Pompeii and the other sites destroyed by Vesuvius include numerous schemes with a mythological picture set in the central pavilion of an architectural composition, or even figures that seem to move freely within the architecture, like actors on a baroque stage set.

The study of Roman painting has progressed remarkably since the mid-nineteenth century. In the eighteenth and nineteenth centuries, when the relentless pace of excavations at Pompeii yielded

Fig. 27.3 Fourth Style wall paintings. Pompeii V 2, 1 (House of Queen Margherita), dining room *r* (east wall) (photo: after coloured lithograph by P. D'Amelio).

house upon house full of murals, interest focused on the mythological pictures, which were regularly cut from the walls to become isolated showpieces in the palaces of the Bourbon kings of Naples. They were seen as reproductions of the lost masterpieces of ancient Greece, and much effort was expended on matching them with works mentioned by Pliny and other writers. Only with the unification of Italy in the 1860s did it become normal to keep the painted schemes intact and to treat them as ensembles, worthy of interest as products of their own age.

Subsequent research has concentrated upon three principal areas:

1. *Chronology*: a milestone was August Mau's identification of four Pompeian styles (1884). Starting with the Italian version of the Hellenistic 'masonry style', which he called the 'First Style', he used the evidence of buildings dated by inscriptions or historical events and minute analysis of the archaeological evidence, together with the architectural writer Vitruvius' account of the development of Roman painting down to the 20s BC, to establish a chronological framework which has remained valid (despite attempts to overthrow it) to the present day. The chronology has been refined by various researchers, particularly the Dutch school of H. G. Beyen, F. L. Bastet and M. de Vos, to the point that most paintings before the volcanic eruption of AD 79 can now be assigned dates to within ten or twenty years. Other scholars, such as H. Diepolder and F. Wirth, have re-examined the panel pictures which formed the centrepieces of wall-decorations (figure 27.4) and shown how they too 'moved with the times'. Even if their compositions went back to famous originals, the supposed replicas constantly varied iconography, setting, brushwork and colour in response to changes of taste. Wirth also tried, with less success, to chart the chronology of painting after Pompeii. But the uneven spread of the evidence and the difficulty of securing sound dates mean that even now the story of

post-Pompeian painting remains vague and controversial.

2. *Decorative programmes*: as early as the 1870s, A. Trendelenberg proposed, on the basis of selected examples, that the subjects of pictures put together in the decoration of a room might have been chosen to embody some form of message or common theme. This idea was picked up by the Swiss Karl Schefold in 1952 and applied to the whole corpus of Pompeian painting. While recognising changes of emphasis over the course of time, he argued that rooms invariably presented intellectual, moral or religious programmes. A particular combination of myths might, for example, turn a room into a 'museum', a shrine of the Muses. Another combination might honour the three deities of nature and fertility, Bacchus (Dionysus), Diana (Artemis) and Venus (Aphrodite). In the Fourth Style, particularly, patrons chose combinations of subjects offering an antithesis of 'hero and sinner', that is, contrasting a myth of a mortal who benefited from the favour of the gods with one in which a transgressor was punished. A similar approach, but on a more pragmatic level, was adopted by the American Mary Lee Thompson, who drew attention to conjunctions of myths focused on common themes. These theories have not been universally accepted; it has been pointed out that, while some combinations of myths are undoubtedly significant, the very multiplicity of combinations that occur militates against there having been consistent patterns of choice such as programmatic intentions would seem to require.
3. *The social dimension*: several recent studies have looked at the distribution of categories of wall

Fig. 27.4 Painting of Odysseus and Penelope. Pompeii VII 9, 4–12 (Macellum), north wall. Third quarter of first century AD, perhaps based on a Greek picture of the fourth century BC. Ht. 82 cm (photo: © R. J. Ling 45/3).

painting according to the functions of space within a house. Thus on the one hand the structure of a decoration can reflect the nature of a room. A scheme focusing upon a central pavilion with a mythological picture would be appropriate for a room such as a dining room or living room where people passed time and could contemplate their surroundings, while a 'paratactic' or repeating scheme in which there was no dominant focus would be suited to spaces of distribution or passage, such as corridors. On the other hand, the degree of elaboration within a decoration may have reflected the importance of a room. The presence of mythological pictures, the use of rich colouring, and the division of the scheme by means of architectural elements – all were factors by which spaces could be privileged. Less important rooms lacked one or more of them. They could feature simpler picture subjects such as landscapes or still lifes, or replace pictures altogether with vignettes of flying Cupids, floating animals, or the like; they could exchange red, black and yellow backgrounds for the white of the plaster; or they could dispense with architectural frameworks, and opt instead for simple schemes of fields separated by candelabra. There was clearly a scale of luxury – a scale which would have been reflected in the costs charged by painters. The richer the patron, the greater number of high-grade decorations he could afford. At the same time there were certain rules of propriety to observe. The most fanciful and avant-garde decorations were often reserved for bedrooms and dining rooms in the inner parts of the house, while grand but more traditional treatments were favoured in the rooms such as the atrium (front hall) where more formal reception took place. In this way the type of decoration chosen could not only define the status of rooms but characterise their role in the house's social life.

Stucco

Stuccowork, in which the plaster coat applied to architectural surfaces was modelled into reliefs, is the forgotten medium of interior decoration. Its chief field was the ceiling or vault, and, since the upper parts of any building are the first to collapse, it has proved more vulnerable to destruction than the other media. However, the lack of surviving evidence also reflects a more restricted usage. The process of working figures and motifs in relief was evidently a more finicky and costly process than applying paint, and it was reserved for a comparatively restricted number of spaces, often the richest rooms in a house or the grandest tombs in a necropolis.

The first stucco decorations were the imitation ashlar walls of late Greek houses already described. Sometimes these contained, at a high level, more elaborate reliefs of architectural elements, such as semi-columns, metopes, triglyphs and crowning cornices. In late republican Italy stucco reliefs moved upwards on to the lunettes (the semi-circular fields at either end of a vaulted room) and on to the vault itself. The first vault-decorations were inspired by the coffers and panels which had decorated the flat stone and wooden ceilings of Greek architecture, but these 'structural' schemes soon dissolved under the liberating influence of the curved surfaces to which they were now applied. Complex systems of square and rectangular panels, enriched with architectural motifs such as leaf patterns or egg-and-dart, and populated with a rich variety of figural and vegetal reliefs, spread in a delicate tracery of ornament over the vault (figure 27.5). During the imperial period, the range of patterns became ever more varied. Polygonal, curvilinear and centralised systems all entered the repertoire. An emphasis on the diagonals reflected the increasing use of groined cross vaults in architecture.

One distinctive feature of stucco reliefs was their reliance on the natural whiteness of the plaster. Backgrounds might be coloured, and panels containing stucco reliefs might be juxtaposed with panels containing painted figures; but the reliefs themselves were never coloured, and the preference was for both reliefs and background to remain uncoloured, relying for effect upon a subtle play of light and shade (figure 27.6).

The scattered and fragmentary nature of the surviving material is compounded by the lack of literary evidence. No ancient author tells us about stuccowork. The most that we have is an ancient

Fig. 27.5 Detail of stucco vault-decoration. Formiae (Formia, Italy), Roman villa in grounds of Villa Colagrosso. Second half of first century AD (photo: © R. J. Ling 36/29).

Fig. 27.6 Stucco relief of a Cupid riding a panther, from Puteoli (Pozzuoli, Italy), tomb in Fondo Fraia. Second half of first century AD. London, British Museum 1956 12-4 10. 31.8 × 34.4 cm (photo: © R. J. Ling 19/7).

term 'opus albarium' (or 'albarium' or 'opus album') used by Vitruvius, but Pliny seems to apply the same term rather to plain whitewash, so usage cannot have been consistent. To Roman writers stucco evidently appeared a subsidiary and artistically insignificant form of architectural decoration, whatever its status in actuality. It has received comparably short shrift from modern researchers, who have produced only a handful of specific studies. In the main these have concentrated on collecting the known material and proposing a chronological sequence; but, more recently, there has been some attempt to put stucco in context, analysing its sources of inspiration and assessing its role within the decorative ensemble. It has been recognised, for example, that many of the patterns used by stucco-workers on vaults were subsequently borrowed by the craftsmen who laid mosaic pavements.

Mosaic

Mosaic, like stucco, is a decorative medium of the Hellenistic and Roman periods (see chapter 24). It developed out of the practice of embedding pebbles into mortar pavements to secure a durable surface. By the fourth century BC such pebble pavements often employed different colours to create decorative patterns, and very soon these patterns were supplemented by figures, generally in grey-white against a black ground. Examples from Pella in Macedonia, dated to the turn of the fourth and third centuries, introduced a greater range of colours and careful grading of size to attain more lifelike effects (figure 27.7). But collecting sufficient natural pebbles of the right sizes and colours posed enormous problems, and from the third century onwards there was an increasing tendency to replace pebbles with specially cut stone cubes (*tesserae*). Those colours which could not be obtained from natural stones could be supplied by cutting tesserae of coloured glass.

From the Greek world *tessera* mosaic passed to Roman Italy. At first, as in the East, figural interest was focused on a central panel inserted in a pavement consisting predominantly of plain or simply patterned surfaces. Such inserted panels, or *emblemata*, were often made of minute tesserae barely 1 or 2 mm square and could attain a refinement of expression almost indistinguishable from that of painting. By the first century BC, however, with the emergence of elaborate forms of wall-decoration, there was a reaction against illusionistic treatments of the floor surface. Centralised schemes focusing upon a pictorial 'window' gave way to all-over abstract patterns, especially ones based on geometric shapes rendered in black and white.

The story of mosaic pavements in the period of the Roman Empire is rich and diverse, with different regions preferring different forms of decoration. In the East, polychrome figure scenes of mythological or allegorical subjects, the legacy of the *emblemata* of the Hellenistic age, remained popular. In Italy and the West, the black-and-white style continued in fashion (figure 27.8), but alongside the purely geometric patterns there emerged a taste for black silhouette figures spreading freely on a white ground, a technique which avoided the more disturbing 'floor-piercing' effects of *emblema* mosaics. At the same time, many mosaicists adopted a new polychrome geometric style in which a leitmotif was the ubiquitous plaited border (guilloche). Where figures were desired, they were frequently set in panels formed by the geometric framework; any effect of spatial recession was once again neutralised by the use of a white background and by the even spread of figures across the floor, with changes of orientation reflecting the changing viewpoint of spectators in different parts of the room. In North Africa, while this type of pavement was common, there were also a large number of distinctive local styles. Particularly popular were all-over polychrome figure compositions depicting scenes of everyday life (figure 27.9) – agricultural operations, hunting, chariot-racing, the contests of the amphitheatre, etc.

The range of mosaic floor-decorations found in the Roman world is remarkable. This reflects the abundance of surviving material. While the superstructures of ancient buildings collapse and the plaster of walls and ceilings is shattered, the pavements remain intact, often protected by the debris lying on top of them. It is usually not until intrusive events take place, such as deep ploughing or the digging of foundations for new buildings, that floor mosaics are threatened. As a result we know far more about mosaics than about paintings and

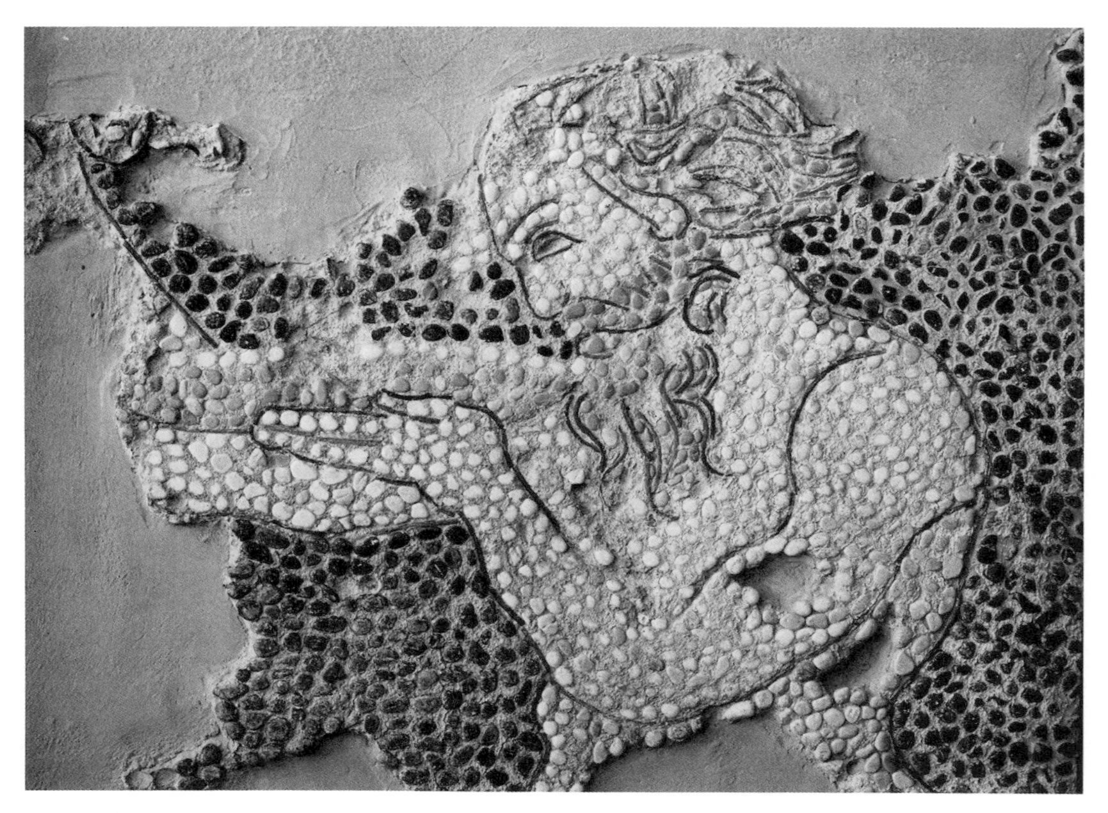

Fig. 27.7 Detail of pebble mosaic: centaur holding plate. Pella (Macedonia), house 1, room C: threshold panel. Last quarter of fourth century BC (photo: © Getty Research Library, Wim Swaan collection, 96.P.21).

Fig. 27.8 Black-and-white geometric mosaic: pavement of a triclinium (three-couch dining room). Tivoli (Italy), Hadrian's Villa, Hospitalia. AD 118–21 (photo: © R. J. Ling 98/5).

Fig. 27.9 Life on a villa estate: so-called Dominus Julius mosaic from Carthage (Tunisia). Second half of fourth century AD. Tunis, Bardo Museum 1 (photo: © R. J. Ling 90/7).

stuccoes. By contrast, the literary evidence – two or three sentences in Pliny, some brief technical instructions in Vitruvius, and scattered references in other authors – is limited (see chapter 59). The decoration of floors, surfaces on which people walked, clearly enjoyed a lower status than that of walls.

Perhaps the greatest challenge presented to modern archaeology is to make the vast mass of material available for study. One of the main objectives of research since the 1950s has therefore been the preparation of catalogues or corpora. Multi-volume publications of the mosaics of France, Tunisia and Spain are already well under way, and a start has been made on similar projects in Turkey, Portugal and Britain. There are also monographs on mosaics in other countries, notably Germany, Switzerland and Hungary, as well as studies on particularly productive sites such as Antioch (in southeastern Turkey), Ostia (the port of Rome), Augst (Switzerland) and Trier (Germany).

Areas of recent study are workshops, techniques and social meaning. The identification of workshops has been a focus of research in Britain, where David Smith has drawn attention to the concentration of certain patterns and motifs in specific parts of the province and argued that each cluster denotes the activity of a close-knit team of craftsmen. With regard to technique, there has been much debate as to whether Roman craftsmen used the so-called 'reverse' technique favoured by their modern counterparts – that is, a method of prefabricating panels by sticking tesserae face down on a template drawn on paper or cloth, then turning the resulting pieces over to install them in the pavement. Opinion is divided, but most experts now believe that the Romans worked only in a direct technique, setting the tesserae face up in the mortar, whether on the floor itself or on a tray in the 'studio'.

Regarding social significance, many of the same controversies have raged as are described above in relation to paintings. Do the subjects of a mosaic pavement or of a group of pavements within a building carry programmatic meanings? Do they reflect the function of the spaces or buildings that they adorned? Or do they, as argued in a recent study by S. Muth on mosaics in Spain and North Africa, create a more general environment for living in which the Greek myths projected the everyday experience of householders into a kind of other world or 'dream world'?

Alongside mosaic pavements, a new field for the mosaic art developed on walls and vaults. Starting from the incrustation of ornamental grottoes and *nymphaea* (shrines of the nymphs) with fragments of pumice, stone chippings and sea-shells, this became the preferred decoration of Pompeian garden fountains and of other installations, including bath buildings, in which water played a prominent role (figure 27.10). Mosaic was regarded as more damp-resistant than painted or modelled plaster, and there were also aesthetic advantages: the water combined with the multifaceted surfaces of the tesserae, here made chiefly of coloured glass, to produce scintillating reflections. The colour schemes of wall- and vault-mosaic were more closely related to mural paintings than to mosaic pavements, with architectural frameworks and coloured backgrounds corresponding to those regularly used in wall decoration. Unfortunately the amount of surviving material from the Roman period is limited, but the legacy of this new branch of mosaic is seen in the soaring blue and gold-ground vault-decorations preserved in early Christian churches in Italy and the Byzantine East. Indeed, there is a continuing tradition of mosaic walls and vaults right through to the eleventh and twelfth centuries. They show a lasting vigour of invention that was not matched by either painting or stucco.

Fig. 27.10 Poseidon (Neptune) and Amphitrite: wall mosaic. Herculaneum (Italy), House of Neptune and Amphitrite, fountain court. Third quarter of first century AD (photo: © R. J. Ling 6/33).

Further reading

K. M. D. Dunbabin, *Mosaics of the Greek and Roman World*, Cambridge: Cambridge University Press, 1999 – full and comprehensive survey.

R. Ling, *Roman Painting*, Cambridge: Cambridge University Press, 1991 – still the only comprehensive survey in English.

R. Ling, *Ancient Mosaics*, London: British Museum Press, 1998 – brief introductory account.

R. Ling, *Stuccowork and Painting in Roman Italy*, Aldershot: Ashgate, 1999 – collection of essays on detailed aspects, important particularly for stuccowork.

H. Mielsch, *Römische Stuckreliefs* (*Mitteilungen des Deutschen Archäologischen Instituts, Römische Abteilung*, Ergänzungsheft 21), Heidelberg: F. H. Kerle, 1975 – the only comprehensive survey of stuccowork available.

J. J. Pollitt, *The Art of Rome: Sources and Documents* (2nd edn), Cambridge: Cambridge University Press, 1983 – translations of ancient sources on Roman painting.

J. J. Pollitt, *The Art of Ancient Greece: Sources and Documents* (2nd edn), Cambridge: Cambridge University Press, 1990 – translations of ancient sources on Greek painting.

K. Schefold, *Pompejanische Malerei: Sinn und Ideengeschichte*, Basel: B. Schwabe, 1952, translated into French as *La Peinture pompéienne: essai sur l'évolution de sa signification* (Collection Latomus 108), Brussels: Latomus, 1972 – presents a controversial but challenging theory of decorative programmes in Pompeian painting.

F. B. Sear, *Roman Wall and Vault Mosaics* (*Mitteilungen des Deutschen Archäologischen Instituts, Römische Abteilung*, Ergänzungsheft 23), Heidelberg: F. H. Kerle, 1977 – basic catalogue.

E. L. Wadsworth, 'Stucco reliefs of the first and second centuries still extant in Rome', *Memoirs of the American Academy in Rome* 4 (1924), 9–102 – out of date but still an important compendium of material, complementing the study of Mielsch.

A. Wallace-Hadrill, *Houses and Society in Pompeii and Herculaneum*, Princeton: Princeton University Press, 1994 – on the social role of wall paintings within the Pompeian house.

28. Pottery and Metalwork

Brian A. Sparkes

Utensils in the Greek and Roman worlds were made of a variety of materials: skins, wood, reeds, clay, bronze, silver, gold, ivory, glass, etc. Some of these containers were fashioned for their contents (both liquid and solid: oil, wine, water, perfume, wheat, fish and so on), others for their usefulness as jugs, cups, bowls etc. Time and the destructive work of human hands have reduced both the bulk and the relative balance of this variety.

Pottery

Baked clay, being indestructible and virtually useless when broken (but see below), now vastly outnumbers the remains of all the other materials. Through excavations that have been conducted in and around the Mediterranean and in the further corners of Greek and Roman penetration, the history of Greek and Roman pottery can be traced from the hand-made shapes of Neolithic times to mass-production at the end of classical antiquity with a precision in dating and geographical spread that is unique. Modern references to Greek fine wares (e.g. figure 28.1) are usually expressed in ways that relate to their decoration, period and/or technique, for example Geometric (from the decoration), archaic (mainly covering the sixth century), black-figure (from the figures fired black against a terracotta background and enhanced by white and red colours and by incision), red-figure (from the technique of reserving the figures within a painted black outline and background, once again but less frequently enhanced by colour), white-ground or mould-made relief ware. Local names of production centres are then added to the categories (e.g. Corinthian, Boeotian, Laconian, Attic or Athenian, Apulian (figure 28.2–28.5).

The different wares of Roman pottery (figure 28.6 for a selection of Roman fine wares) are also complex in their naming, for example Arretine red-gloss, African red-slip, Eastern Sigillata A. Less attention has been paid to the plain and coarse wares that were used in the kitchens or on the farms than to the fine, particularly in the study of Greek pottery, but recent research has improved our understanding of these wares, in both the Greek and Roman periods. The names for shapes used in modern study of Greek pottery have been in part borrowed from ancient texts, often incorrectly (e.g. *pelikē*) or too precisely (e.g. *kylix*, *lēkythos*); Roman pottery studies tend to use modern terms such as bowl, plate, jug.

The basic forms of pottery were largely determined by function: open shapes for drinking and mixing, closed shapes for storage and transport. Being highly malleable in its unbaked state, clay can easily be worked into elaborate shapes and decorated in ways that are not governed by function. Hence the shapes may carry reliefs and appliqués, stamped and incised patterns (figure 28.7), painted designs and figures (see figures 28.2–28.5). Clay was also shaped into hand-held lamps and small figures that were used as toys or given as dedications to the gods or as offerings to the dead.

Pots used in everyday life were often reused later as suitable offerings for sanctuaries and cemeteries (figure 28.4). There are also some which were fashioned in shape and decoration specifically for dedications in sanctuaries or for deposition in graves.

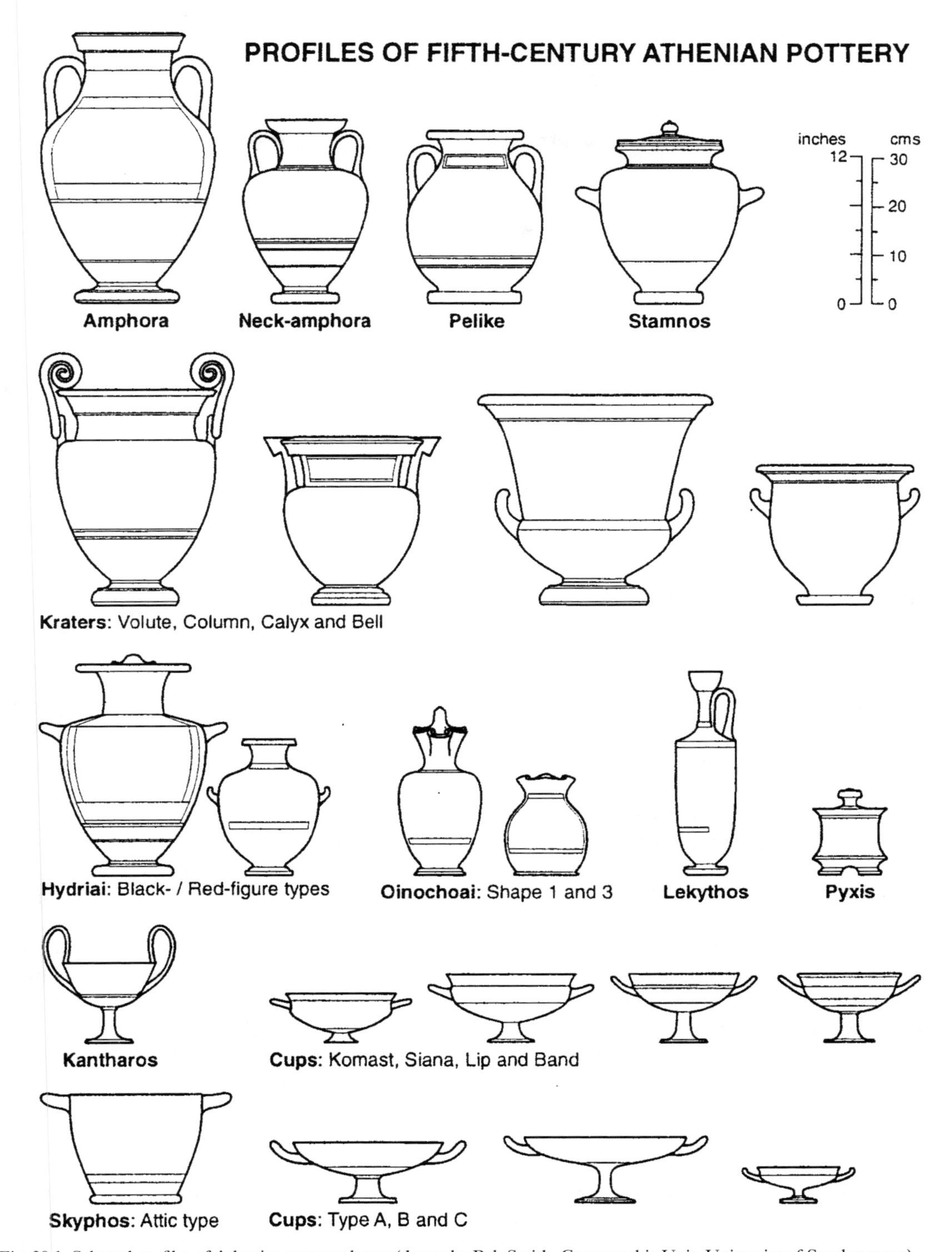

Fig. 28.1 Selected profiles of Athenian pottery shapes (drawn by Bob Smith, Cartographic Unit, University of Southampton).

Fig. 28.2 Black-figure Laconian cup: Bellerophon, Pegasus and the Chimaera, attributed to the Boreads Painter. c. 570 BC. Diam. 14 cm. Malibu, The J. Paul Getty Museum 85.AE.121 (photo: © museum).

Fig. 28.3 Red-figure Athenian *hydria*: Phineus and the Harpies, attributed to the Kleophrades Painter. c. 480 BC. Ht. of vase 39 cm. Malibu, The J. Paul Getty Museum 85.AE.316 (photo: © museum).

Fig. 28.4 Group of vases from a grave in the Athenian Kerameikos cemetery. c. 420 BC. Athens, Kerameikos Museum (photo: © museum).

Fig. 28.5 Red-figure Apulian *loutrophoros*: the dying Alcestis. c. 350 BC. Ht. of vase 129 cm. Basel, Antikenmuseum S 21, Sammlung Ludwig (photo: © museum).

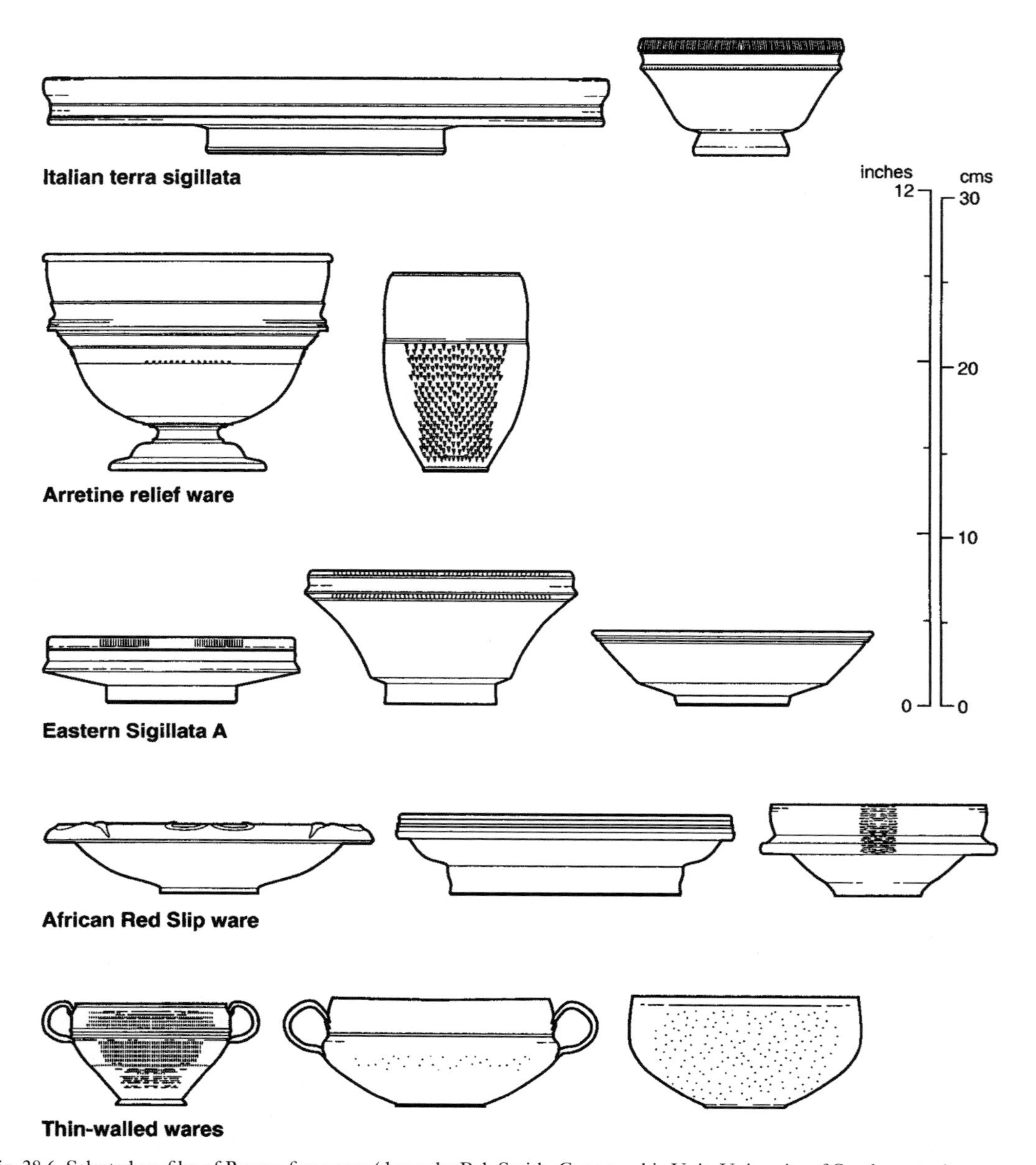

Fig. 28.6 Selected profiles of Roman fine wares (drawn by Bob Smith, Cartographic Unit, University of Southampton).

The study of Greek and Roman pottery has been intense. Here are some of the directions in which this study has moved:

1. *Technique*: the digging of the clay, its preparation and shaping when wet (with hands alone, or on a wheel, or with hammer and anvil), and the application of slip (a mixture of clay and water) have all been closely studied, as has the firing in kilns or on bonfires. Modern technology (e.g. petrographic and chemical analyses, and optical emission spectroscopy) is

Fig. 28.7 Roman handleless cup with incised decoration, from Araines (France). c. AD 150. Ht. 9.5 cm. Oxford, Ashmolean Museum R 244 (photo: © museum).

being increasingly applied to the investigation of the sources of the different clays.

2. *Potteries*: work has been carried out to try to understand the organisation of the potteries: what their layout comprised, how big they were, whether they were part-time household businesses, how many workers were employed, how far their products were distributed and so on.
3. *Shapes*: the manner in which shapes changed over the years, the ways in which potters borrowed shapes from other cultures, the relationship of pottery shapes to shapes in other materials (particularly metal but also wood, reeds, leather etc.), and the basis of the system of proportions are some of the aspects that are continually studied.
4. *Decoration*: apart from the basic wares which served for cooking and storage, and which usually carried either no paint or only a waterproof coating inside, the finer wares were often decorated with paint, reliefs, incisions or stamps, or a combination of them. Paint was the most common method of decoration. Though most pots were merely covered all over with a slip which was fired either black or red, some potters and painters created patterns consisting of geometric, floral or figure designs (see figures 28.2–28.5 above).
5. *Subject*: much detailed research has been devoted to Greek figured pottery, as the decoration carried animal and human figures, and culminated in complex images of myths (see figures 28.2–28.5 above) and of human life and death (see figure 28.4 above). These scenes have been carefully studied, both for the information they give us about popular myths, religion and daily life, and for the comparison that can be made with the extant literary texts in epic verse and drama. The association of mythological images on pottery and the treatment of myths in literature is less frequently pressed than was once the case. In rare instances one can relate the painting on pottery to what is known of missing wall-paintings and other arts.
6. *Painting style*: some painters (e.g. those working in and around Athens, in Corinth, Laconia, Etruria and south Italy and Sicily) exhibit a sufficiently individual style of painting to make it possible to distinguish different hands, even when there are no names of craftsmen written on the pots (see 7 below). The major figures in the work of attribution were Sir John Beazley (1885–1970), who principally studied the painters of Attic and Etruscan pottery, and Dale Trendall (1909–95), who investigated the painters of the Greek pottery of south Italy and Sicily. For some generations there was intense activity in this field, and the map of Greek vase-painting has gradually been given clearer definition by scholars who followed them. However, in recent years attribution has lost its position of scholarly primacy, and even the very validity of this line of research has been questioned. Nonetheless, the territory that such research has secured enables scholars to seek new directions for study.
7. *Lettering*: both Greek and Roman pottery often carry words painted or impressed on the surface of the pots before firing (see chapter 34). Greek inscriptions very occasionally carry the names of the potters and painters; they also name the characters in the myth depicted (e.g. Alcestis on figure 28.5 above) or famous individuals of the time (*kalos*-names), and give greetings to the drinkers, advertisement of the contents etc. Roman fine pottery often carries

stamps giving the name of the potter or factory. There is also lettering that was added after the pots were fired. The painted letters (*dipinti*) usually indicate a commercial notation, but the incised letters (graffiti) have a wider range of reference and are sometimes to be found scratched on fragments of pots already broken. The range covers alphabets, owners' names, shapes, names of deities receiving dedications, curses, messages, prices, shopping lists and so on. In fifth-century Athens there was the particular use made of fragments of broken pottery as voting sherds in the process of ostracism. All these inscriptions, whether painted before firing or added by paint or incision afterwards, help towards a greater understanding of spelling, dialects, common speech, onomastics etc.

8. *Dating*: with such a vast bulk of evidence it is not surprising that much attention has been paid to trying to pinpoint the dates of pottery not only to a relative time-scale but also to a precise and absolute time-scale expressed in BC/AD terms. Pottery is usually the most accurate dating tool for excavated contexts, though some categories of pottery are more difficult to date than others (compare Attic red-figure of the fifth century with the pottery made in the further reaches of Greek influence, and Roman fine wares with the local products from the outer fringes of the Roman Empire).
9. *Contents*: more work is now being done on the residues of organic and other substances to discover what the contents of the various containers might have been.
10. *Findspots*: there are three major contexts in which pottery is found: graves, sanctuaries and households; military sites become more important for pottery in Roman contexts. These findings enable historians to draw conclusions about Greek and Roman regard for the dead, their respect for the gods and the way they used pottery in everyday life. Sanctuaries attracted local potters to set up their workshops nearby; in the same way the arrival of the Roman army persuaded civilian potters to exploit the new market. Attention to the context in which a pot is found, whether near to its place of manufacture or elsewhere in the Mediterranean or beyond, is vital for an understanding of the complex relationship between 'producer' and 'consumer' (see chapter 3). There are Greek pots scattered widely from Persia and Egypt to southern Spain, and Roman pots from northern Britain to India.
11. *Social life*: pots and the scenes they carry can be used to try to calculate the place they had in the lives of the Greeks and Romans: social status, wealth, religion, politics etc.
12. *Economy*: pottery was easy and cheap to make, and methods of distribution ranged from itinerant potters moving from village to village with a load of pots on a donkey to the massive brick factories in the Roman Empire. Pottery which was traded for its own sake had a part to play in the economy and social life of the receiving community. Pottery which served as ballast is a marker for trade routes in other commodities, particularly those which have disintegrated and been lost, such as wood, foodstuffs, clothing (see chapter 3). Some inscriptions on pottery help with understanding the prices of other goods.

There are some pottery containers which stand apart from the others: *pithoi*, *dolia*, *mortaria* and transport amphorae. The Greek *pithoi* were heavy-duty, barrel-shaped Ali-Baba pots that were built up on the spot by hand, perhaps in a courtyard or on a farm, and used for the storage of grain and other foodstuffs. Some early Greek *pithoi* carried incised and relief decoration with complex scenes of myth and ritual; later the shapes lost the embellishment. The Roman *dolia* served similar functions but are much plainer. *Mortaria* are heavy-duty spouted bowls for mixing and grinding. Transport amphorae (figure 28.8) were the large containers for carrying wine, oil, dried fish, fish sauce, pitch and so on. The shape, though it varied from one centre to another, was fairly standard. It had a narrow mouth which could be stoppered, two vertical handles from shoulder to neck, and a full body that curved down to a small pointed toe – these details of shape eased the problems of stacking for transfer on shipboard and of emptying when full and heavy; also the toe could be fixed in the ground when stored. Some

Fig. 28.8 Amphorae at the *thermopolium* of Asellina, Pompeii (XI 11, 2).

amphorae carried painted letters but more usual were stamps that gave names of owners, titles, places of origin, and a pictorial device as a type of logo; these stamps together with observation of the shapes and the use of petrological analysis have enabled the majority of amphora types to be traced to their place of origin. Amphorae survive in large numbers (as at Pompeii (see figure 28.8)), many in fragments (e.g. forming Monte Testaccio, the 'Pottery Mountain', in Rome). Underwater excavations often bring whole amphorae to the surface, and they are used as indicators for maritime and riverine trade throughout both the Greek and the Roman periods (see chapter 22).

Metalwork

The commonest and cheapest metal for the production of containers was bronze; silver was more a luxury item, and gold is even more rarely found as a vase shape. Because metals are intrinsically valuable and can be melted down and reworked, the survival rate is low, as looting and refashioning were common. It is only in special conditions that the metals have survived intact, most often in unrobbed tombs and buried hoards.

Bronze vessels are found in some numbers in Greek and Roman areas, but, as gold and silver vessels gradually ceased to be buried in Greek graves and their place was taken by pottery, it is in the countries bordering the Greek heartlands where this practice continued, with their graves containing imported Greek objects. Burial places in those areas have produced well-preserved examples of gold and silver plate, mainly Macedonia (Derveni), Bulgaria (Thrace: Duvanli, Panagyurishte, Rogozen), Yugoslavia (Trebenishte), south Russia on the Black Sea and interior (Aul Uljap, Semibratny, Kul Oba) and in Etruscan tombs in northern Italy. In the Roman areas Rome has yielded up silver plate (e.g. the Esquiline treasure, a large collection of silver plate

Fig. 28.9 Greek gold *phialē*. Third century BC. Diam. 22.5 cm. New York, Metropolitan Museum of Art, 62.11.1, Rogers Fund 1962 (photo: © museum).

of the late Roman Empire, found at the foot of the Esquiline hill). Pompeii and other towns and villas overwhelmed by the eruption of Vesuvius continue to furnish their share (especially the House of the Menander in Pompeii and the villa at Boscoreale nearby), and hoards of silver buried in the late imperial period have mostly been found by chance in and beyond the northern provinces of the Roman Empire at places such as Hildesheim in south Hanover, Berthouville and Chaourse in France, Kaiseraugst in Switzerland, Mildenhall and Water Newton in England, and Traprain Law in Scotland. The origin of some hoards is uncertain, as it is not unusual for the cache to have reached the art market by illegal routes; the classic example is the late Roman Sevso treasure, said to have been found in Lebanon, a claim disputed by Croatia and Hungary.

The metals were commonly hammered into the form of plates which were soldered or riveted together. Solid cast handles and feet were also attached by soldering or rivets. Decorative work was produced by repoussé reliefs, and also by stamping, chasing and engraving (a technique adopted by potters). The centres of metal production are still not clear. Some objects carry weight inscriptions (see below) and some the names of owners and/or makers, inscribed or stamped. Much attention has recently been paid to the relationship between metal and ceramic shapes and decoration.

Gold objects are mentioned in literary texts and in inventories of temple treasures but are very rare in the archaeological record (the finds of gold in Bronze Age contexts, especially at Mycenae, are exceptional). There were sources of gold in and around Greece, such as the islands of Siphnos and Thasos, Macedonia, Thrace and Asia Minor (where there was a natural alloy of gold and silver (electrum) in the rivers). After Alexander's conquests, supplies of gold from further east became available, and in the period of the Roman expansion the sources, apart from war indemnities, increased with the addition of Spain, southern France and Wales and later the goldfields of the Balkans. Gold was used for jewellery, diadems, plaques, funerary masks, coins and so forth (and, in a few instances, for gold-and-ivory statues, both large and small), but the present number of gold vessels is relatively small, so it is not easy to gauge the prominence of gold plate in society. The few shapes that survive are fluted bowls, deep cups, flasks, mesomphalic *phialai* (shallow dishes with a central boss, for libations (figure 28.9)) and drinking horns.

Silver is also mentioned in temple inventories, where the weight and/or the name of the objects were often given. It was extracted from the ground in some of the same regions as gold, and also there are the important mines at Laurium in Attica. Silver was extracted from lead by smelting and usually alloyed with a little copper to make the metal harder; sometimes gilding was added for patterns or figures, and inlay with niello (black). Particle analysis has gone some way to distinguishing the sources of the silver. Some of the silver vessels found carry inscriptions that relate to

Fig. 28.10 Part of a set of Roman silver from Italy. First century BC. Ht. of *kantharoi* 10.8 cm. New York, Metropolitan Museum of Art, 20.49.2-9, 11, 12, Rogers Fund 1920 (photo: © museum).

the weight of the object and/or the owner's name and the dedication to a deity. Apart from the use of silver as coins and in furniture decoration, the main shapes into which silver (and silver gilt) was made were various (and often elaborate) forms of cups (handled and handleless), dishes, *phialai*, drinking horns, ladles, strainers, perfume bottles, lidded caskets, jugs, saucepans, mirrors, pepper pots. This variety of shapes (figure 28.10) indicates that some were made for domestic use, some for show, and some for religious or funerary purposes.

Bronze was more commonly worked than silver and gold and was more regularly used in everyday life. It was a compound of copper (widely found in Greece, Italy and Spain) and tin (much rarer). Life-size hollow statues of gods, heroes, athletes, generals and emperors were set up in sanctuaries and public areas, and small solid-cast figurines were dedicated as offerings. Of the vase-shapes, the commonest are tripod cauldrons, amphorae, *hydriae*, jugs, plates, *phialai*, pails and lidded chests. Volute-kraters (mixing bowls with handles curling above the rim) are some of the most elaborate products in bronze; the Derveni krater (figure 28.11), which was never filled with wine and water at a party but was only used as an ash-urn, has a Dionysian frieze, with a repoussé scene, cast and chased patterns, and separately cast figures. Besides bronze containers, there was a great variety of bronze objects and hardware: armour and weapons (helmets, breastplates, greaves, shields, swords), inlaid couches, candelabra, mirrors and mirror cases, dress pins etc. Ancient authors distinguish varieties of bronze and their origins, but modern study has failed to clarify the distinctions.

The gold *phialē*, the two silver *kantharoi* and the bronze volute-krater (see figures 28.9–28.11) all carry inscriptions scratched or punctured on them (see chapter 34). The gold *phialē* has part of a Greek name ('Pausi-' – perhaps that of the owner) as well as letters, symbols and numerals in Carthaginian characters (giving the weight of the

Fig. 28.11 Greek bronze volute-krater from Derveni: the myth of Dionysos. c. 325 BC. Ht. 70 cm. Thessaloniki, Archaeological Museum B 1 (photo: © museum).

object); the two silver *kantharoi* with vertical handles record the name of the woman owner ('Sattia, daughter of Lucius') and the weight of the objects in Roman lettering; the bronze krater carries an inscription in silver giving the name of the owner or maker, and his father's name and origin ('Asteiounios, son of Anaxagoras, of Larisa'). It was obviously more prudent to establish ownership of precious objects than of the much cheaper pottery.

Further reading

Pottery

C. Bérard, C. Bron et al., *La Cité des images*, Paris: Fernand Nathan, 1984 (= *A City of Images*, trans. D. Lyons, Princeton: Princeton University Press, 1989) – uses the imagery of Athenian pottery to explore cultural themes.

J. Boardman, *The History of Greek Vases*, London: Thames and Hudson, 2001 – a wide-ranging survey.

R. M. Cook, *Greek Painted Pottery* (3rd edn), London and New York: Routledge, 1997 – an indispensable handbook.

V. Grace, *Amphoras and the Ancient Wine Trade*, Princeton: American School of Classical Studies, 1979 – a useful introductory picture-booklet.

J. W. Hayes, *Handbook of Mediterranean Roman Pottery*, London: British Museum Press, 1997 – a crisp treatment.

R. E. Jones, *Greek and Cypriot Pottery: A Review of Scientific Studies*, Athens: British School of Archaeology at Athens, 1986 – technical studies of a wide range of pottery.

D. P. S. Peacock, *Pottery in the Roman World: An Ethnological Approach*, London: Longman, 1982 – places pottery-making in its varied contexts.

D. P. S. Peacock and D. F. Williams, *Amphorae and the Roman Economy: An Introductory Guide*, London: Longman, 1986 – a catalogue of amphora shapes.

B. A. Sparkes, *Greek Pottery: An Introduction*, Manchester: Manchester University Press, 1991 – summarises the various aspects of Greek pottery under headings such as date, shape, decoration.

Mention should be made of the website that gives access to the archive of Greek pottery built up by Sir John Beazley and enlarged since its acquisition by the Ashmolean Museum to include other material: www.beazley.ox.ac.uk. Users have to register to consult the database of vases listed.

Metalwork

W. Lamb, *Greek and Roman Bronzes*, London: Methuen, 1929 – out of date but still the only handbook to cover the subject.

L. P. B. Stefanelli (ed.), *Il bronzo dei Romani: arredo e suppellettile*, Rome: L'Erma di Bretschneider, 1990.

D. E. Strong, *Greek and Roman Gold and Silver Plate*, London: Methuen, 1966 – a straightforward historical account of classical plate, now somewhat out of date.

M. Vickers and D. Gill, *Artful Crafts: Ancient Greek Silverware and Pottery*, Oxford: Oxford University Press, 1994 – a caustic attack on older views of the relationship between metal and pottery.

29. *Gems, Jewellery and Glass*

Martin Henig

Engraved gems

In both Greek and Roman societies overindulgence in the acquisition and display of luxury objects was regarded as shameful, at least by moralists such as Pliny the Elder. Nevertheless gem-cutting in antiquity achieved a peak of perfection which has never been surpassed, and artists such as Dexamenos in the fifth century BC, Pyrgoteles (said by Pliny [*HN* 37.8] to have been the only man licensed by Alexander the Great to engrave his signet) in the fourth, and Dioscurides (seal-cutter to the emperor Augustus [*HN* 37.8 and 10]) in the first century BC, achieved considerable fame. In fact, there was no contradiction in this desire among the leading men of the time to patronise the best jewellers.

Intaglios

Although engraved gems are generally regarded today as merely a category of jewellery, in antiquity stones cut for use as seals and generally worn on rings were regarded very differently, so much so that they inevitably have primacy in this chapter. Literary sources reiterate the importance of the seal as enshrining the personality of the owner, for with it, if he were a ruler or a magistrate, he would sign laws and decrees, while the private citizen making a contract or a will needed his seal to guarantee his part in the proceedings.

From the archaic period stones were carved with fine tools including lap-wheels, operated by means of a bow-drill. These drills were made of bronze and relatively soft, and so the hard mineral corundum from the island of Naxos was crushed and mixed with olive oil to form a fine paste which was used to provide an abrasive. Techniques of cutting hardly changed over the years. The practitioner, who evidently worked without the aid of a lens, would generally have been short-sighted, a condition that is frequently hereditary and helps to explain how the craft ran in families. Certainly the work always required immense patience and deftness of touch.

Archaic Greek seals at first follow the basic form of Egyptian prototypes, with the backs cut in the shape of scarab-beetles but the flat sealing surfaces recognisably Greek. Worn on swivel-rings, the front, sealing surface was hidden by the finger. At the end of the archaic period and through classical times, the Greeks lost interest in carving the beetle-backs of the scarab seals (although the Etruscans continued the practice) and employed scaraboids, seals of scarab shape but with plain backs. Work was concentrated on the seals and achieved a perfection of artistry that was never to be matched. A few gems are signed. For instance, a chalcedony scaraboid of a youth restraining a lively horse (now in Boston) is signed by someone called Epimenes; equally assured are many anonymous works such as a representation of a youth holding a discus (figure 29.1) on a cornelian scaraboid, fairly close in style to Epimenes, and a study of a satyr drawing his bow on a cornelian scaraboid in Baltimore. In the classical period gems are generally larger, and artists no longer feel constrained to fill the entire surface of the gem. The finest gem-cutter of the age whose works survive is Dexamenos of Chios (c. 450 BC). His most charming signed work is an intimate scene, cut upon a large chalcedony scaraboid. It portrays

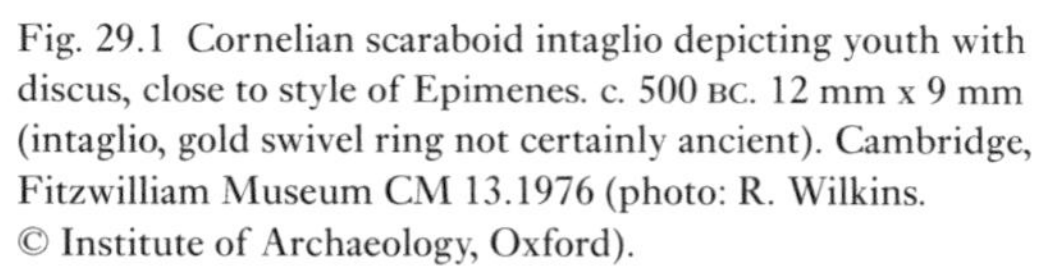

Fig. 29.1 Cornelian scaraboid intaglio depicting youth with discus, close to style of Epimenes. c. 500 BC. 12 mm x 9 mm (intaglio, gold swivel ring not certainly ancient). Cambridge, Fitzwilliam Museum CM 13.1976 (photo: R. Wilkins. © Institute of Archaeology, Oxford).

Fig. 29.2 Chalcedony scaraboid, belonging to Mike and cut by Dexamenos, depicting a domestic scene. Third quarter of fifth century BC. 22 mm x 17 mm. Cambridge, Fitzwilliam Museum B34 (CM) (photo: R. Wilkins. © Institute of Archaeology, Oxford).

a woman called Mikē sitting on a chair being attended by her maid, who holds a mirror to her mistress (figure 29.2); with his portrait of a bearded man in Boston and his two studies of herons in St Petersburg, it deserves to be included in every anthology of masterpieces of Greek art. On a miniature scale we see the same deftness of design as in the other contemporary arts such as sculpture and Attic painted pottery.

The signet ring with a fixed bezel became usual in late classical times (c. 400 BC), and throughout the Hellenistic period we find some of the best work expended on portraits of rulers. As Alexander the Great had opened up the East to Western merchants, new, more precious stones such as tourmalines, garnets, beryls (emeralds and aquamarines) and even sapphires were increasingly used alongside higher-quality amethysts and agates. Portraits of the Ptolemies of Egypt, the Seleucid rulers of Syria and members of other dynasties become regular themes, and, while a very few of these seals perhaps belonged to the persons actually depicted, most will have been worn and used by their advisers, officials and followers. Together, they provide a striking portrait gallery of the leading rulers of the day, comparable to the one to be found on contemporary coins. Examples range from a near-contemporary tourmaline intaglio in the Ashmolean Museum showing Alexander himself, which may give some idea of what Pyrgoteles' lost portraits would have looked like (as mentioned above Pyrgoteles was the official gem-engraver to Alexander the Great), to a sardonyx found in a Roman context in Wroxeter, England, portraying Ptolemy XII. It is possible that the gem was an heirloom, presented to one of his Roman bodyguard by this most frivolous of Egyptian kings who spent much of his reign in exile in Rome, which was in its turn passed on to his successor.

Not surprisingly, there was no discernible break between Hellenistic and Roman imperial gem-cutting. As Roman influence in the Mediterranean world increased in the late Republic, important Romans employed Greek gem-cutters to carve their signets. Several of the gems produced by

Augustus' gem-cutter Dioscurides are extant, beautifully crafted but possibly a little too fussy in execution, bearing comparison with the near-contemporary sculptural works of Pasiteles and his school (leaders of the neoclassical movement in the first century BC). Some intaglios of this time were, however, cut not as seals but for display, like a pair of agate intaglios showing Octavian as Mercury and his sister Octavia as Diana, both in the British Museum.

Co-existing with such imported Hellenistic Greek fashions in gem-cutting were native Italian traditions going back to archaic times, when the practice of using scarab seals was adopted by the Etruscans. Although Rome's contacts with Greece meant that the style was often lively and the subject matter adventurous, these native gems often exhibit a scratchiness and undisguised use of the drill to produce round points or pellets in the cutting comparable to that to be seen on some contemporary coin dies.

From the time of the empire many studios flourished not only in Italy, for example at Aquileia, but throughout the empire. Some of the best evidence comes from Britain, where large numbers of gems have been excavated as site-finds, allowing us to see what Roman soldiers were wearing, in the case of gems lost in the Fortress Baths at Caerleon in south Wales, for example; while, by contrast, the gems from a jeweller's stock-in-trade from Snettisham, Norfolk, tell us about the aspirations of the local farmers, the clientèle of this craftsman, working in the mid-second century AD. A major theme reflected in site-finds everywhere was the need for divine protection, as shown by the gods and goddesses who were so often figured on such seals. A splendid red jasper intaglio found at the Roman villa at Eccles, Kent, depicts the head of Pan (figure 29.3). It is of second-century date and displays the typical textured cutting of the time; no doubt its owner would have looked to Pan to protect his fields from malignant forces. Other devices, such as conjoined human heads and parts of animals, were more strictly amuletic and designed to deflect the baleful influence of the evil eye. In the Greek-speaking East, especially, another large class of stones combines esoteric Eastern deities (such as the god Iao) with magical texts. Everyone seems to have worn a seal of some sort, and the poor would have worn signets cast in glass; wasters (discarded pieces of defective workmanship) from such a workshop have been found in Rome at the Lacus Juturnae.

Many Roman gems reflect historical personages and events; the Hellenistic tradition continues throughout the first century, and overlapping (jugate) portraits of Nero and Poppaea, shown on a cornelian in a private collection, continue the series of Ptolemaic gems, upon which rulers are often shown with their consorts. A more martial theme is represented by some gems of Severan date, a number of which have been found in Britain, making allusion to the victories of Septimius Severus and Caracalla during the great imperial expedition to the province of AD 208–11. They include a green chalcedony from Silchester, in Reading Museum, figuring Caracalla in the guise of the Genius of the Roman people, wearing on his head the corn-measure of the god Serapis and, to emphasise the martial theme, a military trumpet and a *vexillum* in the field. Even more concerned with triumph is a cornelian, found near

Fig. 29.3 Red jasper intaglio depicting a mask of Pan, from Eccles, Kent. Second century AD. 11.5 mm x 9 mm. Eccles Excavation Committee (photo: R. Wilkins. © Institute of Archaeology, Oxford).

Lincoln and still in private hands (figure 29.4), representing Caracalla in the guise of Hercules; he wears a diadem of solar rays and, additionally, accepts a wreath from Victory.

Cameos

Devices of this sort are more familiar to archaeologists and the wider public on cameos because of the fame of a few so-called state cameos, propaganda pieces of fairly large size celebrating the prowess of emperors such as Augustus, Tiberius, Claudius and Septimius Severus. As already noted, intaglios could be used for similar purposes, but their compositions were seldom as ambitious as those of the Gemma Augustea in Vienna, which dates from AD 6–9, or the Grand Camée de France of about AD 17 (in the Cabinet des Médailles, Paris). These slabs of agate were cut to show, in the first case, Augustus and, in the second, Tiberius in the company of divinities, and in the act of welcoming generals from victorious wars. In both gems a lower register depicts vanquished barbarians; the Grand Camée additionally figures the deified Augustus and other imperial *divi* in the heavens above. The idea for such large and luxurious work belongs late in the Hellenistic age, represented best by the large, shallow agate bowl in Naples, the Tazza Farnese, carved on the outside with a Medusa-mask but inside with symbolic figures including the goddess Isis and a sphinx. The composition may honour Cleopatra VII of Egypt, though the meaning of such a composition would only have been fully appreciated within a fairly narrow court circle. Similarly a sapphire, a rare blue-to-purple-coloured stone depicting Aphrodite feeding an eagle (now in the Fitzwilliam Museum, Cambridge), can probably be interpreted as a product of the court of Augustus, making the claim that his imperial power descended from the goddess Venus. More straightforward examples of state propaganda are cameos cut with portraits of deceased rulers, now elevated to the gods, or of new emperors trying to establish a power base of *amici* ('loyal friends'). There are some especially appealing portraits in sardonyx of the teenage Nero dated to AD 54 before overindulgence brutalised his features (figure 29.5).

Fig. 29.4 Cornelian intaglio (set in later bronze brooch) showing Victory crowning Caracalla-Hercules, found near Lincoln. AD 211–12. In private possession (photo: R. Wilkins. © Institute of Archaeology, Oxford).

As in the case of intaglios, the majority of cameos, however, had no political purpose. At one level they were purely decorative, and often served as love-tokens given by men to their girlfriends and wives, who wore them in brooches or in finger-rings. Many simply carry inscriptions - normally in Greek - wishing the wearer 'Good fortune'; others bear the clasped hands and bridal wreath of the marriage contract or a hand tweaking an ear, evoking the memory of an absent lover (Pliny *HN* 9.103; Virgil *Eclogues* 6.34). For instance, one is inscribed with the Greek legend 'Remember me, your dear sweetheart' (figure 29.6). Portraits of women were, likewise, popular, especially in the third century AD. Eros (Cupid) was another frequent theme from late Hellenistic times, as were Dionysus (Bacchus), satyrs and maenads. It would not be totally fair to characterise cameos as useless in contrast to intaglios, because the need for protection by means of amulets was always a vital consideration. Medusa-heads, for example, are very common and were

Fig. 29.5 Sardonyx cameo depicting Nero at age of about 17. c. AD 54 30.3 mm x 28 mm. Derek Content Family Collection (photo: Bruce Frame. © Derek Content)

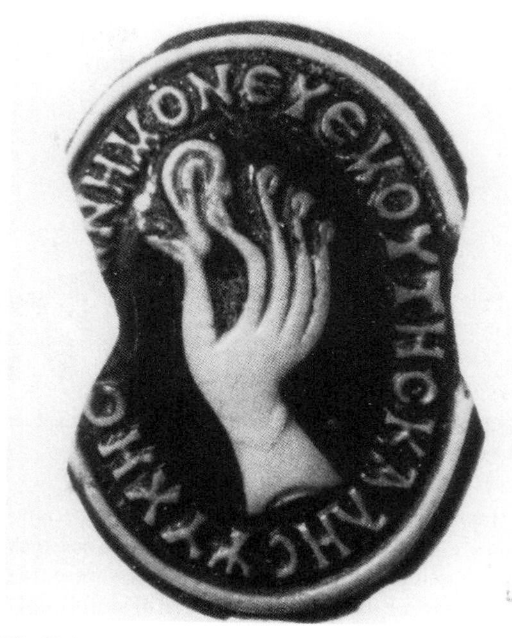

Fig. 29.6 Inscribed onyx cameo depicting a hand pinching an ear in token of remembrance. Third century AD. 14 mm x 6 mm. Oxford, Ashmolean Museum 1966.598 (photo and © Ashmolean Museum)

believed to be efficacious against evil forces. Some deities such as Asclepius (Aesculapius), Athena (Minerva) and Heracles (Hercules) are also commonly found for the same reason. Related to hardstone cameos are carvings in the round on substances regarded as magical, such as amber, that is, fossilised resin obtained from the Baltic but worked among other places at Aquileia at the head of the Adriatic. In addition, jet (fossilised wood) was widely used for pendants, especially in Britain and Germany; in Britain it outcrops at Whitby, and there were certainly workshops at York. Medusa-masks and cupids were fashioned in both media, and interestingly both jet and amber jewellery often found their way into graves.

Jewellery

Jewellery was, of course, worn throughout antiquity, displaying changes in taste and style characteristic of its age. Lack of local gold sources and, possibly, sumptuary legislation concerning extravagance in funerary offerings in many cities, such as Athens, have limited the quantity of surviving jewellery, but there is ample compensation in the many finds of classical jewellery from northern Greece and the semi-barbarian lands where Greeks mixed with Scythians in south Russia. Some of this is of superb quality, like the fifth-century BC necklace from the tomb of a woman buried at Nymphaeum in the Crimea (figure 29.7). With its pendants of naturalistic, hanging acorns, this is a masterpiece of design and execution. Other tombs have yielded similar necklaces and wreaths. A great deal of jewellery has also been found in southern Italy. A recent find from near Crotone was a remarkable diadem made of vine leaves, myrtle leaves and fruit, probably used to deck an image of the goddess Hera and evidently made by a master goldsmith in the mid-sixth century BC. About a century later is a sceptre topped by a delicate capital of leaves and flowers with a shaft covered by a lattice of gold wires, which probably belonged to a priestess of the same goddess at Tarentum. Together with a stylish necklace set with hanging pendants and an elaborate ring, this grave group is now in the British Museum.

Fig. 29.7 Gold necklace with acorn pendants from Nymphaeum in the Crimea. Fifth century BC. L. 31 cm. Oxford, Ashmolean Museum 1885.482 (photo and © Ashmolean Museum).

In the Hellenistic period jewellery became more elaborate, and access to Oriental sources meant that exotic stones such as garnets were frequently incorporated, either carved or simply polished and shaped. A splendid mid-fourth-century gold diadem was found in the 'Tomb of Philip II' at Vergina; other diadems, of about a century later, are recorded from Thessaly in north Greece (Benaki Museum, Athens) and Melos (British Museum) with 'Heracles knots' in the centre, and delicate earrings in the British Museum incorporate amphorae whose bodies are composed of garnets, thus bringing to mind the wine associated with the feast. At such feasts diners would often wear wreaths, and delicate gold wreaths, often incorporating fruit and flowers, are typical of the time; when found in tombs as at Vergina, they are intended to evoke otherworldly feasting.

The Romans were at first very disapproving of such displays of ornament but, surrounded as they were by the gold-loving Etruscans to the north (who had unparalleled skill in filigree and granulation) and Magna Graecia to the south, they had no chance of avoiding the influence of such luxury. By the late republic and early imperial period rich women possessed jewel collections including bracelets, necklaces, rings, earrings, hairpins and hairnets. Many finds of jewellery from Pompeii, and a few surviving wall paintings, can be compared with provincial portraits from Egyptian tombs to show how thoroughly Roman taste had adopted Hellenistic styles. On the peripheries of the empire, in Gaul and Britain for example, brooch-forms of pre-Roman, native Iron Age origin provide some variety. Some, such as the fan-tailed gilt-bronze brooch from Great Chesters (Aesica) on Hadrian's Wall, with its assured curvilinear ornament, are very beautiful and accomplished pieces of jewellery.

A number of new styles can be observed coming into use during the middle years of the empire, with the increasing use of openwork design, of gems chosen for colour and texture rather than for the engraving upon them, and of the incorporation of coins. A rich treasure of gold jewellery dating to Severan times from Lyons conveniently marks the beginning of the new aesthetic, and the gems and bracelets from the Beaurains (Arras) treasure of the end of the third century signal a further development. Some of the most splendid examples of later Roman style are the great cross-bow brooches worn by important Romans, such as those in the treasure of Ténès (Algeria). Other important specimens of late Roman jewellery are to be found in an extraordinary cache of jewellery from Thetford in Norfolk, dedicated to the god Faunus, with its jewelled rings of very varied design, including one in which a wine vessel is supported by a pair of woodpeckers (figure 29.8), while an equally significant jewellery hoard was recovered not very far away from Hoxne, Suffolk. The latter includes a jewelled body chain, such as would be worn by a dancer, and openwork bracelets, one of which seems to have belonged to Domina Iuliana, a great lady whose magnificent appearance would perhaps have anticipated that of the court ladies of

Fig. 29.8 Gold ring with woodpecker supporters on shoulder on either side of a wine vessel, from the treasure found at Thetford, Norfolk. Late fourth or early fifth century AD. 18 mm x 14 mm (internal diameter of ring). London, British Museum 1981.2-1.7 (photo and © British Museum).

the sixth-century Byzantine empress, Theodora, figured on a famous wall mosaic in the sanctuary of the church of San Vitale, Ravenna.

Glass

Modern connoisseurs often place ancient glass high among the arts, but in antiquity it was only the uneducated, like the parvenu Trimalchio (the eponymous character in the section of Petronius' *Satyrica* dealing with the 'Cena Trimalchionis' or 'Dinner with Trimalchio') who would regularly have done so (see Petronius *Sat.* 50.7). The seriously rich naturally aspired to own vessels made of agate, like the so-called Tazza Farnese in Naples and the Cup of the Ptolemies, now in Paris, which are both of late Hellenistic date. Equally, if not more, admired were vessels carved from fluorspar (*myrrhinē*), for which Pliny records values of up to a million sesterces (*HN* 37.18, 20 and 21), or from amber or rock crystal, for which 150,000 sesterces seems to have been a fair price for a single item (*HN* 37.29). Glass was, for the most part, merely a convenient substitute for these, especially the last. The earliest Greek glasses, dating from as early as the archaic period, were small, cast, 'cheap and cheerful' unguent bottles, but in the Hellenistic age a very few vessels were cast and ground down, and layered with thin gold leaf, clearly aiming to achieve the sumptuous effect of crystal inlaid with gold. A similar impression was sometimes achieved in items of jewellery where thin slivers of gold were framed between layers of clear glass.

The advent of glass-blowing in the Levant in the mid-first century BC allowed the production of a wide range of vessels. Some producers like Ennion set up large-scale commercial ventures, and glass vessels stamped with his name and those of other Levantine glass-makers were widely exported. The production of cameo-glasses at the end of the first century BC is like that of the earlier Hellenistic gold glasses, in that it represents another attempt to make glass into a real luxury product, by creating an artificial medium and using colours which do not occur in nature to produce works to rival agate cups. The Portland vase in the British Museum, dated to the end of the first century BC, has even been attributed to Dioscurides, and the Auldjo jug is equally fine (figure 29.9). Later cameo vases are of lower quality, and some were merely cast.

Fig. 29.9 Cameo jug carved white on blue with vine ornament ('Auldjo jug'). Late first century AD. Ht. 22.8 cm. London, British Museum 1840.12-5.41 + 1859.2-16.1 (photo and © British Museum).

During the Empire a great variety of vessels was made wherever there were suitable sands, including, in the northwest of the empire, an important production centre in Cologne. Many of the more interesting works, whether made in Cologne or elsewhere, date quite late in the imperial period, and, as with cameo-glasses, they aimed to imitate the jewelled arts. Some bowls of fourth-century date are cut with Bacchic and hunt scenes, in the manner of intaglios, and include some very pleasing pieces like the Wint Hill Bowl from Banwell, Somerset (figure 29.10). Its inscription, 'Long life to you and yours; drink and good health to you', links it to the inscriptions noted above on cameos. Even greater virtuosity was expended on the *diatreta*, in which the outer layer of a two-layered vessel was laboriously cut away to produce a trellis-like effect. On one vessel, in the British Museum, the myth of Lycurgus and Ambrosia is portrayed on a vase which changes colour depending on whether it is viewed by reflected or transmitted light. Similar vessels with high-relief decoration were carved in hard-stone, like the vase which once belonged to the painter Rubens and is now in Baltimore. Finally the art of gold glasses was revived, generally figured with scenes and devices variously pagan, Jewish or Christian. Many have been found in burial contexts and, beautiful as they are, their real value can only have been relatively modest.

Further reading

Engraved gems

J. Boardman, *Greek Gems and Finger Rings: Early Bronze Age to Late Classical* (2nd edn), London: Thames and Hudson, 2001 – a comprehensive study of Greek glyptics to the end of the classical age.

Fig. 29.10 Vessel of clear glass engraved in imitation of rock-crystal vessel with a hunting scene and an inscription evoking good cheer ('Wint Hill Bowl'), made in Cologne, found at Banwell, Somerset. Diam. 19.3 cm. Oxford, Ashmolean Museum 1957.168 (photo and © Ashmolean Museum).

D. Collon, *7000 Years of Seals*, London: British Museum Publications, 1997, especially chapter 5, pp. 74–87, 'Greek seals' (J. Boardman) and chapter 6, pp. 88–106, 'Roman seals' (M. Henig) – explains the way gems were used, especially for sealing and as amulets.

M. Henig, *The Content Family Collection of Ancient Cameos*, Oxford and Houlton ME: Ashmolean Museum, 1990 – apart from 'state cameos', cameo art has been rather neglected, and this catalogue of a large private collection of mainly personal cameos redresses the balance.

M. Henig, *Classical Gems: Ancient and Modern Intaglios and Cameos in the Fitzwilliam Museum, Cambridge*, Cambridge: Cambridge University Press, 1994 – although a catalogue of one collection, the range of this one is remarkable and contains many masterpieces.

D. Plantzos, *Hellenistic Engraved Gems*, Oxford: Clarendon Press, 1999 – continues where Boardman leaves off.

G. M. A. Richter, *Engraved Gems of the Greeks, Etruscans and Romans*, London: Phaidon, 1970–1 – this two-volume study is the only work in English to survey both Greek and Roman gems.

Jewellery

R. Higgins, *Greek and Roman Jewellery* (2nd edn), London: Methuen, 1980 – the standard work in English.

C. Johns, *The Jewellery of Roman Britain: Celtic and Classical Traditions*, London: UCL Press, 1996 – an exceptionally readable and informative survey of Roman jewellery from a single province.

D. Williams and J. Ogden, *Greek Gold Jewellery of the Classical World*, London: British Museum Publications, 1994 – a comprehensive study of Greek gold jewellery based on an exhibition in the British Museum.

Glass

R. S. Bianchi (ed.), *Reflections on Ancient Glass from the Borowski Collection*, Mainz: Philipp von Zabern, 2002 – a comprehensive catalogue of Roman glass, containing some rare items.

D. B. Harden (ed.), *Glass of the Caesars*, Milan: Olivetti, 1987 – catalogue of a major exhibition staged by the Corning Museum, the British Museum and the Römisch-Germanisches Museum, Cologne.

30. Dress and Textiles

Karen E. Stears

The most common fabrics of the Greek and Roman worlds were wool and linen, but other stuffs were used including hemp, asbestos and leather and, more frequently in the Roman world, silk and cotton. Clothing generally consisted of large rectangular pieces of material draped and pinned in position, although cut and stitched garments were used in the Roman world. Relatively few textiles are preserved from the classical world and much of our evidence is derived from literary and artistic sources. Although the standard Greek and Latin terminology employed by scholars to describe ancient clothing may not be that which was used in antiquity to signify particular items of clothing, it is a useful vocabulary of dress and will be used here.

Production

Textiles were produced both within the household and at industrial centres. In both the Greek and Roman worlds hand-spun woollen and linen yarns were woven on warp-weighted looms which produced large, rectangular pieces, which could be utilised as garments without further cutting (figure 30.1). From the second century AD the two-beam vertical loom was employed to produce narrower woollen cloths and tapestries. Dyestuffs extracted from vegetables (e.g. madder [red], woad [blue] and saffron [yellow]) and animals (e.g. the sea-snail murex [purple] and the insect kermes [red]) produced fabrics in a variety of colours; sulphur bleached garments white. Fulling (treading on garments in tanks containing a mixture of water, urine and fuller's earth) finished newly made fabrics, removing grease and dirt. Archaeological remains of textile production centres have been found at Isthmia (near Corinth), Delos, Pompeii and Ostia. Among the few textile remains, some of the most important are the linen tunic from the Greek Iron Age site of Lefkandi, on the island of Euboea; the decorated funerary textiles from the Seven Brothers tomb groups of the Scythian Kerch region of the Black Sea coast, dating from the fifth and fourth centuries BC; the fourth-century textiles found in the royal Macedonian tombs of Vergina in northern Greece; and the vast number of textile fragments

Fig. 30.1 Black-figure Athenian *lēkythos*; wool-working scene, attributed to the Amasis Painter. c. 560 BC. New York, Metropolitan Museum of Art 31.11.10, Fletcher Fund (photo: © museum).

found in the dumps of the quarry site of Mons Claudianus in Roman Egypt.

Garments

The most simple form of 'dress' was nudity: in Greek society this was the standard 'uniform' of the young male athlete, but clothing was usually worn by all but babies and infants. The basic garment of both the Greek and Roman worlds was the draped mantle (figure 30.2). A large rectangular piece of cloth (Gk. *himation*, Lat. *palla/pallium*) was the traditional garment of Greek men (and after the fifth century BC of Greek women) and of Roman women (Roman men also wore it on informal occasions). It was usually made of wool, but Roman women might wear lighter versions in silk, linen or cotton. The formal dress of Roman men was a semicircular version, the toga (figure 30.3). The *himation/palla* was between 5 and 6 feet (1.5 – 2m) wide and 9 and 10 feet (2.5 – 3m) long; the toga was larger. These mantles were usually plain in colour but the toga might be decorated with a purple border (*praetexta*) to signify high status. The correct arrangement of these large mantles was important, signifying orderly deportment and

Fig. 30.2 Athenian funerary *naiskos* of Damasistrate and Polykleides; variety of Athenian clothing types. Late fourth century BC. Athens, National Museum 743 (photo: © museum).

Fig. 30.3 Ara Pacis Augustae, south frieze; variety of Roman clothing types worn by the imperial family. 13–9 BC. Rome, Campus Martius (photo: © Fototeca Unione 3247 F).

decorum (and probably with the huge toga the ownership of slaves to help the wearer dress); there were various styles of draping, the most common of which was to hold the bulk of the garment with the left arm, thus freeing the right. Folds might be used as pockets. The cumbersome nature of these garments indicates that the wearers would not undertake manual labour. Short cloaks, with or without hoods and fastened at the necks, allowed for easier movement, and were worn by men particularly for travelling and fighting.

A form of woollen mantle worn by Greek women was the *peplos*. It was the main dress of the archaic period but was largely superseded (except in winter) by the *himation* in a change in fashion during the late sixth and fifth centuries. The *peplos* consisted of a rectangular piece of cloth worn folded widthways around the body, with the top third or so folded over lengthways, and then pinned at the shoulders. It continued to be worn by slaves and little girls as it allowed freedom of movement for work or play.

Artistic images often give the impression that mantles were worn, by men especially, without other garments, but this was probably not the case. By the classical period a tunic was regularly worn by both men and women (Gk. *chiton*, Lat. *tunica*). It could be made from a large single piece of cloth, often linen, folded widthways or lengthways around the body and fastened by either brooches or buttons at the shoulders or along the length of the arm, and might, like the *peplos*, also be worn with an overfold and be belted. The garment might also be made from two pieces of cloth, sewn at the sides and then pinned or buttoned at the shoulders. Men wore the tunic short, women wore it long, and in its coarsest and cheapest versions it was the garment of the slave; it was difficult to conceal objects in it, and it used little fabric to produce. Roman versions of the *tunica* for men had sleeves and appear to have been decorated with purple vertical stripes (*clavi*, singular *clavus*), to denote membership of the senatorial or equestrian orders (figure 30.4). Sleeves were sewn on to the later Roman examples of the garment.

Simple loincloths were probably worn by both sexes, and bands of fabric were also used to

Fig. 30.4 Linen tunic with *clavus* from Roman Egypt. Third or fourth century AD. Tunic B, Whitworth Art Gallery, University of Manchester (photo: © museum).

support women's breasts. Belts, simple or crossed more than once over the upper torso, were an essential aid to arranging tunics and keeping clothes or the breasts in place. Greek women regularly wore hairnets (slave-girls the more practical scarf), and men might wear felted hats, but heads were often covered by pulling the mantle up over them; a recent case has been made that Greek women were routinely veiled. Shoes and sandals were made of leather or felt.

Contexts

Dress was a powerful signifier of social statuses such as gender, age, ethnicity, free/slave, citizen/non-citizen, ritual purity, office (whether political, military or religious), and economic class; Roman society especially employed dress in this way. Clothing might also be used to blur, hide or transform social categories, and the inherent danger to social stratification was a matter of complaint for some ancient authors. Social identities might be constructed by means of garment type, colour, decoration, material, cleanliness and the way in which a garment was worn. Accessories such as jewellery, footwear and hairstyles would also contribute to the overall dress effect, and a well-dressed attendant slave might be regarded as an essential accessory for the rich and powerful.

Although the basic garments of the classical world changed relatively little over a long period of time, there was a concept of fashion. This appears to have been focused largely on the level of accessories, notably hairstyles, jewellery, shoes and sandals; and these are the details most commonly employed to construct relative chronologies in Greek and Roman sculpture. However, changes in fashion might also be achieved through crazes for draping, folding, pinning or belting the established garments in new ways, or for elaborating them by means of increasing the amount of material in them or the quality or colour of fabric utilised. Patterns woven into the cloth might also be an area for fashionable display. Occasionally fashion was centred on the import of exotic, usually Oriental, imports, which tended to be cut and sewn garments such as the long-sleeved coat, the *kandys*, in fifth-century Athens, and trousers in the late Roman Empire.

Clothing and other textiles had uses beyond that of dress. In early Greek society they were regarded as cash substitutes in an economy that was not fully monetary. They were also commonly offered as votive and funerary offerings and given as gifts. Even though cloth was produced on a large scale at least from the fifth century BC onward, textiles were ideologically associated with the female domain of the household and with modest feminine industry and decorum; this is a philosophical, a literary and, in the early Roman Empire, a political topos. In myth and literature textiles often serve as plot devices by which women obtain access to power otherwise denied them, be it communication, deception, revelation, murder or suicide. Textiles woven with images are particularly important in these stories.

The study of ancient dress and textiles has been sporadic and fragmentary but is now flourishing. A major strand is the study of yarn and weaves of ancient cloth remains, together with spinning, weaving and dyeing technologies. Reconstructions and experimental archaeology are elements of this approach. The iconography of dress is another major area of research and is of particular use in dating sculpture as well as being a subject in its own right. Dress and textiles in their cultural, social and economic contexts are a growing area of interest, many analyses arising from the relatively new anthropological and sociological disciplines of gender and dress studies.

Further reading

E. J. W. Barber, *Prehistoric Textiles*, Princeton: Princeton University Press, 1991 – a linguistic and technological investigation of Aegean textiles.

L. Cleland, K. E. Stears and G. M. Davies (eds), *Colour in the Ancient Mediterranean World* (BAR International Series 1267), Oxford: Hedges, 2004 – the wider context of colours in antiquity.

L. Cleland, M. Harlow and L. Llewellyn-Jones (eds), *The Clothed Body in the Ancient World*, Oxford: Oxbow, 2005 – essays on the culture of clothing.

A. T. Croom, *Roman Clothing and Fashion*, Stroud: Tempus, 2000 – a study of Roman textiles, especially ways of draping clothing, including the early Christian period.

R. J. Forbes, *Studies in Ancient Technology* (4), Leiden: Brill, 1956 – a detailed examination of classical textile technology.

L. Llewellyn-Jones (ed.), *Women's Dress in the Ancient Greek World*, London: Duckworth and Classical Press of Wales, 2002 – useful collection of essays on cultural studies.

L. Llewellyn-Jones, *Aphrodite's Tortoise: The Veiled Woman of Ancient Greece*, Oxford: Oxbow and Classical Press of Wales, 2003 – an investigation of the use of dress iconography and the veil in particular.

G. Losfeld, *Essai sur le costume grec*, Paris: Editions Boccard, 1991 – exhaustive literary references.

U. Mannering, 'Roman garments from Mons Claudianus', in D. Cardon and M. Feugère (eds), *Archéologie des textiles des origines au Ve siècle: Actes du colloque de Lattes, octobre 1999*, Montagnac: Editions Monique Mergoil, 2000, pp. 283–90 – essential interim study report.

K. D. Morrow, *Greek Footwear and the Dating of Sculpture*, Wisconsin: University of Wisconsin Press, 1985 – controversial study of footwear for establishing sculptural chronology.

A. Pekridou-Gorecki, *Mode in Antiken Griechenland*, Munich: C. H. Beck, 1989 – cursory but useful introduction to clothing and fashion.

J. L. Sebesta and L. Bonfante (eds), *The World of Roman Costume*, Wisconsin: University of Wisconsin Press, 1994 – essential investigations of Roman dress, with good illustrations.

M. Vickers, *Images on Textiles: The Weave of Fifth-Century Athenian Art and Society* (*Xenia* 42), Konstanz: UVK, 1999 – brief introduction to cultural aspects of Athenian textiles.

P. Walton Rogers, L. Bender Jørgensen and A. Rast-Eicher (eds), *The Roman Textile Industry and its Influence: A Birthday Tribute to John Peter Wild*; Oxford: Oxbow Books, 2001 – useful introduction to technical aspects and excellent bibliography.

Website

www.costumes.org, home of the *Costumer's Manifesto* – an excellent resource and gateway to dress and textile sites.

31. *Arms and Armour*

Jon Coulston

There are three principal interconnected areas of evidence for the study of Greek and Roman arms and armour: the artefactual record, iconography, and literary or sub-literary sources. All three have their weaknesses, limitations and biases, but, when employed together with ethnographic parallels and reconstructive experimentation, they may provide a clear overall picture of ancient developments and usage.

Artefacts

Metallic equipment was always inherently valuable, often bound up with the individual's honour and status, and in regular armies soldiers were often accountable for its good order. Thus large items were seldom accidentally 'lost' and it required specific mechanisms to preserve artefacts for the archaeological record. Helmets (figure 31.1), shields and large numbers of missiles were regularly discarded and buried during siegeworks, as at Old Paphos on Cyprus (590 BC), First Jewish War Gamla in Palestine (AD 67), and Dura-Europos in Syria (mid-250s AD). Magazine sites sometimes yield residual stocks, as at Hellenistic Pergamum in Turkey and Aï Khanum in Afghanistan. Occasionally items were deposited through serious mishap, such as when an archaic Greek ship went down near Giglio off southern Italy, or when Vesuvius erupted in AD 79 entombing the arms of soldiers, sailors and gladiators at Pompeii and Herculaneum. Commonly arms and armour survive as votive dedications, either at sacred sites or in funerary contexts. The capture of enemy equipment in battle was an unequivocal proof of victory, and some victors dedicated their own armour as a thank-offering for survival. Thus excavations at panhellenic sites such as Olympia and Isthmia have produced helmets, shields and other armour associated with the Persian and Peloponnesian wars. Horse-harness, armour and weapons were dedicated at temple sites in the Netherlands by local aristocrats who had served with the Roman army. Massive dedications of captured arms and armour were made in Scandinavian sacred lakes following wars between Germanic groups, and these included native equipment, equipment created under Roman influence, and actual Roman items in circulation beyond the imperial frontiers. Greek equipment occurs in quantity where peoples on the fringes of the Greek world practised burial of grave-goods with the aristocratic dead, such as the Scythians, Thracians, Macedonians, Illyrians, Etruscans and Numidians. Similarly, Roman equipment found its way through trade and gift-giving into graves in first-to-fourth century AD Free Germany, or within the Roman Empire through the influx of barbarian groups, into Frankish, Gothic and Hunnic cemeteries.

However, by far the richest context for artefact survival is one peculiar to the Roman army of the first century BC to fourth century AD: the abandonment and demolition of military installations. When frontiers advanced or retreated, bases were dismantled. For unknown reasons valuable metalwork was sometimes not taken away with the military formations concerned, but, with other rubbish (such as fragmentary tents, saddle-covers and shield-leathers), was tidily disposed of in ditches and pits. This usually included unfinished equipment, or damaged items awaiting repair or recycling, all

Fig. 31.1 Copper alloy 'Corinthian'-type helmet, late seventh century BC. Newcastle-upon-Tyne, the University, Shefton Museum of Greek Art and Archaeology 98 (photo: © museum).

surplus to the needs of departing troops. A Hadrianic trunk full of armour and other items found at Corbridge (Northumberland, England), and weapons and sports armour from numerous German forts (e.g. Straubing, Niederbieber, Künzing), fall within this category.

Iconography

The iconographic evidence for Greek and Roman military equipment varies in richness and reliability both chronologically and regionally. For Greek practices reliance is placed on seventh-to-

Fig. 31.2 'Corinthian'-type Greek helmets depicted on an oil-flask of the early fifth century BC. Newcastle-upon-Tyne, the University, Shefton Museum of Greek Art and Archaeology 151 (photo: © museum).

fourth century BC ceramic painting which shows equipment in mythological, heroic military and sporting contexts (figure 31.2). There is an emphasis on heavily armoured hoplites, but in stylised contexts other troops also appear, such as armoured cavalry, light infantry (e.g. Thracian peltasts) and Scythian archers. Depiction of large numbers of combatants over a battlefield was always limited by the painted context. The appearance of hoplites and cavalrymen on carved stone *stēlae* was likewise restrictive in terms of available space. Thus, for example, the depiction of Hellenistic troops with their exceedingly long infantry and cavalry spears (*sarissai*) was particularly problematic; this weapon and the formations it dictated very seldom appeared in Greek art (the Alexander Mosaic from Pompeii, Italy, may be one exception; see chapter 27, figure 27.1). From the later first century BC to the fourth century AD many Roman soldiers chose to be figured on gravestones, principally as standing infantrymen and triumphant horsemen. Soldiers and their equipment appeared in state art from the Hellenistic period onwards, notably on victory monuments. Here the figures were often simplified and homogenised in order to aid visual recognition, as on the Aemilius Paulus monument at Delphi, or on the Columns of Trajan (figure 31.3) and Marcus Aurelius in Rome. Very valuable polychrome evidence is provided by a host of sources, such as painted Hellenistic gravestones from Demetrias in Greece, Sidon in Lebanon and Alexandria in

Fig. 31.3 Detail of Trajan's Column in Rome, depicting Roman troops in segmental plate and mail armour. Early second century AD (photo: © J. C. N. Coulston).

Egypt; numerous frescoes from tombs and other ritual contexts; Romano-Egyptian mummy portraits; and incidental figures in mosaics and manuscript illuminations.

Literary and sub-literary sources

The Greek literary sources make some general reference to hoplite equipment and the constituents of the full provision (*panoplia*), notably with regard to the high expense of armour, the status of its owners, and the ignominy of individuals losing their shields (assumed to have been thrown away in flight). Narrative histories such as those of Herodotus, Thucydides, Xenophon and Polybius provided incidental details relating to equipment but were more likely to dwell on less familiar, non-Greek and barbarian usages. Similarly, Roman sources such as Livy and Tacitus referred to arms and armour in order to make rhetorical points, often with a degree of exaggeration or misunderstanding. Greek and Latin biography incorporated allusions to equipment principally in order to credit individual generals with innovations, in the manner of ancient understanding of how 'inventions' came about, but these now seldom convince modern scholars. From the fourth century BC onwards the vogue for 'technical' treatises did create a context within which the differential arming of various troops in sieges and battles was a major concern (see chapter 59). However, even the most 'specialist' works, such as those on the design of artillery (Heron, Philon, Biton, Vitruvius), must be understood as belonging to recognised literary genres, written from a more or less 'library' perspective, and thus requiring corroboration by archaeological evidence.

Infantrymen

The Graeco-Roman tradition of city-based armies clearly emphasised close-order infantry formations provided at first by wealthy elites, but increasingly over time by mercenary troops and, eventually, by state-armed citizen troops. A Greek tradition may be distinguished of such forces being primarily armed with the spear (*doru*), encompassing the traditional hoplite spearmen (*doruphoroi*) and the Hellenistic pikemen (*sariss-aphoroi*). The sword was only a secondary weapon. Within the Roman orbit an opposing Western model developed of infantry who were primarily

Fig. 31.4 Roman helmet of the later first century AD with crest and plumes, reconstructed by the Ermine Street Guard (photo: © J. C. N. Coulston).

swordsmen with varying types of javelin missiles. The latter model won out when Rome clashed with the Hellenistic kingdoms, and it dominated ancient warfare until the fifth century AD. However, it is clear that ancillary troops were also important, the light infantry and cavalry, the specialist archers and slingers. Many of these were provided by 'outsiders', barbarians whose ecological and cultural backgrounds predisposed them to different methods of waging war which could be employed by Mediterranean states.

Modern studies

Modern scholarship has in the past concentrated on various focused fields such as tracing the development of the hoplite *panoplia*, defining the construction and dimensions of Greek shafted weapons, creating classifications of helmet forms, understanding artillery from the technical treatises, or reconstructing Roman segmental plate armour (*lorica segmentata*). Until the 1980s both Greek and Roman equipment studies suffered from being marginalised within their broader modern military fields, the artefactual evidence rarely being studied seriously, unless as decorated individual artworks, the iconographic and literary sources generally taking precedence. In Greek studies a more professional publication of artefacts has developed in combination with a broader inquiry into the hoplite 'battle experience'. The importance of both the evolution of 'hoplite' warfare as it spread geographically (e.g. to Italy) and the influences of non-Greek cultures have become more fully appreciated. The field of Roman military equipment studies has blossomed through the proceedings of an international conference series, ROMEC, which started in 1983 (*Journal of Roman Military Equipment Studies*). This has created both a forum for the presentation of new discoveries and a platform for thematic inquiries into equipment production and technology (figure 31.4), the archaeological deposition of equipment, and ritual and sociological perspectives. Further questions of warrior and soldier identity are being explored together with the nature of 'Roman' practices, acculturated through contacts within and without the Roman sphere. 'Celtic' traditions of metalworking informed Roman armour and weapon design, and ring-mail spread most widely through its use in Roman armies. Northern European horsemanship developed effective horned saddles which were adopted throughout the Roman world and beyond, the lack of stirrups no longer being considered to have been a serious limitation to ancient cavalry performance. The archery technology of Eastern peoples dominated Roman practice, so that bows of Iranian and Central Asiatic designs were used throughout the Roman Empire, as evidenced by finds of composite bow components in military installations all along the frontiers. Numerous new fittings from catapults have been recovered, and their analysis now allows for a more subtle appreciation not only of how artillery was used, but also of how treatise literature and empirical design interacted.

Further reading

M. C. Bishop and J. C. N. Coulston, *Roman Military Equipment from the Punic Wars to the Fall of Rome*, London: Batsford, 1993 (2nd edn, Oxford: Oxbow, 2006) – definitive work on the subject.

A. Bottini, M. Egg, F.-W. von Hase, H. Pflug, U. Schaaff, P. Schauer and G. Waurick, *Antike Helme: Sammlung Lipperheide und andere Bestände des Antikenmuseums Berlin*, Mainz: Römisch-Germanischen Zentralmuseums, 1988 – well-illustrated catalogue of Greek and Roman helmets.

P. Connolly, *Greece and Rome at War*, London: Greenhill, 1998 – the best overview of Greek and Roman warfare with close attention to the role of arms and armour.

P. Dintsis, *Hellenistische Helme*, Rome: G. Bretschneider, 1986 – well-illustrated catalogue of Greek helmets.

F. Ducrey, *Guerre et guerriers dans la Grèce antique*, Paris: Payot, 1985 – French overview of Greek warfare, heavily illustrated.

M. Feugère, *Casques antiques*, Paris: Editions Errance, 1994 – Greek and Roman helmets in one small volume.

V. D. Hanson, *The Western Way of War*, Oxford: Oxford University Press, 1989 – definitive study of hoplite warfare with due regard to equipment.

Journal of Roman Military Equipment Studies, Oxford: Oxbow, 1–, 1990– (Proceedings of Roman Military Equipment Conference (ROMEC)) – best source for new finds and specialist studies, covering Rome and its enemies.

H. R. Robinson, *The Armour of Imperial Rome*, London: Arms and Armour Press, 1975 – groundbreaking, illustrated study of Roman armour artefacts, although the typologies are superseded.

A. M. Snodgrass, *Arms and Armour of the Greeks* (2nd edn), Baltimore: Johns Hopkins University Press, 1999 – the only detailed overview from the Bronze Age to the Hellenistic period.

32. *Papyri*

Brian McGing

The scope of papyrology

For about 4,000 years, roughly 3000 BC to AD 1000, the people of Egypt made writing-paper out of the papyrus plant (*Cyperus papyrus*), which has given its name to the resulting product ('papyrus' for a single piece of paper, 'papyri' in the plural). The manufacturing process was simple. The outer casing of the triangular stem was removed and the pith cut and peeled away in strips about 30 – 40 cm (12–16 in.) long. These strips were laid vertically side by side and then another layer placed crosswise on top; the two layers were pressed together, dried and rubbed smooth into a writing surface that could be of very high quality. Individual sheets were glued together to create a roll, the standard length of which was twenty sheets (approx. 6–8 m, or 20–6 ft.). The modern book form, the codex (quires of sheets folded in half and stitched along the fold; see chapter 33), was a Roman development that, after its adoption by early Christianity, began to supersede the roll. The ink was for a long time made from water, gum and lampblack (a soot product); in later Roman times, iron gall was added.

The story of this paper is very largely an Egyptian one. In the Mediterranean world it was produced commercially, as far as we can see, only in Egypt, where the plant flourished, particularly in the marshy lands of the Nile delta. Although papyrus writing-paper was exported extensively, to survive it must be kept dry and out of the light. There are some rare survivals in the damp lands on the northern side of the Mediterranean, and the dry spots of the Near East have produced important finds, but overwhelmingly it is Egypt that offers the best conditions for its preservation: the tombs of the pharaohs and Egyptian elite, the use of waste paper as a sort of *papier mâché* (called cartonnage) for human and animal mummies, and the dry desert conditions at the edges of modern settlement have combined to preserve an extraordinary wealth of papyrus documentation: hundreds of thousands of papyri, ranging from whole rolls and books to tiny fragments, survive from Egypt. No other region of the ancient world has preserved a comparable record.

While writing on papyrus had a long and multilingual life, the scholarly discipline known as 'papyrology', which developed at the end of the nineteenth century as a subsection of classical scholarship, has limited itself mainly to the thousands of surviving Greek texts written in Egypt between about 300 BC and AD 700. In its narrowest sense, papyrology's primary task is to decipher and produce editions in readable form of these often fragmentary and difficult texts – in other words, to transform them from raw archaeological artefacts into potentially manageable historical and literary data. It has been the standard practice to write an introduction, translation and commentary on the texts so edited, thus putting them into context, pointing out difficulties and suggesting lines of interpretation as an aid to understanding. In a broader sense, papyrology also seeks to study the world revealed in the texts through works of literary, linguistic and historical analysis.

Such a description, however, needs qualification, as it would not cover all papyrologists or all the work carried out by them: the material, linguistic and geographical scope of the subject is, in

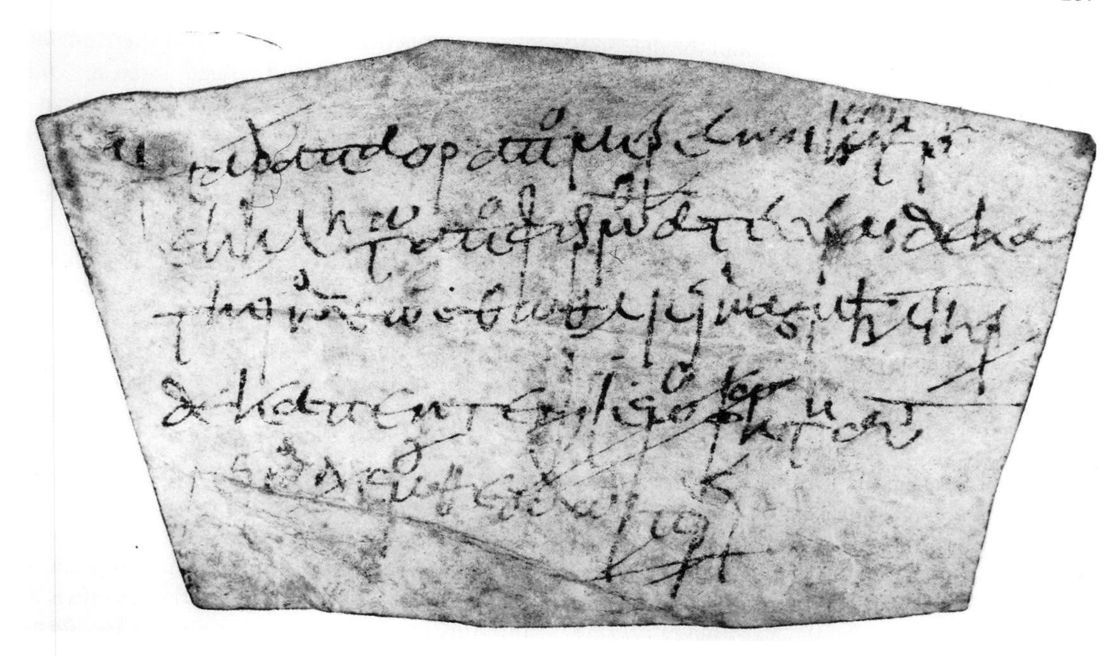

Fig. 32.1 *P. Dub*. 30: rent receipt written on parchment, which began in this period to displace papyrus. Seventh or eighth century AD. Published by kind permission of the Board of Trinity College Dublin.

fact, wider. Writing preserved on *ostraka* (broken pieces of pottery) and on waxed wooden tablets (and, in certain cases, on metal and parchment; figure 32.1) has traditionally come under the aegis of papyrology. The time-span to which I have referred, 300 BC to AD 700, is the Graeco-Roman period of Egyptian history, its beginning marked by Alexander the Great's annexation of Egypt in 332/1 BC, its end by the Islamic conquest in AD 642. During this millennium Greek was the official language of the administration, even after Egypt became a province of the Roman Empire in 30 BC, and most of the surviving documentation is in Greek. There is a small amount of Latin. There are also a large number of texts written in Egyptian, particularly in the cursive form (see also chapter 63) we know as 'demotic'. Traditionally, Egyptologists have studied 'Egyptian' Egypt, taken largely to be the Egypt of the pharaohs, with its writing in hieroglyphs, hieratic (an abbreviated version of the hieroglyphic script) and demotic; and papyrologists (or, more generally, classicists) have studied 'Graeco-Roman' Egypt, the Egypt reflected in the Greek papyri and classical authors of antiquity. This is, however, partly an artificial convenience arising out of two distinctly different modes of modern scholarly training ('classics' and 'Egyptology'), both of them difficult and demanding.

The problem for students of Graeco-Roman Egypt is that the Egyptian people continued to go about their Egyptian business, speaking and writing their language, worshipping their gods, tilling their fields and so on, long after the arrival of the Ptolemies. Egyptian continued to be written down deep into the Roman imperial period (the last dated hieroglyphic inscription comes from AD 394; the last demotic text some fifty years later). Admittedly, even by the first century AD it had become marginalised in most contexts, but in the Ptolemaic period (323–30 BC), especially in its first century, demotic Egyptian is still of central importance; and in the second and third centuries AD the Egyptian language gained a new lease of life when it adapted the Greek alpahabet and developed the form we call Coptic. When looking at the bigger picture, one cannot fully understand Ptolemaic or Byzantine Egypt (AD

284–642) without taking into account the demotic and Coptic material respectively. Although the majority of demotic papyri remains unpublished, a small number of papyrologists have mastered both the Egyptian and Greek languages, and have contributed work of exceptional importance. It might also be noted that the transition from Graeco-Roman to Islamic rule in Egypt, and the nature of that fascinating cultural interaction, can ultimately be assessed only with a mastery of Coptic, Greek and Arabic.

Nor are the potential linguistic demands on the papyrologist limited just to Egypt and its languages: the dry sands of its desert areas may have proved the best preserver of papyrus, but not its only one. A volume of Greek papyri from Petra in Jordan has recently been published, and there have been important discoveries from Dura-Europus on the Euphrates and from the Judaean desert. A recent article (Cotton et al., 'Papyrology') listing documentary papyri from the Roman Near East noted just over 600 texts. The authors comment on the variety of languages used: mostly Greek, but also plenty of Latin (especially in a military context) and Hebrew, Aramaic, Nabataean, Palmyrene, Syriac. A new field of Near Eastern, as opposed to Egyptian, papyrology is developing. The carbonised rolls of papyrus from the remains of Herculaneum, destroyed by the eruption of Vesuvius in AD 79, have created another micro-industry within the general field of papyrology, as have the wooden tablets inscribed in Latin from Vindolanda near Hadrian's Wall in Britain (see also chapter 34). However exciting and important these discoveries are – and there is every reason to expect more such finds, particularly from the Near East – the heart of papyrology still lies in Egypt, if only because there is still so much unpublished material from there: in Greek alone, major papyrological collections such as those in Berlin, Vienna and Oxford have many thousands of unedited texts.

The early history of papyrology

The story of modern papyrology begins to all intents and purposes in the second half of the nineteenth century. It was long known that ancient peoples wrote on papyrus, but it was scarcely appreciated until the discovery in 1752 of many hundreds of papyrus rolls in the ruins of Herculaneum. There was huge interest, and expectation that the world would be given exciting new discoveries of Greek and Latin literature. Wordsworth even wrote a poem about it (No. 28, *Poems of Sentiment and Reflection*). Sadly, the reality was disappointing: very little could be made of the rolls because they were carbonised (modern technology has been able to extract much more from them, and the work still goes on). In 1778 a Danish traveller sent a papyrus roll as a gift to Cardinal Stefano Borgia. It had been one of forty or fifty offered to an unknown merchant, who bought one; the others, so the story went, were burned by Turks who liked the smell. When the text was published it was, if anything, an even bigger disappointment: although it was over 10 feet (3m) long, it contained only a list of men liable for work on the irrigation channels at Tebtunis in the Fayyum region of Egypt in the year AD 192. In the early decades of the nineteenth century, travellers, diplomats, scholars and other interested parties competed to form collections of Egyptian antiquities, and Greek papyri began to turn up. They were almost always finds made by locals, and only in small numbers. Collectors wanted big, spectacular rolls or archives of related texts.

It was the 1870s that really marked the rediscovery of Greek papyri. Farmers had always known that the soil from ancient sites was richer in nitrates, and had used it as fertiliser, but on a relatively small scale. In the 1870s the cultivated area of Egypt expanded and local farmers now needed much larger quantites of this *sebakh* or fertile earth. As they carted it away in huge amounts from the ancient sites, large numbers of papyri, mostly Greek, but also demotic, Coptic and Arabic, were revealed in the dumps where the original inhabitants had thrown them out. The Austrians were the first to take advantage of this new source and many thousands of texts made their way to Vienna, still one of the biggest collections in the world. But other important museums and centres of classical studies soon began to institute purchasing policies. The antiquities market was the first major supplier of papyri for modern collections, but papyri were also being found on archaeological digs, particularly by the British archaeologist Flinders Petrie in the 1880s.

The year 1891 saw the publication of two volumes of Greek papyri that aroused keen interest: the first volume of the Petrie papyri, edited by J. P. Mahaffy of Trinity College Dublin, and the first of the British Museum papyri, edited by Frederick Kenyon. The latter was the more sensational because it contained an edition of a lost work attributed to Aristotle, the *Constitution of the Athenians* (see also chapter 60). And in the 1890s and the early years of the twentieth century, this was still the main reason for the extraordinary excitement generated by papyri: scholars would be able to recover lost masterpieces of Greek literature and philosophy, and Christian texts. That was the motivation behind the decision of the Egypt Exploration Fund to send, in 1895, the first archaeological expedition to Egypt specifically to search for papyri (see also chapter 1). In the following decade, under the leadership of two remarkable British scholars, Bernard Grenfell and Arthur Hunt, huge numbers of papyri were discovered at Tebtunis, at Hibeh and above all at Oxyrhynchus. Oxyrhynchus yielded enormous quantities of papyrus: at the moment nearly 5,000 texts have been published in 67 volumes, and there is much more to come. Other European nations, particularly the Germans, French and Italians, sent their own expeditions in search of papyri, followed later by the Americans.

What they found, and bought on the antiquities market, forms the basis of the modern collections, but it is important to emphasise how arbitrary, both chronologically and geographically, these finds (and purchases) were. From the Fayyum, the ancient Arsinoite nome (administrative region), some hundred kilometres southwest of modern Cairo, we have what is at certain periods probably a good representative sample of the documentation produced in the area. The same holds true for Oxyrhynchus and some sites in Upper Egypt, but in the Nile Delta, the most populous and fertile area of ancient Egypt, but also the dampest, virtually no papyri survive; and, unfortunately, this is also the case for Alexandria, the capital of a highly bureaucratic administration that produced probably millions of rolls of papyrus: the water table is too high to preserve perishable material. We must recognise the limitations this inconsistency places on our knowledge.

The subject matter and importance of papyri

The first volume of Oxyrhynchus papyri was published in 1898 and the first text was something the editors called 'Sayings of Jesus' (it is now recognised as part of the apocryphal Gospel of Thomas). The second text was a third-century AD copy of the opening chapter of Matthew's Gospel, the oldest text of the New Testament known at that time. In 1897 the British Museum published a magnificent papyrus of the fifth-century BC lyric poet Bacchylides (see also chapter 41) and, as we have seen, the Aristotelian *Constitution of the Athenians* had already appeared. So initially expectations of lost literature were not disappointed, but in fact it very soon became clear that the vast majority of texts, probably as many as 95 per cent of them, were not literature but what we call documentary texts: official business, personal correspondence, forms, receipts, contracts, bills – the unselfconscious record of everyday life. This was a disappointment for many, but others realised how hugely important this material could be for our understanding of the social and economic history of the ancient world.

Literary papyri

Although there are subcategories, the division of papyrus texts into 'literary' and 'documentary' remains fundamental. Literary papyri (figure 32.2) can themselves be divided into two main types: those that give us previously unknown works of ancient literature, and those that give us new texts of works already familiar to us through the medieval manuscript tradition.

The most dramatic example of the former is probably the third-century BC comic playwright Menander. Greatly admired in the ancient world as a leading practitioner of Greek New Comedy, his works were known to the modern world only in scattered quotations by ancient writers: papyrus texts have now provided a number of almost complete plays. But there have been many other vital gains; indeed there is scarcely any genre

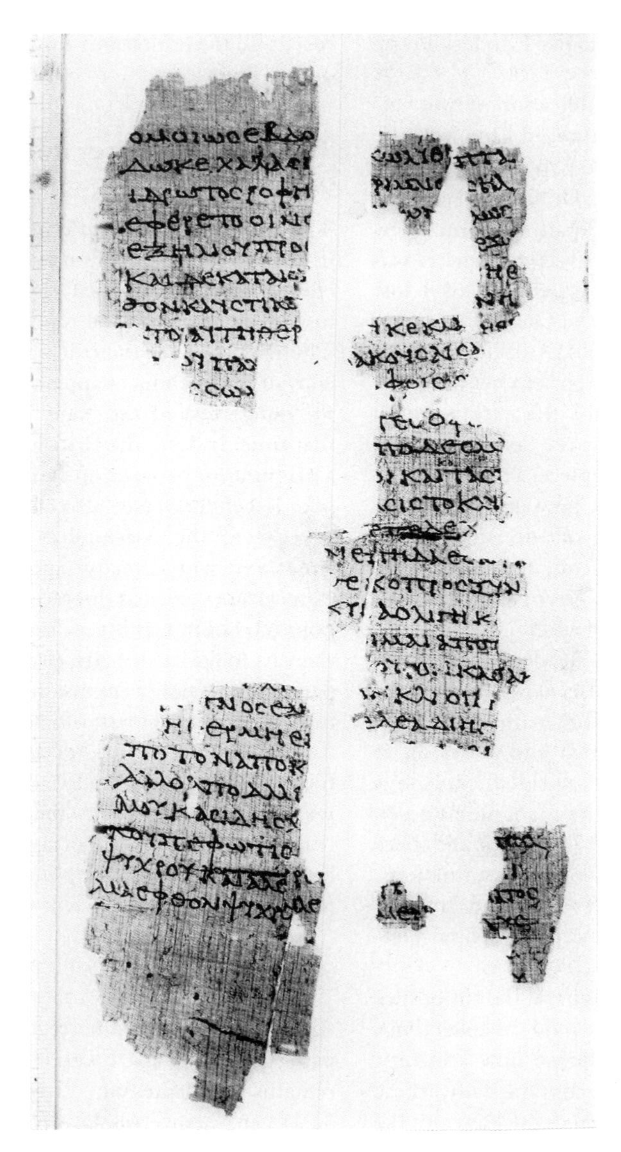

Fig. 32.2 *P. Dub.* 1: Hippocrates, *Epidemics* 7. 80. The handwriting, with the letters separately and neatly written, is characteristic of literary texts. First or second century AD. Published by kind permission of the Board of Trinity College Dublin.

of Greek literature to which papyrus discoveries have not added new material. For instance, new works (often fragmentary), of Archilochus, Sappho, Simonides, Bacchylides and others, have vastly expanded our knowledge of Greek lyric poetry in the archaic age (see also chapter 41). Philosophy has benefited recently with the publication of a new text of the Presocratic philosopher Empedocles, and Herculaneum has, among other gifts to the world, given us fragments of Epicurus' work *On Nature*, and some of the prose writings of Philodemus of Gadara. Hyperides, the fourth-century BC orator, was another entirely lost to literature until papyrological texts led to his rediscovery in the nineteenth century (see also chapter 45). The substantial papyrus fragments of the fourth-century Oxyrhynchus historian, whose name is unknown, undoubtedly represent an important addition to the surviving corpus of Greek history (see also chapter 49). Callimachus and Cercidas are two major beneficiaries among Hellenistic poets. And, lest we forget the Greek literature written by Christian authors (see also chapter 53), part of Origen's *Dialogue with Heraclides* was found on papyrus in 1941, along with extensive remains of the voluminous biblical commentaries of the great fourth-century AD teacher Didymus the Blind. Even Latin literature, although very rarely represented in the finds, gained one startling addition to its ranks, when twelve lines of the Roman elegist Cornelius Gallus were discovered in 1978 (see also chapter 42). There are also many fragments of unknown literary works, to which we cannot assign an author, providing a useful reminder that the canon of Greek literature preserved in the medieval tradition represents only a small proportion of what was actually written in the ancient world.

The primary importance of the second category of literary text mentioned above, where papyri contain works we already know, lies in the enormous contribution they have made to textual criticism, the scholarly task of establishing the most accurate texts of ancient authors. We rely for the survival of ancient literature very largely on the medieval manuscript tradition, which rarely dates much before about the ninth century AD. Papyri, of course, represent a much earlier stage in the transmission of literary works from the ancient world. Our earliest papyri of Homer, for instance, bring us nearly a millennium nearer the original writing down of the Homeric poems than the first complete manuscripts we have. This does not necessarily mean they are 'better', more reliable texts, only that they provide an independent means of checking and assessing the medieval tradition.

While papyri of known works have revolutionised textual criticism, they have also made other important contributions to literary and cultural history. For instance, they have enabled scholars to redate, sometimes quite drastically, the careers of certain ancient writers. The most spectacular examples would include Chariton, author of the novel *Chaereas and Callirhoe* (see also chapter 43), who is now known to have lived in the second century AD, not the fifth or sixth as earlier supposed; Achilles Tatius, author of *The Story of Leucippe and Clitophon*, who also finds himself redated earlier by some 400 years to the mid-second century AD; the epic poet Triphiodorus, who belongs to the third or early fourth century AD, not the fifth.

Another contribution made by literary texts is the way in which their distribution in the towns and villages of the Egyptian countryside gives us a unique insight into small-town Greek life, what Greek-educated people were reading away from the famous centres of Hellenic cultural and intellectual activity. Some of these papyri are clearly school texts and tell us much about the syllabus of Greek education (see also chapter 59). Numbers of surviving papyri indicate just how dominantly popular Homer, particularly the *Iliad*, was: the *Leuven Databank of Ancient Books* lists just over 1,100 papyri of Homer (833 of them from the *Iliad*); in second place, so to speak, comes Euripides with 176 fragments, although the 324 papyri of the New Testament and 431 of the Old Testament give a good indication of Christianity's success in Egypt.

Documentary papyri

As already noted, the vast majority of papyri from Egypt fall into the category identified as 'documentary', covering virtually every imaginable area of public and private life. A list (abbreviated) of subjects represented in the texts collected in a standard primer illustrates the point: administration, adoption, applications, apprenticeship, Christians, complaints, contracts, divorce, foundlings, inheritance, Jews, law suits, leases, letters, loans, magic, marriage, mummies, Nile levels, notifications of birth and death, oracles, property registers, receipts, revolts (figure 32.3), sales, school exercises, slaves, soldiers, taxes, transport, wet-nurses, wills, women (legal rights of). This extraordinary bulk of material, although, as we have observed, not distributed equally over time or location, makes Graeco-Roman Egypt both the best-documented area and the best-documented period in the ancient world.

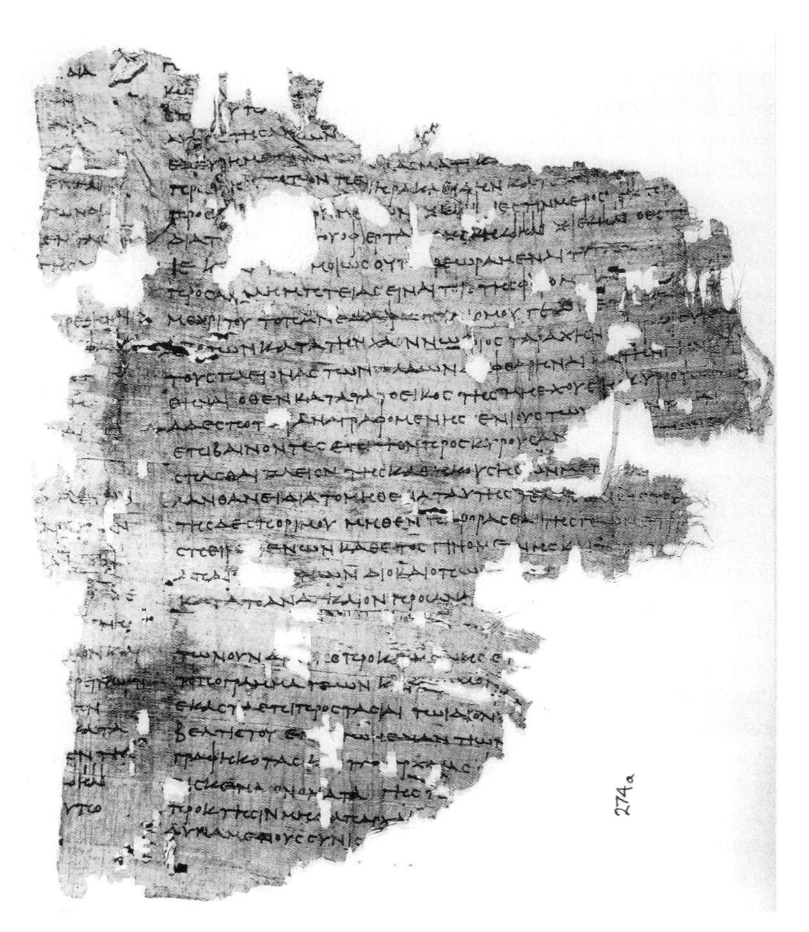

Fig. 32.3 *Pap. Gr. TCD* 274: text containing important historical information on the contemporary revolt in the Thebaid (see *APF* 43 (1997), 273–314). Early second century BC. Published by kind permission of the Board of Trinity College Dublin.

On the whole, papyri do not help us to write a narrative of Egyptian history. They very rarely deal with political events, although the exceptions can be exciting. A recently published papyrus (*P. Bingen* 45), written on 23 February 33 BC, lists various bribes offered to a Roman senator to keep him on the side of Cleopatra and Antony in the coming conflict with Octavian. When first published, it was misidentified and the potential significance of the word at the bottom of the document was not seen by the editor: it is a single Greek word, *genesthoi*, meaning 'make it happen', and the possibility that attracted the world's press, which they soon turned into a virtual certainty, was that it was written by Cleopatra herself. This is quite possible, but it is also possible that it was written by a senior civil servant. The real importance of the text was not who wrote it down, but what it says. It is a rare example of a document originating at the highest levels of the Ptolemaic government and relating directly to the political situation, the cold war in the late 30s BC before the battle of Actium. It is only seldom that something like this appears, or Claudius' famous letter to the Alexandrians (giving his answers to requests made to him and particularly his decision concerning the aftermath of riots between Alexandrians and Jews) (*Select Papyri* 212), and while details about, for instance, senior members of the imperial family and court, or the movements of emperors, or matters pertaining to imperial chronology, crop up from time to time, and will continue to do so, the main importance of documentary papyri lies elsewhere – what they tell us about the administration of the country, its agricultural, tax and legal systems, the military, religion, and the private lives of ordinary people in their relations with the state and with each other.

Although our knowledge of the higher echelons of the Egyptian bureaucracy, the king or governor and other senior officers of state who mostly lived and worked in Alexandria, is rich in comparison with other Hellenistic kingdoms and Roman provinces – official correspondence up and down, and across, the chain of command from the very top to the bottom provides invaluable information – the papyrological record is, so to speak, bottom-heavy: we know much more about middle and lower officialdom and life in the towns and villages of the countryside (see also chapter 60). Here the primary concern of both government and governed was agriculture. The Nile, flooding each summer and leaving behind its rich residue of fertilising silt, made Egypt famously productive. With the grain surplus contributing vitally to the food supply of Rome and, later, Constantinople, the way this great gift of fertility was exploited is, not surprisingly, the subject of thousands of papyri: patterns of landownership, how it was irrigated, who worked it under what conditions, what was grown on it, transport of produce (especially grain), government supervision, survey and modes of official record-keeping, rents (figure 32.4, and see figure 32.1 above) and taxes and other impositions on the farmer. Animal husbandry is also well documented, as is, indeed, the working of all natural resources, animal, vegetable or the valuable mineral deposits. Economic policy is not easy to assess, but some of the mechanics of economic exploitation are reasonably clear, whether it is the monopolistic control of important products such as oil, salt or papyrus in Ptolemaic times, or the Romans' much greater reliance on tax income (see also chapter 5). We certainly do not understand all aspects of the tax system of Roman Egypt, but it is recorded in massive detail; and tax assessments and receipts, along particularly with employment contracts, tell us much about the types of economic activity people engaged in, from doctors to donkey-drivers, weavers to wet-nurses, plumbers to prostitutes.

Mention of contracts brings up the important matter of law, a complicated mixture of Egyptian, Greek and Roman. This is a subject illuminated by various types of papyrus document: royal and imperial edicts, copies of laws and legal texts, court proceedings, official orders and letters, wills, petitions. Some of the most generally informative, from the point of view of social history, are the thousands of petitions that individuals submitted to various officials in their search for legal redress. Because petitioners had to explain the details of their grievance, we learn a great deal not just about the law, but also about the relationship of individuals with each other and with the state. The age-old problems of property and inheritance loom large, just as do marital breakdown and other family disputes; the failure to pay money owed, or to meet other contractual obligations; the disagreements between neighbours; larceny, assault or more organised banditry; and the complaints of unfair treatment by the state, whether its failure to recognise tax and labour exemptions, or the inefficiency and corruption of its officials.

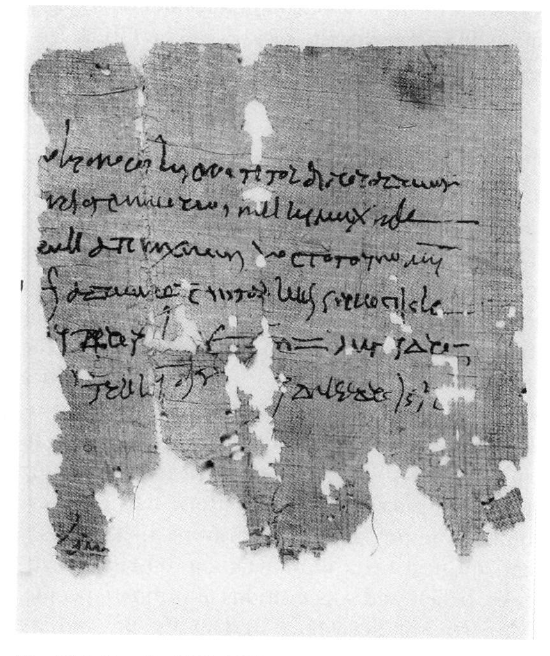

Fig. 32.4 *Pap. Gr. TCD* 107: unpublished receipt from the reign of Antoninus Pius. AD 158/9. Published by kind permission of the Board of Trinity College Dublin.

Petitions highlight problems, when understandings and processes break down or threaten to do so; declarations required by the state and many thousands of private letters are perhaps more neutrally illustrative of social life. Census declarations, for instance, which in Roman times had to be submitted by householders every fourteen years, have made possible modern demographic analysis of household stuctures, gender ratio, life expectancy, the role of disease, age at marriage, sibling marriage. Although private letters are often slightly stiff and formulaic by modern standards, they open a fascinating window onto social conventions and attitudes, and the minutiae of family life. The writers of private letters (and other private documents), although obviously in command of a basic literacy, tended not to be highly educated, and their spelling and syntax, especially the simplifications and 'mistakes' (that is, relative to the 'correct' practice of high literature), constitute one of the most important sources we have for studying the development of the Greek language, as it was spoken and written by ordinary people over a thousand-year period: the documentary papyri in general provide vital evidence in any assessment of ancient literacy, and a whole chapter in the history of the Greek language.

Various texts inform us about religion, Egyptian, Graeco-Roman, Jewish and Christian. Priestly decrees, temple archives and administrative documents tell us much about the important political, economic and religious role of the Egyptian temples and priesthood in the Ptolemaic period. A collection of recently published texts (*P. Polit. Iud.*) concerns the *politeuma* (community) of the Jews in the town of Heracleopolis in the second half of the second century BC. It provides dramatic new evidence about the internal organisation of Jewish communities in Egypt, adding to an already substantial body of texts concerning Jews and Judaism. Private letters, lists of questions to be put to oracles, prayers, spells, curses and magical texts illuminate the religious practices, beliefs and superstitions of ordinary people. Monasticism developed first in Egypt, and we have plenty of documentation with which to trace its organisation and development; indeed, in the Byzantine period there is a mass of material about the monasteries, churches and clergy of Egyptian Christianity.

Such a bald summary neither covers all the subject matter of documentary papyri, nor does justice to the contribution to the study of the ancient world made by this body of material. New inscriptions, coins and archaeological excavations constantly add to our knowledge, and they have the advantage of not being geographically limited, as papyri are to Egypt (at least largely), but papyri constitute the single biggest addition in the modern age to the body of written primary evidence we have from the ancient world.

The future of papyrology

New texts

New texts will continue to emerge, from three sources: existing collections formed in the early years of papyrology, archaeological digs, and the antiquities market.

Of the big existing collections, Oxyrhynchus volumes will no doubt continue to flow off the presses. Editorial leadership has maintained an impressive pace, coupled with the highest quality, of publication. Vienna is another great collection with many thousands of unpublished documents. The Vienna team have had in the past few years a big publication project, with valuable new volumes appearing. On the whole they deal with Egypt in later Roman and Byzantine times. A very recent volume of Berlin papyri resulted from the dismantling of cartonnage from one piece of a coffin, yielding over 100 texts; cartonnage still has a great deal to offer. Smaller collections all over the world will also, presumably, continue to produce new editions, either in volumes, or in article form. I am thinking here of documentary texts, but the same applies to literature. On the whole the main collections have been searched for obviously spectacular literary texts, so it is unlikely that we will find in an existing collection a new text of Bacchylides to match the magnificent British Museum papyrus to which I have already referred. But, as already noted, recently an important new passage from the Greek philosopher Empedocles was recognised in the Strasbourg collection. And the work on the literary material from Herculaneum continues.

Within Egypt, excavations in the late 1980s at ancient Kellis in the Dakleh Oasis in the Western desert uncovered hundreds of papyri, *ostraka* and wooden boards in situ in houses. They were mostly Greek (including a fine wooden codex of works of Isocrates) and Coptic, but some Latin and Syriac. This was an exciting discovery because we had virtually no documentation from the oasis, and the material was found scattered in houses and other buildings, allowing for a careful contextualising (see also chapter 3) of the papyri (in contrast to purchased material, for which the archaeological context has invariably been lost). Kellis is 300 km from the Nile valley, so we might expect to get a slightly different view of life, not, for instance, so dominated by the Nile flood. In fact we seem to have the same sort of general mixture of documents found elsewhere, but it is none the less revealing new material from an area we knew little about before. Another most productive source of new documentation has been the excavations at the Roman quarry site of Mons Claudianus in the Eastern desert, which has yielded thousands of *ostraka*. Other digs are bringing to light more new texts and Near Eastern archaeology, it is hoped, will also continue to discover new papyri.

Purchases on the antiquities market formed the core of many European and American papyrus collections, and although it now operates under much tighter restrictions than a century ago, the market continues to have an important role. The University of Trier in Germany started its papyrus collection only in 1982, but has already built up a small but valuable collection, highlighted by two interesting dossiers: the papers of the second-century BC Ptolemaic official Boethus, and those of the fourth-century AD monastery head Nepherus. The Jewish texts from Heracleopolis, to which I have referred, came from the antiquities market; and it will continue, no doubt, to give us small numbers of new texts.

Editorial work on old texts

Papyri published a long time ago often need re-editing. There has recently appeared the second edition of the first volume of Geneva papyri. They were published first in the years 1896 to 1906, and, as the new editors observe, at that time very few volumes of papyri had been published, so that the parallels we now have available – which are absolutely crucial for our understanding of new texts – did not exist at the time; nor did the dictionaries, lexica and electronic search devices. The result is that some of these early texts were simply not as fully exploited as they now can be. In some cases there was no translation, and sometimes little or no commentary, as in the early volumes of the Berlin papyri. So it can be a very valuable service to re-edit them: it gives underused, or misunderstood, texts a whole new life. The Petrie papyri, published initially in the early 1890s, are a case in point. Even allowing for the absence of parallels and of a developed papyrological methodology, this was a confusing publication, and the systematic republication of these texts currently under way is a valuable new contribution to scholarship. There are other older volumes of papyri that would benefit from a complete republication.

Another way of working with existing editions, which has proved helpful in the past and could be further developed, is the collecting into one place of texts of the same type. Even in the ancient world texts that belonged together became scattered, a process exacerbated by the mostly random way in which modern collections were formed. Modern scholarship can very profitably gather into one publication texts from the same dossier, town or office, or even collect documents that may not have been stored together. There is, for instance, a good collection of wet-nurse contracts; another of texts related to Jews and Judaism; an important one of Ptolemaic ordinances; another on certificates issued to people who had fulfilled their annual obligation to work on the irrigation channels. Other possibilities beckon.

Interpretative studies

If it were possible, or desirable, to devise a grand strategy for the future of documentary papyrology, one of the tensions it might face is between continuing to publish new texts and digesting, or processing in one way or another, what we already have. These are, of course, not mutually exclusive activities; indeed they are interdependent. I am referring only to a matter of emphasis. An argument of diminishing returns might be proposed, that the parameters of subjects identified in the papyrological record so far have been more or less set: another private letter, another tax receipt, another certificate is unlikely to add much to the sum of what we know; scholars should, therefore, try to move more into wider interpretative issues. Even if there were thought to be a certain force in the point, as long as unpublished papyri exist, scholars will want to publish them, if only because it is such an exciting process. And even with a type of document or literary text that is already heavily represented in the published record, there is always something new, however small, in every text. If editorial work (and its attendant service industry of lexical dictionaries, lists of corrections, etc.) has dominated for a century it is hardly surprising. It has, however, left a situation in which there is far more raw material than there is analysis of it.

Much of the broader papyrological analysis so far carried out, the questions it asks and the answers it proposes, have been dictated by traditional concerns arising directly out of the texts themselves and the need to understand them in their own terms. It is difficult to interpret a document involving the state official known as the Royal Scribe without understanding what Royal Scribes did; and a massive new study, of impressive and exacting scholarship, will tell you anything you need to know of this official in the Roman period (T. Kruse, *Der königliche Schreiber und die Gauverwaltung: Untersuchungen zur Verwaltungsgeschichte Ägyptens in der Zeit von Augustus bis Philippus Arabs (20 v. Chr. – 245 n. Chr.)* (*Archiv für Papyrusforschung*, Beiheft 11, 2 vols), Munich and Leipzig: K. G. Saur, 2002). Similar (if usually shorter) treatment has been devoted to other officials, to administrative, religious and military institutions, to different types of document; but there is still a great deal to do, with many 'gaps', so to speak, in the modern coverage of what we might call the traditional approach to historical papyrology – an approach, it should be said, that has yielded rich results. In addition, just as other areas of classical scholarship have been influenced by new theoretical approaches borrowed from other disciplines, so too papyrology has begun to embrace models originating outside the papyri themselves. An already, and justifiably, much-cited example is in the field of demography (Bagnall and Frier, *Demography of Roman Egypt*): we have 300 or so census declarations that survive on papyrus, which give us raw data, the usefulness of which is transformed by the authors' application of modern demographic techniques and models. In the same area, an investigation of disease and demography (Scheidel, *Death on the Nile*) is driven by the same sort of application of modern theory. So too the theoretical underpinnings of a recent book on the structure of land tenure in the Ptolemaic period (Manning, *Land and Power in Ptolemaic Egypt*) pose questions of the papyrological evidence formulated, at least partly, by modern theoretical approaches using comparative data from different periods and other parts of the world.

This type of approach, in placing ancient Egypt in a wider theoretical and evidentiary framework, has the beneficial effect of broadening the applicability of Egypt as a subject of scholarly investigation. For one of the big questions about the nature of papyrological evidence has been its typicality: to what extent can we apply conclusions drawn from the abundant evidence of Egypt to other areas of the Hellenistic and Roman world where we have less, or no, evidence? I think it is fair to say that ancient historians have generally regarded Egypt as exceptional rather than typical, thus isolating it in its own narrow field of studies. A particularly effective case for typicality, or at least for a greater typicality than is often assumed, is made by Dominic Rathbone in his study of the Heroninus archive (*Economic Rationalism and Rural Society in Third Century* AD *Egypt*), a collection of nearly 1,000 papers concerning the running of a large private estate in the Fayyum in the third century AD. From the published material (only about half the total) Rathbone paints a detailed picture of how the estate was run – management, labour, production, transport, the accounting system – but his economic modelling also enabled him to bring the Heroninus material to bear on wider questions of Roman estate management and economic behaviour.

Translation and accessibility of papyri

Papyrology is a very well-organised area of classical scholarship. Very early on in its history, editorial practice was standardised; new lexica, indexing systems and journals were started, along with a standard list of corrections to published texts, and a standard collection of texts published in articles. More recently papyrology was quick to spot the potential of computer technology. Since the late 1980s the *Duke Databank of Documentary Papyri* (available on CD, or online through the Perseus Project, www.perseus.tufts.edu/Texts/papyri.html) has given immediate access to all published documentary texts (including important collections of inscriptions) – a huge advance in working methods, especially when taken with the *Thesaurus Linguae Graecae*, a computerised database of all Greek literature from Homer to AD 1453. And there are a great many more recent electronic developments such as the *Leuven Databank of Ancient Books* (on CD), the Heidelberg catalogue of dated papyri (www.rzuser.uni-heidelberg.de/~gv0/gvz.html) and the creation of digitised images of texts from many papyrus collections around the world. In short, the tools of papyrology are increasingly sophisticated and helpful.

Taking this into account, as well as the extraordinary immediacy and freshness of the material, it may seem surprising that papyrology has in fact developed as a highly specialised, inaccessible area of scholarship. The sheer bulk and complicated detail of the material, coupled with the technical skills necessary to deal with it at first hand, the massive scholarly bibliography that has grown up and the perception of the limited applicability of papyri outside Egypt, have given papyrology a somewhat forbidding aspect. For undergraduate students in the English-speaking world, although a recent and excellent sourcebook on women points the way to future possibilities (Rowlandson, *Women and Society*), there has in the past scarcely been enough material in English to facilitate classical civilisation courses on Graeco-Roman Egypt, attractive as they must surely be. But this is changing. The APIS (Advanced Papyrological Information System) programme now gives computer access to some 18,000 papyrus texts in major American university collections, with bibliography and description, and in many cases with image and English translation (www.columbia.edu/cu/lweb/projects/digital/ apis/index.html). This is a huge addition to the limited body of source material in translation, and a major new scholarly and pedagogical tool.

The study of papyri and of the fascinating world they reveal will, necessarily, continue to be carried out by a small body of 'experts'; but it is far too good a subject to leave entirely to them.

Further reading

Resources

J. F. Oates, R. S. Bagnall, W. H. Willis and K. A. Worp, *Checklist of Editions of Greek, Latin, Demotic and Coptic Papyri, Ostraca and Tablets* (5th edn), Oukville, CT, and Oxford: Oxbow for American Society of Papyrologists, 2001 (web edition at http://scriptorium.lib.duke.edu/papyrus/texts/clist.html) – editions of papyri and all the associated tools of papyrology, abbreviated in scholarly literature in a standard manner.

Sourcebooks

J. Rowlandson, *Women and Society in Greek and Roman Egypt: A Sourcebook*, Cambridge: Cambridge University Press, 1998.

Texts in translation

C. C. Edgar, A. S. Hunt and D. L. Page, *Select Papyri* (3 vols) (Loeb Classical Library), Cambridge MA: Harvard University Press, 1932–41.

Introductions

R. S. Bagnall, *Reading Papyri, Writing Ancient History*, London and New York: Routledge, 1995 – a stimulating appraisal of the nature and use of papyrus as a historical source.

I. Gallo, *Greek and Latin Papyrology*, London: Institute of Classical Studies, 1986.

E. G. Turner, *Greek Papyri*, (2nd edn), Oxford: Clarendon Press, 1980 – the best general work.

Graeco-Roman Egypt

R. S. Bagnall, *Egypt in Late Antiquity*, Princeton: Princeton University Press, 1993.

R. S. Bagnall and B. W. Frier, *The Demography of Roman Egypt*, Cambridge: Cambridge University Press, 1994.

H. I. Bell, *Egypt from Alexander the Great to the Arab Conquest*, Oxford: Clarendon Press, 1956.

A. K. Bowman, *Egypt after the Pharaohs, 332 BC–AD 642: From Alexander the Great to the Arab Conquest*, London: British Museum Press, 1986.

H. M. Cotton, W. E. H. Cockle and F. G. B. Millar, 'The papyrology of the Roman Near East: a survey', *JRS* 85 (1995), 214–35.

N. Lewis, *Life in Egypt under Roman Rule*, Oxford: Clarendon Press, 1983.

N. Lewis, *Greeks in Ptolemaic Egypt*, Oxford: Clarendon Press, 1986.

J. Manning, *Land and Power in Ptolemaic Egypt*, Cambridge: Cambridge University Press, 2003.

D. W. Rathbone, *Economic Rationalism and Rural Society in Third-Century AD Egypt*, Cambridge: Cambridge University Press, 1991.

W. Scheidel, *Death on the Nile: Disease and the Demography of Roman Egypt*, Leiden: Brill, 2001.

Website

Many of the most important links will be found on the site of the International Association of Papyrologists, www.ulb.ac.be/assoc/aip.

33. *Manuscripts*

Helen Dixon

What is a manuscript?

Classical texts have made an almost unimaginable journey: from the author's pen to our modern Loeb, Oxford Classical Text, Teubner or other editions via various media — papyri, tablets, manuscripts and early printed editions. For the greater part of this journey, most classical literature has depended upon copying in manuscripts. The word 'manuscript' derives from the Latin term for a handwritten book, *codex manu scriptus*. As most manuscripts are made of parchment or paper, we have in mind a text written in ink by a scribe or a scholar on one of these materials. In antiquity the earliest writing of Greek and Latin texts in books was executed on papyrus rolls with a reed (see also chapter 32), or on hinged wooden or wax tablets, with a reed or wooden stylus (for texts inscribed in stone see chapter 34). From c. AD 400 manuscripts became the principal medium for transmitting the Latin and Greek classics, from copy to copy, for over a thousand years until Johann Gutenberg used movable type to print the Bible in Latin, and so became the first printer (see also chapter 1).

Establishing the correct text of a literary work, and its transmission, i.e. the history of how each text has survived up to the present day, is not always simple. Like most man-made things, manuscripts (mss.) are impermanent objects, and so the survival of classical and other ancient texts has been at the mercy of time and humankind. If no one at any time had studied and copied manuscripts, we would have hardly any classical texts to read. Indeed, because of lapses in the writing and study of manuscripts, individual lines, whole texts and even some authors' entire output have not survived and are lost forever. Aristotle's *Poetics* spent over a millennium underground until their rediscovery in c. AD 1500. But we will never be able to read the complete historical works of Gaius Iulius Hyginus, Cato the censor and the lost parts of Sallust's *Histories*, for instance, because at some point not enough copies were made. Only citations in other authors, excerpts in anthologies or appearances in medieval library catalogues tell us that these lost works existed. And probably there are still others which have not survived in themselves nor in any other record.

Paradoxically, no extant (existing) text has survived unscarred. When people copy out texts, by virtue of being human they defile the original text with errors of all kinds. For example, a scribe might be unable to read the handwriting in his exemplar (the manuscript he was copying from), might remove titles, words and even whole phrases and replace them with what seemed to him 'better' ones, or might let his attention wander and thus miss out a chunk of text. These alterations would be transmitted by the next copyist, who would probably make changes of his own, as would the next copyist, and so on, producing a pattern of distortion similar to that in the game Chinese whispers. Later readers who had more than one manuscript of a text in their hands often annotated differences between the versions in front of them in margins or between the lines. It follows, then, that the more steps there are between the original and later copies, the less faithful the text preserved.

Thus continual copying ensures the survival of *a* text, but not of *the original* text. The human agency involved in the act of copying out by hand has caused copies to deviate from each other and thus from the original. The new creations thus produced are often of considerable interest in themselves: they may be the work of medieval historians, philosophers, diplomats and other writers, and thus reflect medieval culture in general, as well as showing how a particular classical text influenced education and intellectual thought. Hence the study of manuscripts informs long-established disciplines such as classics, history, theology, English and other modern languages, and new fields (e.g. book history).

However, medieval manuscripts cause problems for anyone who wants to read the speeches that Cicero wrote, instead of the text that medieval scribes rewrote. This is especially problematic with authors such as Catullus, whose text is already corrupt in the earliest manuscripts. Particular interpretations and literary analyses are often at the mercy of individual readings conjectured or picked by scholars from the cacophonic manuscripts. Such choices can sometimes be difficult to support, until an editor tries to establish which manuscripts are the most reliable, and how to detect the correct readings to which they may point back. An editor's job is not a light responsibility. Even so, past editors have often had private agendas, according to whether their objective was to refine textual corruptions using their own norms, or to refind the text that the author penned.

While manuscripts have yielded responsibility for ensuring the survival of classical literature to the printed book, they yet remain any editor's only hope of finding the archetype (the manuscript from which the extant witnesses (i.e. copies) derive) and thus of getting as close as possible to the original. Since printed books are the offspring of manuscripts, they do not denude the manuscript tradition of any text of its fundamental importance. The history of early and later printed editions presents problems similar to those encountered in manuscripts, with the difference that printed books mislead readers, who tend to regard anything in print as authoritative. Editors of printed editions, like their medieval predecessors, weighed up the sources according to evolving sets of criteria to produce new texts. But as time and discoveries progressed, the pool of manuscripts and other resources became ampler: more manuscripts had been discovered and printing facilitated the spread of information. For a modern editor the main role that early printed books play is when an early editor had his hands on a unique lost manuscript, or when individual copies have been annotated by famous scholars.

Materials and book composition

Analysis of the materials of which manuscripts are made and how they are put together is fundamental to our understanding of the transmission of classical literature. The quality of parchment or paper and inks used, watermarks, ruling and even page-numbers often provide crucial clues for solving problems concerning the dates and origins of manuscripts.

While the practice of writing literary texts on papyrus rolls was established by the seventh century BC (see also chapter 32), Diodorus Siculus and Herodotus refer to early uses of leather instead of papyrus for making rolls in Egypt, Persia and Italy. Parchment, known as *membrana* in antiquity, was first produced in bulk and exported from Pergamum in Mysia in the second century AD. Animal hides, sheep or goat (or calf if vellum was desired), were soaked in lime for several days and then flesh and hairs were scraped off. The hide was treated with chemicals, stretched out to dry, and scraped with pumice stone. Hence Catullus (1.2) and [Tibullus] (3.1.9) refer to polished parchment book-covers. The process was refined as new treatments using different chemicals were developed. Traditional parchment-making is still practised today in Europe.

Classical texts were copied onto parchment codices – books composed of leaves as today – as early as the first century BC, to judge by remarks in Horace (*Sat.* 2.3.2), Quintilian (*Inst.* 10.3.3) and Martial (14.184–92), though papyrus rolls remained the standard book material in both the Western and the Eastern parts of the empire. It was only with the copying of Christian texts onto parchment codices from the second century AD that the use of papyrus or parchment codices caught on for classical authors.

The use of parchment codices began with a slow crescendo and came into its own in the fourth century AD when papyrus began to be given up, partly because of its brittleness, but also because from the second century AD the ancient book changed in structure to the codex. The first codices were composed of papyrus, in imitation of wooden panels or wax tablets fastened together with leather thongs. Parchment, far more durable than papyrus or wax, suited the codex better. Parchment codices are composed of gatherings (also called quires): two to six whole sheets of parchment were assimilated in a pile, folded over so as to produce a little booklet and stitched down the middle to produce a number of leaves. The upper page of the leaf is called the recto, the lower page the verso. These terms serve for all manuscripts and early printed books from late antiquity to the Renaissance. Leaves were usually signed by scribes with Roman numerals or letters on the recto of the first leaf in each gathering. Parchment was the sole material used for writing literary texts and official documents in western Europe until the advent of paper.

Paper was introduced first to Spain and exported to Byzantium as early as the thirteenth century by the Arabs, who had learned the art of paper-making from the Chinese in the eighth century. Only in the fifteenth century, however, did paper replace parchment as the most common book-making material, being cheaper and easier to produce. Paper books were affordable for people for whom parchment had previously been prohibitively expensive. Watermarks (studied and reproduced by Briquet, *Les Filigranes*) often provide a useful dating aid for paper manuscripts.

Ink, prepared in the ancient way, was a solution of gum, galls, sepia and iron; and in the Middle Ages of oak-galls, wine and iron. Mixing these solutions with lead and other metals produced inks of different colours. Right through from antiquity to the Renaissance, scribes used brown or black ink for writing texts, and a variety of reds, blues, greens, yellows and even gold and silver ink for decorating title-pages, borders and initials. Pens were of reed from antiquity until the later Middle Ages, when quills were used. Lines were ruled on the parchment or paper, with a knife or pen and ink. Preparatory ruling often included one or two rectangles framing the text space.

Since late antiquity manuscripts have been bound with animal-skin, parchment, paper or cloth, depending on availability and quality of the materials, and how much money buyers wished to spend. While all bindings have the practical function of protecting manuscripts from dirt and damage, the more deluxe productions enhance the aesthetic aspects of high-quality manuscripts, and have therefore begun to be studied as interesting and valuable art historical items in their own right, as have manuscripts which retain vestiges of an old or original binding.

Thanks to codicologists, who study the physical make-up of manuscripts, we are learning more about past book-making processes and are thus better placed to assess the attributes of the manuscript in front of us.

Scripts and bookhands

Editors of classical texts and researchers into transmission need to be able to read, to date and to identify the scripts or bookhands in the manuscripts with which they are faced. This task often requires detective work. First, just as today our handwriting may differ according to where and when we learned to write, so it was for the scribes of our classical manuscripts: sometimes their handwritings are difficult to decipher even for a practised eye. Second, not all scribes and scholars bothered to sign and date their manuscripts. Even when they did, subsequent owners often erased signs of previous possessors. The scientific and historical analysis of handwriting styles and of marks of provenance is a young discipline.

Palaeography, the study of scripts, is inextricably enmeshed with the study of transmission, that is, how the scribes who wrote classical manuscripts handed them on to others, either by lending them to friends or carrying copies from one place to another; this influenced the state of the text of the next copy and perhaps even the script of the transcriber. For example, in the ninth century Irish monks travelling to England, Germany, France, Spain and Italy brought with them handwriting with insular traits. Elements from different contemporary cultural and intellectual environments were thus fused. The study of scribes and scholars, scripts, texts and transmission goes hand in hand.

The scripts or bookhands in which our extant classical Greek manuscripts are written date, with a few late antique exceptions, from the tenth century AD. The scripts in which extant Latin manuscripts are written date from the fourth century AD onwards, and contain many different letter-forms and abbreviations. For example the Latin *et* 'and' was sometimes abbreviated to & or *7*; *enim* 'for' to *n*. or *H*; and *est* 'is' to ÷ or ⌒. The letter *s* was written as either s or ſ, *d* was sometimes formed ð. Many other words were shortened using the common marks of abbreviation: for example, sñia = *sententia* (opinion), dix̄ = *dixit* (said), cā = *causa* (reason). Letter-forms and abbreviations varied according to time and geographical location. The handwriting of a north Italian friar in the eighth century, for instance, may have little in common with that of a German in the ninth century, and neither resembles a French hand in the thirteenth century. When studying a manuscript, we need to be able to identify and read the script and its abbreviations. Given that there is for Greek and Latin scripts a variety of recognised majuscules (capitals) and minuscules (lower case), and many handbooks written on them in the last hundred years, this may seem a daunting prospect. But the best way to learn is to begin.

Just as one acquires a new language by mastering its grammar, syntax and idiom, at the same time exploring how the language works, by reading core texts armed with grammar book and dictionary, so too the different scripts become familiar. The more manuscripts inspected, the more practice gained in identifying the hand, and its likely date and provenance. For Latin manuscripts essential companions are Cappelli, *Dizionario di abbreviature latine ed italiane*, and a general handbook, such as Brown, *A Guide to Western Historical Scripts*, or Thompson, *An Introduction to Greek and Latin Palaeography*, and section B in Bischoff, *Latin Palaeography*, which sets out the main palaeographical milestones, from rustic capitals (s.iv–v, i.e. fourth to fifth centuries) and monumental capitals (s.v), to uncial and half uncial (s.v–vi), insular elements (s.vi–ix), 'Visigothic' and the other experimental pre-Caroline minuscules (s.viii), and from Carolingian or Caroline minuscule (s.ix–xii) to Gothic (s.xii–xiv) and humanist (s.xv) scripts. For Greek manuscripts Wilson, *Medieval Greek Bookhands*, is indispensable. To ascertain more precisely what scripts were being used when, where and by whom, extremely useful are the international series of catalogues of dated and securely datable manuscripts in particular libaries (although some manuscripts are not as datable as editors seem to think); facsimiles of old and rare manuscripts (e.g. Lowe, *Codices Latini antiquiores*, which surveys extant manuscripts before the ninth century); and studies of manuscripts of a particular location, such as Rand, *A Survey of the manuscripts of Tours* 1–2, and Newton, *The Scriptorium and Library at Monte Cassino 1085–1105*, or a particular epoch, such as Derolez, *The Palaeography of Gothic Manuscript Books*. Above all, there is no substitute for inspecting manuscripts yourself.

The massive strides made in palaeography in recent years are of enormous help to editors and transmission researchers in assessing classical manuscripts; for example, palaeographers are often able not only to date unsigned manuscripts but even to attribute them to a scribe. It is to be hoped that detailed modern surveys of manuscripts written at a particular geographical location will continue to be produced. For example, there is much more to learn about the production of classical manuscripts at Lyons. One should be cautious about accepting generalising pronouncements about developments in handwriting in a particular century and region, which do not at the same time acknowledge the variations and differences of writing styles at individual localities. Examples of local varieties at all times must be used to inform our collective impressions.

Texts and transmission: some problems and puzzles

Classical manuscripts and their uses cannot be encompassed within so small an account as the present. It therefore seems useful to consider examples of how manuscripts can answer some of the questions that we would like to ask about the survival of classical texts.

What do manuscripts surviving from late antiquity tell us about early publication?

In addition to what classical authors themselves say about how their works were published, we have a few fourth- and fifth-century manuscripts (in various states of preservation) of Virgil, Terence, Sallust, Cicero and Prudentius. These are among the oldest manuscripts of Latin authors to have survived and give us an idea of antique and late antique editions. The change from papyrus roll to parchment codex does not seem to have affected how Greek and Latin texts were laid out. The Medici Virgil (Florence, Medicea-Laurenziana, plut. 39.1 (+ a single leaf now kept in the Vatican library as Vatican City, Vat. lat. 3225)) was written in beautiful rustic capitals before AD 494, when the consul Turcius Rufius Apronianus Asterius corrected it. Another manuscript of Virgil (Vatican City, Vat. lat. 3256), called the 'Augusteus', was written in the fifth to sixth centuries in monumental capitals modelled on inscriptions. These manuscripts, containing little or no abbreviation, punctuation or spacing between words, are written in professional hands and equal the printed book in regularity of letter-form and quality of production. From them we gain a picture of what ancient books looked like.

The preservation of these authors and not others raises questions not only about book production, but also about early transmission, the late antique canon (i.e. which books were considered classics and widely read in the period) and literary taste throughout the Roman Empire. In addition to what we can infer about influence from the texts of classical authors themselves, what can be inferred from the copying of some authors in antiquity and not others? In answering these questions caution is advisable because the evidence is so scrappy.

Problems of establishing authorship

The manuscripts of a classical author can play an important role together with literary evidence. For example, there is the uncertain authorship of book 3 of Tibullus (divided into two by fifteenth-century Italian scholars). How can we prove that Sulpicia and Lygdamis wrote the poems attributed to them? And what about Pseudo-Cicero, *Rhetorica ad Herennium*, Pseudo-Ovid, *Nux*, and the *Appendices Sallustiana* and *Vergiliana*? Who penned these works? To attempt to answer questions like these we need to consider, in addition to issues of artistic identity and development and of change in mode and subject matter, what light is shed by the manuscripts.

The sparse early manuscript sources and the question of how best to interpret and use them can cause problems. In Tibullus' case (see also chapter 42) the complete text emerged in a manuscript written c. 1380 for Coluccio Salutati (1331–1406), chancellor of Florence, in which all three books are attributed to Tibullus (Milan, Ambrosiana, R 26 *sup*). This manuscript is late and we can prove little about its provenance. Catullus, another casualty of neglect, was said to have returned to Verona from 'exile' (France) by the inscriber of an epigram at the head of a manuscript written at Verona in the 1370s (a copy of the poet Francesco Petrarch's now lost manuscript; see also chapter 1), but there is no evidence that Tibullus did too. Any earlier material that survives therefore assumes monumental importance. First, after antiquity Tibullus' name first surfaces around AD 800 flanked by the names of the poets Claudian and Horace in an important two-page list (Berlin, Diez, B Santen 66, pp. 217–18), once fancied to be the inventory of the court library of the Holy Roman Emperor Charlemagne (c. 742–814), but recently reattributed to the Capitolare library at Verona. Tibullus' appearance in this list with 'lib. II' beside his name has prompted suggestions that a two-book text or a text in which only two books are headed by Tibullus' name circulated in the late eighth century. Since no evidence from the intervening period has survived, can we infer that even earlier lost manuscripts of Tibullus announced him as author of books one and two and *not* book three? Appearances can be deceptive. Until recently few people have asked what the eighth-century list is a list *of*; for it is not clear whether the scribe was itemising a library, or a teaching curriculum, a private reading list or even a book shopping-list. An abbreviated mention in this jotted list, then, is hardly proof that Tibullus only wrote or was transmitted in two books. Second, a medieval manuscript catalogue of the Benedictine Abbey of Lobbes reports three books of Tibullus together with some of Claudian's poems; there are strong reasons to believe that whatever bits of Tibullus and Claudian arrived at Lobbes came from Verona, because in the tenth century a learned bishop of Verona named Ratherius was transferred to Lobbes, and carried many classical manuscripts with him. Third, the medieval manuscripts of excerpts containing Tibullus cause problems of their own (see below). From these and other medieval testimonies it is tempting to infer that the poems in book 3 (whoever wrote them) were originally kept together with Tibullus' poems and were copied with his, and that at some point before the Middle Ages, Tibullus was assumed to have sired them all. When the evidence is slender, any reconstruction should remain tentative, but rather these snippets than nothing at all.

Problems in establishing authenticity of book titles and book divisions

Other questions on which manuscripts may shed light: how do we know if titles and book divisions are authentic? For Lucretius we have titles transmitted from antiquity, since the pedigree of the better of two ninth-century manuscripts has been traced back to the fourth or fifth century. But whether they were Lucretius' own or were supplied by a late antique scholar (as were the prose summaries and titles for Ovid's *Metamorphoses* preserved in some medieval manuscripts) we will never know. For Tibullus we have few controls against the titles in Salutati's manuscript. While the title *Panegyricus Messallae* (panegyric for Messalla) for poem 3.7 (hitherto called the *Laudes Messallae* (praises of Messalla)) crept into a fifteenth-century edition, it is not clear whether the editor knew a manuscript reporting the title, or derived it from an ancient authority, or whether the title owes itself to a fifteenth-century obsession with panegyric writing.

Research on the poem titles and poem division of authors such as Catullus has shown that the manuscripts have an important role to play because the text in the earliest extant manuscripts is mangled, and it seems that the collection was published posthumously without a title.

Gaps in texts and gaps in manuscripts

These do not always amount to the same thing. The text in a mutilated manuscript will obviously be incomplete. On the other hand a manuscript may seem physically complete, while its text may not be. Of Sallust's *Histories*, for example, only four speeches and two letters have survived in full, thanks to an anthology compiled in antiquity; the rest is fragmentary. Conversely, the manuscripts of all authors at some point omit lines or whole passages of text through human error. Even the most assiduous scribe's or scholar's attention sometimes wandered. For example, a scribe's eye might move from one instance of a word to a second soon after, omitting the text in between: this is a common error. Omitting a word one does not know or a topic one does not understand is another unfortunate error. Readers of all centuries including the present have therefore been forced to become editors in order to make good the gaps.

Palimpsest manuscripts

These are fascinating and important witnesses. A palimpest, meaning written twice (from the Greek *palin psao*, 'wipe (smooth) again'), contains two texts, the one superimposed on the other. This occurs when a parchment manuscript has been reused: the original script has been washed off as far as possible, and another text written over it. Palimpsesting was practised with papyri as early as Catullus's time (22.5–6) and with parchment until the eighth century. Thanks to developments in technology, problems in deciphering the underscript (often obscured by the overscript) are allievated. Special photographic equipment and computer software (such as that developed for the European-Union-sponsored Mondo Nuovo Project) can 'lift' the underscript using ultraviolet light.

Manuscripts chosen for palimpsesting in the fourth to eighth centuries, because of lack of either parchment or money, were generally copies of texts no longer read, either because they were considered outmoded or redundant or because of a surplus of copies. Patristic (i.e. written by early Church Fathers) and legal texts were the principal victims, but classical authors were not unscathed. Palimpsested classical manuscripts are important because they constitute some of the earliest witnesses of our authors, for example Sallust's *Histories*, the elder Pliny's *Natural History*, and speeches of Cicero including the *pro Caelio*. All classical Greek manuscripts from late antiquity (including Euripides's *Phaethon*, medical texts and a Greek translation of Virgil) have survived as palimpsests. Sadly a palimpsested manuscript of speeches by Cicero, having been preserved in this way for over 1500 years, was destroyed by fire in 1904.

Scholia and marginalia

The late antique commentators sought to explain allusions and references in much earlier classical texts: examples include Aelius Donatus (on Terence) and Servius (on Vergil). The work of the Homeric scholiasts (scholia, namely glosses or comments) was transmitted or reconstituted in the margins of manuscripts. These men were not the only ancient scholars. If scribes in late antiquity had thought to copy more then perhaps we would possess more. Not much Latin evidence survives, but the study of Greek scholia continues to attract researchers. Marginalia, which should not be confused with scholia, contain later readers' responses to the text (see below).

Are the oldest manuscripts the best?

This is true in many cases, but not always. Because of the non-survival of most manuscripts from late antiquity, the ninth-century and tenth-century manuscripts from the Carolingian period usually constitute the most important witnesses for most classical Latin authors who have been attested throughout the centuries. A common pattern is: a couple of witnesses from the ninth-century renaissance, a lull, another surge in the twelfth century, and then plenty of Renaissance witnesses. Sometimes the ninth-century manuscripts reflect a good early manuscript, and should therefore be an editor's principal focus.

Lucretius is a famous case. Two almost complete ninth-century manuscripts written in Carolingian minuscule, one in Germany (now Leiden, Voss lat. fol. 30 = O) and one in northern France (now Leiden, Voss lat. Q. 94 = Q), have survived, as well as twenty leaves of fragments of another ninth-century manuscript, and mentions in ninth-century German florilegia (lit. 'flower-pickings', extracts of popular passages) and other writings including the library catalogue of Murbach. After the ninth century the complete text of de *Rerum Natura* (*On the Nature of Things*) disappears from view, Lucretius just popping up by name or in a rare citation in the manuscripts of scholars in Belgium, France and Italy. In 1417 somewhere near Constance the Florentine classical scholar Poggio (1380–1459) rediscovered O, had a copy made and sent it to his friend Niccolò Niccoli (1364–1437) in Florence. Since all other manuscripts derive from the copy Poggio sent to Niccoli, we are left with Q and O (the better of the two) to sort the text out.

O was corrected and annotated soon after it was copied by a clever Irishman, named Dungal, in Charlemagne's employ at Pavia and the monastery of Bobbio. Dungal's notes not only help us by improving the text of Lucretius, they also allow us to understand more about him and the context in which he is to be located, ninth-century intellectual and cultural developments, what people were interested in and why. Ninth-century scribes and scholars were more learned than those in the so-called 'Dark Ages' after the Roman Empire had crumbled, and the pursuit of learning with it. Thanks to the improvements and stability of Charlemagne's rule, scribes and scholars knew more Latin, and became interested in preserving classical texts once again. Through Dungal's example we can see how medieval scribes are at the same time editors, because they were often working with manuscripts written in hands they found difficult to read.

So far so good. But when the earliest complete manuscripts of an author date from the twelfth and thirteenth centuries, as in the case of Ovid's *Epistulae Ex Ponto* and *Tristia*, or the end of the fourteenth century in Catullus's case, the text is rarely in a healthy state.

When early witnesses do not abound or exist for only a part of the text (e.g. Catullus 62 in a ninth-century manuscript of excerpts), other witnesses of the text's transmission or circulation become important: old manuscript catalogues, florilegia, and citations in other literature.

The Oriental survival of Greek literature

The survival of Greek literature is largely an Oriental story, and most of our Greek manuscripts date only from the tenth century onwards. The post-antique survival of classical Greek texts at the core of educational curricula in Eastern parts of the Roman Empire was more or less guaranteed. Since the Greek language was used in government administration in the East, classical Greek texts were an indispensible resource for those needing to read and write Greek. In addition, for the early Christian church classical literature proved a useful tool to convert pagans; passages unpalatable for Christians were interpreted allegorically. Alongside biblical and patristic writings, classical authors including Euripides and other dramatists, poets, orators, and Lucian and other Second Sophistic writers remained the staple diet of education in Greek-speaking communities (see also chapter 20). But much non-core literature was lost because of insufficient copying.

From the fourth to the sixth centuries AD, although Greek studies dwindled in the Latin-dominated West, Greek texts continued to be read not only in Constantinople, the capital of the Byzantine Empire, but also in Cappadocia, Antioch, Beirut, Gaza and Alexandria. But during the sixth-to-ninth-century upheaval in Europe there was a decline in learning throughout the eastern Mediterranean: many Greek schools closed, and the Greek language slipped out of use, except in monastic communities. It is not difficult to imagine the devastating consequences for the transmission of classical Greek literature. The scale of the loss is reflected by poor evidence from this time and the fact that many texts were never recovered; for example, of the 123 or so plays written by Sophocles only seven have survived in complete form. The renewed production of Greek manuscripts from the ninth century onwards, however, began to restore Greek literature to the European educational and cultural arena in a number of ways.

Classical Greek texts had been translated into Arabic, Syriac and other Oriental languages from the fourth century onwards. With the rise of Islam, Arab scientists and philosophers turned to the Greek writers on mathematics, medicine and astronomy (see also chapters 54), especially Archimedes, Hippocrates, Galen and Ptolemy, and the philosophers Plato and Aristotle. In the ninth century Arab scholars began to search for manuscripts in the Greek communities in the eastern Mediterranean and Mesopotamia, to compare with and to correct Arabic and Syriac versions of Greek texts, and also to hunt for works not yet translated. In this way some Greek texts (or parts of them) which would not otherwise have survived were preserved, such as Ptolemy's *Planetary Hypotheses*. In other cases extant manuscripts of Arabic translations provide missing passages and correct readings, and thus help modern editors to restore the original Greek text.

The Arab invaders of Byzantine Sicily, southern Italy and Spain in the ninth century brought with them a number of classical Greek authors, including Aristotle and Ptolemy: thus Western medieval knowledge of most of the Aristotelian corpus was owed to the translations of Arab scholars in Spain, and retranslations into Latin. Today a number of Greek texts survive only in Arabic or Latin translations produced in the twelfth and thirteenth centuries by English, Italian, Arab, Spanish and Greek scholars.

After the so-called 'Dark Ages' in Europe the ninth century was for Greek literature in Byzantium a period of revival and renewal, just as for Latin among the Carolingians: scholars set about producing classical Greek texts in manuscripts, in the same way that monks in north Italy were combing libraries for classical Latin manuscripts, and for similar reasons. The university at Byzantium was reopened, and scholars began to hunt for papyri of classical Greek texts in monastic libraries, which they transcribed in parchment and (later paper) manuscripts using new 'minuscule' scripts. To these scholars' manuscripts, and to their mentions of other non-extant texts, the survival of classical Greek literature owes a great debt.

At the beginning of the fifteenth century many Greek scholars travelled to Italy, and after Constantinople fell to the Turks in 1453, there was a stream of Greek refugees bringing Greek texts with them (see also chapter 1). Since the general Italian readership of Greek literature, with the exception of brilliant scholars such as Angelo Poliziano (1454–94), did not master the language for several decades, Greek literature in translation was still the norm. But from the end of the fifteenth century onwards the language became more widely taught in Western Europe and the study of Greek texts has thrived.

Problems with transmission encountered in medieval anthologies and florilegia

Manuscripts of excerpts play an important role for many classical authors, such as Horace, Virgil, Terence, Tibullus, Propertius, Catullus and Lucretius, in order to bridge chasms in the early stages of transmission. But because of their excerptive nature, florilegia do not offer a full text, just what appealed to their compilers' tastes.

Ninth-century anthological manuscripts are for some texts our only testimony: for example, the *Pervigilium Veneris* and the other poems (some of them copied from inscriptions) transmitted in the late antique corpus of poems known as the *Anthologia Latina*, which arrived in Italy from North Africa. The earliest and most impressive copy (Paris, Bibliothèque Nationale, lat. 10308) was written and illuminated in Italy in the eighth century. Problems occur for editors and other researchers because the content of this corpus is fluid and varies from manuscript to manuscript. It seems that, as with any collecting activity, each transcriber included what suited him, omitting and adding at will. Hence some poems appear in all manuscripts, others appear in the earliest and not afterwards, others still (e.g. Catullus 62) make their debut only in ninth-century and later manuscripts.

A similar problem is encountered with tenth- to twelfth-century florilegia. Eleventh- to twelfth-century French manuscripts of the *Florilegium Gallicum* (*FG*) tend to contain more or less similar excerpts from a set range of classical authors. It has therefore been believed that they were copied from a model in contemporary French schools, but their content is too fluid. Sometimes a particular line of an author is available only in one *FG* manuscript. This vexes editors because it is difficult to tell where the *FG* scribe got his extra line from: was it another anthology with more generous extracts, a reference in contemporary writings, hearsay, or did he have a more complete text in front of him? It is generally prudent to incline towards the first and second possibilities.

Another problem with medieval florilegia is that we find the text being changed for reasons of grammatical and rhetorical instruction, editing or taste. Hence a compiler of the *FG* (e.g. in Paris, Bibliothèque Nationale, lat. 7647) made Tibullus and Propertius sound Ovidian. An eleventh-century compiler of a different kind of florilegium at Monte Cassino (Venice, Marciana Z. lat. 497) for some authors listed only brief phrases and single words that pleased him. We need to bear these factors in mind when trying to identify excerpters' potential manuscript sources. How can we trace a lost source when past users have transformed the contents, in some cases almost beyond recognition? Nevertheless these florilegia reveal the teaching tools and students' exposure to classical authors in the Middle Ages. By considering which classical authors have been selected, who has been omitted, and why and how their text has been changed, we can throw light on how a medieval student's approach to a classical author differs from how we interpret classical authors today.

Grammarians and encyclopedic writers including Aulus Gellius, Servius, Priscian, Nonius Marcellus and Isidore of Seville, and for Greek literature the *Suda*, also acted as anthologies and instruments of transmission since they excerpted many classical authors. Isidore's *Etymologiae*, for example, is a collection of classical citations, some of which contain unique textual readings extracted from the manuscripts he used. These writers act *in loco manuscriptorum* (in the place of manuscripts) for the purposes of editing and transmission.

Editing: which is the right reading?

An editor of a classical text begins by drawing up a list of manuscripts and early editions; selecting particular passages where the manuscripts appear to disagree; and inspecting and collating (comparing, noting points of disagreement in) these passages either via a microfilm or a CD-ROM copy or 'in the flesh'. The next step is to establish the manuscript tradition of the text and draw up a family tree of manuscripts (a *stemma*), and to try to draw conclusions about the manuscript to which the extant witnesses can be traced back (the archetype), if indeed they can all be traced back to a single manuscript. This involves making decisions about which textual readings are the right ones and why. As we have seen, the oldest manuscripts are not necessarily the best. Another past principle was that the more difficult reading must be right (*difficilior lectio potior*). But the more difficult reading is not always to be preferred. As we have seen, scribes corrupted the text by poor copying, by omitting words which they did not know or which they could not decipher, or by skipping words owing to lapses of concentration. They have thus transmitted some un-Latin (and thus untranslatable) phrases. Leighton Reynold's article on the problems a modern editor of classical texts finds himself confronting ('Experiences of an editor') is a brilliant illustration of how to go about the task of editing prose texts and contains essential bibliography.

Does a 'closed' or 'contaminated' tradition deprive some manuscripts of value?

If a manuscript contains a text that has inextricably melded readings from more than one branch of the manuscript tradition of an author whose archetype cannot be established from the extant evidence, the manuscript is said to have been contaminated. As such it is usually disregarded by editors unless it imparts any other information that they can use. But this does not necessarily denude the manuscript of value. For example, a medieval manuscript of Ovid's *Tristia* in the British Library turns out to contain plentiful notes by a thirteenth-century German student, and so may offer a window on how the text was being studied and interpreted in Germany in the Middle Ages. Likewise, when a single source is shown to have generated all later extant manuscripts, as in the case of Catullus, Tibullus and Lucretius, for example, the fifteenth-century manuscripts do not constitute witnesses of an independent tradition. But since some of these manuscripts were corrected and annotated by their owners, they may reveal the strategies and capabilities of fifteenth-century editors and the interests of readers. In these ways classical manuscripts provide first-hand evidence of transmission, of the history of classical scholarship and of reception (i.e. who was reading which classical authors when, how and why; see also chapter 11). The influence of classical literature throughout the centuries is debated constantly by historians and other scholars. Yet the notes deposited in the margins of manuscripts by the readers themselves are seldom consulted, still less contextualised, even though some of these readers were as famous as Niccolò Machiavelli.

What does an editor do when only one manuscript of a text survives?

Despite extra problems caused by lack of any control for readings and gaps, an editor is thankful for the one manuscript. If Petronius Arbiter's 'Cena Trimalchionis' ('Dinner with Trimalchio') had not turned up in 1650 on the Dalmatian coast, or if the ninth-century manuscript of Sallust's *Histories* had not entered the Vatican Library in the fifteenth century, we would be completely at a loss for these texts. The saving of an author almost by chance brings home to us the unpredictable element in the survival of texts. Although the calibre of some authors ought to guarantee survival on merit, sadly some of their writings or, in the case of Gaius Cornelius Gallus, their entire ouput has not been saved because not enough manuscripts were copied to ensure survival. This may be due partly to readers' taste and partly to educational curricula in antiquity. For example, while Virgil, Propertius and Ovid thought enough of Gallus to imitate him, he was clearly hard going. The pronouncement of Quintilian (whose judgements became rules of thumb among schoolmasters) that among elegists 'Tibullus seems to be the most polished and elegant; there are those who prefer Propertius; Ovid is naughtier than either, just as Gallus is harsher (or "harder")' may have sealed Gallus' fate. Apart from indirect evidence, we have only a single line and the scrap of papyrus that turned up in 1978 in Egypt.

How do we assess lost manuscripts seen by previous editors?

The value of combing through early printed editions of classical texts cannot be revealed more clearly than when we find a past scholar with his hands on a now lost manuscript that tells a different story from the rest. For example, Joseph Scaliger (1540–1609) saw a unique Tibullan fragment in the library of a French friend, recognised it for what it was, and reported its readings in his 1577 edition. The manuscript disappeared shortly afterwards. The main questions concern whether we can find reasons to believe that the editor is telling the truth, and whether we can use our advances in knowledge and methodology to 'go behind' what the editor says and find out more about his manuscript. In this case we can ascertain that Scaliger had discovered a parchment fragment, perhaps from the twelfth century, containing [Tibullus] 3.4.64-end, Domitius Marsus' *Epigram* and a *Priapeum*, and we can use its readings to emend the text.

Secrets and lies

As we have seen, most manuscripts keep secrets about the exemplars they were copied from, by whom and where, and why. Sometimes manuscripts tell lies because of their corrupt text or the transmission of apocryphal stories about classical authors, such as St Jerome's tale that Lucretius wrote the *de Rerum Natura* after being driven mad by a love potion and committed suicide aged 44. Occasionally a manuscript tells an out-and-out lie: scholarly research has for several centuries been beset by forgeries. Riddles remain aplenty for teasing out by future editor-detectives, although inevitably manuscripts will keep some secrets forever.

Further reading

B. Bischoff, *Mittelalterliche Studien*, Stuttgart: Anton Hiersemann, 1966–81 (= *Manuscripts and Libraries in the Age of Charlemagne*, trans. M. M. Gorman, Cambridge: Cambridge University Press, 1994).

B. Bischoff, *Paläographie des römischen Altertums und des abendländischen Paläographie,* 2nd edn), Berlin: Eric Schmidt, 1986 (= *Latin Palaeography: Antiquity and the Middle Ages*, trans. D. Ganz and D. O'Cronin, Cambridge: Cambridge University Press, 1990).

C. Chavannes-Mazel and M. M. Smith (eds), *Medieval Manuscripts of the Latin Classics: Production and Use*, Anderson Lovelace: Red Gull Press, 1996.

E. R. Curtius, *European Literature and the Latin Middle Ages*, trans. W. R. Trask, Princeton: Princeton University Press, 1990.

M. D. Reeve, 'Classical scholarship', in J. Kraye (ed.) *The Cambridge Companion to Renaissance Humanism*, Cambridge: Cambridge University Press, 1996, pp. 20–46.

L. D. Reynolds (ed.) *Texts and Transmission: A Survey of the Latin Classics*, Oxford: Clarendon Press, 1983.

L. D. Reynolds, 'Experiences of an editor of classical Latin texts', *Revue d'histoire des Textes* 25 (2000), 1–15

L. D. Reynolds and N. G. Wilson, *Scribes and Scholars: A Guide to the Transmission of Greek and Latin Literature* (3rd edn), Oxford: Clarendon Press, 1991.

E. G. Turner, *Greek Manuscripts of the Ancient World* (2nd edn, rev. P. J. Parsons), London: University of London, Institute of Classical Studies, 1987.

M. L. West, *Textual Criticism and Editorial Technique Applicable to Greek and Latin Texts*, Stuttgart: Teubner, 1973.

N. G. Wilson, *Medieval Greek Bookhands* (2 vols), Cambridge MA: Medieval Academy of America, 1973.

Handbooks and reference works

C. Briquet, *Les Filigranes: dictionnaire historique des marques du papier et de leur apparition*, Leipzig: Hiersemann, 1923.

M. Brown, *A Guide to Western Historical Scripts from Antiquity to 1600*, London: British Library, 1990.

A. Cappelli, *Dizionario di abbreviature latine ed italiane* (6th edn), Milan: U. Hoepli, 1990.

A. Derolez, *The Palaeography of Gothic Manuscript Books: From the Twelfth to the Early Sixteenth Century*, Cambridge: Cambridge University Press, 2003.

E. A. Lowe, *Codices latini antiquiores* (12 vols), Oxford: Clarendon Press, 1934–71.

F. Newton, *The Scriptorium and Library at Monte Cassino 1085–1105*, Cambridge: Cambridge University Press, 1999.

E. K. Rand, *A Survey of the Manuscripts of Tours* 1–2, Cambridge MA: Medieval Academy of America, 1929.

E. Maunde Thompson, *An Introduction to Greek and Latin Palaeography*, Oxford: Clarendon Press, 1912.

34. *Inscriptions*

Alison E. Cooley and Graham Oliver

Demystifying inscriptions

It might appear to the uninitiated that experts in inscriptions (who call themselves 'epigraphers') attempt to keep their subject ('epigraphy') in decent obscurity. Consider Charles Dickens's Mr Pickwick, who discovered this curious inscription:

+
BILST
UM
PSHI
S. M.
ARK

Having presented several ingenious interpretations of its meaning, he was elected an honorary member of seventeen learned bodies. The suggestion by a Mr Blotton that the letters represented 'BILL STUMPS, HIS MARK' was dismissed contemptuously, allowing the stone to remain 'an illegible monument of Mr Pickwick's greatness'. How much better to have a text of obscure meaning for scholars to speculate about than a simple graffito by someone with a poor grasp of literacy!

Another common misconception is that if something is 'carved/written in stone', this acts as a guarantee of its authenticity. A supermarket chain cashed in on this by prominently displaying a large 'inscription' declaring 'permanently low prices for ever'. Whatever the merits of this claim, inscriptions, whether fictional or not, are quite capable of misleading the unwary.

Defining inscriptions

An inscription cannot exist without a text, but the text is not its only component. Inscriptions are physical objects, and were often intended to be seen in a particular location. Their texts derived some of their meaning from their context. This can be equally true of impressive public monuments and private graffiti. Below is an outline of the main types of inscription found in the ancient world, considering why inscriptions were produced and how they were used. Then follows an exploration of the issues faced by today's ancient historians wishing to make use of inscriptions as source material.

Types of inscription

Epitaphs

Epitaphs, or funerary inscriptions, are by far the most common inscriptions. Some simply commemorate the name of the deceased, but others, typically in the Roman era, relate career and achievements. Greek funerary inscriptions tend to be simpler and less informative than their Roman counterparts, offering the name of the deceased and sometimes additional information, usually in verse. Unlike modern examples, ancient tombstones do not include the actual dates of birth and death (this sort of information was not readily available), although some give the age at death. Like modern epitaphs, they display formulaic language rather than an everyday response to death. Such formulae (for example, describing the deceased as 'most dear', or 'sweetest') are more typical of the Roman period.

Epitaphs may be inscribed upon simple plaques or *stēlae* – fixed in the ground, or displayed on the walls of a *columbarium* (an underground tomb with multiple similar niches for cinerary urns, named after its resemblance to a dovecote) or catacomb (a less organised underground burial area, usually associated with early Christian cemeteries) – or may belong to elaborate monuments, like that of Niceratus of Histria found at Kallithea, north of Piraeus, Athens (*SEG* 1969: 24.258) or the Pyramid of Cestius at Rome (Keppie, *Understanding Roman Inscriptions*, pp. 104–5). Christian epitaphs, unlike pagan ones, often allude to the deceased's beliefs, including symbols like the *chi-rho* (the first two Greek letters of *Christos*, Christ's name). With Christianisation, a tendency to represent the deceased's relationship with God replaced the previous norm of recording the deceased's relationship with the dedicator of the epitaph.

Sculpted and painted reliefs can provide additional pictorial information (not only on tombstones, but on other types of inscription too). Many Roman tombstones depict the deceased's occupation. Indeed the pictorial element is often the main attraction, to which the inscription adds crucial information such as names, dates or purpose.

Dedications, curses and calendars

People's relationships with the gods inspired many different types of inscription. An individual might offer any type of artefact – a miniature altar, statuette or sculpted relief – to a god, and an inscription on the object demonstrated that both parties had fulfilled their side of a vow, identifying deity and worshipper. Curses against private enemies scratched upon sinister lead tablets were intended only for a deity's eyes: the curse might be written backwards and the tablet folded over before being offered. Notable collections of curses have been found at the sanctuaries of Sulis Minerva at Bath and of Mercury at Uley, both in Roman Britain. Other important religious inscriptions include sacred laws, cult regulations and sacred calendars (*fasti* in Latin). In the Greek world, sacred calendars usually determined what precisely was to be sacrificed to which deities and on which specific days (see also chapter 64).

Inscriptions incorporated into a building

Large inscriptions incorporated into a building identified it and commemorated the benefactor who initially paid for or later restored it. Milestones along Roman roads are a subcategory of building inscription, since they record the road-builder or repairer as well as the distance along the road.

Decrees and laws

Decrees and laws (*psephismata* and *nomoi*; see also chapter 60) form one of the most important categories of inscriptions from the Greek world. Many varied bodies issued decrees, from ad hoc groupings of soldiers to more permanent entities, such as cult groups (*thiasoi* and *genē*), demes or ephebes (young men who had reached the age for military service). Perhaps the most important decrees for political history are those of larger entities. These include cities (poleis) and larger political structures, including confederations of poleis, such as the Boeotian Confederacy, and politico-religious structures, such as the Amphictyonic League at Delphi. Decrees can contain important historical information, such as records of alliances, peace treaties, agreements between poleis, or honours given to important benefactors (such as citizenship; see also chapter 60). Individual laws or collections of various laws cover numerous aspects of life in antiquity from penalties for murder through to protection against counterfeit silver coinage (see also chapter 25).

Likewise in the Roman world, a range of groups, from the state downward, issued decrees. Not only town councils and provincial assemblies but also smaller groups like *Augustales* imitated the way in which the Roman Senate drafted its decrees. These might record measures designed to honour an individual, but also generated separate honorific inscriptions, on bases beneath statues, which summarised the honorand's career (so-called *cursus* inscriptions). Private individuals too set up honorific statues of benefactors.

Other decrees had a legislative function. At Rome, the Roman people ratified laws, but senatorial decrees and imperial edicts came to have similar legal force under the emperors (see also chapter 60). A further distinctive group consists of *diplōmata*, small folded tablets of bronze granting Roman citizenship to auxiliary soldiers on their retirement. One copy was displayed on the Capitol at Rome and another was kept by the individual, and it is these that are found around the empire. The earliest date from the mid-first century AD.

Lists of names

Many inscriptions take the form of, or include, lists of names. Some lists, more typically in Greek epigraphy, are appended to decrees. Lists were inscribed for a variety of purposes and can record, for example, the names of civic magistrates, members of a professional association or town council, or those who had made a religious dedication.

Inscriptions on objects

In addition to monumental inscriptions, just about any object could bear a text. Pottery was often used for inscriptions. Discarded pieces of pottery might carry graffiti, but fine pots also carried writing, often to identify people on scenes, but also to specify the name of the potter. Inscribed pottery served one of the most famous institutions at Athens, ostracism, named after the role played by the *ostraka* (lit. 'pieces of pottery') on which one would write or have written the name of the person one wanted to ostracise, that is, send into non-punitive exile for a fixed period (see also chapters 28 and 60).

Metal was also an important medium for inscriptions. The perceived sinister properties of lead (see above) resulted in its adoption for curse tablets. At Athens, bronze tokens inscribed with an individual's name were used in the law-courts by Athenians serving as jurors. Weights and measures carried inscriptions and were employed by numerous Greek and Roman cities to regulate commercial activities (see also chapters 5 and 62). Money, in the form of coins, also displayed texts, or 'legends', but these are usually studied by numismatists (see also chapter 25). Otherwise, inscriptions on precious metal seldom survive: exceptions are (from Italy) the Pyrgi gold-leaf dedications written in Etruscan and Phoenician to the goddess Astarte, or the fourth-century BC Orphic prayer in Greek found in a Thessalian grave (*SEG* 1977: 27.226 bis).

In the Roman world, the broad range of everyday portable objects bearing inscriptions that may be scratched, painted or stamped onto their surface is known by the term *instrumentum domesticum*. These include abbreviated texts and symbols on transport containers (such as amphorae), fine-ware pottery (see also chapter 28), terracotta lamps, glass vessels, bricks, tiles, lead pipes, wooden barrels and even bread. Many of these texts helped with the organisation of business, providing information relating to production, contents, transport and distribution. Others indicated ownership of personal household possessions, from gems and seals (see also chapter 29) to slave collars, whose inscriptions were designed to deter (or recover) runaways.

Painted inscriptions and graffiti

Painted inscriptions tended to have a short natural lifespan, but the quantity at Pompeii (almost 3,000), where unusual circumstances have led to their preservation, gives some idea of their original number. Graffiti could be etched upon any available surface, even upon a famous statue, such as the colossal statue of Rameses II at the temple of Abu Simbel, where Greek mercenaries carved their names in the early sixth century BC (Fornara, *Translated Documents of Greece and Rome 1*, no. 24 = Meiggs and Lewis, *Greek Historical Inscriptions*, no. 7). Excavations at Vindolanda near Hadrian's Wall have revealed that everyday writing was not only scratched upon the wax of wooden stilus-tablets, such as those found at Pompeii, but also written in ink on slivers of wood.

Why inscribe?

The phrase 'epigraphic habit' was coined by Ramsay MacMullen. He used it to describe the chronological distribution pattern of Latin inscriptions during the principate, climbing to a peak in the early third century AD before declining again. The phrase can be applied equally to the Greek and Roman worlds to define the variable tendency to produce inscriptions. Given that the impetus to inscribe was not equally strong at all times and in all places, the following considerations provide some explanation of epigraphic culture (that is, the cultural habits and constraints governing the tendency to inscribe) in classical antiquity.

The choice of material for a monumental inscription usually depended upon local supply, and the absence of suitable materials could affect the survival of a society's epigraphic culture. Where quarries were nearby, as at Athens and at Aphrodisias in Caria, marble was extensively used. In Republican Rome, local tufas and travertine were mainly used until the marble quarries at Etruscan Luni (Carrara) opened in the first century BC. Consequently, the material used for an inscription can help in judging its date. Marble accommodated the most elegant lettering, whereas a friable stone like volcanic tufa created difficulties for stonecutters. Despite the possibility for recycling marble via the limekiln (using intense heat to break it down to produce building lime for mortar, as often in the Middle Ages and later), stone inscriptions stood a much better chance of survival than metal ones. Although bronze inscriptions are under-represented today since they were so easily melted down, there are still found significant numbers of texts either inscribed upon sheets of bronze or formed from large individual letters affixed to a building. The imprint left by some large bronze letters can even still be seen today, set into a paving surface. Bronze may have been favoured for Roman laws because it invoked ideas of permanency and inviolability, while in the Greek world it may have prevailed in areas where good stone was not readily available.

There may have been several reasons why an inscription was set up. One aim was to teach proper behaviour. An exceptional illustration of this is the lengthy inscription at Oenoanda in Lycia setting out Epicurean philosophical precepts (see also chapter 48). Many inscriptions were commemorative, preserving the memory of an event or person by means of a monument. The act of inscribing itself was designed to defeat the passage of time. The Roman legal code (*Digest* 50.10.2/7; see also chapter 58) stated that if someone had donated a public building, the inscription bearing his or her name should be permanently maintained, even in later phases of rebuilding or repair, when another donor might also set up an inscription. The declared purpose of this was to encourage others to imitate the original donor's generosity. Greek and Roman honorific inscriptions served a similarly exemplary purpose, advertising what sorts of actions were encouraged, particularly acts of public generosity ('euergetism'). A similarly instructive purpose was served by the senatorial decree concerning the Roman senator Piso, accused of civil disobedience in AD 20, in which the Senate presented the behaviour of Piso and of the emperor Tiberius' family as negative and positive role models (see also chapter 50).

Any act of commemoration could be reversed at a later date: an individual's behaviour might be condemned by erasing his name from an inscription (*damnatio memoriae*). In the Roman world, memory of a 'bad' emperor might be removed not only from inscriptions, but also from different commemorative media, with heads being removed from portrait statues and erased from coins. This condemnation was all the more evident if the name remained legible beneath the erasure. Such condemnation is less common in the classical and Hellenistic Greek world, although after Philip V's invasion of Attica in 200 BC, the Athenians removed any reference to him or his ancestors from public monuments. Complete inscriptions might be destroyed by a new government, as when oligarchy replaced democracy in classical Athens (404/3 and 321–319 BC; see also chapter 60). On both of these occasions, though, the succeeding democratic governments re-erected new copies of some decrees.

Creating a monumental inscription and displaying it in public was one way of protecting a text from alteration, but relatively few records were displayed in this fashion. Temporary plaques – 'whitened boards' (in Latin, *alba*) – carried public announcements at Athens and Rome, and archives contained records available for consultation. Other motivations can be found for setting up inscriptions, which might be termed 'symbolic'. Practical record-keeping was not the concern of religious inscriptions (for example, those created by the Arval Brethren, Rome's most ancient college of priests, in their sanctuary just outside Rome) where the actual process of inscribing was itself an element in the observation of cult. In a similar way, the honorific decrees set up in the Agora or on the Acropolis at Athens were never meant to be an archive of public decisions but a token of recognition: the very act of inscribing such a decree was an honour conferred by the state. Symbolic and administrative functions could merge: boundary stones defined the Athenian Agora because some people (e.g. the polluted) were not permitted to enter this public, religious and commercial urban space.

Epigraphical culture depended largely upon the assumption that some people would read an inscription. Such an expectation is expressed in Roman tombstones that address passers-by, exhorting them to 'stay awhile and read'. A comical variation on this theme is presented by Petronius' fictional character Trimalchio, in the *Satyrica* (71). He wanted to force passers-by to read his epitaph by setting a sundial upon his tomb to attract their attention. Readers also seem to be catered for by other measures taken to improve the legibility of inscriptions. Roman laws inscribed on bronze were required to be visible and legible, and they contain clearly marked paragraphs and prominent titles. In the case of stone inscriptions, paint was usually added to their lettering. But the assumption that inscriptions would be read is not unproblematic. It seems unlikely that many people, if any, would actually have spent time reading Roman laws in their inscribed form, given their prohibitive size as monuments. For example, the text of the Flavian municipal law at Irni (Spain) covered ten tablets, in thirty columns containing 1,500 lines of letters only 4–6 mm (¼ inch) high, over a distance of some 9 m (almost 30 ft.).

But the layout of inscriptions may have presented less difficulty than the modern reader imagines. At Athens in the fifth and fourth centuries BC almost all decrees were carved in a *stoichēdon* pattern, an arrangement whereby the letters (always capitals) were cut on the stone as if on a chessboard. Each letter occupies one virtual square, and each letter is uniformly separated by the same space from each adjacent letter (figure 34.1). This distinctive arrangement may not have hindered the reading of the text. Word separators were sometimes used to distinguish word breaks, and, by the Hellenistic period, the ends of lines finish with a complete word. But although the *stoichēdon* style became less common through the third century BC onwards, Greek inscriptions continuedtorunwordstogetherlikethis (*sic*). The *boustrophēdon* style, more common in archaic Greek inscriptions, *may* have made reading more difficult because letters and the inscription were written right to left and left to right alternately. However, contemporary readers may have been more familiar with this format. Indeed, such inscriptions were written as much for their symbolic purpose as for their legibility.

Nevertheless, could people read inscriptions? Literacy levels may well have been very low by modern standards (perhaps under 10 per cent), although it is impossible to measure reading (as opposed to writing) ability in the ancient world. A comment in Petronius' *Satyrica* (58.7), on the ability to read 'engraved capital letters', implies that Romans were aware of different types of literacy. Besides, some inscriptions were rendered accessible even to the illiterate by being read aloud by others, whether through official proclamation by a herald or more informally. At Athens, the dissemination of civic information of public importance through written notices at the Altar of the Ten Eponymous Heroes seems to assume a wide level of at least a minimal level of literacy (such as the ability to recognise one's name). Recent discoveries by M. K. Langdon in the Vari region of southeast Attica of a large number of rock-cut inscriptions suggest that a wide range of people (including shepherds) could not only read but write.

Many inscriptions had administrative and economic functions. Some private inscriptions, notably instructions on the distribution of testamentary wealth, were designed to make others publicly accountable for their actions in a way that archived records could not. Mortgage inscriptions declared that the specific property of a particular person was being used to secure or guarantee

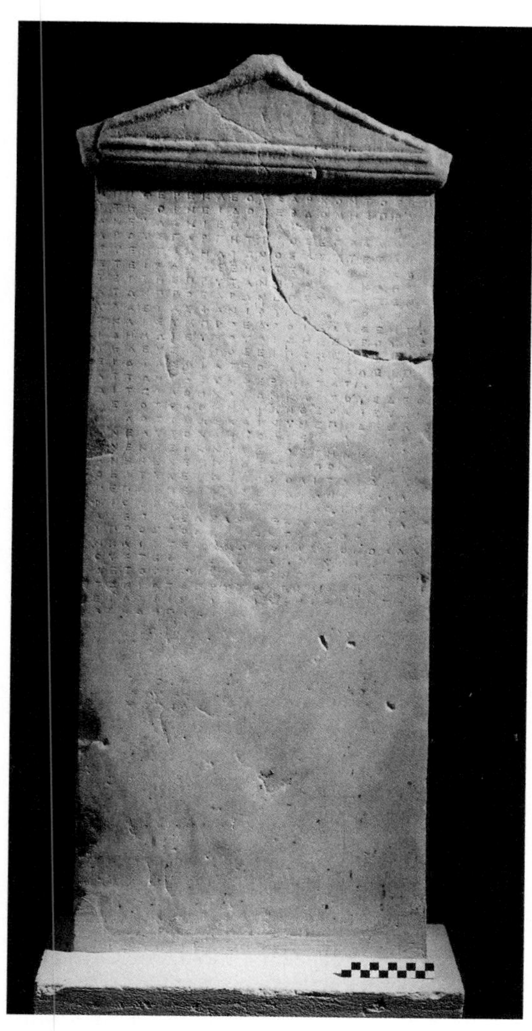

Fig. 34.1 Athenian state decree in honour of Phidias of Rhodes, a doctor, written in *stoichēdon* pattern. 304/3 BC. *IG* ii².483 [EM 7279] courtesy of the Epigraphical Museum, Athens.

loans or debts. In the Roman world, a whole variety of inscriptions served economic activities (see also chapter 5). A single transport-container, or amphora, might bear several inscriptions of different sorts. Painted inscriptions or a stamp on the stopper might describe its contents, weights when full and empty, the persons selling the goods, and the address of the intended recipient. Stamps impressed upon the clay give information about the manufacturing of the vessel, guaranteeing its durability and capacity (see also chapter 28). Finally, the eruption of Vesuvius preserved two large archives of wax tablets. One in Pompeii itself relates to the affairs of the banker Caecilius Iucundus. The other, found just outside the town (the so-called 'Murecine Tablets'), documents business deals brokered at the major harbour-town of Puteoli.

So far we have considered why people set up monumental inscriptions, but it should not be forgotten that graffiti formed a significant part of a society's epigraphic culture. Unlike today, it was not a criminal offence in the ancient world to scratch writing upon walls. Graffiti offer insight into common linguistic usage that is not available from our highbrow literary or monumental epigraphic sources. Although it is rarely possible to know who created the graffiti (and we should avoid modern assumptions about lower-class vandalism and youthful 'graffiti-artists'), we can trace some of the reasons why it was created.

Some graffiti had a subversive, or parodic, intent. It was one way of expressing opposition anonymously under oppressive regimes. One highly literate protest at the emperor Domitian's propensity to award himself triumphal arches consisted of the Latin word for arches, *arci*, in Greek letters meaning 'that's enough' (Suetonius, *Life of Domitian* 13). Politics was not the only sphere to provoke criticism. A rough sketch found on the Palatine at Rome is one of the oldest representations of the crucifixion (mid-third century AD?). It depicts a donkey-headed figure upon the cross, with a figure below raising his arm towards it, as if appealing to it. Alongside this is a text in Greek: 'Alexamenos worships god' (figure 34.2). Other graffiti seem purely for fun, consisting of literary tags, idle sketches, erotic or obscene comments. These give a vivid impression of popular enthusiasms of the time.

The production of monumental inscriptions

Once someone had decided to commission an inscription, how much control could this customer exert over the final product? Petronius' exaggerated picture of the upstart Trimalchio shows him issuing detailed instructions to the stonemason about the inscription and sculptural

Fig. 34.2 Graffito of crucifixion, from the Palatine, Rome.

decoration on his tomb. Here the element of parody probably lay in the nature of the details requested, rather than in the principle that someone might want to control his tomb's appearance. A bilingual shop-sign from Palermo (Sicily) invites private customers to commission inscriptions (*CIL* X.7296 and *IG* xiv.297; see 'How to find out about inscriptions' below).

The quality of the inscription would depend upon the budget: the customer's financial means must have had an impact upon the style of monument (type of stone, care of inscribing, level of literacy, amount of decoration). Some texts may only have been applied by paint. By contrast, public monuments tended to be better funded and so of a more consistent standard, although stone-cutter's errors still appear. Athens produced numerous inscriptions each year, and not only have individual letter-cutters been identified but their careers can be traced sometimes over a twenty- or thirty-year period (see Tracy, *Attic Letter-Cutters*).

But even public monuments could vary in their grandeur. At Athens, the state usually specified the amount of money to be spent on inscribing a decree. Some monumental inscriptions received extra finance. The relatives of Euphron of Sikyon (319/18 BC; *IG* ii².448) subsidised the impressive monument set up in his honour. Arybbas, king of the Molossians, probably added money to the 30 *drachmae* (see also chapter 62) granted to him, in order to pay for one of the tallest Athenian state decrees (*IG* ii².226 = Rhodes and Osborne, no. 70).

Language represented another choice for some customers commissioning their inscriptions. This could be influenced by self-representation as much as by the wish to communicate to others. The inclusion of Palmyrene alongside Latin on a third-century AD tombstone found at South Shields tells us more about the sense of cultural affiliation of its dedicator (a trader from Palmyra) than about the number of Palmyrene speakers in northeast England (*RIB* 1065 = LACTOR 4, 4th edn, no.

204) (figure 34.3). A bilingual inscription such as this one did not necessarily present identical versions of a text in both languages. In this case, the Palmyrene inscription, 'Regina the freedwoman of Barates, alas', contrasts with the formulaic Latin text: 'To the departed spirits of Regina, his freedwoman and wife, a Catuvellaunian, aged 30. Barates of Palmyra'. The sculpted relief on the tombstone also combines Latin and Palmyrene elements, with a prominent place given not only to jewellery (typical of Palmyrene funerary reliefs) but also to wool-working (an archetypal

Fig. 34.3 Tombstone of Regina in Latin and Palmyrene. *RIB* 1065, courtesy of Arbeia Roman Fort, Tyne and Wear Museums.

Fig. 34.4 Digitised image of a squeeze (paper impression of an inscription), a fragment of the Athenian Tribute Lists. 440–439 BC. *IG* i[3].272, lines 1–25. Courtesy of C. V. Crowther, Centre for the Study of Ancient Documents, Oxford.

occupation of the Roman *matrona* or 'lady of the house').

Other examples are less extreme, but many instances can be found of the use of a local language (such as neo-Punic in North Africa) alongside the more universal languages of Latin and Greek. Conventionally, the Roman world is considered to consist of 'Greek East' and 'Latin West' (see also chapters 19 and 20), reflecting those regions' dominant cultural and linguistic characteristics, but some official public inscriptions in the former were set up in Latin, notably in Roman colonies, such as

Pisidian Antioch. Furthermore, parts of the so-called 'Greek East', notably in the Near East, had a complex linguistic profile, with the co-existence of languages like Nabatean, Safaitic and Aramaic (see also chapter 20). Phoenician and Greek inscriptions reflect the strength of Phoenician communities who commissioned inscriptions in prosperous centres such as Delos and Athens. But local diversity is perhaps best observed in the archaic period (see also chapter 16), when Greek inscriptions used local alphabets, often containing distinct letter-forms and characters. The distribution of local alphabets reflects contacts between cities and colonies throughout the Mediterranean and beyond. The diverse local alphabets of archaic Greece gradually disappeared by the fourth century BC, although differences in dialect continued despite the increasing use of 'common Greek' (*koinē*) in the Hellenistic period.

Finally, the location of inscribed monuments could be subject to strict regulation. Although people could set up whatever they liked in private space, public space was subject to official control, particularly in urban areas like the Greek agora or Roman forum, or temples and sanctuaries, where public inscriptions were most commonly set up. Many inscriptions grant honorands the right to set up an inscription in the most visible place, but Athens was unusual in that the people would usually specify more precisely where an inscription should stand.

Uses of inscriptions for the modern ancient historian

Much of our knowledge of ancient history is derived from literary sources, but sometimes an inscription directly sheds light on an episode in political history discussed by an ancient author. Thucydides' *pentacontaetia* (*Histories* 1.89–118) summarises the rise of Athenian power during the mid-fifth century BC and the creation of an empire of tribute-paying allies (see also chapters 16 and 49). Two very large inscriptions set up on the Athenian Acropolis listed the amounts of money that these allies paid to Athena Polias, representing 1/60th of their total tribute payments (LACTOR 1, 4th edn, pp. 86–97). The chance survival of many small fragments of these inscriptions has allowed historians to reconstruct the original monument and so calculate the total tribute paid by the allies for much of the second half of the fifth century (figure 34.4). These inscriptions provide vital information about how Athens ran its empire. Inscriptions can also allow us to evaluate literary sources. Two large bronze tablets found in the provinces illuminate the compositional technique of the Roman historian Tacitus (see also chapter 50). His version of a speech by the emperor Claudius concerning the admission of Gauls to the Senate in AD 48 (*Annals* 11.24) can actually be compared with Claudius' own words, as preserved on a large plaque found in Lyon (*ILS* 212 = LACTOR 8, no. 34). In this case, an inscription illuminates a single speech in Tacitus, but the recent discovery in Spain of the senatorial decree concerning Piso of AD 20 goes even further. This allows us to reassess a whole sequence of episodes recorded by the historian in the light of documentary evidence (*Annals* 2.43–3.19). Furthermore, this decree independently illuminates unexpected elements of social and political history, not hinted at by Tacitus. Other examples could be given, but this should give a taste of some of the possibilities.

Inscriptions can often provide chronological details. The Parian Marble, set up in the third century BC on the Aegean island of Paros, provides a unique time-chart of Greek history dating back from 264/3 BC to events including the Trojan War! Athenian decrees provide the day and date on which the decree was passed. But authenticity and the date of the writing-up must be handled with care. A fourth-century BC decree from Cyrene records what may have been the original founding agreement of the seventh-century BC colony established by Thera (Fornara, no. 18 = Meiggs and Lewis, no. 5). Sometimes inscriptions were updated after they had been set up. At Ostia, a dedication by a prominent magistrate (*Année Épigraphique* 1941.99), Cartilius Poplicola, was updated twice, to record that he had been elected to the town's chief magistracy for a fourth time, and then again for a fifth, a notable achievement obviously thought worthy of being recorded in stone.

Some inscriptions offer interesting historical perspectives on people mentioned only briefly in ancient literary sources, such as the construction by Pontius Pilate of a Tiberieum, arguably a shrine to honour the emperor Tiberius (EDH HD004074). They can provide information on literary figures such as the Hellenistic poet Callimachus, one of many who probably contributed money to a fund to protect the harvest at Athens in 248/7 BC. A short career inscription of even so well-documented a figure as Pliny the younger, who published ten books of letters, covers otherwise unknown aspects of his life (*ILS* 2927 = LACTOR 8, no. 96; see also chapter 44). The study of prosopography, or the 'who's who' of the ancient world, largely depends upon the evidence of inscriptions. Inscriptions, alongside archaeology, can illuminate a way of life not known at all from literature. For example, the writing tablets from Vindolanda cast unexpected light upon many aspects of life in the Roman army at the edge of the empire in the early second century AD (Bowman, *Life and Letters*; LACTOR 4, 4th edn, nos 273–7). They show how soldiers in an auxiliary unit were scattered throughout the province on detachment. Inventories illustrate the soldiers' diet and supplies. Some also give an impression of social life within the camp, with an officer's wife issuing an invitation to her friend for a birthday celebration. But many more ancient voices emerge from the past, including slaves, freedmen, and women. Whereas *Augustales* are mentioned in only a single literary source (Petronius' *Satyrica*), for example, their role in Roman imperial society is illuminated by over 2,000 inscriptions.

Modern responses to ancient inscriptions

Ancient inscriptions have long inspired modern viewers, at least since the fourteenth century when the Roman politician Cola di Rienzo publicly presented the recently discovered 'Law on the powers of Vespasian' in order to support his own political aims. A century later, Cyriacus of Ancona copied out inscriptions he saw during his travels in the Eastern Mediterranean. During the Renaissance, scholars concentrated mainly upon inscriptions as texts, using them as sources of antiquarian detail or as documents of political history. The aesthetic qualities of inscriptions as artistic objects, notably funerary monuments, led to their collection by Italian royalty and by the high society of Europe in the age of the Grand Tour (see also chapter 1). In more modern times, ancient inscriptions have been appropriated for political purposes. The dictator Mussolini created a new inscribed copy of Augustus' *Res Gestae*, carved upon the modern structure he built to house the Altar of Augustan Peace (Ara Pacis; see also chapter 11), in order to legitimise his own fascist rule by evoking imperial Rome.

Dangers faced by the modern ancient historian

There is almost no sphere of ancient history that cannot be illuminated by studying inscriptions, but some words of caution should be borne in mind when tackling them. Above all, they cannot be regarded as impartial historical documents. Inscriptions were not only set up in a selective way, they also survive in a selective way. Not all cultures within the Greek and Roman worlds used stone to create inscribed monuments. Not everyone within inscribing cultures shared the 'epigraphic habit'. Even in the case of Rome, despite the preservation of thousands of inscriptions, less than 1 per cent of the city's inhabitants through the ages are mentioned in the inscriptions surviving today. Where an inscription does survive, the modern reader should always seek out its subjectivity. Inscriptions were always created for a purpose, not in order to provide twenty-first-century historians with documentary evidence. The bias of some inscriptions is immediately obvious, such as the autobiographical account of his achievements which the emperor Augustus had inscribed on his tomb (the *Res Gestae*), in which he carefully disguised the illegitimacy of his early career and rise to power. Less obvious is the career of the late fourth-century BC Aristomedes of Cos, 'friend' of the Hellenistic kings Antigonus Monophthalmus and Demetrius Poliorcetes. The honours given to him by various Greek cities would have gone unnoticed if he had not arranged to have the decrees inscribed at his home town in Cos. These inscriptions express Aristomedes' aspirations as a successful Coan operating on the highest level. Whether carved in stone or on bronze, the intentions and wishes of the composer of the inscription and/or the person who set it up must always be questioned by the historian.

But one of the worst hazards is the tendency of inscriptions to fragment. Not all inscriptions are found in their original complete condition; often they are in pieces, and not all pieces survive. It is common to find that the key phrase needed to interpret the text is missing, where the stone breaks off. In modern editions of inscriptions, words printed inside square brackets – [ ] – are those which have been supplied by the editor in their absence from the inscription itself. The editor is responsible for transcribing the inscribed text and then making sense of it. This can involve assessing and suggesting, where possible, letters and words that no longer exist on the stone ('restorations') especially where the inscription survives only in a fragmentary form. Whether working from the original Latin or Greek, or from translation, ignore square brackets at your peril. Great discussion revolves around what historians believe was preserved on the parts of inscriptions that have not survived, or cannot be read. This is not to say that everything within square brackets is untrustworthy: the formulaic language commonly used in inscriptions does mean that an expression may be paralleled in similar texts, allowing an editor to be reasonably confident in filling in the gaps. This is particularly true of several types of honorific inscription, such as citizenship grants, or of other frequently attested types of decree.

How to find out about inscriptions

The main publications of Latin and Greek inscriptions tend to be rather daunting tomes in the series *Inscriptiones Graecae* (*IG*) and *Corpus Inscriptionum Latinarum* (*CIL*). *Inscriptiones Graecae*, a large project originally designed to collect and publish all Greek inscriptions, covers a number of cities and regions of the Greek world in various volumes. Some of these are in their second or third edition (e.g. Athens and Attica, to 404/3 BC: *IG* i^3; 403/2 BC to AD 267: *IG* ii^2; Laconia and Messenia: *IG* v 1). The massive number of inscriptions from Asia Minor can be found in volumes dedicated to specific sites (e.g. Priene and Pergamum) or as part of the extensive series of inscriptions of Greek states in Asia Minor (*Inschriften griechischer Städte aus Kleinasien* = *IK*). *Corpus Inscriptionum Latinarum* is generally organised geographically (for instance, *CIL* VI: city of Rome), except for its final thematic volumes (e.g. *CIL* XVI: *diplōmata*). Both *IG* and *CIL* are currently undergoing revision, with new editions appearing gradually, but it is unlikely that the projects will see completion even in this century. Besides, new inscriptions are coming to light each year. These are tracked by *Supplementum Epigraphicum Graecum* (*SEG*) and *Bulletin Épigraphique* (*Bull. Ep.*) for Greek texts, and *L'Année Épigraphique* (*AE*) for Roman. Slightly more approachable are extensive selections of inscriptions, such as *Inscriptiones Latinae Selectae* (*ILS*) and *Sylloge Inscriptionum Graecarum* (*SIG* or *Syll.*^{3}), which arrange inscriptions by chronology, region and theme. Regional and chronological selections are also useful, especially since the former are often more up-to-date than the major collections. The *Guide de l'épigraphiste* (eds Bérard et al.) is an invaluable handbook for providing orientation to the morass of epigraphic publications; and an accessible introduction to epigraphy is *Epigraphic Evidence* (ed. Bodel).

Students without knowledge of ancient languages will find many useful sourcebooks giving inscriptions in translation, particularly the LACTOR series (London Association of Classical Teachers Original Records) and *Translated Documents of Greece and Rome* (five volumes from archaic and fifth-century Greece (ed. Fornara) through to the Roman Empire (ed. Sherk)).

Increasingly, the internet provides access to inscriptions in their original languages and in translation, with images of squeezes or photographs. 'Squeezes' are paper impressions of inscriptions. They are made by laying moist heavy filter paper on the stone and then hitting (carefully!) the paper-covered stone with a special brush ('squeeze brush') to push – or 'squeeze' – the paper into the incisions made by the ancient letter-cutter. Once dry, the inscription is imprinted onto the paper. Squeezes have long been the favoured means of preserving an accurate, visual record of an inscription (see figure 34.4 above). The Centre for the Study of Ancient Documents in Oxford provides an excellent gateway to other sites, as well as providing digitised images of squeezes in its own collection: www.csad.ox.ac.uk. Electronic databases also allow searching for any word or part of a word, not possible hitherto in printed indices: the Epigraphische Datenbank Heidelberg (EDH), www.uni-heidelberg.de/institute/sonst/adw/edh/, provides an important online facility for Latin inscriptions. Packard Humanities Institute CD-ROM no. 7, 'Greek documentary texts', is a fully searchable database of most published Greek inscriptions (and papyri) and is distributed on a CD-ROM (The Packard Humanities Institute, 300 Second Street, Los Altos, California, 94022, USA for further information). Such resources provide extensive opportunity for any epigraphical discovery to be studied in ways that Mr Pickwick would never have believed.

Further reading

F. Bérard, D. Feissel, P. Petitmengin, D. Rousset and M. Sève, *Guide de l'épigraphiste: bibliographie choisie des épigraphies antiques et médiévales* (3rd edn, with supplement), Paris: Éditions rue d'Ulm/Presses de l'École normale supérieure, 2000.

J. Bodel (ed.), *Epigraphic Evidence: Ancient History from Inscriptions* (Approaching the Ancient World), London and New York: Routledge, 2001.

A. K. Bowman, *Life and Letters on the Roman Frontier: Vindolanda and its People* (rev. edn), London: British Museum Press, 2003.

C. W. Fornara, *Translated Documents of Greece and Rome 1: Archaic Times to the end of the Peloponnesian War*, Cambridge: Cambridge University Press, 1983.

A. E. Gordon, *Illustrated Introduction to Latin Epigraphy*, Berkeley: University of California Press, 1983.

L. Keppie, *Understanding Roman Inscriptions*, London and New York: Routledge, 2001.

B. H. McClean, *An Introduction to Greek Epigraphy of the Hellenistic and Roman Periods from Alexander the Great down to the Reign of Constantine (323 AD–BC 337)*, Ann Arbor: University of Michigan Press, 2002.

R. MacMullen, 'The epigraphic habit in the Roman Empire', *American Journal of Philology* 103 (1982), 233–46 (online at JSTOR, www.jstor.org).

R. Meiggs and D. Lewis, *A Selection of Greek Historical Inscriptions to the End of the Fifth Century BC* (rev. edn), Oxford: Clarendon Press, 1988.

P. J. Rhodes and R. Osborne, *Greek Historical Inscriptions 403–323 BC*, Oxford: Oxford University Press, 2003.

R. K. Sherk, *Translated Documents of Greece and Rome 6: The Roman Empire: Augustus to Hadrian*, Cambridge: Cambridge University Press, 1988.

S. V. Tracy, *Attic Letter-Cutters of 229 to 86 BC*, Berkeley: University of California Press, 1990.

S. V. Tracy, *Athenian Democracy in Transition: Attic Letter-Cutters of 340 to 290 BC*, Berkeley: University of California Press, 1995.

A. G. Woodhead, *The Study of Greek Inscriptions* (2nd edn), Cambridge: Cambridge University Press, 1981; repr. with new preface, Bristol: Bristol Classical Press, 1992.

Part Three: Texts and Genres

This part introduces the range of literary texts from the Graeco-Roman world, from epic, tragedy and comedy through to the wealth of scientific, medical and 'technical' writings that were produced in classical antiquity. Each chapter surveys not only the surviving texts themselves, but also the contexts of their production, the inter-relationship of different literary genres and, where appropriate, the main trends in modern scholarship. The Further Reading section in each chapter points the way to editions of the surviving Greek and Latin texts as well as to a representative sample of modern scholarship.

35. Greek Epic

Johannes Haubold

Epic may be defined, in the most general terms, as narrative poetry about the deeds of gods and heroes. As an example of the genre, Greek epic is usually approached either as representing the beginning of a distinctly Western literary tradition which comprises, among others, Virgil, Dante, Tasso, Spencer, Milton; or as one of many traditions of poetry known from around the world (e.g. South Slavic epic, African epic, Kirgiz epic). Ancient Greek terms for 'epic' (*epos*, *epea*, *epopoiia*) refer primarily to poetry composed in the hexameter rhythm but also, more narrowly, to heroic poetry, with the *Iliad* and *Odyssey* as the ultimate models.

Epic was one of the most popular genres of ancient Greek literature from the archaic period to late antiquity. During its long history, it changed from a performance genre to one that was transmitted in writing and experienced through reading. In the course of this development, the oldest oral-traditional epics, of which the works of Homer and Hesiod are the most outstanding examples, were never superseded but rather subjected to new editions, adaptations and interpretations. The history of Greek epic as a genre, which is outlined below, concerns not only the variety of known epic texts but also the changing circumstances of transmission (e.g. live performance versus written text), the shifting expectations of ancient audiences (performance culture versus reading culture), and the aesthetic principles underpinning their views of epic as a genre.

Origins

Many of the central themes of Greek epic recur in other literatures of the eastern Mediterranean and ancient Near East. Akkadian poetry of the first millennium BC offers some of the most impressive parallels (e.g. *Enuma Elish*, *Gilgamesh*; see West, *East Face of Helicon*). Elements of traditional Indo-European song played a role in shaping the specifically Greek contribution to Mediterranean narrative culture. The contents of Greek epic are more directly shaped by memories of the Mycenaean era and the collapse of its palace culture.

Archaic epic

Archaic epic has its roots in a long tradition of oral poetry, stretching as far back as the Mycenaean age. The extant songs are composed in a poetic language, a mixture of Ionic and Aeolic, which developed precisely for the purpose of singing the deeds of gods and men. The poems of the archaic period display a similar range of motifs and narrative techniques, and share an overall understanding of the history of the world from its origins, when Earth first mated with Heaven, to life as it is in the present day, the Age of Iron. Written scores of the major poems were current by the late sixth century BC. It is more difficult to say when and why such scores were first produced. Early examples of alphabetic writing (eighth century BC) provide a terminus post quem, but attempts to establish a chronology of textual fixation face some serious difficulties (Janko, *Homer, Hesiod and Hymns*). Regardless of the question of when individual poems were first committed to writing, live performance remained the dominant mode of reception throughout the archaic period.

Epic as described by the earliest surviving texts is 'song', *aoidē*, performed by a 'singer', *aoidos*, to the accompaniment of the *phorminx*, a type of lyre. The singer passes on the *kleos*, 'fame', of gods and heroes to his audience (cf. *Od.* 1.338), instilling pleasure (*terpsis*) and enchanting the listeners (*thelgein*). Ideally, the song is 'truthful' (*etymos*) and proceeds 'as is proper', 'in the correct order' (*kata kosmon*). At the beginning of most songs, the singer asks the Muse(s) to assist him in his task. What follows tends to be a substantial narrative account of events set in the distant past. Much of archaic epic is characterised by a dramatic style of presentation (high proportion of direct speech) and sophisticated narrative techniques (e.g. ring composition, foreshadowing, flashback). Explicit moralising on the part of the narrator is rare in some texts (especially Homeric epic) but more prominent in others (especially Hesiod, *Works and Days*).

The performance contexts for epic song, as described in archaic epic itself, range from symposiastic settings (*Od.* 1.150–5) to public gatherings (*Od.* 8.256ff.), funeral games (*Works and Days* 654–7) and major religious festivals (*Hymn to Apollo* 146ff.). It is tempting to see these as representing different stages in the history of epic performance, but alternative venues are likely to have co-existed at the same time. Archaic epic often incorporates elements drawn from other types of song (e.g. formal laments for the dead), and makes use of a wide variety of registers (e.g. gnomic wisdom, the fable, aetiological narratives). Its character as a genre is determined primarily by its traditional themes, which include the accession to power of Zeus, the exploits of the Olympian gods, the labours of Heracles, the expedition of the Argo, the Calydonian boar hunt, and the Theban and Trojan Wars.

The totality of epic themes constitutes a history of the world, from the births of the gods and the emergence of an ordered universe to the world of humans 'as they are now' (*Il.* 5.304, etc.). Within that history, epic themes may be grouped into different subgenres. Thus, we can distinguish poems about the birth of the gods in the most distant past from poems about the heroic era, and poems about the present and future. Extant examples include the *Theogony* and *Homeric Hymns* (distant past), the *Iliad*, the *Odyssey* and the fragmentary *Catalogue of Women* (heroic age), and the *Works and Days* (present and future). Heroic epic dominates, both in terms of quantity, and in terms of importance and influence. The *Iliad* and *Odyssey* are the longest known examples (c. 15,000 and 12,000 lines respectively), suggesting that epic performances may have lasted more than one day. The average text appears to have been substantially shorter.

The themes of archaic epic are reflected in its traditional language (formulae) and narrative techniques (e.g. type scenes, catalogues). These should not be seen as mechanical means by which the bard composed in the course of a performance (Foley, *Homer's Traditional Art*). Recurrent episodes, such as arming scenes and communal meals, constitute the social and poetic grammar of the genre. Recurrent language reflects the resonant order of the epic universe as a whole and helps to evoke larger narrative structures. For example, Achilles' epithet 'swift-footed' encapsulates his epic persona and evokes, by implication, crucial episodes in his career (e.g. his footrace against Hector in *Il.* 22, his death by being shot in the heel by Apollo). Traditional elements are not static and may stand in a relationship of ironic dissonance with the immediate narrative context (e.g. swift-footed Achilles sitting in his tent for most of the *Iliad*).

From early on, Greek epic is associated with a developed discourse of authorship. Extant texts are attributed to either Homer (*Iliad*, *Odyssey*, *Homeric Hymns*) or Hesiod (*Theogony*, *Works and Days*), but many more poets are mentioned as authors of epic, even if there is little consensus about their oeuvre in the ancient sources (e.g. Orpheus, Musaeus, Stasinus, Arctinus, Lesches, Eumelus). Rather than indicating authorship in the modern sense, these attributions divide epic into subcategories, each with its own narrative scope and register. Thus, major Hesiodic texts outline the history of the universe in the form of extended lists, while the poems of the Homeric tradition dramatise moments of crisis such as the birth of the Olympian gods, or the death of the heroes. The relationship between different traditions of epic was expressed in biographical narratives (e.g. *The Contest between Homer and Hesiod*).

The bulk of lost poems appears to have been comparable in length and scope to the surviving texts (with the exception of the *Iliad* and *Odyssey*, which are longer and more ambitious), though there are indications that the range of tone was wider than the extant sample suggests. Particularly important among the lost works are the poems of the epic cycle, which were edited later than the *Iliad* and the *Odyssey* and were intended to provide a wider context for those two poems: they recounted what happened before and after the events described in the two major Homeric poems. The cycle illustrates a defining principle of archaic Greek epic: any individual song can be seen as a slice from a larger whole. The same tendency towards cyclic accumulation is evident in the fact that archaic epic tends to begin without an elaborate introduction ('in medias res', as Horace puts is at *Ars p.* 148f.), and that the endings of major Hesiodic and Homeric poems (e.g. *Theogony*, *Odyssey*) to this day remain relatively fluid.

Archaic Greek epic was regarded as authoritative on a wide range of issues, and deeply influenced the development of other literary genres such as lyric, drama, philosophy and historiography. The development of epic was in turn influenced by competing performance traditions (e.g. Stesichorus; see chapter 41). Experts on epic developed sophisticated reading strategies (allegory) partly in response to the criticisms voiced by early philosophers (e.g. Xenophanes, Heraclitus). The late archaic period saw an increased trend towards the canonisation and textual fixation of well-known poems. One of the most important developments in this context was the rise of professional performers called rhapsodes, who claimed to be reproducing the works of master poets such as Hesiod and Homer. Political leaders (for example, Hipparchus of Athens) reinforced existing trends towards standardisation by imposing rules regulating public performance (e.g. the so-called 'Panathenaic rule' which prescribed that 'Homer only' should be performed at the Great Panathenaea, and 'in the correct order').

Classical epic

The trend towards canonisation and textual fixation continued during the classical period. There was now mounting pressure to reduce the archaic canon of epic, with thematic consistency serving as a criterion for authenticity (cf. Hdt. 2.117, who claims that the *Cypria* is not by Homer because it gives a different version of Paris' journey to Troy from that found in the *Iliad*). Rhapsodes continued to perform the archaic repertoire (e.g. Plato, *Ion*), but innovation was largely left to other performance traditions (e.g. lyric, tragedy). As a result, the formulaic language of epic gradually came to be experienced as a literary style among others.

Among the epic poets of the classical era, Choerilus stands out for introducing historical epic. Hegemon is credited with the invention of epic parody as a separate genre. An example of it survives in the *Battle of the Frogs and Mice*, of uncertain date. Panyassis composed an influential *Heracleia*. More important was the work of Antimachus, which anticipated, in tone and scope, some of the developments of the Hellenistic era. Antimachus was also a Homeric scholar of some standing, and can therefore be seen as an early exponent of the Hellenistic figure of the *poeta doctus* (or learned poet). The works of Choerilus, Hegemon, Panyassis and Antimachus survive in fragments.

As a cultural force, epic retained its dominant position in the classical period. Homer in particular was invoked, emulated and criticised in a wide variety of contexts. Whole genres reworked epic language and themes (e.g. tragedy, historiography). The sophistic movement explored many subjects through a close engagement with epic (e.g. theories of grammar, cultural history). As a result of the Persian Wars, heroic epic became a vehicle for patriotic sentiment (i.e. the Trojans came to be seen as barbarians). The classical period also witnessed the first attempts to define epic as a literary genre in the modern sense. Alongside the traditional definition as 'song about the deeds of gods and men', a more formal understanding of epic as poetry in the hexameter rhythm became current. Plato saw epic poetry as a form of mimetic art (*Resp.* 598d7ff.). The idea was taken up and refined by Aristotle, who argued that a dramatic plot (*mythos dramatikos*), coherence, a grand scale and an elevated tone (*megaloprepeia*, *onkos*) were central features of epic (*Poet.* 23–4). Aristotle's definition further emphasised existing trends towards viewing Homeric epic (understood primarily as the *Iliad* and *Odyssey*) as a normative model for all epic poetry.

Hellenistic epic

The Hellenistic era marked another step towards the crystallisation and textual fixation of the archaic canon. Zenodotus, Aristophanes and Aristarchus, among others, edited and commented upon the poems of Homer and Hesiod, rejecting as spurious texts that did not conform to strict standards of stylistic and thematic consistency. The transformation of Greek epic into a canon of written texts was underpinned by an aesthetic sensibility which was increasingly removed from the oral-traditional poetics of earlier times. In striking departure from the cumulative approach of archaic epic, Aristarchus sought to explain Homer on the basis of Homer alone. Likewise, the practice of marking repeated passages for deletion (*athetēsis*) shows unease with the resonant patterns of an earlier tradition (see chapter 33). In this climate, Greek epic emerges as a learned, allusive and slimmer genre. Homer remains the dominant model, but imitation is self-conscious and sophisticated: variations on epic themes and epic language are framed by constant, and often explicit, reflections on poetic practice, and are part of a bold mixture of generic models (e.g. epic, lyric, tragedy).

Hellenistic epic influenced Latin poets such as Catullus, Virgil and Ovid, and decisively shaped later perceptions of epic as a genre. Most influential was the poet-scholar Callimachus, who wrote epics in polemical dialogue with other authors. The emphasis is on quality rather than quantity, with the small-scale epic, or epyllion, emerging as the preferred form. Callimachean epic adopts uncanonical models (the *Hymns*), explores traditional themes from unusual angles (*Hecale*), and experiments with aetiological narratives. Generic experimentation of a different kind leads Theocritus to write short epic poems in the Doric dialect (*Idylls*), which inaugurate the tradition of bucolic poetry. The only large-scale heroic epic surviving from Hellenistic times is Apollonius' *Argonautica*, an important model for Virgil's *Aeneid*. A tendency towards the display of arcane learning favours the rise of didactic epics on often obscure topics. Extant examples include Nicander's *Theriaca*, which discusses the bites of poisonous animals, and his *Alexipharmaca*, on poisons and their antidotes. Epic is also used in a panegyric function (e.g. Theocritus, *Idylls* 16 and 17), and placed in the service of philosophical speculation (Cleanthes). Aratus writes the first astronomical epic, opening a long line of similar poems in the Latin tradition. Only fragments survive of the countless historical epics that were composed in Hellenistic times (e.g. Rhianus).

Roman era and late antiquity

The production of Greek epic continued unabated into the Roman era. Some encomiastic epics, now lost, exploited the grandeur of the Homeric style. The genres of historical and didactic epic remained popular. The latter is represented for us by the *Description of the Inhabited World* by Dionysius Periegetes; by Oppian's *Halieutica*, a poem on fishing; and by the *Cynegetica*, on hunting with dogs, which was attributed to Oppian but is not by the same author as the *Halieutica*. Among the mythological epics of the time, the *Posthomerica* by Quintus of Smyrna attempts to revive the idea of an epic cycle by filling the gap between the *Iliad* and *Odyssey*. Lesser poems such as Triphiodorus' *Capture of Troy* and Colluthus' *Abduction of Helen* show that the traditional themes of heroic epic continued to be reformulated well into late antiquity.

The most significant epic of the time is Nonnus' monumental treatment of Dionysus' conquest of India, his *Dionysiaca*. Nonnus aims to rival Homer (48 books = the sum of the books of the *Iliad* and *Odyssey*) by using a strikingly un-Homeric theme and approach (Dionysiac poetics). In the tradition of the Hellenistic poets, Nonnus draws on a wide range of generic models, including the novel. Stylistically, he is known for his rhetorical exuberance and his strict handling of the hexameter verse. Nonnus influenced successive poets such as Musaeus, who composed an account of the love between Hero and Leander. Late antiquity also saw the rise of epic poetry on Christian themes. Nonnus himself wrote a hexameter version of the

Gospel according to John. Among the poems that cast Christian doctrine in epic language, we should note the *Homerocentones* of the empress Eudocia, which make a remarkable use of traditional phraseology in the service of a novel theme.

Further reading

A. W. Bulloch, 'Hellenistic poetry', in P. E. Easterling and B. M. W. Knox (eds), *The Cambridge History of Classical Literature*, vol. 1, part 4, Cambridge: Cambridge University Press, 1985, pp. 541–621 – introductory essay on Hellenistic poetry.

M. Fantuzzi and R. Hunter, *Tradition and Innovation in Hellenistic Poetry*, Cambridge: Cambridge University Press, 2005 – up-to-date discussion of Hellenistic epic.

J. M. Foley, *Homer's Traditional Art*, University Park PA: Pennsylvania State University Press, 1999 – on the way in which early Greek epic conveys its meaning.

J. M. Foley (ed.), *A Companion to Ancient Epic*, Oxford: Blackwell, 2005 – useful reference work; part III is on Greek epic.

A. Ford, *Homer: The Poetry of the Past*, Ithaca NY: Cornell University Press, 1992 – on the generic character of archaic epic.

A. Ford, 'Epic as genre', in I. Morris and B. Powell (eds), *A New Companion to Homer*, Leiden: Brill, 1997, pp. 396–414 – a brief introduction to epic as a genre.

N. Hopkinson, *Greek Poetry of the Imperial Period: An Anthology*, Cambridge: Cambridge University Press, 1994 – selection with introductions and notes of Greek epic from the Roman period (e.g. Quintus of Smyrna, Nonnus).

R. Janko, *Homer, Hesiod and the Hymns*, Cambridge: Cambridge University Press, 1982 – an attempt to establish the relative chronology of extant archaic epics.

A. B. Lord, *The Singer of Tales*, Cambridge MA: Harvard University Press, 1960 – on early Greek epic as a performance medium.

M. Parry, *The Making of Homeric Verse: The Collected Papers of Milman Parry*, ed. A. Parry, Oxford: Oxford University Press, 1971 – fundamental on Greek epic as a traditional genre.

W. G. Thalmann, *Conventions of Form and Thought in Early Greek Epic Poetry*, Baltimore: Johns Hopkins University Press, 1984 – readable introduction to the themes and narrative techniques of early Greek epic.

M. L. West, *The East Face of Helicon: West Asiatic Elements in Greek Poetry and Myth*, Oxford: Oxford University Press, 1997 – on Near Eastern elements in Greek epic.

36. *Roman Epic*

Bruce Gibson

Roman epic poetry presents us with a different dynamic to the history of Greek epic, even though it shares the same interest in subject matter involving heroes and gods. Whereas Greek epic poetry begins with Homer, a poet who was regarded as first not only in terms of chronology but also in terms of literary superiority and position in the literary canon, Roman epic had its paramount poet in the middle of its literary history, Publius Vergilius Maro (70–19 BC), or 'Virgil' as he is usually referred to in English. His *Aeneid*, written in twelve books and still awaiting the final touches from its author at the time of his death, dealt with the departure of the Trojan hero Aeneas from his home at the end of the Trojan War, and his wanderings, which include a visit to Carthage, where Aeneas' decision to leave the Carthaginian queen Dido is presented as the origins of Rome's enmity with Carthage. The second half of the *Aeneid* deals with events subsequent to Aeneas' arrival in Italy, where he fought a war against the Italians which ended in his victory. This victory ends the poem but also anticipates the establishment of the Latin people, which would eventually lead to the foundation of Rome by Romulus and the succession of Roman history down to the time of the first emperor, Augustus, under whom Virgil was writing.

But while Virgil secured primacy for himself in the history of Latin literature, he was not the first or the last epic poet to have written in Latin. However, it was a consequence of Virgil's status that his successors were condemned to stand in his shadow, while his predecessors were not even able to survive in full. Thus epic texts prior to Virgil are known to us through fragments, usually quoted by other ancient authors, who were sometimes grammarians concentrating on archaic features of language; such snippets without proper context can often be hard for us to evaluate or place. This has meant that it is often assumed that Virgil's poem somehow defines Roman epic poetry, whereas in fact it is arguable that many of the features which we associate with Virgil are attested not only after the *Aeneid* but before it as well. But it is perhaps useful first of all to consider the peculiarly Roman dimension of epic poetry written in Latin.

Roman epic?

This chapter is entitled 'Roman Epic'. Yet epic poetry in Latin stands alongside epic poetry written in Greek, and was moreover in many instances composed by poets who were not from the city of Rome, including Virgil himself, who was from Mantua in what is now Lombardy. But it was not just Virgil. Southern Italy furnished epic poets such as Livius Andronicus and Ennius before Virgil, and Statius after Virgil, so that on the surface the designation of epic poetry in Latin as 'Roman' might seem unnecessary. However, the succeeding discussion will aim to show how it might after all be appropriate to think of Latin epic poetry as 'Roman'.

As we have seen, the classic representative of 'Roman epic' is Virgil's *Aeneid*, which makes explicit a temporal relationship between the heroic, pre-Roman past of Homeric times and the later foundation of the historical city of Rome itself (*Aen*. 1.1–7). Within his epic, Virgil also wrote of the battle of Actium (31 BC), which established Augustus in power when he defeated his Roman rival Marcus Antonius and the Egyptian queen Cleopatra, so that the chronological span of the poem thus runs from the heroic age down to the poet's own time. Yet it should not be thought that Virgil was original in making Rome itself part of the subject of his poem. Naevius' *Bellum Poenicum* ('*Punic War*'), written in the second half of the third century BC, had dealt with the First Punic War between Rome and Carthage (264–241 BC), yet the poem also contained the story of Aeneas' departure from Troy, and an appeal from the goddess Venus, Aeneas' mother, to Jupiter to help the Trojans, material which would recur in Virgil's own poem. And after Naevius, the *Annales* of Ennius, who died around 169 BC, would similarly have a grand chronological overview stretching from the fall of Troy and Aeneas' arrival in Italy through the earlier history of Rome down to Ennius' own era, the age of the Second Punic War against Carthage and the wars fought in the Greek East in the first part of the second century BC.

The Virgilian interest in Rome itself and Roman power as subject matter is thus something which can be attested from the earliest times. And Rome also had a role to play in the epics that followed Virgil, even when on occasion the poets wrote of subject matter which on the surface appeared to have no connecton with Rome. Even a work like Ovid's *Metamorphoses*, also written under Augustus, which appears to be no more than a collection of loosely held-together stories from Greek mythology relating to changes of shape, metamorphosis, is framed by references to Augustus near the beginning and, near the end of the poem, to the arrival in Rome of the Greek cult of Aesculapius in the early third century BC and the deification of Julius Caesar following his death in 44 BC (Ov. *Met.* 1.204–5, 15.622–860). Thus Ovid's poem also has a Roman aspect, and it maintains the Virgilian (or Naevian?) device of moving from the earliest times down to contemporary Rome. After Augustus' death, later poets also find themselves writing on Rome, explicitly in the case of Lucan. His epic on the civil war between Julius Caesar and Pompey at the end of the Roman Republic is also a meditation on the Principate that had replaced the Republic, even if there is only one passage directly about Nero (reigned AD 54–68), the emperor under whom Lucan himself was writing, a passage of apparent praise whose potential for subversion (or not) has been argued over by scholars in recent years (Luc. 1.33–66). Other epic poets writing after Lucan would also use the openings of their epics to address the emperor: thus both Valerius Flaccus and Statius, writing under the Flavian dynasty (AD 69–96), address the emperor at the start of poems which take their subject matter from Greek mythology, such as the stories of the Argonauts or the war of the Seven against Thebes. And Silius Italicus, a contemporary of Valerius Flaccus and Statius, whose decision to write about the Second Punic War (218–201 BC) recalls Naevius and Ennius, still managed to combine a subject matter which was far removed from his own time with references to the contemporary Roman world.

Origins

Thus the role of Rome itself as subject matter for Latin epic poets is something which rapidly becomes established, even if, ironically, the very first epic poet to write in Latin, Livius Andronicus, wrote a rendering of Homer's *Odyssey*. Livius can, however, serve as a useful transition to another aspect of Roman epic, its 'Greekness'.

Livius Andronicus, who was said to have been captured from the Greek city of Tarentum in southern Italy and, like Ennius, was referred to by the later critic Suetonius as *semigraecus*, 'half-Greek' (Suet. *Gram.* 1.2), is regarded as the first poet to have written epic poetry in Latin, and was also credited with the foundation of Latin drama by Livy (7.2) and by Cicero (see e.g. *Brutus* 72–3, *Cato maior* 50), who attributed to him the first performance of drama in Rome in 240 BC (see chapter 38). This association of dramatic and epic poetry is indeed worthy of note: other early practitioners of epic poetry such as Naevius and Ennius also composed dramas, so that whereas in Greek literature epic poetry comes first, with drama coming later, in Roman literature the two forms of writing developed alongside one another. But Livius' Latin version of Homer's *Odyssey* seems, from the few fragments which remain, to have displayed both a deep understanding of the original and a willingness to introduce slight variations. This rendering of a Greek text into Latin should not occasion surprise; Greek dramas were rendered into Latin by other poets of this period, such as Ennius and Plautus. However, whereas Greek epic poetry was written in the epic hexameter (which would be used later in Rome as well), it is striking that the earliest epic poets in Latin, Livius Andronicus and then Naevius, used the Saturnian metre, whose origins have been much debated, with some scholars arguing that the metre was native to Italy, while others have affirmed its Greek origins. Whatever the origins of the Saturnian, it is an apparent paradox that this most Greek of all epic poems in Latin did not adopt the metre that had been used by Homer (see chapter 65).

While Naevius also used the Saturnian metre in his poem on the First Punic War, it was Ennius who adopted the Greek hexameter and took it over into Latin, in spite of the fact that the short syllables characteristic of this metre would be more demanding in Latin, which tended to have a higher density of long syllables than Greek. Ennius' adoption of the metre of Homer was accompanied by two even bolder moves. First of all, he used the Greek term 'Musae' in invoking the Muses at the start of his poem instead of the Latin word 'Camenae', which had been used by Livius Andronicus and probably by Naevius as well. Second, he narrated at the start of his first book of *Annales* a dream in which the spirit of the dead Homer had reported to him that his soul had gone through a Pythagorean process of reincarnation before passing over into Ennius himself (Ennius, *Annales* 211 Skutsch = 413 Warmington). Moreover, at the start of the seventh book of the *Annales*, Ennius contrasted his own work with that of his predecessors, notably Naevius, who had used the Saturnian metre, in a passage where Ennius explained that he was not going to write of the First Punic War (*Annales* 206–12 Skutsch = 229–35 Warmington).

In all of this, we should note Ennius' deliberate decision to engage directly with Homer, who becomes the forebear par excellence for Roman epic poetry in spite of the fact that Ennius had serious predecessors in Latin in the shape of Livius Andronicus and Naevius. We thus see the germ of the subsequent interest that Roman epic poets have in both acknowledging their predecessors (including Homer) and sometimes writing them out of literary history. And from Ennius onwards, the hexameter, Homer's metre, was employed by Roman epic poets; there could be no better testimony to the rapid triumph of the hexameter than the fact that we possess hexameter fragments which are said by ancient sources to come from the *Odyssey* of the earlier Livius Andronicus, which was, however, composed, as we have seen, in the Saturnian metre: this would seem to imply that Livius' work was recast in hexameters by some later poet.

The vagaries of the literary tradition have left us knowing little of the epic poetry that was written between the time of Ennius and that of Virgil; this is perhaps a testimony to the continuing primacy of Livius Andronicus (whom the Augustan poet Horace claims to have studied in his youth; Hor. *Epistles* 2.1.69–71), Naevius and Ennius as well as that of Virgil, but the fragmentary figures who precede Virgil are nevertheless important for their continuing interest not only in Roman subject matter, but also in praising leading individuals. Thus Virgil's (limited) praise of Augustus in the course of the *Aeneid*, and the practice already mentioned whereby later poets would praise the emperor at the start of a work, have precedents even in the epic productions of republican literature; it is a further irony that in the fifth century AD, the poet Claudian's panegyric poems on imperial consulates oddly (if unconsciously) look back to what had happened during republican times. This republican tradition of praise is manifested in Ennius' account of the military exploits in Greece of M. Fulvius Nobilior in his *Annales*, and reflects the increasing pervasiveness in Rome of a phenomenon already well established in Greek literature: the use of hexameter poetry to praise kings or other leading figures. Moreover, the fact that from the late third century BC onwards Rome began to intervene militarily in an increasingly wider area of the Mediterranean world meant that the opportunities for composing such poetry could only increase. Thus in the second century BC a poem was composed on a war in Istria in the northern Adriatic by Hostius, while in the first century BC there are examples such as the orator Cicero's poem on the achievements of his own year as consul in 63 BC, and the poems on Caesar's Gallic campaigns in the 50s BC by Furius Bibaculus and Varro of Atax.

Varro of Atax is also of interest, since he was the author of an Argonaut poem which was a Latin version of the *Argonautica* of the Hellenistic Greek poet Apollonius of Rhodes (who wrote in the third century BC; see chapter 35). Varro's range somewhat gives the lie to the notion one gets from poets such as Catullus that there were two types of poets operating in the first century BC (see e.g. Catullus 36, 95): those who wrote hoary and rough epics in the old style, and those who adopted the learning and elegance which is particularly (but not solely) associated by Roman poets with the Hellenistic poet Callimachus. Virgil's *Aeneid* is often seen as an epic poem in the learned manner (and recent work has shown how Virgil is interested not simply in Homer but in other Greek poets as well, such as Apollonius of Rhodes), but this should not be seen as something peculiar to Virgil. As well as Varro of Atax, one should reflect that the tradition of Greek learning goes as far back as Roman epic itself: Livius Andronicus' rendering of Homer's *Odyssey* and Ennius' use of the Pythagorean philosophy of reincarnation, which have already been mentioned, are clear examples of this.

As epic's own history lengthens, however, the potential for learning to include knowledge not only of Greek poets like Homer and Apollonius but also of earlier Latin literature becomes greater. It is a commonplace to associate this kind of thing with Virgil, who in the course of the *Aeneid* shows acquaintance with earlier poets such as Ennius – though our evidence is limited, since the paucity of the fragments of the earlier authors, itself a consequence of Virgil's success, prevents our fullest appreciation of his erudition in this respect. The achievement of later Roman epic poets, however, is in some ways even more impressive, since these poets had to contend with Virgil, whose work became at once a kind of instant classic, as is reflected in the poet Propertius' announcement (2.34.66) that 'something greater than the *Iliad* is being born', written before Virgil's death and hence while the poem was still incomplete.

After Virgil

From Virgil's time onwards, epic poets had to respond to the numinous presence of Virgil as well as Homer. Whether their works would survive must have been a concern to them, given the manner in which Virgil rapidly came to dominate the school curriculum in Latin. There were varying strategies for such poets. Ovid (*Ex Ponto* 4.16.17–18) refers to a Largus who appears to have written of the Trojan Antenor and his arrival in Cisalpine Gaul in northern Italy after the end of the Trojan War, a story which has obvious parallels with that of Virgil's Aeneas. Even more direct engagement with Virgil might be attempted by a poet as ambitious as Ovid himself, who chose to incorporate a version of the *Aeneid* in his *Metamorphoses* (Ov. *Met.* 13.623–14.582).

Other poets, however, chose a different approach to the problem of Virgil. In some cases these responses engaged with Roman history, as Virgil had done, even if the results were quite different. Thus Lucan's *Civil War* dealt with the conflict between Caesar and Pompey at the end of the Roman Republic, just before the rise to ascendancy of Augustus, under whom Virgil had written. A period which was of marginal importance in Virgil's poem (and perhaps a source of some embarrassment too – Virgil refers only briefly to the civil war of Caesar and Pompey at *Aeneid* 6.826–35) was thus made the centre of attention, highlighting the awkwardness of the fact that Augustus too had won the imperial power in another civil war, even if it was the case that Virgil had presented the war of Actium as a foreign war, with the emphasis on Cleopatra and Egypt, rather than on Augustus' Roman opponent Marcus Antonius. And Lucan's approach to the emperor Nero at the beginning of his first book, whether or not it is straightforward praise of Nero, also destabilises the Virgilian version of Roman history, which culminated in Augustus, since history was shown to continue, with Nero as the ultimate focus in the new teleology, in the same way as later poets such as Statius and Valerius Flaccus would address their emperors as well. But in order to establish this revisionist critique of Virgilian history, Lucan was thus required to engage extensively, both on the level of individual words and on the level of whole passages and episodes, with Virgil, and so Lucan's Virgilian erudition, far from being merely a shared poetic language, was thus a crucial part of the poem's fabric and meaning.

The same might well be said for the other epic poems which have survived from the first century AD. Statius' *Thebaid* and his incomplete *Achilleid* superficially appear to have nothing to do with Rome. Yet, as we have already noted, both these poems include addresses to the emperor Domitian (reigned AD 81–96), and moreover it is Statius who directly invokes the *Aeneid* in the epilogue to his *Thebaid*, telling his own poem to follow modestly behind Virgil's. Yet at the same time as he makes this deferential gesture, Statius also remarks that his work is not only being noticed by the emperor but is also being read by the youth of Italy, a statement which seems to establish a claim on Statius' part too for the canonical status enjoyed by Virgil (Stat. *Theb.* 12.810–819). Within the poem, Statius exhibits the same concern to display allusive and learned knowledge of Virgil, as well as a whole range of other poets, both Greek and Latin, including, for example, his own contemporary Valerius Flaccus. Valerius Flaccus' *Argonautica* likewise has a debt to Virgil, whilst at the same time engaging with Apollonius' Greek poem of the same title and also effacing the Argonaut poem that had been written by Varro of Atax in the first century BC (see above), which survives only in fragments. And Silius' *Punica*, on the Second Punic War, declares its interest in Virgil in the first book, with its account of the oath administered by his father to the Carthaginian leader Hannibal, enacting that he should wage everlasting war against the Romans (Sil. 1.81–139). This moment was also described by the Roman historian Livy, but Silius chooses to set it in a temple consecrated to Dido, the Carthaginian queen who in Virgil had loved Aeneas and who had killed herself on his death. Yet strikingly, Silius' poem does not merely respond to Virgil's poem (or to Livy's historiography): his Carthaginian subject matter recalls both Ennius (who is briefly a character in the poem; Sil. 12.387–419) and Naevius; and it has also been shown by recent scholars that he is responding to Lucan's *Civil War*, in terms of his portrayal of discord among the Roman commanders at various points in the course of the poem, or in the uncanny way in which his Hannibal, and perhaps also Scipio Africanus, the Roman commander who defeated Hannibal, unnervingly echo the energetic but destructive Caesar of Lucan.

It is something of an oddity that just as the history of Roman epic begins with fragmentary evidence, so too, after the comparatively lavish provision of complete texts which the first century AD offers us, the evidence for what followed is extremely patchy. In the generation after Statius, the satirist Juvenal complained in his first satire about the profusion of sterile mythological epic being written, but the later second century AD offers us the name of only one epic poet, one Clemens who apparently wrote an epic on Alexander the Great. In the early fifth century AD, we do possess complete poems by Claudian, from Alexandria in Egypt (where he also appears to have written poetry in Greek), who is usually seen as the last pagan poet of Rome (though his patrons in the imperial court were Christian). These poems deal with mythological subjects (such as his poem on *The Rape of Proserpine*) and with contemporary historical events, as well as providing panegyrics of leading figures of the time. Though the world of the fifth century AD was very different from the world of the third century BC, the fact that both Livius Andronicus and Claudian came from Greek cities is a salutary reminder of the manner in which Greek literature is always present in the (near) background in Roman epic poetry. And if Claudian is held to be the last Roman epic poet, writing in the century when the Roman Empire in the West came to an end, this end of Roman epic paradoxically gives life to the long and varied tradition of *Latin* epic poetry, which would continue to be written in different regions of the world throughout the Middle Ages and the Renaissance, often taking as its starting point Roman literature, if not Rome itself.

Further reading

Roman epic poetry is quite well served in terms of translations. There are very many translations of Virgil available: two contrasting highlights are the prose translation by David West (Penguin) and the verse translation by Cecil Day-Lewis (Oxford World's Classics). For the fragments of Livius Andronicus, Naevius and Ennius, see E. H. Warmington's *Remains of Early Latin*, in the Loeb Classical Library series (with parallel Latin and English texts). Convenient parallel texts of post-Virgilian epic poets are also available in the Loeb Classical Library, while for Lucan there is also Susanna Morton Braund's excellent translation for the Oxford World's Classics series. Other fragmentary poets are harder to come by in translation, but there is much useful information on their fragments and background in E. Courtney's *The Fragmentary Latin Poets* (Oxford: Oxford University Press, 1993, paperback 2003).

Critical writing on these poems has often taken the form of commentaries on individual books or more thematic studies of individual poets or poems, but in more recent times there have also been various diachronic studies of epic, which have usefully shown how it is possible to read these poets against (or with) each other. A major concern of much contemporary scholarship has been the study of intertextuality, the manner in which one text may draw on another text as part of its effect and meaning. Finally, epic poetry has recently come to be viewed as a discourse of power, establishing and enforcing hierarchies and ideologies. The items given below reflect the range of some of the approaches being followed today.

A. J. Boyle (ed.), *Roman Epic*, London and New York: Routledge, 1993.

F. Cairns, *Virgil's Augustan Epic*, Cambridge: Cambridge University Press, 1989.

A. Cameron, *Callimachus and his Critics*, Princeton: Princeton University Press, 1995 – contains useful material on the legacy of the Hellenistic Greek poet Callimachus in Rome.

M. Dewar, *Claudian*: Panegyricus de Sexto Consulatu Honorii Augusti, (ed. with intro., trans. and literary commentary), Oxford: Oxford University Press, 1996.

D. C. Feeney, *The Gods in Epic*, Oxford: Oxford University Press, 1991.

S. M. Goldberg, *Epic in Republican Rome*, New York: Oxford University Press, 1995.

P. Hardie, *The Epic Successors of Virgil*, Cambridge: Cambridge University Press, 1993.

S. Hinds, *Allusion and Intertext*, Cambridge: Cambridge University Press, 1998.

A. M. Keith, *Engendering Rome: Women in Latin Epic*, Cambridge: Cambridge University Press, 2000.

D. Nelis, *Vergil's Aeneid and the Argonautica of Apollonius Rhodius*, Leeds: Francis Cairns, 2001.

R. Rees, Romane Memento: *Vergil in the Fourth Century*, London: Duckworth, 2004.

P. Toohey, *Reading Epic: An Introduction to the Ancient Narratives*, London and New York: Routledge, 1992.

37. Greek Tragedy

Pantelis Michelakis

The term 'Greek tragedy' is shorthand for a type of theatrical performance most commonly associated with fifth-century Athens. Its golden age roughly overlaps with that of the city, covering the period from the start of the Persian Wars at the beginning of the fifth century to the very end of the Peloponnesian War in the late 400s. Tragedy is the product of a social, political and intellectual milieu associated with the birth of democracy and the political and military supremacy of Athens over the Greek world. Yet tragedy also had a tremendous impact outside Athens and, in the modern world, it has often been central to aesthetic, ethical, historical and philosophical debates about the nature and origins of Western theatre and culture.

Origins

Tragedy emerged in the late sixth century, relatively late when compared with epic and lyric poetry, but still before historiography, rhetoric and philosophy. Its origins are obscure. Aristotle, who wrote on the subject in the fourth century, related the birth of tragedy to the dithyramb, a type of religious song in honour of the god Dionysus. For Aristotle, tragedy developed from improvisation, when the leaders of the dithyramb started to converse with the singing chorus. This is a plausible explanation, given that in the fifth century tragedy was performed in festivals in honour of Dionysus. The word tragedy itself (in Greek *tragōidia*), which means 'goat-song', may have something to do with the beast-like followers of Dionysus, the satyrs, although it can also be related to songs accompanying the sacrifice of goats, such as those customarily preceding tragic performances in the fifth century. The earliest known tragedian, who is often credited with the invention of the genre and the introduction into it of masks, is the Athenian Thespis. However, tragedy may well have originated outside Athens, and it is not clear when tragedies were first introduced in the festivals of Dionysus. This may have taken place at the very end of the sixth century, in which case it was the newly founded democracy which led to the institutionalisation of tragedy. But tragedy may also have been introduced into the Athenian festivals a little earlier, as part of the ambitious cultural programme of the tyrant Pisistratus.

Form and content

The thirty-two plays that survive today are all attributed to the three tragedians who already at the end of the fifth century were thought to be the greatest of the genre: Aeschylus (c. 545/4–456/5), Sophocles (c. 497/6–406/5) and Euripides (480s–407/6). We have seven plays of Aeschylus: his *Persians* (first performed 472), *Seven Against Thebes* (467), *Suppliant Women* (c. 460s), the *Oresteia* trilogy (458), which consists of *Agamemnon*, *Libation Bearers* and *Eumenides*, and finally *Prometheus*, which may well be the product of another fifth-century tragedian. There are also seven surviving plays of Sophocles: *Ajax* (c. 440s), *Antigone* (c. 445–40), *Women of Trachis* (before 430?), *Oedipus the King* (c. 430–27), *Electra* (c. 410s), *Philoctetes* (409) and *Oedipus at Colonus* (401). The extant plays of Euripides are more numerous, eighteen in total, and more diverse: *Alcestis* (438), often thought of as 'pro-satyric', i.e. less tragic than the rest, *Medea* (431), *Hippolytus* (428), *Children of Heracles* (c. 430–428), *Andromache* (c. 425), *Hecuba* (c. 424), *Suppliant Women* (c. 423), *Trojan Women* (415), *Electra* (before 413?), *Ion* (c. 413), *Iphigenia among the Taurians* (c. 413), *Helen* (412), *Cyclops* (412?), which is the only fully surviving satyr play of fifth-century drama, *Phoenician Women* (c. 409), *Orestes* (408), *Bacchae* (405?), *Iphigenia at Aulis* (405?), and finally *Rhesus*, which, however, may be the product of a fourth-century dramatist. For all their chronological span, thematic diversity and variety of form, these plays are only a small percentage of the total output of the three dramatists and an even smaller part of the overall number of tragic plays produced during their lifetime. The names of other fifth- and fourth-century tragedians, such as Agathon, Ion, Chaeremon and Astydamas, hundreds of titles of lost plays, and five fat volumes of surviving fragments and relevant sources give us a tantalising glimpse into the larger picture of Greek tragedy. They also serve as a reminder of the risks involved in making generalisations about the three most famous tragedians and about tragedy as a genre from the small and, to some extent, random sample of plays that have come down to us.

Tragedies consist of spoken and sung parts. One might think of the average tragedy as having five scenes, each followed by a song sung by the chorus. Such songs combine features of the Attic dialect with elements of Doric, the dialect of lyric poetry, and have complex metrical structures which no doubt reflect their elaborate choreography (see chapter 65). Spoken parts are largely in the dialect spoken in Athens: although close to natural speech they were also in metre (mostly, but not exclusively, iambic trimeter) and, as a result, they must have sounded rather elevated and stylised. The language of tragedy is particularly rich and diverse. This is not due only to the alternation of speech and music, with the metrical and dialectical variations this involves. It is also due to the fact that tragedy systematically draws on the vocabulary of different aspects of contemporary life, including religion, ritual, politics, rhetoric and philosophy, as well as on the language of epic and lyric poetry, incorporating archaisms, colloquialisms and even barbarisms, often switching between registers in the same breath.

The spoken parts of tragedy consist of largely symmetrical but emotionally and/or rhetorically powerful exchanges between characters and/or the chorus leader, which usually take the form of either formal debates or one-line exchanges; long but vivid speeches which summarise the background of the plot or introduce off-stage, often violent, events; and occasional chanting or singing by individual characters, often in exchange with the chorus. The change of emotional register is often marked by the change of metre or the switching between speaking and chanting or singing. The sung parts consist of one or more pairs of stanzas, but they too are very diverse. One of their practical functions is to facilitate the transition from one scene to the next, especially when there is a lapse of time or a change of location or characters. Another important function the chorus performs is to reflect on the conflicts, misfortunes and suffering enacted on stage. Their comments, like those of the characters, are always conditioned by their role and identity and it would be wrong to treat them, as has often been done in the past, as ideal spectators or the mouthpiece of the playwright. The dramatic presence of the chorus in Aeschylus is stronger and their position more integral to the plot than in the plays of the other two dramatists. In some of Euripides' late plays, for instance, the presence of the chorus is not dramatically justified or fully explained, and the function of their songs is rather ornamental. Agathon, a younger contemporary of Euripides, is supposedly the first to have written songs unrelated to the plot of his plays, a practice which probably became more widespread in the fourth century. However, it would be wrong to conclude from that that the chorus lost its appeal. Euripides was also credited with some of the most lyrical songs of Greek tragedy, as well as with some of the most modern ones, drawing on the 'new music' of the last two decades of the fifth century.

Among extant tragedies there is only one which focuses on a historical subject, Aeschylus' *Persians*, which dramatises the aftermath of the naval battle of Salamis. Performed just a few years after the end of the Persian Wars, the play comes surprisingly close to the reality of its spectators. What allows the play to maintain a critical distance from its subject is its emphasis on loss and destruction as experienced from the point of view of the defeated Persians. Twenty years earlier, however, the topicality of the *Capture of Miletus* by Aeschylus' rival Phrynichus had caused deep distress by dramatising a historical event of which the Athenians had personal and bitter experience. Later tragedy does allude to and comment on historical events, but usually indirectly. The scene of Orestes' trial in Aeschylus' *Eumenides*, for instance, relates to the contemporary reality of its audience and especially the reform of the Areopagus council in 462/1. Yet more often than not historical facts are difficult to discern behind the extant plays, and speculation about possible connections between tragic plots and characters and specific events or historical personalities is notoriously untrustworthy as a criterion for dating or interpreting tragedy.

Tragedy draws its subject matter primarily from the world of mythology (see chapter 52). This was a ground very familiar to the spectators from religion, epic and lyric poetry, and art. Most plays focus on episodes from popular mythological cycles, including those of the Trojan War, and of the royal houses of Argos and Thebes. The attitude of the dramatists towards their subject matter is far from reverential. Like other literary and artistic genres, tragedy revises myths of gods and heroes, playing with the expectations of its audience. A good example of the liberties that tragedians could take with the mythological material in their hands is the reunion of Electra and Orestes before they kill their mother Clytemnestra for the murder of Agamemnon, which was treated by all three tragedians. *Prometheus* is unique among extant plays for featuring only divine characters, although *Bacchae* is another play where a god, and in fact the god of the festival (see below), Dionysus, dominates the plot. Usually tragic plays focus on heroes, characters with a literary and mythological background who were often also the object of contemporary cult. The heroes of tragedy are made to act and suffer in ways thought to be paradigmatic of life and human behaviour in general. Decision-making, with the responsibilities it entails, and emotional and physical suffering, with the different responses they generate, are the focus of attention in tragedy. The three tragedians vary in their views and attitudes towards the individual and the world as a whole. At the risk of crude generalisation, one could argue that in Aeschylus dramatic characters are accountable for actions which always have far-reaching consequences not only for themselves, but also for their families and society. In Sophocles dramatic characters act within, and often against, a social and religious framework which may seem opaque or problematic but which ultimately reaffirms itself as a legitimate source of authority and meaning. In Euripides, on the other hand, human action and suffering are set against a fragmented and unpredictable universe, powerful but often devoid of logic or morality.

Even if tragedy maintains some distance from the world outside the theatre, it does not raise large moral and ethical questions within some sort of temporal or socio-political vacuum. The patriotic, pessimist or escapist tone of plays in the last three decades of the fifth century cannot be seen independently of the Peloponnesian War which loomed menacingly over the city of Athens, draining its resources and weakening its self-confidence. The centrality of the issues of gender and ethnicity in many tragic plays cannot be explained without giving consideration to the oppositions between Greeks and Persians or men and women as articulated in other literary and artistic sources of the time. The preoccupation of many plays with horrors such as kin-killing, incest, mutilation and cannibalism cannot be understood without taking into account contemporary concerns and anxieties about the boundaries and limitations of the human body, the body of the family and the body of society at large. Tragedy gives voice not only to gods, heroes, kings, generals and prophets but also to individuals whom Athenian society kept in the margin, which included women, slaves, outcasts, foreigners, adolescents and old people. Through its social hierarchies and value-systems, the world of tragedy does not exactly mirror but rather reimagines and offers a reflection on the world of the audience. The tragedians were thought of as educators, with power and responsibility over the spectators. This is to no small degree related to the dialogical, competitive and confrontational nature of tragedy, which reflects that of Athenian democracy and society as a whole. Tragedy does not aim to subvert society but to reform it. On the one hand it challenges the audience, its values, assumptions and aspirations. On the other hand it promotes self-awareness and, like its institutional framework, to which we will now return, it fosters political and social solidarity.

Festivals

The most renowned of the dramatic festivals where tragedies were performed was the Great Dionysia, or City Dionysia, held in early March each year in honour of Dionysus. Other festivals included the Small or Rural Dionysia in December and the Lenaea in January–February. In the Great Dionysia three playwrights were selected to compete each year. The three playwrights would compete on successive days, each with four plays (a tetralogy), three tragedies followed by a satyr play. Performances would start at dawn. At the time of Aeschylus the plays were thematically related, a convention which was later abolished by Sophocles. The choice of winner was based on a complex voting system designed to ensure impartiality – though not without involving an element of chance: ten judges were chosen by lot from among the Athenian citizens in the audience, one from each of the Attic tribes, but only five votes would eventually count towards the final result. Aeschylus won thirteen victories during his career, having participated in the competition more than twenty times (he is said to have produced ninety plays in total); Sophocles won an impressive eighteen victories in more than thirty competitions (with some 132 plays); and Euripides won only five, one posthumously, having taken part in the competition more than twenty times (with some ninety-two plays). Playwrights had a very busy schedule in the months before the festival. Apart from composing four plays each (well over 5,000 lines), they were responsible for music and choreography, as well as for training their actors and chorus. In the early years there was only one actor but, by the early 450s, the number of actors had increased to three. Aeschylus is credited with the introduction of the second actor and Sophocles with the third. Playwrights stopped acting in their own plays in the 460s. During the second half of the fifth century, and especially after the death of Euripides and Sophocles, the leading actors became the real stars of the competition, collecting prizes, glory and wealth, and even being granted political roles outside the theatre, such as acting as ambassadors for their cities. The chorus initially consisted of twelve members, increased by Sophocles to fifteen. These were chosen from among Athenian citizens, and it is conceivable that they were young men or even, although this is far from certain, adolescents. Each production also had a musician, playing a double pipe, who was the only unmasked figure on stage. The poets themselves, the actors and the musician were paid by the state. The expenses of the choruses were met by rich Athenian citizens (*chorēgoi*) appointed by the state official responsible for the festival. This was an indirect type of taxation, onerous but prestigious, setting the ambitions and wealth of rich individuals at the service of the community at large.

During the fifth century the theatre of Dionysus could accommodate something between 15,000 and 20,000 people. That is approximately half of the number of Athenian citizens, more than twice as many as those usually required in the Assembly for decisions to be taken, and almost one tenth of the total population of Attica. The majority of the audience consisted of adult males of Athenian origin. Other groups would also be present, such as foreign representatives, resident foreigners, slaves and perhaps, although the evidence remains inconclusive, women and children. However, the target audience was the men who constituted the voting and fighting body of fifth-century Athens, a socially and culturally heterogeneous group which was responsible for the well-being of the city in peace and at war and which was invited to the festival to celebrate the power of civic solidarity. The festival included a number of pre-performance ceremonies which fostered cohesion among the spectators, including the display of the annual tax from ally-cities, processions of war orphans, and animal sacrifices. The festival provided an opportunity for the Athenian citizens to see and to be seen, to celebrate the power of democracy and the dominance of their city within the Greek world. It is within this political and institutional framework that tragedy sought to educate its audience.

Performance

The festival of the Great Dionysia was held in the open-air theatre of Dionysus on the east slope of the Acropolis rock, the physical remains of which, probably of Roman times, are still visible today. Initially, the theatre must have had wooden benches for the spectators in the auditorium (*theatron*, lit. 'place for seeing') and a temporary stage building (*skēnē*) in which the actors could dress, separated from each other by a flat, and most probably round, acting area (*orchēstra*). Temporary constructions were gradually replaced by more permanent ones, made of stone, in the course of the fifth and fourth centuries. The actors were also separated from the chorus with the help of a raised platform in front of the stage building. Passages on both sides of the auditorium enabled actors to enter the acting area from opposing directions usually representing different off-stage locations, for instance the city and the countryside. The stage building, which had initially one and later three doors, could be made to represent anything from a palace to a temple, a military hut or a farmhouse. Changes of location within plays suggest that the façade of the stage building was not elaborately decorated, although Sophocles is credited with the invention of scene-painting, and at later stages mechanical devices were used to facilitate quick changes of such paintings. The roof of the stage building was often used for the appearance of the gods, whose physical separation from the human characters below would visualise their superior status. Alternatively, the gods would appear in a basket suspended from a crane called *mēchanē* (meaning 'machine', hence 'deus ex machina', 'god from the machine'). Another piece of theatrical machinery in use in the fifth century was the wheeled platform (*ekkuklēma*), which would be rolled out of the stage building to display scenes which took place inside, often used for the presentation of corpses of characters dying off-stage. At the centre of the acting area there was an altar of Dionysus, which could become part of the setting if the plot required it. Other mobile altars could be brought on stage as well. Among the most impressive props were chariots, which could serve as centre-pieces of processions, but smaller items could also become of focal attention, for instance Ajax's sword, Electra's urn and Philoctetes' bow in the eponymous plays of Sophocles.

The actors and the chorus would wear full masks including wigs, as well as costumes covering their whole body. Masks and costumes would not only enable the actors to play different roles, but would also function as markers for the gender, age and status of the characters. Although naturalistic features would be lost in the wide space of the theatre and the Mediterranean sunlight, body language and voice variations would facilitate the identification of the speaking actor from among the other actors on stage, and also the articulation of the character's changing emotions.

Reception

The impact of tragedy on the cultural and intellectual life of fifth- and fourth-century Athens is clearly manifest in other dramatic, literary and artistic genres, including Aristophanes' comedy, the philosophy of Plato, and vase-paintings. By the end of the fifth century there was a very clear sense that Aeschylus, Sophocles and Euripides constituted the canon of a genre whose golden age was coming to an end. In the 380s a decree was passed which allowed their plays to be revived annually, two generations later Aristotle offered in his *Poetics* what is perceived today as the first critical evaluation of tragedy as a genre, and in the 320s official copies of their plays were made by the state to protect them from accidental or deliberate change through regular revivals. But tragedy was also part of a live performance culture. There were competitions for new playwrights throughout the fourth and third centuries and in the 320s the theatre of Dionysus was built anew, reflecting the central role of drama as a cultural institution of fourth-century Athens.

The fame of tragedy spread very quickly outside Athens. Invited by the tyrant of Syracuse, Hieron, Aeschylus produced plays in Sicily and died there on his last trip. Likewise Euripides is thought to have died in Macedon, in the court of the king Archelaus, where he probably wrote his *Bacchae* and *Iphigenia at Aulis*. Some of the most impressive vase-paintings inspired by tragic productions come from fourth-century southern Italy. With the expedition of Alexander the Great into Asia, numerous cities around the Mediterranean and in Asia drew on the living tradition of tragedy to claim their share in Greek culture and civilisation. Inviting glamorous and hugely expensive actors to perform scenes from their repertoire of tragic roles was thought to be a matter of enormous prestige. Greek tragedy was very influential in Rome as well, with translations and adaptations as early as the third century BC. Among the dramatists who appropriated Greek plays were Ennius, Accius and Seneca. But what accounts for the survival of Greek plays into the modern world is the appeal of Greek tragedy in scholarship and education. The thirty-two tragic plays that survive today are very much the product of a long transmission and canonisation process, which lasted almost without interruption from the era of the Alexandrian editions and commentaries in the third century BC right through to the Byzantine manuscripts of the fourteenth century AD.

The modern world discovered Greek tragedy in the Renaissance with the help of printing and translation into Latin and the main European languages. Aristotle's *Poetics* played a decisive role in rehabilitating Graeco-Roman tragedy as a model for classical French and Italian theatre. Opera emerged in late sixteenth-century Italy as a conscious attempt to recreate Greek tragedy as a theatrical form for the stage rather than solitary reading. In the last five centuries successive generations of translators, playwrights, librettists, composers, directors, actors, dancers, poets, novelists, historians and philosophers have returned to Greek tragedy to celebrate, question and debate what is often perceived as the origin of Western theatre and culture (see chapter 11). Similarly, successive generations of scholars have helped advance our knowledge of the original context and nature of Greek tragedy, while also increasing our awareness of the new meanings with which it has been invested during its long reception history.

Further reading

Texts

R. D. Dawe, *Sophoclis tragoediae* (3rd edn, 7 vols), Stuttgart: Teubner, 1996.

J. Diggle, *Euripides, Fabulae* (3 vols), Oxford: Oxford University Press, 1981–94.

H. Lloyd-Jones and N. G. Wilson, *Sophocles, Fabulae*, Oxford: Oxford University Press, 1990.

D. Page, *Aeschylus, Fabulae*, Oxford: Oxford University Press, 1972.

M. L. West, *Aeschyli tragoediae cum incerti poetae Prometheo*, Stuttgart: Teubner, 1990.

Fragments

C. Collard, M. Cropp and K. H. Lee (eds), *Euripides, Selected Fragmentary Plays*, vol. 1, Warminster: Aris and Phillips, 1995 – texts with introduction, translation and commentary.

B. Snell, S. Radt and R. Kannicht (eds), *Tragicorum Graecorum Fragmenta*, vols 1–5, Göttingen: Vandenhoeck and Ruprecht, 1971–2004 – texts with introduction and notes in Latin.

General studies

E. Csapo and W. J. Slater, *The Context of Ancient Drama*, Ann Arbor: University of Michigan Press, 1994.

P. E. Easterling (ed.), *The Cambridge Companion to Greek Tragedy*, Cambridge: Cambridge University Press, 1997.

S. Goldhill, *Reading Greek Tragedy*, Cambridge: Cambridge University Press, 1986.

A. Lesky, *Greek Tragic Poetry* (German original 1972), New Haven: Yale University Press, 1983.

J. Mossman, *Oxford Readings in Euripides*, Oxford: Oxford University Press, 2003.

A. W. Pickard-Cambridge, *The Dramatic Festivals of Athens* (2nd edn), Oxford: Oxford University Press, 1988.

C. Segal, *Tragedy and Civilization: An Interpretation of Sophocles*, Cambridge MA: Harvard University Press, 1981.

E. Segal, *Oxford Readings in Greek Tragedy*, Oxford: Oxford University Press, 1983.

A. H. Sommerstein, *Aeschylean Tragedy*, Bari: Levante, 1996.

D. Wiles, *Greek Theatre Performance: An Introduction*, Cambridge: Cambridge University Press, 2001.

J. J. Winkler and F. I. Zeitlin (eds), *Nothing to do with Dionysus? Athenian Drama in its Social Context*, Princeton: Princeton University Press, 1990.

38. Roman Tragedy

Roland Mayer

If we may credit Livy's history of Rome (7.2) dramatic entertainments were introduced into Rome from Etruria in 364 BC at the *ludi Romani*; they seem to have been improvisatory in nature, and had a considerable musical element. Over a century later there occurred nothing less than a literary revolution, when, in 240 BC, to mark the successful conclusion of the war against Carthage (the First Punic War) in the previous year, a poet, Livius Andronicus (see chapter 36), was commissioned by the aediles (magistrates in charge of the games) to compose a regular drama for performance instead of, or perhaps in addition to, the traditional musical revue. Rather than create an original plot, Livius chose a Greek script – on that occasion whether it was comic or tragic we do not know; Livius wrote both kinds of drama – and he reworked it in the Latin language using the metres already developed over time for spoken dialogue and song; it is debatable whether he kept the chorus as such. His decision is easily explained by his Hellenic origin (Andronicus is a Greek name); his literary education will have been founded on Homer and Attic drama – and drama, it should be remembered, was still performed in the Greek world. He was brought to Rome as a slave, and his literary skills secured him his manumission (so he took his master's name, Livius). When commissioned to compose a Latin play he would most naturally satisfy his own cultural aspirations by borrowing a plot from the great storehouse of the Greek theatre.

From the Roman point of view, the commission of Livius was equally significant: Rome now makes a bid to be seen as not just a military power, but a cultural centre in the West rivalling Syracuse or Naples. This aspiration was engendered and fostered by the increased contact of Romans during the third century with the developed Hellenic culture of southern Italy and Sicily (where that First Punic War was fought out). Drama therefore appeared in Rome, superficially at least, much as it had appeared at Athens: a public entertainment presented as part of a religious festival under state supervision. But there were two major differences: Roman playwrights did not compete with each other, nor did they compose trilogies or tetralogies; each play stood alone. The *ludi* were paid for out of the public purse, but the aediles might supplement that from private money, since they aimed to secure good will at elections by their generosity in mounting the public games; this motive has, however, been questioned. At any rate, the production of drama, along with all other public entertainments, was firmly controlled by the aristocracy, and, as we shall see, a measure of censorship over what could be mounted was exercised.

Livius was astute and chose to adapt tragedies based upon Greek mythical themes which would be likely to appeal to his audience. The Romans believed that the Trojan Aeneas was involved to some extent in the foundation of their city, and a good number of Livius' plays, and indeed of those of his successors, evoked the myths concerning the Trojan War. That appealed to Roman patriotism, always a strong feature of their national literature, and it also answered a Roman aspiration for a respectable past.

Patriotism lay behind the initiative (if it was that) of Livius' contemporary, Naevius, who ventured upon another kind of serious drama, the plot of which was based upon either Roman legend or contemporary history. This dramatic form, called *fabula praetexta*, in reference to the Roman dress of the characters (cf. Horace's *Art of Poetry* 285–8), is usually treated in literary histories as a subdivision of tragedy. This is arguably mistaken. As a late grammarian, Diomedes, said, tragedy is all about grief, exile and slaughter, events or personal fortunes take a turn for the worse, and the keynote is sadness (*GLK* i.488.16 and 20). Now the *praetexta* by its very nature, and perhaps thanks to the context in which it was performed, was celebratory; success was its theme. As Diomedes saw (*GLK* i.489.25–6), the main similarity between tragedy and *praetexta* was the elevated rank of the personages. It might therefore be fairer to regard the *praetexta* as an independent dramatic kind, not a subdivision of tragedy, but related to it in seriousness, and perhaps formally too. Naevius' traditional position as originator has recently been called into question, and it has been argued that there existed a much older tradition of dramatic re-enactment of national events (see Wiseman, *Roman Drama and Roman History*, chapter 1). If this is so, we might limit Naevius' initiative to the production of written scripts, or to the preservation of the scripts he wrote. What we can say for certain is that the *praetexta* was never a serious rival to the Greek-based tragedy; the eminent poets who wrote tragedies composed very few *praetextae*. The subject matter of this kind of drama generally had a political or propagandistic function. The *Ambracia* of Ennius (?186 BC), for instance, seems to have been designed to justify the disputed triumph celebrated by his patron, M. Fulvius Nobilior, who had captured that city. Much later (c. AD 75), the central figure of Tacitus' *Dialogus*, Curiatius Maternus, is presented as using his tragedies (both mythical and Roman *praetexta*) to suggest criticism of the powerful. The only *praetexta* to have come down to us, the anonymous *Octavia*, was probably composed under Galba or Vespasian with a view to blackening the character of the last of the Julio-Claudians, Nero: his overthrow was justified. This very tendency of the *praetexta* to engage with political issues may have contributed to its marginality: it was too risky for most early playwrights, who were not persons of high status.

The experiment of 240 BC proved successful (albeit much more so for comedy than for tragedy), and gradually, as other religious festivals were added to the Roman calendar, days designated specially for the performance of dramas were included; these were called *ludi scaenici*. Special *ludi* too might involve dramatic performances; these were held by successful generals (Varius' *Thyestes* was certainly performed at Augustus' triumph in 29 BC), or as entertainments at funerals of the aristocracy or at the dedication of temples. Livius had distinguished successors, either as dramatists generally (Naevius, Ennius), or exclusively as tragic poets (Pacuvius, Accius, Pomponius Secundus). But after Accius, who died c. 90 BC, tragedy became the preserve of men of letters (Pollio, Seneca) rather than dedicated dramatists; its retreat from stage to recitation hall, however, ensured its longevity. Recitation in itself need not undermine dramatic impact, but it is undeniable that Seneca's tragedies are works of elite literature in tragic form rather than coherent dramas (contrast Harrison, *Seneca in Performance*).

It would be reasonable to argue that tragedy never did quite succeed at Rome either as an entertainment or as a literary form. Comedy was certainly always more popular, and in due course the regular drama as a whole gave way to the mime and pantomime. Even revivals of classic tragedy were infrequent (Seneca seems to refer to one in *Epist.* 80). More telling still is the engagement of the poet Horace with the problem of drama in two of his epistles (the ones to Augustus and to the Pisones, the latter known as the *Art of Poetry*, especially lines 153–294). It is clear that Horace felt that Roman tragedy had never realised its potential, and those late poems challenge his younger contemporaries to produce a truly national tragedy that would rival the classics of Athens. What factors might induce us to side with Horace, and judge the Romans' experiment in tragedy only a modest success?

First and foremost, there was the subject matter. Greek tragedy was founded on myth, but, the tale of Troy apart, most myths would have been unlikely to engage a Roman audience emotionally; indeed a number of them clearly struck them as strange or even distasteful (see also chapter 52). It is, for instance, significant that plays centred on the myths of Oedipus and Phaedra were not adapted for the stage in the republican period; we find them only in the work of Seneca, who wrote for a small, sophisticated audience. The sexual issues in those tales were unacceptable to the magistrates who commissioned the plays, and a discreet censorship was in operation. For Athenian playwrights myths often involved as well a ritual and religious element. The *Bacchae* or the *Oedipus at Colonus* have a religious intensity that simply could not be conveyed to a Roman audience. But neither could Roman religious sentiment or practice provide an alternative spirit to make good the deficiency.

Second, there were problems of literary technique. Livius borrowed dialogue and song metres from the theatrical entertainments that had existed in Rome for over a century, but no one pretends these measures had the flexibility of those evolved in Athens. Dramatic metres remained comparatively clumsy, and their heaviness is one of the objects of Horace's complaints in his *Art of Poetry* 251–64. Tragic diction too was a matter for concern, especially for the originator, Livius, who had no generic tradition to fall back on. He had to invent a suitable register, and seems to have done the job well. Ennius refined on this technique, but his successor (and nephew) Pacuvius gave tragic speech a more pompous turn (see Cicero, *Orator* 36); such affected language was criticised by the first Roman satirist, Lucilius, and by his successor, Horace, in the *Art of Poetry* 217. Clearly Horace wants a thoroughgoing reform of technique, but by his time it was too late to repel the advance of other popular entertainments. Thus Roman tragic style never achieved the natural flow we find in, say, Euripides.

Third, writing tragedies was not the only literary activity of most of the playwrights referred to above. They experimented with a range of Greek literary kinds, and tragedy was just one string upon their lyre. Consider, on the other hand, Plautus and Terence: comedy was all in all to them, and that concentration of interest upon the one form must have contributed to their success as men of the theatre and as artists (see chapter 40). But the tragic poets, with the exception of Pacuvius and Accius, were not so dedicated, and were not exclusively, or perhaps even primarily, 'men of the theatre'; Naevius and Ennius, for instance, may personally have set more store by their epic poems on national themes. The composition of tragedies may then for them have been something of a sideshow, especially if the writers saw their task as one chiefly of adaptation, rather than original composition. Certainly Varius Rufus had a great success, we are told, with his *Thyestes* early in the reign of Augustus, but he never sought to repeat it; one tragedy sufficed him, as indeed it did Ovid, who wrote an admired *Medea* (he assures us, by the way, that this play was not intended for stage performance).

Finally, there is the issue of sympathy with the tragic concept. However we choose to define tragedy, it is undeniable that in Athens there was a genuine engagement with the suffering of a hero. An Oedipus or an Ajax might fail, in human terms, but there was something special about even that failure which moved the audience. Not so at Rome. In Roman society *uirtus*, excellence in performance and achievement, was the defining characteristic of a man, and one exercised one's *uirtus* on behalf of the *populus Romanus* (Roman people). The individual was so much less than the corporate entity of the Roman state. In such a society, what place was there for a suffering Philoctetes, who would have seemed to a Roman merely self-centred, and not a 'team player'? What the Romans admired was success, not failure, survival, not death. We have only to compare the tragic *Iliad* with the optimistic *Aeneid*; Achilles as much as Hector is a tragic figure, but Aeneas and his Trojans win through with the help of fate. That is arguably what the Romans expected of their role models, who, when all is said and done, created and successfully maintained an empire. The Romans may well have been radically incapable of appreciating the sort of heroic failure we encounter on the Greek (and English) tragic stage.

So what was the appeal of tragedy at Rome? As suggested at the outset, it served to bring Rome culturally into line with other cities of the Italian peninsula. Power alone did not confer prestige, and the arts of peace had to be cultivated as well as those of war. From the audience's point of view, tragedy in Rome as in Athens, and then in the Greek world generally, offered unrivalled spectacle – rather as opera used to do from the baroque period to the end of the nineteenth century. Considerable sums were expended by the magistrates on the productions, and the lust of the eye was satisfied – for some, at any rate: the gigantism of productions in the late republic called down the criticisms of Cicero, who was disgusted by the tasteless display in a revival of Accius' *Clytemnestra* at the opening of Pompey's theatre in August of 55 BC (see *Fam.* 7.1.2), and of Horace in his *Epistle* 2.1.203–7. Though it has been suggested that the audience was not deeply engaged in the plight of the characters, still tragedy presented strong tales of crime and suffering, the sort of thing that continues to entice us to the movies.

Modern critical and historical accounts of Roman tragedy and the *praetexta* are baffled by the complete loss of any scripts dating to the republic. All that has come down to us are the ten plays in the Senecan corpus, one of which, the *praetexta Octavia*, is certainly not by him (others are questioned in whole or in part, and one is incomplete). This skews the picture irretrievably. Most work therefore centres perforce on Seneca, and the issues tend to be the use he made of his Greek models, the mode of presentation (staged or recited), and the presence or absence of philosophical colour (Seneca was a professed Stoic). As regards the issue of staging, those who argue for staging sometimes give the impression that an unstaged (or unstageable) drama must be reckoned faulty or inferior. There seems to be, however, a growing awareness that dramatic form is itself flexible, and a play designed for recitation – rather like a modern radio play – is not dramatically crippled; its effects are simply different.

Further reading

Texts and translations

L. Annaei Senecae Tragoediae, ed. O. Zwierlein, Oxford: Clarendon Press, 1986.

Remains of Old Latin (Loeb Classical Library), ed. E. H. Warmington, Cambridge MA and London: Harvard University Press and William Heinemann, 1935, 1936 – vol. 1 contains translation of Ennius, vol. 2 the other republican tragedians.

Seneca Tragedies (2 vols., Loeb Classical Library), ed. J. G. Fitch, Cambridge MA and London: Harvard University Press, 2002–4; this translation replaces the older one by Frank Justus Miller in the same series.

The Tragedies of Ennius, ed. H. D. Jocelyn, Cambridge: Cambridge University Press, 1969.

Tragicorum Romanorum Fragmenta, ed. O. Ribbeck, Leipzig: Teubner, 1897.

Studies

W. Beare, *The Roman Stage* (3rd edn), London: Methuen, 1964.

H. I. Flower, 'Fabulae praetextae in context: where were plays on contemporary subjects performed in Republican Rome?', *Classical Quarterly* 45 (1995) 170–90.

S. M. Goldberg, 'Dido's Furies', in his *Constructing Literature in the Roman Republic*, Cambridge: Cambridge University Press, 2005, pp. 115–43.

E. S. Gruen, *Studies in Greek Culture and Roman Policy*, Leiden: Brill, 1990, esp. ch. 3.

G. W. M. Harrison (ed.), *Seneca in Performance*, London: Duckworth, 2000.

L. A. Mackay, 'The Roman tragic spirit', *California Studies in Classical Antiquity* 8 (1978) 145–62, esp. pp. 156–62.

T. P. Wiseman, *Roman Drama and Roman History*, Exeter: University of Exeter Press, 1998.

39. Greek Comedy

Ian Ruffell

From a modern perspective, Greek comedy seems at the same time both very familiar and very alien. The modes of humour it deployed over its two centuries of evolution can now be found scattered over many different places in modern comedy.

But the packaging of these elements is something that is difficult for a modern audience to grasp. Performed before an audience of 10,000–15,000 spectators, Greek comedy is truly public popular culture of a kind that cannot be paralleled today outside of a major football match. At the same time, it is presented through means of performance – song, dance and costume – that still flag up its ritual origins. The choral elements of Old Comedy seem to employ kinds of formal patterns that are not well documented elsewhere. Meanwhile, grotesque padding, especially stomach and buttocks, grotesque masks, and the usually very visible presence on male characters of a phallos attached to their tights mark it as highly *other* to modern dramatic forms. Even in the relatively sedate and much more self-consciously modern arena of New Comedy, the relics of these traditional elements are still to be found.

The story of Greek comedy is one of great popularity, creative energy and ferocious evolution, driven partly by competitive energies internal to the competition, partly, perhaps, by historical and cultural change in the period. Comedy as a formal genre was a latecomer to the dramatic contests at Athens, and as such has a claim to be the one truly democratic genre. The first form of comedy developed rapidly and reached its most creative period under the radical democracy of c. 460–405/4. Its popularity was such that an additional dramatic festival was laid on at the winter (January) festival of the Lenaia, where, in contrast to the Great or City Dionysia, *kōmōidia* seems to have been the senior genre. After the fall and re-establishment of the democracy at the end of the fifth century, comedy continued to evolve, and by the third quarter of the fourth century, it had mutated into something rather different.

Taking the realistic elements and contemporary settings of Old Comedy and the escape-plots and melodrama of later tragedy, it now turned to the comedy of character and situation, of mistaken identity, coincidence and accident, with a bit of slapstick thrown in for good measure. As such, New Comedy was a perfect fit for the international market that opened up in the late fourth century following the death of Alexander, just as domestic comment at Athens was becoming less rewarding or, indeed, safe. Though substantially lost until the twentieth century, it is the New Comedy of Greece, largely through its Roman reinterpreters, that has had the more substantial and lasting impact on the dramatic culture of Western Europe (see also chapter 11).

Old Comedy

Athenian Comedy seems to have had its origins in fringe activity and informal performances around the Dionysia. The first victory was won by Khionides (487/6 or 485 BC), about whom we know nothing. The first major figure of Old Comedy was Magnes, who won eleven victories from c. 480. Apart from a few fragments, the evidence for his comedy and the early development of the genre comes largely from the unreliable pen of Aristophanes himself in *Knights* (500–35), with some brief explanations by ancient commentators. The most that we can say is that animal choruses, attested in vase-paintings from Corinth and Athens, seem to have played a major part. Some, at least, of these are padded dancers, and they perhaps show one source for the grotesque costume to be found later. We might also infer that early comedy featured extensive use of the kind of chanted tetrameter verse (*parakatalogē*) that is characteristic of later fifth-century comedy. Even in Aristophanes, songs themselves largely consisted of simple rhythmical patterns, more in the line of popular song, drinking-song and working-song than the complex formal and/or hymnic lyric to be found in fifth-century lyric poetry (Pindar, Bacchylides) or Greek tragedy (see chapter 65).

Kratinos

The theme, content or plot (if any) of early Greek comedy remains obscure. The pivotal figure in the development of the genre was Kratinos (c. 480–c. 420), the dominant playwright of his generation with six victories at the Dionysia (referred to as 6D) and three at the Lenaia (referred to as 3L), and a career that lasted from c. 460 to at least 424/3. Aristophanes gives him the central place in his mini-history of the genre, albeit with many back-handed compliments, before putting the boot in explicitly, claiming that he was, by 424, senile and incontinent, and should be put out to grass. Kratinos, he says, used to be notable particularly for his attacks on contemporaries, especially politicians. But he compares him to a river out of control, taking out everything else en route. In contrast, Aristophanes claims to be rather more subtle. What remains of later criticism expands on Aristophanes, with the rather more specific claim that Kratinos tore apart his plots in his enthusiasm.

The quite substantial fragments of Kratinos' output, including some on papyrus, do seem to bear out some of the story, but they bear out still more the idea that Aristophanes is largely working in a Kratinean tradition. Certainly, there is abundant evidence that Kratinos was political and personal. His career included the periods when Perikles was dominant in Athenian politics, and the treatment that Kleon, in particular, received at the hands of Aristophanes is prefigured in the abuse that Kratinos and his later contemporaries, such as Telekleides (3D, 5L) and, a little younger, Hermippos (1+D, 4L), gave Perikles. Frequent jibes include allusions to Peisistratos, tyrant in the sixth century, and unflattering analogies to Zeus, with similar implications. As well as gleefully pointing out his weirdly shaped head, Perikles' personal connections (such as the courtesan Aspasia, the musician Damon and the general Hagnon) all come under scrutiny for one form or other of bribery, corruption or immorality. But policy as well as personality appears to have figured, not least war policy (*Nemesis*, *Dionysalexandros* and *Wealth-Gods*; so too Hermippos' *Fates*). Significantly, it was during this period of both Periklean ascendancy and vicious attacks that the additional Lenaia competition started.

But it was not just the comic context but also comic techniques that Kratinos (and his contemporaries) pioneered before Aristophanes:

1. 'metatheatrical' confrontation of the audience across the stage/auditorium boundary;
2. large-scale parodic episodes or plots (*Wealth-Gods*, using [Aeschylus], *Prometheus Unbound*);
3. cross-play comic universes (*Wealth-Gods*) and competitive intertextual dialogues with rivals (*Wine-Flask*);
4. a mix of realistic elements or real people with mythological or divine creatures or contexts;
5. explicit engagement with and/or abuse of rival genres and their poets or with rival comedians, or with other rival claimants for public attention and instruction (e.g. *Archilochuses*);
6. utopian elements (*Wealth-Gods* again, further developed by contemporaries, including Aristophanes himself);
7. comic song (Aristophanes himself refers to the contribution that Kratinos made in developing comic lyric).

Perhaps most characteristic of Kratinos is the political use of mythological allegory, with Zeus/Perikles (*Nemesis*) and Dionysos/Paris/Perikles (*Dionysalexandros*) starring in a remake of the Trojan War, and Perikles/Zeus as the evil dictator in *Wealth-Gods*. There is some dispute about how up-front Kratinos' allegory was – and it may well have varied. However, when Aristophanes frames his first play under his own name, *Knights*, as a political allegory, where the people are personified as an old man with problems with the domestic help, this seems to be but the latest twist on an established theme.

Aristophanes

Aristophanes (c. 450–c. 380) is the only exponent of Old Comedy for whom complete plays survive. The eleven that we have cover the range of his career, with most evidence for the 420s. We know little of his life beyond what he says about himself in the plays and some additional material from ancient commentators, which may just be inference on the basis of the text. He did not produce his earliest plays, but used a producer instead, as he was to continue to do at various points in his career. His final play, *Aiolosikon*, was produced by his son Araros, who was a dramatist in his own right. Here is a list, using their most common titles, of plays which survive, or whose dates are known, with festival (if known) and producer.

428/7	*Banqueters*. [?Kallistratos]
427/6	*Babylonians*. Dionysia. [Kallistratos]
426/5	*Acharnians*. Lenaia. [Kallistratos]
425/4	*Knights*. Lenaia.
423	*Clouds*. Dionysia. Our version revised, c. 419–416.
423/2	*Wasps*. Lenaia.
	?Proagon. Lenaia. [Philonides]
422/1	*Peace* I.
415/14	*Amphiaraos*. Lenaia. [Philonides]
	Birds. Dionysia. [Kallistratos]
412/11	*Lysistrata*. ?Lenaia. [Kallistratos]
	Thesmophoriazusae (*Women at the Thesmophoria*). ?Dionysia.
409/8	*Wealth* I.
405	*Frogs*. Dionysia. [Philonides]
?393/2	*Ecclesiazusae* (*Women at the Assembly*). Dionysia.
389/8	*Wealth* II. Dionysia.

Although Aristophanes is for us, as for earlier critics, the major figure of Old Comedy, he did not in his time dominate to the same extent that Kratinos or, especially, Magnes did. It was a tough environment in which to produce: in addition to the still-producing Kratinos, and the mid-career Telekleides and Hermippos, Aristophanes' contemporaries included Eupolis – the third of the great Old Comedians (4D, 3L), who worked in a very similar idiom (see Storey, *Eupolis*).

Plot and structure

Aristophanic (and, as far as we can tell, Eupolidean) comedy tends to follow a broadly similar plot-line: *problem – solution – implementation of solution – results of solution – happy ending*. The opening scenario usually presents a character who is seeking to resolve a problem and/or address a personal obsession. So, in *Peace*, a character obsessed by peace rides a giant fattened-up dung-beetle to heaven to challenge the gods, where he discovers from a shifty Hermes that the goddess Peace is being held prisoner, and then somehow engages the entire Greek world to join in pulling her out of her cave/prison. In *Thesmophoriazusae*, the poet Euripides is going to be sentenced to death by the women of Athens, and needs someone to infiltrate the women-only festival in disguise to plead his case; after trying the camp poet, Agathon (who has more sense), his aged and none-too-pretty relative gets the job, and much cross-dressing chaos and botched Euripidean escapes ensue, until the poet cuts a deal with the women, and the relative escapes singed and plucked, but otherwise unscathed.

The different phases themselves can take up different lengths of time – *Knights* in particular, where a couple of downtrodden slaves seek to displace their master's current favourite with a new arrival, is almost entirely implementation, as their new candidate repeatedly confronts the old. Opposition from other characters (and sometimes the chorus) is encountered in numerous phases, especially the implementation, where it is often (but not always) expressed in terms of a so-called contest (*agon*; a roughly parallel set-piece of recitative and sung elements); and in the results phase, when various (usually unsavoury) characters seek to disrupt or grab a piece of the action. A convenient break in the plot in many plays, allowing for the passage of time and for transition from one phase to the next, is the *parabasis*. This is another formally structured element, where the stage is cleared and the chorus address the audience on issues of dramatic, topical and/or thematic concern. In the earlier plays of Aristophanes, the chorus can speak explicitly on behalf of the poet or even in the poet's own voice; over time, the chorus tend to stay in character, and eventually this element decays altogether.

Within these relatively straightforward and linear plots, there is considerable activity. It is quite episodic. What this means is that there is considerable comic riffing, both on the plot ideas (repeated 'intruders', and so on), and on the basic problem. The plays essentially are sustained comic critiques of an issue, or a related network of issues. Here are some of the main ones.

Democracy and imperialism

Aristophanes' career got off to a flying start, when his play (now lost), the *Babylonians*, got him and/or his producer into serious trouble with Kleon, the pre-eminent populist politician of the time. The problem: that he had besmirched Athens in front of the Athenian allies. What in fact he seems to have done is question the nature of Athenian imperialism. This is something that his rival, Eupolis, would also do in his *Cities* (mid-420s), with the memorable and pointed image of Athenians leering at the female chorus of allied states. In *Birds*, Athenian imperialism is never far from view, whether it is the blockade of the gods that recalls the recent blockade of Melos, or the interruption of this bird-paradise by Athenian imperial officials.

In Aristophanes' plays of the 420s that survive complete, the issue is not the nature of imperialism itself, so much as the effect that empire has on democracy – the introduction of extra resources and their exploitation by politicians. In *Knights* and *Wasps*, this is embedded within the broader question of who runs Athens – and how. Both attack Kleon with a ferocious energy. The domestic setting of *Knights* is an allegory for politics: the old, deaf and initially slightly dense master is ThePeople, and the slaves are politicians. The master's favourite is a barbarian slave-cum-leather-trader, a thinly disguised Kleon, while his rivals and eventual replacement are also market-traders. There is a lot of tactical snobbery here, but there is also a point being made about a quasi-commercial relationship with the people. Compare older Conservatives characterising the Thatcher generation as 'garagistes' (i.e. nouveaux-riches second-hand-car-salesmen). In late fifth-century Athens, the principal means of bribing the people is the money from the Athenians' subject-allies.

In *Knights*, the focus is the Assembly and the council; in *Wasps*, attention turns to the law-courts. Here a father, LoveKleon, is a fanatic for judging cases; his son, HateKleon, urges him to give it up and stay at home, enjoy a comfortable retirement. Just as, ultimately, ThePeople in *Knights* claims to know what he is doing – he is using the politicians – LoveKleon claims that sitting in judgement gives him power and money; a point contested by his son, who argues that the money from the empire is not going towards the people and the people are stooges. The corruption of the law-courts is played out live in the form of another allegorical moment, a domestic trial. HateKleon 'wins' by populist grandstanding and then blatant cheating. But when LoveKleon scandalously joins the leisured classes, it turns out that his private parties are stuffed with the same political players as in public life. *Wasps* is posing the question: 'Where does power lie?'

War and peace

For a number of Aristophanes' plays, this question is embedded in the issue of war and peace. Just as the empire is presented as an excuse for politicians to enrich themselves and con the people, so too is warfare. This is memorably dramatised in the opening scene of *Acharnians*. The central character Dikaiopolis (?= Honest Citizen) tries to discuss peace in the Assembly and is ignored, while time is given to a bunch of useless and/or corrupt ambassadors who have spent the past few years swanning around northern Greece and Persia. Dikaiopolis is thrown out for his pains, forcing him to the desperate remedy of a personal peace treaty. As the play develops, his plans are opposed by the pompous and overblown general Lamachus, at least until he and others like him start wanting a piece of the action. But corrupt politicians versus noble punters is again too easy a story. The really scary opposition for Dikaiopolis is the chorus – men of Akharnai who want payback on the Spartans for trashing their crops. The question that *Acharnians* poses is whether reasoned persuasion can overcome violence or the politics of violent emotion (anger, fear, terror). As we confront that issue in the modern democratic context, the upbeat result is that it can – just. The downside for real-world politics is that Dikaiopolis has to resort to means that are both unconstitutional and impossible *simply to get a hearing*. As an anti-war play, this is a feel-good production, but as a critical reflection on political process, it makes uncomfortable viewing.

Panhellenism and nostalgia

Although there are elements in the other political plays of the mid-420s, the theme of peace resurfaces most explicitly in the first *Peace*, performed just ahead of the Peace of Nikias, which ended the Archidamian War. Although this is an altogether more celebratory effort than *Acharnians*, and a rather different solution is on offer, a number of elements are similar, not least an association of peace with the countryside (the chorus of farmers here support the central character, Trygaios) and the ill-treatment of corrupt figures who have profited from the war. Above all, in the rescue of the goddess, Peace, it stresses and, significantly, *enacts* the idea of the Greeks as a whole coming together - not just making peace but working together for the common good.

This panhellenic ideal is taken up in the *Lysistrata*, the most famous of Aristophanes' peace plays, regularly re-performed since the 1960s whenever the West goes to war. This sees the women of Greece combining to force the men to their knees and to peace negotiations by going on a sex-strike, as well as adopting the more practical short-term measure of seizing the Acropolis of Athens, with the treasuries that funded the war. In addition to this radical approach to united Greek action, the *Lysistrata* evokes the memory of a rather more conventional coalition, that against the Persians. It is something of a minor theme in Aristophanes, from the beginning of *Acharnians* to the denouement of *Frogs*, that the Greeks now go cap in hand to the Persians in order to do each other down, when once they were fighting Persia successfully together. However, from the chorus of *Wasps* to the chorus of *Lysistrata*, that generation are presented as a somewhat hapless bunch of has-beens (understandable, since the Marathon-fighters of *Lysistrata*, if taken literally, would have to be about a hundred years old), and so there is a certain ambivalence, or knowingness, about the past, too. This is comic nostalgia in the fullest sense.

Fantasy and reality

Perhaps the most problematic aspect of Old Comedy is the way that it intertwines realism – often of the crudest sort – with the grotesque and the fantastic. This is perhaps most obvious in the case of the *Birds*, where Peisetairos and Euelpides set out to leave behind all the business of Athens and live among the birds. This, as usual, escalates, and despite the suspicion of the birds, Peisetairos (Persuade-a-friend) convinces them that their birthright is to (1) take the place of the gods, (2) found a city, and (3) stop the gods receiving sacrifice. The grubby realities of politics and Athens as usual, though, are never far from the surface. A similar mix is evident in (at least) *Acharnians* (a personal peace treaty), *Frogs* (rescuing Euripides from Hades), *Peace* (rescuing Peace from Olympos) or *Wealth* (curing blind Wealth). Other plays such as *Wasps*, *Clouds*, *Thesmophoriazusae*, *Lysistrata* and *Ecclesiazusae* adopt measures that are bizarre and implausible, certainly, but not actually *impossible* in a defies-physical-reality kind of way. Even so, the talking dogs and kitchen-utensil-witnesseses of *Wasps* or the personified arguments of *Clouds* are not things you see every day.

Critics have worried about the collision between the apparently serious subject matter of some of these plays and these flights of fancy, not least the central character's obsession and the bizarre or impossible way that he goes about resolving it. They have also worried about these characters themselves, arguing that they are selfish in their eventual good fortune, are mad, are inconsistent, or are otherwise problematic. How, then, can we take these characters' critiques of war or of Athens or of democracy at all seriously? One option adopted is to say that comedy was/is never intended to make a political or social point (Gomme in Segal, *Oxford Readings*; Dover, *Aristophanic Comedy*); another is to say that Aristophanes is satirising people like these extreme characters (Bowie, *Aristophanes*); another is to say that comedy and its characters don't have to be consistent, realistic or practical, and let's not worry about it (de Ste Croix in Segal, *Oxford Readings*; MacDowell, *Aristophanes and Athens*). Even if the last of these is true, though, the really interesting question to ask is what kinds of ideas the implausible plot twists or character elements add to the central issue(s) of the play.

Let's be clear: some of the major characters are pretty awful – most notably Strepsiades (Twister) in *Clouds*, who is trying to blag his way out of his debts. On the other hand, they dominate the stage and are clearly the audience's primary target for identification and empathy (even in an 'oo, isn't he dreadful' kind of way, a feature which has given rise to the idea of the comic hero; Whitman, *Aristophanes and the Comic Hero*). However, in many cases there is an ambivalence about the central character, or even a question of whether there is a single central figure at all. This is most clear in *Wasps*. LoveKleon has much in common with the other comic protagonists of the 420s. He is from a rural background and poorly educated; he is closer in age, though perhaps a bit older; he has the obsession(s) and extreme character; he becomes increasingly the focus of the play; and despite his attachment to Kleon, he is cynical about politicians. HateKleon on the other hand is the man with the plan, and the one who wins over the chorus and (to some extent) his father; as a critic of democracy he expresses many of the elements that come through from the plays of the period. But he is apolitical and entirely prissy and one-dimensional. He also has an unscrupulous side, but that only makes him more of an Aristophanic character.

Sex and gender

It is unsurprising, given the theatrical or social context, that Aristophanes' protagonists tend to be male. However, in two cases, *Lysistrata* and *Ecclesiazusae*, Aristophanes uses a female protagonist. For a predominantly male audience, the direct intervention of Lysistrata and Praxagora in the male realm of politics is considerably more challenging than in the more distanced form of Greek tragedy. Clearly, Aristophanes is no feminist (to use the term would be wildly anachronistic and misleading) and the women's intervention ultimately serves men, solving their problems and restoring the sexual status quo. The main focus of the plays is not on women at all, but on war and on poverty, inequality and a general civic malaise respectively.

However, in order for these issues to get a hearing, Aristophanes is forced to confront Greek constructions of gender in a striking manner. In the trail-blazing *Lysistrata*, tactics include allusions to those few public women in Greece, drawing out the different rules of tragedy, and reinterpreting political problems in terms of women's traditional (household) areas of competence; and to the generally hopeless nature of the men. *Ecclesiazusae* repeats the trick, and has *Lysistrata* fairly clearly in view, but with the added paradoxical twist that the male politicians have lapsed from traditional masculine values to the extent that you might as well get proper women to do the job.

This raises the question: why the use of women at all? The answer has to lie partly in the ever-present pressure to do something new and different, but mostly in the status of women within the Greek polis, especially in Athens. Their ambivalent status as both citizen (for the purpose of procreation and religion) and not-citizen (for anything else) meant that they were in a position to do a systemic critique, from outside the political system but remaining Athenian or Greek, an option that was not available for barbarian and/or slave protagonists. The point can be seen rather more clearly in *Thesmophoriazusae*, which doesn't even uncork the issue of women's role within the polis, let alone try to put the stopper back in. The women here remain separate and marginal, shadowing male political structures in their own space. The dynamics of both space and character mean that the play is far less edgy in terms of gender. For all the male cross-dressing and gender play that take place, this comedy enacts the policing of gender roles, where the audience knows exactly what lies beneath.

Truth and fiction

Issues of gender and issues of genre go hand in hand in *Thesmophoriazusae*. Both the opening scene with the poet Agathon, and Euripides' various escape-schemes (all parodying recent plays), point up the nature of role play in comedy and tragedy. The assault on tragic realism picks up a theme in earlier Aristophanic works. In addition to pervasive use of tragic lines and scenes throughout his work, both *Acharnians* and *Peace* are structured, particularly in their first halves, around parody of Euripidean tragedy. Euripides was both a productive and a threatening source to play off/against, with his innovative plots, controversialist approach to issues, argumentative characters and tendency towards realism. Aristophanes' approach is to use all the good stuff, while gleefully deconstructing the realism by pointing out Euripides' (and tragedy's) use of stage conventions, repeated character types and stereotyped plots. On the expected ad hominem level, allegations that Euripides' mother was a greengrocer and (on the basis of his plots) that he was a misogynist add to the fun. All this is wrapped up in a package that is relentlessly taking the distancing out of drama, emphasises that the real is the domain of comedy, and suggests that for all the surreal elements, the audience always knows what's what.

The treatment of tragedy reaches its apogee in *Frogs*, where Dionysos' fan-boy rescue-mission of Euripides from Hades turns into a dispute between Euripides and Aeschylus over who should get the chair of drama in the underworld. Cue a spectacular send-up of (allegedly) stodgy, traditional, heroic fare and its edgy, too-clever-by-half offspring with its fancy rhythms and loose women: travesties of Aeschylean and Euripidean drama, respectively. Aeschylus wins by a hair, but it is tragedy as a genre that is the loser.

What the rival poets, and the comic chorus, in *Frogs* all agree on is that the major purpose of poetry or drama is to educate its audience. The dispute is really over what is taught or how. Is it patriotic stories and heroic examples we want or a cold, hard look at reality and the development of critical, independent thought?

This places *Frogs* in the same tradition as Aristophanes' earlier *Banqueters* (now lost) and *Clouds*. Although *Clouds* starts out as a full-spectrum display of modern critical inquiry, with all its oddities and cranks, it leads up to a debate between two arguments, the one which *should* win (the Stronger Argument), representing traditional education (*paideia*), and the argument which *should* lose (the Weaker Argument), representing the new. The Weaker Argument uses modern techniques in order to argue for naked shamelessness and self-interest, while the Stronger Argument plaintively upholds traditional values where boys knew their place. The Weaker Argument has the rhetorical and argumentative skills that leave the Stronger Argument floundering, while the latter's claim to the moral high ground is somewhat vitiated by his obsession with his boys' genitalia. As with *Frogs*, this is more than a zero-sum game. It raises the question of whether either the Weaker Argument's effective technique with lack of morals or the Stronger Argument's incompetence with (questionable) morals is the answer. There's more than a hint in both plays that we're being pushed towards the idea of skilful technique and critical engagement *combined with* a strong ethical/political line and an optimistic outlook. That sounds suspiciously like Aristophanic comedy.

Wealth and poverty

Implicit within *Clouds* are questions of wealth and class. The type of education on display is (in contrast to drama) the province of rich young men. Aristophanes' method of placing this under scrutiny is to use an odd-couple approach, with a father, Strepsiades, who is a poor rustic, and a son, Pheidippides (InHockForHorses), who takes after his aristocratic mother. This enables Aristophanes both to use this educational context and to create critical distance from it, a technique that is repeated with the private parties (*symposia*) in *Wasps*.

However, it is only in the final two surviving plays that Aristophanes places wealth in itself centre-stage. Both were composed and performed after Athens' defeat by Sparta, loss of power and loss of income from the subject-allies. In *Ecclesiazusae*, the protagonist, Praxagora (PoliticalActivist), argues that male politicians have ruined the city. Her recipe for success, however, goes way beyond a simple stewardship of the city's resources. Aided by her fellow women (in disguise), who stack the Assembly, she enacts a scheme of communal property and sexual relationships that anticipates Plato's Republic. In *Wealth*, we move from this explicitly political terrain to the mythological, a cure of the blind god, Wealth, which enables him to bestow good fortune on the deserving rather than the undeserving.

Neither play is unrestricted or uncontested wish-fulfilment. In *Ecclesiazusae*, the plan for redistribution is scoffed at by a dissident character who ridicules the idea of altruism, and plans to scrounge from the communal store and not contribute himself; the sexual distribution sees an increasingly grotesque series of old women interrupt a cutesy romance and demand satisfaction from the young man. In *Wealth*, the proposed solution is vigorously opposed by the goddess Poverty, who erupts on stage as a Fury, threatens the activists, and makes the capitalist case that hunger creates innovation and growth. Both plays, then, offer fairly radical statements, but they are developments of elements present in earlier comedy, and like those earlier plays, they are internally contested and dialogic. What are you going to believe?

New Comedy

Already in the last plays of Aristophanes, comedy is changing radically. Although the fantastic plots and socio-political goals of the last plays are familiar from earlier in his career, the formal structures are largely absent, the role of the visible chorus is truncated (probably supplemented at various points with generic material) and metrical variety is much reduced in favour of dialogue. By the time of Menander (320s onwards), this movement had fundamentally shifted the nature of comedy towards a rigid five-act structure, with slots for generic choral songs in the act-divisions. But likewise the range of plots contracted to a much narrower band, focused on paternity, family and, above all, love. Thwarted, frustrated or socially impossible relationships are the key, and resolution involves the creation and resolution of misunderstandings, or the altering of the status of one or more individuals, through recognition by tokens of paternity. In this mix, rape, usually at one of the public festivals where men and women could mix, results in complicating pregnancies or abandoned offspring, whose pasts are the key to resolution of the play.

Just as the range of plots narrowed, so too did character. In place of the extreme individuals, allegorical characters, historical figures (dead or alive) and bolshie women of Old Comedy comes a range of stock characters – the young man in love, the father who misunderstands or objects to a love-match, the slave (cunning, clumsy or comic relief) and the cook (proud of his professional prowess). The lower-class characters in Menander are most often the vehicle for slapstick and more obvious comic relief.

Active female parts are largely restricted to the courtesan (*hetaira*), whose profession and non-Athenian status provide her with motive, means and opportunity for independent action. Given the emphasis on love, the *hetaira's* expertise is often called upon in matters of the heart, although at the same time the *hetairai* themselves are often a complicating factor in the story.

Although characterisation narrowed, in other senses it is much more naturalistic, albeit within fairly restrictive social boundaries. There is also considerable play with the stock characters, with a number of characters clearly constructed as variations on the theme. Extremism in its many forms usually receives its come-uppance, and the kinds of moral perspective on offer are generally seen as reflecting the influence of Aristotle or his pupil Theophrastus, leader of the Peripatetic school. Having said that, the kind of sustained political intervention favoured by our surviving Old Comedy is as absent as the flights of fancy that accompany it there.

Until the twentieth century, New Comedy was known primarily through the Roman comedians Plautus and Terence (late third to second centuries BC), who were, however, adding significant elements themselves or mixing and matching material from a range of authors over a considerable period. New Comedy, specifically that of Menander, is the area of classical literature that has most significantly gained from the discovery of new material on papyrus. This is testament to the enduring popularity of Menander in later antiquity, and his wide appeal. Although Old Comedy did find something of an external market (especially with relatively non-topical comedy like *Thesm.*), it is only with New Comedy that comedy really escapes into the wider Greek world, in terms of both dramatic settings and performance contexts. The still-fragmentary but substantial remains of plays such as the *Samian Woman*, *The Arbitration* (*Epitrepontes*), *The Shield*, *The Sikyonian* and *The Woman from Perinthos* show the general formula.

It is, however, somewhat ironic, that the one play that survives almost complete, *The Old Git* (*Dyskolos*), features a character whose mania for living on his own derives from Old Comic precursors. Rather than an unfortunate accident, the barrier to love here is the old man who rejects society. The wealthy young man who falls in love with his daughter has to find a way round him. Meanwhile the old man's impoverished stepson is highly suspicions of the play-boy's motives, adding still further to the obstacles. Where we end up is familiar territory – the (play)boy gets the girl after rescuing Knemon, the old git, who conveniently falls down a well; the stepson gets the wealth and (as a result) the playboy's sister; Knemon cracks and ends up being tormented by a cook and a servant in a fun comedy ending. All is right with the world. The politics of the play is rather more blatant than elsewhere in Menander, but even though *The Old Git* is a relatively early play, it is a warning that all might not be so familiar in the dramatic world of New Comedy as this account suggests.

How we arrive at Menander in the 320s onwards from late Aristophanes is a complex story and not yet fully understood. The period between the two, which tends to be labelled as Middle Comedy, seems to feature elements familiar from Old Comedy as well as close precursors of Menander in the figure of Alexis. As well as the influence of tragedy (especially the more melodramatic Euripidean plays), and the kind of domestic realism that is an element of *Knights*, *Clouds* or *Wasps*, we have to look at traditions of comedy not well represented in Aristophanes' extant works. From c. 410, parodies of tragedy and/or straight mythological romps (not least featuring the life and loves of Zeus himself) become very fashionable, a movement in which Plato (known as Plato Comicus, to distinguish him from the philosopher) may have been a significant player. But it is becoming increasingly clear that there was a whole series of different types of comedy co-existing with each other in the late fifth century. One line of paternity for a kind of plot-driven domestic comedy appears to be with poets such as Krates – who, according to Aristotle, developed a Sicilian model – and Pherekrates, who was responsible for a series of *hetaira* comedies. Greek comedy, like contemporary popular culture, was and continued to be a complex ecosystem, whose dynamics we are still learning to read.

Further reading

Aristophanes

J. Henderson, *Aristophanes* (4 vols), Cambridge MA: Harvard University Press, 1998–2000 – text and translation.

A. H. Sommerstein, *Aristophanes: The Complete Plays* (12 vols), Warminster: Aris and Phillips, 1980–2001 – text with parallel translation, and increasingly detailed commentary.

The best modern texts (with commentary) are in the Oxford series by various hands on individual plays.

Fragments

W. G. Arnott (ed.), *Alexis: The Fragments*, Cambridge: Cambridge University Press, 1996.

R. Kassel and C. Austin (eds), *Poetae Comici Graeci*, Berlin and New York: de Gruyter, 1983–.

I. C. Storey, *Eupolis: Poet of Old Comedy*, Oxford: Clarendon Press, 2003.

Menander

W. G. Arnott (ed.), *Menander* (3 vols), Cambridge MA: Harvard University Press, 1979–2000.

A. W. Gomme and F. H. Sandbach, *Menander: A Commentary*, Oxford: Clarendon Press, 1973.

F. H. Sandbach, *Menandri reliquiae selectae*, Oxford: Clarendon Press, 1990.

General works

A. M. Bowie, *Aristophanes: Myth, Ritual, Comedy*, Cambridge: Cambridge University Press, 1993.

K. J. Dover, *Aristophanic Comedy*, Berkeley and Los Angeles: University of California Press, 1972.

R. L. Hunter, *The New Comedy of Greece and Rome*, Cambridge: Cambridge University Press, 1985.

D. Konstan, *Greek Comedy and Ideology*, Oxford: Clarendon Press, 1995.

D. M. MacDowell, *Aristophanes and Athens*, Oxford: Clarendon Press, 1995.

J. F. McGlew, *Citizens on Stage: Comedy and Political Culture in the Athenian Democracy*, Ann Arbor: University of Michigan Press, 2002.

E. Segal (ed.), *Oxford Readings in Aristophanes*, Oxford: Clarendon Press, 1996.

M. S. Silk, *Aristophanes and the Definition of Comedy*, Oxford: Clarendon Press, 2000.

C. H. Whitman, *Aristophanes and the Comic Hero*, Cambridge MA: Harvard University Press, 1964.

D. Wiles, *The Masks of Menander: Sign and Meaning in Greek and Roman Performance*, Cambridge: Cambridge University Press, 1991.

J. Wilkins and F. D. Harvey (eds), *The Rivals of Aristophanes*, London: Duckworth, 2000.

For general works on ancient Greek theatre, see chapter 37.

40. Roman Comedy

Alison Sharrock

Rome was a spectacular society – a society, that is, of performance and public display. When we read the fragments of scripted drama which have come down to us as texts (this includes whole plays, but it is still only a tiny proportion of the original output), we should see them as one small aspect of a greater whole, which was the very public Roman world of politics, religion, entertainment and the expression of identity. Although drama flourished for many centuries throughout the Roman world (see chapter 38), a relatively short period in the middle republic saw the production of the plays which soon became the canonical texts of 'Roman comedy', the influence of which was to be felt on comic drama and other genres right up to the present day.

During this period of production, there was no permanent theatre at Rome. That came later, in a different political climate. In the republic, the aristocratic backers of dramatic performances (usually as part of their official state functions) paid for elaborate but temporary theatrical structures. The next time, some other backer would have the chance to perform, by creating his own magnificent edifice. The plays were produced as part of regular religious festivals such as the *ludi Romani* in honour of Jupiter Best and Greatest, or at special events such as the dedication of the temple of the Great Mother, in 191 BC, for which Plautus' *Pseudolus* was written, or funeral games like those for Lucius Aemilius Paullus in 160 BC, at which the *Adelphoe* and the *Hecyra* of Terence were performed.

These two playwrights are the most important survivors to the present day, although others such as Caecilius were at least as famous in antiquity. Plautus produced his plays, twenty-one of which survive (although some are incomplete), between around 205 and 184 BC, whereas Terence wrote, between 166 and 160 BC, the six plays which are all extant. All these plays belong to the genre *fabula palliata*, or 'comedy wearing a little Greek cloak'. The characters and settings are Greek (although perhaps we should say, 'Greek', for they often tell us more about Roman perceptions of Greeks than about Greeks themselves, and their underlying Romanness sometimes peeks through). The plays themselves are in some sense translated from the plays of Greek New Comedy, which flourished in the Hellenistic age and is most famously represented by Menander. But the idea of translation is misleading. Both Plautus and Terence developed and adapted their models, and hybridised them with native Italian dramatic forms to produce this very Roman Republican genre. Nor was their relationship with their 'Greek originals' always the same: we know that there are some passages which constitute near-translations of Greek lines, while others are free invention, and it seems very likely that a similar variation applies also to whole plays. The plays are written in verse: mostly iambic senarii (a form of spoken verse which is evocative of everyday speech) and trochaic septenarii (a verse-form sometimes described as 'recitative'), but also including a dazzling range of other metres in the sung parts (*cantica*) of the plays. Terence's limpid, clear Latin meant that his plays became school texts from antiquity onwards. The language of Plautus, by contrast, is at first difficult for modern readers, being not only archaic and to some extent colloquial but also spectacular and magnificent, an essential vehicle of his humour. It repays the effort.

Both comfortable recognition and surprising reversals of expectation are creative sources of humour, and both were employed to good effect by the Roman comedians. Plautus and Terence used what we, perhaps unhelpfully, call 'stock plots' and 'stock characters' to people their plays, relying on the audience's enjoyment of seeing old favourites like the dopey young lover, the braggart warrior, the angry old man, and most of all the clever slave whose job it is to deceive his master and stage-manage the play. The dramatists relied also on the audience being able to make a fair stab at how the play would turn out in the end, even when they were not told the story either through the common inheritance of myth (as was usual with Greek tragedy) or by an expository prologue (as was common in Greek New Comedy and used occasionally by Plautus). You can be fairly sure that lovers will get together, that slaves will triumph (or at least, will not suffer even if their plan slips), and that social roles will not undergo any lasting subversion, however much they may be disrupted during the play-time. Within these bounds of friendly familiarity, however, the playwrights constantly provoke laughter by the unexpected: the conventional 'running slave' routine is performed instead by a god pretending to be a slave (Plautus *Amphitruo*); a neatly planned trick is undermined by the young lover, who was meant to be the beneficiary, changing his mind about his love-object (Plautus *Epidicus*); warning is given of a deceit-plot, in which the very warning itself constitutes part of the deceit (Plautus *Pseudolus*); the best-laid plans of clever slave and angry father are both blown to pieces by a plot-twist which has been hinted at, but in such a way that no one has believed it (Terence *Andria*); a supposedly clever slave is tricked by a woman slave in the other house into confessing all to the master (Terence *Eunuchus*); or simply a verse posing as expressing proper Roman morality is undercut at its ending by a grammatical surprise, and a reversal of intention (Plautus *Bacchides*).

Critics of Roman comedy sometimes imply that the existence of 'stock plots' means that the plays are 'all the same'. It is very tempting, particularly in a short, introductory essay like this, to offer a 'typical' plot, but although it is true that plot-elements are repeated and some plays conform to general 'types', in fact there is no 'typical plot' of a Roman comedy. Some of the more common elements, however, with examples in each case are these: a young man wants to enjoy a prostitute, but lacks the money to pay her keeper, so his slave finds some way of cheating the lover's father of the money (Plautus *Pseudolus*, *Bacchides*; Terence *Heauton Timoroumenos*); a young man is in love with a girl who is not legally or socially available for marriage, until it conveniently turns out that she is the long-lost daughter of a citizen, sometimes the man next door, and so the marriage can go ahead (Plautus *Poenulus*, *Rudens*; Terence *Andria*, and many variants); children may be lost by abduction (Plautus *Menaechmi*, *Captivi*), by exposure (Plautus *Cistellaria*; Terence *Heauton Timoroumenos*), or by illegitimacy (Plautus *Epidicus*; Terence *Phormio*); a soldier is a rival to the young lover, and is often accompanied by a parasite who flatters and amuses him, while also exposing him (the soldier) to the audience's ridicule (Plautus *Miles Gloriosus*; Terence *Eunuchus*); some old fathers are anti-comic characters (agelasts) who try to stop their sons having fun, but others are ridiculous old would-be lovers themselves, and act as rivals to their sons (Plautus *Asinaria*, *Casina*, *Mercator*); their wives are often formidable characters, or 'nagging old bags' (depending on your point of view), who bring a rich dowry and so control their husbands (the three just mentioned, plus Terence *Phormio*). In general, however, these stock elements are just the substantial building blocks out of which the comic and dramatic essence of the play is created.

One of the most entertaining and important aspects of a Roman comedy is its emphasis on disguise, deceit and implied questions of identity. Very many plays involve a trick of some sort: persuade a dupe that his eyes deceive him, and that the girl he thought he saw kissing her lover was not his own master's concubine but her twin sister (Plautus *Miles Gloriosus*); intercept a letter which releases a prostitute from the pimp (Plautus

Pseudolus); pretend that someone is a stranger hunting his long-lost daughters (Plautus *Poenulus* – a nice one, this, in that it turns out that the stranger really *is* hunting his lost daughters, but the controlling clever slave thinks he is just a good actor!); dress up a male slave as the young bride who is to be 'married' to the old master's slave so that the old master can get in first (Plautus *Casina* – the old master gets a predictably nasty shock!); dress up a young man as a eunuch-slave who is presented as a gift to his older brother's prostitute-mistress, so that the younger man can get close to the beautiful girl he has just seen arriving at the prostitute's house (Terence *Eunuchus*). This last example is a shocking one to modern sensibilities, because the young man rapes the girl in the middle of the play, off-stage of course, and although rape and seduction are frequent plot-elements in Roman comedies this is the only instance of such an act taking place during the play itself. The young man marries his victim in the end, as sophisticated Roman theatregoers will have anticipated, when the girl is recognised as a citizen. The movement from disguised eunuch to adolescent rapist to legal husband dramatises for this young man the process of growing up and finding an adult, stable identity: the story of coming to adulthood is a favourite not only of this genre but of many others, including Greek tragedy, which is an important intertext for Roman comedy.

All these deceits have a long history in trickster-narratives in drama and other genres before and after Plautus and Terence. Part of their power for comedy derives from the humour of misunderstanding, which some theorists have seen as an inherent aspect of what makes something funny: the audience laughs out of a sense of superiority towards the confusion of the poor dupes on the stage. One particularly popular version of the comedy of misunderstanding is that which hinges on double identities, which Plautus played out in detail in two 'twinning' plays, *Amphitruo* and *Menaechmi*, later to become the models for Shakespeare's *The Comedy of Errors*. *Amphitruo* is, in my view, the funnier play. There are (as in Shakespeare's play) two sets of doubles: the gods Mercury and Jupiter take on the appearance and identity of the Theban hero Amphitruo and his slave Sosia, so that Jupiter can pursue an affair with Amphitruo's wife Alcmena without her consciousness of adultery. A further set of twins will ensue, because Alcmena is pregnant twice over, once from her husband and once from mighty Jove, whose child will be Hercules. The play ends with the miraculous birth of the hero and Amphitruo's acceptance of the situation and reconciliation with his wife. This play is unusual for being the only *palliata* to have a mythological theme, to involve gods as main characters, and to show an adulterous wife (albeit unknowingly so). In other ways, however, it is typical Plautus, with larger-than-life characters, magnificent vocabulary, and a great big mess of confusion which all comes right in the end.

All the plays of Plautus and Terence end in reconciliation and celebration, often including a marriage or pseudo-marriage. It can sometimes be difficult for modern readers to see what was funny about Roman comedy, but even without the music, the spectacle, the choreography and the entire cultural setting, the bare texts still give us a taste of the comic spirit which pervaded these plays.

Further reading

The Latin texts of Plautus and Terence are available in OCT. The Cambridge Greek and Latin Classics at present contains editions of Plautus *Amphitruo* (D. Christenson, 2000), *Casina* (W. T. MacCary and M. M. Willcock, 1976), and *Menaechmi* (A. S. Gratwick, 1993), plus Terence *Adelphoe* (R. H. Martin, 1976) and *Eunuchus* (J. A. Barsby, 1999). Translations of all the plays are available in the series edited by D. R. Slavitt and P. Bovie, *The Complete Roman Drama in Translation* (Baltimore: Johns Hopkins University Press, 1995).

R. C. Beacham, *The Roman Theatre and its Audience*, London and New York: Routledge, 1991.

S. Goldberg, *Understanding Terence*, Princeton: Princeton University Press, 1986.

E. S. Gruen, *Culture and National Identity in Republican Rome*, London: Duckworth, 1993.

R. L. Hunter, *The New Comedy of Greece and Rome*, Cambridge: Cambridge University Press, 1985.

D. Konstan, *Roman Comedy*, Ithaca: Cornell University Press, 1983.

A. R. Sharrock, *Fabulous Artifice: Poetics and Playfulness in Roman Comedy*, forthcoming.

N. W. Slater, *Plautus in Performance: The Theatre of the Mind* (2nd edn), Amsterdam: Harwood Academic, 2000.

41. Greek Lyric Verse: Melic, Elegiac and Iambic

Emily Greenwood

The diverse types of ancient Greek song that fall outside of epic and tragedy are referred to collectively as 'lyric' poetry. Unlike the English adjective 'lyric' and its synonym 'lyrical', which can mean 'expressing deep personal emotion', in the context of ancient Greek literature 'lyric' translates the Greek adjective *lyrikos*, meaning poetry that was sung in accompaniment to the lyre (*lyra* in ancient Greek). However, this is already a problematic definition because not all poetry that we refer to as lyric was accompanied by the lyre; sometimes a reed instrument called the *aulos* was used, and sometimes no musical accompaniment was involved. Traditionally, scholars held that this poetry – in contrast to the recited narrative of epic – was poetry that expressed the subjective emotions of an individual, hence the connotations of the English adjectives 'lyric' and 'lyrical'. Now scholars are more likely to treat the personal voices in these poems as personae that do not necessarily bear any relation to the emotions of the poets who composed them.

Lyric poetry subdivides into 'melic' poetry, which basically means sung poetry; 'elegy', which is defined by metrical form – elegy makes use of a two-line unit called the elegiac couplet in which a line of dactylic hexameter is followed by a shorter line; and 'iambus', which was written primarily in the iambic trimeter, but the name of the metre probably derives from the genre iambus, and not the other way around (see chapter 65). These categories are unsatisfactory, in that elegy and iambus could be sung and hence could also be described as 'melic' poetry. Furthermore, the different categories are not comparable since they point to different aspects of the poetry: 'melic' is a musical definition, 'elegy' is a metrical definition, whereas 'iambus' refers to a genre and its characteristic subject matter. A further way in which lyric poetry is subdivided is to distinguish between poems that were performed by a solo singer (monody), and poems that were composed for performance by choruses (choral lyric). However, poets such as Stesichorus and Ibycus (see table 41.1) appear to have composed monody which may have featured the participation of a chorus in performance, to 'act out' the song. Hence the distinction between monody and choral lyric does not account for all the Greek lyric poetry that survives. The fact that these categories are artificial and potentially misleading should prompt us to approach Greek lyric poetry with an open mind, without preconceptions about what 'type' of poetry we are reading. The poems themselves are invariably much better guides to this question than abstract typologies such as 'melic', 'elegaic' or 'sympotic elegy'.

This dissatisfaction with invented, generic labels is reflected in recent scholarship in ancient Greek lyric poetry, which increasingly tends to focus on the more inclusive notion of Greek 'song culture', a category that highlights the similarities and continuities between different kinds of poetry. Homeric epic, choral lyric, lyric monody and Attic tragedy all share myths, and show awareness of the broader tradition of Greek culture and song to which they belong. Approaching Greek poetry in terms of 'song culture' allows us to think about these poems in close relation to the contexts in which they may have been performed, with all that this implies. Who was in the audience? What was the location of the performance? Were the

Table 41.1 Overview of Greek lyric poets

Melic		→	← Elegaic	← Iambic
Choral	(Solo singer + chorus)	Monody		
			Callinus (Ephesus) 7th century	Archilochus (Paros-Thasos) c. 680–640
			Tyrtaeus (Sparta) mid-7th century	
Alcman (Sparta) c. 650–600	Stesichorus (Southern Itlay) c. 630–550	Sappho (Lesbos) c. 630–after 595	Mimnermus (Colophon) 7th century	Semonides (Amorgos) c. 650–600
		Alcaeus (Lesbos) c. 630–570	Solon (Athens) c. 640–560	
	Ibycus (Rhegium–Samos) c. 6th century	Anacreon (Teos) c. 570–500	Xenophanes (Colophon) c. 565–473	
		Simonides (Ceos) c. 557/6–468/7	Theognis (Megara) 6th century; but the *Theognidea* 7th–5th centuries	Hipponax (Ephesus) second half of 6th century
Bacchylides (Ceos) c. 520–440				
Pindar (Boeotia) c. 520–440		Timocreon (Rhodes) 5th century		

All dates are BC. The arrows (←→) in the first row indicate that the divisions between melic, elegiac and iambic are fluid, and that several poets spanned these categories. This table is not exhaustive; I have stuck to the most important, canonical poets. We know of other poets, such as Susarion, Euenus, Praxilla, Cydias, Pratinas, Telesilla and Lamprocles, but in some cases their identity is not certain, the attribution of fragments is disputed, and the context of their poems is obscure.

songs performed for a specific occasion? And how did all these different factors shape the verse? Emphasising 'song culture' also reminds us that the notion of poetry as we know it had yet to be invented; in fact, these poems are part of the process of invention. Two excellent studies that focus on the performance of Greek lyric poetry are Eva Stehle's *Performance and Gender in Ancient Greece* and Andrew Ford's *Origins of Criticism* (chs 1–3). The latter gives especial prominence to the notion of 'song culture'.

In this chapter I have chosen to highlight themes that are central to contemporary debates about Greek lyric poetry. In privileging this thematic approach it has not been possible to mention every 'lyric' poet whose works survive, or to offer comprehensive discussions of the poets that I do mention.

Innovation

It is often said that all literature is about other literature, and that every work of literature begins with previous works of literature. Literary genealogy tries to detect the flow of influence between different types or families of literature. However, to speak of 'genealogies' is misleading, because there is nothing natural about literary genres. While every archaic Greek poem might conform to type in part, the poems also proclaim their innovativeness. Hence, although it is important to be alert to the generic type that might lurk behind a poem (the *epithalamium* or wedding song behind fragment 105a of Sappho, for example), we must acknowledge that individual poets do not simply 'use' or 'follow' these types, but instead transform them. Thus genre can never be a sufficient guide to the interpretation of a poem, but it can serve to highlight the presence of both tradition and innovation within a poem.

All of the poets whose works I will refer to in this chapter were conscious of the fact that they were not performing epic, but epic was still a prominent part of the cultural landscape, and poetry continued to take its bearings from epic. One could argue that to concretise 'epic' as a genre is itself an artificial invention, since Homeric epic bears traces (whether actual or potential) of other genres (tragedy, invective, satire, didactic poetry). There are no 'pure' genres. Archaic Greek lyric poets signal their awareness of existing mythological traditions and the way in which different poets have handled them. The poet Alcaeus from the island of Lesbos (c. 630–570 BC) refers to the version of the Trojan War that we find in Homer's *Iliad* with the phrase 'as the story tells' (Alcaeus fr. 42). Conversely, Stesichorus – a poet from southern Italy who composed his poetry in roughly the same period – famously revoked the Homeric tradition about Helen of Troy's adultery in his 'palinode' (*palinōidia* meant 'recantation', or 'reverse song' in ancient Greek):

> That story is not true:
> you did not go on the well-benched ships,
> nor did you reach Troy's citadel.
>
> (Stesichorus fr. 192)

In the course of his first 'Olympian' ode – an epinikian (victory) choral lyric poem composed to celebrate a victory at the Olympic games by Hieron in 476 BC – the poet Pindar proclaims that he will not follow previous accounts of the myth of Pelops, son of Tantalus: 'contrary to earlier accounts I shall proclaim . . .' (line 36). In fact, Pindar underscores his uniqueness by alienating himself from the existing tradition:

> For me, however, it is impossible to call
> any of the blessed gods a glutton: I stand apart.
>
> (*Olympian* 1, lines 52–3)

We can interpret this claim as both a literary and an ethical statement; what is important is that innovation, or the uniqueness of a particular poem, only emerges within the context of a pre-existing tradition. In the case of lyric poetry this tradition frequently looks back to epic poetry.

Winged words: poetry travelling

Although scholars have attempted to clarify the original circumstances and contexts for the performances of Greek lyric poetry, it is important to appreciate that even during the poets' own lifetimes these poems travelled. Sometimes they travelled quite literally, in the sense that the poets themselves performed their poems all over the Greek world. The poet Simonides (from the Cycladic island of Ceos) travelled to Athens to benefit from the patronage of Hipparchus, the brother of Hippias, who was tyrant of Athens at the time. Similarly, the poet Anacreon of Teos was poet in residence at the court of Polycrates, tyrant of Samos, and subsequently in Athens, also at the invitation of Hipparchus (c. 520 BC). Perhaps the best example of 'travelling' poetry is the poet Pindar, who accepted commissions to compose 'epinician' odes in celebration of athletic victors from all over the Greek world. The theme of travel is an important theme in these odes, as Pindar describes his role as being to compose a poem that will accompany the victors home and publish their fame at home and abroad (see Kurke, *Traffic in Praise*, chs 1–2).

However, the poems also circulated independently in an early form of 'publication' whereby the poems of Archilochus, or Sappho, or Solon, or Tyrtaeus could be taken up and performed by other singers, both in their lifetimes, and in subsequent generations (re-performance). Consequently, it is misleading to speak of a single, original performance context for Greek lyric poetry; instead, we must think of a variety of performances and occasions for performance in the ancient Greek world, some of which were far removed from their original context. One of the implications of such travel is that it makes it difficult to appeal to a single interpretative community in order to make sense of the poems. It is significant that many studies that privilege the performance context of Greek lyric poetry do not consider the question of reperformance.

There is yet another sense in which these were 'travelling' poems: some of the poets whose works survived clearly envisaged a literary afterlife for themselves. One of the many formulaic phrases that recurs in Homeric epic is 'winged words' (*epea pteroenta*). The neuter noun *epea* means words, but also whole utterances and, ultimately, whole poems. The conceit of 'winged words' can be understood in different ways, both spatially and temporally: first, words carry on the voice and news spreads geographically through 'word of mouth' – the ability of words to travel in this way makes them metaphorically 'winged'. Second, words get passed down from generation to generation, by oral tradition, and so words travel across time. These two aspects are encompassed in the concept of *kleos* (fame, glory, recognition), which has been explained as the 'acoustic renown' that men (it was not usually thought appropriate for women to aspire to *kleos*) gained as a result of great deeds, whether on the battlefield, in politics, in the athletics arena or for pious acts. This familiar idea is reworked by the sixth-century poet Theognis, from the polis of Megara, who informs Cyrnus – the addressee of several of his fragments – that he has 'given him wings' (lines 237–9):

> To you I have given wings, on which you may fly aloft
> above the boundless sea and all the earth
> with ease.

He then goes on to claim that Cyrnus will gain immortality (or infamy, given the ambivalent tone of the poem) through having his name repeated in Theognis' poetry (lines 251–2):

> . . . even to those who are not yet born, you will be
> alike a theme of song, so long as earth and sun exist.

The lure of the fragment

The majority of surviving Greek lyric poetry is fragmentary, and this fragmentariness heightens the complexity of the poetry. The fact that we have scant idea about the performance context for these poems seems trivial when confronted with a two-line fragment, which could be described as lines missing a poem, let alone missing a performance context. However, it is sometimes the shortest fragments that have elicited the most extensive and intense scholarly discussions. Precisely because fragments are 'out of context' they allow more scope for interpretation – the reader has to work hard to supply a context that will explain the fragment. The best example of the lure of the fragment is the poetry of Sappho, a sixth-century poet from Lesbos. Sappho is also enticing as a result of the fact that hers is one of the few surviving female voices in Greek literature; consequently her fragments have been subjected to close, intimate scrutiny.

In antiquity it was thought that fragment 105a of Sappho belonged to an *epithalamium* – a wedding song that anticipates the wedding night:

> Like the sweet apple that reddens on the highest bough,
> high on the highest bough, and the apple gatherers have forgotten it –
> no, they have not forgotten it completely, but they could not reach it.

The apple furnishes a comparison for the nubile young bride – supposedly the addressee or 'object' of the wedding song – who, like the apple, is 'ripening'. However, for some contemporary readers of Sappho this generic explanation, while not wrong exactly, has seemed pedestrian. Anne Carson proposes that fragment 105a is a comment on Sappho's understanding of the psychology of erotic love: the apple that eludes the apple-pickers is a metaphor for what Carson calls 'the reach' of love – the notion that love is characterised by longing, striving and incompleteness (see Carson, *Eros the Bittersweet*, pp. 26–9). If we look outside of this fragment at Sappho's oeuvre as a whole, then the sweetness of the apple might suggest Sappho's famous description of love (*erōs*) as 'sweetbitter' (*glukupikros*): love starts sweet and then becomes bitter (fr. 130). The apple then becomes a symbol for a beguiling object of desire whose sweetness will fade, and which will evoke a dream of love that will prove unattainable.

This little fragment epitomises what I have referred to as 'the lure of the fragment'. Its incompleteness and the fact that the circumstances and occasion for its performance are unclear invite imaginative acts of interpretation, but these interpretations are frustrated by the realisation that they are provisional and partial. This point can be made of all literary interpretation, in so far as the meanings of poems are continually negotiated and renegotiated, but in the case of poetic fragments the incompleteness is literal, as opposed to metaphorical.

The best interpretations of such fragments neither seek to ignore the historical context of the fragments by treating the poems as free-floating artefacts, nor consider 'historical' readings of the poems a sufficient end. Furthermore, there are two different kinds of history to consider: the historical context of the fragment (including the occasion for its composition, and the circumstances of its performance) and its reception history – the way in which different readers have read and interpreted this fragment throughout history. Both 'histories' are relevant and important. It is possible to entertain the view that Sappho's self-conscious preoccupation with similes is a comment on the inadequacy of language as a way of representing the world, while acknowledging that these similes were influenced by cultural and generic conventions at the time of composition.

Authorship and authority

In the previous section we have seen the potential for fragments of a few lines' length to entice scholars into complex interpretations. Through a process of continuous reading by diverse cultures in different periods of history, the fragments of Greek lyric poetry have accrued many different meanings. A similar process occurs when we turn to the subject of authorship. The literary critics associated with the library of Alexandria assembled a canon of Greek lyric poetry that recognised nine poets: Alcman, Alcaeus, Sappho, Stesichorus, Ibycus, Anacreon, Simonides, Bacchylides and Pindar (this canon is attested in the first century BC). However, the reputation of these poets was established well before the existence of the library of Alexandria, and it seems likely that these big names attracted poems composed by others. Not every fragment in the corpus of Sappho's poetry was composed by Sappho; there are several fragments whose authorship is disputed. More strikingly, the reputation of the elegiac poet Theognis seems to have absorbed the poems of other singers. Theognis is thought to have lived in the sixth century BC, but some of the lines in the *Theognidea* (the name given to the corpus of poetry attributed to Theognis, which runs to 1,400 lines of verse) can be dated to the seventh century, and others to the fifth century, spanning (roughly) the period 625 BC to 479 BC – an unfeasible lifespan for a single poet. Although we can point to an historical author called Theognis whose poetry forms the core of the so-called *Theognidea*, the name 'Theognis' also acts as an 'author function' – a successful author who attracts emulation and to whom subsequent generations attributed poems that appeared to be 'in the manner of Theognis'.

This idea of the 'author function' has been well documented in the case of Shakespeare, whose reputation for literary genius has meant that a single playwright has been accredited with plays and poems that were sometimes written collaboratively, if not by other people altogether. The related concept of the 'genius' of the author feeds back into the way in which readers interpret the fragments. Every single fragment has to justify the genius of its author – this is another reason why fragments, such as that of Sappho discussed above, evoke highly complex interpretations.

In the case of Theognis this development is particularly ironic, since one of the surviving fragments addresses the very issue of how to 'fix' one's words, to ensure that they will not be appropriated or altered:

> Kyrnos, as I work my craft let a seal be set upon
> these words of mine, and they will never be
> stolen unremarked,

nor will anyone change the good that is there to
something worse;
(Theognis lines 19–21)

Although there is no clear consensus about what is envisaged by the 'seal', and although we may be dealing with concepts of ownership rather than 'authorship' (see the excellent discussion by Ford, 'Seal of Theognis'), the poet clearly seeks a way of protecting the identity and integrity of his poetry as his possession, perhaps in response to the wide circulation of his poems in his lifetime.

One of the problems with looking for concepts of authorship in archaic Greek lyric poetry is that there was then no analogous term, and arguably no analogous idea. Instead of looking for signs of authorship as such, we can look for claims to authority and expertise. Since the notion of authorship is premised on the idea of authority, claims to authority can point us towards the conception that Greek lyric poets had of their role and standing in society; it can inform us of their self-image as producers and performers of knowledge.

When we speak of the poet's voice in archaic Greek lyric, we need to consider the extent to which poets had a voice, in the metaphorical sense. Did their voices count, and what kind of social presence did they have? The bards (*aoidoi*) and later rhapsodes who recited epic poetry had a literal voice, in that they related stories, myths and traditions to communities all over the Greek world, and in this played a crucial role in sustaining and also inventing social and cultural memory. However, they did not fulfil this function in their own voice. Although the narrators of Greek epic poetry can be self-reflexive, they are self-effacing in comparison to the lyric poets. Individual authorship (I use this term with the proviso outlined above) is much more pronounced in archaic Greek lyric poetry.

We gain an insight into the contest for recognition in which poets were implicated when we read fragment 2.11–14 of the sixth-century poet Xenophanes (a fragment in elegiac couplets), which protests about the disproportionate amount of attention and honour paid to victorious athletes, contrasted with society's failure to appreciate his specialist wisdom (*sophiē*):

. . . for superior to the strength
of men and of horses is the expertise (*sophiē*)
that I lay claim to.
But thought on this point is very haphazard, and it
is not right
to give preference to strength over serviceable
expertise (*sophiē*).

Xenophanes is a good example of the breadth of poetry in this period, and the inappropriateness of modern notions of the poet. Xenophanes' works have been preserved and studied both as examples of early Greek philosophy (so-called 'Presocratic' philosophy), and as 'poetry' (see chapter 48). Both 'philosophy' and 'poetry' are potentially misleading terms in this context. The Greek noun *philosophia* originally meant a passion for knowledge and the pursuit of knowledge, and the Greek verb *poiein*, from which 'poetry' derives, meant 'to make'. So we could say that Xenophanes made verses in the quest for knowledge and about the quest for knowledge, and used his poetry to showcase his knowledge.

Contexts

Ancient Greek lyric poetry is not read solely, or even primarily, as poetry, in the sense that we understand this word; instead, many scholars of ancient Greece seek to relate the poetry to its historical context and the institutional context in which it was performed. Some scholars go so far as to say that this poetry is about social performance(s), and that the poetry is the medium for the performance. Hence, in order to understand the poetry, we need to understand, where, how and for whom it was performed. One of the most important institutions for the understanding of the context of Greek non-dramatic poetry is the symposium, which can be loosely translated as 'drinking party'. The symposium was an institution that covered a spectrum of different gatherings: religious celebrations, military messes (see the performance of Tyrtaeus' elegies in Spartan messes mentioned below), public (civic) meals and private parties. In turn, these private parties combined various flavours: ranging from political intrigue, cultural performance and intellectual debate to gratuitous hedonism. All symposia were political, in that they all took place within polis communities. However, some symposia seem to have acted as a focus for factions whose political interests were not shared by the community at large (the 'self-defining interest group'; Stehle, *Performance and Gender*, p. 214).

In much of the poetry of Alcaeus, the symposium is an occasion for venting political grievances and revolutionary designs against an individual called Pittacus, who was the tyrant of Mytilene 590–580 BC (Alcaeus represents Pittacus as a power-seizing tyrant, but Aristotle *Politics* 1285a29ff records that Pittacus was an *aisumnētēs* – an elected tyrant). The geographer Strabo, writing in the first century BC, tells us that the political poems of Alcaeus were referred to as *stasiōtika* (revolutionary poems). However, we cannot assume that the audiences of Alcaeus' stasiotic poems were invariably like-minded. One of the concerns of politically charged poetry is how to distinguish your true friends from your enemies, and your rightful peers from social upstarts. This is a recurrent theme in the elegies of Theognis of Megara, for example. In lines 681–2 of the *Theognidea*, the poet describes his verses as *ainigmata* (riddles), which carry a veiled message for 'the noble'. The reference to encoded messages implies that there were potentially many different audiences or 'interpretative communities' for sympotic elegy (elegy performed at a symposium).

The symposium was also a locus for politics of a different kind; one of the elegiac fragments of the poet Anacreon discusses the *literary* politics of the symposium, by dismissing quarrels and war as inappropriate subject matter for this context:

> I don't like the man who, while drinking beside the
> full mixing bowl,
> talks about quarrels and warfare with its tears,
> but rather one who mingles the Muses' and
> Aphrodite's splendid gifts
> together and so keeps the charms of festivity in
> mind.
>
> (Anacreon elegy 2)

This fragment can be read as a *recusatio* (a later Latin term for the trope where a poet rejects other genres in favour of the one that he is about to sing): quarrels and war are fine for epic, but not for sympotic elegy. However, it also prescribes a particular agenda for the symposium, by promoting festivity at the expense of heavy political themes. Andrew Ford has called this kind of literary politics 'sympotic ethics', in which the context and protocol of the symposium determine the nature of the poetry (see Ford, *Origins of Criticism*, ch. 1).

This fragment tells us about Anacreon's preferred symposium, or the kind of sympotic atmosphere that his poems promote; other examples of sympotic elegy are overtly martial in tone. The poetry of Tyrtaeus, who lived in Sparta in the second half of the seventh century BC, is often referred to as 'martial' elegy, since it speaks tirelessly of war and exhorts its Spartan audiences to pursue courage in battle. Although poems travelled throughout the Greek world, the primary audience for Tyrtaeus' poetry is a Spartan one, and the original historical backdrop for the poems was a struggle known as the Second Messenian War. Some fragments, such as fragment 11 of Tyrtaeus, suggest that they were actually performed in the midst of battle:

> Feel no fear before the multitude of men, do not
> run in panic,
> but let each man bear his shield straight toward
> the fore-fighters.

The Athenian politician Lycurgus supports this tradition; in a speech delivered in 330 BC, he tells his audience that it is a law in Sparta that when Spartans take to the field, they are summoned to the king's tent to hear a rendition of Tyrtaeus' poetry to inspire them for the battle ahead (Lycurgus *Against Leocrates* 107). Notwithstanding Lycurgus' testimony, Ewen Bowie has argued convincingly that what we have here is not so much a poetic briefing in the field of war as a poem sung in a dining mess or a symposium (Bowie, 'Miles ludens?').

Similar questions about context are raised by the poetry of Solon, who held the archonship of Athens in the year 594/3 BC, and is studied both as an Athenian politician and lawgiver and as a poet. Fragments 1–3 of Solon allegedly relate to an incident when Athens was at war with Megara over territorial rights to the island of Salamis. The most extensive account of this incident is found in Plutarch's *Life of Solon* (chapter 8), which was written some 600 years after the events it describes. According to Plutarch, Solon pretended to be mad (to get around a prohibition which prescribed the death penalty for inciting the Athenians to fight for Salamis), and, disguised as a herald, recited a poem in the Agora urging the Athenians to fight for Salamis. The ancient biographical tradition about Solon asks us to believe that Solon's 'Salamis Elegy' was actually delivered in the agora to an audience of citizens. When we turn to the poem itself, the poet proclaims:

> I myself have come as a herald from lovely Salamis,
> having arranged words into song in place of a public speech.

The poem is held out as a substitute for a public speech. So rather than interpreting this to mean that Solon rushed into the Agora and sang a song in place of a conventional speech, we could equally interpret this as meaning that Solon circulated a song, instead of speaking in public. The account given by Plutarch may be true, but it might also be an elaborate tradition woven around a kernel of truth, or inferred from the poem itself. At any rate, we should not assume that such accounts are true; often they derive from the attempt to make sense of poems that had been passed down from archaic and classical Greece, just as we attempt to make sense of these poems now, in different ways.

Biography

Once Greek lyric poetry ceased to be performed in its original contexts, and once it became divorced from the religious and social institutions that helped to make sense of it, a fallacious biographical tradition set in, whereby – to put it crudely – any first-person utterances in the poems were presumed to reflect the direct voice and the biographical reality of the poet. This fallacy has been most fiercely challenged in the case of choral lyric. In choral lyric there is a discrepancy between the (singular) poet who composed the song and the (plural) chorus who performed it. A further complication is introduced by the fact that this chorus, in the plural, can refer to itself in the first person, either collectively or through the chorus leader. In the case of Alcman, a poet who wrote a series of *partheneia* (songs for performance by choruses of young women at religious festivals), this led to the tradition that he was obsessed with young girls, since in many of the poems a first-person voice expresses desire for a woman in the chorus. Conversely, scholars such as Claude Calame have argued that these maiden-choruses were united by homoerotic desire, often expressed towards the chorus leader, and that the 'I' is the voice of the chorus, not the poet (see Calame, *Choruses of Young Women in Ancient Greece*). In the case of Pindar's choral lyric, where the first person voice in the poem shifts between first–person singular and first-person plural pronouns, Mary Lefkowitz has suggested that we regard the 'I' in Pindar as an 'autobiographical fiction' – a performance-related persona or invention (Lefkowitz, 'First person in Pindar reconsidered'). This distinction between the poet/ author and the first person 'I' is sometimes referred to as 'deauthorisation'.

The biographical debate also applies to monody, which was performed by a solo singer. In fact, ancient biographers were particularly eager to probe poems in which individual poets appeared to discuss their love-lives, or private vendettas, in order to infer who Sappho loved and how, or the relationship of the poet Archilochus to the objects of his abuse, for example. One indication that we may be dealing with a typecast depiction of the psychology of love and erotic desire, rather than an incident from the biography of the poet, is the recurrent phrase 'once again'. This suggests a common, repeated experience, which the audience can relate to. The poet's persona, rather than the poet himself or herself, plays up or enacts the drama of love. Take, for example, some of the lyrics of Anacreon of Teos: '*Once again* Love has beaten me like a blacksmith' (fr. 413), or '*Once more* tossing a purple ball / at me, Love with the golden hair/ points to a girl . . .' (fr. 358). Sappho does it too in fr. 130:

> *Once again* Love drives me on, that loosener of limbs,
> bittersweet creature against which nothing can be done.

To borrow a phrase from Anne Pippin Burnett, the world depicted in these poems is a 'song-created world (which may or may not reflect the real)' (*Three Archaic Poets*, p. 6).

Biographical fictions have also been detected in so-called iambus. Iambic poetry has ritual connections with the celebration of Demeter and Dionysus. It is typically scatalogocial and offensive; to take Hipponax – a sixth-century poet from Ephesus – as an example (although, on the basis of the fragments that survive, Hipponax's iambus is more lewd than that of Archilochus and Semonides), his poems contain copious references to prostitutes, shit, anal sex, cursing and punch-ups – all depicted in graphic language and with graphic imagery. Some scholars draw an analogy between the genre of iambus and the modern musical genre of rap, which is notorious for its explicit and transgressive lyrics, but which is 'heard' differently by its primary audiences, for whom such rude lyrics are an inalienable part of the genre.

Iambus is characterised by invective, sometimes directed at a group of people and sometimes at named individuals: in the case of poem 7 of Semonides (a misogynistic satire) women are the object of abuse, but in Hipponax and Archilochus individuals are singled out for ridicule and scorn. In several surviving fragments Hipponax vents his spleen on a sculptor called Bupalus, and Archilochus attacks the family of Lycambes, primarily by claiming to expose the easy sexual availability of Lycambes' daughters. The ancient biographical tradition recorded that the ferocity of this poetic invective had led both Bupalus and Lycambes and his daughters to commit suicide. However, it is now believed that these named individuals are fictional characters who only exist in the poems, and that the professed enmity is contrived to satisfy the expectations of iambus. Again, such fictional enmity is a well-attested phenomenon in rap music; see, for example the song 'Ms. Jackson' by the group Outkast (from the album *Stankonia*, Arista Records, 2000).

Poetry and history

Another consequence of the fragmentariness of Greek lyric poetry is that the corpus is provisional; every so often new works surface which force us to revise our understanding (or misunderstanding) about the range of lyric poetry and its potential subject matter. In the twentieth century, the best example of a find that forced scholars to reconceptualise ancient Greek poetry was the publication of a papyrus fragment (originally many, piecemeal papyrus fragments) from Oxyrhynchus containing an elegy on the battle of Plataea (479 BC) by the poet Simonides (elegy 11). This fragment (*P. Oxy.* 3965) is referred to as 'the New Simonides'.

As it stands, this poem relates the struggle of the Spartans and their allies at Plataea to the epic struggle of the Trojan War. Hitherto the narrative of the battle of Plataea had been associated with the prose history of Herodotus (see book 9 of Herodotus' *Histories*), so it is intriguing to find the same historical battle treated in a poetic medium, in a radically different genre. This find has forced classicists to think more carefully about the relationship between prose and poetry, as co-existing media that could discuss the same events. It is likely that Simonides was commissioned to compose the poem and this, too, throws an interesting light on the position of a Herodotus or a Thucydides, both of whom attempted to write free-thinking accounts of past and contemporary, or near-contemporary, events (see chapter 49). If poets were commissioned to tailor narratives of these same events to the interests and glory of different audiences, this makes the task of the historians all the more countercultural. Unlike the new prose genre of history, Simonides' 'Plataea Elegy' is not apologetic about viewing the present in terms of the mythical past, since he is writing within a continuous poetic tradition reaching back to Homeric epic, in language that echoes Homeric language.

Further reading

Translations

When reading literature in translation, especially poetry, it is a good idea to consult more than one translation. The following are recommended (the translations used in this chapter are taken from Miller's anthology):

A. Miller, *Greek Lyric: An Anthology in Translation*, Indianapolis: Hackett, 1996.

M. L. West, *Greek Lyric Poetry: Translated with an Introduction and Notes*, Oxford: Oxford University Press, 1993.

Critical works

E. Bowie, 'Miles ludens? The problem of martial exhortation in early Greek elegy', in O. Murray (ed.), *Sympotica: A Symposium on the Symposion*, Oxford: Oxford University Press, 1990, pp. 221–9.

A. P. Burnett, *Three Archaic Poets: Archilochus, Alcaeus, Sappho*, London: Duckworth, 1983.

C. Calame, *Choruses of Young Women in Ancient Greece* (trans. D. Collins and J. Orion), Lanham MD: Rowman and Littlefield, 1997.

A. Carson, *Eros the Bittersweet*, Princeton: Princeton University Press, 1986.

P. E. Easterling and B. M. W. Knox (eds), *Cambridge History of Classical Literature. Vol. 1: Greek Literature*, Cambridge: Cambridge University Press, 1985.

A. L. Ford, 'The seal of Theognis: the politics of authorship in archaic Greece', in T. Figueira and G. Nagy (eds), *Theognis of Megara: Poetry and the Polis*, Baltimore: Johns Hopkins University Press, 1985, pp. 82–95.

A. Ford, *The Origins of Criticism: Literary Culture and Poetic Theory in Classical Greece*, Princeton: Princeton University Press, 2002.

D. E. Gerber (ed.), *A Companion to the Greek Lyric Poets*, Leiden, New York, and Cologne: Brill, 1997.

L. Kurke, *The Traffic in Praise: Pindar and the Poetics of Social Economy*, Ithaca NY: Cornell University Press, 1991.

M. K. Lefkowitz, 'The first person in Pindar reconsidered – again', *Bulletin of the Institute of Classical Studies* 40 (1995), 139–50.

E. Stehle, *Performance and Gender in Ancient Greece: Nondramatic Poetry in its Setting*, Princeton: Princeton University Press, 1997.

42. Latin Poetry other than Epic and Drama

Alison Sharrock

Poetry flourished throughout the ancient Roman world. As is the case in many pre-modern societies, literature in verse form had a very high profile within the wider cultural ambience of ancient Rome, from the earliest times until (and beyond) the transition to the medieval world. Indeed, it would probably be fair to say that the single biggest change marking the end of 'ancient' Roman poetry was not any seismic shift in content or genre (although shifts certainly happened, gradually, erratically and incompletely), but the transition from quantitative metres to verse structures based on word stress. Ancient Latin versification worked by the arrangement of long and short syllables in metrical patterns; medieval Latin (and vernacular) verse, by contrast, was structured without regard to the lengths of syllables but on the basis of rhythmic stresses, in the manner of most modern verse (see chapter 65).

The genre of Roman poetry which is best known, then and now, is epic: a genre in which the poet adopts the position of a bard, acting as a conduit for the divine song of the muses, telling the stories of great heroes and battles, and effacing his own role and personality (except, of course, in so far as his role is precisely that of 'bard', and when the intrusion of his own personality has particular emotive effect – but that's another story; see chapter 36). The epic poet recounts the deeds of others. Second in honour is drama (always in verse), in which, still more than in epic, the poet occludes his own position in order to present 'people doing things', and to offer the characters' stories to the audience without an explicit teller as intermediary (see chapters 38 and 40). Roman poets paid lip-service to the notion that tragedy was an important genre, and treated it as such in their theorising and imagistic statements about the nature of their poetry, but tragedy does not play a major role in the history of Latin poetry as we know it. In practice, both epic and dramatic poets find metaphorical ways of writing themselves into their work, but they do so indirectly.

There were, however, many other genres of Roman poetry, with diverse aims and styles – lyric, satire, invective, elegy, didactic, pastoral, iambic, the verse epistle, panegyric, and all manner of occasional poetry (from the highly literary to crude graffiti): it is perhaps not too much of a generalisation to distinguish and collate the non-epic, non-dramatic poetry as the 'I-genres'. By this term, I mean to indicate that the poets of these genres more or less explicitly placed themselves in their work, and took a 'point of view' which they sought to present to the reader. This should not be taken as meaning that the poets wrote sincerely and straightforwardly about their own personal concerns, versifying their feelings independently of literary tradition, generic expectation or rhetorical pose: rather, their manner of presenting their poetry was to a considerable extent by means of what one scholar, with regard to Greek poetry, has called 'first-person fictions' (Lefkowitz, *First-Person Fictions*). I shall follow the story of Roman poetry through some of its most important components, from the late republic until the early empire. This restricted scope reflects the common practice of our modern reading, but we should remember that we are jumping in and out partway through the process, not watching it from beginning to end.

During the lively and troubled later years of the Republic, a craze arose for a kind of poetry which presented itself as new, clever (even abstruse), sophisticated and delicate (even dilettantish). (These poets were clearly seen as 'new' in their own day. Cicero makes several references to 'new poets', and compares traditional Roman poets favourably with these modern 'chanters of Euphorion', *Tusc.* 3.45.) 'Neoteric' is the term now applied to this poetic movement. Neoteric poetry took its aesthetic code, in part, from the erudite poetic traditions of the Hellenistic Greek scholar-poets, particularly Callimachus, along with whom it stressed its own 'littleness', both of scale and of style, but emphatically not of effort. This poetry, for all its abstraction and erudition, often presented itself as rooted in the real lives of contemporary upper-class Romans: an example of how this works in practice is the slippage between poetic and personal values, such as the use of the term *sal* (salt) to apply to wittiness and good taste in both social behaviour and poetic effectiveness (Catullus 13.5, 14.16, 86.4).

Today, the best-known representative of the neoteric movement is Catullus (c. 84–54 BC), whose collected poems did a great deal to shape the pattern of 'I-poetry' in the Roman world and beyond. We seem to see a man obsessed – obsessed, famously, with a beloved woman whom he calls Lesbia, with his own inner feelings, with his troubled sense of identity as a Roman elite male and as a struggling and suffering lover; obsessed too with poetry, with artistry, with friendships and enmities. This poet of the 'self' actually offers us multiple 'selves' – violent and gentle, learned and flippant, political and disengaged, urbane and obscene. The poems themselves fall roughly into three groups (which some scholars believe represent three 'books' arranged as such by the poet himself). First come the poems (1–60) in a variety of lyric and iambic metres, including Sapphics (stanzas in the manner of the Greek female poet Sappho of Lesbos) and hendecasyllables (continuous eleven-syllable lines). Most of these poems range in length from ten to thirty lines. Next comes a group of longer poems, again in a variety of metres, where the learned Hellenistic ancestry (never absent) is foregrounded. Among these is the *epyllion* ('little epic'), poem 64, 408 lines of hexameters recounting the mythical marriage of the Argonaut Peleus with the sea-nymph Thetis. The central panel of the poem is an *ekphrasis* (rhetorical description) of the coverlet on their marriage bed, on which is woven the story of Ariadne abandoned on Naxos by Theseus, after she had helped him defeat the Minotaur. The inserted story 'comes to life', to the point where we almost forget that it is just a picture on a bedspread. Although this poem takes us as far as Catullus gets from the norms of the 'I-genres', such is the force of his self-presentation that many readers want to see an implied identification between the abandoned Ariadne and the suffering lover-poet himself. The final group is constituted by forty-eight short poems in elegiac couplets, which range from love poems (e.g. 70, 72, 76, 85 – a famous two-liner) to spectacular examples of obscene abuse (e.g. 80, 88, 93 – another famous two-liner, 94).

At around the same time as Catullus was presenting this passionate persona to the public, Lucretius (c. 94 BC to between c. 55 and 51 BC) was expressing another great passion in a different kind of verse. Its object was Epicurean philosophy, and the genre was 'didactic' or 'teaching poetry'. Because all literature had a strongly didactic bent throughout Greek and Roman antiquity, there is considerable fuzziness around the boundaries of the didactic genre itself. For the Romans, Lucretius was instrumental in shaping the style and topoi (or motifs) of the genre, but no one afterwards matched the impression of personal commitment and evangelistic zeal which he conveys. (It may be that Lucretius was indeed personally committed to his Epicurean creed; it is more important here, however, that he chose to and managed to convey the impression (he 'constructed the persona') of personal commitment and high purpose.)

The poem is written in six quite long books of continuous hexameters, and displays other connections with epic in addition to the metre, such as a strong sense of teleology (being purposefully directed towards an ultimate goal) and narrative direction, as well as some elevated diction. Unlike in epic, however, here the poet and his reader are active participants in the process. Lucretius seeks to persuade his reader (concentrated and simplified into the direct addressee, the contemporary Roman aristocrat Memmius) that the world is wholly explicable by physics, that the gods live a blessed life apart and are not concerned with the affairs of humans, that there is no life after death, that the universe is infinite, that everything is made up of atoms, and that the duty of humanity is to be happy, which is achieved by removal of the fear of death. (It sounds more modern than it is.) Many readers of Lucretius have experienced an uneasy sense of paradox in his work, not least in the contrast between the dry subject matter of atomic theory and the sublimely beautiful poetic imagery that makes fire bloom from wood (1.900, 4.450), atoms nearly split their sides laughing at the joke of atoms being able to discourse on philosophy (2.976), and dancing motes in a sunbeam hold the clue to the universe (2.112–41).

The next character in my brief history of Roman non-epic poetry is actually the star of the epic story: Virgil. On his way towards that masterpiece of Roman epic, the *Aeneid*, Virgil produced important works in both the fields described above, neoteric poetry and the didactic genre. Virgil's first extant and reliably authentic work (that is, work that is surviving and which we are sure was actually written by him) is the *Eclogues*, a collection of ten fairly short pastoral poems, in which shepherds serenade their loved ones, pay scant attention to their sheep, and engage in singing contests with other shepherds, while, underneath, political forces darkly threaten turmoil and promise peace. The poems stretch my attribution of the non-epic, non-dramatic genres to a class of 'I-genres', because most are more like dramatic vignettes than they are personal statements by the poet, and yet the personal point of view is foregrounded even here, albeit by the master of self-effacement. The poems are consciously 'neoteric', written in the tradition of Callimachus (especially *Eclogue* 6) and more importantly the Hellenistic pastoral poet Theocritus, whose *Idylls* constitute a close model which – in true Virgilian fashion – the *Eclogues* derive from and transcend.

After pastoral comes didactic: Virgil's next endeavour was a poem on farming, the *Georgics*, written in the tradition of the archaic Greek didactic poet Hesiod, and of Rome's own Lucretius. Again, the existence of strong models may seem to undermine the originality of the work, until one understands how Virgilian intertextuality functions. Virgil made out of the (Greek and Greek-influenced) didactic tradition a poem which is not only supremely beautiful but also wholly Roman, and highly political, for it was written against the historical background of the early attempts by Octavian (the future Augustus) to reconstruct the land of Italy in the face and the aftermath of the civil wars. A poem on how to run a farm cannot be politically neutral in Rome. The horrors of plague (book 3), the glories of rural Italy (book 2), the noble art of bee-keeping (book 4) in which the language itself seems to soar through the air and dip into the flowers like the bees which are its subject: all these are witness to the power of didactic poetry and its political import. But many readers find most moving a section of the poem which is not overtly didactic: the 'digression' on Orpheus and Eurydice in book 4, which tells of how the farmer Aristaeus lost his bees in punishment for the attempted rape of Eurydice which caused her death, and how he regained them by the practice of *bougonia* (sacrifice of a bull by beating). Readers have not been able to resist seeing a political allegory here.

Another poetic genius of the early Augustan period was Horace (65–8 BC). Unlike the self-effacing Virgil, Horace presents us with a vast array of first-person roles in his wide-ranging poetic corpus. It is possible to arrange the Horatian oeuvre in two parallel groups (Henderson, *Fighting for Rome*, p. 108): first a polymetric group, containing the iambic *Epodes*, the lyric *Odes*, and the hymn commissioned by Augustus for his *ludi saeculares* in 17 BC; second a hexameter group comprising the *Satires* and the two books of *Epistles*, culminating in the *Ars Poetica*. It would be wrong to push too far the differing characteristics of the two groups, since there is arguably as much both of variation and of overlap within as there is between them, but a few generalisations might not go amiss. The polymetric group plays out roles derived partly from the lyric and iambic poetry of archaic and Hellenistic Greece. Although Horace's poems, with the exception of the hymn, were probably not designed for ritual or other public performance, they none the less construct the persona of the poet as lyric bard, a public speaker who channels and directs the values of his society and performs the celebration and vituperation which police those values. Horace sometimes seems like a court poet, writing (brilliant) propaganda for his imperial master. The so-called 'Roman Odes' (*Odes* 3.1–6) may be taken as the finest exposition of this Horatian voice. But there are other voices also: there is the understated eroticism of love poems like *Odes* 1.5, the delicate beauty of 'nature poetry' like *Odes* 1.9, reflections on the nature of the poetic art (e.g. *Odes* 3.25), drinking songs such as the (highly political) *Odes* 1.37, and the misogynistic obscenity of poems like *Epodes* 8 and 12. The hexameter group, by contrast, constructs the persona of a poet in his study, reflecting on the failings of the world, and occasionally its joys, considering how the world might be made a better place, and communicating those reflections for the 'private' edification of his addressee. There is a strongly didactic and moralising bent to the hexameter group. Its culmination is the verse epistle addressed to the aristocratic Piso brothers, in which Horace lays out the aesthetics and practicalities of poetic theory. This 'Ars Poetica' is written consciously in the tradition of Aristotle's *Poetics*, but it has one important difference from its Greek predecessor: the *Ars Poetica* is itself a poem.

In contrast to the polymath Horace, a group of poets who were his contemporaries seem almost obsessively focused on one kind of poetry. These were the elegists, the most famous of whom were Propertius (between 54 and 47 BC to sometime after 16 BC), Tibullus (between 55 and 48 BC to 19 BC), the rare female poet Sulpicia (probably a younger contemporary), and Ovid (43 BC–AD 17) – who managed to drag himself away from that obsession. Because they form so clear a group, critics from antiquity onwards have been inclined to make comparisons between them (Quintilian *Inst.* 10.1.93), comparisons which should be taken (as mine should) as useful starting points rather than final words. Propertius is intense, passionate and difficult; Tibullus is elegant, gentle and dreamy; Sulpicia is hardly noticed, being considered to be part of the Tibullan corpus until the early modern period, but is actually remarkable for providing what may be a female expression of her own desire; and Ovid is the cynical, clever trickster, who is more in love with art (especially his own) than with any particular beloved. Roman elegy is primarily love poetry, although in fact it also touches on other themes. It is 'I-poetry' par excellence, and is closely focused on the internal turmoil of the lover-poet, for whom poetry is a means both to express his feelings and to pursue his affair. Poetry is (or so the lover likes to believe) the magic spell which can open the door of the beloved mistress. It should not be thought, however, that elegy simply translates real lives wholesale into verse, without the mediation of intertextual erudition and artistry. There is passion and 'raw emotion', certainly, but there is also a strong sense of the role of the love poet as being subject to aesthetic choice, and also of poetic ancestry, particularly in Hellenistic and neoteric poetry. In fact, the first elegist was the neoteric poet Gallus, who was celebrated in Virgil's tenth *Eclogue*, but his work is lost except for a few lines. The slippage between emotion and artistry is so great that recent readers have seen the possibility of reading the beloved woman as some sort of metaphor for the poetic process itself.

Roman love elegy had considerable influence, albeit indirectly, over the development of the subjective expression of first-person emotion in poetry – the feature which was to become perhaps the defining characteristic of poetry in the modern world. But some of the aspects of its discourse which it passed down through the Middle Ages to the modern world were actually considerably more problematic in their original context than they later became. We might take as an example the pose of the elegist as a humble lover, dominated by his beloved whom he views as a mistress in both modern senses of the word. This notion was played out for the Romans in the imagery of the 'slavery of love' (*servitium amoris*). To most modern readers, who know too little about slavery but are influenced by medieval and later notions of 'courtesy' and a potentially strong ethic of humility, the idea that the lover might 'be a slave' may seem less odd than it should. To the Romans, slave-owning, status-conscious and fairly up-front about their low estimation of women, the idea that the lover would enjoy being enslaved to a mistress, and would be quite happy to be considered lazy as long as he could be with the beloved (e.g. Tib. 1.1.57–8), was rather shocking. The pose these poets took up was deliberately counter-cultural.

By the time Ovid came to write, the elegiac tradition was already well developed. What he did with the tradition of self-display was to drive it to extremes – but constantly to tease the reader over the question of whether he means what he says, whether he is talking about love or about poetry, and what is the connection between himself as poet and the speaker as lover (Sharrock in P. R. Hardie (ed.) *The Cambridge Companion to Ovid*, Cambridge, Cambridge University Press, 2002). His collection of love elegies, the *Amores*, begins with a programmatic joke in which he claims to have been about to write an epic when Cupid (god of love) came along and stole one metrical foot from every second line, thus turning continuous hexameters into elegiac couplets (alternating hexameter and pentameter). In this way, he confronts the Propertian notion that love for a particular woman drives the lover to become an elegiac poet, and neatly inverts it such that the poet is forced into elegy by means of a metrical accident, and then has to find a subject matter, sharpish, to fit his metre.

Subject matters he found, in abundance. As well as the *Amores* and various bits and pieces, Ovid produced elegiac verse epistles (*Heroides*) which purported to be letters from abandoned heroines to their deserting lovers; a (spoof?) didactic poem on how to be a good lover (*Ars Amatoria*) and another on how to fall out of love when required (*Remedia Amoris*); an elegiac poem on the Roman calendar (*Fasti*); and two collections of poems from exile (*Tristia* and *Epistulae ex Ponto*), after Augustus had him relegated to Tomi on the shores of the Black Sea in AD 8. In addition, Ovid tried his hand at both the genres excluded from this chapter: there was a tragedy, *Medea*, which is lost, and there is a major epic (albeit problematically so), the *Metamorphoses*. Ovid was crucial in mediating the first wave of Latin poetry to the later Roman and medieval worlds. Modern classical studies used to like to group Roman poetry into 'Golden' and 'Silver' ages, and although this periodisation has been questioned in recent years, we can still see Ovid as something of a bridge between different worlds.

In the 'Silver' period of Latin literature (first and early second centuries AD), poetry went to two extremes. The formal voice manifested itself in a minor flurry of epics, while the 'I-genres' developed the lightest and generically 'lowest' end of the earlier poetic heritage. Two main 'low' groups flourished, and transmitted something of themselves to posterity: occasional poetry, and satire. Poetry in the 'I-voice' reflects (and, to some extent, creates) the tensions and anxieties of imperial society, being shot through with both satire and sycophancy; and with a kind of impotent despair about the state Rome was in, sitting alongside lively celebrations of its minutiae.

One imperial poet adopted both the high-epic and the low-'I' voices in his poetry. Statius (late 40s AD to c. 96) was the author of two epics, a *Thebaid* and an unfinished *Achilleid*, but also of a collection of light, occasional poems called the *Silvae*. The collection consists of shortish poems, mostly in hexameters, which mark special occasions or celebrate aspects and moments in the lives of upper-class and powerful 'friends', or offer admiration, thanks, or indeed requests to actual or potential patrons. They are deceptively informative about the life and times of their author (and constitute the main source for our apparent knowledge about Statius' biography).

A near-contemporary, and equally eager to tell us about himself and his world, was Martial (between AD 38 and 41 to between 101 and 104), but surprisingly, perhaps, he and Statius determinedly ignore each other. Martial produced fifteen poetry books which are extant: a *Liber Spectaculorum* celebrating the inauguration of the Flavian amphitheatre (the Colosseum); *Xenia* and *Apophoreta*, which are books of mostly two-line tags purportedly attached to guest-presents and take-away gifts ('carry-outs') respectively, with a strongly Saturnalian tone and setting; and twelve books of *Epigrams*. Martial's epigrams hold to their poetic ancestry in the epigram poetry of Greece, with its origins in inscriptions on graves, monuments, or dedications in temples ('epigram' means 'written on'), but they range widely in subject matter and stylistic technique. There are hendecasyllables and scazons (limping iambics) as well as the more familiar elegiac couplets. Several poems make explicit references to or are closely modelled on the epigrams of Catullus, such as 1.7, which neatly states Martial's programmatic position by imitating the 'comparison' poems of Catullus (36 and 49: joking stuff about Cicero as worst/best advocate, Catullus as worst/best poet, and Lesbia as worst/best woman), while symbolising the point of comparison (Martial's and Catullus' poems) through the metaphor of birds, in which the Catullan exemplar is the *passer* ('sparrow') which is the subject of the notorious Catullan poems 2 and 3. There are poems about poetry, sex, dinner parties (a common theme, shared by the light poem and the literary letter), Martial's Spanish home, Bilbilis (e.g. 1.49: a long poem for Martial, at forty-two lines), Rome, the relationship between town and country, poems of praise, begging poems, insulting poems. Unlike the republican aristocrat Catullus, however, Martial does not explicitly attack people who are both living and eminent, but rather makes his targets out of general 'types', as did his contemporaries in the satiric genre.

The scholar Quintilian famously said, in his potted history of Roman literature, that 'Satire is wholly ours' (*Inst.* 10.1.93). It may or may not be wholly Roman, but what exactly it *is* remains a bone of contention among scholars. As far as our two imperial poets are concerned, the poetic pedigree for satire comes from the republican poet Lucilius through the Augustan Horace, and turns up in the Neronian Persius (AD 34–62) as a genre requiring medium-length poems in hexameters, fulminating at the failures of society at large, usually by means of types or non-entities, rather than major political figures (except perhaps in hints). Persius in fact begins his collection of hexameter poems with a preface in scazons, which, as a metre associated with violent abuse, sets a tone of more explicit invective than the poems actually maintain. There is plenty of violent language (and, one might say, 'violence to language', for the Latin is deliberately difficult and distorted), but the discourse is short on specifics. Persius adopts a Stoic voice, quite possibly from genuine philosophical conviction, but offers less a moral programme than a tirade of disgust at the moral failings of others, and indeed of himself.

Around fifty years later, another 'Disgusted of Rome' found it 'difficult not to write satire' (*Satire* 1.30) when he saw around him all the failings of the once-great people. Juvenal wrote his sixteen extant *Satires* probably in the first quarter of the second century AD, in the reigns of Trajan and Hadrian, around the same time, therefore, as Tacitus and the younger Pliny were composing their various great works. Juvenal takes up the hint inherent in the use of the hexameter for Roman satire, and gives his discourse something of the 'grand style' of epic, a great, bloated bombardment of abuse in heroic style – but a heroic failure. The rhetorical position which the satirist adopts is inscribed with its own impotence: no one, it seems, not even the satirist, can actually do anything about the moral cancer afflicting Rome. But the rhetoric of excess is such that the audience can see the gaps, and, at one level, see the whole thing as a (telling) joke. This discourse may have a moral purpose, but it is primarily entertainment.

Further reading

Latin texts of the authors mentioned are available in the Oxford Classical Texts series or the Teubner series of classical texts. Translations in the Oxford World's Classics and the Penguin Classics series exist (even if not currently in print) for most of the poets, although Martial and Statius are incomplete. The Loeb Classical Library offers the most complete translation-series.

S. Braund, *The Roman Satirists and their Masks*, Bristol: Bristol Classical Press, 1996.

G. B. Conte, *Latin Literature: A History* (rev. edn), Baltimore: Johns Hopkins University Press, 1999.

J. W. Henderson, *Fighting for Rome*, Cambridge: Cambridge University Press, 1998.

M. R. Lefkowitz, *First-Person Fictions*, Oxford: Oxford University Press, 1991.

R. O. A. M. Lyne, *The Latin Love Poets from Catullus to Horace*, Oxford: Oxford University Press, 1980.

A. Sharrock, 'Ovid and the Discourses of Love: The Amatory Works', in P. R. Hardie (ed.), *The Cambridge Companion to Ovid*, Cambridge: Cambridge University Press, 2002, pp. 150–62.

A. Sharrock and R. Ash, *Fifty Key Classical Authors*, London and New York: Routledge, 2002.

43. The Novel

Jason König

What are the defining features of the ancient novel 'genre' (as far as the word 'genre' is appropriate for texts which had no established place within ancient theorisations of literature)? Can the different ancient 'novel' texts be analysed as a unit? How do they relate to each other and to their wider literary and social contexts? All of these are questions which have occupied a great deal of energy within modern work on the novel texts of the Greek and Roman world. If they have provoked a bewildering range of different answers that is partly because these are texts which show tantalising signs of interconnection, but which nevertheless do not survive in sufficient volume to make a clear picture attainable. It is also, however, a consequence of effects which the novels themselves orchestrate in deliberate and artful ways. These are challenging, elusive texts (as Jack Winkler has importantly shown for the work of Apuleius and Heliodorus; Winkler, *Auctor and Actor*, and in Swain, *Oxford Readings*). They constantly make it difficult for us to be sure of their own generic affiliations, their own seriousness or otherwise. They constantly set puzzles for us to solve, constantly offer us models of failed or only partially successful communication and interpretation. The difficulty many modern commentators have had in categorising them and characterising them is fully appropriate to the way in which the problems of misapprehension and miscommunication, hybrid and insecure identity, are thematised within the texts themselves.

That said, it is not difficult to see that the stories of love and adventure which many of these texts offer to their readers tend to cluster around a number of distinctive narrative features. The five fully surviving Greek 'novels' (if we follow conventional categorisation – although there are many other texts which could conceivably qualify) seem to have been written between the first century BC and third century AD, although none of them is easy to date. These texts are Chariton *Chaireas and Callirhoe*; Xenophon of Ephesus *Ephesiaka*; Longus *Daphnis and Chloe*; Achilles Tatius *Leukippe and Kleitophon*; and Heliodorus *Aithiopika* (all of these translated in Reardon, *Collected Ancient Greek Novels*). They all draw on standard plot patterns and reshape them with varying degrees of ingenuity: enforced separation of prodigiously beautiful and chaste hero and heroine; accounts of the travels and dangers and ordeals they must face in the course of that separation, which see them not only falling into the clutches of predatory pirates and bandits, who threaten their mutual commitment to fidelity, but also often stumbling into involvement in events of political and military crisis; and then final reconciliation. Standard 'generic' features like these are summarised with monotonous regularity at the beginning of modern works on the ancient novel, in conformity with the long-outdated cliché that the ancient novel is a neglected area of study. This summary is included here in the hope that it will obviate the need for this kind of opening, rather than encouraging it! The two surviving Latin novels – Apuleius' *Metamorphoses* and Petronius' *Satyrica* (the second of which survives only in part) – replay many of the same themes, although neither of them is based on a heterosexual relationship between hero and heroine: the hero of Apuleius' novel, for example, is turned into a donkey, and only returned to human form – reunited not with a heroine figure, but rather with his old self – in the closing book of the novel.

All of these texts revel in their imitation and transformation of the canonical genres of classical Greek and Latin literature – epic, tragedy, new comedy, historiography, bucolic – often combining generic markers in ways which deliberately make it difficult for us to judge which should be given more weight. In that sense they have a great deal in common with many other comic texts which were contemporary with them, most obviously with the anarchic parody of Greek literary traditions in Lucian's *True Histories*. The narrator of Petronius' *Satyrica*, for example, regularly draws on epic and tragic clichés in his account of his own low-life adventures, but those clichés are contaminated through the absurdity and vulgarity of the events he describes, and through the reminiscence of other less elevated genres like mime. The capacity of these ancient novels to swallow up and reshape so many different genres has often been associated with Mikhail Bakhtin's theorisation of the novel as a 'polyphonic' genre (see chapter 8). That sometimes oversimplified insight has been nuanced by Dan Selden (in Tatum, *Search for the Ancient Novel*), who argues provocatively that the novels are united by their obsession with figures and events which perform more than one function, display more than one identity at the same time. By that account, the trope of hybridity and double logic is central to the world of the novel, thematised not only in the uncategorisable generic mixtures of the texts themselves, but also in the inherent multivalence of even the smallest details of characterisation and description.

The contrast between idealising Greek novel traditions and grotesque, parodic Roman ones has long been commonplace, but it has recently been challenged by the discovery of papyrus fragments from other Greek novels (text and translation in Stephens and Winkler, *Ancient Greek Novel*), many of which are packed with erotic and sensational material. For example, the surviving fragments from Lollianos' *Phoinikika* offer vivid description of loss of virginity, bandits disguised as ghosts, and cannibalism, all compressed within a very small stretch of surviving text. On that basis one might be tempted to draw a further boundary-line between an idealising and a non-idealising Greek tradition, but even that distinction is hard, on closer inspection, to uphold. The idea that the surviving Greek novels are idealising, moralising texts is one which has long bedevilled their interpretation. They do undeniably exhibit some of the trappings we would at first sight associate with moralising writing – chastity rewarded, wickedness punished – but there has also been a general failure to notice the eroticisation which is always lying just beneath the respectable surfaces of their narratives. The novels suggest a correlation between beauty and chastity on the one hand and elite identity on the other, but they nevertheless also, always, leave open the possibility that those links may be fragile, impossible to guarantee. The heroes and heroines of the novels are repeatedly brought close to degradation and anonymity, even though they always ultimately, often miraculously, escape from it.

That obsession with the integrity of the elite body and elite bonds of mutual fidelity is in line with a number of features of imperial-period Greek society: for example, the way in which proper deportment and physical appearance was used obsessively in this period as a marker of identity for elite men and women alike; and the move towards increasing valorisation of heterosexual relations and especially marriage within Roman Empire elite society, related, as many have suggested, to the development of new Christian ideals of chastity. But the novels are very far from being solemn celebrations of these ideological trends. Instead – like so many other texts from the same period – they constantly joke about the difficulties of keeping bodily integrity intact, not least in the repeated trope whereby the heroes or heroines flirt with the possibility of infidelity, or even commit infidelities in ways which they later attempt to justify or explain away, with varying degrees of sophistic absurdity (most obviously in Achilles Tatius *Leukippe and Kleitophon* book five).

Discussion of these issues has often centred on debate about the degree to which some of these texts themselves parody the ancient novel 'genre'. It has long been argued, for example, that the novels of Apuleius and Petronius are dedicated to the task of debunking the standard conventions of the Greek novel; and it is certainly hard to deny that the Latin texts contain a number of bizarre distortions of narrative features which are common in their Greek equivalents, as I suggested above. It has also long been argued that the more 'sophisticated' of the Greek novelists (as they are standardly but misleadingly categorised) – Longus, Achilles Tatius, Heliodorus – take pleasure in undermining generic norms which the more 'simplistic' authors Chariton and Xenophon follow in more solemn ways. Longus, for instance, offers an ingeniously bucolic version of the novelistic clichés; for example, in his humorous representation of the way in which his shepherdess heroine Chloe maintains her chastity not out of any moral scruples but simply as a result of her unsophisticated, rustic ignorance about how the mechanics of love work. However, there is a danger in that approach of giving too much weight to a false dichotomy between formulaic early novels and sophisticated late ones, a danger of underestimating the extent to which even Chariton and Xenophon playfully manipulate the generic expectations of their audience. Xenophon's novel has often been derided as a clichéd, almost subliterary production, but more sensitive recent analysis has started to reveal the complexity and humour with which he parodies the assumptions on which his own work is based; for example, by his persistent strategy of juxtaposing mention of the unmistakable beauty of his hero and heroine with examples of the way in which they are misrecognised as soon as they are removed from familiar contexts; and by his strategy of lurching between snapshot images of novelistic clichés in an extravagantly disjointed and exhilaratingly bewildering fashion. Self-parody, it seems, was a part of the novel genre in all its forms.

Who, then, were the novels written for? Much nineteenth- and early twentieth-century scholarship, in line with its general denigration of the Greek literature of the Roman Empire, assumed that these were texts written for women, unworthy of the attention of the highly educated and philosophically minded male elite of that period. As those stereotypes have been broken down there has been an increasing willingness to recognise the fact that these are sophisticated, allusive texts, many of which hint at philosophical and theological depths (more on that in a moment) – although that fact should not of course be allowed to lead to the opposite assumption, that they would therefore have been unsuitable for female readers. Many of the novels in fact oscillate between male and female focalisation, hinting at a new equality between male and female protagonists, unparalleled within earlier literary traditions; while nevertheless undermining that impression of equality in a variety of ways, for example by objectifying their female protagonists through conspicuously male ways of looking – most obviously in the predatory gaze of the first-person male narrator of Achilles Tatius' novel; or else, conversely, by making the female heroines of the novel conspicuously more spirited and cunning than their male lovers, in ways which might well have been appealing to female readers or listeners. That effect is achieved most notably and humorously in Heliodorus' *Aithiopika*, where the hero Theagenes, despite being descended from Achilles (so he claims), cannot come close to matching his beloved Charikleia's poise and intelligence.

Once again, then, it may be closer to the truth to suggest that the novels deliberately stop short of giving us an easy answer to the problem of readership. They flirt with a number of different possible readers, hinting at a number of different levels of sophistication and gender positions from which one might read, but without ever allowing us to settle on any one of them as the 'right' one. They generate questions, in other words, about the self-positioning of their readers (or listeners) through the experience of reading.

The novels' play with the theme of identity is particularly conspicuous in their obsessive interest in the theme of travel to exotic lands – which draws on the ethnographical traditions of the *Odyssey* and Herodotus (see chapters 35 and 49), but which also reshapes those traditions in ways which are particularly appropriate for the audiences for which they were written. The Roman Empire brought about increasingly routine contact between different parts of the Mediterranean world, in ways which not only led to an intensified investment in local, civic identities, combined with an intensified fascination with the variety of cultures united under Roman power, but also prompted increasingly frequent claims about the way in which the whole of the known world had been united by the common influences of a shared Greek cultural heritage. The Greek novels reflect those contradictory strands in a number of different ways. Many of them emphasise the importance of the native city of their hero and heroine – in Chariton's *Chaireas and Callirhoe*, for instance, the Sicilian hero and heroine are represented as favourites of their fellow citizens in the opening book, but are then wrenched away from that comforting environment, before finally returning there to scenes of communal celebration in book eight. Others show a fascination with the edges of the Greek-speaking world, or even with what lies beyond those edges, in ways which throw doubt on assumptions of Greek cultural centrality. Heliodorus' *Aithiopika*, for example, tells the story of Charikleia (who is initially presented to us as an archetype of Hellenic beauty, in her role as priestess of Delphi, at the very centre of the Greek world) and her journey back to what she discovers is her birthplace in Ethiopia, where she was born, by a strange freak of conception, from black parents. The novel's discovery of Greekness beyond the boundaries of the Mediterranean world at first sight seems to support contemporary ideas about the universal relevance of Hellenic culture. But it also throws a comically disturbing light on the ideal of authentic Hellenic learning and identity as something which has spread out from the centres of traditional Greek territory. The images of hybridity with which Charikleia – like so many other characters in the novel – are characterised are also applied by Heliodorus to his own text, which parades its own bastardised cultural and intellectual heritage (see Whitmarsh in Hunter, *Studies in Heliodorus*).

The novels also offer a promising place for thinking through the mutual influence and implication of Greek and Latin cultural ideals and literary traditions. That is true most conspicuously of all for Apuleius, whose work is a translation and adaptation of an original Greek text, set in mainland Greece with Greek characters speaking, via Apuleius' text – in Latin. How far, Apuleius seems to be asking us, does translation bring cultural transformation? How far has the original been latinised? Is translation enough to alter cultural affiliation? Those questions are paralleled within the bodily transformations of the text. The narrator leaves behind his human self in book three, a change which is followed by constant anxiety about the degree to which he is able to hold on to his old, human identity when he enters his new, donkey's body. The text challenges us to decide how far changes of form (whether bodily or linguistic) bring change of inner identity. It is hard to avoid the impression that these thematic preoccupations are related to Apuleius' own self-positioning, as an orator and philosopher who performed in both Greek and Latin, and who elsewhere (especially in the *Apology*) proclaims his own ability to switch between different cultural affiliations and linguistic competences at will. It is less easy to find engagements with Latin literature and the Roman political world within the Greek novels which survive, although it is tempting to feel that the cultural and political realities of the Roman Empire make themselves felt even when they are not given explicit mention. The Greek texts, for example, are repeatedly interested in exploring the relation between private passion and public crisis, as the domestic, inward-looking mutual obsession of their protagonists' early encounters is unable to protect them from the influence of political and military happenings. Is it ever possible, these texts seem to be asking, to tell a story which is truly private, a story which is removed from the harsh realities of the public world (which for the original readers of the novel is of course an unavoidably Roman world)?

The recurring scenes of dangerous and unpredictable travel – forced on the protagonists against their will – are also a concrete feature of the novels' obsession with the impression that there may be some shadowy divine presence controlling their storylines. The divine machinery of the novels' universe is rarely made explicit, but the characters themselves repeatedly appeal to the gods for help, blaming the gods for their predicaments, and for many of the novels the repeatedly invoked goddess Fortune (*Tychē*) seems to be their guiding divinity. However, some of these texts hint at the possibility that they may have more profound divine secrets encoded within them, although characteristically they always refuse to yield up those secrets in any unequivocal way.

For example, Heliodorus' labyrinthine plot frequently leaves the impression that it has some divine controller hovering behind it. Some have seen the text as an elaborate advertisement for the cult of the sun-god Helios, who is given conspicuous attention in the climactic final chapters (and who also makes an implicit appearance, so a second-time reader might notice, in the description of a sunrise in the very opening sentence of the work), but it seems wrong to suggest that this is a solemn piece of religious propaganda, or that the final revelation of Helios' involvement can satisfyingly account for all of the vagaries of the plot which have come before. It is tempting, in fact, to give more weight to Heliodorus himself as a quasi-divine, controlling authorial force, a suspicion which might be reinforced by the very final sentence of the work where he advertises his own connections with the sun god, revealing his own name for the first time (Heliodorus means 'Gift of the Sun') and the fact that he is a member of the Clan of Descendants of the Sun. In a sense Heliodorus himself is the godlike presence who hides behind the action, the final answer to the text's riddles, revealed in its final sentence.

Divine influence is even more unmistakable in Apuleius' *Metamorphoses*, which follows a similar pattern to Heliodorus' text in introducing its deus ex machina only in the final book. There the narrator Lucius is turned back to human form by the favour of the goddess Isis, and then becomes a devoted worshipper of her, a development which is narrated with a solemnity which seems out of place by comparison with the grotesque humour of previous books. There has been much debate about the degree to which this final book makes the *Metamorphoses* a 'religious' text. Those who argue in favour of that view make much of the detail that Apuleius was himself an initiate of Isis, as well as being a famous Platonic philosopher. Others argue that the final book is itself parodic of the Isis cult, a sly continuation of the absurdities of the opening book, with a narrator who is no more reliable and intelligent than he was in his time as a donkey. It seems more likely, however, that the difficulty of making that judgement is itself precisely the point. Whenever we incline too far towards one view or the other Apuleius pulls the rug from under our feet, exploiting the fine line between religious revelation and trickery which is a preoccupation of so much writing about religious knowledge in this period.

There has, finally, been a great deal of work done on the reception of the novel in later periods; for example, on its adaptation by Byzantine novelists from the eleventh century onwards, and on the enormous influence of these texts over the formation of the modern novel. The best of this work has shown vividly how thematic preoccupations which are central to the original texts are recast in distinctive forms to answer to related anxieties and preoccupations within the societies which imitate them.

Analysis of the ancient novels has tended (albeit with many notable exceptions) to be presented either through survey accounts of the 'genre' as whole, often involving extensive summary of individual texts, or within volumes of collected essays, a format which is no doubt appropriate for such a diverse subject, but which sometimes proves frustrating by the provisional, self-contained nature of the studies it tends to produce. Despite the popularity of the ancient novel as an object of study in the last few decades, there is still a pressing need for more ambitious and also more intricate work both on individual texts, and on the way in which these novels relate to other areas of cultural production and social preoccupation in the imperial period; and also on the way in which imitation of the ancient novels relates to 'borrowing' of other forms of ancient literature and ancient thought within the work of later authors and periods.

Further reading

Ancient Narrative – regular journal, published on paper and at www.ancientnarrative.com; includes five collections of essays to date.

S. Bartsch, *Decoding the Ancient Novel: The Reader and the Role of Description in Heliodorus and Achilles Tatius*, Princeton: Princeton University Press, 1989.

G. B. Conte, *The Hidden Author: An Interpretation of Petronius'* Satyricon, Berkeley: University of California Press, 1996.

S. Goldhill, *Foucault's Virginity: Ancient Erotic Fiction and the History of Sexuality*, Cambridge: Cambridge University Press, 1995.

Groningen Colloquia on the Novel (9 vols), 1988–98.

S. Harrison (ed.), *Oxford Readings in the Roman Novel*, Oxford: Oxford University Press, 1999.

N. Holzberg, *The Ancient Novel: An Introduction*, London and New York: Routledge, 1994.

R. L. Hunter (ed.), *Studies in Heliodorus*, Cambridge: Cambridge University Press, 1998.

H. Morales, *Vision and Narrative in Achilles Tatius*, Cambridge: Cambridge University Press, 2004.

J. R. Morgan and R. Stoneman (eds), *Greek Fiction: The Greek Novel in Context*, London: Routledge, 1994.

B. Reardon (ed.), *Collected Ancient Greek Novels*, Berkeley: University of California Press, 1989.

V. Rimell, *Petronius and the Anatomy of Fiction*, Cambridge: Cambridge University Press, 2002.

G. Schmeling (ed.), *The Novel in the Ancient World*, Leiden: Brill, 1996.

S. Stephens and J. Winkler (eds), *The Ancient Greek Novel: The Fragments*, Princeton: Princeton University Press, 1995.

S. Swain (ed.), *Oxford Readings in the Greek Novel*, Oxford: Oxford University Press, 1999.

J. Tatum (ed.), *The Search for the Ancient Novel*, Baltimore: Johns Hopkins University Press, 1994.

T. Whitmarsh (ed.), *The Cambridge Companion to the Greek and Roman Novel*, Cambridge: Cambridge University Press, forthcoming.

T. Whitmarsh, *Reading the Self in the Ancient Novel*, Cambridge: Cambridge University Press, forthcoming.

J. J. Winkler, *Auctor and Actor: A Narratological Reading of Apuleius's* The Golden Ass, Berkeley: University of California Press, 1985.

44. Letters

Michael Trapp

Varieties of letter

At first sight, the four dry, formulaic lines of an invitation to a religious festival somewhere in Egypt in the third or fourth century AD, and the fifty-eight polished elegiac couplets in which Penelope complains to Odysseus about the slowness of his return from Troy, seem to have very little indeed in common. Yet both of these pieces of writing – *Oxyrhynchus papyrus* 112 and Ovid *Heroides* 1 – are letters. Together, they mark points towards the extremes of the spectrum of material to which this name can be given, and begin to suggest its diversity in form, circumstances of origin and modes of preservation.

P. Oxy. 112 is – to use a popular but tendentious distinction, which needs some deconstructing – a 'real', utilitarian piece of correspondence: a written message of modest length, made to be conveyed between physically separate parties, and framed by conventional formulae of salutation and farewell. It is written in unsophisticated style by and to correspondents otherwise entirely unknown to history; it survives as an individual item, in the original form in which it was first sent; and it is known to us as a result of archaeological research and excavation. Thousands of examples of this category of letter survive, embracing private, business and low-level administrative concerns; most are in Greek but there are some in Latin. The majority are on papyrus (see chapter 32), discovered in Egypt from the 1890s onwards, and dating from between the third century BC and the sixth century AD. Others, including the oldest yet known, are incised on thin sheets of lead; others still are on wood and potsherds (*ostraka*). A number of more public communications, from kings, emperors and governors, survive as inscriptions (see chapter 34), carved copies on stone set up to publicise their contents to the communities addressed. In general, these archaeologically recovered letters share the characteristic that they are primarily functional items, never intended for a general readership distinct from their original recipients.

Heroides 1, in contrast, is a highly sophisticated exercise in literary creativity, meant from the start for the delectation of a reading public. In a clever variation on the declamatory *suasoria* (invented speech in character), Ovid imagines what character X might have said to character Y, but at a point in their story where they could not meet face to face and had to communicate via the written word instead; and he does so not in the standard epistolary medium of prose but in the most elegantly pointed of verse. This too stands for a larger category, that of 'fictitious' epistolography. Greek authors working in this field, all somewhat later than Ovid, and all writing in prose rather than verse, include Alciphron (second to third century AD), with his corresponding fishermen, farmers, parasites and courtesans (imitated from the characters and episodes of New Comedy and pastoral poetry); Aelian (third century AD), with his rustics; and Philostratus (third century AD) and Aristaenetus (fifth century AD), with their lovers. In all these works it is obvious that the element of fiction embraces both the characters and a fortiori the sending of their supposed missives, even when the characters and situations are not strictly invented, but inherited from traditional mythology.

In between these two extremes, so to speak (though too strict an attempt to plot everything along a single axis is questionable), come other equally substantial and significant categories of letter. Springing most readily to mind – perhaps most people's immediate association when 'ancient letters' are mentioned – is the ('real') correspondence of great historical figures, collected and published for a general readership, perhaps with some editorialising and improvement of the contents, either by the writers themselves or by their admirers: the collections of Cicero, Pliny and Fronto (second century AD) in Latin, of the emperor Julian and Libanius (fourth century AD) in Greek, and of great early Christian figures such as Basil (fourth century AD), Augustine and Jerome (both fourth to early fifth centuries). Some such collections are general and miscellaneous in character, intended to show off their author in a number of different guises (including those of fine writer and of actor in great historical events). Others have a narrower focus, in particular on didactic aims: the prime cases here are those of Epicurus and the authors of the New Testament epistles, above all St Paul; whether Seneca's *Moral Epistles* to Lucilius belong in exactly the same category depends on whether they are thought to have begun as individual missives actually sent to their ostensible recipient, or to have been planned from the start as a set and for a broader readership.

If not in fact deriving from a real original correspondence, Seneca's *Epistles* exemplify another more widespread phenomenon, the use of letter-form to clothe kinds of communication equally or more commonly found in non-epistolary guise. So the critic Dionysius of Halicarnassus casts some of his essays in literary history and criticism as *Epistles* to Ammaeus and Gnaeus Pompeius, or Plutarch one of his sets of consolatory commonplaces as a letter to Apollonius. On a smaller scale, a number of authors (e.g. Martial at the beginning of some of his books of epigrams) cast their prefaces as dedicatory epistles.

Then there is the class of *pseudepigrapha*, sets of letters purporting to be by real historical personages, and dealing more-or-less realistically with their careers and thoughts, but in fact the work of much later, now unknown authors. Such sets, which masquerade as 'the collected correspondence' on the model of Cicero's or Aristotle's or Epicurus', blend historicising fiction with moralising elements, in different proportions in different cases; some also have ambitions to serve as models of epistolographic technique. Certainly belonging to this category are the letters of Phalaris, Themistocles, Hippocrates, Socrates and the Socratics, Diogenes, Crates and Chion of Heraclea (this last constituting the one generally agreed instance of the 'epistolary novel' in antiquity). The status of those assigned to Plato, Isocrates and Demosthenes is more controversial.

Finally, there are further examples of the transposition of letter-form into verse, to set beside *Heroides*. Practically unknown in Greek, this manoeuvre seems to have appealed particularly to Roman poets. Lucilius (fragmentary), Catullus and Propertius all provide isolated examples, with Horace and Ovid making the major contributions. Horace in *Epistles* book I follows Epicurus and anticipates Seneca in using the letter as a vehicle for moral-philosophical musing and advice, while in *Epistles* II and the *Ars Poetica* he turns to literary criticism and the model of the epistolary essay. Ovid's contribution, besides *Heroides*, also includes his verse letters from exile, in *Tristia* and *Ex Ponto*.

Reading letters: historical inquiry and aesthetic pleasure

'The letter' is clearly a very large and diverse category (large and diverse enough to raise teasing questions about where exactly its outer boundaries should be set, and how exactly it is best subdivided). The ways in which they can be studied and used, and the kinds of interest that can be found in them, are correspondingly numerous. In the first place, they make an extraordinarily rich body of historical evidence (taking 'historical' in its broadest sense). The letters of both famous and obscure individuals illuminate the events they lived through, as active participants or observers, and at least give the appearance of doing so from a privileged vantage-point, valuably different in kind from that adopted by high-style narrative history. At the same time such letters – above all in substantial collections – give a sense of introducing us to the correspondents themselves with an intimacy not matched by any other kind of material. Similarly, letters illuminate social and intellectual life, at all levels of society, from the cultivated elite responsible for the major, 'literary' letter collections down to the humble (but still modestly educated) landowners, soldiers and traders who penned the items on papyrus, lead and wood. The study of the provincial society and economy of Graeco-Roman Egypt has been created over the last century by papyrus finds, among which letters form a specially important category; other areas onto which letters open valuable windows are women's life, and the social setting of the Roman army. And on yet another level, letters – especially those by socially undistinguished correspondents – cast light on the history of the Greek and Latin languages, showing in vivid detail how the spelling, grammar and pronunciation of their everyday versions *(koinē* Greek and 'vulgar Latin') differed from those of the high-style literary language; here too, as with historical events and persons, letters give a sense of bringing us into more direct contact with the realities of ancient life.

In addition to all this, letters can offer great aesthetic satisfaction: they are a good read, in ways that cut across boundaries between 'reality' and 'fiction' and high and low style. All letters, however naive or sophisticated, whether encountered in isolation or as part of a collection, can offer the pleasures and the puzzles of eavesdropping, the challenge to reconstruct the situation to which the letter relates, and the states of mind of sender and recipient. This potential can be deliberately exploited by the compilers of collections and the crafters of literary fictions, in whose hands sequences of letters may become vehicles for an intriguingly different mode of narrative. The letters of sophisticated correspondents (again, whether real or fictitious) offer the additional pleasure and challenge of fine writing, both on the level of verbal style and on that of effective rhetorical strategy and structure. And in all cases, letters may be enjoyed – as ancient epistolary theory already acknowledged – as presentations of their senders' (and sometimes recipients') characters.

Reading letters: sincerity, manipulation and issues of communication

But whatever the interests and purposes of the reader, letters (as much as any other written structures) require to be read alertly, even with suspicion. In both its literary and its functional guises, the letter may present itself as a transparent and unproblematic form, but this is far from being straightforwardly so. The sense of letters as an intimate, benevolent and therefore particularly *sincere* form of writing, giving a true and candid view of both the events they spring from and comment on, and the personality of their writers, is a powerfully seductive one; letter-writers themselves (and authors of epistolary fictions) often exploit it. But it needs to be resisted, in the interests both of the realistic use of letters as historical evidence, and of a properly sophisticated approach to them as literary texts.

Letters are a thoroughly subjective and thoroughly interested form of communication, shaped not by any consistent desire for objective reporting, but by the forwarding of their writers' own plans and desires at the time of writing. The views of the world they offer are closely tied to those of particular individuals at particular points in time, shaping what they have to say to their immediate circumstances and their relationships with their addressees. This includes the representation of the writer's own character. Letter-writers – especially naive correspondents – may indeed give themselves away in their correspondence, exposing their characters by inadvertence. But they may also – all the more the more sophisticated their education and rhetorical training – use letters to construct personae for themselves: not what they are, but what they aspire to be, or what they think it prudent to appear to be to their correspondents of the moment.

Alertness to this slippery quality in letters makes for better use of them in historical study, and more satisfying because more complicated reading of them as literary texts. It also points us towards yet another reason for finding them interesting: their capacity to stimulate thought on issues of writing and communication more generally. Not only questions of subjectivity, selectivity and self (mis-)representation, but also issues of empathy, the attempted control of reader-response, absence and presence, and the slipping of meaning between sender and receiver can be focused with particular vividness and immediacy in the reading of letters.

Modern scholarship

Modern scholarship on ancient epistolography is somewhat patchy. There are good editions of most major literary letter collections (though still no comprehensive replacement for Hercher's *Epistolographi Graeci*); letters on papyrus, lead, wood, pottery and stone have to be hunted through specialist publications, with the help of some anthologies. Promising recent literary-critical studies of Cicero's correspondence, and of Greek fictional epistolography, point to exciting possibilities for future work.

Further reading

M. Beard, 'Ciceronian correspondences: making a book out of letters', in T. P. Wiseman (ed.), *Classics in Progress*, Oxford: Oxford University Press, 2002, pp. 103–44.

C. D. N. Costa, *Greek Fictional Letters*, Oxford: Oxford University Press, 2001.

R. Cribiore, 'Windows on a woman's world: some letters from Roman Egypt', in A. Lardinois and L. McClure (eds), *Making Silence Speak: Women's Voices in Greek Literature and Society*, Princeton: Princeton University Press, 2001, pp. 223–39.

R. Hercher, *Epistolographi Graeci* (with Latin trans.), Paris: Didot, 1873.

G. O. Hutchinson, *Cicero's Correspondence: A Literary Study*, Oxford: Oxford University Press, 1998.

A. J. Malherbe (ed.), *Ancient Epistolary Theorists*, Atlanta: Scholars Press, 1988.

J. T. Reed, 'The epistle', in S. E. Porter (ed.), *Handbook of Classical Rhetoric in the Hellenistic Period, 330 BC–AD 400*, Leiden and New York: Brill, 1997, pp. 171–93.

P. A. Rosenmeyer, *Ancient Epistolary Fictions: The Letter in Greek Literature*, Cambridge: Cambridge University Press, 2001.

C. E. W. Steel, *Reading Cicero: Genre and Performance in Republican Rome*, London: Duckworth, 2004.

M. Trapp, *Greek and Latin Letters: An Anthology*, Cambridge: Cambridge University Press, 2003.

J. L. White, *Light from Ancient Letters*, Philadelphia: Fortress Press, 1986.

45. Rhetoric

Alastair Blanshard

'Rhetoric' is hard to pin down (cf. Quintilian *Institutio oratoria* 2.15). At its simplest, it is the art of persuasive speaking. Yet such a definition tells us little. It embraces almost every act of communication. When is a speaker not trying to persuade the listener of something? Even the most basic questions or statements carry with them implicit claims about the character and disposition of the speaker. Bound up in a simple statement such as 'I love you' are a whole series of statements that the speaker wishes the listener to believe (e.g. 'Trust me', 'I'm sincere', 'I know what love is', 'I want you to love me in return'). The communication of these ancillary messages is often just as important as the primary message (sometimes even more so). Body language, tone of voice, timing, environment and surrounding context are all utilised to facilitate communication, and form part of its rhetoric. Famously, it was declared that 'The only thing that isn't rhetorical are tidal waves.' To which one critic replied, 'Why not tidal waves?'

The study of the rhetoric of antiquity involves the study of society at its broadest and most diverse. It embraces everything that contributes to the creation and transmission of beliefs. Rhetoric transcends genre. It can be found in everything from the most baroque of Hellenistic epigrams to the crudest of Pompeian graffiti. Studying the rhetoric of a culture opens up a window onto its values, desires and anxieties.

However, there is a second and narrower sense in which rhetoric can be studied. This involves the study of those moments singled out by the ancients themselves as moments when rhetoric (*rhētorikē*; 'the art of the *rhētōr* – the speaker') is foregrounded. These events vary considerably in their format. They include, among other things, political meetings, court proceedings and funeral eulogies. However, they all share the same underlying structure. These are moments when the speaker and audience came together and a social contract was formed. In coming together, both parties agreed that there was a topic on which the audience needed to be persuaded. They agreed that certain individuals would have the task of doing the persuading. They agreed on roughly the form that this persuading would take. They agreed a system of criteria by which it was possible to determine who was the most persuasive. Finally, they agreed that consequences would flow from this act of persuasion. These stylised events come to dominate the public life of the city. Policy was decided by these events. Justice was determined and administered. Minds were educated, and beliefs instilled. It is the study of these formalised performances that concerns the rest of this chapter on rhetoric.

The origins of rhetoric

The Greeks attributed the birth of rhetoric to two figures from Sicily, Corax and Tisias, and they keenly preserved a number of stories about them. Two are famous. They both involve a paradox and a dispute. The first story recounts the marvellous rhetorical example that they devised to demonstrate the strength and versatility of arguments based on probability (Aristotle *Art of Rhetoric* 1402a18–21; Plato *Phaedrus* 273a–b). The example is based on a hypothetical fight between a big man and a small man. In the ensuing court-case, the small man is advised to argue that 'Is it likely that I, a small man, would start a fight with a large man, when it is obvious that I would be soundly beaten?' However, this argument is countered by the big man, who turns the logic of probability on its head and argues 'Is it likely that I, a big man, would start a fight with a small man, when it is obvious that blame would fall on me?' We find a similarly insoluble argument contained in the other famous story told about these two Sicilians (Sextus Empiricus *Against the Professors* 2.96–9). This one involves a dispute over a bill. Corax claims that Tisias owes him money for the teaching that Tisias has received from him. To recover the money Corax takes his student to court. However, this strategy falls apart when Tisias argues that if he cannot persuade the jury of his case, then the rhetorical instruction that he has received from Corax was worthless, and so he needn't pay. Conversely, if he can persuade the jury of the rightness of his case, he wins the case and doesn't have to pay. In either case, the consequence of each premise is that Tisias avoids his debts.

Such stories are clearly fictional. The Greeks created numerous anecdotes about imaginary inventors. Corax and Tisias are as real as Daedalus and his wings or Orpheus and his alphabet. We have little reason to believe that Corax or Tisias existed or that they developed in isolation a marvellous system of linguistic tricks that they called 'rhetoric'. Nevertheless, what these stories do indicate are some of the ways in which the Greeks thought about rhetoric. In particular, these stories are educative about the conditions in which the Greeks thought rhetoric thrived and the uses to which rhetoric could be put, and they highlight some of the anxieties which rhetoric generated in the Greeks.

Let's start by examining the place in which these stories located the birth of rhetoric – the state of Syracuse on the island of Sicily. This island, located on the Western edge of the Greek world, was famous for a number of things. But one thing in particular stands out – its volatile and innovative political climate. Sicily was the place where some of the first and most important experiments in government occurred. The development of rhetoric in ancient Greece seems to be inextricably linked with the development of political consciousness within the community. It thrives when values exist in a state of flux. According to tradition, Corax's teaching takes off in the immediate aftermath of the overthrow of tyranny in Syracuse, and the institution of democracy. Rhetoric, as we shall see, can quite happily operate during periods of authoritarian rule. However, it is most useful when you need to persuade a community or its representatives of a course of action. It is during their attempts to persuade gatherings and assemblies (cf. *Iliad* 2.278–335) that the heroes of the *Iliad* are at their most rhetorical, not in their communications with one another. Rhetoric works best at that moment when community consultation feels legitimate and appropriate. Rhetoric is born with franchise.

The second thing to note about the stories involving Corax and Tisias is that they both involve legal disputes. Written law was one of the by-products of the politicisation of the community. No longer was justice dependent on the whim of rulers or magistrates. Such a move was a catalyst for the growth of rhetoric. The act of translating abstract written statutes into concrete justice provides an opportunity for rhetoric. Self-interest on the part of the litigants combined with the judge's belief in his deliberative capacities creates the ideal environment for rhetoric to flourish. Rhetoric became the lubricant that oiled the machinery of justice. It is telling that the moment represented in the trial scene on the 'Shield of Achilles' (our earliest literary reference to a legal proceeding) is not the moment of judgement, but the moment when the parties are pleading their cause (*Iliad* 18.497–508). Rhetoric had quickly become the law-courts' most distinctive feature.

The final thing to note about the stories concerning Corax and Tisias is the way in which they undermine the utility of rhetoric. Rhetoric claims to assist in the discovery of truth ('Who started the fight?') and justice ('In what circumstances should damages be paid?'). In practice, these stories show that rhetorical techniques lead only to paradox and confusion. From the moment that people became conscious about the art of persuasion, they began to feel anxious about it. Rhetoric is something that needs to be watched and thought about. It is destined to have a life as much in theory as in practice.

Rhetoric in the classical city

Given these features, it is no accident that rhetoric came to thrive in one place in particular: a city famed for the enfranchisement of its citizen-body, its litigiousness and its love of theory; a city whose 'constitution lay in speeches' (Demosthenes *On the Crown* 184) – Athens.

According to Thucydides, the politician Cleon once berated the Athenian populace for their love of rhetoric. He criticised their strange passion that saw them embrace novelty in argumentation even at the expense of their empire (Thucydides 3.38.3–7). Whatever the validity of Cleon's criticisms, they do point to an important truth about Athenian civic life. This was a polis where large-scale rhetorical displays were important and regular events.

Public policy was determined through debate in the Assembly. There were at least forty meetings of this body a year, and the audience routinely numbered at least six thousand. It was a volatile environment in which politicians faced heckling opponents and an audience not afraid to voice its disagreement or displeasure. There were no political parties, just a myriad of constantly changing factions. It was an environment where any attempt to wield political power required skilful speaking. For the speaker (Gk. *rhētōr)* the rewards were great. Civic honours were routinely offered to the most prominent advisors. The potential to influence events was large. Indeed, Cleon's criticisms about the Athenian love of rhetoric come midway through a debate that demonstrates this potential. In 428 BC, the city of Mytilene had revolted from Athens. In this, it was unsuccessful, and the following year it surrendered to Athenian forces. The Mytileneans' fate was decided by debate in the Assembly. Or rather, two debates (Thucydides 3.36–49). On the first day, the argument was won by advocates (of which Cleon was one) who favoured the total extermination of Mytilene. However, on the following day, the debate was reopened and the Assembly was persuaded to precisely the opposite conclusion, namely that this was a moment to show some clemency, not brutality. Such a volte-face, famous both in antiquity and later, is testament to the power of persuasion, the potential fickleness of the audience, and the importance of the stakes in Assembly debates. Rhetoric could be all that separated life from death.

The only venue that could rival the Assembly for rhetorical display was the law-court. Indeed, throughout the fourth century BC, political disagreements often spilled out into the law-court as rival politicians launched high-profile legal suits against each other. The size of Athenian juries (no fewer than 201, and often numbering a few thousand; cf. *The Constitution of Athens* 53.2–3), the absence of a judge, and the lack of overly prescriptive rules of procedure or evidence meant that Athenian legal proceedings encouraged dramatic presentation rather than dry legalistic argument. It also encouraged litigants to seek help in writing their speeches. We have over 100 surviving examples of speeches given in the Athenian law-court. Almost all of these are written by professional speechwriters (*logographoi*). Speechwriting was a lucrative and high-profile profession open to both citizens and foreigners. The most famous Athenian orators were all speechwriters for the law-court.

Perhaps the most distinctively Athenian rhetorical performance in the city was the funeral oration given for the war-dead. The practice is unparalleled elsewhere. The most gifted speaker was chosen from among the citizen body to deliver a patriotic eulogy for all those who had died in battle in the previous year. The most celebrated of these is the funeral oration given by Pericles in 431 BC (Thucydides 2.34–46). However, we have a number of other examples delivered over the course of the fourth century. In the funeral oration, history and myth are strained through a philosophy of civic obligation to create texts that construct an idealised Athens for general contemplation.

Collections of each of these various types of speeches were assembled by Hellenistic scholars for study and imitation. Ten speechwriters were selected to form a representative canon of the best of Attic oratory. The largest collection of speeches in this canon belongs to the fourth-century politician and statesman Demosthenes (384–322 BC). A staunch opponent of Philip of Macedon, a number of his speeches to the Athenian Assembly survive. The most highly regarded are the *Philippics* and the *Olynthiacs*. These speeches, written between 351 BC and 341 BC, chart his attempts, often unsuccessful, to persuade the Athenian people that they should adopt a policy of vigorous opposition to Macedonian expansion. A student of the leading orator Isaeus (c. 420–c. 340 BC), Demosthenes was also a talented writer for the law-court. He first came to prominence in his prosecution of his guardians for their administration of his inheritance (*Against Aphobus* 1–4; cf. *Against Onetor* 1 and 2). The speeches that he wrote for his clients encompass a wide range of legal topics including cases involving contractual obligations (*Against Lacritus*), inheritance (*Against Macaratus*), assault (*Against Meidias*; *Against Conon*), false testimony (*Against Euergus and Mnesibulus*) and mining law (*Against Pantaenetus*). Behind a significant number of these apparently private legal actions lurks a wider political agenda. The proposals of political opponents were often indicted in the law-court (e.g. *Against Timocrates* and *Against Aristocrates*). Two of Demosthenes' most important speeches arose through his political feud with another of the canonical orators, Aeschines (c. 397–c. 322 BC). Their dispute preserves our only sets of speeches from both sides of a case (Aeschines *On the Embassy*, Demosthenes *On the Embassy*; Aeschines *Against Ctesiphon* and Demosthenes *On the Crown*). Demosthenes' political activities also form the basis of another group of surviving speeches, namely the prosecution speeches written by Dinarchus (c. 360–c. 290 BC) and Hyperides (c. 389–c. 322 BC) when Demosthenes was charged with receiving the bribes in the so-called 'Harpalus affair'.

After Demosthenes, the best-represented author is Lysias, a metic whose family originally came from Syracuse. Between them Lysias and Demosthenes represent the bulk of our surviving Attic oratory. We have only a few speeches or fragments of speeches by other orators. The majority of Lysias' speeches were written for clients involved in private legal proceedings. His clients range from members of some of the wealthiest and most distinguished Athenian families to a poor disabled man who is forced to defend his right to a state pension. These speeches have proven very popular with social and cultural historians because they provide a useful insight into the social and political environment of the early fourth century – a period in which Athens came to terms with the legacy of 'The Thirty', the oligarchic regime imposed by Sparta on Athens after the end of the Peloponnesian War. Indeed, Lysias' family suffered terribly under this regime. His brother was murdered and their property was confiscated. The details of the abuse they received are detailed in his most celebrated speech, *Against Eratosthenes*, in which he indicted a member of 'The Thirty' for the crimes committed during their rule. Stylistically, Lysias was praised for his simple style, which is characterised by short sentences, simple syntax and regular Attic diction. He was also praised for his *ethopoiia*, the ability to portray a sympathetic and believable character.

It is important to note that rhetoric was not only performed in Athens, it was also staged and stylised. Critique of rhetoric is one of the constant themes of drama. The contemporary teaching of rhetoric is one of Aristophanes' targets in the *Clouds*. His *Wasps* parodies forensic rhetoric in a ludicrous scene involving the trial of a dog for stealing some cheese. In Aeschylus' *Eumenides*, the law-court again features on stage. On this occasion the dramatist bases his play on the very first trial in Athens, the trial of Orestes for the murder of his mother. To hear this case, Athena establishes the Athenian homicide court, the Areopagus. Aeschylus builds the performance of rhetoric into the myth-history of the city. Rhetoric joins agriculture as one of Athena's gifts to the city.

It was a gift bestowed on the rest of Greece as well. Athens may be our best-documented case of the important role of rhetoric in public life, but there is plenty of evidence to suggest that Athens was not unusual in its arrangements. We have a law-court speech written for performance in Aegina (Isocrates *Aegineticus*) that is just as sophisticated as any produced for an Athenian audience. Foreign schools of rhetoric are known. Famously, only 'laconic' Sparta remained immune to the charms of speech.

The science of classical rhetoric

Given such enthusiasm, there was clearly a market for teachers to make the secrets of persuasion available to a paying audience. From the fifth century onwards, we find numerous references to travelling teachers of rhetoric, a number of whom seem to have written handbooks on the topic. None of the early handbooks survive. Some of them were collected together by Aristotle, but that collection is lost. From references in later works, it seems that their content was basic. Speeches were divided up into their constituent parts, and rules about the order of these parts were established. There seems to have been little concern with logic or argumentation. Discussion of style seems to have been minimal. The majority of teaching seems to have occurred through the process of requiring students to learn exemplary speeches by rote.

However, towards the end of the fifth century, we notice an increase in sophistication as various authors explore different aspects of the art of persuasion. In doing so, they not only up the ante for their competitors, but assist in the process by which rhetoric becomes a distinct discipline with its own rules and specialised vocabulary. The orator Antiphon is a good example of this type of figure, keen to explore the boundaries of rhetoric. Three of his surviving speeches are conventional law-court speeches. However, among his speeches survives a collection of exercises designed to test the limits of conventional rules of argumentation.

These exercises, known as 'the Tetralogies', comprise four speeches on the topic of an imaginary homicide. The case is opened by a prosecutor, who outlines the facts and presents his arguments. He is answered by the defendant, who protests his innocence and rebuts the arguments of the prosecutor. In the process, he often adds some new arguments. The prosecutor then adds a reply, and the defendant is allowed to conclude the proceedings with a final speech. Through this dialectical procedure, Antiphon gives the rules of evidence a good workout. Each exercise takes a hypothetical situation in which the justice of the situation is far from clear, and the speeches serve only to make the waters muddier. Evidentiary problems such as 'deathbed' confessions, the allocation of responsibility for accidents ('Who is to blame when a boy accidentally walks in front of a javelin?'), and the rules for 'self-defence' are presented from opposing angles with no clear resolution. In making their cases, the fictional litigants use the full range of argumentation available to them. Antiphon shows us how to construct arguments based on probability, logic and fact. These exercises offer a rich sample of techniques of proof.

While Antiphon was working on argument, others were concerned with style. In 427, when Gorgias (c. 483–376 BC) arrived in Athens as an ambassador from Leontini, he gave, according to legend, such an impressive speech to the Assembly that the city was completely awe-struck. From his surviving works, the *Encomiun of Helen*, the *Defence of Palamedes* and the *Epitaphios* ('funeral oration'), we can construct a sense of his distinctive and influential style. His speeches are elaborate constructions. There is constant antithesis and word-play. He often balances his clauses with the same number of syllables, and rhymes the last words of clauses and phrases. With Gorgias, we see prose begin to challenge poetry in artistry.

When examining Gorgias and Antiphon, it is important to remember that we are only dealing with the tip of the iceberg. The types of experiments in argumentation and style that they were conducting were being replicated throughout the Greek world. In a passage of Plato's *Phaedrus* (266d–267d), the youth Phaedrus gives a brief discussion of rhetorical teaching. The account is studded with names. The practitioners of the new science of rhetoric were establishing themselves in positions of power and influence.

Clearly, they were successful enough to upset Plato (427–347 BC). In a number of places, he expressed his dissatisfaction with the work of these sophists. He accused them of selling tricks that did not lead to justice or the good. The good should be determined by reason, not by resorting to clever speaking. Plato's distinction between rhetoric and philosophy was to be extremely influential. However, it is an opposition that has a tendency to be overstated. Plato's position on rhetoric is not entirely negative. He presided over the Academy when Aristotle first offered lectures on the topic of rhetoric. Even in the *Gorgias*, a work that sets out his theoretical opposition to rhetoric, Plato concedes that a philosophically valid rhetoric is possible (503a–504e). In the

Phaedrus, he expands on this idea (277b–c). In order for the rhetoric to be valid, the speaker must be an expert in the topic for discussion, make use of logical proof, adapt his argument to his audience, and most importantly be aiming to instil a notion of justice and truth. Admittedly, this expects more from rhetoric than it could, in practice, provide. However, it does show that even the most seemingly hostile critics found it difficult to escape the lure of rhetorical theory.

It was Plato's successor, Aristotle, who was to have the most influence on the science of persuasive speaking (see chapter 48). He first gave lectures on the topic of rhetoric around 355 BC as a member of Plato's Academy. The topic was presumably one that he taught Alexander during his period as his tutor in the 340s. His notes on rhetoric were subsequently revised into the *Rhetoric* some time before his return to Athens in 335. There is much in the *Rhetoric* that is not new, and it does bear a number of striking resemblances to another rhetorical textbook from the same period, the *Rhetoric for Alexander*, a work attributed to Anaximenes of Lampsacus (c. 380–320 BC). Nevertheless, it is hard to overstate the significance of Aristotle's *Rhetoric*. Its value lies in its establishment of a framework for the discussion and development of rhetoric. Aristotle was a compulsive taxonomist. For the first time, the whole discipline is laid out into almost all its constituent parts. Aristotelian divisions dominate the study of rhetoric for the next two and a half millennia.

Among all the divisions in the *Rhetoric*, three are the most prominent and influential. The first is Aristotle's division of speeches into three genres: deliberative speeches (those concerned with determining an advantageous course of action, normally political), forensic speeches (those whose main concern is determining justice and past actions, normally given in the law-court), and epideictic speeches (display speeches whose main concern are honourable things; examples include speeches such as encomia or funeral orations).

The second important division is that of types of proof into artistic proofs (arguments from probability or logic, emotive arguments etc.) and inartistic proofs (factual proofs established through witness statements, laws etc.). This division underpins all subsequent discussion of argumentation and evidence.

The final division, and perhaps the most important, is that of the subject of rhetoric into a number of parts. These parts provide the headings under which rhetoric is subsequently discussed and theorised. They are the building blocks of rhetorical theory.

The first division or part is 'invention' (Gk. *heuresis*, Lat. *inventio*). This area of rhetoric is involved with determining the subject matter of the speech, the question at issue and the theme of the speech. Once these have been determined, the speaker can identify the range of arguments that can be used to support the main claim of the speech. This part also involves discussion of the types of proof that can be used in making these arguments.

The second part is 'arrangement' (Gk. *taxis*, Lat. *dispositio*). Under this head comes discussion of the various parts of the speech and the best arrangement of those parts. The most common divisions are (in order): the introduction (Gk. *prooimion*, Lat. *exordium*); a narration of all the relevant facts and background (Gk. *diēgēsis*, Lat. *narratio*); a presentation of proofs to support your argument (Gk. *pistis*, Lat. *probatio*); and a conclusion (Gk. *epilogos*, Lat. *peroratio*).

The third area that Aristotle discusses is 'style' (Gk. *lexis*, Lat. *elocutio*). This discussion involves both the choice of individual words, and the arrangement of those words. From these apparently simple concerns blossoms a large body of literary theory. In a world obsessed with one's public persona, style makes man.

These three parts are the most important ones for Aristotle. However, he does acknowledge that there is another area that concerns the speaker and that is the area of delivery (Gk. *hypocrisis*, Lat. *pronuntiatio*). This topic gets discussed at the beginning of book 3 and represents the fourth part of rhetoric. It includes such things as stance, use of gestures and the control of the voice.

To these four headings, a fifth was later added in the Hellenistic period. This is the area of memory (Gk. *mnēmē*, Lat. *memoria*). Remembering the arguments and structure of a speech was a difficult task in itself, and a number of mnemonic devices were developed to assist the speaker remember his lines. These devices still form the basis of most modern mnemonic systems.

The division of rhetoric into these five subject areas set the agenda for the development of the subject in the Hellenistic and later periods. Rhetoricians developed new theories and exercises under these headings. A generic series of questions was developed to assist in determining the subject matter of the speech. The subdivisions of a speech were further subdivided and refined. Different styles were categorised. All this activity was done within an Aristotelian framework. The subject grew larger and more ornate, but its essential structure remained the same.

Rhetoric in Roman life

Rhetoric was always conceived as a foreign import to Rome. It was a by-product of empire, another commodity that flooded into Rome in the wake of its expansion into the Hellenistic East. Like other such perceived 'imports' (e.g. philosophy, medicine and pederasty), rhetoric often found itself occupying a slightly uneasy position in Roman cultural life. In particular, it seemed antithetical to, and potentially dangerous for, traditional notions of the self-sufficient Roman citizen who persuaded not through clever words, but through his own integral authority. This perceived threat was the basis of a number of criticisms of rhetoric that circulated throughout the republican and early imperial periods.

Yet, alongside such antagonism, we also find an active engagement with rhetoric. The censors might occasionally expel teachers of rhetoric from Rome, as they did in 161 and 92 BC (Suetonius *On Grammarians and Rhetoricians* 25.2; Aulus Gellius 15.11.2). However, these expulsions were never for long (our two earliest Latin treatises date from a few years after the edict of 92), and arose only because of the extreme popularity of the subject. Rhetoric could be made to feel extremely Roman. Livy saw few problems in populating his history of early Rome with statesmen that all speak like properly trained orators. Even Cato the Censor, famous in antiquity for his blustering anti-Hellenism, produced speeches whose style and structure would stand as models of classical rhetoric.

Cicero records an infamous episode that highlights the complex interchange between notions of rhetoric and the anti-rhetorical stance of aspects of Roman ideology (*de Oratore* 2.124, 188, 194–6; cf. Livy *Periochae* 70, Quintilian *Institutio oratoria* 2.15.7). It concerns the trial for extortion of Manius Aquilius (consul 101 BC). In this notorious case, the defendant is acquitted not on account of the quality of his argument (he is reluctant even to make a defence), but because his advocate strips off his client's shirt and exposes the numerous scars that Aquilius had incurred during his years of military service. On the face of it, the story looks like a perfect example of the limitations of rhetoric in Rome. All the eloquent arguments of Aquilius' accusers count for nothing in the face of this silent body (cf. Sallust *Jugurthine War* 85.26–37 for similar sentiments). However, a closer analysis of the story demonstrates the way in which rhetoric is absolutely crucial to making this moment work. Aquilius succeeds not because the audience is hostile to rhetoric, but rather because they have so assimilated its techniques and systems of thought that the rhetoric of the display passes as unmarked.

Such anti-rhetorical displays will only work if everybody else is using rhetoric. If both sides abandon rhetoric, we are left with two silent scarred bodies facing each other off in the law-court. No side has any advantage, and the process descends into farce. Anti-rhetorical stances need rhetoric, and are evidence of rhetoric's influence. In many ways, these stances are just as rhetorical. They share one of the main concerns of rhetoric, namely the portrayal of character. Along with creating and arranging types of argumentation, one of rhetoric's greatest concerns was the creation of a credible and sympathetic character (*ethopoiia*) and encouragement of sympathy (*pathos*) in the audience. It would be better to see this display not as a contest between rhetoric and personal integrity, but as one between 'argument' and 'character'. It is just a contest between different limbs of rhetoric. Indeed, such physical displays were so complementary to ideas of rhetorical theory that later rhetoricians would even advocate the technique of stripping off to show your scars in their handbooks on rhetoric. It is no accident that the brains behind this move turns out not to be Aquilius, but his advocate, the skilled orator, Marcus Antonius. So in many ways, this is not a story about the failure of rhetoric, but one about the ability of rhetorical training to secure success even without words. Rhetoric didn't undermine Roman values. It articulated and reinforced them. Sometimes silence speaks volumes.

This story is also useful for illustrating part of the reason for the success of rhetoric in Rome – its utility to elite life in Rome. Just as in the city-states of Greece, participation in the civic life of the Roman Republic required the art of persuasive speaking. It was inevitable that an ex-consul and long-serving general like Manius Aquilius would be adept at a few rhetorical tricks. Few politicians could hope to avoid encounters with the law-court or the assemblies.

The political life of the Roman Republic is dominated by formal and informal group meetings. The technical names (e.g. *comitia*, *contiones*) and the functions of these assemblies may vary. What doesn't change is the importance of rhetoric. The rostra in the Forum became one of the important places for public gatherings. These meetings (*contiones*), which were convened by magistrates or priests, provided an opportunity for political leaders to lay out their legislative programmes, discuss contemporary events, or rally opposition to the proposals of their enemies. Technically, any citizen could address these gatherings, if they had the permission of the convening magistrate. In practice, it was a foolish idea unless you were not only well connected, but also well skilled in the art of public speaking. A similar situation obtains in the most august of the republican decision-making bodies, the Senate. Whilst public speaking was not a prerequisite for holding any of the offices that would lead to membership of the Senate, participation in senatorial deliberations required a reasonably high degree of oratorical ability. It was no accident that the Senate was regularly the venue for some of the finest oratorical displays of the Roman Republic. Its members had trained in rhetoric since adolescence, and regarded the skill as one of the necessary accomplishments of the public man. There is some truth in Tacitus' romanticisation of the republican past as a time when the more competent a man was at speaking the more easily he would find political office, and once in office the more he would outstrip his peers in honours and gain influence with the powerful, achieve the respect of the Senate, and obtain glory from the people (cf. Tacitus *Dialogus* 36.4).

The other important venue for rhetorical display was the law-court. Proceedings were held in the open air and often attracted large crowds of interested spectators. Legal proceedings lasted much longer in Rome than in Athens. It was possible for an Athenian jury to hear up to four legal cases in a sitting. Even the longest cases took no longer than a day. In contrast, Roman legal proceedings often took a number of days to conclude, and consisted of a number of speeches by the opposing parties. In addition to being longer and more complex than their Greek counterparts, Roman legal proceedings differed in the more prominent role played by specialist advocates. Under Roman law, it was possible for parties to legal proceedings to be represented in court by an advocate. Although such advocates were prevented from charging fees for such services, they were able to benefit through the relationships of patronage that such service established. For talented and ambitious individuals, the law-court provided a mechanism to increase their prestige and assist their pursuit of political office.

This opportunity for social and political advancement combined with the sophistication of the proceedings to encourage a class of individuals for whom rhetoric was not merely an addition to a series of accomplishments, but constituted their livelihood, and guaranteed their status. For advocates such as Cicero and Hortensius, their rhetorical skill could be parleyed into power that previously could only be achieved on the basis of military or political skill.

It is traditionally argued that such opportunities ended with the fall of the republic. The shift from public debate to private intrigue, from dramatic legal contests to empty political 'show trials', is routinely presented as a factor that contributed to the decline of Roman rhetoric. In fact, there is no decline in the volume, sophistication or importance of rhetoric in the Roman Empire. Tacitus' *Dialogus* (c. AD 97) begins with his interlocutors complaining about the contemporary decline in rhetoric, but what their ensuing discussion demonstrates is just how nuanced and sophisticated is their understanding of the subject.

During the empire, new forms are developed and adapted. For example, the imperial panegyric, elements of which can be traced back to the Hellenistic period, arguably reaches its high point of refinement during this period. The *XII Panegyrici Latini* provides us with a collection of these speeches. They include the *Panegyricus* of Pliny the Elder (AD 61–112). This speech, one of the finest examples of post-Ciceronian oratory, contrasts the virtues of the emperor Trajan with his despotic predecessor Domitian. Other later examples include Claudius Mamertinus' speech of praise for the emperor Julian and a collection of speeches in praise of Constantine by anonymous Gallic orators.

One of the greatest benefits to the dissemination of rhetoric was the empire's establishment of a homogeneous elite culture. With rhetoric as one of its key elements, we find schools, practitioners and displays of rhetoric firmly entrenched from Gaul to the borders of the Parthian Empire. Virtuoso rhetoricians could travel the empire entertaining crowds and demanding huge fees. Chairs of rhetoric were established as gifts to grateful cities. Donations of rhetoric had joined donations of water and grain as one of the ways by which one demonstrated one's philanthropy. It had become one of the staples of civic life.

Declamation was the most distinctive feature of this rhetorical landscape. Originally devised as an exercise in rhetorical training, it grew in importance to become an established art form in its own right. Two distinct types are recognised. The first is the *suasoria* (pl. *suasoriae*), which required the orator to compose a speech offering advice to an historical character or assembly (e.g. 'Should Athens hand Demosthenes over to Philip?'; 'Should Cicero burn his books to save his life?'). Although grounded in the practice of deliberative rhetoric, *suasoriae* tended to be merely opportunities for orators to demonstrate their sophistication of language and phraseology. The second type was the *controversia* (pl. *controversiae*). These involved arguments based on imaginary court-cases (e.g. 'A law provides that in the case of rape a woman may demand either the death of her seducer or marriage without dowry. A certain man rapes two women in one night; one now demands his death, the other demands marriage'; Seneca *Controversiae* 1.5). The subjects chosen for these cases are always elaborate, exotic and melodramatic. Pirates, suicides, patricide, adultery, rape and kidnapping are regular features. Their relationship with actual Roman law and real practice are only tangential. Their purpose was to provide entertainment and mental stimulation rather than legal training, a fact reflected in the anecdotes about popular declaimers who prove useless when having to defend themselves in real trials.

Conversion starts with persuasion. One area in which the science of rhetoric had a large impact was in the public performances of the early Christian church (see chapter 53). Skilled orators are regularly found among the most important bishops, and sermons and homilies provide one of the major ways in which church teaching was transmitted. Augustine (AD 354–430) devoted the second half of *de Doctrina Christiana* ('On the Christian Scriptures') to the topic of rhetoric and its utility for expounding Christian teaching. Famously, Jerome (AD 348–420) dreamt that God castigated him for being more of a Ciceronian than a Christian (Jerome *Letters* 22.30). It was Christian appropriation of classical models of rhetoric that helped ensure the transmission of large volumes of rhetorical works through late antiquity and the medieval period.

Writing Roman rhetoric

The most complete of the early Latin works on rhetoric is the *Rhetoric for Herennius*, written sometime between 86 and 82 BC. The author of the work is unknown. During the medieval period, it was transmitted as a work of Cicero, but this notion was dispelled at the beginning of the Renaissance. From indications within the text, we can identify the author only as a wealthy member of the Roman elite who was well disposed towards Greek scholarship in both philosophy and rhetoric. The work purports to be a response to Herennius' request for information about rhetoric. The work corroborates the general impression of the sophisticated level of rhetorical scholarship in the republic. It adopts the five standard divisions of classical rhetoric, and many of the subdivisions found in Hellenistic Greek writing. Its discussion on delivery, memory and style are some of the best- and earliest-preserved writings on this topic.

The *Rhetoric for Herennius* is also important because it helps to provide some of the context for the most important of the Latin writers of rhetoric, Cicero (106–43 BC). Cicero's rhetorical writings are voluminous. We possess numerous forensic speeches, which represent versions of speeches that Cicero delivered in court and subsequently wrote up for publication. As a result they often omit important details such as the examination of witnesses. Indeed, sometimes the speeches were not even delivered. Such was the case with most of Cicero's speeches against the corrupt governor Verres who fled into exile after Cicero's first speech against him.

Cicero's first major public trial was his defence of Sextus Roscius on the charge of parricide (*pro Sexto Roscio Amerino*). Although the language is a little overblown, the speech shows many of the trademark features of Cicero's forensic oratory, especially in its argumentation and its unflattering depiction of the figure whom Cicero blamed for the conspiracy against his client, the freedman Chrysogonus. Indeed, this taste for invective (Lat. *vituperatio*) can be seen in a number of Cicero's speeches, most notably his attack on L. Calpurnius Piso (see also *in Verrem* and the *Second Philippic* against Marcus Antonius). Cicero was also skilled in characterisation and could vary his tone to suit the subject matter, both features which critics have singled out for praise in his defence of Marcus Caelius (*pro Caelio*).

We also possess a number of Cicero's political speeches to both the Senate and various *contiones*. These include his speech in support of Pompey's command against Mithradates (so-called *pro Lege Manilia*) and his important intervention on behalf of Caesar (*de Provinciis consularibus*). From his time as consul in 63 BC, we possess seven speeches, the most famous being his four against the conspiracy of Catiline. Through this collection of consular speeches, we can see Cicero developing a distinct consular ethos based on his desire to achieve *concordia ordinum* – that is, a balance between the political interests of the factions of the Senate, the equestrians (*equites*) and the people. It is this vision that unifies Cicero's consular rhetoric whether he is opposing the introduction of ill-conceived land reform (*de Lege agraria* I and II), reminding the people of the dignity due to equestrians (*Att.* 2.1), or using the context of a treason trial to defend the authority of the Senate (*pro Rabirio*). Throughout his political speeches, Cicero's model was Demosthenes. Indeed, this imitation can be seen most clearly in his so-called '*Philippics*' against Antony, all of which were published and circulated as a pamphlet. They apparently so angered Antony that he eventually demanded Cicero's hands and head to be hung from the rostra in the Forum.

Cicero also wrote works on rhetorical theory. Comparison between the *Rhetoric for Herennius* and Cicero's earliest work on rhetoric, *de Inventione* ('On Invention') displays a number of similarities in content, and suggests a reasonably widespread and standardised rhetorical curriculum. It was a curriculum with which Cicero would later express some dissatisfaction (cf. *de Oratore* 1.5, 2.75), and to which he would desire to make some lasting reforms.

Cicero's writings on rhetoric fall into two categories. The first are technical treatises that summarise and schematise previous rhetorical writings. *De Inventione*, a summary of techniques of constructing rhetorical argument, is Cicero's first attempt at such a work. In addition to this, he wrote *Partitiones oratoriae* ('The Parts of Rhetoric'), a dialogue in which Cicero's son quizzes his father about the various heads of rhetoric, the *Topica* (44 BC), a summary of Aristotle's work by the same name which was purportedly written from memory during a sea-voyage to educate a travelling companion, and *de Optimo Genere Oratorum* ('On the Best Kind of Orator') which purports to be an introduction to a translation of two of the most famous Athenian forensic speeches, those given by Aeschines against his great rival Demosthenes.

Cicero's most influential contribution to Roman rhetoric, however, was not these summaries, but rather his three non-technical treatises *de Oratore* (55 BC), *Brutus* and the *Orator* (both 46 BC).

De Oratore is a dialogue in three books on the general topic of oratory. It is addressed to Cicero's brother Quintus and is offered as advice on how to become the ideal orator, a figure who corresponds closely to the figure of the ideal statesman found in the political writings of Cicero. The *Brutus* also shares the dialogue form, but its content consists of a historical survey of Roman rhetoric set against the background of civil strife. Along with the *Orator* it is part of Cicero's intervention in the debates about style that were raging throughout the late republic.

This body of material would become the standard works on rhetoric for the rest of the Roman Empire. All successors acknowledged the supremacy of Cicero, and all claimed to be his heirs and working within his tradition. However, while Cicero was regarded as providing the best words on rhetoric, he was not permitted to provide the last word. Throughout the empire, rhetoricians continued to publish handbooks on specific points and exemplary speeches for imitation.

Volume is always encouraging to the critical spirit. It allows a person to make a mark through systemisation and resolution of academic debates. So it was that Quintilian (c. AD 40–c. 96) ensured his fame through the *Institutio oratoria* ('Education of the Orator'). As he works through the five traditional headings of rhetoric, Quintilian summarises the mass of material that had been accumulated through the work of generations of scholars of rhetoric. He establishes his authority through negotiating disputes in practice and theory. Quintilian not only writes up a tradition, he also adds to it. Importantly, he expands the field of rhetoric to include everything that contributes to the education of the orator. Music, philosophy and mathematics are all subsumed within the discipline. In the *Institutio oratoria*, Quintilian lays the groundwork for Renaissance humanism.

Quintilian's reputation lead to a number of speeches being attributed to him. Two collections survive known as the *Declamationes Maiores* ('Greater Declamations') and *Declamationes Minores* ('Lesser Declamations'). The former, a collection of nineteen declamations, almost certainly constitutes spurious imitations from the fourth century. More debatable is the collection of 'Lesser Declamations'. It is possibly a collection of notes published by one of Quintilian's students. The work is a testament to the influence of this teacher and the cachet of his name.

This imitation of Quintilian is also a reflection of the fact that he is the last Latin writer on rhetoric who commands universal respect. Handbooks continue to be written, and a number of these are collected in the work known as the *Rhetores Latini Minores* ('The Lesser Latin Rhetoricians'). They demonstrate a diversity of approaches, and show the continued enthusiasm for the topic. As long as Roman culture continued so did rhetoric. The import had become integral.

Further reading

Texts and Translations

Texts and translations of the major speeches by Greek and Roman orators are available in the Loeb Classical Library series. This series also includes texts and translations of the most important rhetorical handbooks and treatises on rhetoric. For the text and translation of imperial panegyrics, see C. E. V. Nixon and B. S. Rodgers (eds), *In Praise of Later Roman Emperors*, Berkeley: California University Press, 1994. Translations of the Attic orators are available in the *Oratory of Classical Greece* series published by the University of Texas Press.

Modern discussions

M. L. Clarke, *Rhetoric at Rome: A Historical Survey* (3rd edn), London: Routledge, 1996 – a useful historical sweep of developments in Roman rhetoric.

T. Cole, *The Origins of Rhetoric in Ancient Greece*, Baltimore and London: Johns Hopkins University Press, 1991.

W. J. Dominik (ed.), *Roman Eloquence: Rhetoric in Society and Literature*, London: Routledge, 1997.

G. A. Kennedy, *A New History of Classical Rhetoric*, Princeton: Princeton University Press, 1994 – provides a useful summary of Kennedy's voluminous scholarship on the topic.

H. Lausberg, *Handbook of Literary Rhetoric: A Foundation for Literary Study*, eds D. E. Orton and

R. Dean Anderson, Leiden: Brill, 1998 – an English translation of a classic German handbook. Contains useful explanations of almost all technical terms used in rhetorical writings.

J. M. May (ed.), *Brill's Companion to Cicero: Oratory and Rhetoric*, Leiden and Boston: Brill, 2002 – an important collection of essays that examines almost every aspect of Cicero's oratory and rhetorical writings.

D. A. Russell, *Greek Declamation*, Cambridge: Cambridge University Press, 1983.

E. Schiappa, *The Beginnings of Rhetorical Theory in Classical Greece*, New Haven and London: Yale University Press, 1999.

I. Worthington (ed.), *Persuasion: Greek Rhetoric in Action*, London: Routledge, 1994 – a helpful collection of articles that covers theory, practice and contemporary approaches to Greek rhetoric.

46. *Literary Criticism*

Donald Russell

There are three famous books of classical literary criticism: Aristotle's *Poetics*, Horace's *Ars Poetica* and the treatise *On Sublimity* attributed to Longinus. All three have had immense influence on modern thinking about literature, the first two since the Renaissance, the last since Nicolas Boileau's French translation of 1674. But they are, as it were, the highest peaks of a complex and largely submerged mountain range: just how complex we are seeing a little more clearly since the recent improved decipherment and interpretation of the Herculaneum papyri of the Epicurean philosopher Philodemus, a contemporary of Virgil and Horace (see chapter 32). In fact, the three books represent three distinct modes in which ancient criticism was expressed: Aristotle was a philosopher, Horace a poet, 'Longinus' a teacher of rhetoric. There is a fourth mode, which we may call the grammatical or exegetic. This is a useful way of mapping our subject.

Poetical

Let us take the poetical mode first, for the first critics were the poets themselves: 'bard envies bard' (Hesiod *Works and Days* 26). The singers Phemius and Demodocus are characters in Homer's *Odyssey*. Pindar's Odes contain much comment: claims to be the spokesman (*prophātās*) of the Muses, contempt for plodding and uninspired contemporaries, and a critical view of the improprieties of myth. Aristophanes, especially in *Frogs*, deploys much sophistication to describe and parody the metre, style and content of contemporary tragedy (see chapter 39). The tradition continued in Hellenistic times: Callimachus, scholar as well as poet, was advocate and exemplar of a delicate perfectionism, and denigrated the expansiveness and loose construction of rivals. The Roman literary world inherited this sort of partisanship: Catullus, Virgil and Ovid were all in a sense critics, concerned with the relationship of art and inspiration, or of grandeur and neatness, always with an inclination to the Callimachean side (see chapter 42). The most explicit critic is Horace, not only in *Odes* and *Satires*, but especially in the literary epistles, of which *Ars Poetica* is the most elaborate. As a lyric poet, he claims inspiration and public usefulness, but also delicate art: he cannot and will not rival Pindar (*Odes* 4.2). In the *Epistles*, he emphasises the progress made in his own time, the technical development that makes him and his contemporaries superior to the age of Ennius and Plautus. The *Ars* represents the same position, but it is not wholly explicable in terms of the poets' tradition of criticism: it is a didactic poem which professes not only to advise would-be dramatists, but to versify theory and communicate insights due to philosophical writing in the tradition of Aristotle. It is therefore time to turn to this line of development.

Philosophical

Plato tells us that there was an 'ancient quarrel' between poetry and philosophy (see chapter 48). In his predecessors, this was mainly a moral matter: the objectionable fables about the gods offended the common conscience, and to interpret them allegorically (which meant attributing deeper knowledge to the poet) was not convincing to all, and certainly not to Plato. (Allegorical interpretation, however, played an important part in later culture – Stoics and Neoplatonists devised different forms of it – and is one of the most extraordinary legacies of Greek learning to the Christian world.) Plato's complaint too was primarily moral: exposure to poetical myth and the pretence involved in playing a part in drama were bad for the character. He therefore preferred epic to drama, and epic with the least possible amount of direct speech. But he linked this perception with his metaphysical view that the world we see is only a shadow of the real world of 'ideas', so that the imitative ('mimetic') arts, visual as well as verbal or musical, can give us only a shadow of a shadow.

It is usually held, and there is much truth in it, that Aristotle's *Poetics* is a response to Plato, and propounds a view of poetry that would make it intellectually more respectable. But this is not all that this book does. It is the first systematic attempt to set *poiētikē* (this 'art of poetry' is not exclusively confined to verse, but defined rather by its fictionality) in the context of other skills, as a 'mimetic' art using speech, with or without rhythm or music. It is crucial to his argument that *mimesis* is seen as a natural activity of intelligent and curious human beings, and as a means of expressing general truths about life. Though tragedy had, by Aristotle's time, long passed its peak, it is tragedy as a fully developed genre which is his main subject, and his discussion of plot, character, emotional effect and language is based for the most part on Sophocles and Euripides, both of whom had died more than twenty years before he was born. Epic, for Aristotle, is a less perfect genre, because it is more diffuse and lacks the kind of unity which he saw in the best tragedies, such as Sophocles' *Oedipus Tyrannus*.

Aristotle's successors in the philosophical tradition are less well known. His pupil Theophrastus followed up his master's speculations about style (to be found in Aristotle's *Rhetoric III*, not in *Poetics*), and it is largely from him that the dominant interest in types of style (*charactēres*, *genera dicendi*) which we find in the Roman period derives: this interest does, however, become the concern rather of the rhetorical and exegetical traditions than of philosophers. Our ideas of Hellenistic poetics are nowadays in flux. They depend a great deal on the fragmentary writings of Philodemus, himself both an Epicurean philosopher and a competent poet, who reported and criticised the views of various Stoic and Peripatetic predecessors, mostly mere names to us. Between them, these thinkers present us with an astonishing range of answers to the question 'what makes a good poem?' Is it its content, morally useful or pleasurably fanciful? Is it the arrangement of words in metre, or even the sounds themselves? Or is it some combination of these factors?

These essentially philosophical speculations naturally interested and influenced critics of a more rhetorical or grammatical type; and when, in the late first century BC, we once again encounter complete texts, for example Cicero's *de Oratore* or Dionysius of Halicarnassus' *Arrangement of Words*, we are aware of great sophistication in the minute discussion of sound and style, and a vast range of reference, from oratory to lyric poetry. In the later times, the philosophical school which contributed most to theoretical criticism and to aesthetics generally was the Neoplatonic. Faced with the need to reconcile Plato with Homer, and with the problem of interpreting Plato's dialogues, the Neoplatonists developed elaborate allegorical structures. Thus the dialogue was represented as an analogue of the kosmos, and Plato (and indeed Homer before him) is said to have been aware that there were several kinds of poetry, not all equally valuable: some poetry was inspired, some was commendable because it communicated wisdom and good advice, and some was 'imitative', whether realistic or mere *skiagraphia*, 'shadow-drawing', with no higher aim than to stimulate the emotions. Systems like this (which comes from Proclus) seem very bizarre; but Neoplatonic allegory is historically important because of its influence on Christian study of the Bible.

Rhetorical

Rhetoric, which gives us our third mode, was the practical skill of persuasive speech, or rather the conceptual framework which made this skill teachable. It was the subject of many treatises (mostly lost) written in the fifth and fourth centuries, culminating in Aristotle's *Rhetoric*. Even in its earliest phases, it went far beyond 'hints for public speakers'; it developed not only an elaborate theoretical structure, a central feature of which was a sharp distinction between content and verbal form, but also a critical function applicable to literature generally, not only oratory. The reason for this was the educational context. Young people knew their Homer and went to the theatre. Teachers of rhetoric therefore naturally drew on poetical material to illustrate the principles of persuasion. Poetry was specially relevant to 'display' oratory ('epideictic') which aimed not at persuading a jury or advocating a political action but at giving public praise or creating a mood of patriotic pride, or simply at giving amusement. Some later rhetoricians in fact reckoned all poetry to be part of the 'epideictic' branch of oratory. In such an approach to literature the reader is not simply a passive judge, but a would-be practitioner who wants to learn by imitation. The reader must therefore focus clearly on the writer's intention, and analyse the means by which it is fulfilled.

The great bulk of surviving Greek and Roman criticism is of this kind. Thus the *Art of Rhetoric* attributed to Dionysius of Halicarnassus, but actually of the second or third century AD, examines at length a number of speeches in Homer under the head of 'figured speeches' – that is, speeches in which the orator's real intention is quite different from what it appears to be (ed. L. Radermacher, pp. 311–42). Again, Quintilian's survey of the literature of both languages (*Institutio oratoria* 10.1), which looks superficially like literary history, is really concerned only to recommend authors whose techniques provide useful models for the budding orator. *On Sublimity* itself makes it clear at the beginning that the author's hope is to say something 'useful' for orators. In his vast range of examples, both prose and poetry, 'Longinus' matches particular features of style or thought with the effect they produce on the reader, with the implication that this is what you must do if you want this result. But 'sublimity', unlike the stylistic qualities identified by other ancient critics (e.g. Demetrius, Hermogenes), does not depend primarily on choice or arrangement of words, important as these are, but on a special quality of thought and feeling: it requires the writer's mind to be fixed on great matters, and to be deeply moved. 'Longinus', though he distances himself from philosophers (44.1), and is certainly a teacher of rhetoric, is also a moralist, with a high ideal of the reach of the human mind, and a deep admiration for Plato.

Grammatical or exegetic

We come finally to the *grammatikos*, the expert in exegesis. Already in classical times many words in Homer were unintelligible, and teachers had to explain them as best they could. The ancient texts also were often ambiguous and self-contradictory; they gave rise to problems (*problēmata*) which cried out for solutions (*luseis*). Aristotle's *Poetics* already engages with earlier work of this kind. The Hellenistic commentators on Homer, and especially Aristarchus, were the great developers of this type of scholarship. Their work survives mainly in the 'scholia', (that is, marginal notes in medieval manuscipts), brief and sometimes cryptic. From them, a certain type of exegesis, current for nearly a millennium, can be inferred. Apart from difficult words and 'problems', the *grammatikos* might comment on moral issues, on history and antiquities, on the appropriateness of the passage to the character speaking or to the fictional situation, on figures of speech and rhetorical moves, or even on the life of the poet and its relation to his work. (Little was really known of poets' lives, so that the biography was usually constructed out of hints in the poems.) The *grammatikos* would not necessarily have a clear theoretical position concerning the nature and excellence of poetry, but he would usually be an educator. In the prevailing educational system of Hellenistic and Roman times he taught children who were not ready for rhetoric or philosophy.

Perhaps the best examples of commentaries which we have are some Latin ones from late antiquity: Servius on Virgil, Donatus on Terence. But as a final illustration of this mode, let us take a text which is not a commentary, but a book of advice for parents and teachers: Plutarch's *How the Student should Read Poetry*. Plutarch was himself not a *grammatikos* or a rhetorician, but a teacher of philosophy; but here he addresses himself to pre-philosophical education and asks how a boy reading the poets can learn useful lessons from them without absorbing wrong or immoral notions. To answer this, and so offer his own response to Plato's rejection of poetry in the *Republic*, he draws on the whole repertoire of exegetical techniques: philological knowledge, study of context, insights into the poets' distant and remote world. What is perhaps most interesting about this is that it is all relatively undogmatic. Plutarch seems to want to stimulate the student's critical reactions, not simply to tell him what to think, though of course he has no doubts about the moral principles to which the young man must conform, and he recognises that the reader he is addressing is 'a lover of beauty and honour, who approaches poems not for amusement but for education', and has quite different concerns from the scholar and the rhetorician.

So, after all, the great works we have chosen to represent those four 'modes' of criticism all break the bounds of this classification. This is what distinguishes them and makes them specially interesting. It is of course not surprising that a thousand years of thinking about literature should have produced such diversity, both within and outside the world of education. Grammar, rhetoric and philosophy all went to the making of literary understanding, and the best minds drew on them all. The combined achievement is astonishing, and it is right that it should be a major theme of modern scholarship.

Futher reading

Translations:

S. Halliwell, *The Poetics of Aristotle*, London: Duckworth, 1987.

D. A. Russell and M. Winterbottom, *Ancient Literary Criticism: The Principal Texts in New Translations*, Oxford: Clarendon Press, 1972.

Loeb Classical Library editions of Longinus and Demetrius; Dionysius of Halicarnassus.

Surveys

G. A. Kennedy (ed.), *Cambridge History of Literary Criticism. Vol. 1: Classical Criticism*, Cambridge: Cambridge University Press, 1989.

D. A. Russell, *Criticism in Antiquity* (2nd edn), Bristol: Bristol Classical Press, 1995.

Other works

C. O. Brink, *Horace on Poetry* (3 vols), Cambridge: Cambridge University Press, 1963–82.

A. Ford, *The Origins of Criticism*, Princeton: Princeton University Press, 2002.

S. Halliwell, *Aristotle's Poetics*, London: Duckworth, 1986.

G. A. Kennedy, *The Art of Persuasion in Greece*, Princeton: Princeton University Press, 1963.

G. A. Kennedy, *The Art of Rhetoric in the Roman World*, Princeton: Princeton University Press, 1972.

M. R. Lefkowitz, *The Lives of the Greek Poets*, London: Duckworth, 1981.

R. Meijering, *Literary and Rhetorical Theories in Greek Scholia*, Groningen: Egbert Forsten, 1987.

D. Obbink (ed.), *Philodemus and Poetry*, Oxford: Oxford University Press, 1995.

47. *Grammar and Linguistics*

Philip Burton

Defining ancient grammar

While various cultures have developed more or less formal studies of language, the Graeco-Roman tradition has been by far the most influential in the formation of the modern field of linguistics (see chapter 7). This is partly a matter of historical contingency; the massive importance of English as a world language has given a special prominence to the Graeco-Roman linguistic tradition compared to (say) the Chinese or even the Indian tradition. However, it is also partly because of the sheer depth of that tradition – some 1,000 years of it – and partly also because of its success in providing a theoretical model for describing languages other than Greek and Latin.

Such triumphalist statements, however, risk hiding another truth: that the Greeks and Romans had no single word or intellectual class for what we would call linguistics. The closest equivalent is what in Greek is called *grammatikē*, and in Latin *grammatica*, *litteratura*, *scientia litterarum* or similar, translated here as 'grammar'. This category, however, covers several fields which would not normally be considered part of modern linguistics, while other questions which would be considered part of linguistics are not normally included under 'grammar'. Moreover, the discipline of grammar itself is formed only after a long period of intellectual debate, and continues to evolve throughout antiquity and beyond. Much of our knowledge of ancient grammar comes indirectly, through sources significantly later and often with a different agenda. This account, then, begins with a consideration of some areas of linguistic inquiry which either pre-date the formalisation of grammar as a discipline, or in some sense stand aside from it.

Linguistics before grammar: phonetics, etymologies and glosses

The development of the Greek alphabetical system of classical times is in itself a considerable achievement in applied phonetics. Although most of the shapes and values of the characters are based on the ancient North Semitic script, the adaptation is subtle and economical. In the distinctions it makes within the consonant system it is vastly superior to the Bronze Age Linear B script (though that also was based on a valid de facto phonological analysis); and, unlike its Semitic prototype, it was equipped with seven vowel symbols (a e h i o u w) to reflect the ten vowels of the classical language (the vowel symbols a i u each representing both long and short vowel sounds).

By the classical period further analysis of the sounds of Greek had clearly taken place. Plato (*Cratylus* 393E, 424C) distinguishes 'vocalised' (*phōnēenta*, i.e. 'vowel' sounds) from 'non-vocalised' (*aphōna*) sounds, and refers to further subdivisions of the vowel category made by 'specialists in the field'. Aristotle adds a further class of 'half-vocalised' or 'semivowel' sounds (*hēmiphōna*). The meanings of these terms correspond fairly closely with those in use today, but not exactly: the ancient class of semivowels included not only the resonants (in modern terminology; see appendix to this chapter) *l r m n*, but also the fricative *s* and the clusters *ks* (the Greek letter ξ, Latin *x*), *ps* (Greek ψ), and *sd* (Greek ζ).

In other words, the category of semivowels was closer to that now described as continuants.

The quest for etymologies or 'true meanings' of words goes back to our earliest Greek literature; compare, for instance, the story given to account for Odysseus' name in *Odyssey* 19.406–8. The vogue for etymology is parodied (probably) in Plato's *Cratylus*, in which Socrates gives a master-class in the art of the improbable; for instance, giving six unlikely etymologies for the name Apollo. Underlying this, however, is a serious philosophical debate about how far language exists 'naturally' and how far 'by convention'. The latter seems to have been Plato's belief, and was certainly Aristotle's; and for those who accepted it, much of the imperative to discover 'true meanings' disappeared. Etymology remains important, however, in the growth industry of literary scholarship; scholars based in the revival Hellenistic literary centres of Alexandria and Pergamum alike sought to explain unfamiliar words in Homer and other ancient texts with reference to archaism, dialect and borrowing from non-Greek sources.

The Stoic input

Much of the progress in linguistic thought between the fourth and third centuries was made by the Stoic school of philosophy (see chapter 48). Our knowledge of Stoic linguistics is almost entirely second-hand, but there are enough references in later authors to establish its importance. The Stoic Chrysippus is credited with having identified five 'parts of speech' or 'parts of the sentence' (*merē tou logou*); it is within Stoicism that we first find the different case-forms of the Greek noun identified (with the possible exception of the vocative); we also have the traces of theory dealing with the distinction between tense and aspect in the Greek verbal system. Much of the Stoic work on language was done in the field of semiotics, in which they developed a four-fold distinction between the thing signified; the 'sayable' (*lekton*), that is, the mental conception of the thing in the mind of the speaker or hearer; the word as a physical utterance; and the 'act of saying' (*lexis*), consisting of the word plus the sayable. Such an approach could, and did, lead equally into phonetics or into semantic theory.

The invention of grammar: Greek writers

The growth of grammar as a separate field of inquiry was, then, neither natural nor inevitable; and it is worth while asking what exactly the earliest grammarians thought they were doing. One of our main sources is a hostile one. At some point in the second or early third century AD, the Greek philosopher Sextus Empiricus composed a work entitled *Against the Grammarians*, in the course of which he argued that the conceptions of grammar current in his day were internally incoherent and mutually exclusive. He begins by reiterating a familiar distinction, between grammar as basic literacy on the one hand, and on the other hand more advanced literary or linguistic study. He then proceeds to list some of the definitions in use. Having listed Crates of Mallus, Aristophanes of Byzantium and Aristarchus of Samothrace (collectively later second to mid-first century BC) as founders of the discipline, he then takes his starting point from the definition of grammar given by the first-century BC grammarian Dionysius Thrax: 'practical knowledge of the things generally said by the poet and prose-writers'. There were, according to Sextus, those who criticised Dionysius's characterisation of grammar as 'practical knowledge' (*empeiria*), claiming this deprived it of its status as a field of expert skill (*technē*). Another grammarian, Chaeris, defines it as 'a skill (*hexis*) which distinguishes on the basis of expertise (*technē*) and research (*historia*)'. This debate seems to rumble on well into the Byzantine era; a fourteenth-century commentary on Dionysius Thrax distinguishes 'practical knowledge' (*empeiria*) from 'knowledge' (*epistēmē*), 'expertise' (*technē*), and 'experience' (*peira*), with 'expertise' itself divided into four – and so on. Others again, according to Sextus, protested against Dionysius' definition on the ground that the study of grammar should include everyday speech as well as literary language; and at least one other grammarian thought that the subject should include the 'things thought' as well as the 'things said'. Sextus is doubtless playing up the differences, but they must reflect a real debate over the nature of grammar in relation to other systems of knowledge.

So much for the definitions. What of the content? Greek grammarians divide their subject in various ways, but the most influential (possibly going back to the first-century BC grammarian Tyrannio) distinguishes four separate activities: reading aloud, interpretation, textual criticism and overall 'judgement' (*krisis*) on a passage. Sextus Empiricus records a tripartite scheme, consisting of the 'technical' dimension (largely concerned with the language), the 'historical' (explanation of historical and mythical elements), and what he calls the 'special' part, a combination of textual and literary criticism; his scheme, therefore, corresponds largely to the canonical four-way division, but with the third and fourth elements combined. In Dionysius Thrax we find a division of grammar into six parts: skill in reading aloud, interpretation of the figures of speech, accounting for unusual words and 'historical' details, etymology, accounting for the pattern of speech (*analogia*), and 'judgement' (*krisis* again). In practice, then, there is a general consensus among the Greek grammarians about the divisions of their subject, and about the overall sequence of the different divisions, even if their account of different subdivisions varies.

The practical goal of the Greek grammarians being to enable their students to read aloud the classics of Greek literature, their main focus is on the relationship between the written text and its realisation in speech. This does not preclude a concern with overall literary judgement on a passage, but according to Dionysius, it is from the reading that we are able to understand and form our judgements on a passage. The importance of the relationship between written text and oral performance is clear from the prominence he gives early on to accent and punctuation (on which he is our earliest source); only in this context do they make sense. The remainder of his work is taken up largely with material on letters (both the signs and the sounds they represent), syllable quantity (important for scanning verse texts correctly) and the different 'parts of speech'. These he counts as eight: the noun, verb, participle, article, pronoun, preposition, adverb and conjunction. This taxonomy – a development of the Stoic system – corresponds closely to modern analyses. However, his subdivisions are less modern-looking. Nouns, for instance, are grouped not on primarily inflectional grounds, into the 'declensions' familiar to modern readers, but rather on a mixture of morphological and semantic grounds.

Two features of Dionysius' definition are particularly notable. First, there is the search for 'patterns of speech' (*analogiae*). The period between the Stoic Chrysippus and the first century BC saw a lively debate between those who sought as far as possible to regularise linguistic use, and those who argued instead that such matters should be determined by common usage (Greek *sunētheia*, Latin *consuetudo*, *usus*). The proponents of regularity or analogy (*analogia*) are presented in our sources as arguing against such irregular patterns as (to take a Latin example) the positive form of the adjective *magnus*, the comparative *maior* and the superlative *maximus*, or the similar set *bonus* 'good', *melior* 'better', *optimus* 'best'. These 'analogists', most notably Aristophanes of Byzantium and Aristarchus of Samothrace, are sometimes grouped together in modern thought as the 'Alexandrian school', because of their association with the Ptolemaic royal library at Alexandria. These scholars are particularly known for their work on the text of Homer, and their advocacy of analogy probably springs in part from the desire to clarify obscurities in the transmitted text by identifying the regular patterns underlying word-forms which were opaque in their day. Their opponents support the principle of anomaly (*anōmalia*), and recognised such irregularity as a fact not only of linguistics but of every other category of knowledge. The anomalist school is said to claim as its founders Chrysippus the Stoic and Crates of Mallos; they are particularly associated with the Attalid royal capital of Pergamum, Alexandria's rival as the capital city of Hellenistic cultural world. The debate on whether grammar is a science (*technē*) or some form of practical experience (*empeiria*) to some extent maps onto the analogy/anomaly question. In the wrong hands, this controversy could drift into mere pedantry; and it has in any case been conventional in recent years to see our ancient sources as schematic, derivative or both. However, it anticipates some of the key questions and theories of modern linguistics. The anomalist emphasis on practicality, clarity and brevity in some ways prefigures the 'co-operative principle' of language put forward by the twentieth-century philosopher H. P. Grice. Modern historical phonologists share the analogists' interest in patterns such as *magnus/maior/maximus*, though for different reasons; such 'morphophonemic alternations' can be used as a means for establishing earlier forms of words and the processes of sound-change they subsequently underwent.

The other notable feature of Dionysius' definition of grammar is the absence of any serious concern with syntax. This is typical of much ancient grammar, which begins at the atomic level of letters, works up to the molecular levels of syllables and words, but seldom considers what constitutes a clause (*kōlon*, Latin *membrum*) or sentence (*logos*, *noēma*, Latin *sententia*). This is not primarily an intellectual failure in ancient linguistics, since these concepts are familiar in the rhetorical and dialectical writers. It is simply the case that works on grammar tend to work at the level of the very short linguistic unit. Dionysius himself works up the scale from letters to syllables to words, but, though he defines the sentence as 'a combination of words . . . conveying a meaning complete in itself', he does not take the question further. The most notable Greek syntactician is Apollonius Dyscolus (second century AD), who in his *Syntax* devotes considerable attention to the principles underlying what makes a particular utterance grammatically correct or not.

Latin writers

The crystallisation of grammar as a distinct field of intellectual inquiry in the second century BC coincided with an intense growth of interest in Greek ideas among Roman intellectuals. It is not surprising, therefore, that our earliest Latin grammar and grammarians appear shortly afterwards. Suetonius (*de Grammaticis* 2.1) relates that it was Crates of Mallos who showed the way: sent by King Attalus of Pergamum on an embassy to Rome, he broke his leg falling into a sewer-hole, and spent his convalescence giving lectures on grammar. However, Suetonius emphasises also that the class of grammarian did not arrive overnight: into the first century BC, a distinction was made between the *litterator* 'elementary teacher' and the *litteratus* 'man of literary culture'; the latter group also taught rhetoric. Greek seems to have remained the accepted language even for Latin studies until the mid-20s of the first century BC. Of these earlier grammarians the most influential was Remmius Palaemon (second quarter of the first century AD), a colourful character who is credited with creating the canonical eight parts of Latin speech by replacing the article (not found in Latin) with the interjection (classed in Greek as an adverb). The earliest Latin grammatical work to survive may well be a handbook on orthography, ascribed to the second-century AD grammarian Terentius Scaurus.

By this time one of the most important studies of Latin linguistics had already been published. Marcus Terentius Varro's *On the Latin Language* (*de Lingua Latina*), probably published in 43 BC, ran to twenty-five books, of which books 5–10 are more or less well preserved. These show Varro less as a grammarian and more as a theorist of language, interested in etymology and in syntax, which (as in the Greek tradition) is largely considered as a branch of logic. The extant portions deal extensively with the analogy/anomaly debate, which he may exaggerate. Varro is one of several major Latin authors who stand outside the grammatical tradition, yet provide valuable information on it and on language theory at Rome generally: others include Quintilian (AD 35 to late first century), perhaps a pupil of the Roman grammarian Remmius Palaemon; Aulus Gellius, the second-century literary antiquarian; Augustine of Hippo (354–430), the Christian bishop whose works include a tractate on grammar as well as a developed theory of semiotics, notably expounded in his work *On Christian Teaching* (*de Doctrina Christiana*); and Macrobius, the fifth-century polymath who, in addition to his better-known *Saturnalia*, also composed an essay in contrastive linguistics on the Greek and Latin verb systems.

From later antiquity and the early Middle Ages

we have a considerable volume of grammatical works proper. These are often pseudonymous and hard to date; they do, however, reflect an intellectual tradition which was not always the passing down of received ideas. Two authors are particularly notable: Donatus, the Roman grammarian of the fourth century AD whose *Ars Minor* ('Shorter Art') and *Ars Maior* ('Longer Art') are the most influential grammars of the early Middle Ages; and Priscian (fifth-sixth century), the Latin grammarian of the Greek city of Constantinople. Priscian's *Institutio de nomine et pronomine et verbo* ('Teaching on the Noun, Pronoun, and Verb') was also highly influential in the earlier Middle Ages; but his masterpiece is the immense *Institutiones* ('Teachings'), a summation of previous Graeco-Roman linguistic thought, particularly notable for his application to Latin of the second-century AD Greek grammarian Apollonius Dyscolus' writings on syntax.

Grammar and society

But why did grammar matter? Who became a professional grammarian, how, and why? Who studied under them? And why did ancient society countenance the existence of people whose economic contribution as producers was not immediately apparent? It is clear that the early study of grammar was seen as a province of what was originally called sophistry; pre-dating the sober accounts in Plato and Aristotle cited above, and the advances made by the Stoic school, are the sort of proto-analogist speculations which Aristophanes puts into the mouth of the Sophist Socrates (*Clouds* 658–92). And to some extent grammar retains its links with philosophy. However, there is little doubt that from around the first century BC the study and teaching of grammar are professionalised and set aside from other branches of knowledge. At first the new trade is largely taught by slaves and freedmen, but from the first century AD at least, grammarians are already conceptualising their trade in semi-hieratic terms. By late antiquity, the entrance to their schools is typically depicted as covered by a curtain, acting as a veil to the mysteries practised within. According to the compelling account put forward by Kaster (*Guardians of Language*), the grammarian's classroom became the single most important influence outside the family on the influential classes of the Roman Empire, in the Greek world displacing the gymnasium as the civic space where young elite males went to compete with each other. Some grammarians enjoyed stellar careers: Ausonius of Bordeaux was plucked from his schoolroom in the mid-360s to become tutor to the future emperor Gratian, who later rewarded him with a praetorian prefecture and ultimately with a consulship. More often, however, the grammarian is glimpsed on the edge of the groups of the powerful, but seldom taking a prominent position among them.

Appendix

Characters in square brackets are phonetic symbols as distinct from letters; so b is the letter b, [b] the sound made at the start of *bit*.

aspect form expressing features of an event such as beginning, duration, completion or repetition (whereas tense expresses distinctions of time)
continuant produced by incompletely closing the vocal tract (the passage from lungs to mouth) to give a continuous flow of air, such as [s], [z], [l]
fricative produced by constricting the vocal tract (the passage from lungs to mouth) without complete closure to give a noisy flow of air, such as [f], [s], [v]
resonant consonant capable of functioning as the nucleus of a syllable, such as the final [l] in bottle; resonants are sometimes divided into liquids ([l] and [r]), nasals ([m] and [n]) and semi-vowels ([w] and [y]).

Further reading

Texts

D. L. Blank, *Sextus Empiricus*, Against the Grammarians, Oxford: Clarendon Press, 1998 – introduction, commentary and notes on a key text.
R. Kaster (ed.), *Suetonius*, de Grammaticis et Rhetoribus, Oxford: Clarendon Press, 1995 – introduction, text, notes and commentary on this key work.
H. Keil (ed.), *Grammatici Latini* [*GLK*], Leipzig:

Teubner, 1855–80 – indispensable collection of the key Latin texts.

G. Uhlig et al. (eds), *Grammatici Graeci*, Leipzig: Teubner, 1867–1910 – indispensable collection of the key Greek texts.

Secondary works

S. Everson (ed.), *Language*, Cambridge: Cambridge University Press, 1994 – collection of specialist essays specifically on ancient linguistics and philosophy of language.

R. Kaster, *Guardians of Language: The Grammarian and Society in Late Antiquity*, Berkeley: University of California Press, 1988 – a breakthrough book in integrating the grammar and the wider culture of the ancient world.

V. Law, *Grammar and Grammarians in the Early Middle Ages*, London: Longman, 1997 – covers a slightly later period, but with plenty of classical overlaps; crisp and lucid.

V. Law, *The History of Linguistics in Europe: From Plato to 1600*, Cambridge: Cambridge University Press, 2003 – ideal introduction.

V. Law and I. Sluiter (eds), *Dionysius Thrax and the Techne Grammatike*, Munster: Nodus, 1995 – useful studies on a central text.

P. Matthews, 'Greek and Latin Linguistics', in G. Lepschy (ed.), *History of Linguistics. Vol. II: Classical and Medieval Linguistics*, London: Longman, 1994 – dense and authoritative.

R. H. Robins, *A Short History of Linguistics* (4th edn), London: Longman, 1997 – everything one would expect from a book in its fourth edition since publication in the mid-1960s.

I. Sluiter, *Ancient Grammar in Context: Contributions to the Study of Ancient Thought*, Amsterdam: VU University Press, 1990 – good orientation in the subject.

D. J. Taylor (ed.), *The History of Linguistics in the Classical Period*, Amsterdam and Philadelphia: John Benjamins, 1987 – not a systematic history, but a serviceable collection of papers. Contains a translation of Dionysius Thrax.

48. Philosophy

Catherine Osborne

The heading 'philosophy' covers intellectual activity of a theoretical kind, not including the practical or exact sciences (for which see chapters 54 and 56). However, in the early period it is not easy to divide philosophy from science, so there is some overlap with the origins of science in the Presocratic period. The material can be divided into six sections: Presocratic philosophy, Socrates and the Sophists, Plato, Aristotle, Hellenistic philosophy, and late antique and early Christian philosophy.

Presocratic philosophy

Philosophy is usually regarded as beginning in the city of Miletus, on the coast of Asia Minor, in the sixth century BC. We can find hints of speculation about the nature and origin of the world, and about the meaning of human life and death, in earlier literature and myth (including both Homer and Hesiod). But the Greeks themselves identified Thales of Miletus as founder of the search for 'wisdom' (*sophia*), which later came to be called the love of wisdom (*philo-sophia*).

The Presocratic philosophers mostly precede Socrates both in date and in outlook, although the later Presocratics overlap Socrates's life chronologically. Geographically, the phenomenon of early Greek philosophy is not Athenian. Some of the thinkers come from Ionia in the East, some from Magna Graecia (southern Italy and Sicily) in the West. Only Anaxagoras is known to have worked in Athens, but he too was not Athenian.

A standard list of the main thinkers of the period would include:

A. Sixth-century thinkers:

1. the three Milesian philosophers, namely Thales, Anaximander and Anaximenes;
2. Xenophanes of Colophon;
3. Pythagoras of Samos.

B. Turn of the sixth to fifth century:

4. Heraclitus of Ephesus;
5. Parmenides of Elea.

C. Fifth-century thinkers:

6. Zeno of Elea;
7. Anaxagoras of Clazomenae;
8. Empedocles of Acragas;
9. Melissus of Samos;
10. Democritus of Abdera and his associate Leucippus;
11. Fifth-century followers of Pythagoras;
12. Diogenes of Apollonia.

Accurate dates are not available for most of these; for some we can hardly determine who published before whom. It is often assumed that Parmenides was reacting against thinkers (1) to (4), and that thinkers (6) to (10) were directly influenced by Parmenides and either loved him or hated him. But in practice there is precious little evidence in their work that any of them were in conversation with any of the rest.

Locating, studying and citing the texts of the Presocratics

The texts for the Presocratics are not complete. Very little remains of any written works that they produced. We use three main sources of evidence:

1. testimonia (ancient reports about the philosophers);
2. extracts from their writings quoted by other ancient writers (known as 'fragments');
3. in rare cases, small quantities of readable material that occasionally turn up on papyrus, either in recent excavations, or in museum collections.

In the case of (1) and (2) what we are really reading is the text of the ancient author who is telling us about, or quoting from, the original philosopher. These ancient authors range from Plato, in the fourth century BC, to Neoplatonic writers of the sixth century AD and even some Byzantine texts. In the case of (3), papyrus fragments, it might appear that we have access to the original text, but this is not strictly true since the papyrus will be a copy, normally from the Roman period, and often badly damaged.

It is customary to read the texts in a Presocratic philosophy sourcebook which has excerpted the passages to make a collection of resources relevant to a particular philosopher. Usually the resources are separated into those considered to be genuine quotations (fragments) and those which are just reports and paraphrases (testimonia), and in some cases the sourcebook will give you *only* the words that are taken to be quotations and none of the context or surrounding words. Alternatively the supposedly genuine words may be put in a different typeface from the surrounding context.

The standard reference work for the study of Presocratic philosophy is *Die Fragmente der Vorsokratiker* by Hermann Diels in the sixth edition revised by Walther Kranz. This three-volume work in Greek and German is known affectionately as Diels-Kranz, and the numbering system adopted by Diels-Kranz for the fragments and testimonia is cross-referenced in every edition and translation that has appeared since. Most new sourcebooks rearrange the fragments into their own order, but it is always possible to find a particular text by using the Diels-Kranz reference numbers.

Diels-Kranz reference numbers come in the form of a number, a letter and a number, often abbreviated to the letter and the last number. The first number identifies the philosopher in question: it refers to the chapter in Diels-Kranz. Xenophanes, for instance, is chapter 21 in Diels-Kranz, so all Xenophanes texts have 21 as their first number. You don't need to include this number if writing solely about Xenophanes, or if you have said that the fragment is by Xenophanes. The letter is normally either A (to indicate a testimonium or ancient report about the philosopher, that is, our category (1) above) or B (indicating that Diels-Kranz identified the words as a genuine quotation, a fragment, belonging to our category (2) above). The letter C you will scarcely meet: it identifies material regarded as not genuine. For Pythagoras there is no letter, neither A nor B, since there are thought to be no genuine writings. Where genuine papyrus material has been found, it will appear as a B fragment, but most of this material has turned up too recently to appear in Diels-Kranz. Third, the fragment has a number, its place in the A list of testimonia or the B list of fragments in Diels-Kranz's collection. For B fragments this number can be used by itself. For instance, to identify number 112 in the list of Empedocles' fragments one could say 'DK 31 B 112' (where DK stands for Diels-Kranz) or one could just say 'Empedocles fragment 112'. If you refer to a fragment by just a number in this way, you should always use the DK number, never the number assigned in some textbook that you happen to have for your course.

A brief survey of the period

Philosophy begins when Thales suggests that the earth is held aloft by floating on water and that water might be the fount and source of everything. The important breakthrough here is not so much the theories, which are perhaps a little naive, but rather the idea that we need to ask and answer questions about origins, and answer them with an appeal to natural forces that have relevant explanatory power (not just gods and their emotions). The tradition passes to Thales' fellow citizens, Anaximander and Anaximenes, who suggest more elaborate solutions to the same kinds of problems. Anaximander is particularly notable for his brilliant suggestion that a world poised in equilibrium might need no support to hold it stationary in mid-space.

Xenophanes, Parmenides and Empedocles were poets as well as philosophers; indeed poetic output seems to have been a normal way to publish one's teachings in any field in the sixth century. Xenophanes' best work is in theology (arguments against polytheism and gods in human form) and in theory of knowledge (drawing the distinction between true belief and genuine knowledge). Parmenides is notorious for arguing that plurality, motion, change and all kinds of variation are impossible, resulting in an uncompromising monism (the doctrine that there is just one undifferentiated reality). It is not just his conclusion that is important: indeed we might think that his conclusion must be wrong. It is also his attempt to defend his conclusion by a meticulous proof, based on a worry about whether it makes sense to say of something that 'it is not'. Logic was in its infancy (although Xenophanes had produced some fine informal arguments) and Parmenides' method of examining how the word 'is' functions, to see what we can and can't say about reality, is an important development (with a long and distinguished subsequent history).

Zeno and Melissus are usually classified as members of an 'Eleatic School' along with Parmenides, since they also adhered to varieties of monism. Zeno is famous for some elegant paradoxes to prove that ideas such as motion, division and plurality are absurd. These include the well-known paradox of Achilles and the tortoise, reported in not quite those terms by Aristotle.

Heraclitus' outlook on the world was the very opposite of Parmenides', although he must have been at work at the very same time, in another part of the Greek world. While Parmenides argued for his conclusions, Heraclitus presented his proposals in enigmatic utterances. While Parmenides is famed for discounting all motion, Heraclitus is reputed to have made motion and change fundamental to the structure of the universe. 'Everything flows' is his most famous dictum, and many of his extant fragments focus on puzzles about opposites.

Empedocles, and his shadowy but more famous guru Pythagoras, represent another alternative tradition to Parmenides, though they, like Parmenides, were based in the south of Italy. Their interests included life after death, reincarnation, the morality of meat-eating and techniques for achieving spiritual well-being, together with (in the case of the school of Pythagoras) a fascination with numbers and geometry and (in the case of Empedocles) a complex theory about the physical world based on a cycle of alternating periods of love (unity) and strife (disunity).

Anaxagoras developed a theory of the structure and composition of the world that was designed to allow for apparent change by mixture and remixture of existing materials, without any new stuff ever developing. To permit this and explain biological and chemical processes, Anaxagoras suggested that there were many kinds of material, perhaps infinitely many, and that some of every kind of material was present in minute quantities in every ordinary piece of matter, however small. Infinite divisibility is an essential commitment, allowing that however we divide something, it will always contain a full set of yet smaller parts of all the basic materials. Anaxagoras also attempted to explain the presence of intelligence (mind) in some organisms, and to attribute the origin of order in the cosmos to a cosmic mind. Leucippus and Democritus are famous for inventing the idea of the atom: a small, uncuttable body too small to see. The world, they suggested, is entirely composed of such microscopic bodies, moving around in empty space, the void (which, despite being 'nothing', is allowed to exist as a second kind of reality). Phenomena as we perceive them are the effects of macroscopic collections of atoms on our senses. The theory raises interesting issues about the reliability of sense perception, and Democritus made important contributions in the field of epistemology (theory of knowledge). His extensive writings on ethics are less intensively studied.

Socrates and the Sophists

Fifth-Century Sophists

The Sophists were a group of itinerant teachers providing private education for ambitious young men in the second half of the fifth century BC. It was a time when the increasingly sophisticated political and civic life in the Greek cities meant that power and influence depended upon acquiring a range of skills in public debate.

A list of the main Sophists would include:

1. Protagoras of Abdera;
2. Gorgias of Leontini;
3. Hippias of Elis;
4. Prodicus of Ceos;
5. Antiphon the Sophist (who may be the same person as Antiphon of Rhamnous);
6. the unknown author of the *Dissoi Logoi* ('Twofold Arguments');
7. and a number of otherwise unknown characters portrayed by Plato, including Callicles (in the *Gorgias*) and Thrasymachus (in the *Republic*).

As with the Presocratics, the Sophists' work has to be reconstructed from other people's reports: collections of their fragments appear in volume 2 of Diels-Kranz (see above under 'Presocratic philosophy') and in some, but not all, recent Presocratics sourcebooks in translation. Alternatively the work of the Sophists is usefully gathered in Gagarin and Woodruff, *Early Greek Political Thought.*

As with the earlier Presocratics, texts for the Sophists can be cited according to the numbering in Diels-Kranz. Use this method for the fragments of Protagoras, Prodicus and Hippias. Other works are preserved more extensively and can be cited by author, title and chapter or paragraph numbers. For instance, there is a separate edition of the *Dissoi Logoi* (T. M. Robinson, New York: Arno Press, 1979) and of Gorgias's *In Praise of Helen* (D. M. Macdowell, Bristol: Bristol Classical Press, 1982). Part of Antiphon's work *On Truth* is preserved in a papyrus from Oxyrhynchus, *P. Oxy* 1364 (for which the recommended edition is the *Corpus dei Papyri Filosofici Greci e Latini* vol. 1, eds G. Bastianini and F. Decleva Caizzi, Florence: L. S. Olschki, 1989). Gorgias's *On What Is Not* is reconstructed from extensive citations/summaries in two authors, Sextus Empiricus *Adv. Math.* 7 65–87 and pseudo-Aristotle *On Melissus, Xenophanes and Gorgias* chapters 5 to 6, 979a11–980b21. You may wish to use either or both of these texts directly, or access them via the extracts provided in a Presocratic philosophy sourcebook.

In discussing the Sophists we also appeal to evidence in Plato's dialogues, where Plato portrays the Sophists in conversation with Socrates and other characters. The most relevant texts are *Protagoras* (for Protagoras, Hippias, Prodicus), *Theaetetus* (for Protagoras), *Gorgias* (for Gorgias and Callicles) and *Republic* book 1 (for Thrasymachus). Extracts from these dialogues are often included in sourcebooks on Presocratic philosophy. They should be cited according to the conventions for handling Plato (see below).

Aside from their shared interests in the hot topics of the day, including the debate about nature and convention (*nomos* and *physis*), there is no particular reason to see the Sophists as a school of thought. They are treated together largely because Plato portrayed them as Socrates' typical opponents. For this reason (and also for their pragmatic and amoral attitude to their business of teaching the young to succeed in the world) they have been regarded with some suspicion and are usually excluded from the canon of first-rate philosophers.

Socrates

Socrates (c. 470–399 BC), by contrast, is one of the most original and inspiring figures in the history of humankind. Although he wrote nothing, his life, his strange and compelling thoughts, his uncompromising moral vision and, above all, his death in 399 at the hands of the Athenian democracy have had an influence on subsequent generations that is paralleled perhaps only by Jesus Christ (whose life and death took a rather similar course). Because Socrates wrote nothing himself, we are not in a position to reconstruct his thoughts from his own words, even in fragments, unless his own spoken words are preserved in other authors.

Evidence for the teachings of Socrates: Xenophon's Socrates and Plato's Socrates

But are Socrates' speeches preserved in other authors? Two authors have been quarried for evidence: Xenophon and Plato. Xenophon wrote a memoir of the life of Socrates (*Memorabilia*) in which he portrays Socrates (whom he knew personally) in conversation with his friends. Plato wrote a large number of individual dialogues in which a character called Socrates figures, appearing in conversation with other Athenians and with visitors to Athens from the time of the historical Socrates. Plato had been a pupil of Socrates in his youth and was clearly profoundly influenced by him. Plato's dialogues are often grouped into early-, middle- and late-period works (see below) and it is often felt that works of the early period portray Socrates much as he was in real life, with views very like those he really held.

However, there is some discrepancy between the Socrates of Xenophon's memoirs and the Socrates in Plato's dialogues. Plato's Socrates is more exciting philosophically than Xenophon's. We might reach one of three conclusions: (1) Xenophon's picture is more accurate, whereas Plato enriches his portrait with insights too profound to be realistic; (2) Plato's picture is more accurate whereas Xenophon was too stupid to see Socrates' subtleties; or (3) both Xenophon and Plato saw and portrayed sides of Socrates that were true to life, but as always happens, each saw what mattered most to himself in the relationship.

Another factor worth noting is that many other writers produced 'Socratic dialogues' in the period after the death of Socrates, when Plato and Xenophon were writing. Hence both authors belong to a wider genre, much of it lost or ignored. It seems that works in this genre formed a kind of philosophical exercise written as historical fiction. How accurate did the historical portrait need to be? Doubtless the author aimed primarily to amuse and intrigue his reader, and to honour the memory of Socrates. Even works like the *Apology*, Plato's version of Socrates' defence speech at his trial, may be imaginatively enhanced for the readers.

The Socratic Paradoxes

Socrates is famous for his irony, and for certain neat sayings that reflect his characteristic approach to life. These 'Socratic paradoxes' look stupid or false at first sight. They invite a hasty response of derision from the listener. But once the background has been filled in they turn out to be undeniable, Socrates triumphs and one's own dismissive response is shown up as stupid.

1. 'No one does wrong willingly' (because if you knew which was the better thing to do, you would choose to do it).
2. 'It is always better to suffer wrong than to do wrong' (because doing wrong is corruption in oneself, and hence is the most harmful damage one can inflict upon oneself, whereas suffering wrong does no damage to one's character).
3. 'A good man can never be harmed' (because only moral corruption is any kind of harm to oneself at all).
4. 'It is better to suffer punishment than to get away with injustice' (because punishment is the means to free oneself from the corruption that is the only source of harm).

All these are closely related, and turn round the crucial thesis that moral corruption is to be avoided at all costs. In addition, Socrates is known for the claim, voiced in Plato's *Apology*, that he knew that he knew nothing (from which it followed that he was, despite appearances to the contrary, the wisest man around).

It follows from the Socratic paradoxes that success depends upon knowledge: one is powerless to avoid doing wrong unless one knows what is best. And those who appear successful may be the least powerful and least fortunate of all, if their apparent success comes from morally corrupt behaviour.

The Socratic Elenchus

Socrates's notorious method of inquiry is known as the *elenchus* (meaning 'scrutiny'). It is illustrated in Plato's early dialogues. Socrates tests his fellow citizens on their understanding of fundamental concepts of morality (courage, sobriety, respect, or virtue in general), so as to show that they do not know what they are talking about. The process is primarily negative: Socrates elicits a proposed definition from his companion ('the interlocutor') rather than offering one of his own. He draws the interlocutor into analysis of the suggested definition, and shows up flaws or inconsistencies in the interlocutor's commitments. The interlocutor himself recognises these as intolerable.

Socrates is reticent about offering proposals himself, and although he encourages the interlocutor to withdraw his original proposal, Socrates does not commit himself to any preferred view. This purely negative pose fits with the claim to know nothing (or solely that one does not know). But it seems to clash with Socrates' sincere commitment to the moral thesis grounding his paradoxes, and, in particular, with his confidence that injustice can never be worthwhile, no matter what the stakes. In Plato's portrait, these deep commitments emerge as conceptual truths that each interlocutor finds he cannot deny: conventional morality falls apart whereas the Socratic paradoxes emerge unscathed, to the surprise of interlocutors who were unaware that they believed them. What survives this *elenchus* is the paradoxical set of doctrines set out above. We then have to ask whether this counts as knowledge. Or is it just the only thing left to live by, once the *elenchus* has destroyed everything else?

Plato

Plato (427–347 BC) was about 30 when Socrates died, and had been a disciple of Socrates since his teens. His philosophical interests continue from Socrates' concerns with moral philosophy and theory of knowledge, and from the Socratic search for definitions of terms. In Plato's work this develops into an interest in metaphysics.

Plato's published works

Because of his eminent place in the history of philosophy, Plato's published oeuvres have been preserved complete and with a good manuscript tradition. In antiquity thirty-four dialogues, the speech called the *Apology* and a set of epistles were ascribed to Plato, and these thirty-six items were arranged into nine groups of four (called tetralogies) by Thrasyllus of Alexandria (died AD 36) and Dercyllides, during the reign of Tiberius. Not all of the thirty-six works included in the tetralogies are Plato's beyond question. In addition a number of spurious works are added after the ninth tetralogy in the main manuscripts and Greek editions.

Stephanus references

The Thrasyllan tetralogies still appear as the organising principle for modern editions (e.g. the Oxford Classical Texts). References to Plato's works, however, are always given according to the 1578 Geneva edition of Plato's works by Henri Estienne, known as Stephanus. A typical Stephanus reference looks like this: Plato *Gorgias* 458b3. In other words, it includes:

1. the name of the author, Plato;
2. the name of the dialogue, *Gorgias*;
3. a number, 458, indicating the page number in Stephanus's edition;
4. a letter, here 'b', indicating the second section of the Stephanus page (each page has five sections, about ten lines each, lettered a to e);
5. a line number, 3, indicating the third line of Greek text in section b.

If the reference is to be less precise the line number may be omitted, and consecutive sections can be strung together. For instance, *Gorgias* 458bc would refer to a passage spanning sections b and c of 458.

Stephanus' edition came in three volumes and the page numbers started afresh in each volume. This means that the same Stephanus page number recurs in different dialogues of Plato. Thus while there is a reference 458c3 in the *Gorgias* (which was in volume I of Stephanus), there is also a reference 458c3 in the *Republic* (which was in volume II).

Stephanus references are included in the margin of all good editions and translations of Plato's works and are invariably used to give references in works of scholarship. They should also be used in all student essays.

Unwritten doctrines

Besides the published dialogues, there is some evidence, largely derived from Aristotle, for oral teachings that are not in Plato's published dialogues. Plato would have delivered these esoteric doctrines in lectures in the school that he established in Athens, called the Academy. They included theories about mathematics, about the nature of mathematical objects and about the derivation of number from a pair of principles called the One and the Indefinite Dyad. Interest in these rather specialised aspects of Plato's teaching is confined to a minority of scholars. In Britain and the United States, the study of Plato invariably means the study of Plato's written works, and this will be the focus of what follows.

Early, middle and late works of Plato

Plato's dialogues are commonly divided into three groups on grounds of style and content. It is likely that the division roughly reflects the sequence in which Plato wrote the works, if we assume that changes in style and apparent developments in the ideas expressed are a record of Plato's changing interests and manner of writing. That assumption may be overconfident, however, since the purpose of the dialogues varies and they are never a simple record of Plato's latest ideas. Indeed Plato himself never speaks in any of his works, and the subject matter, dramatic settings and vividly characterised interlocutors contribute to the variety in style and structure. Nevertheless most scholars concede some validity to stylometric tests that have yielded this general division into three periods.

Early dialogues

The first group, early dialogues or Socratic dialogues, includes the *Apology* (Plato's reconstruction of Socrates' speech at his trial) and several relatively simple dialogues, in which Socrates plays a major part, often investigating the virtues in ways that seem to be authentically Socratic. Typical early Socratic dialogues include:

1. *Euthyphro*;
2. *Charmides;*
3. *Laches;*
4. *Crito.*

Socrates is often shown reaching no conclusion by the end of the dialogue: all the proposed solutions to a puzzle are found wanting. Such dialogues are called *aporetic dialogues*, because they result in *aporia* or impasse.

Middle dialogues

This is where *classic Platonism* is to be found. The middle group includes dialogues in which the subjects under discussion are more Platonic than Socratic: not just ethics but also politics, knowledge, the soul (or mind), and the nature of truth and reality. Middle-period dialogues usually offer positive doctrines for consideration, and Socrates often leads the way by suggesting the theories for consideration. Some of these theories have been taken to be Plato's own ideas put into the mouth of Socrates (who is still the main character in all the dialogues).

The middle period dialogues include:

1. *Phaedo*;
2. *Republic* (in ten books);
3. *Phaedrus*;
4. *Symposium.*

All the famous Platonic doctrines are sketched out in these dialogues and ascribed to the character 'Socrates'. These include:

1. the theory of recollection;
2. the tripartite soul;
3. the ideal state mapped out in the *Republic*;
4. the Theory of Forms.

These theories will be explained briefly below.

Late dialogues

In the late dialogues, or 'critical dialogues', the notable feature is a critical attitude towards the classic Platonic theories. It is as though the mature Plato became less convinced by his supposed solutions to the problems than he had been in his prime. Most striking is the dialogue called *Parmenides*, which opens with a sustained refutation of the most famous middle-period doctrine, the Theory of Forms. Other dialogues in this group tend either to ignore or to avoid the subject of Forms, or, in turning their attention to new problems of logic and language, they modify the notion of Forms to answer a different set of questions.

The *Sophist* and *Statesman* introduce a new dialectical method of 'collection and division', which appears to replace the hypothetical method developed in the middle period. The *Laws* develops a political model that is notably more down to earth and realistic than the *Republic*.

Dialogues of this period are less likely to make Socrates the lead character. Some give the main part to an unnamed visitor from Elea.

Transitional works and misfits

Not all the dialogues fit neatly into the three-fold analysis described here. Between the early and middle periods we need to include:

1. *Protagoras* and *Gorgias*: more complex and subtle than most Socratic dialogues, but still on ethical problems and largely Socratic in style;
2. *Meno*: appeals to a theory of recollection but not to the Forms in analysing the idea that virtue is knowledge.

In the late period there are two or three misfits, in particular the following:

1. The *Theaetetus* is aporetic and written in Socratic style; it investigates knowledge without explicit appeal to either Forms or recollection, but it is unclear whether it avoids those doctrines deliberately.
2. The *Timaeus* is late by stylistic tests; the main speaker is not Socrates; its sequel, the *Critias*, remains unfinished, which might indicate that it was in progress when Plato laid down his pen for the last time. But the *Timaeus* makes heavy use of the theory of Forms with no hint of negative judgement.

Key Platonic theories

As we have seen, Plato explores his philosophical ideas by means of dialogue. He does not dictate doctrines in dogmatic treatises. He explores objections not just to others' views but also to his own previous proposals. We should not assume that Plato ever unquestioningly endorsed those theories we now know as classic Platonism. Still, those theories have become permanently associated with his name and should be outlined here.

The theory of recollection: anamnesis

In order to explain some features of our ability to grasp and use concepts, Plato makes Socrates suggest (in the *Meno* and the *Phaedo*) that 'all learning is recollection'. 'Recollection' here means 'being reminded of *x* by *y*', where *x* and *y* might be any two items in the world. Socrates appeals to this idea to explain how we can understand and use certain concepts without being taught them, apparently picking them up from experience. When we 'pick something up from experience', he suggests, we are not actually acquiring the concept for the first time but reawakening latent knowledge already stored in the mind (= soul, *psuchē*). Our latent knowledge is awakened by objects and events around us, things which remind us of the concept that is already within us, and so it appears that we learn the concept from experiencing those objects.

In the *Meno* Socrates illustrates this idea by prompting an uneducated slave boy to deploy his latent grasp of geometrical truths so as to propose and scrutinise possible answers to a problem. The boy is shown coming to reject the false answer and accept the correct one, on the basis of his own innate conceptual resources. In the *Phaedo* Socrates links the recollection theory to the Theory of Forms, suggesting that the latent knowledge is of the Forms. Using the mathematical concept of absolute equality, he shows that we need not, or indeed cannot, have learned the concept from physical objects, but must rather have been reminded of it by their closeness to, and falling short of, the ideal of absolute equality. Since we have always been in a position to use the concept of equality spontaneously, in judging the shortcomings of physical items that are supposedly equal (or, indeed, unequal), we must have possessed the concept from our earliest days. Concepts of this sort, Socrates suggests, were once acquired, but in a period before birth, when our intellect encountered the immaterial Forms directly.

The tripartite soul

The term 'soul' translates the Greek term *psuchē*, which means 'mind' or 'self'. The *psuchē* is all those aspects of yourself that are lost from your material remains at death; for instance, your character, emotions, intellect, desires, passions, will, and so on. Hence we can analyse the human person into some mental aspects (soul) and some physical aspects (body).

Plato's analysis of the human person shifts slightly between different dialogues of the middle period. The main difference is the dividing line between physical aspects (body) and mental aspects (soul). Do the physical appetites, desires and emotions belong to our physical make-up or to our mental life? In the *Phaedo* the term 'soul' (*psuchē*) is reserved for the intellect, that is, the capacity for conceptual knowledge and inquiry, whereas all other faculties, emotions and desires are treated as aspects of the body. The dialogue emphasises the ideal of separation of soul from body, by which it means detaching intellectual pursuits from the distractions of physical pleasures and temporal commitments.

In the *Republic* and *Phaedrus* Plato expresses things slightly differently. Rather than call the bodily desires 'body', he suggests that they are distinct parts or functions of the 'soul'. The soul thus conceived has three parts, each with its own enthusiasms and desires. They are *logistikon*, which loves reason and theory; *thumoeides*, which is honour-loving and affectionate; and *epithumētikon*, characterised by appetites for simple pleasures such as food, drink and sex. This tripartite soul allows Plato to develop a more positive attitude than he had in the *Phaedo* to emotions and appetites as collaborating contributors, along with intellect, in a happy and successful human life.

The ideal state mapped out in the republic

The tripartite soul is sketched out in the *Republic* as part of a twofold project, analysing both morality in the individual and justice in the state, as analogous states of harmony among competing factions. In both, Plato suggests, the best state involves co-operation of the various elements towards the achievement of shared goals, and those goals should be set by reference to what is genuinely good and not a distorted set of values.

Analogous to the three parts of the soul, Plato envisages a society comprising three basic types of individual: rational philosophers, spirited fighters and those whose primary focus is satisfaction of appetites. In the ideal society each individual must be given scope to develop his or her talent in the appropriate direction, and to use it towards genuinely good goals. In order to discover those perfect goals the rational philosophers must investigate goodness. The others must listen to and respect the philosophers' conclusions. The political structure is based on consensus, but the rulers (who invent the policy) will be those philosophers who have actually *achieved* what no one in this world has ever achieved – perfect understanding of the absolute good. This is what is meant by 'Philosopher Kings', though it must be remembered that Plato also meant there to be Philosopher Queens.

To avoid some common errors in understanding the *Republic*, we need to stress its imaginary status. As a blueprint for a real society it is useless: people do not have just one talent; no one has discovered absolute goodness and if they did it would not map onto achievable reality; and breaking down the family ties and inherited privilege that stand in the way of Plato's ideal – of equal opportunities for all – would generate a massive revolt from those who currently enjoy undeserved status. But remember that Plato is not saying that people who *claim* to know what is good should rule. He says that those who *do* know what is good (and believe in it) should rule. He is not saying that people should be unfairly assigned to classes that determine their life opportunities. He says that opportunities should be matched to abilities and inclinations, regardless of birth or wealth.

Plato explores the mechanisms that would be needed to enable such things to happen: mechanisms to select children for their best role in life by ability not birth, mechanisms to provide a perfect education for the most gifted children. It is a beautiful society without corruption, to match the beautiful life of the morally perfect individual. Most of the objections brought against the *Republic* amount to the claim that we cannot, in fact, imagine a society in which those in power are not corrupted by evil desires.

THE THEORY OF FORMS

The Theory of Forms is not really a theory. Rather Forms are a multi-purpose tool for explaining several things. Plato invokes them in various dialogues for the following purposes:

1. as objects of knowledge (when they are the things we can know, as opposed to physical objects, which we perceive, and as opposed to opinions, which could be erroneous);
2. as standards of value (when what is fair, for instance, serves as the standard we use when judging whether an action or social practice is fair);
3. as concepts for analysing the world, as when the notion of 'equal' figures in a judgement about whether two sticks are of equal length.

Forms are independently real intellectual objects. They are not invented by humans. Rather the concepts exist, whether or not humans exist, whether or not we choose to use them, whether or not there are any things that participate in them. The relation between a thing that falls under a Form (say a large thing) and the Form (say Largeness) is known as 'participation'.

Plato's Theory of Forms helps to explain a wide range of philosophical issues:

1. In morality, perfect goodness, fairness, justice and courage do not go away or cease to stand as ideals, just because no one is at present good, fair, just or courageous.
2. In aesthetics, perfect beauty may not be instantiated in any existing body, but it may be what the painter aims to achieve, and against which we measure his or her achievement.
3. In mathematics and measurement, what is large for a mouse is not large for an elephant, but the notion of largeness we can understand as the same in both cases.
4. In logic, we collect items under the general description 'beds' but they need not all match each other exactly; what they share is adequate conformity with the abstract notion of what it is, ideally, to be a bed.

Forms are immaterial concepts or ideals. We might think that the physical objects are more real than these ideas. But for Plato the reverse is true: the world of Forms is reality, whereas the bits and pieces we meet are transient and unreliable, muddled and impure.

Aristotle

Aristotle (384–322 BC) began his career as a student in Plato's Academy. His writings fall into two categories: (1) exoteric works, written for publication early in his career: these no longer survive and have to be reconstructed from fragments quoted by other writers; and (2) school works, which are records of Aristotle's lecture courses delivered to students in the Lyceum. In what follows we shall deal with the school works. These are what we usually study when we study Aristotle today.

Bekker references

References to Aristotle's works are standardly made by page and line of the edition of the Greek text produced by Immanuel Bekker in 1831. Bekker references are included in the margin of all good editions of the Greek text (such as the Oxford Classical Texts) and in reputable translations of Aristotle's works. They are invariably used to give references in works of scholarship. They should also be used in all student essays.

A typical Bekker reference looks like this: Aristotle *On Generation and Corruption* 2.7, 334a26–31. In other words, it includes:

1. the name of the author, Aristotle;
2. the name of the work, *On Generation and Corruption*; the title may be in its Latin form (in this case *de Generatione et Corruptione*) or abbreviated (in this case often *GC*);
3. the number of the book, here book 2 – it is conventional to denote the books by Greek letters, so you might find a B (*Beta*) for book 2 here;
4. the number of the chapter (in this case chapter 7) – this is not strictly required since the Bekker page will fix the reference;
5. a number, 334, indicating the page in Bekker's edition;

6. a letter, here 'a', indicating the left column on the Bekker page (each page has two columns, about 30–2 lines each, lettered a or b);
7. line numbers, 26–31, indicating lines 26–31 of the Greek text in column a.

Every page of the Bekker edition is uniquely numbered, so there are not (as in Plato) similar references referring to different works. 334a26–31 occurs in *On Generation and Corruption* only, and nowhere else.

Since Bekker's edition, newer and more authoritative editions have been published, so you will not actually use the text as edited by Bekker. The Bekker referencing system is occasionally – but only occasionally – confusing where a later edition has relocated portions of text to a different place in the same work.

The *Constitution of Athens*, attributed to Aristotle, was discovered on a papyrus at the end of the nineteenth century, too late for Bekker's edition, so there are no Bekker references for this work. References are to the sections marked out by the first editor.

Aristotle's philosophical writings

Aristotle had an immense range of interests, and the remains of his lecture courses (surviving in the form of collections of notes) touch on most of the areas of philosophy recognised today – although the divisions do not always line up exactly with our current ways of dividing the subject.

Besides what we think of as philosophy, Aristotle was an enthusiast for natural science. Some of his most significant work was in biology, including detailed observation of the structure and behaviour of organisms. The *Historia Animalium* and the *Parts of Animals* are a treasure house of amazing discoveries, many of which have been confirmed only since the invention of the microscope.

On more strictly philosophical topics, Aristotle's work covers the following:

1. Questions about mind, soul, perception, and the movement of living things; for these see *de Anima*, *de Motu Animalium* and the short works known as *Parva Naturalia*.
2. Physics, including questions about the behaviour of matter and cosmology; for these see the *Physics*, *de Caelo*, *Meteorologica*, *de Generatione et Corruptione*.
3. Metaphysics, including the analysis of time, place, motion, reality and god; for these topics see the *Physics*, *Metaphysics*, *de Caelo*.
4. Philosophy of language, including the distinction between various categories of predication; see in particular *Categories*, *de Interpretatione*, *Topics*, *Rhetoric*.
5. Logic, especially deductive reasoning. The main works are *Prior Analytics*, *Posterior Analytics*, *Sophistici Elenchi*, *Rhetoric*.
6. Ethics, for which the classic text is the *Nicomachean Ethics* named after Aristotle's son Nicomachus (Nikomachos). Note the two possible spellings. There are also two other ethical treatises extant, (a) the *Eudemian Ethics*, which is closely related to the *Nicomachean Ethics*: indeed three books of the *EE* are duplicated in the *NE*; and (b) the *Magna Moralia*, whose authenticity is disputed.
7. Political philosophy, covered in the *Politics*, a continuation of Aristotle's work in ethics.

In addition the *Poetics*, of which only the first book survives, is a study of drama – tragic drama in particular – and its psychological effects. This work, together with parts of the *Rhetoric*, belongs to literary theory, psychology and sociology.

How to read Aristotle

Most of Aristotle's work is very compressed in style. To understand what he is saying one must fill out the allusions in the sentences. He often spends several pages setting out other people's views and raising difficulties and potential responses from the other thinker, before indicating (in the sketchiest way) how he himself wishes to resolve the difficulties. It is therefore very dangerous to read short extracts out of context, since it is usually far from clear whether Aristotle agrees with the view he is outlining: often he is setting up the opposition view, or indeed giving it the most charitable defence available, prior to demolishing it thoroughly some chapters later.

Because the works are so allusive and need much interpretative elucidation, translations are interpretations of the text and works of philosophical scholarship. It is not possible to give a mere rendering into another language. Beginners who lack much knowledge of Aristotelian philosophy will find it hard to read the Greek unaided, even if your Greek language is at advanced postgraduate level: you should use a good commentary, such as the classic ones by W. D. Ross, and refer to a recent translation by a reputable Aristotelian scholar, alongside the Greek text, to help to embed the English equivalents for Aristotle's elaborate technical terminology. Avoid the Loeb translations (except for the *de Caelo*).

Aristotle as a philosopher

Although it has been suggested that Aristotle was a Platonist in early life, most of his mature work diverges substantially from the doctrines associated with middle-period Plato (although not so far from the views explored in Plato's later works). The key difference is that where Plato is distinctly otherworldly, Aristotle tends to be more this-worldly.

Whereas Plato posited transcendent Forms – to be the meaning of words, to be universals, to be the objects of knowledge – Aristotle tries to be less extravagant in his metaphysics. There are immanent forms: objects manifest a form, and that form is common to others like it, but there is no otherworldly exemplar, no transcendent type. So language – including the use of universal terms – and epistemology – including knowledge of universals – must all work by abstraction of the common form from the particulars that manifest the form. Forms can be permanent but not independent of particular substances. For Aristotle, 'substance' (a conventional translation of his technical term *ousia*, i.e. 'what has being') is first and foremost the individual things we meet in this world, composed of form and matter. This may seem common sense, but it radically diverges from Plato's claim that particular things in this world are not really real.

For Aristotle, the soul (*psuchē*) is the form of an organic body (such as a plant or animal, its form being its ability to function in the ways living bodies function). Since form cannot exist without matter, it must follow that the soul cannot survive without the body. The soul just is the activity of a body equipped with functioning organs for life. Souls come in various sorts: the more complex and multi-functional an organism is, the more complex and multi-functional its soul: animals have some or all of the five senses, and powers of locomotion, that plants lack; humans have an additional capacity, for intellectual thought. Aristotle occasionally suggests that this last capacity might not be a bodily function. For pure thought is the activity of god, and god does not require a body to do it. So might that aspect of a human soul be separable?

Should Aristotle have included god in his metaphysics? The device appears to be vital to his account of the entire structure of the world. To account for motion in the heavens, Aristotle posits an unmoved mover, which causes other beings to move without itself engaging in any movement. The ultimate cause of movement is the god who does nothing but be perfectly desirable. Everything else is then moved to desire it, as the object of their love, and this is what causes movement in the heavens and every process towards goodness in the world.

Hence the whole universe is teleological, structured towards good results. But this is achieved without the intervention of any craftsman-creator or law-giving deity. Aristotle's ethical theory depends upon this cosmology, in that it identifies the ideal human life with the well-functioning human being. The value of conventional civic and private virtues, as recognised in a well-ordered society, is secured by humans' natural tendency to desire the good. And since human beings tend naturally to social co-operation and political organisation, we can also deduce truths in political science, by observing which political orders bring out the best in human achievements. Thus we can understand why Aristotle's project included a collection of constitutions, among them the *Constitution of Athens*.

This amazing edifice of systematic Aristotelian theory was hugely influential on the late medieval world and (via the scholastic tradition) on modern Western philosophy. In addition Aristotle's treatises on syllogistic (the *Analytics*) and language (the *Categories*) served as the classic textbooks in the field until relatively recently.

Hellenistic philosophy

After Aristotle, the period up to and including the first century AD is characterised by a tendency for philosophers to form into schools, with a tradition of school doctrines handed down, with modifications, from the founder. The most important traditions in this period are (1) the Stoics, (2) the Epicureans and (3) sceptics of various kinds, not all of the same school.

Source materials

In contrast with the well-preserved texts for Plato and Aristotle, we are back to reconstructing lost works, as for the Presocratic philosophers. Philosophers of the Hellenistic period wrote thousands of books, far more than the Presocratics did. The remnants, though numerous and often long, are a pitiful record of what must have been intricate and elaborately defended systems of thought.

From the early period, a few documents survive intact. For Epicurus we have several summaries of his teachings:

1. Epicurus *Letter to Herodotus:* this is an epitome of Epicurus' physical doctrines, and is preserved in Diogenes Laertius *Lives of the Philosophers* book 10, 35–83.
2. Epicurus *Letter to Pythocles*, again preserved in Diogenes Laertius 10.84–116, immediately after the *Letter to Herodotus*. This is an epitome of Epicurus' doctrines concerning astronomical and meteorological phenomena.
3. Epicurus *Letter to Menoeceus* preserved in Diogenes Laertius 10.122–35. This is an epitome of doctrines in ethics.
4. Epicurus' *Kuriai Doxai* ('Key Doctrines'): a set of maxims forming a kind of creed for Epicureanism. These are reproduced by Diogenes Laertius in the last fifteen chapters of his life of Epicurus (10.139–54), and another set known as the *Sententiae Vaticanae* survives in its own right.

For the complete texts of the works preserved by Diogenes Laertius, consult his *Life of Epicurus* (Oxford Classical Text or vol. II of the Loeb edition). Extracts are given in Long and Sedley.

For the Stoics, nothing survives complete from Zeno of Citium, founder of the school. The earliest surviving work is a Hymn to Zeus by Cleanthes, the second head of the school. This comes down to us via Stobaeus *Anthology* 1.25.3–1.27.4. Text and translation are provided by Long and Sedley.

However, where we lack evidence for the earliest founders of a school, much is filled in by later adherents to the same school, who continued to develop the school doctrines on the basis of tenets accepted from the founder. This factor makes Hellenistic philosophy very different from the Presocratic period. Instead of relying solely on fragmentary quotations from the original founders (although there are some of those), we have extensive surviving works from later thinkers whose task it is to expound and explain the school position.

Chief among these are:

1. for the Epicureans, the elegant poetry of Lucretius, *de Rerum Natura*. This renders Epicurean doctrine into Latin for readers of the first century BC. It appears that it is faithful to Epicurus' original in many of its qualities.
2. for the Stoics, the letters, essays and tragedies of Seneca, a Stoic of the first century AD writing in Latin; the *Discourses* of Epictetus, a Stoic of the first to second century AD; and the *Meditations* of Marcus Aurelius, a stoic philosopher of the second century AD (and Roman emperor AD 161–80).
3. for the Academic sceptics, extensive works by Cicero (writing in Latin in the first century BC).
4. for the Pyrrhonian sceptics, the *Outlines of Pyrrhonism* and the *Adversus Mathematicos* by Sextus Empiricus (writing in Greek, second century AD). These provide a systematic account of the way of life identified as Pyrrhonism, with a critique of other schools.

Aside from their value as testimony to their own school of thought, both Cicero and Sextus Empiricus provide extensive information about the Stoics and Epicureans with whom they entered into debate.

Besides these substantial bodies of text, there is also an increasing quantity of fragmentary material being recovered from papyrus remains (particularly from Herculaneum) and from the inscriptions recording the work of the Epicurean philosopher Diogenes of Oenoanda.

Sourcebook: Long and Sedley

The most accessible and reliable way to access a suitable body of excerpted material for the study of this period of philosophy is via the collection of source material in A. A. Long and D. N. Sedley, *The Hellenistic Philosophers*. There are two volumes: Volume 1 provides translations of extracts from the principal sources, arranged by topic, with philosophical commentary, indices, and brief notes on the sources and philosophers of the period; volume 2 provides original text (Greek or Latin) for the same extracts (plus a few more that are not translated in volume 1) and an extensive annotated bibliography indicating where to go for pursuing further work on the topics covered.

Themes and characteristics of Hellenistic philosophy

There is not space in a brief chapter such as this to do justice to the extensive systems of thought developed over a period of hundreds of years by the Hellenistic schools. One common thread is clear, however: all three schools set out to deliver happiness, in the form of individual peace of mind (tranquillity, *ataraxia*).

Epicureans

Epicureanism is noted first for its physics, namely a comprehensive form of atomism, designed to explain all phenomena, including the senses and intellectual thought, in terms of the movement and interactions of atoms. Second, Epicurean theology concludes that the gods have no interest in human affairs. This is crucial for ethics, since there is no punishment or reward after death, so that our conduct in this life is all that matters. Since death holds no fear for the Epicurean, one learns peace of mind, free from the false fears that frighten other folk. To live well, one needs only the few simple pleasures recommended by nature. Despite widespread misunderstanding, Epicureans do not pursue a life of hedonistic indulgence.

Stoics

Stoicism also emphasises the need to understand which things are valuable and which not. A Stoic sage (i.e. a notional person who has achieved perfect understanding – a practically unattainable ideal) would not be troubled by the lack of things of no real importance, or by apparent disasters. Many apparent evils are in fact 'indifferent': that is, neither good nor bad in themselves. Hence the Stoic will not fear death, or the loss of a loved one: for peace of mind comes from knowledge of what matters, and what matters is basically moral virtue, not natural occurrences. Indeed, the Stoic believes that all events follow a predetermined plan; the world is a providentially organised material organism. What happens to each of us is part of the plan, and we must be content to go along with it.

Because understanding the rational basis of the world yields the right attitude, the Stoics placed a high priority on investigations in the field of logic and reasoning.

Sceptics

Academic scepticism: The complex history of the Academy after Plato's death includes a period (the Middle Academy) under the leadership of Arcesilaus (316/5–242/1 BC) characterised by investigations in Socratic style, typically concluding that knowledge was unattainable.

Pyrrhonian scepticism: Later sceptics of the Pyrrhonian school rejected the Academy's dogmatic scepticism. Pyrrhonian sceptics led by Aenesidemus (first century BC) claimed to revive a method of Pyrrho (c. 365–275 BC) for achieving peace of mind by non-committal resignation. Their method involved balancing opposing arguments to any proposed thesis, on any subject, until you reach a state of *epochē* or suspended judgement – the point where there seems no secure reason to assent to either conclusion, and you just settle for neither. The Pyrrhonian sceptic simply gets on with ordinary life, undisturbed by unproven philosophical theories.

Late antique and early Christian philosophy

Over the first six centuries AD the Hellenistic schools declined in importance, giving way to two other movements: Christianity, on the one hand,

and Platonism – dominating both pagan and Christian philosophy – on the other.

Middle Platonism

Middle Platonism comes between the sceptical academy of Arcesilaus and the full-blown Neoplatonism of the period from Plotinus. It is characterised by a reaffirmation of Platonist teaching, with an eclectic infiltration of Stoic thought. It originates with Antiochus of Ascalon, head of the Academy in the first century BC. Cicero, who studied under Antiochus, is a source of evidence for the early period. The school became prominent in the first century AD, and the chief extant Middle Platonist writers are, from the first and second centuries AD, Plutarch of Chaeronea (whose *Moralia* are the largest and most complete body of extant Middle Platonist philosophy); Apuleius (an eccentric philosopher-cum-poet: see especially the *Metamorphoses* and *de Deo Socratis*; there is also a rather uninspired work *de Dogmate Platonis,* of disputed authorship), Alcinous (the otherwise unknown author of the handbook called *Didaskalikos* – Alcinous is the name given in the manuscripts and is now preferred (commentary by J. Dillon, Oxford: Clarendon Press, 1993), though earlier editions attributed the work to Albinus), Albinus (whose extant remains are now confined to the *Eisagōgē*, an introduction to the reading of Plato), and Numenius (preserved only in fragments).

Many Christian authors show influence from Middle Platonism: see especially Origen and Clement of Alexandria, and note also the extensive writings of Philo Judaeus, a Jewish philosopher and exegete (interpreter of texts), also from Alexandria.

For the study of Middle Platonism it is best to start with the texts of Plutarch's *Moralia*, which are a collection of gently philosophical essays on a range of topics, some of them more trivial than others, or by approaching the period through John Dillon's *The Middle Platonists.*

Neoplatonism

Neoplatonism is conventionally supposed to start with its greatest exponent, Plotinus (AD 205–269/70), although for any idea associated with Neoplatonism there are always precursors to be found in the Middle Platonism of the second century. Ammonius Saccas (third century AD), a teacher in Alexandria who taught both Plotinus and the Christian Platonist Origen, was probably also a key catalyst for the rise of Neoplatonism.

Neoplatonism is characterised by an amalgam of Platonic and Aristotelian ideas, by the doctrine that Plato and Aristotle agreed on all matters of importance, and by an elaborate metaphysical theory invoking a supreme principle, known as the One. This assimilates Aristotle's Unmoved Mover and Plato's Form of the Good and provides the source of being and reality for the entire world of plurality (which emerges from the One by a process of falling away from the One). The further things are from the One, the less their reality. For both mind and world the fall away from the One is a decline into chaos, so that turning back towards the One and reassimilating with the next higher level of reality is a choice-worthy process; supremely choice-worthy is total absorption into the One itself.

Plotinus' *Enneads* are a collection of essays assembled by his pupil Porphyry and published as six sets of nine treatises, each set on a related series of topics. The essays in *Ennead* 1 deal with ethics and aesthetics, those in 2 and 3 with physics and cosmology, in 4 with the soul, in 5 and 6 with metaphysics, logic and epistemology. The texts are difficult to read (Plotinus apparently wrote as he thought and without revising his work for publication) but the ideas have inspired many great thinkers. The major critical edition is by Paul Henry and Hans Rudolf Schwyzer (Paris: Desdée de Brouwer, 1951–73). They also edited the *Oxford Classical Text* (1969–82), which has a useful apparatus of philosophical sources and parallels. The most famous translation is that by Stephen MacKenna (London: Penguin, 1991), which has become a classic in its own right. It is, however, rather too free for the purposes of detailed scholarship.

The second and third generation of Neoplatonists include Porphyry, Iamblichus and Proclus. Later still the Neoplatonic commentators of the fifth and sixth centuries AD are a major source of evidence, not only for Neoplatonic philosophy and for the interpretation of Aristotle (often their explicit focus) but also for an immense range of other information on Greek philosophy from the Presocratics onwards. These commentators include Syrianus, Ammonius, Damascius, Simplicius, Philoponus and Olympiodorus. Many of these texts are now being translated into English for the first time. A three-volume sourcebook of material from the ancient commentators edited by Richard Sorabji (*Philosophy of the Commentators*) provides easy access to a representative sample of important extracts, and there is a complete list of the ancient commentators, with dates, list of extant works, editions and bibliography, in Sorabji, *Aristotle Transformed*.

Besides the pagan tradition of Neoplatonism two key Christian thinkers, writing in Latin, assimilated Neoplatonic thought seamlessly into Christian philosophy (see also chapter 53). Augustine of Hippo (AD 354–430) describes his own conversion to Christianity and Platonism, as a single event, in the *Confessions*. Augustine's vast published output employs philosophical resources creatively in the effort to resolve ecclesiastical disputes of the day. Boethius (c. AD 480–524) wrote his famous *Consolation of Philosophy* in prison while awaiting execution. He also wrote commentaries on Aristotle and on Porphyry's *Isagōgē*. Like Augustine, Boethius recognises no distinction between Christian and Neoplatonic thought. Among the Greek commentators, Philoponus in the sixth century was a Christian, and, from the seventh century, all the Alexandrian commentators after Olympiodorus were Christians: that is Elias, David, pseudo-Elias and Stephanus.

The four pagan philosophical schools in Athens were closed by the Christian emperor Justinian in AD 529, but there is some evidence that Damascius and Simplicius decamped to Harran, where continuing Neoplatonist activity can be traced as late as 943, and that a vast fund of knowledge of Greek philosophy was transmitted thence to Baghdad and the Arab world. The school in Alexandria may have continued to 640, but there is then a gap before the revival of the commentary tradition in the late Byzantine period (Eustratius and Michael of Ephesus, eleventh and twelfth centuries AD).

Further reading

Aristotle, *The Complete Works* (rev. Oxford translation, ed. J. Barnes), Princeton: Princeton University Press, 1984.

H. Diels and W. Kranz, *Die Fragmente der Vorsokratiker* (6th edn, 3 vols), Berlin: Weidmann, 1951–2 (5th edn trans. K. Freeman, *Ancilla to Pre-Socratic Philosophers: A Complete Translation of the Fragments of Diels*, Fragmente der Vorsokratiker, Cambridge MA: Harvard University Press, 1983).

J. Dillon, *The Middle Platonists: A study of Platonism 80 BC to AD 220*, London: Duckworth, 1977.

J. Ferguson (ed.), *Socrates: A Source Book* (compiled and in part trans. John Ferguson), London: Macmillan for the Open University, 1970.

M. Gagarin and P. Woodruff (eds), *Early Greek Political Thought from Homer to the Sophists*, Cambridge: Cambridge University Press, 1995.

J. Gregory, *The Neoplatonists: A Reader* (2nd edn), London: Routledge, 1999.

G. S. Kirk, J. E. Raven and M. Schofield, *The Presocratic Philosophers* (2nd edn), Cambridge: Cambridge University Press, 1983.

A. A. Long and D. N. Sedley, *The Hellenistic Philosophers. Vol.1: Translations of the Principal Sources with Philosophical Commentary*, Cambridge: Cambridge University Press, 1987.

A. A. Long and D. N. Sedley, *The Hellenistic Philosophers. Vol. 2: Greek and Latin Texts with Notes and Bibliography,* Cambridge: Cambridge University Press, 1987.

Plato, *Complete Works* (in translation; ed. with intro. and notes J. M. Cooper; associate ed. D. S. Hutchinson), Indianapolis: Hackett, 1997.

Plato, *Four Texts on Socrates: Plato's* Euthyphro, Apology, *and* Crito, *and Aristophanes'* Clouds (trans. with notes T. G. West and G. S. West; intro. T. G. West; rev. edn), Ithaca: Cornell University Press, 1998.

R. Sorabji, *Aristotle Transformed,* London: Duckworth, 1990.

R. Sorabji, *The Philosophy of the Commentators, 200–600 AD: A Sourcebook in Three Volumes,* London: Duckworth, 2004.

Xenophon, *Conversations of Socrates* (trans H. Tredennick, ed. R Waterfield), London: Penguin, 1990.

49. Greek Historiography

Thomas Harrison

The story of Greek historiography is easily told as a succession of 'great historians': Herodotus, the historian of the Greek–Persian Wars and their background, dubbed the 'father of history'; Thucydides, the first great 'scientific' historian, whose topic was the Peloponnesian War between Athens and Sparta and their respective allies; and finally Polybius, the archetypal soldier-historian representing (ambivalently) Roman conquest to his fellow Greeks. Such a narrative has something to be said for it. These three figures stand out, not only for the scale and magnificence of their surviving works, but also for their self-conscious reflection – most explicit in the case of Polybius – on the nature of 'history-writing' itself. Undoubtedly also, as Thucydides responded to (and tacitly corrected) the work of Herodotus, Polybius saw himself as the inheritor of a tradition of serious history-writing.

Writing the history of historiography

Inevitably, however, the development of Greek history-writing is a much more complex story. First, there are difficulties – especially at the start of the story – in distinguishing any clear genre of historiography. Herodotus recorded his *historiae*, literally his 'inquiries'. Though the term is suggestive of a critical attitude essential to history-writing, Herodotus' canvas includes much material – mythical traditions, for example, or accounts of the customs of foreign peoples recorded as if in a timeless present – that is not evidently historical to a modern audience. Though subsequent historians develop an increasingly self-conscious attitude to their tasks, the boundaries of history remain permeable: are we to classify the moralising biographies of Plutarch as history, to take just one example? Any attempt to trace the history of Greek historiography is bedevilled, then, by the problem of defining what we are looking at: whether to focus on the major works of military-political history, the so-called tradition of 'great historiography' (Marincola, *Authority and Tradition*), or to take a more catholic approach that also embraces biography, ethnography, and local history (the approach of Felix Jacoby).

Second, and as a consequence of this lack of any clear disciplinary borderline, ancient historians were influenced by and reacted against a great number of writers, not all historians. (A full story of Greek historiography, then, would need to take in much, much more.) Herodotus did not create history in a vacuum, but was influenced by and reacted to not only previous ethnographic or geographical work, but Homeric epic, or other poetic sources such as Simonides' narrative elegy on the battle of Plataea (see also chapter 41). Thucydides' famous description of his own work as a 'possession for all time' rather than a 'competition piece for the immediate moment' fails to mention Herodotus by name, and surely refers to a broader number of writers; modern scholarship has emphasised his familiarity (and indeed Herodotus') with Hippocratic medical writings, and (more recently) with the poet Pindar (S. Hornblower, *Thucydides and Pindar*, Oxford: Oxford University Press, 2004). By the time that we reach Polybius (200–118), the number of models for emulation and rejection – local historians, ethnographers, 'universal historians' – has multiplied. Though we can meaningfully distinguish strands in ancient historiography – often by tracing the influence of particular earlier historians, so distinguishing the relative influence of Thucydidean and Herodotean models of history – and though some generalisations are possible (such as that war is the subject par excellence of ancient historians), no clear story, either of progress or of decline, can be imposed on this mass of writers.

A third complication is that many of these historians, indeed the vast majority, exist only in 'fragments', i.e. in quotations from others' works (for how to access these historians, see Further Reading below). Since predecessors were usually quoted only for scathing criticism, it is very hard to get an accurate sense of these historians' own agendas. What we can deduce, however, from the lengths to which their successors went – for example, from Polybius' devotion of a whole book to the faults of the historian of Sicily, Timaeus of Tauromenium (condemned as an armchair historian) – is that they were sufficiently sizeable figures to require such treatment, and that our picture of the development of Greek history is consequently a skewed one.

Another consequence of these facts of survival – this time for the use of sources as historical evidence, rather than for our tracing its development – is worth outlining at the start. A second-century AD writer, Arrian of Nicomedia, might be thought a poor source for the history of (the late fourth century BC) Alexander the Great – except for the fact that he relies in large part on the accounts of two contemporaries of Alexander, Ptolemy (later ruler of Egypt) and Aristobulus. In this case we are lucky that Arrian declares his policy of relying on these two sources upfront. In most other such cases, such reliance is not so openly revealed, with the result that the historian needs to assess the (non-extant) sources of our surviving source before judging its worth as historical evidence.

This technique of 'source criticism' is not an exact science (see also chapter 50). If an early writer is mentioned in passing by a later one, it is a jump to presume that his entire account depends on that earlier writer (though it is certainly evidence of some familiarity, and that jump may – tentatively – be a reasonable guess). We can compare an account without a named source with another that does name one or more earlier writers – but again it is a jump to presume an *even* reliance on that earlier writer throughout a work (given that the points of overlap may be fairly brief). Later writers also shape their material to varying extents and in varying ways. The first-century BC 'universal historian' (see below) Diodorus Siculus is thought to have relied, predominantly at least, on single historians in turn: so, for example, his account of the fifth century BC relies on the fourth-century BC Ephorus of Cyme, while his version of the early period of the successors to Alexander derives from the (highly rated) lost work of Hieronymus of Cardia. (Still, one cannot simply speak of his account as if it *were* Ephorus' or Hieronymus' account unmediated.) Plutarch's biographies, by contrast, contain quotations from a large number of earlier writers, embedded within his own moralising framework (his *Parallel Lives* make comparisons, for example, explicit and implicit, between one Roman and one Greek life). The anecdotes preserved in Plutarch's lives can constitute historical gems for the historian, but it is important to recognise that they are selected for inclusion by criteria very different to our own.

Herodotus and the origins of history

It was once fashionable to look for a 'Herodotus before Herodotus', a key figure whose work explained how Herodotus could have written the work he did. Herodotus' clearest precursor is Hecataeus of Miletus, whose ethnographic and genealogical work (the *Periodos gēs*, or 'Journey Around the World', and *Genealogies*) clearly underlie some aspects of Herodotus' later account, in particular of Egypt. Deflecting the question of how history was invented from Herodotus, whose text survives intact, to a fairly shadowy figure who survives only in fragments now looks a fairly curious strategy, however – as do old attempts to trace Herodotus' evolution, for example from ethnographer to historian, by looking for the awkward joins in his text. Recent work by contrast, has tended to assume the integrity of the *Histories* (i.e. that they reflect a unified purpose) and to look at the structuring motifs of the work as a whole. By isolating Herodotus' critical vocabulary and comparing it to the fragments of his contemporaries and predecessors (for example, Hecataeus, Hellanicus of Lesbos, Xanthus of Lydia or Hippias of Elis), this work has also shown how Herodotus formed part of a movement of other 'proto-historians', all striving unevenly towards a critical attitude to the past or to telling the story of other cultures (Fowler, 'Herodotus and his contemporaries').

What is clear is that Herodotus combined the geographical and ethnographic focus of Hecataeus within an overarching narrative framework, that of the growth of Persia's power and its clash with Greece. His canvas, as a consequence, is a vast one – and Herodotus' value as a historical source is consequently enormous. Not only is he the main literary source (supplemented by fragments of poetry, later literary traditions, and most importantly material remains) for the archaic period of Greek history, but he is also a key source in the reconstruction of many of the foreign cultures he describes – not least, those of Persia or Egypt. It is wise not to take his stories at face value, however. Leaving aside his own, often ironical, shaping of his material, the oral traditions that he relays have already undergone a long period of 'deformation' (see O. Murray, 'Herodotus and Oral History', in N. Luraghi (ed.), *The Historian's Craft in the Age of Herodotus*, Oxford: Oxford University Press, 2001, pp. 16–44) and come, as it were, ready packaged with the biases of those that have transmitted them. Herodotus' claims to autopsy (i.e. to have seen things with his own eyes) have also been contested hotly – not least his claim of travel in Egypt. More recently, however, modern attention has focused on other themes: his intellectual context, in particular his affinities with medical and scientific writers, the narrative patterns of his work and Herodotus' own narration, and the value of the *Histories* as evidence of cultural presuppositions, for example concerning the gods or foreign peoples. Herodotus is now also, in general, seen within a late fifth-century context: writing under the shadow of the conflict between Athens and Sparta and, far from being dazzled by the bright lights of Periclean Athens (as in previous scholarship), offering a cynical angle on the origins of Athens' imperial power (e.g. Fornara, *Herodotus*).

Thucydides

Thucydides' work in many ways appears to mark a reaction against Herodotus. His work is contemporary history – that of the Peloponnesian War, which he lived through, and indeed participated in. Though he picked up (at least in his preamble in book 1) from the point at which Herodotus left off, the end of the Persian Wars, and though some of the themes of his work echo Herodotus' (the importance of control of the sea, for example), his work also appears more austere in style, his narrative is more linear (following the seasons of campaigning with occasional pauses in the action for deliberative speeches or set-piece descriptions, for example of the Athenian Plague or the Corcyraean revolution), and two classes of characters are largely missing from his work (whether this is the result of a deliberate decision, or simply a reflection of his different subject matter): women and the gods.

The story of scholarship on Thucydides in some ways also reverses that of Herodotus: as Herodotus has gone from (being presented as) a raconteur devoid of serious purpose, Thucydides has made the reverse journey: from austere fact-grubber to, if not a frivolous storyteller, at least a much more self-consciously literary figure. In addition to the continuing studies of the value of his work as evidence for Athenian imperialism, there has been a new stress on his subtlety as a narrator (T. Rood, *Thucydides: Narrative and Explanation*, Oxford: Clarendon Press, 1998), on literary intertexts, for example with Herodotus, or on the 'tragic structure' of his work. (Why did he give such a disproportionate emphasis to the Athenian expedition to Sicily, books 6–7, unless he wanted to tell a story of the fall of Athens? See Kallet, *Money and the Corrosion of Power*; Rood, 'Thucydides' Persian Wars'.) Thucydides' sometimes seemingly unvarnished style is now seen as intentionally so.

Hand in hand with this greater stress on Thucydides' artfulness as a narrator is a greater wariness not only of his historical judgements, but even of our ability to deduce what those judgements are. Crucially, the long speech sections included in his work can *never* be taken as standing for the views of their author, but need to be seen in complex relationship with one another and with the surrounding narrative. So, for example, Thucydides' view of the origins of the Peloponnesian War cannot be reduced to simple judgement of who started it on the basis of a single passage (the late revelation, for example, that the Spartans felt responsible for breaking the truce between themselves and the Athenians: 7.18). Rather, we should look at the sum total of his presentation of the causes of war: the reason why he gives us so many positions together is to show precisely how the responsibility for war cannot be simply allocated, to reveal (almost in slow motion) how war becomes inevitable. Perhaps the greatest problem in approaching Thucydides, however, is our almost exclusive reliance on him: with rare exceptions (Herodotus' more cynical account of the beginnings of Athenian imperialism, Athens' imperial decrees recorded on inscriptions, the few relevant chapters of the Aristotelian *Constitution of Athens*, or the evidence of contemporary Greek drama), we are largely forced to try to correct or nuance Thucydides' account from the evidence that he himself provides.

The fourth century

Any expectation that history after Thucydides simply continued in the same vein, rejecting myth and the gods in favour of steely scientific history, will be largely disappointed. There *were* continuators of Thucydides: most prominently, the *Hellenica* (lit. 'Greek affairs') of Xenophon or Theopompus, which took Thucydides' narrative on from the moment that it ceased in mid-sentence (in 411/10) to 362 and 394 respectively, or the anonymous (and, like Theompompus, fragmentary) Oxyrhynchus historian, so called because his text was found on papyrus in the Egyptian town of that name. But as the careers of both Theompompus and Xenophon reveal, neither Herodotus nor Thucydides had stamped any clear hierarchy on the types of historical writing that were possible. In addition to his *Hellenica*, Theopompus also wrote an epitome of Herodotus and the *Philippica* (see below). Xenophon's other more or less historical works include his biographical account of the Spartan *Agesilaus*, his memoir of the *Anabasis* (or 'Journey Up-Country' into the Persian Empire of the 10,000 Greek mercenaries in the service of Cyrus the Younger), and his fantastic reconstruction of the life of the elder Cyrus, the founder of the Persian Empire (onto whom he projects all the characteristics of the ideal monarch) in the *Cyropaedia*.

Nevertheless, we can distinguish a number of strands in the historical work of the fourth century. In addition to *Hellenica*, there continued to be local histories, notably the histories of Attica (or *Atthides*, singular: *Atthis*) of the Atthidographers (most famously, Androtion and the third-century Philochorus). Ctesias, Dinon and Heracleides continued the concerns of fifth-century writers by undertaking *Persica*, or histories of Persia (variously credible: Ctesias, a doctor in the court of the Persian king, has often been valued poorly because of his salacious anecdotes and, for example, confusing the order of the battles of the Persian Wars). But at the same time, there were newer developments. Ephorus of Cyme's universal history, the first of its kind, took the history of the Greek world from the mythical return of the sons of Heracles down to 340 BC; he was subsequently a prime source for the universal history of Diodorus. A word should be said for Aristotle as a historian – though his works scarcely constitute history by his own definition in the *Poetics* ('what Alcibiades did and suffered') – his comparative analysis of constitutions in the *Politics* or the schematic account (first narrative, then a description) of the *Constitution of Athens* (probably by one of his pupils) might be counted as history by modern standards. Finally, another work of Theopompus, the *Philippica*, foreshadows one aspect of the historians of the Hellenistic age, in particular the chief historians of Alexander, in its focus on a single individual: the Macedonian king, and father of Alexander, Philip II.

The Hellenistic world and beyond

The changed landscape of the Hellenistic world with its dominant monarchs did not, however, bring uniformity to the writing of history. The histories of Alexander, for example, range from the apparently sober (and admiring) accounts of Ptolemy and Aristobulus, the so-called 'official' tradition (preserved by Arrian), to the more romantic 'Vulgate' tradition, the main figure in which is Clitarchus (a key source for Diodorus, and the son of Dinon), apparently more popular in its approach and more cynical towards its protagonist. The expansion of Greek influence also gave a renewed impetus to ethnographic writing (e.g. Megasthenes, Hecataeus of Abdera; see chapter 51), and hence to the popularity of Herodotus, as well as giving rise to the recording of local traditions in Greek by non-Greeks: most prominently, the Egyptian Manetho, the Babylonian Berossus, or the Roman Fabius Pictor (see also chapter 50). In terms of our ability to reconstruct a narrative of Hellenistic history, however, with the end of Diodorus' continuous account in 302 BC we are – except for some passages of Plutarch's lives derived from Duris of Samos, Phylarchus and others – largely in the dark until the account of Polybius begins in earnest in 220 BC.

Polybius of Megalopolis (200–118) is the outstanding figure of the historiography of the Hellenistic age – even though, of the forty books of his history, only the first five survive in full. Like Herodotus before him, integrating the history of the Greek world with that of its neighbours, Polybius' breadth of scope is crucial to his achievement. He set out to show 'how and by what sort of government in less than fifty-three years the Romans came to conquer and rule almost the whole inhabited world'. Rome's conquests did not only give him a story to tell, however, but by their unification of the whole 'inhabited world' (or *oikoumenē*) also gave him his own vision of history: previous history, as he says, had consisted of so many disparate episodes, but from 220 (the beginning of the fifty-three years) onwards, history is an 'organic whole'; the expansion of Roman power is at the same time incremental and rationally explicable and guided by providence (or *tychē*, fortune). In keeping with the grandeur of his theme, Polybius is dismissive of the limited focus (Timaeus) as well as the rhetorical effects (Phylarchus) of his predecessors (though he is himself capable of the latter) and fond of laying out his procedure in elaborate detail. So, for example, a change of mind leads him to continue his story from the completion of Rome's conquests in 168/7 in order to reveal 'how they exercised their worldwide supremacy, and . . . the impressions and judgements which the rest formed concerning their rulers'.

The most fascinating aspect of Polybius' work (and the most discussed in modern scholarship) is the mixture of attitudes he reveals to Roman expansion. Here his personal biography cannot be kept separate, as he was himself a participant in the events that he describes. His father Lycortas had held the chief magistracy of the Achaean League; after the League's defeat, he was one of a thousand hostages transported to Italy as a guarantee of good behaviour. His friendship with the young P. Scipio Aemilianus (later, the destroyer of Carthage in 146) leads, however, to a curious ambivalence towards Rome: at times, nostalgic for a free Greek past, at times almost a proponent of Roman *mores*. This can be seen, especially, in his lengthy – and somewhat schematic – account of the Roman constitution in book 6. Developing the Greek idea of the mixed constitution, he finds that Rome's supposed balance of aristocratic, democratic and monarchic elements makes it immune to the decline that affects other constitutions.

The position of the Greek world under Roman rule is crucial to much of the historiographical work that follows: not least to the *Parallel Lives* (and other historical essays, contained within his *Moralia*) of Plutarch with their merging of Roman and Greek virtues, or the *Geography* and lost *History* of Strabo (first century BC to first century AD) or the *Roman Antiquities* of Dionysius of Halicarnassus (first century BC to first century AD), both seeking in different ways to reconcile the Greeks with Rome. The Egyptian Appian of Alexandria (second century AD) took the history of different regions down to the point of integration within Rome, while the Jewish Josephus wrote both *Jewish Antiquities* (on the model of Dionysius of Halicarnassus) and an account of the Jewish revolt against Rome (66–70), in which he himself changed to the Roman side. Other historians themselves held high Roman office: the historian of Alexander, the Greek Arrian, was governor of Nicomedia, while the half-Greek Cassius Dio (second to third century AD), author of a Roman history in eighty books written in Attic Greek, was a senator.

Dio's 'atticising', characteristic of the broader literary and cultural movement known as the Second Sophistic, is also representative of a strand in Greek historiography that continues into late antiquity and beyond. Just as the Latin historian Ammianus Marcellinus (himself a Greek from Antioch) saw his *Res Gestae* as summing up the whole of Graeco-Roman historiography, so a number of historians in Greek (often termed 'classicising') returned to earlier models. This number includes both fragmentary figures such as Priscus, Malchus, Eunapius of Sardis, or Olympiodorus (see Blockley, *Fragmentary Classicising Historians*) as well as Procopius' accounts of the Persian, Vandalic and Gothic wars of the sixth-century emperor Justinian.

At the same time, however, Christian historiography, by foregrounding the story of the triumph of Christianity over all others, marked a significant departure. The effective founder of Christian historiography was Eusebius (third to fourth century AD), bishop of Caesarea, apologist of the first Christian emperor, Constantine, and author of (among other works) a *Life of Constantine*, a chronicle, and a *Church History*. But there were other models of Christian 'historical' writing. Hagiography (i.e. the writing of saints' lives) was initiated by Athanasius' life of the pioneer of Egyptian monasticism, St Anthony (c. AD 360). A more eccentric model of historical writing, finally, is the Panarion (or 'medicine chest') of Epiphanius, bishop of Salamis on Cyprus: a history of eighty heresies (for the eighty concubines of the Song of Solomon), 'exposing their unlawful deeds like poisons and toxic substances, matching the antidotes with them at the same time'.

Further reading

Texts

Texts and translations of all the major surviving Greek historians are widely available (Herodotus in good Penguin, World's Classics and University of Chicago translations, Thucydides in a good Penguin translation); the only full translation of Polybius into English is that of the Loeb Classical Library. Excellent commentaries on Thucydides (by A. W. Gomme and others, and more recently by Simon Hornblower) and on Polybius (by F. W. Walbank) exist. Herodotus is less well served in English: Cambridge University Press have begun a series of commentaries (Flower and Marincola on book IX is already published), and a translation of the Italian Lorenzo Valla commentaries is in progress for publication by Oxford University Press.

Fragments

The fragmentary Greek historians are collected in the monumental *Die Fragmente der griechischen Historiker* (1923–), initiated by Felix Jacoby. The organisation of this work is complex. Historians (a category interpreted broadly) are classed by genres. Jacoby's original plan envisaged six parts, of which he completed the first three (in seventeen volumes of texts, commentaries and notes): (1) genealogy and mythography, (2) military political history (or *Zeitgeschichte*) and (3) horography (i.e. local histories) and ethnography. An individual writer is given a number (or, in some cases more than one: there are 856 in all). Then we are given their testimonia (i.e. ancient biographical details excerpted from other texts) and their fragments (in practice it is hard to ascertain where a fragment begins and ends: Jacoby's text indicates his estimate by marking the 'quotation' with a more spaced typeface). Testimonia and fragments are given in numbered sequence as T1, F1 and so on, so that a reference to the first testimonium or fragment of Hecataeus would look as follows: *FGrHist* 1 T 1, or *FGrHist* 1 F 1.

Like the Forth Bridge, Jacoby's work is being revised before it has even been finished. While part IV, 'Biography and Antiquarian Literature', is still in the course of publication, new versions of parts I–III are now being prepared, as *Brill's New Jacoby*, with a facing translation and new commentary (under the general editorship of Ian Worthington). Jacoby's original work is now also available electronically, with a three-volume index by Pierre Bonnechère. For an account of Jacoby's work, and its methodological underpinning, see Guido Schepens, 'Jacoby's *FGrHist*: problems, methods, prospects', in Glenn W. Most (ed.), *Collecting Fragments – Fragmente sammeln* (Aporemata: Kritische Studien zur Philologiegeschichte 1), Göttingen: Vandenhoeck and Ruprecht, 1997.

An excellent collection of late Roman 'classicising' historians, edited with translation, can be found in R. C. Blockley's *The Fragmentary Classicising Historians of the Later Roman Empire* (2 vols), Liverpool: Cairns, 1981.

Surveys of Greek historiography

C. W. Fornara, *The Nature of History in Ancient Greece and Rome*, Berkeley: University of California Press, 1983.

S. Hornblower, *Greek Historiography*, Oxford: Oxford University Press, 1994, esp. pp. 7–71.

J. Marincola, *Authority and Tradition in Ancient Historiography*, Cambridge: Cambridge University Press, 1998.

A. Momigliano, *Essays in Ancient and Modern Historiography*, Oxford: Blackwell, 1977.

Studies of particular historians

E. Bakker, I. de Jong and H. van Wees (eds), *Brill's Companion to Herodotus*, Leiden: Brill, 2002.

A. Cameron, *Procopius and the Sixth Century*, London: Duckworth, 1985.

K. Clarke, *Between Geography and History: Hellenistic Constructions of the Roman World*, Oxford: Oxford University Press, 1999 – on Polybius, Strabo and Posidonius.

W. R. Connor, *Thucydides*, Princeton: Princeton University Press, 1984.

B. Croke and A. Emmet (eds), *History and Historians in Late Antiquity*, Sydney: Pergamon Press, 1983.

M. A. Flower, *Theopompus of Chios: History and Rhetoric in the Fourth Century BC*, Oxford: Oxford University Press, 1994.

C. W. Fornara, *Herodotus: An Interpretative Essay*, Oxford: Oxford University Press, 1971.

R. Fowler, 'Herodotus and his Contemporaries', *JHS* 116 (1996), 62–87.

J. Gould, *Herodotus*, London: Weidenfeld and Nicolson, 1989.

S. Hornblower, *Thucydides*, London: Duckworth, 1987.

L. Kallet, *Money and the Corrosion of Power in Thucydides: The Sicilian Expedition and its Aftermath*, Berkeley: University of California Press, 2002.

T. Rood, 'Thucydides' Persian Wars', in C. S. Kraus (ed.), *The Limits of Historiography*, Leiden: Brill, 1999, pp. 141–68.

D. A. Russell, *Plutarch*, London: Duckworth, 1972.

K. Sacks, *Diodorus Siculus and the First Century*, Princeton: Princeton University Press, 1990.

C. J. Tuplin (ed.), *Xenophon and his World*, Stuttgart: F. Steiner, 2004.

F. W. Walbank, *Polybius*, Berkeley: University of California Press, 1972.

F. W. Walbank, *Polybius, Rome and the Hellenistic World: Essays and Reflections*, Cambridge: Cambridge University Press, 2002.

M. Whitby, 'Greek historical writing after Procopius: variety and vitality', in A. Cameron and L. Conrad (eds), *The Byzantine and Early Islamic Near East*, vol. 1, Princeton: Darwin Press, 1992, pp. 25–80.

50. Roman Historiography

Edward Bispham

Telling it how it was?

Roman (like Greek) historians made much of 'telling it how it was', but in the telling lay much which altered how things had been. Roman historical writing ranged from the serious and analytical to the racy and frothy; all variants, however, drew on a repertoire of techniques which were shared by oratory and poetry. Historical narrative aimed to preserve the past; but also to entertain, to move and to instruct. Instruction was of two kinds: moral – the presentation, through events and above all individuals, of praiseworthy and reprehensible conduct, to be imitated or avoided; and political – justifying Roman expansion, and the Roman character, underlining Rome's special relationship with the gods, and advocating or attacking particular forms of political or social activity.

Roman historians were mainly senators. Their social status is important: probably no other ancient community had its history (and Roman history is a peculiar type of local history) treated over and over again by so many of its own elite. That Roman historiography was senatorial historiography links it tightly to the competition between aristocratic families for status and glory which marked the civic and especially the military spheres. This competition is framed within a normative account of the fundamental values and customs which the ruling elite shared and which in turn helped to justify their position within society; but to whom? The audience must in fact have been rather limited, but wider than the sons of senators, and have embraced the upper classes of both Rome and the Italian cities.

Roman historical narratives, then, were always political, and often partisan; inevitably they contradicted each other. They also suffered as do all attempts to represent multiple contemporary actions in any medium: they necessarily had a singular point of view, and thus were inevitably *selective*. It was impossible to record everything; writers needed to pick and order material, in order to be intelligible, be readable, and make a point.

It cannot be simple to work out 'what happened' from ancient histories: they are not 'archival' records of the past, they are narratives. The past itself is no longer directly accessible; what we have is a historiographically constituted past, a series of stories. Even achieving reconciliation between divergent accounts is not to reach the truth, but to make judgements about narratives. All of this, of course, makes the whole endeavour of interrogating Roman histories about the past more challenging, and more fun.

To appreciate what Roman historians were trying to do when they turned the past into narrative, we need to examine the traditions and influences within which they operated, the development of historiography at Rome, and ideological and practical constraints on the genre.

A fragmented tradition

One of the most paradoxical characteristics of the Roman historical tradition is its *incompleteness*, as a whole, and in its parts. Think of an iceberg: it may look big, but what we see is dwarfed by what we cannot see, hidden, invisible below the water. The surviving writings of, say, Sallust and Livy are only the 'tip of the iceberg'; most of what they wrote has been lost beneath the waves of time, with the loss of the manuscripts containing their texts. Of Sallust's *Histories* almost all is lost, and only thirty-five of Livy's 142 books have come down to us.

We could extend the iceberg analogy further. Icebergs once formed part of an icecap, but ended up floating free in the ocean. Roman historical texts are also isolated remnants, broken off from a wide and varied land-mass of historical writing, the broader tradition of Roman historiography. This is known to us only in sketchy outlines, through passing references in surviving writers, characterising in general terms the work of authors now lost in whole or in part. The size of this 'lost continent' of Roman histories is considerable. Some forty historians who wrote during the Roman Republic now survive only in tiny snippets; their demise is partly to be blamed on Livy's history, which drew on them heavily, but was more readable. All that we know about them consists of brief quotations (or more often paraphrases of the original content, made with no pretence as to accuracy) in later writers. These are usually, but inaccurately, referred to as fragments. Their heterogeneity is striking. For example, the 140-odd 'fragments' of Cornelius Sisenna are mostly phrases illustrating unusual or archaic diction in the works of later grammarians. Such citations are very different from passages where Livy tells that he is giving the version of, say, a battle found in his predecessor Claudius Quadrigarius. They tease but frustrate our understanding of the historical tradition as a whole, and give inevitable but perhaps undue prominence to the big 'bergs' of the surviving writers.

In studying fragmentary historians, emphasis used to be placed on reconstructing the entire historical edifice from the few remains surviving. Such approaches now seem very insecure, and a less prescriptive approach is being adopted, with greater agnosticism about the ordering and significance of the fragments, and more emphasis on flexibility in interpretation.

Sometimes late writers allow some level of reconstruction of missing texts. Sections of the imperial histories of Florus and Orosius can be compared with surviving books of Livy; it seems fairly clear that both drew on him in such a way that where Livy's text is lost, *some idea* of what was in it can be gained from the relevant passages of Florus (second century AD) and Orosius (fifth century AD); both were compressing Livy, which complicates the exercise. A related area of study (often referred to by its German name, *Quellenforschung*) is a more ambitious form of source criticism. It analyses surviving texts in order to discover their sources, and thus to evaluate their reliability, and to allow for bias or defects absorbed from the sources. This approach has declined in popularity: it depended upon a rather naive approach; most attributions to this source or that were little more than conjecture, often with no basis in the text.

For example, *Quellenforschung* might argue that all mentions of the city of Antium in Livy must derive from his predecessor Valerius Antias, whose *cognomen* shows he was from Antium, and must therefore have had an interest in his home town. This assumes that Valerius came from Antium – there is no evidence either way, and in that case it is futile to speculate whether he had an interest in Antium (if he did, we might expect to know more about it from Livy than we do); it also assumes that none of Antias' predecessors was moved to write anything about this strategically important city. Similar weaknesses affect claims that all mentions of Fabii in the first thirty books of Livy are drawn from the first Roman historian, Fabius Pictor; such a claim is bold even when made of *favourable* mentions of Fabii. Comparison of what we have with what we do not have is, to say the least, problematic; and the quest for sources makes no allowance for creative adaptation by the surviving writer, let alone intervening writers.

History today

More recent scholarship has tended to look at surviving writers more for their own sake and on their own terms than for their possible sources, and it is here that the interests of historians and literary specialists have begun to converge. One important result to emerge in recent years is also tied to developments in literary theory (see also chapter 8). The medium is increasingly recognised to be inseparable from the message:

we cannot simply admit that Tacitus has an insinuating and oblique way of talking about his subjects, and then weed out what we think are the facts from this treatment, like prising gemstones from a setting.

Let us consider Livy again. First, his understanding of the past depended primarily on his reading of his (now lost) predecessors, but he certainly often reshaped this material, using his rhetorical training, to suit his own ends, rather than unthinkingly copying earlier writers. Second, the resulting stories about the past were necessarily told for his contemporary Augustan audience, which had its own interests, worries and agendas, and which valued the past not so much for its own sake as for what it could do to entertain and instruct them. Livy's history is the past which mattered for Augustan readers, making it count in the present. In the same way, while Orosius drew on Livy, he was a Christian: thus his work (*Histories Against the Pagans*) is not just an abridgement of Livy's, but a history which stresses the disasters suffered by pagans. By telling us what they do, and in the ways in which they do, both Livy and Orosius tell us as much about their present as about their past.

It follows, that to understand any writer's history, we need to understand his age and its preoccupations, and also the literary traditions within which he operated. For the latter, some idea of the breadth and variety of Roman historical writing is essential. Here a number of factors need serious consideration.

Annals and annalists

The Romans distinguished between two types of history: *annales* and *historia*, which often appear as titles of historical works. They were said to be, respectively, ancient and contemporary history, but this distinction finds little support in the content of the works so titled. The history and concept of *annales* are controversial, and need discussion.

By contrast with Greek historiography, the Roman historical tradition is a neophyte. Greek historical writing began in the fifth century (see chapter 49); Greek writers had known about Rome since the fourth century, but not written seriously about it until the third. Importantly, they were followed by home-grown historical narratives only at the end of the third century: Fabius Pictor was a contemporary of the Second Punic War, and wrote Rome's first history c. 200 BC at the latest. How on earth did Pictor find out more than the bare outlines of early Roman history, with only limited material written by outsiders available? It must be that there is a high proportion of fiction in Pictor's account of early Roman history, whether invented by him, or current in oral tradition, or represented on the stage at the *ludi* (games). For us the construction of a narrative which might reflect real events is correspondingly more difficult than it is in well-documented periods.

This leads to a second problem. Romans were making some records of notable events in the human and in the divine spheres from an early period. Several writers refer to an annual priestly record, made on a whitened board, and known as the *annales maximi* (or 'annals of the highest (priest)'). It seems to have been, to judge from criticisms of it, sparse and tedious – giving names of magistrates and major civil and military events, as well as eclipses and corn shortages, according to the second-century BC writer Cato the Elder (but we do not have the end of this quotation from Cato). The *annales maximi* are much discussed by scholars: how important are they?

They are probably responsible for the particular way in which Roman historical writing was structured, namely recording events year by year, in a record headed by the names of the chief Roman magistrates (usually consuls). Thus the individual *year* became the fundamental structural unit for narrating the past: when it ended, the narrative broke off, to resume under new magistrates in the next year. This year-by-year structure also occurs in Greek histories, especially in local histories. Yet in Roman historiography it was for over two hundred years the dominant form for prose (and verse) narratives about the past, and subsequently gave a poignant shape to the works of Tacitus, who knowingly exploited with a bitter nostalgia the historical narrative form of the free republic to sharpen his history of life under Rome's first emperors. Yet it is uncertain whether the first generation of Roman historians, starting with Fabius Pictor, wrote like this (annalistically); and we know that some, such as Cato the Elder, so disparaging about the *annales maximi*, did not.

If Pictor was not influenced by the *form* of the *annales maximi*, did he exploit their *content*? They would have provided a 'hard core' of dates and events, names and actions, something which most scholars assume to lie behind Pictor and his successors. Yet it is difficult to find material in Livy for which a strong, rather than a circular, case can be made for derivation from the priestly annals; and if there is no obviously priestly material in Livy, was there any in the earlier writers on whom he drew? The Elder Cato suggests that there was: he said that it was not his intention to write the kind of material found in the *annales maximi*, implying other writers did just that; and Dionysius of Halicarnassus implies that Polybius calculated the foundation date of Rome from them. Beyond this we can only assume, and not prove, that some material from the *annales maximi* found its way into the oldest level of the annalistic tradition. By the end of the second century BC the *annales maximi* were no longer being compiled, and any consultation had probably ceased. In the Augustan period a work entitled *Annales Maximi* was published in an edition of eighty books, but its relation to the earlier priestly chronicle is unknown.

If Pictor did not use the *annales maximi*, the question about his sources becomes more acute. We have already noted the probability that he (like his successors) resorted to invention, and that he must have depended on oral tradition. Roman historians (as opposed to those interested in the history of places, rituals, institutions and language, known as antiquarians, of whom Varro is the most famous) seem to have a poor record for consulting documents; other possible sources not already mentioned include the traditions of the great aristocratic families, oral and written, among the latter the family trees (*stemmata*) which decorated, in gloomy profusion, the atria of their houses. Various writers used these ingredients in varying combinations, giving rise to a plurality of traditions in Roman history; among these the survival of Livy's work has made one strand canonical. 'Annalist', a term used to describe the creators of these historical traditions, has become a dirty word, implying an inventive, exaggerated but unsophisticated account of Roman history. Although we are much better able to judge Livy than his predecessors, he is often excused where they are blamed, or credited with turning the annalists' base metal to gold. If this is true, it is a matter of style and not content; Livy stands at the end of the annalistic tradition, is effectively the last of the republican annalists, and must be judged on the same terms as the others.

Before Livy

Cicero (*de Legibus* 1.6, *de Oratore* 2.51–3) seems to have had a low view of earlier historians; but this was a stylistic judgement. Critical scholars often point to exaggeration of numbers, or blatantly partisan treatment of individual families. Another way in which writers found material was in the retrojection of the issues of their own day into the past. A structural outcome of the need to put flesh on the bare bones of Roman history was that the diet of free invention (what Badian called the 'expansion of the past'; 'Early historians', pp. 11–13) was successful beyond expectation: Roman history expanded, and in the case of the ninety-seven-plus-volume monster of Cn. Gellius, became obese. Here, the process of inventing the past was linked to an increasingly volatile present: from the time at which Fabius wrote, increasing elite competition was beginning the processes which would tear the Roman Republic apart (see also chapter 18).

Many scholars have tried to identify major developments in historiography in this period. Examples include the growing interest in monographs, shorter and more focused works than the standard total histories of Rome (such as Coelius Antipater's work on the Hannibalic War, and Sallust's surviving works); and the rise of antiquarian inquiry (perhaps beginning with Calpurnius Piso in the late second century BC).

Given the exiguous remains of earlier writers, little can be said with certainty. Denigration of Livy's predecessors is a cheap shot. Some points about them should be made, however. The first is the breadth of the Roman historical traditions: we would be wrong to try to separate out too firmly separate strands of annalistic history, antiquarianism, ethnography and so on; to do so would be to ignore the richness and complexity of the historical endeavour. This breadth finds interesting expression in the mixture of short universal history with extended imperial panegyric of Velleius Paterculus, an army officer writing in the reign of Tiberius.

Second, Cicero's criticisms should not lead us to believe that early Roman historians were unsophisticated. Fabius Pictor was clearly sensitive to the nature of Hellenistic historiography. He wrote in Greek, which was *the* literary language for prose writing just as, in the early modern period, Italian was the language of choice for opera, whatever the composer's nationality. Fabius sought to situate Romans in the complex world of myth and identity in the Hellenistic Mediterranean: to show who they were, where they had come from, and perhaps to 'debarbarise' them: he was engaging with Greek culture, but writing for Greeks and Romans. Polybius drew attention to Fabius' partiality, and it seems that his contemporary history was aimed in part at justifying Rome's wars with Carthage; he possibly wished to elevate these wars to an epic status, to rival the great wars of Greek history.

After Pictor, Roman history changed in important ways within a couple of generations. In the middle of the second century Latin supplanted Greek as the language of composition. A Latin cultural identity had crystallised under the influence of, and in reaction to, 'hellenisation' (see also chapter 18). There are two protagonists here. First, there is Cato the Elder, whose *Origines* in part recorded the traditions of non-Roman communities in Italy, an endeavour at once patriotic, and redolent of Hellenistic antiquarian research (and indeed unthinkable without it). Second, there is Ennius, whose hexameter poem *Annales* may be the earliest work to use the annalistic structure. Apart from one or two literary showpieces, Roman history-writing in Greek was from now on abandoned to Greeks (such as Polybius, Diodorus Siculus, Dionysius of Halicaranssus and Dio Cassius; see also chapter 49).

Some scholars have seen a decline in the social status of Roman historians in the first century BC, culminating in the 'outsider' Livy (born a non-Roman in Patavium in north Italy). The evidence for this claim is slim. In fact, there is an increasing tendency for the protagonists in great events to write autobiographical memoirs, telling their side of the story: the dictator Sulla's was one such; Caesar's *Commentarii* are a similar exercise; Augustus too wrote an autobiography of his early years, stopping when the end of the Civil Wars left no more rivals, nothing more to explain away, no one to whom he was accountable. His *Res Gestae*, or achievements, is a very different kind of narrative, inscribed on bronze and stone; it reminds us of the historiographical importance of inscriptions.

From the later first century BC we have some works surviving whole or in large part. Sallust's monographs on the Catilinarian conspiracy and the Jugurthine War show an interest in the abuse of power by small factions for their own ends, and the corruption and inadequacy of Roman society. Sallust's pessimistic take on the late Republic, in common with much historical writing, foregrounded a moralising interpretation in terms of luxury and decadence at the expense of other types of analysis (although he was aware of socio-economic factors too). Sallust also represents a historiographical tendency, from the later second century onwards, to seek *the* turning point for the republic, the point at which the rot set in. The paradigm of decline was taken up by Livy, who explores the redemptive possibilities afforded by the *exempla* of Rome's past greatness, in the face of present moral deficiencies, most clearly manifested by civil wars. Livy cannot simply be labelled as an Augustan partisan – he stopped the history at a troubled, not a triumphant, point: the unexpected death of the elder Drusus, Augustus' stepson, in Germany in 9 BC. Nevertheless, his very traditional concerns do largely overlap with those also expressed in the golden age of early Augustan poetry, and to that extent buttress the programme of the regime.

'Court tittle-tattle'?

The great German historian Theodor Mommsen decided not to publish his history of the Roman emperors: 'what is there beyond court tittle-tattle?', he asked. While this is unfair, it is true that the advent of imperial monarchy in Rome made the writing of history difficult, as it was hard to find out what had happened; dangerous, if it was too independent or critical; or trivial, if too adulatory, as Tacitus famously pointed out. Further, what happened, and why, became more opaque for historians – autocracies are naturally secretive – causing further difficulties (see Dio Cassius 53.19, 54.15.1–4). Tacitus blamed autocracy for bringing to an end the traditional diet of senatorial historiography (overseas conquest and political competition), and would have us believe that he was reduced to recording the uninspiring record of imperial cruelty to an aristocracy sunk in servility (*Annals* 4.32; compare 3.65). Although a main Tacitean concern was how to reconcile personal liberty for the elite with the demands imposed by the principate, he was not nevertheless short of traditional material either.

Once dead, emperors' characters encouraged the natural disposition of much ancient historical writing to explain history in terms of interpersonal dynamics and the moral failings or strengths of individuals. Tacitus himself, writing in the reign of Hadrian, certainly failed to write, as he claimed, 'without anger and partisan spirit'. His work seems, in the light of epigraphic discoveries (the *senatus consultum* (see also chapter 34) about the trial for murder of Cn. Piso the elder, and Claudius' speech on the entry of Gallic aristocrats to the Senate), to be reliable, if jaundiced. His imperial predecessors, rivals and successors have perished almost utterly. No large-scale Latin history was attempted until the fourth century AD, when a Greek, Ammianus Marcellinus, starting, significantly, at the point where Tacitus' *Histories* finished, wrote, in Latin, a huge narrative history down to his own day. What survives of his work suggests little use of the Greek historians Herodian or Cassius Dio (both early third-century AD writers, generally of good quality, whose work reflects the fact that in a truly worldwide empire, Roman history had become everyone's property). Instead, inferior Latin sources were used, including a lost imperial history known as the *Kaisergeschichte* ('emperor-history'); its existence was theorised in Germany in the nineteenth century, on the basis of very similar passages in the *Historia Augusta* (below), Eutropius and Aurelius Victor.

These works apart, the dominant form of historical writing in Latin after Tacitus seems to have been (auto)biography, exemplified by Suetonius, and continued through (the lost) Marius Maximus to the peculiar *Historia Augusta* in the fourth century AD. Such writing was in a sense the natural outcome of interest in the single dominating figure of the emperor, although intellectual currents, such as the Second Sophistic in Greece, interested in the virtues and vices of great men and their protreptic implications (i.e. for encouraging morally sound behaviour), also encouraged the biographical trend, not least in Suetonius' contemporary Plutarch. The pagan revival of the fourth century, represented by savants like Macrobius and Servius, the commentator on Virgil, or the anonymous author of the *Origo Gentis Romanae*, shows that some of the earlier traditions had survived, if little read outside the pagan intellectual elite. It is perhaps salutary to note that the most widely read histories were not the past masters, but brief, carelessly excerpted epitomes like the *Breviarium* of Eutropius and the *Periochae* of Livy, which often doomed the works from which they were taken to fatal neglect. That, though, was the past; the future belonged to Christian writers like Eusebius and Orosius. Against their continuing debt to pagan classical culture must be set a fundamentally new outlook and agenda. A new chapter in history-writing had begun.

Further reading

Collections of fragments

H. Beck and U. Walter, *Die frühen römischen Historiker* (2 vols), Darmstadt: Wissenschaftliche Buchgesellschaft, 2001, 2004 – republican historians; texts, with translation and commentary in German.

M. Chassignet, *L'Annalistique romaine* (3 vols), Paris: Association G. Budé, 1996, 1999, 2004 – republican historians (except Cato the Elder); texts, with translation and notes in French.

T. Cornell et al., *Fragments of the Roman Historians*, Oxford: Oxford University Press, forthcoming – republican and imperial historians; texts, with introduction, translation and commentary in English.

H. Peter, *Historicorum Romanorum Reliquiae* (2 vols),

Leipzig: Teubner, 1914; rev. edn Stuttgart: Teubner, 1967 – first serious edition of the fragments of lost Roman historians; texts, with introduction and notes in Latin.

Secondary reading

E. Badian, 'The early historians', in T. A. Dorey (ed.), *Latin Historians*, London: Routledge and Kegan Paul, 1966, pp. 1–38.

E. H. Bispham, 'Literary sources', in R. Morstein-Marx and N. S. Rosenstein (eds), *A Companion to the Roman Republic*, Oxford: Blackwell, 2006, pp. 29–50.

B. W. Frier, *Libri Annales Pontificum Maximorum* (2nd edn), Ann Arbor: Michigan University Press, 1999.

C. S. Kraus and A. J. Woodman, *Latin Historians* (*Greece and Rome* New Surveys in the Classics 27), Oxford: Oxford University Press, 1997.

J. M. Marincola, *Authority and Tradition in Ancient Historiography*, Cambridge: Cambridge University Press, 1997.

E. Rawson, *Intellectual Life in the Late Roman Republic*, London: Duckworth, 1985, ch. 15.

E. Rawson, 'Prodigy lists and the use of the *Annales Maximi*', in E. Rawson, *Roman Culture and Society: Collected Papers*, Oxford, Oxford University Press, 1991, pp. 1–15.

M. Toher, 'Augustus and the evolution of Roman historiography', in K. A. Raaflaub and M. Toher (eds), *Between Republic and Principate: Interpretations of Augustus and his Principate*, Berkeley and Los Angeles: University of California Press, 1990, pp. 139–54.

T. P. Wiseman, *Clio's Cosmetics: Three Studies in Greco-Roman Literature*, Leicester: Leicester University Press, 1979.

T. P. Wiseman, *Historiography and Imagination: Eight Essays on Roman Culture*, Exeter: Exeter University Press, 1994.

A. J. Woodman, *Rhetoric in Classical Historiography*, London: Routledge, 1988.

51. Geography and Ethnography

Kai Brodersen

Geography and ethnography, 'writing about the world and its people', define a genre of literature in the ancient world, and, more widely, a field of ancient knowledge. (The even wider non-technical usage of 'geography' as referring to the 'real' locations of places on the surface of the earth is not what this chapter is about, but the recent *Barrington Atlas*, edited by R. Talbert, provides up-to-date information.) In general, the ancient term *geographia* refers to writing about world *and* people alike; the distinction which our modern use of two different words, geography and ethnography, implies was not usually made in antiquity, neither was there a contradiction between 'imagined' or 'mythical' and 'real' geography: the journeys of the Argonauts and the wanderings of Odysseus were as much part of what *geographia* dealt with as were more recent endeavours to explore and meet, or conquer, the world and its people. Accordingly, the 'first geographer' the ancient tradition (e.g. Strabo 1.1.2) acknowledged was Homer, whose works indeed demonstrate an interest both in the world and in its people, in the Greek homelands (as represented, e.g., in the catalogue of ships from Greece, *Iliad* 2) as well as beyond (most notably in the *Odyssey*).

The expansion of the Greek world in the archaic period was facilitated by, and/or led to, a recording of the names of places and peoples in the order in which they appear to a coastal voyager on a boat, with a view to providing practical information for travellers, be it traders, soldiers, settlers, envoys or pilgrims. The growth of interest in 'the other' in the wake of the Persian Wars and beyond, early voyages of exploration and, more intensively, the truly marvellous conquests of Alexander the Great in the East, and Roman generals in the South, West and North of the Mediterranean world, made geographical and ethnographical literature appeal to even wider audiences. At the same time, such writings were increasingly embellished with information on, and stories about, places, peoples and wonders within and even outside the known world, producing works capable of inventing alternative worlds inhabited by very different peoples, from classical and Hellenistic *Persica* and *Indica* to the *Marvels beyond Thule* by Antonius Diogenes in the second century AD. Even ancient utopias are firmly set in the traditional framework of geography and ethnography.

Practical geography and ethnography

The practicalities of moving around in the world and among its peoples are at the root of the so-called *periplus* (sea-voyage around) which lists places and people along the shores of the Mediterranean, and sometimes those of the 'outer' limits of the world. Obviously, neither the hinterland nor islands in the middle of the sea can easily be included in such linear descriptions of continuous coastlines, and they are either ignored or described separately. The *periplus* type of geographical and ethnographical literature continued to provide the basic structure for later geographies and ethnographies well into the Roman Empire: witness the elder Pliny's books 3–6 of his *Natural History*, Strabo's *Geography*, Pomponius Mela's *Chorography* or Dionysius of Alexandria's *Periegesis*, but also the archaeological evidence at the *Sebasteion* (precinct for a cult of the Roman emperor) in Aphrodisias, where the representations of peoples in the Roman world appear to have been placed in a *periplus*-like order, and separately from the representations of islands (Smith, '"Simulacra gentium"'). As in other works of *geographia*, the interest in places *and* people in the *periplus* is obvious.

The coastal hinterland, and larger land-masses, were similarly explored, and conceptualised, along routes across the land, in *periēgēseis* (leadings around) and *itineraria* (itineraries, descriptions of ways) recording stations along routes, and distances between them. Unlike routes travelled along on the sea, where distances between individual places on the coast were difficult to assess, roads and other routes across the country could easily be measured, and the distances thus be recorded for the benefit of future travellers. There is plenty of evidence for the practical use of *itineraria*: inscriptions name the names of, and list the distances to, stations along a route, and to places in a province (e.g. the newly discovered 'stadiasmus provinciae Lyciae' in Patara; see Işik et al., *Miliarium Lyciae*); portable objects record stations on a long-distance route (like the so-called Vicarello goblets with their record of stations and distances on the roads from Gades/Cadiz to Rome, or vessels naming stations along Hadrian's walls; see Dilke, *Greek and Roman Maps*); and manuscripts transmit the 'Itinerarium Antonini', a list of stations and distances along roads (and rivers) both across the land-mass of the Roman provinces (and beyond) and along the Mediterranean coastline ('Itinerarium Maritimum'). Finally, *itineraria picta*, 'painted itineraries', were known by late antiquity and seem to have converted the information in the text-bound *itineraria* into images which are perhaps best compared with the well-known London Underground maps: disregarding real distances and angles, they present a network of routes and thus provide a practical tool to check routes, stations along them, and places where these routes cross each other (see Brodersen, *Terra Cognita*). While a papyrus, of which only parts have been published so far, may present such a diagram already in the first century BC (see Brodersen, 'Mapping the ancient world'), certainly the most impressive *itinerarium pictum* is the so-called *Tabula Peutingeriana*, a twelfth-century 'map' presumably based on Roman material (see Talbert in Talbert and Brodersen, *Space in the Roman World*).

The theory of geography and ethnography

Beyond the practicalities, theoretical reflection on the world and its people was developed: what was the place of the world and its peoples, or the *oikoumenē* (inhabited world), on the face of the earth and in the wider cosmos? (See chapter 14.)

Such theoretical reflections on the wider world in writings are being referred to as *periodos gēs* (walk around the world) and, again, conceptualise the world and its people in a linear description of places and peoples along routes, but also attempting a graphic representation. Works of this kind by Anaximander of Miletus and Hecataeus of Miletus are lost to us but for a few fragments, which, however, allow us to conclude that they presented the *oikoumenē* as surrounded by the ocean, and divided into four parts by the Mediterranean and the Phasis river from west to east, and the Tanais (Don) and Nile rivers from north to south. The world beyond the *oikoumenē* was, or so the ancient tradition claimed, first referred to as a globe by Parmenides of Elea, and divided into five zones: two extreme cold ones at the margins, one extremely hot one in the middle, and two temperate ones in between, with one of these two being the zone of our *oikoumenē* (and the other one inhabited by the *antipodes* or *antichthones*). Further theoretical reflection, and especially the discovery of the use of *climata*, the 'leanings' or angles of the sun's rays on the surface of the earth varying with the latitude (longitude was difficult to measure exactly well until the eighteenth century), led to a more refined theory, culminating in the work of Eratosthenes of Cyrene in the third century BC, which allowed this scholar to define the globe's circumference, and devise a map-like representation of the *oikoumenē* (see Geus in Talbert and Brodersen, *Space in the Roman World*).

The most comprehensive attempt at summing up geographical theory, and at presenting estimated latitudes and longitudes for more than

8,000 places and peoples, was the *Geography*, presented by the second-century scholar Ptolemy of Alexandria. While it was, for all we know, ignored by contemporaries and later antiquity alike, it played a major role in the Renaissance revival of geography as a science.

Practical versus theoretical geography and ethnography

A connection of the 'down-to-earth' descriptions of routes on the sea or across the land in the *periplus* and *itinerarium* and their more developed literary forms, on the one hand, and the 'high-brow' theoretical reflections on the *oikoumenē* and the globe, on the other hand, is not something antiquity seems to have achieved, or even to have tried to achieve. While Egypt, for example, was for obvious practical reasons considered a unity in the *periplus* and *itinerarium* type of literature, theoretical geography saw the Nile as the boundary of the two continents Africa and Asia, thus, as it were, dividing Egypt into two parts on separate continents, without ever referring to the conceptual difficulties involved (which would have been apparent from a map). This is true for later authors, as well, including Pomponius Mela (who gives a *summa*, or comprehensive account of theoretical geography with a divided Egypt, before presenting a *periplus* with a unified one) and Dionysius of Alexandria, and even for the large-scale geographical works of Strabo and the elder Pliny, where the theoretical chapters remain conceptually unconnected with the detailed descriptions of the places and people in the *oikoumenē* in the *periplus*-like main body of the text.

It is not easy today to understand this 'split' view of practical and theoretical geography (and ethnography) in the ancient world, but one reason might be the different approaches, and very different sizes, of the audiences of the two different kinds of text: the very 'practical' geography and ethnography, as accessible in *periplus* or *itinerarium*, could be useful indeed for many travellers, and was able to serve its purpose without any reference to wider issues of theory. The latter, on the other hand, seem to have been discussed by only a small group of learned men over long time-spans (second-century authors readily acknowledge the contributions made to this kind of scholarship by authors half a millennium before) – the sort of 'veneer' of a tiny and generation-spanning group of scholars keeping knowledge alive, and developing it, which is typical for a pre-industrial society. And this knowledge was accessible only to the best scholars, anyway, as not even Cicero would claim that he understood theoretical geography (see e.g. his *Letter to Atticus* 2.6.1: *Hercule sunt res difficiles ad explicandum*, 'By Hercules, these things are difficult to explain!').

Trends in recent scholarship on geography and ethnography

Ancient geography and ethnography have been widely studied. Editions of the relevant sources, 'practical' and 'theoretical' alike, started to be published soon after the invention of printing (they soon played a major role in shaping the developing science of geography) and continue to be revised in the light of recent textual research. While the major texts are accessible in reliable editions, the sheer size of Strabo's *Geography* – seventeen ancient books – has, as yet, prevented the publication of a complete modern edition, as has the sheer boredom of the more than 8,000 names of places and peoples with their geographical data in Ptolemy's *Geography* (see Stueckelberger in Talbert and Brodersen, *Space in the Roman World*). For both works, however, reliable editions are on their way: Stefan Radt in Groningen (Netherlands) has started a new complete and critical edition of Strabo, and Alfred Stueckelberger in Berne (Switzerland) has mustered a team of scholars to tackle a fresh, and for the first time critical, complete edition of Ptolemy's *Geography*.

While 'theoretical' geography and ethnography were the focus of research in the nineteenth and up to the middle of the twentieth century (see e.g. the histories of ancient geography of Bunbury and Thomson), the 'practical' side has become a hotly debated topic for research only since the 1980s (Janni, *La mappa e il periplo*; Nicolet, *Space, Geography, and Politics*; Brodersen, *Terra Cognita*; Adams and Laurence, *Travel and Geography*): how are we to understand the 'linear' perception, and presentation, of space in lists of places and peoples along a route in *periplus* or *itinerarium*? What are the implications of this for how the ancient world conceptualised the world at large? And what about the geography and ethnography concerning the edges of the earth in ancient thought (Romm, *Edges of the Earth*)?

At the same time, the question of ancient 'map consciousness' has been discussed, with opinions ranging from an approach postulating that, in spite of the lack of clear evidence, the classical world simply 'must have had, and used, maps' (see e.g. Harley and Woodward, *History of Cartography*), to trying to understand why the lack of evidence for maps may point to a different mode of conceptualising space by reducing information to what is actually needed when planning a journey or march (a concept which has become a familiar feature of any 'routing' software translating the information found in a – virtual – map into an itinerary list to be used when driving). The debate is still going on, and has led to a renewed interest in the (only supposedly 'boring') subliterary text of the *periplus* and *itinerarium* kind. Their – as yet underrated – contribution to the ancient writing about the world and its people may well be expected to lead to a better understanding of ancient geography and ethnography.

Further reading

Primary sources

Strabo and Pliny the elder are available in the Loeb Library, Pomponius Mela in a new translation by F. E. Romer (Ann Arbor: University of Michigan Press, 1998), while the latest English version of Dionysius' *Periēgēsis* is that of John Free (in his *Tyrocinium geographicum Londinense*, 1789; available via www.gale.com/Eighteenth-Century). Antonius Diogenes' *Marvels beyond Thule* are translated in S. A. Stephens and J. J. Winkler (eds), *Ancient Greek Novels: The Fragments*, Princeton: Princeton University Press, 1995. The fullest collection of Greek geographical fragments is still C. Müller (ed.), *Geographi Graeci minores*, Paris: Didot, 1855–61, repr. Hildesheim: Olms 1990; for the Roman itineraries see O. Cuntz and J. Schnetz (eds), *Itineraria Romana*, Leipzig: Teubner, 1929–40, repr. Stuttgart: Teubner 1990.

Secondary

C. Adams and R. Laurence (eds), *Travel and Geography in the Roman World*, London and New York: Routledge, 2001 – a collection of essays mainly on the 'practical' side of the topic.

K. Brodersen, *Terra Cognita*, Hildesheim and New York: George Olms Verlag, 1995, 2nd edn. 2003 – a study of the evidence for, and implications of, linear modes of conceptualizing space versus 'maps'.

K. Brodersen, 'Mapping the ancient world', *Ad familiares: Journal of the Friends of Classics* 17 (1999), 2–4 – on the newly discovered 'map' in a papyrus of the first century BC.

E. H. Bunbury, *A History of Ancient Geography* (2 vols), London: Murray, 1879 – a dated but still useful survey of ancient theoretical geography.

O. A. W. Dilke, *Greek and Roman Maps*, London: Thames and Hudson, 1985 – a traditional survey of maps, predating the discussion of 'map consciousness'.

J. B. Harley and D. Woodward (eds.), *The History of Cartography I: Cartography in Prehistoric, Ancient, and Medieval Europe and the Mediterranean*, Chicago and London: University of Chicago Press, 1987 – a monumental survey of ancient mapping and geography.

F. Işik, H. Işkan and N. Çevik, *Miliarium Lyciae* (*Lykia*, 4 (1998/9)), Ankara: Anadolu akdeniz kültürleri, 2001 – publication of the 'stadiasmus provinciae Lyciae'.

P. Janni, *La mappa e il periplo*, Rome: Bretschneider, 1984 – on the *periplus* as a mode of conceptualising space.

C. Nicolet, *Space, Geography, and Politics in the Early Roman Empire*, Ann Arbor: University of Michigan Press, 1991 – an influential study on the uses of geography in Rome.

J. S. Romm, *The Edges of the Earth in Ancient Thought: Geography, Exploration, and Fiction*, Princeton: Princeton University Press, 1992.

R. R. R. Smith, '"Simulacra gentium": the "ethne" from the Sebasteion at Aphrodisias', *Journal of Roman Studies* 78 (1998), 50–77 and pl. 1–9.

R. J. A. Talbert (ed.), *Barrington Atlas of the Greek and Roman World* (atlas and 2-volume map-by-map directory), Princeton: Princeton University Press, 2000 – a great research tool for finding out the 'real' location of places and people.

R. J. A. Talbert and K. Brodersen (eds), *Space in the Roman World: Its Perception and Presentation*, Münster and New York: LIT, 2004 – a collection of essays on theoretical and practical geography, and on the *Tabula Peutingeriana* (by R. J. A. Talbert); with a survey of the new edition of Ptolemy's geography.

J. O. Thomson, *History of Ancient Geography*, Cambridge: Cambridge University Press, 1948 – a survey of theoretical geography.

52. *Mythology*

Eva Parisinou

A brief history of terms

Any modern discussion on mythology should begin by highlighting its association with oral tradition. The structure of the Greek compound word *mythologia* is but a small reminder of this. Its constituent parts, *mythos* and *logos*, bear direct reference to the deliberate act of oral dissemination. *Logos*, an etymological derivative of the verb *legō*, meaning to narrate, to tell, to recite, sets the frame within which to understand the nature and the functions of a *mythos*. Both *mythos* and its Roman counterpart, the *fabula*, literally refer to a speech, a narration which presupposes the existence of a hearing and responding audience. Yet one must fully acknowledge the breadth and complexity of meanings that *mythoi* comprised in culturally and temporally distinct communities.

At its simplest, a myth is a traditional story which expresses human perceptions of, and reactions to, a variety of aspects of the world. *Mythologia*, therefore, as a collective noun, may be understood as a standard body of myths which were created, recited and/or understood within a community. The term is also used to denote the scholarly orientation, ancient or modern, which focuses on the study of myths of human societies and their mutual cultural borrowings.

Content, use and function of myths

What can a myth be about? Generally speaking, myths have encompassed a broad variety of themes that are of relevance to the life and everyday operations of a human community. These include: (1) cosmological concerns – ideas about the beginnings of the world, the structure and order of the universe; (2) religious and metaphysical beliefs regarding the nature and capacities of the divine, the place of humans in the creation, death and afterlife; (3) beliefs and practices about life-cycles, such as adolescence, preparation for marriage, family life and becoming a soldier or a citizen; (4) traditions about the foundation of cities, ethnic entities, states, institutions, but also cults and rituals – these may often relate to further myths of gods, heroes or groups of people who were involved in the process; and (5) stories about individuals who played an important role in the life of a community (positive or negative).

Most (if not all) of these themes tend to converge between cultures regardless of temporal and geographical barriers. Should this be taken to suggest the existence of sets of cross-cultural links underlying the organisation and basic needs of pre-industrial and pre-literate societies who relied upon mythology as a means for their survival? Careful consideration of the nature and role of these popular mythological themes in the life of human communities points to a positive answer. It seems that myth did not merely contribute substantially to the self-definition of a community on a cultural and social level but also justified and validated its institutions and hierarchical structures. Furthermore, it set the boundaries of human existence within the natural world and towards the supernatural. These roles were performed through myths' aetiological functions, which often account for the beginnings or the first cause of natural phenomena, rituals, states, institutions or customs.

But how did this transmission of shared values or culture actually work? It is true that the reception of myths by the members of a community cannot have been a formal process with respect to the manner, occasion, content and agent(s) or media of their transmission. This would rather be contingent on constantly changing parameters relating to the specific temporal, spatial and cultural context of the narrative, and the function that it is called to perform in response to human needs. As products of collective imagination and popular wisdom, myths are generally not associated with the specific name of a single or collective creator and do not have a fixed written content, as is the case with written stories. Myths are told and retold over the generations, following a flexible way of transmission whereby narratives may slightly alter or on occasions even transform, if circumstances so require. Yet the main plotlines tend to remain unchanged, despite the constant mutation and manipulation of their parts. This inseparable bond between a myth and the social reality or realities in which the former is created, or simply used, articulate the main reason for the timeless value and topicality of myths and their message to the people (moral, symbolic or other).

Ancient perceptions of myth

Perceptions of myth fluctuated substantially over the centuries of the classical past. They ranged from firm collective acceptance of mythical tradition through the reminiscence of a heroic past, to highly critical expressions of the effectiveness of mythology as a medium by which to understand and to explain the world.

Early Greek poetry, notably the works of Homer and Hesiod, are thronged with mythical narratives. Their strong religious orientation is reflected in themes about the nature of the pantheon, the creation of the world, and the life and deeds of heroised mortals and demi-gods. The earliest myths (for example, the Trojan expedition, the Calydonian Hunt or the Argonauts) were performed orally by poets before an audience on particular social or religious occasions. In spite of the fluidity and often lack of accuracy of these mythical narratives, it would be unfair to say that their content was substantially questioned by the early Greek-speaking, pre-literate communities. This was partly because of people's trust in the authority of the poet, whose inspiration was believed to be a divine gift. In this way, a vivid memory was preserved of a distant, shared past among the community.

The introduction and gradual spread of alphabetic writing in the eighth century BC opened the way for more sophisticated, fixed systems of communication. This marked the beginning of a definitive, yet gradual, transformation in the patterns of transmission of mythical tradition. Popular imagination in seventh-century BC Greece continued to draw inspiration from myths not only through oral dissemination, but also through artworks. Mythical narratives are securely identified (often accompanied by explanatory inscriptions) in the figurative arts of the period.

At about the same time, new literary genres began to appear alongside poetry, initiating fresh approaches and perceptions of the world. Among the earliest such manifestations are the prose works of natural philosophers from Ionia (east Aegean), which exhibit significant new intellectual trends: they attempt reinterpretations of the beginnings of the universe, leaving aside mythological explanation. For example, Thales of Miletus, Anaximander and Anaximenes for the first time shifted the focus of cosmological thought from oral mythological traditions (such as the *Theogony* of Hesiod) to natural elements, namely water, the infinite element and air (see chapter 48). Their lead was soon followed by later generations of natural philosophers (such as Xenophanes, Parmenides, Zeno of Elea and Heraclitus), who in turn prepared the ground for the birth of moral philosophy and science in mainland Greece. A new age of rationalism elevating the value of reason (*logos*) was progressively gaining ground at the expense of *mythos* in its old-fashioned form as a kind of proto-history.

From the late fifth century BC onwards, an intellectual revolution with Athens at its centre rose decidedly against anything that represented mythical tradition. This movement is best represented by the scientific and philosophical literature of the times (e.g. Hippocrates, Plato,

Aristotle) as well as by forensic speeches and large-scale historical accounts produced by both local and foreign advocates of the new age. Although interest in mythology never faded out completely, its credibility was fundamentally challenged because of its inherent incompatibility with truth and reality. In this context of a Greek 'enlightenment', the latter concepts were firmly grounded in rational thinking and were expressed by demonstrative argument, which could prove or disprove previously unshakeable 'truths', convictions and hierarchies. *Logos* refers to the power of the human mind to reorganise and reinterpret the real world or facts (*erga*) using a variety of rational avenues. Advocates of this movement included the sophist Protagoras of Abdera, who vehemently denied the existence of absolute or universal truths and claimed that everything is subject to multiple, equally valid interpretations or *logoi* (quoted by Diogenes Laertius 9.51). This notion of *logos* is no longer suited to mythological narrative, the veracity of which cannot be tested.

Thucydides, the first Greek 'scientific' historian, in the fifth century BC was a firm supporter of the new rationalism. He condemns *mythoi* as products of the remote past, the authorities of which cannot be checked, and speaks with contempt about poetic exaggeration. Instead, he praises the virtues of conciseness and accuracy as a means to reach the safest conclusions in historical accounts (1.21). In this way he distinguishes his work from that of his predecessors, and most notably Herodotos, who essentially based his historical 'inquiry' (as he named his history) on oral tradition. It must be admitted, however, that Thucydides was ultimately unable to keep his history entirely clear of oral material, as he often depends on the latter in the absence of other evidence.

Despite these critical and derogatory attitudes to myths, there were prose authors who saw scope in preserving them. Hecataeus of Miletus (c. 550–480 BC), for example, first 'rationalised' myths by trying to extract elements of reality from them (see chapter 49). This trend was to become popular in antiquity, as was also that of 'allegorisation', whereby myths were considered not as literal stories but as tokens of allegorical truths. The earliest advocate of the allegorical use of myths was Theagenes of Rhegion in the late sixth century BC. The contribution of these ancient initiatives was enormous, even if they were but by-products of the intellectual interests of their times. Further to rescuing large parts of the Greek mythical tradition, a significant precedent was set which was to be followed by later scholarship. Examples include the extensive mythographic collections of the Hellenistic and early imperial period (c. 250 BC–AD 150), such as the work of Apollodorus (1st c. AD) known as *The Library* (and its abridgement *The Epitome*), and theme-specific collections, like the love stories collected by the first-century BC poet and grammarian Parthenius. The function of myths as key to understanding ancient literature and particularly poetry was recognised by commentators of late antiquity; their work is known as scholia (commentaries) on the poems of Homer, Pindar, the tragedians and others.

The Greek mythological heritage survived to exercise substantial influence on later mythologies during Roman antiquity – alongside strong native traditions, but also other external influences from the north, notably Gaul and Germania. The Greeks had a strong presence in Italy originally as traders and, from the ninth century BC onwards, as settlers of the south coasts of the peninsula and of Sicily. Perhaps the most striking instance of borrowing from Greek mythology is the array of gods who assumed Latin names in accordance with native traditions. On the other hand, native myths shaped early perceptions of major events in early Roman history, such as the foundation of Rome in 753 BC. This appears in fragmentary narratives of the third-century BC Roman historian Quintus Fabius Pictor, and later in the work of Livy (59 BC-AD 17). Both wrote about the shadowy periods of the foundation of Rome, with its legendary gods and heroes, and the beginnings of institutions that were to last in the city for many centuries. The popularity of this theme is further reflected in works of authors writing in Greek, including Dionysius of Halicarnassus' *Roman Antiquities*, and Plutarch's extensive biographies, the *Parallel Lives of Greeks and Romans* (AD 46–after 120; lives of Romulus and Numa, as well as Publius Valerius Publicola and Coriolanus). Related mythological content is found in poetic texts, notably Virgil's (70–19 BC) epic the *Aeneid*, which focused on the return of Aeneas from Troy, his arrival in Italy and union with the Italic populations. Ovid (43 BC–AD 17), too, employed mythological material in his works *Metamorphoses* and *Fasti*; in the latter he told of the mythological origins of sacred rites and festivals in the Roman year.

Such traditions were cultivated and disseminated throughout Roman antiquity and they undoubtedly formed part of imperial propaganda. Christianity was apparently unable completely to eliminate popular support and trust in mythological tradition, despite intense polemic against paganism and all that it represented. Hostile attitudes to myths are expressly attested in the works of Eusebius, Hippolytus, Lactantius, Arnobius and others, who, in their attempt to discredit particular myths, unintentionally contributed to the preservation of a great part of mythological material (see chapter 53).

Modern approaches in the study of mythology

Extensive theoretical approaches to myths in nineteenth-century Europe evolved around their origins and meaning in human society. Although interest in these topics was not really a novelty considering, for example, the rationalising approach to myth of Euhemerus (early third century BC), it opened the way to substantial scholarly debate. Some of the earliest views were expressed by the German philologist Max Müller and by scholars of the British anthropological school, such as Sir E. B. Tylor and, towards the turn of the century, Sir J. G. Frazer; these scholars highlighted the role of natural forces in the creation of mythological traditions. Müller considered mythical figures as symbolic representations of nature, and especially the sun. Tylor, on the other hand, highlighted the dependence of myths upon dreams in an attempt to explain the latter. He supported the idea of animism (ie that all natural elements had a soul) in the creation of the first myths. Expanding on this, Frazer linked the origins of myth-making with the natural cycles of birth, growth, decay and death, drawing his inspiration from an ancient Italic ritual conducted at Nemi, near Rome. Criticism of the views of the British anthropological school came from scholars such as Ludwig Deubner and Martin Nilsson, who argued against the previously supported coherence in the content of the various mythological narratives; instead, they saw myth as a medium through which to explain religious ritual.

Further links between ritual and myth were identified by the ritualist school, a chief representative of which was Jane Ellen Harrison. This school posited that myths were born from ritual acts and functioned as the 'script' or explanation of the latter. Whilst this theory is no longer accepted today, modern research still acknowledges a relationship between myths and religious rites in specific cultural contexts. An example has been offered by the French philologist Georges Dumézil within an Indo-European frame; he argued that three basic social functions (sovereignty, force and fertility) underlie certain Greek rituals and mythical narratives. Even so, one cannot postulate whether it is myth or ritual that has priority.

Within the field of British anthropological research of the early twentieth century, and contrary to the earlier trends expressed by Tylor and his followers, the Polish-born Bronislaw Malinowski became the chief representative of the functionalist trend in the study of mythology. He emphasised the psychological conditions that lead to the creation of myths, with the latter considered as culturally relevant explanations of what failed to be understood logically in a prescientific society. Related views, but significantly expanded and theoretically informed, were put forward by Sigmund Freud and his followers (known as the school of psychoanalysts), who saw myths as reflections of the workings of the human soul (*psychē*). They, too, found a connection between dreams, myths and folktales, holding that, since dreams were triggered by wishes, myths reflected the collective wishes of a society. In this context, scholars like Karl Abraham placed myths in the period of the childhood of humankind, while Swiss psychoanalyst Carl Jung noted certain sets of archaic patterns or archetypes which the human mind tends to reproduce in myths.

Further theoretical approaches depended on methods previously developed by linguists, such as structuralism, in order to unravel the ways myth functioned as a commonly understood sign system in society. The French anthropologist Claude Lévi-Strauss is the best-known advocate of this trend. He explained myth as a composition made up of interdependent units which assume different meanings in combination with each other in different societies. Building on the work of earlier scholars in the field, notably that of the Russian scholar V. J. Propp, Lévi-Strauss emphasised the role of myth in responding to fundamental questions or stages of human life, which often take the form of binary oppositions, such as wild-tame or life-death. Originally focusing on the myths of the Americas, Lévi-Strauss's theory was applied to the mythical traditions of Oceania, India, Australia, Africa and ancient Greece. Followers of Lévi-Strauss, but also of semioticians like Roland Barthes, include Jean-Pierre Vernant and Marcel Detienne, who turned their attention to culture-specific social structures (with a particular interest in ancient Greece) responsible for the nature of myths in different areas. The semiotic method considered myths as a metalinguistic secondary sign system built on the primary sign system of the language.

Alongside the French school, recent, poststructuralist trends in the study of mythology have fully recognised the significance of the historical and social conditions within which myths were formed and functioned in different localities and periods. Furthermore, the comparative aspect of a wealth of the world's mythological tradition has been recognised and extensively explored, highlighting useful links between cultures in their historical context. The chief representatives of these trends include Jan Bremmer, H. S. Versnel, Fritz Graf, Peter Wiseman and Charles Segal. Specific areas of interest include the relationship between myth and religion, particularly with regard to the aetiological (i.e. explanatory) function of myths (Walter Burkert), the value of their narratological analysis (Claude Calame) for the understanding of specific cultural and ethnological systems, and the construction and influence of visual narratives in art (Thomas Carpenter, H. A. Shapiro and Christiane Sourvinou-Inwood).

Further reading

Introductory

L. Bruit Zaidman and P. Schmitt Pantel, *Religion in the Ancient Greek City* (trans. P. Cartledge), Cambridge: Cambridge University Press, 1992, esp. pt. III.12 (1st edn Paris, 1989) – good introductory discussion.

F. Graf, *Greek Mythology: An Introduction* (trans. T. Marier), Baltimore: Johns Hopkins University Press, 1993 – the best introduction to issues of terminology, review of scholarship and the place of myth in Greek literature and poetry.

M. P. O. Morford and R. J. Lenardon, *Classical Mythology* (6th and 7th edns), Oxford: Oxford University Press, 1999, 2002 – excellent, updated introduction including relevant source material and a related study-guide containing useful further links: *Classical Mythology*, www.oup-usa.org/sc/0195143388.

More advanced

D. Braund and C. Gill (eds), *Myth, History and Culture in Republican Rome: Studies in Honour of T. P. Wiseman*, Exeter: University of Exeter Press, 2003 – good, updated discussions and bibliography on Roman myths and their relationship with early historical narratives.

J. N. Bremmer (ed.), *Interpretations of Greek Mythology*, London, Sydney and Totowa NJ: Barnes and Noble Books, 1987 – covers matters of definition, modern theories and interpretative approaches of myths.

J. N. Bremmer and N. M. Horsfall, *Roman Myth and Mythology* (*BICS Supplement* 52), London: Institute of Classical Studies, 1987 – analytical and comparative approaches of Roman myths with other traditions.

T. H. Carpenter, *Art and Myth in Ancient Greece*, London: Thames and Hudson, 1991 – good discussions on mythological representations in art, excellent illustrations.

L. Edmunds (ed.), *Approaches to Greek Myth*, Baltimore: Johns Hopkins University Press, 1990 – analysis of myths and interpretative theories, including discussion on folklore.

R. L. Gordon (ed.), *Myth, Religion and Society: Structuralist Essays by M. Detienne, L. Gernet, J.-P. Vernant and P. Vidal-Naquet*,

Cambridge and Paris: Cambridge University Press, 1981 – interpretative essays on ancient myths in their social context by leading authorities in the field.

G. S. Kirk, *The Nature of Greek Myths*, London: Penguin, 1990 – overview of modern theories and major problems with them.

H. A. Shapiro, *Myth into Art: Poet and Painter in Classical Greece*, London and New York: Routledge, 1994 – comparative approach of mythological narratives in poetry and art; role of pottery as medium for dissemination of mythical tradition.

J.-P. Vernant, *Myth and Society in Ancient Greece*, London, Brighton and Atlantic Highlands NJ: Harvester Press, 1980 (French original, 1974, trans. J. Lloyd) – essay on Greek myths in their social context.

T. P. Wiseman, *Historiography and Imagination: Eight Essays on Roman Culture* (*Exeter Studies in History* 33), Exeter: University of Exeter Press, 1994 (repr. 1999) – on Roman self-perception and the contribution of mythological narratives to early Roman history.

53. Christian Literature

Clifford Ando

Christian literature has not traditionally figured in curricula and reading lists in classical studies. That should surprise: Christianity is undoubtedly the most influential legacy to Europe of ancient Greece and Rome, and – bracketing the problem of their authors' religious affiliation – a very significant majority of extant Greek and Latin texts were written by authors who would have identified themselves as Christian. The lack of interest of classicists in Christian texts therefore requires explanation. It arises from a convergence of interests, both ancient and modern, religious and racial. On the one hand, Christian historians and theologians have long sought to describe Christianity itself as somehow immaculately conceived, the result of a providential disruption in human history and certainly not the product of any particular social and intellectual context. Classicists for their part, whether Reformation, Enlightenment, Romantic or modern, long desired to study a world uncorrupted by currents Eastern or Semitic. The few remarkable scholars who have ignored these boundaries – Eduard Norden and Richard Reitzenstein above all, and from different eras Arthur Darby Nock and David Daube – are the exceptions who prove the rule.

The complicity of classics in this segregation is doubly ironic, for scholars might well have studied, rather than merely respected, the Christian community's efforts to present itself as insulated from 'the classical world'. What is more, the increasing sophistication and depth of Christian literature's engagement with classical thought offers one useful method for periodising it. That periodisation, based on Christianity's interactions with what it saw as the outside world, harmonises in significant ways with one we might construct with reference to developments within the Christian community. For as the Christian population grew, diversified and spread, groups and individuals within it came to use literature alongside other disciplinary mechanisms to police the internal orderings of their communities.

Christianity's first literary products have a special claim to separation from the classical, which is to say, the pagan, by virtue of being sacred. I refer, of course, to the texts that came to be included in the Bible: the Gospels, Acts, the letters of Paul, and the apocalyptic and eschatological books with which it closes. Alongside these – which reached something like their present form between the late first and late second centuries AD – must be set that vast range of texts, the so-called Apocrypha, which, though kindred in origin, date and genre, came to be excluded from the orthodox canon.

Already diverse in style and generic affiliation, these products of Christian literature's long first century range from texts that bear witness to the life of a charismatic leader, whose closest classical kin is Euripides' *Bacchae*, to a sort of prose-poetry best exemplified now in the Sibylline Oracles. Most of these texts are concerned with the formation of a Christian community, or with one such among many, and thus with circumscribing a (form of) Christian identity. In general, the earlier texts display the community's profound investment in the moment of its foundation; they gaze insistently towards Christianity's roots in the intensely Jewish world of first-century Palestine, with the canonical books in particular seeking to distinguish Christianity from it.

The later texts of the New Testament and its Apocrypha come rapidly to reflect and regard its embeddedness in the network of Greek cities that comprised the Eastern Mediterranean under Roman rule. As a group, those later texts – together with the works of the so-called Apostolic Fathers – seek through letters and narratives of direct contact to connect the outposts of a population that had spread rapidly along the routes of commerce and migration in a world empire. Typical of these is the story of Paul and Thecla – an appendix to Acts that tells of Paul's journey to Iconium and his encounter there with Thecla, a young woman who converts and is later ordained by Paul. At one level, the story is the product of a desire on the part of one among many isolated churches to legitimate and fortify itself by declaring a direct connection to the apostolic mission. On another, its obsession with Thecla's efforts to preserve her chastity against the advances of assorted pagan men (and animals!) becomes a metaphor for the Christian community itself, a small, self-conscious and conscientiously continent body of people, forever aware of the allure and physical power of the pagan world in which they lived. The works of this period thus provide a remarkable portrait of one constituency's developing self-perception, in the enormously complicated fabric of legal, religious, ethnic and political cultures of one corner of the Mediterranean world – a portrait to be read alongside that provided by the contemporaneous essays and orations of Plutarch, Lucian, Dio Chrysostom and Aelius Aristides. The latter regarded the rulership of cities as their birthright; the former saw the so-called Greek city as its context.

By the middle of the second century, Christianity had fairly thoroughly penetrated the ranks of the educated Graeco-Roman elite. At the same time, the sheer number of Christians had grown, both at a local level and across the empire. This expansion and diversification brought with it a need to draw and protect boundaries of many kinds, both between Christians and others and within the Christian population itself. The tools deployed for this work were varied and included ritual and dress, along with literature. Many of the most characteric forms of those literatures have close analogues in contemporaneous pagan culture – though not infrequently it is the Christian exemplar of any given genre that has been best preserved. Apologetic literature, for example, came into its own in this period, though the name is somewhat misleading, not least by being too general. Works subsumed in that category are occasionally defensive, to be sure, but the majority of second- and early third-century apologies are addressed to Roman governors or emperors and take the form of petitions (e.g. Justin's first *Apology*) or epistles (e.g. Tertullian's *To Scapulus*) and occasionally of speeches (e.g. Athenagoras' *Plea*). (Exceptions include those open letters addressed 'to the non-Christians': Tatian's *Oration to the Greeks*, Tertullian's *To the Nations*, Clement's *Protrepticus*, and numerous much later works, including several attributed to Justin.) They thus share structural and rhetorical features with both legal petitions and literary epistles, but the overwhelming majority of non-Christian petitions are preserved on stone and hence rarely complete; of literary epistles and speeches offering advice to emperors, on the other hand, much survives, including such varied works as Arrian's *Periplus*, Dio's *Kingship* orations, and a number of speeches in the corpus of Aelius Aristides.

Apologies were formally addressed to non-Christians and so constructed the Christian community as a unity. But the fault-lines that had divided Christianity already at its infancy – and which are abundantly visible in Acts – had since multiplied, and by the late second century the project of defining orthodoxy had begun in earnest. For many years, at the level of literature this project proceeded not through positive formulations of the basic tenets of the faith, but negatively, through reactionary treatises (whose titles always begin 'Against', as, for example, Tertullian's *Against Marcion*) and catalogues of heresies (of which that by Irenaeus of Lyon is the first to survive). In this context we must acknowledge that the original works of such 'heretics' as Valentinus, Montanus and Marcion, to name but three, were rigorously censored already in antiquity and so are known today only through the interrelated processes of quotation and refutation by the orthodox. Nevertheless, at a time when Greek philosophers (see chapter 48) were producing an enormous amount of doxographic literature – Arius Didymus's *Summary of Stoic Ethics*, Alcinous's *Handbook of Platonism*, Apuleius's *On Plato* or, from a later date, Porphyry's *Introduction* – Christian thinkers devoted much of their energies to an essentially destructive polemics. Clement's fascinating *Paedagogus* might seem an exception to this rule, but it treats problems of ethics and not those of doctrine per se.

Within that group of communities that would emerge victorious in these debates – the self-declared orthodox – the late second and early third centuries likewise witnessed dramatically heightened efforts of a disciplinary nature, through treatises seeking to establish and enforce a normative order within the Christian community. Like the sumptuary legislation and moralising literature of earlier eras, these tend to invoke standards against any who, by virtue of being seen or heard, would violate traditional class- and sex-based orderings of society. Sometimes, as with certain of Cyprian's essays *To Quirinus*, the aim was quite literally to silence: he might allow in one essay that 'No one is without error or sin'; he could nevertheless insist in another that 'women' – and women alone – 'should be silent in church'. Such works can be profitably juxtaposed not only with heresiological tracts (i.e. writings condemning heresies), but also with texts on martyrdom, such as those by Cyprian and Commodian, in reflecting ongoing struggles for authority within towns, churches and the church.

Finally, though Christians had been persecuted as early as the reign of Nero, only in the latter half of the second century did they begin to record the circumstances of the deaths of martyrs. Scholars have perhaps emphasised too little the heterogeneity of the martyr acts as a corpus. But we may nevertheless invoke them as exemplifying three related developments in Christian literature and the historical self-consciousness of the Christian community more generally. First, while the martyr acts de facto advanced the historical vision of Christian literature beyond rewritings of its foundational narrative, they did so largely by placing the martyrs within what we might loosely call a prophetic metanarrative, in which the martyr quite literally 'bears witness' to some foundational truth that itself hearkens back to the Christ story. Second, the martyr acts are the precursor of later ecclesiastical historiography in promoting a vision of Christian history as one of latent and periodically violent conflict between the Christian and the powers and principalities of this world. Third, by closely mimicking the form and protocols of actual court proceedings, the martyr acts paradoxically invoke the rationality and authority of the Roman government as guarantor of their truth-content.

There is much of interest in Christian literature that a chronological accounting of its achievements – its embracing of new genres and engagement with classical thought – will not reveal. Perhaps foremost is the remarkable opportunity afforded us to study the development of truly regional bodies of work – an opportunity not often available to classicists and little exploited even when it is, as with, say, Spanish Latin of the first century. In the West, Africa contributes quite literally millions upon millions of words between the mid-second and mid-fifth centuries, by authors as diverse as Tertullian, Cyprian, Arnobius, Lactantius, Optatus, Augustine, Quodvultdeus and Possidius – to whom we might add immigrants such as Orosius. At the other end of the Mediterranean, one might study the relatives and students of Procopius of Gaza. Himself the author of *ekphraseis* (rhetorical descriptions of works of art or nature), letters, philosophical polemics and biblical exegesis (interpretation), his brother Zacharias became bishop of Mytilene and wrote an ecclesiastical history, biographies, and treatises against contemporary Aristotelians, while his student Choricius wrote a panegyric for his teacher, *ekphraseis* of churches, and a defence of mime. As a consequence, we know – we *could* know – Gaza and its educated class between 470 and 550 better than we know the literary culture of any classical city other than Rome or Athens. Of course, that is true so long as we retain that usage of 'classical' that excludes the Christian; otherwise, we should have to set Gaza alongside Antioch, Constantinople and Alexandria, to name only three, as cities generating each on its own several thousand pages of (classical) texts.

At the same time, excessive attention to what is classical in Christian literature risks occluding its distinctive contributions to the culture of the high and late imperial Mediteranean. Foremost among those contributions must be the development of the sermon. Now it is of course true that public speaking had always been a dominant form of literary archievement, but what had often been celebrated in rhetorical texts of the second century, say, was precisely the gap that separated the educated speaker and his peers from the mass of the population that formed their audiences. In that regard, the sermons of Christian homilists – most famously Augustine in Latin and John Chrysostom in Greek – represent nothing less than a revolution in the politics of literary production, a democratisation theorised, in fact, by Augustine himself, in the fourth book of his work *On Christian Doctrine*. For where the economy of praise in the second and third centuries privileged a form of speech distinct from the everyday, Christian preachers were under a corresponding compulsion to make themselves understood and thus to cultivate what Augustine called *sermo humilis*, 'a humble form of speech'.

Likewise distinctive and important are the developments in philology advanced by Christian scholars. For there can be little doubt, whatever the achievements of Alexandrian, Roman and Jewish textual criticism and literary exegesis – and they were considerable – that these disciplines came together with a deeper intensity and new horizons in Christian scholarship of the third century and beyond. For what Christians ultimately could not avoid was the linguistic and cultural heterogeneity at the heart of their sacred texts. So while Christian commentators on the Old Testament occasionally knew and disputed Jewish readings of those books, or learned parts of their craft from pagan grammarians and writers on Homer and Virgil, for example, they could never naturalise their position in relation to Hebrew Scripture in particular or, in the case of Western readers, to the Greek New Testament, either. As a result, a very significant portion of Christians' intellectual energies found its outlet in the practice and theory of transmitting, translating and reading texts – from Marcion to Origen to Tyconius to Augustine and Jerome. The sheer volume of their writings, set beside the commentaries and exegeses of Donatus, Servius and Lactantius Placidus in the West, and the allegories of Neoplatonists in the East, makes it all the more lamentable that so little effort has been devoted to studying the relationship between classical and Christian hermeneutics in late antiquity.

One genre of text thoroughly classical in origin but almost uniformly Christian in surviving examples is the record of the proceedings of a deliberative body. As with martyr acts, so with the proceedings of councils, Christians largely adopted the protocols and mechanics for conducting and recording meetings developed by the organs of Roman government. But to say that is to pretend that in identifying the origins of an idea we have exhausted our curiosity. For the proceedings of councils of the church, both ecumenical and local, constitute the best surviving evidence for the actual forms and functioning of speech and argument in the ancient world. Speakers are introduced; their words are recorded – purportedly verbatim!; and they are dismissed; texts are read aloud, their contents and meaning disputed; cajoling, wheedling, invective; the languages of law and religion, spite and sentiment, passion and personality, are all abundantly on display. For those left unmoved by the pretensions of bucolic poetry or the clash of egos in epic, the proceedings of church councils may well be the antidote. In them, lives are shattered; communities are torn asunder. These are heart-breaking texts.

Finally, Christians in the ancient world produced any number of ultimately unclassifiable masterpieces, of the sort one fears to demean through pallid summary or even praise. I mention two. Augustine's *Confessions*, written in the final years of the fourth century, tells the story of how he came to be a Christian in the world, and likewise describes his understanding of the world in which he found himself. That the first tale unfolds in part as an intellectual journey, while the second is mediated by Scripture, are themselves facts whose explanation Augustine himself seeks to discover. But he also seeks to understand the place of mother, son, lover and friend in the confessional relationship and world at large, and in so doing offers by far the truest evocations of love and loss to survive from the ancient world. Boethius' *Consolation of Philosophy* is a very different but no less moving text. Writing in prison shortly before his execution, Boethius marshalled the resources of classical culture with unnerving control and tragic discipline, to achieve that mastery of emotions and the self that Socrates a thousand years before had displayed almost with condescension. These two works are the highest achievement, as the latter is the end, of classical literature.

Further reading

Texts

A great deal of Christian literature is available in English, whether electronically or in print. On the web, see the Christian Classical Ethereal Library, the École Initiative, and the Internet Ancient History Sourcebook. In print, readers should turn first to one set, two series and a publisher: the set is the thirty-eight volumes of the Ante-Nicene, Nicene and post-Nicene Fathers, a nineteenth-century project oft-reprinted; the two series are 'The Fathers of the Church' and 'Ancient Christian Writers'; and the publisher is the Society for the Promotion of Christian Knowledge. Greek and Latin texts of these authors can be somewhat harder to locate: in keeping with the traditional boundaries of classics outlined above, no Christian text has merited publication as an 'Oxford Classical Text', and few have appeared in the Loeb Classical Library. Instead, students must generally turn to one of six series published outside the Anglophone world: Die griechischen christlichen Schriftsteller der ersten Jahrhunderte, Patristische Texte und Studien, the Corpus Scriptorum Ecclesiasticorum Latinorum, the Corpus Christianorum, Sources Chrétiennes, and the Collection des Universités de France. New Testament Apocrypha present a particular challenge: translations with bibliographic information regarding texts may be found in J. K. Elliott, *The Apocryphal New Testament*, Oxford: Clarendon Press, 1993.

Secondary

V. Burrus, *'Begotten, not Made': Conceiving Manhood in Late Antiquity*, Stanford: Stanford University Press, 2000.

G. E. Caspary, *Politics and Exegesis: Origen and the Two Swords*, Berkeley: University of California Press, 1979.

H. Chadwick, *Early Christian Thought and the Classical Tradition: Studies in Justin, Clement and Origen*, Oxford: Clarendon Press, 1966.

E. R. Dodds, *Pagan and Christian in an Age of Anxiety*, Cambridge: Cambridge University Press, 1965.

B. D. Ehrman, *The Orthodox Corruption of Scripture*, New York: Oxford University Press, 1993.

S. G. MacCormack, *The Shadows of Poetry: Vergil in the Mind of Augustine*, Berkeley: University of California Press, 1998.

B. L. Mack, *A Myth of Innocence: Mark and Christian Origins*, Philadelphia: Fortress Press, 1991.

H. G. Snyder, *Teachers and Texts in the Ancient World: Philosophers, Jews and Christians*, New York: Routledge, 2000.

D. E. Trout, *Paulinus of Nola: Life, Letters and Poems*, Berkeley: University of California Press, 1999.

J. Wyrick, *The Ascension of Authorship*, Harvard: Harvard University Press, 2004.

54. *Science and Mathematics*

T. E. Rihll

Ancient science is a label for a wide variety of intellectual pursuits of the Greeks and Romans from the sixth century BC to the sixth century AD. Most of the work was done in Greek by Greeks, though a significant number of them lived under Roman rule, and a few of them were very well connected in the highest echelons of Roman society.

The Greeks and Romans did not have a clear definition of science (ours is not undisputed, but is clearer than theirs) and therefore there is some disagreement among modern scholars as to what ancient work counts as science and what does not. What is indisputable is that ancient individuals of the highest scientific calibre also worked in areas which we would call unscientific, such as astrology. But this is also true of Isaac Newton, and does not advance the argument very far.

If we took our major scientific categories to be, in alphabetical order, astronomy, biology, chemistry, (physical) geography, mathematics and physics, then one could easily find significant ancient work in all these areas but one, namely chemistry. To give just one example from each field, Ptolemy's astronomy was what Nicolaus Copernicus and Johann Kepler had to overcome; Aristotle is known, with good reason, as the father of biology; Eratosthenes calculated the circumference of the earth to within a few per cent of the figure we think correct today; Euclid is still the basis of our geometry (including non-Euclidean geometry, which differs only in rejecting Euclid's fifth postulate, but that has large consequences); and Aristotle's physics was what Galileo Galilei had to argue against. But neither Aristotle's nor any other ancient's thoughts on chemical combination were a serious impediment for Antoine Lavoisier.

Ancient science is difficult to characterise because even that portion of it that survives is so diverse. By modern standards the vast majority of it is very accessible. That is to say, very few technical terms or units of measurement are used, texts are not peppered with algebra or other specialised notations and short-hands, and what few experiments and tests the reader is advised to do can usually be performed with household utensils and the unassisted human senses (eye, ear, nose, finger, tongue). It can also be brilliant; *simply* brilliant. Indeed, often, the more simple it is, the more brilliant it is; its brilliance *lies* in its simplicity.

The origins of science are attributed to the Presocratics. What survives of their work is very fragmentary, often poetical, and open to numerous interpretations (see chapter 48). What is significant about it in the context of the development of science, and what is shared by these authors, is that their works appear to be trying to explain natural phenomena in natural terms. That is to say, they try to explain things in the world around us, and about us ourselves, without reference to gods or other supernatural sources. This leads in due course to an explanation for lightning, for example, being caused by something other than Zeus throwing bolts from above, or illness by something other than Apollo firing arrows at people. The 'other' in question may have been completely wrong, but it was god-free. To think thus may seem, in this secular age, like a small step, but in the context of human history, it was a giant leap. As far as we know, no earlier people ever suggested that it was not the gods that were responsible for light, or earthquakes, or sickness, or humankind, or whatever. The Presocratics were the first to suggest that these things were a pure consequence of the natural behaviour of natural phenomena. And believing that they were such, the Presocratics and their successors set out to try to find out, or work out, what *is* the natural behaviour of natural phenomena, and what are the natural causes of these perceptible phenomena and behaviours. This is not to say that they were by definition atheists; most seem to have believed in the divine in some guise or another (as there are today cosmologists or biologists who do not believe, say, in the Creation as told in the Bible but who do believe in a modern notion of God). What the Presocratics did not believe in is anthropomorphic gods of the epic or tragic style interfering in the world and our lives.

This trend towards natural explanations started early – traditionally with the Milesian philosopher Thales (c. 624–548 BC) – but it needs to be noted that 'Presocratics' is a very misleading term, since the 'pre' does not mean prior in a temporal sense, which is the sense in which it is normally used in English. Most 'Presocratics' were actually contemporaries of Socrates. They belong to the fifth century BC, not a century or two earlier. They were active when Pericles was active, when the Peloponnesian War was being fought, when Euripides and Aristophanes were writing; most of them do *not* belong to the archaic period.

Progress was quite quick in some areas. For example, Aristophanes' *Clouds* famously lampoons mid- to late fifth-century thinking on the causes of rain, among other things, yet what we call the water cycle (in very simple form: water evaporates from the surface of the earth, in the air it cools and condenses into cloud, thence falls back to the surface as rain) had been fully worked out by Aristotle's time, in the mid-to-late fourth century, and his explanation of rainbows is essentially the same as ours today. He even describes a method to create a rainbow at home, so that one can easily check the veracity of some of what he says about them.

Progress was dramatic in the person of Aristotle, and in that of his friend, colleague and successor at the Lyceum, Theophrastus (see chapter 48). They were both outstanding naturalists, in the sense that they examined nature carefully and thought about it deeply. 'Physics' is the almost unavoidable but nevertheless misleading translation of the Greek word *phusis*, which means 'nature' in contrast with man-made things such as law and civil society and conventions. Aristotle's *Physics* therefore concerns the phenomena and behaviour of basically everything in nature. Here he discusses in general terms – with lots of examples – what things are made of, how they change, and why they change. Explanation is his aim, and the cosmos and everything in it is his subject. A significant portion of it, as the need or opportunity arises from the material, is concerned with trying to refute atomism, which had been developed by Leucippus and Democritus in the first half of the fifth century, and would be carried further by Epicurus in his Garden in the fourth century (see below and chapter 48).

Together Aristotle and Theophrastus worked on biology, Aristotle gathering vast amounts of data on animals (terrestrial and marine), Theophrastus on plants, and each tried to sort their data into coherent groups and patterns. They also worked on what we would call physical geography, tackling earthquakes, volcanoes, minerals, and probably fossils (relevant work, *On things turned to stone*, lost). Aristotle also worked a little (by his voluminous standards) on astronomy and mathematics, and Theophrastus on meteorology and much else. (Among other things they also both worked on politics, ethics and topics which are now called philosophy.) Both thought deeply about methodology, especially sense perception and its reliability, or lack thereof, and about how the mind or soul receives and processes the information from the senses. This is what we might classify today as psychology. They also thought – Aristotle especially – about valid and invalid reasoning, and Aristotle wrote brilliantly about the principles of logic. Since their work had a strong empirical element, and the sceptical movement was developing during the time that they lived and worked and taught, this was crucial from a theoretical *and* a pragmatic perspective.

It would be wrong, however, to assume that scientific progress marched onwards and upwards and that the next generation built on the achievements of the fledgling Lyceum. Aristotle may have founded a school which lasted until AD 529, but large-scale original work on many non-mathematical and astronomical topics – even inside the Lyceum – appears to have more or less stopped within a generation of Theophrastus' death. What we see instead is development at the margins or micro-level, and what might be called the development of dogmas. The Academy, the Lyceum, the Stoa and the Garden were all 'schools' in competition for hearts, minds, and paying customers. They all offered different explanations for the world and everything in it. They all offered training for the intellect. They all argued with one another on points of method and theory. Plato and Aristotle and Zeno (the founder of Stoicism) and Epicurus were all regarded as very clever men; but they did not agree, even on the fundamentals. It should not then be surprising that scepticism developed, and attracted intelligent followers. The sceptics' arguments generally undermined any claims to certain knowledge, and those then running the schools seem to have taken refuge in their founding fathers' respective teachings. There was, it seems, a loss of nerve and confidence. Instead of collecting new data about natural phenomena and analysing it, as Aristotle, Theophrastus and to some extent Plato had done, their intellectual heirs seem to have invested most of their energy in filling in the gaps and joining the dots left by their founders, or in preserving the inheritance, or cultivating 'soft' subjects like ethics which did not rely on sense perception, or abstract subjects like logic which likewise were independent of sense perception.

The following two centuries (the third to second BC) witnessed so many outstanding contributions to science that they are sometimes called 'the golden age' of Greek science. It is noticeable, however, that the really big contributions (see below for examples) are largely confined to mathematics and astronomy – the 'exact sciences' – and their applications, such as mechanics, optics, pneumatics and astrology. The exact sciences, with their very solid foundations in the axiomatic method and the production of proofs or demonstrations, escaped more or less (but not completely) unscathed from the attacks of the sceptics. It is also noticeable that most of the 'great' contributions are achieved by people who do not come from or live in Athens and therefore had, at most, only intermittent exposure to the Athenian schools with their current interests and priorities.

Now we find – to pick out just the highest lights of the highest achievers in this 'golden age' of ancient science – Eratosthenes (third century BC) who calculated the circumference of the earth, solved some other serious mathematical problems, invented a 'sieve' for finding prime numbers, invented the system of dating by Olympiads, was librarian at Alexandria, and edited literary texts. Here is Euclid (late third century to early second century) synthesising his predecessors' achievements into something far greater than the sum of its parts, namely his thirteen books on the basics (elements) of geometry, and working on optics, harmonics (see chapter 55), and other mathematically oriented subjects. Here is Aristarchus (c. 320–250 BC, sometimes called 'the ancient Copernicus') suggesting that the changing seasons are caused by the earth going round the sun and not vice versa, and calculating the size and distance of the sun and moon from earth. Here is Archimedes (287–212 BC) devising some stunning mathematics whilst discovering specific gravity ('eureka!') and keeping the Romans out of his home town, Syracuse, with wondrous wooden machines which moderns have conspicuously failed to reproduce adequately. So, too, to this age belongs the greatest ancient astronomer, Hipparchus (c. 190–120), who among other things discovered the precession of the equinoxes and worked out the length of the year to such accuracy that if *his* calendar (instead of Sosigenes') had been followed by Caesar then we would still be working with the Julian calendar and Pope Gregory would not have had to obliterate the 5th–14th October in AD 1582 (see chapter 64). Each of these men did far more than I have mentioned, and there were many others working wonders in mathematics, astronomy, and mathematically-based topics, and anatomy (see chapter 56).

During Roman imperial times scientific work was more patchy. Original contributions were relatively few and far between, and most were undertaken by Greeks in Greek. Whatever their cultural roots and native tongue, all were fully paid-up members of the Roman world, and some were part of the cultural elite, being personally acquainted with famous generals and emperors. So, for example, we find, in the first century BC, the great polymath and Stoic Posidonius, who, among other things, was the first to relate the movement of the tides to the movement of the moon, and who taught, among other people, Pompey and Cicero. In the same period (probably) Dioscorides produced a comprehensive *Herbal* which formed the basis for all Western herbals thereafter; and Lucretius went to extraordinary lengths to preserve and promote the teachings of the founder of the Garden, Epicurus. In the first century AD (probably) Diophantus produced what is often called the first algebra, and Seneca developed a special interest in physical geography. In the second century AD Galen wrote voluminously on medicine (10 per cent of *all* surviving works in Greek were written by Galen; see chapter 56), and Ptolemy wrote the *Almagest*, which was *the* astronomical text in Europe and the Middle East for the next 1,500 years. There are also a number of writers who are not considered scientists but whose works, often encyclopedic in scope, preserve what little we know of scientific thought and advances made sometime before they record them. For example, Pliny wrote very comprehensively on natural history and human exploitation of the natural environment; Frontinus grappled with the hydraulic engineering of the Roman water-supply; Plutarch wrote extensively on animals (he was an evangelical vegetarian) and a little on physics and astrophysics, and makes a statement which comes closer than anything else in all ancient literature to the notion of gravity; Vegetius wrote on agriculture, animal health and military science; and finally, to conclude this all too brief overview, in the late antique period, Simplicius, Philoponus and others less famous argued from a pagan and a Christian perspective respectively about the meaning and implications of Aristotle's corpus as they knew it.

Modern approaches and problems

The ease of accessing this material is as variable as the range is great. There is an extensive body of modern literature on the exact sciences in antiquity, and many of the relevant texts have been translated into English at least in part (usually the 'best' part from the history of science perspective). At the other end of the scale, there is almost nothing on ancient veterinary works, and the first book on ancient meteorology for almost a hundred years appeared in 2003. Some ancient scientists, including two of the best (Hipparchus and Eratosthenes), still await an editor to collect together all the fragments and testimonia, but there are quite understandable reasons for such omissions (see below). There are a number of sourcebooks on ancient science which offer the reader a taste of the range and scope of the surviving texts in English translation, and have bibliographies that are a good place to start further reading. Irby-Massie and Keyser, *Greek Science of the Hellenistic Era*, is the most recent at the time of writing. Its principal predecessor is Cohen and Drabkin, *Sourcebook in Greek Science*. Santillana, *Origins*, has fewer, but longer, extracts.

There are also collections of translations in specific areas: Heath for astronomy; Thomas for mathematics; Barker for music; Warmington for geography; there is also a great deal of relevance to many fields in Hankinson, *Cause*. The late commentators on Aristotle are the subject of a large project to translate their works into English.

The survival of all this material is very variable, as is to be expected with such a large and diverse topic. What is certain is that it is only a tiny part of what was originally produced. Equally certain is that it is not always (or even often?) the best part. For example, the only work of the great astronomer Hipparchus that survives (and then only in fragmentary state) is his critique of a popular (poetical) account of the constellations by Aratus and the work of Eudoxus on which that poem was based. For some texts we are indebted to Arab scholars, who appear to have tried to find and translate into one or another Arabic language whatever ancient scientific texts they could, possibly from as early as the third century AD and certainly by the eight century AD. In striking contrast to the Medieval West, Arab scholars were not interested in Greek literature, and were interested in Greek science and mathematics. In some cases the only surviving copy of a text or part of a text is in Arabic, e.g. Theophrastus' *Meteorology*. In others, Arabic texts constitute a vital element in the manuscript tradition for a work which also survives in whole or in part in Greek or in Latin translation, e.g. the medical works of Rufus of Ephesus. The importance of the Arabic tradition in the transmission of ancient scientific texts is well illustrated by the fact that the second most important of all ancient scientific treatises (after Euclid's *Elements*) is far better known by its Arabic title, the *Almagest*, than it is by its Greek name, the *Mathematical Syntaxis*.

What needs to be lodged in the mind is that hardly any of these old manuscripts (that is to say, the manuscripts as physical items) are actually ancient (see chapter 33). Only a tiny part of 1 per cent of 'surviving' texts, in the sense of sheets of papyrus, was produced before the tenth century AD. These are basically those surviving as scraps and tatters preserved in the dry sand of Egypt or toasted and buried in Philodemus' library at Herculaneum. All the rest of our 'old' manuscripts are copies of works, the originals for which were written a very long time before our copies were made. For example, there are more than fifty copies of Ptolemy's *Geography*, not one of which pre-dates the thirteenth century AD. In other words, the oldest existing copy of that work was written about one thousand two hundred years after Ptolemy wrote it. That temporal gap is as large as AD 800 is from today. The assumption – easily made and rarely recognised – that anachronisms did not creep in along the way of transmission is more optimistic than realistic. A lot changes in 1,200 years, not least language, concepts and modes of thought. This inevitably presents huge potential difficulties in the interpretation of such material.

In some areas of ancient science, especially mathematics, the subject itself can help to eliminate some of the errors that have crept in during the long centuries of transmission. Numbers are peculiarly liable to corruption in the process of copying. Whereas a scribe copying a literary text might use his understanding of the context to decide what a faint letter or word should be, there is often no such context to help interpret a faint number. Additionally, the development of a set of unique symbols for numbers (1, 2, 3 and so on) and operations (+, –, = and so on) was a very slow process extending way beyond antiquity ('=' first appeared in AD 1557, for example, invented by a Welshman called Robert Recorde). The majority of ancient mathematical texts use letters to stand for numbers, alpha for 1, beta for 2 and so on, according to a system recognised by those educated in it. But not everyone then, and certainly very few people in late antiquity and the Middle Ages, were so educated. As a result there is the potential for confusion over whether a set of symbols is a word or a number.

Some errors are obvious to one who understands what the original author was talking about, even if the person copying the text out in, say, the twelfth century AD did not (as they sometimes did not; in extreme cases the scribe seems to be copying a Greek text with no knowledge at all of the language). For example, one copyist of Heron's *Metrica* understood the content of the work so poorly that the modern editor was prompted to pepper his commentary with exclamation marks. At one point (1.17) the hapless scribe took the word 'lemma' as the continuation of the previous number instead of the first word of the next section. Anyone who knows something about mathematics would recognise 'lemma' as a word and would understand what it was doing at that precise place in the text. That is an extreme example, but even at the other extreme, when dealing with an ancient of outstanding mathematical ability, errors still arose in the original, and can sometimes be corrected, by moderns with the appropriate mathematical skills. These errors are more interesting in that they sometimes reveal that the author did not just round but massaged his computations, apparently in order to make the results seem more rigorous and tidy.

The same basic problem exists to this day, because very few people have both the linguistic skills necessary to tackle an ancient text in the original and the scientific knowledge to understand what the text is talking about. Some translations of ancient scientific texts into a modern language were done by classicists who had no difficulty rendering the Greek into English but understood the meaning of those words little better than the medieval scholars who preserved them.

One approach to this problem has been teamwork: a classicist to provide a 'raw' translation, and a scientist of the appropriate topic to explain what it might mean. Joint-authored translations, with or without texts, are often of this type. In the case of the polymath Theophrastus or the encyclopedist Pliny, the team needs to be very large. As on an archaeological dig a numismatist will be called in to explain the coin finds, so in dealing with texts like this the services of a specialist scientist might be needed to understand what the author is actually saying. Every topic has much more depth to those interested and experienced in it than it does to the casual passer-by. So D'Arcy Thompson, a late nineteenth-/early twentieth-century classicist with a strong background in biology, wanted to and was able to examine all (or almost all) references to fish and to birds in ancient sources, and work out a more precise and accurate translation for most relevant words, and say that some words seemed to be generic and not to identify specific species and so on. A similar exercise could be carried out with profit by someone interested in, for example, minerals, or drugs, or meteorological phenomena, to pick just three examples at random.

Unless and until such research is performed, we are necessarily dealing with a lot of uncertainties in the details of what ancient sources said about these things, and that can have implications far beyond the matter of getting the details right. For example, we cannot know if 'the Memphis stone' works as an anaesthetic until we know what the Memphis stone *is* in modern (geological) terms, and, once identified, it has been chemically analysed and empirically tested to see if it works in any way other than as a placebo. Until that happens we do not know whether or not the ancients had an effective local anaesthetic.

Further reading

Texts and sourcebooks

A. Barker, *Greek Musical Writings* (2 vols), Cambridge: Cambridge University Press, 1984.

M. R. Cohen and I. E. Drabkin (eds), *A Sourcebook in Greek Science*, Cambridge MA: Harvard University Press, 1948.

W. W. Fortenbaugh, R. W. Sharples, M. G. Sollenberger, P. M. Huby and D. Gutus, *Theophrastus of Eresus: Sources for his Life, Writings, Thought and Influence* (2 vols), Leiden: Brill, 1992.

T. L. Heath (ed.), *Greek Astronomy*, New York: AMS Press, 1969 (orig. pub. 1932).

G. Irby-Massie and P. T. Keyser (eds), *Greek Science of the Hellenistic Era: A Sourcebook*, London and New York: Routledge, 2002.

G. de Santillana (ed.), *The Origins of Scientific Thought, from Anaximander to Proclus 600 BC–AD 500*, New York: University of Chicago Press, 1961.

I. Thomas (ed. and trans.), *Greek Mathematical Works* (2 vols), Cambridge MA: Harvard University Press, 1939–41.

G. J. Toomer (trans. and annotated), *Ptolemy's Almagest*, London: Duckworth, 1984.

E. Warmington (trans.), *Greek Geography*, London: Dent, 1934.

The 'Late Commentators on Aristotle' series is edited by R. Sorabji and published by Duckworth.

Secondary

There are articles on many ancient scientists in C. C. Gillispie (ed.), *Dictionary of Scientific Biography* (16 vols), New York: Scribner, 1970–80.

J. Evans, *The History and Practice of Ancient Astronomy*, Oxford: Oxford University Press, 1998.

D. Fowler, *The Mathematics of Plato's Academy* (2nd corr. edn), Oxford: Oxford University Press, 1990.

D. Furley (ed.), *From Aristotle to Augustine* (Routledge History of Philosophy vol. 2), London and New York: Routledge, 1997.

R. Hankinson, *Cause and Explanation in Ancient Greek Thought*, Oxford: Oxford University Press, 1998.

G. E. R. Lloyd, *Methods and Problems in Greek Science*, Cambridge: Cambridge University Press, 1991.

T. E. Rihll, *Greek Science*, Oxford: Oxford University Press, 1999.

L. Taub, *Ancient Meteorology*, London and New York: Routledge, 2003.

C. J. Tuplin and T. E. Rihll, *Science and Mathematics in Ancient Greek Culture*, Oxford: Oxford University Press, 2002.

55. Music

David Creese

Music, a form of human expression as basic as speech, was cultivated with great zeal in Greek and Roman antiquity. It played an integral role in the civic, religious and educational life of Graeco-Roman culture, from the singing of Homeric epic in the archaic period to the singing of hymns in the early church.

There are four main sources of evidence for the study of Greek and Roman music: artistic representations of musicians and instruments, the often fragmentary remains of surviving instruments, texts and inscriptions, and a number of musical scores whose melodies may still be sung or played.

Artistic representations

Musicians and instruments were artistic subjects for the earliest Bronze Age cultures of the Aegean: we have Cycladic marble figurines of harpists and pipers, and Minoan painting and pottery depicting a variety of instruments, including lyres, pipes and a range of percussion instruments. It appears that the Mycenaeans were heirs to at least some of the musical resources of the Minoans, although there is no unequivocal evidence that they possessed any instrument but the lyre. We are far from any safe generalisations about Mycenaean music; the sum total of our evidence consists of seven (or perhaps eight) finds, five of them artistic representations of lyres.

In Greek and Roman art we find musical instruments of three main types: stringed, wind and percussion. They are depicted in nearly every art form, but most abundantly in painted ceramic.

The stringed instruments represented in Greek art are lyres, harps and lutes. Lyres have strings of roughly equal length, stretched across a resonant soundbox and made fast to a crossbar held by two arms. Harps have strings of unequal length, attached to a soundbox at one end and to a curved or obliquely angled neck at the other. Lutes have strings of equal length, stretched across a soundbox and along a neck against which they can be stopped by the fingers to change their pitch.

Lyres are by far the most commonly occurring stringed instruments in Greek art. There are four main varieties: the *phorminx* and *kithara* (the 'box-lyres'), and the *lyra* and *barbitos* (the 'bowl-lyres').

The *phorminx*, the lyre of Homeric epic, first appears in eighth-century art. It is a round-based lyre, often shown with four strings. Seven-stringed *phorminges* appear more regularly from the seventh century on. The classical form of the instrument is represented in Greek art by around thirty-five sixth- and fifth-century Attic vase-paintings; it also appears in over a dozen contemporary Etruscan and Anatolian examples.

By 600 BC the *phorminx* had become less common in art than a newer, square-based lyre, the *kithara* (figure 55.1). Its larger size and apparently hollow composite arms indicate a greater dynamic range than that of the *phorminx*. The *kithara* is most frequent in black-figure ceramic. From the fourth century it is less prominent and detailed, and in Hellenistic and Roman art it appears as a much simplified, more neatly rectangular instrument, without any of the complex curlicues in the arms. Competition is often assumed in many black-figure representations of the *kithara*: Nike (victory) is not infrequently seen nearby – or, as in figure 55.1, holding the instrument herself. Normally *kithara*-players are male.

Fig. 55.1 *Nike* holding *kithara*. Red-figure amphora by the Nikon Painter. Madrid, Museo Arqueológico Nacional, inv. 11104.

The smaller, lighter tortoise-shell lyre (figure 55.2) begins to appear in Greek art in the late eighth century. With slender, solid wooden arms and a soundbox which is often depicted so as to exhibit clearly its tortoise-shell markings, the *lyra* becomes very frequent from the sixth century: over 385 detailed depictions of it appear on Greek vases from the period 500–420 BC alone. It appears in many contexts, from the more public (procession, sacrifice, dance) to the more private (school, symposium, home); it is also played by famous musicians of myth (Orpheus, Achilles, Paris). We

Fig. 55.2 Symposium scene including two *lyrai* (front and back views). Column *kratēr* by Athana Painter. Corinth. 590–575 BC. Paris, Musée du Louvre, E629.

see it in both divine and human hands (Apollo, the Muses, Hermes; men, women, children).

A longer-stringed (and hence deeper-voiced) bowl-lyre appears in Greek ceramic from the late sixth century BC. The *barbitos* (or *barbiton*) was also built from a tortoise-shell soundbox, but had longer arms which curved inward near the top. Unlike the *kithara*, it is more common in red-figure than in black-figure, and after less than a century of popularity it gradually disappears from Attic ceramic by about 400, though it does appear intermittently in Apulian and Etruscan art until about 350. In art the *barbitos* is associated with poetry and, more especially, with revelry.

Harps do not appear in Greek art until the mid-fifth century BC. Three main varieties are discernible, all of which are roughly triangular in shape, with an elongated soundbox along the oblique, curved or arched upper side. The harp rests on the player's knee and is plucked with the bare fingers (unlike the lyres, whose strings were struck with a plectrum). The number of strings depicted ranges from nine to thirty-two. The players are almost always female; domestic scenes are common. Harps are much less frequent in Greek art than lyres (there are, for example, only eighteen extant depictions from the fifth century BC).

Lutes were known in many ancient Near Eastern cultures, but are not seen in Greek art until the fourth century BC. The artistic evidence for the instrument is very limited, and begins around the time of Alexander's Persian campaigns. Between 330 and 200 there are only around a dozen surviving representations of the instrument in Greek art, mostly terracottas. The player is normally female, though Eros also appears. The instrument is always held with the neck to the player's left; she stops the strings with the fingers of her left hand, and either plucks the strings with her right, or strikes them with a plectrum held in her right hand.

Wind instruments of three main types (flutes, reed-pipes and 'brass' instruments) were known

Fig. 55.3 *Hetaira* playing *auloi*. Red-figure *kylix* by Oltos. 525–500 BC. Madrid, Museo Arqueológico Nacional, inv. 11267.

to the Greeks and Romans; of these, reed-pipes were by far the most common.

The Greek reed-pipe, called the *aulos* (or *auloi* (plural), because it was played in pairs; see figures 55.3 and 55.4) begins to appear in art in the late eighth century BC. Frequently mistranslated 'flute', the *aulos* had a double-reed mouthpiece similar to those of modern oboes and bassoons, fitted into a segmented pipe; the pitch was varied by means of finger-holes – usually four, when these are shown in the vase-paintings. The aulete blows into both pipes simultaneously; sometimes he wears a leather strap (the *phorbeia*) around his face to support his cheeks. Usually the vase-paintings indicate identical fingering on both pipes. Depictions of *auloi* show significant variation in length, and textual sources confirm that there were several types which differed mainly in pitch. The instrument is portrayed in a very wide variety of contexts (ritual, competitive, dramatic, sympotic, domestic), where it is played by nearly every possible type of performer (divine, human; male, female; old, young; slave, free). Auletes are often shown accompanying dancing and revelry, and the instrument is very frequent in sympotic scenes, where it is often played by boys or *hetairae* (see figure 55.3). Its central role in the musical/poetic life of Greece is reflected in its association with the Muses in art (see figure 55.4).

The *aulos* was known in Italy as well, where it appears in Etruscan and Roman art. The *tibia* (as it was called in Latin) accompanied many civic events in Rome, and *tibicines* (pipers) are depicted at sacrifices, dramas, weddings and funerals.

The so-called 'brass' instruments are represented in Greek art by the *salpinx*, a kind of straight, round-belled trumpet. It appears in vase-paintings, normally in military contexts, and is usually at least as long as the player's outstretched arm. Roman art presents a wider range of 'brass' instruments: the *tuba*, a straight trumpet with a flared bell; the *lituus* (which also appears in Etruscan art), a straight horn widening to an upturned end; and the *bucina* or *cornu* (figure 55.5), a large horn with a lunate curve, braced with a cross-piece that also serves as a handle. All three instruments are seen in military contexts, but the *lituus* and *cornu* also appear in other settings, such as funeral and wedding processions, where they may be played with the *tibia*.

Flutes and panpipes are much rarer in Greek and Roman art. Both cultures possessed a species of transverse flute similar in size and shape to the

Fig. 55.4 Melpomene, Muse of tragedy, playing *auloi*. Red-figure *oinochoē* by Methyse Painter. Athens. 455–440 BC. Paris, Musée du Louvre, G440.

Fig. 55.5 Soldier playing *cornu*. Limestone relief. Osuna (Spain). Early first century BC. Madrid, Museo Arqueológico Nacional.

modern military fife, called *plagiaulos* in Greek and *obliqua tibia* in Latin. The panpipe (Greek *syrinx*, Latin *fistula*) makes rare appearances in Greek vase-painting, often in pastoral contexts, where it is frequently associated with its divine inventor, Pan. It appears in Etruscan art from the late sixth century, and later in Roman art. The classical Greek form of the instrument was constructed from reeds of equal length bound together; pitch variation was achieved (textual sources tell us) by blocking each pipe with wax to a different speaking length. In Etruscan, Roman and later Greek depictions its pipes are of unequal length; the instrument's shape thus resembles a bird's wing, as the second-century AD grammarian Pollux puts it (4.69).

The organ (*hydraulis*), an invention of the third-century BC Alexandrian engineer Ctesibius, is associated in mosaics with arena sports such as beast fights and gladiatorial displays. The organist stands behind it, and can be seen over the top of the pipes, which may number from seven to fifteen.

In art, as in literature, percussion instruments are associated primarily with revelry and mystery cults. Among them are *krotala* (clappers) and *kumbala*, small cymbals rarely much bigger than the player's open hand. The *tympanon* (Latin *tympanum*), a kind of frame drum, appears in art from Greek red-figure to Roman relief. Particularly associated with the cults of Dionysus and Cybele, it is found in orgiastic scenes of many kinds, often with the *aulos* and in the company of dancers or maenads. In the vase-paintings it appears as a circle with minimal depth, its diameter approximately equal to the length of the (often female) player's forearm. She holds it in her left hand by the bottom of the rim, and strikes it in the centre with the flat of her right hand.

Singing is also portrayed, usually in association with instruments (most commonly the *aulos*, sometimes lyres). Often the singer's head is thrown back, at an angle which could only have produced a tighter, sharper vocal sound than that preferred in most modern Western music. Several red-figure vases show singers with letters streaming out of their mouths – either words or merely a string of meaningless letters or circles. One of these shows Alcaeus and Sappho playing *barbitoi*; Alcaeus' name is written above his head, and, in a gently curving line between his mouth and the crossbar of his *barbitos*, the letters 'o o o o o'.

Surviving instruments

Of Mycenaean instruments there are only two (or perhaps three) finds, all of them from lyre-type instruments. They range in date from Late Helladic I at Mycenae to Late Helladic III at Menidi (Attica).

Several substantial *lyra* remains survive. Among the most important are tortoise-shell soundboxes from Argos, Reggio and Bassae (Arcadia). The species most commonly used, *Testudo marginata*, now produces a carapace of 22–30 cm in length and 10–13 cm in depth (roughly the dimensions suggested by the vase-paintings), but surviving tortoise-shell soundboxes are substantially smaller (15–18 cm). Two *lyra* arms and a crossbar are preserved in the British Museum (the 'Elgin lyre').

At least eighteen *auloi*/*tibiae* are extant, and a greater number of fragments as well. They range in date from the seventh century BC to the first century AD, and in location from Asia Minor in the East to Italy in the West, and to Egypt in the South. The varying sizes of the *aulos* indicated in artistic and textual sources are reflected in the surviving pipes, which range from 33 to 59 cm in length, with cylindrical bores of 5–10 mm in diameter. They are constructed in sections, and in some cases the joints are scored, suggesting the use of waxed thread to make the seal between sections. Most are wooden, others are of bone; some have been partially encased in metal. They have between five and fifteen finger-holes, usually with one or two on the underside. The earliest examples (the Brauron, Elgin, Louvre and Copenhagen *auloi*) have the fewest finger-holes (5–9), and the latest (four *tibiae* from Pompeii) have the most (10–15).

Flute-type instruments have not fared as well in the archaeological record, but 'brass' instruments are rather better represented. Some nearly complete examples of the Greek *salpinx* survive, and several Roman instruments as well, including at least one *tuba*, and some *cornua* from Pompeii. An Etruscan *lituus* from Caere (near Rome) measures 160 cm – much longer than the instrument appears in any extant artistic representation. Two Roman *litui* from Germany are both shorter than the Caere *lituus* (70 and 74 cm).

An early third-century AD organ has been discovered at Aquincum (Hungary). It has fifty-two bronze pipes arranged in four ranks of thirteen, but they are not sufficiently well preserved to allow a certain identification of the pitches they once sounded.

Some percussion instruments also survive. There are three pairs of *kumbala* (cymbals) and a number of unpaired examples, the earliest dating from the fifth or fourth century BC. They range from 5 to 18 cm in diameter. Several *seistra* (Latin *sistra*, rattles) have also been found; those from the Pompeian temple of Isis closely resemble surviving examples of the Egyptian form of the instrument.

Textual and epigraphical evidence

Music is well documented in Greek and Roman literature. By far the largest quantity of evidence about the subject comes from textual sources, which fall into four main groups: (1) Greek and Latin verse originally composed to be sung (a group which includes early Greek epic and lyric, and much of Greek and Roman drama; these texts often contain clues to the musical aspects of their performance, as well as other occasionally detailed references to music); (2) prose works which provide evidence about music, by either evaluation, criticism, description or musical exemplum; (3) specialised musicological literature, in which the history, forms and underlying structures of music were analysed and debated; (4) inscriptions which supply valuable evidence about the contexts, details, dates and locations of certain types of musical performances, and in some cases even the notated musical compositions themselves.

From these sources we learn more about the instruments – sometimes merely things which are also suggested by the artistic and archaeological evidence, but often the kind of information only texts can provide. Our impression of the *kithara*, for instance, as a professional's instrument which first appeared in the seventh century BC is supported by the statements of Aristotle (*Pol.* 1341ᵃ18–19) and the author of the pseudo-Plutarchian *de Musica* (1133c). That lyre-strings were made from twisted sheep-gut, on the other hand (*Od.* 21.408, *Hom. Hymn Herm.* 51), is the type of detail that art and archaeology do not supply. Scientific texts such as Theophrastus' *Historia plantarum* record important details about the materials used in the manufacture of instruments (e.g. *aulos*-reeds, 4.11.1–7). Instrument names, which are only very rarely indicated in art, are supplied in (often confused) abundance by the textual sources. Later authors such as Athenaeus, Pollux and Hesychius list so many names of instruments and their parts, in fact, as to outnumber the types of instruments known from the artistic sources. Authors of specialist works sometimes provide detailed descriptions of instruments as well (e.g. the organ by Heron of Alexandria (*Pneum.* 42) and Vitruvius (*de arch.* 10.8)). There were in addition several technical works (now lost) which would have shed further light on instruments and their manufacture: Athenaeus reports that Aristoxenus wrote a treatise on *aulos*-boring, for example

(634e-f). Finally, the musical uses of the voice and the activity of singing are more fully documented in literature than they could have been in any other medium.

Descriptions of the sounds ancient instruments made are the unique preserve of literature, though the value of such testimony is limited. The *lyra*, for example, is 'sweet-sounding' (Pind. *Ol.* 10.93–94), the *aulos* makes a 'sweet clamour' (Soph. *Aj.* 1202), and *tympana* are 'deep-thundering' (Eur. *Bacch.* 156). Occasionally onomatopoeia is used: Ennius' *tuba* emits a frightening '*taratantara*' (*Ann.* 140), and Aristophanes' Euripides mocks Aeschylus with the *kithara*-imitating refrain '*phlattothrattophlattothrat*' (*Ran.* 1281–95).

Musical scenes are often described in ways that parallel the mythical, ritual or festival associations implied by the artistic evidence: the *tympanon*, for example, with the cult of the Great Mother (Hdt. 4.76, Eur. *Bacch.* 59, Catull. 63.8–9). Some associations are reinforced through myth, such as that of Apollo with the lyre and satyrs with the *aulos* in the popular story of Apollo and Marsyas (Apollod. *Bibl.* 1.4.2). There are invention-myths for many of the instruments (e.g. Hermes and the lyre, Athena and the *auloi*). These and other stories, such as those about Orpheus (Verg. *G.* 4.453–529, Ov. *Met.* 10–11), serve not only to associate extraordinary musical talent with particular geographical regions, but also to portray it as a powerful supernatural force, not to be trivialised or misused.

Music was always a popular subject: there were, for example, comedies with such titles as Magnes' *Barbitos-players*, Anaxilas' *Lyre-maker* and Menander's *Kithara-player*. Moralising discourse about music and its effects occurs both in Greek comedy and in the philosophical works of Plato, Aristotle and others, where ethical theories of music, first advanced in the fifth century, were more fully developed. The notion that certain instruments and music composed in certain attunements could affect the character of the listener or performer was later challenged by Epicureans such as Philodemus.

Attempts to analyse the structures which underlie music and musical sound had begun by the fifth century BC, but no musicological writings survive independently from that period (see chapter 54). Authors of works in the Pythagorean tradition quoted by later writers show attempts at harmonic analysis by appeal to the parallel manipulation of mathematical ratios. The elements of this 'mathematical harmonics' (Arist. *APo.* 79a1–2) were perhaps best stated in the Euclidean *Sectio canonis* ('Division of the Monochord'), a short mathematical document of disputed date and authorship. A more discursive attempt to summarise the discipline's basic doctrines is presented by Nicomachus of Gerasa in his *Handbook of Harmonics* (early second century AD).

Aristotle's pupil Aristoxenus took a different approach to musical theory, rejecting ratio-based analysis in favour of a method that quantified the intervals of the many attunements of Greek music in tones and fractions of a tone. His work was later summarised in Aristoxenian handbooks, such as those of Cleonides (perhaps second century AD) and Bacchius Geron (third-fourth century AD).

From at least the time of Eratosthenes (third – early second century BC), attempts were made to integrate these two fundamentally antithetical approaches to harmonics, and the works of Gaudentius and Aristides Quintilianus both incorporate Aristoxenian and mathematical analysis. Claudius Ptolemy, whose rigorous scientific account of harmonics relies primarily on the ratio-based theory of the Pythagoreans, was none the less reluctant to sacrifice the richness, diversity and committed appeal to sense-perception offered by Aristoxenus' approach to the subject, and for all his criticisms of Aristoxenus, Ptolemy is heavily indebted to him. Fragments of the writings of several other important musicological authors are preserved by Theon of Smyrna, and by Porphyry in his commentary on Ptolemy's *Harmonics*. Among the Latin authors who wrote about music the most influential was Boethius, whose *de Institutione Musica* was an ambitious attempt to translate and summarise the work of his Greek predecessors.

Rhythmics, another important branch of musical theory in antiquity, received attention from Aristoxenus, Bacchius, Aristides Quintilianus and St Augustine. Physical acoustics was also investigated by ancient authors. Archytas theorised about the causes of sound in the early fourth cen-

Natural History are available in the Loeb series. Other medical writers are more difficult to locate. Aretaeus and Paul of Aegina were last translated into English in 1856 and 1844–7 respectively, and Caelius Aurelianus and Soranus in the 1950s. The recent editions and translations of the fragments of Diocles (P. J. van der Eijk, 2000–1) and of the Methodists (M. M. Tecusan, 2004) mark a great advance in our knowledge of medicine in the period between Hippocrates and Galen. But many less familiar authors or texts deriving from Oriental sources are extremely hard to locate even in a major library. Medical papyri are listed by M. H. Marganne, and the Greek epigraphic sources have been collected by E. Samama: both volumes have an accompanying French translation of the texts.

Further reading

E. J. Edelstein and L. Edelstein, *Asclepius: Collection and Interpretation of the Testimonies* (repr.), Baltimore: Johns Hopkins University Press, 1998.

W. Haase and H. Temporini (eds), *Aufstieg und Niedergang der römischen Welt. II Principat. Band 37. Teilband 1–3. Medizin und Biologie*, Berlin and New York: de Gruyter, 1993–6.

R. Jackson, *Doctors and Diseases in the Roman World*, London: British Museum Publications, 1988.

J. Jouanna, *Hippocrates*, Baltimore: Johns Hopkins University Press, 1999.

G. E. R. Lloyd, *In the Grip of Disease: Studies in the Greek Imagination*, Oxford: Oxford University Press, 2003.

M. H. Marganne, *Inventaire analytique des papyrus grecs de médecine*, Geneva: Droz, 1981.

V. Nutton (ed.), *The Unknown Galen (BICS Supplement 77)*, London: Institute of Classical Studies, 2002.

V. Nutton, *Ancient Medicine*, London: Routledge, 2004.

G. Sabbah, P. P. Corsetti and K. D. Fischer, *Bibliographie des textes médicaux latins*, St Etienne: Université de St Etienne, 1987; *Premier Supplément: 1986–1999*, St Etienne: Université de St. Etienne, 2000.

E. Samama, *Les Médecins dans le monde grec*, Geneva: Droz, 2003.

P. N. Singer, *Galen: Selected Works*, Oxford: Oxford University Press, 1997.

W. D. Smith, *The Hippocratic Tradition*, Ithaca: Cornell University Press, 1979.

M. M. Tecusan, *The Fragments of the Methodists*, Leiden: Brill, 2004.

P. J. van der Eijk, *Diocles of Carystus: A Collection of the Fragments with Translation and Commentary*, Leiden: Brill, 2000–1.

57. Greek Legal Texts

Benet Salway

Legal texts generally fall into three basic categories: pronouncements issued by some public authority; private legal documents such as contracts, wills or manumission agreements (agreements for freeing a slave from slavery); and works of legal commentary or theory written by private individuals. Examples of all three genres exist in ancient Greek, but the pattern of original production and subsequent survival of these different types was not uniform across the Greek world or throughout antiquity. Our knowledge of the actual texts of legislation is largely dependent upon the survival of individual pronouncements inscribed on stone (see chapter 34). We are thus best informed on this aspect for those regions and times when the epigraphic habit was most marked, for example Attica in the classical era and Asia Minor in the Hellenistic and Roman periods. In contrast, the vast majority of private legal documents in Greek that survive come from Egypt under Ptolemaic and Roman rule, simply because environmental conditions have been favourable for the preservation of the papyrus on which they are written. However plentiful these scattered remains, they cannot be used to reconstruct a coherent system of 'Greek law' because there never was a unified system, even after the political unification of much of the Greek world under Hellenistic and then Roman rule. Indeed *autonomia*, the right to be governed according to one's own *nomoi* (laws, social norms), was a defining element of the independent Greek political community (polis) from the classical period onwards. The eventual political absorption of most Greek communities by Rome, including the extension of the Roman private civil law to all free inhabitants of the empire by the emperor Caracalla's grant of Roman citizenship in AD 212 and the homogenisation of the political statuses of communities in late antiquity, put an end to these independent traditions and would have rendered obsolete much legislation and legal literature that existed.

It is rare that a body of legal texts pertaining to the same community and time survives that is sufficient to reconstruct the outlines of any one legal system. Many of the public decrees that do survive do not establish or confirm general principles of law but rather are ad hoc motions to grant privileges or honours to individuals or communities. Indeed much modern understanding of the Athenian legal system of the classical period is derived not from documentary sources but from contemporary literature, most notably speeches delivered in the law-courts by the Attic orators, whose works were, of course, preserved as models of style, not for the interest of their legal content (see chapter 45). However, even where the speaker would appear to be presenting a verbatim quotation of the text of a particular law (e.g. the law on intestate succession cited in Demosthenes 43.51), given the forensic context, one has to be cautious in using such evidence to reconstruct the original text of any law. The best overview of the legal system of any Greek community is in fact provided by the sequence of laws, the earliest dating back to the sixth century, that began to be inscribed in the early fifth century at Gortyn in Crete on public buildings around the Agora and continued to be added to until some time in the third century (*IC* IV 1–162, 165).

The manner of this inscription, with the text running on in a sequence of parallel columns, is quite unlike the civic *stēlē* format associated with the publication of individual decrees, as at Athens. In fact the layout strongly suggests that the text was transferred to the medium of stone from pre-existing papyrus scrolls. The bulk of the text belongs to two phases: the 'Lesser Code' (*IC* IV 41), inscribed in the early fifth century, and the 'Great Code' (*IC* IV 72) of c. 450 BC. Even these subsections do not comprise a uniform text composed at one moment but rather a compilation of many individual laws. So while not a systematic collection, the laws do cover many areas of life, including family relations and property, slaves, sureties, gifts, mortgages and court procedure, among other things. The public display of these laws in the Agora was clearly a strong (re)statement by the community of its normative rules, though the texts do need to be treated cautiously as historical evidence for how things worked in practice. After all, the weakness of Greek legal systems, including the Athenian, was the difficulty of enforcing a verdict once obtained (a problem still prevalent for civil cases under the English common law).

Some debate surrounds the initial emergence of written law in the Greek world. Legal texts are certainly among the very earliest public inscriptions. Some have seen the influence of Near Eastern models behind the phenomenon; others see the enactment of written laws as an indigenous product of archaic Greek culture, whether in response to the growing demands of international commerce, or to the need to establish a socio-political consensus as the emerging institutions of the polis superseded more narrowly based monarchical and oligarchic regimes, or to the spread of literacy itself (Gagarin, *Early Greek Law*). Ancient literary tradition (Aristotle, *frag.* 548 Rose), confirmed by the epigraphic record, suggests that from the mid-seventh century BC communities throughout the Greek world began to enact public written laws. The earliest written laws are attributed to Zaleucus, the lawgiver to Epizephyrian Locri in southern Italy in 662 BC, and the earliest legal inscription known is that from Dreros in Crete, now dated c. 650–600 BC (ML 2). The first written laws at Athens are attributed to Draco in c. 621/0 BC, though according to Aristotle, even before this legal officers (*thesmothetae*) had recorded decisions (*thesmia*) in writing and kept them for judging future disputes, an example of which probably survives in the later tyranny law of Solon (*Ath. Pol.* 16.10). Other than a substantial fragment of the law on homicide preserved epigraphically (reissued in a version from 409/8 BC: *IG* I^3.104), none of the original text of Draco's legislative programme survived the later codification by Solon of 594/3 BC (also largely lost), whose own programme was published on wooden boards (*axones*).

But what was the nature and purpose of written law in archaic Greece? Whether historical or not, it is striking that ancient tradition commonly attributed the authorship of these founding sets of laws to a single authorised legislator (*nomothetēs*) rather than a commission (e.g. Solon at Athens, Zaleucus at Locri, Charondas at Catania), often supposedly appointed after a period of civil discord. It may also be significant that outsiders were often chosen, such as Demonax of Mantinea for Cyrene, Andromadas of Rhegium for Thracian Chalcis, Philolaus of Corinth for Thebes. These written laws regulated several areas of conflict, notably the area of procedure. The publication of law in this way may have led to the expanded use and increased regulation of the judicial process. The written laws of archaic Greece gave individual magistrates less control over the judicial process and increased the role of legal procedure at the expense of traditional means of self-help. Also the extension of law over areas previously governed by traditional customs (e.g. family affairs) increased the power of the impersonal polis over its inhabitants, as did the stipulation of specific penalties, even when these simply enshrined those derived from custom, as it reduced variation between different judges or from case to case. The establishment of written laws plausibly reflects a general weakening of the power and autonomy of aristocratic families and the growth of the idea of the state and citizenship. That life at Sparta remained governed by the oral regulations (*rhētrae*) attributed to Lycurgus may indicate that this famously conservative society had not undergone the kinds of developments that stimulated the establishment of written laws elsewhere, rather than being the result of a *rhētra* forbidding the writing down of legal texts, as claimed by Plutarch (*Lyc.* 13.1–4). In any case by the mid-sixth century, with the exception of Sparta, most cities had written laws.

Although little survives of the laws of the archaic period, a certain amount can be ascertained about form and content. The Dreros text shares with Draco's Athenian homicide law, Solon's law of theft (Demosthenes 24.105), and other sixth-century texts from Chios (ML 8) and Eretria (*IG* XII.9 1273–74) a characteristic literary form comprising third-person singular conditional sentences in prose. Moreover, although legend might ascribe lawgiving to divine inspiration and the wrath of the gods might be invoked as a sanction, the actual texts of Greek laws that survive do not represent themselves as divine instructions, unlike the Mosaic law. To judge from the surviving texts, the archaic lawgivers did not attempt comprehensive prescriptions of the constitution (*politeia*) but tended to cover four basic categories: tort laws (relating to damage or injury); family and property; public laws (religious, economic, political); and procedural laws – though there was no contemporary systemisation of this sort. For example, Draco's homicide law and Solon's law of theft both combine substantive provisions with procedural innovations (indeed the main purpose of Draco's law seems to be the detailed elaboration of a procedure for settling disputes arising out of a homicide).

Fixed penalties were commonly included for torts; indeed Draco's supposed application of the death penalty for all offences has made the severity of his legislation proverbial. Solon's legislation seems to have been particularly comprehensive on public matters of business, religion and politics, though it contained a good deal of family law (as did the legislation of Philolaus at Thebes). In contrast to the tort laws, these family laws do not seem to have contained explicit penalties. Private enforcement by the head of the household may have been envisaged, or the remedy was not stated because it was assumed obvious that it would be a private legal suit (*dikē*) brought by the victim or relatives to enforce compliance. But some of Solon's laws, where the victims may have been rendered unable to bring a case (because sold into slavery, for example), also allowed third parties to bring a case by means of a new procedure called a *graphē*, the name of which implies the submission of a written accusation. Procedural regulation and innovation such as this may have been the most significant part of the work of Zaleucus and his fellow archaic lawgivers, rather than the formulation of general principles that were probably already established by custom.

From the fifth century onwards, as government by citizen assembly (*ecclēsia*) and council (*boulē*) became the standard pattern among the Greek poleis, so the resolutions of these organs of government became the dominant form for the enactment of new legislation as well as other official pronouncements with legal force, such as treaties with other states, grants of privilege etc. These motions, approved by majority vote (*psēphisma*), commonly followed the formula 'It was resolved by the *boulē* and/or *dēmos* that . . .'; they continued to be used throughout the Greek world into late antiquity, and form the vast majority of surviving official inscriptions (Rhodes and Lewis, *Decrees of the Greek States*). Often decrees originated from an initial proposal put forward by the council (*probouleuma*), whose wording is sometimes preserved in the final document. At Athens, already by 410 BC, the number and overlapping validity of these individual decrees had become so confusing that all existing laws were revised and inscribed on stone. Thereafter only those laws with an epigraphic archive copy were considered authoritative, while new decrees were meant not to override general laws (*nomoi*), whose formulation was henceforth entrusted to a panel of *nomothetae*. With the advent of the Hellenistic kingdoms and then later Roman domination, Greek communities had to contend with new forms of public document with legal force: the letter or edict from an external superior authority, to which they often responded with civic decrees and which were often memorialised in stone in the same manner (e.g. the dossier collected by Ma, *Antiochos III*, pp. 284–372).

The importance of the written text was not confined to matters of public law. The introduction of legal systems governed by written texts was accompanied (some would argue, even preceded) by the employment of written memoranda for private transactions, which might then be produced as evidence in court should arrangements fail. Indeed, at Athens in the classical period commercial cases (*dikai emporikai*) could only be brought in instances when a specifically written contract (*syngraphē*), drawn up in the Athenian trading centre (*emporion*) or concerning voyages to or from the *emporion*, had been contravened by one or other of the parties (Todd, *Shape of Athenian Law*, pp. 334–7). The penetration of such written documentation to the very fringes of the Greek world at an early date is suggested by the trading contract on a lead sheet in c. 450 BC and recovered from Pech-Maho on the coast of Provence (Wilson, 'The "Illiterate trader"?'). The Greek papyri from the rubbish dumps of Ptolemaic and Roman Egypt are replete with private legal instruments such as contracts and wills, and from the Black Sea region survive records of manumission incorporating contracts for continued obligations (*paramonē*) by the freed person to the ex-master (Gibson, *Jewish Manumission Inscriptions*).

The one area of literary endeavour in which Greece lags behind Rome is that of legal theory and commentary. Nevertheless Plato's longest and last dialogue, the *Laws* (*Nomoi*), written towards the middle of the fourth century BC, is a major work of legal philosophy and is supremely valuable as a record of at least one contemporary ancient opinion of the role of law. Plato views law as a product of reason; reason provides knowledge of eternal truths, and human laws are the counterpart amongst men of the divine order governing the cosmos; so an adequate legal system cannot be produced by piecemeal legislation but should be the result of the single unified vision of a wise legislator. It is argued that the true aim of law is not simply peace but virtue (*aretē*), for which an essential prerequisite is self-discipline (*sophrosynē*), so any system of laws should be framed to produced this. The ideal general framework for this would be a self-restraining constitution that combined elements of both monarchy and democracy, and laws should be given preambles designed to persuade citizens to obey laws of their own free will rather than through fear of the penalty. Plato upholds the principle of the paramount sovereignty of the law, before describing his ideal legal code, which largely comprises features borrowed from existing Greek cities, chiefly Athens and Sparta.

The *Laws* in fact represents a systematic attempt to codify and reform Greek practice in the light of a clear vision of the ultimate purpose of law. However, the only works of analysis and commentary of real legal systems known before the arrival of Rome were generated by members of the Peripatetic movement. The only surviving example is the *Athenaion Politeia* (*Constitution of the Athenians*), ascribed to Aristotle, but Theophrastus (c. 370–287 BC), Aristotle's successor, is known to have written a comparative work entitled *Laws*, and a certain Craterus, who may be the same as the Macedonian governor of Attica in the 270s and 260s, compiled a collection of Athenian decrees (*Psephismatōn synagōgē*) in at least nine books, organised chronologically and focusing on the fifth century. It was only at Rome that the study of law as an independent discipline was really to develop.

Further reading

I. Arnaoutoglou, *Ancient Greek Laws: A Sourcebook*, London: Routledge, 1998.

L. Foxhall and A. D. E. Lewis (eds), *Greek Law in its Political Setting: Justifications not Justice*, Oxford: Oxford University Press, 1996.

M. Gagarin, *Early Greek Law*, Berkeley: University of California Press, 1986.

M. Gagarin and D. Cohen (eds), *The Cambridge Companion to Ancient Greek Law*, Cambridge: Cambridge University Press, 2005.

M. J. Geller and H. Maehler, with the collaboration of A. D. E. Lewis (eds), *Legal Documents of the Hellenistic World*, London: Warburg Institute, 1995.

E. L. Gibson, *The Jewish Manumission Inscriptions of the Bosporan Kingdom* (Texts and Studies in Ancient Judaism 75), Tübingen: Mohr Siebeck, 1999.

E. M. Harris and L. Rubinstein (eds), *The Law and the Courts in Ancient Greece*, London: Duckworth, 2003.

J. Ma, *Antiochos III and the Cities of Western Asia Minor* (rev. edn), Oxford: Oxford University Press, 2002.

P. J. Rhodes, 'Public documents in the Greek states: archives and inscriptions', *Greece and Rome* n.s. 48 (2001), 33–44 and 136–53.

P. J. Rhodes with D. M. Lewis, *The Decrees of the Greek States*, Oxford: Clarendon Press, 1997.

R. F. Stalley, *An Introduction to Plato's Laws*, Oxford: Blackwell, 1983.

S. C. Todd, *The Shape of Athenian Law*, Oxford: Oxford University Press, 1993.

R. F. Willetts, *The Law Code of Gortyn* (Kadmos supplement 1), Berlin: de Gruyter, 1967.

J.-P. Wilson, 'The "illiterate trader"?', *BICS* 42 (1997–8), 29–56.

58. Latin Legal Texts

Simon Corcoran

Whereas so many Latin literary forms owed a heavy debt to Greek paradigms, there was little Greek precedent in the area of jurisprudence, and the Romans developed a strong and innovative tradition of their own, regarded as typically Roman inasmuch as juristic writing was highly practical rather than purely philosophical. Cicero's *Republic* and *Laws*, named in homage to Plato, are not typical works. The *Laws*, in as far as it survives (three incomplete books out of six), outlines a code of essentially constitutional law for an idealised although Roman-style republic. In contrast, the greatest achievements of Roman legal writers were in the area of civil law, in the sense of the law governing private relations between citizens.

The main difficulty for the modern scholar is that both legislative enactments and juristic commentaries usually survive as edited extracts in later compilations. Legal texts were created for current use, which meant that older ones had a tendency to obsolescence, with more recent writings superseding but also subsuming their predecessors. Thus the earlier texts, not being fixed in an unchanging canon, either do not survive or only do so as selectively quoted by later writers. This is best illustrated from the simple fact that most of our knowledge of Roman law comes from the great work of compilation carried out at the command of the emperor Justinian (AD 527–65), which produced the *Digest* and the *Justinian Code*, both made up of edited extracts from earlier texts, texts which in their original forms were simultaneously rendered obsolete and invalid.

Legislation in the Republic and early Empire

The early defining moment for Roman law is the compilation of the Twelve Tables in 451/0 BC, which codified and made public the core of the Roman civil law. Despite its venerable status, the text has not survived intact, but has to be reconstructed from later discussions and quotations (usually in 'modernised' Latin), particularly from Cicero, Festus and Gellius. The Twelve Tables were presented to an assembly, the *comitia centuriata*, for ratification, and henceforth all laws (*leges*) would be proposed by a magistrate and then passed by one of the popular assemblies, including the *concilium plebis* (from which patricians were excluded), whose 'plebiscites' (*plebiscita*) were binding from 287 BC. *Leges* continued to be passed into the early imperial period, whether proposed by emperors or by other magistrates. Augustus' social legislation (on marriage, and on manumission of slaves) included laws proposed directly by himself (e.g. *Lex Iulia de maritandis ordinibus*, c.18 BC) but also by the consuls of the day (e.g. *Lex Papia Poppaea*, AD 9). Formal use of the popular assemblies to pass legislation seems to have withered away by the end of the first century AD.

Decrees of the Senate *(senatus consulta, SC*), which had often formed the basis for a bill laid before the people by a magistrate during the republic, acquired the force of law under the early empire (in effect the final stage of the legislative process was simply being dropped) and became an important avenue for law-making. However, since the decrees themselves came to be little more than embodiments of an imperial speech (*oratio*), they in turn ceased to be legally significant from the early third century AD.

Some legal works were solely devoted to discussing particular laws or decrees. For instance, Gaius, Paul and Ulpian all wrote works on the Augustan marriage laws under the title 'Lex Iulia et Papia', and similarly, Paul wrote on the *SC Silanianum* of AD 10, which dealt with the consequences of a slave murdering his master. But although much of the content and sometimes the wording is recoverable from the later legal commentaries, texts of *leges* and *senatus consulta* (as with the Twelve Tables), especially those concerned with private law, do not survive in anything like an intact state. It is in Frontinus' administrative handbook that we find verbatim quotation of six *senatus consulta* of 11 BC (*De Aquaeductu Urbis Romae* 100–8 and 125–7; Johnson et al., *Ancient Roman Statutes* (*ARS*) no. 141). We are otherwise largely dependent upon permanent contemporary copies created to meet political or administrative concerns. This is most famously demonstrated by officially inscribed documents relating to the aftermath of the death of Germanicus in AD 19: the *Lex Aurelia Valeria*, which contained posthumous honours (Crawford, *Roman Statutes* (*RS*) no. 37), and the *senatus consultum* on the elder Piso of AD 20, which recounted and celebrated the latter's disgrace and death for his conduct surrounding the prince's demise (Rowe, *Princes and Political Cultures*).

Magistrates could also make law by edict, but the most significant such activity for the development of the civil law was that of the urban praetor, in charge of litigation between Roman citizens. Each year the praetor would issue an edict, laying out which sort of actions and remedies he would allow, and by the late second century BC this had become an important and flexible way of modifying and innovating in law. Each praetor would generally take over his predecessor's edict, but might add, delete or modify clauses. A good deal of evidence for the edict in the late republic comes from the writings of Cicero, but the edict continued to change on into the imperial period, although it is presumed that it became increasingly stable. Finally, the jurist Salvius Julianus at the request of the emperor Hadrian 'codified' the edict into a fixed form in AD 131. The edict, even in its final form, does not survive as an intact text, although its shape and content are generally well known, given the extensive and lengthy commentaries written on it. Its structure provided one of the chief organising principles for later legal works, including the imperial codes. The text of the edict is reconstructed in Lenel, *Das Edictum Perpetuum* (trans. as *ARS* no. 244).

Juristic writing

Although the Twelve Tables and other laws (and eventually the praetor's edict) were fixed texts, they did not and could not provide for all situations. The question of 'what the law was' always retained a degree of uncertainty, and interpretation and those who offered it came to enjoy a considerable eminence. By the last century of the republic these experts did not simply answer queries put to them, but had started to write in a more systematic way, producing works that ranged from large multi-book treatments of the entire civil law or the praetor's edict, to monographs dealing with individual topics. Some works were made up entirely of answers (*responsa*) given by the jurist to particular problems. Jurists do not generally worry about what we would call 'jurisprudence' or the philosophy of law to any significant degree, although questions of general principle are raised and developed. The works, however, are to a considerable extent grounded in actual practice, as can easily be seen from the way in which judgements in real cases or responses to genuine queries are frequently cited. Theoretical examples are also much used and sometimes seem to suggest a delight in solving a difficult problem that has not (yet at least) arisen, but the sense of connection to the real world of litigation and the courts is never far away. The Augustan jurist Antistius Labeo is recorded as spending half the year in Rome answering queries put to him by litigants or pupils, and the other half on his estates writing legal works (*Digest* I.2.2.47). The world of the jurists, however, is that of the wealthy and landed elite, to which they and their intended audience belong, and the shape of the law largely reflects the concerns and needs of the upper class.

As was normal for governors and other judges, the emperor himself would routinely include jurists in his *consilium* and ask for their advice when conducting legal business. But legal expertise could also lead to more formal appointments. In the early third century, two of the most outstanding jurists, Papinian (d. 212) and Ulpian (d. 223), each held a series of 'palatine' offices, culminating in the praetorian prefecture. However, the tendency for all matters to come before the emperor meant that authoritative opinions on points of law, such as would once have been given by a jurist, now increasingly came from the emperor in the form of rescripts (although usually written by an expert jurist in the emperor's name). By the late third century, innovative or substantive legal works ceased to be written. Thus the most important work of Hermogenian, one of the last known classical jurists and Diocletian's praetorian prefect, was his Code, a collection of imperial rescripts, which had been formally issued in the names of Diocletian and his colleagues, but in fact written by himself (Honoré, *Emperors and Lawyers*).

The works of the juristic writers do not survive intact, but generally only in excerpts. The one authentic and virtually complete work we have is the *Institutes* of Gaius (mid-second century AD), known from its chance survival in a fifth-century palimpsest in Verona, and which therefore gives us an unfiltered account of the Roman law of the 'classical period'. Otherwise we are heavily dependent on the *Digest*. In the first half of the twentieth century much scholarly effort was devoted to detecting 'interpolations' in the *Digest* (and the Justinianic Code), a task performed with such a degree of scepticism that it often seemed that little of any original text had survived the attentions of Justinian's commissioners. The contemporary view is more accepting and has tried to be rather more systematic in judging how far editorial changes were made. None the less, it must always be remembered that Justinian was attempting to produce generally consistent and current law for his own time and that the source material has been through a sixth-century filter. This effect is enhanced as we attempt to look further back in time. For instance, the *Digest* is dominated by the works of Ulpian, which comprise about 40 per cent, but themselves contain quotations from and discussions of earlier laws and writers. By contrast, few works of republican date were extracted directly, only surviving if already present within the later writers. This layering or 'onion' effect means that the oldest texts may have been filtered or altered more than once. Despite this, we are fortunate that the *Digest* and other surviving works are so explicit in citing their sources, giving details of author, work and even the book number within a work. Thus they can be used to reconstruct otherwise lost writings. The most comprehensive such attempt was Lenel's *Palingenesia Iuris Civilis*, which reordered the legal writings according to their original authors and works. Despite the Justinianic filter, these jurists' writings give us both an impressive quantity of Latin prose, and a rich source for the social and intellectual history of the principate.

Imperial legislation and late antiquity

From the start of the principate, the emperor was always influential in the making or development of law, although at first working through existing procedures. However, by the time of Gaius (mid-second century), virtually any pronouncement or decision of the emperor had come to have the force of law, and during the course of the third century this became a monopoly. The enactment of new *leges* and *senatus consulta* had ended, and authoritative juristic writing also ceased (although existing law and writings remained valid). This change is marked by the issue in the 290s under Diocletian of two works, the Gregorian and Hermogenian Codes (called codes because in *codex*, i.e. book, form, not because they 'codified' in a modern sense; see chapter 33). Although named after their compilers, these contained exclusively imperial rescripts (spanning the period from Hadrian to Diocletian), issued in the names of emperors, even if written by juristically able office-holders. It is also from this period onwards that substantial and largely intact legal texts are preserved. These are often attested in only a few manuscripts (or even a single one), and are generally anonymous, or at least pseudonymous. Thus the *Sententiae* attributed to the Severan jurist Paul date in fact to c. AD 300 (although best preserved in the early sixth-century version given in the Breviary of Alaric). Other notable survivals include: the *Fragmenta Vaticana* (early fourth century), the *Mosaicarum et Romanarum legum collatio* ('Comparison of Roman and Mosaic Laws'; late fourth century), and the *Consultatio veteris cuiusdam iurisconsulti* ('Consultation of some ancient Jurist'; mid-fifth century). In contrast to Gaius' *Institutes*, our sole authentic intact text of the classical period, these works resemble the codes, being little more than compilations of already existing texts (whether the classical juristic writings or imperial rescripts) with minimal intervention by the author. This authorial reticence has the advantage for us that quotations are both direct and unedited, and so provide important 'control' texts for the reliability of the Justinianic Corpus, where passages are present in both. Contrast the lengthy edict of Diocletian on incest as given in the *Collatio* VI.4 with the short extract in the Justinianic Code (V.4.17).

The two Diocletianic codes do not themselves survive, but the next act of code-making does. This is the Theodosian Code, issued in 438 by the emperor Theodosius II, containing edited extracts from imperial laws (generally as letters to officials, often the praetorian prefect) from the time of Constantine (AD 313) up to Theodosius. The text we have is substantially complete, with two early manuscripts preserving between them full versions of books VI–XVI. The first five books are incompletely reassembled from later epitomes and other sources. This was the last great legislative act of the undivided empire. There also survive some other near-contemporary sets of imperial constitutions: the so-called *Sirmondian Constitutions*, concerned with ecclesiastical matters (sixteen texts, covering a similar period to the Theodosian Code), and sets of 'Novels' (*Novellae constitutiones* = new constitutions) of emperors from both East and West between 438 and 468. These are particularly rich as a source, since their unabbreviated texts often give for an enactment the background otherwise excised in codified versions (e.g. Valentinian III, *Nov.* 21.1, by which mutual wills between spouses are validated, the issue having arisen from a specific case). The continual intervention of the late Roman state in religious affairs also means that imperial legislative texts are frequently preserved in Christian sources, such as Eusebius, Augustine, and proto-canonical collections like the *Collectio Avellana* (Coleman-Norton, *Roman State and Christian Church*).

The next important codification is that of the Visigothic King Alaric II, who issued his 'Breviary' in 506 to provide a slimmed-down code for his Roman subjects in Gaul and Spain. This survives intact, and contains abbreviated versions of the Theodosian Code, the 'Novels', the Gregorian and Hermogenian Codes (unhelpfully brief), Gaius' *Institutes*, Paul's *Sententiae* and a fragment of Papinian. The manner of 'abbreviation' was generally to select a limited number of texts, but take them over intact, while frequently adding an explanatory *interpretatio*. The standard modern edition of the Theodosian Code and its English translation is in reality a combination of the original code and the Breviary, since it includes all surviving *interpretationes*.

Finally, we come to Justinian, whose work of compilation is largely responsible for the survival of so much Roman legal writing, even if in an edited form. Becoming emperor in 527, almost immediately he set about trying to bring the unruly mass of Roman legal texts, both the imperial and the juristic, into a coherent whole (a plan originally conceived by Theodosius II). His timing was crucial, since the truncated empire had been left largely Greek in terms of language, culture and increasingly administration, and only the edifice of Roman law kept Latin as a vital language, supported by two major law-schools in Beirut and Constantinople. This was probably the last point, therefore, at which Latin legal culture remained sufficiently strong to fulfil the task that Justinian set. Various commissions were created for the purpose, in which the key figure was the jurist Tribonian, and the first resultant publication was the Justinian Code in 529. This twelve-book work contained cannibalised versions of the three existing codes (Gregorian, Hermogenian, Theodosian) together with more recent legislation, including the early legislation of Justinian himself. Then in 533 there followed the *Institutes*, a four-book introduction to Roman law closely modelled on Gaius, and the more substantial *Digest* in fifty books, a recompilation of the large corpus of juristic writings produced between Augustus and Diocletian, and of which an intact sixth-century manuscript survives. As a result of this project and the legal ferment it had created, the Code was expanded with much new legislation and issued in a revised edition in 534. This second edition is the one we have. Even after his codification was completed, Justinian continued to legislate, if with decreasing frequency, although the surviving collections of his 'Novels' are late and unofficial (550s/570s). Despite the size of the Justinianic Corpus, it was still a great deal more compact than the sprawling mass of works that had formed its source material. In the empire, it was soon rendered into Greek, and later recompiled in its turn into the *Basilica* in the ninth century. But the original Latin versions survived in Italy, and became a major focus of study and use from the turn of the first millennium, thus providing the basis for the legal culture of much of Western Europe down to the present age.

Documentary sources

The juristic writings and imperial laws form the bulk of our Roman legal knowledge. But as already noted, they tend to survive only in later forms, so that the earlier the period, the less extensive and reliable the source material. Further, although many legal writings arose in a context of real practice (if with an upper-class bias), their continued existence and use made them 'normative', guides to what should rather than did happen. Surviving contemporary documents, therefore, are a vital complement to the main legal works. As already noted, inscriptions are an important source for *leges* and *senatus consulta* (see chapter 34). Particularly significant is the *Lex Irnitana* from southern Spain, the longest known Latin bronze inscription, and the fullest known version of an identikit municipal charter issued to various cities in Baetica under the Flavians (*AE* 1986.333). This sets out their constitutional and legal arrangements, throwing light on legal procedure in the first century. Also important for this period are tablets from Pompeii and Herculaneum preserved as a result of the eruption of Vesuvius, which provide examples of real litigation documents (e.g. *TPSulp.*; Metzger, *Litigation*, appendix). Throughout the imperial period papyri, principally from Egypt, provide examples of wills, sales and contracts, court transcripts, and even texts that directly match the juristic sources, such as some important passages of Gaius' *Institutes*, which supplement defective parts of the palimpsest, or a rescript (reply by an emperor) of Severus Alexander to the Bithynians known from the *Digest* (XLIX.1.25; *P. Oxy*. XVII 2104; XLIII 3106). Similarly, epigraphy provides an intact text of an edict, of which only short extracts attributed to Constantine appear in the Codes (CTh IX.5.1; CJ IX.8.3; *ARS* no. 302). We can also see how imperial rescripts were used in practice, as with the inscribed copy erected by the villagers of Scaptopara in Thrace of the apparently unhelpful rescript they received from Gordian III (*ARS* no. 287), or the citation in court of a rescript of Constantine a decade after its issue, but not by its original recipient or for its original purpose (*Columbia Papyri* VII no. 175). Even from marginal Britain there is a small number of legal documents, including a land conveyance, a slave sale and a will (*RIB* 2504.29; *Britannia* 34 (2003), 41–51, and 35 (2004), 347–8). Given that our most substantial legal sources are relatively late, the documentary sources help by providing material that contrasts in both type and date, and thus enable a fuller picture to emerge of the Roman legal system in theory and practice.

Further reading:

P. Birks and G. McLeod (trans.), *Justinian's Institutes*, London: Duckworth, 1987.

P. R. Coleman-Norton, *Roman State and Christian Church: A Collection of Legal Documents to AD 535*, London: SPCK, 1966.

G. Comodeca, *Tabulae Pompeianae Sulpiciorum* [*TPSulp.*] (Vetera 12), Rome: Edizioni Quasar, 1999.

M. H. Crawford (ed.), *Roman Statutes* [*RS*] (2 vols, British Institute of Classical Studies Supplement 64) London: Institute of Classical Studies, 1996 – vol. 1 contains *leges* from inscriptions, vol. 2 those from literary/legal sources

J. A. Crook, *Law and Life of Rome*, London: Thames and Hudson, 1967.

W. M. Gordon and O. F. Robinson (trans.), *The Institutes of Gaius*, London: Duckworth, 1988.

T. Honoré, *Emperors and Lawyers* (2nd edn), Oxford: Oxford University Press, 1994.

T. Honoré, *Ulpian* (2nd edn), Oxford: Oxford University Press, 2002.

M. Hyamson (ed. and trans.), *Mosaicarum et Romanarum Legum Collatio*, London: Oxford University Press, 1913; repr. Buffalo: W. S. Hein, 1997.

A. C. Johnson, P. R. Coleman-Norton and F. C. Bourne (trans.), *Ancient Roman Statutes* [*ARS*], Austin: University of Texas Press, 1961; repr. Clark, NJ: Lawbook Exchange, 2003 – includes *leges*, *senatus consulta*, the praetor's edict, and imperial constitutions from inscriptions and papyri.

O. Lenel, *Palingenesia Iuris Civilis*, Leipzig: Bernhard Tauchnitz, 1889; repr. with supplement, Graz: Akademische Druck- und Verlagsanstalt, 1960.

O. Lenel, *Das Edictum Perpetuum* (3rd edn), Leipzig: Bernhard Tauchnitz, 1927.

J. F. Matthews, *Laying Down the Law: A Study of the Theodosian Code*, New Haven: Yale University Press, 2000.

E. Metzger, *Litigation in Roman Law*, Oxford: Oxford University Press, 2005.

C. Pharr (ed.), *The Theodosian Code and Novels and the Sirmondian Constitutions*, Princeton: Princeton University Press, 1952; repr. Union, NJ: Lawbook Exchange, 2001.

J. G. F. Powell and J. A. North (eds), *Cicero's Republic* (*BICS Supplement* 76), London: Institute of Classical Studies, 2001.

S. Riccobono et al., *Fontes Iuris Romani Anteiustiniani* (3 vols., 2nd edn), Florence: S. A. G. Barbèra, 1940–3 – one-stop-shop for pre-Justinianic material (other than the Theodosian Code); contains vol. 1, *Leges*: laws primarily from inscriptions and papyri; vol. 2, *Auctores*: juristic works and fragments; vol. 3, *Negotia*: example documents such as contracts, wills etc.

O. F. Robinson, *The Sources of Roman Law*, London and New York: Routledge, 1997.

G. Rowe, *Princes and Political Cultures: The New Tiberian Senatorial Decrees*, Ann Arbor: University of Michigan Press, 2002.

A. Watson, *Law Making in the Later Roman Republic*, Oxford: Oxford University Press, 1974.

A. Watson (ed.), *The Digest of Justinian* (4 vols), Philadelphia: University of Pennsylvania Press, 1985; rev. 2-vol. paperback, 1998.

59. *Technical Writing*

Alice König

Many surveys of Greek and Latin literature end with a section on technical writing. In so doing, they often give the impression that the extant 'technical' treatises of the ancient world together represent a discrete and homogeneous body of works; few such surveys, however, agree on what should or could be defined as 'technical literature', thereby raising questions about the nature and coherence of that 'genre' even as they summarise it.

All sorts of ancient texts contain technical information, from works of history to poetry, from philosophical treatises to speeches. Very broadly speaking, however, 'technical handbooks' might be loosely defined as texts whose primary (or at least ostensible) purpose is to describe, discuss or teach a specific *technē* ('skill'). Of course, this very general definition potentially includes some medical, mathematical, musical and rhetorical treatises which have already been discussed elsewhere in this companion, and the fact that they have been discussed in chapters of their own offers an important insight into prevailing attitudes to ancient technical writing, for, while many ancient texts could be loosely described as 'technical', the umbrella term 'technical literature' tends to be reserved for the 'handbooks' that are left over when more highly regarded branches of *technē* and learning – like medicine and mathematics – have been dealt with.

Surveys of ancient 'technical literature', then, often bring together texts that have been overlooked by others, presenting them in the process – without always meaning to do so – as marginalia, the remnants of Greek and Latin literature. Many writers have gone on to compound this by dismissing these treatises as stylistically impoverished, even 'unliterary' works; by focusing primarily on their technical discussions and failing, in so doing, to appreciate their social, cultural and political involvement; and by interpreting them, as a result, as straightforwardly functional works, specialised but otherwise uncomplicated instruction manuals to which only like-minded specialists would now ever want to turn. In short, such surveys tend to write ancient 'technical handbooks' off as texts that are to be referenced but not really read.

This chapter aims to encourage a different approach, for it will underline the enormous variety of works which are regularly brought together under the heading 'technical literature'; it will stress their complexity, and the need to read them in greater depth than many have been read to date; and it will also insist on their wider importance for the study of ancient literature and society more generally. With such a huge number of texts to cover, however, it will only be able to touch upon each very briefly.

Agriculture

A range of authors, both Greek and Latin, wrote about agriculture in the ancient world. Hesiod, for example, includes some practical advice on farming in his *Works and Days* (Greek; thought to be c. 700 BC). Virgil's *Georgics* (Latin; c. 29 BC) also appears – at least on the surface – to offer practical instruction on agricultural topics. Few scholars, however, would categorise either work as a 'technical handbook'. Texts which *are* regularly classified as technical 'manuals', though, include

Cato the Censor's *de Agri Cultura* (c. 160 BC); Varro's *de Re Rustica* (c. 37 BC); and Columella's *de Re rustica* (c. AD 60–65).

Cato's *de Agri Cultura* is often cited as our earliest extant example of Latin prose writing. It seems to be addressed to the owner, or overseer, of a small farm, and gives advice on a huge range of issues – from choosing soil and grafting fig trees to keeping weevils out of the grain and letting land to tenants; it focuses in particular on wine and olive oil production. It is striking in part for its unsystematic arrangement, for, although it hints at some organisation in places, advice on the treatment of diseases, the planting of crops, the care of animals and so on are all interspersed almost at random. Further, in addition to offering practical guidance, this text also idealises farm work, turning it (in its opening chapter) into the bravest, most respected and most secure of professions. Although practical in focus, therefore, the treatise touches upon potentially wider issues.

Varro's *de Re Rustica* is addressed to his wife, and discusses agriculture in general (in book I), the rearing of cattle and sheep (book II) and smaller livestock (book III). In contrast to Cato's, it is organised systematically, and casts each separate discussion as a didactic dialogue. Also unlike Cato, Varro sets his work in the context of (and, indeed, in competition with) other writing, for at the beginning of book I he lists a huge number of authors who had apparently also published treatises on agriculture (mainly in Greek), claiming that his handbook will be briefer. This work, then, is not simply another in a long line of agricultural treatises, but one which is conscious of the body of writing that already exists and even intends to improve upon it.

Columella's twelve-book treatise is perhaps the most thorough agricultural manual to survive from antiquity; it is also, however, one of the most perplexing. For, in addition to giving advice on the organisation of the farm, arable cultivation, viticulture, the rearing of animals, fish and game, and so on, it turns, in book X, from prose to poetry, claiming that one of its aims is to 'complete' Virgil's *Georgics*. Thus it not only sets itself alongside other 'technical' writing, but also attempts to compete with – or at least be read in the context of one of – Rome's canonical poets. Like Cato's *de Agri Cultura* and Varro's *de Re Rustica*, this text has long been regarded by most critics as a purely practical handbook; it goes out of its way, however, to test the boundaries of that category of writing.

As both Varro and Columella testify, many other authors wrote about agriculture before them; those authors' works no longer survive. However, a few later treatises are still extant, including part of Gargilius Martialis' *de Hortis* ('On Gardens') and Palladius' *de Re Rustica* (a fifteen-book work, written in the mid-fifth century AD, which uses both Columella and Gargilius Martialis as sources).

Architecture and civil engineering

Vitruvius' *de Architectura* (c. 27 BC) is the only architectural 'handbook' to survive from antiquity (like Varro, Vitruvius mentions a number of earlier works on the subject, but they have all been lost). 'Architectural' is a rather misleading adjective to use in relation to this treatise, for its ten books cover much more than what we would think of as 'architecture' today, from town-planning and public building to the water-supply, astronomy, and civil and military machinery. It is dedicated to Octavian, and promises him in its preface that it will support him in his own building work by enabling him to inform himself about buildings which have already been completed and ones which may be begun in the future. It does much more than that, however, for not only is it encyclopedic in its coverage (as it claims, it brings all aspects of the 'discipline' together within its pages), but it also elevates architecture above all other 'sciences' and exalts architects over every other profession. This is another competitive treatise, in other words, which is concerned as much with self-promotion as it may be with practical instruction.

Like the *de Architectura*, Sextus Julius Frontinus' *de Aquis* (c. AD 98) is unique: nothing like it survives from antiquity. This short treatise constitutes an account of the construction and administration of Rome's water-supply system from the origins of the city to Frontinus' day, and some critics argue that it is more of an administrative than a technical treatise, since it focuses more upon management issues than it does on hydraulic engineering. Its author claims to have written it when he was appointed *curator aquarum* (officer in charge of the water-supply) in order to instruct himself – not others – about his new post. However, it was clearly written at least for the attention, if not for the benefit, of a wider readership than Frontinus claims, and for that reason is a much more complicated text than it appears at first glance. Indeed, in the process of discussing the management of Rome's aqueduct network, this 'handbook' appears to explore the rhetoric and currency of specialised know-how, and the nature and appeal of technical writing itself, reflecting on several different aspects of Roman imperial politics as it does so. It has been described in the past as 'one of the driest [works] ever written' (A. T. Hodge, *Roman Aqueducts and Water-Supply*, London: Duckworth, 1992, p. 16); the fascinating games which it plays with knowledge, literature and politics, however, must render it not only interesting but also extremely important for the study of Flavio-Trajanic Rome more generally.

Land surveying

Land surveying was a particularly Roman practice, and a number of Latin technical treatises were written on the subject. These works, which were collected into one edition in the sixth century AD and are now collectively known as the *Corpus Agrimensorum*, were written by a range of authors from the first century AD until the sixth, including Sextus Julius Frontinus, Agennicus Urbicus, Hyginus and Siculus Flaccus. Between them, they discuss the nature, practice and history of land settlement, and some of the works are accompanied by illustrations, which suggests that their primary purpose may have been practical, perhaps even didactic (although it is not clear if all of the illustrations are original). As with many other technical texts, however, they are not all as straightforward or as exclusively technical as they seem. At the same time as outlining the origins of the discipline, the different categories of land, the different types of dispute which a surveyor might come across, and the 'art' of surveying itself, Frontinus' four fragmentary essays on the subject, for example, seem to reflect not only on the difficulties involved in but also perhaps on the ideals (of 'justice' and 'truth') underpinning land measurement, and on the relationship between the rules which they set out and the reality of the terrain which they are supposed to be able to master. These essays at least, in other words, seem to be exploring the rhetoric, as well as setting out some of the principles, of Roman land surveying (in much the same way as the same author's *de Aquis* not only explained but also explored its own subject and presentation).

Mechanics

Up to this point, the technical handbooks under discussion have all been Latin. That is not because no such handbooks were written in Greek but rather because many Greek technical treatises have been lost. However, a significant number of Greek works on mechanics survive (see chapter 54). The 'Peripatetic' *Mēchanica* (c. 280 BC), which is sometimes (though probably wrongly) ascribed to Aristotle, is one of the earliest of these. It is a largely theoretical work, and it discusses a range of mechanical questions by using the principle of the lever (the principle that the further away from an object the lifting force is, the smaller the force needed) as its paradigm. Ctesibius, who invented a number of devices including a pump, the first accurate water-clock and a military catapult, wrote what is thought to have been the first work on pneumatics in antiquity (c. 270 BC), but this is no longer extant. A number of Archimedes' works survive, however. Archimedes (c. 287–212 BC) became well known in antiquity for a series of ground-breaking inventions (which included the war machines used against the Romans during the siege of Syracuse, and the water screw), but most of his literary output had a more mathematical bent; one mechanical treatise of his which does survive, though, is his *Method of Mechanical Theorems*, which discusses his method for finding the areas and volumes of shapes like the parabola and sphere by mechanical, as opposed to mathematical, means. Philon of Byzantium (fl. c. 200 BC), meanwhile, brought all sorts of aspects of mechanics together in an encyclopedic work on the subject. Only three of a possible nine books survive intact: book IV, which discusses the construction of military catapults; book V (which survives only in Arabic), on siphons and other pneumatic devices; and book VIII, on other types of war and siege machinery.

As Archimedes' work underlines in particular, many of these mechanical treatises have considerable overlaps with some of the mathematical writing which has been examined in chapter 54. Some of them also overlap with a subcategory of 'technical handbooks' which this chapter will look at next – military treatises – for, in addition to Philon, Biton (third or second century BC) wrote a short treatise on the construction of war machines (in particular, catapults, scaling ladders and siege towers), and, as noted above, Vitruvius also discussed military machinery in the final book of his *de Architectura*. Finally, Heron of Alexandria (fl. c. AD 60) touched on both mathematics and military machinery in his writings, which include a work on pneumatics (*Pneumatica*), one on theatrical automata (*On Automata-Making*), a treatise on the 'dioptra' (a measuring instrument) (*Dioptra*), a work on the construction of military catapults (*Belopoeica*), several works on geometry (not all of which are now thought to have been by him), and one three-book treatise on the general principles of mechanics (*Mēchanica*), which survives only in Arabic.

In the process of writing on similar subjects, many of these authors engaged with and responded to each other in their treatises, and for this reason they are often studied alongside each other. It is not just other mechanical writings which these texts interact with, however. We have already seen that some of Archimedes' output, for example, lies at the interface between mathematics and mechanics (this is true also of a much later mathematician, Pappus of Alexandria (fl. c. AD 320), who writes about mechanics in his collection of treatises on mathematical sciences). Recent research on the output of Heron of Alexandria, meanwhile, has revealed that in addition to engaging with earlier mechanical writings, he sets his work in a competitive relationship to a range of other disciplines, in particular to contemporary philosophy. Far from being narrowly focused, therefore, many of these treatises – like so many other so-called 'technical handbooks' – set their discussions in wider contexts and must consequently be studied not in a mechanical vacuum but rather in relation to the cultural, social and political backgrounds with which they engaged.

Warfare

As Brian Campbell notes (Campbell, 'Teach yourself how to be a general'), ancient military manuals tend to fall into two categories: technical accounts of drills and weaponry, and strategic handbooks. We have already met a number of works which fall into the former category: the military books of Philon, Biton, Vitruvius and Heron. Others include Aeneas Tacticus' *Poliorcētica* ('On Siege-craft', written in the mid-fourth century BC); Asclepiodotus' *Tactica* (first century BC), which discusses the organisation and disposition of the ideal phalanx; the Greek *Tactica* of Aelianus (first–second century AD), which discusses, among other things, the different subdivisions of the phalanx, the arrangement of infantry troops, the use of chariots and elephants, and marching formations; and Arrian's *Tactica* (c. AD 130), which analyses weapons and equipment, troop formations, battle manoeuvres, marching formations, and techniques for giving orders successfully.

Onasander's treatise on 'generalship' (the *Stratēgicos*, which was written c. AD 50) falls more neatly into the second category, offering guidance, as it does, on the character and qualities required in a successful commander. Similary, Frontinus' late first-century AD *Stratēgēmata* (as its title implies) is more 'strategic' than technical. This treatise is one of only two extant military manuals written in Latin, and it sets out hundreds of examples of successful military stratagems, from both Greek and Roman history, in order, it claims, to furnish future army commanders with inspiration and support. Polyaenus' *Stratēgēmata* (c. AD 162) also presents a huge array of successful military stratagems, although it arranges them in a rather more random fashion than Frontinus. Vegetius' *Epitoma Rei Militari* (c. AD 383; the other extant Latin military 'handbook'), meanwhile, collates information taken from several of these authors (in particular, Frontinus, and also a lost work on warfare by the elder Cato), and discusses the responsibilities of a commander (specifically: maintaining discipline and morale, keeping order, organising a camp, planning the campaign, preparing tactical manoeuvres, and using stratagems).

Campbell argues that most of these texts had a primarily practical purpose: to provide practical guidance, perhaps even training, for army commanders. However, he also acknowledges that some may have had other aims too: 'Partly they were intended to entertain – the ancient concept of a textbook was certainly not like ours' (p. 27). Even this acknowledgement only scratches the surface of this body of writing, though, for in addition to teaching and/or entertaining, many engaged with political and literary issues, as so many other technical treatises seem to have done. Aelianus' *Tactica*, for example, reflects on Roman military supremacy over the Greeks; Vegetius' *Epitoma* epitomises existing epitomes, and also ponders on the relevance of ancient paradigms for fourth-century Roman military activities; and Frontinus' *Stratēgēmata* (which teases out its relationship to another of Frontinus' texts, now lost, the *de Re Militari*) plays games with didactic literature, ancient history-writing, and the Roman ideal of military 'disciplina'. Like the agricultural, architectural, gromatic (i.e. land surveying) and mechanical 'handbooks' of antiquity, then, the body of military writing that survives is more complex, more varied, and in need of closer reading than many scholars to date have appreciated.

Encyclopedias

Several of the works which we have looked at in the course of this survey have had 'encyclopedic' ambitions: Vitruvius' *de Architectura*, for example, attempts to bring all intellectual disciplines under the umbrella of architecture; Philon's work on mechanics, too, seems to have been encyclopedic in its scope, in the sense that it tries to bring together *all* aspects of mechanics. Perhaps the most impressive 'encyclopedia' of antiquity, however, is Pliny the elder's *Naturalis Historia*, a thirty-seven-book compendium of all contemporary knowledge about the animal, vegetable and mineral worlds. It is not an encyclopedia as we might define one today (that is, a reference book which one can look up all sorts of different facts in), but it certainly contains a lot of factual information (on agriculture, medicine, the techniques of metallurgy and so on), and has consequently been much referenced by all sorts of historians in search of such data, in particular specifically technical data. For that reason, although it does not focus on one particular *technē*, it tends to find itself dumped at the end of surveys of ancient technical writing, because surveyors are not quite sure what else to do with it. It is appropriate that this survey does end with this text, though, for it vividly dramatises one important feature of all sorts of 'technical' and knowledge-based writing, and that is its concern not simply to pass on but also to experiment with the organisation and presentation of knowledge: for in the process of detailing thousands of facts and figures, this text teases its readers with their inaccessibility, with their relationship to each other, with the question of what they all add up to when brought together, and engages in the process with Roman imperial 'encyclopedic' activities (on the physical and political, rather than the intellectual, level).

Pliny the Elder's *Naturalis Historia*, in other words, drives home the point that apparently technical works may be much more than they seem, invariably require closer scrutiny than critics have tended to assume, and can offer fascinating and important insights into the worlds in which they were composed. Further, it underlines the fact that, although this encyclopedic *Edinburgh Companion* appears to organise its various sections on purely objective, practical criteria, it too presents its material in subjective, sometimes loaded, sometimes prejudiced ways: technical writing comes last among texts and genres yet again, but it is to be hoped that as these treatises are studied in greater depth, the genre itself, as well as the individual works, will be re-evaluated.

Further reading

B. Campbell, 'Teach yourself how to be a general', *Journal of Roman Studies* 77 (1987), 13–29.

B. Campbell, *The Writings of the Roman Land Surveyors: Introduction, Text, Translation and Commentary* (Journal of Roman Studies Monographs 9), London: Roman Society, 2000.

S. Cuomo, 'Divide and rule: Frontinus and Roman land-surveying', *Studies in the History and Philosophy of Science* 31 (2000), 189–202.

A. G. Drachmann, *The Mechanical Technology of Greek and Roman Antiquity: A Study of the Literary Sources*, Copenhagen: Munksgaard; Madison: University of Wisconsin Press, 1963.

M. Formisano, *Tecnica e scrittura: Le letterature tecnico-scientifiche nello spazio letterario tardolatino*, Rome: Carocci, 2001.

P. Gros, *Le Projet de Vitruve: objets, destinaires et réception du* De Architectura (Collection de l'école française de Rome, vol. 192), Rome, 1994.

J. F. Healy, *Pliny the Elder on Science and Technology*, Oxford: Oxford University Press, 1999.

J. Henderson, 'Columella's living hedge: the roman gardening book', *Journal of Roman Studies* 92 (2002), 110–33.

E. W. Marsden, *Greek and Roman Artillery: Technical Treatises*, Oxford: Oxford University Press, 1971.

C. Nicolet, (ed.), *Les Littératures techniques dans l'antiquité romaine: status, public et destination, tradition* (Fondation Hardt, Entretiens sur l'Antiquité classique 42), Geneva, 1996.

C. Santini, and N. Scivoletto (eds), *Prefazioni, prologhi, proemi di opere tecnico-scientifiche latine,* vols I and II, Rome: Herder, 1990, 1992.

Part Four: Essential Information and Systems of Reference

This part of the Companion aims to introduce the reader to some fundamentals which underlie all discussions of the classical world: the Greek and Latin alphabets, for example; ancient naming systems; the ancient calendar; and ancient weights and measures. Scholars writing in their own fields often refer to or use such systems in passing, assuming a knowledge of them which the student is far from likely to have. As well as demystifying the iambic trimeter and the Roman trinominal system, the section aims to give some sense of the historical development of names, of the calendar, of political institutions and so on. There is also a series of time-charts, which list the major monarchic lines of antiquity, from Persian kings to Roman emperors, and provide 'spot dates' for important events from the political to the cultural, not only across antiquity, but into the present day (the latter illustrate the reception of classical culture, and the history of classical studies, for example). A glossary of ancient and modern terms is designed to help with the more detailed aspects of the present work, and to be of wider use; and the list of abbreviations will allow the student to navigate the world of journals, reference collections and scholarly editions which lie concealed behind scholarly acronyms.

60. Politics

Edward Bispham

'Politics; from *poly* = many and *tics* = parasites.' (trad.)

The Political Animal

Politics today can be defined as the way power is acquired, structured and applied (also the ways in which power is extended into social relations, e.g. sexual politics). This includes the establishment of institutions for the administrative needs of the community (legislation, justice, foreign relations etc). Politics also covers the positions adopted by individuals on questions related to the running of the community; how individuals and groups achieve their goals without recourse to violence; the actions of those in government and in opposition to the government; and attempts to gain public support for those actions. More broadly, politics is the establishment or validation of modes of group or individual behaviour, and the regulation of disputes between social groups. Finally, politics refers to the study of these phenomena (or political science).

Ancient politics must be understood equally broadly. For Aristotle, famously, man was a *politikon zōon*, a political animal (*Pol.* 1252b9–53a39): what distinguished man from other animals was that he alone lived in a polis, a community. Political theory debated the good life for citizens of this community, its best constitution, and its best citizen. Aristotle's *Politics* (probably meant to be read after his *Nichomachean Ethics*) explicitly sought to examine how by living in a polis man might fulfil his proper end (*telos*), and achieve *eudaimonia* (happiness).

Greek politics (*ta politika*) were all those things pertaining to the life of the polis: administration, justice, disputes over policy and competition for office. Yet the Greek term for 'constitution' (*politeia*) also meant citizenship, and the life of citizen and community in the broadest sense; ancient writers frequently stress how it is the community, i.e. the citizens, that constitutes the polis, not the physical fabric of the city. Indeed, consideration of any ancient community must include its rural territory as well as the urban centre(s); different forms of exploitation of, and settlement in, the landscape are closely related to the character of the political institutions of the communities in question (Osborne, *Classical Landscape with Figures*, pp. 113–36, 193–7). City and countryside do not mean much without their inhabitants, or without each other.

Most of our material for the study of ancient politics is from watching it 'in action' in the historical and oratorical texts. There are also theoretical discussions by philosophers (Plato, Aristotle; and Cicero) and descriptions of the political systems of individual communities (Polybius for Rome; the *Athēnaiōn Politeia* attributed to Aristotle for Athens; Xenophon's *Lakedaimoniōn Politeia* for Sparta). Note that Aristotle's theories engage with current practice, and how heavily influenced Polybius is by earlier theoretical analyses. As ever, much is missing: almost all the polis constitutions written for Aristotle are lost; and despite all the ancient (largely elite) discussions of democracy, ranging from the critique of the Old Oligarch to Attic drama, no ancient theory of democratic politics was ever formulated, for example. Finally, from the seventh century onwards, we possess inscribed laws (see also chapters 34, 57 and 58), although these tend to concentrate as much on procedure (who could do what when) and regulating elite competition as on substance (what is and what is not allowed).

Ancient writers on politics were preoccupied with political *stability*. This reflects the fact that class conflict (*stasis*, which can denote anything from political unrest to open civil war: see Thuc. 3.82 for the classic discussion of extreme *stasis* on Corcyra) was endemic in the ancient world. The long-term stability of Athens, Sparta and Rome should not lead us to underestimate tensions there: constitutional change was regular and controversial: the *Ath. Pol.* (*Constitution of the Athenians*) 41 lists eight major constitutional turning points in Athens in the sixth and fifth centuries alone. Most other communities regularly flip-flopped between constitutions.

Here, the extent to which power was concentrated or shared out was the crucial variable: rule could be exercised by the one, the few or the many. Hence the differing political organisations of the ancient world: democracies (classical Athens, Syracuse), oligarchies (e.g. Massilia, Corinth, and to a degree republican Rome) and absolute rule (Greek tyrants, Hellenistic kings, Roman emperors). Much political conflict within communities was defined by the dynamic of oscillation between these positions, as individuals, narrow groups and the masses sought to (re)gain or defend a dominant position (Arist. *Pol.* 1310a3–10). Some class conflict was instrumental, a struggle by the poor to improve their lot. This is reflected, for instance, in a desire on the part of the poor for war, and the rich for peace (eg Ar. *Eccl.* 197–8); the latter claimed that the former took irresponsible decisions as they had little or nothing to lose. In archaic Athens and Rome, the poor sought escape from debt, or debt-bondage, and land-hunger (see Pl. *Leg.* 648d–e, 736c–e for the rallying calls). In extreme cases we witness the expulsion of the leaders (and even supporters) of one group by another, and even mass murder, as at Argos in 370 BC (Diod. Sic. 15.58).

The constant fear of 'regime change' is reflected in two interesting phenomena. The first is the obsession of ancient theorists with the 'mixed constitution', one which, by combining elements of the three core types of constitution (monarchy, oligarchy and democracy), prevented alternation between them, thus engendering political stability. Communities admired for their mixed constitutions were Sparta and Rome; Polybius (book 6) developed the theory of the mixed constitution as applied to Rome, propounding a theory of cyclical change between constitutions (*anacyclōsis*), and suggested how Rome had, temporarily at least, extracted itself from the cycle. Polybius' theorising, however, ignored some areas which modern scholars have seen as crucial to Roman politics, such as the structural advantages enjoyed by the nobility within Roman society (see also chapter 18).

The second area, also reflecting the traditional nature of ancient societies, is praise of the past, and its power as a legitimating force in the present. Statesmen of all persuasions, from democrat to autocrat, disguised reforms as a return to the ancestral constitution (Greek *patrios politeia*), or by reference to the practice of earlier generations (Latin *mos maiorum*); opponents sought to undermine proposals by demonstrating that they were revolutionary and *new*. Continuity was thus important as a framework for managing even radical change; yet continuity was whatever the speaker wanted it to be on the day; the interpretation of the past, and thus of the present to which it had given rise, lay in the hands of the powerful, not of the masses, and was often used to resist, rather than effect, change. The appeal to the past can be linked to two further points. One is the emphasis by autocrats (and aristocratic families, especially in Rome) on dynastic legitimacy, where the quality of the ancestors validated the current generation. The other is the lack of any objectively fixed content to the *patrios politeia* or *mos maiorum*. Something similar can be observed in the flexible and contingent nature of political slogans. Thus *isonomia* in Athens meant equality before and through the law to democrats, but power-sharing restraint to oligarchs; in Rome *libertas* meant free and open competition for real power to aristocrats, but freedom from arbitrary and autocratic rule to the masses. The slipperiness of these terms was noted, for example, by Thucydides and Sallust.

Phenomena and epiphenomena

Discussion of ancient politics is in danger of falling between two stools: of failing to do justice both to the broad similarities and differences between societies across time, and to the enormous variety of constitutional arrangements and political processes. Before we look at three major political systems (Athens, Graeco-Roman Egypt and Rome, below), let us consider the broader picture.

First, variety: this can be illustrated by magisterial titulature, often recorded in official documents, and in the Roman world on tombstones (see also chapter 34). Cretan cities had chief magistrates called *kosmoi*; *aisymnētēs* is the title of chief magistrates in many East Greek cities, but also in Megara; and inland Arcadian cities like Orchomenos and Mantinea had *thearoi*; but the magistracy is also found on the Aegean islands of Thasos and Ceos. And each individual city had various magistracies (from early on, see *SEG* 30. 380 for archaic Tiryns); in Hellenistic Italy we see the supplementing of indigenous magistracies like the Oscan *meddíss tuvtiks* with specialised officials modelled on Roman ones: for example, the Roman censor appears as the Oscan *kenstur*. On the other hand, new political conditions could bring standardisation. Under the Roman Empire, local magistracies persist not only in the Greek East, but also in the form of the Punic *suffes* and the Celtic *vergobret*; yet in the communities of the western Empire we find mostly one or more pairs of magistrates exercising judicial and executive functions.

Recent studies of ancient politics have moved away from the study of institutions, towards ideologies of power and the discourses which expressed them. Magisterial titles are in one sense *epiphenomena*, that is, they rest on the surface of political phenomena, and in themselves give scant indication of the contexts in which they functioned, which are far more important. Despite the diversity noted above, some underlying common threads can be picked out.

Control could be exercised by a number of institutional means (as well as by intimidation or bribery); annual magistracies formed only a part of the political anatomy. Equally important were the council and popular assembly, which together with the magistrates (the executive) were common, in various permutations, to almost all ancient societies; even autocrats, with their courtiers and retinues, could not do without administrative organs (magistrates and council). The strength of these elements varied from place to place, reflecting local political dynamics.

Although scholars tend, especially in Greek history, to take the independent polis or city-state as the fundamental unit of political analysis, the politics of conquest and international relations created political machinery operating on a number of different, sometimes overlapping, scales. Indeed, the question of scale may be properly asked of city-states themselves: what makes a polis a polis? When is a community not a polis? And why? The second century AD Greek traveller Pausanias was indignant that Phocian Panopeus could be called a polis (10.4.1), lacking public buildings and amenities (he ignores its impressive fortifications). Yet a polis it was: it had an independent political existence. The high populations of classical Athens and of Hellenistic cities like Alexandria, Antioch and Rome were atypical. The major cities numbered a few dozen, but there were some four or five hundred much smaller communities like Panopeus, which enjoyed political independence at one time or another, had political institutions, a citizen body, and aristocrats in competition for magistracies, and claim the title of polis (see Hansen and Nielsen, *An Inventory of Archaic and Classical Poleis*).

Two aspects of this vast spectrum of communities are problematic: one is the 'cut-off' point at the bottom. Take the example of the tiny community excavated at Vroulia on the southern tip of Rhodes: it was delimited by a wall, outside which lay the cemetery, containing the burials of some 120 individuals, spanning roughly the period 625–575 BC, and a sanctuary; within the walled area were another sanctuary and two straight parallel streets onto which opened at least fifty rooms, configured into house plots in various ways. Nothing is known of its administration, or its brief history. Polis or not? Whatever the answer, in the majority of communities in the Greek world, from Spain to the Black Sea, politics operated in a context not much more substantial than that represented by Vroulia. The 6,000 citizens who constituted a quorum (mininum level of attendance needed for business to proceed) for some assemblies at Athens represent a gross deviation from the norm of Greek politics.

The second problem is the tendency of polis-centred writers to police entitlement to polis status, and to push onto the 'sidelines' other types of communal organisation which did not fit squarely into the (self-defined) polis model. This mainly affects inland or geographically 'marginal' parts of old Greece, which were organised (probably only from the classical period) into federal leagues (see also chapter 17). Here, constituent communities submerged their individual autonomy to create larger political entities with federal magistrates, council and assembly. Greek writers characterised such areas as *ethnē*, and the term 'tribal' is sometimes used to describe their political organisation, connoting for us, as *ethnos* did for writers like Thucydides, backwardness and dispersed settlement. While areas like Aetolia and Arcadia clearly fell into the *ethnos* category, other cases were less clear cut: Boeotia contained about a dozen poleis of different sizes, but from the sixth century onwards passed through repeated federal episodes, with communities represented in proportion to their size in the federal institutions. This allowed Thebes, the largest Boeotian polis, to dominate the federal structure and thus the smaller cities.

Certainly the areas of Greece characterised by the *ethnos* label were not consistently organised into more or less stable territorial blocks, centred on a single polis to which smaller settlements are subordinated. It is, perhaps, no coincidence that of the 150-odd 'constitutions' attributed to Aristotle, of which only the Athenian survives, few concern communities from the *ethnos* areas, though Punic Carthage *was* included (Arist. *Pol.* 1272b24–1273b26); similar ideas may underlie Polybius' treatment of kingdoms. Yet much written in ancient sources about these areas is prejudice: some of their communities were, from the Geometric or early archaic periods, large central places with monumental buildings, complex social and economic organisation, law codes and high art; they seem to have passed through the same struggles as the rest of archaic Greece (and for that matter Rome), whereby the community gradually asserted its values and power over those of aristocrats (see also chapters 15 and 16). Their conceptions of themselves, however, allowed two (or more) different levels of political identity, the local and the regional, to co-exist more easily than in poleis (where broader identities like 'Dorian' and 'Ionian' were nevertheless manipulated beside polis ones). The understanding of Greek politics needs to take into account interlocking levels of identity which transcended those of the community of origin.

The polis model, nevertheless, works for much of the non-Greek Mediterranean, within limits: the East coast of Spain, Western Italy and North Africa, for example. Yet, despite the proliferation of Greek cities in the East after Alexander, the city-state represents only one form of political organisation: it existed beside villages and temple estates (see also chapter 12). Further, Greek cities (and even leagues) had to accommodate themselves to the Hellenistic kingdoms. The problem of how to conduct political life safely but without complete surrender of autonomy was not unique to the Greek cities of the Hellenistic period, but persisted after the kingdoms were absorbed into the Roman Empire (see also chapters 19 and 20).

The politics of subject cities have sometimes been viewed as not worth study, since no real power resided in the cities themselves; and the politics of the Roman Principate have been termed 'paltry' (Finley, *Politics in the Ancient World*, p. 117) because of the end of real popular participation. This misses the point. Political life in the subject cities hardly bored the inhabitants, to judge from the epigraphic record (see also chapter 34 of this volume), or from the burgeoning rhetorical culture of the Second Sophistic. Indeed, politics in cities under the Roman Empire posed unusually complicated dilemmas for the elites of the Greek East, aware both of their glorious political heritage and of being subjects of the Caesars: reconciling these two political imperatives was a considerable challenge (see Finley, *Politics in the Ancient World*, p. 52f., citing Plut. *Mor.* 813d-e). Equally, the politics of autocracy are not uninteresting because secrecy characterised decision-making at the highest levels. Our sources (such as Tacitus, unduly influential here – see also chapter 50) reflect major changes in political methods: autocracies take decisions privately and unaccountably. Yet the particular conditions of imperial politics (the threat of imperial displeasure or tyranny, and the 'double-speak' of political discourse, as well as the lack of opportunity for taking decisions which really mattered) did not deter wealthy, ambitious and even able figures from all corners of the empire from seeking political advancement which would put them, or their descendents, in the Roman Senate. Traditional thirst for distinction and power still fuelled political ambition.

Finally, typical vs. atypical: we are unusually well-informed about political developments in Roman and Athens. For other states our evidence is patchy: there is little of it and its chronological distribution is uneven. The Roman consulship illustrates the dangers of reading too much into too little. Two elected 'ordinary' consuls, the supreme Roman magistrates following the expulsion of the kings, entered office on 1 January every year (with brief intermission in times of crisis, when a dictator was elected, and replaced between 444 and 367 BC by another magistracy with consular powers) until AD 527. The longevity of the consulship masks huge changes in its powers and function: it was, at various times, the instrument of patrician domination; the pinnacle of influence and power for the patricio-plebeian nobility of the Republic; weakened under Augustus; and largely ceremonial from the later third century AD onwards with the prolonged absences of emperors from Rome. In the case of most other cities the known points of institutional and political history are scattered across time: do they represent change or continuity? The evidence is bitty and heterogeneous; yet historians still try to join up the few surviving dots to make a picture, often guesswork and pseudo-history. Let us now look briefly at three of the cases where we can say something with confidence.

Democratic Athens

In the archaic period Athens was ruled by a closed circle of aristocratic families (the Eupatridae), who competed to be elected one of the nine *archōns* (the eponymous (see also chapter 64), the *basileus* and the polemarch; and six *thesmothetai* or junior *archōns*); after a year as archōn came life membership of the aristocratic council, the Areopagus. As elsewhere in archaic Greece, aristocrats from outside the ruling circle increasingly demanded more power, leading to *stasis*. In 594 BC Solon was elected eponymous *archōn*, to deal with political tension as well as socio-economic problems. He broke the existing monopoly on political power, substituting wealth for birth as the criterion for office, probably gave more power to the Assembly and instituted a council to prepare its business (a procedure known as *probouleusis*). Although later Athenians often looked on him as the father of democracy, he neither ended political competition between aristocrats nor reduced the power of the archonship and Areopagus over the people. Competition culminated in some fifty years of tyranny, after which (508 BC) another aristocrat, Cleisthenes, cut the Gordian knot of aristocratic squabbling by giving substantial power to the people: this was democracy (whatever Cleisthenes' intentions at the time).

Cleisthenes created ten new tribes, which eclipsed the four traditional ones; each tribe drew its membership from new geographical divisions (*trittyes* or thirds) of Attica: coast, inland and city (i.e. Athens and environs). Thus each tribe represented a cross-section of Athenian society. At the core of the system, carefully grouped into tribes via the *trittyes* (thus ensuring equality of size and geographical diversity), were the demes, the villages of Attica. Every Athenian's membership of his deme was hereditary, whether he lived there or not; it was at deme level that his citizenship was confirmed, and in the deme assemblies that many had their first taste of politics; after Cleisthenes the official name (see also chapter 61) of each Athenian as recorded in public documents was 'x of deme y', rather than 'x son of z'. The demes were tied directly to the centre of politics via the new council (the *boulē*) of 500 (50 from each tribe), with which Cleisthenes replaced the old council of 400. Demes contributed, in proportion to their size, the members of this crucial feature of the democracy. The *boulē* represented all of Attica, its members were chosen by lot, and they could only serve twice, which meant that many Athenians would at one time or another sit on the council. Cleisthenes thus made the countryside an integral part of the democracy. As deme members Athenians had access to the privileges and responsibilities of the polis. In polis contexts, whether in the army or the major dramatic festivals, they were representatives of their tribe.

Cleisthenes' complicated reforms undermined traditional loyalties by mixing up Attica, and allowing new ways of imagining the political community; the losers were the aristocratic families. Other archaic poleis combined tribal and territorial reform with political change: Corinth, Sicyon (under Cleisthenes' grandfather) and Cyrene. What seems to be unique in the Athenian case is the power of the *ekklēsia*, which made the people (*dēmos*) the winners. Further reforms in the 460s and 450s pushed Athens along the road to radical democracy: stripping the Areopagus of most of its powers, with corresponding increases in the power of the Assembly, *boulē* and jury-courts (*dikastēria*), and then introducing pay for the juries; all candidates for all offices were scrutinised for suitability beforehand (*dokimasia*) and had to account for their tenure at the end of the year (*euthunē*).

It seems that from the outset Cleisthenes intended the Assembly to be stronger than the magistrates and the council. Even the introduction (in 501 BC) of important new magistrates, the ten *stratēgoi* or generals, one from each tribe, with military and civic responsibilities, did not weaken the hand of the Assembly. The generalship remained an elective office, while the archōnship became sortitive (chosen by lot); generals could also hold office in consecutive years, and build up prestige through success. They might be given privileged access to council or assembly, and co-operate with the former in introducing motions in wartime. Their role changed in the fourth century, with growing specialisation in both war and politics. The punishment (sometimes with death) of generals by the Assembly for failing to carry out the wishes of the *dēmos* shows, however, who had the whip hand; even Pericles was rejected at the polls after years in office, and fined, before the *dēmos* relented (Thuc. 2.65.2–4).

The *ecclēsia* met forty times a year, with extra meetings in emergencies. There were mandatory agenda items, which came up at particular meetings. The first meeting (called the *kuria ecclēsia*) of each prytany (the year was divided into ten prytanies; see also chapter 64), for example, discussed whether to depose any of the current magistrates, the corn supply and national security; lists of confiscated property and of heiresses were read; informers could be censured or accusations of treachery made. The *ecclēsia*'s agenda was prepared by the *boulē*, which introduced matters for discussion and proposals for the vote (*probouleumata*); matters not on the agenda could not be discussed, but the *ecclēsia* was sovereign (even 'unlimited' powers sometimes given to generals and envoys were delegated from the Assembly), and always debated and voted on contentious and important policy; on routine, uncontroversial matters the *boulē* would sometimes give the *ecclēsia* a steer. Discussion in the Assembly was open to anyone (the principle of *isēgoria*), and amendments could be proposed; private citizens might also propose a motion asking the *boulē* to bring a *probouleuma* at a later stage, often for honorific decrees.

Within these parameters the fifth-century assembly was able 'to do what ever it wished' (Xen. *Hell.* 1.7.12); it is sometimes argued that it became less sovereign in the fourth century, and that popular rule mutated into the rule of the laws (*nomoi*), which became fixed, and had greater power than the decrees or *psēphismata* of the people. This distinction does come in after the codification of Athens' laws in the late fifth century, yet it seems hard to sustain the view that this made Athens somehow less democratic than it had been: the codification and the new procedures were designed to *protect* the democracy after two oligarchic coups (411 and 404 BC); participation remained wide, at both polis and deme level. In the fifth century, laws could be proposed by *probouleuma* of the council, or as amendments in the *ecclēsia*; in the fourth century, this became impossible. Under the later system the *thesmothetai* had to make an annual review of the laws and flag up contradictions; the resolution of these was the job of a special assembly (Aeschin. 3.38–40). By a cumbersome process, laws could in the fourth century be changed: the old laws were read out once a year, and, if any were not approved again, new laws could be proposed and voted on in a special legislative assembly (that of the *nomothetai*).

The assembly was sovereign, but it could not have operated without the *boulē*, which prepared its business, drafting decrees without trying to predetermine the outcome of debate: when the Four Hundred oligarchs in 411 BC wanted to disable the democracy they dismissed the *boulē* and replaced it themselves, rather than trying to impose constitutional restrictions on the power of the Assembly; Alcibiades equally insisted on the restoration of the *boulē* and the dissolution of the Four Hundred, saying nothing about the Assembly (Thuc. 8.86.6). The *boulē* had oversight of many areas of public business, from annual review of the (elite) cavalry to monitoring the outcome of the Assembly's orders for trireme building. It cooperated in most of the routine work of the magistrates, and generally coordinated the running of the city; it received overseas envoys; and it had some punitive powers. The terms of service and the complete turnover of personnel every year made it impossible for the council to develop its own corporate identity (as the Roman Senate did). It sat every day except for festivals; each of the ten monthly presidencies fell to one of the tribal contingents of fifty, who were in residence throughout their prytany; they summoned the full *boulē* when necessary, and the *ecclēsia*. Any citizen (and for that matter any foreign envoy) could approach the *boulē* and ask for particular measures to be put on the agenda; not all proposals had to be put on the agenda: the *boulē* had a duty to stop illegal proposals being made.

Athens had hundreds of annual *archai* or magistracies, many of them paid, and most open to and (apparently) held by ordinary Athenians. Most, from the superintendents of dockyards to the magistrates who oversaw festivals, such as the *hieropoioi*, were chosen by lot (Arist. *Pol.* 1365b30–31); many operated as boards of ten (one from each tribe). Finance was an area of particular complexity, with a number of boards operating in a highly atomised way, each with very specific areas of competence (and all accepting or disbursing monies as ordered by the Assembly); the complexity of financial management worked both to decrease fraud, and to encourage the spread of power from the few to the many (a basic reason for the proliferation of Athenain *archai*). In the later fourth century some important financial officials began to be *elected*: a military treasurer and the overseer of the 'theoric' fund. Originally this was set up to pay for citizens to view spectacles, but it quickly came to control peacetime revenues. Lycurgus held a powerful financial office in the last years of the democracy; it effectively ran public revenues, having some oversight, for example, of fiscal boards like the *pōletai* (sellers) and *apodektai* (receivers); despite limits on re-election, Lycurgus seems one way or another to have controlled Athens' revenues for twelve years. All magistrates who handled public money were audited by *logistai*, with further oversight by the *boulē* (where the buck probably stopped when it came to balancing the books). There were also, in the fifth century, a large number of magistrates needed for the running of Athens' empire, whose roles concerned both the collection of the tribute paid to Athens by its subjects, and the maintenance of loyalty and, where they had been imposed, democratic institutions. The *dēmos* took as close an interest in the running of the empire as in that of the polis.

After the reforms of the mid-fifth century, the paid jury courts became important in politics; they heard cases such as the *graphē paranomōn*, an often politically motivated charge against proposers of laws which conflicted with an existing law, or were procedurally flawed or illegal; they also heard charges for treason, fraud and bribery, as well as civil suits. Juries could be over a thousand strong, and were chosen by lot from a panel of 6, 000 citizens; these were paid for their service, and seem from the evidence of Aristophanes often to have been humble and elderly.

The democracy was dissolved as a punishment for Athens' revolt from Macedonian overlordship after Alexander's death, and was never fully reinstituted, although many institutions, such as the ten tribes and the *archōns*, survived unaltered for centuries.

Ptolemaic and Roman Egypt

The wealth of papyrological evidence on Egypt, especially from the reign of Ptolemy II onwards, and again in the second and third centuries AD, allows us an unprecedented view of the detailed running of a Hellenistic kingdom, and, later, a Roman province, and to observe the changes brought about in the transition from one to the other, despite an apparently high level of institutional continuity (see also chapter 32). The temporal bias in the distribution of the papyri is matched by a geographical one: most papyri come from the Fayyum region.

Ptolemaic Egypt, a highly centralised 'top-down' system, could not be more different from Athens: in the middle of the third century BC the *dioikētēs* Apollonius wrote to one of his subordinates 'no one has the right to do as he likes' (*P. Tebt.* 703 = Austin, *The Hellenistic World* (1st edn, 1981) no. 256). The Ptolemaic system was only marginally predicated on cities, unlike the neighbouring Seleucid kingdom, for example; more important were the Egyptian temples, which were given donations of land by the king; their power grew as the monarchy weakened, before waning again under Roman control. Another major and unusual element in the socio-political mix of Ptolemaic Egypt was the cleruchs, prisoners of war and Graeco-Macedonian immigrants settled on crown land, who were expected to fight for the king in wartime. Yet above all the Ptolemaic system depended on the control of the villages which formed the main settlement pattern of Egypt, and of the agricultural output of the inhabitants.

The Ptolemaic political economy, if such a term can be applied, was not centrally planned from scratch, but was a centralised system of exploitation in large part inherited from the Pharoahs. The system was complex, and, requiring literacy at all levels, was serviced by scribes, who at village level were local Egyptians (who continued to enjoy religious freedom and their own law codes); overall it required 'an army of officials' (Thompson, 'The Ptolemies and Egypt', p. 111). The aim of the system was partly fiscal, for the king to maximise his revenue from his domains (to this end the Ptolemies began a far-reaching monetarisation of Egypt), and partly for the maintenance of security. The importance of the fiscal motive explains the gradual increase in the power of the king's chief financial officer, the *dioikētēs*, based in Alexandria. Egypt was divided into some forty administrative areas or *nomes*, inherited from the Pharonic setup, with names changed by the Ptolemies. These were subdivided into *topoi* and *kōmai* (villages); they were run by, respectively, nomarchs, toparchs and komarchs. In addition there was a kingdom-wide garrison system run by generals (*stratēgoi*), and there were the cleruchs. Over time power devolved increasingly to the *stratēgoi*, until in the second century their military duties passed to new officials: *epistratēgoi*.

The Ptolemaic exchequer was run by *oikonomoi*, who operated under the auspices of the *dioikētēs*: they collected rents and taxes, trying not to alienate the indigenous peasants, as well as checking that everything, including types of crops grown and numbers of cattle, ran according to a centrally imposed schedule. This in turn was based on a detailed land survey; the *oikonomoi* had to update the documentation where necessary. Besides the collection of taxes the Ptolemies derived substantial revenues from a royal monopoly on oil-producing plants and their processing (this was relaxed in the Roman period), and fixed prices and licences for other types of agriculture and production.

Roman control depoliticised Egypt, moving the centre of power away from Alexandria to Rome, and later Constantinople. Like the Ptolemies, the emperors were interested in assuring Egypt's security, and thus its considerable revenue, as well as the corn supply for the *annona*, or free grain distributions, for Rome. Egypt at once assumed a unique position among Roman provinces. Senators and important members of the equestrian order were banned from entering it without imperial permission; unlike other large provinces it was run by an equestrian *praefectus* who normally held office for three years, had legions at his disposal, and was directly answerable to the *princeps*. Below the prefect were other equestrian procurators, some in posts which were essentially those of the Ptolemaic system, and others in new ones, such as the *iuridicus*, and the powerful controller of the *idios logos* (the personal account of the *princeps*, a restructured Ptolemaic institution, whose remit is known from its code or *Gnomon*, surviving on papyrus).

In Hadrian's reign the *dioikētēs* reappears, now responsible for the agricultural economy; the *epistratēgoi* now have judicial functions; and the whole system is marked by a sharper division between Roman and native officials. At nome level the key positions in tax collection, and in making Roman rule work in general, were those of the *stratēgos* and the Royal Scribe. Under Roman rule nomes acquired capitals (*mētropoleis*) where the administration was based; these communities acquired more magistrates and greater self-government.

These offices were the preserve of the so-called Greek 'gymnasial class'; until the Severan period no *mētropolis* had a *boulē*. At the bottom of the scale were still the *kōmai*, run by the village scribe and the elders. Another important Roman innovation was the transformation of the Ptolemaic liturgy system, mixing voluntary and compulsory liturgies (duties) covering everything from magistracies for the 'gymnasial class' to irrigation construction for the peasants. Egypt's few cities (notably Alexandria), effectively Greek *poleis*, stood outside this system; within the cities, and also outside them, were *politeumata*: under the Ptolemies these had been separate communities for different, often military, ethnic groups. The most famous is that of the Jews, in Alexandria, whose religious privileges and pseudo-public institutions aroused jealousy and even violence from the city's Greek population.

Rome

After the expulsion of the kings in 509 BC, sovereignty passed into the hands of the people, but much power remained with the families on which the kings had drawn for their councils: the patricians. They alone held the priesthoods and magistracies and sat on the Senate, where tenure was for life (only in the late fourth century BC was its membership made subject to review and regulation). The Senate was the advisory council for the magistrates, and its decrees (*senatus consulta*) were issued in response to questions put to it by the presiding magistrate, and took the form of advice. Yet the Senate, partly owing to the influence (*auctoritas*) of ex-magistrates from whom it was largely recruited, was always more powerful than its technical constitutional role would suggest; from the Hannibalic War (218 BC) onwards it became almost supreme within the commonwealth (*res publica*), and its decrees commanded obedience; it, not the priests, mediated between men and gods. The undermining of its authority was co-extensive with the collapse of the Republic. Ironically, under the empire, senatorial decrees gained the force of law which they had never technically possessed before, and the Senate found itself paradoxically less powerful but busier than ever before, for example acting as a court in many high-profile cases, especially treason trials.

The sacral and political functions of the kings were transferred to new positions. Priesthoods were held for life, and until the late Republic (and then again under the empire) were filled by co-option, not election. Magistrates were generally elected in pairs, to serve for one year, although a dictator (appointed in emergency for specific tasks) usually served for six months, and censors – magistrates who conducted the census (and periodic ritual renewal) of the population, as well as regulating the membership of the Senate and letting state contracts – were elected every five years and served for eighteen months. Traditionally the first consuls were elected immediately after the expulsion of the kings, but the reality was probably less tidy. By the middle of the fourth century, the classic magisterial organisation was in place: two consuls, who provided civic and military leadership; two praetors, who had oversight of the judiciary, as well as deputising for the consuls; ten tribunes of the plebeians (ie all those who were not patricians) – not technically magistrates of the Roman people; aediles, who had responsibility for games and festivals, and for the upkeep of the city's infrastructure; and quaestors, whose responsibilities included the treasury, record-keeping, and assisting the consuls on campaign (usually in charge of army pay).

Two important developments mark the magistracies during the Republic. One is the battle fought by the plebeians for political equality with the patricians and an end to the patrician monopoly on power; this is known as the Struggle of the Orders, and lasted over two centuries, until in the early third century the Hortensian law (*lex Hortensia*) guaranteed that resolutions of the plebeian assembly (*plebei scita*, plebiscites) would be treated as equal in validity to laws (*leges*) passed by the whole people (*populus*); this completed a long transition which had slowly seen all the magistracies and priesthoods opened up to plebeian aristocrats. The second development was a gradual increase in the numbers of magistrates within colleges, starting with the appointment of two more praetors in 227 BC to govern Rome's first provinces, Sicily and Sardinia/Corsica. These increases, which affected all regular higher magistracies except the consulship, were one of the few responses which the Romans made to the demands placed on their polis administrative structures by the acquisition of an empire for which they were not designed.

Increasing competition for power, fed by the rapidly expanding profits of empire, led to (180 BC) a regularisation of the magistracies into a formal career path with specified intervals and rules restricting repeated tenure; in 82/81 BC Cornelius Sulla, as dictator, reintroduced these rules, as well as increasing the number of praetors to eight (with extremely important implications for the intensity of competition between ex-praetors for two consulships) and quaestors to twenty. The quaestorship (men became eligible at the age of 30) was the bottom rung of the ladder, followed by the aedileship and the praetorship, and then the consulship, to be held no earlier than three years after the praetorship, at a minimum age of 42; the tribunate could be held by plebeians at any stage, but was generally held before or after the aedileship. This order of magistracies (the cursus honorum) remained fixed into the imperial period, although the minimum ages were lowered for members of the imperial family, and those who satisfied the Augustan marriage legislation by fathering three children, for example. Under Augustus we also find extra consulships introduced, with the 'ordinary' consuls being replaced by 'suffects', at first for six months, then for shorter periods, to allow more men to attain the coveted office.

Magistrates often acted on the 'advice' of the Senate: perhaps most importantly for legislation, where consuls, tribunes or occasionally praetors proposed laws to the popular assemblies, after debate in the Senate. Individual magistrates were expected to seek the *auctoritas patrum*, senatorial sanction, before approaching the people with a legislative bill. Refusal to do so, while not illegal, was highly controversial, as shown in the case of Ti. Gracchus' agrarian law (133 BC), and subsequent popular legislation. Tribunes were perhaps the most likely to clash with senatorial consensus, and could interpose a veto to block political business; this was supposed to operate in the interests of poor plebeians, but many tribunes were aristocrats with conservative sympathies, taking orders from senior figures in the Senate.

Roman assemblies could not meet without a magisterial summons; whether they met to vote for new magistrates or on laws, there could be no discussion of what was before them. Only in trials before the people were opposing arguments heard. No intervention was allowed from the floor, and the only role for the people was to vote for *a* rather than *b* to be elected, or to vote 'yes' or 'no' to a proposed law. There were four assemblies operating under the republic; all used complicated group-voting procedures, rather than a simple majority of hands as in Athens. One, the *comitia curiata*, had by the late republic become a rubber-stamp, with thirty lictors (magistrates' assistants) standing in for the people. In two other assemblies, the *comitia tributa* (tribal assembly) and the *concilium plebis* (plebeian assembly), the voting units were geographical: the four urban and thirty-one rural tribes (after 241 BC). These assemblies passed laws, elected lesser magistrates (tribunes and plebeian aediles could be elected only in the *concilium plebis*, from which patricians were banned), and heard some trials. The fourth assembly was the *comitia centuriata* (assembly of centuries), where votes on war and peace were taken, where alliances were confirmed, where capital cases were tried (until the late Republic, when elite jury courts gradually took over), and where the highest magistrates (consuls and praetors, who were accorded the sacrally imbued power of command, *imperium*) were elected; some legislation also passed through this assembly. The centuries from which this assembly took its name were originally military units, but they evolved to become voting units spread across five property-classes, in such a way that the rich not only held a numerical advantage but voted first.

Magistrates (and priests) could also summon informal meetings called *contiones* to discuss matters of current concern. These were often the means by which upcoming legislation was discussed, but magistrates also used them to disseminate information (as Cicero's *Third Catilinarian* speech announces to the people the capture of the 'conspirators' at the Milvian Bridge in 63 BC), or to ask public figures to give an account of their conduct. Yet the presiding magistrate controlled discussion, and only those whom he summoned to speak were heard (although the masses were not averse to heckling in order to make their views known).

The empire changed things radically; all real decisions were taken by the emperor, who, however much he might seek consensus, was accountable to no one. We have seen that the Senate, while stripped of real power, was kept busy. The magistrates too remained outwardly as they had been under the republic, and 'good' emperors liked to preserve the fiction of 'normal service' in the political arena, sometimes accepting the consulship themselves. The real losers were the people, whose assemblies did not outlive the Augustan period as significant functioning entities; even the *space* for popular politics in the Roman Forum, the *comitium*, was effectively cancelled out in the Augustan rebuilding programme. Under the empire new structures emerged, or remained partially hidden, through which the emperor exercised control; important among these are his freedmen and slaves, who could be trusted as few senators could, and who owed the *princeps* everything; and the equestrian procurators who looked after his possessions (*patrimonium*) in the provinces. Under the republic the acquisition of overseas territories had been met with an increase in magistrates; further needs for manpower were met by the extension of the *imperium* of serving magistrates by a year (or more) to allow them to go as governors to the provinces. Under the principate the same system was continued, with two important developments: first, emperors themselves, by virtue of their *imperium*, had their own provinces, which were governed by trusted senators acting as their legates or deputies; and second, there was an increasing use of equestrians, both as financial officials responsible for tax collection (procurators), and as governors of smaller provinces, as well as in Egypt. Emperors tended to have a laissez-faire attitude as long as provinces were peaceful and paid their taxes, although Rome remained suspicious of local democracies. The politics of the subject cities were the concern of the governor, and of the emperor, who reacted to problems with the aid of precedent where available, and where there was none, by trying to balance equity with such overriding Roman interests as might be at stake in any outcome (Plin. *Ep.* book 10).

It ain't what it used to be . . .

There are some fundamental differences between ancient and modern politics; they illustrate some of the peculiar characteristics of ancient practice. A major problem is the assimilation of ancient societies to modern nation-states, i.e. the assumption that there is much in common between the political organisation of the modern states with which we are familiar and that of ancient communities. Yet the nation-state (a nineteenth-century phenomenon) has only limited relevance to the ancient world, and many of the functions and attributes characteristically predicated of it are anachronistic when applied to antiquity. Indeed, some scholars reject the term 'city-state' as a translation for polis, as carrying too much modernist baggage; I have tried to use the term 'community' where possible. Nevertheless, those working at the transition from prehistory to history, where societies are supposed to be transformed from kin-based tribes or chiefdoms to communities organised around stable political structures and laws, have found the concept of 'state-formation' a fruitful one (see also chapter 13).

Modern states, unlike ancient communities, have a far-reaching political economy, as a part of which they tax to spend on education and welfare, which no ancient community did; in antiquity indiscriminate taxation was the mark of the tyrant, and *direct* taxation of the citizen body was rare and limited to imposts on the rich in emergencies; even Ptolemaic and Roman Egypt had a political economy only in the weakest sense, by our standards, and revenues were directed to the purse of the ruling power. Again, modern states are structured around a formal separation of military and civil, of church and state, of state and government, and of 'powers', ie keeping separate the legislature, executive and judiciary; in ancient societies this was not the case. Modern states achieve this separation partly through large, expensive bureaucracies. Ancient communities met most bureaucratic requirements, and those of policing, with a limited staff of public slaves (and thus a very low administrative cost burden; see *Ath. Pol.* 47.5, 48.1, for the considerable responsibilities of Athenian public slaves, crucial, for example, in the work of the *pōletai* and *apodektai*). Even in Rome in the early empire, with a population of about a million, the slaves and ex-slaves (freedmen) assigned to maintaining order and fighting fires can be numbered only in the hundreds.

Very few ancient communities had standing armies, and these, like Rome from the early empire onwards, were generally autocratic ones, where the necessary tax revenues could be exacted; Sparta was, as often, an exception. The attempt by the Roman Republic to confront the pressures of running a large territorial empire with what were essentially the administrative structures of a polis has often been used to explain the collapse of the republican system; but it has been pointed out that the subsequent administration of the earlier Roman emperors was not, in quantitative or qualitative terms, notably more complex than its predecessor. The concentration of power in the hands of a single individual (the emperor), and the addition of the remarkable fiscal and human resources of his own household, were the significant new factors here.

Some relatively complex bureaucracies did emerge, for example in Ptolemaic/Roman Egypt, and the later Roman and Byzantine empires; and we have seen that Athens' financial management was very complicated. Further, while Athens' bureaucracy was cheap, the maintenance of (by the fourth century) the Assembly, *boulē*, courts and *archai* on state pay was a major drain on resources (Dem. 24.97–9; the possibility of shortfall: Dem. 24.99, 39.17, 45.4).

In place of bureaucracies, ancient communities allowed considerable latitude to private intervention; indeed they expected and needed it from the wealthy. Much of what we would regard as the business of the state was wholly or partly in private hands, for example tax collection; and the shipment of grain to Rome for the state-subsidised distributions was done by private shippers, to whom emperors (themselves the ultimate benefactors) offered various incentives. Munificent expenditure for the community (a ritualised form of inequality known as euergetism; see also chapters 17, 19 and 34) was a way both of cementing or reinforcing the dominant position of the wealthy in ancient society (see Arist. *Pol.* 1321a31–42 on the desirability of euergetism for oligarchies), and of diffusing class tensions created by socio-economic inequalities. Euergetism took a wide range of forms, from public feasts commemorating the donor, to public buildings and infrastructure, to entertainment (games and theatrical competitions: there were some hundred 'liturgical' appointments a year connected to providing the festivals of classical Athens, and 177 days devoted to state-funded games by the later Roman Empire), to military contributions (eg trierarchy, where a rich Athenian paid to equip a trireme), to disaster relief (such as the ransoming of citizens kidnapped by pirates in the Hellenistic world, or the relief of famine). The competition between, and honouring of, these civic benefactors (*euergetai*) is a major component in the political discourse of ancient communities.

Correspondingly, the weakness of the community in many areas hindered investigation of crime and reaction to social disorder. In the Bacchanalian religious 'crisis' (186 BC; Livy 39.8–19) we see the limited machinery of the Roman authorities in action, supplemented by the use of private citizens as informers. In the 50s BC the Senate and magistrates were for some years powerless to stop Clodius Pulcher using gangs of poor citizens to control the city through organised rioting, and until the imposition of martial law by Pompey, it was by private enterprise alone, in the form of gangs of gladiators organised by the senator Milo, that disorder was combated.

Generosity to the whole community by individuals shaded into support for smaller groups of dependents by powerful men, or patronage. As a social phenomenon patronage has a higher profile in Roman than in Greek society; this is largely a reflection of the particular language, and ethical sensibilities, which developed around Roman patron–client relations, which were unique in one respect, namely the large role played by slaves who, when freed, entered their masters' patronage on rather strict terms (see also chapter 18). Nevertheless, this mutual, if asymmetric, relationship is, as a broader sociological phenomenon, characteristic of the hierarchical nature of all ancient societies. In some instances state 'patronage' might combat the private influence of individual members of the elite: jury pay in Athens or the *annona* in Rome fall into this category. Finally, there was occasional state intervention in the Hellenistic world and in republican Rome to protect the interests of the poor indirectly, for example the fixing of grain prices to prevent speculation by the rich.

The often numerically tiny executive was not a professional class of politicians. In Athens those who spoke often in the Assembly were called simply *rhētores* (speakers – the proposer of a motion was technically said to 'speak' it); by contrast, in Rome the Senate was explicitly concerned with politics, unlike the *equites*. Members of local aristocracies were elected to positions for which their suitability came down to little more than good birth, leisure for training in public speaking, wealth to engage in acts of patronage or undue influence, as well as ownership of slaves to gather facts and remember who was who. Especially in the Hellenistic kingdoms, and in Rome, 'friends' of the ruler or magistrate were important, acting (always unpaid, but not without prospect of eventual reward) as advisors, or as governors' staff in the Roman provinces. The 'friends' (*philoi*) of Hellenistic kings constituted a select, trusted group for whom merit offered opportunities for social and geographical mobility; over time gradations of 'friendship' appeared ('first friend' and so on; see also chapter 17). Democratic regimes allowed for wider participation, and thus a politicisation of society; this led, however, to no real evolution of political skills or a political class; no more did popular participation in the Athenian courts end legal amateurism. There were some 'specialists', men whose previous experience fitted them to advise or act in certain areas, especially in the field of foreign policy, and in some areas of domestic policy; and note the importance placed on detailed technical knowledge of revenues and other technicalities by Socrates: Xen. *Mem.* 3. 6. Athenian 'demagogues' have sometimes been seen as technocrats, holding a detailed working knowledge of Athenian finances in the Peloponnesian War.

Popular participation, so familiar from Athenian democracy, is also problematic. The size of even tiny nation-states makes representative (thus *indirect*) democracy essential. In Europe today only three Swiss cantons preserve what was the order of the day in most ancient communities which were not autocratically ruled: *direct* participation in decision-making. In such communities, sovereignty lay with the Assembly of citizens, which typically met regularly throughout the year, and took decisions on matters put to it by the council or magistrates, in some cases after discussion, on matters ranging from honorific decrees for benefactors to votes for war. This highly ritualised, direct involvement is a key feature of ancient politics. Participation could be restricted, however, not by apathy, but by the physical difficulty for some rural citizens of travelling to vote. Attica (a large polis territory by Greek standards) was not so large that attendance was completely ruled out for those who dwelt furthest from Athens, *if* they could afford to be away from their livelihoods for a day or two up to four times a month. The distances and times involved for rural citizens wishing to vote in Rome, especially in the first century BC, often meant that attendance at the assemblies was restricted to members of the urban *plebs* and richer rural landowners. In the Roman assemblies which voted by geographical tribes, a few rural votes might count disproportionately strongly (see also chapter 18). And while the Athenian political landscape after Cleisthenes encouraged wide participation on the *boulē* and in other activities organised through the ten tribes, Rome sought no such structural cohesion to remedy the problems of a dispersed citizen body.

So while the ordinary citizen could have a direct say on matters which might have a critical impact on him, in larger communities *total* participation was an illusion. Furthermore, ancient politics had no room for women (except at an ideological level, as in Pericles' law of 451 BC, whereby no one could be an Athenian citizen unless both parents were Athenians); and even among men there were gradations of political empowerment. As with the modern nation-state, citizenship of a community was an important marker of status and privilege. The citizen could own land in his home community where the resident alien (*metoikos*, or metic, in Athens, *incola* in the Roman world) could not; the citizen enjoyed advantages at law over the non-citizen, in matters of marriage, inheritance and business transactions; nevertheless, the resident alien was not immune from taxation, for example in Athens.

Yet citizenship of a community was itself a spectrum. At one end, the value of the citizenship and the freedom of the citizen were defined against the widespread institution of slavery, in democracies as under other systems (and we must understand the ideological attraction of this state of affairs in its own terms, despite our repugnance).

Membership of the citizen body itself did not automatically bring full citizen rights. Sparta is an interesting case: unfree (but not enslaved) Messenians (the Spartans' neighbours) were constrained to perform agricultural labour as 'helots'. Classical Sparta's citizen body was an elite whose internal ideological equality was framed not only against the helots, but against other subject neighbours (*perioikoi*, 'dwellers-around') and a bewildering array of ex-helots and Spartiate citizens who had lost their full citizen rights (including the 'inferiors', 'bastards' and 'tremblers'). In Rome, the plebeian response to patrician exclusiveness was not only to seek equality, but also to form a state within a state. In the fourth to second centuries BC a number of Roman communities in Italy held a half-citizenship, the *civitas sine suffragio*, which allowed access to Roman law, for example, and required service in the legions, but entailed no right to vote. Freedmen were disabled by a restrictive form of citizenship, although their sons suffered no such disadvantage.

More interestingly, citizenship was not always co-extensive with political rights: while it often (but not always) involved the right to vote, it did not always, especially in oligarchies, involve full political rights, such as that to hold office. Thus when an oligarchy seized power in Athens in 411 BC, one of its first actions was to abolish the system of pay for office and restrict the holding of magistracies to those able to provide their own armour, i.e. the hoplite class, or an approved list of 5,000 of them. The restriction of full political rights to a subset of the citizen group is what counts here, not what that group then did with those powers. Such groups *always* included those at the upper end of the socio-economic scale, and *varied* only in how far down the existing social structure political privilege was extended. In Rome, the *comitia centuriata* was weighted in favour of the rich, who, despite their marked numerical inferiority with respect to the rest of the population, held almost half of the centuries: since decisions required a simple majority, a near unanimous vote by the upper-class centuries, which voted first, meant that often the poor did not vote at all. And while citizenship is paramount on the polis model, in other situations, such as membership of a federal league or under the Roman Empire, where (as opposed to the republic) local and Roman citizenship could be held simultaneously, both making demands on the holder, accommodation was needed between different levels of identity. Finally, one citizenship could be temporarily or permanently exchanged with another (a potential grant of citizenship known as *isopoliteia*, usually actuated by moving to the granting community), or merged with that of another community on an equal basis (*sympoliteia*); the Hellenistic period saw a proliferation of honorary citizenships given by Greek communities to poets, actors etc.

The oligarchic coup of 411 and the Roman centuriate assembly both illustrate a crucial characteristic of ancient politics, which was only slowly eroded, and which enjoyed continued importance in ancient thought long after its formal expressions had been watered down. This is the timocratic ideal, where political and social worth were interdependent. The idea was that the wealthier element in society, essentially small farmers upwards, were rich enough to provide their own armour and weapons; could be expected to fight (as a seasonal militia) to protect their land; could be liable for taxation on the basis of their wealth (in Rome); and could be expected not to take irresponsible political decisions which might have disastrous consequences, since their property would thereby be out at risk. *On that basis* this group was often given political rights, either absolutely or relatively greater than those of the mass of citizens. This boils down to more power and influence for the wealthy, and a politics broadly tailored to the interests of the landowner.

Rome was unique in the extent to which it fetishised the classification of its citizens into wealth bands with concomitant political clout and financial liability; but most ancient states, as far as our evidence allows us to see, had basic divisions of wealth within the citizen body which were mapped onto the landscape of political power. Democratic Athens dispensed with most of the restrictions on the political opportunities of the lower wealth classes of the *dēmos*, but significantly never sought to abolish the classes themselves. Nor did the Romans, even when gradual proletarianisation and professionalisation of the Roman army in the last two centuries of the republic had rendered obsolete the concept of a timocratically based citizen militia, culminating in the creation of a standing army, which robbed the census of one of its core functions. The division of ancient societies into various categories of 'have' and 'have-not' was figured (by the 'haves', naturally) in moral terms; those to whom more of the political cake had been given justified the inequality by appropriating for themselves language connoting moral goodness, and imputing moral failings to the masses. Thus we find the elites called *hoi aristoi*, *beltistoi* (the best), *chrēstoi* (the worthy) – Greek – and *boni* (good), *optimates* (the best men) – Latin; and the masses called *ponēroi* (the worthless), *improbi* (the wicked), and *plebs sordida* (the dirty *plebs*). References to the poor sought to deny to them any of the distinctiveness, in terms of virtue or birthright, which marked out aristocrats.

The importance of timocracy cannot be understood without grasping the centrality of war to ancient society. War was a regular occurrence in Greece, more so in Rome, and in both tied closely to religion and society. The citizen militia's political force derived from the probability that it *would* fight regularly: to protect the land of the peasant farmer and thus the community borders in classical Greece, while in Roman Italy there was the added incentive of conquest and resettlement (itself linked to Rome's unique pragmatism in the extension of its citizenship). The close ties between city and territory, between agricultural production, war and political power, were reflected in the link between the ideologies of political autonomy and of autarky (self-sufficiency) which 'forced the city to be countrified' (Osborne, *Classical Landscape with Figures*, p. 196); in turn this nexus of ideas and needs put the citizen peasant-farmer at the centre of politics. Equally, changes to polis autonomy in the fourth century led to a professionalisation not only of the soldier's role (as a mercenary, a stateless individual), but of those of urban citizen and the rural peasant, further undermining the timocratic ideal.

Striking too is the absence of political parties: although there were ideological differences which caused sharp and sometimes violent disagreements, politics remained focused on individuals. Political careers remained in general the preserve of the wealthy. Leading families sought to retain, and if possible advance, their position with respect to competitors, and it is impossible to pull apart the political and social threads of this hunger for power and influence. Sons of leading families (especially in Rome) were expected to follow in their fathers' steps; they could profit from ancestral achievements. Members of different families might combine on the basis of marriage connections, shared values or naked self-interest. Such combinations might be issue-driven or tied to broader ideological preferences, but they were not fixed or long-lived, and could be temporarily, intermittently or permanently overwritten by other ties, influences or goals. Attempts to prove the existence of stable political groupings (factions) do not fit the evidence available, or probability. More extreme applications of prosopography (who was who, and to whom they were related) and of patron–client models to Roman politics have also proved unworkable: the ties of family were powerful, but not inviolate (witness the common practice of giving sons in adoption to other families); and the idea that the vote could be 'got out' by particular aristocrats passing instructions down the pyramid of their dependents and dependents' dependents implies an inflexible and deterministic process which does not reflect the subtleties of patronage relations as visible in the evidence, and could not have survived in the real political ecosystem.

There were, however, aristocratic clubs, particularly in the Greek world, formed for social purposes, but inculcating and replicating shared political values, mainly through the institution of the *symposium*, and sometimes taking political action, as with the mutilation of the Herms in Athens in 415. The (perceived) dangers for public order of permanent associations in parts of the Roman Empire were such that Trajan forbade the creation of a corporation of fire-fighters in Nicomedia in Pontus (Plin. *Ep*. 10.33–34; compare 10.92–93).

Our political systems allow occasional rags-to-riches, 'log cabin to the White House', political trajectories. In antiquity by contrast, as we have seen, much political power remained in the hands of the rich, and the poor never attained outright control. For Aristotle (*Pol*. 1279b6–40) it was the opposition between rich and poor which underpinned the tension between the 'few' and the 'many', a view which has been adopted by Marxist scholars in particular. Even when the many took power, they were led and organised by members of the elite: the brothers Gracchi were Roman nobles; and despite the claims of Aristophanes that Cleon was the son of a tanner, he was an aristocrat, his father had been a wealthy man, and he had married into an aristocratic family.

In republican Rome assemblies precluded any discussion, and *contiones* were rigidly controlled. In democratic Athens proposals could be discussed in the Assembly, with all citizens enjoying an equal right to speak. Such 'open floor' meetings tended to happen only in the second meeting of every prytany (*Ath. Pol.* 43.6) and in special assemblies; and those who spoke in the Athenian assembly in the fourth century were often the 'usual suspects', a limited number of elite *rhētores* who proposed laws and went on embassies (see Dem. 18.169–79 on the summoning and functioning of the Assembly; on this occasion as on others, Demosthenes did not speak off the cuff but came prepared – no *probouleuma* had been introduced; also Dem. 22.36–7, 24.147, Aeschin. 3.9 for *rhētores* on the *boulē*). Others occasionally spoke, the so-called 'private speakers'; the very name is revealing. In practice, if not in theory, then, voters in both Athens and Rome could regularly expect to hear policy formulated or criticised by members of the elite; in Athens there were exceptions to the rule, in Rome never. Of course, the political elite of Athens was very different from the largely self-perpetuating and exclusive nobility of the Roman Republic. Perhaps because of the possibility for repeated tenure of the generalship, there was no magisterial 'career structure' as there was in Rome, where the annuality of office tenure placed an emphasis both on attaining the office and on achieving *auctoritas* (authority or influence) to endure beyond office-holding. Yet *structurally* the dominance of the elite in political life is analogous.

The control of the elite extended to an ability to politicise social conflict, and in some cases to identify the interests of the community with those of a small fraction of it: an extreme form of this is the extension of the Roman law of treason (*maiestas*) from physical offences against the community to verbal offences against the ruling emperor or his family. Elites also controlled legal systems and the administration of justice in most cases (democracies were an exception, although elite logographers wrote speeches for defence and prosecution; see also chapter 45): legal systems may embody prevailing social inequalities, and be instruments of social control, despite impartial administration.

Elites also dominated the religious institutions of most communities (see also chapter 4), although this area of life fell more clearly under popular control in democracies. In our secular Western societies, where church and state are separated and agnosticism or atheism common, it is very hard to imagine how intimately religion and politics were bound together in the ancient world. This does not mean that religion was ever used *explicitly* to legitimate policy or political control. No ancient politician claimed anything like the divine right of English Tudor and Stuart kings, despite phenomena like the cult offered to some Hellenistic kings (especially the Ptolemies) and Roman emperors; religious law existed, but was of very restricted application. On the other hand, the creation and organisation of loyalty to the emperor were largely achieved across the empire, at least among the ruling classes, through systematic acts of worship of the emperor. All political meetings started with prayers (and at Athens curses against those seeking to overthrow the democracy), and in Rome on consecrated ground; important actions required the consent of the gods, and any act could be stopped by the announcement of unfavourable omens. It is important to remember that outside democratic communities the priests, those who interpreted signs of divine favour and displeasure, and who offered advice on how to maintain relations with the gods, were the elite. Polybius (6.56.6) believed that the Roman elite exploited the extraordinary superstitious piety of ordinary citizens as a form of social control (implying that this would be strange to his Greek readers); closer to the truth is the notion that the Roman elite, while as a class they used religious process for their own ends, felt themselves as individuals just as much bound by the way religion impinged on the political process and structured authority as did the poor.

Ninety per cent or more of ancient populations lived and worked in the countryside, and this structural continuity is one factor which allows meaningful generalisations to be drawn across the range of ancient societies; there was nothing in antiquity like the Industrial Revolution which acted as a catalyst for enormous change in society and the organisation of power within it. Combining this with the structural deficit which the poor faced in politics compared with the elite, we might wonder whether the poor played any real part at all in the political life of their communities. Yet it is clear that in Athens the rich had either to sulk at home inactive or to play a part in the running of the democracy, whatever they thought of it (Xen. *Hell.* 2.3.15). Democratic ideology, honed and sustained through the rhetoric of public debate in the courts, the Assembly and even the theatre, imposed powerful constraints on the private as well as the public persona of the wealthy man, who was forced to weave his discrepant socio-economic status into the ideological fabric of equality, to appear both extraordinary and unthreateningly ordinary. The wealthy were more open than others to attack, especially by sykophants, or professional informers, and even the spectre of financial shortages for state pay might mean the risk of attacks on the wealthy, to increase revenue by confiscations. Small wonder that Plutarch describes the Athenian general Nikias as always seeming afraid of the *dēmos* (*Nic.* 2, 5; contrast Thuc. 6.14).

To ask whether Rome was a democracy or not, as a lively current debate does, is unhelpful, since there is no agreement on what constitutes democracy for the purposes of the exercise (see also chapter 18). Yet it is also clear that it is inadequate to describe it as an oligarchy. Despite all the limitations on the exercise of popular participation and sovereignty, the last two centuries of the Republic (which also saw the gradual introduction of a secret ballot) saw a considerable emphasis on speaking in front of the people, on taking oaths in front of them about observing laws they had voted for, and even, in the last century of the republic, a notable flexing of popular muscle to control magistrates. Even under the empire, a ruler could afford to ignore the venues for public interaction, and to receive public approbation or jeers, only at risk to himself. The emperor Tiberius became hugely unpopular for avoiding the games. The remarkable outbreaks of mob violence witnessed in the circus at Constantinople in the late empire testify to the enduring importance of the *plebs* in Roman politics, but it would be a mistake, under the Republic at least, to see their ability to act meaningfully as limited to the arena of rioting.

Finally, we should not forget *where* politics happened: to discuss Roman politics without an understanding of the micro-topography of the Forum Romanum, or to analyse Athenian politics with no grasp of how the Agora or the Pnyx worked, is to tell only half the story; to read a play but never to see it staged. The importance of place is further enhanced by the 'face-to-face' nature of ancient societies, where rulers and ruled might see and interact with each other regularly, even in huge cities like Rome; related to personal interaction is the importance of oral culture and the spoken word to ancient society, which lacked mass literacy, and had no mass media other than coinage.

Further reading

Sourcebooks

M. M. Austin, *The Hellenistic World from Alexander to the Roman Conquest: A Selection of Ancient Sources in Translation* (2nd edn), Cambridge: Cambridge University Press, 2006.

B. M. Levick, *The Government of the Roman Empire: A Sourcebook* (2nd edn), London and New York: Routledge, 2000.

Aristotle

D. Keyt and F. D. Miller (eds), *A Companion to Aristotle's* Politics, Oxford: Blackwell, 1991.

Politics: general

M. I. Finley, *Politics in the Ancient World*, Cambridge: Cambridge University Press, 1983 – a classic discussion which will stimulate agreement and disagreement.

The polis, the state and beyond

R. Brock and S. Hodkinson (eds), *Alternatives to Athens: Varieties of Political Organization and*

Community in Ancient Greece, Oxford: Oxford University Press, 2000.

M. H. Hansen, *Polis and City State: An Ancient Concept and its Modern Equivalent (Acts of the Copenhagen Polis Centre 6)*, Copenhagen: KDVS, 1998.

M. H. Hansen and T. H. Nielsen, *An Inventory of Archaic and Classical* Poleis, Oxford: Oxford University Press, 2004.

N. F. Jones, *Public Organisation in Ancient Greece: A Documentary Study*, Philadelphia: American Philosophical Society, 1987.

C. Morgan, *Early Greek States Beyond the Polis*, London and New York: Routledge, 2003.

I. Morris, *Death Ritual and Social Structure in Classical Antiquity*, Cambridge: Cambridge Universty Press, 1992, ch. 7 – Vroulia.

R. G. Osborne, *Classical Landscape with Figures: The Ancient Greek City and its Countryside*, London: George Philip, 1987.

Democratic Athens

M. H. Hansen, *The Athenian Democracy in the Age of Demosthenes: Structure, Principles, and Ideology*, London: Bristol Classical Press, 1999.

A. H. M. Jones, *Athenian Democracy*, Oxford: Blackwell, 1969, pp. 99–133.

J. Ober, *Mass and Elite in Democratic Athens: Rhetoric, Ideology and the Power of the People*, Princeton: Princeton University Press, 1989.

P. J. Rhodes (ed.), *Athenian Democracy*, Edinburgh: Edinburgh University Press, 2003.

Hellenistic kingdoms

J. Ma, *Antiochos III and the Cities of Western Asia Minor*, Oxford: Oxford University Press, 1999.

D. J. Thompson, 'The Ptolemies and Egypt', in A. Erskine (ed.), *A Companion to the Hellenistic World*, Oxford: Blackwell, 2003, pp. 105–20, esp. 108–11.

The Roman Republic and Roman 'Democracy'

F. G. B. Millar, *The Crowd in the Late Roman Republic*, Ann Arbor: University of Michigan Press, 1998.

R. Morstein-Marx, *Mass Oratory and Political Power in the Late Roman Republic*, Cambridge: Cambridge University Press, 2004.

C. Nicolet, *The World of the Citizen in Republican Rome*, trans. P. S. Falla, Berkeley: University of California Press, 1992.

The Roman Republic and Empire

A. K. Bowman, 'Egypt', in A. K. Bowman, E. Champlin and A. W. Lintott (eds), *The Cambridge Ancient History* X (2nd edn), Cambridge: Cambridge University Press, 1996, pp. 676–702.

J. E. Lendon, *Empire of Honour*, Oxford: Oxford University Press, 1997.

A. W. Lintott, Imperium Romanum: *Politics and Administration*, London and New York: Routledge, 1993.

A. W. Lintott, *The Constitution of the Roman Republic*, Oxford: Oxford University Press, 1999.

F. G. B. Millar, *The Emperor in the Roman World: 31 BC–AD 337* (2nd edn), London: Duckworth, 1992.

J. R. Patterson, *Political Life in the City of Rome*, London: Bristol Classical Press, 2000.

P. Veyne, *Bread and Circuses: Historical Sociology and Political Pluralism*, London: Penguin, 1990 – classic discussion of euergetism.

T. P. Wiseman (ed.), *Roman Political Life 90 B.C.–A.D. 69*, Exeter: Exeter University Press, 1985.

61. Names and Naming Systems

Clive Cheesman

Greek and other non-Roman naming patterns

Most inhabitants of the ancient Mediterranean world had or used only one name each. To minimise the chances of confusion, people often appended supplementary labels to their names. The most widespread was the simple patronymic: the father's name, in the genitive case (ie 'of *x*'). Thus a panel of arbitrators from Priene around 190 BC was formally listed as Meniscus [son] of Metrodorus, Agias [son] of Simus, and Molon [son] of Diagoras. Less common but still widespread was the adjectival patronymic, where the father's name was put into adjectival form: thus Phyllica Parmenisceia, a Thessalian woman living around 300 BC, was Phyllica daughter of Parmeniscus (lit. 'Parmeniscian Phyllica'); and Cletonymus Mnastocleius, from Lato on Crete around 100 BC, was son of Mnastocles. In private inscriptions a patronymic is often pursued back several generations, giving the father's patronymic, *his* father's patronymic and so on (with abbreviations used to indicate the reappearance of the same name). Much rarer, but occasionally found, are metronymics (also present in Etruscan names): the mother's name, in the genitive case or adjectival form.

Specifying a person's geographical origin or residence was also common. It was natural to refer to outsiders or newcomers by their place of origin, and at all times Greeks could be designated in this way. But *within* many communities a specialised version of this method developed, whereby a citizen was designated by membership of some unit that was, at least in origin, geographically defined. In democracies some such method could conveniently amount to a statement of full participation in the polis. At Athens, for instance, every citizen was inscribed in a deme (see also chapters 16 and 60); Callistratus Marathonius, Callimachus Hagnosius and Phrasitelides Icarieus were demesmen respectively of Marathon, Hagnous and Icarion.

By-names were also ever-present. Often introduced by a formula such as *ho kai* ('the one also [known as]') or *ho epikaloumenos* ('the one surnamed'), or indeed occasionally by no formula at all (as on the coinage of Smyrna, for instance), the by-name was not always restricted to a background role and sometimes took over from its 'real' counterpart: a story told about Plato the philosopher relates that his name was in origin a nickname ('sturdy') given him by his wrestling master, which came to eclipse his original name, Aristocles.

The structure and meaning of names

The names bestowed by speakers of Greek and other Indo-European languages (see also chapter 63) were a mixture of simple and compound forms. It has often been thought that the simple names result from ad hoc shortenings of compound names, and in many cases this will be true. Pet names ('hypocoristics') formed from long names have a habit of sticking and becoming independent name forms in their own right. But there are too many simple forms, stretching too far back historically, for them all to be accounted for in this way. Indeed simple names such as *Simus* ('snub-nosed') and *Glaucus* ('grey'), both very frequent throughout later classical history and beyond, seem to be represented in the syllabic Linear-B texts of Mycenaean Greek (see also chapter 63). Greek also provides a mass of highly visible simple names that are 'theophoric', that is, based on divine names: *Dionysius*, *Apollonius*, *Athenaeus* and the like.

The majority of Greek personal names, however, like Celtic, Germanic and Iranian ones, can be broken down into two distinct elements, usually noun- or verb-stems but sometimes adverbs or prepositions. Examples in Greek are legion; the basic pattern is illustrated by the following:

Aristophanes (*aristo-* 'best' + *phan-* 'appear', 'shine forth')
Agathocles (*agatho-* 'good' + *kleo-* 'renown')
Aleximbrotus (*alexi-* 'protect' + *mbroto-* 'mortal man')
Philippus (*philo-* 'loving' + *hippo-* 'horse')
Demophilus (*demo-* 'people' + *philo-* 'loving')
Periandrus (*peri* 'around' + *andro-* 'man')

Many compounds were theophoric, especially ones including stems indicating birth or giving: *Diogenes*, *Athenodoros*, *Herodotus*. These names ('born of Zeus', 'gift of Athena', 'given by Hera') seem to make a kind of internal sense, as do many of the non-theophoric compounds; but many names, perhaps the majority, cannot be 'translated' in this way.

In the Semitic (Near Eastern) languages (such as Phoenician and Hebrew) the situation was very similar. A great proportion of names were compound, mostly theophoric, and many having the sentence form familiar from the Bible. Thus Punic gives us 'SMN'MS ('Esmun has raised [him]'), ŠM'MLK ('the king has heard [him]'), and ḤNB'L (*Hannibal*, 'Ba'al has given'); while Palmyrene gives us BL'QB ('Bel has protected') and ZBDL' ('gift of God'). These were liable to hypocoristic shortening, producing a stock of simple names: thus ḤNB'L and other names with the same prefix gave rise to ḤN' (*Hanno*, '[*x*] has given'), and names like ZBDL' led to ZBD' ('gift of [*x*]'; cf. biblical *Zebedee*). There were also many other simple names that probably did not originate this way, some with unexpected meanings: Palmyrene yields BQY ('bottle'), YTM' ('orphan') and KLB' ('dog', the same as the biblical *Caleb*).

Complex names in ancient Italy

One area of the ancient Mediterranean where things seem radically different is Italy. Soon after the Italic and Etruscan epigraphic record (see also chapter 34) starts we find that individuals have two names, and that the separate names in use are neither compounds nor easily comprehensible. Usually, furthermore, the form of the name found in second place in these binominal (ie two-name) complexes is different from that of the forename, and it is frequently consistent: thus in Paelignian and Marrucine inscriptions it often ends in *-ies*, in Umbrian in *-is* and in Oscan in *-iis* or *-iís*. Something similar seems to be going on in Etruscan at an early date, with the second name regularly taking one of several adjectival forms. Despite this, forenames and second names do frequently bear some resemblance. The simplest explanation is that the second name is some kind of patronymic adjective (see above), formed from the father's name; sometimes this is perhaps true. But often there is a straightforward patronymic as well, giving the father's forename in the genitive (see above). What we have is in fact a kind of hereditary surname, perhaps formed on the basis of the given name of an ancestor, perhaps preserving some entirely different element.

This is the context in which Roman names need to be seen. The male Roman had a complex name of at least two parts, of which the second is, indeed, a hereditary surname with a regular formal ending in *-ius*. How something so different from the Indo-European and Semitic norms arose is much discussed. The need for a secondary name may have been prompted by the small variety offered by the few, simple forms used as forenames. But why the solution should have been a *hereditary* name is not clear; it has been linked with the growth of Etruscan urbanism in the eighth century BC, with the development of inherited family property, with a new sense of genealogical solidarity thought to be seen in archaeological evidence such as 'ancestral' tomb complexes at Osteria dell'Osa and elsewhere in Latium. None of this is entirely satisfactory, but it is clear that the use of the hereditary name at Rome had ancestral connotations and was extremely important for the definition of a particularly Roman institution, the *gens* (a descent group – real or fictive in origin – with cult and legal responsibilities; cf. the Attic *genos*).

The Roman *'tria nomina'* scheme

The standard phrase for the Roman naming system is the *tria nomina*, which means simply 'three names', but is better read as 'the three sorts of name', of which a freeborn male Roman always possessed two, one received soon after birth (the *praenomen*) and one inherited (the *nomen* or *nomen gentilicium*); of these, a free woman had in general only the latter. The third type of name was the *cognomen*, a late addition to the other two, which it followed in the name structure; optional for many generations, but eventually eclipsing the two other name types totally, partly because it shared important characteristics with both of them.

The *praenomen* was generally chosen from a very restricted selection, each with a conventional abbreviation. The most common were:

Gaius (C.)	Tiberius (Ti.)	Decimus (D.)
Lucius (L.)	Sextus (Sex.)	Appius (Ap.)
Marcus (M.)	Gnaeus (Cn.)	Spurius (Sp.)
Publius (P.)	Aulus (A.)	Numerius (N.)
Quintus (Q.)	Manius (M'.)	Caeso (K.)
Titus (T.)	Servius (Ser.)	Mamercus (Mam.)

These names are clearly simple in structure, some being plain ordinal numbers (*quintus* = 'fifth', *decimus* = 'tenth'), and they are strikingly different from given names in the Greek world. It has often been suggested that they are pet forms of lost compound names with two elements like Greek names; if so, the loss of the originals was impressively complete, and had surprisingly close parallels across the Italic world, where many language groups are to be found using simple forenames (often clearly equivalent to the Latin ones) from an early date. There were other *praenomina* not listed here in occasional use and it is important to understand that the category was not firmly bounded either by law or by convention. At the end of the republic and in the first two generations of the empire some Roman noble families experimented with showier, more varied *praenomina*. But in overwhelming practice Romans restricted themselves to the first few names given above; at all times in Roman history the six most popular *praenomina* tended to represent about 80 per cent of those in use, while *Gaius* and *Lucius* specifically each account for a fifth of named men over time. This is noteworthy conservatism, but far from unparalleled.

The *nomen* or *nomen gentilicium* was the name that indicated its bearer's *gens* membership. Like that membership, it passed by male-line inheritance and certain forms of patronage: all the sons of a man shared his *nomen*, as did his freed slaves (*liberti*), and anyone who acquired citizenship under his authority; from the first century BC on, the latter two groups also took their patron's *praenomen*. By the later republic powerful and successful Romans might manumit hundreds of slaves and enfranchise thousands of new citizens, so that certain *praenomen–nomen* pairings became extremely widespread.

The *nomen*'s most obvious formal characteristic was, as indicated above, that it almost always ended in the adjectival termination *-ius* (feminine form *-ia*): hence *Iulius, Valerius, Cornelius*. Other terminations existed (deriving from non-Latin languages of Italy where similar naming practices had developed) but they too were adjectival. Thus in early usage a person called (for instance) *Marcus Tullius* is to be understood as 'the Tullian Marcus', the Marcus who belongs to the *gens Tullia*. All sorts of other people and property – slaves, freedmen, clients, estates – could be described in the same way, and by extension the undertakings and enterprises of *gens* members were named similarly: laws (eg *lex Acilia*), roads (*via Aemilia*), aqueducts (*aqua Marcia*), markets (*forum Cornelium*) and other constructions (*circus Flaminius*). This usage cannot, however, be described as current after the first century AD.

In theory, since the *gentilicium* indicated *gens*-membership, it was possible to have only one, since one could only belong to one *gens*. With the decreasing importance of that institution under the early principate it became common for nobles to display second and third *gentilicia* in reference to maternal ancestry or testamentary inheritances from outside their male-line kindred. With these multiple *nomina* they often adopted multiple *cognomina* and even *praenomina*. The Hadrianic consul C. Bruttius Praesens L. Fulvius Rusticus is an example. Polyonymy (the adoption of multiple names) of this sort was pursued with gusto by some senatorial families in the second century AD.

The third type of name was the *cognomen*. This might not be present in an individual's name at all, or might be represented several times over. Some *cognomina* were hereditary, and functioned as family-designations within the broader context of the *gens*; thus the name *Scipio* was borne by one family branch of Cornelii, *Sulla* by another. Other *cognomina* were specific to individuals. Either way, many clearly began as personal descriptions – *Longus* ('tall'), *Calvus* ('bald'), *Capito* ('big head'), *Pulcher* ('handsome'), *Brutus* ('dumb' or 'dull') – and in other cases such as *Cicero* ('chick-pea') and *Murena* ('lamprey'), where we understand the Latin but do not know the origin of the name, it is easy to see it starting out as a personal nickname or epithet. This was the standard Roman interpretation too, regularly offered in explanation of prominent but more or less opaque *cognomina*, such as *Scipio* or *Caesar*.

As will already have been seen, many *cognomina* are rather unflattering in a lexical sense, and this (perceived as another sharp disinction between Roman and Greek naming habits) has led to a largely fruitless debate on how and why they came to be used voluntarily by the Romans. One influential suggestion is that they originated in the crude insults and mockery applied by the mob to those who sought their votes or harangued them in political contexts. This leaves open the question of why the mob's targets (and their heirs) were so happy to retain them. In fact, many *cognomina* are neutral at worst and it is hopeless and unnecessary to provide a single account for the origin of such a wide category.

One sort of *cognomen* was definitely and specifically complimentary. This was the name assumed by a victorious general to commemorate a triumph (see also chapter 18) over a people: thus P. Cornelius Scipio *Africanus* (for his Carthaginian triumph of 201 BC), L. Mummius *Achaicus* (for his victory in Achaea in 146) and Q. Caecilius Metellus *Creticus* (for his victory in Crete in 67). Dubious precedents for this appear in the sources back to the earliest days of the republic, but it was really a practice of the third to first centuries BC, when it died out for all but the *princeps* (see also chapter 19), since all military triumphs, deserved or not, were thereafter ascribed to him; thus emperors and their families accumulated strings of names like *Dacicus*, *Parthicus*, *Britannicus* and *Germanicus*.

On this 'traditional' account of the *tria nomina* women lacked any clear equivalent to the given name; recorded examples of feminine versions of the *praenomina* listed above are so few as to be insignificant. The great majority of republican women are known to us only by the feminine form of their family's *nomen gentilicium*, perhaps with a hereditary cognomen as well: *Claudia*, *Calpurnia*, *Scribonia*; *Caecilia Metella*. To distinguish them from their sisters, aunts and cousins we hear only of the occasional use of colourless, functional epithets such as *Maior* (elder) or *Minor* (younger), *Prima* (first), *Secunda* (second) and the like. The explanation that women lacked any legal or civic personality and therefore needed no individuating name seems inadequate; it does not address practicalities, and it was precisely in the home, not the public sphere, that an individuating name might have been of use.

Part of the answer lies in the structural make-up of the traditional Roman name, on which women's names shed much light. Though adjectival in form, the *nomen* was the fulcrum on which the other names hinged. *Praenomen* and *cognomen* alike were seen as qualifying (i.e. adding to, saying more about) the *nomen*, and a personal *cognomen*, even if consisting of no more than a plain ordinal number, did the job just as well as an obscure archaic *praenomen*. There was no sharp line in Latin usage between proper nouns (names of people and places) and common ones (names of objects), and a woman called *Acilia Secunda*, the second or younger Acilia, was just as effectively individuated and named as her brother *Quintus Acilius*. Indeed in ordinary usage her *cognomen* might migrate to leading position, as in *Quarta Hostilia*. Add to this a wide range of descriptive words (*Paulla* 'little one', *Rufa* 'redhead') and the increasing use in the late Republic and beyond of derived forms of ancestral *cognomina*, and it seems perfectly possible to see how women were catered for. Their apparent onomastic (i.e. related to names, hence onomastics is the study of names) poverty derives from their general absence from the written record and the lack of that 'system' which has in any case been exaggerated in regard to men's names.

The basic form of *praenomen* + *nomen* in *-ius* and *cognomen* was not only replicated by citizens throughout the empire but loosely copied by non-citizens (despite occasional attempts to curb this). However, only citizens used certain abbreviated onomastic adjuncts (i.e. additions to the names) which gave their names the final, formal touch: the filiation (an indication of whose son or daughter they were), and an indication of which of the thirty-five voting tribes they were enrolled in (see also chapters 18 and 60). Filiation was expressed by means of the father's *praenomen*, with *f* for *filius* or *filia* (son or daughter), and tribe by one of the three- or four-letter conventional abbreviations (eg *Clu* for Clustumina, *Tro* for Tromentina). Both, tellingly, were inserted in the name after the *nomen* and before the formally less fixed *cognomen*. These adjuncts gave formations such as *M. Cassius M.f. Cam. Tenax*, where *Cam(illa tribu)* indicates enrollment in the Camillan tribe. In certain contexts, the *praenomina* of the grandfather and even the great-grandfather might be added, with *nep[os]* (grandson) and *pronep[os]* (great-grandson) respectively. Freedmen, however, did not refer either to a voting tribe or, in official contexts, to natural parentage, and instead they inserted the *praenomen* of their patron, with the abbreviation *l.* or *lib.* for *libertus/liberta*; thus Cicero's secretary and freedman *M. Tullius M. lib. Tiro* (Marcus Tullius, freedman of Marcus (Tullius), Tiro. His *cognomen*, like that of the newly enfranchised citizen, was the name he had held previously as a single personal name.

The Roman world at large

The speed and indiscriminate nature of the way in which large populations in the provinces and in Italy were absorbed into the citizenship make it wise to mistrust the onomastic apparel in which the Roman world is soon clothed. By the mid-third century practically all men possessed the *tria nomina*; indeed large numbers of them had the same *praenomen* and *nomen*, 'Marcus Aurelius', which they had received from Caracalla along with citizenship under the *Constitutio Antoniniana* of AD 212 (see also chapter 19). For most purposes people continued to live in a one-name culture, however. This is obvious from considerations of practicality: what use is a *praenomen* if all the male members of your family, village and locality have the same one? But such arguments can be overstated, and what really tells is the seamless way in which old onomastic practices carried on. Papyri show that people still signed letters (even formal ones), addressed each other and referred to third parties by one name only, the *cognomen*, their old personal name. Furthermore the acquisition of two bureaucratic labels in the form of a *praenomen* and *nomen* did not increase variety or variability at all. Just as they had done before becoming Romans, people continued to use alternative names and epithets. Thus the old Greek usage of *x* 'who is also [called]' *y* is replicated precisely in Latin inscriptions by the formulae *qui et* and *quae et* ('he who is also *x*', 'she who is also *y*'). Alternatively, a nickname or by-name might be introduced by the word *signo* (lit. 'by sign'), suggesting that it was the name of reference, or simply appended without explanation. Particularly common were names formed from Greek or Latin words given an ending in *-ius*, like the old *gentilicium*, with which they had little in common otherwise. These names often appear on tombstones in the vocative form (the inflection – that is, the form – of the noun used to address individuals) only, as if being used to address the departed, and men's and women's forms are often identical despite the strict requirements of grammar. Examples from the Christian community are *Eupsychius*, *Eudromius* and *Gregorius*. Such names placed in the vocative end up resembling the imperative (ordering) form of a verb, and thus can be mistaken for the sort of 'acclamation' or parting-shot that also frequently appears on late antique tombs (see also chapter 20): *Eupsychi* could mean 'keep your spirits up', *Eudromi* 'run the good race' and *Gregori* 'wake up'. This ambiguity was doubtless fully intended.

Another telling evolution (and a genuine case of 'bottom-up' change) is the gradual mutation of certain *nomina* (*Flavius*, *Aurelius* and occasionally *Valerius*) into status designations rather than true names. Arising from their appearance as imperial dynastic names, borne by scores of imperial freedmen and other prominent clients across the Roman world, these names became associated with dignitary rank. The result was that from the fourth century AD on scribes and junior officials automatically ascribed these names to their peers and superiors (and even their wives) whether or not they were entitled to them as names. Though the upper classes resisted at first, by the fifth century usages such as *Fl(avius) Venantius*, with the status designation added to a single name, were widely accepted at all levels with any pretensions to status. For the less eminent, *cognomina* (and a few ancient *nomina* and *praenomina* that were used like *cognomina*) sufficed; these were the names that were to survive into the Middle Ages. Despite a reflowering of showy and unsystematic polyonymy among aristocrats of the late fifth and sixth centuries, a one-name culture had been re-established.

Further Reading

M. Dondin-Payre and M.-T. Rapsaet-Charlier (eds), *Noms: identités culturelles et romanisation sous le Haut-Empire*, Brussels: Timperman, 2001.

S. Hornblower and E. Matthews (eds), *Greek Personal Names: Their Value as Evidence*, Oxford: Oxford University Press/British Academy, 2000.

M. Kajava, *Roman Female Praenomina* (*Acta Instituti Romani Finlandiae* 14), Rome: Finnish Institute, 1994.

E. A. Meyer, 'Epitaphs and citizenship in Classical Athens', *Journal of Hellenic Studies* 113 (1993), 99–121.

L'Onomastique latine: actes du colloque internationale organisé à Paris du 13 au 15 Octobre 1975, Paris: Editions CNRS, 1977.

O. Salomies, 'Names and identities: onomastics and prosopography', in J. Bodel (ed.), *Epigraphic Evidence: Ancient History from Inscriptions*, London and New York: Routledge, 2001, pp. 73–94.

B. Salway, 'What's in a name? A survey of Roman onomastic practice *c.* 700 BC to AD 700', *Journal of Roman Studies* 84 (1994), 126–45.

C. J. Smith, *The Roman Clan: The* Gens *from Ancient Ideology to Modern Anthropology*, Cambridge: Cambridge University Press, 2005.

S. Wilson, *The Means of Naming: A Social and Cultural History of Personal Naming in Western Europe*, London: UCL Press, 1998.

62. Measures, Weights and Money

Brian A. Sparkes

In antiquity cheating over measures in the market-place was commonplace, as measures could not be made as accurately as we demand. The modern measurements given below should be treated as over-precise approximations. There were localised systems of metrology (measurement) and variation in dialects between the Greek city-states and between different communities in Italy (between Latin-speaking Rome and Oscan-speaking Pompeii, for example), so the spelling also varied. The terms were used for centuries, but the denominations, values and weights do not correspond throughout antiquity. It should also be noted that many words such as *pous*, *digiti*, *chous*, *amphora*, *urna* have other everyday meanings and in most contexts do not carry the technical meaning.

Measures

Length

Both Greeks and Romans used parts of the body (foot, forearm, hand, palm) to signify length. The foot was the basic measurement, but there were various local Greek measures (Olympic (320 mm = 12.6″), Pergamene (330 mm = 13″), 'Aeginetan' (333 mm = 13.1″), Attic (295.7 mm = 11.64″)), whereas the Roman measures were more standardised.

2 *daktyloi* (finger's breadths)	=	1 *kondylos* (middle joint of finger)
4 *daktyloi*	=	1 *palastē* or *dōron* ('palm')
10 *daktyloi*	=	1 *lichas* (lesser 'span' between thumb and forefinger)
12 *daktyloi*	=	1 *spithamē* ('span' between thumb and little finger)
16 *daktyloi*	=	1 *pous* ('foot')
18 *daktyloi*	=	1 *pygmē* (short 'cubit', from elbow to start of fingers)
20 *daktyloi*	=	1 *pygōn* (short 'cubit', from elbow to first joint of fingers)
24 *daktyloi*	=	1 *pēchys* ('cubit', from elbow to fingertips)
2½ *podes*	=	1 *bēma* ('pace')
6 *podes*	=	1 *orgyia* ('fathom', length of outstretched arms to fingertips)
10 *orgyiai*	=	1 *amma* ('chain')
10 *ammata*	=	1 *stadion* (192 m = 210 yds)
100 *podes*	=	1 *plethron*
600 *podes*	=	1 *stadion* (192 m = 210 yds)

The Greeks borrowed some foreign measures, e.g. 30 *stadia* = 1 *parasang* (a *farsang*, a Persian measure) and 60 *stadia* = 1 *schoinos* (an Egyptian measure, though this was an unstable equivalence).

In Roman numeration the foot (*pes/pedes*) is slightly smaller (296 mm = 11.65″) than the English foot; the Oscan foot was smaller still (275 mm = 10.83″).

4 *digiti* (finger's breadths	=	1 *palma* (width of the 'palm')
16 *digiti*	=	1 *pes* ('foot')
12 *unciae* (inches)	=	1 *pes*
1½ *pedes*	=	1 *cubitum* ('cubit', from elbow to fingertips)
5 *pedes*	=	1 *passus* (double 'pace')
125 *passus*	=	1 *stadium*
1,000 *passus*	=	*mille passuum* (1 mile, 1.61 km)

Area

The calculation of area by the amount that could be ploughed in a day by a yoke of oxen emphasises the agricultural basis of life; the English word 'acre' is the equivalent measure. The equivalent Greek term *plethron* meant both 100 feet in length and 100 × 100 feet = 10,000 square feet. In Latin the terms were:

2 *actus quadrati*	=	1 *iugerum* or *as* (240 × 120 Roman feet, 0.67 acres)
2 *iugera*	=	1 *heredium*
100 *heredia*	=	1 *centuria*

Capacity

In both Greek and Latin a division was made between dry (corn) and liquid (wine) measures. In Greek the dry measures were:

6 *kyathoi*	=	1 *kotylē* (a quarter of a litre or under half a pint)
4 *oxybapha*	=	1 *kotylē*
4 *kotylai*	=	1 *choinix* (a day's ration, a little more than a litre, a little less than a quart)
8 *choinikes*	=	1 *hekteus*
6 *hekteis*	=	1 *medimnos*

and the liquid measures were:

6 *kyathoi*	=	1 *kotylē*
4 *oxybapha*	=	1 *kotylē*
2 *kotylai*	=	1 *xestēs*
12 *kotylai*	=	1 *chous* (c. 3 litres or three-quarters of a gallon)
12 *choes*	=	1 *amphoreus* or *metrētēs* (9 gallons, cf. 'bushel' = 8 gallons)

At Rome for dry and liquid measures the *sextarius* (over half a litre) was the standard unit. The dry measures were:

16 *sextarii*	=	1 *modius* (2 imperial gallons, 1 'peck')
6 *modii*	=	1 *medimnus*

and in liquid measures one *sextarius* ('dram') was equal to 1 British pint:

12 *cyathi*	=	1 *sextarius* or *as*
2 *heminae*	=	1 *sextarius*

6 *sextarii*	= 1 *congius* (6 pints)
12 *heminae*	= 1 *congius*
4 *congii*	= 1 *urna*
8 *congii*	= 1 *amphora*
2 *urnae*	= 1 *amphora* or *quadrantal* (26 litres, 6 gallons)
20 *amphorae*	= 1 *culleus* (120 gallons)

An army *modius* ('bushel') is estimated to have been 1.3 to 1.5 times larger than a regular *modius*.

Weights

Values of goods and services, when not bartered in kind, were traded in the form of weights of metal or stone. The major Greek standards for weights were the Aeginetan and Attic-Euboic (the Attic-Euboic are the weights given below). The terms used for weights gave their names to the denominations of coins: *obolos* was the word for a cooking spit or nail, and *drachmē* was a handful.

6 *oboloi*	= 1 *drachmē* (4.31 grams)
100 *drachmai*	= 1 *mna* ('mina', 436 grams; 1 lb is 454 grams)
60 *mnai*	= 1 *talanton* ('talent', half a hundredweight)

In Latin terminology a pound weight was a *libra* or *as*.

24 *scripula*	= 1 *uncia* ('ounce', c. 27 grams)
12 *unciae*	= 1 *libra* or *as* (327.45 grams, 0.721 lb)

Other divisions of the *libra* were the *deunx* (= 11 *unciae*), the *dextans* (= 10 *unciae*) and so on to *sextans* (= 2 *unciae*).

Money

The material of Greek coins was mainly silver, with gold valued much more highly. The weights and the relation between the coins are based on the names and relations of weights. A skilled labourer could earn a drachma a day in fifth-century Athens, an unskilled worker half that amount.

6 *oboloi*	= 1 *drachmē* (4.3 grams of silver)
2 *drachmai*	= 1 *didrachmon*
4 *drachmai*	= 1 *tetradrachmon*
100 *drachmai*	= 1 *mna* ('mina', a sum of money, not a coin; 430 grams, c. 1 lb silver)
60 *mnai*	= 1 *talanton* ('talent', a sum of money, not a coin; 26 kg, 57 lb)

The *Dareikos* (Daric, thought erroneously to be named after the Persian king Darius) was used as a noun or an adjective (qualifying the noun *statēr*, a standard coin in various metals) and was the name given to the standard Persian gold coin. Another Persian coin that has a Greek name is *siglos* (at one time worth seven and a half Attic *oboloi*). *Philippeioi* was the name given to gold didrachms issued originally by Philip II of Macedon.

The Latin word for money (*pecunia*) was derived from *pecus* (cattle), showing the pastoral basis of bargaining before coinage was used. Exchange was originally by means of rough lumps of bronze/copper (*aes rude*), then standard rectangles of bronze with an animal in relief on top (elephant, pig) (*aes signatum*; 1.5 kg, 3.3 lb). These were replaced by circles of bronze (*aes grave*), which came to be called simply *aes* or *as/asses* (weighing about one Roman pound). One *as* was equivalent to 2 *semis*, 3 *trientes*, 4 *quadrantes*, 6 *sextantes*, 12 *unciae*.

When the Romans adopted silver as a medium for coins, the basic coins were *sestertii* (sesterces – the commonest coin used in Roman currency) and *denarii*, and all equivalences varied over time through devaluation.

2½ (or later 4) *asses*	=	1 *sestertius* (short for *Semis-tertius*, i.e. 'half for the third time' = 2½; it was abbreviated to IIS, i.e. II + S (emis), with the first two strokes joined to read HS)
4 *sestertii*	=	1 *denarius*
16 *asses*	=	1 *denarius*
25 *denarii*	=	1 *aureus* (gold coin)

In equating Greek and Roman coinage, 1 *drachmē* = 1 *denarius*.

Appendix

There are some actual measures that survive. The excavations of the Athenian Agora have unearthed bronze and clay measures of capacity that have the word *dēmosios/dēmosion* ('public') on their sides (fifth and fourth centuries BC). Some lead weights from the same site and from other sites are in the form of square plaques with a badge and sometimes a denomination of the issuing city or an official guarantee in relief on top. From Thasos there is a standard wine measure with hollows for a quarter and a half amphora (first century BC). A well-preserved *mensa ponderaria* (weighing table) survives from Pompeii, with a dozen different-sized cavities in it for measuring dry weights – the *mensa* is adjacent to the Forum Holitorium, the vegetable market; the measures had to be adjusted from the Oscan to the Roman standard after the city gained Roman citizenship, as an inscription records. Commercial amphorae were often of a fixed capacity. There are also metrological reliefs with the parts of the human body, foot, etc. (in Oxford, Ashmolean Museum (Michaelis 83), from East Greece, fifth century BC (figure 62.1), and in Piraeus Museum (5352), from Salamis, late fourth century BC (figure 62. 2)). A relief from Lepcis Magna displays linear measures (Augustan period). One might also mention a bronze corn measure (*modius*) in Chesters Museum; the inscription declares its capacity as exactly 17½ sextarii (from Magnis (Carvoran) on Hadrian's Wall, first century AD). Some Greek temples in Asia Minor have left traces of scale plans (e.g. at Didyma). For coins, see chapter 25.

Fig. 62.1 Greek metrological relief from East Greece, with measures by fathom (outstretched arms) and foot. C. 450 BC. Ht. 62 cm, length 2.09 m. Oxford, Ashmolean Museum Michaelis 83 (photo: © museum).

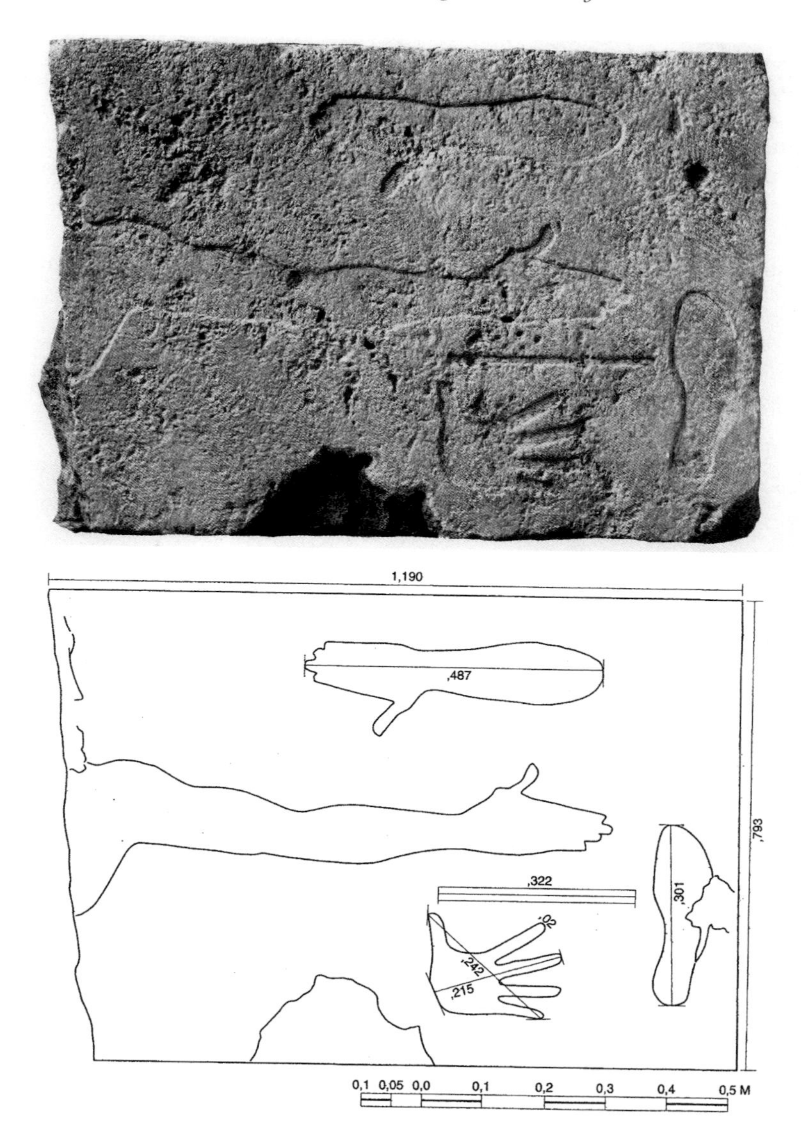

Fig. 62.2a–b Photograph and drawing of a fragmentary Greek metrological relief from Salamis, with measures by outstretched arm, forearm, foot, and palm and fingers. Fourth century BC. Piraeus Museum 5352 (photo: © museum).

Further reading

C. Corti and N. Giordani (eds), *Pondera: pesi e misure nell'antichità*, Modena: Museo della Bilancia Libra 93, 2001.

O. A. W. Dilke, *Mathematics and Measurement*, London: British Museum Publications, 1987.

T. Figueira, *The Power of Money*, Philadelphia: University of Pennsylvania, 1998, esp. ch. 11.

M. C. Howatson (ed.), *The Oxford Companion to Classical Literature* (2nd edn), Oxford: Oxford University Press, 1980, *s. v.* under 'money and coins', 'weights and measures'.

F. Hultsch, *Griechische und römische Metrologie* (2nd edn), Berlin: Weidmann, 1882.

M. Lang and M. Crosby, *The Athenian Agora*, X: *Weights, Measures and Tokens*, Princeton: American School of Classical Studies at Athens, 1964.

J. Melville Jones, *A Dictionary of Ancient Greek Coins*, London: Seaby, 1986.
J. Melville Jones, *A Dictionary of Ancient Roman Coins*, London: Seaby, 1990.
Oxford Classical Dictionary (3rd edn), Oxford: Oxford University Press, 1996 *s. v.* 'Coinage' (Rutter and Crawford), 'Finance' (Millett and Burton), 'Measures' (Vickers), 'Wages' (Millett), 'Weights' (Gill).
W. F. Richardson, *Numbering and Measuring in the Classical World* (rev. edn), Bristol: Bristol Phoenix Press, 2004.

63. *Writing Systems*

J. H. W. Penney

Both the Greeks and the Romans were dependent on others for the introduction of writing into their cultures, borrowing writing systems and adapting them (with varying success) to the needs of their own languages. For the Greeks, there were two quite separate processes of borrowing from different sources, while the Romans owe their alphabet ultimately to the Greeks but through Etruscan mediation.

Linear B and the Cypriot syllabary

The earliest recorded Greek texts (c. 1400–1200 BC), mainly on clay tablets found in the ruins of Mycenaean palaces on Crete and on the mainland, are written in a script known as Linear B. This belongs to a family of scripts developed on Crete: Cretan pictographic, Cretan hieroglyphic, Linear A and Linear B. The names were assigned by Sir Arthur Evans, the excavator of Knossos, to reflect a perceived progression from a pictorial to a more linear style of forming signs. Inscriptions in the first three of these remain essentially undeciphered, and it is not known what the language of the texts might be, but the Linear B script was successfully decoded by Michael Ventris in 1952, and the language of the tablets shown to be an early form of Greek, now known as Mycenaean Greek.

The signs of the script fall into three groups. These are (i) numerals, which are easily recognised; (ii) ideograms, conventional signs for various commodities such as barley or oil, for animals such as sheep or horses, for people (distinguishing men and women), for units of measurement – which often, but not invariably, bear some pictorial resemblance to what they represent (the signs in both these groups convey no linguistic information, since they could effectively be read in any language, just as the numeral 3 today may be read around the world as *three*, *trois*, *drei*, *üç*, *tiga* etc). Finally (iii), and more helpful, there are syllabic signs, which have sound values (figure 63.1): they represent syllables normally consisting either of a vowel alone (*a*, *e*, *i*, *o*, *u*) or of a consonant followed by a vowel (*ta*, *te*, *ti*, *to*, *tu*, *ra*, *re* etc); a few have more complex values, and some remain undeciphered. It was the successful reading of these syllabic signs that allowed the language of the texts to be recognised as Greek.

As a system for writing Greek, the Linear B syllabary (the set of syllabic signs) has certain drawbacks, due to a shortage of signs and to the impossibility of writing a consonant without a following vowel:

1. Greek distinguishes between the plain voiceless stops [p], [t] and [k], their aspirated counterparts [pʰ], [tʰ] and [kʰ] and their voiced counterparts [b], [d] and [g] (see appendix to this chapter): the later Greek alphabet has separate signs for all of these (Π Τ Κ; Φ Θ Χ; Β Δ Γ) but in the Linear B script distinctions of aspiration are completely ignored and a distinction of voice only indicated in the case of the *d*-signs. So *pa*, for instance, can stand for [pa] or [pʰa] or [ba], *te* can stand for [te] or [tʰe], but *de* only for [de].
2. No distinction can be made in the script between [r] and [l], so *ro* stands for either [ro] or [lo] etc.

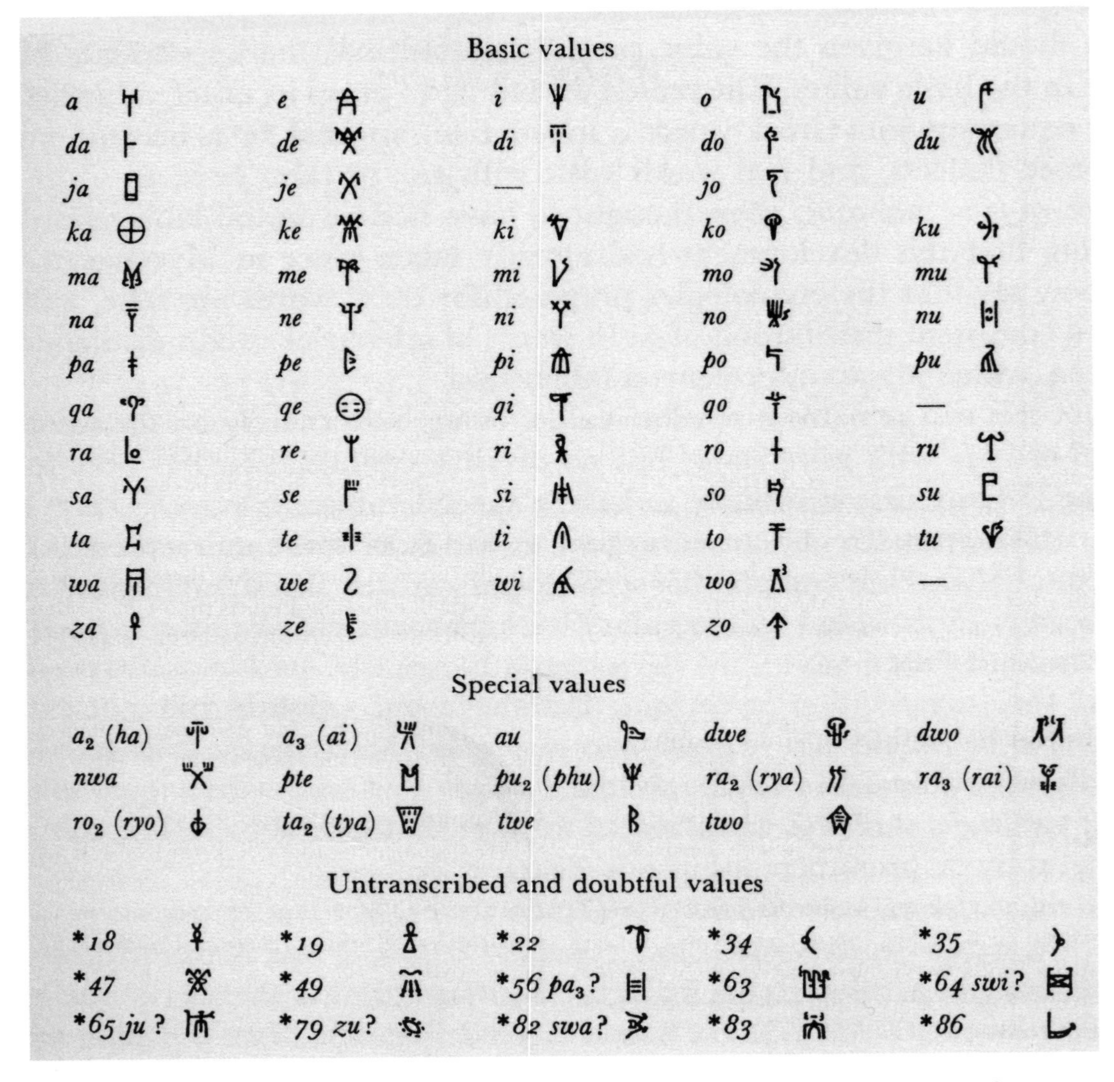

Fig. 63.1 The Mycenaean Greek syllabary (Linear B). Reprinted from M. Ventris and J. Chadwick, *Documents in Mycenean Greek* (2nd edn), Cambridge: Cambridge University Press, 1973, p. 385.

3. There are no distinctions made in writing between long and short vowels.
4. The second element of the diphthongs [ei], [ai] and [oi] is not normally written, so *pa* can also stand for [pai] etc.
5. Syllable-final nasals [m] and [n], liquids [r] and [l], and sibilants [s] are not written internally or finally, so eg *ko-wo* stands for [korwos], cf. Homeric κοῦρος 'boy', and *i-jo-te* for [iyontes], cf. classical ἴοντες 'going' (masc. nom. pl.).
6. Initial consonant clusters, and some internal ones, are written with signs containing the vowel that is eventually to follow the cluster, so *ti-ri-* for [tri-]; cf. *ko-to-na* for [ktoina] (a plot of land), *e-ko-to* for [Hektōr] (a man's name). Thus more vowels have to be written than are actually pronounced.
7. The signs transliterated *ja*, *je* etc. are to be read as [ya], [ye], but in many cases the [y] is simply an automatic glide, cf. *i-jo-te* above.

In addition it should be noted that Mycenaean Greek still retains (and consistently writes) a sound [w] which is lost in classical Attic and Ionic; cf. *wo-no* [woinos] beside classical οἶνος 'wine' etc. Another archaic feature contributing to the unfamiliar look of some words is the survival of a sound [k^w] (with aspirated [k^{wh}] and voiced [g^w]) represented by the *q*-series of signs; these sounds merge with other consonants in the post-Mycenaean period: cf. *-qe* [k^we] beside classical τε 'and', *qa-si-re-u* [g^wasileus] beside classical βασιλεύς 'king'.

The difficulties inherent in the writing system and in its interpretation may be illustrated by a final example: *a-re-ku-tu-ru-wo e-te-wo-ke-re-we-i-jo* is a man's name, to be read [Alektruōn Etewoklewehios], 'Alektruōn son of Eteoklēs'.

The Linear B script seems not to have survived the collapse of the Mycenaean world, and there are no written texts from Greece or the Aegean for several centuries (see also chapter 15). Greater continuity, however, is found on Cyprus, where in the second millennium BC versions of a syllabic script labelled 'Cypro-Minoan' were in use, related to the Cretan family of scripts. These remain undeciphered, but a later development of one of them was used to write Greek and this can be read. An isolated early text dates to the eleventh century, but throughout the archaic and classical period Greek was written on Cyprus using this syllabic script. There are local variations, but the underlying system is clearly the same for all of them. The inventory of signs is somewhat different from that of Linear B, e.g. [r] and [l] have separate sets of signs, the *d*-series does not exist, nor the *q*-series. The difficulties of writing Greek with a syllabic system remain, but the spelling conventions are a little more sympathetic than those of Linear B: diphthongs are written in full and syllable-final consonants (except [m] and [n]) are notated – final consonants being written using the signs with inherent *e*-vocalism, eg *po-to-li-ne* [ptolin], cf. Homeric πτόλιν 'city' (acc. sg.).

The Greek alphabet

In the late second millennium, a script had been devised for the writing of various West Semitic languages of the Levant (see also chapter 12), and one important variant of this was the Phoenician alphabet, consisting of twenty-two signs, representing consonants only, with no signs for vowels. This was the source of the Greek alphabet (see also chapter 15).

There was a well-established Greek tradition that their alphabet was borrowed from the Phoenician alphabet: Herodotus (5.58–61) expresses the thought mythologically when he speaks of Kadmos, the Phoenician, having brought their writing system to Greece; more prosaically, the term φοινικήια 'Phoenician things' for 'letters' is found in inscriptions, and from archaic Crete an inscription offers the terms ποινικαστάς for 'scribe' and ποινικάζεν for 'to write' (lit. 'to do Phoenician things').

This Greek tradition is confirmed by several facts. The letters of the early Greek alphabets patently resemble those of the Phoenician alphabet and they occur in the same order (figure 63.2). The names of the letters are also clearly borrowed from the Semitic names (the exact form of the Phoenician versions of these is unknown): cf. Greek *alpha*, *bēta*, *gamma*, *delta* etc. beside *'ālep̱*, *bêṯ*, *gīmel dāleṯ* etc.

The most important of the changes introduced by the Greeks, when they borrowed the alphabet, was the conversion of some of the Phoenician consonantal signs into signs for vowels. A, E, I, O all continue signs that in the Phoenician alphabet represent consonants; the Phoenician letter *wāw* survived with its value [w] as the Greek digamma F, but a variant of it, Y, was introduced as a separate sign for the vowel [u] and added at the end of the alphabet (the usual place for new letters). The regional alphabets of archaic Greece differ considerably in their inventories of letters and in the shapes of some letters, but this major adaptation is common to all, which is the crucial argument in favour of postulating a single original borrowing and modification of the Phoenician alphabet and not a series of separate events.

The Phoenician alphabet, borrowed in its full form, contained several letters that were scarcely needed for the writing of Greek, and these were dealt with variously. The letter *qōp* (Ϙ) was borrowed as *qoppa* and used in archaic alphabets

Phoenician		Crete	Attica	Ionia
ʾ	𐤀	Α Α	Α 𐤀	Α
b	𐤁	Β ᑭ	Β	Β
g	𐤂	Λ Γ	Γ	Γ
d	𐤃 𐤃	Δ	Δ	Δ
h	𐤄	Ε Ε	Ε	Ε
w	𐤅 𐤅	Ϝ F	F	
z	𐤆	Ι	Ι	Ι
ḥ	𐤇	Η	Η	Η H
ṭ	⊗	⊗ ⊕	⊗ ⊕	⊗ ⊕
y	𐤉	S	Ι	Ι
k	𐤊	Κ	Κ	Κ
l	𐤋	Λ Γ	Λ	Γ
m	𐤌	Μ	Μ	Μ
n	𐤍	Ν	Ν	Ν
s	𐤎			Ξ
ʿ	Ο	Ο	Ο	Ο
p	𐤐	Γ ᑭ	Γ	Γ
ṣ	𐤑	Μ		
q	Φ Ϙ	Φ Ϙ	Ϙ	Ϙ
r	𐤓	Ρ	Ρ Ρ	Ρ
š	𐤔		Σ	Σ Σ
t	+ 𐤕	Τ	Τ	Τ
		Υ V	Υ	Υ V
			Φ	Φ
			Χ	Χ
				Ψ Ψ
				Ω

Fig. 63.2 The Phoenician alphabet and some early Greek alphabets. Adapted from A. Heubeck, 'Schrift', in *Archaeologica Homerica* III.x, Gottingen: Vandenhoeck and Ruprecht, 1979, p. 102.

simply as a substitute for *kappa* for writing [k] before the vowels [o] and [u] (the names of the letters seem to have prompted this distribution) but was later abandoned. There were more signs for sibilants than Greek needed, and all versions of the Greek alphabet abandoned one or more of them, making different choices.

The date and place of the creation of this first Greek alphabet are fiercely disputed. The first known inscriptions date from the early eighth century BC, and much depends on whether this is taken to prove that the period of creation cannot have been much earlier or whether an accidental gap in attestation can be assumed. As to location, given that both the Greeks and the Phoenicians traded throughout the Mediterranean, there are countless possibilities (depending on the chronology) for encounters between them that might have resulted in the transfer of writing skills; suggestions include Al Mina in Syria, Cyprus, Rhodes, Crete and Euboea, but there is no agreement.

The Greek alphabet that forms the common core of all the archaic Greek alphabets must originally have ended with the invented *upsilon*, since new letters are normally added at the end of an alphabet. Most archaic alphabets, however, already show the additional signs Φ, X, and Ψ, the so-called 'supplementals', which differ somewhat in their use and values from place to place. In Crete they are not used in writing Greek (cf. ποινικάζεν above for what would in Attic be φοινικάζειν), which has been taken to be a sign of the archaism of the Cretan alphabet. Elsewhere Φ stands regularly for [p^h], but there is fundamental disagreement on the representation of [k^h]: some alphabets use the sign X, whereas in others this has the value [ks] and the sign Ψ is used for [k^h]; where X is used for [k^h], Ψ has the value [ps]. Attempts have been made to reduce this variation to a single process of creation and diffusion, but much remains obscure. It is noteworthy that the Ionic alphabet – that is, the alphabet of Eastern Ionia, the one most familiar to classicists – uses X with value [k^h], but the Euboean alphabet, which was exported to Italy, uses X with the value [ks], which eventually appears in the Latin alphabet (see below).

In Ionia, the sound [h] was lost quite early, and the letter H, which until then had been used to write this sound, acquired a new value. Formerly it had been used to write not only [h] but also an initial sequence [hę̄], as in HRA [Hę̄rā], the name of the goddess, by a form of shorthand writing using the sign to write the first syllable of the letter-name *hēta* rather than just the first sound; after the loss of [h], the letter would be simply *ēta* and came to stand simply for the long vowel. A companion sign *omega* (Ω) for the long vowel [ō] was then created, and duly added at the end of the alphabet. Since the Ionic dialect had also lost the sound [w], the digamma was no longer needed and fell out of use. These changes resulted in the alphabet that has become familiar as 'the Greek alphabet', as it indeed became after it was adopted throughout the Greek world – in Athens officially in 403/2 (though it was in unofficial use earlier) and in most other regions by the end of the fourth century BC: Α Β Γ Δ Ε Ζ Η Θ Ι Κ Λ Μ Ν Ξ Ο Π Ρ Σ Τ Υ Φ Χ Ψ Ω.

Other developments in the fifth century led to further improvements in the representation of vowels. In early Attic inscriptions, the letter E can stand for short [e] or either of two long vowels, [ẹ̄] (the product of contraction of two short [e] sounds and of various lengthening processes) and [ę̄], an inherited long vowel (with which the inherited [ā] also eventually merged in a change common to Attic and Ionic). Similarly O can stand for short [o] or either of two long vowels [ọ̄] and [ǭ]. At this early period there also existed two diphthongs [ei] and [ou], written EI and OY, but during the fifth century, by a change common to Ionic too, these diphthongs changed into the long vowels [ẹ̄] and [ọ̄], falling together with the already existing vowels of that quality; the spellings EI and OY now came to represent the sounds [ẹ̄] and [ō] (from whatever source). At Athens from 403/2, with the help of the newly introduced *ēta* and *ōmega*, it was now possible to distinguish E = [e], EI = [ẹ̄], H = [ę̄], O = [o], OY = [ọ̄], Ω= [ọ̄]. A, I and Y continued to stand for both long and short vowels.

The older Attic alphabet had used H with the value [h]. The Ionic alphabet provided no symbol for this sound and (apart from a few examples where H is still to be read [h]) it was not represented in Attic inscriptions (breathings, like accents, were invented in Alexandria during the Hellenistic period; see also chapter 47).

The alphabet in Italy: the Etruscan alphabet

The Greek alphabet was brought to Italy by Greek traders and settlers. One group of these, from Euboea (see also chapter 15), established themselves in the early eighth century BC in northern Campania, where they came into contact with the Etruscans; by this route the Greek alphabet, in a Chalcidian form, was introduced into Etruria, and from there it spread to other parts of central and northern Italy. The history and development of the Latin alphabet can only be understood against this background.

The earliest full representation of the alphabet borrowed by the Etruscans appears, written from right to left, on a miniature ivory writing-tablet (see also chapter 34) from Marsiliana d'Albegna (early seventh century BC; figure 63.3). It shows the following letters (in the conventional transliteration): *a b c d e v z h θ i k l m n* $\overset{+}{s}$ *o p ś q r s t u ṡ φ χ*. From this it can be seen that a very full form of the alphabet (twenty-six letters) was transmitted, with all the Phoenician sibilants (here transliterated *z* $\overset{+}{s}$ *ś s ṡ*), with *qoppa* (*q*) and with three supplementals following the *upsilon*; it is clear from Etruscan texts that X must have been borrowed with a value close to [ks], since it is used to write sibilants, while Ψ represents [kʰ] – in line with Euboean practice. The third letter, transliterated *c*, continues the Greek *gamma* (see below); the sixth is the Greek *digamma*, transliterated *v* and standing for [w]; *z*, to judge from its value in some other alphabets derived from the Etruscan, probably represented an affricate [tˢ] or a sequence of sounds [ts].

Such a complete alphabet was obviously the one taught and learned, but for practical purposes a number of letters were superfluous and do not appear in the writing of Etruscan texts: the language did not distinguish between [o] and [u], so *o* was not needed; Etruscan seems not to have distinguished between voiceless and voiced consonants (eg between [p], [t], [k] and [b], [d], [g]), so *b* and *d* are not used in writing Etruscan. The Greek *gamma* (*c*), on the other hand, came to be used with the value [k], alongside *k* and *q*: these were originally distributed according to the following vowel, with sequences *ce*, *ci*, *ka*, *qu* (in all of which the consonant is [k]). This is clearly modelled on the archaic Greek use of *qoppa* before [o] and [u] but *kappa* elsewhere (see above); the incorporation of the *gamma* into this system became possible once it was no longer required to write a voiced consonant [g], and its adoption specifically before front vowels may have been determined by the

Fig. 63.3 Miniature ivory writing-tablet with early Etruscan alphabet from Marsiliana d'Albegna. Early seventh century BC. Reprinted from M. Pandolfini and A. L. Prosdocimi, *Alfabetari e insegnamento della scrittura in Etruria e nell'Italia antica*, Florence: Olschki, 1990, p. 20.

name of the letter if this was, as has been plausibly suggested, in the first instance *gemma* rather than *gamma*. This system of triple representation of a single sound [k] (often referred to as the C/K/Q convention) appears only in the oldest inscriptions and was simplified by the sixth century, with *c* being generalised in southern Etruria and *k* in the north.

Etruscan distinguished two sibilants (the exact difference being a matter for debate) and the four signs (including X) provided in the model alphabet were clearly too many. In the earliest inscriptions a variety of spellings, involving different choices of letter, is attested, but simplification followed, with *s* and *ś* alone being used (although with reversed values in northern and southern areas).

These practicalities had in due course an effect on the alphabet as it was taught and learned, and a reduced version of nineteen letters was adopted, with otiose signs removed: cf. the sixth-century alphabet from Perusia (modern Perugia): *a e v z h θ i k l m n p ś r s t u φ χ*.

Etruscan had a sound [f] for which there was no suitable letter in the Greek alphabet, and this was at first spelled with a combination of letters *vh*. In the late sixth century the Etruscans adopted a sign 8 for [f] (probably taken from another central Italian alphabetic system) and added this to their alphabet – in final position.

The Latin alphabet

The Romans seem to have borrowed the alphabet from the Etruscans at a very early period, when the Etruscan alphabet was still being taught in its fullest form. This is the most likely explanation for the fact that the Latin alphabet has B, D and O with their Greek values [b], [d] and [o], even though these letters are not used in Etruscan inscriptions and eventually drop out of the Etruscan alphabet, as noted above. It is of course possible that the Romans also had some direct acquaintance with the Greek alphabet, but appeal to this as an explanation is less satisfactory in the light of the fact that the original Greek *gamma* in the Latin alphabet has the value [k] not [g]. This can readily be explained as being taken over from the Etruscan alphabet together with the C/K/Q convention (see above). In the earliest Latin inscriptions there are some slight traces of the C/K/Q convention being applied, although there are many inconsistencies, but it is clear from later Latin spellings that it was once operative: the letter K survives in the Latin alphabet but is used only in a few fossilised spellings like *kalendae* (see also chapter 64) and *Karthago* or as the abbreviation for the name *Kaeso*, always before [a], and Q is used in combination with V to write [kw] in words like *quis* ('who'), but in republican inscriptions still also to write [k] before [u], e.g. *pequnia* for classical *pecunia* (money). Further striking evidence for the adoption of the convention comes from the variant vowels in the names of the letters: *cē*, *kā*, *qū*. Apart from the survivals noted, C was generalised fairly early as the normal spelling (just as in southern Etruria).

Another feature of the Latin alphabet that speaks for an Etruscan mediation is the notation of [f]. It seems that originally the Romans adopted the Etruscan digraph spelling FH (rendered as *vh* in transliterations of Etruscan texts), the first letter being the original digamma. There is just one Latin attestation of this in a seventh-century

Fig. 63.4 Earliest full Latin alphabet, on an early third-century BC dish from Monteroni di Palo. Reprinted from M. Cristofani (ed.), *Civiltà degli etruschi*, Milan: Electa, 1988, p. 343.

inscription on a gold brooch from Praeneste in the form FHEFHAKED [fefaked] ('made'); doubts have been cast on the authenticity of the object and its inscription, but perhaps needlessly. At all events the former existence of such digraph spellings provides the simplest explanation of how F could come to stand for [f] in the Latin alphabet, by being used on its own as a simplification of the digraph FH. That meant that F could no longer represent [w], with the consequence that V was used with both vocalic and consonantal values, both for [u] and for [w].

Otiose signs such as Θ, Φ and Ψ – the Latin language did not make distinctions of aspiration in its stop system – were discarded; of the sibilant signs, S alone is used for [s] from the earliest inscriptions. The letter X, occasionally used by the Etruscans to write one of their sibilants, has the value [ks] in Latin, just as in the Euboean Greek model: this again might be explained by preservation of the original value through the practice of reciting the full alphabet as part of the process of learning it.

The earliest attestation of the Latin alphabet written out as such is on an early third-century BC clay dish from Monteroni di Palo: A B C D E F Z H I K L M N O P Q R S T V X (figure 63.4). A striking feature of this is the presence of Z as the seventh letter, in accordance with the Graeco-Etruscan model, although this letter is not used in writing Latin. At some time in the third century, Z was replaced by G: the latter was an invention (presumably a simple modification of the letter C) and provided at last a way of writing [g], hitherto written C; the Z, which was not needed, was dropped. According to Roman tradition, the invention of G was the work of a schoolmaster, probably a Greek from Tarentum. This is an unusual example of a new letter being inserted into the alphabet instead of being added at the end, but its substitution for Z made it possible to achieve this without breaking the rhythm of recitation.

In the later Republic, there was manifestly a desire to represent borrowed Greek words more precisely. This can be seen in the adoption of the spellings PH, TH and CH to write the Greek aspirated consonants (written Φ, Θ and X in classical Greek), whereas previously P, T and C had sufficed. It also led to the addition of two new letters to the Latin alphabet, simply taken from the Greek alphabet and added at the end (in the usual manner). These were Y and Z, with their contemporary Greek values [ü] and [z] respectively, found in words like *Zephyrus*.

The end result of these processes was the familiar Latin alphabet: A B C D E F G H I K L M N O P Q R S T V X Y Z (the introduction of J and W, as well as the separation of U and V, are much later Western European developments).

The Latin alphabet did not provide a perfect system for representing the language. No distinction could at any stage be made in writing between [i] (as in *iter* 'way') and consonantal [y] (as in *iam* 'now'); once F had acquired the value [f], there was equally no way of distinguishing vocalic [u] (as in *ullus* 'any') from consonantal [w] (as in *uetera* 'old'). There were no separate symbols for long and short vowels: from c. 135 to 75 BC, there are inscriptions in which long vowels are written double (e.g. *paastores*, shepherds), but this practice (no doubt borrowed from the Oscans in southern Italy) failed to become established. A notation EI for [ī], distinct from I for [i], is found in the late republic and early empire, and it arose as follows: Latin once had a diphthong [ei], which was written EI; in the third century BC this diphthong became a long vowel [ẹ̄] and was then written either E or conservatively EI; around the mid-second century BC this [ẹ̄] became [ī], indistinguishable from existing [ī] in words like *uita* ('life'), and this vowel was now spelled I or still conservatively EI; the EI spelling now represented [ī], whatever the origin of the sound, and so could be used even in words that never had an original diphthong, whence spellings like VEITA (these spellings are never entirely consistent). In the first century BC one may find in inscriptions the so-called 'I *longa*', a particularly tall version of I, used for [i], but in the imperial period this acquires other functions.

Appendix

Characters in square brackets are phonetic symbols as distinct from letters; so b is the letter b, [b] the sound made at the start of *bit*.

aspirate stop pronounced with an audible release of breath, such as the sound at the start of *pit*; the sound [h]
front vowels vowels produced with the tongue at the front of the mouth, such as [i]
stop produced with lips, tongue, etc. completely blocking the flow of air from the lungs, such as [k], [t]
voiced produced with vocal fold vibration, like the [z] in *hazy* or the sound at the start of *thy*
voiceless produced without vocal fold vibration, like the [s] in *miss* or the sound at the start of *thigh*

Further reading

Mycenaean and Greek Alphabets

W. S. Allen, *Vox Graeca: A Guide to the Pronunciation of Classical Greek* (3rd edn), Cambridge: Cambridge University Press, 1987.

J. Chadwick, *Linear B and Related Scripts*, London: British Museum Press, 1987.

A. Heubeck, *Schrift* (*Archaeologica Homerica* III.x), Göttingen: Vandenhoeck and Ruprecht, 1979.

L. H. Jeffery, *The Local Scripts of Archaic Greece* (rev. edn with supplement by A. W. Johnston), Oxford: Clarendon Press, 1990.

R. Wachter, 'Alphabet', in *Brill's New Pauly* 1 A–Ari, Leiden and Boston: Brill, 2002, pp. 529–41.

The Etruscan alphabet

M. Cristofani, 'Recent advances in Etruscan epigraphy and language', in D. Ridgway and F. R. Ridgway (eds), *Italy Before the Romans*, London, New York and San Francisco: Academic Press, 1979, pp. 373–412.

The Latin alphabet

W. S. Allen, *Vox Latina: A Guide to the Pronunciation of Classical Latin* (2nd edn), Cambridge: Cambridge University Press, 1989.

R. Wachter, *Altlateinische Inschriften: Sprachliche und epigraphische Untersuchungen zu den Dokumenten bis etwa 150 v. Chr.*, Bern, Frankfurt, New York and Paris: P. Lang, 1987, pp. 7–54.

R. Wallace, 'The origins and development of the Latin alphabet', in W. M. Senner (ed.), *The Origins of Writing*, Lincoln NE: University of Nebraska Press, 1989, pp. 121–35.

64. The Ancient Calendar

Thomas Harrison and Edward Bispham

No single calendar was ever adopted as standard in the ancient world. Instead there was a proliferation of local systems of dating, with years beginning in different months in different parts of the ancient world (in July in Athens, and in Rome initially in March, and then in January). Moreover, states and other collective bodies which had calendars sometimes chose to mark significant events by beginning a new era, that is starting the calendar again from scratch from the point being celebrated, or by moving New Year's Day to the relevant date; an example of the latter is the decree of the *koinon* of the Roman province of Asia from 9 BC, whereby New Year was moved in all the cities of Asia to 23 September, to fall on Augustus' birthday, marking the benefits he had brought to all mankind (Sherk, *Translated Documents of Greece and Rome 4*, no. 101).

In the Greek world, the best-known calendar is the Athenian. In the Roman world, the (solar) Julian calendar was exported across the empire; even then, however, Greek cities continued to use their own lunar calendars alongside it, or to merge the two (so, for example, giving local names to the solar months). Neither calendars nor precisely fixed times of day were ever internalised to anything like the extent current today. Instead, the practical and the symbolic character of calendars is at the forefront: their role is to ensure the regularity of the agricultural year, of festivals or of civic institutions (even the term 'calendar' is derived from a Latin term for 'debt register'), but also to demarcate the cycle of the seasons and to regulate the worship of the gods.

Years

Years were dated in antiquity by the names of a city's chief magistrate(s) or priests (hence in Athens by '*archōn* year', or in Rome by the consuls) or by regnal year (e.g. in the case of the Hellenistic monarchies, or the Roman emperors, who exploited the annual renewal of their tribunician power for this purpose (see also chapter 19). The problem that arises from this multiplicity of dating systems is how to relate events dated by different systems.

A number of responses were adopted. In the fifth century BC, Herodotus used a system of 'generations' to establish synchronisms between geographically distant events (and so to establish a makeshift relative chronology for archaic history). Hellanicus of Lesbos used the list of priestesses of Hera at Argos as a basis, while Thucydides adopted more than one local dating system in combination. From the Hellenistic period onwards, more robust attempts were made to establish relative chronologies, attempts associated with Eratosthenes and Timaeus. The use of Olympiads (the four-year periods between Olympic festivals) is one example, where the regularity of the games, and the fixing of the first Olympic victory to 776 BC, established an internationally recognised dating system (see also chapter 49). Another is the foundation date of Rome, with years numbered as *ab urbe condita*, 'from the foundation of the city' (see also chapter 50). (The foundation date itself was first dated by reference to Olympiads. Timaeus started the ball rolling by suggesting the thirty-eighth year before the first Olympiad, what we call 813 BC, also his date for the foundation of Carthage; he was followed by Roman writers opting for a number of dates in the eighth century – see Dionysius of Halicarnassus, *Ant. Rom.* 1.74 – before Varro finally fixed it to the year we call 753 BC.) At the same time, however, dating by generations (which could be of thirty, thirty-three or forty years) continued. Hand in hand with this went a persistent temptation to date by educated guesswork: so, for example, to date births in relation to the *acmē* or high point (or just a known dated event) of an individual's career. So, for example, the traditional date for Herodotus' birth, 484 BC, is fixed forty years earlier than his known participation in the foundation of the city of Thurii – the year at which he is deemed to have 'flourished'.

A new impetus was given to the search for a universal dating system by the rise of Christianity (hence the chronological system of Eusebius of Caesarea's *Chronicle*). An important advance was made in 526 by Dionysius Exiguus ('Little Dennis'), who had been charged by the papacy with finding a date for Easter on which all Christians could agree, and which avoided the prevailing system; that system based its calculation on the day of accession of the emperor Diocletian, famously unfriendly to the Christians (see also chapters 19 and 20). Dionysius' new starting point involved establishing the birthdate of Christ as equivalent to the year 754 *ab urbe condita*, that is, what we call AD 1, a synchronism still widely accepted, although it did not catch on in Dionysius' lifetime.

Months and days

Already by the fifth century BC, Greek astronomers knew the length of the 'tropical' year (365¼ days) and of the month (29½ days) (see also chapter 54). The problem in devising any calendar is to square this with a roughly regular dating system (hence the leap year adjusts for four missing quarter-days by adding an additional day in every fourth year). A number of similar expedients were devised in antiquity, both by astronomers (so e.g., according to two schemes, by the addition of extra or 'intercalary' months in particular years on eight- or nineteen-year cycles) and more arbitrarily at a political level.

The Greek world

The Greek year was based on lunar months (ie months according to the waxing and then the waning of the moon, with the full moon at the middle point of the month). Months were named after divinities or festivals, though from the Hellenistic period onwards they could also be named after kings or other powerful individuals (with the names of months changing sometimes at a bewildering pace, depending on the course of events). Named months are attested as early as the Mycenaean period.

In the case of the Athenian calendar, the year began with the first new moon after the summer solstice. The year was identified by the name of the chief (the so-called 'eponymous') *archōn*; hence the archonship of Solon, say, is identified today as 594/3, that is, it ran from midsummer 594 to midsummer 593. In the following list of Athenian months, Hecatombaeon corresponds roughly to July and so on:

1. Hecatombaeon
2. Metageitnion
3. Boedromion
4. Pyanopsion
5. Maemacterion
6. Posideon
7. Gamelion
8. Anthesterion
9. Elaphebolion
10. Munychion
11. Thargelion
12. Scirophorion

Some months had 29 days and others 30. The year was of 354 (plus or minus one) days. To keep the months in step with the seasons, an occasional thirteenth month was introduced (this followed Posideon, ie after the winter solstice – the shortest day of the year), creating a year of 384 (plus or minus one) days.

Within each month, counting of days was not straightforwardly sequential. After the first day of the month (the new moon, *noumēnia*), the next nine days were counted as the first, second, third etc. days of the 'waxing moon'; from the twenty-second until the thirtieth day (*triakas*) the days were counted backwards, so, for example, the fourth day of the 'waning month'. In months of 29 rather than 30 days (so called 'hollow' months), the 'second day of the waning month' (ie the 29th) was simply omitted.

In Athens, the year was also split into ten units (prytanies), each prytany being the term for which a one-tenth portion of the Athenian *boulē* or council of 500 (again termed a prytany: 50 men from a single tribe) took charge of the day-to-day administration of the city. The first four prytanies were 36 days in length, the last six 35 days. The Aristotelian *Constitution of Athens* (see also chapter 60) describes in detail what political institutions were reserved for what assembly meeting in this institutional calendar.

The other major calendar in use in the East before and during the Roman period was the Egyptian, which, with Macedonian equivalents (in parentheses below) added to the months in 119/118 BC, lasted through to the end of the empire, attested on thousands of papyri:

Thoth (Dius)	Phamenoth (Artemisius)
Phaophi (Apellaeus)	Pharmouthi (Daisius)
Hathyr (Audnaeus)	Pachon (Panemus)
Choiach (Peritius)	Payni (Loius)
Tybi (Dystrus)	Epeiph (Gorpiaeus)
Mecheir (Xandiucs)	Mesore (Hyperberetaeus)

The Roman world

The Roman year was initially 355 days long, with March, May, July (Quintilis) and October 31 days long, February 28, and the remaining months 29. The names of the months (some again based on the names of deities, e.g. Martius or Junius, others merely numerical, i.e. September onwards) are the basis of today's Western months:

1. Ianuarius	7. Quintilis (later: Iulius)
2. Februarius	8. Sextilis (later: Augustus)
3. Martius	9. September
4. Aprilis	10. October
5. Maius	11. November
6. Iunius	12. December

From 153 BC, the year began on the first of January (rather than, as earlier, the first of March).

Dating within the months was done by reference to marker days: Kalends (the beginning of a month), Nones, and Ides (the middle of the month). The position of these varied depending on the length of the month: the Nones were in short months five days, and in long months seven days, after the Kalends; the Ides (nine days later, counting inclusively) were correspondingly on the thirteenth day of short months and the fifteenth day of long months. Dates were calculated by working backwards from these marker days (abbreviated respectively as Kal., Non., and Id.; thus IV Kal. Mart. means four days before the Kalends of March, ie 25 February; pr. stands for *pridie*, 'the day before').

To intercalate (in order to marry this calendar with the seasons), a month of 27 days could be added at the end of February but with that month shortened to 23 (or in a leap year 24) days. (This was often politically motivated as a way of delaying events tied to a fixed calendar date.

By the time of Julius Caesar, however, the year was baldly out of kilter with the seasons, and a big readjustment was needed: the year 45 BC was 445 days long (with an additional 67 days). Thereafter, a solar calendar was adopted, with a year of 365 days, longer months, and an additional day in February (between the 23rd and 24th) in leap years.

As in Athens, one major function of the Roman calendar was to divide time between sacred and secular activities (although antiquity did not distinguish between these two categories as sharply as we do today; see also chapter 4). A number of inscribed calendars survive from Italy and elsewhere in the empire, and they reveal how anniversaries of events important in the imperial house (birthdays, accessions, victories etc.) were added into calendars, beside the existing entries marking the traditional republican religious festivals. A similar process can be seen with the Christianisation of the Roman imperial calendar, which during the fourth and fifth centuries became a hybrid, with the addition of Christian festivals including, as well as festivals like the Nativity and Easter, the anniversaries of martyrdoms. The finest example is the codex-calendar known as the *Calendar of 354*, also the *Calendar of Filocalus*, after its creator; there were more specific Christian liturgical calendars too, starting with the *feriale* (festival calendar) of AD 336. Although there have been further reforms (the

Gregorian reforms of Pope Gregory XIII in 1582, and the Orthodox reforms of 1924), the Julian calendar (named after Caesar) is the basis of our modern Western calendar.

Weeks, days and hours

The Roman calendar seems from the beginning to have recognised eight-day cycles, which separated regular market days or *nundinae*; these are marked with the letters A to H in the inscribed calendars. At the same time a number of influences, from astrology to Judaism, seem to have led to the informal adoption in the Hellenistic world of a seven-day cycle, with individual days named after deities, which passed into usage in the Roman West. The deities are (in Roman nomenclature) Saturn, Sol, Luna, Mars, Mercury, Juppiter, Venus: these names have passed into modern usage through the Romance languages, with *dies Lunae* becoming *lundi* in French, *lunedi* in Italian etc.; and in translated form, Monday = Moon's day (see A. Degrassi, *Inscriptiones Italiae* XIII, Rome: Libreria dello Stato, 1963, 2 no. 53, from Pompeii = Sherk, *Translated Documents of Greece and Rome 6*, no. 198). Christians seem from at least the second century to have taken the *dies Solis* (the sun's day) as sacred, and from the time of Constantine the Great it became equated with the *dies dominicus* or Lord's day. The church retained the seven-day cycle, and the names of the days of the week, despite pagan and Jewish associations; while the old pagan republican eight-day cycle survives on the *Calendar of 354* beside the seven-day cycle, the former was probably obsolescent by this time.

According to Herodotus, the division of the day into twelve portions came, with the sundial, from the Babylonians (Hdt. 2.109). These hours, calculated by sundial, varied according to the length of daylight. At night-time, the equivalent division could only be performed by means of a water clock (*klepsydra*), but it was only in the third century BC that a means was devised to ensure an even flow of water (by the engineer Ctesibius, who is also supposed to have invented dials with moving pointers). An increased sophistication in the distinction between times of day seems to have developed in response to the needs of bureaucracy, especially in Egypt and Rome: Suetonius, for example, claims that it was Augustus who was responsible for the addition of the time of day to written documents (see also chapter 60).

Further reading

E. J. Bickerman, *Chronology of the Ancient World* (rev. edn), London: Thames and Hudson, 1980.

G. Dohrn-van Rossum, *History of the Hour: Clocks and Modern Temporal Orders*, Chicago: University of Chicago Press, 1996.

R. Hannah, *Greek and Roman Calendars: Constructions of Time in the Classical World*, London: Duckworth, 2005.

B. Lancon, *Rome in Late Antiquity*, Edinburgh: Edinburgh University Press, 2000, ch. 10.

A. K. Michels, *The Calendar of the Roman Republic*, Princeton: Princeton University Press, 1967.

M. R. Salzman, *On Roman Time: The Codex-Calendar of 354 and the Rhythms of Urban Life in Late Antiquity*, Berkeley: University of California Press, 1990.

A. E. Samuel, *Greek and Roman Chronology: Calendars and Years in Classical Antiquity*, Munich: Beck, 1972.

R. K. Sherk, *Translated Documents of Greece and Rome 4: Rome and the Greek East to the Death of Augustus*, Cambridge: Cambridge University Press, 1984.

R. K. Sherk, *Translated Documents of Greece and Rome 6: The Roman Empire: Augustus to Hadrian*, Cambridge: Cambridge University Press, 1988.

65. *Metre*

Armand D'Angour

This chapter gives an overview of the elements of Greek and Latin metre, introduces the main technical terms and symbols used, and offers some suggestions for learning and for further study. It is written to be read continuously; technical terms are indicated in **bold** when they are first introduced or explained, and later paragraphs assume a grasp of the explanations given in previous paragraphs.

The music of poetry

Poetry is distinguished from prose in respect of sound no less than expression. The earliest Greek poems (including the epics of Homer and the compositions of the lyric poets) were songs. The melody would be accompanied by a lyre or *aulos* (reed-pipe), and the words were sung in predetermined patterns of rhythm based on movement and dance. The melodies are not preserved; but since each syllable of a Greek word has a natural spoken duration that may be measured as either short or long (like the dots and dashes of Morse Code), the patterns of verse rhythm are preserved in the actual words of the poems. From the fifth century BC most Greek poetry was no longer composed to be sung, but the Greeks continued to regard poetry not just as words, but as music (*mousikē* is derived from the Muses, goddesses of poetry, music and dance). Roman poets, who from the third century BC imitated the metres used in Greek poetry (displacing earlier Italian traditions such as **Saturnian** verse) and adapted them for use with Latin, followed this convention; Virgil's *Aeneid*, for instance, begins with the words *arma virumque cano*, 'Arms and the man I *sing*'. The music survives in the memorable, and measurable, rhythms of ancient poetry: metre (from Greek *metron*) means 'measure'. Since metre is thus integral to both Greek and Latin verse, and is used with great effectiveness and skill, some knowledge of how it works is essential to the proper understanding and enjoyment of classical poetry. The terminology and notation used for the formal description of ancient metres may seem daunting, but for practical and scholarly purposes they are unavoidable. The technical aspect of metre can, indeed, hold a fascination of its own; but the study of metre should above all help us appreciate something of the music of ancient poetry.

Quantitative metre

Ancient metre differs significantly from modern in that it depends on measuring *syllables* rather than *accents* (or *stresses*). In English, the rhythm of poetry comes from stressing certain syllables to create a regular pattern of beats. Take the first two lines of William Blake's poem *The Tiger* ('beats' are marked with ´):

> Tíger! Tíger! búrning bríght
> Ín the fórests óf the níght.

The beat is preserved even if we increase the number of syllables as, for example, in

> Tíger! Tíger! búrning bríght,
> Féarsomely sílent in the fórests of the níght.

Within each beat each syllable has approximately the same duration; we do not dwell twice as long on the stressed syllables as the unstressed. By contrast, the metres of Greek poetry (and Roman poetry, insofar as it adopts Greek principles) are created from sequences of syllables, each of which has a measurable duration that is either **long** or **short**. The time-value assigned to a syllable is called its **quantity**. Quantity is standardly indicated by these symbols: – for long, ⏑ for short. In theory the duration of the long was double that of the short (even if in practice this ratio is less precise): short and long may therefore be considered equivalent to quaver (♪) and crotchet (♩) in modern musical notation. The metrical term for the single time-unit is a **mora**, so a long syllable comprises two **morae**; in many cases two short syllables (⏑⏑) may be substituted for a long one (this is called **resolution** – the long syllable is **resolved**) or one long syllable for two short ones (**contraction**). If we artificially extend the stressed syllables of Blake's *Tiger* to twice the length of the unstressed ones, they present the following metrical pattern:

– ⏑ – ⏑ – ⏑ – (♩ ♪ ♩ ♪ ♩ ♪ ♩)

Since such patterns are simply symbolic indications of time-values, it is more accurate to speak of long and short **positions**, each of which may be filled by a syllable; but for convenience we may occasionally refer simply to syllables. Sometimes a position permits *either* a long or short syllable; if so, it is called **anceps** (pronounced *án-seps*) and indicated by the symbol × (equivalent to ⏓ or ⏒). The syllable which fills an anceps position may itself be determined as being either long or short (when ambiguous, it is called **syllaba anceps**). The metrical symbols are most easily read by using *dum* for the long syllable (–) and *di* for the short (⏑) as follows:

dum di dum di dum di dum

Bear in mind that we tend out of habit to stress the heavier syllables (*dúm di dúm di dúm di dúm*) rather than to lengthen them as ancient readers would have. *NB* The accent marks placed on ancient Greek words do not indicate stress as here (and as they do in modern Greek), but are used to mark alterations in vocal *pitch*; in spoken ancient Greek, the voice rose on syllables marked with the acute ´, rose slightly less on the grave `, and rose and fell on the circumflex ˆ.

Scansion and prosody

Repeatable rhythmic units of the type described above form the identifiable sequences, the **metres**, of Greek poetry. In antiquity, metres were assigned generic names related to features such as their provenance (eg the **Ionic** metre is related to Ionia and **Aeolic** metres are derived from poetry in the Aeolic dialect) or their structure; for example, **hexameters** consist of six metra (Greek *hex* = six) and **hendecasyllables** of eleven syllables (*hendeka* = eleven). Specific sequences were often identified by names derived from poets with whom the metres were particularly associated, such as **Sapphics** from the poetess Sappho, **Alcaics** from Alcaeus. The key to identifying a metre is to scan correctly each given line of verse, **scansion** being the term used for the analysis of metrical quantities. The system of principles that determine quantity is called **prosody** (pronounced *prós-o-dee*), and includes rules about when vowels were pronounced long or short **by nature** (just as we 'naturally' pronounce *o* short in 'holiday' and long in 'holy') and when syllables with short vowels are long **by position**. Greek alphabetic characters exist for long *e* (*ēta*) and *o* (*ōmega*), though the other vowels (*a, i or u*) may be pronounced either long or short. No Latin vowels indicate natural quantities, but these can often be inferred from the position of a word in a metrical sequence (e.g. to fit the hexameter, the *i* of 'primus' in *Aeneid* 1.1 must be long by nature, and the *u* short). The first line of Virgil's *Aeneid* ends with the word *oris*, the third line begins with the word *litora*: how are they pronounced and scanned? The natural vowel-quantities are sometimes indicated in modern texts by printing *ōrīs* and *lītora*. The bars on top of the *o* and *i*, called **macrons** (from the Greek for 'long'), indicate that these vowels are here long by nature (*ō* as in English 'or', *ī* as in 'police'). They should accordingly be scanned long: *ōrīs* is two long syllables (– –), and *lītora* is a long followed by two shorts (– ⏑⏑).

Principles of prosody

The vowels in *ōrīs* and *lītora* precede at most a *single* consonant; in such circumstances vowels that are *not* long by nature (i.e. the *o* and *a* in 'litora') will be both pronounced and scanned short. A vowel followed by *two or more* consonants (including at the beginning of a following word) or by a double-consonant such as Latin x and Greek ψ (*psi*) will usually be scanned long by position, even if it is not long by nature. The exception to this principle is that particular groups of double-consonants such as *tr* and *pl* (as in Latin *pa*<u>*tr*</u>*is* and Greek *ha*<u>*pl*</u>*os*) permit a short vowel preceding them to remain short; the basic rule is that the combination of a **mute** consonant – *c*, *p*, *t* – and a **liquid** consonant – *l*, *m*, *n*, *r* – permit this shortening (**packet** of **minerals** may serve as a mnemonic). Principles of prosody overlap in Greek and Latin, but each language has distinct features. In both, for instance, **elision** of vowels takes place when a short vowel at the end of a word is followed by a vowel or aspirate (*h*) at the beginning of the following word. This is marked in Greek by an apostrophe, for example *muri' Achaiois* for *muria Achaiois*; but elision is not so marked in Latin, where word-endings such as *um* are also elided, as in *mult*(*um*) *ille* (for purposes of scansion, the elided element may be bracketed in this way). Diphthongs (e.g. *ae*, *oe*) are always scanned long in Latin; but diphthongs in Greek (eg *ai*, *au*, *eu*, *oi*) may sometimes be shortened, as may a naturally long vowel, before a vowel or aspirate. This is called **correption**, and occurs particularly between words (e.g. *eipe kai hēmin*, scanned – ⏑ ⏑ – –), though it may also occur within a word (eg *toioutos*, scanned ⏑ – –).

The colon

Scholars in antiquity subdivided bodies of metre such as verses and stanzas into smaller units for analysis, naming some subdivisions after anatomical terms such as *kōlon* 'limb' (Latinised as 'colon'), *pous* 'foot' ('pes'), and *daktylos* 'finger' (or 'toe'). But ancient poets composed in rhythm, not to metre; and **cola** (plural of **colon**) are the shortest units of metre that would have been viable for purposes of composition (most cola have between five and eleven syllables). The seven-syllable sequence we encountered above – *dum di dum di dum di dum* – is found as a colon in Greek poetry, and was named a **lēkythion** (pronounced *le-kíth-i-on*), meaning 'little oil-bottle', on account of an amusing literary association. The rhythmical sequence is repeatedly used in a scene of Aristophanes' comedy *Frogs*, in which the tragedian Aeschylus claims that he can substitute the ends of verses written by his rival Euripides with the phrase *lēkuthion apōlesen* (– ⏑ ⏑⏑ ⏑ – ⏑ –), which constitutes a lekythion with the second long resolved, meaning 'lost his bottle of oil, he did' (the translation mimics the metre). The comic effect may be suggested by making a similar substitution in Blake's lines:

> Tiger! Tiger! burning bright
> *Lost his bottle of oil, he did!*

Dochmiacs

Many commonly used cola are identified by-names based either on intrinsic features or on literary associations. The **dochmiac** colon is named from a Greek word meaning 'askew', because of the jerky movement of the sequence of short and long syllables:

> ⏑ – – ⏑ – *di dum dum di dum*

Dochmiacs are regularly found in the lyric choruses of Greek tragedies, and always associated with agitation or distress (virtually all other metres have no such emotional association but are used for a variety of emotional expression). The following mnemonic (memory-aid) for dochmiacs was invented by Gilbert Murray, the Regius Professor of Greek at Oxford 1908–36 (I have slightly changed his second line):

> The wise kangaroos
> Prefer boots to shoes.

Mnemonics are helpful for recalling the sequence of longs and shorts in cola or longer units of metre. However, they are likely to misrepresent the true nature of the rhythms (in due course one should learn by heart representative verses in the original languages). An English-speaker would tend to utter the above using four beats as follows:

The wíse kángaróos ´
Prefér bóots to shóes ´

Here the fourth and eighth stress-marks fall on a silent beat that would be marked by a rest in a musical score; but there is no evidence that sequences of dochmiacs in Greek admitted a silent beat of this kind. The little evidence we by chance possess shows that a dochmiac colon might have been heard as having essentially *two* principal beats as follows:

⏑ –́ – ⏑́ –

A suitable mnemonic in this case (proposed by Oxford undergraduate Gail Trimble in 2001) might be:

That ól' man ríver,
he jús' keeps róllin' . . .

The dochmiac metre shows a degree of flexibility found in few other metres in the licence allowed for the basic sequence to be resolved and for the substitution of longs for shorts. All three longs may be resolved into two shorts, and either short of the basic dochmiac may be replaced by a long (**'dragged'**) – which may in turn be resolved. With just the last long of the basic dochmiac resolved, one gets the rhythm ⏑ – – ⏑ ⏑⏑ 'The Regius Professor'! ('Regius' has two syllables as in 'region'). With all three long syllables resolved, we get eight short syllables as follows (it helps to bunch the resolved syllables together, visibly and audibly):

⏑ ⏑⏑ ⏑⏑ ⏑ ⏑⏑

That is, 'The wise kangaroos prefer boots to shoes – *in any regular leather*'.

Feet and metra

Units smaller than cola are artificial subdivisions, constructed for the purpose of metrical analysis; no poet ever composed by adding such small units of metre together. A **foot** may consist of two or three syllables (e.g. – –, – ⏑⏑); so a whole line (or **verse**) may be analysed as a series of feet in varying sequences. Feet with different metrical shapes are assigned names of their own: thus a foot consisting of two longs, *dum dum* (– –), is called a **spondee** (easy to remember because 'spondee' itself has two long syllables), while one consisting of a long followed by two shorts (– ⏑⏑) is a **dactyl** (from the Greek word for 'finger' and 'toe', which similarly consist of a long section attached to two short ones). In many metrical contexts, dactyl and spondee are interchangeable; in terms of duration, the unit-measure (or **metron**) of a dactyl (1 long + 2 shorts) is equivalent to that of a spondee (2 longs). An **iambic** (*i-ám-bic*) foot is traditionally defined as *di dum* (⏑ –) with two positions (the English 'iambic pentameter', as used in sonnets, has five iambs, eg in Shakespeare's 'Shall I compare thee to a summer's day'). For iambic and other metres, however, the metron is a different, and more useful, unit of analysis than the foot. In the **iambic trimeter**, for instance, which is used for speeches in Greek drama (Aristotle decribed iambics as 'most like speaking'), a spondee, dactyl, and even **anapaest** (⏑⏑–) might occur in place of ⏑ – ; the system is more economically mapped out by the iambic metron (× – ⏑ –), consisting of four positions beginning with long or short (anceps) and permitting numerous possible resolutions (in Greek comedy even the short syllable may be resolved). Thus the basic iambic trimeter may be simply represented as three similar *metra* as follows (a single vertical line is used to mark off the metra):

× – ⏑ – | × – ⏑ – | × – ⏑ – ||

A passage of iambic trimeters consists of verses like this, variously resolved, following one another in serried ranks, with a **pause** (marked with two vertical lines as above) at the end of each line and the same metrical sequence starting afresh at the beginning of each line. The term for such forms of verse is **stichic** (*stíck-ic*, from Greek *stichos* 'rank'). It contrasts with **lyric** metres in which lines often quite different from each other in metrical form flow continuously into each other without pause (such continuity is called **synapheia**, pronounced *sin-a-fée-a*).

The hexameter

Students often begin (and, regrettably, sometimes end) their study of metre with another regular stichic metre, the **dactylic hexameter**. This is one of the most abundantly employed metres in both Greek and Latin, used in epics of Homer and Virgil (so it is also called the **epic hexameter**, or simply abbreviated to 'hexameters') and in didactic and pastoral poetry. As its name indicates, the metre may be analysed into six dactylic metra:

1 2 3 4 5 6
– ⏖ | – ⏖ | – ⏖ | – ⏖ | – ⏖ | – – ||

'High on a branch of a tree sat a woodpecker watching a weevil' mimics the rhythm (or with spondaic fourth foot 'Everyone knows that *Survive* is a song by Gloria Gaynor'). If a regular pulse (or **ictus**) occurs on the first long of each foot (the **princeps**), the conflict of ictus with the natural stress accent of Latin words may be used to great poetic effect (see Wilkinson 1963). Each metron except the last consists of either a dactylic or spondaic foot; the final metron always has two long positions, in the second of which the syllable may be either long or short. Thus in *Aeneid* 1.2, the *it* of the last word *vēnit* is short; and since *dum di* (– ⏑) is traditionally called a **trochee** (*tróe-key*), the resulting foot is notionally trochaic (though a trochaic *metron*, – ⏑ – ×, is a reduplicated foot on the same lines as the iambic metron). But in hexameters such a short final syllable is better described as **brevis in longo**, that is, 'a short syllable in a long position'; the same applies to a short syllable in the final long of the iambic trimeter. In practice, the penultimate (fifth) foot of the hexameter is usually a dactyl, thus providing a satisfying impetus to end the line with the sequence – ⏑⏑ – – (called an **adonean** colon in lyric metre, after the ritual cry *ō ton Adōnin*, 'Oh for Adonis!').

The caesura

Poets in both Greek and Latin avoided making a strong word-break in the very centre of the hexameter line (i.e. at the end of the third foot), thus avoiding the jingle effect created by splitting the line into two halves of similar length and rhythm (compare 'High on a branch of a fir-tree, watchfully woodpeckers idled'). Instead, a significant word-break invariably occurs close to either side of this central point, allowing for the line to be divided according to a more rhythmically effective ratio (the same principle applies to the iambic trimeter). The resulting near-to-central-word break that occurs in the third or fourth foot of the hexameter (after either the first long or first short syllable) is called a **caesura** (pronounced *se-zyú-ra*); there may indeed be caesurae in both feet, but the one that constitutes the more significant break in sense or rhythm will be the *principal* or *main* caesura. Thus the three words with which the *Aeneid* begins allow for a strong word-break in the third foot after the first long (a **strong caesura**): 'arma virumque cano' – 'Arms and the man I sing.' For purposes of scansion, quantities are marked above each syllable, with the main caesura indicated by a short vertical double line:

– ⏑ ⏑ – ⏑ ⏑ – || – – – – ⏑ ⏑ – – ||
arma vi|rumque ca|no Troi|ae qui|primus ab|oris

'Arma virumque cano' itself constitutes a colon called a **hemiepes** (*hem-e-é-pez*, and meaning 'half [*hemi*] an epic hexameter [*epos*]' – in fact it is just *under* half). In choosing a dactylic hemiepes pregnant with programmatic meaning to begin his great epic, Virgil was consciously imitating Homer, whose incomparable *Iliad* also begins with three weighty words in the same rhythm, *Mēnin a|eide the|ā* ('[Of] anger sing, goddess'). To read hexameters fluently, it helps first to practise reading lines up to the main caesura, and identifying the words that constitute the – ⏑ ⏑ – – of the last two feet (eg *primus ab oris*), over a series of lines. The so-called **pentameter**, a line which alternates with the hexameter in the couplets (or **distichs**) of **elegiacs**, is simply two hemiepes cola in sequence. In developed Latin elegiacs, the second half of the pentameter is always fully dactylic, thus:

– ⏖ – ⏖ – | – ⏑⏑ – ⏑⏑ – ||

Additional remarks and symbols

Each metre has its own complexities and peculiarities. Aeolic metres, for instance, as originally used in Greek by Sappho and Alcaeus and brilliantly employed in Latin by Horace, use a variety of different cola notionally based on the **choriambic** foot (– ⏑ ⏑ –), such as **glyconics** (× × – ⏑ ⏑ – ⏑ –) and **pherecrateans** (× × – ⏑ ⏑ – –). The cola are usually arranged in stanzas, and in synapheia; they may be lengthened by internal additions (**expansion**) of either choriambs or dactyls: thus × × – ⏑ ⏑ – ⏑ ⏑ – ⏑ – is a glyconic expanded by a dactyl (underlined). Pindar uses Aeolic and other cola, such as **dactylo-epitrite** (mainly hemiepes cola linked to **epitrites** – ⏑ –, which in other contexts are called **cretics**). These are combined into larger structures which end with a clear metrical break called **periods** (period end is marked with |||); and periods in turn are built up into **triads**, sequences of three stanzas called **strophe** (*stróe-fee*), **antistrophe** (*an-tís-tro-fee*) and **epode**. In this arrangement, strophe and antistrophe use an identical metrical pattern (they are in **responsion**) while the epode is in a different pattern; but the precise metrical sequence of each triad may then be repeated (Pindar's fourth *Pythian* ode spans thirteen such triads). For convenience, modern metricians use abbreviations for the names given to metra and cola; of those we have encountered above, the lekythion is notated *lk*, dochmiac d, dactyl *da* (so hexameter = 6*da*), iambic metron *ia* (so iambic trimeter = 3*ia*), anapaestic metron (⏒– ⏒–) *an*, trochaic metron *tr*, adonean *ad*, hemiepes *D* (so a pentameter is *DD*), choriamb *cho*, glyconic *gl*, pherecratean *pher*, glyconic expanded by a dactyl gl^{da}, epitrite *e*, cretic *cr*. This notation is particularly useful when distinct cola are found mixed together in long sequences, as in the lyrics of Greek tragedy; Latin metres are more uniform. Armed with such terms and symbols, one may proceed to analyse metres and assimilate their complex patterns with economy and accuracy, and in due course hope to recreate in one's reading something of the vital rhythms of ancient verse.

Further reading

M. L. West, *Greek Metre*, Oxford: Oxford University Press, 1982 – authoritative and comprehensive, but not always easy reading.

L. P. Wilkinson, *Golden Latin Artistry*, Cambridge: Cambridge University Press, 1963.

66. Time-charts

Brian A. Sparkes

The volumes of *Cambridge Ancient History* (2nd edn, 1970–) and E. J. Bickerman, *Chronology of the Ancient World* (2nd edn, 1980), provide some of the fullest data. The chronology of the classical world is constantly being revised, usually in small ways, in the face of new evidence and new interpretations of old evidence. Through lack of historical support the dates relating to the earlier centuries are the least precise, but those at the close of antiquity also suffer from a similar lack of data. Against many of the dates in these lists 'c.' for 'circa' has been inserted, but the abbreviation could have been attached to many more. The death dates, and particularly the birth dates, of many of the major figures of classical antiquity cannot be ascribed to a precise year.

All dates in this book are expressed as BC ('before Christ') and AD ('anno domini') rather than the more recent BCE ('before common era') and CE ('common era').

Kings and Emperors

The dates in the following lists of kings and emperors refer to the years of their rule. Where the dates overlap, there was joint rule; in the Hellenistic period the territory that kings ruled might contract and/or expand in relation to their (lack of) success against neighbouring kingdoms. In the list of Roman emperors the names in capital letters give those now in common use.

Kings and Emperors

Kings of Achaemenid Persia

- 559–530 Cyrus
- 530–522 Cambyses, son of Cyrus
- 522 Smerdis (Bardiya), brother of Cambyses
- 522–486 Darius I, son of Hystaspes
- 486–465 Xerxes, son of Darius
- 465–424 Artaxerxes I, son of Xerxes
- 424 Xerxes II, son of Artaxerxes I
- 424–404 Darius II (Ochus), son of Artaxerxes I
- 404–359 Artaxerxes II (Arsakes), son of Darius II
- 359–338 Artaxerxes III (Ochus), son of Artaxerxes II
- 338–336 Artaxerxes IV (Arses), son of Artaxerxes III
- 336–331 Darius III (Artashata), son of Arsames who was grandson of Artaxerxes II

Kings of Macedon

- d. c. 498 Amyntas I, son of Alketas
- c.498–454 Alexander I, son of Amyntas I
- 454–413 Perdiccas II, son of Alexander I
- 413–399 Archelaus, son of Perdiccas II
- 399–396 Orestes, son of Archelaus
- 396–c. 393 Aeropus II
- c. 393 Amyntas II, son of Archelaus
- c. 393 Pausanias, son of Aeropus II
- c. 393–370 Amyntas III, great-grandson of Alexander I
- c. 390 Argaeus
- 370–368 Alexander II, son of Amyntas III
- c. 368–c. 365 Ptolemaeus Alorites, son of an Amyntas
- c. 365–359 Perdiccas III, son of Amyntas III
- 359–336 Philip II, son of Amyntas III
- 336–323 Alexander III the Great, son of Philip II
- 323–317 Philip III Arrhidaeus, son of Philip II
- 323–310 Alexander IV, son of Alexander III

The Antigonids

- 306–301 Antigonus I Monophthalmus
- 306–283 Demetrius I Poliorcetes, son of Antigonus I
- 283–239 Antigonus II Gonatas, grandson of Demetrius I
- 239–229 Demetrius II, son of Antigonus II
- 229–221 Antigonus III Doson, greatgrandson of Demetrius I
- 221–179 Philip V, son of Demetrius II
- 179–168 Perseus, son of Philip V

Antigonus I reigned only in various parts of Asia Minor and Syria; Demetrius I reigned during the years 294–287 in many parts of Greece, the islands and Macedonia; Antigonus Gonatas began his reign in Macedonia in 277. He and the other Antigonids were kings of Macedonia.

The Seleucids

- 305–281 Seleucus I Nicator, son of Antiochus
- 281–261 Antiochus I Soter, son of Seleucus I
- 261–246 Antiochus II Theos, son of Antiochus I
- 246–225 Seleucus II Callinicus, son of Antiochus II
- 225–223 Seleucus III 'Ceraunus', son of Seleucus II
- 223–187 Antiochus III the Great, son of Seleucus II
- 187–175 Seleucus IV Philopator, son of Antiochus III
- 175–164 Antiochus IV Epiphanes, son of Antiochus III
- 164–162 Antiochus V Eupator, son of Antiochus IV
- 162–150 Demetrius I Soter, son of Seleucus IV
- 150–145 Alexander Balas, pretended son of Antiochus IV
- 145–140 Demetrius II Nicator, son of Demetrius I
- 145–142 Antiochus VI Epiphanes, son of Alexander Balas
- 139/8–129 Antiochus VII Sidetes, son of Demetrius I
- 129–125 Demetrius II Nicator, son of Demetrius I
- 126 Cleopatra Thea
- 125–121 Cleopatra Thea and Antiochus VIII 'Grypus', son of Demetrius I
- 125 Seleucus V
- 121–96 Antiochus VIII 'Grypus', son of Demetrius I
- 115–95 Antiochus IX Cyzicenus
- 96–95 Seleucus VI Epiphanes Nicanor
- 95–88 Demetrius III Philopator
- 95–83 Antiochus X Eusebes
- 95 Antiochus XI Philadelphus
- 94–84 Philip I Philadelphus
- 87 Antiochus XII Dionysus
- 83–69 (Tigranes of Armenia)
- 69–64 Antiochus XIII Asiaticus
- 65–64 Philip II

The Ptolemies

- 304–283 Ptolemy I Soter, son of Lagus
- 285–246 Ptolemy II Philadelphus, son of Ptolemy I
- 246–221 Ptolemy III Euergetes I, son of Ptolemy II
- 221–204 Ptolemy IV Philopator, son of Ptolemy III
- 204–180 Ptolemy V Epiphanes, son of Ptolemy IV
- 180–145 Ptolemy VI Philometor, son of Ptolemy V
- 170–163 Ptolemy VIII Euergetes II ('Physkon'), son of Ptolemy V
- 170–164 and 163–116 Cleopatra II, daughter of Ptolemy V
- 145 Ptolemy VII Neos Philopator, son of Ptolemy VI
- 145–116 Ptolemy VIII, son of Ptolemy V
- 139–101 Cleopatra III, daughter of Ptolemy VI, wife of Ptolemy VIII
- 116–107 Ptolemy IX Soter ('Lathyrus'), son of Ptolemy VIII
- 107–88 Ptolemy X Alexander I, son of Ptolemy VIII
- 101–88 Cleopatra Berenice, daughter of Ptolemy IX
- 88–81 Ptolemy IX, son of Ptolemy VIII
- 80 Cleopatra Berenice, daughter of Ptolemy IX
- 80 Ptolemy XI Alexander II, son of Ptolemy X
- 80–58 Ptolemy XII Neos Dionysus ('Auletes'), son of Ptolemy IX
- 58–55 Berenice IV, daughter of Ptolemy IX
- 56–55 Archelaos, husband of Berenice IV
- 55–51 Ptolemy XII, son of Ptolemy IX
- 51–47 Ptolemy XIII, son of Ptolemy XI
- 51–30 Cleopatra VII Philopator, daughter of Ptolemy XI
- 47–44 Ptolemy XIV, son of Ptolemy XI
- 36–30 Ptolemy XV ('Caesarion'), son of Julius Caesar and Cleopatra VII

The Attalids

- 283–263 Philetaerus
- 263–241 Eumenes I, nephew of Philetaerus
- 241–197 Attalus I Soter, cousin and adopted son of Eumenes I
- 197–159/8 Eumenes II Soter, son of Attalus I
- 159/8–139/8 Attalus II, son of Attalus I
- 139/8–133 Attalus III, son of Eumenes II

[• 133–129 (Aristonicus ('Eumenes III'), bastard son of Eumenes II.]

Roman Emperors

- 27 BC–AD 14 C. Julius divi f(ilius) Caesar AUGUSTUS
- 14–37 TIBERIUS Julius Caesar Augustus
- 37–41 GAIUS Julius Caesar (CALIGULA)
- 41–54 Tiberius CLAUDIUS Caesar Germanicus
- 54–68 NERO Claudius Caesar Germanicus
- 68–9 Ser. Sulpicius GALBA Caesar
- 69 M. Salvius OTHO Caesar

- 69 A. VITELLIUS (Germanicus)
- 69–79 (T. Flavius) Imperator Caesar VESPASIANus
- 79–81 TITUS (Flavius) Vespasianus
- 81–96 Imp. Caesar DOMITIANus Augustus
- 96–8 M. Cocceius NERVA
- 98–117 M. Ulpius Nerva TRAJANus
- 117–38 (P. Aelius) Trajan HADRIANus
- 138–61 T. Aelius Hadrianus ANTONINUS PIUS
- 161–9 L. Aurelius VERUS
- 161–80 MARCUS AURELIUS Antoninus
- 176–92 (L.) Aurelius COMMODUS
- 193 P. Helvius PERTINAX
- 193 M. Didius JULIANUS
- 193–211 L. Septimius SEVERUS Pertinax
- 198–217 M. Aurelius Antoninus (CARACALLA)
- 209–12 P. Septimius GETA
- 217–18 M. Opellius MACRINUS
- 218–22 M. Aurelius Antoninus (ELAGABALUS)
- 222–35 M. Aurelius SEVERUS ALEXANDER
- 235–8 D. Iulius Verus MAXIMINUS ('Thrax')
- 238 M. Antoninus GORDIANUS I
- 238 M. Antoninus GORDIANUS II
- 238–44 M. Antoninus GORDIANus III, grandson of Gordianus I
- 244–9 M. Julius Philippus (PHILIP THE ARAB)
- 249–51 C. Messius Quintus TRAJANus DECIUS
- 251–3 C. Vibius TREBONIANUS GALLUS and C. Vibius Afinius Gallus Veldumnianus VOLUSIANus
- 253 M. Aemilius AEMILIANus
- 253–8 P. Licinius GALLIENUS
- 253–60 P. Licinius VALERIANus and P. Licinius GALLIENUS
- 268–9 M. Aurelius CLAUDIUS (II, GOTHICUS)
- 269 M. Aurelius QUINTILLUS
- 270–5 M. Domitius AURELIANus
- 275–6 M. Claudius TACITUS
- 276 M. Annius FLORIANus
- 276–82 M. Aurelius PROBUS
- 282–3 M. Aurelius CARUS
- 283–4 M. Aurelius Numerius NUMERIANus
- 283–5 M. Aurelius CARINUS
- 284–305 Gaius Aurelius Valerius DIOCLETIANus
- 286–305 Marcus Aurelius Valerius MAXIMIANus
- 293–306 Flavius Valerius CONSTANTIUS I (CHLORUS)
- 293–311 GALERIUS Valerius Maximianus
- 305–13 MAXIMINus DAIA
- 306–12 MAXENTIUS
- 306–37 Flavius Valerius CONSTANTINUS I (CONSTANTINE)
- 308–24 Valerius Licinianus LICINIUS
- 317–40 Flavius Claudius CONSTANTINUS II
- 324–61 Flavius Julius CONSTANTIUS II
- 333–50 Flavius Julius CONSTANS
- 361–3 Flavius Claudius JULIANUS (JULIAN the Apostate)
- 363–4 Flavius JOVIANus
- 364–75 Flavius VALENTINIANus I
- 364–78 Flavius VALENS
- 367–83 Flavius GRATIANus
- 375–92 Flavius VALENTINIANus II
- 379–95 Flavius THEODOSIUS I

Western Empire	Eastern Empire
• 393–423 HONORIUS	
	• 395–408 Flavius ARCADIUS
	• 408–50 THEODOSIUS II
• 423–55 VALENTINIANus III	
	• 450–7 MARCIANUS
• 455 MAXIMUS	
• 455–6 Eparchius AVITUS	
	• 457–74 LEO I
• 457–61 Julius Valerius MAJORIANus	
• 461–5 SEVERUS	
• 467–72 ANTHEMIUS	
• 472 OLYBRIUS	
• 473–4 GLYCERIUS	
	• 473–4 LEO II
	• 474–5 and 476–91 ZENO
• 474–91 (deposed 476) ROMULUS AUGUSTUS ('AUGUSTULUS')	
	• 491–518 ANASTASIUS
	• 518–27 JUSTINUS I
	• 527–65 Flavius Petrus Sabbatius JUSTINIANus

The Julio-Claudians

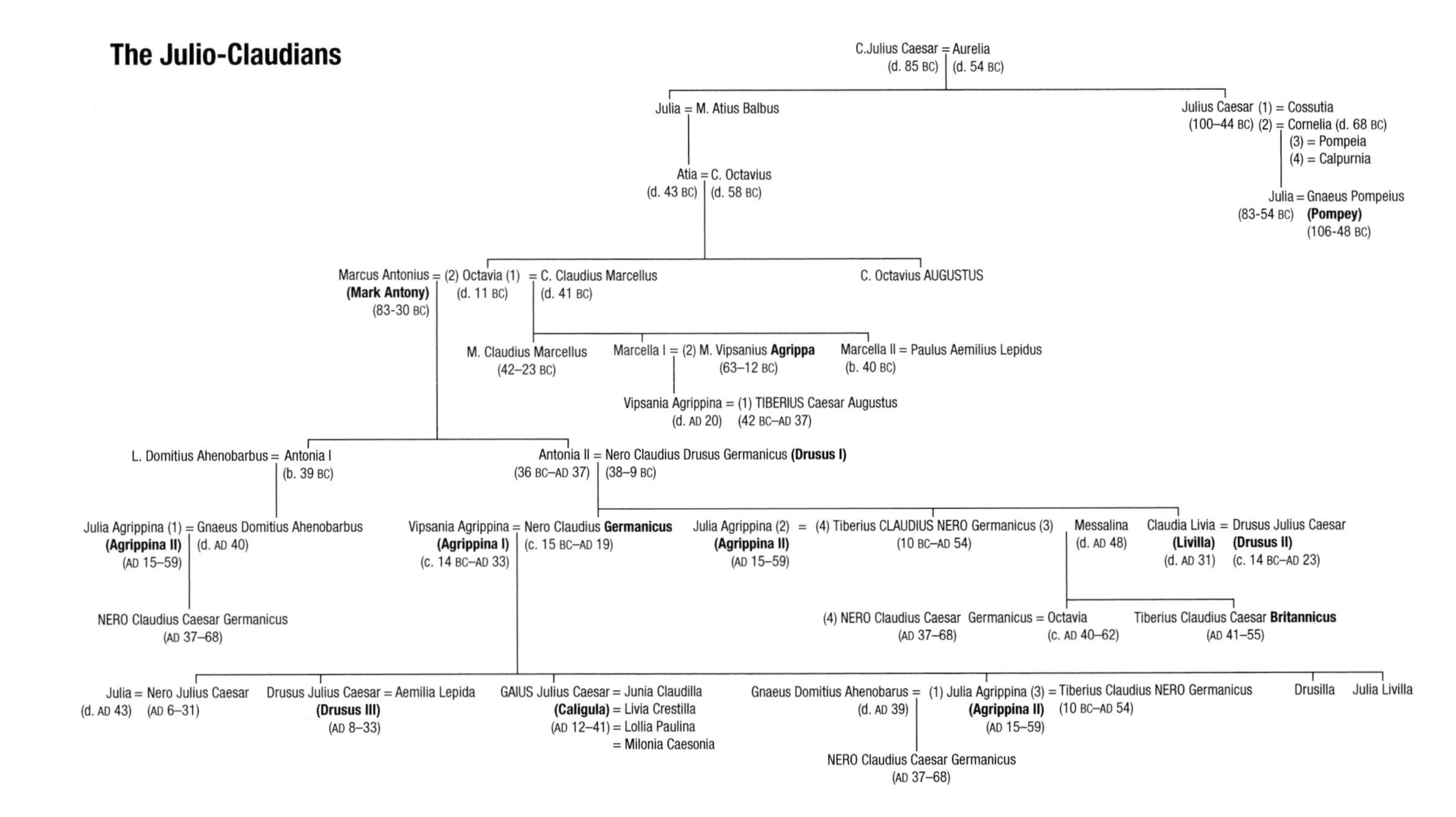

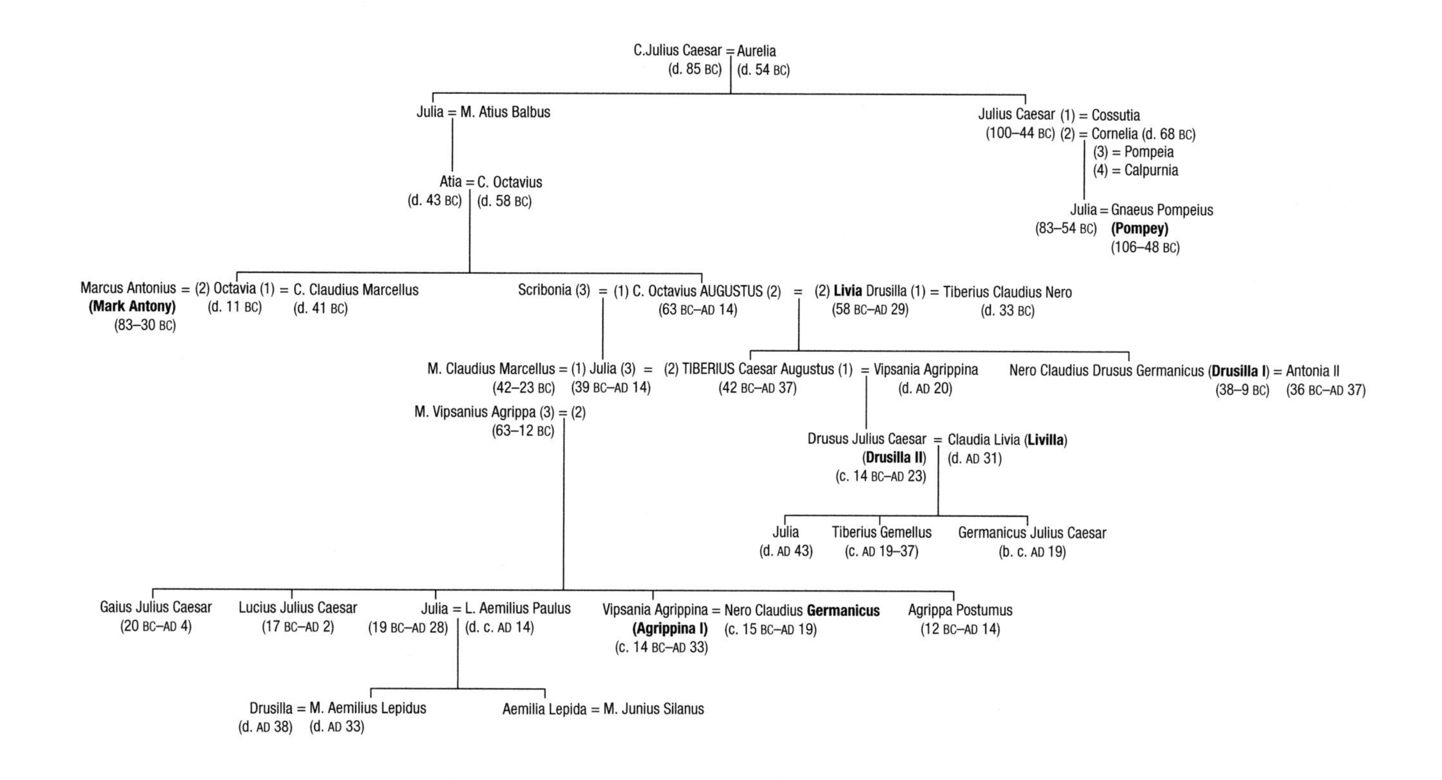
C.Julius Caesar = Aurelia
(d. 85 BC) (d. 54 BC)
Julia = M. Atius Balbus
Julius Caesar (1) = Cossutia
(100–44 BC) (2) = Cornelia (d. 68 BC)
(3) = Pompeia
(4) = Calpurnia
Atia = C. Octavius
(d. 43 BC) (d. 58 BC)
Julia = Gnaeus Pompeius
(83–54 BC) **(Pompey)**
(106–48 BC)
Marcus Antonius = (2) Octavia (1) = C. Claudius Marcellus
(Mark Antony) (d. 11 BC) (d. 41 BC)
(83–30 BC)
Scribonia (3) = (1) C. Octavius AUGUSTUS (2) = (2) **Livia** Drusilla (1) = Tiberius Claudius Nero
(63 BC–AD 14) (58 BC–AD 29) (d. 33 BC)
M. Claudius Marcellus = (1) Julia (3) = (2) TIBERIUS Caesar Augustus (1) = Vipsania Agrippina
(42–23 BC) (39 BC–AD 14) (42 BC–AD 37) (d. AD 20)
Nero Claudius Drusus Germanicus (**Drusilla I**) = Antonia II
(38–9 BC) (36 BC–AD 37)
M. Vipsanius Agrippa (3) = (2)
(63–12 BC)
Drusus Julius Caesar = Claudia Livia (**Livilla**)
(Drusilla II) (d. AD 31)
(c. 14 BC–AD 23)
Julia
(d. AD 43)
Tiberius Gemellus
(c. AD 19–37)
Germanicus Julius Caesar
(b. c. AD 19)
Gaius Julius Caesar
(20 BC–AD 4)
Lucius Julius Caesar
(17 BC–AD 2)
Julia = L. Aemilius Paulus
(19 BC–AD 28) (d. c. AD 14)
Vipsania Agrippina = Nero Claudius **Germanicus**
(Agrippina I) (c. 15 BC–AD 19)
(c. 14 BC–AD 33)
Agrippa Postumus
(12 BC–AD 14)
Drusilla = M. Aemilius Lepidus
(d. AD 38) (d. AD 33)
Aemilia Lepida = M. Junius Silanus

Military

Prehistoric–1200 BC

- c. 1400 Mycenaeans take control of palace sites on Crete; palace at Cnossus destroyed
- c. 1270 Destruction of Troy VIIA
- c. 1230 Disaster (earthquake?) at Mycenae

'Dark age' 1200–770 BC

- 1200–1125 Destruction of Mycenae, Pylos and other Mycenaean centres; Sea Peoples marauding in Mediterranean
- 1184 Date computed in antiquity for fall of Homeric Troy

Political and social

Prehistoric–1200 BC

- c. 3500–2000 Early Bronze Age (Helladic, Minoan, Cycladic)
- c. 2000–1600 Middle Bronze Age (Helladic, Minoan, Cycladic)
- c. 1600–1100 Late Bronze Age (Helladic, Minoan, Cycladic)
- c. 1500–1450 Volcanic eruptions on Thera (Santorini)
- c. 1500–1200 'Apennine' culture in Western central Italy
- c. 1300 Ulu Burun wreck
- c. 1300–1100 Phoenicians develop their own alphabet

'Dark age' 1200–770 BC

- c. 1125– Abandonment of most mainland Greek sites
- c. 1100–825 Settlement at Lefkandi (on Euboea)
- c. 1050 Renewal of Greek contacts with Cyprus
- c. 1050–950 Greeks settle on coast of Asia Minor
- c. 1000 Dorians settle Sparta and Laconia; settlements on hills of Rome
- c. 975 Hero's tomb at Lefkandi
- 930 Reputed start of Spartan king list of Agiads

Cultural and religious

Prehistoric–1200 BC

- c. 2200– Middle Minoan Palace culture on Crete
- c. 2000 Compilation of the *Epic of Gilgamesh* in Sumeria
- 1760 Archives of Sumerian city of Mari throw light on politics of Western Asia
- c. 1700– Second Palace culture on Crete; Linear A script on Crete (undeciphered)
- c. 1675–1550 Grave Circle B at Mycenae
- c. 1610–1490 Grave Circle A at Mycenae
- c. 1550– Development of Mycenaean culture on mainland Greece
- c. 1525–1450 Early tholos and chamber tombs
- c. 1450– Linear B script at Cnossus (deciphered as an early form of Greek)
- c. 1400 'Treasury of Atreus' built
- c. 1300 Linear B script at Mycenae and Pylos

'Dark age' 1200–770 BC

- c. 1050 Sub-Mycenaean pottery
- c. 1025–900 Protogeometric pottery
- c. 900–700 Geometric pottery

Archaic period 770–479 BC

- c. 740–720 Spartan conquest of neighbouring Messenia
- 740–605 Assyrian empire at its height
- c. 720–710 Lelantine war between Chalcis and Eretria on Euboea
- c. 670 Messenian Helots revolt from Sparta; start of Second Messenian War
- 669 Traditional date for defeat of Spartans by Argives at battle of Hysiae
- 615–605 End of Assyrian empire with the defeat of the Assyrians by the Babylonians at the battle of Carchemish (605)
- c. 612 Athenians take Salamis from Megara
- 586 Sack of Jerusalem and exile of Jews to Babylon
- 557– Rise of Persian Empire under Cyrus
- 550 Persians under Cyrus defeat Medes
- 546/5 Persians under Cyrus defeat Croesus of Lydia and Ionian Greeks of Asia Minor; fall of Sardis
- 539 Persians under Cyrus destroy state of Babylon

- 890 Reputed start of Spartan king list of Eurypontids
- c. 850 Euboeans involved in trade with Near East
- c. 850–600 'Villanovan' culture in Western central Italy
- 814 Traditional date of foundation of Carthage by Phoenicians
- c. 800 Town of Sparta is enlarged to include Amyclae
- c. 800–700 Celtic culture spreads to Spain and Britain

Archaic period 770–479 BC

- c. 775 Beginning of Greek settlement in Italy by Euboeans at Pithekoussai on island of Ischia
- 754 Beginning of *ephor* list in Sparta
- 753 Traditional date for foundation of Rome by Romulus
- 753–509 Period of kings at Rome
- 735 Traditional date for first Greek settlement in Sicily at Naxos
- 733 Traditional date for foundation of Syracuse by Corinthians
- c. 725 Settlement at Cumae on west coast of Italy
- c. 706 Sparta founds Taras (Taranto)
- c. 700 Settlement of Black Sea area by Greeks
- c. 700–600 Lycurgan reforms at Sparta (*rhētra*)
- c. 700–500 Etruscan civilisation in Italy
- c. 685 Beginning of Greek settlements in Hellespont and Black Sea
- 683/2 Beginning of lists of archōns in Athens
- c. 680 Kingdom of Lydia (Asia Minor) founded by Gyges (687–652)

Archaic period 770–479 BC

- 776 Traditional date of first recorded victor in Olympic Games
- c. 750–700 Phoenician (Semitic) alphabet adapted for writing Greek
- c. 750–690 Increase of bronze offerings in sanctuaries
- c. 725 First stone temple of Artemis Orthia, Sparta
- c. 725–630 Protocorinthian pottery at Corinth; 'Orientalising' period
- c. 700 Homer and Hesiod active
- c. 700 Protoattic pottery developed in Attica
- c. 675–640 Archilochus of Paros, poet, active
- c. 670 Spartan poet Tyrtaeus active; *Iliad* and *Odyssey* reach their 'final' form
- c. 670–620 'Daedalic' sculpture in vogue
- c. 660 First stone temple of Apollo, Corinth
- c. 630–600 Early Corinthian pottery begins; Semonides and Alcman poets active
- c. 625 Attic black-figure pottery begins; tiled roofs on Greek temples

Military

• 525 Persians under Cambyses conquer Egypt; Spartans depose Polycrates, tyrant of Samos
• 524 Etruscans defeated at battle of Cumae
• c. 513 Darius I in Thrace mounts inconclusive expedition against Scythia
• 511–510 Hippias expelled from Athens by Cleomenes I; war between Sybaris and Croton in South Italy; Sybaris destroyed
• c. 499 Latins defeated by Romans at battle of Lake Regillus
• 499–494 Unsuccessful Ionian Revolt against Persia
• 494 Ionians defeated at battle of Lade; Miletus sacked; Cleomenes I defeats the Argives at the battle of Sepeia
• 493 'Cassian' treaty between Rome and Latins
• 490 Persians sack Eretria (Euboea); Athenians and Plataeans win battle of Marathon
• 481–480 Xerxes' invasion of Greece; battles of Artemisium, Thermopylae and Salamis; Gelon defeats Carthaginians at battle of Himera (Sicily)
• 479 Battles of Plataea and Mycale (Asia Minor) with victory for Greeks; Carthaginians defeated in their attack on Sicily; 'Oath of Plataea' sworn

Political and social

• c. 680–660 Pheidon tyrant at Argos
• 664 Foundation of Saïte dynasty in Egypt under Psamtek (Psammetichos) I (664–610)
• c. 660 Foundation of Byzantium by Megara
• 657–585 Tyranny of Cypselids at Corinth
• 655–555 Tyranny of Orthagorids at Sikyon
• c. 650 Reforms attributed to Spartan Lycurgus; Greek settlement at Olbia (Bug Estuary)
• c. 640 Theagenes becomes tyrant at Megara; beginning of coinage in Asia Minor
• 632 Attempted tyranny of Cylon at Athens and exile of Alcmaeonids
• 630 Greek settlement at Cyrene (North Africa) founded by Theraeans
• c. 620 Draco lawgiver at Athens; Greek trading-post established at Naucratis in Nile delta
• 616–579 Traditional dates for rule of Etruscan Tarquinius Priscus at Rome
• c. 610 Tyranny of Thrasybulus at Miletus (Asia Minor)
• 607/6 Athens and Mytilene (on Lesbos) dispute over Sigeum
• c. 600 Tyranny of Pittacus at Mytilene; foundation of Massilia (Marseilles) by Phocaeans; draining of Roman forum and creation of urban centre
• c. 600–590 First Sacred War over Delphi
• c. 594 Solon archōn and lawgiver at Athens; establishment of classes according to wealth
• 579–534 Traditional dates for Servius Tullius, king of Rome; military reforms and creation of *comitia centuriata*; treaty with

Cultural and religious

• c. 610–575 Sappho and Alcaeus, poets, active on Lesbos
• c. 600 Temples of Hera at Olympia and on Samos built; first marble kouroi statues, under influence of Egypt; Hebrew scriptures consolidated
• c. 590–575 Solon active as poet
• 585 Thales, Milesian philosopher, predicts eclipse of sun
• 582–573 First Pythian Games at Delphi (582), Isthmian Games (581), Nemean Games (573)
• c. 580 Temple of Artemis, Corcyra (Corfu); first major temple on Athenian Acropolis
• c. 570 'François' vase made in Athens
• c. 570–550 Anaximander and Anaximenes, Milesian philosophers, active
• 566 Reorganisation of Panathenaic festival in Athens
• c. 550–530 Amasis Painter and Exekias active as vase-painters in Athens
• 548 Temple of Apollo at Delphi destroyed
• c. 545/4 Birth of Aeschylus
• 534 First tragedy performed at City Dionysia in Athens
• c. 530 Red-figure painted pottery replaces black-figure as main output in Attica
• c. 525 Pythagoras of Samos active in Southern Italy; Siphnian treasury built at Delphi
• c. 520–470 Simonides, poet, active
• c. 510–480 Technique of making hollow-cast bronzes perfected
• 509 Foundation of temple of Jupiter on Capitoline, Rome
• c. 500 Heraclitus, Parmenides and Hecataeus active
• c. 500–490 Temple of Apollo at Eretria built

Latins and foundation of temple of Diana on the Aventine
• 575–550 Beginning of coinage in Ionia and mainland Greece
• 570–526 Amasis Pharaoh of Egypt
• c. 561–560 First tyranny of Pisistratus at Athens
• c. 560–546 Croesus king of Lydia
• 559 Cyrus the Great becomes first king of Achaemenid Persian empire
• 546 Pisistratus tyrant again in Athens

• 540 Etruscans and Phoenicians expel Phocaeans from Alalia (on Corsica)
• 540–522 Tyranny of Polycrates on Samos
• 539 Jews released from exile in Babylon; some return to Judaea and rebuild Jerusalem and the temple
• 534–509 Tarquinius Superbus king at Rome
• 530 Death of Cyrus; accession of his son, Cambyses
• c. 528/7 Death of Pisistratus; Hippias and Hipparchus succeed their father as tyrants

• 525/4 Cleisthenes archōn at Athens
• 522 Darius I seizes power in Persia and overthrows Polycrates
• 520 Cleomenes I becomes king of Sparta
• 514 Hipparchus assassinated by Harmodius and Aristogeiton
• 509 Traditional date of expulsion of kings and foundation of Roman Republic; first treaty with Carthage
• 508/7 Expulsion of Isagoras from Athens; reforms of Cleisthenes

---

• 498 First preserved ode by Pindar (*Pythian* 10)
• c. 497/6 Birth of Sophocles
• c. 490–485 Treasury of Athenians at Delphi
• 487/6 or 485 First comedy performed at City Dionysia in Athens
• 484 First victory of Aeschylus, tragic poet, at Dionysia
• 480 Birth of Euripides

Military

Classical period 479–323 BC

- 478–466 Delian League under Athenian leadership continues war against Persia
- 474 Hieron of Syracuse defeats Etruscans off Cumae (Campania)
- c. 470 Naxos tries to secede from Delian League and is forced to rejoin
- c. 467/6 Greeks under Cimon defeat Persians at Eurymedon (Asia Minor)
- 465 Unsuccessful revolt of Thasos from Delian League
- 464 Earthquake at Sparta and helot revolt in Messenia

Political and social

- 501 First election of ten generals (*stratēgoi*) in Athens; first republican dictator in Rome
- 494 First secession of plebeians in Rome
- 494–287 Struggle of the Roman Orders
- 493/2 Themistocles archōn at Athens; port established at Piraeus
- c. 491 Gelon becomes tyrant of Gela and later of Syracuse
- 487 First ostracism at Athens
- 487/6 Athenian archōns chosen by lot
- 486 Death of Darius I; accession of his son Xerxes

- 483/2 Rich find of silver at Laurium mines (Attica); Athenian navy increased

Classical period 479–323 BC

- 479–478 Rebuilding of walls of Athens
- 478/7 Foundation of Delian League under Athens
- c. 471 Ostracism of Themistocles; rise of influence of Cimon
- 471 Tribunes and Plebeian Council (*concilium plebis*) officially recognised at Rome
- 464 Earthquake at Sparta
- 463 Democracy established at Syracuse
- 462/1 Constitutional reforms of Ephialtes at Athens

Cultural and religious

Classical period 479–323 BC

- 479 Dedication of the Serpent Column at Delphi
- 478 Bronze charioteer dedicated by Polyzelus at Delphi
- 477–476 Second set of statues of the Tyrant-slayers set up in Athens
- 472 *Persae* of Aeschylus first performed
- c. 470 Birth of Socrates and Democritus
- c. 470–460 Polygnotus, painter, active
- 468 First victory of Sophocles at City Dionysia; death of Simonides

- 462 Spartans appeal for help from Athens; Egypt revolts from Persian rule
- 461 Athens breaks alliance with Sparta
- 461–446 'First Peloponnesian War' between Athens and Sparta
- 460 End of helot revolt in Messenia; Athenian expeditionary force to Egypt
- 457 Battle at Tanagra and Athenian conquest of Boeotia
- 457/6 Athenian conquest of Aegina
- 454 Athenian defeat in Egypt and collapse of Egyptian revolt

- 451 Five Years Truce between Athens and Sparta
- 450 Rome on the offensive against neighbouring tribes
- 449 Possible peace treaty between Athens and Persia
- 449–447 Second Sacred War over Delphi
- 447 Athens loses Boeotia
- 446 Revolts of Euboea; Spartan invasion of Attica
- 446/5 Thirty Years Peace between Athens and Sparta
- 441–439 Revolt and surrender of Samos

- 435–433 War between Corinth and Corcyra (Corfu)
- 433 Athenian alliance with Corcyra; naval battle of Sybota
- 432 Revolt of Potidaea
- 431 Peloponnesian War begins; first Peloponnesian invasion of Attica
- 428–427 Revolt of Mytilene (Lesbos); civil war on Corcyra
- 427–424 Athenian campaign in Sicily
- 425 Athenians defeat Spartans at Pylos (Messenia)

- 461 Ephialtes assassinated; Cimon ostracised
- 457 Building of Long Walls at Athens
- 454 Delian treasury moved to Athens; growth of Athenian empire
- 453 First Tribute Quota List erected on Athenian Acropolis
- 451/0 Citizenship law at Athens limits citizenship to those whose parents are both citizens; codification of the Laws of the Twelve Tables at Rome
- 449 Secession of plebs at Rome

- 443 Athens founds colony at Thurii in southern Italy
- 443–429 Pericles' annual election as *stratēgos* (general) in Athens
- 437/6 Foundation by Athenians of city of Amphipolis (Thrace)
- 432 Megarian decree passed in Athens
- 430–426 Plague at Athens
- 429 Death of Pericles
- 425 Reassessment of tribute in Delian League
- 420 Statue of Nike (Victory) erected at Olympia

- 411–410 Oligarchic coup of the Four Hundred at Athens overthrows democracy
- 410 Full democracy restored at Athens
- 409 Foundation of city of Rhodes
- 405–367 Dionysius tyrant of Syracuse
- 404 The Thirty Tyrants come to power
- 403 Fall of the Thirty Tyrants; democracy restored at Athens
- 399 Trial and execution of Socrates

- 468–456 Building of temple of Zeus at Olympia
- c. 460–450 Riace bronzes
- c. 460–440 Myron, sculptor, active
- 458 *Oresteia* of Aeschylus first performed
- 456 Anaxagoras comes to Athens
- c. 456/5 Death of Aeschylus
- 455 First production by Euripides; birth of Thucydides
- c. 450 Zeno of Elea's paradoxes; birth of Hippocrates
- c. 450–430 Phidias and Polyclitus, sculptors, active

- 447–432 Periclean building programme under direction of Phidias on Athenian Acropolis
- 445 Birth of Aristophanes
- c. 445–426 Herodotus, historian, active
- 442 Comedy added to Lenaea Festival
- 440–430 Leucippus and Democritus claim all matter is made up of atoms
- 438 Phidias' Athena Parthenos consecrated in the Parthenon
- c. 435 Phidias' Zeus Olympios erected at Olympia
- c. 433 Protagoras in Athens

- 431 *Medea* of Euripides first performed; Thucydides starts his *History*
- c. 430 Attic classical grave-reliefs start
- 427 Gorgias, orator, in Athens; birth of Plato
- c. 425–395 Zeuxis and Parrhasius, painters, active
- 423 *Clouds* of Aristophanes first performed
- 420 Nike of Paeonius erected at Olympia
- c. 420–410 Balustrade of Athena Nike temple erected on Athenian Acropolis

Military

- 424 Athenian defeat at Delium (Boeotia); Spartan Brasidas captures Amphipolis (Thrace)
- 422 Death of Cleon and Brasidas in battle at Amphipolis
- 421 Peace of Nicias; fifty years' alliance between Athens and Sparta
- 420 Athenian alliance with Argos, Mantinea and Elis; Alcibiades general
- 418 Battle of Mantinea
- 416 Athenians crush the island of Melos
- 415–413 Athenian forces attack Sicily and are disastrously defeated
- 413 Spartans invade Attica and fortify Decelea
- 412–411 Revolt and siege of Chios; Sparta receives Persian money to rebuild its navy
- 410 Athens wins naval battle of Cyzicus (Hellespont)
- 409–406 Carthaginian campaign in Sicily
- 406 Athenian victory at naval battle of Arginusae (Asia Minor)
- 405 Athenian naval disaster off Aegospotami (Hellespont); siege of Athens by the Spartan Lysander
- 405–396 Siege and capture of Etruscan city of Veii by Romans
- 404 Capitulation of Athens and destruction of its Long Walls
- 401–400 Expedition of Cyrus the Younger against Persia; retreat of the Ten Thousand Greeks led by Xenophon
- 397–395 Agesilaus' campaign to free the Greeks in Asia Minor from the Persians
- 396 Roman conquest of Etruria begins
- 395–386 Corinthian War instigated by Persia, which regains control of Ionian Greeks

Political and social

- 399–360 Agesilaus king of Sparta
- 385–370 Jason rules Pherae (Thessaly)
- 379/8 Athens forms Second Athenian League
- 377–353 Mausolus ruler of Caria
- 370 Foundation of Messene
- c. 369 Foundation of Megalopolis (Arcadia)
- 367 First plebeian consul at Rome
- 359 Philip II becomes ruler of Macedon
- 357–355 Collapse of Second Athenian Alliance
- 356 Birth of Philip's son Alexander
- 336 Philip assassinated at Aegeae (Vergina); Alexander succeeds to his father's position as king and Leader of the Corinthian League
- 335 Alexander sacks Thebes; accession of Darius III as king of Persia
- 331 Alexander founds Alexandria (Egypt) and visits oracle of Ammon at Siwah
- 327 Alexander marries Roxane; introduction of *proskynesis* by Alexander
- 324 Unrest in Alexander's empire; Alexander returns to Susa via Indus and Makram desert; decree on restoration of Greek exiles; death of Hephaestion
- 323 Death of Alexander in Babylon

Cultural and religious

- 415 Mutilation of the Hermae and parody of the Eleusinian Mysteries
- 409–406 Erechtheion in Athens completed
- c. 407/6 Death of Euripides
- c. 406/5 Death of Sophocles
- 405– *Frogs* of Aristophanes first performed; Euripides' *Bacchae* produced posthumously
- 403 Adoption of Ionic alphabet as standard Greek spelling
- 401 Sophocles' *Oedipus at Colonus* produced posthumously
- c. 400 Building of temple of Apollo at Bassae
- 399 Trial and execution of Socrates
- 394 Gravestone of Dexileos erected in Athenian Kerameikos cemetery
- c. 390–354 Xenophon, writer, active
- 387 Plato founds Academy in Athens
- 384 Birth of Aristotle and Demosthenes
- c. 380–360 Temple of Asclepius built at Epidaurus
- c. 370–330 Praxiteles and Scopas, sculptors, active
- c. 360–315 Lysippus, sculptor active
- 358–330 Theatre built at sanctuary of Asclepius at Epidaurus
- 352–351 Mausoleum at Halicarnassus built
- c. 350–320 Apelles, painter, active
- 347 Death of Plato
- 346–325 Rebuilding of temple of Apollo, Delphi
- 343 Aristotle becomes tutor to Alexander
- 342–341 Birth of Menander and Epicurus

- 394 Persians under Conon of Athens defeat Spartan fleet off Cnidus (Asia Minor)
- 386 King Artaxerxes of Persia imposes the 'King's Peace'/Peace of Antalcidas on Greeks and controls Asia Minor; sack of Rome by Gauls
- 386–385 Sparta reduces Mantinea
- 382 Spartans seize Thebes
- 371 Thebans under Epaminondas destroy Spartan hegemony at battle of Leuctra (Boeotia)
- 370–369 Messenia liberated from Sparta
- 362 Battle of Mantinea, Epaminondas killed
- 362–361 General Peace (Koine Eirene) in Greece
- 359–336 Philip of Macedon gradually takes over Greece
- 357–355 Allies revolt from Athens ('Social War')
- 353–346 Sacred War of Philip over Delphi
- *348* Philip captures Olynthus (Chalcidice)
- *346* Peace of Philocrates between Athens and Philip
- 343–341 First Samnite War
- 340 Philip besieges Perinthus and Byzantium and seizes Athenian corn-fleet; Athens declares war on Philip
- 340–338 Rome takes over control of Latium and Campania
- 338 At battle of Chaeronea (Boeotia), Philip defeats Athens and Thebes; foundation of Corinthian League under Philip
- 337 Corinthian League declares war on Persia
- 335 Alexander campaigns in Thrace and Illyria and sacks and destroys Thebes

---

- 338 Death of Isocrates
- 335 Aristotle founds Lyceum (Peripatetic school) in Athens; Diogenes the Cynic supposedly meets Alexander in Corinth

Military

• 334 Alexander crosses Hellespont; battle of Granicus (Troad); conquest of Asia Minor; Alexander winters at Gordium
• 333 Defeat of Darius III at the battle of Issus (Cilicia)
• 332 Siege and capture of Tyre (Phoenicia) and conquest of Syria
• 332/1 Alexander captures Egypt without opposition
• 331 Battle of Gaugamela (Mesopotamia); capture of Babylon, Susa and Persepolis
• 330 Alexander destroys Persepolis (Iran); Bessus murders Darius III; end of Achaemenid Persian Empire
• 329 Alexander reaches Hindu Kush (Bactria)
• 328 Murder of Cleitus; capture of Sogdian Rock (Sogdiana)
• 328–304 Second Samnite War in the central Appenines
• 327 Alexander at Baktra; conspiracy of the Pages
• 326 Alexander reaches India; battle of the Hydaspes (Punjab); defeat of Porus; mutiny of Alexander's troops at the Hyphasis
• 323 Death of Alexander at Babylon

Political and social

Cultural and religious

Hellenistic and Roman Republican period 323–31 BC

- 323–322 Revolt of Greeks in Greece (Lamian War)
- 321 Romans defeated by Samnites at the Caudine Forks
- 311 Peace Treaty between the Successors of Alexander
- 310–306 Invasion of North Africa by Agathocles of Syracuse
- 305–304 Siege of Rhodes by Demetrius (Poliorcetes)
- 301 Battle of Ipsus; Antigonus defeated and killed
- 298–290 Third Samnite War leads to crushing of Samnites
- 295 Battle of Sentinum
- 294 Demetrius captures Athens
- 281 Battle of Corupedium; Seleucus takes over Asia Minor
- 280–275 Pyrrhus, king of Epirus, in a bid to assist Greeks of south Italy fails to defeat Romans
- 279 Gauls invade Macedonia and are repulsed at Delphi
- 277 Antigonus Gonatas defeats Gauls
- 274–217 Four Syrian Wars between Seleucids and Ptolemies; battle of Raphia in Egypt sees close of Wars
- 272 Romans capture Tarentum (Taras)
- 267–262 Chremonidean War, in which Ptolemy supports Athenian bid for independence from Macedonia
- 264–241 First Punic War between Rome and Carthage
- 240 War of the Mercenaries against Cathage
- 238 Rome occupies Corsica and Sardinia
- 238–227 Attalus of Pergamum wars against the Gauls and becomes master of Asia Minor

---

Hellenistic and Roman Republican period 323–31 BC

- 323 Ptolemy satrap of Egypt
- 323–281 Alexander's 'Successors' divide his empire
- 321 Seleucus satrap of Babylonia
- 320 Settlement at Triparadisus; recognition of status of Ptolemy and Seleucus; Antigonus given supreme command of army in Asia
- 317 Demetrius of Phaleron established in power at Athens; Philip III Arrhidaeus, half-brother of Alexander the Great, murdered
- 315 Olympias, mother of Alexander, murdered
- 314–168 Delos independent
- 312 Via Appia, first great Roman road, and Aqua Appia, first aqueduct into Rome, built
- 310 Roxane and Alexander IV, son of Alexander the Great, murdered
- 306–304 Antigonus, Ptolemy and Seleucus all assume royal titles
- 301 Three major kingdoms emerge: Ptolemaic, Antigonid and Seleucid
- 300 Foundation of Antioch by Seleucus I
- 297–272 Pyrrhus king of Epirus
- 294 Demetrius, son of Antigonos, king of Macedon
- 290 Aetolian League emerges as important political force in central Greece
- 289 Roman mint established
- 284 Foundation of Achaean League in Peloponnese
- 283 Death of Demetrius; his son, Antigonus Gonatas, takes royal title
- 277 Antigonus Gonatas becomes king of Macedon

Hellenistic and Roman Republican period 323–31 BC

- 322 Death of Aristotle and Demosthenes; Theophrastus becomes head of Lyceum
- 321–293 Menander, comic dramatist, active
- c. 320 End of Athenian red-figure; Pytheas of Massilia circumnavigates Britain
- 317 Sculptured tombs banned in Athens
- 310 Zeno of Citium founds Stoic school in Athens
- 307 Epicurus founds his philosophical school in Athens
- 300 Ptolemy I of Egypt founds Museum and Library of Alexandria; Euclid active; Dicaearchus of Messenia produces first world map; foundation of Antioch-on-the-Orontes
- 295 Colossus of Rhodes and Tyche of Antioch erected
- 293 Death of Menander
- c. 287 Death of Theophrastus
- c. 270 Callimachus and Theocritus, poets, active; Aristarchus of Samos proposes heliocentric theory of universe; Manetho, priest, compiles list of Egyptian dynasties
- 264 First gladiatorial games in Rome
- 263–241 Building programme at Pergamum
- 260 Apollonius of Rhodes, head of Library at Alexandria, writes *Argonautica*; Herophilus of Chalcedon and Erasistratus of Ceos experiment on human body
- c. 260–212 Archimedes, mathematician, active
- 246 Eratosthenes becomes head of Library at Alexandria; he calculates the circumference of the earth correctly

Military

• 229–219 Romans fight two Illyrian wars
• 225 Gallic invasion of Italy
• 221 Hannibal takes over command of Carthaginian forces in Spain
• 218 Siege and capture of Saguntum in Spain by Hannibal
• 218–201 Second Punic War; Hannibal invades Italy; battle of Trebia
• 217 Hannibal defeats Romans at Lake Trasimene (Umbria)
• 216 Hannibal defeats Romans at Cannae (Apulia)
• 215 Philip V of Macedon allies with Carthage against Rome; Hannibal in South Italy
• 214–205 First Macedonian War between Rome and Philip V
• 213–211 Siege of Syracuse by Roman general Marcellus
• 211 Hannibal marches on Rome but fails to capture city; Capua and Syracuse fall to Romans
• 211–206 Scipio Africanus defeats Hasdrubal in Spain
• 209 Attalus I of Pergamum allies with Rome against Philip
• 204 Scipio lands in Africa
• 202 Scipio defeats Hannibal at battle of Zama; peace made with Carthage; triumph of Scipio
• 202–200 Fifth Syrian War
• 202–191 Roman conquest of Gallia Cisalpina
• 200 Palestine falls under Seleucid rule
• 200–197 Second Macedonian War between Rome and Philip V
• 197 Romans defeat Philip V of Macedon at Cynoscephalae
• 197–133 Rome conducts wars in Spain
• 192–188 Syrian War between Rome and Antiochus III

Political and social

• 269 Beginning of Roman silver coinage
• 263–241 Eumenes I of Pergamum succeeds Philetaerus and establishes a separate kingdom
• 260 Rome builds navy
• 251 Aratus unites Sicyon with Achaean League
• 248–247 Parthian era begins under Arsacids
• 241–197 Attalus I rules Pergamum
• 238– City of Pergamum built
• 235–222 Cleomenes III king of Sparta; reform of Spartan state
• 227 Sicily and Sardinia (with Corsica) made Roman provinces; revolution at Sparta
• 221 Philip V ruler of Macedon
• 197 Spain divided into two provinces
• 196 Flamininus proclaims ‘Freedom of Greece’
• 192 Sparta joins Achaean League
• 189 Cities of Aetolian League become subject allies of Rome
• 179 Philip V dies and is succeeded by his son Perseus
• 171–138 Reign of Mithridates I
• 167 Delos successful as free port
• 146 Provinces of Macedonia and Africa created
• 133 Tribunate of Tiberius Gracchus; Attalus III of Pergamum bequeaths his kingdom to Rome; Tiberius Gracchus murdered
• 129 Kingdom of Pergamum becomes Roman province of Asia
• 123 First tribunate of Gaius Gracchus
• 121 First use of *senatus consultum ultimum*; Gaius Gracchus killed
• 120–63 Mithridates VI king of Pontus

Cultural and religious

• c. 240–207 Livius Andronicus, earliest Roman poet and playwright, active
• 228 Romans admitted to Isthmian Games
• 221 Circus Flaminius built in Rome
• 211 First influx of Greek art into Rome from Syracuse
• c. 205–184 Plautus, comic dramatist, active
• c. 205–169 Ennius, poet, active at Rome
• c. 200 Fabius Pictor writes first prose history of Rome in Greek; Aristophanes of Byzantium becomes head of Library at Alexandria; Apollonius of Perge, mathematician, active
• 196 Rosetta Stone inscribed with trilingual inscription
• 186 Greek-style games held in Rome; Bacchanalian rites in Italy suppressed
• 184 Cato as censor campaigns against influence from East
• c. 170 Ennius writes epic poem of history of Rome
• 168–167 Victory monument to Aemilius Paulus built at Delphi
• 167 Polybius, Greek historian, arrives in Rome and writes his *History*
• 166–159 Great Altar of Zeus and Athena built at Pergamum
• 166–139 Comedies of Terence produced
• c. 160 Cato’s *Origines* in Latin prose
• 155 Visit of Carneades and other Greek philosophers to Rome causes sensation
• c. 150 Stoa of Attalus built in Athens
• c. 120 Temple of Fortune built at Praeneste

• 191 Rome completes conquest of Cisalpine Gaul
• 188 Apamea Peace Treaty
• 171–168 Third Macedonian War between Rome and Perseus
• 170–168 Sixth Syrian War between Syria and Egypt
• 168 Start of revolt of Maccabees in Judaea; Romans under Aemilius Paulus end kingdom of Macedonia at Pydna
• 155–133 Wars in Spain leave Rome in charge
• 149–146 Third Punic and Fourth Macedonian Wars

• 146 War against Achaean League; Corinth and Carthage destroyed by Romans
• 136–132 First Sicilian Slave War
• 133 Fall of Numantia to Romans under Scipio Aemilianus
• 130 Antiochus VII dies fighting the Parthians
• 112–106 Jugurtha of Numidia fights Rome and is defeated by Marius
• 104–100 Second Sicilian Slave War
• 104– Marius reforms the Roman army

• 102–101 Marius defeats the Teutoni at Aquae Sextiae and, together with Catulus, the Cimbri near Vercellae
• 91–88 'Social War' between Rome and its Italian allies
• 89–85 Mithridates VI of Pontus massacres Romans and Italians in Asia and tries to free Greeks from Rome
• 88 Sack of Delos
• 88–82 Civil war between Marius and Sulla
• 87 Marius seizes Rome

• 118 Gallia Narbonensis becomes Roman province
• 107–100 Marius consul six times
• 82–80 Sulla dictator of Rome; proscriptions at Rome
• 74 Nicomedes of Bithynia bequeaths his kingdom to Rome
• 70 First consulship of Crassus and Pompey
• 64 End of Seleucid kingdom; establishment of provinces of Bithynia, Cilicia and Syria
• 63 Consulship of Cicero; Catilinarian conspiracy in Rome
• 60 Agreement between Pompey, Crassus and Caesar ('First Triumvirate'); Pompey marries Caesar's daughter Julia
• 59 Consulship of Caesar
• 56 Dynasts renew agreement at Luca
• 55 Second consulship of Crassus and Pompey
• 52 Pompey sole consul
• 49–44 Caesar holds dictatorships
• 47 Second consulship of Caesar; Pompey murdered in Egypt; Caesar sets up Cleopatra and her brother as joint rulers
• 46 Caesar refounds Corinth as Roman colony and celebrates his successes with four triumphs

• 44 Caesar assumes dictatorship for life; Caesar assassinated
• 43 Agreement between Antony, Lepidus and Octavian ('Second Triumvirate'); proscriptions; Cicero murdered
• 40 Herod made king of Judaea by Roman Senate
• 38 Octavian marries Livia
• 37 Antony marries Cleopatra at Antioch
• 34 Antony and Cleopatra celebrate a triumph at Alexandria

• 106 Cicero born
• c. 94 Lucretius born
• 84 Catullus born
• 78 Tabularium built on Capitoline at Rome
• 70 Virgil born; Cicero delivers his orations against Verres
• 65 Horace born
• 59 Livy born
• 59–54 Catullus' poems to Lesbia; neoterics active
• 55 Pompey has first stone theatre in Rome built
• c. 55 or 51 Death of Lucretius and publication of his *de Rerum Natura*

• 55–43 Cicero's work on Roman rhetoric, politics and philosophy transforms Latin language; Varro active
• 46 Forum of Caesar begun in Rome
• 44 Cicero attacks Antony in his *Philippics* speeches
• 44–AD 21 Strabo, geographer, active
• 43 Ovid born
• 39 First public library built in Rome
• 38 Virgil's *Eclogues* published
• 29 Virgil's *Georgics* completed; Horace's *Epodes* published

• 28–23 Mausoleum of Augustus begun; two public libraries established by Augustus; programme of urban renewal in Rome; Vitruvius writes his *de Architectura*

Military

- 86 Athens and Piraeus sacked by Romans under Sulla in war with Mithridates
- 85 Peace of Dardanus pauses Mithridatic war
- 83–82 Second Mithridatic War
- 82 Sulla returns to Italy; civil war
- 80–72 Sertorius gains control of Spain; Pompey is sent to recover the territory
- 74 M. Antonius given power to deal with pirates; Mithridates declares war on Rome and invades Bithynia
- 74–63 Third Mithridatic War
- 73–71 Slave revolt of Spartacus put down by Crassus and Pompey
- 72 Lucullus victorious over Mithridates in Pontus
- 67 Pompey given extraordinary command against pirates, whom he clears from Mediterranean
- 66 Pompey finally defeats Mithridates
- 64–63 Pompey successful in Syria
- 58–51 Caesar campaigns in Gaul
- 55–54 Caesar's invasion of Britain
- 54 Crassus in the East
- 53 Crassus killed by Parthians at the battle of Carrhae
- 52 Rising in Central Gaul under Vercingetorix
- 51 Parthian invasion of Syria
- 49 Caesar crosses the Rubicon, starting Civil War; Pompey goes east
- 48 Caesar defeats Pompey at battle of Pharsalus (Greece)
- 46 Caesar campaigns in Africa
- 42 Republicans defeated at battle of Philippi (Greece); Brutus and Cassius commit suicide
- 41–40 Perusine War in Italy
- 41–32 Antony in the East

Political and social

- 30 Defeat and suicide of Antony and Cleopatra at Alexandria; Egypt made Roman province
- 29 Triple triumph of Octavian at Rome

Cultural and religious

- 40 Parthians capture Jerusalem; Rome backs Herod the Great as king of Judaea
- 36 Antony's invasion of Parthia ends in disaster; Octavian defeats Pompey at Naulochus
- 32 Final breach between Antony and Octavian
- 31 Octavian defeats Antony and Cleopatra at battle of Actium

Roman Empire 31 BC–AD 500

- 19 Parthians return Roman standards
- 16–13 Augustus in Gaul
- 13–9 Roman control extended to the Danube

Roman Empire 31 BC–AD 500

- 28–27 First constitutional settlement in Rome creates principate; Octavian takes the name Augustus; further settlements in 23 and 19
- 22 Augustus refuses dictatorship
- 21 Marriage of Agrippa and Augustus' daughter Julia
- 20 Roman diplomatic triumph in Parthia
- 19 Social reforms in Rome
- 17 Augustus adopts his grandsons Gaius and Lucius
- 12 Death of Marcus Agrippa

- 6 Tiberius, Augustus' stepson, retires to Rhodes
- 2 Augustus is made *pater patriae*

Roman Empire 31 BC–AD 500

- 24–23 First three books of Horace's *Odes* published
- 20 Building of temple of Mars Ultor in Rome begun
- 19 Death of Virgil; Augustus saves *Aeneid* from destruction
- 16– AD 3 Maison Carrée at Nîmes built
- 13–11 Theatre of Marcellus built
- 12 Augustus becomes *pontifex maximus*
- 9 Dedication of Ara Pacis Augustae
- 8 Death of Horace

- 4 Birth of Jesus
- 2 Dedication of Forum of Augustus

Military

AD

• 6–9 Revolt in Pannonia
• 9 Defeat of Varus by Arminius in Germany with loss of three legions; Rhine and Danube become frontier
• 14 Revolt of legions in Pannonia and Germany; Germanicus crosses the Rhine
• 16 Germanicus again invades Germany
• 17 Germanicus celebrates a triumph and goes east
• 43 Invasion of Britain under Aulus Plautius; Claudius visits Britain for final victory
• 58–62 Conquest and loss of Armenia
• 60/1 Revolt in Britain under Boudicca
• 66–74 Jewish revolt against Roman rule put down
• 68–9 Civil War
• 70 Titus, Vespasian's elder son, captures Jerusalem and sacks the temple
• 73–4 Fall of Masada
• 78–84 Campaigns by Agricola as governor of Britain
• 86–92 Domitian's wars against the Dacians
• 101–6 Trajan conquers Dacia; Dacia made a Roman province
• 114–17 Trajan's war in Parthia; Armenia and Mesopotamia annexed
• 115–17 Jewish revolt in Cyrenaica
• 132–5 Second Jewish revolt under Bar Kochba and final dispersal of Jews
• 157–8 Operations against Dacian tribes
• 162–6 Parthian Wars
• 168–75 Wars in Germany successfully turn back German invaders

---

Political and social

AD

• 2 Tiberius returns from Rhodes, given no part in public affairs; death of Lucius Caesar
• 4 Death of Gaius Caesar; Tiberius adopted by Augustus and given *tribunicia potestas*
• 6 Judaea made Roman province
• 14 Death of Augustus; accession of Tiberius to Principate
• 19 Death of Germanicus at Antioch
• 23 Death of Tiberius' son Drusus
• 26 Pontius Pilate appointed governor of Judaea; Tiberius retires to Capri
• 29 Death of Livia, widow of Augustus and mother of Tiberius
• 31 Sejanus, praetorian prefect and virtual ruler of empire, put to death
• 37 Death of Tiberius; accession of Gaius ('Caligula') to Principate
• 41 Murder of Gaius; accession of Claudius to Principate
• 48 Messalina, Claudius' wife, put to death; Claudius marries Agrippina
• 49 Roman *colonia* founded at Colchester
• 53 Marriage of Nero, Agrippina's son, and Octavia, Claudius' daughter
• 54 Claudius poisoned by Agrippina; accession of Nero
• 59 Murder of Agrippina on Nero's orders
• 62 Nero divorces Octavia and marries Poppaea
• 64 Fire in Rome
• 65 Death of Poppaea
• 68 Death of Nero; accession of Galba

Cultural and religious

AD

• 2–4 Publication of Ovid's *Metamorphoses*
• 17 Death of Livy and Ovid
• 30 Traditional date for the crucifixion of Jesus in Jerusalem
• 37/8 Josephus, Jewish Greek historian, born
• 42–54 Letters of Paul to early Christian churches
• 48 Plutarch born
• 60–230 Rise of cultural 'hellenism' in the 'Second Sophistic'
• 64–8 Building of Nero's Golden House; heyday of 'Silver' Latin
• 65 Suicides of Seneca and Lucan; death of St Paul in Rome
• 65–100 Gospels and Acts of the Apostles written
• 70 Titus has treasures brought to Rome from Jerusalem
• 79 Pliny the Elder dies in eruption of Vesuvius
• 80 Inauguration of Flavian Amphitheatre (Colosseum) in Rome; Domitian's palace built on Palatine
• 81 Arch of Titus built in Rome
• 86–98 Martial composes his epigrams
• 98–120 Tacitus and Suetonius write their histories; Pliny the Younger's letters written, also Plutarch's *Lives*
• 100 Codex starts to replace roll for pagan books
• 101 Birth of Herodes (Atticus)
• 110–17 Juvenal writes his satires
• 112–13 Dedication of Forum of Trajan and Trajan's Column
• 118–28 Pantheon built in Rome in place of building erected by Agrippa in 27 BC
118–38 Hadrian builds his palatial villa at Tibur (Tivoli)
• c. 120 Death of Plutarch

• 197 Severus campaigns in Parthia
• 224 Sasanid dynasty takes over in Persia
• 232 Alexander Severus defeats the Sassanid Ardashir II
• 235–84 'Third-century crisis'
• 252 European provinces sacked by Goths and others
• 256 Destruction of Dura-Europos
• 260 Emperor Valerian captured by Sasanians
• 267 Heruli invade Greece and sack Athens; Goths invade Asia Minor; Zenobia gains power in Palmyra

• 271 Romans invade Dacia
• 273 Palmyra destroyed by Aurelian
• 297 Defeat of Sasanians gives peace to frontier
• 312 Constantine wins victory at the Milvian Bridge (Rome)
• 378 Battle of Adrianople; emperor Valens killed in battle against the Visigoths
• 406–7 Invasion of Vandals, Suebi and Alamanni into the empire; Vandals reach southern Spain
• 410 Sack of Rome by Alaric the Goth; Honorius withdraws all troops from Britain

• 429–39 Vandals move into North Africa and occupy Carthage
• 445 Attila becomes leader of the Huns and attacks the empire
• 451 Attila invades Italy but dies two years later
• 455 Vandals sack Rome
• 458 Sicily captured by Vandals
• 472 Capture of Rome by Ricimer
• 490 Theodoric invades Italy

• 69 Year of the Four Emperors (Galba, Otho, Vitellius, Vespasian); Vespasian victorious
• 79 Death of Vespasian; accession of Titus; eruption of Vesuvius buries Pompeii and Herculaneum
• 80 Fire at Rome; destruction of Capitoline temple
• 81 Death of Titus; accession of his brother Domitian
• 96 Assassination of Domitian; accession of Nerva
• 98 Death of Nerva; accession of Trajan
• 100 Timgad in North Africa founded for veterans

• 106 Arabia (ancient Nabataean kingdom) made Roman province
• 117 Death of Trajan; accession of Hadrian
• 122 Hadrian visits Britain; Hadrian's Wall built across north Britain
• 130 Antinoöpolis founded by Hadrian in Middle Egypt
• 132–5 Revolt of Bar Kokhba in Palestine put down; Hadrian makes Jerusalem a Roman colony
• 138 Death of Hadrian; accession of Antoninus Pius
• 139–42 Antonine Wall built in Britain

• 161 Death of Antoninus Pius; accession of Marcus Aurelius and Lucius Verus
• 166 Marcus Aurelius and Lucius Verus celebrate joint triumph
• 176 Marcus Aurelius and his son Commodus hold triumph in Rome
• 180 Death of Marcus Aurelius; accession of Commodus
• 192 Murder of Commodus
• 193 Septimius Severus wins struggle to succeed Commodus
• 199–200 Septimius Severus in Egypt

• 132–9 Hadrian's mausoleum built in Rome
• c. 140–70 Ptolemy of Alexandria, geographer, active
• 141 Inauguration of temple of Antoninus and Faustina in Rome
• 145 Temple of Divine Hadrian consecrated in Rome
• 150 Galen, court physician, and Pausanias, travel-writer, active; revival of art of Greek oratory
• c. 165 Apuleius' *Golden Ass* published
• 174–80 *Meditations* of Marcus Aurelius
• 190 Death of Lucian

• 193 Column of Marcus Aurelius in Rome completed
• 200 Mishnah, Rabbinic compilation of 'oral' law, written down
• 202 Dio Cassius begins his Roman history
• 203 Arches of Septimius Severus erected in Rome and Lepcis Magna
• 211–17 Baths of Caracalla in Rome built
• 235 Philostratus publishes his *Lives of the Sophists*
• 244 Plotinus uses Plato's ideas in Neoplatonism

• 249–51 Emperor Decius begins major persecution of Christians
• 257 Valentinian's persecution of Christians
• 262 Last celebration of 'Secular Games'
• 271 Aurelian Walls built round Rome
• 298–306 Diocletian's baths in Rome built
• 303–5 Last major persecution of Christians
• 311 Edict of Milan promotes religious toleration, leading to Christianisation of empire at official level

Military

Political and social

• 211 Death of Septimius Severus at York; Caracalla kills his brother Geta and succeeds his father
• 212 Citizenship granted to all free inhabitants of the empire
• 217 Assassination of Caracalla near Carrhae
• 218–22 Elagabalus emperor
• 222 Murder of Elagabalus; Severus Alexander becomes emperor
• 226 Sasanian empire established in place of Parthian
• 235 Death of Severus Alexander; Maximinus becomes emperor
• 247 Millennary celebrations of founding of Rome
• 271 Emperor Aurelian begins construction of new walls round Rome
• 284–306 Diocletian gains central power, becomes emperor and establishes the tetrarchy (two Augusti and two Caesars); imperial capitals established at Trier, Milan, Sirmium and Nicomedia
• 286 Maximian given rank of Augustus
• 293 Constantius and Galerius appointed Caesars in the West and East
• 301 Diocletian's price edict
• 305 Diocletian and Maximian abdicate, succeeded by Constantius and Galerius as Augusti
• 306 Death of Constantius at York; his son Constantine declared emperor of the West
• 324 Constantine becomes sole Augustus; Byzantium begins to be transformed into Constantinople
• 330 Constantinople (the 'New Rome') becomes official seat of emperor
• 337 Death of Constantine
• 361–3 Julian the Apostate emperor

Cultural and religious

• 313–22 First Christian basilica built in Rome
• 314–15 Arch of Constantine erected in Rome
• 325 First Ecumenical Council in Nicaea
• 378 Ammianus Marcellinus writes his history of the empire
• 380–420 Jerome translates Old and New Testaments into Latin
• 391 Edict of Theodosius I closes pagan shrines; destruction of Library and Serapeum in Alexandria
• 394 Olympic Games abolished by Theodosius I
• 397–400 Augustine writes his *Confessions*
• 413–26 Augustine writes *City of God*
• 425 Earliest mosaics in Ravenna, in mausoleum of Galla Placidia
• 430 Death of Augustine in Hippo while under siege from Vandals

- 379–95 Theodosius (I) the Great emperor
- 382 Goths allowed independent status within the Roman Empire
- 395 Death of Theodosius; division of empire between his sons, Arcadius in the East, Honorius in the West; revolt of Alaric and the Visigoths
- 402 Imperial court moved to Ravenna
- 475–6 Romulus Augustulus last emperor in the West
- 476 End of Roman Empire in the West with deposition of Romulus Augustulus; Odoacer becomes king of Italy
- 490 Ostrogothic kingdom of Italy founded

After antiquity

- 524 Boethius' *Consolation of Philosophy*
- c. 525 Dionysius Exiguus devises current system of reckoning dates (AD 1 = *ab urbe condita* 754)
- 526 Death of Theodoric
- 527–34 Justinian's law code
- 529 Justinian closes Academy in Athens
- 532–7 Church of Santa Sophia built
- 532–47 San Vitale, Ravenna, built
- 533 Justinian regains North Africa from Vandals
- 537 Dedication of new church of Santa Sophia, Constantinople
- 540 Cassiodorus founds the monastery of Vivarium, Southern Italy
- 547–54 Procopius writes of Justinian's wars and his *Secret History* and *Buildings*
- 554 Justinian takes over control of Italy
- 555 Fifth Ecumenical Council at Constantinople
- 565 Death of Justinian
- 570–636 Isidore of Seville, author of various theological and historical works and compiler of the influential *Etymologiae*
- 622 Hegira: flight of Prophet Muhammad from Medina
- 672–735 Venerable Bede, English historian and scholar, author of *Ecclesiastical History of the English People*
- 680 Sixth Ecumenical Council condemns Monotheletism
- 700–20 Monasteries built at Farfa, San Vincenzo and Montecassino
- 715 Great Mosque at Damascus decorated with mosaics
- 716–843 Period of Iconoclasm (interrupted 780–813)
- 768–814 Reign of Charlemagne
- 782 Alcuin invited to head palace school for Charlemagne
- 9th c. Uncial script replaced by minuscule
- 810–93 Photius, scholar and patriarch of Constantinople
- 860 St Cyril's mission to Khazans
- 10th c. *Suda*, dictionary and encyclopedia, published
- 11th c. Paper used for imperial archives at Constantinople; monastic churches built (Hosios Loukas, Nea Moni, Daphni); revival of Montecassino, mother monastery of Benedictine order
- 1079–1142 Peter Abelard, French dialectician and theologian
- 1095–9 First Crusade
- 1098 Jerusalem taken by Crusaders; foundation of Cistercian Order
- 1115–95 Eustathius, archbishop, scholar and commentator on Homer
- 1147–9 Second Crusade
- 1148 Anna Comnena's *Alexiad* completed
- c. 1150 Beginnings of universities of Paris and Oxford
- 1189–92 Third Crusade
- 1204 Fourth Crusade; sack of Constantinople and foundation of Latin Empire
- 1209 Beginning of Cambridge University
- 1215 Fourth Lateran Council in Rome
- 1216 Dominican Order founded
- 1261 Byzantine authority recaptures Constantinople
- 1265–1321 Dante Alighieri, Italian poet, author of *La Vita Nuova* and *La Divina Commedia*
- 1304–74 Francesco Petrarch, Italian book collector, scholar and poet
- 1309–77 Popes at Avignon
- 1314–21 Dante's *Divine Comedy*
- mid 14th c. Latin works of e.g. Cicero, Augustine, Boethius, Aquinas translated into Greek
- 1378–1417 'Great Schism' of Roman church
- 1380–1400 Geoffrey Chaucer's *Canterbury Tales*
- 1397 Beginning of Greek studies in Western Empire
- 1453 Constantinople taken by Turks under Mehmet II
- 1465 Printed edition of Cicero's *de Officiis*
- 1468–1540 Guillaume Budé, first great classical scholar of France
- c. 1478 Sandro Botticelli's 'Primavera'
- 1488 Printed edition of Homer
- c. 1490 Nero's Golden House discovered
- 1494–1515 Aldus Manutius sets up publishing house in Venice to print Greek and Latin texts
- 1495–7 Leonardo da Vinci's 'Last Supper'
- 1506 Statue of Laocoon found in Rome
- 1507 First Greek book printed in France
- 1508–12 Michelangelo Buonarroti paints ceiling of Sistine Chapel
- 1516 Desiderius Erasmus publishes his first edition of New Testament
- 1532 Niccolò dei Machiavelli's *Il Principe* published
- 1547–1606 Justus Lipsius professor of history at Leiden University
- 1598–1600 George Chapman's translation of Homer's *Iliad*
- late 16th c. Christopher Plantin and Elzevier family, printers, in Netherlands
- 1660 Royal Society founded
- 1687 Parthenon damaged during Venetian siege
- 1697 John Dryden's translation of Virgil's *Aeneid*
- 1699 Richard Bentley publishes his *Dissertation upon the Epistles of Phalaris* (written in English) and postulates existence of letter digamma in ancient Greek
- 1707 Society of Antiquaries founded
- 1710 Digging starts at Herculaneum
- 1715–20 Alexander Pope's translation of Homer's *Iliad*
- 1725–6 Pope's translation of Homer's *Odyssey*

• 1732 Society of Dilettanti founded
• 1748 Systematic excavation of Pompeii begins
• 1753 British Museum founded
• 1759–1808 Richard Porson, outstanding Greek scholar at Cambridge
• 1764 Johann Joachim Winckelmann's *Geschichte der Kunst des Altertums*
• 1766 Gotthold Lessing's *Laocoon* published
• 1766–88 Edward Gibbon's *Decline and Fall of the Roman Empire*
• 1768 Royal Academy founded
• 1768–88 Johann Wolfgang von Goethe's tour of Italy
• 1769 Robert Wood publishes his *Essay on the Original Genius of Homer*
• 1771 Josiah Wedgwood and Thomas Bentley open pottery factory in Etruria, Stoke-on-Trent
• 1772 British Museum acquires Sir William Hamilton's first vase collection
• 1776 American Declaration of Independence
• 1789 French Revolution begins
• 1795 Wolf's *Prolegomena ad Homerum*
• 1795–1815 Napoleonic Wars
• 1817 August Boeckh's *Die Staatshaushaltung der Athener*
• 1821 Greek War of Independence begins
• 1822 Rosetta Stone deciphered
• 1824 B. G. Teubner editions of Greek and Latin texts begin
• 1827 Battle of Navarino
• 1833 Johann Gustav Droysen's *History of Hellenism*
• 1837 University of Athens established
• 1841 George Grote's *History of Greece*
• 1854–5 Theodor Mommsen's *History of Rome*
• 1867–94 Karl Marx's *Das Kapital*
• 1870 Unification of Italy
• 1871 Unification of Germany; Heinrich Schliemann begins digging at Troy
• 1872 Friedrich Nietzsche's *Birth of Tragedy*
• 1878–86 Carl Humann excavates at Pergamum
• 1884 August Mau identifies four Pompeian styles of wall-painting
• 1890–1915 J. G. Frazer's *Golden Bough*
• 1891 First modern edition of [Aristotle's] *Athenian Constitution*
• 1897 First papyri found at Oxyrhynchus
• 1903 Jane Harrison's *Prolegomena to the Study of Greek Religion*
• 1912–27 K. J. Beloch's *Griechische Geschichte*
• 1914–18 World War I
• 1926 M. I. Rostovtzeff's *Social and Economic History of the Roman Empire*
• 1939–45 World War II
• 1941 M. I. Rostovtzeff's *Social and Economic History of the Hellenistic World*
• 1952 Decipherment of Linear B as Mycenaean Greek

67. Maps

Brian A. Sparkes

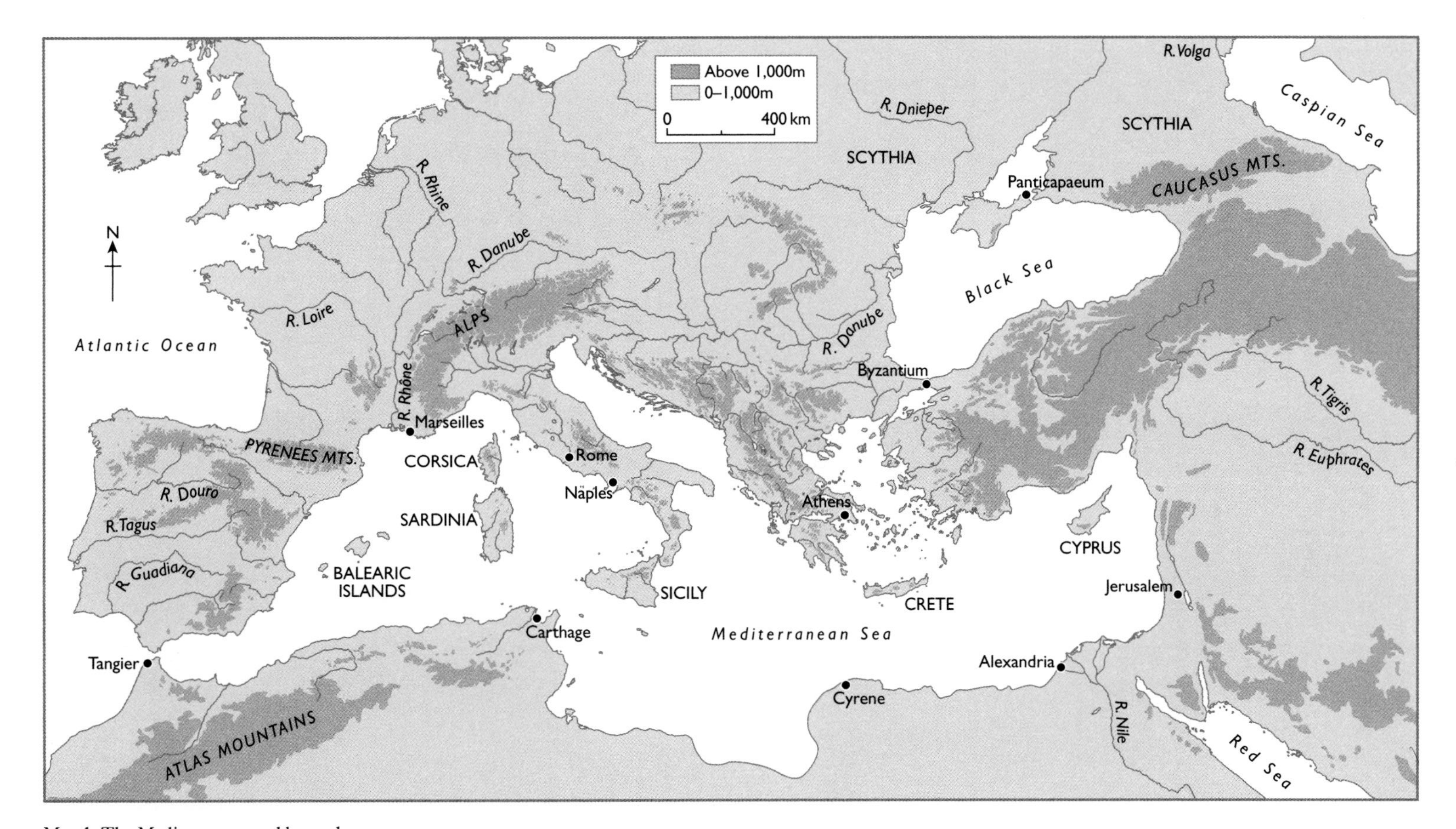

Map 1 The Mediterranean and beyond

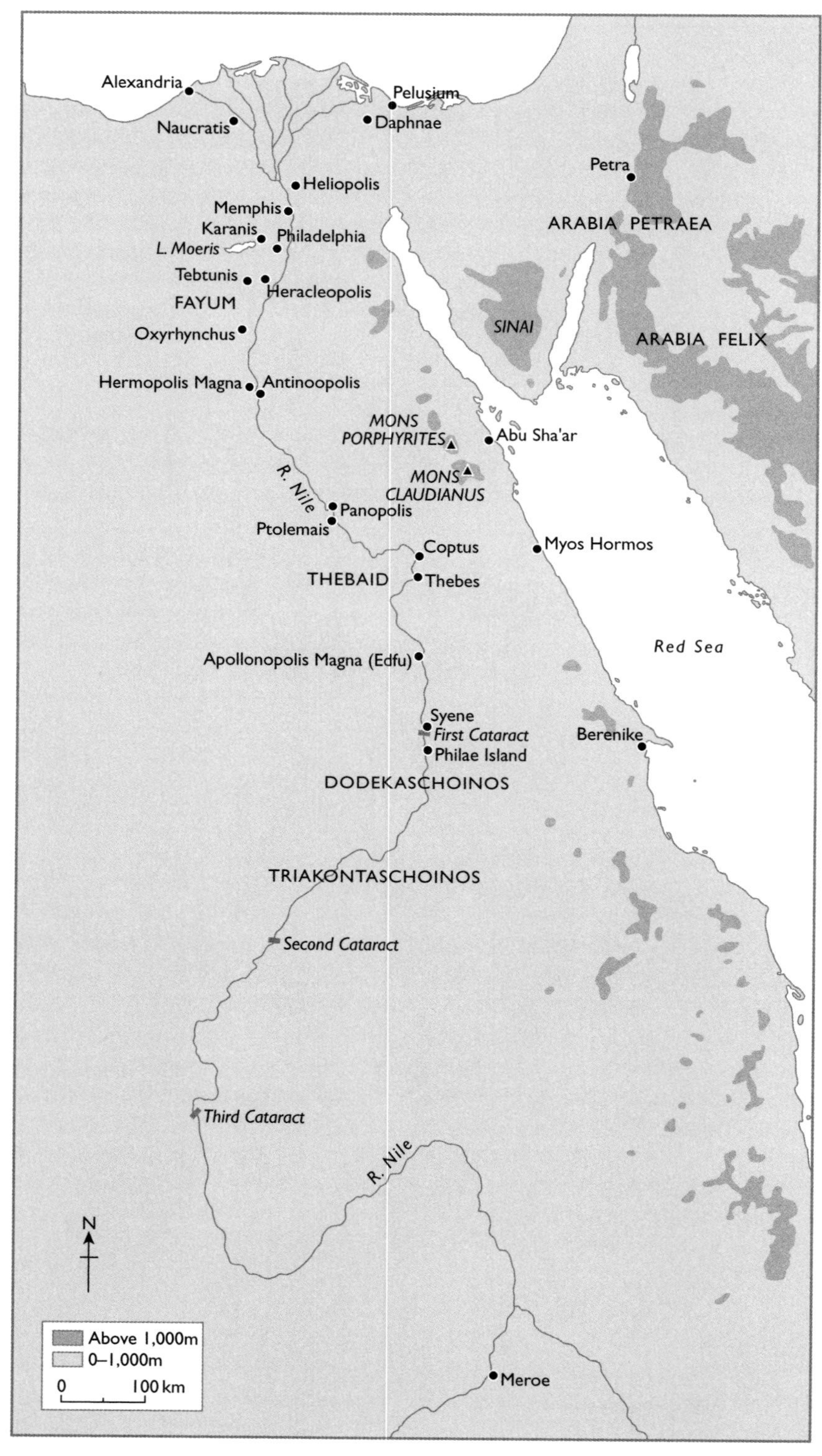
Alexandria
Naucratis
Pelusium
Daphnae
Petra
Heliopolis
Memphis
Karanis
Philadelphia
L. Moeris
ARABIA PETRAEA
Tebtunis
Heracleopolis
FAYUM
SINAI
Oxyrhynchus
ARABIA FELIX
Hermopolis Magna
Antinoopolis
MONS PORPHYRITES
Abu Sha'ar
MONS CLAUDIANUS
R. Nile
Panopolis
Ptolemais
Coptus
Myos Hormos
THEBAID
Thebes
Red Sea
Apollonopolis Magna (Edfu)
Syene
First Cataract
Berenike
Philae Island
DODEKASCHOINOS
TRIAKONTASCHOINOS
Second Cataract
Third Cataract
R. Nile
N
Above 1,000m
0–1,000m
0
100 km
Meroe

Map 2 Egypt

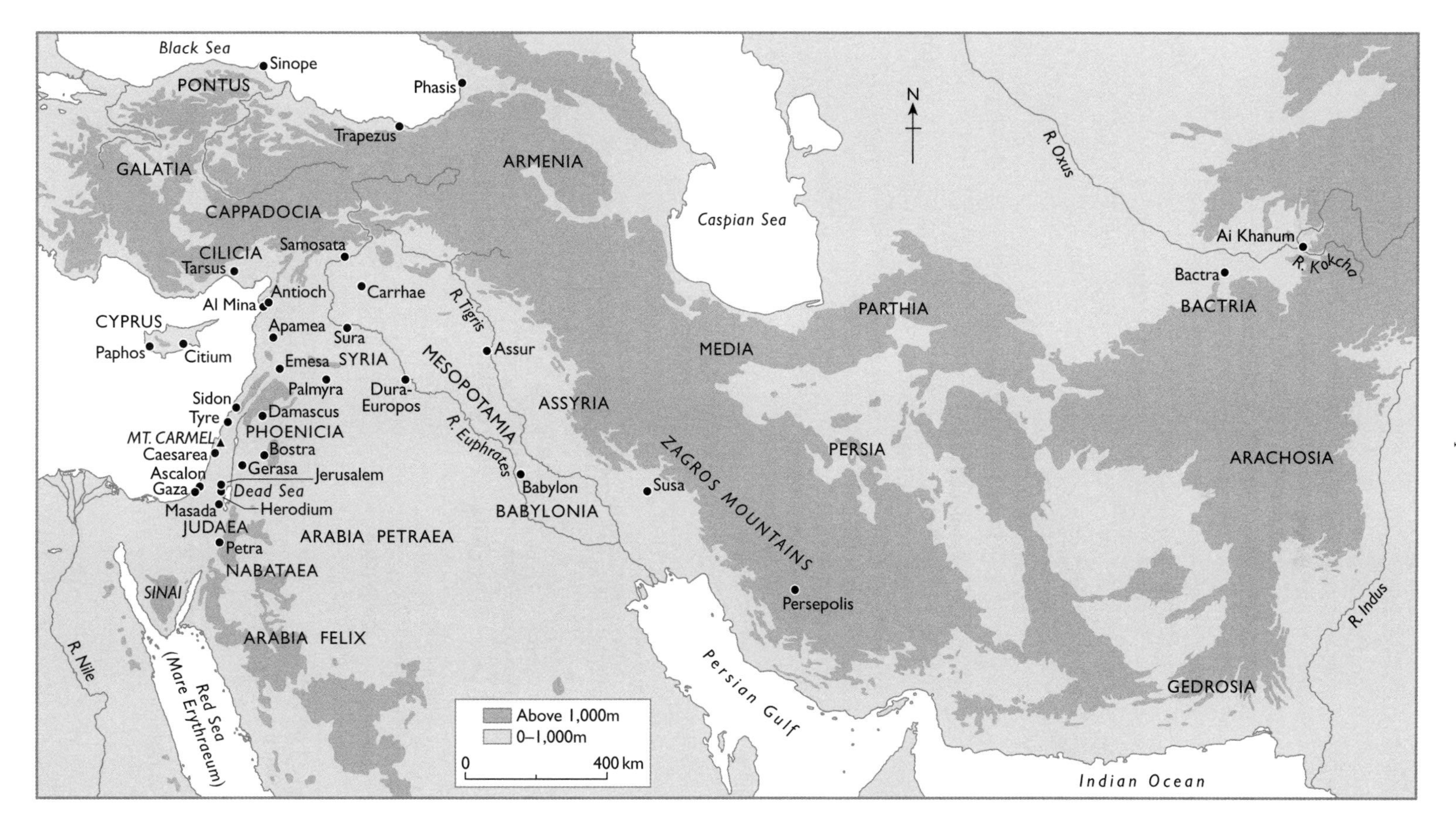

Map 3 The Near East

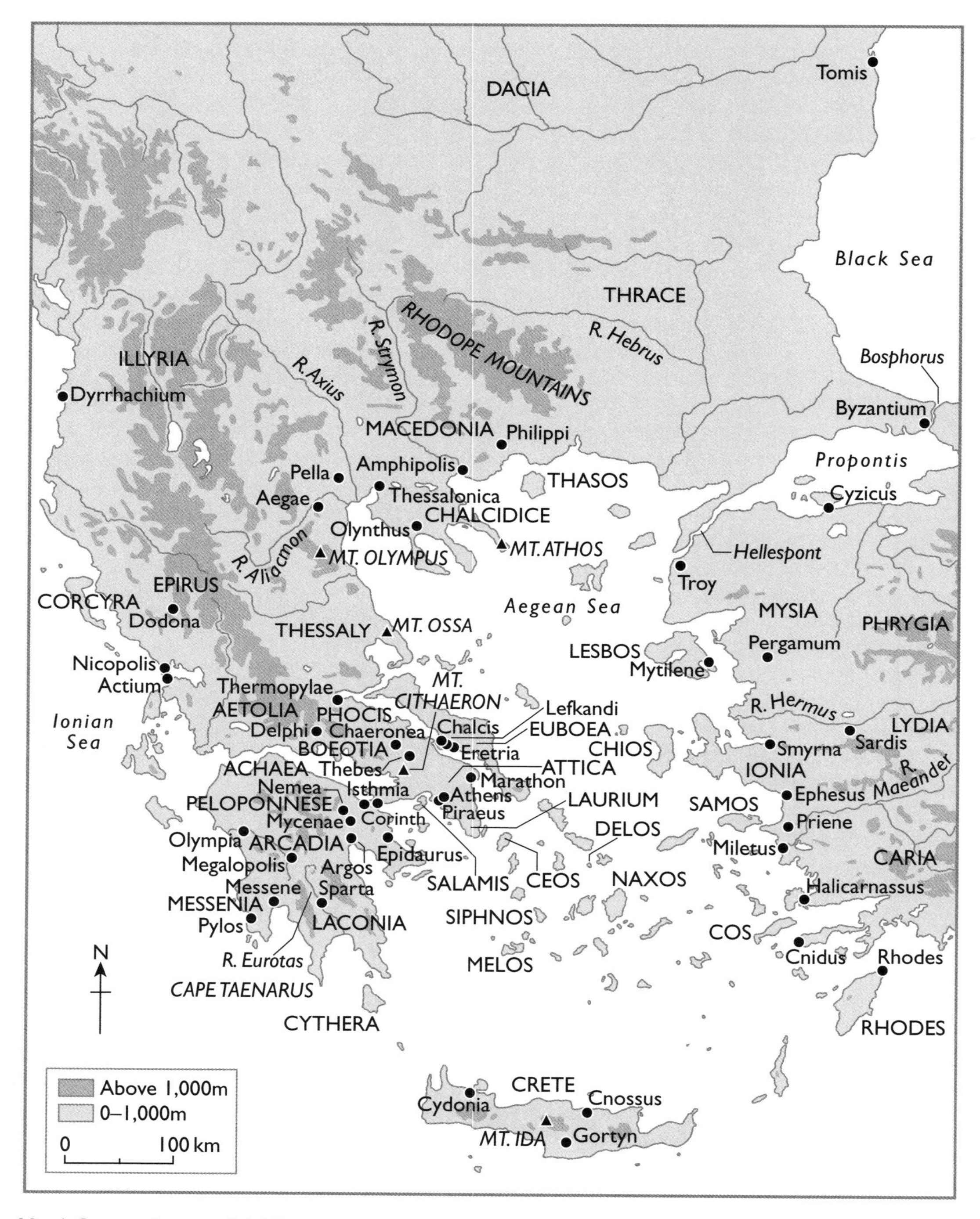

Map 4 Greece and western Asia Minor

Map 5 Italy and Sicily

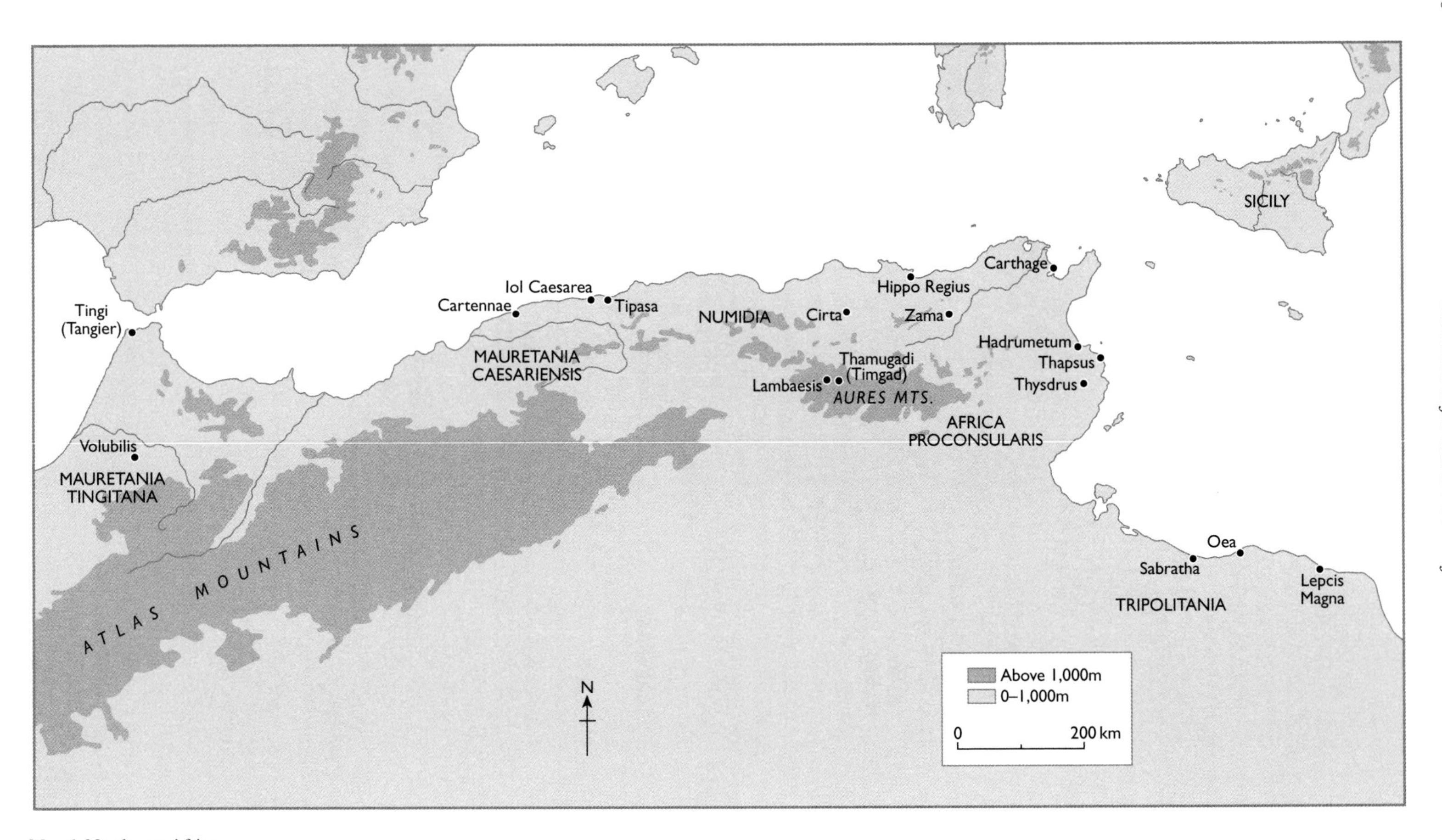

Map 6 Northwest Africa

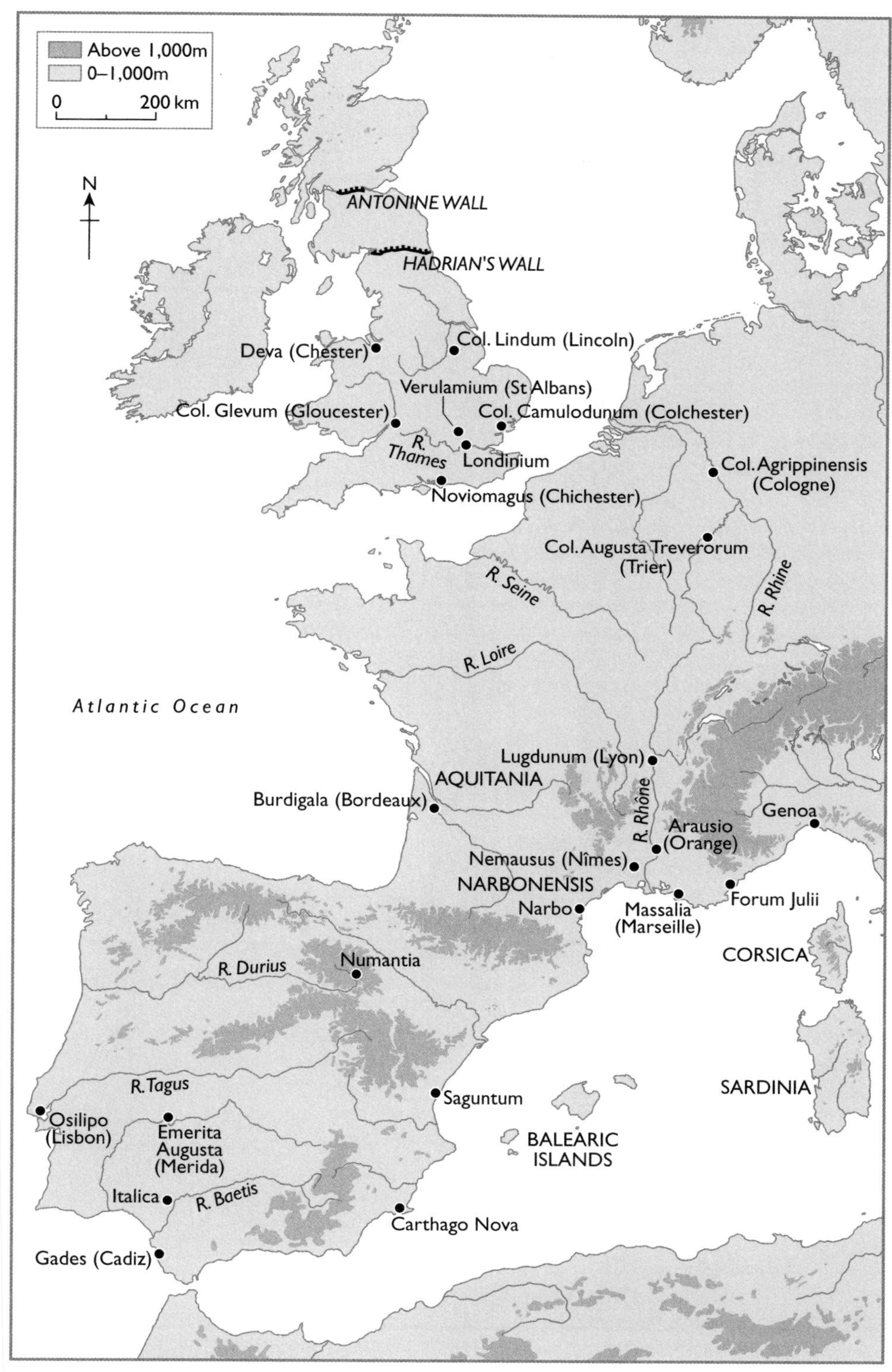

Map 7 The western provinces

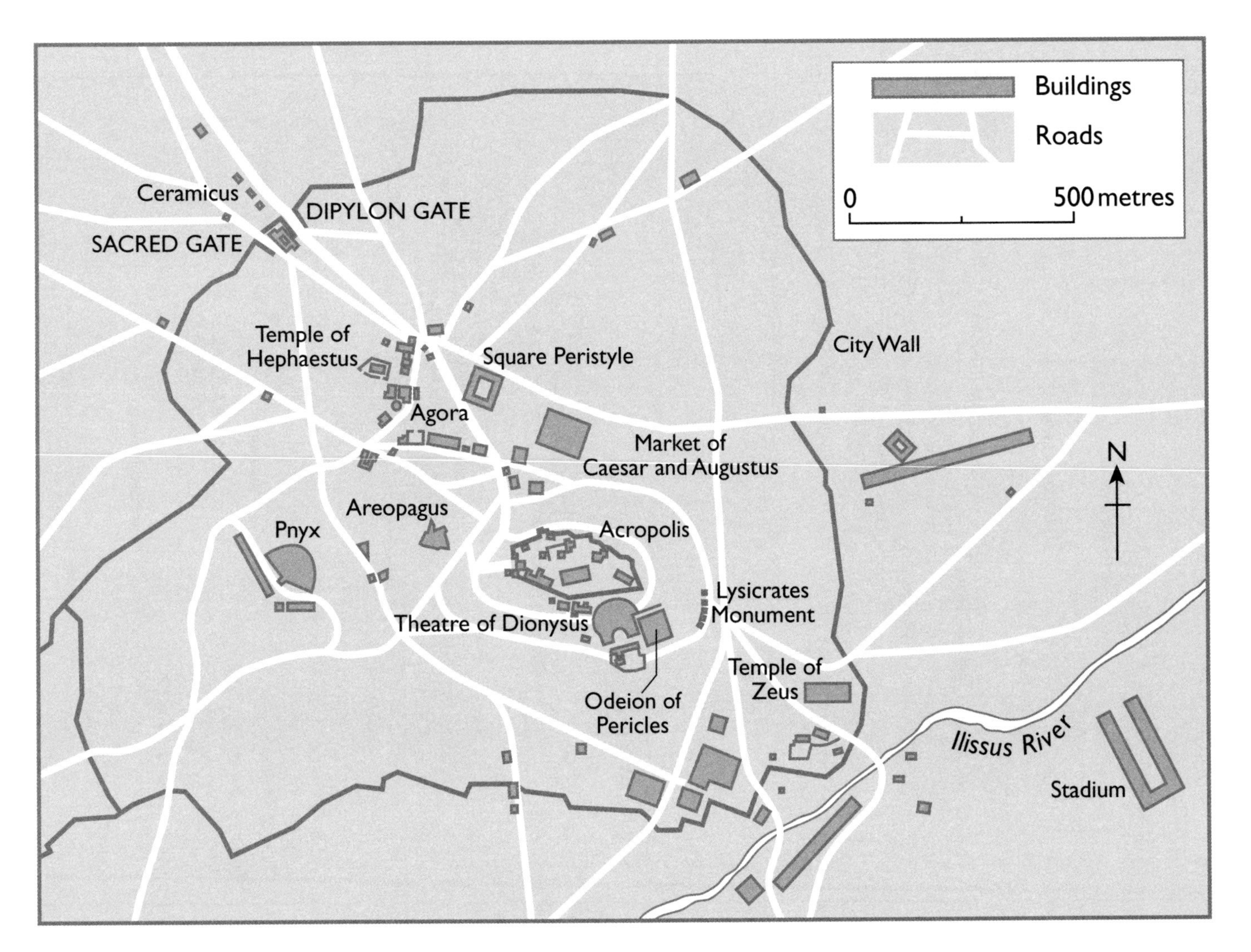

Map 8 Plan of Athens

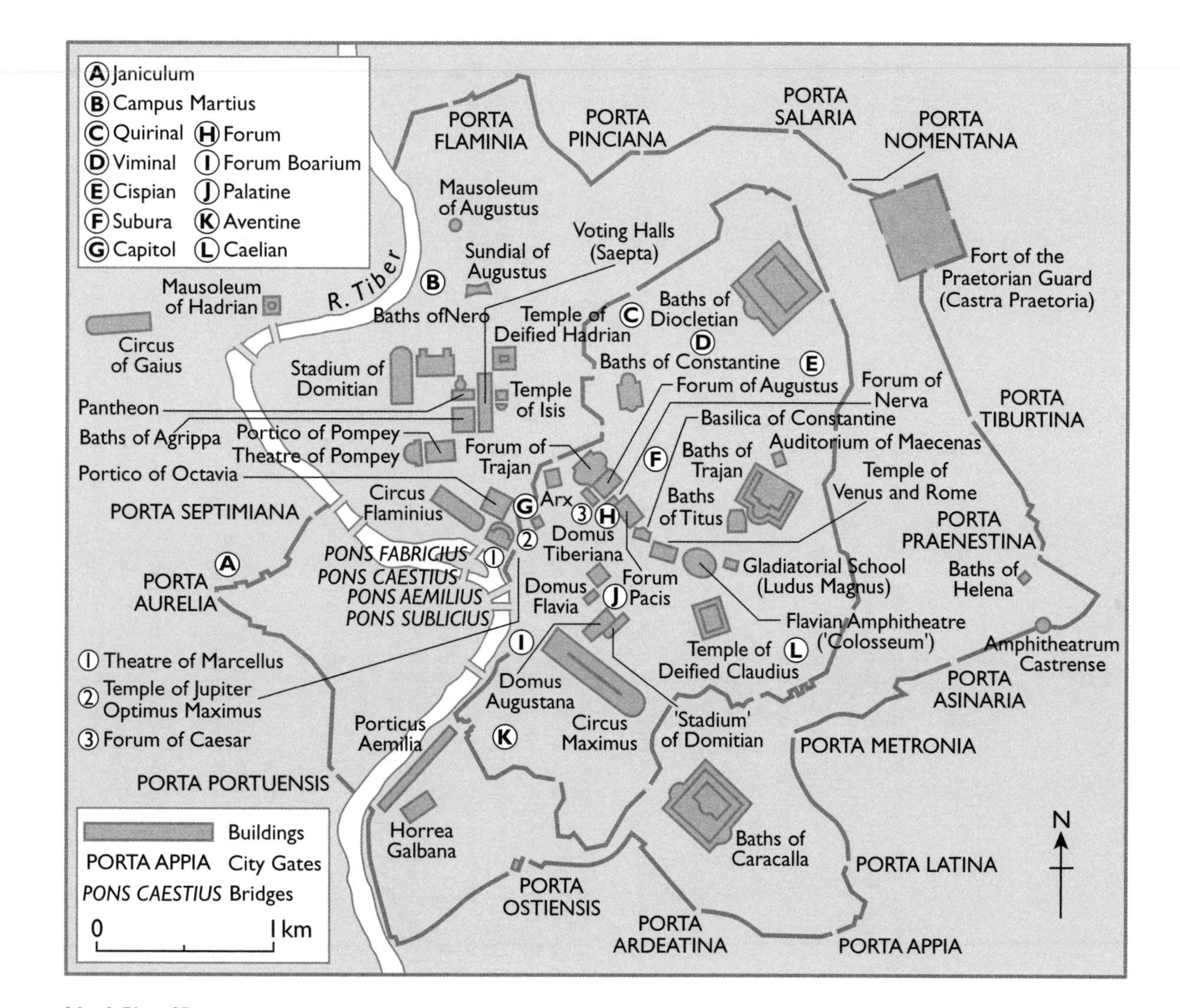

Map 9 Plan of Rome

68. Glossary of Ancient and Modern Terms

Thomas Harrison

This glossary comprises ancient terms, modern theoretical or literary terms with particular relevance to the ancient world, and select Latin and Greek phrases in common usage in English. No glossary can be comprehensive; this one seeks only to give brief definitions of terms that are likely to appear unexplained in books and articles on the ancient world. Where there is a fuller discussion of a given term elsewhere in the Companion, reference is given to the page of that discussion.

Since alternative transliterations of Greek terms are possible, readers are advised to check under alternative spellings; in general c is preferred to k. If readers do not find help on a given topic here, they should also consult the index (which includes e.g. every proper name referred to in the Companion) or a relevant dictionary or reference work (see chapter 69).

a fortiori lit. 'by the stronger' (Latin); all the more, with stronger reason
a posteriori lit. 'from what is after' (Latin); used of an argument that deduces a cause from the result, or knowledge which derives from experience alone
a priori lit. 'from what is before' (Latin); used of knowledge that is independent of all particular experience (in contrast to a posteriori knowledge)
ab initio lit. 'from the beginning' (Latin)
ab urbe condita lit. 'from the founding of the city' (Latin); the foundation of Rome, traditionally 753 BC, from which dates were reckoned
acmē lit. 'high point'; e.g. date at which an individual is deemed to have flourished; used to establish notional year of birth (see p. 486)
acropolis lit. 'the highest point in the city' (Greek); citadel used e.g. of the Acropolis of Athens
acroterium (plural: ***acroteria***) sculptural figure or ornament at the corners and apex of a pediment
ad hoc lit. 'for the immediate purpose' (Latin)
ad hominem lit. 'to the person' (Latin); used of arguments addressed to the author rather than the work
adlocutio address, e.g. of commander to troops (Latin)
adventus formalised arrival (of an emperor) (Latin)
aedes lit. 'dwelling' (Latin); temple building
aediles (Roman) magistrates responsible for civic affairs (e.g. water-supply or markets) (see pp. 455–6)
aetiological (e.g. of myth) tracing the origins or explanation of something (e.g. how the leopard got his spots)
agathos (plural: ***agathoi***) lit. 'good' (Greek); used of people of high social status
agōgē Spartan system of education
agōn lit. 'contest' (Greek); a formal debate within Greek drama (see p. 301)
agora central open space in the (Greek) city: a focus for political as well as social and religious life (see pp. 266, 428–9)
alabastron small flask for oils and perfumes
album senatorium roll (i.e. list) of senators drawn up by censors every five years (Roman)
alliteration repetition of the same sound in two or more words
Altertumswissenschaft study of the whole of Graeco-Roman culture, not only literary texts (see pp. 4–5)

amphictyony association of Greek poleis with common responsibility for a religious sanctuary (most famously Delphi)
amphitheatre arena for gladiatorial contests (e.g. the Colosseum in Rome)
amphora large, two-handled storage jar (see pp. 52, 145, 212–13)
anachōrēsis abandonment of one's place of work to avoid taxation (common in Ptolemaic Egypt)
anacolouthon lack of grammatical sequence within a sentence (often intended)
anacyclōsis theory of cyclical change between political constitutions (see p. 448)
analepsis flashback (in narrative) to an earlier time
anaphora repetition of a word or phrase at the beginning of successive clauses or phrases
andrōn men's room in Greek house
annales annual account of events in Rome drawn up by priests
Annales school school of thought associated with the journal *Annales* (and with the historians Marc Bloch, Fernand Braudel and Lucien Febvre)
annona public food supply in Rome
antefix ornament along the eaves of a tiled roof
anthropomorphic in human shape (e.g. of gods)
apella Spartan popular assembly
aporia lit. 'no way through', (Greek); impasse, used of philosophical stalemate with which some Platonic dialogues end (see pp. 43, 367)
apostrophe turn from the general audience to address a specific group, person, object, or abstract entity
apotheosis elevation to divine status (formalised into ceremony in Rome)
apse semi-circular recess with a half-domed roof
archaic used of the period approximately from the development of writing and the origin of the Greek *polis* (eighth century) to the Persian Wars (490–479 BC) (see pp. 92–4)
archaism use of an older turn, phrase or style; self-conscious throwback; hence 'archaising'
archēgētes founder of a (Greek) city
archetype (in textual transmission) the MS to which the surviving manuscripts can be traced back (see pp. 252, 259–60)
architrave (in architecture) lit. 'main beam'; lowest part of entablature; lintel or beam that rests on the capitals of columns in e.g. Greek temple
archōn magistrate (Greek); the 'eponymous' *archōn* in Athens was the magistrate after whom the year was named (see p. 451)
arena central area of an amphitheatre (Latin)
Areopagus hill west of the Athenian Acropolis, hence name given to the council of former *archōns* who met there in democratic Athens
aretē virtue, excellence (Greek)
aries (Roman) battering ram
aristos (plural: ***aristoi***) lit. 'the best' (Greek); used of people of the highest social status
armilla (Roman) bracelet given as military medal
aroura square measure (of land) in Graeco-Roman Egypt, equivalent to c. 2,760 square metres
artaba measure of corn (e.g. used in Graeco-Roman Egypt)
arx defensible hill, fortress (Latin)
aryballos small, usually round, flask for oils and perfumes (Greek)
as (Roman) bronze coin (see p. 474); also a Roman measure of weight and area (see pp. 472–3)
assonance repetition of the same sounds in two or more words
asty (Greek) city (the *asty* and the *chōra* together constitute the polis)
asylia status of inviolability (i.e. freedom from attack) claimed by Greek cities
asyndeton lack of conjunctions between clauses (e.g. 'I came, I saw, I conquered')
atrium (Roman) hall
Atthis a history of Athens
Attic of the city and territory of Athens
Attica territory of the city of Athens
auctoritas moral authority (Latin)
augures (or augurs) (Roman) college of priests with responsibility for the observation of auspices (or omens)
aula regia imperial audience chamber
aulētēs musician who plays the *aulos*
aulos Greek reed-pipe, equivalent to the Roman *tibia* (see pp. 416, 418–19)
aureus Roman gold coin (see p. 474)

auspicium (or **auspice**) omen, e.g. unusual pattern of birds' flight, taken as sign of divine approval or disapproval of human action
autonomia (Greek) the right to be governed according to one's own *nomoi* or laws
axones wooden boards on which the Athenian reformer Solon's legislative programme was published

ballista (Roman) stone-throwing military engine
balneum (Roman) bath
barbarian (Greek: *barbaros*, plural: *barbaroi*); Greek term for foreign peoples
basileus (plural: ***basileis***) Greek term for 'king', used especially of foreign kings such as the Great King of Persia; also the name for magistrates in some Greek cities; in the Mycenaean period used of local rulers
basilica large (Roman) public hall, later used as model for early churches (see p. 166)
bibliothēkē/bibliotheca (Greek, Roman) public library
black-figure Greek pottery technique in which figures are fired black against a terracotta background, enhanced by incisions and by white and red colours (see pp. 206, 208, 226, 413, 415)
bona fide lit. 'in good faith' (Latin)
boulē (Greek) council (e.g. in Athens, the council of the 500 and the council of the Areopagus); hence *bouleutai*, members of a *boulē*, or *bouleutērion*, council-chamber (see pp. 430, 451–2)
boustrophēdon lit. 'as the ox turns' (Greek); style of writing (used e.g. in early Greek inscriptions) in which the writing runs from right to left and then from left to right in alternate lines (see p. 266)
Bronze Age traditional term for the period c. 3000–1000 BC
bucchero Etruscan pottery with black shiny finish

caduceus staff carried by Roman public heralds or ambassadors as symbol of peace
caesura break in a line of verse
Campus Martius the field of Mars; space outside the city of Rome for army musters
capital top of a column (e.g. Doric, Ionian or Corinthian)
capite velato lit. 'with the head veiled' (Latin); pose of officiating Roman priests
Capitoline Triad Jupiter, Juno and Minerva
capitolium temple of the Capitoline Triad
cartonnage mass of papyri used in mummification of humans or animals in Egypt, the source of many newly discovered papyri (see pp. 238, 246)
caryatid female figure supporting an entablature (e.g. at the Erechtheion on the Acropolis)
castra (Roman) military camp
catachresis extreme metaphor
cella inner or main chamber of a temple
censor (Roman) magistrate with responsibility, every five years, for the census and *album senatorium*
centurion leader of a company of (Roman) infantry (each maniple had two centurions, 'prior' and 'posterior', or senior and junior)
cheirotonia vote by show of hands (Greek)
chiasmus two corresponding pairs (e.g. of words) arranged in inverted order (a-b-b-a) rather than alternately (a-b-a-b)
chitōn tunic worn by Greek men and women (equivalent to Roman *tunica*) (see p. 228)
chlamys a short rectangular cloak worn by cavalry and by ephebes (Greek)
chōra rural hinterland of a (Greek) city-state
chorēgia sponsorship of a chorus at the Athenian musical or dramatic festivals (a form of 'liturgy') (see p. 291)
chorēgus sponsor of Greek dramatic performances (see p. 291)
chorography the study or description of regions (see p. 131)
choryphaeus chorus leader (in Greek drama)
chous small squat jug (Greek)
chryselephantine (of statues) made of gold and ivory
chthonic of the earth (e.g. used of certain class of deities)
cinaedus Greek term for effeminate (or sexually passive) male (see p. 28)
circa approximately (used especially of dates)
circus maximus (Roman) arena
civilis princeps term for Roman emperor as between citizen and ruler
classical reception study of the various appropriations of, and responses to, classical works in different historical contexts (as distinct from classical tradition) (see pp. 1, 57–62)
classical tradition transmission of classical

culture through history (as distrinct from classical reception) (see pp. 3–8, 57)

clavi vertical purple stripes on sleeves of Roman *tunica*, which denoted membership of the senatorial or equestrian classes

closure completeness, sense of finality, of a literary work

codex (plural: **codices)** manuscript (in book form) (see pp. 238, 253, 435)

codicology study of manuscripts (codices) as objects in their own right (in contrast to palaeography) (see p. 253)

cognomen Roman third name, sometimes hereditary, sometimes indicating a personal attribute or military triumph (see pp. 467–70)

cohors (or **cohort**) unit of Roman army, comprising three maniples: one legion comprises ten cohorts

coin hoard collection of coins taken out of circulation in antiquity with a view to later recovery (see p. 175)

colonia (Roman) colony (see pp. 000–00)

colossus oversize statue (Latin)

columbarium structure designed in the style of a dovecote, to hold the remains of the dead (Roman)

comitia assemblies of the Roman people (see p. 456), including *comitia centuriata* (which elected senior magistrates and voted on laws; voting was by 'centuries', a system which favoured the wealthy), *comitia curiata* (with a limited religious role), and *comitia tributa* (plebeian assembly which elected aediles, quaestors and tribunes; voting was by tribe)

concordia concord, unity (Latin)

confer lit. 'compare' (Latin); usually abbreviated as cf. in footnotes

connoisseurship method for identifying individual artists by analysis of minute details (see p. 50)

consul senior magistrate of the Roman Republic (two in each year) (see pp. 102–3, 451)

contio (plural: *contiones*) non-voting popular assembly in Rome

contrapposto (of sculpture) balanced pose in which the weight is unevenly distributed and the shoulders and hips slope in opposite directions (see p. 187)

controversia (plural: *controversiae*) Roman rhetorical form involving arguments based on an imaginary law-court-case (see pp. 000–00)

convivium dinner party (Latin), equivalent to Greek symposium

Corinthian order most ornate of the architectural orders or styles, distinguished especially by capitals decorated with leaves (see pp. 161, 163–4)

cornice (in architecture) set of mouldings that crown an entablature (see p. 199)

cryptoporticus hidden (usually underground) corridor

cubiculum bedroom of Roman house

cuneiform lit. 'wedge-shaped' (Latin); Near Eastern script (see p. 69)

curia assembly hall of the (Roman) senate; also, a voting group within the *comitia curiata*

cursus honorum career ladder of public offices in Rome up which an aspiring politician sought to climb, culminating in the consulship (see p. 456)

curule (chair) folding seat reserved for magistrates (Roman)

Daedalic traditional term given to early Greek pottery and other artefacts (especially of the seventh century BC)

damnatio memoriae eradication of someone's memory from official records and buildings

Daric Persian coin (see p. 473)

Dark Age(s) traditional term for period, 1200–700 BC, between the collapse of the Mycenaean palace system and the rise of the Greek *polis* (see pp. 87–91)

de facto lit. 'in reality' (Latin); used in oppsition to de jure

de jure lit. 'in law' (Latin); used in opposition to de facto

decemvirs board of ten Roman magistrates (see p. 23)

deconstruction approach to analysis of texts which dismantles what it sees as unquestioned assumptions and contradictions in language

decumanus east-west street in a Roman town

Delian League modern term for the fifth-century BC hegemony of Athens

deme a village or neighbourhood (Greek), a subset of the city (and by extension of those who live there) (see p. 451)

demography study of human populations
denarius (plural: *denarii)* Roman silver coin, equivalent to four *sestertii* (see p. 474)
dentils (in architecture) rectangular blocks occupying the place of a frieze and representing the ends of the joists (see pp. 000–00); (in numismatics) toothlike device around rim of coins
deuteragonist second actor (in Greek drama)
devotio ceremony whereby a Roman commander offered himself and his men to the Manes and the Earth to secure victory
Diadochi successors (e.g. successor kings); term given to the kingdoms and rulers who succeeded Alexander and inherited the different areas of his rule (see pp. 98–9)
diagramma royal decision (of Hellenistic monarchs)
dictator magistrate with extraordinary powers elected (in Roman Republic) for a maximum period of six months to deal with emergency
die hard metal punch used to strike coinage (engraved to give pattern to a coin) (see p. 173)
digamma early letter of the Greek alphabet, which became obsolete; pronounced as w, written approximately as F (see p. 487)
Digest compilation of Roman civil law in fifty volumes (published in AD 533) (see pp. 435–7)
dikastērion (plural: *dikastēria*) law-court (see pp. 000–00)
dikē justice (Greek); also used of private law suit (in contrast to *graphē*, public suit)
dinos large round-bottomed bowl (Greek)
diocese administrative division within Roman Empire
dioikētēs (Greek) chief financial officer of Ptolemaic Egypt (see p. 454)
dipinti writing painted onto fired pottery (see p. 212) or written on walls
diplōmata small (c. 6.5 × 5″;16×12 cm) hinged folding bronze tablets mainly issued to auxiliary soldiers on retirement from service, recording the grant to them of Roman citizenship on discharge (see p. 264)
divus (fem.: *diva*; plural: *divi*/*divae*) title of deified emperors and members of the imperial family
dokimasia scrutiny of the qualifications for office of a prospective magistrate (in democratic Athens) (see p. 452)
dolium (plural: *dolia*) large Roman earthenware vessel, used for storage and fermentation (see p. 212)
dominate the rule of Diodetian and his successors; the term indicates a hardening of imperial rule, in which the emperor is *dominus* (master and not *princeps* (first citizen) – contrast with 'principate'
Doric order simplest of the three architectural orders or styles, with plain round capitals (see pp. 160–1)
drachma (plural: **drachmae**) Greek silver coin, equivalent to six obols (see p. 473)
Dressel typological classification system for Roman amphorae (named after the German scholar Heinrich Dressel)

ecclēsia assembly of adult male citizens in democratic Athens
eccyclēma platform wheeled on to Greek dramatic stage (e.g. for magnificent entrances)
eisangelia denunciation; legal procedure in democratic Athens
eisodos (plural: *eisodoi*) passageways leading to the *orchēstra* in Greek drama
eisphora form of taxation (used in Greek cities, especially when at war)
ekphora **lit.** 'carrying out' (Greek); used of a body for burial; a stage in the Greek funeral
elenchus lit. 'refutation' (Greek); philosophical procedure associated with Socrates (see pp. 365–6)
eleutheria (Greek) freedom
ellipsis (in narrative) information left out
emblēma (plural: *emblēmata*) inserted panel of mosaic pavement (see p. 201)
emporion trading centre (Greek)
encaustic technique for painting using heated wax (see p. 194)
entablature (in architecture) a superstructure, originally wooden, set up over columns in e.g. Greek temples; consisting of architrave, frieze and cornice
entasis (in architecture) the slight bulge towards the middle of a column, used to correct the illusion that straight columns are concave (see pp. 161–2)
epeisodion (plural: *epeisodia*) 'episode', a section of a Greek drama

ephēbeia institution whereby Greek men newly come of age (ephebes) performed national service for two years
ephēmeridai daily records; also used of royal diaries
ephor one of five annually elected Spartan magistrates
epigraphy study of texts inscribed on buildings, stone *stēlae* or other surfaces (see pp. 15, 47, 273)
epiklēros heiress (Greek)
epistratēgos military governor in Ptolemaic Egypt with authority over a number of nomes (administrative districts)
epithalamium wedding song
epithet an adjective or descriptive phase; also used of the titles of gods and goddesses (e.g. Athena Polias)
eponymous lending his or her name to something (e.g. the eponymous *archōn* is the magistrate in Athens after whom the year is named) (see pp. 451, 486)
epulones seven Roman priests with responsibility for sacred banquets
eques (plural: ***equites***) cavalryman, member of the equestrian order (Latin)
erastēs male lover (Greek)
ergo lit. 'therefore' (Latin)
erōmenos male beloved (Greek)
erratum (plural: **errata**) lit. 'error/errors' (Latin); used to refer to corrections made to an article or book after publication
ethnos ethnic group, people (Greek) (see p. 450)
euergetēs benefactor (Greek), a title bestowed on an individual by a city, hence 'euergetism', aristocratic funding of e.g. public buildings, festivals, grain (see p. 458)
eusebeia reverence, conduct in conformity with the wishes of the gods
euthunai inquiry into a magistrate's conduct in democratic office
evocatio lit. 'calling forth' (Latin); ritual in which Rome invited the guardian deity of an enemy city to come to Rome
ex(h)edra (in architecture) an open-fronted recess, e.g. in a portico
exempli gratia lit. 'by way of example' (Latin); abbreviated to 'e.g.'
exodos final section of a Greek drama
ex post facto lit. 'from what is done afterward' (Latin); used especially of arguments

fabula palliata lit. 'comedy wearing a little Greek cloak' (Latin); form of Roman (comic) drama, (see p. 309)
fabula praetexta form of Roman drama (called '*praetexta*' in reference to the Roman dress of the characters) (see pp. 295–6)
fasces bundle of rods bound together; symbol of authority of Roman magistrates
fetiales (sing.: ***fetialis)*** (Roman) college of priests, with responsibility e.g. for declarations of war
fibula brooch used for fastening clothing (Latin)
flamen (plural: ***flamines)*** priests of certain deities; e.g. Jupiter (the *flamen dialis*), Mars (*Martialis*), Quirinus (*Quirinalis*)
florilegium (plural: **florilegia**) collection of literary 'flowers'; anthology (see p. 259)
floruit-date date at which an individual is deemed to have 'flourished'; used to establish notional year of birth (see p. 486)
focaliser person through whom a narrative is 'seen' (either a narrator or a character); hence 'focalisation', the construction of a narrative through a character or narrator's point of view
folio one leaf (i.e. two pages) of a codex (see p. 253)
forum open square or market-place at heart of Roman towns (and of Rome itself)
fratres arvales (Roman) college of priests, with responsibility e.g. for the festival of the goddess Dea Dia and agriculture
frieze (in architecture) wide central section of entablature, often sculpted in relief (see pp. 160, 185, 188)
frigidarium cold room in Roman baths (see pp. 169–70)

genius deified abstraction of an individual man's characteristics, or of a place (Latin)
genos (plural: ***genē***) Greek cult group who claimed descent from a common ancestor
gens (plural: ***gentes***) Roman 'clan'; a group of families that claimed descent from a common ancestor

gentilicius name held by all members of a given Roman *gens*
Geometric term given to the period from c. 900 to 770 BC (from the geometric patterns of pottery)
gerousia Spartan council of elders
glosses synonyms or explanations of words added by scribes or scholiasts
graffiti writing scratched onto fired pottery or *ostraka* (see pp. 264, 267)
graphē (plural: ***graphai***) public law suit in Athens (which, by contrast to a *dikē* or private law suit, anyone was able to bring)
graphē paranomōn charge brought against someone (in democratic Athens) for introducing an illegal proposal
Great Dionysia Athenian dramatic festival
gymnasium public building for athletic (and more broadly ethical and intellectual) training

harmost Spartan governor of foreign cities
haruspex (plural: ***haruspices***) Etruscan diviner(s) consulted in Rome
heliaea Athenians sitting as a court of appeal
Helladic term given to the Greek Bronze Age
Hellenistic term used of the period from the death of Alexander (323 BC) to the death of Cleopatra (31 BC) (see pp. 98–101)
Hellenotamiae treasurers of the Delian League
Hellespont passage of sea between the Greek mainland and Asia Minor, the boundary between Asia and Europe
helots subject people of the Spartans
hendiadys expression of a single idea through two nouns connected by a conjunction (e.g. 'he did not come because of the rain and weather' rather than 'because of the rainy weather')
herm stone pillar (topped with a figure of Hermes with exaggerated features) that marked the boundary of a Greek *oikos*
hero figure to whom (semi-divine) honours were paid after death (Greek); heroes could be historical or figures from myth (especially the Trojan War period)
hērōon shrine to a hero (Greek)
hetaira (Greek) courtesan
hetaireia association of citizens (Greek) formed with a view to political collaboration
hetairos companion; used e.g. of Macedonian noblemen serving in the army
himation traditional garment of Greek men, and of Greek women from fifth century BC; made from large rectangular piece of cloth (equivalent to Roman *palla* or *pallium*) (see pp. 227–8)
holocaust sacrifice in which the entire offering is burnt
homoios (plural: ***homoioi***) lit. 'equal' (Greek); one of the Spartan citizens or Spartiates
homoioteleuton common error in the transmission of texts in which two words, phrases or lines end with the same sequence of letters and the scribe accidentally skips to the second, and so omits the intervening words
homonoia lit. 'oneness of mind' (Greek); political ideal of unity, especially in the Hellenistic period
honorand recipient of honours (e.g. as recorded in honorific decrees)
hoplite heavily armed soldier (Greek) (see pp. 232–6)
horos boundary stone marking debt on land
humanitas liberal education and culture (Latin)
hybris arrogance often leading to violence (Greek)
hydria large, three-handled jar used for water (Greek)
hypocoristic pet name (see pp. 465–6)
hypomeiones inferiors; a marginal group of non-citizens within Sparta
hypothesis summary of the plot of a play (found together with the texts in manuscripts)
hysteron proteron lit. 'later-earlier' (Greek); inversion of the actual sequence of events (in narrative)

iambic metrical form (associated, at least in the archaic Greek period, with invective)
Ides ninth day after the Nones of each month in the Roman calendar, counting inclusively (see p. 487)
imago image, representation (Latin); plural: ***imagines*** ancestor portraits
imperator title of Roman commander, later used as title for emperors
imperium power of command of legitimate Roman rulers (see pp. 108, 456–7)
impluvium pool in the centre of an atrium of a Roman house where rainwater collected
in medias res lit. 'into the middle of things' (Latin); used of a narrative that begins in the middle of the story

in situ lit. 'in the original place' (Latin)
in toto lit. 'entirely' (Latin)
in vacuo lit. 'in a vacuum' (Latin); in the absence of any other factors or circumstances
instrumentum domesticum everyday portable object bearing inscriptions, scratched, painted or stamped onto its surface
intaglio design carved into a surface (e.g. stone, metal, gem) (see 217–20)
interpolation insertion of a word or passage into an ancient text (see p. 435)
Ionic order order or style of architecture distinguished especially by capital with two scrolls (see pp. 161, 162)
ipso facto lit. 'by that very fact' (Latin)
Iron Age traditional term for post-Bronze Age period (see pp. 72–7, 87, 89)
isēgoria equal right to speak (Greek), e.g. before the Athenian Assembly
isonomia equality before the law (Greek) See p. 448)
isopoliteia **lit.** 'equal citizenship' (Greek); i.e. an arrangement whereby the citizens of two (or more) cities could enjoy the rights of citizenship of the other(s) (see p. 460)
ithyphallic lit. 'with erect phallus' (Greek)
itinerarium (plural: *itineraria*) (Greek) itinerary (see p. 392)
iugerum Roman square measure (equivalent to c. 2,500 square metres) (see p. 472)

janiform two heads joined back to back (named after Roman god Janus)

kakos (plural: *kakoi*) lit. 'base, bad' (Greek); used of people of low social status
Kalends (or *kalendae*) first day of the Roman month (see p. 487)
kalpis jar for water (Greek)
kandys sleeved coat used in fifth-century Athens (copied from Persia)
kantharos drinking cup with two high handles (Greek)
klērotērion allotment machine used in democratic Athens
koinē common Greek language which superseded the various dialects (Attic, Doric etc.) in the Hellenistic period (see pp. 33, 337)
koinon alliance (Greek)
kōmē village, country town
kommos mournful exchange between actor(s) and chorus in Greek drama
Kopienkritik method for identifying features of an original Greek sculpture by comparing a number of later (Roman) copies (see p. 52)
korē (plural: *korai*) girl; hence archaic Greek statue of a young woman (see p. 186)
kottabos game played at symposium involving flicking of wine at a target (Greek)
kotylē (plural: *kotylai*) Greek liquid measure (equivalent to c. 0.25 litre) (see p. 472)
kouros (plural: *kouroi*) young man; hence archaic Greek statue of a young man (see pp. 186, 190–2)
kratēr large vessel for diluting wine (Greek)
krypteia Spartan institution whereby young Spartiates performed secret duties
kylix wide, shallow drinking cup with two handles (Greek)

lacuna gap (i.e. missing words) in a text (e.g. a MS or inscription), sometimes filled by conjecture on the basis of parallels
Lares (Roman) household gods
Late Helladic the period between c. 1600 and c. 1100 BC
latifundium (plural: *latifundia*) large (Roman) estate or farm (see p. 155)
laudatio eulogy, panegyric (Roman)
legatus (or **legate**) Roman ambassador
legend inscription on a coin (see pp. 176–8)
legion largest unit of Roman army (comprising between 4,200 and 6,000 infantry and a small cavalry force)
lēkythos flask for oils (Greek)
lemma keyword(s) in commentary or dictionary
Lenaia Athenian dramatic festival
lex (plural: *leges*) (Roman) law
lexicology study of the word-stock of a language (see p. 31)
libertus a freed slave (Latin)
libra (Roman) weight, equivalent to c. 11 oz or 327 g (see p. 473)
lictors attendants to Roman magistrates who carried the fasces
limen threshold of Roman building
Linear A Minoan script (see p. 477)
Linear B Mycenaean script (see pp. 477–8)

litotes understatement, for intensification, by denying the contrary of the thing being affirmed (e.g. 'not the worst cricketer in the world')
liturgy Athenian institution whereby wealthy individuals undertook e.g. the sponsorship of choruses or of triremes as a form of taxation and self-advertisement
logographos (plural: ***logographoi***) professional speechwriter employed in Athenian law-courts
lorica segmentata Roman segmental plate armour (see p. 236)
ludi (Roman) public festivals (often including dramatic performances (e.g. *ludi saeculares, ludi Romani, ludi scaenici* (dramatic festivals)
Lupercalia annual (Roman) festival
lustratio performance of a ritual of purification (Roman)
lustrum five-yearly *lustratio* carried out by the (Roman) censor on completion of the census

maenad female follower of Dionysus
magi (sing.: ***magus***) Persian priestly caste, magicians
Magna Graecia lit. 'Great Greece' (Latin); southern Italy and Sicily, inhabited by Greeks
Manes benevolent spirits (Roman)
maniple a unit of a Roman legion, c. 160 men (a cohort consisted of three maniples)
manumission procedure for freeing a slave
mechanē/machina (Greek, Latin) crane used in drama e.g. for the appearance of divinities (hence the expression 'deus ex machina', 'the god from the machine')
medimnos Attic corn measure of c. 54.5 litres (see p. 472)
merismos allocation of public revenue in classical Athens
metic citizen of another (Greek) city resident in Athens; hence *metoikion*, metic tax
metonymy substitution of one word for another which it suggests; part for the whole (e.g. 'Downing Street' for 'the British government')
metopes panels, either plain or sculpted, which alternate with triglyphs on friezes of (Doric) Greek temples (see p. 160)
metrētēs Greek liquid measure of c. 30.4 litres (see p. 472)
mētropolis (plural: ***mētropoleis***) lit. 'mother-city' (Greek); city from which a colony originates
mimesis lit. 'imitation' (Greek); crucial term in Greek aesthetics (see p. 352)
Minoan Aegean civilisation c. 3500–1100 BC, named after Minos, mythical king of Knossos
missorium large dish (Latin)
mna (or ***mina***, plural: ***mnae***) Greek monetary unit (and unit of weight), equivalent to 100 *drachmae* (see p. 473)
modius Roman corn measure of c. 8.62 litres (see p. 472)
modus operandi lit. 'manner (or method) of working' (Latin)
monody lyric verse sung by single actor in Greek drama (see p. 313)
morphology study of the forms of words in a language (see p. 31)
mortaria (sing.: ***mortarium***) heavy-duty spouted Roman bowls used for mixing and grinding (see p. 212)
mos maiorum (plural: ***mores maiorum***) lit. 'way of our forebears' (Latin); traditional Roman virtues
motif repeated theme
municipium town given Roman citizenship
munus (plural: ***munera***) gift, benefaction (Latin), either by an individual to a city (equivalent to Greek idea of euergetism) or to the dead
murmillones heavily armed gladiators
Musaeum sanctuary of the Muses, hence centre of cultural activity
mutatis mutandis **lit.** 'with necessary changes having been made' (Latin); used in argument to mean 'taking into account different conditions and circumstances'

naos (Greek) temple
narratology theory of narrative, that seeks to identify features common to all narratives (e.g. focalisation, prolepsis etc.) (see p. 38)
naumachia staged naval battle
necropolis lit. 'city of the dead' (Greek); cemetery
neoteric group of Roman poets (including Catullus) influenced by traditions of Hellenistic Greek poetry (see pp. 324–5)
ne plus ultra lit. 'the highest point' (Latin); e.g. 'the ne plus ultra of wickedness'
New Criticism school of literary criticism

emphasising close textual criticism and eschewing historical or biographical approaches (see p. 36)
Nikē winged female personification of victory (Greek)
nome administrative district in Graeco-Roman Egypt
nomen (or ***nomen gentilicium***) Roman name indicating its bearer's membership of a particular *gens* (see pp. 466–7, 468–9)
nomos (plural: ***nomoi***) law, custom, convention (Greek)
nomothetēs Greek lawgiver
non sequitur lit. 'it does not follow' (Latin); used in argument of a statement that does not follow rationally from the previous one
Nonae (or **Nones**) fifth or seventh day before the Ides of each (Roman) month, counting inclusively (see p. 487)
nothos (plural: ***nothoi***) illegitimate (Greek); the *nothoi* were a marginal group in Sparta
numen (plural: ***numina***) divine power (Roman)
numismatics study of coins (see pp. 15, 173–5)
nundina Roman market day (see p. 488)
nymphaeum shrine of the nymphs, fountain-house

obol Greek monetary unit, equivalent to one-sixth of a drachma (see p. 473)
odeum/odeion (Latin, Greek) concert hall, roofed theatre
oikos (Greek) household
oikoumenē inhabited world (Greek) (see p. 392)
oinochoē wine jug (Greek)
oligarchy rule by the few (see pp. 451–3)
olpē round-lipped jug (Greek)
Olympiad period between successive Olympic games; a common basis for dating (see pp. 485–6)
onomatopoeia use of words to imitate natural sounds; approximation of sound to sense
opisthodomos the porch at the rear of a temple *cella*
oppidum (fortified) town (Latin); used of Iron Age settlements (see pp. 76–7)
optimates conservative Roman political tendency; opposed to *populares* (see p. 461)
opus africanum architectural structure with upright pillars framing sections of smaller stones or rubble
opus latericum wall-facing of bricks
opus quadratum wall made of dressed stone
opus reticulatum wall-facing of small tufa blocks placed in a net pattern
opus sectile wall or floor-facing made from pieces of coloured stone
opus signinum mortar including crushed pottery or brick
opus spicatum paving of bricks to form herring-bone pattern
opus tesselatum tessellation
opus vermiculatum technique of mosaic which involves using minute pieces to create pictures
orchēstra lit. 'dancing floor' (Greek); area in front of the *skēnē* in Greek drama where the chorus danced (see pp. 167, 192)
Orientalising revealing Eastern influence; used of the art of the Greek world (and hence the period) of c. 725–630 BC
orthogonal planning (e.g. of masonry or streets) based on right angles
ostracism Athenian institution by which a prominent individual is voted into exile for a period of ten years
ostraka small potsherds used in antiquity for writing (especially for receipts in Egypt and for ostracism in democratic Athens) (see pp. 238–9)
otium (Latin) (lifestyle of) leisure

palaeobotany biological study of plant remains in archaeological record
palaeography study of the text of manuscripts, e.g. writing hands (in contrast to codicology) (see pp. 253–4)
palaistra/palaestra (Greek, Latin) wrestling school
palimpsest manuscript in which one text has been partially erased and a subsequent text written over it (see pp. 256–7)
palla item of clothing worn mainly by Roman women (equivalent to Greek *himation*) (see pp. 227–8)
Palladion sacred image of goddess Athena
pallium item of clothing, worn mainly by Roman men (equivalent to Greek *himation*) (see pp. 227–8)
panegyric address (in prose or verse) praising an individual (see pp. 256, 284, 347)
panhellenic literally 'of all the Greeks' (Greek); used e.g. of festivals open to all Greeks

panhellenism ideology seeking to unite Greeks (often in opposition to the barbarian)
papyrology study of texts written on papyrus (see pp. 238–49)
parabasis formal section in Old Comedy in which the *choryphaeus* and chorus address the audience directly (see pp. 301–2)
paradeisos Persian park
paradigm ideal example of something
paramonē legal agreement whereby the manumission of a slave was subject to conditions of continued service to the ex-master
paraprosdokian unexpected ending of a phrase or series
paronomasia etymological word-play; use of similar-sounding words with different meanings
patera saucer-shaped dish used for libations (Roman); architectural decoration of same pattern
paterfamilias head of a Roman household and family
patria potestas authority of a *paterfamilias* over his household (Latin)
patricians aristocratic class of Roman citizens
pax deorum good relations between gods and men (Latin)
pediment the triangular area under the roof at either end of a Greek temple
pelikē pear-shaped amphora
peltast lightly armed Greek soldier
peplos woollen mantle worn by Greek women (see p. 228), hence the *peplos* used to clothe the cult statue of Athena in Athens
per se lit. 'in itself' (Latin)
peraea mainland territory belonging to an island polis
periēgēsis (plural: ***periēgēseis***) lit. 'leading around' (Greek); itinerary (see p. 392)
periodos gēs lit. 'journey around the world' (Greek), hence account of a journey (see p. 392)
perioikos (plural: ***perioikoi***) lit. 'one who lives nearby' (Greek); name given to inhabitants neighbouring Sparta who were free but without Spartan citizen rights
periplus sea-voyage around (Greek) (see pp. 391–2)
peripteral of a building supported by exterior columns
peristyle of a building with surrounding columns
pes lit. 'foot' (Latin); Roman measure of distance, made up of twelve *unciae* or inches (see p. 472)
phalanx formation of heavily armed infantry (hoplites) with spears and overlapping shields
phialē (plural: ***phialai***) shallow Greek dish, used for libations (see pp. 214–16)
philoi (sing.: ***philos***) lit. 'friends' (Greek); name given to members of the entourage of the kings of the Hellenistic period
philology systematic study of language (see pp. 4–5, 30–3)
phoneme basic unit of sound in a language (see p. 31)
phonetics study of the sounds of language (see p. 30)
phonology study of the distribution of sounds in a language (see pp. 30–1)
phoros lit. 'burden, tribute' (Greek); name given to tribute owed to Athens by its fifth-century BC allies
phratry lit. 'brotherhood' (Greek); a social and religious organisation that claimed descent from a common ancestor
phylē (plural: ***phylai***) tribe; organisational unit within Greek polis
pietas lit. 'piety' (Latin); duty towards parents
pithos (plural: ***pithoi***) barrel-shaped Greek pot made for storage of e.g. grain (see p. 212)
plebs the mass of Roman citizens, hence 'plebeian' (in contrast to 'patrician')
pleonasm use of superfluous words (whether for rhetorical effect or unintentionally)
plethron Greek measure of area (100 feet by 100 feet), equivalent to the English term 'acre' (see pp. 471–2)
plinth a pedestal supporting a column
polis (plural: **poleis**) Greek city-state, i.e. the city or *asty* and its *chōra* or rural hinterland (see pp. 19–20, 93, 449–50)
politeia constitution of a Greek city (see p. 448)
pomerium sacred boundary of the city of Rome
pontifex (plural: ***pontifices***) member of the most important college of Roman priests; the post of *pontifex maximus* (i.e. high priest) was, from the time of Augustus onwards, held by the emperor
populares Roman political grouping who pur-

ported to act on behalf of the people; opposed to *optimates* (see p. 461)
pornē (Greek) prostitute
portico a roofed porch or walkway supported by columns
positivism an approach based on the presumption of absolute truths or knowledge (as opposed to relativism, in which knowledge is seen as dependent on an individual's point of view and understanding)
post hoc, ergo propter hoc lit. 'after, therefore because of' (Latin); used of a fallacy in argument
potestas authority of a (Roman) magistrate, inferior to *imperium* (see p. 108)
praefectus praetorio prefect (i.e. commander) of the praetorian guard (for the protection of the Roman emperor)
praefectus urbi lit. 'prefect of the city' (Latin); magistrate with responsibility for maintaining order in Rome
praenomen Roman first name (see pp. 466–9)
praeteritio figure of speech whereby emphasis is given to a point by pretending not to mention it (e.g. 'there is no need to mention . . .')
praetexta (Latin) decorated with a purple border; used on Roman toga to signifly high social status
praetor Roman magistrate (from 367 BC, junior to the consuls) with military and judicial responsibilities in the republican period; in the imperial period only with a judicial role
praetoriani the praetorian guard, responsible for protecting the emperor
prima facie lit. 'at first appearance' (Latin)
primus inter pares lit. 'first among equals' (Latin)
princeps title for the Roman emperor, connoting that he was first among equals
princeps iuventutis leader of the (Roman) aristocratic youth
princeps senatus leader of the (Roman) senate
principate the rule of the Roman emperors from Augustus to Carinus, in which the emperor is nominally no more than *princeps* (first citizen) – contrast with 'dominate'
probouleuma preliminary resolution, e.g. of the Athenian *boulē* or council, then passed to the Assembly for debate; hence the 'probouleutic function' of the *boulē* (see pp. 430, 452)
proconsul magistrate holding office in place of a consul outside Rome
procurator overseer of imperial properties and of collection of taxes in provinces
prolepsis (in narrative) flashforward to an event later in time
pronaos entrance hall to the *cella* of a temple
propylaea monumental entrance, e.g. to the Acropolis
proskynēsis gesture of respect reserved for the Persian King (misunderstood by Greeks as a sign of worship)
prosopography collection of all known information about individuals and their relationships in a particular historical context (see p. 461)
protagonist leading actor in Greek drama
prothesis laying out of a body in a Greek funeral
Protoattic seventh-century BC style of Athenian vase-painting
Protocorinthian late eighth-century BC style of Corinthian vase-painting
proxenos citizen of one (Greek) *polis* with responsibility for the well-being of the citizens of another *polis* resident in his own city (cf. modern consul)
psēphisma (plural: *psēphismata*) decree, resolution made by vote (Greek)
publicani individuals who bid for the rights to gather revenue on behalf of the (Roman) state

quadriga a four-horse chariot (Roman)
quaestor Roman magistrate with largely financial responsibilities (usually in the provinces)
Quellenforschung scholarship focusing on the hunt for sources (see pp. 36, 385)
quindecimviri (*sacris faciundis*) college of (Roman) priests with responsibility for Sybilline prophecies, Apollo and foreign cults
quire gathering of two to six pieces of parchment folded and stitched to form part of a codex or manuscript (see pp. 238, 253)
quorum minimum number of participants required to give binding force to the decisions of an assembly or other meeting

reader-response criticism school of literary criticism according to which a poem or other work is co-operatively produced by reader and text (see p. 35)

recto top (that is, right-hand) page of a leaf of parchment in a codex or manuscript (see p. 253)
recusatio lit. 'refusal' (Latin); literary trope whereby a writer professes to reject a genre or approach
red-figure Greek pottery technique in which the background is painted black and the figures take on the colour of the clay (see pp. 206–7)
regia home of the kings of Rome (and later the *pontifex maximus*)
relativism view that the truth of a proposition is relative, dependent on its context, rather than absolute
reliefs sculptures in which figures project from, but are attached to, a background (see pp. 184–5, 199–201)
repoussé technique for creating a relief design in metal by hammering or pressing the reverse side (see pp. 214–15)
res gestae lit. 'things done, achievements' (Latin)
res publica lit. 'public property, public affairs' (Latin); (Roman) commonwealth
retiarius lightly armed gladiator, with net and trident
rhapsode bard, reciter of verse (Greek)
rhētor (plural: *rhētores*) orator and politician (Greek)
rhētra (plural: *rhētrae*) oral laws of the city of Sparta; archaic Greek laws
rhyton drinking horn (Greek)
ring-composition form in which the end of a passage of narrative reiterates the beginning
rostra platform from which speakers addressed the people in the Roman Forum

Salii (or **Salians**) (Roman) priests of Mars and Quirinus
salutatio formal meeting between Roman client and patron (Latin)
sarcophagus lit. 'flesh-eating' (Greek); a stone coffin, often elaborately sculpted
sarisa (plural: *sarissai*) spear or pike used by Macedonian and Hellenistic armies
satrap provincial governor of the Persian Empire
Saturnalia annual midwinter religious festival (Roman)
satyr half-man, half-beast figure from Greek mythology
scholia marginal notes added to early manuscripts (the authors of which are called 'scholiasts') (see p. 257)
Sebasteion temple of imperial cult
Second Sophistic term given to the revival of Greek culture under the Roman Empire (and the period associated: late first century AD to mid-third century AD) (see pp. 382, 389, 450)
seisachtheia lit. 'shaking off of burdens' (Greek); name given to the Athenian reformer Solon's cancellation of debts
semiotics study of signs, and of how meaning is indicated and understood
senatus (Roman) Senate; in the republican period, responsible for all domestic and foreign policy; in the imperial period, membership was a prerequisite for senior office-holding
senatus consultum (plural: *senatus consulta*) decree of the (Roman) Senate (see pp. 433–4)
sestertius (plural: *sestertii*) (Roman) base metal coin, worth a quarter of a *denarius* (see p. 474)
simile scene or image, often drawn from the natural world, introduced by way of comparison ('just as . . ., so did . . .')
sine qua non lit. 'that without which not' (Latin); an essential condition for something
skēnē stage building of Greek drama (see p. 292)
skyphos drinking cup with small side-handles (Greek)
sodalis (plural: *sodales*) member of a *sodalitas*, a religious fraternity dedicated to the worship of a particular (Roman) cult
solidus (Roman) gold monetary unit (introduced by Diocletian) (see p. 474)
sōphrosynē virtue of self-discipline (Greek)
Spartiate a Spartan with full citizen rights
squeeze paper impression of an inscription (see pp. 270, 273–4)
stadion (or **stade**) Greek measure of distance equivalent to c. 177 metres or 600 feet (see p. 471)
stadium (plural: **stadia**) race-course
stamnos wine vessel with wide mouth and short neck (Greek)
stasimon (plural: *stasima*) lyric ode sung by chorus in Greek drama
stasis civil war, factional strife within a (Greek) *polis* (see p. 448)

stēlē (plural: *stēlae*) or **stēla** (plural: **stēlai**) upright piece of stone, used for inscriptions and/or for carved reliefs (see pp. 184, 263)
stemma family tree of the manuscript tradition of a text (see pp. 259–60)
stereobate base of a building (below the stylobate)
stichomythia rapid dialogue between two characters in Greek drama
stoa long colonnade (Greek)
stoichēdon style of inscription in which the letters form a neat grid, each letter occupying one virtual square, and each letter separated by the same (or a similar) space from each adjacent letter (see p. 266)
stratēgos (plural: *stratēgoi*) general (Greek)
stratiotic fund army fund of democratic Athens
structuralism approach to analysing narrative, discourse or culture on the basis of an assumed underlying and invariant structure
stucco plaster modelled into reliefs (see pp. 199–201)
stylobate masonry on which a column rests
suasoria (plural: *suasoriae*) Roman rhetorical form of invented speech in character (see p. 347)
successors term given to the kingdoms and rulers who succeeded Alexander and inherited the different areas of his rule, e.g. 'successor kings' (see pp. 98–9)
survey archaeology archaeological technique for assessing settlement patterns over a wide area through examination of the remains on/near the surface (see pp. 19, 82–3)
sycophant malicious prosecutor in Greek lawcourts
symmory group of men liable to pay taxation in Athens
sympoliteia union of two or more (Greek) poleis
symposium elite male drinking party (Greek), equivalent to Roman *convivium* (see pp. 318–19)
syncretism identification of gods from different religious systems with one another
synecdoche using the part of something in place of the whole (e.g. referring to a car as 'wheels')
syngeneia kinship (Greek)
synoecism unification of a number of towns or villages into a single (Greek) polis
syntax study of the organisation of words into complex units (see p. 31)
syntaxis financial contribution (implicitly more voluntary than *phoros*) (Greek)
syssition (plural: *syssitia*) dining group to which all Spartan citizens (Spartiates) belonged and to which they paid contributions

tablinum reception room of a (Roman) house
talent (Greek) monetary unit (and unit of weight) made up of 6,000 drachmae (see p. 473)
taurobolium sacrifice of a bull (Latin)
technē craft (Greek)
temenos shrine (Greek), i.e. including temple and surrounding land
terminus ante quem lit. 'point before which' (Latin); the latest possible time of an event (used in establishing a relative chronology on the basis of a few dated events)
terminus post quem lit. 'point after which' (Latin); the earliest possible time of an event (used in establishing a relative chronology on the basis of a few dated events)
terra sigillata lit. 'figured clay' (Latin); red-slipped Roman tableware (see pp. 16, 18–19)
tesserae cut pieces of coloured stone that make-up mosaic (see pp. 201–4)
testudo lit. 'tortoise' (Latin); military formation used by Roman army
theatron lit. 'place for seeing' (Greek); auditorium of Greek theatre (see p. 292)
theologeion position from which divinities speak in Greek drama
theophoric name name based on a divine name (e.g. Dionysius from Dionysus) (see p. 466)
theōria pilgrimage (Greek)
theriomorphic in animal shape
thermae (Roman) baths (see pp. 168–70)
thiasos (plural: *thiasoi*) a Greek religious association
tholos round, columned building used as tomb, temple or public building
thyrsos wand carried by devotees of god Dionysus (Greek)
tibia Roman reed-pipe, equivalent to the Greek *aulos* (see pp. 416, 418–19)
timē honour (Greek)
toga formal dress of Roman men, made

from large, semi-circular piece of cloth (see pp. 227–8)
togate dressed in a toga (used of figures in statues)
topos (plural: **topoi**) lit. 'place' Greek ; a commonplace or motif, e.g. in poetry
tribuni militum (or **military tribunes**) military officers, six to each legion
tribuni plebis (or **tribunes of the people**) magistrates who act on behalf of the plebs
tribunicia potestas lit. 'authority of the tribunes of the people' (Latin); from the time of Augustus, this authority was claimed by the emperor (see p. 108)
triclinium dining room of a (Roman) house
triglyphs rectangles decorated with vertical grooves (alternating with metopes) on friezes of Doric Greek temples (see p. 160)
tripod three-legged stand, to support seat or bowl (but used to refer to both stand and bowl)
trireme Greek warship with 3 banks of oars
tritagonist third actor in Greek drama
trittys (plural: ***trittyes***) regional unit of the city of Athens (a *trittys*, or 'third', comprised a variable number of demes; each of ten tribes consisted of three *trittyes*, one from each of three regions)
triumphator Roman general who had won a major victory and was given permission for a triumph (a religious procession celebrating victory)
triumvirate magistracy of 3 people
trophy enemy's arms set up to commemorate victory
tumulus burial mound
tunica tunic worn by Roman men and women (equivalent to Greek *chitōn*) (see p. 228)
typology classification according to type; in philology, the study of common features across a number of languages (see p. 32)
tyrant (or ***tyrannos***) autocratic ruler, used especially of archaic and classical rulers of Greek cities

uncia Roman measure, equivalent to one inch; twelve *unciae* make-up a *pes* (or foot); also measure of weight (see pp. 472–3)

velatium awning over amphitheatre
verbatim lit. 'word for word' (Latin)
verso bottom (that is, left-hand) page of a leaf of parchment in a codex or manuscript (see p. 253)
vestales (or **vestal virgins**) six priestesses of the Roman goddess Vesta, required to maintain strict sexual abstinence
vexillatio temporary military detachment (Roman)
vexillum Roman military standard
vicarius (or **vicar**) in charge of a diocese in Roman Empire
vici settlements that grew up outside the walls of (Roman) cities
villa rustica (Roman) farm

wanax Mycenaean Greek term for king, also used as divine title (see p. 87)
white-ground (of pottery) technique of vase-painting in which a pot, especially a *lēkythos*, is painted white and then decorated

xoanon wooden statue, usually of deity (Greek)

69. Resources

Brian A. Sparkes

The following pages list some of the varied methods of access to information about the classical world

Libraries

United Kingdom and Ireland

For libraries in the UK and Ireland, see L. Franklin and J. York, *Libraries and Information Services in the United Kingdom and the Republic of Ireland 2003* (29th edn), London: Facet Publishing, 2002. Access to most libraries that have comprehensive holdings of books on the classical world is through membership, either of a university or of a society.

There are six copyright libraries (i.e. libraries that stock a copy of all books published in the UK and Ireland):

The British Library, 96 Euston Road, London NW1 2DB, www.bl.uk
The Bodleian Library, Broad Street, Oxford OX1 3BG, www.bodley.ox.ac.uk
Cambridge University Library, West Road, Cambridge CB3 9DR, www.lib.cam.ac.uk
The National Library of Scotland, George IV Bridge, Edinburgh EH1 1EW, www.nls.uk
The National Library of Wales, Aberystwyth, Ceredigion SY23 3BU, www.llgc.org.uk
The National Library of Ireland, Kildare Street, Dublin 2, Republic of Ireland, www.nli.ie

Libraries in the UK that specialise in works on the classical world and for which a membership card is needed are:

The Sackler Library, Beaumont Street, Oxford OX1 2LG, www.saclib.ox.ac.uk
The Warburg Institute, Woburn Square, London WC1H 0AB, www.sas.ac.uk/warburg
The Joint Library of the Hellenic and Roman Societies (with the Library of the Institute of Classical Studies), Senate House, Malet Street, London WC1E 7HU, www.sas.ac.uk/icls
The Institute of Archaeology, 31–34 Gordon Square, London WC1H 0PY, www.ucl.ac.uk/archaeology

Most British higher education libraries belong to UK Libraries Plus, a co-operative venture that enables students to borrow from other libraries; see www.lisa.sbu.ac.uk/uklibrariesplus.

Worldwide

For a guide to libraries worldwide, see H. Lengenfelder, *World Guide to Libraries* (7th edn), Munich: Saur, 1986.

Museums

The following museums hold major collections of classical antiquities:

United Kingdom

The British Museum, Great Russell Street, London WC1B 3DG, www.thebritishmuseum.ac.uk
The Fitzwilliam Museum, Cambridge CB2 1RB, www.fitzwilliam.cam.ac.uk

The Museum of Classical Archaeology, Sidgwick Avenue, Cambridge CB3 9DA, www.classics.cam.ac.uk/art.html

The Ashmolean Museum, Beaumont Street, Oxford OX1 2PH, www.ashmol.ox.ac.uk

The Sir John Soane Museum, 13 Lincoln's Inn Fields, London WC2A 3BP, www.soane.org

The Shefton Museum of Greek Art and Archaeology, The University, Newcastle upon Tyne NE1 7RU, www.ncl.ac.uk/shefton-museum

The Ure Museum of Greek Archaeology, The University of Reading, Whiteknights, Reading RG6 6AA, www.reading.ac.uk/Ure

For museums displaying Romano-British material, see R. J. A. Wilson, *A Guide to the Roman Remains in Britain* (4th edn, compiled M. Symonds), London: Constable, 2002, pp. 665–72.

Worldwide

For a full list of museums worldwide, see M. Zils (ed.), *Museums of the World* (9th edn), 2 vols, Munich: Saur, 2002. For details of museums (and sites) in Greece, see www.culture,gr, and for Italy see www.beneculturali.it.

Classical societies

United Kingdom

The main societies in the United Kingdom for the study of the classical world are:

The Society for the Promotion of Hellenic Studies, Senate House, Malet Street, London WC1E 7HU (publication of the *Journal of Hellenic Studies* and *Archaeological Reports*), www.hellenicsociety.org

The Society for the Promotion of Roman Studies, Senate House, Malet Street, London WC1E 7HU (publication of the *Journal of Roman Studies* and *Britannia*), www.romansociety.org

The Classical Association, Senate House, Malet Street, London WC1E 7HU (publication of *Classical Quarterly*, *Classical Review*, *Greece and Rome*, and *CA News*), www.classicalassociation.org

Joint Association of Classical Teachers (JACT), Senate House, Malet Street, London WC1E 7HU (publication of the *Journal of Classics Teaching* and *Omnibus*), www.jact.org

Friends of Classics, Jeannie Cohen, 51 Achilles Road, London NW6 1DZ, and Peter Jones, 28 Akenside Terrace, Newcastle upon Tyne NE2 1TN (publication of *ad familiares*)

The Association for Latin Teaching (ARLT), Senate House, Malet Street, London WC1E 7HU, www.arlt.co.uk (also mentions resources for Greek teaching, language, literature, etc.)

Classical departments in British Universities

For these, see *Classicists in British Universities*, issued by the Classical Association and obtainable from The Classical Association, Senate House, Malet Street, London WC1E 7HU (office@classicalassociation.org). The latest version can be accessed online at www.classicalassociation.org/CLASSICI.

Reference volumes and general books

Publishers who maintain an interest in the classical world often issue books in series, e.g. Blackwell ('Blackwell Introductions to the Classical World', 'Interpreting Ancient History'), Cambridge University Press (besides the *Cambridge Ancient History*, there are series entitled 'Key Themes in Ancient History', 'Cambridge Companions to Literature' and 'Landmarks in World Literature'), Classical Association ('Greece and Rome: New Surveys in the Classics'), Edinburgh University Press ('Edinburgh Readings on the Ancient World'), Fontana ('Fontana History of the Ancient World'), Oxford University Press ('Oxford Readings'), Routledge ('The Routledge History of the Ancient World', 'Approaching the Ancient World' and 'Classical Foundations'). More and more books are now appearing on the web as eBooks, to be read online or downloaded.

A. Classical world

1. General and history

C. Andresen, K. Bartels and L. Huber *Lexikon der Alten Welt*, Zurich and Stuttgart: Artemis, 1965.

M. Avi Yonhah and J. Shatzman, *Illustrated Encyclopaedia of the Classical World*, Maidenhead: Sampson Low, 1976.

M. Beard and J. Henderson, *Classics: A Very Short Introduction*, Oxford: Oxford University Press, 1995.

H. Bengston, *Einführung in die alte Geschichte* (7th edn), Munich: Beck, 1975 (= *Introduction to Ancient History*, trans. of 6th edn by R. I. Frank and F. D. Gilliard, Berkeley, Los Angeles and London: University of California Press, 1970).

E. J. Bickerman, *Chronology of the Ancient World* (rev. edn), London: Thames and Hudson, 1980.

J. Boardman, J. Griffin and O. Murray (eds), *The Oxford History of the Classical World*, Oxford: Oxford University Press, 1986.

G. W. Bowersock, P. Brown and O. Grabar (eds), *Late Antiquity: A Guide to the Postclassical World*, Cambridge MA: Harvard University Press, 1999.

F. Braudel, *The Mediterranean in the Ancient World*, Harmondsworth: Penguin, 2002.

Cambridge Ancient History (2nd edn, 14 vols and 7 plate vols), Cambridge: Cambridge University Press, *1970–*.

H. Cancik, H. Schneider and M. Landfester (eds), *Der Neue Pauly: Enzyklopädie der Antike* (15 vols + index vol.), Stuttgart: Metzler, 1996–2003.

H. Cancik, H. Schneider and M. Landfester (eds), *Brill's New Pauly: Encyclopaedia of the Ancient World* (20 vols), Leiden, Boston and Cologne: Brill, 2002–.

M. Cary, *The Geographic Background of Greek and Roman History*, Oxford: Clarendon Press, 1949.

M. Crawford (ed.), *Sources for Ancient History*, Cambridge: Cambridge University Press, 1983.

C. Daremberg and E. Saglio (eds), *Dictionnaire des antiquités* (9 vols), Paris: Hachette, 1877–1919.

M. Grant, *A Guide to the Ancient World: A Dictionary of Classical Place Names*, New York: H. W. Wilson, 1986.

M. Grant and R. Kitzinger (eds), *Civilization of the Ancient Mediterranean: Greece and Rome* (3 vols), New York: Charles Scribner & Sons, 1988.

Handbuch der Altertumswissenschaft, Munich: Beck, 1897– – a massive series of handbooks grouped under topics such as history, archaeology, language, religion; some in English.

K. Hopwood, *Ancient Greece and Rome: A Bibliographical Guide*, Manchester and New York: Manchester University Press, 1995.

S. Hornblower and A. Spawforth (eds), *Oxford Companion to Classical Civilization*, Oxford: Oxford University Press, 1998.

S. Hornblower and A. Spawforth (eds), *Who's Who in the Classical World*, Oxford: Oxford University Press, 2000.

S. Hornblower and A. Spawforth (eds), *Oxford Classical Dictionary* (3rd edn rev.), Oxford: Oxford University Press, 2003.

F. Jacoby, *Die Fragmente der griechischen Historiker*, Leiden: Brill, 1923–58 – this collection is now in the process of being completed; a new version, with English translations of all texts, is also under way: *Brill's New Jacoby*, ed. I. Worthington. The original volumes are available on CD-ROM.

F. W. Jenkins, *Classical Studies: A Guide to the Reference Literature*, Englewood CO: Libraries Unlimited, 1996.

J. Marouzeau, J. Ernst et al., *L'Année philologique: bibliographie critique et analytique de l'antiquité gréco-latine*, Paris: Les Belles Letters, 1928– – see online version p. 557.

A. Pauly, G. Wissowa, W. Kroll et al. (eds), *Paulys Real-Encyclopädie der classischen Altertumswissenschaft*, Stuttgart: Metzler and Munich: Druckenmüller, 1894–1980 – for an index to the supplements and supplementary volumes, see H. Gärtner and A. Wünsch, *Register der Nachträge und Supplemente*, Munich: Druckenmüller, 1980, J. P. Murphy,

Index, Chicago: Ares, 1980, and T. Erler, *Gesamtregister*, Stuttgart: Metzler, 1997–.

P. Petit, *Guide de l'étudiant en histoire ancienne* (3rd edn), Paris: Presses Universitaires de France, 1969.

B. Radice, *Who's Who in the Ancient World* (rev. edn), Harmondsworth: Penguin, 1973.

J. E. Salisbury, *Encyclopedia of Women in the Ancient World*, Santa Barbara: ABC-Clio, 2001.

A. E. Samuel, *Greek and Roman Chronology: Calendars and Years in Classical Antiquity*, Munich: Beck, 1972.

W. Smith, *A Dictionary of Greek and Roman Biography and Mythology* (new edn with intro. by C. Stray), London: I. B. Tauris, 2005 – also available online at www.ancientlibrary.com/smithbio

W. Smith, *A Dictionary of Greek and Roman Geography* (new edn with intro. C. Stray), London: I. B. Tauris, 2005.

G. Speake (ed.), *Dictionary of Ancient History*, Oxford: Blackwell, 1994 (= *The Penguin Dictionary of Ancient History*, Harmondsworth: Penguin, 1995).

G. Whitaker, *A Bibliographical Guide to Classical Studies*, Hildesheim, Zurich and New York: Olms-Weidmann, 1977–.

K. Ziegler and W. Sontheimer (eds), *Der Kleine Pauly: Lexikon der Antike* (5 vols), Stuttgart: A. Druckenmüller, 1964–75.

2. Literature and scholarship

W. W. Briggs, Jr, and W. M. Calder III (eds), *Classical Scholarship: A Biographical Encyclopedia*, New York and London: Garland, 1990.

L. Casson, *Libraries in the Ancient World*, New Haven CT: Yale University Press, 2001.

M. Grant, *Greek and Latin Authors 800 BC–AD 1000*, New York: H. W. Wilson, 1980.

M. Howatson (ed.), *The Oxford Companion to Classical Literature* (2nd edn), Oxford: Oxford University Press, 1989.

T. J. Luce (ed.), *Ancient Writers: Greece and Rome* (2 vols), New York: Charles Scribner & Sons, 1982.

R. Pfeiffer, *History of Classical Scholarship: From the Beginnings to the End of the Hellenistic Age*, Oxford: Clarendon Press, 1968.

R. Pfeiffer, *History of Classical Scholarship: From 1300 to 1850*, Oxford: Clarendon Press, 1976.

L. D. Reynolds and N. G. Wilson, *Scribes and Scholars: A Guide to the Transmission of Greek and Latin Literature* (3rd edn), Oxford: Clarendon Press, 1991.

R. Rutherford, *Classical Literature: A Concise History*, Oxford: Blackwell, 2004.

A. Sharrock and R. Ash, *Fifty Key Classical Authors*, London and New York: Routledge, 2002.

O. Taplin (ed.), *Literature in the Greek and Roman Worlds: A New Perspective*, Oxford: Oxford University Press, 2000.

R. B. Todd (ed.), *The Dictionary of British Classicists, 1500–1960* (3 vols), Bristol: Thoemmes Continuum, 2004.

3. Mythology and religion

R. E. Bell, *Women of Classical Mythology: A Biographical Dictionary*, New York and Oxford: Oxford University Press, 1991.

M. Grant, *Myths of the Greeks and Romans*, London: Weidenfeld and Nicolson, 1962.

M. Grant and J. Hazel, *Who's Who in Classical Mythology* (rev. edn), London and New York: Routledge, 2001.

P. Grimal, *The Dictionary of Classical Mythology*, Oxford: Blackwell, 1986.

S. I. Johnston (ed.) *Religions of the Ancient World: A Guide*, Cambridge MA: Harvard University Press, 2004.

L. Kahil et al. (eds), *Lexicon Iconographicum Mythologiae Classicae* (8 double vols and 2 vols of indices), Zurich: Artemis, 1981–99.

J. March, *Cassell Dictionary of Classical Mythology*, London: Cassell, 1998.

M. P. O. Morford and R. J. Lenardon, *Classical Mythology* (7th edn), Oxford: Oxford University Press, 2002.

S. Price and E. Kearns, *The Oxford Dictionary of Classical Myth and Religion*, Oxford: Oxford University Press, 2003.

J. D. Reid, *The Oxford Guide to Classical*

Mythology in the Arts, 1300–1990s (2 vols), New York and Oxford: Oxford University Press, 1993.

W. H. Roscher (ed.), *Ausführliches Lexikon der griechischen und römischen Mythologie* (6 vols and 4 supplements), Leipzig: Teubner, 1884–1937.

Thesaurus Cultus et Rituum Antiquorum, Los Angeles: J. Paul Getty Museum, 2005–.

4. Philosophy

J. Annas, *Ancient Philosophy: A Very Short Introduction*, Oxford: Oxford University Press, 2000.

A. H. Armstrong, *An Introduction to Ancient Philosophy* (3rd edn), London: Methuen: 1957.

T. Irwin, *Classical Thought*, Oxford and New York: Oxford University Press, 1989.

5. Art and archaeology

R. B. Bandinelli et al., *Enciclopedia dell'Arte Antica: Classica e Orientale* (7 vols with supplements and atlases), Rome: Istituto Poligrafico dello Stato, 1958–97.

J. Boardman (ed.), *The Oxford History of Classical Art*, Oxford: Oxford University Press, 1993.

N. T. de Grummond (ed.), *An Encyclopedia of the History of Classical Archaeology*, London: Greenwood, 1996.

R. Stillwell (ed.), *The Princeton Encyclopedia of Classical Sites*, Princeton NJ: Princeton University Press, 1976 – now available in shortened form via Perseus; see p. 557.

R. Vollkommer (ed.), *Künstlerlexikon der Antike*, Munich: Saur, 2001–4.

B. Greece

1. General and history

L. Adkins and R. A. Adkins, *Handbook to Life in Ancient Greece*, New York: Facts on File, 1997.

J. Boardman, J. Griffin and O. Murray (eds), *The Oxford Illustrated History of Greece and the Hellenistic World*, Oxford: Oxford University Press, 1986.

J. Boardman, J. Griffin and O. Murray (eds), *The Oxford History of the Classical World: Greece and the Hellenistic World*, Oxford: Oxford University Press, 1988.

D. Bowder (ed.), *Who Was Who in the Greek World, 776 BC–30 BC*, Ithaca NY: Cornell University Press, 1982.

R. Browning (ed.), *The Greek World: Classical, Byzantine and Modern*, London: Thames and Hudson, 1985.

P. Cartledge (ed.), *The Cambridge Illustrated History of Ancient Greece*, Cambridge: Cambridge University Press, 1998.

J. K. Davies, *Athenian Propertied Families*, Oxford: Clarendon Press, 1971.

P. Devambez, R. Flacelière, P. -M. Schuhl and R. Martin, *A Dictionary of Greek Civilization*, London: Methuen, 1967.

J. Hazel, *Who's Who in the Greek World*, London and New York: Routledge, 2000.

A. P. Kazhdan (ed. in chief), *Oxford Dictionary of Byzantium* (3 vols), New York: Oxford University Press, 1991.

C. Mango (ed.), *The Oxford History of Byzantium*, Oxford: Oxford University Press, 2002.

D. Sacks, *Encyclopedia of the Ancient Greek World*, New York: Facts on File, 1995.

D. Sacks and O. Murray, *Dictionary of the Ancient Greek World*, Oxford: Oxford University Press, 1997.

G. Speake (ed.), *Encyclopedia of Greece and the Hellenic Tradition* (2 vols), London and Chicago: Fitzroy Dearborn, 2000.

2. Literature and scholarship

P. E. Easterling and B. M. W. Knox, *The Cambridge History of Classical Literature. Vol.1: Greek Literature*, Cambridge: Cambridge University Press, 1985.

T. Whitmarsh, *Ancient Greek Literature*, Cambridge: Polity, 2004.

3. Mythology and religion

R. E. Bell, *Place-Names in Classical Mythology: Greece*, Santa Barbara: ABC-Clio, 1989.

L. Bruit Zaidman and P. Schmitt Pantel, *Religion in the Ancient Greek City* (trans. P. Cartledge), Cambridge: Cambridge University Press, 1992.

W. Burkert, *Greek Religion* (trans. J. Raffan), Oxford: Blackwell, 1985.

R. Buxton, *The Complete World of Greek Mythology*, London: Thames and Hudson, 2004.

P. E. Easterling and J. V. Muir, *Greek Religion and Society*, Cambridge: Cambridge University Press, 1985.

T. Gantz, *Early Greek Myth: A Guide to Literary and Artistic Sources*, Baltimore and London: Johns Hopkins University Press, 1993.

F. Graf, *Greek Mythology: An Introduction* (trans. T. Marier), Baltimore: Johns Hopkins University Press, 1993.

R. Hard, *The Routledge Handbook of Greek Mythology*, London and New York: Routledge, 2003.

H. W. Parke, *Festivals of the Athenians*, London: Thames and Hudson, 1977.

L. Preller, *Griechische Mythologie* (5th edn, rev. C. Robert), Berlin and Zurich: Weidmann, 1964–7.

4. PHILOSOPHY AND SCIENCE

J. Barnes, *The Presocratic Philosophers*, London and Boston: Routledge and Kegan Paul, 1979.

H. Diels and W. Kranz (eds), *Die Fragmente der Vorsokratiker* (6th edn, 3 vols), Berlin: Weidmann, 1951–2. (5th edn trans. K. Freeman, *Ancilla to Pre-Socratic Philosophers: A Complete Translation of the Fragments in Diels*, Fragmente der Vorsokratiker, Cambridge MA: Harvard University Press, 1983).

E. R. Dodds, *The Greeks and the Irrational*, Berkeley and Los Angeles: University of California Press, 1951.

W. K. C. Guthrie, *A History of Greek Philosophy* (6 vols), Cambridge: Cambridge University Press, 1962–81.

G. S. Kirk, J. E. Raven and M. Schofield, *The Presocratic Philosophers* (2nd edn), Cambridge: Cambridge University Press, 1983.

G. E. R. Lloyd, *Early Greek Science*, London: Chatto and Windus, 1970.

G. E. R. Lloyd, *Greek Science after Aristotle*, London: Chatto and Windus, 1973.

A. A. Long, *Hellenistic Philosophy* (2nd edn), London: Duckworth, 1986.

A. A. Long and D. N. Sedley, *The Hellenistic Philosophers* (2 vols), Cambridge: Cambridge University Press, 1987.

T. E. Rihll, *Greek Science* (*Greece and Rome* New surveys in the Classics 29), Oxford: Oxford University Press, 1999.

5. ART AND ARCHAEOLOGY

M. Beard and J. Henderson, *Classical Art: From Greece to Rome*, Oxford: Oxford University Press, 2001.

D. Leekley and R. Noyes, *Archaeological Excavations in the Greek Islands*, Park Ridge NJ: Noyes Press, 1975.

D. Leekley and R. Noyes, *Archaeological Excavations in Southern Greece*, Park Ridge NJ: Noyes Press, 1976.

D. Leekley and R. Noyes, *Archaeological Excavations in Central and Northern Greece*, Park Ridge NJ: Noyes Press, 1980.

F. Matz and H. G. Buchholz (eds), *Archaeologica Homerica*, Gottingen: Vandenhoek and Ruprecht, 1967–.

R. Osborne, *Archaic and Classical Greek Art*, Oxford: Oxford University Press, 1998.

M. Robertson, *A History of Greek Art*, Cambridge: Cambridge University Press, 1975.

M. Robertson, *A Shorter History of Greek Art*, Cambridge: Cambridge University Press, 1981.

J. Travlos, *Pictorial Dictionary of Ancient Athens*, London: Thames and Hudson, 1971.

J. Travlos, *Bildlexikon zur Topographie des antiken Attika*, Tübingen: Wasmuth, 1988.

C. Rome

1. GENERAL AND HISTORY

L. Adkins and R. A. Adkins, *Handbook to Life in Ancient Rome*, New York: Facts on File, 1994.

J. Boardman, J. Griffin and O. Murray (eds), *The Oxford Illustrated History of the Roman World*, Oxford: Oxford University Press, 1986.

J. Boardman, J. Griffin and O. Murray (eds), *The Oxford History of the Classical World: The Roman World* (2nd edn), Oxford: Oxford University Press, 2001.

D. Bowder (ed.), *Who Was Who in the Roman World, 753 BC–AD 476*, Ithaca NY: Cornell University Press, 1980.

M. Bunson, *Encyclopedia of the Roman Empire* (rev. edn), New York: Facts on File, 2002.

M. Grant, *The Roman Emperors: A Biographical Guide to the Rulers of Imperial Rome, 31 BC–AD 476*, New York: Scribner's, 1985.

J. Hazel, *Who's Who in the Roman World*, London and New York: Routledge, 2001.

P. Matyszak, *Chronicle of the Roman Republic: The Rulers of Ancient Rome, from Romulus to Augustus*, London: Thames and Hudson, 2003.

C. Scarre, *Chronicle of the Roman Emperors*, London: Thames and Hudson, 1995.

H. Temporini and W. Haase (eds), *Aufstieg und Niedergang der römischen Welt*, Berlin and New York: de Gruyter, 1972– – articles in German, English, French or Italian, e.g. on political history, law, religion, language and literature, philosophy and sciences.

G. Woolf (ed.), *The Cambridge Illustrated History of the Roman World*, Cambridge: Cambridge University Press, 2004.

2. Literature and scholarship

E. Kenney and W. V. Clausen, *The Cambridge History of Classical Literature: Latin Literature*, Cambridge: Cambridge University Press, 1982.

S. Harrison (ed.), *A Companion to Latin Literature*, Oxford, Blackwell, 2004.

3. Mythology and religion

L. Adkins and R. A. Adkins, *Dictionary of Roman Religion*, New York: Facts on File, 1996.

M. Beard, J. North and S. Price, *Religions of Rome* (2 vols), Cambridge: Cambridge University Press, 1998.

J. N. Bremmer and N. M. Horsfall, *Roman Myth and Mythography* (*BICS Supplement* 52), London: Institute of Classical Studies, 1987.

J. Ferguson, *The Religions of the Roman Empire*, London: Thames and Hudson, 1970.

M. Grant, *Roman Myths*, London: Weidenfeld and Nicolson, 1971.

R. MacMullen, *Paganism in the Roman Empire*, New Haven CT: Yale University Press, 1981.

J. Scheid, *An Introduction to Roman Religion* (trans. J. Lloyd), Edinburgh: Edinburgh University Press, 2003.

H. H. Scullard, *Festivals and Ceremonies of the Roman Republic*, London: Thames and Hudson, 1981.

R. Turcan, *The Cults of the Roman Empire* (trans. A. Nevill), Oxford: Blackwell, 1996.

R. Turcan, *The Gods of Ancient Rome* (trans. A. Nevill), Edinburgh: Edinburgh University Press, 2000.

T. P. Wiseman, *The Myths of Rome*, Exeter: University of Exeter Press, 2004.

4. Philosophy and science

M. L. Clarke, *The Roman Mind*, London: Cohen and West, 1956.

5. Art and archaeology

Corpus Signorum Imperii Romani, Great Britain 1–8, Oxford: Oxford University Press for the British Academy, 1977– – the British section of a multi-national corpus of Roman sculpture.

J. Elsner, *Imperial Rome and Christian Triumph: The Art of the Roman Empire AD 100–450*, Oxford: Oxford University Press, 1998.

M. Henig (ed.), *A Handbook of Roman Art: A Survey of the Visual arts of the Roman World*, Oxford: Phaidon, 1983.

E. Nash, *Pictorial Dictionary of Ancient Rome* (rev. edn), London: Thames and Hudson, 1968.

L. Richardson, Jr, *A New Topographical Dictionary of Ancient Rome*, Baltimore and

London: Johns Hopkins University Press, 1992.
E. M. Steinby (ed.), *Lexicon Topographicum Urbis Romae* (6 vols), Rome: Edizioni Quasar, 1993–2001.
S. Walker, *Roman Art*, London: British Museum Press, 1991.
P. Zanker, *The Power of Images in the Age of Augustus* (trans. A. Shapiro), Ann Arbor: University of Michigan Press, 1988.

Writing, language and dictionaries

A. Classical world

R. S. Bagnall, *Reading Papyri, Writing Ancient History*, London and New York: Routledge, 1995.
F. Bérard, D. Feissel, P. Petitmengin, D. Rousset and M. Séve, *Guide de l'épigraphiste: bibliographie choisie des épigraphies antiques et médiévales* (3rd edn, with supplement), Paris: Éditions rue d'Ulm/Presses de l'École normale supérieure, 2000.
W. V. Harris, *Ancient Literacy*, Cambridge MA: Harvard University Press, 1989.
N. Lewis, *Papyrus in Classical Antiquity*, Oxford: Clarendon Press, 1974.

B. Greek

W. S. Allen, *Vox Graeca: A Guide to the Pronunciation of Classical Greek* (3rd edn), Cambridge: Cambridge University Press, 1987.
P. Chantraine, *Dictionnaire étymologique de la langue grecque: histoire des mots*, Paris: Klincksieck, 1968–80.
P. Easterling and C. Handley, *Greek Scripts: An Illustrated Introduction*, London: Society for the Promotion of Hellenic Studies, 2001.
P. M. Fraser and E. Matthews (gen. eds), *A Greek Lexicon of Personal Names.* (1) P. M. Fraser and E. Matthews (eds), *The Aegean Islands, Cyprus, Cyrenaica.* (2) M. J. Osborne and S. G. Byrne (eds), *Attica.* (3A) P. M. Fraser and E. Matthews (eds), *Peloponnese, Western Greece, Sicily and Magna Graecia.* (3B) P. M. Fraser and E. Matthews (eds), *Central Greece,* Oxford: Clarendon Press, 1987–2000.
G. Horrocks, *Greek: A History of the Language and its Speakers*, London and New York: Longman, 1997.
Inscriptiones Graecae, Berlin and New York: de Gruyter, 1873-; 2nd edn 1913-; 3rd edn 1981-.
G. W. H. Lampe, *A Patristic Greek Lexicon*, Oxford: Clarendon Press, 1961.
H. G Liddell and R. Scott, *An Intermediate Greek-English Lexicon*, Oxford: Oxford University Press, 1899 – a new edition is in preparation.
H. G. Liddell, R. Scott and H. S. Jones, *Greek-English Lexicon* (10th edn), Oxford: Clarendon Press, 1996, including a *Revised Supplement,* eds E. A. Barber et al.
R. Meiggs and D. Lewis, *A Selection of Greek Historical Inscriptions to the End of the Fifth Century* (rev. edn), Oxford: Clarendon Press, 1988.
L. R. Palmer, *The Greek Language*, London: Faber and Faber, 1980.
W. Pape and G. Benseler, *Wörterbuch der griechischen Eigennamen* (3rd edn, 2 vols), Brunswick: Vieweg and Son, 1911 (unrev. repr. Graz: Akademische Druck und Verlaganstalt, 1959).
P. J. Rhodes and R. Osborne, *Greek Historical Inscriptions 404–323 BC*, Oxford: Oxford University Press, 2003.
B. Snell et al. (eds), *Lexikon des frühgriechische Epos*, Gottingen: Vandenhoek and Ruprecht, 1979–.
H. Solin, *Die griechischen Personnamen in Rom: Ein Namenbuch*, 3 vols, Berlin and New York: de Gruyter, 1982.
Thesaurus Linguae Graecae, Graz: Akademische Druck u. Verlaganstalt, 1829; 1954 – see CD-ROM, p. 558)
R. Thomas, *Literacy and Orality in Ancient Greece*, Cambridge: Cambridge University Press, 1992.
E. G. Turner, *Greek Papyri* (2nd edn), Oxford: Clarendon Press, 1980.
A. G. Woodhead, *The Study of Greek Inscriptions* (2nd edn), Cambridge:

Cambridge University Press, 1981; repr. with new Preface, Bristol: Bristol Classical Press, 1992.

C. Latin

W. S. Allen, *Vox Latina: A Guide to the Pronunciation of Classical Latin* (2nd edn), Cambridge: Cambridge University Press, 1989.

Corpus Inscriptionum Latinarum, Berlin and New York: de Gruyter, 1893–.

A. Ernout and A. Meillet, *Dictionnaire étymologique de la langue latine: histoire des mots* (4th edn), Paris: Klincksieck, 1959.

P. G. W. Glare et al., *Oxford Latin Dictionary*, Oxford: Clarendon Press, 1968–82.

T. Janson, *A Natural History of Latin* (trans. and adapted N. Vincent and M. Sorenson), Oxford: Oxford University Press, 2004.

C. T. Lewis and C. Short, *A Latin Dictionary*, Oxford: Oxford University Press, 1879.

L. R. Palmer, *The Latin Language*, London: Faber and Faber, 1954.

Prosopographia Imperii Romani, Berlin and New York: de Gruyter, 1933–.

Thesaurus Linguae Latinae, Munich and Leipzig: Saur, 1900– – see CD-ROM, p. 558.

Sourcebooks in translation

A. Classical world

The London Association of Classical Teachers publishes a series of sourcebooks ('LACTOR' = 'London Association of Classical Teachers – Original Records'); some are included below.

W. Cotter, *Miracles in Greco-Roman Antiquity: A Sourcebook*, London: Routledge, 1999.

H. Mac L. Currie, *The Individual and the State*, London: Dent and Toronto: Hakkert, 1973.

J. Ferguson (ed.), *Greek and Roman Religion: A Sourcebook*, Park Ridge NJ: Noyes Press, 1980.

J. F. Gardner, *Leadership and the Cult of the Personality*, London: Dent and Toronto: Hakkert, 1974.

T. K. Hubbard, *Homosexuality in Greece and Rome: A Sourcebook of Basic Documents*, Berkeley, Los Angeles and London: University of California Press, 2003.

J. W. Humphrey, J. P. Oleson and A. N. Sherwood, *Greek and Roman Technology: A Sourcebook*, London and New York: Routledge, 1998.

M. Johnson and T. Ryan, *Sexuality in Greek and Roman Society and Literature: A Sourcebook*, London and New York: Routledge, 2005.

M. Joyal, J. Yardley and I. Mc Dougall, *Greek and Roman Education Sourcebook*, London and New York: Routledge, 2006.

R. S. Kraemer, *Women's Religions in the Greco-Roman World: A Sourcebook*, Oxford: Oxford University Press, 2004.

A. D. Lee, *Pagans and Christians in Late Antiquity: A Sourcebook*, London and New York: Routledge, 2000.

M. R. Lefkowitz and M. B. Fant, *Women's Life in Greece and Rome: A Source Book in Translation* (3rd edn), London: Duckworth, 2005.

L. A. McClure (ed.), *Sexuality and Gender in the Classical World: Readings and Sources*, Oxford: Blackwell, 2002.

F. Meijer and O. van Nijf, *Trade and Society in the Ancient World*, London and New York: Routledge, 1992.

C. Rodewald, *Democracy: Ideas and Realities*, London: Dent and Toronto: Hakkert, 1974.

J. Rowlandson, *Women and Society in Greek and Roman Egypt: A Sourcebook*, Cambridge: Cambridge University Press, 1998.

K. D. White, *Country Life in Classical Times*, London: Elek, 1977.

T. Wiedemann, *Greek and Roman Slavery: A Sourcebook*, London and New York: Routledge, 1980.

M. H. Williams, *The Jews among the Greeks and Romans: A Diasporan Sourcebook*, London: Duckworth, 1998.

B. Greece

I. Arnaoutoglou, *Ancient Greek Laws: A Sourcebook*, London: Routledge, 1998.

M. M. Austin, *The Hellenistic World from*

Alexander to the Roman Conquest: A Selection of Ancient Sources in Translation (2nd edn), Cambridge: Cambridge University Press, 2006.

M. M. Austin and P. Vidal-Naquet, *Economic and Social History of Ancient Greece: An Introduction*, London: Batsford, 1977.

R. Bagnall and P. Derow, *The Hellenistic Period: Historical Sources in Translation* (2nd edn), Oxford: Blackwell, 2003.

A. Barker, *Greek Musical Writings* (2 vols), Cambridge: Cambridge University Press, 1984–9.

J. Binder, *The Monuments and Sites of Athens: A Sourcebook*, forthcoming.

S. M. Burstein, *Translated Documents of Greece and Rome 3: The Hellenistic Age from the Battle of Ipsos to the Death of Kleopatra VII*, Cambridge: Cambridge University Press, 1985.

M. R. Cohen and I. E. Drabkin, *A Source Book of Greek Science*, Cambridge MA: Harvard University Press, 1948.

M. Crawford and D. Whitehead, *Archaic and Classical Greece: A Selection of Ancient Sources in Translation*, Cambridge: Cambridge University Press, 1983.

E. Csapo and W. J. Slater, *The Context of Greek Drama*, Ann Arbor: University of Michigan Press, 1994.

M. Dillon and L. Garland, *Ancient Greece: Social and Historical Documents from Archaic Times to the Death of Socrates (c. 800–399 BC)* (rev. edn), London and New York: Routledge, 2000.

J. Ferguson and K. Chisholm, *Political and Social Life in the Great Age of Athens*, London: Ward Lock Educational, 1978.

N. R. E. Fisher, *Social Values in Classical Athens*, London: Dent and Toronto: Hakkert, 1976.

C. W. Fornara, *Translated Documents of Greece and Rome 1: Archaic Times to the End of the Peloponnesian War*, Cambridge: Cambridge University Press, 1983.

P. Harding, *Translated Documents of Greece and Rome 2: From the End of the Peloponnesian War to the Battle of Ipsus*, Cambridge: Cambridge University Press, 1985.

W. Heckel and J. C. Yardley, *Alexander the Great: Historical Sources in Translation*, Oxford: Blackwell, 2003.

G. L. Irby-Massie and P. T. Keyser, *Greek Science of the Hellenistic Era: A Sourcebook*, London and New York: Routledge, 2002.

N. Lewis, *The Fifth Century BC: Greek Historical Documents*, Toronto: Hakkert, 1971.

J. Longrigg, *Greek Medicine from the Heroic to the Hellenistic Age: A Sourcebook*, London: Duckworth, 1988.

S. G. Miller, *Arete: Greek Sports from Ancient Sources*, Berkeley, Los Angeles and London: University of California Press, 1979.

J. M. Moore, *Aristotle and Xenophon on Democracy and Oligarchy* (new edn), London: Chatto and Windus, 1983.

R. Osborne, *The Athenian Empire* (LACTOR 1, 4th edn), London: London Association of Classical Teachers, 2000 – Sources translated from Index III of Hill's *Sources for Greek History*.

D. Phillips, *Political Oratory from Classical Athens: a Sourcebook*, London and New York: Routledge, 2003.

E. Pöhlmann and M. L. West, *Documents of Ancient Greek Music*, Oxford: Oxford University Press, 2001.

J. J. Pollitt, *The Art of Ancient Greece: Sources and Documents* (2nd edn), Cambridge: Cambridge University Press, 1990.

P. J. Rhodes, *The Greek City States: A Sourcebook*, London and New York: Routledge, 1986.

D. G. Rice and J. E. Stambaugh, *Sources for the Study of Greek Religion*, Missoula MT: Scholars Press, 1979.

J. W. Roberts, *Athenian Radical Democracy 461–404 BC* (LACTOR 5), London: London Association of Classical Teachers, 1998.

E. W. Robinson, *Ancient Greek Democracy: Readings and Sources*, Oxford: Blackwell, 2003.

M. M. Sage, *Warfare in Ancient Greece: A Sourcebook*, London and New York: Routledge, 1996.

G. R. Stanton, *Athenian Politics c. 800–500 BC: A Sourcebook*, London and New York: Routledge, 1990.

C. Rome

M. Beard, J. North and S. Price, *Religions of Rome. Vol. 2: A Sourcebook*, Cambridge: Cambridge University Press, 1998.

C. B. Champion, *Roman Imperialism: Readings and Sources*, Blackwell: Oxford, 2003.

D. Cherry (ed.), *The Roman World: A Sourcebook*, Oxford: Blackwell, 2001.

M. G. L. Cooley, *The Age of Augustus* (literary texts trans. B. W. J. G. Wilson; LACTOR 17), London: London Association of Classical Teachers, 2003.

J. Gardner, *The Roman Household: A Sourcebook*, London and New York: Routledge, 1990.

S. Ireland, *Roman Britain: A Sourcebook*, London and New York: Routledge, 1996.

B. Levick, *The Government of the Roman Empire: A Sourcebook* (2nd edn), London: Routledge, 2000.

N. Lewis and M. Reinhold (eds), *Roman Civilization Select Readings 1: The Republic and the Augustan Age; 2: The Empire* (3rd edn), New York: Columbia University Press, 1990.

K. Lomas, *Roman Italy 338 BC–AD 200: A Sourcebook*, London: UCL Press, 1996.

M. R. Maas, *Readings in Late Antiquity: A Sourcebook*, London and New York: Routledge, 2000.

J. C. Mann and R. G. Penman (eds), *Literary Sources for Roman Britain* (LACTOR 11), London: London Association of Classical Teachers, 1977.

V. A. Maxfield and B. Dobson (eds), *Inscriptions of Roman Britain* (LACTOR 4, 3rd edn), London: London Association of Classical Teachers, 1995.

J. J. Pollitt, *The Art of Rome: Sources and Documents* (2nd edn), Cambridge: Cambridge University Press, 1983.

J. -A. Shelton, *As the Romans Did: A Sourcebook in Roman Social History* (2nd edn), Oxford: Oxford University Press, 1997.

R. K. Sherk, *Translated Documents of Greece and Rome 4: Rome and the Greek East to the Death of Augustus*, Cambridge: Cambridge University Press, 1984.

R. K. Sherk, *Translated Documents of Greece and Rome 6: The Roman Empire: Augustus to Hadrian*, Cambridge: Cambridge University Press, 1988.

Maps and atlases

For ancient maps, see O. A. W. Dilke, *Greek and Roman Maps*, London: Thames and Hudson, 1985.

Sheet maps

H. Kiepert, *Formae Orbis Antiqui*, Berlin: D. Reimer, 1893–1914 (repr. Rome: Quasar, with intro. R. Talbert, 1996, and repr. of 25 plates by J. Paul Getty Museum Publications, 1998).

Map of Roman Britain (4th edn), Ordnance Survey, 1978.

N. Postgate, *Classical Wall Maps: The Ancient Near East and Lands of the Bible*, London and New York: Routledge, 1991.

R. Stoneman and R. Wallace, *Classical Wall Maps: Ancient Greece and the Aegean*, London and New York: Routledge, 1989.

R. Stoneman and R. Wallace, *Classical Wall Maps: Roman Italy*, London and New York: Routledge, 1989.

R. Stoneman and R. Wallace, *Classical Wall Maps: Alexander's Empire*, London and New York: Routledge, 1991.

R. Stoneman and R. Wallace, *Classical Wall Maps: Roman Empire*, London and New York: Routledge, 1991.

Tabula Imperii Romani – a map of the Roman Empire based on the international 1:1,000,000 map of the world, 1954–.

Atlases

H. Bengtson and V. Milojčić (eds), *Grosser Historischer Weltatlas, I: Vorgeschichte und Altertum* (6th edn), Munich: Bayerischer Schulbuch, 1978–95.

M. Grant, *Routledge Atlas of Classical History* (5th edn), London and New York: Routledge, 1994.

G. B. Grundy, *Murray's Classical Atlas* (2nd edn), London: J. Murray, 1917.

N. Hammond, *Atlas of the Greek and Roman World in Antiquity*, Park Ridge NJ: Noyes Press, 1981.
R. Muir and G. Philip (eds), *Philip's Atlas of Ancient and Classical History*, London: George Philip and Son, 1938.
A. Philippson and E. Kirsten, *Die griechische Landschaften: Eine Landeskunde* (4 vols), Frankfurt: Klöstermann, 1950–59.
R. J. A. Talbert (ed.), *Barrington Atlas of the Greek and Roman World*, Princeton: Princeton University Press, 2000.

There are also books that use maps as the basis for the presentation of aspects of the classical world, sometimes alongside text and photographs:

T. Cornell and J. Matthews, *Atlas of the Roman World*, Oxford: Phaidon, 1982.
M. I. Finley (ed.), *Atlas of Classical Archaeology*, London: Chatto and Windus, 1977.
M. Grant, *Ancient History Atlas 1700 BC to AD 565* (4th edn), London: Weidenfeld and Nicolson, 1989.
M. Grant, *The Routledge Atlas of Classical History* (5th edn), London and New York: Routledge, 1994.
J. Haywood, *The Cassell Atlas of World History: The Ancient and Classical Worlds*, vol. 1, London: Cassell, 2000.
A. A. M. van der Heyden and H. H. Scullard, *Atlas of the Classical World*, London: Nelson, 1959.
B. Jones and D. Mattingly, *An Atlas of Roman Britain*, Oxford: Blackwell, 1990; Oxford: Oxbow Books, 2002.
P. Levi, *Atlas of the Greek World*, Oxford: Phaidon, 1980.
C. McEvedy, *The New Penguin Atlas of Ancient History* (2nd edn), Harmondsworth: Penguin, 2001.
R. Morkot, *The Penguin Historical Atlas of Ancient Greece*, Harmondsworth: Penguin, 1996.
R. J. A. Talbert (ed.), *Atlas of Classical History*, London and Sydney: Croom Helm, 1985.

Websites

The easiest way to access websites is through a search engine (a programme that searches for a word or phrase that you enter) or a directory (this gives categorised listings of web links). The most popular search engines are Altavista (www.altavista.digital.com), Google (www.google.com) and Yahoo (www.yahoo.com). http://bubl.ac.uk/link provides access to selected internet resources covering all academic subjects, and www.humbul.ac.uk gives access to subjects in the humanities (follow the links to Archaeology and Classics). To ensure you receive only the complete subject you are requesting and not its individual elements, it is best to use quotes round a phrase when searching, e.g. "National Library of Scotland". The number of websites is now apparently limitless and increasing rapidly. System requirements vary, and access to some of the sites is by licence or subscription (individual and corporate), some by password.

A helpful guide to Greek sites on the net is Roberto M. Danese, *Kybernetes: Il greco classico in rete*, Rimini: Guaraldi, 2004 (with diskette of websites and emails); see also the general sites listed under (A) below. See also the subject-specific lists of websites in chapters. 22, 28, 30, 32, 34, 52, and 53.

A. General

Below are listed some websites that may be of general help to students of the classics; many provide useful links:

www.aclclassics.org – American Classical League
www.classics.ac.uk – the Classical Association
www.classicsinfo.org – a gateway site with information for students on classics departments, seminars, conferences, etc.
www.classicsnet.plus.com – a gateway site to classics
www.classicspage.com – popular classics website
www.hca.ltsn.ac.uk – the Subject Centre for History, Classics and Archaeology
www.kirke.hu-berlin.de/ressourc/ressourc.html – extensive German list of classical web resources

www.trentu.ca/ahc/resources.html#dir – a lengthy list of classical web resources

B. Text-Searching Websites

http://classics.mit.edu/ – a searchable collection of over 400 classical Greek and Latin texts (in English translation) with user-provided commentary
www.tlg.uci.edu – a digital library of Greek literature

C. Bibliographic Websites

www.aim25.ac.uk – includes access to information about the archives of the Joint Library of the Hellenic and Roman Societies and the Library of the Institute of Classical Studies.
www.annee-philologique.com/aph/ – online version of *L'Année philologique* (1959–)
www.dyabola.de – a collection of German catalogues and bibliographies
www.gnomon.ku-eichstaett.de/ – updates to the CD-ROM of *Gnomon*

D. A selection of archaeological sites

http://ibis.cch.kcl.ac.uk/eala/2004/index.html – Aphrodisias (focusing on inscriptions)
www.agathe.gr/ – American School of Classical Studies site on the Athenian Agora excavations
www.bsr.ac.uk/BSR/sub_arch/BSR_Arch_02 Pomp.htm – British School at Rome site on Pompeii
www.davidgill.co.uk/attica/default.htm – a selection of sites from Attica
www.nyu.edu/projects/aphrodisias/home.ti.htm – Aphrodisias (focusing on the site itself)
www.perseus.tufts.edu/PR/platner.ann.html – the *Topographical Dictionary of Ancient Rome*
www.simulacraromae.org – French, Italian and Spanish sites on e.g. Rome, Narbonne, Cartagena and other Roman remains
www.unc.edu/awmc/web-princetonencyclopediaofclassicalsites.html – the *Princeton Encyclopedia of Classical Sites*

E. A Selection of Subject-based Websites

http://didaskalia.open.ac.uk – site for ancient theatre and drama in performance
www.apgrd.ox.ac.uk - archive of performances of Greek and Roman drama
www.atm.ox.ac.uk/rowing/trireme – the Greek trireme
www.beazley.ox.ac.uk – a wide-ranging set of illustrated articles on sculpture, gems and pottery, with an explanation of the photographs in the Beazley Archive in the Ashmolean Museum, Oxford
www.classicalstudies.co.uk – a website run by Theatre Odyssey
www.csad.ox.ac.uk – website of the Centre for the Study of Ancient Documents
www.cvaonline.org – an illustrated catalogue of over 100,000 vases of the *Corpus Vasorum Antiquorum*
www.lamp.ac.uk/classics/mathos – a website for learning Ancient Greek
www.logs.com and www.libronix.com – electronic versions of multilingual Bibles and dictionaries, including Liddell-Scott-Jones's *Greek-English Lexicon*, with the 1996 supplement integrated into the body of the dictionary
www.perseus.tufts.edu – a multimedia database which began as a learning resource for Ancient Greece but which has been extended to include a selection of Latin literature
www.pompeii.co.uk – an introduction to the Pompeii Interactive CD
www.roman-emperors.org – self-explanatory
www.stoa.org – an American consortium on a variety of subjects such as democracy, women, Trajan's Column, with useful links

Software/Databases

A small sample of available CD-ROMs is listed below; some are subscription-based.

A. General

Oxford Classical Dictionary (3rd edn, 2000)

Perseus 2.0 – a massive database of Greek culture, available in a comprehensive (4 CD-ROMs) and a concise (1 CD-ROM) edition

B. Texts

Bibliotheca Teubneriana Latina (*BTL*[3]) – over 500 classical Latin texts published by Saur

F. Jacoby, *Die Fragmente der griechischen Historiker* – the original volumes (1923–58)

Library of Christian Latin Texts (used to be called *CETEDOC*) – Christian Latin texts of the *Corpus Christianorum Series Latina*

Musaios – search software for *TLG* and *Packard Humanities Institute*

Oxford Text Archive, produced by Oxford University Computing Service

Packard Humanities Institute – Latin literary texts (PHI 5.3) with word and phrase searches for Latin literature and documentary papyri and inscriptions (PHI 7.0); further information from the Packard Humanities Institute, 300 Second Street, Los Altos, California 94022, USA

Patrologia Latina – full text of Migne's *Patrologia Latina*

Thesaurus Linguae Graecae (*TLG*) – word and phrase search of Greek literary texts (this is available online to subscribers, www.tlg.uci.edu)

Thesaurus Linguae Latinae (*TLL*[3]) – word and phrase search of Latin literary texts

Workplace for Windows – another search software for *TLG* and *Packard Humanities Institute*

C. Bibliographies

Dyabola – a collection of German catalogues and bibliographies, e.g. a subject catalogue of the German Archaeological Institute in Rome, a databank of Attic grave-reliefs and a census of antique art and architecture known to the Renaissance

Gnomon Bibliographische Datenbank – a bibliographic database of the leading German review journal, together with data from some other journals and entries from *ANRW*, *CAH* and *OCD* (with English user interface)

70. Abbreviations

Thomas Harrison

The purpose and scope of this section

Classics, more than many disciplines, employs a huge number of abbreviations: ancient authors and their works, modern journals, or modern editions or collections of ancient texts, are all routinely referred to in abbreviated form; classicists also continue to employ a number of other traditional abbreviations (usually derived from Latin terms) that are less common in other disciplines. Though modern authors tend to follow the conventions of one of a number of major works (for example, the *Oxford Classical Dictionary*), there is no single authoritative list of abbreviations; instead a number of variants are commonly used.

Such conventions may have the virtue of saving space, but they can also be a block to understanding, preventing the uninitiated from following up references in footnotes or endnotes. This section is intended to provide a single alphabetical list of abbreviations used in classical works. It comprises abbreviations of ancient authors, journals, collections of authors and texts, and all other common abbreviations. It is not broken up into sections – for the simple reason that it may not be obvious that an abbreviation refers, for example, to a classical text or a journal. It does not aim to be comprehensive. In particular, it does not give full details of publication for any journal or collection, but only sufficient material for it to be found through an electronic library catalogue; not all the works of a given author are necessarily listed (especially where a standard system of numeration is used); it also does not include journals (such as *Antiquity*, *Metis* etc.) where the main title is not commonly further abbreviated; variant abbreviations are included where the alternative is not easily recognisable. Where the authorship of a work is questionable, this is signalled by an asterisk after the name of the work.

For other lists of abbreviations, see especially the *Oxford Classical Dictionary* (3rd edn), Liddell and Scott's *Greek-English Lexicon*, revised edn, or the *Oxford Latin Dictionary* (especially for ancient authors and works), or any recent edition of the bibliographical journal *L'Année philologique* (for the titles of journals).

Using abbreviations

Primary texts (i.e. the works of ancient writers) are standardly referred to in the format: Author *Work* 1–999. In other words, the abbreviated name of the author is given in Roman (i.e. non-italic) type, followed by the name of the work in italic type, and by a numerical reference. In the case of some major authors of only one surviving work (for example, Herodotus or Thucydides: Hdt., Thuc.), the name of the work is not necessary. The numerical reference may refer to book, chapter, or – in the case of verse writings, inscriptions and papyri – line number. (In the case of each major author, there is a conventional system of numeration.) Square brackets around the name of the author signify that the authorship of the work is open to question. A modern name or initial(s) after the reference signifies the editor of the specific edition being referred to (reference systems often vary between editions; editors' names are also often abbreviated to initials, such as DK for Diels-Kranz). Some authors choose to give equivalent reference in another edition too. So, for example:

Hdt. 7.129 = Herodotus book 7, chapter 129;
Soph. *Ant.* 1202–12 = Sophocles *Antigone* lines 1202–12;
[Arist.] *Ath. Pol.* 13.2 = the Aristotelian *Athenaion Politeia* chapter 13, subsection 2;
Enn. *Ann.* 206–12 Skutsch (= 229–35 Warmington) = Ennius *Annales* 206–12 in Skutsch's edition, or 229–35 in Warmington's edition

There are two major conventional systems for referring to *secondary scholarship* (i.e. modern works): 'short titles' and the 'name-date' (or Harvard) system. Versions of both systems differ in details of order and punctuation of items.

In the *short-title system*, reference in the footnotes or endnotes is made to a shortened version of the article or book, and to specific page numbers, as in the following examples:

Walbank, 'The problem of Greek nationality', p. 60.
Dench, *From Barbarians to New Men*, pp. 20–32.
Goldhill, 'Modern critical approaches', p.. 324.

The corresponding bibliography then lists the full details as follows:

F. W. Walbank, 'The problem of Greek nationality', *Phoenix* 5 (1951), 41–60.
Emma Dench, *From Barbarians to New Men: Greek, Roman and Modern Perceptions of Peoples from the Central Apennines*, Oxford: Oxford University Press, 1995.
S. D. Goldhill, 'Modern critical approaches to Greek tragedy', in P. E. Easterling (ed.), *The Cambridge Companion to Greek Tragedy*, Cambridge: Cambridge University Press, 1997, pp. 324–47.

Some bibliographies list only the place of publication; others the place of publication and the name of the publisher. In the case of some journal articles that employ the short title system, there is no bibliography: instead, an item of bibliography is referred to in full at its first citation in a footnote, and then (if cited again) a reference is made to the footnote at which it was cited in full: so, for example, Walbank, 'The problem of Greek nationality' (n. 2), p. 60.

In the *name-date system*, reference in footnotes is made to the name of the author, the date of publication and specific page numbers, as in the following examples:

Walbank 1951: 60
Dench 1995: 20–32
Goldhill 1997: 324

In some cases, the date of publication (and the page number(s)) are put in rounded brackets: so e.g. Walbank (1951: 60).

The corresponding bibliography then lists the full details as follows:

Walbank, F. W. (1951), 'The problem of Greek nationality', *Phoenix* 5, 41–60.
Dench, Emma (1995), *From Barbarians to New Men. Greek, Roman and Modern Perceptions of Peoples from the Central Apennines* (Oxford: Oxford University Press).
Goldhill, S. D. (1997) 'Modern critical approaches to Greek tragedy', in P. E. Easterling (ed.), *The Cambridge Companion to Greek Tragedy* (Cambridge: Cambridge University Press), 324–47.

Where two or more items of bibliography published in the same year by the same author are cited, they are distinguished as e.g. Smith 2005a and Smith 2005b.

Abbreviations

A&A	*Antike und Abendland*
AA	*Archäologischer Anzeiger*
AAA	*Athens Annals of Archaeology*
AAHG	*Anzeiger für die Altertumswissenschaft*
AAntHung	*Acta Antiqua Academiae Scientiarum Hungaricae*
AArch	*Acta Archaeologica*
AArchHung	*Acta Archaeologica Academiae Scientiarum Hungaricae*
AASO	*Annual of the American Schools of Oriental Research*
AAWM	*Abhandlungen der Akademie der Wissenschaften in Mainz*
ABAW	*Abhandlungen der Bayerischen Akademie der Wissenschaften*
Abh.	*Abhandlungen* (of Academy or Society, e.g. *der Akademie der Wissenschaften in Mainz*)
ABSA	*Annual of the British School at Athens*
ABull	*Art Bulletin*
ABV	*Attic Black-Figure Vase-Painters*
AC	*L'Antiquité classique*
Ach. Tat.	Achilles Tatius
AClass	*Acta Classica*
A&Cr	*Antigüedad y cristianismo*
ActaHyp	*Acta Hyperborea*
Act. Ir.	*Acta Iranica*
AD	*Archaiologikon Deltion*
A.D.	Apollonius Dyscolus
ADAJ	*Annual of the Department of Antiquities of Jordan*
ADAW	*Abhandlungen der Deutschen Akademie der Wissenschaften zu Berlin*
adesp.	Gk. adespota, i.e. unattributed or anonymous (used of fragments)
ad loc.	Lat. ad locum, i.e. at the place in question (used esp. of commentaries in referring to discussion of a particular line or chapter)
AE	*L'Année Épigraphique*; also *Archaiologike ephemeris*
AEHE	*Annuaire de l'École pratique des hautes études*
Ael.	Aelian, *Ep[istulae]*, *[de] N[atura] A[nimalium]*, *Tact[ica]*, *V[aria] H[istoria]*
AEMΘ (also *AEMT*)	*Archaiologiko Ergo ste Makedonia kai Thrake*
Aen.	*Aeneid*
Aen. Tact.	Aeneas Tacticus
Aeol.	Aeolic (i.e. dialect)
AEph	*Archaiologike ephemeris*
Aesch. (also A.)	Aeschylus, *Ag[amemnon]*, *Cho[ephoroe] = Libation Bearers*, *Eum[enides]*, *Pers[ae] = Persians*, *P[rometheus] V[inctus]* = Prometheus Bound*, *Sep[tem Contra Thebas] = Seven Against Thebes* (also *Th.*), *Suppl[ices] = Suppliants*
Aeschin.	Aeschines, *[against] Ctes[iphon]*, *Tim[archus]* (or speeches referred to by number)
AFB	*Anuari de filologia (de la Universitat de Barcelona)*
AFC	*Anales de filologia clásica*
AFL	*Annali della Facoltà di lettere [e filosofia]*: e.g. *AFLB* (*di Bari*), *AFLC* (*di Cagliari*), *AFLL* (*di Lecce*), *AFLM* (*Università di Macerata*), *AFLN* (*di Napoli*), *AFLPer* (*di Perugia*), *AFLS* (*di Siena*)

AfrIt	*Africa Italiana*
AfrRom	*Africa Romana*
Agath.	Agathias
AH	*Ancient History*
A^{1}H	Inscription of Artaxerxes 1 at Hamadan (see Kent, *Old Persian*)
A^{2}H	Inscription of Artaxerxes 2 at Hamadan (see Kent, *Old Persian*)
AHAM	*Anales de historia antigua y medieval*
AHAW	*Abhandlungen der Heidelberger Akademie der Wissenschaften*
AHB	*Ancient History Bulletin*
AHistHung	*Acta Historica Academiae Scientiarum Hungaricae*
AHR	*American Historical Review*
AHRC	Arts and Humanities Research Council
AI	*Acta Iranica*
AION	*Annali dell'Istituto universitario orientale di Napoli*
AIPhO	*Annuaire de l'Institut de philologie et d'histoire orientales et slaves*
AIV	*Atti dell'Istituto veneto*
AJ	*Archaeological Journal*
AJA (also *AJArch*)	*American Journal of Archaeology*
AJAH	*American Journal of Ancient History*
AJN	*American Journal of Numismatics*
AJPh (also *AJP*, *AJPhil*)	*American Journal of Philology*
AK	*Antike Kunst*
Alc.	Alcaeus
Alcm.	Alcman
Alex. Aphr.	Alexander of Aphrodisias
Alex. Trall.	Alexander of Tralles
AM	*Athenische Mitteilungen* (= *MDAI(A)*)
Amer. Acad. Rome	*Memoirs of the American Academy at Rome*
Amer. Hist. Rev.	*American Historical Review*
AMI	*Archäologische Mitteilungen aus Iran*
Amm. Marc.	Ammianus Marcellinus
Ammon.	Ammonius Grammaticus
Anacr.	Anacreon
Anat. St.	*Anatolian Studies*
Anaxag.	Anaxagoras (see DK)
Anaximand.	Anaximander (see DK)
Anaximen.	Anaximenes (see DK)
AncPhil	*Ancient Philosophy*
Anc. Soc.	*Ancient Society*
AncW	*Ancient World*
And.	Andocides
Androt.	Androtion
Anecd. Bach.	*Anecdota Graeca* (ed. L. Bachmann)
Anecd. Bekk.	*Anecdota Graeca* (ed. I. Bekker)
Anecd. Ox.	*Anecdota Graeca* (from Oxford ms., ed. J. A. Cramer)
Anecd. Par.	*Anecdota Graeca* (from Paris ms., ed. J. A. Cramer)
Annales (ESC)	*Annales: Économies, sociétés, civilisations*
Annales (HSS)	*Annales: Histoire, sciences sociales*
ANRW	*Aufstieg und Niedergang der römischen Welt*

ANSMusN	*American Numismatic Society Museum Notes*
Ant. Af.	*Antiquités africaines*
AntTard	*Antiquité tardive*
Ant. Class.	*L'Antiquité classique*
Anth. Lat.	*Anthologia Latina* = *Latin Anthology*
Anth. Lyr. Graec.	*Anthologia Lyrica Graeca* (ed. E. Diehl)
Anth. Pal.	*Anthologia Palatina* = *Palatine Anthology*
Anth. Plan.	*Anthologia Planudea*
Antiph.	Antiphon
AntJ	*Antiquaries Journal*
Anz.	*Anzeiger/Anzeigen* (of Academy or Society, e.g. *der Österreichischen Akademie der Wissenschaften in Wien*)
AO	*Archiv orientalni*, also *Athenian Officials* (ed. R. Develin)
aor.	aorist
Ap.	Apuleius, *Apol[ogia]*, *Asclep[ius]*, *de deo Soc[ratico]*, *de dog[mate] Plat[onis]*, *Flor[ida]*, *Met[amorphoses]*
ap.	Lat. *apud*, i.e. quoted in (used to refer to source of ancient fragment or quotation)
A^{1}P	Inscription of Artaxerxes I at Persepolis (see Kent, *Old Persian*)
A^{3}P	Inscription of Artaxerxes III at Persepolis (see Kent, *Old Persian*)
APA	American Philological Association
APB	*Acta Patristica et Byzantina*
APF	*Athenian Propertied Families*
APh	*L'Année philologique*
Apollod.	Apollodorus, *Bibl[iotheca]*, *Ep[itome]*
App.	Appian, *B[ella] Civ[ilia]*, *Gall[ica]*, *Hann[ibalica]*, *Hisp[anica]*, *Ill[yrica]*, *Mac[edonica]*, *Mith[ridatica]*, *Num[idica]*, *Pun[ica]*, *Sam[nitika]*, *Sic[ilica]*, *Syr[iaca]*
app. crit.	Lat. apparatus criticus, i.e. critical apparatus (details of textual variants, published at foot of page of edition)
Ap. Rhod.	Apollonius of Rhodes, *Arg[onautica]*
AR	*Archaeological Reports*
Ar.	Aristophanes, *Ach[arnians]*, *Av[es]* = *Birds*, *Eccl[esiazusae]* = *Assemblywomen*, *Eq[uites]* = *Knights*, *Lys[istrata]*, *Nub[es]* = *Clouds*, *Pax* = *Peace*, *Plut[us]* = *Wealth*, *Ran[ae]* = *Frogs*, *Thesm[ophoriazusae]*, *Vesp[ae]* = *Wasps*
A.R.	Apollonius Rhodius
A&R	*Atene e Roma*
Arat.	Aratus, *Phaen[omena]*, *Progn[ostica]*
Arch. Ael.	*Archaeologica Aeliana*
Arch. Anz.	*Archäologischer Anzeiger* in *Jahrbuch des deutschen archäologischen Instituts*
Arch. Class.	*Archeologica Classica*
Archil.	Archilochus
Archim.	Archimedes, *Method of Mechanical Theorems*
Arch. Journ.	*Archaeological Journal*
ArchN	*Archaeological News*
ArchOrient	*Archiv orientalni*
Arch. Pap.	*Archiv fur Papyrusforschung*
Arch. Rep.	*Archaeological Reports*
ARID	*Analecta Romana Instituti Danici*

Arist.	Aristotle, *An[alytica] Post[eriora]* (also *APo*), *An[alytica] Pr[iora]* (also *APr*), *Ath[ēnaiōn] Pol[iteia]* = Athenian Constitution* (also known as *Constitution of the Athenians*), *[de] Cael[o]*, *Cat[egoriae]*, *[de] Col[oribus]*, *de An[ima]*, *de Audib[ilibus]**, *de Motu An[imalium]* (also *MA*), *de Spir[itu]*, *[de] Div[inatione per] Somn[ia]*, *Eth[ica] Eud[emia]* = *EE*, *Eth[ica] Nic[omachea]* = *EN*, *[de] Gen[eratione] An[imalium]* (also *GA*), *[de] Gen[eratione et] Corr[uptione]* (also *GC*), *Hist[oria] An[imalium]* (also *HA*), *[de] I[ncessu] A[nimalium]* (also *IA*), *[de] Insomn[iis]*, *[de] Int[erpretatione]*, *[de] Iuv[entute]*, *[de] Lin[eis] ins[ecabilibus]**, *[de] Long[aevitate]*, *Mag[na] Mor[alia]* (also *MM*)*, *Mech[anica]**, *[de] Mem[oria]*, *Metaph[ysica]*, *Mete[orologica]*, *Mir[abilia]*, *[de] Mund[o]**, *Oec[onomica]**, *[de] Part[ibus] An[imalium]* (also *PA*), *Parv[a] nat[uralia]*, *Ph[ysica]*, *Phgn* = *Physiognomica**, *Poet[ica]*, *Pol[itica]*, *Pr[oblemata]**, *[de] Resp[iratione]*, *Rh[etorica]*, *Rh[etorica ad] Al[exandrum]**, *[de] Sens[u]*, *[de] Somn[o et] Vig[ilia]*, *Soph[istici] el[enchi]* (also *SE*), *Top[ica]*, *[de] V[irtutibus et] V[itiis]*, *[de]Xen[ophane]**
Aristid.	Aristides, *Or[ations]*
Aristid. Quint.	Aristides Quintilianus
Aristox.	Aristoxenus, *Fr[agmenta] hist[orica]*, *Harm[onica]*, *Rhythm[ica]*
Arn.	Arnobius, *Adv[ersus] Nat[iones]*
ARP	*Accordia Research Papers*
Arr.	Arrian, *[Expeditio contra] Alan[os]*, *Anab[asis]*, *Cyn[egeticus]*, *Epict[eti] diss[ertationes]*, *Ind[ica]*, *Parth[ica]*, *Peripl[us] M[aris] Eux[ini]*, *Tact[ica]*
Artem.	Artemidorus
ARV	*Attic Red-Figure Vase-Painters*
AS	*Anatolian Studies*, also *Assyriological Studies*
A^{2}S	Inscription of Artaxerxes 2 at Susa
ASAA	*Annuario della Scuola archeologica di Atene e delle Missioni Italiane in oriente*
ASAE	*Annales du Service des antiquités de l'Égypte*
ASAW	*Abhandlungen der Sachsischen Akademie der Wissenschaften zu Leipzig*
Asc.	Asconius, *Corn.* = *Commentary on Cicero,* pro Cornelio, *In Tog[a] Cand[ida]*, *Mil.* = *Commentary on Cicero,* pro Milone, *Pis.* = *Commentary on Cicero,* in Pisonem, *Verr.* = *Commentary on Cicero,* in Verrem
Ascl.	Asclepiodotus
ASNP	*Annali della Scuola normale superiore di Pisa*
Ath.	Athenaeus
Ath. Pol.	*Athēnaiōn Politeia* = *Athenian Constitution* (see Arist. and Xen.)
ATL	*Athenian Tribute Lists*
Att.	Attic (i.e. dialect)
August.	Augustine, *[Expositio of Epist.] Ad Rom[anos]*, *C[ontra] Acad[emicos]*, *Conf[essions]*, *De civ[itate] D[ei]* = *City of God*, *[De]div[ersis] quaest[ionibus]*, *[Tractatus] in Evang[elium] Iohan[nis]*, *Ep[istulae]*, *Retract[ationes]*, *Serm[ones]*
Aul. Gell.	see Gell.
Aur. Vict.	Aurelius Victor, *Caes[ares]*, *de vir[is] Ill[ustribus]*
Auson. (also Aus.)	Ausonius
AW	*Antike Welt*
AWE	*Ancient West and East*

B.	Bacchylides
Bab.	Babylonian
BABesch	*Bulletin antieke Beschaving*
Babr.	Babrius
Bacchyl.	Bacchylides
BAGB	*Bulletin de l'Association Guillaume Budé*
BAR	*British Archaeological Reports*
BASO	*Bulletin of the American Schools of Oriental Research*
BASP	*Bulletin of the American Society of Papyrologists*
BAssBudé	*Bulletin de l'Association Guillaume Budé*
Batr.	*Batr[achomyomachia]*
BCH	*Bulletin de correspondance hellénique*
BCTH	*Bulletin du Comité des travaux historiques et scientifiques*
BdA	*Bollettino d'arte*
BdArch	*Bollettino di archeologia*
BE	*Bulletin épigraphique* (published in *REG*)
BES	*Bulletin of the Egyptological Seminar*
BGU	*Berliner Griechische Urkunden*
BICS	*Bulletin of the Institute of Classical Studies of the University of London*
BIDR	*Bollettino dell'Istituto di diritto romano*
BIE	*Bulletin de l'Institut d'Égypte*
BIFAO	*Bulletin de l'Institute français d'archeologie orientale*
BiOr	*Bibliotheca Orientalis*
BJ	*Bonner Jahrbücher*
BJRL	*Bulletin of the John Rylands Library, University of Manchester*
BKT	*Berliner Klassikertexte*
BM	British Museum
BMC	*British Museum Catalogue*
BMCR (also *BMCRev*)	*Bryn Mawr Classical Review (online)*
BNJ	*British Numismatic Journal*
Bnum	*Bollettino di numismatica*
BO	*Bibliotheca Orientalis*
BRL	*Bulletin of the John Rylands Library, University of Manchester*
BSA	*Annual of the British School at Athens*
BStudLat	*Bollettino di studi latini*
BTCGI	*Bibliografia topografica della colonizzazione greca in Italia e nelle isole tirreniche*
Budé	Collection des Universités de France (published in association with l'Association Guillaume Budé)
ByzF	*Byzantinische Forschungen*
ByzZ	*Byzantinische Zeitschrift*
CA	Classical Association
CAAP	*Commentary on the Aristotelian* Athenaion Politeia (ed. P. J. Rhodes)
Caes.	Caesar, *B[ellum] Afr[icanum]*, *Bell[um] Alex[andrinum]*, *B[ellum] Civ[ile]*, *B[ellum] Gall[icum]*
CAF	*Comicorum Atticorum Fragmenta* (ed. T. Kock)
CAH	*Cambridge Ancient History*
Callim.	Callimachus, *Aet[ia]*, *[Hymnus in] Ap[ollinem]*, *[Hymnus in] Cer[erem]*, *[Hymnus in] Del[um]*, *[Hymnus in] Dian[am]*, *Epigr[ammata]*, *Hec[ale]*,

	Hymn (1–6), *Ia[mbics]*, *[Hymnus in] Iov[em]*, *Lav[acrum] Pall[adis]*, *Sos[ibii Victoria]*
Calp.	Calpurnius Siculus, *Ecl[ogues]*
CArchJ	*Cambridge Archaeological Journal*
Carm.	*Carmen/Carmina*, so e.g. *Carmen arvale*, *Carmina epigraphica*, *Carmen popularia*, *Carmen Saliare*
Cass. Dio	Cassius Dio
Cassiod.	Cassiodorus, *Inst[itutiones]*, *Var[iae]*
Cato	*[de] Agr[icultura]*, *Orig[ines]*
Catull.	Catullus
CB	*Classical Bulletin*
CCAG	*Catalogus Codicum Astrologorun Graecorum*
CCC	*Civiltà classica e cristiana*
CCGS	*Corpus Christianorum, series Graeca*
CCSL	*Corpus Christianorum, series Latina*
CE	*Chronique d'Égypte*
CEA	*Cahiers des études anciennes*
CEG	*Carmina Epigraphica Graeca* (ed. P. A. Hansen)
Cels.	Celsus
CErc	*Cronache ercolanesi*
cf.	Lat. *confer*, i.e. compare
CFC	*Cuadernos de filología clásica*
CGF	*Comicorum Graecorum Fragmenta* (ed. G. Kaibel)
CGFP	*Comicorum Graecorum Fragmenta in papyris reperta* (ed. C. Austin)
Chalcid.	Chalcidius, *In [Platonis] Tim[aeum]*
CHCL	*Cambridge History of Classical Literature*
ChHist	*Church History: Studies in Christianity and Culture*
CHI	*Cambridge History of Iran*
Chron d'E	*Chronique d'Égypte*
Chrysipp.	Chrysippus
CIA	*Corpus Inscriptionum Atticarum*
Cic.	Cicero, *Acad[amicae Quaestiones]*, *Acad[emica] Post[eriora]*, *Acad[emica] Pr[iora]*, *[Epistulae] ad Brut[um]*, *[de] Amic[itia]*, *[pro] Arch[ia]*, *[Epistulae ad] Att[icum]*, *[pro] Balb[o]*, *Brut[us]*, *[pro] Caec[ina]*, *[pro] Cael[io]*, *[in] Cat[ilinam]*, *[pro] Clu[entio]*, *[pro] Corn[elio]*, *de Imp[erio] Gn. Pomp[eii]*, *[pro Rege] Deiot[aro]*, *de Or[atore]*, *[de] Div[inatione]*, *Div[inatione in] Caec[ilium]*, *[de] Dom[o sua]*, *[Epistulae ad] Fam[iliares]*, *[de] Fat[o]*, *[de] Fin[ibus]*, *[pro] Flac[co]*, *[pro] Font [eio]*, *[de] Har[uspicum] Resp[onso]*, *[de] Inv[entione] Rhet[orica]*, *[de] Leg[ibus]*, *[de] Leg[e] Agr[aria]*, *[pro] Leg[e] Man[ilia]* = *de Imp[erio] Gn. Pomp[eii]*, *[pro] Lig[ario]*, *Luc[ullus]* = *Acad[emica] Post[eriora]*, *[pro] Marc[ello]*, *[pro] Mil[one]*, *[pro] Mur[ena]*, *[de] Nat[ura] D[eorum]* (also *ND*), *[de] Off[iciis]*, *Orat[or ad M. Brutum]*, *Part[itiones] or[atoriae]*, *[Orationes] Phil[ippicae]* (= *Philippics), [in] Pis[onem]*, *[pro] Planc[io]*, *[de] Prov[inciis] cons[ularibus]*, *[Epistulae ad] Q[uintum] Fr[atrem]* (also *QF*), *[pro] Quinct[io]*, *[pro] Rab[irio] Post[umio]*, *[post] Red[itum ad] Pop[ulum]*, *[post] Red[itum in] Sen[atu]*, *[de] Rep[ublica]*, *[pro] Rosc[io]*, *[pro Sexto] Rosc[io] Am[erino]*, *[pro] Scaur[o]*, *[de] Sen[ectute]*, *[pro] Sest[io]*, *Somn[ium Scipionis]*, *[pro] Sull[a]*, *[Oratio in Senatu in] Tog[a] cand[ida]*, *Top[ica]*, *Tusc[ulanae Disputationes]*, *[in] Verr[em]*

Cicero (Quintus)	*Comment[ariolum petitionis]*
CIE	*Corpus Inscriptionum Etruscarum*
CIJ	*Corpus Inscriptionum Judaicarum*
CIL	*Corpus Inscriptionum Latinarum*
CISA	*Contributi dell'Istituto di storia antica dell'Università del Sacro Cuore*
CISem	*Corpus Inscriptionum Semiticarum*
CJ	*Classical Journal*
CJ	Codex Justinianus (Justinianic Code)
cj.	conjectured by (used of textual changes)
ClAnt	*Classical Antiquity*
ClassStud	*Classical Studies*
Claud.	Claudianus, *[De] cons[ulatu] Hon[orii]*, *[De] cons[ulatu] Stil[ichonis]*
CLE	*Carmina Latina Epigraphica* (eds F. Bücheler and E. Lommatzsch)
Clem.	Clemens Alexandrinus, *Paed[agogus]*, *Protr[epticus]*, *Strom[ateis]*
C&M	*Classica et Mediaevalia*
CMa	Inscription ascribed to Cyrus at Pasargadae (Murghab) (see Kent, *Old Persian*)
CMG	*Corpus Medicorum Graecorum*
CML	*Corpus Medicorum Latinorum*
CNRS	Centre National de Recherche Scientifique
CO	*Classical Outlook*
Cod.	Codex
Cod. Iust.	Codex Iustinianus (Justinianic Code)
Cod. Theod.	Codex Theodosianus (Theodosian Code)
Colum.	Columella, *[de re] rust[ica]*
comm.	Commentary
Corn.	Cornutus
Corp. Herm.	Corpus Hermeticum
CPF	*Corpus dei papiri filosofici Greci e Latini*
CPh (also *CP*, *C Phil*)	*Classical Philology*
CPL	*Corpus Poetarum Latinorum*
CQ	*Classical Quarterly*
CR	*Classical Review*
CRAI (also *CR Acad Inscr.*)	*Comptes rendus de l'Académie des inscriptions et belles-lettres*
CRDAC	*Atti del Centro Ricerche e documentazione sull'antichità classica*
CretStud	*Cretan Studies*
CRF	*Comicorum Romanorum Fragmenta* (ed. O. Ribbeck)
CronASA	*Cronache di archeologia e di storia dell'arte*
Cron. Erc.	*Cronache ercolanesi*
CRR	*The Coinage of the Roman Republic* (ed. E. A. Sydenham)
CSCA	*California Studies in Classical Antiquity* (now *ClAnt*)
CTh	Codex Theodosianus (Theodosian code)
Curt.	Q. Curtius Rufus
CVA	*Corpus Vasorum Antiquorum*
CW	*Classical World*
Cyril.	Cyrillus, *Adv[ersus] Iul[ianum]*
DA	*Dissertations Abstracts* (microfilms: University of Michigan)
Dam.	Damasius, *[Vita] Isid[ori]*, *[de] princ[ipiis]*

DArch	*Dialoghi di archeologia*
DB	Inscription of Darius I at Bisitun (see Kent, *Old Persian*)
D.C.	Dio Cassius
DCB	*Dictionary of Christian Biography*
D. Chrys.	Dio Chrysostom
DCPP	*Dictionnaire de la civilisation phénicienne et punique*
DdA	*Dialoghi di archeologia*
DE	Inscription of Darius I at Elvend (see Kent, *Old Persian*)
Def. tab.	*Defixionum tabellae* (curse tablets)
Dem.	Demosthenes, *De cor[ona]*(= *on the Crown*), *Epit[aphios]*, *[Against] Lept[ines]*, *[Against] Meid[ias]* (other texts are also referred to by standard numeration)
Demad.	Demades
Democr.	Democritus (see DK for text)
De vir. Ill.	*De viris illustribus* (author unknown)
DFA[3]	*Dramatic Festivals of Athens* (A. W. Pickard-Cambridge, rev. J. Gould and D. M. Lewis)
DH	Inscription of Darius I at Hamadan (see Kent, *Old Persian*)
D.H.	see Dion. Hal.
DHA	*Dialogues d'histoire ancienne*
Dial. di Arch.	*Dialoghi di archeologia*
Did.	Didymus
Diels-Kranz, also DK	*Fragmente der Vorsokratiker* (eds H. Diels and W. Kranz)
Din.	Dinarchus
Dio Cass.	Dio Cassius
Dio Chrys.	Dio Chrysostom (= Dio Cocc[eianus]), *Or[ationes]*
Diod. Sic.	Diodorus Siculus
Dion. Hal.	Dionysus of Halicarnassus, *Ant[iquitates] Rom[anae]* (= *Roman Antiquities*), *[De] comp[ositione verborum]*, *De imit[atione]*, *[On] Dem[osthenes]*, *[On] Isoc[rates]*, *[On] Lysias*, *[Epistula ad] Pomp[eium]*, *[Ars] Rhet[orica]*, *[On] Thuc[ydides]*, *[De] vet[erum] cens[ura]*
Dion. Thrax	Dionysius Thrax
Dionys. Per.	Dionysius the Periegete
DK (also Diels-Kranz)	*Fragmente der Vorsokratiker* (eds H. Diels and W. Kranz)
D.L.	Diogenes Laertius
DNa	Inscription of Darius at Naqs-i-Rustam, numbered a, b etc. (see Kent, *Old Persian*)
DNP	*Der Neue Pauly* (see *RE*)
Donat.	Donatus, *Vit[a] Verg[ilii]*
DOP	*Dumbarton Oaks Papers*
Dor.	Doric (i.e. dialect)
Dox. Graec.	*Doxographi Graeci* (ed. H. Diels)
DP	Inscription of Darius I at Persepolis (see Kent, *Old Persian*)
DS	Daremberg and Saglio, *Dictionnaire des antiquités grecques et romaines*
D.S.	Diodorus Siculus
DSa	Inscription of Darius at Susa, numbered a, b etc. (see Kent, *Old Persian*)
DTC	*Dictionnaire de théologie catholique*

E.	see Eur.
EA	*Electronic Antiquity*, also *Epigraphica Anatolica*
EAA	*Enciclopedia dell'arte antica*
ECAGR	*Edinburgh Companion to Ancient Greece and Rome*
EClás	*Estudios clásicos*
EDH	Epigraphische Datenbank Heidelberg
ed. maior/minor	full or shorter edition
EEC	*Encyclopaedia of the Early Church*
EGF	*Epicorum Graecorum Fragmenta* (ed. M. Davies), also *Epicorum Graecorum Fragmenta* (ed. G. Kinkel)
Einzelschr.	Einzelschriften (i.e. monographs supplementary to a journal)
El.	Elamite (language of some Persian documents)
ElectronAnt	*Electronic Antiquity*
EMC	*Échos du monde classique (Classical Views)*
Emped.	Empedocles (see DK)
Enc. Ir.	*Enciclopedia Iranica*
Enn.	Enn[ius], *Ann[ales]*
Ep.	*Epistles*
Ep. Anat.	*Epigraphica Anatolica*
Epicharm.	Epicharmus
Epict.	Epictetus, *Ench[iridion]*, *Gnom[ologium]*
Epicurus	*Ep[istulae]*, *Ep[istula ad] H[ero]d[o]t[um]*, *Ep[istula ad] Men[oeceum]*, *Ep[istula ad] Pyth[oclem]*, *[de Rerum] Nat[ura]*, *Sent[entiae] Vat[icanae]*, *R[arae] S[ententiae]*
Epigr. Gr.	*Epigrammata Graeca ex lapidibus conlecta* (ed. G. Kaibel)
Epiph.	Epiphanius, *Adv[ersus] haer[eses]*
epit.	epitome
Epit. de Caes.	*Epitome de Caesaribus* (in Teubner ed. of Aurelius Victor)
Epit. Oxyrh.	*Epitome Oxyrhynchia* (of Livy)
Eratosth.	Eratosthenes
EstAnt	*Estudios de la antigüedad*
et al.	and others
Et. de Pap.	*Études de papyrologie*
Et. Magn.	*Etymologicum Magnum*
EtrStud	*Etruscan Studies*
Euc.	Euclid
Eudem.	Eudemus
Eunap.	Eunap., *V[itae] S[ophistarum]* (= *Lives of the Sophists*)
Eup.	Eupolis
Eur. (also E.)	Euripides, *Alc[estis]*, *Andr[omache]*, *Bacch[ae]*, *Cyc[lops]*, *El[ectra]*, *Hec[uba]*, *Hel[en]*, *Heracl[idae]*, *H[ercules]F[urens] (= Her[acles])*, *Hipp[olytus]*, *I[phigenia in] A[ulis]*, *I[phigenia in] T[auris]*, *Med[ea]*, *Or[estes]*, *Phoen[issae]*, *Rhes[us]**, *Suppl[ices]*, *Tro[ades]*
Eus.	Eusebius, *Chron[ica]*, *H[istoria] E[cclesiastica]*, *Praep[aratio] evang[elica]*, *Vit[a] Const[antini]*
Eust.	Eustathius, *[ad] Il[iadem]*, *[ad] Od[ysseam]*, *Prooem[ium commentariorum] Pind[aricorum]*
Eutocius	*In Arch[imedis] circ[uli] dim[ensionem]*
Eutr.	Eutropius
E&W	*East and West*

f., ff.	next, following (e.g. of pages or lines)
FA	*Fasti Archaeologici*
FCG	*Fragmenta Comicorum Graecorum* (ed. A. Meinecke)
FD	*Fouilles de Delphes*
Fest.	Festus
FGE	*Further Greek Epigrams* (ed. D. L. Page)
FGrHist	*Fragmente der griechischen Historiker* (ed. F. Jacoby)
FHG	*Fragmenta Historicorum Graecorum* (ed. C. Müller)
Firm. Mat.	Firmicus Maternus
fl.	Lat. *floruit*, (i.e. 'flourished' (conventional date of individual's prime)
Flor.	L. Annaeus Florus
FLP	*The Fragmentary Latin Poets* (ed. E. Courtney)
FOR	*Forma Orbis Romanae*
FPG	*Fragmenta Philosophorum Graecorum*
FPL	*Fragmenta Poetarum Latinorum*
FPR	*Fragmenta Poetarum Romanorum* (ed. E. Baehrens)
fr. (also F)	fragment (i.e. of author)
Front.	Frontinus, *[De] Aq[uae ductu urbis Romae]*, *Strat[egemata]*
Fronto	Fronto, *Ep[istulae]*
Fulg.	Fulgentius, *Myth[ologiae tres libri]*
FUR	*Forma Urbis Romae*
Gai.	Gaius, *Inst[itutiones]*
Gal.	Galen
GB	*Grazer Beiträge*
GCS	*Die griechischen christlichen Schriftsteller der erstern Jahrhunderte*
GDI	*Sammlung der griechischen Dialektinschriften* (eds H. Collitz et al.)
Gell.	Aulus Gellius, *N[octes] A[tticae]*
GeogrAnt	*Geographia Antiqua*
German.	Germanicus, *Arat[ea]*
GGM	*Geographici Graeci Minores* (ed. C. Müller)
GHI	*Greek Historical Inscriptions*: see ML, RO, Tod
GIFC	*Giornale italiano di filologia classica*
Gk.	Greek
GL, also *GLK*	*Grammatici Latini* (ed. H. Keil)
GLP	*Greek Literary Papyri* (ed. D. L. Page), also *Greek Lyric Poetry* (ed. M. L. West)
Gorg.	Gorgias, *Hel[en]*, *Pal[amedes]*
G&R	*Greece and Rome*
Gramm. Lat.	*Grammatici Latini* (ed. H. Keil)
GRBS	*Greek, Roman and Byzantine Studies*
GVI	*Griechische Vers-Inschriften* (ed. W. Peek)
H.	Homer, *Il[iad]*, *Od[yssey]*
Harp.	Harpocration
Harv. Stud.	*Harvard Studies in Classical Philology*
Harv. Theol. Rev.	*Harvard Theological Review*
HCA	*Historical Commentary on Arrian's* History of Alexander (ed. A. B. Bosworth)
HCP	*Historical Commentary on Polybius* (ed. F. W. Walbank)

HCT	*A Historical Commentary on Thucydides* (eds A. W. Gomme, A. Andrewes and K. J. Dover)
Hdn.	Herodianus
Hdt.	Herodotus
Hel.	Heliodorus, *Aeth[iopica]*
Hell. Oxy.	*Hellenica Oxyrhynchia*
Heraclid. Pont.	Heraclides Ponticus
Heraclit.	Heraclitus (see DK)
Hermog.	Hermogenes, *[peri] Id[eōn logou]*, *[de] Inv[entione]* (= *peri eureseōs*), *[peri tōn] stas[eōn]* (on Issues), *[peri] meth[ōdou demotētos]*, *Prog[ymnamata]*
Herod.	Herodas
Heron	Heron of Alexandria, *Pneum[atica]*
Hes.	Hesiod, *Cat[alogue of Women]*, *Op[era et Dies]* (= *Works and Days*), *Sc[utum Herculis]*, *Theog[ony]*
Hesp.	*Hesperia*
HHD	*Homeric Hymn to Demeter* (*HHA* = *Homeric Hymn to Apollo* etc.)
Hieron.	see Jer.
Hippoc., also *Hp.*	Hippocrates, *[de diaeta in morbis] acut[is]*, *[de] aer[a, aquis, locis]* (=*A[irs], W[aters], P[laces]*), *Epid[emiae]*, *[de] morb[o] sacr[o]* (= *On the Sacred Disease*), *[de] mul[ierum affectibus]*, *[de] virg[inibus morbis]*, *[de] v[etere] m[edicina]* (for questions of authorship see p. 424)
Hippol.	Hippolytus, *[Refutatio omnium] haer[esium]*
Hist.	*Historia*
Hist. Aug.	*Historia Augusta* (see SHA)
HM	*History of Macedonia* (by N. G. L. Hammond et al.)
Hom.	Homer, *Il[iad]*, *Od[yssey]*
Hom. Hymn Herm.	*Homeric Hymn to Hermes*
Hor.	Horace, *Ars p[oetica]*, *Carm[ina]* (= *Odes*), *Carm[en] saec[ulare]*, *Epist[ulae]*, *Epod[es]*, *Sat[ires]*
HRF	*Historicorum Romanorum Fragmenta* (ed. H. Peter)
HRRel	*Historicorum Romanorum Reliquiae* (ed. H. Peter)
HS	sesterce(s)
Hsch.	Hesychius
HSPh, also *HSCP*	*Harvard Studies in Classical Philology*
H&T	*History and Theory*
HThR	*Harvard Theological Review*
Hyg.	Hyginus
Hymn. Hom. Ap.	*Homeric Hymn to Apollo* etc. (see *HHD*)
Hymn. Mag.	*Hymni Magici*
Hymn. Orph.	*Hymni Orphici*
Hyp.	Hyperides, *[against] Ath[enagoras]*, *[against] Dem[osthenes]*, *Epit[aphios]*, *[for] Eux[enippus]*, *[for] Lyc[ophron]*, *[against] Phil[ip]*
hyp.	hypothesis
IA	*Iranica Antiqua*
i.a.	Lat. *inter alia*, i.e. among other things
Iamb.	Iamblichus, *[On the] Myst[eries]*, *Protr[epticus]*, *V[ita] P[ythagorae]*
ib., ibid.	Lat. ibidem, i.e. in the same work, in the same passage
Ibyc.	Ibycus

IC	*Inscriptiones Creticae*
ICS	*Illinois Classical Studies*
IDélos	*Inscriptions de Délos*
IE	Indo-European
IEG	*Iambi et Elegi Graeci* (ed. M. L. West)
IEJ	*Israel Exploration Journal*
IF	*Indogermanische Forschungen*
IFAO	*Institut français d'archéologie orientale au Caire*
IG	*Inscriptiones Graecae*
IGBulg	*Inscriptiones Graecae in Bulgaria repertae*
IGRom, also *IGRRP*	*Inscriptiones Graecae ad res Romanas pertinentes*
IJCT	*International Journal of the Classical Tradition*
IK	*Inschriften griechischer Städte aus Kleinasien*
ILabraunda	*Labraunda Swedish Excavations and Researches: The Greek Inscriptions* (ed. J. Crampa)
ILAlg	*Inscriptions latines de l'Algérie*
I. l. de Gaulle	*Inscriptions latines des trois Gaulles*
ILLRP	*Inscriptiones Latinae Liberae Rei Republicae*
ILS	*Inscriptiones Latinae Selectae* (ed. H. Dessau)
IMagn	*Die Inschriften von Magnesia am Maeander*
IMylasa	*Die Inschriften von Mylasa*
Inscr. Ital.	*Inscriptiones Italiae*
Inst. Iust.	*Institutiones Iustiniani* (Institutions of the Emperor Justinian)
Ion.	Ionic (i.e. dialect)
IPE	*Inscriptiones orae septentrionalis Ponti Euxini*
IranMitt	*Archäologische Mitteilungen aus Iran*
IrAnt	*Iranica Antiqua*
Is., also Isae.	Isaeus
ISestos	*Die Inschriften von Sestos und der Thrakischen Chersones*
Isid.	Isidorus, *de vir[is]ill[ustribus]*
Isoc.	Isocrates, *Bus[iris]*, *Panath[enaicus]*, *Paneg[yricus]* (other texts are also referred to by standard numeration)
IVO (or *IvO*)	*Inschriften von Olympia*
J.	see Joseph.
JA	*Journal asiatique*
JAC (= *ZAC*)	*Journal of Ancient Civilization*, also *Journal of Ancient Christianity*
JACT	Joint Association of Classical Teachers
Jahrb. f. cl. Phil.	*Jahrbücher fur classische Philologie*
JAOS	*Journal of the American Oriental Society*
JARCE	*Journal of the American Research Center in Egypt*
JbAC	*Jahrbuch für Antike und Christentum*
JBL	*Journal of Biblical Literature*
JCS	*Journal of Classical Studies*
JDAI	*Jahrbuch des Deutschen Archäologischen Instituts*
JEA	*Journal of Egyptian Archaeology*
JECS	*Journal of Early Christian Studies*
Jer.	Jerome, *ab Ab[raham]*, *Chron[ica]*, *de vir[is]ill[ustribus]*, *Ep[istles]*
JEurArch	*Journal of European Archaeology*

JFA	*Journal of Field Archaeology*
JGRS	*Journal of Greco-Roman Studies*
JHI	*Journal of the History of Ideas*
JHS	*Journal of Hellenic Studies*
JIES	*Journal of Indo-European Studies*
JKAF	*Jahrbuch für kleinasiatische Forschung*
JMA	*Journal of Mediterranean Archaeology*
JNES	*Journal of Near Eastern Studies*
JNG	*Jahrbuch für Numismatik und Geldgeschichte*
JNStud	*Journal of Neoplatonic Studies*
JÖAI	*Jahrshefte des österreichischen archäologischen Instituts in Wien*
JÖB	*Jahrbuch des österreichischen Byzantinistik*
Jord.	Jordanes, *Get[ica]*
Joseph.	Joseph[us], *A[ntiquitates] J[udaicae]* (= *Jewish Antiquities*), *[Contra] Ap[ionem]*, *B[ellum] J[udaicum]* (= *Jewish War*), *Vit[a]*
JRA	*Journal of Roman Archaeology*
JRMES	*Journal of Roman Military Equipment Studies*
JRS	*Journal of Roman Studies*
JSTOR	Journal Storage: The Scholarly Journal Archive
JThS	*Journal of Theological Studies*
Jul.	Julian (emperor), *Apophth[egmata]*, *Ep[istles]*, *Mis[opogon]*, *Or[ationes]*
Just. *Epit.*	Justin, *Epitome*
Justin, *Apol.*	Justin Martyr, *Apologia*
Juv.	Juvenal
JWI	*Journal of the Warburg and Courtauld Institutes*
K-A	R. Kassel and C. Austin (eds), *Poetae Comici Graeci*
KlPauly	*Der Kleine Pauly*
Kl. Schr.	*Kleine Schriften* (i.e. collected papers, of various authors)
Lactant.	Lactantius, *de Mort[ibus] Pers[ecutorum]*, *Div[inae] Inst[itutiones]*
LACTOR	*London Association of Classical Teachers – Original Records*
Lat.	Latin
LCM	*Liverpool Classical Monthly*
LEC	*Les Études classiques*
LGPN	*Lexicon of Greek Personal Names*
Lib.	Libanius
LibAnt	*Libya Antiqua*
LibStud	*Libyan Studies*
LIMC	*Lexicon Iconographicum Mythologiae Classicae*
LivAAA	*Liverpool Annals of Anthropology and Archaeology*
Liv. Andron.	Livius Andronicus, *Od[yssia]*
Livy	*Epit[ome]*, *Per[iochae]*
Longin. (also Long.)	Longinus, *[Ars] Rh[etorica]*
LP	E. Lobel and D. L. Page, *Poetarum Lesbiorum Fragmenta*
LSAG	*Local Scripts of Archaic Greece* (eds L. Jeffery and A. W. Johnston)
LSAM	*Lois sacrées de l'Asie Mineure*
LSCG	*Lois sacrées des cités grecques*
LSJ	Liddell and Scott (rev. H. Stuart Jones), *Greek-English Lexicon*

LSS	*Lois sacrées des cites grecques. Supplément*
Luc.	Lucan
Lucian	Lucian, *Alex[ander]*, *Anach[arsis]*, *Apol[ogia]*, *Cal[umniae non temere credendum]*, *Catapl[us]*, *Demon[ax]*, *de mort[e] peregr[ini]*, *Dial[ogi] d[eorum]*, *Dial[ogi] meret[ricii]*, *Dial[ogi] mort[uorum]*, *Her[odotus]*, *Hermot[imus]*, *[Quomodo] hist[oria] conscr[ibenda] sit*, *[Adversus] ind[octum]*, *Iupp[iter] trag[oedus]*, *[de] luct[u]*, *Macr[obii]*, *Nigr[inus]*, *Philops[eudes]*, *Pseudol[ogista]*, *[de] Salt[atione]*, *Scyth[a]*, *Somn[ium]*, *Symp[osium]*, *[de] Syr[ia] d[ea]*, *Tox[aris]*, *Trag[oedopodagra]*, *Ver[a] Hist[oria]* (1–2), *Vit[arum] auct[io]*
Lucil.	Lucilius
Lucr.	Lucretius
LXX	Septuagint
Lyc.	Lycurgus, *[Against] Leoc[rates]*
Lycoph.	Lycophron, *Alexandra*
Lydus	Lydus, *[de] mag[istratibus]*, *[de] mens[ibus]*
lyr. adesp.	lyrica adespota, i.e. anonymous lyric poems
Lys.	Lysias
MAAR	*Memoirs of the American Academy in Rome*
Macrob.	Macrobius, *[Commentarius ex Cicerone] in Somn[ium Scipionis]*, *Exc[erpta Grammatica]*, *Sat[urnalia]*
MadMitt	*Madrider Mitteilungen* (= *MDAI(M)*)
MAMA	*Monumenta Asiae Minoris Antiquae*
Man.	Manetho
Marcellin.	Marcellinus
Mart.	Martial, *Spect[acula]*
Mart. Cap.	Martianus Capella
M. Aur.	Marcus Aurelius, *Med[itations]*
MCSN	*Materiali e contributi per la storia della narrativa greco-latina*
MD	*Materiali e discussioni per l'analisi dei testi classici*
MDAI	*Mitteilungen des Deutschen Archäologischen Instituts* (different volumes for Athens (A), Rome (R), Madrid (M), Cairo (K), Istanbul (I))
MedArch	*Mediterranean Archaeology*
MediterrAnt	*Mediterraneo antico*
MEFR	*Mélanges d'archéologie et d'histoire de l'École française de Rome*
MEFRA	*Mélanges de l'École française de Rome. Antiquité*
Men.	Menander, *Dysk[olos]*, *Epit[repontes]*, *Georg[os]*, *Hēr[ōs]*, *Kith[aristēs]*, *Kol[ax]*, *Kon[eazomenai]*, *Mis[oumenoi]*, *Per[inthia]*, *Phasm[a]*, *P[eri]k[eiromenē]*, *Sam[ia]*
Men. Rhet.	Menander Rhētor
MH	*Museum Helveticum*
MHA	*Memorias de historia Antigua*
MHR	*Mediterranean Historical Review*
MIFAO	*Mémoires de l'Institut français d'archéologie orientale*
Mimn.	Mimnermus
Min. Fel.	Minucius Felix, *Oct[avius]*
Mir. Ausc.	*De mirabilibus auscultationibus* (author unknown)
ML	R. Meiggs and D. Lewis, *A Selection of Greek Historical Inscriptions to the End of the Fifth Century* BC

Mnemos.	*Mnemosyne*
MNIR	*Mededelingen van het Nederlandsch historisch Instituut te Rome*
Mosch.	Moschus, *Ep[itaphios] Bion[is]*
MRR	*Magistrates of the Roman Republic* (ed. T. R. S. Broughton)
MS (plural: MSS)	manuscript
MusHelv	*Museum Helveticum*
Muson.	Musonius Rufus
MW	M. McCrum and A. G. Woodhead, *Select Documents of the Flavian Emperors*
M-W	R. Merkelbach and M. L. West, *Fragmenta Hesiodea*
Naev.	Naevius
NC	*Numismatic Chronicle*
NECJ	*New England Classical Journal*
NECN	*New England Classical Newsletter*
Nemes.	Nemesianus, *Cyn[egetica]*, *Ecl[ogae]*
Nep.	Cornelius Nepos
Nic.	Nicander, *Alex[ipharmaca]*, *Ther[iaca]*
Nic. Dam.	Nicolaus of Damascus
Non.	Nonius
Nonn.	Nonnus, *Dion[ysiaca]*
Not. Dign.	*Notitia dignitatum*
Not. Scav., also *NSc*, *NSA*	*Notizie degli scavi di antichità*
NP	*Der Neue Pauly (see* RE*)*
NT	Novum Testamentum = New Testament
NTS	*New Testament Studies*
Num. Chron.	*Numismatic Chronicle*
Numen.	Numenius
NZ	*Numismatische Zeitschrift*
OA	*Oriens Antiquus*
OAth	*Opuscula Atheniensia*
OCD	*Oxford Classical Dictionary*
OCT	Oxford Classical Texts (of specific authors, so e.g. OCT of Aeschylus)
ODB	*Oxford Dictionary of Byzantium*
ODCC	*Oxford Dictionary of the Christian Church*
OGIS	*Orientis Graeci Inscriptiones Selectae*
OJA	*Oxford Journal of Archaeology*
Olymp.	Olympiodorus
OP	Old Persian
Op. Arch.	*Opuscula Archaeologica*
Op. Ath.	*Opuscula Atheniensia*
Or.	*Oration*
ORF	*Oratorum Romanorum Fragmenta*
ORom	*Opuscula Romana*
Oros.	Orosius
Orph.	Orphica, *A[rgonautica]*, *H[ymns]*, *L[ithica]*
OSAPh	*Oxford Studies in Ancient Philosophy*
OT	Old Testament

OTerr	*Orbis Terrarum*
Ov.	Ovid, *Am[ores]*, *Ars am[atoria]*, *Fast[i]*, *Hal[ieuticon liber]*, *Her[oides]*, *Ib[is]*, *Medic[amina faciei]*, *Met[amorphoses]*, *[Epistulae ex] Pont[o]*, *Rem[edia] am[oris]*, *Trist[ia]*
P. or *P.*	Papyrus: so e.g. *P. Berol.*, *P. Tebt.*, *P. Oxy.*, *P. Petr.*, *P. Grenf.* etc., usually named after a place (Berlin, Oxyrhynchus, Tebtunis) or an individual (Petrie, Grenfell)
PA	*Prosopographia Attica* (ed. J. Kirchner)
PACA	*Proceedings of the African Classical Association*
PalEQ	*Palestine Exploration Quarterly*
Parm.	Parmenides (see DK)
ParPass	*see PP*
Parth.	Parthenius
PAS	*Proceedings of the Aristotelian Society*
Paulus, *Sent.*	Iulius Paulus, *Sententiae*
Paus.	Pausanias
PBA	*Proceedings of the British Academy*
PBSR	*Papers of the British School at Rome*
PCA	*Proceedings of the Classical Association*
PCG	*R. Kassel and C. Austin, Poetae Comici Graeci*
PCIA	*Popoli e civiltà dell'Italia antica*
PCPhS (also PCPS)	*Proceedings of the Cambridge Philological Society*
PECS	*Princeton Encyclopedia of Classical Sites*
PEQ	*Palestine Exploration Quarterly*
Pers.	Persius
Petron.	Petronius, *Sat[yrica]*
PFT	*Persepolis Fortification Texts* (ed. R. T. Hallock)
PGM	*Papyri Graecae Magicae* (eds K. Preisendanz et al.)
Ph.	Philo
Pherec.	Pherecydes
Philostr.	Philostratus, *Her[oicus]*, *Imag[ines]*, *V[ita] A[pollonii]*, *V[itae] Soph[istarum]*
Phil. Wochenschr.	*Philologische Wochenschrift*
Phld.	Philodemus
Phleg.	Phlegon of Tralles
Phot.	Photius, *Bibl[iotheca]*
PIE	Proto-Indo-European
Pind. (also Pi.)	*Isthm[ian Odes]*, *Nem[ean Odes]*, *Ol[ympian Odes]*, *Pae[ans]*, *Pyth[ian Odes]*
PIR	*Prosopographia Imperii Romani*
Pl.	Plato, *Alc[ibiades]**, *Am[atores]**, *Ap[ology]*, *Ax[iochus]**, *Ch[a]rm[ides]*, *Clit[ophon]**, *Crat[ylus]*, *Cri[to]*, *Criti[as]*, *Def[initiones]**, *Demod[ocus]**, *Epin[omis]**, *Er[y]x[ias]**, *Euth[y]d[emus]*, *Euth[y]phr[o]*, *G[o]rg[ias]*, *Hipparch[us]**, *H[ip]p[ias] mai[or]**, *H[ip]p[ias] min[or]*, *Ion*, *Lach[es]*, *Leg[es]* (= *Laws*), *Ly[sis]*, *Menex[enus]*, *Men[o]*, *Min[os]**, *Ph[ae]d[o]*, *Ph[ae]dr[us]*, *Ph[i]l[e]b[us]*, *P[o]l[i]t[icus]* (= *Statesman*), *P[a]rm[enides]*, *Pr[o]t[agoras]*, *Resp[ublica]* (= *Republic*), *Sis[yphus]**, *Soph[ist]*, *Symp[osium]*, *Th[ea]g[es]**, *Th[eae]t[etus]*, *Ti[maeus]*, *[de] Virt[ute]**

Platon.	Platonius, *[de] Diff[erentia] Com[oediarum]*
Plaut.	Plautus, *Amph[itruo]*, *Asin[aria]*, *Bacch[ides]*, *Capt[ivi]*, *Cas[ina]*, *Cist[ellaria]*, *Curc[ulio]*, *Men[aechmi]*, *Merc[ator]*, *Mil[es gloriosus]*, *Most[ellaria]*, *Poen[ulus]*, *Pseud[olus]*, *Rud[ens]*, *Stich[us]*, *Trin[ummus]*
Plin.	Pliny (the elder), *H[istoria] N[aturalis]* Pliny (the younger), *Ep[istles]*, *Pan[egyricus]*, *[Epistulae ad] Tra[ianum]*
PLM	*Poetae Latini Minores*
PLRE	*Prosopography of the Later Roman Empire* (eds A. H. M. Jones, J. R. Martindale and J. Morris)
Plut.	Plutarch, *Aem[ilius Paulus]*, *Ages[ilaus]*, *Alc[ibiades]*, *Alex[ander]*, *Ant[onius]*, *Arat[us]*, *Arist[ides]*, *Artox[erxes]*, *Brut[us]*, *Caes[ar]*, *Cam[illus]*, *Cat[o] Mai[or]*, *Cat[o] Min[or]*, *C[aius] Gracch[us]*, *Cic[ero]*, *Cim[on]*, *Cleom[enes]*, *Comp[aratio]* (of two subjects of parallel lives), *Crass[us]*, *Demetr[ius]*, *Dem[osthenes]*, *Eum[enes]*, *Fab[ius]*, *Flam[ininus]*, *Galb[a]*, *Luc[ullus]*, *Lyc[urgus]*, *Lys[ander]*, *Mar[ius]*, *Marc[ellus]*, *Mor[alia]* (including a number of smaller works with short titles), *Nic[ias]*, *Num[a]*, *Oth[o]*, *Pel[opidas]*, *Per[icles]*, *Phil[opoemen]*, *Phoc[ion]*, *Pomp[eius]*, *Publ[icola]*, *Pyrrh[us]*, *Rom[ulus]*, *Sert[orius]*, *Sol[on]*, *Sull[a]*, *Them[istocles]*, *Thes[eus]*, *Ti[berius] Gracch[us]*, *Tim[oleon]*, *Vit[ae Parallelae]* (paired lives of a Roman and a Greek)
PMG	*Poetae Melici Graeci* (ed. D. L. Page)
PMGF	*Poetarum Melicorum Graecorum Fragmenta* (ed. M. Davies)
Poet. Rom. Vet.	*Poetarum Romanorum Veterum Reliquiae* (ed. E. Diehl)
Poll.	Pollux, *Onom[asticon]*
Polyaen.	Polyaenus, *Strat[egemata]*
Polyb.	Polybius
Pomp.	Pomponius
Porph.	Porphyry, *[de] abst[inentia]*, *de antr[o] nymph[arum]*, *[Vita] Plot[ini]*
PP	*La parola del passato*
P&P	*Past and Present*
PPF	*Poetarum Philosophorum Graecorum Fragmenta* (ed. H. Diels)
praef.	*praefatio*
PRIA	*Proceedings of the Royal Irish Academy*
Prisc.	Priscian, *Inst[itutiones] gramm[aticae]*, *[Institutio] de nom[ine et] pron[omine et] verb[o]*
Procl.	Proclus, *Hypotyp[osis]*, *in [Platonis] R[espublicam] Commentarii*, *in [Platonis] Ti[maeum] Commentarii*
Procop.	Procopius, *[de] Aed[ificiis]*, *[Historia] Arc[ana]* (= *Secret History*), *[de Bello] Goth[ico]*, *[de Bello] Pers[ico]*, *[de Bello] Vand[alico]*
Prop.	Propertius
Protag.	Protagoras (see DK)
Prudent.	Prudentius, *Cath[emerina]*, *C[ontra] Symm[achum]*, *Perist[ephanon]*
Ps.-	Pseudo-
Ptol.	Ptolemy (mathematician), *Alm[agest]*, *Geog[raphia]*, *Harm[onica]*, *Tetr[abiblos]*
PVS	*Proceedings of the Virgil Society*
PW	see *RE*
PW	*Philologische Wochenschrift*
Pythag.	Pythagoras (see DK)
QS	*Quaderni di storia*

QUCC	*Quaderni urbinati di cultura classica*
Quint.	Quintilian, *Ep[istula] ad Tryph[onem]*, *Inst[itutio] oratoria*
Quint. Smyrn.	Quintus Smyrnaeus
RA	*Revue archéologique*
RAC	*Rivista di archeologia cristiana*
RAL	*Rendiconti della Classe di scienze morali, storiche e filologiche dell'Accademia dei Lincei*
RBPh	*Revue belge de philologie et d'histoire*
RE	*Realencyclopädie der classischen Altertumswissenschaft* (shorter and new versions are *Der Neue Pauly* – an English translation of which is in progress – and *Der Kleine Pauly*)
REA	*Revue des études anciennes*
REByz	*Revue des études Byzantines*
REC	*Revista de estudios clásicos*
REG	*Revue des études grecques*
REgypt	*Revue d'égyptologie*
REL	*Revue des études latines*
RELat	*Revista de estudios latinos*
RendLinc	*Rendiconti della Classe di scienze morali, storiche e filologiche dell'Accademia dei Lincei*
rev.	revised
Rev. Arch.	*Revue archéologique*
Rev. Et. Anc.	*Revue des études anciennes*
Rev. Et. Grec.	*Revue des études grecques*
Rev. Et. Lat.	*des études latines*
Rh. Mus. (also *RhM*)	*Rheinisches Museum für Philologie*
RHR	*Revue de l'histoire des religions*
RIB	*The Roman Inscriptions of Britain*
RIC	*Roman Imperial Coinage* (H. Mattingly, E. A. Sydenham et al.)
RIL	*Rendiconti dell'Istituto lombardo, Classe di lettere, scienze morali e storiche*
Riv. Fil.	*Rivista di Filologia*
RivStPomp	*Rivista di studi pompeiani*
RM	*Rheinische Museum*
RN	*Revue numismatique*
RO	*Greek Historical Inscriptions 404–323* B.C. (eds P. J. Rhodes and R. Osborne)
RO	*Römisches Österreich*
RömMitt	*Römische Mitteilungen* (= *MDAI(R)*)
RPh	*Revue de philologie, de littérature et d'histoire anciennes*
RPhA	*Revue de philosophie ancienne*
RRC	*Roman Republican Coinage* (ed. M. H. Crawford)
RSA (also *RStAnt*)	*Rivista storica dell'antichità*
RSC	*Rivista di studi classici*
SAGT	*Studies in Ancient Greek Topography* (ed. W. K. Pritchett)
Sall.	Sallust, *[Epistulae] ad Caes[arem] sen[em]**, *[Bellum] Cat[ilinae]*, *Hist[oriae]*, *[Bellum] Iug[urthinum]*
Sapph.	Sappho
Satyr.	Satyrus, *Vit[a] Eur[ipidis]*

SAWW	*Sitzungsberichte der Österreichischen Akademie der Wissenschaft in Wien*
SBAW	*Sitzungsberichte der Bayerischen Akademie der Wissenschaften*
SC	*senatus consultum*
sc.	Lat. scilicet, i.e. that is to say, namely
schol.	scholiast (i.e. commentator on ancient author)
SCI	*Scripta Classica Israelica*
SCO	*Studi Classici e Orientali*
Scol. Anon.	*Scolia Anonyma* (in *Anth. Lyr. Graec.*)
Scol. Att.	*Scolia Attica* (in *Anth. Lyr. Graec.*)
Scymn.	Scymnus
SDAW	*Sitzungsberichte der Deutschen Akademie der Wissenschaften zu Berlin*
SE	*Studi etruschi*
SEG	*Supplementum Epigraphicum Graecum*
Semon.	Semonides
Sen.	Seneca (the elder), *Con[troversiarum] ex[cerpta]*, *Controv[ersiae]*, *Suas[oriae]* Seneca (the younger), *Apocol[ocyntosis]*, *[de] Ben[eficiis]*, *[de] Clem[entia]*, *[De] Const[antia sapientis]*, *Dial[ogi]*, *Ep[istulae]*, *Epigr[ammata super exilio]*, *[Ad] Helv[iam]*, *Med[ea]*, *[de] Prov[identia]*, *Q[uaestiones] nat[urales]*, *[de] Tranq[uillitate animi]*
Serv.	Servius
SHA	Scriptores Historiae Augustae, *Ael[ius]*, *Alex[ander] Sev[erus]*, *Ant[oninus] Pius*, *Aurel[ian]*, *Avid[ius] Cass[ius]*, *Clod[ius]*, *Comm[odus]*, *Did[ius] Iul[ianus]*, *Hadr[ian]*, *Heliogab[alus]*, *M[arcus Aurelius] Ant[oninus] (= Caracalla)*, *Marc[us]*, *Max[iminus]*, *Pert[inax]*, *Pesc[ennius] Nig[er]*, *Prob[us]*, *Sev[erus]*, *Tyr[anni] Trig[inta]*, *[Lucius] Verus*
SHAW	*Sitzungsberichte der Heidelberger Akademie der Wissenschaften*
Sid. Apoll.	Sidonius Apollinaris, *Carm[ina]*, *Ep[istles]*
SIFC	*Studi italiani di filologia classica*
SIG	*Sylloge Inscriptionum Graecarum* (= *Syll*[3])
Sil.	Silius Italicus, *Pun[ica]*
Simon.	Simonides
Simpl.	Simplicius
Sitz.	*Sitzungsberichte* (of Academy or Society, *e.g. der Österreichischen Akademie der Wissenschaft in Wien*)
SMEA	*Studi micenei ed egeo-anatolici*
SNG	*Sylloge Nummorum Graecorum*
SO	*Symbolae Osloenses*
Socrates, *Hist. Eccl.*	*Historia Ecclesiastica*
Solin.	Solinus
Soph.	Sophocles, *Aj[ax]*, *Ant[igone]*, *El[ectra]*, *O[edipus at] C[olonus]*, *O[edipus] T[yrannus]*, *Phil[octetes]*, *Trach[iniai]*
Sor.	Soranus, *Gyn[aeceia]*
Sozom.	Sozomen, *Hist[oria] eccl[esiastica]*
Speus.	Speusippus
SSR	*Socratis et Socraticorum Reliquiae* (ed. G. Giannantoni)
SStor	*Storia della storiografia*
Stat.	Statius, *Achil[leis]*, *Silv[ae]*, *Theb[ais]* (= *Thebaid*)
Steph. Byz.	Stephanus Byzantinus
StEtr	*Studi Etruschi*

StIran	*Studia Iranica*
Stob.	Stobaeus, *Ecl[ogai]*, *Flor.* = *Anthologion*
Str.	Strabo
str.	Strophe
StSard	*Studi Sardi*
StudClas	*Studii clasice*
Suet.	Suetonius, *[Divus] Aug[ustus]*, *[Gaius] Calig[ula]*, *[Divus] Claud[ius]*, *Dom[itian]*, *Galb[a]*, *[de] Gram[maticis]*, *[Divus] Iul[ius]*, *Ner[o]*, *[de] Poet[is]*, *Rel[iquiae]*, *[de] Rhet[oribus]*, *Tib[erius]*, *[Divus] Tit[us]*, *Vesp[asian]*, *Vit[ellius]*, *Vita Hor[atii]*, *Vita Luc[ani]*
Supp. Aesch.	*Supplementum Aeschyleum* (ed. H. J. Mette)
Suppl. Hell.	*Supplementum Hellenisticum* (eds H. Lloyd-Jones and P. Parsons)
s.v.	Lat. *sub verbo*, i.e. under the heading of (used esp. of ancient encyclopedias such as the Suda)
SVF	*Stoicorum Veterum Fragmenta* (ed. H. von Arnim)
Syll[3]	*Sylloge Inscriptionum Graecarum* (= *SIG*)
SyllClass	*Syllecta Classica*
Symm.	Symmachus, *Ep[istulae]*, *Rel[ationes]*
T	Lat. *testimonium*, i.e. piece of (ancient) evidence (concerning an author)
Tab.	Lat. *Tabula*, i.e. table or law, hence Twelve Tables or e.g. *Tab[ula] Agn[oniensis]*
Tac.	Tacitus, *Agr[icola]*, *Ann[als]*, *Dial[ogus de oratoribus]*, *Germ[ania]*, *Hist[oriae]*
TAPhA (also *TAPA*)	*Transactions of the American Philological Association*
TAPhS	*Transactions of the American Philosophical Society*
Ter.	Terence, *Ad[elphoe]*, *An[dria]*, *Eun[uchus]*, *H{e}aut[on timorumenos]*, *Hec[yra]*, *Phorm[io]*
Tert.	Tertullian, *Ad nat[iones]*, *Adv[ersus] Valent[inianos]*, *Apol[ogeticus]*, *de [testimonio] anim[ae]*, *de bapt[ismo]*, *de monog[amia]*, *de praescr[iptione] haeret[icorum]*, *de spect[aculis]*
Test.	Lat. *testimonium*, i.e. piece of (ancient) evidence (concerning an author)
TGF	*Tragicorum Graecorum Fragmenta* (eds A. Nauck et al.)
Them.	Themistius, *Or[ationes]*
Theoc.	Theocritus, *Epig[rammata]*, *Id[ylls]*
Theoph.	Theophilus, *Ad Autol[ycum]*
Theophr.	Theophrastus, *[de] Caus[is] Pl[antarum]* (also *CP*), *Char[acters]*, *Hist[oria] Pl[antarum]* (also *HP*), *[de] Ign[e]*, *[de] Lap[idibus]*, *[de] Lass[itudine]*, *Metaph[ysica]*, *[de] Od[oribus]*, *Phys[icorum] Op[iniones]*, *[de] Sens[ibus]*, *[de] Sign[is Tempestatum]*, *[de] Sud[ore]*, *[de] Vent[is]*, *[de] Vert[igine]*
Theopomp.	Theopompus
Thgn.	Theognis
Thphr.	see Theophr.
Thuc.	Thucydides
Tib.	Tibullus
Tim.	Timotheus, *Pers[ae]*
TIR	*Tabula Imperii Romani*
TLG	*Thesaurus Linguae Graecae*
TLL	*Thesaurus Linguae Latinae*

TLS	*Times Literary Supplement*
Tod	M. N. Tod, *Greek Historical Inscriptions*
TPhS	*Transactions of the Philological Society*
TRF	*Tragicorum Romanorum Fragmenta* (ed. O. Ribbeck)
TrGF	*Tragicorum Graecorum Fragmenta* (eds B. Snell et al.)
Tzetz.	Tzetzes, *[Historiarum variarum] Chil[iades]*
Ulp.	Ulpian
Val. Max.	Valerius Maximus
Varro	Varro, *[de] ling[ua] Latina*, *[de re] rust[ica]*, *Sat[urae] Men[ippeae]*
Vatin.	Vatinius
VDI	*Vestnik drevnej istorii (Revue d'histoire ancienne)*
Veg.	Vegetius, *[de re] mil[itari]*
Vell. Pat.	Velleius Paterculus
Verg., also Virg.	Virgil, *Aen[eid]*, *Catal[epton]*, *Ecl[ogues]*, *G[eorgics]*
Vett. Val.	Vettius Valens
Vig. Christ.	*Vigiliae Christianae*
Vit.	Lat. *Vita*, i.e. Life, hence *Vit[a] Aesch[yli]*, *Vit[a] Eur[pidi]* etc. (see respective OCT editions for texts)
Vitr.	Vitruvius, *de Arch[itectura]*
Vopiscus, *Cyn.*	Vopiscus, *Cynegetica*
VT	*Vetus Testamentum* (= *Old Testament*)
WdF	*Wege der Forschung*
WS	*Wiener Studien*
XE	Inscription of Xerxes at Elvend (see Kent, *Old Persian*)
Xen.	Xenophon, *Ages[ilaus]*, *Anab[asis]*, *Apol[ogia]*, *Ath[enaion] Pol[iteia]**, *Cyn[egeticus]*, *Cyr[opaedia]*, *[de] eq[uitandi ratione]*, *[de] eq[uitum] mag[istro]*, *Hell[enica]* (also *HG*), *Hier[o]*, *Lac[edaimoniōn] Pol[iteia]* (= *Constitution of the Spartans*), *Mem[orabilia]*, *Oec[onomicus]*, *Symp[osium]*, *[de] vect[igalibus]* (= *Por[oi]*)
XH	Inscription of Xerxes at Hamadan
XPa	Inscription of Xerxes at Persepolis, numbered a, b, c etc. (see Kent, *Old Persian*)
XSa	Inscription of Xerxes at Susa, numbered a, b, c etc. (see Kent, *Old Persian*)
YClS	*Yale Classical Studies*
ZAC	*Zeitschrift für antikes Christentum* (=*JAC*)
ZDMG	*Zeitschrift der Deutschen Morgenländischen Gesellschaft*
Zen.	Zenobius
ZfA	*Zeitschrift für Archäologie*
Zonar.	Zonaras
Zos.	Zosimus
ZPE	*Zeitschrift für Papyrologie und Epigraphik*

Contributors

Editors

Edward Bispham teaches Ancient History at Brasenose and St Anne's Colleges, Oxford. He has published a number of articles on Roman public inscriptions, and on early Roman colonisation. He edited (with Christopher Smith) *Religion in Archaic and Republican Rome and Italy* (2000) and is currently editing volumes on Pliny and on the Roman Empire, as well as forming part of a collaborative project on the fragmentary Roman historians. Monographs on Italy after the Social War, and on the Roman Republic, are in press or forthcoming. He is co-director of a landscape archaeology project and field school (with Prof. S. Kane) in central Italy (the Sangro valley). Ongoing research includes a biography of the emperor Macrinus (with Robert Coates-Stephens).

Thomas Harrison is Rathbone Professor of Ancient History and Classical Archaeology at the University of Liverpool; he was formerly a British Academy Postdoctoral Fellow at University College London, and Lecturer in Ancient History at the University of St Andrews. His publications include *Divinity and History: The Religion of Herodotus* (2000), *The Emptiness of Asia: Aeschylus'* Persians *and the History of the Fifth Century* (2000), (as editor) *Greeks and Barbarians* (2002) and *Greek Religion: Belief and Experience* (2007).

Brian A. Sparkes studied at King's College London and the British School of Archaeology at Athens. He worked for the Agora Excavations in Athens and recently retired from the post of Professor of Classical Archaeology at Southampton University. His publications include *Black and Plain Pottery of the 6th, 5th, and 4th centuries* BC (with Lucy Talcott, 1970), *Greek Pottery: An Introduction* (1991), *Greek Art* (1991) and *The Red and the Black* (1996). He was Honorary Secretary of the Society for the Promotion of Hellenic Studies 1995–2004, President of the Joint Association of Classical Teachers 2001–3 and President of the Classical Association 2004–5.

Other contributors

Clifford Ando is Associate Professor of Classics, History and Law at the University of Southern California. He writes on the history of law, religion and culture in the Roman world. He is author of *Imperial Ideology and Provincial Loyalty in the Roman Empire* (2000), and editor of *Roman Religion* (2003).

Alastair Blanshard is a lecturer in Ancient History at the University of Sydney. He has published on aspects of ancient democracy, rhetoric, sexuality and classical reception; his *Hercules: Scenes from a Heroic Life* was published in 2005.

Lisa Bligh was formerly Lecturer in Ancient History at St Hilda's College, Oxford. After undergraduate studies in her native New Zealand, she completed a doctorate at Edinburgh University in 1999, and was subsequently a Junior Research Fellow at Worcester College, Oxford.

Tom Boiy is a Postdoctoral Fellow of the Fund for Scientific Research – Flanders (Belgium) at the Department of Oriental Studies, Katholieke Universiteit Leuven. He specialises in Early Hellenistic, Seleucid and Parthian Babylonia; his *Late Achaemenid and Hellenistic Babylon* was published in 2004.

Kai Brodersen is Professor of Ancient History at the Universitaet Mannheim, and has been a Visiting Fellow at both Newcastle upon Tyne and St. Andrews. He has published on Greek and Roman historiography, geography and paradoxography, on ancient cartography and conceptualisations of space, and on popularising the classics.

Philip Burton is Senior Research Fellow in Theology in the University of Birmingham, and Lecturer in Greek and Latin in the University of St Andrews. His works include *The Old Latin Gospels* (2000) and a translation of Augustine's *Confessions* (2001). He is currently working on an edition of the Old Latin manuscripts of the Gospel according to John, and a book on language in Augustine's *Confessions.*

Clive Cheesman, Rouge Dragon Pursuivant at the College of Arms, was formerly a curator in the Department of Coins and Medals of the British Museum and has lectured at Birkbeck College London. His Ph.D. thesis was on Roman onomastics, on which he is writing a book, and his research interests include the history of antiquarianism, and ancestry and genealogical memory in the Roman world.

Alison E. Cooley, Lecturer in Classics and Ancient History, University of Warwick, has edited several books about inscriptions, including *The Afterlife of Inscriptions* (2000) and *Becoming Roman, Writing Latin?* (2002). She is joint series editor of Oxford Studies in Ancient Documents. She is the author of *Pompeii* (2003) and *Pompeii: A Sourcebook* (2004), and is currently working on a new edition of the *Res Gestae* (with G. J. Oliver) and *The Cambridge Handbook to Latin Epigraphy*.

Simon Corcoran is Research Fellow in the Department of History, University College London, working on the Volterra Roman Law projects (www.ucl.ac.uk/history/volterra). He is the author of *The Empire of the Tetrarchs: Imperial Pronouncements and Government* AD *284–324* (rev edn 2000).

Jon Coulston is a lecturer in the School of Classics at the University of St Andrews. His research concerns military history, the Roman army, military equipment, Roman sculpture and the archaeology of the city of Rome. Numerous publications include (with M. C. Bishop) *Roman Military Equipment from the Punic Wars to the Fall of Rome* (1993, 2nd edn 2006). He is at present preparing a monograph on Trajan's Column.

David Creese is Assistant Professor of Classics at the University of British Columbia. His primary research interest is Greek and Roman music, especially Greek harmonic theory, and music and Graeco-Roman society. He is currently completing a book on the monochord and its place in the development of Greek harmonic science.

Armand D'Angour is Fellow and Tutor in Classics at Jesus College, Oxford. He has published articles on ancient Greek music and on Roman poetry, and was commissioned by the International Olympic Committee to compose a Pindaric *Ode to Athens* for the 2004 Olympic Games. He is currently completing a book on ancient Greek responses to novelty and innovation, and plans to write a truly accessible guide to ancient metre.

Helen Dixon, currently a British Academy Postdoctoral Fellow at the Warburg Institute, University of London, specialises in Latin palaeography, the transmission of Latin texts and the history of classical scholarship. She has published articles on manuscripts of Tibullus and contributed to *A Catalogue of Books Printed in the Fifteenth Century Now Kept in the Bodleian Library*. She is now writing a book on the Renaissance scholar Giulio Pomponio Leto.

Bruce Gibson is Lecturer in Classics at the University of Liverpool, and a specialist in the literature of the Roman Empire. His edition, translation and commentary on Statius, *Silvae* 5, will be published in 2006, and he is currently working on Pliny's *Panegyricus*. His publications include articles on Catullus, Horace, Ovid, Statius, Tacitus and Apuleius.

Mark Golden is Professor of Classics, University of Winnipeg. He is the author of *Children and Childhood in Classical Athens* (1990), *Sport and Society in Ancient Greece* (1998) and *Sport in the Ancient World from A to Z* (2003), and the co-editor (with Peter Toohey) *of Inventing Ancient Culture* (1997) and *Sex and Difference in Ancient Greece and Rome* (2003).

Richard Gordon was a pupil of M. I. Finley at Cambridge, lectured in Ancient Civilisation at the University of East Anglia (1970–88), and is now a private scholar in Germany. He has worked mainly on Graeco-Roman religions and magic. His publications include *Image and Value in the Graeco-Roman world* (1996) and 'Imagining Greek and Roman magic' in B. Ankarloo & S. Clark (eds), *The Athlone History of Witchcraft and Magic in Europe, 2: Ancient Greece and Rome* (1999), pp. 159–275.

Emily Greenwood is a lecturer in Greek Literature at the University of St Andrews. She has published articles on Derek Walcott, the reception of classics in the Caribbean, and Greek historiography. Her *Thucydides and the Shaping of History* was published by Duckworth in 2006.

Lorna Hardwick teaches in the Department of Classical Studies at the Open University, where she is Professor of Classical Studies and Director of the Research Project on the Reception of Classical Texts and Images in Modern Poetry and Drama (www2.open.ac.uk/ClassicalStudies/GreekPlays). Her publications include *Reception Studies* (*Greece and Rome* New Surveys in the Classics 33) (2003).

Johannes Haubold is Leverhulme Lecturer in Greek Literature at the University of Durham. He is the author of *Homer's People: Epic Poetry and Social Formation* (2000) and co-author of *Homer: The Resonance of Epic* (2004).

Olivier Hekster is Van der Leeuw Professor in Ancient History at the Radboud University, Nijmegen, and was previously Fellow and Tutor in Ancient History at Merton College, Oxford. He is author of *Commodus: An Emperor at the Crossroads* (2002) and co-editor of *Representation and Perception of Roman Imperial Power* (2004) and *Imaginary Kings: Royal Images in the Ancient Near East, Greece and Rome*. His research focuses on Roman ideology.

Martin Henig is Visiting Lecturer in Roman Art at the University of Oxford and Supernumerary Fellow of Wolfson College, Oxford. He has been Honorary Editor of the British Archaeological Association since 1985. Among his publications on ancient art and society are (as editor) *A Handbook of Roman Art* (1985), *Classical Gems in the Fitzwilliam Museum, Cambridge* (1994), *The Art of Roman Britain* (1995), *The Heirs of King Verica* (2002) and (with Arthur Macgregor) *Catalogue of the Engraved Gems and Finger-Rings in the Ashmolean II, Roman* (2004).

J. D. Hill is Curator at the British Museum responsible for the British and European Iron Age, and has carried out fieldwork in Denmark and Britain. He has published widely on different aspects of Iron Age society, religion and material culture.

Alice König is a Lecturer in Latin and Classical Studies at the University of St Andrews. She is a specialist in Latin technical writing, ancient geography and travel-writing, and in technical and scientific knowledge in the Roman Empire.

Jason König is Lecturer in Greek and Classical Studies at the University of St Andrews. He has written a range of articles on the Greek literature and culture of the Roman Empire, and is the author of *Athletics and Literature in the Roman Empire* (2005). He is currently working on a book on narrative representations of consumption and the symposium in the first to fifth centuries AD.

David Konstan is the John Rowe Workman Distinguished Professor of Classics and Professor of Comparative Literature at Brown University. Among his books are *Roman Comedy* (1983), *Sexual Symmetry: Love in the Ancient Novel and Related Genres* (1994), *Greek Comedy and Ideology* (1995), *Friendship in the Classical World* (1997) and *Pity Transformed* (2001). He was President of the American Philological Association in 1999.

Irene Lemos is Reader in Classical Archaeology at Merton College, Oxford, and a specialist in early Greek archaeology. She is the author of *The Protogeometric Aegean: The Archaeology of the Late Eleventh and Tenth Centuries BC* (2003), and is director of the Lefkandi-Xeropolis excavations on Euboea.

Richard Lim is Associate Professor in the Department of History, Smith College, Massachusetts, and a specialist in the history of late antiquity. His publications include *Public Disputation, Power and Social Order in Late Antiquity* (1995) and (as editor with Carole Straw) *The Past Before Us: The Challenge of Historiographies of Late Antiquity* (2004). He is currently writing a book on public spectacles and civic transformation in late Roman cities.

Roger Ling is Professor of Classical Art and Archaeology in the University of Manchester. His special interest is Roman archaeology. In addition to excavations in Britain and survey work in Turkey, he has directed a project in the Insula (city-block) of the Menander at Pompeii, in course of publication as a five-volume monograph.

Roland Mayer is Professor of Classics at King's College London, and a specialist in Roman literature and culture. His publications include, most recently, *A Commentary on Tacitus'* Dialogus (2001) and *Seneca: Phaedra* (2003). He is currently writing a commentary on Horace *Odes* 1, and is researching the Roman value-concept of *gloria*.

Andrew Meadows is Curator of Greek coins in the Department of Coins and Medals in the British Museum. He is the co-editor, with Kirsty Shipton, of *Money and its Uses in the Ancient World* (2001).

Brian McGing is Professor in the School of Classics, Trinity College Dublin, and a specialist in Graeco-Roman Egypt and in the history of Judaism and of Asia Minor in the Hellenistic and early Roman periods. His publications include *The Foreign Policy of Mithridates VI Eupator King of Pontus* (1986) and *Greek Papyri from Dublin* (P. Dub.) (1995).

Pantelis Michelakis is Lecturer in Greek Language and Literature at the University of Bristol. He is the author of *Achilles in Greek Tragedy* (2002) and *Euripides: Iphigenia in Aulis* (2006), and co-editor of *Homer, Tragedy and Beyond: Essays in Honour of P. E. Easterling* (2001) and *Agamemnon in Performance, 458 BC–2004 AD* (2005).

Zahra Newby is a lecturer in the Department of Classics and Ancient History at the University of Warwick. Her published articles explore the art and culture of the Roman Empire and the treatment of works of art in the Greek literature of the imperial period. Her *Greek Athletics in the Roman World: Victory and Virtue* was published in 2005.

Vivian Nutton is Professor of the History of Medicine at the Welcome Trust Centre for the History of Medicine, University College London. He specialises in the history of the classical tradition in medicine, from antiquity to the present, particularly in Galen and in medicine in the Renaissance. His publications include *From Democedes to Harvey: Studies in the History of Medicine* (1988), *Galen's* On My Own Opinions (1999) and *Ancient Medicine* (2004).

Graham Oliver is Lecturer in Ancient Greek Culture at the University of Liverpool, and a specialist in Greek history and epigraphy. He is completing a new fascicle of Athenian decrees and laws, 321–301 BC, for *Inscriptiones Graecae*, volume II (3rd edn). Recent publications include (as editor) *The Epigraphy of Death: Studies in the History and Society of Greece and Rome* (2000).

Catherine Osborne has been lecturing in Philosophy at the University of East Anglia since 2003. Before that she was Reader in Ancient Greek Culture at the University of Liverpool. She is the author of *Rethinking Early Greek Philosophy* (1987) and *Eros Unveiled: Plato and the God of Love* (1994). Her latest book, *Presocratic Philosophy: A Very Short Introduction*, was published in 2004.

Robin Osborne is Professor of Ancient History in the University of Cambridge and a Fellow of King's College. He was President of the Society for the Promotion of Hellenic Studies from 2002 to 2006. His books include *Greece in the Making c.1200–479 BC* (1996), *Archaic and Classical Greek Art* (1998) and *Greek History* (2004).

Eva Parisinou teaches Greek and Roman history and material culture at the Open University and Birkbeck College London. She is the author of *The Light of the Gods: The Role of Light in Archaic and Classical Greek Cult* (2000) and has published extensively in the areas of Greek visual culture as reflected in figurative art and ancient technology, with particular focus on lighting technology.

Anthony Parker recently retired from the University of Bristol, where he was Senior Lecturer in the Department of Archaeology and Director of the Centre for Maritime Archaeology and History. His research involves many aspects of Roman material culture and has concentrated on ancient shipwrecks and the methodology of maritime archaeology.

J. H. W. Penney is University Lecturer in Classical Philology at the University of Oxford and a Fellow of Wolfson College. His research interests include Indo-European phonology and morphology, the languages of pre-Roman Italy, and Tocharian. He has published on these topics, including a chapter in *The Cambridge Ancient History* IV (2nd edn, 1988) on 'The Languages of

Italy'. He is currently at work on a handbook on the development of Latin and the other Italic languages from Indo-European.

Mark Pobjoy is Senior Tutor at Magdalen College, Oxford, having formerly been Fellow and Tutor in Ancient History at the College. His interests range from Latin epigraphy and classical historiography to the poetry of Virgil, while his principal speciality is the political history of Roman Italy. His publications include articles on Latin inscriptions and the coinage of the Social War, while his major current project is a work on the history of Capua under Roman rule.

Nicholas Purcell is Fellow and Tutor in Ancient History at St John's College, Oxford. He works on ancient (especially Roman) cultural, social and economic history, and is particularly interested in gardens in antiquity and the history of the Mediterranean landscape. He has recently written (with Peregrine Horden) *The Corrupting Sea: A Study of Mediterranean History* (2000).

T. E. Rihll is a lecturer in the Department of Classics and Ancient History at the University of Wales Swansea. She has published *Greek Science* (*Greece and Rome* New Surveys in the Classics 29) (1999), and edited (with C. J. Tuplin) and contributed to *Science and Mathematics in Ancient Greek Culture* (2002). She also publishes on Greek history.

Ian Ruffell is Lecturer in Classics at the University of Glasgow, and works on Greek comedy, cultural theory and gender. He has published articles on Old Comedy and on Roman satire and is preparing books on the absurd in Aristophanes and on the *Prometheus Bound.*

Donald Russell is an Emeritus Fellow of St John's College, Oxford, and Emeritus Professor of Classical Literature, University of Oxford. His works include an edition of Longinus, *On Sublimity* (1964), *Criticism in Antiquity* (2nd edn, 1995), and (with M. Winterbottom) *Ancient Literary Criticism: The Principal Texts in New Translation* (1972). He has also edited Quintilian in the Loeb Classical Library (2001).

Benet Salway is Lecturer in Ancient History at University College London and Director of the AHRC project *Law and the End of Empire*. Before that he was a lecturer in the Classics Department of the University of Nottingham. His research interests include travel and the perception of geography in the Roman world and later Roman social and political history.

Alison Sharrock is Professor of Classics at the University of Manchester. She is the author of *Seduction and Repetition in Ovid's* Ars Amatoria 2 (1994), co-author of *Fifty Key Classical Authors* (2002), and co-editor of *Intratextuality: Greek and Roman Textual Relations* (2000) and of *The Art of Love: Bimillennial Essays on Ovid's* Ars Amatoria *and* Remedia Amoris (forthcoming). She is currently working on a book entitled *Fabulous Artifice: Poetics and Playfulness in Roman Comedy* and on a project on Lucretius.

Karen E. Stears was formerly a lecturer in Ancient History at the University of Edinburgh. Her interests are centred on social and economic Greek history and classical Athenian art. She now lives and works in Italy.

Peter Stewart is Senior Lecturer in Classical Art at the Courtauld Institute of Art. He has worked widely in the fields of classical art and cultural history and specialises in the study of Roman sculpture. His publications include *Statues in Roman Society: Representation and Response* (2003) and *Roman Art (Greece and Rome* New Surveys in the Classics 34) (2004).

Christopher Stray is Honorary Research Fellow in the Department of Classics and Ancient History, University of Wales Swansea. His publications on the history of classical education and scholarship include *The Living Word: W.H.D. Rouse and the Crisis of Classics in Edwardian England* (1992) and *Classics Transformed: Schools, Universities, and Society in England 1830–1960* (1998).

Richard Tomlinson was an assistant in the Department of Greek at the University of Edinburgh before moving to the Department of Ancient History and Archaeology at the University of Birmingham, eventually becoming Professor and Head of Department. He then became Director of the British School at Athens in 1995, retiring in 1997. He has written books on Greek and Roman architecture, as well as a study of the nineteenth-century photographs of Athens collected by the Victorian artist Sir Lawrence Alma-Tadema.

Michael Trapp is Professor of Greek Literature and Thought at King's College London. His publications include *Maximus Tyrius:* Dissertationes (1994), *Maximus of Tyre: The Philosophical Orations* (1997) and *Greek and Latin Letters: An Anthology* (2003).

James Whitley is an archaeologist specialising in early Iron Age and archaic Greece, and is currently Director of the British School at Athens. Publications include *Style and Society in Dark Age Greece* (1991) and *The Archaeology of Ancient Greece* (2001), which won the Runciman prize for 2002. Since 1992 he has been directing a survey in and around the site of Praisos in Eastern Crete.

Jonathan Williams is the curator of Iron Age and Roman coins in the Department of Coins and Medals in the British Museum. He is the author of *Beyond the Rubicon: Gauls and Romans in Republican Italy* (2001), and the co-editor of *Coin Hoards from Roman Britain Vol. XI* (2002).

Index

Note: Page numbers in *italics* denote illustrations or tables. Spelling of Greek and Latin names may vary (see pp. ix–x for detailed information). For ancient and modern technical terms, consult chapter 68.